Investment Analysis and Portfolio Management

Fifth Edition

Investment Analysis and Portfolio Management

Fifth Edition

Frank K. Reilly
University of Notre Dame

Keith C. Brown
University of Texas at Austin

The Dryden Press
Harcourt Brace College Publishers

Fort Worth   Philadelphia   San Diego   New York   Orlando   Austin   San Antonio
Toronto   Montreal   London   Sydney   Tokyo

Executive Editor: Mike Reynolds
Associate Editor: Shana Lum
Project Editor: Sandy Walton
Production Manager: Carlyn Hauser
Executive Product Manager: Craig Johnson
Art Director: Sue Hart
Art & Literary Rights Editor: Adele Krause
Cover Illustration: Ken Reid/FPG International
Project Management: Elm Street Publishing Services, Inc.
Compositor: Shepard Poorman Communications Corporation
Text Type: 10/12 Times Roman

Some material in this work previously appeared in INVESTMENT ANALYSIS AND PORTFOLIO MANAGEMENT, Fourth Edition, copyright © 1994, 1989, 1985, 1979 by The Dryden Press. All rights reserved.

Address for Editorial Correspondence
The Dryden Press, 301 Commerce Street, Suite 3700, Fort Worth, TX 76102

Address for Orders
The Dryden Press, 6277 Sea Harbor Drive, Orlando, FL 32887
1-800-782-4479, or 1-800-433-0001 (in Florida)

ISBN: 0-03-018683-8

Library of Congress Catalog Card Number: 96-83161

CFA Examinations used throughout the text are reprinted with permission from The Institute of Chartered Financial Analysts, Charlottesville, Virginia.

Printed in the United States of America
8 9 0 1 2 3 4 5 032 9 8 7 6 5 4 3

The Dryden Press
Harcourt Brace College Publishers

To my best friend and wife,
Therese,
and our greatest gifts and
sources of happiness,
Frank K. III, Charlotte, and Lauren
Clarence R. II
Therese B.
Edgar B., Michele, and Kayleigh

F. K. R.

To Sheryl, Alexander, and Andrew,
who make it all worthwhile

K. C. B.

The Dryden Press Series in Finance

Amling and Droms
Investment Fundamentals

Berry and Young
Managing Investments: A Case Approach

Bertisch
Personal Finance

Boone, Kurtz, and Hearth
Planning Your Financial Future

Brigham
Brigham's Interactive Guide to Finance

Brigham
Fundamentals of Financial Management
Seventh Edition

Brigham, Aberwald, and Gapenski
Finance with Lotus 1-2-3
Second Edition

Brigham and Gapenski
Cases in Financial Management: Dryden Request

Brigham and Gapenski
Cases in Financial Management: Module A

Brigham and Gapenski
Cases in Financial Management: Module C

Brigham and Gapenski
Financial Management: Theory and Practice
Eighth Edition

Brigham and Gapenski
Intermediate Financial Management
Fifth Edition

Brigham and Houston
Fundamentals of Financial Management:
The Concise Edition

Chance
An Introduction to Derivatives
Third Edition

Clark, Gerlach, and Olson
Restructuring Corporate America

Cooley
Advances in Business Financial Management:
A Collection of Readings
Second Edition

Dickerson, Campsey, and Brigham
Introduction to Financial Management
Fourth Edition

Eaker, Fabozzi, and Grant
International Corporate Finance

Evans
International Finance: A Markets Approach

Fama and Miller
The Theory of Finance

Gardner and Mills
Managing Financial Institutions:
An Asset/Liability Approach
Third Edition

Gitman and Joehnk
Personal Financial Planning
Seventh Edition

Greenbaum and Thakor
Contemporary Financial Intermediation

Harrington and Eades
Case Studies in Financial Decision Making
Third Edition

Hayes and Meerschwam
Financial Institutions: Contemporary Cases in the Financial
Services Industry

Hearth and Zaima
Contemporary Investments: Security and Portfolio Analysis

Johnson
Issues and Readings in Managerial Finance
Fourth Edition

Kidwell, Peterson, and Blackwell
Financial Institutions, Markets, and Money
Sixth Edition

Koch
Bank Management
Third Edition

Leahigh
Pocket Guide to Finance

Maisel
Real Estate Finance
Second Edition

Martin, Cox, and MacMinn
The Theory of Finance: Evidence and Applications

Mayes and Shank
Advanced Financial Analysis with Microsoft Excel

Mayes and Shank
Financial Analysis with Lotus 1-2-3 for Windows

Mayes and Shank
Financial Analysis with Microsoft Excel

Mayo
*Financial Institutions, Investments, and Management:
An Introduction*
Fifth Edition

Mayo
Investments: An Introduction
Fifth Edition

Pettijohn
PROFIT+

Reilly and Brown
Investment Analysis and Portfolio Management
Fifth Edition

Reilly and Norton
Investments
Fourth Edition

Sears and Trennepohl
Investment Management

Seitz and Ellison
Capital Budgeting and Long-Term Financing Decisions
Second Edition

Siegel and Siegel
Futures Markets

Smith and Spudeck
Interest Rates: Principles and Applications

Stickney
*Financial Reporting and Statement Analysis:
A Strategic Perspective*
Third Edition

Weston, Besley, and Brigham
Essentials of Managerial Finance
Eleventh Edition

Preface

The pleasure of authoring a textbook comes from writing about a subject that you enjoy and find exciting. As an author, you hope that you can pass on to the reader not only knowledge but also the excitement that you feel for the subject. In addition, writing about investments brings an added stimulant because the subject can affect the reader during his or her entire business career and beyond. We hope what readers derive from this course will help them enjoy better lives through managing their resources properly.

The purpose of this book is to help you learn how to manage your money so that you will derive the maximum benefit from what you earn. To accomplish this purpose, you need to learn about the investment alternatives that are available today and, what is more important, to develop a way of analyzing and thinking about investments that will remain with you in the years ahead when new and different investment opportunities become available.

Because of its dual purpose, the book mixes description and theory. The descriptive material discusses available investment instruments and considers the purpose and operation of capital markets in the United States and around the world. The theoretical portion details how you should evaluate current investments and future opportunities to develop a portfolio of investments that will satisfy your risk–return objectives.

Preparing this fifth edition has been challenging for two reasons. First, many changes have occurred in the securities markets during the last few years in terms of theory, new financial instruments, and trading practices. Second, as mentioned in the prior edition, capital markets have become global. Consequently, very early in the book we present the compelling case for global investing. Subsequently, to ensure that you are prepared to function in this new global environment, almost every chapter discusses how investment practice or theory is influenced by the globalization of investments and capital markets. This completely integrated treatment is to ensure that you leave this course with a completely global mindset on investments that will serve you well into the twenty-first century.

INTENDED MARKET

This text is addressed to both graduate and advanced undergraduate students who are looking for an in-depth discussion of investments and portfolio management. The presentation of the material is intended to be rigorous and empirical, without being overly quantitative. A proper discussion of the modern developments in investments and portfolio theory must be rigorous. The detailed discussion of numerical empirical studies reflects the belief that it is essential for our theories to be exposed to the real world and be judged on the basis of how well they help us understand and explain reality

KEY FEATURES OF THE FIFTH EDITION

When planning the fifth edition of *Investment Analysis and Portfolio Management,* we wanted to retain its traditional strengths and capitalize on new developments in the investments area to make it the most comprehensive investments textbook available.

First, the fifth edition maintains its unparalleled international coverage. Investing knows no borders, and although the total integration of domestic and global investment opportunities may seem to contradict the need for separate discussions of international issues, it in fact makes the need for specific information on non-U.S. markets, instruments, conventions, and techniques even more compelling. Sections of chapters that deal with international topics are designated by this icon 🌐 for easy identification.

Second, today's investing environment includes derivative securities not as exotic anomalies but as standard investment instruments. We felt that *Investment Analysis and Portfolio Management* must reflect that situation. Consequently, our four chapters on derivatives have been completely rewritten to provide an even more intuitive, clear discussion of the different instruments, their markets, valuation, trading strategies, and general use as risk management/return enhancement tools.

The introductory derivatives chapter appears early in the book as Chapter 11 in the section on "Developments in Investment Theory." We kept this placement from the previous edition because we are still committed to the philosophy that every investments student needs to be exposed to the basics of derivative instruments, markets, and usage. Our Chapter 11 provides this overview.

For instructors who want to get into more detail on derivative pricing, valuation, and strategies, we have three separate chapters near the end of the book. Chapter 23 discusses forwards and futures contracts first, before options, because typically investors consider forward/futures positions before they turn to options to hedge risk. Chapter 24 then covers option contracts, which are variations of forwards and futures. Part 4 concludes with a chapter on swaps, warrants, convertibles, and structured notes. Chapter 25 is an in-depth discussion of these more "advanced" derivative types.

Third, we have reordered Chapter 10, "Extensions and Testing of Asset Pricing Theories," to follow immediately after the introductory chapter on asset pricing models. We felt that instructors who wanted to teach this chapter would do so in this order, not as a final chapter as it appeared in the previous edition.

Fourth, we have added many new questions and problems to the end-of-chapter material, including a significant number of CFA exercises, to provide more student practice on executing basic computations and then applying them to more sophisticated investment problems.

Finally for the fifth edition, we have added two new chapters, Chapter 2, "Asset Allocation," and Chapter 22, "Equity Portfolio Management Strategies." The addition of both of these chapters reflects our commitment to the *application* of investment concepts through the creation of portfolios and their management.

MAJOR CONTENT CHANGES IN THE FIFTH EDITION

The text has been thoroughly updated for currency. In addition to these time-related revisions, we have also made the following specific changes to individual chapters:

Chapter 2	A new chapter on global asset allocation describing the portfolio management process and matching investors' goals with investment strategies
Chapter 3	Increased description of international bond markets and an in-depth discussion of real estate instruments, such as REITs and CREFs
Chapter 4	Discussion of emerging national markets in such countries as China and Hungary. A summary description of developed and emerging markets
Chapter 5	Description of the Brinson Partners Global Security Market Index and a full update on bond market indexes. A summary description of dozens of indexes from around the world
Chapter 6	Detailed section on obtaining bond information. Expanded discussion of new online information sources

Chapter 7	Discussion of studies examining the BV/MV ratio as a determinant of return potential
Chapter 8	Use of two new companies, Coca-Cola Company and Exxon, to explain the concepts of portfolio theory
Chapter 10	Placed immediately following the introductory chapter on asset pricing models and includes a new discussion of recent studies on the relationship of beta to rates of return and on the benchmark error problem in testing the CAPM
Chapter 11	Completely rewritten chapter introducing derivative securities and markets and provides payoff diagrams, describes the relationships among different derivative types, and illustrates their use as risk management tools
Chapter 12	Introduces the importance of the GAAP and considers the quality of financial statements and the value of analyzing them, as well as including a description of cross-sectional ratio analysis
Chapter 14	Includes recent studies on the effect of consumer sentiment and expectations on the business cycle
Chapter 15	New discussion of credit card receivables as an asset-backed security
Chapter 16	A detailed explanation of bond price–yield curves to begin the chapter, while the rest of the chapter thoroughly examines derivation of the theoretical spot rate curve and the use of spot rates in valuing bonds and includes a much-expanded discussion of Macaulay, modified, and effective duration including the impact of embedded options.
Chapter 18	Adds an analysis of estimating the equity risk premium while considering the implications of the dividend payout ratio as either an active or passive management decision
Chapter 20	Includes a thoroughly updated company analysis of Walgreen with a description of their competitive strategies and a new discussion considering the computation and use of EVA, MVA, and the franchise factor in a company analysis
Chapter 21	Expands the discussion of the moving-average line using Cisco Systems, as an example
Chapter 22	A new chapter detailing active and passive equity portfolio management strategies
Chapter 23	Completely new chapter on futures and forwards, their valuation and applications
Chapter 24	Completely new chapter on option contracts including hedging strategies and option pricing models
Chapter 25	Completely new chapter describing three additional types of derivative instruments, swaps, warrants and convertibles, and structured notes
Chapter 27	Covers the important topic of performance attribution analysis including a detailed example and discussion of measuring market timing skills

SUPPLEMENT
PACKAGE

The preparation of the fifth edition provided the opportunity to reconsider the supplement products offered to instructors and students who use *Investment Analysis and Portfolio Management.* The result of this examination is a greatly improved package that provides more than just basic answers and solutions. We are indebted to the supplement writers who devoted their time, energy, and creativity to making this supplement package the best it has ever been.

THE INSTRUCTOR'S MANUAL AND TEST BANK   The *Instructor's Manual,* written by Ladd Kochman of Kennesaw State College, contains a brief outline of each chapter's key concepts and equations that can be easily copied and distributed to students as a reference tool. The *Instructor's Manual* contains a set of 150 transparency masters that are tables and figures from the main text.

Taking into consideration that, after four editions, the *Test Bank* would need a dramatic infusion of new and fresh testing material, Jeffrey A. Manzi of Ohio University prepared an excellent set of new questions and problems for the fifth edition's *Test Bank.* Full solutions to the testing material are also included.

For instructors who would like to prepare their exams via computer, The Dryden Press will provide a Microsoft Word diskette with the complete *Test Bank* for easy test compilation.

THE SOLUTIONS MANUAL   This separate volume, which can be purchased by students if instructors wish, contains all the answers to the end-of-chapter questions and solutions to end-of-chapter problems. Again, Ladd Kochman was ever diligent in the preparation of these materials, ensuring the most error-free solutions possible.

POWERPOINT PRESENTATION SOFTWARE   Jeffrey A. Manzi went beyond the call of duty in the creation of a full set of chapter files in Microsoft PowerPoint. For each chapter, Dr. Manzi has developed a self-contained presentation that covers all the key concepts, equations, and examples of the chapter. The files can be used as is for an innovative, interactive class presentation. Instructors who have access to Microsoft PowerPoint can modify the slides in any way they wish, adding or deleting materials to match their needs.

In addition, PowerPoint has an added feature that Dr. Manzi has utilized—instructor's notes pages. In addition to reprinting the slide, the notes page will indicate when the instructor should "click" for additional text and will provide additional explanations and examples. This value-added material will add depth to any class presentation and discussion.

DATA DISK   With this edition, we have prepared a disk containing economic data and stock information from U.S. and foreign companies, over a 20-year period. This data disk is offered free to adopters.

PORTFOLIO MANAGER FOR THE PERSONAL COMPUTER   This software program, developed by Jim Pettijohn and Joe Evans, provides routines for students to apply the concepts and techniques presented in the text. Students can build a portfolio from a database of real companies and perform analyses on their investments. The routines are cross-referenced to the text for additional information. This package is available free to adopters.

STUDY GUIDE   A student *Study Guide,* prepared by David Leahigh of King's College, includes the following for each chapter: a reference outline of definitions and equations; a brief concept outline; extensive exercises, including true-false, fill-in-the-blank, multiple-choice, and short-answer questions; a set of problems that provide additional practice; and answers to all of these exercises. The *Study Guide* is an excellent resource for all students wanting additional information and practice.

MANAGING INVESTMENTS: A CASE APPROACH   Co-authored by Michael A. Berry of James Madison University and S. David Young of Tulane University, this book contains 36 Harvard-style cases and 10 technical notes. Based on real-world problems, the text gives students hands-on experience in applying theoretical principles and models to decisions faced by individual investors and portfolio managers. Adopters of *Managing Investments* have access to a comprehensive *Instructor's Manual,* which includes detailed teaching notes for the cases.

The Dryden Press will provide complimentary supplements or supplement packages to those adopters qualified under our adoption policy. Please contact your sales representative to learn how you may qualify. If as an adopter or potential user you receive supplements you do not need, please return them to your sales representative or send them to:

Attn: Returns Department
Troy Warehouse
465 South Lincoln Drive
Troy, MO 63379

ACKNOWLEDGMENTS So many people have helped us in so many ways that we hesitate to list them, fearing that we may miss someone. Accepting this risk, we will begin with the University of Notre Dame and the University of Texas at Austin because of their direct support. Also, we must thank the Bernard J. Hank Family, who have endowed the Chair that helped bring Frank Reilly back to Notre Dame and has provided support for our work.

Reviewers for this edition were:

John Alexander
Clemson University

Robert E. Brooks
University of Alabama

Charles Cao
Pennsylvania State University

Atreya Chakraborty
Brandeis University

Robert Clark
University of Vermont

James D'Mello
Western Michigan University

William Dukes
Texas Tech University

Davinder Malhotra
Philadelphia College of Textiles and Science

Iqbal Mansur
Widener University

Thomas W. Miller, Jr.
University of Missouri–Columbia

Henry Oppenheimer
University of Rhode Island

Laurie Prather
University of Tennessee at Chattanooga

Murli Rajan
University of Scranton

Steve Rich
Baylor University

Shekar Shetty
University of South Dakota

Premal Vora
King's College

Robert Weigand
University of South Florida

We were fortunate to have the following excellent reviewers for earlier editions:

Robert Angell
East Carolina University

George Aragon
Boston College

Brian Belt
University of Missouri–Kansas City

Omar M. Benkato
Ball State University

Arand Bhattacharya
University of Cincinnati

Carol Billingham
Central Michigan University

Susan Block
University of California–Santa Barbara

Gerald A. Blum
Babson College

Robert J. Brown
Harrisburg, Pennsylvania

Dosoung Choi
University of Tennessee

John Clinebell
University of Northern Colorado

Eugene F. Drzycimski
University of Wisconsin–Oshkosh

John Dunkelberg
Wake Forest University

Eric Emory
Sacred Heart University

Thomas Eyssell
University of Missouri–St. Louis

James Feller
Middle Tennessee State University

Eurico Ferreira
Clemson University

Michael Ferri
John Carroll University

Joseph E. Finnerty
University of Illinois

Harry Friedman
New York University

R. H. Gilmer
University of Mississippi

Stephen Goldstein
University of South Carolina

Steven Goldstein
Robinson-Humphrey/American Express

Keshav Gupta
Oklahoma State University

Sally A. Hamilton
Santa Clara University

Ronald Hoffmeister
Arizona State University

Ron Hutchins
Eastern Michigan University

A. James Ifflander
Arizona State University

Stan Jacobs
Central Washington University

Kwang Jun
Michigan State University

Jaroslaw Komarynsky
Northern Illinois University

Danny Litt
Century Software Systems/UCLA

Miles Livingston
University of Florida

Christopher Ma
Texas Tech University

Stephen Mann
University of South Carolina

George Mason
University of Hartford

John Matthys
DePaul University

Michael McBain
Marquette University

Dennis McConnell
University of Maine

Jeanette Medewitz
University of Nebraska–Omaha

Jacob Michaelsen
University of California–Santa Cruz

Nicholas Michas
Northern Illinois University

Lalatendu Misra
University of Texas–San Antonio

Michael Murray
LaCrosse, Wisconsin

John Peavy
Southern Methodist University

George Philippatos
University of Tennessee

George Pinches
University of Kansas

Rose Prasad
Central Michigan University

George A. Racette
University of Oregon

Bruce Robin
Old Dominion University

James Rosenfeld
Emory University

Stanley D. Ryals
Investment Counsel, Inc.

Katrina F. Sherrerd
Association of Investment Management and Research

Frederic Shipley
DePaul University

Douglas Southard
Virginia Polytechnic Institute

Harold Stevenson
Arizona State University

Kishore Tandon
The City University of New York–Baruch College

Donald Thompson
Georgia State University

David E. Upton
Virginia Commonwealth University

E. Theodore Veit
Rollins College

Bruce Wardrep
East Carolina University

Rolf Wubbels
New York University

Valuable comments and suggestions have come from former graduate students at the University of Illinois: Paul Fellows, University of Iowa; Wenchi Kao, DePaul University; and David Wright, University of Wisconsin–Parkside. Once more, we were blessed with bright, dedicated research assistants when we needed them the most. This includes Maria Vivero, Kevin Poppink, and most recently Arunas Leonavicius, who has been extremely careful, dependable, and creative.

Current and former colleagues have been very helpful: Yu-Chi Chang, Bill McDonald, Rick Mendenhall, Bill Nichols, Juan Rivera, and Norlin Rueschhoff, University of Notre Dame; C. F. Lee, Rutgers University; and John M. Wachowicz, University of Tennessee. As always, some of the best insights and most stimulating comments continue to come during too-infrequent runs with a very good friend, Jim Gentry of the University of Illinois.

We are convinced that a professor who wants to write a book that is academically respectable, relevant, as well as realistic requires help from the "real world." We have been fortunate to develop relationships with a number of individuals (including a growing number of former students) whom we consider our contacts with reality.

We especially want to thank Robert Conway, who was the managing director of the London office of Goldman, Sachs & Company, for suggesting several years ago that it was essential to have the book reflect the rapidly evolving global market. This important advice has had a profound effect on this book over time.

The following individuals have graciously provided important insights and material:

Sharon Athey
Brown Brothers Harriman

Joseph C. Bencivenga
Bankers Trust

Lowell Benson
Robert A. Murray Partners

David G. Booth
Dimensional Fund Advisors, Inc.

Gary Brinson
Brinson Partners, Inc.

Charles K. Brown
Goldman, Sachs & Co.

Roy Burry
Kidder, Peabody & Co.

Tom Butler
Dean Witter Discover

Abby J. Cohen
Goldman, Sachs & Co.

Thomas Coleman
Adler, Coleman and Co. (NYSE)

Robert Conway
Goldman, Sachs & Co.

Robert J. Davis
Crimson Capital Co.

Robert J. Davis, Jr.
Merrill Lynch Pierce Fenner & Smith

Philip Delaney, Jr.
Northern Trust Bank

Steven Einhorn
Goldman, Sachs & Co.

Sam Eisenstadt
Value Line

Frank J. Fabozzi
Yale University

Paul Feldman
Goldman, Sachs & Co.

Kenneth Fisher
Forbes

John J. Flanagan, Jr.
Lawrence, O'Donnell, Marcus & Co.

Martin S. Fridson
Merrill Lynch Pierce Fenner & Smith

Richard A. Grasso
New York Stock Exchange

William J. Hank
Moore Financial Corporation

Rick Hans
Walgreen Corp.

Lea B. Hansen
Consultant

W. Van Harlow
Fidelity Management and Research

Jim Johnson
Options Clearing Corporation

John W. Jordan II
The Jordan Company

Andrew Kalotay
Kalotay Associates

Luke Knecht
Russell Reynolds Assoc.

Warren N. Koontz, Jr.
Loomis, Sayles & Co.

Mark Kritzman
Windham Capital Management

C. Prewitt Lane
ICH Companies

Martin Leibowitz
TIAA-CREF

Douglas R. Lempereur
Templeton Investment Counsel, Inc.

Robert Levine
Nomura Securities

Michael Lipper
Lipper Analytical

Amy Lipton
Bankers Trust

Scott Lummer
Ibbotson Associates

John Maginn
Mutual of Omaha

Scott Malpass
University of Notre Dame

Richard McCabe
Merrill Lynch Pierce Fenner & Smith

Michael McCowin
State of Wisconsin Investment Board

Terrence J. McGlinn
McGlinn Capital Markets

Robert Milne
Duff & Phelps

Robert G. Murray
First Interstate Bank of Oregon

Ian Rossa O'Reilly
Wood Gundy, Inc.

Robert Parrino
University of Texas

John J. Phelan, Jr.
New York Stock Exchange

Philip J. Purcell III
Dean Witter Discover

Jack Pycik
Consultant

Chet Ragavan
Merrill Lynch Pierce Fenner & Smith

John C. Rudolf
Summit Capital Management

Stanley Ryals
Investment Counsel, Inc.

Ron Ryan
Ryan Labs, Inc.

Sean St. Clair
Duff & Phelps

Robert F. Semmens
The Beacon Group

Brian Singer
Brinson Partners

Donald J. Smith
Boston University

William Smith
Dean Witter Reynolds

William M. Stephens
Ameritech

James Stork
Duff & Phelps

Masao Takamori
Tokyo Stock Exchange

Kevin Terhaar
Brinson Partners

Anthony Vignola
Kidder, Peabody & Co.

William M. Wadden
Stein, Roe & Farnham

Sushi Wadhwani
Goldman, Sachs & Co.

Jeffrey M. Weingarten
Goldman, Sachs & Co.

Ken Wiles
Fulcrum Financial Group

Robert Wilmouth
National Futures Association

Richard S. Wilson
Ryan Labs, Inc.

We continue to benefit from the help and consideration of the dedicated people who are or have been associated with the Institute of Chartered Financial Analysts, which is a part of the Association for Investment Management and Research: Tom Bowman, Whit Broome, Bob Luck, Pete Morley, Sue Martin, Katie Sherrerd, Clay Singleton, and Donald Tuttle.

Professor Reilly would like to thank his assistant, Cheri Gray, who had the unenviable task of keeping his office and his life in some sort of order during this project. Barbara Campbell was the understanding project editor who put up with both of our schedules and brought the book from messy manuscript and sloppy exhibits to bound volume with incredibly good humor.

As always, our greatest gratitude is to our families—past, present, and future. Our parents gave us life and helped us understand love and how to give it. Most important are our wives who provide love, understanding, and support throughout the day and night. We thank God for our children and future grandchildren who ensure that our lives are full of love, laughs, and excitement.

Frank K. Reilly
Notre Dame, Indiana

Keith C. Brown
Austin, Texas

October 1996

About the Authors

Frank K. Reilly is the Bernard J. Hank Professor of Business Administration and former dean of the College of Business Administration at the University of Notre Dame. Holding degrees from the University of Notre Dame (B.B.A.), Northwestern University (M.B.A.), and the University of Chicago (Ph.D.), Professor Reilly has taught at the University of Illinois, the University of Kansas, and the University of Wyoming in addition to the University of Notre Dame. He has several years of experience as a senior securities analyst as well as experience in stock and bond trading. A Chartered Financial Analyst (CFA), he has been a member of the Council of Examiners, the Research Foundation, the Council on Education and Research, the Education Committee, and the CFA Grading Committee, and is currently on the Board of Trustees of the Institute of Chartered Financial Analysts. Professor Reilly has been president of the Financial Management Association, the Midwest Business Administration Association, the Eastern Finance Association, the Academy of Financial Services, and the Midwest Finance Association. He is or has been on the board of directors of the First Interstate Bank of Wisconsin, Norwest Bank of Indiana, the Investment Analysts Society of Chicago, Brinson Global Funds, Fort Dearborn Income Securities, Greenwood Trust Co., Discover Finance Corporation, NIBCO, Inc., Battery Park Funds, Inc., Certified Financial Planners Board of Standards, and the Association for Investment Management and Research.

As the author of more than one hundred articles, monographs, and papers, Professor Reilly has written for numerous publications including *Journal of Finance, Journal of Financial and Quantitative Analysis, Journal of Accounting Research, Financial Management, Financial Analysts Journal, Journal of Fixed Income, Financial Review,* and *Journal of Portfolio Management.* In addition to *Investment Analysis and Portfolio Management,* fifth edition, Professor Reilly is the coauthor of another textbook, *Investments,* fourth edition (The Dryden Press, 1995), with Edgar A. Norton.

Professor Reilly was named on the list of *Outstanding Educators in America* and has received the University of Illinois Alumni Association Graduate Teaching Award, the Outstanding Educator Award from the M.B.A. class at the University of Illinois, and the Outstanding Teacher Award from the M.B.A. class at Notre Dame. He also received the C. Stewart Sheppard Award from the Association of Investment Management and Research (AIMR) for his contribution to the educational mission of the Association. He is editor of *Readings and Issues in Investments, Ethics and the Investment Industry,* and *High Yield Bonds: Analysis and Risk Assessment,* and is or has been a member of the editorial boards of *Financial Management, European Journal of Finance, The Financial Review, The Financial Services Review, The Journal of Applied Business Research, Journal of Financial Education,* and *Quarterly Review of Economics and Business.* He is included in *Who's Who in Finance and Industry, Who's Who in America, Who's Who in American Education,* and *Who's Who in the World.*

Keith C. Brown holds the position of Allied Bancshares Centennial Fellow and Associate Professor of Finance at the Graduate School of Business, University of Texas. He received his B.A. in Economics from San Diego State University, where he was a member of the Phi Beta Kappa, Phi Kappa Phi, and Omicron Delta Epsilon honor societies. He received his M.S. and Ph.D. in Financial Economics from the Krannert Graduate School of Management at Purdue University. Since leaving school in 1981, he has specialized in teaching Investments, Derivatives, and Capital Markets courses at the M.B.A. and Ph.D. levels and has received five awards for teaching innovation and excellence. In addition to his academic responsibilities, he is also vice president of The M.B.A. Investment Fund, L.L.C., a privately funded investment company managed by graduate students at the University of Texas.

Professor Brown has published more than forty articles, monographs, chapters, and papers on topics ranging from asset pricing and investment strategy to financial risk management. His publications have appeared in such journals as *Journal of Finance, Journal of Financial Economics, Journal of Financial and Quantitative Analysis, Review of Economics and Statistics, Financial Analysts Journal, Financial Management, Advances in Futures and Options Research, Journal of Fixed Income, Journal of Applied Corporate Finance,* and *Journal of Portfolio Management.* In addition to his contributions to *Investment Analysis and Portfolio Management,* fifth edition, he is a coauthor of *Interest Rate and Currency Swaps: A Tutorial,* a textbook published in 1995 through the Association for Investment Management and Research (AIMR). He received a Graham and Dodd Award from the Financial Analysts Federation as an author of one of the best articles published by *Financial Analysts Journal* in 1990.

In August of 1988, Professor Brown received his charter from the Institute of Chartered Financial Analysts (ICFA). He has served as a member of AIMR's CFA Candidate Curriculum Committee and Education Committee, and on the CFA Examination Grading staff. He is the research director of the Research Foundation of the ICFA, from which position he guides the development of the research portion of the organization's worldwide educational mission. For the past several years, he has also been associate editor for both *Financial Analysts Journal* and *CFA Digest.* In other professional service, Professor Brown has been a regional director for the Financial Management Association and has served as the applied research track chairman for that organization's annual conference.

Professor Brown is the cofounder and senior partner of Fulcrum Financial Group, a portfolio management and investment advisory firm located in Austin, Texas, and Charlotte, North Carolina, that currently oversees portfolios holding a total of $60 million in fixed-income securities. From May 1987 to August 1988 he was based in New York as a senior consultant to the Corporate Professional Development Department at Manufacturers Hanover Trust Company. He has lectured extensively throughout the world on investment and risk management topics in the executive development programs for companies such as Chase Manhattan Bank, Chemical Bank, Lehman Brothers, Union Bank of Switzerland, Shearson, Texas Commerce Bank, The Beacon Group, Motorola, and Halliburton. He also spent 13 months as a senior planner with a California-based financial planning firm.

Brief Contents

Part 1 The Investment Background 2
Chapter 1 The Investment Setting 4
Chapter 2 Asset Allocation 37
Chapter 3 Selecting Investments in a Global Market 66
Chapter 4 Organization and Functioning of Securities Markets 105
Chapter 5 Security-Market Indicator Series 151
Chapter 6 Sources of Information on Global Investments 178

Part 2 Developments in Investment Theory 206
Chapter 7 Efficient Capital Markets 208
Chapter 8 An Introduction to Portfolio Management 251
Chapter 9 An Introduction to Asset Pricing Models 277
Chapter 10 Extensions and Testing of Asset Pricing Theories 305
Chapter 11 An Introduction to Derivative Markets and Securities 333

Part 3 Valuation Principles and Practices 372
Chapter 12 Analysis of Financial Statements 374
Chapter 13 An Introduction to Security Valuation 429
Chapter 14 The Analysis of Alternative Economies and Security Markets:
The Global Asset Allocation Decision 460

Part 4 Analysis and Management of Bonds 488
Chapter 15 Bond Fundamentals 490
Chapter 16 The Analysis and Valuation of Bonds 525
Chapter 17 Bond Portfolio Management Strategies 591

Part 5 Analysis of Common Stocks 638
Chapter 18 Stock-Market Analysis 640
Chapter 19 Industry Analysis 679
Chapter 20 Company Analysis and Stock Selection 714
Chapter 21 Technical Analysis 771
Chapter 22 Equity Portfolio Management Strategies 802

Part 6 Derivative Security Analysis 824
Chapter 23 Forward and Futures Contracts 826
Chapter 24 Option Contracts 872
Chapter 25 Swap Contracts, Convertible Securities, and Other
Embedded Derivatives 916

Part 7 Investment Companies and Evaluating Portfolio Performance   964

Chapter 26   Investment Companies   966
Chapter 27   Evaluation of Portfolio Performance   993

Appendix A   How to Become a Chartered Financial Analyst   1036
Appendix B   Code of Ethics and Standards of Professional Conduct   1039
Appendix C   Interest Tables   1041
Appendix D   Standard Normal Probabilities   1047
Glossary   1049
Name/Company Index   1069
Subject Index   1074

Contents

Part

1   *The Investment Background*   2

Chapter 1
The Investment Setting   4

WHAT IS AN INVESTMENT?   4
    Investment Defined   5

MEASURING RETURN AND RISK   6
    Measuring Historical Rates of Return   6
    Computing Mean Historical Returns   8
    Calculating Expected Rates of Return   11
    Measuring the Risk of Expected Rates of Return   14
    Risk Measures for Historical Returns   15

DETERMINING REQUIRED RATES OF RETURN   16
    The Real Risk-Free Rate   17
    Factors Influencing the Nominal Risk-Free Rate   17
    Risk Premium   20
    Risk Premium and Portfolio Theory   22
    Fundamental Risk versus Systematic Risk   23
    Summary of Required Rate of Return   23

RELATIONSHIP BETWEEN RISK AND RETURN   24
    Movements along the SML   25
    Changes in the Slope of the SML   25
    Changes in Capital Market Conditions
      or Expected Inflation   27
    Summary of Changes in the Required Rate of Return   27

OUTLINE OF THE BOOK   28

    Chapter 1 APPENDIX
    Computation of Variance and Standard Deviation   33

Chapter 2
Asset Allocation   37

INDIVIDUAL INVESTOR LIFE CYCLE   37
    Pre-Investment Needs   38
    Life Cycle Investment Strategies   38
    Life Cycle Investment Goals   40

THE PORTFOLIO MANAGEMENT PROCESS   40

THE NEED FOR A POLICY STATEMENT   41
    Understand and Articulate Investor Goals   41
    Portfolio Performance Standards   42

INPUT TO THE POLICY STATEMENT   43
    Investment Objectives   43
    Investment Constraints   46
    Constructing the Policy Statement   51

OBJECTIVES AND CONSTRAINTS OF
INSTITUTIONAL INVESTORS   51
    Mutual Funds   51
    Pension Funds   51
    Endowment Funds   53
    Insurance Companies   53
    Banks   54
    Institutional Investor Summary   55

THE IMPORTANCE OF ASSET ALLOCATION   55
    Real Investment Returns after Taxes and Costs   56
    Returns and Risks of Different Asset Classes   57
    Asset Allocation Summary   61

ASSET ALLOCATION AND CULTURAL DIFFERENCES   61

Chapter 3
Selecting Investments in a Global Market   66

THE CASE FOR GLOBAL INVESTMENTS   67
    Relative Size of U.S. Financial Markets   68
    Rates of Return on U.S. and Foreign Securities   69
    Individual Country Risk and Return   71
    Risk of Combined Country Investments   71

GLOBAL INVESTMENT CHOICES   77
    Fixed-Income Investments   78
    Equity Instruments   82
    Special Equity Instruments: Options   84
    Futures Contracts   84
    Investment Companies   85
    Real Estate   86
    Low-Liquidity Investments   87

HISTORICAL RISK/RETURNS ON ALTERNATIVE
INVESTMENTS   89
    Stocks, Bonds, and T Bills   89
    World Portfolio Performance   91
    Art and Antiques   94
    Real Estate   95

    Chapter 3 APPENDIX
    Covariance and Correlation   102

Chapter 4
Organization and Functioning of Securities Markets 105

WHAT IS A MARKET? 106
CHARACTERISTICS OF A GOOD MARKET 106
ORGANIZATION OF THE SECURITIES MARKET 107

PRIMARY CAPITAL MARKETS 108
GOVERNMENT BOND ISSUES 108
MUNICIPAL BOND ISSUES 108
CORPORATE BOND AND STOCK ISSUES 109
PRIVATE PLACEMENTS AND RULE 144A 111

SECONDARY FINANCIAL MARKETS 111
WHY SECONDARY MARKETS ARE IMPORTANT 111
SECONDARY BOND MARKETS 112
FINANCIAL FUTURES 113
SECONDARY EQUITY MARKETS 113

REGIONAL EXCHANGES AND THE OVER-THE-COUNTER MARKET 120

DETAILED ANALYSIS OF EXCHANGE MARKETS 125
EXCHANGE MEMBERSHIP 125
TYPES OF ORDERS 126
EXCHANGE MARKET MAKERS 131

CHANGES IN THE SECURITIES MARKETS 134
EVIDENCE AND EFFECT OF INSTITUTIONALIZATION 134
NEGOTIATED COMMISSION RATES 135
THE IMPACT OF BLOCK TRADES 136
INSTITUTIONS AND STOCK PRICE VOLATILITY 137
NATIONAL MARKET SYSTEM (NMS) 137
NEW TRADING SYSTEMS 140
GLOBAL MARKET CHANGES 141
FUTURE DEVELOPMENTS 143

Chapter 4 APPENDIX
Characteristics of Developed and Developing Markets around the World 148

Chapter 5
Security-Market Indicator Series 151

USES OF SECURITY-MARKET INDEXES 152

DIFFERENTIATING FACTORS IN CONSTRUCTING MARKET INDEXES 153
THE SAMPLE 153
WEIGHTING SAMPLE MEMBERS 153
COMPUTATIONAL PROCEDURE 153

STOCK-MARKET INDICATOR SERIES 153
PRICE-WEIGHTED SERIES 153
VALUE-WEIGHTED SERIES 156

UNWEIGHTED PRICE INDICATOR SERIES 157
GLOBAL EQUITY INDEXES 160

BOND-MARKET INDICATOR SERIES 165
INVESTMENT-GRADE BOND INDEXES 165
HIGH-YIELD BOND INDEXES 167
GLOBAL GOVERNMENT BOND MARKET INDEXES 167

COMPOSITE STOCK—BOND INDEXES 167
MERRILL LYNCH—WILSHIRE U.S. CAPITAL MARKETS INDEX (ML—WCMI) 168
BRINSON PARTNERS GLOBAL SECURITY MARKET INDEX (GSMI) 168

COMPARISON OF INDEXES OVER TIME 169
CORRELATIONS AMONG MONTHLY EQUITY PRICE CHANGES 169
CORRELATIONS AMONG MONTHLY BOND INDEXES 169
ANNUAL STOCK PRICE CHANGES 171
ANNUAL BOND RATES OF RETURN 171

Chapter 5 APPENDIX
Foreign Stock-Market Indexes 177

Chapter 6
Sources of Information on Global Investments 178

AGGREGATE ECONOMIC ANALYSIS 179
U.S. GOVERNMENT SOURCES 179
BANK PUBLICATIONS 180
NON-U.S. ECONOMIC DATA 181

AGGREGATE SECURITY-MARKET ANALYSIS 182
GOVERNMENT PUBLICATIONS 182
COMMERCIAL PUBLICATIONS 183
BROKERAGE FIRM REPORTS 186

INDUSTRY ANALYSIS 188
INDUSTRY PUBLICATIONS 188
INDUSTRY MAGAZINES 188

INDIVIDUAL STOCK AND BOND ANALYSIS 190
COMPANY-GENERATED INFORMATION 190
COMMERCIAL PUBLICATIONS 191
BROKERAGE FIRM REPORTS 194

INVESTMENT MAGAZINES 194

OBTAINING INFORMATION ON BONDS 197
REQUIRED INFORMATION 197
SOURCES OF BOND QUOTES 198

SOURCES OF INFORMATION ON MUTUAL FUNDS 198

THEORETICAL AND EMPIRICAL ANALYSIS 200
ACADEMIC JOURNALS 200

COMPUTERIZED DATA SOURCES 202
DATA BANKS 202
ONLINE DATABASES 203

Part
2   Developments in Investment Theory   206

Chapter 7
Efficient Capital Markets   208

WHY SHOULD CAPITAL MARKETS BE EFFICIENT?   209

ALTERNATIVE EFFICIENT MARKET HYPOTHESES   210
Expected Return or Fair Game Model   210
Weak-Form Efficient Market Hypothesis   211
Semistrong-Form Efficient Market Hypothesis   211
Strong-Form Efficient Market Hypothesis   212

TESTS AND RESULTS OF ALTERNATIVE EFFICIENT MARKET HYPOTHESIS   212
Weak-Form Hypothesis: Tests and Results   212
Semistrong-Form Hypothesis: Tests and Results   215
Strong-Form Hypothesis: Tests and Results   234

IMPLICATIONS OF EFFICIENT CAPITAL MARKETS   241
Efficient Markets and Technical Analysis   241
Efficient Markets and Fundamental Analysis   242
Efficient Markets and Portfolio Management   244
Efficiency in European Equity Markets   246

Chapter 8
An Introduction to Portfolio Management   251

SOME BACKGROUND ASSUMPTIONS   252
Risk Aversion   252
Definition of Risk   253

MARKOWITZ PORTFOLIO THEORY   253
Alternative Measures of Risk   253
Expected Rates of Return   254
Variance (Standard Deviation) of Returns for an Individual Investment   254
Variance (Standard Deviation) of Returns for a Portfolio   255
Standard Deviation of a Portfolio   261
A Three-Asset Portfolio   268
Estimation Issues   269
The Efficient Frontier   270
The Efficient Frontier and Investor Utility   270

Chapter 8 APPENDIXES
A. Proof That Minimum Portfolio Variance Occurs with Equal Weights When Securities Have Equal Variance   275
B. Derivation of Weights That Will Give Zero Variance When Correlation Equals –1.00   276

Chapter 9
An Introduction to Asset Pricing Models   277

CAPITAL MARKET THEORY: AN OVERVIEW   278
Background for Capital Market Theory   278
Risk-Free Asset   280
The Market Portfolio   283

THE CAPITAL ASSET PRICING MODEL: EXPECTED RETURN AND RISK   287
The Security Market Line (SML)   288

ARBITRAGE PRICING THEORY (APT)   297
Empirical Tests of the APT   300

Chapter 10
Extensions and Testing of Asset Pricing Theories   305

RELAXING THE ASSUMPTIONS   305
Differential Borrowing and Lending Rates   306
Zero–Beta Model   307
Transactions Costs   308
Heterogeneous Expectations and Planning Periods   309
Taxes   309

EMPIRICAL TESTS OF THE CAPM   310
Stability of Beta   310
Comparability of Published Estimates of Beta   311

RELATIONSHIP BETWEEN SYSTEMATIC RISK AND RETURN   312
Effect of Skewness on the Relationship   314
Effect of Size, P/E, and Leverage   314
Effect of Book-to-Market Value: The Fama-French Study   315
Summary of CAPM Risk–Return Empirical Results   315

THE MARKET PORTFOLIO: THEORY VERSUS PRACTICE   317

ARBITRAGE PRICING THEORY (APT)   322
Empirical Tests of the APT   325
Roll-Ross Study   325
Extensions of the Roll-Ross Tests   326
The APT and Anomalies   327
The Shanken Challenge to Testability of the APT   329

Chapter 11
An Introduction to Derivative Markets and Securities   333

OVERVIEW OF DERIVATIVE MARKETS   334
The Language and Structure of Forward and Futures Markets   334
The Language and Structure of Option Markets   336

INVESTING WITH DERIVATIVE SECURITIES 338
The Basic Nature of Derivative Investing 338
Basic Payoff Diagrams for Forward Contracts 340
Basic Payoff Diagrams for Call and Put Options 341
Option Payoff Diagrams: An Example 344

THE RELATIONSHIP BETWEEN FORWARD AND
OPTION CONTRACTS 347
Put-Call-Spot Parity 347
Put-Call Parity: An Example 349
Creating Synthetic Securities Using Put-Call Parity 350
Adjusting Put-Call-Spot Parity for Dividends 351
Put-Call-Forward Parity 352

APPLICATIONS OF DERIVATIVES IN PORTFOLIO
MANAGEMENT 354
*Restructuring Asset Portfolios with Forward
  Contracts* 354
Protecting Portfolio Value with Put Options 356
Altering Portfolio Payoffs with Call Options 360

Part
3   *Valuation Principles and Practices* 372

Chapter 12
Analysis of Financial Statements 374

MAJOR FINANCIAL STATEMENTS 374
Generally Accepted Accounting Principles 375
Balance Sheet 375
Income Statement 375
Statement of Cash Flows 376
Alternative Measures of Cash Flow 380
Purpose of Financial Statement Analysis 381

ANALYSIS OF FINANCIAL RATIOS 381
Importance of Relative Financial Ratios 381

COMPUTATION OF FINANCIAL RATIOS 383
Common Size Statements 383

EVALUATING INTERNAL LIQUIDITY 383
Internal Liquidity Ratios 383

EVALUATING OPERATING PERFORMANCE 388
Operating Efficiency Ratios 389
Operating Profitability Ratios 390

RISK ANALYSIS 396
Business Risk 398
Financial Risk 399

ANALYSIS OF GROWTH POTENTIAL 406
Importance of Growth Analysis 406
Determinants of Growth 406

EXTERNAL MARKET LIQUIDITY 408
Market Liquidity Defined 408
Determinants of Market Liquidity 408

COMPARATIVE ANALYSIS OF RATIOS 409
Internal Liquidity 409
Operating Performance 409
Financial Risk 409
Growth Analysis 411

ANALYSIS OF NON-U.S. FINANCIAL STATEMENTS 411
Accounting Statement Format Differences 411
Differences in Accounting Principles 411
International Ratio Analysis 412

THE QUALITY OF FINANCIAL STATEMENTS 417
Balance Sheet 417
Income Statement 418

THE VALUE OF FINANCIAL STATEMENT ANALYSIS 418

USES OF FINANCIAL RATIOS 418
Stock Valuation Models 419
Financial Ratios and Systematic Risk 419
Financial Ratios and Bond Ratings 420
Financial Ratios and Insolvency (Bankruptcy) 421
Limitations of Financial Ratios 421

Chapter 13
An Introduction to Security Valuation 429

AN OVERVIEW OF THE VALUATION PROCESS 430

WHY A THREE-STEP VALUATION PROCESS? 431
General Economic Influences 431
Industry Influences 432
Company Analysis 433
Does the Three-Step Process Work? 433

THEORY OF VALUATION 434
Stream of Expected Returns 434
Required Rate of Return 435
*Investment Decision Process: A Comparison of
  Estimated Values and Market Prices* 435

VALUATION OF ALTERNATIVE INVESTMENTS 436
Valuation of Bonds 436
Valuation of Preferred Stock 437
Valuation of Common Stock 438
Infinite Period DDM and Growth Companies 443
Valuation with Temporary Supernormal Growth 443
Earnings Multiplier Model 445

ESTIMATING THE INPUTS: THE REQUIRED RATE
OF RETURN AND THE EXPECTED GROWTH RATE
OF DIVIDENDS 447
Required Rate of Return (k) 447

ESTIMATING THE REQUIRED RETURN FOR FOREIGN
SECURITIES 449
EXPECTED GROWTH RATE OF DIVIDENDS 453
ESTIMATING DIVIDEND GROWTH FOR FOREIGN STOCKS 455

Chapter 13 APPENDIX
Derivation of Constant Growth Dividend
Discount Model (DDM) 458

Chapter 14
The Analysis of Alternative Economies and
Security Markets: The Global Asset
Allocation Decision 460

ECONOMIC ACTIVITY AND SECURITY MARKETS 461

CYCLICAL INDICATOR APPROACH TO
FORECASTING THE ECONOMY 462
CYCLICAL INDICATOR CATEGORIES 463
ANALYTICAL MEASURES OF PERFORMANCE 466
LIMITATIONS OF THE CYCLICAL INDICATOR APPROACH 466
LEADING INDICATORS AND STOCK PRICES 467
OTHER LEADING INDICATOR SERIES 467

MONETARY VARIABLES, THE ECONOMY,
AND STOCK PRICES 470
MONEY SUPPLY AND THE ECONOMY 470
MONEY SUPPLY AND STOCK PRICES 471
OTHER ECONOMIC VARIABLES AND STOCK PRICES 472
INFLATION, INTEREST RATES, AND SECURITY PRICES 473
SUMMARY OF MACROECONOMIC ANALYSIS 476

ANALYSIS OF WORLD SECURITY MARKETS 477
INFLATION AND EXCHANGE RATES 477
CORRELATIONS AMONG RETURNS 479
INDIVIDUAL COUNTRY STOCK PRICE CHANGES 480
INDIVIDUAL COUNTRY ANALYSIS 480
WORLD ASSET ALLOCATION 482

Part
4 Analysis and Management of Bonds 488

Chapter 15
Bond Fundamentals 490

BASIC FEATURES OF A BOND 490
BOND CHARACTERISTICS 491
RATES OF RETURN ON BONDS 493

THE GLOBAL BOND-MARKET STRUCTURE 494
PARTICIPATING ISSUERS 495
PARTICIPATING INVESTORS 497
BOND RATINGS 497

ALTERNATIVE BOND ISSUES 500
DOMESTIC GOVERNMENT BONDS 500
GOVERNMENT AGENCY ISSUES 502
MUNICIPAL BONDS 505
CORPORATE BONDS 507
INTERNATIONAL BONDS 516

OBTAINING INFORMATION ON BOND PRICES 517
INTERPRETING BOND QUOTES 517

Chapter 16
The Analysis and Valuation of Bonds 525

THE FUNDAMENTALS OF BOND VALUATION 526
THE PRESENT VALUE MODEL 526
THE YIELD MODEL 528

COMPUTING BOND YIELDS 529
NOMINAL YIELD 530
CURRENT YIELD 530
PROMISED YIELD TO MATURITY 530
PROMISED YIELD TO CALL 534
REALIZED (HORIZON) YIELD 535

CALCULATING FUTURE BOND PRICES 536
REALIZED (HORIZON) YIELD WITH DIFFERENTIAL
REINVESTMENT RATES 538
PRICE AND YIELD DETERMINATION ON NONINTEREST DATES 540
YIELD ADJUSTMENTS FOR TAX-EXEMPT BONDS 540
BOND YIELD BOOKS 541

BOND VALUATION USING SPOT RATES 541

WHAT DETERMINES INTEREST RATES? 543
FORECASTING INTEREST RATES 544
FUNDAMENTAL DETERMINANTS OF INTEREST RATES 545
TERM STRUCTURE OF INTEREST RATES 548

CALCULATING FORWARD RATES FROM THE
SPOT-RATE CURVE 554

TERM-STRUCTURE THEORIES 556
YIELD SPREADS 560

WHAT DETERMINES THE PRICE VOLATILITY
FOR BONDS? 561
TRADING STRATEGIES 564
DURATION MEASURES 565
MODIFIED DURATION AND BOND PRICE VOLATILITY 568
BOND CONVEXITY 569
DURATION AND CONVEXITY FOR CALLABLE BONDS 576
LIMITATIONS OF MACAULAY AND MODIFIED DURATION 578

Chapter 17
Bond Portfolio Management Strategies 591

ALTERNATIVE BOND PORTFOLIO STRATEGIES 591
PASSIVE MANAGEMENT STRATEGIES 592

ACTIVE MANAGEMENT STRATEGIES 593
A GLOBAL FIXED-INCOME INVESTMENT STRATEGY 605
MATCHED-FUNDING TECHNIQUES 607
CONTINGENT PORTFOLIO STRATEGIES 616

IMPLICATIONS OF CAPITAL MARKET THEORY
AND THE EMH ON BOND PORTFOLIO
MANAGEMENT 623
BONDS AND TOTAL PORTFOLIO THEORY 623
BONDS AND CAPITAL MARKET THEORY 624
BOND PRICE BEHAVIOR IN A CAPM FRAMEWORK 624
BOND-MARKET EFFICIENCY 627

Part
5   Analysis of Common Stocks 638

Chapter 18
Stock-Market Analysis 640

APPLYING THE VALUATION MODEL TO
THE MARKET 641
TWO-PART VALUATION PROCEDURE 642
IMPORTANCE OF BOTH COMPONENTS OF VALUE 642

ESTIMATING EXPECTED EARNINGS PER SHARE 645
ESTIMATING GROSS NATIONAL PRODUCT 645
ESTIMATING SALES PER SHARE FOR A MARKET SERIES 645
ALTERNATIVE ESTIMATES OF CORPORATE NET PROFITS 647
ESTIMATING AGGREGATE OPERATING PROFIT MARGIN 648
ESTIMATING DEPRECIATION EXPENSE 652
ESTIMATING INTEREST EXPENSE 652
ESTIMATING THE TAX RATE 653
CALCULATING EARNINGS PER SHARE: AN EXAMPLE 654

ESTIMATING THE EARNINGS MULTIPLIER FOR A
STOCK-MARKET SERIES 655
DETERMINANTS OF THE EARNINGS MULTIPLIER 655
ESTIMATING AN EARNINGS MULTIPLIER: AN EXAMPLE 665
CALCULATING AN ESTIMATE OF THE VALUE FOR THE
MARKET SERIES 669

CALCULATING THE EXPECTED RATE OF
RETURN ON COMMON STOCKS 669

ANALYSIS OF WORLD MARKETS 671
INDIVIDUAL COUNTRY ANALYSIS 672

Chapter 19
Industry Analysis 679

WHY DO INDUSTRY ANALYSIS? 680
CROSS-SECTIONAL INDUSTRY PERFORMANCE 681
INDUSTRY PERFORMANCE OVER TIME 682
PERFORMANCE OF THE COMPANIES WITHIN AN INDUSTRY 682
DIFFERENCES IN INDUSTRY RISK 682
SUMMARY OF RESEARCH ON INDUSTRY ANALYSIS 683

ESTIMATING INDUSTRY RATES OF RETURN 683

ESTIMATING EARNINGS PER SHARE 684
FORECASTING SALES PER SHARE 684
FORECASTING EARNINGS PER SHARE 689

COMPETITION AND EXPECTED INDUSTRY
RETURNS 689
BASIC COMPETITIVE FORCES 689
INDUSTRY PROFIT MARGIN FORECAST 691
AN INDUSTRY EARNINGS ESTIMATE EXAMPLE 694

ESTIMATING AN INDUSTRY EARNINGS
MULTIPLIER 696
MACROANALYSIS OF AN INDUSTRY MULTIPLIER 697
MICROANALYSIS OF AN INDUSTRY MULTIPLIER 698
WHY THE DIFFERENCE? 705
ESTIMATING THE FUTURE 705

GLOBAL INDUSTRY ANALYSIS 706
THE EUROPEAN CHEMICAL INDUSTRY 706

APPENDIX 19A
Preparing an Industry Analysis 711

Chapter 20
Company Analysis and Stock Selection 714

ANALYSIS OF COMPANIES VERSUS THE
SELECTION OF STOCK 715
GROWTH COMPANIES AND GROWTH STOCKS 715
OTHER COMPANY–STOCK COMPARISONS 716

ESTIMATING THE VALUE OF A COMPANY 717

ESTIMATING COMPANY EARNINGS PER SHARE 718
COMPANY SALES FORECAST 718
ESTIMATING THE COMPANY PROFIT MARGIN 721

IDENTIFYING AND SELECTING COMPETITIVE
STRATEGIES 721
LOW-COST STRATEGY 722
DIFFERENTIATION STRATEGY 722
FOCUSING A STRATEGY 722

WALGREEN COMPETITIVE STRATEGIES 722
THE INTERNAL PERFORMANCE 723

ESTIMATING COMPANY EARNINGS MULTIPLIERS 726
MACROANALYSIS OF THE EARNINGS MULTIPLIER 726
MICROANALYSIS OF THE EARNINGS MULTIPLIER 727
MAKING THE INVESTMENT DECISION 732

ADDITIONAL MEASURES OF RELATIVE VALUE 734
PRICE/BOOK VALUE (P/BV) RATIO 735
PRICE/CASH FLOW (P/CF) RATIO 738

MEASURES OF VALUE-ADDED   739
   Economic Value-Added (EVA)   740
   Market Value-Added (MVA)   742
   Relationships between EVA and MVA   742
   The Franchise Factor   742

GLOBAL COMPANY ANALYSIS   743
   Earnings per Share Analysis   743
   Profitability and Financial Strength   744
   Common Stock Statistics   744
   Share Price Performance   746
   Individual Company Analysis   747

ANALYSIS OF GROWTH COMPANIES   747
   Growth Company Defined   749
   Actual Returns above Expected Returns   749
   Growth Companies and Growth Stocks   750
   Growth Companies and the Dividend Discount Model 750
   Alternative Growth Models   750
   No-Growth Firm   750
   Long-Run Growth Models   751
   The Real World   754
   Growth Duration   754
   A Flexible Growth Stock Valuation Model   758
   An Example of the Flexible Growth Model   760

Chapter 21
Technical Analysis   771

UNDERLYING ASSUMPTIONS OF
TECHNICAL ANALYSIS   772

CHALLENGES TO TECHNICAL ANALYSIS   774
   Challenges to Technical Analysis Assumptions 774
   Challenges to Technical Trading Rules   774

ADVANTAGES OF TECHNICAL ANALYSIS   775

TECHNICAL TRADING RULES AND INDICATORS   776
   Contrary-Opinion Rules   777
   Follow the Smart Money   781
   Other Market Environment Indicators   784
   Stock Price and Volume Techniques   788
   Technical Analysis of Foreign Markets   795
   Technical Analysis of Bond Markets   797

Chapter 22
Equity Portfolio Management Strategies   802

PASSIVE VERSUS ACTIVE MANAGEMENT   802

AN OVERVIEW OF PASSIVE EQUITY PORTFOLIO
MANAGEMENT STRATEGIES   803
   Index Fund Construction Techniques   804

AN OVERVIEW OF ACTIVE EQUITY PORTFOLIO
MANAGEMENT STRATEGIES   805

USING FUTURES AND OPTIONS IN EQUITY
PORTFOLIO MANAGEMENT   810
   Modifying Portfolio Risk and Return: A Review 810
   The Use of Futures in Asset Allocation   812
   The Use of Derivatives in Equity Portfolios 812
   Hedging Portfolio Inflows   812
   Hedging Portfolio Outflows   814
   The Standard & Poor's 500 Index Futures Contract 814
   *Using Futures in Passive Equity Portfolio
Management*   816
   *Using Futures in Active Equity Portfolio
Management*   817
   *Modifying the Characteristics of an International
Equity Portfolio*   818

ASSET ALLOCATION STRATEGIES   819
   Integrated Asset Allocation   819
   Strategic Asset Allocation   819
   Tactical Asset Allocation   819
   Insured Asset Allocation   820
   Selecting an Allocation Method   820

Part
6   Derivative Security Analysis   824

Chapter 23
Forward and Futures Contracts   826

AN OVERVIEW OF FORWARD AND
FUTURES TRADING   827

HEDGING WITH FORWARDS AND FUTURES   830
   Hedging and the Basis   830
   Calculating the Optimal Hedge Ratio   832

FORWARD AND FUTURES CONTRACTS: BASIC
VALUATION CONCEPTS   834
   Valuing Forwards and Futures   834
   The Relationship between Spot and Forward Prices 835

FINANCIAL FORWARDS AND FUTURES: APPLICATIONS
AND STRATEGIES   837
   Interest Rate Forwards and Futures   837
   Long-Term Interest Rate Futures   838
   Short-Term Interest Rate Futures   843
   Stock Index Futures   849
   Currency Forwards and Futures   854

APPENDIX 23A
A Closed-Form Equation for Calculating Duration   867

APPENDIX 23B
Calculating Money Market Implied Forward Rates   868

Chapter 24

Option Contracts 872

AN OVERVIEW OF OPTION MARKETS AND
CONTRACTS 873
OPTION MARKET CONVENTIONS 873
PRICE QUOTATIONS FOR EXCHANGE-TRADED OPTIONS 874

OPTION TRADING STRATEGIES 880
STRADDLES, STRIPS, AND STRAPS 881
STRANGLES 883
CHOOSER OPTIONS 884
SPREADS 884
RANGE FORWARDS 887

THE FUNDAMENTALS OF OPTION VALUATION 889
THE BASIC APPROACH 889
IMPROVING FORECAST ACCURACY 891
THE BINOMIAL OPTION PRICING MODEL 893
THE BLACK-SCHOLES VALUATION MODEL 897
ESTIMATING VOLATILITY 900

OPTION VALUATION: EXTENSIONS AND
ADVANCED TOPICS 902
VALUING EUROPEAN-STYLE PUT OPTIONS 902
VALUING OPTIONS ON DIVIDEND-BEARING SECURITIES 903
VALUING AMERICAN-STYLE OPTIONS 905
OTHER EXTENSIONS OF THE BLACK-SCHOLES MODEL 907

Chapter 25

*Swap Contracts, Convertible Securities,
and Other Embedded Derivatives* 916

OTC INTEREST RATE AGREEMENTS 917
FORWARD RATE AGREEMENTS 917
INTEREST RATE SWAPS 919
CAPS AND FLOORS 925
COLLARS 926
SWAP OPTIONS ("SWAPTIONS") 928

SWAP CONTRACTING EXTENSIONS 931
CURRENCY SWAPS 931
EQUITY INDEX–LINKED SWAPS 935
COMMODITY SWAPS 937

WARRANTS AND CONVERTIBLE SECURITIES 939
WARRANTS 939
CONVERTIBLE SECURITIES 941
CONVERTIBLE PREFERRED STOCK 941
CONVERTIBLE BONDS 942

OTHER EMBEDDED DERIVATIVES 945
DUAL CURRENCY BONDS 947
EQUITY INDEX–LINKED NOTES 948
COMMODITY-LINKED BULL AND BEAR BONDS 952
SWAP-LINKED NOTES 953

Part

*7 Investment Companies and Evaluating
Portfolio Performance* 964

Chapter 26

Investment Companies 966

WHAT IS AN INVESTMENT COMPANY? 967

MANAGEMENT OF INVESTMENT COMPANIES 967

CLOSED-END VERSUS OPEN-END
INVESTMENT COMPANIES 968
CLOSED-END INVESTMENT COMPANIES 968
OPEN-END INVESTMENT COMPANIES 971
FUND MANAGEMENT FEES 973

TYPES OF INVESTMENT COMPANIES BASED
ON PORTFOLIO MAKEUP 973
COMMON STOCK FUNDS 973
BALANCED FUNDS 973
BOND FUNDS 973
MONEY MARKET FUNDS 974
BREAKDOWN BY FUND CHARACTERISTICS 974

PERFORMANCE OF INVESTMENT COMPANIES 976
ANALYSIS OF OVERALL PERFORMANCE 976
IMPACT OF FUND OBJECTIVES 977
MARKET TIMING ABILITY 978
CONSISTENCY OF PERFORMANCE 979
WHAT PERFORMANCE STUDIES MEAN TO YOU 980

SOURCES OF INFORMATION 981

GLOBAL INVESTMENT COMPANIES 990

Chapter 27

Evaluation of Portfolio Performance 993

WHAT IS REQUIRED OF A PORTFOLIO MANAGER? 994

COMPOSITE PORTFOLIO PERFORMANCE
MEASURES 995
PORTFOLIO EVALUATION BEFORE 1960 995
TREYNOR PORTFOLIO PERFORMANCE MEASURE 995
SHARPE PORTFOLIO PERFORMANCE MEASURE 998
JENSEN PORTFOLIO PERFORMANCE MEASURE 1000

APPLICATION OF PORTFOLIO
PERFORMANCE MEASURES 1002
COMPONENTS OF INVESTMENT PERFORMANCE 1006

PERFORMANCE ATTRIBUTION ANALYSIS 1010
ASSET CLASS ATTRIBUTION ANALYSIS: AN EXAMPLE 1011
PERFORMANCE ATTRIBUTION EXTENSIONS 1013

MEASURING MARKET TIMING SKILLS 1015

FACTORS THAT AFFECT USE OF
PERFORMANCE MEASURES   1016
  BENCHMARK ERRORS AND GLOBAL INVESTING   1017

A DEMONSTRATION OF THE GLOBAL
BENCHMARK PROBLEM   1018
  IMPLICATIONS OF BENCHMARK PROBLEMS   1019
  RELIABILITY OF PERFORMANCE MEASURES   1021

EVALUATION OF BOND PORTFOLIO
PERFORMANCE   1021
  A BOND MARKET LINE   1021
  DECOMPOSING PORTFOLIO RETURNS   1024
  ANALYZING SOURCES OF RETURN   1026
  CONSISTENCY OF PERFORMANCE   1028
  REQUIRED CHARACTERISTICS OF BENCHMARKS   1028

APPENDIX A
How to Become a Chartered Financial Analyst   1036

APPENDIX B
Code of Ethics and Standards of Professional Conduct   1039

APPENDIX C
Interest Tables   1041

APPENDIX D
Standard Normal Probabilities   1047

Glossary   1049

Name/Company Index   1069

Subject Index   1074

Part 1

THE INVESTMENT BACKGROUND

Chapter 1   The Investment Setting

Chapter 2   Asset Allocation

Chapter 3   Selecting Investments in a Global Market

Chapter 4   Organization and Functioning of Securities Markets

Chapter 5   Security-Market Indicator Series

Chapter 6   Sources of Information on Global Investments

The chapters in this section provide a background for your study of investments by answering the following questions:

- Why do people invest?
- How do you measure returns and risks for alternative investments?
- What factors should be considered when making your asset allocation decision?
- What investments are available?
- How do securities markets function?
- How and why are securities markets in the United States and around the world changing?
- How can you evaluate the market behavior of common stocks and bonds?
- What are the factors that cause differences among stock and bond market indexes?
- How can you get relevant information to learn about and evaluate potential investments?

In the first chapter we consider why an individual would invest, how to measure the rates of return and risk for alternative investments, and what factors determine an investor's required rate of return on an investment. The latter point will be very important in subsequent analyses when we work to understand investor behavior, the markets for alternative securities, and the valuation of various investments.

Because the ultimate decision that must be made by an investor is the makeup of his or her portfolio, Chapter 2 deals with the very important asset allocation decision. This includes specific steps that should be included in the portfolio management process and the factors that influence the makeup of an investor's portfolio over its life cycle.

To minimize risk, investment theory asserts the need to diversify. To explore investments available to investors, we begin Chapter 3 by making the overpowering case for why investors should invest globally rather than limit choices to only U.S. securities. Building on this premise, we discuss several investment instruments found in global markets. We conclude the chapter with a review of the historical rates of return and measures of risk for a number of alternative asset groups.

In Chapter 4 we examine how markets work in general, and then focus on bond and stock markets specifically. During the 1980s, significant changes occurred in the operation of the securities market, including a trend toward a global market. After discussing these changes and the globalization of these markets, and the rapid development of capital markets around the world, we can envision how global markets will continue to expand available investment alternatives.

These initial chapters provide the framework for you to understand various securities, the markets where they are bought and sold, and how you might manage a collection of investments in a portfolio. Specific portfolio management techniques are described in later chapters.

Investors, market analysts, and financial theorists often gauge the behavior of securities markets by evaluating changes in various market indexes. The performance of these indexes is also used to make asset allocation decisions. We examine and compare a number of stock-market and bond-market indexes for the domestic and global markets in Chapter 5.

Finally, Chapter 6 describes sources of information for investors seeking to learn more about various investment opportunities. The information ranges from macroeconomic data to individual company reports.

Chapter

1

The Investment Setting

This chapter answers the following questions:

- Why do individuals invest?
- What is meant by an investment?
- How do investors measure the rates of return on alternative investments?
- How do investors measure the risks related to alternative investments?
- What factors contribute to the rates of return that investors require on an investment?
- What macroeconomic and microeconomic factors contribute to changes in the required rates of return for individual investments and investments in general?

This chapter discusses several topics that are basic to subsequent chapters. We begin with a consideration of what is an investment and the returns and risks related to investments. This leads to a presentation of how to measure the expected and historical rates of return for an individual asset or a portfolio of assets. In addition, we consider how to measure the risk not only for an individual investment, but also for an investment that is part of a portfolio.

The third section of the chapter discusses factors that determine the required rate of return for an individual investment. The factors discussed include those that contribute to an asset's *total* risk. Because most investors have a portfolio of investments, it is necessary to consider how to measure the risk of an asset when it is a part of a large portfolio of assets. The risk that prevails when an asset is part of a portfolio is referred to as its *systematic* risk.

The final section deals with what causes changes in an asset's required rate of return over time. Changes occur because of both macroeconomic events that affect all investment assets and microeconomic events that affect the specific asset.

WHAT IS AN INVESTMENT?

For most of your life, you will be earning and spending money. Rarely, though, will your current money income exactly balance with your consumption desires. Sometimes you may have more money than you want to spend; at other times you may want to purchase more than you can afford. These imbalances will lead you either to borrow or to save to maximize the benefits from your income.

When current income exceeds current consumption desires, people tend to save the excess. They can do any of several things with these savings. One possibility is to put the money under a mattress or bury it in the backyard until consumption desires exceed current income. When they retrieve their savings from the mattress or backyard, they would have the same amount they saved.

Another possibility is to give up immediate possession of these savings for a larger amount of money that will be available for future consumption. This tradeoff of *present* consumption for a higher level of *future* consumption is the reason for saving. What you do with the savings to make them increase over time is *investment*.[1]

Those who give up immediate possession of savings (i.e., defer consumption) expect to receive a greater amount than they gave up. Conversely, those who consume more than their current income (i.e., borrow) must be willing to pay back more than they borrowed.

The rate of exchange between *future consumption* (future dollars) and *current consumption* (current dollars) is the *pure rate of interest*. Both willingness to pay this difference for borrowed funds and the desire to receive a surplus on savings give rise to an interest rate referred to as the *pure time value of money*. This interest rate is established in the capital market by a comparison of the supply of excess income available (savings) to be invested and the demand for excess consumption (borrowing) at a given time. If you can exchange $100 of certain income today for $104 of certain income 1 year from today, then the pure rate of exchange on a risk-free investment (i.e., the time value of money) is said to be 4 percent (104/100 − 1).

The investor who gives up $100 today expects to consume $104 of goods and services in the future. This assumes that the general price level in the economy stays the same. This price stability has rarely been the case during the past several decades when inflation rates have varied from 1.1 percent in 1986 to 13.3 percent in 1979, with an average of about 5.65 percent a year from 1970 to 1995. If investors expect a change in prices, they will require a higher rate of return to compensate for it. For example, if an investor expects a rise in prices (i.e., inflation) at the rate of 2 percent during the period of investment, he or she will increase the required interest rate by 2 percent. In our example, the investor would require $106 in the future to defer the $100 of consumption during an inflationary period (the investor wants a 6 percent interest rate instead of 4 percent). This required rate is referred to as the *nominal risk-free rate*.

Further, if the future payment from the investment is not certain, the investor will demand an interest rate that exceeds the pure time value of money plus the inflation rate. The uncertainty of the payments from an investment is the *investment risk*. The excess amount added to the nominal risk-free interest rate is called a *risk premium*. In our previous example, the investor would require more than $106 1 year from today to compensate for the uncertainty. As an example, if the required amount were $110, $4, or 4 percent, would be considered a risk premium.

INVESTMENT DEFINED   From our discussion we can specify a formal definition of investment. Specifically, an **investment** is the current commitment of dollars for a period of time to derive future payments that will compensate the investor for (1) the time the funds are committed, (2) the expected rate of inflation, and (3) the uncertainty of the future payments. The investor can be an individual, a government, a pension fund, or a corporation. Similarly, this definition includes all types of investments, including investments by corporations in plant and equipment and investments by individuals in stocks, bonds, commodities, or real estate. This text emphasizes investments by financial institutions and individual investors. In all cases, the investor is trading a *known* dollar amount today for some *expected* future stream of payments that will be greater than the current outlay.

At this point, we have answered the questions about why people invest and what they want from their investments. They invest to earn a return from savings due to their deferred

---

[1] In contrast, when current income is less than current consumption desires, people borrow to make up the difference. Although we will discuss borrowing on several occasions, the major emphasis of this text is how to invest savings.

consumption. They want a rate of return that compensates them for the time, the expected rate of inflation, and the uncertainty of the return. This return, the investor's **required rate of return,** is discussed throughout this book. A central question of this book is how investors select investments that will give them their required rates of return.

The next section of this chapter describes how to measure the expected or historical rate of return on an investment and also how to quantify the uncertainty of expected returns. You need to understand these techniques for measuring the rates of return and the uncertainty of these returns to evaluate the suitability of a particular investment. Although our emphasis will be on financial assets such as bonds and stocks, we will refer to other assets such as art and antiques. Chapter 4 discusses the range of financial assets and also considers some nonfinancial assets.

MEASURING RETURN AND RISK

Choosing among alternative instruments requires that you estimate and evaluate the expected risk–return tradeoffs for the alternative investments available. Therefore, you must understand how to measure the rate of return and the risk involved in an investment accurately. To meet this need, we examine how to quantify return and risk and how to measure *historical* and *expected* rates of return and risk.

We consider historical measures of return and risk because this book and other publications provide numerous examples of historical average rates of return and risk measures for various assets, and understanding these presentations is important. In addition, these historical results are often used by investors when attempting to estimate the *expected* rates of return and risk for an asset class as part of the asset allocation decision.

The first measure is the historical rate of return on an individual investment over the time period the investment is held (i.e., its holding period). Next, we consider how to measure the *average* historical rate of return for an individual investment over a number of time periods. The third section considers the average rate of return for a *portfolio* of investments.

Given the measures of historical rates of return, we will present the traditional measures of risk for a historical time series of returns (i.e., the variance and standard deviation).

Following the presentation of measures of historical rates of return and risk, we turn to estimating the *expected* rate of return for an investment. Obviously, such an estimate contains a great deal of uncertainty, and we present measures of this uncertainty or risk.

MEASURING HISTORICAL RATES OF RETURN

When you are evaluating alternative investments for your portfolio, you will often be comparing investments with very different prices or lives. As an example, you might want to compare a $10 stock that pays no dividends to a stock selling for $150 that pays dividends of $5 a year. To properly evaluate these two investments, you must accurately compare their historical rates of return.

When we invest, we defer current consumption to add to our wealth so that we can consume more in the future. Therefore, when we talk about a return on an investment, we are concerned with *the change in wealth* resulting from this investment. This change in wealth can be due either to cash inflows such as interest or dividends or to a change in the price of the asset (positive or negative).

If you commit $200 to an investment at the beginning of the year and you get back $220 at the end of the year, what is your return for the period? The period during which you own an investment is called its *holding period*, and the return for that period is the **holding period return (HPR).** In this example, the HPR is 1.10, calculated as follows:

$$\text{HPR} = \frac{\text{Ending Value of Investment}}{\text{Beginning Value of Investment}}$$

$$= \frac{\$220}{\$200} = 1.10$$

This value will always be zero or greater; that is, it can never be a negative value. A value greater than 1.0 reflects an increase in your wealth, which means that you received a positive rate of return during the period. A value less than 1.0 means that you suffered a decline in wealth, indicating a negative return during the period. An HPR of zero indicates that you lost all of your money.

Although HPR helps us express the change in value of an investment, investors generally evaluate returns in *percentage terms on an annual basis*. This conversion to annual percentage rates makes it easier to directly compare alternative investments that have very different characteristics. The first step in converting an HPR to an annual percentage rate is to derive a percentage return, referred to as the **holding period yield (HPY).** The HPY is equal to the HPR minus 1.

$$\text{HPY} = \text{HPR} - 1$$

In our example:

$$\text{HPY} = 1.10 - 1 = 0.10$$
$$= 10\%$$

To derive an *annual* HPY, you compute an *annual* HPR and subtract 1. Annual HPR is found by:

$$\text{Annual HPR} = \text{HPR}^{1/n}$$

where:

n = number of years the investment is held

Consider an investment that cost $250 and is worth $350 after being held for 2 years:

$$\text{HPR} = \frac{\text{Ending Value of Investment}}{\text{Beginning Value of Investment}} = \frac{\$350}{\$250}$$

$$= 1.40$$
$$\text{Annual HPR} = 1.40^{1/n}$$
$$= 1.40^{1/2}$$
$$= 1.1832$$
$$\text{Annual HPY} = 1.1832 - 1 = 0.1832$$
$$= 18.32\%$$

In contrast, consider an investment of $100 held for only 6 months that earned a return of $12:

$$HPR = \frac{\$112}{\$100} = 1.12 \ (n = .5)$$

$$\text{Annual HPR} = 1.12^{1/.5}$$
$$= 1.12^2$$
$$= 1.2544$$
$$\text{Annual HPY} = 1.2544 - 1 = 0.2544$$
$$= 25.44\%$$

Note that we made some implicit assumptions when converting the HPY to an annual basis. This annualized holding period yield computation assumes a constant annual yield for each year. In the 2-year investment, we assumed an 18.32 percent rate of return each year, compounded. In the partial year HPR that was annualized, we assumed that the return is compounded for the whole year. That is, we assumed that the rate of return earned during the first part of the year is likewise earned on the value at the end of the first 6 months. The 12 percent rate of return for the initial 6 months compounds to 25.44 percent for the full year.[2]

Remember one final point: The ending value of the investment can be the result of a change in price for the investment alone (e.g., a stock going from $20 a share to $22 a share), income from the investment alone, or a combination of price change and income. Ending value includes the value of everything related to the investment.

COMPUTING MEAN HISTORICAL RETURNS

Now that we have calculated the HPY for a single investment, we want to consider **mean rates of return** for a single investment and for a portfolio of investments. Over a number of years, a single investment will likely give high rates of return during some years and low rates of return, or possibly negative rates of return, during others. Your analysis should consider each of these returns, but you also want a summary figure that indicates this investment's typical experience, or the rate of return you should expect to receive if you owned this investment over an extended period of time. You can derive such a summary figure by computing the mean rate of return for this investment over some period of time.

Alternatively, you might want to evaluate a portfolio of investments that may include similar investments (e.g., all stocks, or all bonds) or a combination of investments (e.g., stocks, bonds, and real estate). In this instance, you would calculate the mean rate of return for this portfolio of investments for an individual year or for a number of years.

SINGLE INVESTMENT   Given a set of annual rates of return (HPYs) for an individual investment, there are two summary measures of return performance: the arithmetic mean return and the geometric mean return. To find the **arithmetic mean (AM),** the sum (Σ) of annual yields is divided by the number of years (n) as follows:

$$AM = \Sigma HPY/n$$

where:

$\Sigma\textbf{HPY}$ = the sum of annual holding period yields

An alternative computation, the **geometric mean (GM),** is the nth root of the product of the HPRs for n years.

$$GM = (\Pi HPR)^{1/n} - 1$$

---

[2] To check that you understand the calculations, determine the annual HPY for a 3-year HPR of 1.50. (Answer: 14.47 percent.) Compute the annual HPY for a 3-month HPR of 1.06. (Answer: 26.25 percent.)

where:

ΠHPR = the product of the annual holding period returns as follows:

$$(HPR_1) \times (HPR_2) \times \ldots \times (HPR_n)$$

To illustrate these alternatives, consider an investment with the following data:

Year	Beginning Value	Ending Value	HPR	HPY
1	100.0	115.0	1.15	0.15
2	115.0	138.0	1.20	0.20
3	138.0	110.4	0.80	−0.20

$$
\begin{aligned}
AM &= [(.15) + (.20) + (-.20)]/3 \\
&= 0.15/3 \\
&= 0.05 = 5\% \\
GM &= [(1.15) \times (1.20) \times (0.80)]^{1/3} - 1 \\
&= (1.104)^{1/3} - 1 \\
&= 1.03353 - 1 \\
&= 0.03353 = 3.353\%
\end{aligned}
$$

Investors are typically concerned with long-term performance when comparing alternative investments. GM is considered to be a superior measure of the long-term mean rate of return because it indicates the compound annual rate of return based on the ending value of the investment versus its beginning value.[3] Specifically, using the prior example, if we compounded 3.353 percent for 3 years, $(1.03353)^3$, we would get an ending wealth value of 1.104.

The geometric mean of annual rates of return for an asset or portfolio of assets is also referred to as the time-weighted rate of return (TWRR). As will be discussed in the chapter on the evaluation of portfolio performance (Chapter 27), TWRR is generally considered to be the appropriate measure of return performance.

Although the arithmetic average provides a good indication of the expected rate of return for an investment during a future individual year, it is biased upward if you attempt to measure an asset's long-term performance. This is very obvious for a volatile security. Consider, for example, a security that increases in price from $50 to $100 during year 1 and drops back to $50 during year 2. The annual HPYs would be:

Year	Beginning Value	Ending Value	HPR	HPY
1	50	100	2.00	1.00
2	100	50	0.50	−0.50

[3] Note that the GM is the same whether you compute the geometric mean of the individual annual holding period yields or the annual HPY for a 3-year period, comparing the ending value to the beginning value, as discussed earlier under annual HPY for a multiperiod case.

This would give an arithmetic mean rate of return of:

$$[(1.00) + (-0.50)]/2 = 50/2$$
$$= 0.25 = 25\%$$

This investment brought no change in wealth over the two-year period and therefore no return, yet the arithmetic mean rate of return is computed to be 25 percent.

The geometric mean rate of return would be:

$$(2.00 \times 0.50)^{1/2} - 1 = (1.00)^{1/2} - 1$$
$$= 1.00 - 1 = 0\%$$

This answer of a 0 percent rate of return accurately measures the fact that there was no change in wealth from this investment.

When rates of return are the same for all years, the geometric mean will be equal to the arithmetic mean. If the rates of return vary over the years, the geometric mean will be lower than the arithmetic mean. The difference between the two mean values will depend on the year-to-year changes in the rates of return. Larger annual changes in the rates of return, that is, more volatility in annual returns, will result in a greater difference between the alternative mean values. This relationship will be demonstrated in Chapter 3.

An awareness of both methods of computing mean rates of return is important because published accounts of long-term investment performance or descriptions of financial research will use both the AM and the GM as measures of average historical returns. Also, both will be used throughout this book.

A PORTFOLIO OF INVESTMENTS   The mean historical rate of return (HPY) for a portfolio of investments is measured as the weighted average of the HPYs for the individual investments in the portfolio, or the overall change in value of the original portfolio. The weights used in computing the averages are the relative *beginning* market values for each investment; this is referred to as dollar-weighted or value-weighted mean rate of return. This technique is demonstrated by the examples in Table 1.1. As shown, the HPY is the same (9.5 percent) whether you compute the weighted average return using the market value weights or if you compute the overall change in the total value of the portfolio.

The purpose of this section has been to help you understand how you can properly measure the historical rates of return on alternative investments in order to compare them.

TABLE 1.1   **COMPUTATION OF HOLDING PERIOD YIELD FOR A PORTFOLIO**

Investment	Number of Shares	Beginning Price	Beginning Market Value	Ending Price	Ending Market Value	HPR	HPY	Market Weight	Weighted HPY
A	100,000	$10	$ 1,000,000	$12	$ 1,200,000	1.20	20%	0.05	0.01
B	200,000	20	4,000,000	21	4,200,000	1.05	5	0.20	0.01
C	500,000	30	15,000,000	33	16,500,000	1.10	10	0.75	0.075
Total			$20,000,000		$21,900,000				.095

$$HPR = \frac{21,900,000}{20,000,000} = 1.095$$

$$HPY = 1.095 - 1 = .095$$
$$= 9.5\%$$

Although the analysis of historical performance is very useful, selecting investments for your portfolio requires you to predict the rates of return you *expect* to prevail. The next section discusses how you would derive such estimates of expected rates of return. We will also recognize that there is great uncertainty regarding these future expectations, and we will discuss how one measures this uncertainty that is referred to as the risk of an investment.

CALCULATING
EXPECTED RATES
OF RETURN

Risk is the uncertainty that an investment will earn its expected rate of return. In the examples in the prior section, we examined *realized* historical rates of return. In contrast, an investor who is evaluating a future investment alternative expects or anticipates a certain rate of return. The investor might say that he or she *expects* the investment will provide a rate of return of 10 percent, but this is really the investor's most likely estimate, also referred to as a *point estimate*. Pressed further, the investor would probably acknowledge the uncertainty of this point estimate return and admit the possibility that, under certain conditions, the annual rate of return on this investment might go as low as −10 percent or as high as 25 percent. The point is, the specification of a larger range of possible returns from an investment reflects the investor's uncertainty regarding what the actual return will be. Therefore, a larger range of expected returns makes the investment riskier.

An investor determines how certain the expected rate of return on an investment is by analyzing estimates of expected returns. To do this, the investor assigns probability values to all *possible* returns. These probability values range from zero, which means no chance of the return, to 1, which indicates complete certainty that the investment will provide the estimated rate of return. These probabilities are typically subjective estimates based on the historical performance of the investment or similar investments modified by the investor's expectations for the future. For example, an investor may know that about 30 percent of the time the rate of return on this particular investment was 10 percent. Using this information, along with future expectations regarding the economy, one can derive an estimate of what might happen in the future.

The *expected* return from an investment is defined as:

$$\text{Expected Return} = \sum_{i=1}^{n} (\text{Probability of Return}) \times (\text{Possible Return})$$

$$E(R_i) = [(P_1)(R_1) + (P_2)(R_2) + (P_3)(R_3) + \ldots + (P_nR_n)]$$

$$E(R_i) = \sum_{i=1}^{n} (P_i)(R_i)$$

Let us begin our analysis of the effect of risk with an example of perfect certainty wherein the investor is absolutely certain of a return of 5 percent. Figure 1.1 illustrates this situation.

Perfect certainty allows only one possible return, and the probability of receiving that return is 1.0. Few investments provide certain returns. In the case of perfect certainty, there is only one value for P_iR_i:

$$E(R_i) = (1.0)(0.05) = 0.05$$

In an alternative scenario, suppose an investor believed an investment could provide several different rates of return depending on different possible economic conditions. As an example, in a strong economic environment with high corporate profits and little or no

FIGURE 1.1

PROBABILITY DISTRIBUTION FOR RISK-FREE INVESTMENT

inflation, the investor might expect the rate of return on common stocks during the next year to reach as high as 20 percent. In contrast, if there is an economic decline with a higher-than-average rate of inflation, the investor might expect the rate of return on common stocks during the next year to be −20 percent. Finally, with no major change in the economic environment, the rate of return during next year would probably approach the long-run average of 10 percent.

The investor might estimate probabilities for each of these economic scenarios based on past experience and the current outlook as follows:

Economic Conditions	Probability	Rate of Return
Strong economy, no inflation	0.15	0.20
Weak economy, above average inflation	0.15	−0.20
No major change in the economy	0.70	0.10

This set of potential outcomes can be visualized as shown in Figure 1.2.

The computation of the expected rate of return [$E(R_i)$] is as follows:

$$E(R_i) = [(0.15)(0.20)] + [(0.15)(-0.20)] + [(0.70)(0.10)]$$
$$= 0.07$$

Obviously, the investor is more uncertain about the expected return from this investment than about the return from the prior investment with its single possible return.

A third example is an investment with ten possible outcomes ranging from −40 percent to 50 percent with the same probability for each rate of return. A graph of this set of expectations is shown in Figure 1.3. In this case, there are numerous outcomes from a wide range of possibilities. The expected rate of return [$E(R_i)$] for this investment would be:

$$E(R_i) = (0.10)(-0.40) + (0.10)(-0.30) + (0.10)(-0.20) + (0.10)(-0.10) + (0.10)(0.0)$$
$$+ (0.10)(0.10) + (0.10)(0.20) + (0.10)(0.30) + (0.10)(0.40) + (0.10)(0.50)$$
$$= (-0.04) + (-0.03) + (-0.02) + (-0.01) + (0.00) + (0.01) + (0.02) + (0.03)$$
$$+ (0.04) + (0.05)$$
$$= 0.05$$

The *expected* rate of return for this investment is the same as the certain return discussed in the first example, but in this case, the investor is highly uncertain about the *actual* rate of return. This would be considered a risky investment because of that uncertainty. We would anticipate that an investor—faced with the choice between this risky investment and the certain case—would select the certain alternative. This expectation is based on the belief

---

FIGURE 1.2

PROBABILITY DISTRIBUTION FOR RISKY INVESTMENT WITH THREE POSSIBLE RATES OF RETURN

FIGURE 1.3

PROBABILITY DISTRIBUTION FOR RISKY INVESTMENT WITH TEN POSSIBLE RATES OF RETURN

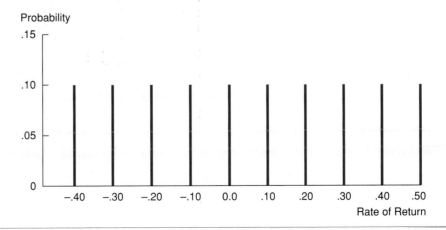

that most investors are **risk averse,** which means that if everything else is the same, they will select the investment with less uncertainty.

MEASURING THE RISK
OF EXPECTED RATES
OF RETURN

We have shown that we can calculate the expected rate of return and evaluate the uncertainty, or risk, of an investment by identifying the range of possible returns from that investment and assigning each possible return a weight based on the probability that it will occur. Although the graphs help us visualize the dispersion of possible returns, most investors want to quantify this dispersion using statistical techniques. These statistical measures allow you to compare the return and risk measures for alternative investments directly. Two possible measures of risk (uncertainty) have received support in theoretical work on portfolio theory: the *variance* and the *standard deviation* of the estimated distribution of expected returns.

In this section, we demonstrate how variance and standard deviation measure the dispersion of possible rates of return around the expected rate of return. We will work with the examples discussed earlier. The formula for variance is as follows:

$$\text{Variance } (\sigma^2) = \sum_{i=1}^{n} (\text{Probability}) \left(\begin{array}{c} \text{Possible} \\ \text{Return} \end{array} - \begin{array}{c} \text{Expected} \\ \text{Return} \end{array} \right)^2$$

$$= \sum_{i=1}^{n} (P_i)[R_i - E(R_i)]^2$$

VARIANCE   The larger the **variance** for an expected rate of return, the greater the dispersion of expected returns and the greater the uncertainty, or risk, of the investment. The variance for the perfect-certainty example would be:

$$(\sigma^2) = \sum_{i=1}^{n} P_i[R_i - E(R_i)]^2$$

$$= 1.0(0.05 - 0.05)^2 = 1.0(0.0) = 0$$

Note that in perfect certainty, there is *no variance of return* because there is no deviation from expectations, and therefore *no risk,* or *uncertainty.* The variance for the second example would be:

$$(\sigma^2) = \sum_{i=1}^{n} P_i[R_i - E(R_i)]^2$$

$$= [(0.15)(0.20 - 0.07)^2 + (0.15)(-0.20 - 0.07)^2 + (0.70)(0.10 - 0.07)^2]$$
$$= [0.010935 + 0.002535 + 0.00063]$$
$$= .0141$$

STANDARD DEVIATION   The **standard deviation** is the square root of the variance:

$$\text{Standard Deviation} = \sqrt{\sum_{i=1}^{n} P_i[R_i - E(R_i)]^2}$$

For the second example, the standard deviation would be:

$$\sigma = \sqrt{0.0141}$$
$$= 0.11874$$

A RELATIVE MEASURE OF RISK   In some cases, an unadjusted variance or standard deviation can be misleading. If conditions are not similar, that is, if there are major differences in the expected rates of return, it is necessary to use a measure of *relative variability* to indicate risk per unit of expected return. A relative measure of risk that is widely used is the **coefficient of variation,** which is equal to:

$$\text{Coefficient of Variation (CV)} = \frac{\text{Standard Deviation of Returns}}{\text{Expected Rate of Return}}$$

$$= \frac{\sigma_i}{E(R)}$$

The CV for the example above would be:

$$CV = \frac{0.11874}{0.07000}$$

$$= 1.696$$

This measure of relative variability and risk is used by financial analysts to compare alternative investments with very different rates of return and standard deviations of returns. As an illustration, consider the following two investments:

	Investment A	Investment B
Expected Return	.07	.12
Standard Deviation	.05	.07

Comparing absolute measures of risk, investment B appears to be riskier because it has a standard deviation of 7 percent versus 5 percent for investment A. In contrast, the CV figures show that investment B has less risk per unit of return as follows:

$$CV_A = \frac{0.05}{0.07} = 0.714$$

$$CV_B = \frac{0.07}{0.12} = 0.583$$

RISK MEASURES FOR HISTORICAL RETURNS   To measure the risk for a series of historical rates of returns, we use the same measures as for expected returns (variance and standard deviation) except that we consider the historical holding period yields (HPY) as follows:

$$\sigma^2 = \sum_{i=1}^{n} [HPY_i - E(HPY)]^2/n$$

where:

σ^2 = **the variance of the series**
HPY_i = **the holding period yield during period** *i*
$E(HPY)$ = **the expected value of the holding period yield that is equal to the arithmetic mean of the series**
n = **the number of observations**

The standard deviation is the square root of the variance. Both measures indicate how much the individual observations over time deviated from the expected value of the series. An example computation is contained in the appendix to this chapter. As we will see in subsequent chapters where we present historical rates of return for alternative asset classes, presenting the standard deviation as a measure of risk for the series is fairly common. In some cases, the coefficient of variation for a series is also included.

DETERMINING REQUIRED RATES OF RETURN

In this section, we continue our consideration of factors that you must consider when selecting securities for an investment portfolio. You will recall that this selection process involves finding securities that provide a rate of return that compensates you for: (1) the time value of money during the period of investment, (2) the expected rate of inflation during the period, and (3) the risk involved.

The summation of these three components is called the *required rate of return*. This is the minimum rate of return that you should accept from an investment to compensate you for deferring consumption. Because of the importance of the required rate of return to the total investment selection process, this section contains a discussion of the three components and what influences each of them.

The analysis and estimation of the required rate of return for an investment alternative is complicated by the behavior of market rates over time. First, a wide range of rates are available for alternative investments at any time. Second, the rates of return on specific assets change dramatically over time. Third, the difference between the rates available (i.e., the spread) on different assets changes over time.

The yield data in Table 1.2 for alternative bonds demonstrates these three characteristics. First, even though all of these securities have promised returns based on bond contracts, the promised annual yields during any year differ substantially. As an example, during 1993 the average yields on alternative assets ranged from 3.33 percent on T-bills to 7.93 percent for Baa corporate bonds. Second, the changes in yields for a specific asset are shown by the 3-month Treasury bill rate that went from 8.11 percent in 1989 down to 3.33 percent in 1993. Third, an example of a change in the difference between yields over time (referred to as a yield spread) is shown by the Baa–Aaa spread. The yield spread in 1988 was 112 basis points (10.83 − 9.71), but it was only 16 basis points in 1993 (7.93 − 7.77). (A basis point is 1/100 of a percent.)

Because differences in yields result from the riskiness of each investment, you must understand the risk factors that affect the required rates of return and include them in your assessment of investment opportunities. The required returns on all investments change over time, and large differences separate individual investments. Therefore, you must be aware of the several components that determine the required rate of return, starting with the risk-free rate. The discussion in this chapter considers the three components and briefly

TABLE 1.2	PROMISED YIELDS ON ALTERNATIVE BONDS							
Type of Bond	1988	1989	1990	1991	1992	1993	1994	1995
U.S. government 3-month Treasury bills	6.67%	8.11%	7.50%	5.38%	3.43%	3.33%	4.25%	5.49%
U.S. government long-term bonds	8.98	8.58	8.74	8.16	7.52	6.59	7.37	6.93
Aaa corporate bonds	9.71	9.26	9.32	8.77	8.14	7.77	7.97	7.59
Baa corporate bonds	10.83	10.18	10.36	9.80	8.98	7.93	8.63	7.83

Source: *Federal Reserve Bulletin*, various issues.

discusses what affects these components. The presentation in Chapter 13 on valuation theory discusses the factors that affect these components in greater detail.

THE REAL RISK-FREE RATE

The **real risk-free rate (RFR)** is the basic interest rate, assuming no inflation and no uncertainty about future flows. An investor in an inflation-free economy who knew with certainty what cash flows he or she would receive at what time would demand the real risk-free rate on an investment. Earlier we called this the *pure time value of money,* because the only sacrifice the investor made was deferring the use of the money for a period of time. This real risk-free rate of interest is the price charged for the certain exchange between current goods and future goods.

Two factors, one subjective and one objective, influence this exchange price. The subjective factor is the *time preference* of individuals for the consumption of income. When individuals give up $100 of consumption this year, how much consumption do they want a year from now to compensate for that sacrifice? The strength of the human desire for current consumption influences the rate of compensation required. Time preferences vary among individuals, and the market creates a composite rate that includes the preferences of all investors. This composite rate changes gradually over time because it is influenced by all the investors in the economy whose changes in preferences may offset one another.

The objective factor that influences the real risk-free rate is the set of *investment opportunities* available in the economy. The investment opportunities are determined in turn by the long-run *real growth rate* of the economy. When an economy is growing rapidly, there are more and better opportunities to invest funds and experience positive rates of return. A change in the economy's long-run real growth rate causes a change in all investment opportunities and a change in the required rates of return on all investments. Just as investors supplying capital should demand a higher rate of return when real growth is higher, those looking for funds to invest should be willing and able to pay a higher rate because of the higher growth rate. Thus, a *positive* relationship exists between the real growth rate in the economy and the real RFR.

FACTORS INFLUENCING THE NOMINAL RISK-FREE RATE

Earlier, we observed that an investor would be willing to forgo current consumption to increase future consumption at a rate of exchange called the *risk-free rate of interest*. This rate of exchange was measured in real terms because the investor wanted to increase the consumption of actual goods and services rather than consuming the same amount that had cost more money. Therefore, when we discuss rates of interest, we need to differentiate between real rates of interest that adjust for changes in the general price level, as opposed to *nominal* rates of interest that are stated in money terms. That is, nominal rates of interest are determined not only by real rates of interest, but also by factors that will affect the nominal rate of interest that prevails in the market.

Investors view T-bills as a prime example of a default-free investment because the government has unlimited ability to derive income from taxes or the creation of money from which to pay interest. Therefore, rates on T-bills should change only gradually. In fact, the data in Table 1.3 show a very erratic pattern. Specifically, T-bill rates were below 5 percent in 1976, and increased to over 14 percent in 1981 before declining to less than 6 percent in 1986 and 3.33 percent in 1993. In sum, T-bill rates almost tripled in 5 years and then declined by about 75 percent in 12 years. Clearly, the nominal rate of interest on a default-free investment is not stable in the long run or the short run, even though the underlying determinants of the real RFR are quite stable. The point is, two other factors influence the *nominal* risk-free rate: (1) the relative ease or tightness in the capital markets, and (2) the expected rate of inflation.

| TABLE 1.3 | THE 3-MONTH TREASURY BILL YIELDS AND RATES OF INFLATION |

Year	3-Month T-Bills	Rate of Inflation	Year	3-Month T-Bills	Rate of Inflation
1976	4.98%	5.80%	1986	5.98%	1.10%
1977	5.27	6.50	1987	5.78	4.40
1978	7.19	7.70	1988	6.67	4.40
1979	10.07	11.30	1989	8.11	4.60
1980	11.43	7.70	1990	7.50	6.10
1981	14.03	10.40	1991	5.38	3.10
1982	10.61	6.10	1992	3.43	2.90
1983	8.61	3.20	1993	3.33	2.75
1984	9.52	4.00	1994	4.25	2.67
1985	7.48	3.80	1995	5.49	2.54

Source: *Federal Reserve Bulletin,* various issues; *Economic Report of the President,* various issues.

CONDITIONS IN THE CAPITAL MARKET   You will recall from prior courses in economics and finance that the purpose of capital markets is to bring together investors who want to invest savings with companies or governments who need capital to expand or to finance budget deficits. The cost of funds at any time (the interest rate) is the price that equates the current supply and demand for capital. A change in the relative ease or tightness in the capital market is a short-run phenomenon caused by a temporary disequilibrium in the supply and demand of capital.

As an example, disequilibrium could be caused by an unexpected change in monetary policy (e.g., a change in the growth rate of the money supply) or fiscal policy (e.g., a change in the federal deficit). Such a change in monetary policy or fiscal policy will produce a change in the nominal risk-free rate of interest, but the change should be short-lived because in the longer run, the higher or lower interest rates will affect capital supply and demand. As an example, a decrease in the growth rate of the money supply (a tightening in monetary policy) will reduce the supply of capital and increase interest rates. In turn, this increase in rates will cause an increase in the supply due to savings and a decrease in the demand for capital by corporations or individuals. These changes will bring rates back to the long-run equilibrium, which is based on the long-run growth rate of the economy.

EXPECTED RATE OF INFLATION   Previously it was noted that, if investors expected the price level to increase during the investment period, they would require the rate of return to include compensation for the inflation rate. Assume that you require a 4 percent real rate of return on a risk-free investment, but you expect prices to increase by 3 percent during the investment period. In this case, you should increase your required rate of return by this expected rate of inflation to about 7 percent $[(1.04 \times 1.03) - 1]$. If you do not increase your required return, the $104 you receive at the end of the year will represent a real return of only 1 percent, not 4 percent. Because prices have increased by 3 percent during the year, what previously cost $100 now costs $103, so you can consume only about 1 percent more at the end of the year $[(\$104/103) - 1]$. If you had required a 7.12 percent nominal return, your real consumption could have increased by 4 percent $[(\$107.12/103) - 1]$. Therefore, an investor's nominal required rate of return on a risk-free investment should be:

$$\text{Nominal RFR} = (1 + \text{Real RFR})(1 + \text{Expected Rate of Inflation}) \quad 1$$

Rearranging the formula, you can calculate the real rate of return on a risk-free investment as follows:

$$\text{Real RFR} = \left[\frac{(1 + \text{Nominal Risk-Free Rate of Return})}{(1 + \text{Rate of Inflation})} \right] - 1$$

To see how this works, assume that the nominal return on U.S. government T-bills was 9 percent during a given year, when the rate of inflation was 5 percent. In this instance, the real risk-free rate of return on these T-bills was 3.8 percent, as follows:

$$\text{Real RFR} = [(1 + 0.09)/(1 + 0.05)] - 1$$
$$= 1.038 - 1$$
$$= 0.038 = 3.8\%$$

This discussion makes it clear that the nominal rate of interest on a risk-free investment is not a good estimate of the real RFR, because the nominal rate can change dramatically in the short run in reaction to temporary ease or tightness in the capital market or because of changes in the expected rate of inflation. The significant changes in the average yield on T-bills shown in Table 1.3 were generally caused by large changes in the expected rate of inflation during this period. Table 1.3 also shows the volatility of annual rates of inflation. The time-series plot in Figure 1.4 shows a strong, but not perfect relationship between the two series. The lack of perfect correlation is because the T-bill yield series is the average

---

FIGURE 1.4   **THE 3-MONTH T-BILL YIELDS AND RATES OF INFLATION**

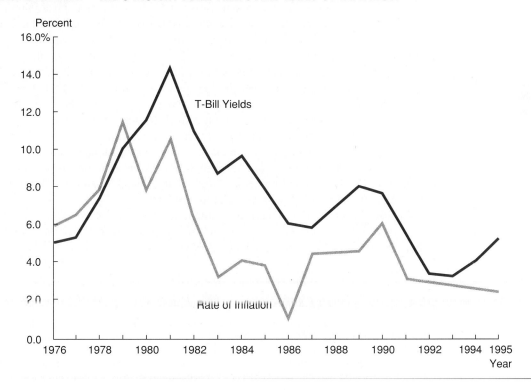

for the year, while the rate of inflation is the actual rate that is derived at the end of the year. It appears that investors are not perfect forecasters of inflation; however, they are apparently using their imperfect forecasts.

THE COMMON EFFECT   All the factors discussed thus far regarding the required rate of return affect all investments equally. Whether the investment is in stocks, bonds, real estate, or machine tools, if the expected rate of inflation increases from 2 percent to 6 percent, the investor's required return for *all* investments should increase by 4 percent. Similarly, if there is a decline in the expected real growth rate of the economy that causes a decline in the real RFR of 1 percent, then the required return on all investments should decline by 1 percent.

RISK PREMIUM   A risk-free investment was defined as one for which the investor is certain of the amount and timing of the expected returns. The returns from most investments do not fit this pattern. An investor typically is not completely certain of the income to be received or when it will be received. Investments can range in uncertainty from basically risk-free securities such as T-bills to highly speculative investments such as the common stock of small companies engaged in high-risk enterprises.

Most investors require higher rates of return on investments to compensate for any uncertainty. This increase in the required rate of return over the nominal risk-free rate is the **risk premium.** Although the required risk premium represents a composite of all uncertainty, it is possible to consider several fundamental sources of uncertainty. In this section we identify and discuss briefly the major fundamental sources, including business risk, financial risk (leverage), liquidity risk, exchange rate risk, and country risk.

Business risk is the uncertainty of income flows caused by the nature of a firm's business. The more uncertain the income flows of the firm, the more uncertain the income flows to the investor. Therefore, the investor will demand a risk premium that is based on the uncertainty caused by the basic business of the firm. As an example, a retail food company would typically experience very stable sales and earnings growth over time and would have low business risk compared to a firm in the auto industry, where sales and earnings fluctuate substantially over the business cycle, implying high business risk.[4]

Financial risk is the uncertainty introduced by the method by which the firm finances its investments. If a firm uses only common stock to finance investments, it incurs only business risk. If a firm borrows money to finance investments, it must pay fixed financing charges (in the form of interest to creditors) prior to providing income to the common stockholders, so the uncertainty of returns to the equity investor increases. This increase in uncertainty because of fixed-cost financing is called *financial risk* or *financial leverage,* and causes an increase in the stock's risk premium.[5]

Liquidity risk is the uncertainty introduced by the secondary market for an investment.[6] When an investor acquires an asset, he or she expects that the investment will mature (as with a bond) or that it will be salable to someone else. In either case, the investor

---

[4] In Chapters 18 and 19, we discuss factors that contribute to business risk—sales volatility and operating leverage. For a discussion of business risk, see Eugene F. Brigham and Louis C. Gapenski, *Financial Management: Theory and Practice,* 8th ed. (Ft. Worth, TX: The Dryden Press, 1997), Chapter 13.

[5] For a discussion of financial leverage, see Eugene F. Brigham, *Fundamentals of Financial Management,* 7th ed. (Ft. Worth, TX: The Dryden Press, 1995), 441–442.

[6] You will recall from prior courses that the overall capital market is composed of the primary market and the secondary market. Securities are initially sold in the primary market and then all subsequent transactions take place in the secondary market. These concepts are discussed in Chapter 4.

expects to be able to convert the security into cash and use the proceeds for current consumption or other investments. The more difficult it is to make this conversion, the greater the liquidity risk. An investor must consider two questions about liquidity when assessing the liquidity risk of an investment: (1) How long will it take to convert the investment into cash? (2) How certain is the price to be received? Similar uncertainty faces an investor who wants to acquire an asset: How long will it take to acquire the asset? How uncertain is the price to be paid?

Uncertainty regarding how fast an investment can be bought or sold, or the existence of uncertainty about its price, increases liquidity risk.

A U.S. government Treasury bill has almost no liquidity risk because it can be bought or sold in minutes at a price almost identical to the quoted price. In contrast, examples of illiquid investments include a work of art, an antique, or a parcel of real estate in a remote area. Such an investment may require a long time to find a buyer, and the selling price could vary substantially from expectations. Investors will increase their required rates of return to compensate for liquidity risk. This could be a significant consideration when investing in foreign securities depending on the country and the liquidity of its stock and bond markets.

Exchange rate risk is the uncertainty of returns to an investor who acquires securities in a currency different from his or her own. The likelihood of incurring this risk is becoming greater as investors buy and sell assets around the world, as opposed to only assets within their own countries. A U.S. investor who buys Japanese stock denominated in yen must consider not only the uncertainty of the return in yen, but also any change in the exchange value of the yen relative to the U.S. dollar. That is, in addition to the foreign firm's business and financial risk and the security's liquidity risk, the investor must consider the additional uncertainty of the return when the return in yen must be converted to U.S. dollars.

As an example of exchange rate risk, assume that you buy 100 shares of Mitsubishi Electric at 1,050 yen when the exchange rate is 100 yen to the dollar. The dollar cost of this investment would be about $10.50 per share (1,050/100). A year later, you sell the 100 shares at 1,200 yen when the exchange rate is 110 yen to the dollar. When you calculate the HPY in yen, you find the stock has increased in value by about 14 percent (1,200/1,050), but this is the HPY for a Japanese investor. A U.S. investor receives a much lower rate of return because during this time period the yen has weakened relative to the dollar by about 10 percent (i.e., it requires more yen to buy a dollar—110 versus 100). At the new exchange rate, the stock is worth $10.91 per share (1,200/110). Therefore, the return to you as a U.S. investor would be only about 4 percent ($10.91/$10.50) versus 14 percent for the Japanese investor. Clearly, the exchange rate could have gone in the other direction, the dollar weakening against the yen. In this case, as a U.S. investor you would have experienced the 14 percent return measured in yen as well as a gain from the exchange rate change.

The more volatile the exchange rate between two countries, the more uncertain you would be regarding the exchange rate, the greater the exchange rate risk, and the larger would be the exchange rate risk premium you would require.[7]

Country risk, also called *political risk,* is the uncertainty of returns caused by the possibility of a major change in the political or economic environment of a country. The

---

[7] An article that examines the pricing of exchange rate risk in the U.S. market is Philippe Jorion, "The Pricing of Exchange Rate Risk in the Stock Market," *Journal of Financial and Quantitative Analysis* 26, no. 3 (September 1991): 363–376.

United States is acknowledged to have the smallest country risk in the world because its political and economic systems are the most stable. Nations with high country risk include Russia, because of its political and economic instability since 1992, and China, as a result of unrest in 1989. On a single day, June 5, 1989, the Hong Kong stock market declined over 20 percent following student–military confrontations in China.[8] Individuals who invest in countries that have unstable political–economic systems must add a country risk premium when determining their required rates of return.

When investing globally, investors must consider these additional uncertainties: How liquid are the secondary markets for stocks and bonds in the country? Are any of the country's securities traded on major stock exchanges in the United States, London, Tokyo, or Germany? What will happen to exchange rates during the investment period? What is the probability of a political or economic change that will adversely affect your rate of return? Exchange rate risk and country risk differ among countries. A good measure of exchange rate risk would be the absolute variability of the exchange rate relative to a composite exchange rate. The analysis of country risk is much more subjective and must be based on the history and current environment of the country.

This discussion of risk components can be considered a security's *fundamental risk* because it deals with the intrinsic factors that should affect a security's standard deviation of returns over time. In subsequent discussion, the standard deviation of returns is referred to as a measure of the stock's *total risk*.

$$\text{Risk Premium} = f(\text{Business Risk, Financial Risk, Liquidity Risk,}$$
$$\text{Exchange Rate Risk, Country Risk})$$

RISK PREMIUM AND PORTFOLIO THEORY

An alternative view of risk has been derived from extensive work in portfolio theory and capital market theory by Markowitz, Sharpe, and others.[9] These theories are dealt with in greater detail in Chapters 8 and 9, but their impact on the risk premium should be mentioned briefly at this point. Markowitz and Sharpe indicated that investors should use an *external market* measure of risk. Under a specified set of assumptions, all rational, profit-maximizing investors want to hold a completely diversified market portfolio of risky assets, and they borrow or lend to arrive at a risk level that is consistent with their risk preferences. Under these conditions, the relevant risk measure for an individual asset is its *comovement with the market portfolio*. This comovement, which is measured by an asset's covariance with the market portfolio, is referred to as an asset's **systematic risk.** This is the portion of an individual asset's total variance attributable to the variability of the total market portfolio. In addition, individual assets will have variance that is not related to the market portfolio but is due to unique features. This nonmarket (unique) variance is called *unsystematic risk* and is generally considered to be unimportant because it is eliminated in a large, diversified portfolio. Therefore, under these assumptions, *the risk premium for an*

---

[8] Russell Todd and Robert Sherbin, "Hong Kong Stocks Plunge 22% on China Unrest; Other Asia Markets Fall; London Shares Drop," *Wall Street Journal,* June 6, 1989, C10. This country risk for Hong Kong stocks related to events in China is because Hong Kong will revert back to China in 1997. During 1993–1995, the uncertainty continued because of political conflicts between the British Governor of Hong Kong and Chinese officials.

[9] These works include Harry Markowitz, "Portfolio Selection," *Journal of Finance* 7, no. 1 (March 1952): 77–91; Harry Markowitz, *Portfolio Selection—Efficient Diversification of Investments* (New Haven, CT: Yale University Press, 1959); and William F. Sharpe, "Capital Asset Prices: A Theory of Market Equilibrium Under Conditions of Risk," *Journal of Finance* 19, no. 3 (September 1964): 425–442.

individual earning asset is a function of the asset's systematic risk with the aggregate market portfolio of risky assets. The measure of an asset's systematic risk is referred to as its *beta:*

$$\text{Risk Premium} = f(\text{Systematic Market Risk})$$

FUNDAMENTAL RISK VERSUS SYSTEMATIC RISK

Some might expect a conflict between the market measure of risk (systematic risk) and the fundamental determinants of risk (business risk, etc.). A number of studies have examined the relationship between the market measure of risk (systematic risk) and accounting variables used to measure the fundamental risk factors such as business risk, financial risk, and liquidity risk. The authors have concluded that *there is generally a significant relationship between the market measure of risk and the fundamental measures of risk.*[10] Therefore, the two measures of risk can be complementary. This consistency seems reasonable because the market measure of the risk should reflect the fundamental risk characteristics of the asset. For example, a firm that has high business risk and financial risk might have an above-average beta. At the same time, as we will discuss in Chapter 20, a firm that has a high level of fundamental risk and a large standard deviation (i.e., high total risk) can have a lower level of systematic risk because its variability of earnings and stock price is not related to the aggregate economy or the market portfolio of risky assets. Therefore, one can specify the risk premium for an asset either as:

$$\text{Risk Premium} = f(\text{Business Risk, Financial Risk, Liquidity Risk,}$$
$$\text{Exchange Rate Risk, Country Risk})$$

or

$$\text{Risk Premium} = f(\text{Systematic Market Risk})$$

SUMMARY OF REQUIRED RATE OF RETURN

The overall required rate of return on alternative investments is determined by three variables: (1) the economy's real RFR, which is influenced by the investment opportunities in the economy (i.e., the long-run real growth rate); (2) variables that influence the nominal RFR, which include short-run ease or tightness in the capital market and the expected rate of inflation (the first two sets of variables are the same for all investments); and (3) the risk premium on the investment. In turn, this risk premium can be related to fundamental factors including business risk, financial risk, liquidity risk, exchange rate risk, and country risk, or it can be a function of the asset's systematic market risk (beta).

MEASURES AND SOURCES OF RISK   In this chapter we have examined both measures and sources of risk arising from an investment. The *measures* of risk for an investment are:

- Variance of rates of return
- Standard deviation of rates of return
- Coefficient of variation of rates of return (standard deviation/mean)
- Covariance of returns with the market portfolio (beta)

---

[10] A brief review of some of the earlier studies is contained in Donald J. Thompson II, "Sources of Systematic Risk in Common Stocks," *Journal of Business* 49, no. 2 (April 1976): 173–188. There is a further discussion of specific variables in Chapters 9 and 20.

The *sources* of risk are:

- Business risk
- Financial risk
- Liquidity risk
- Exchange rate risk
- Country risk

RELATIONSHIP BETWEEN RISK AND RETURN

Previously, we showed how to measure the risk and rates of return for alternative investments, and we discussed what determines the rates of return that investors require. This section discusses the risk–return combinations that might be available at a given point in time and illustrates the factors that cause *changes* in these combinations.

Figure 1.5 graphs the expected relationship between risk and return. It shows that investors increase their required rates of return as perceived risk (uncertainty) increases. The line that reflects the combination of risk and return available on alternative investments is referred to as the **security market line (SML).** The SML reflects the risk–return combinations available for all risky assets in the capital market at a given time. Investors select investments that are consistent with their risk preferences; some consider only low-risk investments, whereas others welcome high-risk investments.

Beginning with an initial security market line, three changes can occur. First, individual investments can change positions on the SML because of changes in the perceived risk of the investments. Second, the slope of the SML can change because of a change in the attitudes of investors toward risk; that is, investors can change the returns they require per unit of risk. Third, the SML can experience a parallel shift due to a change in the real RFR or the expected rate of inflation. These three possibilities are discussed in this section.

FIGURE 1.5   **RELATIONSHIP BETWEEN RISK AND RETURN**

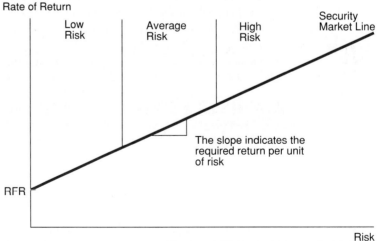

FIGURE 1.6   **CHANGES IN THE REQUIRED RATE OF RETURN DUE TO MOVEMENTS ALONG THE SML**

MOVEMENTS ALONG THE SML   Investors place alternative investments somewhere along the SML based on their perceptions of the risk of the investment. Obviously, if an investment's risk changes due to a change in one of its fundamental risk sectors (business risk, etc.), it will move along the security market line. For example, if a firm increases its financial risk by selling a large bond issue that increases its financial leverage, investors will perceive its common stock as riskier and the stock will move up the SML to a higher risk position. If this happens, investors will require a higher rate of return. As the common stock becomes riskier, it changes its position on the SML. Any change in an asset that affects its fundamental risk factors or its systematic risk (i.e., its beta) will cause the asset to move *along* the SML as shown in Figure 1.6. Note that the SML does not change, only the position of assets on the line.

CHANGES IN THE SLOPE OF THE SML   The slope of the security market line indicates the return per unit of risk required by all investors. Assuming a straight line, it is possible to select any point on the SML and compute a risk premium (RP) through the equation:

$$RP_i = R_i - RFR$$

where:

> RP_i = **risk premium for asset** *i*
> R_i = **the expected return for asset** *i*
> **RFR = the expected return on a risk-free asset**

If a point on the SML is identified as the portfolio that contains all the risky assets in the market (referred to as the *market portfolio*), it is possible to compute a *market risk premium* as follows:

$$RP_m = R_m - RFR$$

where:

> RP_m = **the risk premium on the market portfolio**
> R_m = **the expected return on the market portfolio**
> **RFR = the expected return on a risk-free asset**

This market risk premium is *not constant* because the slope of the security market line changes over time. Although we do not understand completely what causes these changes

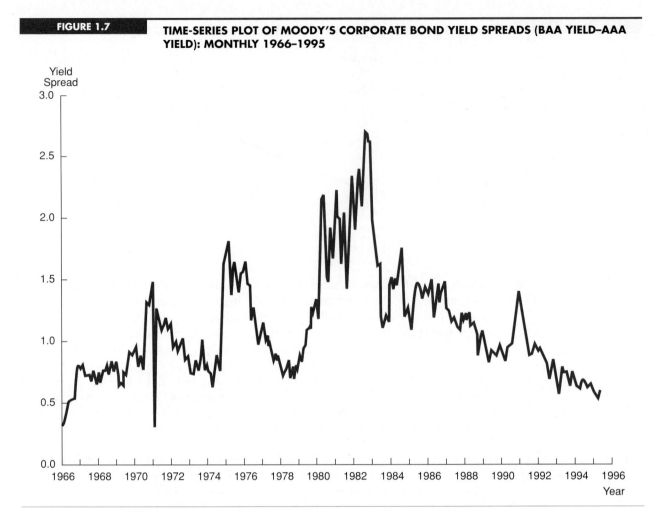

FIGURE 1.7

TIME-SERIES PLOT OF MOODY'S CORPORATE BOND YIELD SPREADS (BAA YIELD–AAA YIELD): MONTHLY 1966–1995

Source: © Moody's Investor's Services.

in the slope, we do know that there are changes in the yield differences between assets with different levels of risk even though the inherent risk differences are relatively constant.

These differences in yields are referred to as **yield spreads,** and these spreads change over time. As an example, if the yield on a portfolio of Aaa-rated bonds is 7.50 percent and the yield on a portfolio of Baa-rated bonds is 9.00 percent, we would say that the yield spread is 1.50 percent.[11] This 1.50 percent is referred to as a risk premium because the Baa-rated bond is considered to have higher credit risk, that is, greater probability of default. This Baa–Aaa yield spread is *not* constant over time. For an example of changes in a yield spread, note the substantial difference in the yield spread between Aaa-rated and Baa-rated bonds shown in Figure 1.7.

Although the underlying risk (i.e., the probability of default) for the portfolio of bonds in the Aaa-rated bond index and the Baa-rated bond index would probably not change

---

[11] Bonds are rated by rating agencies based on the credit risk of the securities, that is, the probability of default. Aaa is the top rating Moody's (a prominent rating service) gives to bonds with almost no probability of default. (Only U.S. Treasury bonds are considered to be of higher quality.) Baa is a lower rating Moody's gives to bonds of generally high quality that have some possibility of default under adverse economic conditions. These ratings are discussed in detail in Chapter 15.

FIGURE 1.8   **CHANGE IN MARKET RISK PREMIUM**

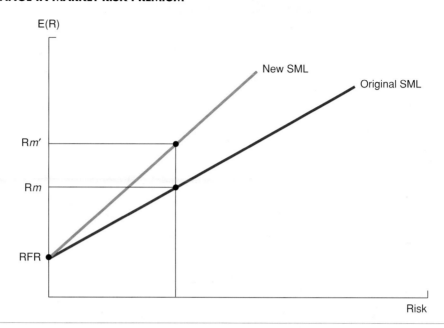

dramatically over time, it is clear from the time-series plot in Figure 1.7 that the difference in yields has experienced changes of over 100 basis points (1 percent) in a short period of time (e.g., see the increase in 1974 to 1975 and the dramatic decline in 1983 to 1984). Such a change in the yield spread during a period where there is no change in the risk characteristics of Baa bonds relative to Aaa bonds would imply a change in the market risk premium. Specifically, although the risk levels of the bonds remain relatively constant, investors have changed the yield spreads they demand to accept this difference in risk.

This change in the risk premium implies a change in the slope of the security market line. Such a change is shown in Figure 1.8. The figure assumes an increase in the market risk premium, which means that there is an increase in the slope of the market line. Such a change in the slope of the SML will affect the required rate of return for all risky assets. The point is, regardless of where an investment is on the original SML, its required rate of return will increase, although its individual risk characteristics remain unchanged.

CHANGES IN CAPITAL MARKET CONDITIONS OR EXPECTED INFLATION

The graph in Figure 1.9 shows what happens to the SML when there are changes in one of the following factors: (1) expected real growth in the economy, (2) capital market conditions, or (3) the expected rate of inflation. For example, if there is an increase in expected real growth, temporary tightness in the capital market, or an increase in the expected rate of inflation, the SML will experience a parallel shift upward. The parallel shift occurs because changes in expected real growth, in capital market conditions, or in the expected rate of inflation affect all investments no matter what their levels of risk.

SUMMARY OF CHANGES IN THE REQUIRED RATE OF RETURN

The relationship between risk and the required rate of return for an investment can change in three ways:

1. A movement *along* the SML is caused by a change in the risk characteristics of a specific investment, such as a change in its business risk, its financial risk, or its systematic risk (its beta). This change affects only the individual investment.

FIGURE 1.9   **CAPITAL MARKET CONDITIONS, EXPECTED INFLATION, AND THE SECURITY MARKET LINE**

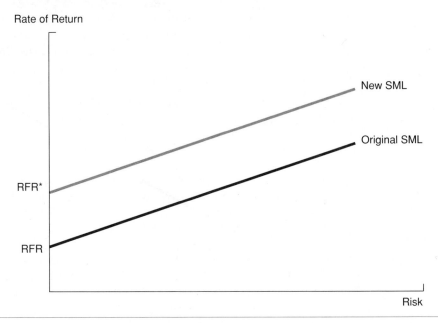

*RFR = Nominal risk-free rate.

2. A change in the *slope* of the SML occurs in response to a change in the attitudes of investors toward risk. Such a change demonstrates that investors want either higher or lower rates of return for the same risk. This is also described as a change in the market risk premium (R_m – RFR). A change in the market risk premium will affect all risky investments.

3. A *shift* in the security market line reflects a change in expected real growth, in market conditions such as ease or tightness of money, or a change in the expected rate of inflation. Again, such a change will affect all investments.

OUTLINE OF THE BOOK

As discussed earlier, Part 1 of the book provides an investment background by concentrating on why and how individuals invest, why the asset allocation decision is important and what factors affect this decision during alternative phases of your life cycle, the alternative investments that are available, the functioning of the markets for bonds and stocks, the indexes that track the performance of the major investments, and the sources of information for the investment process.

Part 2 considers four theoretical topics that are critical to the analysis and investment process. Specifically, there is a discussion of the concept of **efficient markets** and a review of the empirical evidence that supports this theory and some evidence at odds with the theory. Another major development in investment theory is **portfolio theory,** which is at the core of why investors diversify and how they should diversify. Building on this theory, several authors have developed an asset pricing theory referred to as the **capital asset pricing model,** which implies a risk measure applicable to all risky assets. There is also a consideration of an alternative asset pricing model referred to as **arbitrage pricing theory.** This is followed by a chapter on extensions and testing of these models. Finally, the past decade has witnessed explosive growth in **derivative securities,** such as options and futures that allow investors additional risk–return configurations. These instruments and markets are introduced in this section.

These important topics (efficient markets, portfolio theory, capital asset pricing models, and derivative securities) are introduced in these early chapters because they are central to the subsequent analysis and portfolio management discussion.

Part 3 delves into valuation principles and practices. We begin by discussing how to analyze financial statements and how this analysis can be applied to bonds and stocks. The following chapter contains a discussion of general valuation principles and how they are used to value stocks and bonds. Finally, there is a presentation on macroeconomic analysis and how it might be used to determine how to allocate assets in a global market environment.

Part 4 initiates the detailed analysis of investments beginning with fixed-income securities (bonds) because the valuation process for bonds is easier. Specifically, assuming that the issuer does not default, the investor receives a specified set of income flows and can concentrate on estimating the required rate of return. The first chapter deals with describing the fundamental characteristics and markets for bonds. The second chapter discusses the valuation and analysis of bonds. The final chapter considers numerous bond portfolio strategies, including several new techniques for managing a portfolio of bonds.

Part 5 emphasizes the analysis of common stocks using the top-down, fundamental approach. Specifically, we build on the macroeconomic analysis in Chapter 13 with a microvaluation of the stock market in Chapter 18. The subsequent chapters discuss industry analysis and how to examine individual companies within an industry and the stocks of these firms. In contrast to evaluating investments based on fundamental economic factors, some investors feel that the securities market is its own best predictor and, therefore, you need to examine only trends in alternative market series. This approach to investment analysis is called *technical analysis* and is considered in the fourth chapter of this section. The section concludes with a chapter on principles and techniques employed in equity portfolio management.

Besides the trend toward global markets, the other major development in capital markets has been the creation of new investment instruments. The chapters in Part 6 build on the introduction to derivatives contained in Chapter 11. Specifically, there are individual chapters on forwards and futures, stock options, and warrants and convertibles. These are followed by a chapter that considers advanced applications of these instruments.

Finally, Part 7 contains a chapter on investment companies (also known as *mutual funds*) as an alternative to direct investment. This includes a discussion of how to analyze and select a fund. The book concludes with a chapter on the evaluation of portfolio performance. This includes the selection of an appropriate benchmark and the attribution of performance for global portfolios.

In summary, the purpose of the book is to help you to understand why you invest, what investments are available to you, how you evaluate investments and make investment decisions, how you combine alternative investments into a portfolio, and how you evaluate the performance of your investment portfolio to determine if it is meeting your objectives.

Summary

The purpose of this chapter is to provide a background for subsequent chapters. To achieve that goal, we cover several topics:

- We discuss why individuals save part of their income and why they decide to invest their savings. We define *investment* as the current commitment of these savings for a period of time to derive a rate of return that compensates for the time involved, the expected rate of inflation, and the uncertainty.

- We examine ways to quantify historical return and risk to help analyze alternative investment opportunities. We consider two measures of mean return (arithmetic and geometric) and apply these to a historical series for an individual investment and to a portfolio of investments during a period of time.
- We consider the concept of uncertainty and alternative measures of risk (the variance, standard deviation, and a relative measure of risk—the coefficient of variation).
- Prior to discussing the determinants of the required rate of return for an investment, we note that the estimation of the required rate of return is complicated because the rates on individual investments change over time, because there is a wide range of rates of return available on alternative investments, and because the differences between required returns (e.g., the yield spreads) on alternative investments likewise change over time.
- We examine the specific factors that determine the required rate of return: (a) the real risk-free rate, which is based on the real rate of growth in the economy; (b) the nominal risk-free rate, which is influenced by capital market conditions and the expected rate of inflation; and (c) a risk premium, which is a function of fundamental factors such as business risk or the systematic risk of the asset relative to the market portfolio (i.e., its beta).
- We discuss the risk–return combinations available on alternative investments at a given point in time (illustrated by the SML) and the three factors that can cause changes in this relationship. First, a change in the inherent risk of an investment (i.e., its fundamental risk or market risk) will cause a movement along the SML. Second, a change in investors' attitudes toward risk will cause a change in the required return per unit of risk, that is, a change in the market risk premium. Such a change will cause a change in the slope of the SML. Finally, a change in expected real growth, in capital market conditions, or in the expected rate of inflation will cause a parallel shift of the SML.

Based on this understanding of the investment environment, you are prepared to consider the asset allocation decision. This is the subject of Chapter 2.

Questions

1. Discuss the overall purpose people have for investing. Define investment.
2. Divide a person's life from ages 20 to 70 into 10-year segments and discuss the likely saving or borrowing patterns during each of these periods.
3. *The Wall Street Journal* reported that the yield on common stocks is about 3 percent, whereas a study at the University of Chicago contends that the annual rate of return on common stocks since 1926 has averaged about 10 percent. Reconcile these statements.
4. Some financial theorists consider the variance of the distribution of expected rates of return to be a good measure of uncertainty. Discuss the reasoning behind this measure of risk and its purpose.
5. Discuss the three components of an investor's required rate of return on an investment.
6. Discuss the two major factors that determine the market nominal risk-free rate (RFR). Explain which of these factors would be more volatile over the business cycle.
7. Briefly discuss the five fundamental factors that influence the risk premium of an investment.
8. You own stock in the Gentry Company, and you read in the financial press that a recent bond offering has raised the firm's debt/equity ratio from 35 percent to 55 percent. Discuss the effect of this change on the variability of the firm's net income stream, other factors being constant. Discuss how this change would affect your required rate of return on the common stock of the Gentry Company.
9. Draw a properly labeled graph of the security market line (SML) and indicate where you would expect the following investments to fall along that line. Discuss your reasoning.
   a. Common stock of large firms
   b. U.S. government bonds
   c. United Kingdom government bonds
   d. Low-grade corporate bonds
   e. Common stock of a Japanese firm
10. Explain why you would change your nominal required rate of return if you expected the rate of inflation to go from zero (no inflation) to 5 percent. Give an example of what would happen if you did not change your required rate of return under these conditions.

11. Assume the long-run growth rate of the economy increased by 1 percent and the expected rate of inflation increased by 4 percent. What would happen to the required rates of return on government bonds and common stocks? Show graphically how the effects of these changes would differ between these alternative investments.

12. You see in *The Wall Street Journal* that the yield spread between Baa corporate bonds and Aaa corporate bonds has gone from 350 basis points (3.5 percent) to 200 basis points (2 percent). Show graphically the effect of this change in yield spread on the SML and discuss its effect on the required rate of return for common stocks.

13. Give an example of a liquid investment and an illiquid investment. Discuss why you consider each of them to be liquid or illiquid.

14. *CFA Examination III (1981)*

    As part of your portfolio planning process, it is suggested that you estimate the real long-run growth potential of the economy.

    a. Identify and explain three major determinants of the economy's real long-run growth. [5 minutes]

    b. Briefly discuss the outlook for each of these three determinants of long-term growth. Present approximate estimates for each of these components and calculate the composite real growth potential for the next 5 years. (You should provide a calculation, but emphasize the process rather than specific numbers.) [10 minutes]

Problems

1. On February 1, you bought Cheri Corporation stock for $34 a share and a year later you sold it for $39 a share. During the year you received a cash dividend of $1.50 a share. Compute your HPR and HPY on this stock investment.

2. On August 15, you purchased Computer Corporation stock at $65 a share and a year later you sold it for $61 a share. During the year, you received dividends of $3 a share. Compute your HPR and HPY on this investment.

3. At the beginning of last year, you invested $4,000 in 80 shares of the Chang Corporation. During the year, Chang paid dividends of $5 per share. At the end of the year, you sold the 80 shares for $59 a share. Compute your total HPY on these shares and indicate how much was due to the price change and how much was due to the dividend income.

4. At the beginning of 1995, you bought 100 shares of the Lauren Corporation at $30 a share. At the end of 1997, you sold the 100 shares for $55 a share. Assuming Lauren did not pay any dividends, compute your annual HPY on this investment.

5. The rates of return computed in Problems 1, 2, 3, and 4 are nominal rates of return. Assuming that the annual rate of inflation was 4 percent, compute the real rates of return on these investments. Compute the real rates of return if the inflation rate was 8 percent.

6. During the past 5 years, you owned two stocks that had the following annual rates of return:

Year	Stock T	Stock B
1	0.19	0.08
2	0.08	0.03
3	−0.12	−0.09
4	−0.03	0.02
5	0.15	0.04

a. Compute the arithmetic mean annual rate of return for each stock. Which is more desirable by this measure?

b. Compute the standard deviation of the annual rate of return for each stock. (Use Chapter 1 appendix if necessary.) By this measure, which is the preferable stock?

c. Compute the coefficient of variation for each stock. (Use the appendix if necessary.) By this relative measure of risk, which stock is preferable?

  d. Compute the geometric mean rate of return for each stock. Discuss the difference between the arithmetic mean return and the geometric mean return for each stock and relate the differences in mean return to the standard deviation of the return for each stock.

7. You are considering acquiring shares of common stock in the Light and Dry Beer Corporation. Your rate of return expectations are as follows:

Possible Rate of Return	Probability
−0.10	0.30
0.00	0.10
0.10	0.30
0.25	0.30

Compute the expected return [$E(R_i)$] on this investment.

8. A stockbroker calls you and suggests that you invest in the Cheryl Computer Company. After analyzing the firm's annual report and other material, you feel that the distribution of rates of return is as follows:

Possible Rate of Return	Probability
−0.60	0.05
−0.30	0.20
−0.10	0.10
0.20	0.30
0.40	0.20
0.80	0.15

Compute the expected return [$E(R_i)$] on this stock.

9. Without any formal computations, do you consider Light and Dry Beer in Problem 7 or Cheryl Computer in Problem 8 to present greater risk? Discuss your reasoning.

10. During the past year, you had a portfolio that contained U.S. government T-bills, long-term government bonds, and common stocks. The rates of return on each of them were as follows:

U.S. government T-bills	5.50%
U.S. government long-term bonds	7.50
U.S. common stocks	11.60

During the year, the consumer price index, which measures the rate of inflation, went from 160 to 168 (1982–1984 = 100). Compute the rate of inflation during this year. Compute the real rates of return on each of the investments in your portfolio based on the inflation rate.

11. You read in *Business Week* that a panel of economists has estimated that the long-run real growth rate of the U.S. economy over the next 5-year period will average 3 percent. In addition, a bank newsletter estimates that the average annual rate of inflation during this 5-year period will be about 4 percent. What nominal rate of return would you expect on U.S. government T-bills during this period?

12. What would your required rate of return be on common stocks if you wanted a 5 percent risk premium to own common stocks, given what you know from Problem 11? If common stock investors became more risk averse, what would happen to the required rate of return on common stocks? What would be the impact on stock prices? Draw a graph of the SML and show what would happen.

13. Assume that the consensus required rate of return on common stocks is 14 percent. In addition, you read in *Fortune* that the expected rate of inflation is 5 percent and the estimated long-term real growth rate of the economy is 3 percent. What interest rate would you expect on U.S. government T-bills? What is the approximate risk premium for common stocks implied by these data?

References

Fama, Eugene F., and Merton H. Miller. *The Theory of Finance*. New York: Holt, Rinehart and Winston, 1972.

Fisher, Irving. *The Theory of Interest*. New York: Macmillan, 1930; reprinted by Augustus M. Kelley, 1961.

Chapter 1
APPENDIX

COMPUTATION OF VARIANCE AND STANDARD DEVIATION

Variance and standard deviation are measures of how actual values differ from the expected values (arithmetic mean) for a given series of values. In this case, we want to measure how rates of return differ from the arithmetic mean value of a series. There are other measures of dispersion, but variance and standard deviation are the best known because they are used in statistics and probability theory. Variance is defined as:

$$\text{Variance } (\sigma^2) = \sum_{i=1}^{n} (\text{Probability}) (\text{Possible Return} - \text{Expected Return})^2$$

$$= \sum_{i=1}^{n} (P_i)[R_i - E(R_i)]^2$$

Consider the following example, as discussed in the chapter:

Probability of Possible Return (P_i)	Possible Return (R_i)	$P_i R_i$
0.15	0.20	0.03
0.15	−0.20	−0.03
0.70	0.10	0.07
		$\Sigma = 0.07$

This gives an expected return [$E(R_i)$] of 7 percent. The dispersion of this distribution as measured by variance is:

Probability (P_i)	Return (R_i)	$R_i - E(R_i)$	$[R_i - E(R_i)]^2$	$P_i[R_i - E(R_i)]^2$
0.15	0.20	0.13	0.0169	0.002535
0.15	−0.20	−0.27	0.0729	0.010935
0.70	0.10	0.03	0.0009	0.000630
				$\Sigma = 0.014100$

The variance (σ^2) is equal to 0.0141. The standard deviation is equal to the square root of the variance:

$$\text{Standard Deviation} = \sqrt{\sum_{i=1}^{n} P_i[R_i - E(R_i)]^2}$$

Consequently, the standard deviation for the preceding example would be:

$$\sigma = \sqrt{0.0141} = 0.11874$$

In this example, the standard deviation is approximately 11.87 percent. Therefore, you could describe this distribution as having an expected value of 7 percent and a standard deviation of 11.87 percent.

In many instances, you might want to compute the variance or standard deviation for a historical series to evaluate the past performance of the investment. Assume that you are given the following information on annual rates of return (HPY) for common stocks listed on the New York Stock Exchange (NYSE):

Year	Annual Rate of Return
19__1	0.07
19__2	0.11
19__3	−0.04
19__4	0.12
19__5	−0.06

In this case, we are not examining expected rates of return, but actual returns. Therefore, we assume equal probabilities, and the expected value (in this case the mean value, $\overline{R}$) of the series is the sum of the individual observations in the series divided by the number of observations, or 0.04 (0.20/5). The variance and standard deviation are:

Year	R_i	$R_i - \overline{R}$	$(R_i - \overline{R})^2$	
19__1	0.07	0.03	0.0009	$\sigma^2 = 0.0286/5$
19__2	0.11	0.07	0.0049	$= 0.00572$
19__3	−0.04	−0.08	0.0064	
19__4	0.12	0.08	0.0064	$\sigma = \sqrt{0.00572}$
19__5	−0.06	−0.10	0.0110	$= 0.0756$
			$\Sigma = 0.0286$	

We can interpret the performance of NYSE common stocks during this time period by saying that the average rate of return was 4 percent and the standard deviation of annual rates of return was 7.56 percent.

COEFFICIENT OF VARIATION   In some instances, you might want to compare the dispersion of two different series. The variance and standard deviation are *absolute* measures of dispersion. That is, they can be influenced by the magnitude of the original numbers. To compare series with very different values, you need a *relative* measure of dispersion. A measure of relative dispersion is the coefficient of variation, which is defined as:

$$\text{Coefficient of Variation (CV)} = \frac{\text{Standard Deviation of Returns}}{\text{Expected Rate of Return}}$$

A larger value indicates greater dispersion relative to the arithmetic mean of the series. For the previous example, the CV would be:

$$CV_1 = \frac{0.0756}{0.0400} = 1.89$$

It is possible to compare this value to a similar figure with a very different distribution. As an example, compare this investment to another investment that has an average rate of return of 10 percent and a standard deviation of 9 percent. The standard deviations alone indicate that the second series has greater dispersion (9 percent versus 7.56 percent) and might be considered to have higher risk. In fact, the relative dispersion for this second investment is much less.

$$CV_1 = \frac{0.0756}{0.0400} = 1.89$$

$$CV_2 = \frac{0.0900}{0.1000} = 0.90$$

Considering the relative dispersion and the total distribution, most investors would probably prefer the second investment.

PROBLEMS   1. Your rate of return expectations for the common stock of Floppy Disc Company during the next year are:

Possible Rate of Return	Probability
−0.10	0.25
0.00	0.15
0.10	0.35
0.25	0.25

  a. Compute the expected return $[E(R_i)]$ on this investment, the variance of this return (σ^2), and its standard deviation (σ).

  b. Under what conditions can the standard deviation be used to measure the relative risk of two investments?

  c. Under what conditions should the coefficient of variation be used to measure the relative risk of two investments?

2. Your rate of return expectations for Turk Computer Company stock during the next year are:

Possible Rate of Return	Probability
−0.60	0.15
−0.30	0.10
−0.10	0.05
0.20	0.40
0.40	0.20
0.80	0.10

a. Compute the expected return $[E(R_i)]$ on this stock, the variance (σ^2) of this return, and its standard deviation (σ).

b. On the basis of expected return $[E(R_i)]$ alone, discuss whether Floppy Disc or Turk Computer is preferable.

c. On the basis of standard deviation (σ) alone, discuss whether Floppy Disc or Turk Computer is preferable.

d. Compute the coefficients of variation (CVs) for Floppy Disc and Turk Computer and discuss which stock return series has the greater relative dispersion.

3. The following are annual rates of return for U.S. government T-bills and United Kingdom common stocks.

Year	U.S. Government T-Bills	United Kingdom Common Stock
19__4	.063	.150
19__5	.081	−.043
19__6	.076	.374
19__7	.090	.192
19__8	.085	−.106

a. Compute the arithmetic mean rate of return and standard deviation of rates of return for the two series.

b. Discuss these two alternative investments in terms of their arithmetic mean rates of return, their absolute risk, and their relative risk.

c. Compute the geometric mean rate of return for each of these investments. Compare the arithmetic mean return and geometric mean return for each investment and discuss this difference between the mean rates of return as related to the standard deviation of each series.

Chapter

2

Asset Allocation

This chapter answers the following questions:

- What are the four steps in the portfolio management process?
- What is the role of asset allocation in investment planning?
- Why is a policy statement important to the planning process?
- What objectives and constraints should be detailed in a policy statement?
- How and why do investment goals change over a person's lifetime and circumstances?
- What influences the investment strategies of institutional investors?
- Why do asset allocation strategies differ across national boundaries?

The previous chapter indicated that the expected return on an asset or a portfolio is dependent on the risk involved—i.e., *risk drives return*. Therefore, the practice of investing funds and managing portfolios should focus on managing risk rather than on managing returns.

This chapter examines some of the practical implications of risk management in the context of asset allocation. **Asset allocation** is the process of deciding how to distribute an investor's wealth among different countries and asset classes for investment purposes. We will see that, in the long run, the highest compounded returns accrue to those investors with larger exposures to risky assets. We will also see that although there are no shortcuts or guarantees to investment success, maintaining a disciplined approach to investing will increase the likelihood of investment success over time.

The asset allocation decision should not be done in isolation; rather, it is a component of a portfolio management process. In this chapter, we present the four-step portfolio management process. The first step in this process is to develop an investment policy statement that will guide all future decisions. Much of the asset allocation strategy is based on the investor's policy statement.

What is meant by an "investor" can range from an individual to a corporation's multibillion dollar pension fund, a university endowment, or an insurance company. Regardless of who the investor is or how simple or complex his or her investment needs, it is necessary to develop an investment policy statement prior to making long-term investment decisions. We begin this chapter with a review of an investor's life cycle and the implications of this for investment strategy. This feeds into a review of financial planning and policy statements in the context of the individual investor. Later, we discuss applications to institutional investors. We also review historical data to show the importance of the asset allocation decision prior to concluding with an examination of asset allocation strategies across national borders.

INDIVIDUAL INVESTOR LIFE CYCLE

Investment needs change over a person's life cycle. How individuals structure their financial plans should be related to their age, financial status, future plans, and needs.

PRE-INVESTMENT NEEDS   Before embarking on an investment program, other needs must be satisfied. An investment plan should not be started until adequate income exists to cover living expenses and to provide a safety net for unexpected needs.

INSURANCE   Life insurance should be a component of any financial plan because it protects loved ones against financial hardship should death occur before financial goals are met. The death benefit paid by the insurance company can help pay off medical bills and funeral expenses and provide a lump sum of cash the family can use to maintain their lifestyle. A financial plan should not begin without adequate life insurance coverage. Experts suggest life insurance coverage that is equal to seven to ten times an individual's annual salary.

Insurance can also help meet long-term goals such as retirement planning. For example, when you reach retirement age, you can receive the cash value of your life insurance policy and use the proceeds to supplement your retirement lifestyle or for estate planning purposes.

Several basic life insurance contracts are available. *Term life insurance* provides only a death benefit; the premium to purchase the insurance changes every renewal period. Term insurance is the least expensive life insurance to purchase, although the premium increases as you age (reflecting the increased probability of death). *Universal* and *variable life policies,* although technically different from each other, are similar because both provide a death benefit and a savings plan. The premium paid on such policies exceeds the death benefit cost to the insurance company, so the excess premium is invested as the policyholder chooses from a number of investment vehicles. The cash value of the policy grows, based on the performance of the underlying investment funds. Insurance companies may restrict the ability to withdraw funds from these policies before the policyholder reaches a certain age.

Insurance also provides protection against other uncertainties. Health insurance helps to pay medical bills. Disability insurance provides continuing income if you are unable to work. Automobile and home (or rental) insurance provides protection against accidents and damage to cars or residences.

Although no one ever expects to use their insurance coverage, a first step in a sound financial plan is to have adequate coverage "just in case." Lack of insurance coverage can ruin the most well-planned investment program.

CASH RESERVE   Emergencies, job layoffs, and unforeseen expenses happen, and good investment opportunities emerge. Therefore, it is important to have a cash reserve to help meet these occasions. In addition to providing a safety cushion, a cash reserve reduces the likelihood of being forced to sell investments at inopportune times to cover unexpected expenses. Most experts recommend a cash reserve of about 6 months' worth of living expenses. Notably, the cash reserve funds should be in investments that are easily converted to cash with little chance for a loss in value. Money market mutual funds and bank accounts are appropriate vehicles for the cash reserve.

An investor's insurance and cash reserve needs will change over his or her life. As noted, a retired person may "cash out" a life insurance policy to supplement income and the need for disability insurance declines at retirement. At the same time, supplemental Medicare coverage or nursing home insurance may become more important.

LIFE CYCLE INVESTMENT STRATEGIES   After the basic insurance and cash reserves needs are met, individuals can begin planning a serious investment program. Because of changes in their net worth and risk tolerance, individuals' investment strategies will change over their lifetime. Below, we review vari-

FIGURE 2.1

RISE AND FALL OF A PERSON'S NET WEALTH OVER HIS OR HER LIFETIME

ous phases in the investment life cycle. Although each individual's needs and preferences are different, there are some general traits that affect most investors over the life cycle. There are generally four life cycle phases, as shown in Figure 2.1.

ACCUMULATION PHASE   Individuals in the early-to-middle years of their working careers are in the **accumulation phase,** wherein they attempt to accumulate assets for satisfying fairly immediate needs (e.g., a down payment for a house) or longer-term goals (e.g., children's college education). Typically, during this phase, their net worth is small, and debt from car loans or their own past college loans may be heavy. Because they typically have long investment time horizons and growing earning ability, individuals in the accumulation phase generally make fairly high-risk investments in the hopes of making above-average nominal returns.

CONSOLIDATION PHASE   Individuals in the **consolidation phase** are typically past the midpoint of their careers, have paid off most of their outstanding debts, and might have the assets to pay their children's college bills. Earnings exceed expenses, so the excess can be invested to provide for future retirement or estate planning needs. The typical investment horizon is still long (20 to 30 years), so moderate-risk investments are still attractive. Still, they do not want to take large risks that may jeopardize their current nest egg.

SPENDING PHASE   The **spending phase** typically begins when individuals retire. Living expenses are covered by Social Security income and income from prior investments, including employer pension plans. Since their earning years have concluded (although some retirees take part time positions or do consulting work), they seek greater protection of their capital. Still, they must balance their desire to preserve the nominal value of their savings with the need to protect themselves against inflation. The average 65-year-old person in the United States has a life expectancy of about 20 more years. Thus, although their portfolio may be less risky than in the consolidation phase, they still need some risky growth investments (such as common stocks) for inflation protection.

GIFTING PHASE　The **gifting phase** is similar to, and may be concurrent with, the spending phase. In this stage, some individuals have sufficient income to cover their expenses as well as a reserve for uncertainties. For these individuals, excess assets can be used to provide financial assistance to relatives or friends, set up charitable trusts, or construct trusts as an estate planning tool to minimize estate taxes.

LIFE CYCLE INVESTMENT GOALS　During the investment life cycle, individuals have a variety of financial goals. **Near-term, high-priority goals** are shorter-term financial objectives, such as a house down payment, a new car, or a trip. Parents with teenage children may need to accumulate funds to help pay college expenses. Due to their short time horizon, high-risk investments are usually not recommended as a means for achieving these goals.

Long-term, high-priority goals typically include the ability to retire at a certain age. Because of their long-term nature, higher-risk investments can be used to help meet these objectives.

Lower-priority goals are not critical. Examples include buying a new car every few years, redecorating the home with expensive furnishings, or taking a long, luxurious vacation.

THE PORTFOLIO MANAGEMENT PROCESS　The first step in the portfolio management process, as seen in Figure 2.2, is for the investor to construct a **policy statement.** The policy statement specifies the types of risks the investor is willing to take and his or her investment goals and constraints. All investment decisions should be consistent with the investor's policy statement. We will examine the process of constructing a policy statement later in this chapter. Since investor needs change over time, the policy statement must be periodically reviewed and updated.

FIGURE 2.2　　**THE PORTFOLIO MANAGEMENT PROCESS**

1. Policy statement
   Focus: Investor's short-term and long-term needs, familiarity with capital market history, and expectations

2. Examine current and project financial, economic, political, and social conditions
   Focus: Short-term and intermediate-term expected conditions to use in constructing a specific portfolio

3. Implement the plan by constructing the portfolio
   Focus: Meet the investor's needs at minimum risk levels

4. Feedback loop: Monitor and update investor needs, environmental conditions, portfolio performance

The process of investing looks for strategies that offer the best possibility of meeting the policy statement guidelines. In the second step of the portfolio management process, the investor studies current financial and economic conditions and attempts to forecast future trends. The investor's needs—as reflected in the policy statement—and the financial market expectations will jointly determine the investment strategy. Because economies are dynamic, the portfolio will have to be constantly monitored and updated to include asset reallocations to reflect changes in financial market expectations.

The third step of the portfolio management process is to construct the portfolio. Based on the investor's policy statement and financial market forecasts, the investor determines how to allocate available funds across different countries, asset classes, and securities. This involves constructing a portfolio that will minimize the investor's risks while meeting the return needs specified in the policy statement. (The theory of portfolio construction is discussed in Chapter 8, and some of the practical aspects of selecting portfolio investments are discussed in Parts 4 and 5.)

The fourth step in the portfolio management process is to continually monitor the investor's needs and capital market conditions. When necessary, an updated policy statement is written and the investment strategy is modified accordingly. A component of the monitoring process is to evaluate a portfolio's performance and compare the results to the expectations and requirements as specified in the policy statement. The evaluation of portfolio performance is discussed in Chapter 27.

THE NEED FOR A POLICY STATEMENT

As noted above, a policy statement guides the investment process. Constructing a policy statement is an invaluable planning tool that will help the investor understand his or her own needs better as well as assist an advisor or portfolio manager in managing a client's funds. While it does not guarantee investment success, a policy statement provides discipline on the investment process and reduces the possibility of inappropriate decisions. There are two important reasons for constructing a policy statement: first, it helps the investor decide on realistic investment goals, and second, it creates a standard by which the performance of the portfolio manager can be judged.

Understand and Articulate Investor Goals

When asked what their investment objective is, most people will likely say, "to make a lot of money." Such an objective has two drawbacks: it may not be appropriate for the investor and it is too open-ended to provide meaningful guidance. Such an objective is well suited for going to the racetrack or buying lottery tickets, but it is not an appropriate investment objective for investing funds in financial and real assets.

An important purpose of writing a policy statement is to help investors understand their own needs, objectives, and investment constraints by learning about financial markets and the risks of investing. This should prevent them from making inappropriate investment decisions and increase the possibility of satisfying their specific, measurable financial goals.

Thus, the policy statement helps the investor to specify realistic goals and become better informed about the risks and costs of investing. The market values of stocks, bonds, or real estate can fluctuate dramatically. A review of market history shows that it is not unusual for asset prices to decline by 10 percent to 20 percent over several months. Investors typically focus on a single statistic, such as the 10 percent long-run average annual rate of return on stocks, and expect the market to rise 10 percent every year. Such thinking ignores the risk of stock investing. A policy statement requires that the investor become familiar with the risks of investing because we know there is a strong positive relationship between risk and return.

One investment expert recommends that investors should think about the following set of questions and explain their answers as part of the process of constructing an investment policy statement:[1]

1. What are the real risks of an adverse financial outcome, especially in the short run?
2. What would be my reaction to an adverse financial outcome (e.g., −15% return)?
3. How knowledgeable am I about investments and markets?
4. What other capital or income sources do I have? How important is this particular portfolio to my overall financial position?
5. Are there any legal restrictions that may affect my investment needs?
6. Are there any unanticipated consequences of interim fluctuations in portfolio value that might affect my investment policy?

In summary, constructing a policy statement is mainly the responsibility of the investor. It is a process whereby investors articulate their realistic needs and goals and become familiar with financial markets and investing risks. Without this information, investors cannot adequately communicate their needs to the portfolio manager. In turn, the portfolio manager needs this input to construct a portfolio that will satisfy clients' needs.

PORTFOLIO PERFORMANCE STANDARD
The policy statement is also the basis for judging the performance of the portfolio manager. Performance cannot be judged without an objective standard, which is provided by the policy statement. The point is, the portfolio's performance should be compared to guidelines specified in the policy statement rather than be judged on the portfolio's overall return. For example, if a portfolio's performance is poor relative to a stock market index, the portfolio manager should not necessarily be fired, especially if the stock market has higher risk than the client desires. Many times the policy statement will include a **benchmark portfolio,** which is the appropriate comparison standard. The risk of the benchmark, and the assets included in the benchmark, will be in agreement with the client's risk preferences and investment needs. Therefore, the portfolio manager's performance should be compared to an appropriate benchmark portfolio. An investor specifying low-risk investments in the policy statement should compare the portfolio manager's performance against a low-risk benchmark portfolio. In contrast, an investor seeking high-risk, high-return investments should compare the portfolio's performance against a high-risk benchmark.

Since it sets an objective performance standard, the policy statement acts as a starting point for periodic portfolio review and client communication with managers. Managers should mainly be judged by whether they consistently followed the client's policy guidelines. Therefore, even deviations that result in higher portfolio returns can be grounds for the manager's dismissal.

Thus, we see the importance of the client constructing the policy statement: the client must first understand his or her own needs before communicating them to the portfolio manager; in turn, the portfolio manager must understand the client's desires and implement them by following the investment guidelines. As long as policy is being followed, shortfalls in performance should not be a major concern. Remember that the reason for the policy statement was to impose an investment discipline on the client and portfolio manager. As questions (1) and (6) indicate, clients must enter the investment arena with their

---

[1] Adapted from Charles D. Ellis, *Investment Policy: How to Win the Loser's Game* (Homewood, IL: Dow Jones Irwin, 1985): 25–26.

eyes open. The less knowledgeable they are, the more likely it is that clients will inappropriately judge the performance of the portfolio manager.

The construction of a policy statement helps to protect the client against inappropriate investments or unethical behavior by the portfolio manager. Without clear, written guidance, some managers may invest in high-risk investments that are inappropriate, given the investor's needs and risk preferences. Though legal recourse is a possibility against such action, a clear and unambiguous policy statement should help avoid such unethical behavior by a portfolio manager.

Another consideration is a change in a manager. It is possible that your portfolio manager may be promoted, dismissed, or take a better job offer. Therefore, you may find that your funds are being managed by an individual you do not know and who does not know you. To prevent costly delays during a manager transition, you want the new manager to "hit the ground running" in the management of your funds. A clearly written policy statement will help ensure that there are no delays in monitoring and rebalancing your portfolio and that there can be a seamless transition from one money manager to another.

A clearly written policy statement helps the portfolio manager construct an appropriate portfolio. In summary, the policy statement acts as an objective measure for portfolio performance, helps guard against ethical lapses by the portfolio manager, and aids in the transition between money managers. Therefore, before beginning any investment program, whether for an individual or a multi-billion-dollar pension fund, you should construct a policy statement that satisfactorily answers the following questions:[2]

1. Is the policy carefully designed to meet the specific needs, risk constraints, and objectives of this particular investor?
2. Is the policy statement written so clearly and explicitly that a competent stranger could manage the portfolio in conformance with the client's needs (that is, in case of a manager transition, could the new manager using this policy statement handle your portfolio in accordance with your needs)?
3. Would the client have been able to remain committed to the policies during the capital market experiences of the past 50 to 60 years—particularly the past 10 years (that is, does the client fully understand investment risks and the need for a disciplined approach to the investment process)?
4. Would the portfolio manager have been able to follow the policy over the same period? (That is, we do not want the portfolio manager to change strategies because of a disappointing market.)
5. Would the policy, if implemented, have achieved the client's objectives?

INPUT TO THE POLICY STATEMENT

Before constructing a policy statement, there needs to be an exchange of information, ideas, fears, and goals. The client and advisor need to discuss the client's investment objectives and constraints. To help illustrate this, we will discuss the investment objectives and constraints that may confront "typical" 25-year-old and 65-year-old investors.

Investment Objectives

The **objectives** of the investor are his or her investment goals, expressed in terms of both risk and return. The goals cannot be expressed only in terms of returns because we know there is a relationship between risk and returns. Expressing goals only in terms of returns

---

[2] Adapted from Charles D. Ellis, *Investment Policy: How to Win the Loser's Game* (Homewood, IL: Dow Jones-Irwin, 1985): 62.

can lead to inappropriate investment practices by the portfolio manager, such as the use of high-risk investment strategies or account "churning" (i.e., excessive short-term trading).

For example, a person may have a stated return goal such as "double my investment in five years." Before such a statement becomes part of the policy statement, the client must understand investment risks, including the possibility of loss. *A careful analysis of the client's risk tolerance should precede any discussion of return objectives.* Investment firms survey clients to gauge their risk tolerance. For example, Merrill Lynch has asked its clients to place themselves in one of the four categories in Figure 2.3. Sometimes investment magazines or books contain tests that can help individuals evaluate their risk tolerance (see Figure 2.4).

FIGURE 2.3   **SELECTED RISK CATEGORIES AND SUGGESTED INITIAL ASSET ALLOCATIONS FOR MERRILL LYNCH'S CLIENTS**

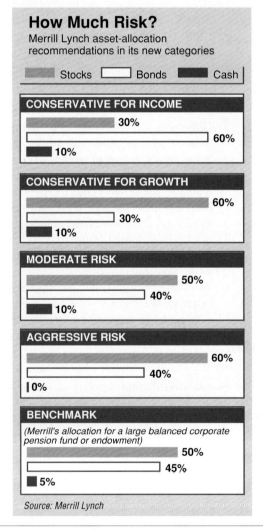

Source: William Power, "Merrill Lynch to Ask Investors to Pick a Risk Category," *The Wall Street Journal,* July 2, 1990, C1

How much risk is right for you?

You've heard the expression "no pain, no gain"? In the investment world, the comparable phrase would be "no risk, no reward."

How you feel about risking your money will drive many of your investment decisions. The risk-comfort scale extends from very conservative (you don't want to risk losing a penny regardless of how little your money earns) to very aggressive (you're willing to risk much of your money for the possibility that it will grow tremendously). As you might guess, most investors' tolerance for risk falls somewhere in between.

If you're unsure of what your level of risk tolerance is, this quiz should help.

1. You win $300 in an office football pool. You:
   a) spend it on groceries b) purchase lottery tickets
   c) put it in a money market account d) buy some stock.

2. Two weeks after buying 100 shares of a $20 stock, the price jumps to over $30. You decide to: a) buy more stock; its obviously a winner b) sell it and take your profits c) sell half to recoup some costs and hold the rest d) sit tight and wait for it to advance even more.

3. On days when the stock market jumps way up, you: a) wish you had invested more b) call your financial adviser and ask for recommendations c) feel glad you're not in the market because it fluctuates too much d) pay little attention.

4. You're planning a vacation trip and can either lock in a fixed room-and-meals rate of $150 per day or book standby and pay anywhere from $100 to $300 per day. You: a) take the fixed-rate deal b) talk to people who have been there about the availability of last-minute accommodations c) book stand-by and also arrange vacation insurance because you're leery of the tour operator d) take your chances with stand-by.

5. The owner of your apartment building is converting the units to condominiums. You can buy your unit for $75,000 or an option on for $15,000. (Units have recently sold for close to $100,000, and prices seem to be going up.) For financing, you'll have to borrow the down payment and pay mortgage and condo fees higher than your present rent. You: a) buy your unit b) buy your unit and look for another to buy c) sell the option and arrange to rent the unit yourself d) sell the option and move out because you think the conversion will attract couples with small children.

6. You have been working three years for a rapidly growing company. As an executive, you are offered the option of buying up to 2% of company stock— 2,000 shares at $10 a share. Although the company is privately owned (its stock does not trade on the open market), its majority owner has made handsome profits selling three other businesses and intends to sell this one eventually. You: a) purchase all the shares you can and tell the owner you would invest more if allowed b) purchase all the shares c) purchase half the shares d) purchase a small amount of shares.

7. You go to a casino for the first time. You choose to: a) play quarter slot machines b) $5 minimum-bet roulette c) dollar slot machine d) $25 minimum-bet blackjack.

8. You want to take someone out for a special dinner in a city that's new to you. How do you pick a place? a) read restaurant reviews in the local newspaper b) ask co-workers if they know of a suitable place c) call the only other person you know in this city, who eats out a lot but only recently moved there d) visit the city sometime before your dinner to check out the restaurants yourself.

9. The expression that best describes your lifestyle is: a) no guts, no glory b) just do it! c) look before you leap d) all good things come to those who wait.

10. Your attitude toward money is best described as: a) a dollar saved is a dollar earned b) you've got to spend money to make money c) cash and carry only d) whenever possible, use other people's money.

SCORING SYSTEM: Score your answers this way: 1) a-1, b-4, c-2, d-3 2) a-4, b-1, c-3, d-2 3) a-3, b-4, c-2, d-1 4) a-2, b-3 c-1, d-4 5) a-3, b-4, c-2, d-1 6) a-4, b-3, c-2, d-1 7) a-1, b-3, c-2, d-4 8) a-2, b-3, c-4, d-1 9) a-4, b-3, c-2, d-1 10) a-2, b-3,c-1, d-4.

What your total score indicates:

■ 10-17: You're not willing to take chances with your money, even though it means you can't make big gains.

■ 18-25: You're semi-conservative, willing to take a small chance with enough information.

■ 24-32: You're semi-aggressive, willing to take chances if you think the odds of earning more are in your favor.

■ 33-40: You're aggressive, looking for every opportunity to make your money grow, even though in some cases the odds may be quite long. You view money as a tool to make more money.

Risk tolerance is a function of an individual's psychological makeup as well as other factors, including a person's current insurance coverage and cash reserves. Risk tolerance is affected by an individual's family situation (e.g., the number and ages of children) and by age. We know that older persons generally have shorter investment time frames with which to make up any losses. Risk tolerance is also influenced by one's current net worth and income expectations. Specifically, individuals with higher incomes are more likely to undertake risk, since their incomes can help cover any shortfall. Likewise, individuals with larger net worths can afford to place some assets in risky investments while the remaining assets provide a cushion against losses.

A person's return objective may be stated in terms of an absolute or relative percentage return, or it can be stated as a general goal, such as capital preservation, current income, capital appreciation, or total return.

Capital preservation means investors want to minimize their risk of loss, usually in inflation-adjusted terms. Generally, this is a strategy for very risk-averse investors.

Capital appreciation is an appropriate objective when investors want the portfolio to grow in real terms over time to meet some future need. This is a very aggressive strategy for investors willing to take on risk to meet their objective.

When **current income** is the objective, investors want the portfolio to concentrate on generating income rather than capital gains. This relatively low-risk strategy is chosen by investors who want to supplement their earnings with income generated by their portfolio to meet their living expenses.

The **total return** strategy is similar to capital appreciation; namely, investors want the total value of the portfolio to grow over time to meet a future need. Whereas the capital appreciation strategy does this through capital gains, the total return strategy seeks to increase the portfolio value by both capital gains and reinvesting current income. Since the total return strategy has both income and capital gains components, its risk exposure lies between that of the current income and capital appreciation strategies.

Investment objective: 25 year old   What is an appropriate investment objective for our typical 25-year-old investor? Let's assume he holds a steady job, is a valued employee, has adequate insurance coverage, and an appropriate cash reserve. Let's also assume that his current long-term, high-priority investment goal is to build a retirement fund. Depending on his risk preferences, he can select a moderate to high risk strategy because his job income will probably grow over time. Further, given his young age and income growth potential, a low-risk strategy is inappropriate for his retirement fund goal; a total return or capital appreciation objective would be most appropriate.

Investment objective: 65 year old   Assume our typical 65-year-old investor has adequate insurance coverage, a cash reserve, and is retiring this year. This individual will want less risk exposure than the 25-year-old investor, since her earning power from employment will soon be ending; she will not be able to recover any investment losses by saving more out of her paycheck. Depending on her income from Social Security and a pension plan, she may need some income from her retirement portfolio to meet current living expenses. Because she can be expected to live an average of another 20 years, she will need protection against inflation. A risk-averse investor will choose a combination current income and capital preservation strategy; a more risk tolerant investor will choose a combination of current income and total return in an attempt to have principal growth outpace inflation.

INVESTMENT CONSTRAINTS   In addition to having risk–return investment objectives, certain constraints will also affect the investment plan. Investment constraints include liquidity needs, an investment time horizon, tax factors, legal and regulatory constraints, and unique needs and preferences.

LIQUIDITY NEEDS   As discussed in Chapter 1, an asset is **liquid** if it can be quickly converted to cash at a price close to fair market value. Treasury bills are a very liquid security; life insurance contracts, real estate, and venture capital are not.

Investors may have liquidity needs that the investment plan must consider. For example, an investor may have a primary long-term goal, but also several important near-term goals. Thus, funds will have to be available to satisfy the near-term goals. For example, wealthy individuals with sizable tax obligations should have adequate liquidity to pay their taxes without upsetting their investment plan.

Our typical 25-year-old investor probably has little need for liquidity as he focuses on his long-term retirement fund goal. This constraint may change, however, should he become unemployed or if near-term goals, such as honeymoon expenses or a house down payment, enter the picture. Should any changes occur, the investor needs to revise his investment policy statement and financial plans accordingly.

Our soon-to-be-retired, 65-year-old investor needs liquidity more than the younger investor. Although she may receive regular checks from her pension plan and Social Security, they will probably not equal her working paycheck. She will want some of her portfolio in liquid securities to meet unexpected expenses or bills.

TIME HORIZON   We know that an investor's time horizon is an investment constraint. There is also a relationship between an investor's time horizon, liquidity needs, and ability to handle risk. Investors with long investment horizons generally require less liquidity and can tolerate greater portfolio risk. Less liquidity is needed because these funds are not usually needed for many years; greater risk tolerance is possible because any losses can be overcome by returns in subsequent years. Investors with shorter time horizons generally favor less risky investments because losses are harder to overcome during a short time frame.

Although our 25-year-old investor has a longer investment time horizon than our 65-year-old investor, this does not mean the 65-year-old should put all her money in short-term CDs, because she needs the inflation protection that long-term investments such as common stock can provide. Still, the time horizon constraint means that the 25-year-old will probably have a greater proportion of his portfolio in equities, including stocks in small firms or international firms, than the 65-year-old.

There can be an intergenerational conflict regarding the time horizon constraint in a personal trust. A **personal trust** is money set aside by a grantor that is often managed by a third party (the trustee) who is typically an investment advisor of a bank trust department. Often the trusts are constructed so that one party (perhaps the grantor and/or the surviving spouse) receives income from the trust's investments while another party (the "remainderperson") receives the residual value of the trust after the income beneficiaries' death. Usually, the income beneficiaries are late-stage investors and the remainderpersons are younger and generally interested in growth of the principal. This conflict between short- and long-term investment objectives is usually resolved in favor of the near-term income beneficiaries. Such trusts typically focus on maintaining income while ignoring the long-term priority needs of the remainderperson.

Most trust agreements allow the income beneficiaries to receive some of the principal as needed to maintain an income stream. Thus, an alternative strategy would be to maximize the trust's after-tax total return while maintaining the trust's desired risk exposure. This way the remainderperson's desires for principal growth can probably be met over time while the income beneficiaries enjoy their income stream.

TAX CONCERNS   Investment planning is complicated by the tax code, and can be further complicated if international investments are part of the portfolio. Taxable income from

| TABLE 2.1 | MARGINAL TAX RATES, 1996 |

Individual Tax Rate Schedules

	Taxable Income	Tax	Percent on Excess
Married filing jointly	$0	$0	15%
	40,100	6,015	28
	96,900	21,919	31
	147,700	37,667	36
	263,770	79,445	39.6
Single	$0	$0	15
	24,000	3,600	28
	58,150	13,162	31
	121,300	32,738	36
	263,750	84,020	39.6
Head of household	$0	$0	15
	32,150	4,822	28
	83,050	19,074	31
	134,500	35,024	36
	263,750	81,554	39.6
Married filing separately	$0	$0	15
	20,050	3,007	28
	48,450	10,959	31
	73,850	18,833	36
	131,875	39,722	39.6

Corporate Tax Rate Schedules

Taxable Income	Tax	Percent on Excess
$ 0	$ 0	15%
50,000	7,500	25
75,000	13,750	34
100,000	22,250	39
335,000	113,900	34
10,000,000	3,400,000	36
15,000,000	5,150,000	38
18,333,333	6,416,667	36

interest, dividends, or rents is taxable at the investor's marginal tax rate. Table 2.1 shows the marginal tax rates for different levels of taxable income. As of 1996, the top federal marginal tax rate is 39.6 percent. State taxes make the tax bite even higher.

Capital gains are taxed differently. The capital gains tax rate is either 0 percent, 15 percent, or 28 percent, depending on the investor's income level and other factors. **Unrealized capital gains** reflect the price appreciation of currently held assets that have not been sold; taxes on unrealized capital gains can be deferred indefinitely. Capital gains only become taxable after the asset has been sold for a price higher than its cost or the asset's **basis.** If appreciated assets are passed on to an heir, the basis of the assets is their value on the date of the holder's death. The heirs can then sell the assets and not pay the capital gains tax. **Realized capital gains** occur when an appreciated asset has been sold.

There is sometimes a trade-off between taxes and diversification needs. If entrepreneurs have much of their wealth concentrated in equity holdings of their firm, or if employees have purchased substantial amounts of their employer's stock through payroll deductions over their working life, the portfolio may contain a large amount of unrealized capital gains. In addition, the portfolio may be quite risky because it is concentrated in a single company. The decision to sell some of the company stock to diversify the portfolio by reinvesting the proceeds in other assets must be balanced against the resulting tax liability.

Another tax factor is that some sources of income are exempt from federal and state taxes. Interest on federal securities, such as Treasury bills, notes, and bonds, is exempt from state taxes. Interest on municipal bonds is exempt from federal taxes. Further, if the investor purchases municipal bonds issued by the state in which he or she lives, the interest is exempt from both state and federal income tax. Thus, high income individuals have an incentive to purchase municipal bonds to reduce their tax liabilities.

Other means to reduce tax liabilities are available to the investor. Contributions to an IRA (individual retirement account) may result in a deduction from taxable income if certain conditions are met. Notably, the investment returns of the IRA investment, including any income, are deferred until the funds are withdrawn from the account. The benefits of tax-deferral can dramatically compound over time. Figure 2.5 illustrates how $1,000 invested at a tax-deferred rate of 8 percent grows compared to funds invested in a taxable investment, which returns 8 percent pre-tax. For an investor in the 28 percent tax bracket, a taxed investment grows at an after-tax rate of 5.76 percent. After 30 years, the value of the tax-deferred investment has grown nearly twice as large as the taxable investment.

Other tax-deferred investments include cash values of life insurance contracts; they accumulate tax-free until the funds are withdrawn. Employers may offer employees 401(k) or 403(b) plans, which allow the employee to reduce taxable income by making tax-

| FIGURE 2.5 | **EFFECT OF TAX-DEFERRAL ON INVESTOR WEALTH OVER TIME** |

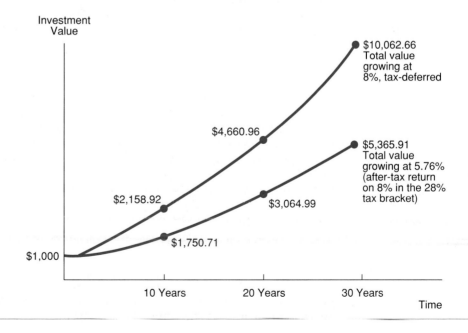

deferred investments. Employee contributions often are matched by employer donations (up to a specified limit), thus allowing the employees to double their investment with little risk!

Our typical 25-year-old investor probably is not in a very high tax bracket, so detailed tax planning will not be a major concern and tax-exempt income, such as municipals, will also not be considered. Nonetheless, he should still invest as much as possible into tax-deferred plans such as an IRA or 401(k). The liquidity drawback to such investments, however, is that early withdrawals (before age 59½) are taxable and subject to an additional 10 percent early withdrawal tax.

Our 65-year-old retiree may face a different situation. If she is in a high tax bracket prior to retiring—and therefore sought tax-exempt income and tax-deferred investments—her situation may change shortly after retirement. Without regular paychecks, the need for tax-deferred investments or tax-exempt income decreases. Taxable income may now offer higher after-tax yields than tax-exempt municipals due to the investor's lower tax bracket. Should her employer's stock be a large component of her retirement account, careful decisions must be made regarding the need to diversify versus the cost of realizing large capital gains (in her lower tax bracket).

LEGAL AND REGULATORY FACTORS   At times, legal and regulatory factors constrain the investment strategies of individuals and institutions. In our discussion about taxes, we mentioned one such constraint: funds removed from an IRA account or 401(k) plan before age 59½ are taxable and subject to an additional 10 percent withdrawal penalty. You may also be familiar with the tag line in many bank CD advertisements—"substantial interest penalty upon early withdrawal." Such regulations and rules make these investments unattractive for investors with substantial liquidity needs.

Regulations can also constrain investments that can be made by someone in a **fiduciary** role. A fiduciary is someone who supervises an investment portfolio of a third party, such as a trust account or discretionary account.[3] The fiduciary or trustee must make investment decisions in accordance with the owner's wishes; a properly written policy statement assists this process. In addition, trustees of a trust account must meet the "prudent man" standard, which means that *they must invest and manage the funds as a prudent person would manage his or her own affairs.* Notably, the prudent man standard is based on the composition of the entire portfolio, not each individual asset in the portfolio.[4]

All investors must respect some laws, such as insider trading prohibitions. Insider trading involves the purchase and sale of securities on the basis of important information that is not publicly known. Typically, people possessing inside information are the firm's managers, who have a fiduciary duty to their shareholders. Security transactions based on inside information violate the fiduciary trust between shareholders and management, since the managers seek personal financial gain from their privileged position as agents for the shareholders.

For our typical 25-year-old investor, legal and regulatory matters are not going to be a major concern, with the possible exception of insider trading laws and penalties for early withdrawal of funds from tax-deferred retirement accounts. His financial advisor would have to obey the regulations pertinent to a client–advisor relationship.

---

[3] A discretionary account is one in which the fiduciary, many times a financial planner or stockbroker, has the authority to purchase and sell assets in the owner's portfolio without first receiving the owner's approval.

[4] As we will discuss in Chapter 8, it is sometimes wise to hold assets that are individually risky in the context of a well-diversified portfolio, even if the investor is strongly risk averse.

Similar concerns confront our 65-year-old investor. In addition, if she wants to do some estate planning with trust accounts, she should seek legal and tax advice to ensure her plans are properly implemented.

UNIQUE NEEDS AND PREFERENCES   This category covers individual concerns of each investor. Some investors may want to exclude certain investments for personal or social consciousness reasons. For example, they may request that no firms that manufacture or sell tobacco, alcohol, pornography, or environmentally harmful products be included in their portfolio.

Some of the points raised in discussing other constraints can also be considered unique needs and preferences. For example, consider the businessperson with a large portion of his wealth tied up in his firm's stock. Although it may be financially prudent to sell some of the firm's stock and reinvest the proceeds for diversification purposes, it may be hard for the individual to approve such a strategy due to emotional ties to the firm. Further, if the stock holdings are in a private company, it may be difficult to find a buyer unless shares are sold at a discount from their fair market value.

Because each investor is unique, the implications of this final constraint differ for each person; there is no "typical" 25-year-old or 65-year-old investor. Each will have to decide for himself—and then communicate his desires in his policy statement.

CONSTRUCTING THE POLICY STATEMENT

A policy statement should incorporate an investor's objectives (risk and return) and constraints (liquidity, time horizon, tax factors, legal and regulatory constraints, and unique needs and preferences). The policy statement allows the investor to determine what factors should be reflected in the investment plan. Communicating these needs, goals, or aspirations to the investment advisor gives the advisor a better chance of constructing an investment strategy that will satisfy the investor's objectives and constraints. The first important step in the investing process is to construct the policy statement.

OBJECTIVES AND CONSTRAINTS OF INSTITUTIONAL INVESTORS

Institutional investors include mutual funds, pension funds, insurance firms, endowments, and banks. In this section, we review the characteristics of several different institutional investors and discuss their typical investment objectives and constraints.

MUTUAL FUNDS

A mutual fund pools together sums of money from investors, which are then invested in financial assets. Each mutual fund has its own investment objective, such as capital appreciation, high current income, or money market income. A mutual fund will state its investment objective, and investors, as part of their own investment strategies, choose the appropriate funds in which to invest. Two basic constraints face mutual funds: those created by law to protect mutual fund investors, and those that represent choices made by the mutual fund's managers. Some of these constraints will be discussed in the mutual fund's prospectus, which must be given to all prospective investors before they purchase shares in a mutual fund. Mutual funds are discussed in Chapter 26.

PENSION FUNDS

Pension funds are a major component of retirement planning. Basically, a firm's pension fund receives contributions from the firm and/or its employees. The funds are invested with the purpose of giving workers either a lump sum payment or the promise of an income stream after their retirement. A pension plan's objectives and constraints depend on whether the plan is a defined benefit plan or a defined contribution plan. We review each below.

Defined benefit pension plans promise to pay retirees a specific income stream after retirement. The size of the benefit is usually based on factors that include the worker's salary and/or time of service. The company will contribute a certain amount each year to the pension plan; the size of the contribution will depend on actuarial assumptions concerning the age and composition of the workforce, future salary increases, and the rate of return to be earned on the plan's assets. Under a defined benefit plan, the company carries the risk of paying the future pension benefit to retirees; should investment performance be poor, or should the company not be able to make adequate contributions to the plan, the shortfall will have to be made up in future years. "Poor" investment performance means the actual return on the plan's assets fell below the assumed **actuarial rate of return.** The actuarial rate is used to find the present value of the plan's future obligations and thus determines the size of the firm's annual contribution to the pension plan.

A defined benefit plan's risk tolerance depends on the plan's funding status and its actuarial rate. For **underfunded plans** (where the present value of the fund's liabilities to employees exceeds the value of the fund's assets), a more conservative approach toward risk is taken to assure that the funding gap is closed over time. This may entail a strategy whereby the firm makes larger plan contributions and assumes a lower actuarial rate. For **overfunded plans** (where the present value of the pension liabilities is less than the plan's assets), a more aggressive investment strategy can be taken, in which the firm reduces its contributions and increases the risk exposure of the plan. The objective is to meet the plan's actuarial rate of return, which is set by actuaries who estimate future pension obligations based on assumptions about future salary increases, current salaries, retirement patterns, worker life expectancies, and the firm's benefit formula. The actuarial rate also affects the size of the firm's plan contributions over time.

The liquidity constraint on defined benefit plans is mainly a function of the average age of employees. A younger employee base means less liquidity is needed; an older employee base generally means more liquidity is needed to pay current pension obligations to retirees. The time horizon constraint also is affected by the average age of employees, although some experts recommend using a 5- to 10-year horizon for planning purposes. Taxes are not a major concern since pension plans are exempt from paying tax on investment returns. The major legal constraint is that the plan must be managed in accordance with ERISA, the Employee Retirement Income Security Act. Also, investments must satisfy the "prudent man" standard when evaluated in context with the overall pension plan's portfolio.

Defined contribution pension plans do not promise set benefits; rather, the benefit received by a worker is affected by the size of the contributions made to the pension fund and the returns earned on the fund's investments. Notably, the allocation of the funds among assest classes is made by the employee. Thus, the plan's risk is borne by the employees. Unlike a defined benefit plan, employees' retirement income is not an obligation of the firm.

Because the individual worker decides how his contributions to the defined contribution plan are to be invested, objectives and constraints depend on the individual. As noted, the worker carries the risk of inadequate retirement funding rather than the firm. Studies have shown consistently that defined contribution plans are generally conservatively invested. Specifically, it has been contended that employees tend toward very conservative asset allocation. If, however, the plan is an estate planning tool for a wealthy founder or officer of the firm, a higher risk tolerance and return objective is appropriate because most of the plan's assets will ultimately be owned by the individual's heirs.

The liquidity and time horizon needs for the plan differ depending on the average age of the employees and the degree of employee turnover within the firm. Similar to defined benefit plans, defined contribution plans are tax-exempt and are governed by the provisions of ERISA.

ENDOWMENT FUNDS Endowment funds arise from contributions made to charitable or educational institutions. Rather than immediately spending the funds, the organization invests the money to provide a future income stream to the organization. The investment policy of an endowment fund is impacted by a "tension" between the organization's need for current income and the desire to create a growing income stream to protect against future inflation.

To meet the institution's operating budget needs, the fund's return objective is often set by adding the required spending rate (the amount taken out of the funds each year) and the expected inflation rate. Funds that have more risk-tolerant trustees may have a higher spending rate than those overseen by risk-averse trustees. Since a total return approach is usually used to meet the return objective over time, the organization is generally withdrawing both income and capital gains returns to meet budgeted needs. The risk tolerance of an endowment fund is largely affected by the collective risk tolerance of the organization's trustees.

Due to the fund's long-term time horizon and hopefully a steady flow of new contributions, there are only minor liquidity requirements, except for the need to spend part of the endowment each year and maintain a cash reserve for emergencies. Many endowments are tax-exempt, although income from some private foundations can be taxed at either a 1 percent or 2 percent rate. Short-term capital gains are taxable, but long-term capital gains are not. Regulatory and legal constraints arise on the state level, where most endowments are regulated. Unique needs and preferences may affect investment strategies by college or religious endowments, which sometimes have strong preferences about social investing issues.

INSURANCE COMPANIES The investment objectives and constraints for an insurance company depend on whether it is a life insurance company or a nonlife (such as property and casualty) insurance firm.

LIFE INSURANCE COMPANIES   Except for firms dealing only in term life insurance, life insurance firms collect premiums during a person's lifetime, which must be invested until a death benefit is paid to the beneficiaries. At any time, the insured can turn in his or her policy and receive its cash surrender value. Discussing investment policy for an insurance firm is complicated by the insurance industry's proliferation of insurance and quasi-investment products.

Basically, an insurance company wants to earn a positive "spread"—the difference between the rate of return on investment minus the rate of return it credits its policyholders. This concept is similar to a defined benefit pension fund that tries to earn a rate of return in excess of its actuarial rate. If the spread is positive, the insurance firm's surplus reserve account rises; if not, the surplus account declines by an amount reflecting the negative spread. A growing surplus is an important competitive tool for life insurance companies. Attractive investment returns allow the company to advertise better policy returns than those of their competitors. A growing surplus also allows the firm to offer new products and expand insurance volume.

Since life insurance companies are quasi-trust funds for savings, fiduciary principles limit the risk tolerance of the invested funds. The National Association of Insurance Commissioners (NAIC) establishes risk categories for bonds and stocks; companies with excessive investments in higher-risk categories must set aside extra funds in a mandatory securities valuation reserve (MSVR) to protect policyholders against losses.

Insurance companies' liquidity needs have increased over the years due to policy surrender increases and product-mix changes. A company's time horizon depends on its specific product mix. Life insurance policies require longer-term investments, while guaranteed insurance contracts (GICs) and shorter-term annuities require shorter investment time horizons.

Tax rules changed considerably for insurance firms in the 1980s. For tax purposes, investment returns are divided into two components: (1) the policyholder's share, which is the return portion covering the actuarially assumed rate of return needed to fund reserves; and (2) the balance that is transferred to reserves. Unlike pensions and endowments, life insurance firms pay income and capital gains taxes at the corporate tax rates on this second component of return.

Except for the NAIC, most insurance regulation is on the state level. Regulators oversee the eligible asset classes and the reserves (MSVR) necessary for each asset class, and enforce the "prudent man" investment standard. Audits ensure that various accounting rules and investment regulations are followed.

NONLIFE INSURANCE COMPANIES   Cash outflows are somewhat predictable for life insurance firms, based on their mortality tables. In contrast, the cash flows required by major accidents, disasters, and lawsuit settlements are not as predictable for nonlife insurance firms.

Due to their fiduciary responsibility to claimants, risk exposures are low to moderate. Depending on the company and competitive pressures, premiums may be affected by both the probability of a claim and the investment returns earned by the firm. Typically, casualty insurance firms invest their insurance reserves in bonds for safety purposes and to provide needed income to pay claims; capital and surplus funds are invested in equities for their growth potential. As with life insurers, property and casualty firms have a stronger competitive position when their surplus accounts are larger than competitors'. Many insurers now focus on a total return objective as a means to increase their surplus accounts.

Because of uncertain claim patterns, liquidity is a concern for property and casualty insurers who also want liquidity so they can switch between taxable and tax-exempt investments as their underwriting activities generate losses and profits. The time horizon for investments is typically shorter than that of life insurers, although many invest in long-term bonds to earn higher yields. Investing strategy for the firm's surplus account focuses on long-term growth.

Regulation of property and casualty firms is more permissive than for life insurers. Similar to life companies, states regulate classes and quality of investments for a certain percentage of the firm's assets. But beyond this restriction, insurers can invest in many different types and qualities of instruments, although some states limit the proportion of real estate assets.

BANKS   Pension funds, endowments, and insurance firms obtain virtually free funds for investment purposes. Not so with banks. To have funds to lend, banks must attract them in a competitive interest rate environment. They compete for funds against other banks and against other investment vehicles, from bonds to common stocks. The success of a bank is primarily due to its ability to generate returns in excess of its cost of funds.

A bank tries to maintain a positive spread between its cost of funds and its returns on assets. If banks anticipate falling interest rates, they will try to invest in longer-term assets to lock in the returns while seeking short-term deposits, whose interest cost is expected to fall. When banks expect rising rates, they will try to lock in longer-term deposits with fixed-interest costs, while investing in short-term securities to capture rising interest rates. The risk of such strategies is that losses may occur if a bank incorrectly forecasts the direction of interest rates. The aggressiveness of a bank's strategy will be related to the size of its capital ratio and the oversight of regulators.

Banks need substantial liquidity to meet withdrawals and loan demand. A bank has two forms of liquidity. Internal liquidity is provided by a bank's investment portfolio that includes highly liquid assets that can be sold to raise cash. A bank has external liquidity since it can borrow from the federal funds markets (where banks lend reserves to other banks), from the Federal Reserve Bank's discount window, or it can sell certificates of deposit at attractive rates.

Banks have a short time horizon for several reasons. First, they have a strong need for liquidity. Second, because they want to maintain an adequate interest revenue–interest expense spread, they generally focus on shorter-term investments to avoid interest rate risk and to avoid getting "locked in" to a long-term revenue source. Third, since banks typically offer short-term deposit accounts (demand deposits, NOW accounts, etc.), they need to closely match the maturity of their assets and liabilities to avoid taking undue risks.[5]

Banks are heavily regulated by numerous state and federal agencies.[6] The Federal Reserve Board, the Comptroller of the Currency, and the Federal Deposit Insurance Corporation all oversee various components of bank operations. The Glass-Steagall Act restricts the equity investments that banks can make. Unique situations that affect each bank's investment policy depend on their size, market, and management skills in matching asset and liability sensitivity to interest rates. For example, a bank in a small community may have many customers who deposit their money with it for the sake of convenience. A bank in a more populated area will find its deposit flows are more sensitive to interest rates and to competition from nearby banks.

INSTITUTIONAL INVESTOR SUMMARY

There are a great variety of institutions, and each institution has its "typical" investment objectives and constraints. This discussion has provided a flavor of the differences that exist between types of institutions. Similar to individual investors, "cookie-cutter" policy statements are inappropriate for institutional investors. The specific objectives, constraints, and investment strategies must be determined on a case-by-case basis. Our discussion in this section has attempted to indicate some of the major issues confronting alternative institutional investors.

THE IMPORTANCE OF ASSET ALLOCATION

A major reason why policy statements are developed is to determine an overall investment strategy. Although a policy statement does not indicate which specific securities to purchase and when they should be sold, policy statements should provide guidelines as to the asset classes that should be included in the portfolio and the relative proportions of the investor's funds that should be invested in each class. How funds are divided into different asset classes is the process of asset allocation. Rather than present strict percentages, asset allocation *ranges* are provided which allow the investment manager some freedom—based on his reading of capital market trends—to invest toward the upper or lower end of the

---

[5] An asset/liability mismatch is what caused the ultimate downfall of savings and loan associations. They attracted short-term liabilities (deposit accounts) and invested in long-term assets (mortgages). When interest rates became more volatile in the early 1980s and short-term rates increased dramatically, S&Ls suffered large losses.

[6] At the time of this writing, Congress was considering proposals to reduce the duplication of regulations among federal bank regulatory agencies.

ranges. For example, suppose a policy statement stipulates that common stocks be 60 percent to 80 percent of the value of the portfolio and that bonds should be 20 percent to 40 percent of the portfolio's value. If the manager is particularly bullish about stocks, he will increase the allocation of stocks toward the 80 percent upper end of the equity range and decrease bonds toward the 20 percent lower end of the bond range. Should he be more optimistic about bonds, the manager may shift the allocation closer to 40 percent of the funds invested in bonds with the remainder in equities.

A review of historical data and empirical studies indicates the importance of the asset allocation decision and the entire investment policy statement process. In general, four decisions are made when constructing an investment strategy: First, what asset classes will be considered for investment; second, what normal or policy weights will be assigned to each eligible asset class; third, what are the allocation ranges that are allowed from the policy weights; and fourth, what specific securities will be purchased for the portfolio. Studies on investment performance over time have come to the following significant conclusion: 85 percent to 95 percent of overall investment returns arise from the first and second decisions that are concerned with the long-term asset allocation decisions.[7] Good stock or bond pickers may add some value to portfolio performance, but the major source of investment return and risk over time is the asset allocation decision. A well-constructed policy statement helps ensure that an appropriate asset allocation decision is implemented. Although the following data review will focus primarily on U.S. securities, in Chapter 3 we will present a strong case for global asset allocation.

REAL INVESTMENT RETURNS AFTER TAXES AND COSTS

Figure 2.6 shows how an investment of $1 would have grown between 1969 and 1994. It also examines, using fairly conservative assumptions, how investment returns are affected by taxes and inflation.

Focusing first on stocks, funds invested in 1969 in the S&P 500 would have averaged an 10.1 percent annual return by the end of 1994. Unfortunately, this return is unrealistic because if the funds were invested over time, taxes would have to be paid and inflation would erode the real purchasing power of the invested funds. As shown, incorporating taxes into the analysis lowers the after-tax average annual return of a stock investment to 7.0 percent.

But the major reduction in the value of our investment is due to inflation. The real after-tax annual average return on stock investments was only 1.2 percent, which is much less than our initial unadjusted 10.1 percent return!

The results for bonds and bills purchases in Figure 2.6 show something even more surprising. After adjusting for taxes, long-term bonds did not maintain their purchasing power; T-bills *lost* value in real terms. One dollar invested in long-term government bonds in 1969 gave the investor an annual average after-tax real return of 0.6 percent. An investment in Treasury bills *lost* an average of 1.5 percent after taxes and inflation. Municipal bonds, because of the protection they offer from taxes, earned an average annual real return of 8 percent over this time frame.

The results of this historical analysis imply that, for taxable financial investments, the only way to maintain purchasing power over time is to invest in common stocks. An asset allocation decision for a taxable portfolio that does not include a substantial commitment to common stocks may make it difficult for the portfolio to maintain real value over time.[8]

---

[7] See Gary P. Brinson, Brian D. Singer, and Gilbert L. Beebower, "Determinants of Portfolio Performance II: An Update," *Financial Analysts Journal* 47, no. 3 (May–June 1991): 40–48.

[8] Of course, other equity-oriented investments, such as venture capital or real estate, may also provide inflation protection after adjusting for portfolio costs and taxes.

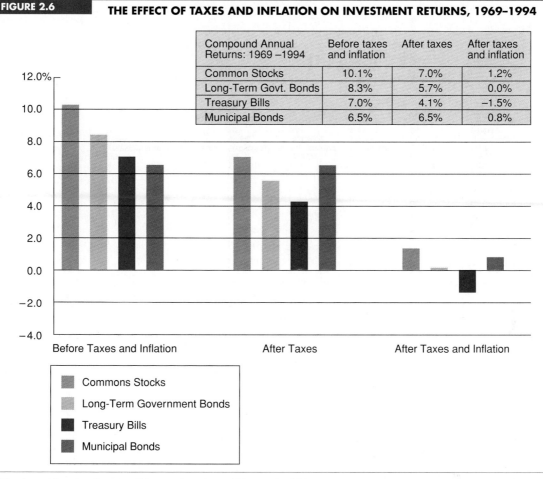

FIGURE 2.6

THE EFFECT OF TAXES AND INFLATION ON INVESTMENT RETURNS, 1969–1994

Compound Annual Returns: 1969–1994	Before taxes and inflation	After taxes	After taxes and inflation
Common Stocks	10.1%	7.0%	1.2%
Long-Term Govt. Bonds	8.3%	5.7%	0.0%
Treasury Bills	7.0%	4.1%	−1.5%
Municipal Bonds	6.5%	6.5%	0.8%

Before Taxes and Inflation   After Taxes   After Taxes and Inflation

- Commons Stocks
- Long-Term Government Bonds
- Treasury Bills
- Municipal Bonds

Source: *The Asset Allocation Decision,* Ibbotson Associates, Chicago, IL 1993. Updated by authors using Ibbotson Associates data.

RETURNS AND RISKS OF DIFFERENT ASSET CLASSES

By focusing on returns we have ignored its partner—risk. We would expect that assets with higher long-term returns have these returns to compensate for their risk. Table 2.2 illustrates returns (unadjusted for costs and taxes) for several asset classes over time. As expected, the higher returns available from equities come at the cost of higher risk where risk is measured by an asset's standard deviation of returns. This difference in risk for alternative asset classes is precisely why a policy statement is needed and why the investor and the money manager must understand the capital markets and have a disciplined approach to investing. There will be times when safe Treasury bills will outperform equities. And, because of their higher risk, there will be times when common stocks lose value, sometimes quite substantially. During these times, undisciplined and uneducated investors sell their stocks at a loss and vow never to invest in equities again. In contrast, during these times, disciplined investors stick to their investment plan, consider the decline as a buying opportunity, and position their portfolio for the next bull market.[9] By holding on to their stocks and perhaps purchasing more at depressed prices, the equity portion of the portfolio will experience a substantial future increase.

_____

[9] Newton's law of gravity seems to work two ways in financial markets. What goes up must come down; it also appears over time that what goes down will come back up.

TABLE 2.2   **HISTORICAL AVERAGE ANNUAL RETURNS AND RETURN VARIABILITY, 1926–1995**

	Geometric Mean	Arithmetic Mean	Standard Deviation	Distribution
Large company stocks	10.2%	12.2%	20.3%	
Small company stocks	12.2	17.4	34.6	*
Long-term corporate bonds	5.4	5.7	8.4	
Long-term government bonds	4.8	5.2	8.8	
Intermediate-term government bonds	5.1	5.2	5.7	
U.S. Treasury bills	3.7	3.7	3.3	
Inflation	3.1	3.2	4.6	

Distribution scale: −90%   0%   90%

*The 1933 Small Company Stock Total Return was 142.9 percent.

Source: © *Stocks, Bonds, Bills, and Inflation 1996 Yearbook,*™ Ibbotson Associates, Chicago (annually updates work by Roger G. Ibbotson and Rex A. Sinquefield). Used with permission. All rights reserved.

FIGURE 2.7   **EQUITY RISK: LONG-TERM AND SHORT-TERM PERSPECTIVES**

Historically, the S&P 500 Has Posted Healthy Gains. . .

Total returns, by decade, including share price gains and reinvested dividends, in percent

*Through Dec. 31, 1994

. . .But Getting There Can Be Rough

Annual total returns including share price gains and reinvested dividends, in percent

Sources: "Why It's Risky Not to Invest More in Stocks," *The Wall Street Journal,* February 11, 1992, C1, and Ibbotson Associates, Inc. Updated by authors, using Ibbotson Associates data.

The asset allocation decision determines to a great extent both the returns and the volatility of the portfolio. Table 2.2 indicates that stocks are riskier than bonds or T-bills. Figure 2.7 illustrates the year-by-year volatility of stock returns. It also shows that stocks have sometimes earned returns lower than those of T-bills for extended periods of time. By sticking with an investment policy and riding out the difficult times, attractive long-term rates of return can be earned.

The asset allocation decision specified in the policy statement can also help reduce the volatility of portfolio returns. For reasons that are fully discussed in Chapter 8, diversifying by combining different asset classes in a portfolio reduces overall portfolio volatility. Figure 2.8 shows that a portfolio comprised of equal weightings of U.S. stocks, bonds, and T-bills experienced an average rate of return similar to that of U.S. stocks, but with much lower volatility than a U.S. stock portfolio.

A popular measure of risk is the standard deviation or variance of annual rates of return for an asset class. By this measure, stocks are risky and T-bills are not. An alternative and intriguing measure of risk is the probability of *not* meeting your investment return objec-

FIGURE 2.8   **THE BENEFITS OF DIVERSIFICATION**

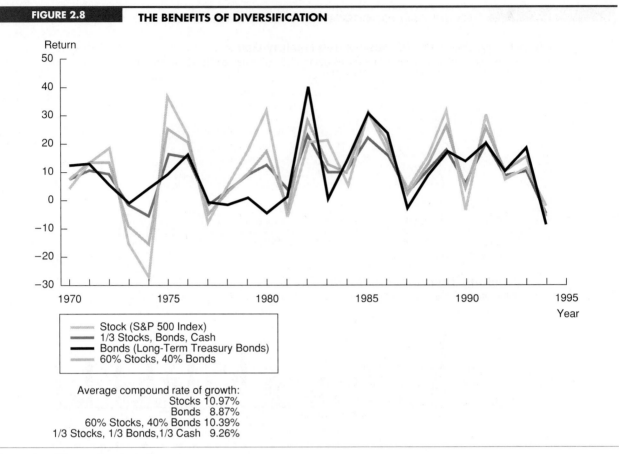

Average compound rate of growth:
Stocks 10.97%
Bonds 8.87%
60% Stocks, 40% Bonds 10.39%
1/3 Stocks, 1/3 Bonds, 1/3 Cash 9.26%

Data source: Ibbotson Associates, Inc.

Source: Adapted from Tom Herman, "Diversified Portfolios Are More Restful," *The Wall Street Journal,* January 25, 1990, C1. Updated by authors, using Ibbotson Associates data.

tive. From this risk perspective, if the investor has a long time horizon, the risk of equities is small and that of T-bills is large because of their differences in expected returns.

Focusing solely on return variability as a measure of risk ignores a risk of significance for income-oriented investments such as Treasury bills or certificates of deposit. T-bills and CDs can suffer from reinvestment risk, which is the risk that interim cash flows or the principal paid at maturity will be reinvested in a lower-yielding security. The year 1994 was particularly hard on T-bill investors because their T-bill income fell 37 percent from 1993 levels due to lower interest rates. Table 2.3 compares the variability of income payouts from common stocks (measured by the dividends from the S&P 500), and T-bills. Between 1926 and 1995, dividend income from stocks rose 57 times compared to 41 times for T-bills. The income from stocks fell only 11 times, while T-bill rollovers resulted in an income loss 28 times. The worst 1-year drop in stock income, 39.0 percent in 1932, was not as severe as the largest decline, 76.6 percent, in T-bill income, which occurred in 1940. In addition, the growth rate of income from stocks far outpaced that of inflation and the growth of income from T-bills. Between 1926 and 1995, stock dividends rose over 1,700 percent, inflation rose 700 percent, and T-bill income rose only 7 percent. The point is, when one considers the growth in principal that

TABLE 2.3

COMPARISON OF INCOME PAYOUTS FROM COMMON STOCKS AND TREASURY BILLS, 1926–1995

Over the past 69 years, stocks have been a more reliable source of income than either bonds or Treasury bills. The figures below presume that each year an investor spent all dividend and interest income kicked off by the securities, but left the capital intact.

	Years When Payout Rose	Years When Payout Fell	Worst One-Year Drop in Income	1926 to 1995	
				Change in Value of Income	Change in Value of Principal
Stocks	57	11	−39.0%	1,738.1%	3,170.3%
20-year Treasury bonds	38	31	−9.5	49.8	−25.7
5-year Treasury bonds	40	29	−36.9	105.9	22.9
Treasury bills	41	28	−76.6	7.3	—

Table data source: Ibbotson Associates, Inc.

Source: "T-Bill Trauma and the Meaning of Risk," *The Wall Street Journal,* February 12, 1993, C1. Updated by authors, using Ibbotson Associates data.

stocks offer, we see that "conservative," income-oriented T-bill investors are really exposed to substantial amounts of risk.

ASSET ALLOCATION SUMMARY

A carefully constructed policy statement determines the types of assets that should be included in a portfolio. The asset allocation decision, not the selection of specific stocks and bonds, determines most of the portfolio's returns over time. Although seemingly risky, investors seeking capital appreciation, income, or even capital preservation over long time periods should include a sizable allocation to equities in their portfolio. As noted in this section, a strategy's risk may depend on the investor's goals and time horizon. At times, investing in T-bills may be a riskier strategy than investing in common stocks.

ASSET ALLOCATION AND CULTURAL DIFFERENCES

Thus far, our analysis has focused on U.S. investors. Non-U.S. investors make their asset allocation decisions in much the same manner. At the same time, because they face different social, economic, political, and tax environments, their allocation decisions will be different from those of U.S. investors. Figure 2.9 shows the portfolio mixes of institutional investors in the United States, the United Kingdom, Germany, and Japan. In the United States, both foreign and domestic equities comprise about 45 percent of invested assets. In the United Kingdom, equities make up 72 percent of assets; in Germany, equities are only 11 percent of the typical portfolio; and in Japan, equities are 24 percent of assets.

National differences in environment can explain much of the divergent portfolio strategies. Of these four nations, the average age of the population is highest in Germany and Japan and lowest in the United States and the United Kingdom, thus helping to explain the greater use of equities in the latter countries. Government privatization programs during the 1980s in the United Kingdom encouraged equity ownership among individual and institutional investors. In Germany, regulations prevent insurance firms from having more than 20 percent of their assets in equities. Both Germany and Japan have strong banking sectors that invest privately in firms and whose officers sit on corporate boards. Since 1960, the United Kingdom's cost of living has increased at a rate more than 4.5 times that of Germany; this inflationary bias in the U.K. economy favors equities in U.K. asset allocations.

| FIGURE 2.9 | **PORTFOLIO MIXES, VARIOUS COUNTRIES, 1990–1991** |

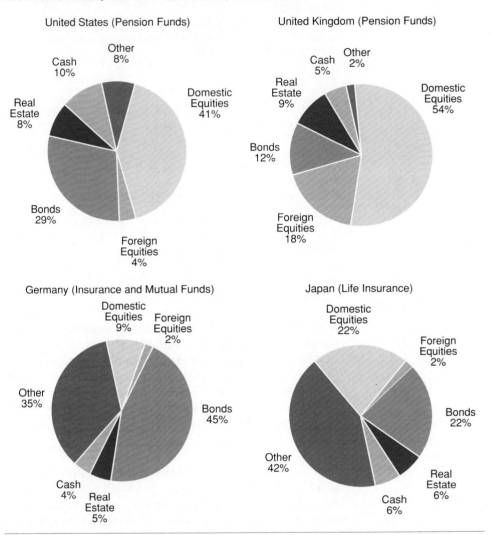

Source: "Culture and Portfolio Mixes, Various Countries, 1990–1991." Reprinted with permission, from the *Investing Worldwide III* seminar proceedings, 1992. Copyright 1992, Association for Investment Management and Research, Charlottesville, VA. All rights reserved.

Asset allocation policy and strategy is determined in the context of the investor's objectives and constraints. This discussion indicates that among the factors to consider is the investor's political and economic environment.

Summary

- The chapter reviewed the importance of developing an investment policy statement prior to implementing a serious investment plan. Because investors are required to examine their needs, risk tolerance, and familiarity with the capital markets, they will do a better job of identifying their objectives and constraints. Individual and institutional investment plans depend on the accurate formulation of a policy statement.

- We reviewed the importance of the asset allocation decision in determining long-run portfolio investment returns and risks. Since the asset allocation decision is made after the objectives and constraints are determined, it should be re-emphasized that the success of the investment program depends on the construction of the policy statement.
- There are many opportunities to invest in both domestic and international assets. The next chapter reviews investment choices and makes a strong case for including global assets in the asset allocation decision.

Questions

1. Compare and contrast the investment objectives and constraints of a bank and an insurance company.
2. Compare and contrast the investment objectives and constraints of an insurance company and a defined benefit pension fund.
3. "Young people with little wealth should not invest money in risky assets such as the stock market because they can't afford to lose what little money they have." Do you agree or disagree with this statement? Why?
4. Your healthy 63-year-old neighbor is about to retire and comes to you for advice. She indicates that she is planning on taking all the money out of her company's retirement plan and investing it in bond mutual funds and money market funds. What advice should you give her?
5. Discuss how an individual's investment strategy may change as he or she goes through the accumulation, consolidation, spending, and gifting phases of life.
6. What is included in a policy statement and why is it important?
7. How do the objectives and constraints differ between a defined contribution pension plan and a defined benefit pension plan?
8. Use the questionnaire in the "Check Your Risk Tolerance" box (Figure 2.4) to determine your risk tolerance. Use this information to help write a policy statement for yourself.
9. Suppose your first job pays you $35,000 annually. What percentage should be in your cash reserve? Approximately how much life insurance should you carry if you are unmarried? How much should you have if you are married with two young children?
10. What is the marginal tax rate for a couple, filing jointly, if their taxable income is $20,000? $40,000? $60,000? What is their tax bill for each of these income levels?
11. What is the marginal tax rate for a single individual if his taxable income is $20,000? $40,000? $60,000? What is his tax bill for each of these income levels?
12. *CFA Examination I (1990)*

    You are being interviewed for a junior portfolio manager's job at Progressive Counselors, Inc., and are eager to demonstrate your grasp of portfolio management basics.

    a. Portfolio management is a process whose *four* key steps are applicable in all investment management situations. List these *four* key steps.

    An endowment fund has a conservative Board of Trustees. The Board establishes an annual budget that relies on gifts at well as investment income. Gift income is unpredicable, having represented from 10 to 50% (averaging 30%) of annual spending over the past 10 years. If the gift component of any year's total income falls short of this average level, the shortfall is met from liquidity reserves.

    b. List and briefly discuss the objectives and contraints that must be considered in developing an Investment Policy Statement for this endowment fund.
13. *CFA Examination III (1995)*

    The Board has agreed in principle to add bonds denominated in non-U.S. currencies to BI's portfolio. The question of how to regard such bonds from an asset allocation point of view has arisen. Donovan requests opinions from two different advisory firms.

    The first firm responds as follows:

    "In our opinion, domestic investors should view non-U.S. bonds as securities that may, for mispricing reasons, be attractive for inclusion in the portfolio from time to time. Non-U.S.

bonds should not be viewed as a separate asset class eligible for inclusion as a permanent portfolio asset."

a. Briefly discuss the validity of this advisor's statement.

The second firm responds as follows:

"Decision-making about the use of non-U.S. bonds in BI's pension plan starts with the Board and may eventually involve the management of its fixed-income portfolio."

b. Briefly explain the difference between strategic (policy level) and tactical (operating level) decision-making for asset allocation in the context of the above statement.

Problems

1. a. Someone in the 36 percent tax bracket can earn 9 percent on her investments in a tax-exempt IRA account. What will be the value of a $10,000 investment in 5 years? 10 years? 20 years?

   b. Suppose the above 9 percent return is taxable rather than tax-deferred. What will be the after-tax value of the $10,000 investment after 5, 10, and 20 years?

2. a. Someone in the 15 percent tax bracket can earn 10 percent on his investments in a tax-exempt IRA account. What will be the value of a $10,000 investment in 5 years? 10 years? 20 years?

   b. Suppose the above 10 percent return is taxable rather than tax-deferred. What will be the after-tax value of the $10,000 investment after 5, 10, and 20 years?

Use the following information for the next four questions:

The geometric average rate of return is as follows for the asset classes specified:

Long-term government bonds	6.00%
Long-term corporate bonds	7.00%
Large-cap common stocks	10.00%
Small-cap common stocks	12.00%
International common stocks	14.00%
Emerging market common stocks	16.00%

3. You are 25 years old and expect to retire in 40 years. You have a 401(k) program that allows you to invest $2,000 a year, and all returns are tax-exempt. Compute the ending value of this fund in 40 years, assuming the following asset allocation:

   a. 80% Long-term government bonds
      20% Large-cap common stock

   b. 50% Long-term government bonds
      50% Large-cap common stock

   c. 20% Long-term government bonds
      80% Large-cap common stocks

4. You are 35 years old, expect to retire in 30 years, and have fairly low risk aversion. Assume a 401(k) program where your employer matches your contributions up to $1,500 a year and all the returns are tax-exempt. Assume you invest $1,500 a year with the employer match. Compute the ending value with the following asset allocation:

   a. 20% Long-term corporate bonds
      80% Large-cap common stocks

   b. 10% Long-term corporate bonds
      40% Large-cap common stocks
      50% Small-cap common stocks

   c. 10% Long-term corporate bonds
      90% Small-cap common stocks

5. You are 45 years old, expect to retire at age 70, and have a very low risk aversion (you realize you don't have as long to accumulate your retirement fund). Your employer has a 401(k) program that matches your contribution up to $2,000 a year and all returns are tax-exempt.

Compute the ending value of the fund if you invest $2,000 a year with the following asset allocation:

a. 10% Long-term corporate bonds
   30% Large-cap common stocks
   60% Small-cap common stocks

b. 20% Large-cap common stocks
   30% Small-cap common stocks
   50% International common stocks

c. 20% Small-cap common stocks
   30% International common stocks
   50% Emerging market common stocks

6. You are 30 years old and just had your first child. You assume that you will need about $200,000 in 20 years to pay for most of the cost of your child's education. Compute how much you will need to invest every year if you invest the money as follows:

a. 100% Long-term government bonds

b. 80% Long-term government bonds
   20% Large-cap common stocks

c. 20% Long-term government bonds
   80% Large-cap common stocks

d. 100% Small-cap common stocks

e. 100% Emerging market common stocks

References

Bhatia, Sanjiv, ed. *Managing Assets for Individual Investors* (Charlottesville, VA: Association for Investment Management and Research, 1995).

Ellis, Charles D. *Investment Policy: How to Win the Loser's Game.* Homewood, IL: Dow Jones-Irwin, 1985.

Logue, Dennis E. *Managing Corporate Pension Plans.* New York: HarperBusiness Publishers, 1991.

Peavy, John W. *Cases in Portfolio Management.* Charlottesville, VA: Association for Investment Management and Research, 1990.

Peavy, John W., ed. *Investment Counsel for Private Clients* (Charlottesville, VA: Association for Investment Management and Research, 1992).

Chapter

3

Selecting Investments in a Global Market

This chapter answers the following questions:

- What are the several reasons why investors should have a global perspective regarding their investments?
- What has happened to the relative size of U.S. and foreign stock and bond markets?
- What are the differences in the rates of return on U.S. and foreign securities markets?
- How can changes in currency exchange rates affect the returns that U.S. investors experience on foreign securities?
- Is there an additional advantage of diversifying in international markets beyond the benefits of domestic diversification?
- What alternative securities are available? What are their cash flow and risk properties?
- What are the historical return and risk characteristics of the major investment instruments?
- What is the relationship among the returns for foreign and domestic investment instruments and what is the implication of these relationships for portfolio diversification?

Individuals are willing to defer current consumption for many reasons. Some save for their children's college tuition or their own; others wish to accumulate down payments for a home, car, or boat; others want to amass adequate retirement funds for the future. Whatever the reason for an investment program, the techniques we used in Chapter 1 to measure risk and return will help you evaluate alternative investments.

But what are those alternatives? Thus far, we have said very little about the investment opportunities that are available in financial markets. In this chapter, we address this issue by surveying investment alternatives. This background is needed for making the asset allocation decision discussed in Chapter 2 and for later chapters where we analyze several individual investments such as bonds, common stock, and other securities. It is also important when we consider how to construct and evaluate portfolios of investments.

As an investor in the 1990s, you have an array of investment choices that were not available a few decades ago. Together, the dynamism of financial markets, technological advances, and new regulations have resulted in numerous new investment instruments and expanded trading opportunities.[1] Improvements in communications and relaxation of international regulations have made it easier for investors to trade in both domestic and global markets. Telecommunications networks enable U.S. brokers to reach security exchanges in London, Tokyo, and other European and Asian cities as easily as those in New York, Chicago, and other U.S. cities. The competitive environment in the brokerage industry and

---

[1] For an excellent discussion of the reasons for the development of numerous financial innovations and the effect of these innovations on world capital markets, see Merton H. Miller, *Financial Innovations and Market Volatility* (Cambridge, MA: Blackwell Publishers, 1991).

the deregulation of the banking sector have made it possible for more financial institutions to compete for investor dollars. This has spawned investment vehicles with a variety of maturities, risk–return characteristics, and cash flow patterns. In this chapter we examine some of these choices.

As an investor, you need to understand the differences among investments so you can build a properly diversified **portfolio** that conforms to your objectives. That is, you should seek to acquire a group of investments with different patterns of returns over time. If chosen carefully, such portfolios minimize risk for a given level of return because low or negative rates of return on some investments during a period of time are offset by above-average returns on others. The goal is to build a balanced portfolio of investments with relatively stable overall rates of return. A major goal of this text is to help you understand and evaluate the risk–return characteristics of investment portfolios. An appreciation of alternative security types is the starting point for this analysis.

This chapter is divided into three main sections. As noted earlier, investors can choose securities from financial markets around the world. Therefore, in the first section we look at a combination of reasons why investors *should* include foreign as well as domestic securities in their portfolios. Taken together, these reasons provide a compelling case for global investing. We continue the investigation of where to invest in Chapter 4 when we examine securities markets around the world in more detail.

In the second section of this chapter, we discuss securities in domestic and global markets, describing their main features and cash flow patterns. From this discussion, you will see that the varying risk–return characteristics of alternative investments suit the preferences of different investors. Some securities are more appropriate for individuals, whereas others are better suited for financial institutions such as insurance companies and pension funds.

The third and final section contains an assessment of the historical risk and return performance of several investment instruments from around the world and examines the relationship among the returns for many of these securities. An understanding of these relationships will provide further support for global investing.

THE CASE FOR GLOBAL INVESTMENTS

Ten years ago, the bulk of investments available to individual investors consisted of stocks and bonds sold on U.S. securities markets. Now, however, a call to your broker gives you access to a range of securities sold throughout the world. Currently, you can purchase stock in General Motors or Toyota, U.S. Treasury bonds or Japanese government bonds, a mutual fund that invests in U.S. biotechnology companies, a global growth stock fund or a German stock fund, or options on a U.S. stock index or on the British pound along with innumerable other investments.

Several changes have caused this explosion of investment opportunities. For one, the growth and development of numerous foreign financial markets such as those in Japan, the United Kingdom, and Germany have made these markets accessible and viable for investors around the world. Numerous U.S. investment firms have recognized this opportunity and established and expanded facilities in these countries. This expansion was aided by major advances in telecommunications technology that made it possible to maintain constant contact with offices and financial markets around the world. In addition to the efforts by U.S. firms, foreign firms and investors undertook counterbalancing initiatives with wealth derived from oil sales and from foreign exchange provided by surpluses in balances of payments. As a result, investors and investment firms from around the world found it desirable and possible to trade securities worldwide. Thus, investment alternatives are available from the traditional U.S. financial markets and from security markets around the world.[2]

There are three interrelated reasons U.S. investors should think of constructing global investment portfolios. They can be summarized as follows:

1. When investors compare the absolute and relative sizes of U.S. and foreign markets for stocks and bonds, they see that ignoring foreign markets reduces their choices to less than 50 percent of available investment opportunities. Because more opportunities broaden your range of risk–return choices, it makes sense to evaluate foreign securities when selecting investments and building a portfolio.
2. The rates of return available on non-U.S. securities often have substantially exceeded those for only U.S. securities. The higher returns on non-U.S. *equities* can be justified by the higher growth rates for the countries where they are issued. These superior results have continued to prevail even when the returns were risk-adjusted.
3. One of the major tenets of investment theory is that investors should diversify their portfolio. Because the relevant factor in attempting to diversify is low correlation between asset returns, it can be shown that diversification with foreign securities can help to substantially reduce portfolio risk.

In this section, we analyze these reasons to demonstrate why there should be a growing role of foreign financial markets for U.S. investors and to assess the benefits and risks of trading in these markets.

RELATIVE SIZE OF U.S. FINANCIAL MARKETS

Prior to 1970, the securities traded in the U.S. stock and bond markets comprised about 65 percent of all the securities available in world capital markets. Therefore, a U.S. investor selecting securities strictly from U.S. markets had a fairly complete set of investments available. Under these conditions, most U.S. investors probably felt it was not worth the time and effort to expand their investment universe to include the limited investments available in foreign markets. That situation has changed dramatically over the last 25 years. Currently, investors who ignore foreign markets limit their investment choices substantially.

Figure 3.1 shows the breakdown of securities available in world capital markets in 1969 and 1995. Not only has the overall value of all securities increased dramatically (from $2.3 trillion to $44 trillion), but the composition has also changed. Concentrating on proportions of bond and equity investments, the figure shows that U.S. dollar bond and equity securities made up 53 percent of the total value of all securities in 1969 versus 28.4 percent for nondollar bonds and equity. By 1995, U.S. bonds and equities accounted for 40.3 percent of the total securities market versus 51.4 percent for nondollar bonds and stocks. These data indicate that if you consider only the stock and bond market, the U.S. proportion of this combined market has declined from 63 percent of the total in 1969 to about 44 percent in 1995.

The U.S. security markets now include a smaller proportion of the total world capital market, and it is likely that this trend will continue. The faster economic growth of many other countries compared to the United States will require foreign governments and individual companies to issue debt and equity securities to finance this growth. Therefore, U.S. investors should consider investing in foreign securities because of the current and future overall importance of these securities in world capital markets. Not investing in foreign

[2] In this regard, see Scott E. Pardee, "Internationalization of Financial Markets," Federal Reserve Bank of Kansas City, *Economic Review* (February 1987), 3–7.

| FIGURE 3.1 | **TOTAL INVESTABLE CAPITAL MARKET: 1969 AND 1995** |

1969
$2.3 Trillion

1995 (Preliminary)
$44.0 Trillion

Source: Brinson Partners, Inc., Chicago, IL.

stocks and bonds means you are ignoring almost 60 percent of the securities that are available to you.

RATES OF RETURN ON U.S. AND FOREIGN SECURITIES

An examination of the rates of return on U.S. and foreign securities not only demonstrates that many non-U.S. securities provide superior rates of return, but also shows the impact of the exchange rate risk discussed in Chapter 1.

GLOBAL BOND MARKET RETURNS   Table 3.1 reports annual compound rates of return for several major international bond markets for 1987–1993. The *domestic return* is the rate of return an investor within the country would earn. In contrast, the return in U.S. dollars is what a U.S. investor would earn after adjusting for changes in the currency exchange rates during the period.

| TABLE 3.1 | **INTERNATIONAL BOND MARKET COMPOUND ANNUAL RATES OF RETURN: 1987–1993** |

	COMPONENTS OF RETURN		
	Total Domestic Return	Total Return in U.S. $	Exchange Rate Effect
Canada	11.47	12.14	0.60
France	11.44	12.69	1.12
Germany	7.58	9.14	1.45
Japan	7.03	12.49	5.10
United Kingdom	13.65	13.58	−0.01
United States	9.23	9.23	—

Source: Frank K. Reilly and David J. Wright, "Global Bond Markets: An Analysis of Alternative Benchmarks and Risk–Return Performance," Midwest Finance Association (March 1995). Based on data from Merrill Lynch Bond Indexes.

An analysis of the domestic returns in Table 3.1 indicates that the performance of the U.S. bond market ranked fourth out of the six countries. When the impact of exchange rates is considered, the U.S. experience was fifth out of six. A difference in relative performance for domestic versus U.S. dollar returns means that the exchange rate effect for a U.S. investor was almost always positive (i.e., the U.S. dollar was weak) and added to the domestic performance.

As an example, the domestic return on Japanese bonds was 7.03 percent compared with the return for U.S. bonds of 9.23 percent. The Japanese foreign exchange effect was 5.10 percent, which increased the return on Japanese bonds converted to U.S. dollars to 12.49 percent, which was above the return for U.S. bonds. The point is, investors in non-U.S. bonds from several countries could experience rates of return close to or above those of investors who limited themselves to the U.S. bond market.

GLOBAL EQUITY MARKET RETURNS   Table 3.2 shows the compound growth rate of prices in local currencies and in U.S. dollars for 12 major equity markets, four areas of the world, and the total world for the period from 1986 to 1994. The performance in local currency indicated that the U.S. market was ranked seventh of the total 17 countries and areas or was the seventh of 12 countries. The performance results in U.S. dollars indicate that the currency effect was positive for 10 of the 11 foreign countries (the U.S. dollar was weak relative to these currencies). The currency effect hurt the U.S. dollar returns for only Sweden. Overall, in U.S. dollar returns, the U.S. market was ranked fifteenth of the 17 countries and areas or eleventh of 12 countries.

| TABLE 3.2 | FT-ACTUARIES WORLD EQUITY PRICE PERFORMANCE: AVERAGE YEARLY RETURNS IN LOCAL CURRENCY AND U.S. DOLLARS, 1986–1994 |

	Local Currency		U.S. Dollars	
	Percent	Rank[a]	Percent	Rank[a]
Australia	10.6	4 (4)	12.4	8 (6)
Canada	4.5	17 (12)	4.7	17 (12)
France	12.0	3 (3)	15.5	5 (4)
Germany	5.3	16 (11)	9.6	14 (10)
Italy	9.6	6 (6)	11.2	11 (8)
Japan	8.5	12(T) (8)	18.7	1 (1)
The Netherlands	8.3	14 (9)	13.1	7 (5)
Spain	14.9	2 (2)	17.8	3 (2)
Sweden	18.0	1 (1)	17.6	4 (3)
Switzerland	7.2	15 (10)	11.5	10 (7)
United Kingdom	10.3	5 (5)	11.1	13 (9)
United States	9.4	7 (7)	9.4	15 (11)
Europe	8.6	11	11.1	12
Pacific Basin	9.2	8	18.6	2
Europe and Pacific	8.7	10	14.8	6
North America	9.1	9	9.1	16
World	8.5	12(T)	11.5	9

[a]Based on rank within 17 countries and areas (rank for only the 12 countries). (T) indicates a tie in the ranking.

Source: "Anatomy of World Markets" (London: Goldman Sachs International, Ltd., October 1991). (Updated through December 1994 by authors.) Reprinted by permission of Goldman Sachs.

Like the bond market performance, these results for equity markets around the world indicate that investors who limited themselves to the U.S. market experienced rates of return below those in many other countries. This is true for comparisons that considered both domestic returns and rates of return adjusted for exchange rates.

INDIVIDUAL COUNTRY
RISK AND RETURN

As shown, most countries experienced higher compound returns on bonds and stocks than the United States. A natural question is whether these superior results are attributable to higher levels of risk for securities in these countries.

Table 3.3 contains the returns and risk measures for six major bond markets in local currency and U.S. dollars, along with a composite ratio of return per unit of risk. The results in local currency are similar to the rate of return results—the U.S. bond market ranked fourth of the six countries. The results when returns and risk are measured in U.S. dollars were quite different. Specifically, although the return almost always increased because of the weak dollar, the risk measures typically increased dramatically (i.e., the average risk for the five non-U.S. countries went from 5.15 percent to 12.73 percent). As a result, the returns per unit of risk declined significantly and the U.S. performance ranked first. Beyond the impact on the relative results in U.S. dollars, these significant increases in the volatility for returns in U.S. dollars are evidence of the exchange rate risk discussed in Chapter 1.

Figure 3.2 contains the scatter plot of local currency equity returns (the compound growth rate of price) and risk for the 12 individual countries, four regions of the world, and the total world for 1986 to 1994. The risk measure is the standard deviation of daily returns as discussed in Chapter 1. Notably, the U.S. market experienced one of the lowest risk values. The return-to-risk position above the line of best fit indicates that the U.S. performance in local currency was tied for first out of 17, mainly because of the very low measure of risk. The results in U.S. dollars in Figure 3.3 show similar risk results. Measuring return and risk in U.S. dollars, the U.S. return/risk performance is ranked third of 17. While most countries or areas experienced higher returns in U.S. dollars, the risk measures increased substantially due to the exchange rate risk.

RISK OF COMBINED
COUNTRY INVESTMENTS

Thus far, we have discussed the risk and return results for individual countries. In Chapter 1, we considered the idea of combining a number of assets into a portfolio and noted that investors should create diversified portfolios to reduce the variability of the returns over time. We discussed how proper diversification reduces the variability (our measure of risk) of the portfolio because alternative investments have different patterns of returns over time. Specifically, when the rates of return on some investments are negative or below

| TABLE 3.3 | INTERNATIONAL BOND MARKET RETURN–RISK RESULTS: LOCAL CURRENCY AND U.S. DOLLARS, 1987–1993 |

Country	LOCAL CURRENCY			U.S. DOLLARS		
	Return	Risk	Return/Risk	Return	Risk	Return/Risk
Canada	11.47	6.41	1.79	12.14	9.02	1.35
France	11.44	4.30	2.66	12.69	12.10	1.05
Germany	7.58	3.41	2.22	9.14	13.07	0.70
Japan	7.03	4.82	1.46	12.49	14.18	0.88
United Kingdom	13.65	6.81	2.00	13.58	15.30	0.89
United States	9.23	4.70	1.96	9.23	4.70	1.96

FIGURE 3.2

ANNUAL RATES OF RETURN AND RISK FOR MAJOR STOCK MARKETS IN LOCAL CURRENCY: 1986–1994

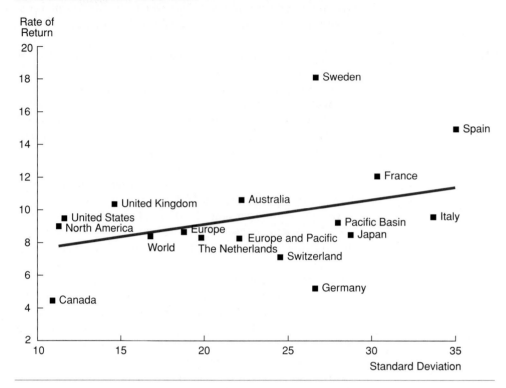

average, other investments in the portfolio will be experiencing above-average rates of return. Therefore, if a portfolio is properly diversified, it should provide a more stable rate of return for the total portfolio (i.e., it will have a lower standard deviation and therefore less risk). Although we will discuss and demonstrate portfolio theory in detail in Chapter 8, we need to consider the concept at this point to fully understand the benefits of global investing.

The way to measure whether two investments will contribute to diversifying a portfolio is to compute the correlation coefficient between their rates of return over time. Correlation coefficients can range from +1.00 to −1.00. A correlation of +1.00 means that the rates of return for these two investments move exactly together. Combining investments that move together in a portfolio would not help diversify the portfolio because they have identical rate of return patterns over time. In contrast, a correlation coefficient of −1.00 means that the rates of return for two investments move exactly opposite to each other. When one investment is experiencing above-average rates of return, the other is suffering through similar below-average rates of return. Combining two investments with large negative correlation in a portfolio would contribute much to diversification because it would stabilize the rates of return over time, reducing the standard deviation of the portfolio rates of return and hence its risk. Therefore, if you want to diversify your portfolio and reduce your risk, you want an investment that has either *low positive* correlation, *zero* correlation, or, ideally, *negative correlation* with the other investments in your portfolio. With this in

FIGURE 3.3

**ANNUAL RATES OF RETURN AND RISK FOR MAJOR STOCK MARKETS
IN U.S. DOLLARS: 1986–1994**

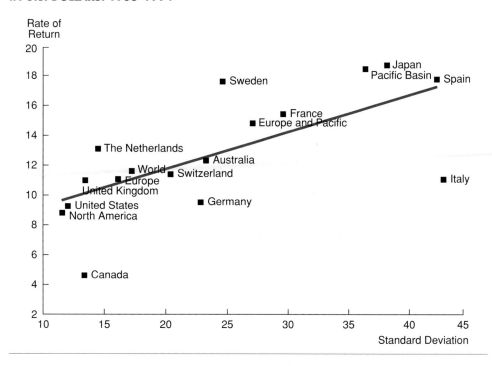

mind, the following discussion considers the correlations of returns among U.S. bonds and stocks with returns on foreign bonds and stocks.

GLOBAL BOND PORTFOLIO RISK   Table 3.4 lists the correlation coefficients between rates of return for bonds in the United States and bonds in major foreign markets in domestic and U.S. dollar terms from 1987 to 1993. Notice that only one correlation between domestic rates of return is above 0.50. For a U.S. investor, the important correlations are between the rates of return in U.S. dollars. In this case, all the correlations between returns in U.S. dollars are lower than the correlations among domestic returns and there is

TABLE 3.4

**CORRELATION COEFFICIENTS BETWEEN RATES OF RETURN ON BONDS IN THE
UNITED STATES AND MAJOR FOREIGN MARKETS: 1987–1993 (MONTHLY DATA)**

	Domestic Returns	Returns in U.S. Dollars
Canada	0.68	0.51
France	0.41	0.34
Germany	0.36	0.32
Japan	0.40	0.23
United Kingdom	0.29	0.19

Source: Frank R. Reilly and David J. Wright, "Global Bond Markets: An Analysis of Alternative Benchmarks and Risk–Return Performance," Midwest Finance Association Meeting (March 1995).

only one correlation above 0.34. Notably, while the individual volatilities increased substantially when returns were converted to U.S. dollars, the correlations with U.S. returns declined.

These low positive correlations mean that U.S. investors have substantial opportunities for risk reduction through global diversification of bond portfolios. A U.S. investor who bought bonds in any market except Canada would substantially reduce the standard deviation of the well diversified portfolio.

Why do these correlation coefficients for returns between U.S. bonds and those of various foreign countries differ? That is, why is the U.S.–Canada correlation 0.51 whereas the U.S.–United Kingdom correlation is only 0.19? The answer is because the international trade patterns, economic growth, fiscal policies, and monetary policies of the countries differ. We do not have an integrated world economy, but rather a collection of economies that are related to one another in different ways. As an example, the U.S. and Canadian economies are very closely related because of their geographic proximity, similar domestic economic policies, and the extensive trade between them. Each is the other's largest trading partner. In contrast, the United States has less trade with the United Kingdom, and the fiscal and monetary policies of the two countries differ dramatically.

A country between these extremes is Japan. The United States has a strong trade relationship with Japan, but each has a fairly independent set of economic policies. Therefore, the U.S.–Japan correlation falls between those with Canada and the United Kingdom. The point is, macroeconomic differences cause the correlation of bond returns between the United States and each country to likewise differ. These differing correlations make it worthwhile to diversify with foreign bonds, and the different correlations indicate which countries will provide the greatest reduction in the standard deviation (risk) of returns for a U.S. investor.

Also, *the correlation of returns between a single pair of countries changes over time* because the factors influencing the correlations such as international trade, economic growth, fiscal policy, and monetary policy change over time. A change in any of these variables will produce a change in how the economies are related and in the relationship between returns on bonds. As an example, the correlation between bond returns in the United States and Japan before 1980 was quite low, reflecting limited trade and independent economic policies. During the 1980s, international trade between the two countries increased substantially and so did the correlation between returns on bonds.

Figure 3.4 shows what happens to the risk–return tradeoff when we combine U.S. and foreign bonds. A comparison of a completely non-U.S. portfolio (100 percent foreign) and a 100 percent U.S. portfolio indicates that the non-U.S. portfolio has both a higher rate of return and a higher standard deviation of returns than the U.S portfolio. Combining the two portfolios in different proportions provides a very interesting set of points.

As discussed in Chapter 8, the expected rate of return is a weighted average of the two portfolios. In contrast, the risk (standard deviation) of the combination is *not* a weighted average, but also depends on the correlation between the two portfolios. In this example, the risk levels of the combined portfolios decline below those of the individual portfolios. Therefore, by adding non-correlated foreign bonds to a portfolio of U.S. bonds, a U.S. investor is able to not only increase the expected rate of return, but also reduce the risk of a bond portfolio.

GLOBAL EQUITY PORTFOLIO RISK   The correlation of world equity markets resembles that for bonds. Table 3.5 lists the correlation coefficients between monthly equity returns of each country and the U.S. market (in both domestic and U.S. dollars) for the 15-year period

FIGURE 3.4

RISK–RETURN TRADEOFF FOR INTERNATIONAL BOND PORTFOLIOS

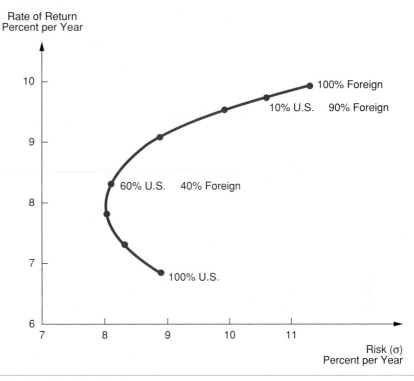

Source: Kenneth Cholerton, Pierre Piergerits, and Bruno Solnik, "Why Invest in Foreign Currency Bonds?" *The Journal of Portfolio Management* Vol. 12 No. 4 (Summer 1986) pp. 4–8. This copyrighted material is reprinted with permission from *The Journal of Portfolio Management,* a publication of Institutional Investor, Inc., 488 Madison Avenue, NY, NY 10022.

TABLE 3.5

CORRELATION COEFFICIENTS BETWEEN PRICE RETURNS ON COMMON STOCKS IN THE UNITED STATES AND MAJOR FOREIGN STOCK MARKETS: 1981–1995 (MONTHLY DATA)

	Local Currency Price Returns	U.S. Dollar Price Returns
Australia	0.48	0.40
Canada	0.74	0.75
France	0.52	0.43
Germany	0.44	0.34
Italy	0.33	0.27
Japan	0.39	0.28
The Netherlands	0.63	0.57
Spain	0.42	0.33
Sweden	0.46	0.39
Switzerland	0.66	0.52
United Kingdom	0.70	0.56

Source: "Anatomy of World Markets" (London: Goldman Sachs International, Ltd., October 1991). Updated by the authors using data provided by Goldman Sachs. Reprinted by permission of Goldman Sachs.

from 1981 to 1995. About one-half of the correlations between local currency returns top 0.50. The correlations among rates of return adjusted for exchange rates were always lower; only 4 of the 11 correlations between U.S. dollar returns exceed 0.50, and the average correlation was only 0.44.

These relatively small positive correlations between U.S. stocks and foreign stocks have similar implications to those derived for bonds. Investors can reduce the overall risk of their stock portfolios by including foreign stocks.

Figure 3.5 demonstrates the impact of international equity diversification. These curves demonstrate that as you increase the number of randomly selected securities in a portfolio, the standard deviation will decline due to the benefits of diversification *within your own country*. This is referred to as domestic diversification. After a certain number of securities (30 to 40), the curve will flatten out at a risk level that reflects the basic market risk for the domestic economy. The lower curve illustrates the benefits of international diversification. This curve demonstrates that adding foreign securities to a U.S. portfolio to create a global portfolio enables an investor to experience lower overall risk because the non-U.S. securities are not correlated with our economy or our stock market, so you are able to eliminate some of the basic market risks of the U.S. economy.

To see how this works, consider, for example, the effect of inflation and interest rates on all U.S. securities. As discussed in Chapter 1, all U.S. securities will be affected by these variables. In contrast, a Japanese stock is mainly impacted by what happens in the Japanese economy and will typically not be affected by changes in U.S. variables. Thus, adding

FIGURE 3.5

RISK REDUCTION THROUGH NATIONAL AND INTERNATIONAL DIVERSIFICATION

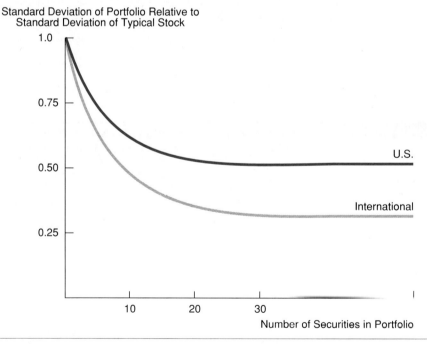

Source: B. H. Solnik, "Why Not Diversify Internationally Rather than Domestically?" *Financial Analysts Journal* (July–August 1974): 48–54. Reprinted by permission of the *Financial Analysts Journal*.

Japanese, German, and French stocks to a U.S. stock portfolio reduces the portfolio risk of the global portfolio to a level that reflects only worldwide systematic factors.

SUMMARY ON GLOBAL INVESTING   At this point, we have considered the relative size of the market for non-U.S. bonds and stocks and found that it has grown in size and importance, becoming too big to ignore. We have also examined the rates of return for foreign bond and stock investments and determined that, in most instances, their rates of return per unit of risk were superior to those in the U.S. market. Finally, we discussed constructing a portfolio of investments and the importance of diversification in reducing the variability of returns over time, which reduces the risk of the portfolio. It was noted that in order to have successful diversification an investor should combine investments with low positive or negative correlations between rates of return. An analysis of the correlation between rates of return on U.S. and foreign bonds and stocks indicated a consistent pattern of low positive correlations. Therefore, the existence of relatively high rates of return on foreign securities combined with low correlation coefficients indicates that adding foreign stocks and bonds to a U.S. portfolio *will almost certainly reduce the risk of the portfolio and can possibly increase its average return.*

As promised, there are several rather compelling reasons for adding foreign securities to a U.S. portfolio. Therefore, developing a global investment perspective is important because such an approach has been shown to be justified, and because this current trend in the investment world will continue in the future. Implementing this new global investment perspective will not be easy because it requires an understanding of new terms, instruments (e.g., Eurobonds), and institutions (e.g., non-U.S. stock and bond markets). Still, the effort is justified because you are developing a set of skills and a way of thinking that will carry you into the next century and beyond.

The next section presents an overview of investment alternatives from around the world, beginning with fixed-income investments and progressing through numerous alternatives.

GLOBAL INVESTMENT CHOICES

This section provides an important foundation for subsequent chapters where we describe techniques to value individual investments and combine alternative investments into properly diversified portfolios that conform to your risk–return objectives. In this section, we briefly describe the numerous investment alternatives available and provide a brief overview of each.

The investments are divided by asset classes. Specifically, in the first subsection, we describe fixed-income investments, including bonds and preferred stocks. In the second subsection, we discuss equity investments, while the third subsection contains a discussion of special equity instruments such as warrants and options, which have characteristics of both fixed-income and equity instruments. In subsection four, we consider futures contracts that allow for a wide range of return–risk profiles. The fifth subsection considers investment companies.

All these investments are called *financial assets* because their payoffs are in money. In contrast, there are *real assets* such as real estate, which is discussed in the sixth subsection. We conclude with assets that are considered *low liquidity investments* because of the relative difficulty in buying and selling them. This includes art, antiques, coins, stamps, and precious gems.

The purpose of this survey is to briefly introduce each of these investment alternatives so you can appreciate the full spectrum of alternatives. The final section of the chapter describes the historical return and risk patterns for many individual investment alternatives and the correlations among the returns for these investments. This additional background and perspective will help you evaluate individual investments in order to build a properly diversified portfolio of investments from around the world.

FIXED-INCOME
INVESTMENTS

Fixed-income investments have a contractually mandated payment schedule. Their investment contracts promise specific payments at predetermined times, although the legal force behind the promise varies and this affects their risks and required returns. At one extreme, if the issuing firm does not make its payment at the appointed time, creditors can declare the issuing firm bankrupt. In other cases (e.g., income bonds), the issuing firm must make payments only if it earns profits. In yet other instances (e.g., preferred stock), the issuing firm does not have to make payments unless its board of directors votes to do so.

Investors who acquire fixed-income securities (except preferred stock) are really lenders to the issuers. Specifically, you lend some amount of money, the *principal,* to the borrower. In return, the borrower promises to make periodic interest payments and to pay back the principal at the maturity of the loan.

SAVINGS ACCOUNTS   You might not think of savings accounts as fixed-income investments, yet an individual who deposits funds in a savings account at a bank or savings and loan association (S&L) is really lending money to the institution and, as a result, earning a fixed payment. These investments are generally considered to be convenient, liquid, and very low-risk because almost all are insured. Consequently, their rates of return are generally low compared with other alternatives. Several versions of these accounts have been developed to appeal to investors with differing objectives.

The passbook savings account has no minimum balance, and funds may be withdrawn at any time with very little loss of interest. Due to its flexibility, the promised interest on passbook accounts is relatively low.

For investors with larger amounts of funds who are willing to give up liquidity, banks and S&Ls developed **certificates of deposit (CDs),** which require minimum deposits (typically $500) and have fixed durations (usually 3 months, 6 months, 1 year, 2 years). The promised rates on CDs are higher than those for passbook savings, and the rate increases with the size and the duration of the deposit. An investor who wants to cash in a CD prior to its stated expiration date must pay a heavy penalty in the form of a much lower interest rate.

Investors with large sums of money ($10,000 or more) can invest in Treasury bills (T-bills)—short-term obligations (maturing in 3 to 12 months) of the U.S. government. To compete against T-bills, banks and S&Ls issue money market certificates, which require minimum investments of $10,000 and have minimum maturities of 6 months. The promised rate on these certificates fluctuates at some premium over the weekly rate on 6-month T-bills. Investors can redeem these certificates only at the bank of issue, and they incur penalties if they withdraw their funds before maturity.

CAPITAL MARKET INSTRUMENTS   **Capital market instruments** are fixed-income obligations that trade in the secondary market, which means you can buy and sell them to other individuals or institutions. Capital market instruments fall into four categories: (1) U.S. Treasury securities, (2) U.S. government agency securities, (3) municipal bonds, and (4) corporate bonds.

U.S. Treasury securities   All government securities issued by the U.S. Treasury are fixed-income instruments. They may be bills, notes, or bonds depending on their times to maturity. Specifically, bills mature in 1 year or less, notes in over 1 to 10 years, and bonds in over 10 years from time of issue. U.S. government obligations are essentially free of credit risk because there is little chance of default and they are very liquid.

U.S. government agency securities   Agency securities are sold by various agencies of the government to support specific programs, but they are not direct obligations of the Treasury. Examples of agencies that issue these bonds include the Federal National Mortgage Association (FNMA or Fannie Mae), which sells bonds and uses the proceeds to purchase mortgages from insurance companies or savings and loans; and the Federal Home Loan Bank (FHLB), which sells bonds and loans the money to its 12 banks, which in turn provide credit to savings and loans and other mortgage-granting institutions. Other agencies are the Government National Mortgage Association (GNMA or Ginnie Mae), Banks for Cooperatives, Federal Land Banks (FLBs), and the Federal Housing Administration (FHA).

Although the securities issued by federal agencies are not direct obligations of the government, they are virtually default-free because it is inconceivable that the government would allow them to default. Also they are fairly liquid. Because they are not officially guaranteed by the Treasury, they are not considered riskless. Also, because they are not as liquid as Treasury bonds, they typically provide slightly higher returns than Treasury issues.

Municipal bonds   Municipal bonds are issued by local government entities as either general obligation or revenue bonds. General obligation bonds (GOs) are backed by the full taxing power of the municipality, whereas revenue bonds pay the interest from revenue generated by specific projects (e.g., the revenue to pay the interest on sewer bonds comes from water taxes).

Municipal bonds differ from other fixed-income securities because they are tax-exempt. The interest earned from them is exempt from taxation by the federal government and by the state that issued the bond, provided the investor is a resident of that state. For this reason, municipal bonds are popular with investors in high tax brackets. For an investor having a marginal tax rate of 35 percent, a regular bond with an interest rate of 8 percent yields a net return after taxes of only 5.20 percent [$0.08 \times (1 - 0.35)$]. Such an investor would prefer a tax-free bond of equal risk with a 6 percent yield. This allows municipal bonds to offer yields that are lower than yields on comparable taxable bonds, generally by about 25 to 30 percent.

Corporate bonds   Corporate bonds are fixed-income securities issued by industrial corporations, public utility corporations, or railroads to raise funds to invest in plant, equipment, or working capital. They can be broken down by issuer, in terms of credit quality (measured by the ratings assigned by an agency on the basis of probability of default), in terms of maturity (short term, intermediate term, or long term), or based on some component of the indenture (sinking fund or call feature).

All bonds include an **indenture,** which is the legal agreement that lists the obligations of the issuer to the bondholder, including the payment schedule and features such as call provisions and sinking funds. **Call provisions** specify when a firm can issue a call for the bonds prior to their maturity, at which time current bondholders must submit the bonds to the issuing firm, which redeems them (that is, pays back the principal and a small premium). A **sinking fund** provision specifies payments the issuer must make to redeem a given percentage of the outstanding issue prior to maturity.

Corporate bonds fall into various categories based on their contractual promises to investors. They will be discussed in order of their seniority.

Senior secured bonds are the most senior bonds in a firm's capital structure and have the lowest risk of distress or default. They include various secured issues that differ based on the assets that are pledged. **Mortgage bonds** are backed by liens on specific assets such as land and buildings. In the case of bankruptcy, the proceeds from the sale of these assets are used to pay off the mortgage bondholders. **Collateral trust bonds** are a form of mortgage bond except that the assets backing the bonds are financial assets such as stocks, notes, and other high-quality bonds. Finally, **equipment trust certificates** are mortgage bonds that are secured by specific pieces of transportation equipment such as locomotives and box cars for a railroad and airplanes for an airline.

Debentures are promises to pay interest and principal, but they pledge no specific assets (referred to as *collateral*) in case the firm does not fulfill its promise. This means that the bondholder depends on the success of the borrower to make the promised payment. Debenture owners usually have first call on the firm's earnings and any assets that are not already pledged by the firm as backing for senior secured bonds. If the issuer does not make an interest payment, the debenture owners can declare the firm bankrupt and claim any unpledged assets to pay off the bonds.

Subordinated bonds are similar to debentures, but in the case of default, subordinated bondholders have claim to the assets of the firm only after the firm has satisfied the claims of all senior secured and debenture bondholders. That is, the claims of subordinated bondholders are subordinate to those of other bondholders. Within this general category of subordinated issues, you can find senior subordinated, subordinated, and junior subordinated bonds. Junior subordinated bonds have the weakest claim of all bondholders.

Income bonds stipulate interest payment schedules, but the interest is due and payable only if the issuers earn the income to make the payment by stipulated dates. If the company does not earn the required amount, it does not have to make the interest payment and it cannot be declared bankrupt. Instead, the interest payment is considered in arrears and, if subsequently earned, it must be paid off. Because the issuing firm is not legally bound to make its interest payments except when the firm earns it, an income bond is not considered as safe as a debenture or a mortgage bond, so income bonds offer higher returns to compensate investors for the added risk. Although there are a limited number of corporate income bonds, these income bonds are fairly popular with municipalities because municipal revenue bonds are basically income bonds.

Convertible bonds have the interest and principal characteristics of other bonds, with the added feature that the bondholder has the option to turn them back to the firm in exchange for its common stock. For example, a firm could issue a $1,000 face-value bond and stipulate that owners of the bond could turn the bond in to the issuing corporation and convert it into 40 shares of the firm's common stock. These bonds are very appealing to investors because they combine the features of a fixed-income security with the option of conversion into the common stock of the firm, should the firm prosper.

Because of their desirability, convertible bonds generally pay lower interest rates than nonconvertible debentures of comparable risk. The difference in the required interest rate increases with the growth potential of the company because this increases the value of the option to convert the bonds into common stock. These bonds are almost always subordinated to the nonconvertible debt of the firm, so they are considered to have higher credit risk and are rated lower.

An alternative to convertible bonds is a debenture with warrants attached. A **warrant** allows the bondholder to purchase the firm's common stock from the firm at a specified price for a given time period. The specified purchase price for the stock set in the warrant is typically above the price of the stock at the time the firm issues the bond but below the expected future stock price. The warrant makes the debenture more desirable, which lowers its required yield. The warrant also provides the firm with future common stock capital when the holder exercises the warrant and buys the stock from the firm.

Unlike the typical bond that pays interest every 6 months and its face value at maturity, a **zero coupon bond** promises no interest payments during the life of the bond but only the payment of the principal at maturity. Therefore, the purchase price of the bond is the present value of the principal payment at the required rate of return. For example, the price of a zero coupon bond that promises to pay $10,000 in 5 years with a required rate of return of 8 percent is $6,756. To find this, assuming semiannual compounding (which is the norm), use the present value factor for 10 periods at 4 percent, which is 0.6756.

Preferred stock   Preferred stock is classified as a fixed-income security because its yearly payment is stipulated as either a coupon (e.g., 5 percent of the face value) or a stated dollar amount (e.g., $5 preferred). Preferred stock differs from bonds because its payment is a dividend and therefore not legally binding. For each period, the firm's board of directors must vote to pay it, similar to a common stock dividend. Even if the firm earned enough money to pay the preferred stock dividend, the board of directors could theoretically vote to withhold it. Because most preferred stock is cumulative, the unpaid dividends would accumulate to be paid in full at a later time.

Although preferred dividends are not legally binding as the interest payments on a bond are, they are considered *practically* binding because of the credit implications of a missed dividend. Because corporations can exclude 80 percent of intercompany dividends from taxable income, preferred stocks have become attractive investments for financial corporations. For example, a corporation that owns preferred stock of another firm and receives $100 in dividends can exclude 80 percent of this amount and pay taxes on only 20 percent of it ($20). Assuming a 40 percent tax rate, the tax would only be $8 or 8 percent versus 40 percent on other investment income. Due to this benefit, the yield on high-grade preferred stock is typically lower than that on high-grade bonds.

INTERNATIONAL BOND INVESTING   As noted earlier, over half of all fixed-income securities available to U.S. investors are issued by firms in countries outside the United States. Investors identify these securities in different ways: by the country or city of the issuer (e.g., United States, United Kingdom, Japan); by the location of the primary trading market (e.g., United States, London); by the home country of the major buyers; and by the currency in which the securities are denominated (e.g., dollars, yens, pounds sterling). We identify foreign bonds by their country of origin and include these other differences in each description.

A **Eurobond** is an international bond denominated in a currency not native to the country where it is issued. Specific kinds of Eurobonds include Eurodollar bonds, Euroyen bonds, Eurodeutschemark bonds, and Eurosterling bonds. A Eurodollar bond is denominated in U.S. dollars and sold outside the United States to non-U.S. investors. A specific example would be a U.S. dollar bond issued by General Motors and sold in London. Eurobonds are typically issued in Europe, with the major concentration in London.

Eurobonds can also be denominated in yen or deutschemarks. For example, Nippon Steel can issue Euroyen bonds for sale in London. Also, if it appears that investors are looking for foreign currency bonds, a U.S. corporation can issue a Euroyen bond in London.

Yankee bonds are sold in the United States, denominated in U.S. dollars, but issued by foreign corporations or governments. This allows a U.S. citizen to buy a bond of a foreign firm or government but receive all payments in U.S. dollars, eliminating exchange rate risk.

An example would be a U.S. dollar-denominated bond issued by British Airways.[3] Similar bonds are issued in other countries, including the Bulldog Market, which involves British sterling-denominated bonds issued in the United Kingdom by non-British firms, or the Samurai Market, which involves yen-denominated bonds issued in Japan by non-Japanese firms.

International domestic bonds are sold by an issuer within its own country in that country's currency. An example would be a bond sold by a Japanese corporation in Japan denominated in yen. A U.S. investor acquiring such a bond would receive maximum diversification, but would incur exchange rate risk.

EQUITY INSTRUMENTS   This section describes several equity instruments, which differ from fixed-income securities because their returns are not contractual. As a result, you can receive returns that are much better or much worse than what you would receive on a bond. We begin with common stock, the most popular equity instrument and probably the most popular investment instrument.

Common stock represents *ownership* of a firm. Owners of the common stock of a firm share in the company's successes and problems. If, like Wal-Mart Stores, McDonald's, Microsoft, or Intel, the company does very well, the investor receives very high rates of return and can become very wealthy. In contrast, the investor can lose money if the firm does not do well or even goes bankrupt, as the once formidable Penn Central, W. T. Grant, and Interstate Department Stores all did. In these instances, the firm is forced to liquidate its assets and pay off all its creditors. Notably, the firm's preferred stockholders and common stock owners receive what is left. Investing in common stock entails all the advantages and disadvantages of ownership and is a relatively risky investment compared with fixed-income securities.

COMMON STOCK CLASSIFICATIONS   When considering an investment in common stock, people tend to divide the vast universe of stocks into categories based on general business lines and by industry within these business lines. The division gives classifications for industrial firms, utilities, transportation firms, and financial institutions. Within each of these business lines, there are industries. The most diverse group—the industrial group—includes such industries as automobiles, industrial machinery, chemicals, and beverages. Utilities include electrical power companies, gas suppliers, and the water industry. Transportation includes airlines, trucking firms, and railroads. Financial institutions include several categories of banks, savings and loans, and credit unions.

An alternative classification scheme might separate domestic (U.S.) and foreign common stocks. We will avoid this division because the business line industry breakdown is more appropriate and useful when constructing a diversified portfolio of common stock investments. With a global capital market, the focus of analysis should include all the companies in an industry viewed in a global setting. For example, when considering the automobile industry, it is necessary to go beyond General Motors, Ford, and Chrysler and consider auto firms from throughout the world such as Honda Motors, Porsche, Daimler Benz, Nissan, and Fiat.

Therefore, our subsequent discussion on foreign equities concentrates on how you buy and sell these securities because this procedural information has often been a major impediment. Many investors may recognize the desirability of investing in foreign common stock

---

[3] For a discussion of the growth of this market related to stocks, see Michael Siconolf, "Foreign Firms Step Up Offerings in U.S." *The Wall Street Journal,* June 1, 1992, C1, C2.

because of the risk and return characteristics, but they may be intimidated by the logistics of the transaction. The purpose of the next section is to alleviate this concern by explaining the alternatives available.

ACQUIRING FOREIGN EQUITIES   Currently, there are several ways to acquire foreign common stock:

1. Purchase or sale of American Depository Receipts (ADRs)
2. Purchase or sale of American shares
3. Direct purchase or sale of foreign shares listed on a U.S. or foreign stock exchange
4. Purchase or sale of international mutual funds

Purchase or sale of American Depository Receipts   The easiest way to acquire foreign shares directly is through **American Depository Receipts (ADRs).** These are certificates of ownership issued by a U.S. bank that represent indirect ownership of a certain number of shares of a specific foreign firm that are held on deposit in a bank in the firm's home country. ADRs are a convenient way to own foreign shares because the investor buys and sells them in U.S. dollars and receives all dividends in U.S. dollars. This means that the price and returns reflect both the domestic returns for the stock and the exchange rate effect. Also, the price of an ADR can reflect the fact that it represents multiple shares—for example, an ADR can be for 5 or 10 shares of the foreign stock. ADRs can be issued at the discretion of a bank based on the demand for the stock. The shareholder absorbs the additional handling costs of an ADR through higher transfer expenses, which are deducted from dividend payments.

ADRs are quite popular in the United States because of their diversification benefits.[4] By the end of 1994, 216 foreign companies had stocks listed on the New York Stock Exchange (NYSE) and over 150 of these were available through ADRs, including all the stock listed from Japan, the United Kingdom, Australia, Mexico, and the Netherlands. In addition, there are 65 foreign firms listed on the American Stock Exchange (AMEX) with most of the non-Canadian stocks available through ADRs.

Purchase or sale of American shares   American shares are securities issued in the United States by a transfer agent acting on behalf of a foreign firm. Because of the added effort and expense incurred by the foreign firm, a limited number of American shares are available.

Direct purchase or sale of foreign shares   The most difficult and complicated foreign equity transaction takes place in the country where the firm is located because it must be carried out in the foreign currency and the shares must then be transferred to the United States. This routine can be cumbersome. A second alternative is a transaction on a foreign stock exchange outside the country where the securities originated. For example, if you acquired shares of a French auto company listed on the London Stock Exchange (LSE), the shares would be denominated in pounds and the transfer would be swift, assuming your broker has a membership on the LSE.

Finally, you could purchase foreign stocks listed on the NYSE or AMEX. This is similar to buying a U.S. stock, but only a limited number of foreign firms qualify for—and are willing to accept—the cost of listing. Still, this number is growing. At the end of 1994, over 60 foreign firms (mostly Canadian) were directly listed on the NYSE, in addition to the

---

[4] For evidence of this, see Dennis T. Officer and Ronald Hoffmeister, "ADRs: A Substitute for the Real Thing?" *Journal of Portfolio Management* 13, no. 2 (Winter 1987): 61–65; and Mahmoud Wahab and Amit Khandwala, "Why Not Diversify Internationally with ADRs?" *Journal of Portfolio Management* 19, no. 2 (Winter 1993): 75–82.

firms that were available through ADRs. Also, there are many foreign firms traded on the National Association of Securities Dealers Automatic Quotations (NASDAQ) system.

Purchase or sale of international mutual funds   Numerous investment companies invest all or a portion of their funds in stocks of firms outside the United States. The alternatives range from *global funds,* which invest in both U.S. stocks and foreign stocks, to *international funds,* which invest almost wholly outside the United States. In turn, international funds can: (1) diversify across many countries, (2) concentrate in a segment of the world (e.g., Europe, South America, the Pacific basin), (3) concentrate in a specific country (e.g., the Japan Fund, the Germany Fund, the Italy Fund, or the Korea Fund), or (4) concentrate in types of markets (e.g., emerging markets, which would include stocks from countries such as Thailand, Indonesia, India, and China). A mutual fund is a convenient path to global investing, particularly for a small investor, because the purchase or sale of one of these funds is similar to a transaction for a comparable U.S. mutual fund.[5]

Special Equity Instruments: Options   In addition to common stock investments, it is also possible to invest in equity-derivative securities, which are securities that have a claim on the common stock of a firm. This would include **options**—rights to buy or sell common stock at a specified price for a stated period of time. The two kinds of option instruments are (1) warrants and (2) puts and calls.

WARRANTS   As mentioned earlier, a warrant is an option issued by a corporation that gives the holder the right to acquire a firm's common stock from the company at a specified price within a designated time period. The warrant does not constitute ownership of the stock, only the option to buy the stock.

PUTS AND CALLS   A **call option** is similar to a warrant because it is an option to buy the common stock of a company within a certain period at a specified price called the *striking price.* A call option differs from a warrant because it is not issued by the company but by another investor who is willing to assume the other side of the transaction. Options also are typically valid for a shorter time period than warrants. Call options are generally valid for less than a year, whereas warrants extend for over 5 years. The holder of a **put option** has the right to sell a given stock at a specified price during a designated time period. Puts are used by investors who expect a stock price to decline during the specified period or by investors who own the stock and want protection from a price decline.

Futures Contracts   Another instrument that provides an alternative to the purchase of an investment is a **futures contract.** This is an agreement that provides for the future exchange of a particular asset at a specified delivery date (usually within 9 months) in exchange for a specified payment at the time of delivery. Although the full payment is not made until the delivery date, a good faith deposit, the *margin,* is made to protect the seller. This is typically about 10 percent of the value of the contract.

The bulk of trading on the commodity exchanges is in futures contracts. The current price of the futures contract is determined by the participants' beliefs about the future for the commodity. For example, in July of a given year, a trader could speculate on the Chicago Board of Trade for wheat in September, December, March, and May of the next year. If the investor expected the price of a commodity to rise, he or she could buy a futures contract on one of the commodity exchanges for later sale. If the investor expected the price to fall, he or she could sell a futures contract on an exchange with the expectation of buying similar contracts later when the price had declined to cover the sale.

---

[5] Mutual funds in general and those related to global investing will be discussed in Chapter 26.

There are several differences between investing in an asset through a futures contract and investing in the asset itself. One is the use of borrowed funds to finance the futures purchase, which increases the volatility of returns. Because an investor puts up only a small portion of the total value of the futures contract (10 to 15 percent), when the price of the commodity changes, the change in the total value of the contract is large compared to the amount invested. Another unique aspect is the term of the investment: Although stocks can have infinite maturities, futures contracts typically expire in less than a year.

FINANCIAL FUTURES   In addition to futures contracts on commodities, a recent innovation has been the development of futures contracts on financial instruments such as T-bills, Treasury bonds, and Eurobonds. For example, it is possible to buy or sell a futures contract that promises future delivery of $100,000 of Treasury bonds at a set price and yield. The major exchanges for financial futures are the Chicago Mercantile Exchange (CME) and the Chicago Board of Trade (CBOT). These futures contracts allow individual investors, bond portfolio managers, and corporate financial managers to protect themselves against volatile interest rates. There are currency futures that allow individual investors or portfolio managers to speculate on or to protect against changes in currency exchange rates. Finally, there are futures contracts on stock market series such as the S&P (Standard & Poor's) 500, the *Value Line* Index, and the Nikkei Average on the Tokyo Stock Exchange.

INVESTMENT COMPANIES   The investment alternatives described so far are individual securities that can be acquired from a government entity, a corporation, or another individual. However, rather than directly buying an individual stock or bond issued by one of these sources, you may choose to acquire these investments indirectly by buying shares in an investment company, also called a *mutual fund,* that owns a portfolio of individual stocks, bonds, or a combination of the two. Specifically, an **investment company** sells shares in itself and uses the proceeds of this sale to acquire bonds, stocks, or other investment instruments. As a result, an investor who acquires shares in an investment company is a partial owner of the investment company's portfolio of stocks or bonds. We distinguish investment companies by the types of investment instruments they acquire. Discussions of some of the major types follow.

MONEY MARKET FUNDS   **Money market funds** are investment companies that acquire high-quality, short-term investments (referred to as *money market* instruments) such as T-bills, high-grade commercial paper (public short-term loans) from various corporations, and large CDs from the major money center banks. The yields on the money market portfolios always surpass those on normal bank CDs because the investment by the money market fund is larger and the fund can commit to longer maturities than the typical individual. In addition, the returns on commercial paper are above the prime rate. The typical minimum initial investment in a money market fund is $1,000, it charges no sales commission, and minimum additions are $250 to $500. You can always withdraw funds from your money market fund without penalty (typically by writing a check on the account), and you receive interest to the day of withdrawal.

Individuals tend to use money market funds as alternatives to bank savings accounts because they are generally quite safe (although they are not insured, they typically limit their investments to high-quality, short-term investments), they provide yields above what is available on most savings accounts, and the funds are readily available. Therefore, you might use one of these funds to accumulate funds to pay tuition or for a down payment on a car. Because of relatively high yields and extreme flexibility and liquidity, the total value of these funds has grown to over $700 billion in 1995.

BOND FUNDS   Bond funds generally invest in various long-term government, corporate, or municipal bonds. They differ by the type and quality of the bonds included in the portfolio as assessed by various rating services. Specifically, the bond funds range from those that invest only in risk-free government bonds and high-grade corporate bonds to those that concentrate in lower-rated corporate or municipal bonds, called *high-yield bonds* or *junk bonds*. The expected rate of return from various bond funds will differ, with the low-risk government bond funds paying the lowest returns and the high-yield bond funds expected to pay the highest returns.

COMMON STOCK FUNDS   There are numerous common stock funds that invest to achieve stated investment objectives, which can include aggressive growth, income, precious metal investments, and international stocks. Such funds offer smaller investors the benefits of diversification and professional management. To meet the diverse needs of investors, numerous funds have been created that concentrate in one industry or sector of the economy such as chemicals, electric utilities, health, housing, and technology. These funds are diversified within a sector or an industry, but are not diversified across the total market. Investors who participate in a sector or an industry fund bear more risk than an investor in a total market fund because the sector funds will tend to fluctuate more than an aggregate market fund that is diversified across all sectors. Also, as noted earlier, there are international funds that invest outside the United States or global funds that invest in the United States and in other countries. These funds offer opportunities for global investing by individual investors.[6]

BALANCED FUNDS   Balanced funds invest in a combination of bonds and stocks of various sorts depending on their stated objectives.

REAL ESTATE   Like commodities, most investors view real estate as an interesting and profitable investment alternative but believe that it is only available to a small group of experts with a lot of capital to invest. In reality, some feasible real estate investments do not require detailed expertise or large capital commitments. We will begin by considering low-capital alternatives.

REAL ESTATE INVESTMENT TRUSTS (REITS)   A **real estate investment trust** is an investment fund designed to invest in various real estate properties. It is similar to a stock or bond mutual fund, except that the money provided by the investors is invested in property and buildings rather than in stocks and bonds. There are several types of REITs.

Construction and development trusts lend the money required by builders during the initial construction of a building. Mortgage trusts provide the long-term financing for properties. Specifically, they acquire long-term mortgages on properties once construction is completed. Equity trusts own various income-producing properties such as office buildings, shopping centers, or apartment houses. Therefore, an investor who buys shares in an equity real estate investment trust is buying part of a portfolio of income-producing properties.

REITs have experienced periods of great popularity and significant depression in line with changes in the aggregate economy and the money market. Although they are subject

---

[6]For a study that examines the diversification of individual country funds, see Warren Bailey and Joseph Lim, "Evaluating the Diversification Benefits of the New Country Funds," *Journal of Portfolio Management* 18, no. 3 (Spring 1992): 74–80.

to cyclical risks depending on the economic environment, they offer small investors a way to participate in real estate investments.[7]

DIRECT REAL ESTATE INVESTMENT   The most common type of direct real estate investment is the purchase of a home, which is the largest investment most people ever make. Today, according to the Federal Home Loan Bank, the average cost of a single-family house exceeds $100,000. The purchase of a home is considered an investment because the buyer pays a sum of money either all at once or over a number of years through a mortgage. For most people, who are not in a position to pay cash for a house, the financial commitment includes a down payment (typically 10 to 20 percent of the purchase price) and specific mortgage payments over a 20- to 30-year period that include reducing the loan's principal and paying interest on the outstanding balance. Subsequently, a home-owner hopes to sell the house for its cost plus a gain.

Raw land   Another direct real estate investment is the purchase of raw land with the intention of selling it in the future at a profit. During the time you own the land, you have negative cash flows because it is necessary to make mortgage payments, maintain the property, and pay taxes on it. An obvious risk is the possible difficulty of selling it for an uncertain price. Raw land generally has low liquidity compared to most stocks and bonds. An alternative to buying and selling the raw land is the development of the land into a housing project or a shopping mall.

Land development   Typically, land development involves buying raw land, dividing it into individual lots, and building houses on it. Alternatively, buying land and building a shopping mall would also be considered land development. This is a feasible form of investment, but requires a substantial commitment of capital, time, and expertise. Although the risks can be high because of the commitment of time and capital, the rates of return from a successful housing or commercial development can be significant.[8]

Rental property   Many investors with an interest in real estate investing acquire apartment buildings or houses with low down payments, with the intention of deriving enough income from the rents to pay the expenses of the structure, including the mortgage payments. For the first few years following the purchase, the investor generally has no reported income from the building because of tax-deductible expenses including the interest component of the mortgage payment and depreciation on the structure. Subsequently, rental property provides a cash flow and an opportunity to profit from the sale of the property.[9]

LOW-LIQUIDITY INVESTMENTS   Most of the investment alternatives we have described are traded on securities markets. Except for real estate, most of these securities have good liquidity. Although many investors view the investments we discuss in this section as alternatives to financial investments, financial institutions do not typically acquire them because they are considered to be fairly

---

[7] For recent discussions, see Eric S. Hardy, "The Ground Floor," *Forbes,* August 14, 1995, 185; and Susan E. Kuhn, "Real Estate: A Smart Alternative to Stocks," *Fortune,* May 27, 1996, 186.

[8] For a review of studies that have examined returns on real estate, see William Goetzmann and Roger Ibbotson, "The Performance of Real Estate as an Asset Class," *Journal of Applied Corporate Finance* 3, no. 1 (Spring 1990): 65–76; C. F. Myer and James Webb, "Return Properties of Equity REITs, Common Stocks, and Commercial Real Estate: A Comparison," *Journal of Real Estate Research* 8, no. 1 (1993): 87–106; and Stephen Ross and Randall Zisler, "Risk and Return in Real Estate," *Journal of Real Estate Financial Economics* 4, no. 2 (1991): 175–190. For an analysis of the diversification possibilities, see Susan Hudson-Wilson and Bernard L. Elbaum, "Diversification Benefits for Investors in Real Estate," *Journal of Portfolio Management* 21, no. 3 (Spring 1995): 92–99.

[9] For a discussion of this alternative, see Diane Harris, "An Investment for Rent," *Money,* April 1984, 87–90.

illiquid and have high transaction costs compared to stocks and bonds. Many of these assets are sold at auctions, causing expected prices to vary substantially. In addition, transaction costs are high because there is generally no national market for these investments, so local dealers must be compensated for the added carrying costs and the cost of searching for buyers or sellers. Given these liquidity risk considerations, many financial theorists view the following low-liquidity investments more as hobbies than investments, even though studies have indicated that some of these assets have experienced substantial rates of return.

ANTIQUES   The investors who earn the greatest returns from antiques are dealers who acquire them at estate sales or auctions to refurbish and sell at a profit. If we gauge the value of antiques based on prices established at large public auctions, it appears that many serious collectors enjoy substantial rates of return. In contrast, the average investor who owns a few pieces to decorate his or her home finds such returns elusive. The high transaction costs and illiquidity of antiques may erode any profit that the individual may earn when selling these pieces. The subsequent discussion of rates of return on various assets will provide some evidence on the returns.

ART   The entertainment sections of newspapers or the personal finance sections of magazines often carry stories of the results of major art auctions, such as when Van Gogh's *Irises* and *Sunflowers* sold for $59 million and $36 million, respectively.

Obviously, these examples and others indicate that some paintings have increased significantly in value and thereby generated large rates of return for their owners. However, investing in art typically requires substantial knowledge of art and the art world, a large amount of capital to acquire the work of well-known artists, patience, and an ability to absorb high transaction costs. For investors who enjoy fine art and have the resources, these can be satisfying investments, but for most small investors, this is a difficult area in which to get returns that compensate for the uncertainty and illiquidity. This was especially true between 1989 and 1994 when there was a bear market in art.[10]

COINS AND STAMPS   Many individuals enjoy collecting coins or stamps as a hobby and as an investment. The market for coins and stamps is fragmented compared to the stock market, but it is more liquid than the market for art and antiques. Indeed, the volume of coins and stamps traded has prompted the publication of weekly and monthly price lists.[11] An investor can get a widely recognized grading specification on a coin or stamp and, once graded, a coin or stamp can usually be sold quickly through a dealer.[12] It is important to recognize that the difference between the bid price the dealer will pay to buy the stamp or

---

[10] For a discussion of art sold at auction, see Jerry E. Patterson, "A Dazzling Year," *Institutional Investor,* International Edition, September 1987, 324–339; Peter C. DuBois, "Not a Pretty Picture," *Barron's,* November 12, 1990, 14; Judith H. Dobrzynski, "The Art Market Is Not a Pretty Picture," *Business Week,* November 13, 1990, 57; Alexandra Peers, "With Spring Auction, Shaky Art Market Faces Flood of Less-than-Stellar Works," *The Wall Street Journal,* April 29, 1992, C1, C16; and "Market Is Picture of Optimisim in Flux," *The Wall Street Journal,* April 26, 1996, C1.

[11] A weekly publication for coins is *Coin World,* published by Amos Press, Inc., 911 Vandermark Rd., Sidney, OH 45367. There are several monthly coin magazines, including *Coinage,* published by Behn-Miller Publications, Inc., Encino, CA. Amos Press also publishes several stamp magazines, including *Linn's Stamp News* and *Scott Stamp Monthly.* These magazines provide current prices for coins and stamps.

[12] For an article that describes the alternative grading services, see Diana Henriques, "Don't Take Any Wooden Nickels," *Barron's,* June 19, 1989, 16, 18, 20, 32. For an analysis of commemorative coins, see R. W. Bradford, "How to Lose a Mint," *Barron's,* March 6, 1989, 54, 55.

coin and the asking or selling price the investor must pay the dealer is going to be fairly large compared to the difference between the bid and ask prices on stocks and bonds.

DIAMONDS   Diamonds can be and have been good investments during many periods. Still, investors who purchase diamonds must realize that: (1) diamonds can be very illiquid, (2) the grading process that determines their quality is quite subjective, (3) most investment-grade gems require substantial investments, and (4) they generate no positive cash flow during the holding period until the stone is sold. In fact, during the holding period the investor must cover costs of insurance and storage. Finally, there are appraisal costs before selling.[13]

In this section, we have described the most common investment alternatives to introduce you to the range of investments available. We will discuss many of these in more detail when we consider how you evaluate them for investment purposes. You should keep in mind that new investment alternatives are constantly being created and developed. You can keep abreast of these by reading business newspapers and magazines.

In our final section, we will present some data on historical rates of return and risk measures for a number of these investments to provide some background on their historical return–risk performance. This should give you some feel for the returns and risk characteristics you might expect in the future.

HISTORICAL RISK/RETURNS ON ALTERNATIVE INVESTMENTS

How do investors weigh the costs and benefits of owning investments and make decisions to build portfolios that will provide the best risk–return combinations? To help individual or institutional investors answer this question, financial theorists have examined extensive data and attempted to provide information on the return and risk characteristics of various investments.

Many theorists have studied the historical rates of return on common stocks, and a growing interest in bonds has caused investigators to assess their performance as well. Because inflation has been so pervasive, many studies include both nominal and real rates of return on investments. Still other investigators have examined the performance of such assets as real estate, foreign stocks, art, antiques, and commodities. This section reviews some of the major studies that provide background on the rates of return and risk for these investment alternatives. This should help you to make decisions on the alternatives you might want to examine when building your investment portfolio and the allocation to the various asset classes.

STOCKS, BONDS, AND T-BILLS

A set of studies by Ibbotson and Sinquefield (I&S) examined historical nominal and real rates of return for six major classes of assets in the United States: (1) large company common stocks, (2) small capitalization common stocks,[14] (3) long-term U.S. government bonds, (4) long-term corporate bonds, (5) U.S. Treasury bills, and (6) consumer goods (a

---

[13] For a discussion of problems and opportunities, see "When to Put Your Money into Gems," *Business Week,* March 16, 1981, 158–161.

[14] Small capitalization stocks were broken out as a separate class of asset because several studies have shown that firms with relatively small capitalization (stock with low market value) have experienced rates of return and risk that were very different from those of stocks in general. Therefore, it is felt that they should be considered a unique asset class. We will discuss these studies in Chapter 7, which deals with the efficient markets hypothesis. The large company stock returns are based upon the S&P Composite Index of 500 stocks—i.e., the S&P 500.

measure of inflation).[15] For each asset, the authors calculated total rates of return before taxes or transaction costs.

These investigators computed geometric and arithmetic mean rates of return and computed nine series derived from the basic series. Four of these series were net returns reflecting different premiums: (1) a *risk premium,* which I&S defined as the difference in the rate of return that investors receive from investing in large company common stocks (as represented by the stocks in the S&P 500 Index that is described in Chapter 5) rather than in risk-free U.S. Treasury bills; (2) a *small stock premium,* which they defined as the return on small capitalization stocks minus the return on large company stocks; (3) a *horizon premium,* which they defined as the difference in the rate of return received from investing in long-term government bonds rather than short-term U.S. Treasury bills; and (4) a *default premium,* which they defined as the difference between the rates of return on long-term risky corporate bonds and long-term risk-free government bonds. I&S also computed the real inflation-adjusted rates of return for common stocks, small capitalization stocks, Treasury bills, long-term government bonds, intermediate-term government bonds, and long-term corporate bonds.

A summary of the rates of return, risk premiums, and standard deviations for the basic and derived series appears in Table 3.6. As discussed in Chapter 1, the geometric means of the rates of return are always lower than the arithmetic means of the rates of return, and the difference between these two mean values increases with the standard deviation of returns.

Over the period from 1926 to 1995, large company common stocks returned 10.5 percent a year, compounded annually. To compare this to other investments, the results show that common stock experienced a risk premium of 6.6 percent and inflation-adjusted real returns of 7.2 percent per year. In contrast to all common stocks, the small capitalization stocks (which are represented by the smallest 20 percent of stocks listed on the NYSE measured by market value) experienced a geometric mean return of 12.5 percent, which was a premium compared to all common stocks of 1.8 percent.

Although common stocks and small capitalization stocks experienced higher rates of return than the other asset groups, their returns were also more volatile as measured by the standard deviations of annual returns.

Long-term U.S. government bonds experienced a 5.2 percent annual return, a real return of 2.0 percent, and a horizon premium (compared to Treasury bills) of 1.4 percent. Although the returns on these bonds were lower than those on stocks, they were also far less volatile.

The annual compound rate of return on long-term corporate bonds was 5.7 percent, the default premium compared to U.S. government bonds was 0.5 percent, and the inflation-adjusted return was 2.5 percent. Although corporate bonds provided a higher return, as one would expect, the volatility of corporate bonds was slightly lower than that experienced by long-term government bonds.

The nominal return on U.S. Treasury bills was 3.7 percent a year, whereas the inflation-adjusted return was 0.6 percent. The standard deviation of nominal returns for T-bills was the lowest of the series examined, which reflects the low risk of these securities and is consistent with the lowest rate of return.

---

[15] The original study was Roger G. Ibbotson and Rex A. Sinquefield, "Stocks, Bonds, Bills, and Inflation: Year-by-Year Historical Returns (1926–1974)," *Journal of Business* 49, no. 1 (January 1976): 11–47. Although this study was updated in several monographs, the current update is contained in *Stocks, Bonds, Bills, and Inflation: 1996 Yearbook* (Chicago: Ibbotson Associates, 1996). A seventh asset class (intermediate term U.S. Government bonds) was not part of the original studies but was added during the last decade.

TABLE 3.6

BASIC AND DERIVED SERIES: HISTORICAL HIGHLIGHTS (1926–1995)

Series	Annual Geometric Mean Rate of Return	Arithmetic Mean of Annual Returns	Standard Deviation of Annual Returns
Large company stocks	10.5%	12.5%	20.4%
Small capitalization stocks	12.5	17.7	34.4
Long-term corporate bonds	5.7	6.0	8.7
Long-term government bonds	5.2	5.5	9.2
Intermediate-term government bonds	5.3	5.4	5.8
U.S. Treasury bills	3.7	3.8	3.3
Consumer price index	3.1	3.2	4.6
Equity risk premium	6.6	8.6	20.3
Small stock premium	1.8	3.4	18.3
Default premium	0.5	0.5	3.0
Horizon premium	1.4	1.7	8.5
Large company stock—inflation adjusted	7.2	9.2	20.6
Small capitalization stock— inflation adjusted	9.1	14.1	33.7
Long-term corporate bonds— inflation adjusted	2.5	3.0	10.0
Long-term government bonds— inflation adjusted	2.0	2.5	10.6
Intermediate-term government bonds—inflation adjusted	2.1	2.3	7.1
U.S. Treasury bills—inflation adjusted	0.6	0.7	4.2

Source: © *Stocks, Bonds, Bills, and Inflation: 1996 Yearbook*™, Ibbotson Associates, Chicago (annually updates work by Roger G. Ibbotson and Rex A. Sinquefield). Used with permission. All rights reserved.

This study reported the rates of return, return premiums, and risk measures on various asset groups in the United States. The rates of return were generally consistent with the uncertainty (risk) of annual returns as measured by the standard deviations of annual returns.

WORLD PORTFOLIO PERFORMANCE

Expanding this analysis from domestic to global securities, Ibbotson, Siegel, and Love examined the performance of numerous assets, not only in the United States, but around the world.[16] Specifically, for the period from 1960 to 1984 they constructed a value-weighted portfolio of stocks, bonds, cash (the equivalent of U.S. T-bills), real estate, and precious metals from the United States, Northern and Western Europe, Japan, Hong Kong, Singapore, Canada, and Australia. They computed annual returns, risk measures, and correlations among the returns for alternative assets. Table 3.7 shows the geometric and arithmetic average annual rates of return and the standard deviations of returns for that period.

ASSET RETURN AND RISK   The results in Table 3.7 generally confirm the expected relationship between annual rates of return and the risk of these securities. The riskier assets—those that had higher standard deviations—experienced the highest returns. For

[16]Roger G. Ibbotson, Laurence B. Siegel, and Kathryn S. Love, "World Wealth: Market Values and Returns," *Journal of Portfolio Management* 12, no. 1 (Fall 1985): 4–23.

| TABLE 3.7 | WORLD CAPITAL MARKET: TOTAL ANNUAL RETURNS (1960–1984) |

	Geometric Mean	Arithmetic Mean	Standard Deviation[a]	Coefficient of Variation[b]
Equities				
United States	8.81%	10.20%	16.89%	1.66
Foreign				
Europe	7.83	8.94	15.58	1.74
Asia	15.14	18.42	30.74	1.67
Other	8.14	10.21	20.88	2.04
Equities total	9.08	10.21	15.28	1.46
Bonds				
United States				
Corporate[c]	5.35	5.75	9.63	1.67
Government	5.91	6.10	6.43	1.05
United States total	5.70	5.93	7.16	1.21
Foreign				
Corporate domestic	8.35	8.58	7.26	0.85
Government domestic	5.79	6.04	7.41	1.23
Crossborder	7.51	7.66	5.76	0.75
Foreign total	6.80	7.01	6.88	0.98
Bonds total	6.36	6.50	5.56	0.86
Cash equivalents				
United States	6.49	6.54	3.22	0.49
Foreign	6.00	6.23	7.10	1.14
Cash total	6.38	6.42	2.92	0.45
Real estate[d]				
Business	8.49	8.57	4.16	0.49
Residential	8.86	8.93	3.77	0.42
Farms	11.86	12.13	7.88	0.65
Real estate total	9.44	9.49	3.45	0.36
Metals				
Silver	9.14	20.51	75.34	3.67
Gold	9.08	12.62	29.87	2.37
Metals total	9.11	12.63	29.69	2.35
U.S. market wealth portfolio	8.63	8.74	5.06	0.58
Foreign market wealth portfolio	7.76	8.09	8.48	1.05
World market wealth portfolio				
Excluding metals	8.34	8.47	5.24	0.62
Including metals	8.39	8.54	5.80	0.68
U.S. inflation rate	5.24	5.30	3.60	0.68

[a]Standard deviation from arithmetic mean.
[b]Coefficient of variation equals standard deviation/arithmetic mean.
[c]Including preferred stock.
[d]United States only.

Source: *The Journal of Portfolio Management* Vol. 12 No. 1 (Fall 1985) pp. 4–23. This copyrighted material is reprinted with permission from *The Journal of Portfolio Management,* a publication of Institutional Investor, Inc., 488 Madison Avenue, NY, NY 10022.

example, silver had the highest arithmetic mean rate of return (20.51 percent) but also the largest standard deviation (75.34 percent), whereas risk-free U.S. cash equivalents (T-bills) had low returns (6.49 percent) and the smallest standard deviation (3.22 percent). The data amassed by Ibbotson et al. could be used to assess the relative risk of assets in a portfolio, as well as risk and return values for each asset

RELATIVE ASSET RISK   Calculating the coefficients of variation (CVs), which measure relative variability, Ibbotson et al. found a wide range of values. The lowest CVs were experienced by the cash equivalents (T-bills) and real estate investments. Silver had the highest CV value because of its very large standard deviation, and corporate bonds the next highest because of a relatively small mean return. The CVs for stocks ranged from 1.46 to 2.04, with U.S. stocks about in the middle (1.66). Finally, the world market portfolios had rather low CVs (0.62 and 0.68), demonstrating the benefits of global diversification.

CORRELATIONS BETWEEN ASSET RETURNS   Table 3.8 is a correlation matrix of selected U.S. and world assets. The first column shows that U.S. equities have a reasonably high correlation with European equities (0.640) and other foreign equities (0.807), but low correlation with Asian equities (0.237). Also, U.S. equities show a negative correlation with U.S. government bonds (−0.006), farm real estate (−0.171), and gold (−0.088). You will recall from our earlier discussion that you can use this information to build a diversified portfolio by combining those assets with low positive or negative correlations.

TABLE 3.8

CORRELATION MATRIX OF WORLD CAPITAL MARKET SECURITY RETURNS

	U.S. Equities	U.S. Market Portfolio	World Market, Including Metals
U.S. equities	1.000	0.917	0.757
Europe equities	0.640	0.605	0.706
Asia equities	0.237	0.209	0.351
Other equities	0.807	0.754	0.753
Foreign total: equities	0.672	0.626	0.732
World total: equities	0.964	0.886	0.805
U.S. corporate bonds and preferred stock	0.323	0.393	0.207
U.S. government bonds	−0.006	0.152	−0.023
U.S. total: bonds	0.166	0.284	0.093
Foreign domestic corporation bonds	0.050	0.153	0.380
Foreign domestic government bonds	−0.024	0.171	0.426
Foreign total: bonds	0.052	0.191	0.429
World total: bonds	0.124	0.172	0.389
U.S. cash equivalents (T-bills)	0.079	0.130	−0.004
Foreign cash equivalents	−0.386	−0.233	0.105
World total: cash equivalents	−0.238	0.103	0.046
Business real estate	0.164	0.394	0.390
Residential real estate	0.125	0.442	0.552
Farm real estate	−0.171	−0.019	0.133
U.S. total: real estate	0.054	0.371	0.531
Gold	−0.088	0.104	0.427
Silver	0.116	0.291	0.283
World total: metals	−0.086	0.111	0.427
U.S. market wealth portfolio	0.917	1.000	0.873
Foreign market wealth portfolio	0.510	0.533	0.727
World market wealth portfolio (excluding metals)	0.861	0.925	0.924
World market wealth portfolio (including metals)	0.757	0.873	1.000

Source: *The Journal of Portfolio Management* Vol. 12 No. 1 (Fall 1985) pp. 19–21. This copyrighted material is reprinted with permission from *The Journal of Portfolio Management,* a publication of Institutional Investor, Inc., 488 Madison Avenue, NY, NY 10022.

ART AND ANTIQUES   Unlike financial securities, where the results of transactions are reported daily, art and antique markets are very fragmented and lack any formal transaction reporting system. This makes it difficult to gather data. The best-known series that attempt to provide information about the changing value of art and antiques were developed by Sotheby's, a major art auction firm. These value indexes cover 13 areas of art and antiques and a weighted aggregate series that is a combination of the 13.

Reilly examined these series for the period from 1975 to 1991 and computed rates of return, measures of risk, and the correlations among the various art and antique series.[17] Figure 3.6 shows these data and compares them with returns for 1-year Treasury bonds, the Lehman Brothers Government/Corporate Bond Index, the Standard & Poor's 500 Stock Index, and the annual inflation rate.

These results vary to such a degree that it is not possible to generalize about the performance of art and antiques. As shown, the average annual compound rates of return (measured by the geometric means) ranged from a high of 16.8 percent (modern paintings) to a low of 9.99 percent (English silver). Similarly, the standard deviations varied from 21.67 percent (Impressionist–Post Impressionist Paintings) to 8.74 percent (American furniture). The relative risk measures (the coefficients of variation) varied from a high of 1.33 (continental silver) to a low value of 0.71 (English furniture). The annual rankings likewise changed over time.

| FIGURE 3.6 | **GEOMETRIC MEAN RATES OF RETURN AND STANDARD DEVIATION FOR SOTHEBY'S INDEXES, S&P 500, BOND MARKET SERIES, 1-YEAR BONDS, AND INFLATION: 1976–1991** |

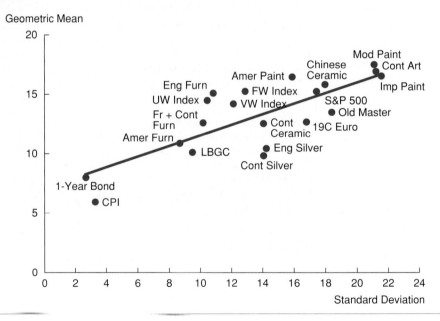

Source: Adapted from Frank K. Reilly, "Risk and Return on Art and Antiques: The Sotheby's Indexes," Eastern Finance Association Meeting, May 1987. (Updated through September 1991.)

---

[17] Frank K. Reilly, "Risk and Return on Art and Antiques: The Sotheby's Indexes," Eastern Finance Association Meeting, April 1987. The results reported are a summary of the study results and have been updated through September 1991.

Although there was a wide range of mean returns and risk, the risk–return plot in the figure indicates that there was a fairly consistent relationship between risk and return during this 16-year period. Comparing the art and antique results to the bond and stock indexes indicates that the stocks and bonds experienced results in the middle of the art and antique series.

Analysis of the correlation matrix of these assets in Table 3.9 using annual rates of return reveals several important relationships. First, the correlations among alternative antique and art categories (e.g., paintings and furniture) vary substantially from over 0.90 to some negative correlations. Second, the correlations between rates of return on art/antiques and bonds are generally negative. Third, the correlations of art/antiques with stocks are typically small positive values. Finally, the correlation of art and antiques with percentage changes in the CPI (i.e., the rate of inflation) indicates that several of the categories have been fairly good inflation hedges since they were positively correlated with inflation (e.g., Chinese ceramics), and they were clearly superior inflation hedges compared to long bonds and common stocks.[18] This would suggest that a properly diversified portfolio of art, antiques, stocks, and bonds might provide a fairly low-risk portfolio. It is important to reiterate the earlier observation that most art and antiques are considered to be quite illiquid and the transaction costs are fairly high compared to the financial assets we have discussed.

REAL ESTATE   Somewhat similar to art and antiques, returns on real estate are difficult to derive because there are a limited number of transactions and there is not a national source of data for the transactions that allows one to accurately compute rates of return. In the study by Goetzmann and Ibbotson, the authors gathered data on commercial real estate through REITs and Commingled Real Estate Funds (CREFs).[19] They estimated returns on residential real estate from a series created by Case and Shiller.[20] The summary of the real estate returns compared to various stock, bond, and an inflation series is contained in Table 3.10. As shown, the two commercial real estate series reflected very different results. The CREFs had lower returns and very low volatility, while the REIT index had higher returns and risk. Notably, the REIT returns were above common stocks, but the risk measure for real estate was lower (there was a small difference in the time period). The residential real estate series reflected lower returns and very low risk. The longer-term results indicate that all the real estate series experience lower returns than common stock, but they also had much lower risk.

Table 3.11 shows the correlations among annual returns for the various asset groups. The results indicate a relatively low positive correlation between commercial real estate and stocks. In contrast, there was negative correlation between stocks and residential real estate and farm real estate. This negative relationship with real estate was also true for 20-year government bonds.

---

[18] These results for stocks are very consistent with several prior studies that likewise found a negative relationship between inflation and rates of return on stocks, which indicates that common stocks have generally been very poor inflation hedges. In this regard, see Eugene F. Fama, "Stock Returns, Real Activity, Inflation and Money," *American Economic Review* 71, no. 2 (June 1981). 545–565, and Jeffrey Jaffe and Gershon Mandelker, "The 'Fisher Effect' for Risky Assets: An Empirical Investigation," *Journal of Finance* 31, no. 2 (June 1976): 447–458.

[19] William N. Goetzmann and Roger G. Ibbotson, "The Performance of Real Estate as an Asset Class," *Journal of Applied Corporate Finance* 3, no. 1 (Spring 1990): 65–76.

[20] Carl Case and Robert Shiller, "Price of Single Family Homes Since 1970: New Indexes for Four Cities," National Bureau of Economic Research, Inc., Working Paper No. 2393 (1987).

TABLE 3.9

CORRELATION COEFFICIENTS AMONG ANNUAL RATES OF RETURN FOR ART, ANTIQUES, STOCKS, BONDS, AND INFLATION: 1976–1991 (SEPTEMBER YEAR END)

	Old Mast.	19C Euro.	Impr. Pt.-Im.	Mod. Paint.	Cont. Art	Amer. Paint.	Cont. Ceram.	Chin. Ceram.	Engl. Silver	Cont. Silver	Ameri. Furn.	Fr. & Cont. Furn.	Engl. Furn.	Fix Wt. Index	Unwtd. Index	Pr. W. Index	1-yr. T Bond	LBGC Bond	S&P 500	CPI
Old masters painting	*																			
19th-century European paintings	0.948	*																		
Impressionist–post impressionist paintings	0.442	0.467	*																	
Modern paintings	0.403	0.473	0.969	*																
Continental art	0.780	0.652	0.566	0.476	*															
American paintings	0.599	0.515	0.464	0.386	0.674	*														
Continental ceramics	0.589	0.584	0.200	0.191	0.227	0.498	*													
Chinese ceramics	0.447	0.419	0.279	0.267	0.279	0.561	0.708	*												
English silver	0.394	0.497	0.117	0.186	0.057	-0.012	0.295	0.098	*											
Continental silver	0.628	0.709	0.354	0.404	0.301	0.054	0.600	0.270	0.729	*										
American furniture	-0.176	-0.204	0.185	0.165	-0.071	0.012	-0.251	-0.167	0.122	-0.168	*									
French and continental furniture	0.648	0.755	0.116	0.192	0.310	0.143	0.622	0.459	0.541	0.764	-0.379	*								
English furniture	0.234	0.328	0.548	0.605	-0.016	0.433	0.471	0.449	0.105	0.222	0.043	0.178	*							
Fixed-weight index	0.817	0.835	0.851	0.838	0.727	0.637	0.536	0.525	0.359	0.622	0.001	0.525	0.550	*						
Unweighted index	0.859	0.872	0.740	0.731	0.700	0.677	0.666	0.611	0.450	0.686	-0.017	0.620	0.540	0.977	*					
Price weighted index	0.828	0.826	0.791	0.776	0.733	0.723	0.610	0.593	0.397	0.611	0.000	0.536	0.555	0.984	0.990	*				
1-year Treasury bond	-0.331	-0.376	-0.089	-0.131	0.159	-0.109	-0.570	-0.269	-0.103	-0.302	0.130	-0.248	-0.612	-0.269	-0.309	-0.258	*			
LBGC bond index	-0.169	-0.182	-0.280	-0.308	-0.173	-0.308	-0.422	-0.318	0.052	-0.210	-0.159	-0.328	-0.351	-0.332	-0.366	-0.359	-0.080	*		
S&P 500	0.038	-0.026	-0.082	-0.134	-0.097	-0.127	-0.041	-0.015	-0.031	-0.058	0.144	-0.113	-0.030	-0.075	-0.080	-0.121	-0.224	0.127	*	
Consumer Price Index	0.008	0.010	0.064	0.056	0.161	0.283	0.290	0.462	0.127	0.085	0.118	0.338	-0.024	0.141	0.224	0.227	0.496	-0.647	-0.322	*

Source: Frank K. Reilly, "Risk and Return on Art and Antiques," July 1992.

TABLE 3.10

SUMMARY STATISTICS OF COMMERCIAL AND RESIDENTIAL REAL ESTATE SERIES COMPARED TO STOCKS, BONDS, T-BILLS, AND INFLATION

Series	Date	Geometric Mean	Arithm. Mean	Standard Deviation
Annual Returns in the Last 20 Years				
CREF (Comm.)	1969–87	10.8%	10.9%	2.6%
REIT (Comm.)	1972–87	14.2	15.7	15.4
C&S (Res.)	1970–86	8.5	8.6	3.0
S&P (Stocks)	1969–87	9.2	10.5	18.2
LTG (Bonds)	1969–87	7.7	8.4	13.2
TBILL (Bills)	1969–87	7.6	7.6	1.4
CPI (Infl.)	1969–87	6.4	6.4	1.8
Annual Returns over the Long Term				
I&S (Comm.)	1960–87	8.9%	9.1%	5.0%
CPIHOME (Res.)	1947–86	8.1	8.2	5.2
USDA (Farm)	1947–87	9.6	9.9	8.2
S&P (Stocks)	1947–87	11.4	12.6	16.3
LTG (Bonds)	1947–87	4.2	4.6	9.8
TBILL (Bills)	1947–87	4.9	4.7	3.3
CPI (Infl.)	1947–87	4.5	4.6	3.9

Source: William N. Goetzmann and Roger G. Ibbotson, "The Performance of Real Estate as an Asset Class," *Journal of Applied Corporate Finance* (Spring 1990, Vol. 3 No. 1) pp. 65–76. Reprinted with permission.

TABLE 3.11

CORRELATIONS OF ANNUAL REAL ESTATE RETURNS WITH THE RETURNS ON OTHER ASSET CLASSES

	I&S	CREF	CPI Home	C&S	Farm	S&P	20-Yr. Gvt.	1-Yr. Gvt.	Infl.
I&S	1								
CREF	0.79	1							
CPI Home	0.52	0.12	1						
C&S	0.26	0.16	0.82	1					
Farm	0.06	−0.06	0.51	0.49	1				
S&P	0.16	0.25	−0.13	−0.20	−0.10	1			
20-Yr. Gvt.	−0.04	0.01	−0.22	−0.54	−0.44	0.11	1		
1-Yr. Gvt.	0.53	0.42	0.13	−0.56	−0.32	−0.07	0.48	1	
Infl.	0.70	0.35	0.77	0.56	0.49	−0.02	−0.17	0.26	1

Note: Correlation coefficient for each pair of asset classes uses the maximum number of observations, i.e., the minimum length of the two series in the pair.

Source: William N. Goetzmann and Roger G. Ibbotson, "The Performance of Real Estate as an Asset Class," *Journal of Applied Corporate Finance* (Spring 1990, Vol. 3 No. 1) pp. 65–76. Reprinted with permission.

These results imply that returns on real estate are equal to or slightly lower than common stocks, but real estate possesses very favorable risk results. Specifically, real estate had much lower standard deviations as unique assets, and either low positive or negative correlations with other asset classes in a portfolio context.

Summary

- Investors who want the broadest range of choices in investments must consider foreign stocks and bonds in addition to domestic financial assets. Many foreign securities offer investors higher risk-adjusted returns than domestic securities. In addition, the low positive or negative correlations between foreign and U.S. securities makes them ideal for building a diversified portfolio.

- Figure 3.7 summarizes the risk and return characteristics of the investment alternatives described in this chapter. Some of the differences are due to unique factors that we discussed. Foreign bonds are considered riskier than domestic bonds because of the unavoidable uncertainty due to exchange rate risk and country risk. The same is true for foreign and domestic common stocks. Investments such as art, antiques, coins, and stamps require very heavy liquidity risk premiums. You should divide consideration of real estate investments between your personal home, on which you do not expect as high a return because of nonmonetary factors, and commercial real estate, which requires a much higher rate of return due to cash flow uncertainty and illiquidity.

- Studies on the historical rates of return for common stocks and other investment alternatives (including bonds, commodities, real estate, foreign securities, and art and antiques) point toward two generalizations:[21]

  1. A positive relationship typically holds between the rate of return earned on an asset and the variability of its historical rate of return. This is expected in a world of risk-averse investors who require higher rates of return to compensate for more uncertainty.

  2. The correlation among rates of return for selected alternative investments is typically quite low, especially for U.S and foreign stocks and bonds and between these financial assets and real assets, as represented by art, antiques, and real estate. This confirms the advantage of diversification among investments from around the world.

- In addition to describing many direct investments, such as stocks and bonds, we also discussed investment companies that allow investors to buy investments indirectly. These can be very impor-

---

FIGURE 3.7   **ALTERNATIVE INVESTMENTS—RISK AND RETURN CHARACTERISTICS**

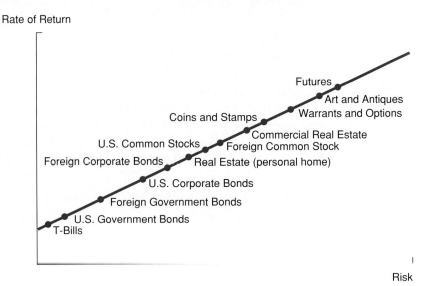

---

[21] A recent book that provides an excellent discussion of global investing and contains extensive analysis of returns and risks for alternative asset classes is Roger G. Ibbotson and Gary P. Brinson, *Global Investing* (New York: McGraw-Hill, 1993).

tant to investors who want to take advantage of professional management but also want instant diversification with a limited amount of funds. With $10,000, you may not be able to buy many individual stocks or bonds, but you could acquire shares in a mutual fund, which would give you a share of a diversified portfolio that might contain 100 to 150 different U.S. and international stocks or bonds.

- Now that we know the range of domestic and foreign investment alternatives, our next task is to learn about the markets in which they are bought and sold. That is the objective of the next chapter. The discussion in Chapter 4 will help us understand how markets match buyers and sellers of investments. Later chapters will describe how investors evaluate the risk and return characteristics of alternative investments to build diversified portfolios that are consistent with their objectives.

Questions

1. What are the advantages of investing in the common stock rather than corporate bonds of the same company? Compare the certainty of returns for a bond with those for a common stock. Draw a line graph to demonstrate the pattern of returns you would envision for each of these assets over time.

2. Discuss three factors that cause U.S. investors to consider including global securities in their portfolios.

3. Discuss why international diversification reduces portfolio risk. Specifically, why would you expect low correlation in the rates of return for domestic and foreign securities?

4. Discuss why you would expect a *difference* in the correlation of returns between securities from the United States and from alternative countries (e.g., Japan, Canada, South Africa).

5. Discuss whether you would expect any *change* in the correlations between U.S. stocks and the stocks for different countries. For example, discuss whether you would expect the correlation between U.S. and Japanese stock returns to change over time.

6. When you invest in Japanese or German bonds, what are the major additional risks you must consider besides yield changes within the country?

7. Some investors believe that international investing introduces additional risks. Discuss these risks and how they can affect your return. Give an example.

8. What alternatives to direct investment in foreign stocks are available to investors?

9. You are a wealthy individual in a high tax bracket. Why might you consider investing in a municipal bond rather than a straight corporate bond, even though the promised yield on the municipal bond is lower?

10. You can acquire convertible bonds from a rapidly growing company or from a utility. Speculate on which convertible bond would have the lower yield and discuss the reason for this difference.

11. Compare the liquidity of an investment in raw land with that of an investment in common stock. Be specific as to why and how they differ. (Hint: Begin by defining *liquidity*.)

12. What are stock warrants and call options? How do they differ?

13. Discuss why financial analysts consider antiques and art to be illiquid investments. Why do they consider coins and stamps to be more liquid than antiques and art? What must an investor typically do to sell a collection of art and antiques? Briefly contrast this procedure to the sale of a portfolio of stocks that are listed on the New York Stock Exchange.

14. You have a fairly large portfolio of U.S. stocks and bonds. You meet a financial planner at a social gathering who suggests that you diversify your portfolio by investing in gold. Discuss whether the correlation results in Table 3.8 support this suggestion.

15. You are an avid collector/investor of American paintings. Based on the information in Figure 3.6, describe your risk–return results during the period from 1976 to 1991 compared to U.S. common stocks.

16. *CFA Examination I (1993)*

    Chris Smith of XYZ Pension Plan has historically invested in the stocks of only U.S. domiciled companies. Recently, he has decided to add international exposure to the plan portfolio.

    a. Identify and briefly discuss *three* potential problems that Smith may confront in selecting international stocks that he did not face in choosing U.S. stocks.

17. *CFA Examination III (1993)*

TMP has been experiencing increasing demand from its institutional clients for information and assistance related to international investment management. Recognizing that this is an area of growing importance, the firm has hired an experienced analyst/portfolio manager specializing in international equities and market strategy. His first assignment is to represent TMP before a client company's investment committee to discuss the possibility of changing their present "U.S. securities-only" investment approach to one including international investments. He is told that the committee wants a presentation that fully and objectively examines the basic, substantive considerations on which the committee should focus its attention, including both theory and evidence. The company's pension plan has no legal or other barriers to adoption of an international approach, no non-U.S. pension liabilities currently exist.

a. Identify and briefly discuss *three* reasons for adding international securities to the pension portfolio and *three* problems associated with such an approach.

b. Assume that the committee has adopted a policy to include international securities in its pension portfolio. Identify and briefly discuss *three* additional *policy-level* investment decisions the committee must make *before* management selection and actual implementation can begin.

Problems

1. Calculate the current horizon (maturity) premium on U.S. government securities based on data in *The Wall Street Journal.* The long-term security should have a maturity of at least 20 years.

2. Using a source of international statistics, compare the percentage change in the following economic data for Japan, Germany, Canada, and the United States for a recent year. What were the differences, and which country or countries differed most from the United States?
a. Aggregate output (GDP)
b. Inflation
c. Money supply growth

3. Using a recent edition of *Barron's*, examine the weekly percentage change in the stock price indexes for Japan, Germany, Italy, and the United States. For each of three weeks, which foreign series moved most closely with the U.S. series? Which series diverged most from the U.S. series? Discuss these results as they relate to international diversification.

4. Using published sources (e.g., *The Wall Street Journal, Barron's, Federal Reserve Bulletin*), look up the exchange rate for U.S. dollars with Japanese yen for each of the past 10 years (you can use an average for the year or a specific time period each year). Based on these exchange rates, compute and discuss the yearly exchange rate effect on an investment in Japanese stocks by a U.S. investor. Discuss the impact of this exchange rate effect on the risk of Japanese stocks for a U.S. investor.

5. *CFA Examination (Adapted)*

The following information is available concerning the historical risk and return relationships in the U.S. capital markets:

U.S. CAPITAL MARKETS TOTAL ANNUAL RETURNS, 1960–1984

Investment Category	Arithmetic Mean	Geometric Mean	Standard Deviation of Return[a]
Common stocks	10.28%	8.81%	16.9%
Treasury bills	6.54	6.49	3.2
Long government bonds	6.10	5.91	6.4
Long corporate bonds	5.75	5.35	9.6
Real estate	9.49	9.44	3.5

[a]Based on arithmetic mean.

Source: Adapted from R. G. Ibbotson, Laurence B. Siegel, and Kathryn S. Love, "World Wealth: Market Values and Returns," *Journal of Portfolio Management* 12, no. 1 (Fall 1985): 4–23.

a. Explain why the geometric and arithmetic mean returns are not equal and whether one or the other may be more useful for investment decision making. [5 minutes]

b. For the time period indicated, rank these investments on a risk-adjusted basis from most to least desirable. Explain your rationale. [6 minutes]

c. Assume the returns in these series are normally distributed.
   1. Calculate the range of returns that an investor would have expected to achieve 95 percent of the time from holding common stocks. [4 minutes]
   2. Suppose an investor holds real estate for this time period. Determine the probability of at least breaking even on this investment. [5 minutes]

d. Assume you are holding a portfolio composed entirely of real estate. Discuss the justification, if any, for adopting a mixed asset portfolio by adding long-term government bonds. [5 minutes]

6. You are given the following long-run annual rates of return for alternative investment instruments:

U.S. government T-bills	4.50%
Common stock	12.50
Long-term corporate bonds	5.80
Long-term government bonds	5.10
Small capitalization common stock	14.60

a. On the basis of these returns, compute the following:
   1. The common stock risk premium
   2. The small firm stock risk premium
   3. The horizon (maturity) premium
   4. The default premium

b. The annual rate of inflation during this period was 4 percent. Compute the real rate of return on these investment alternatives.

References

Beidleman, Carl, ed. *The Handbook of International Investing.* Chicago: Probus Publishing, 1987.

Brick, John R., H. Kent Baker, and John A. Haslem, eds. *Financial Markets Instruments and Concepts.* 2d ed. Reston, VA: Reston Publishing, 1986.

Elton, Edwin J., and Martin J. Gruber, eds. *Japanese Capital Markets.* New York: Harper & Row Publishers, 1990.

European Bond Commission. *The European Bond Markets.* Chicago: Probus Publishing, 1989.

Fabozzi, Frank J., ed. *The Japanese Bond Markets.* Chicago: Probus Publishing, 1990.

Fisher, Lawrence, and James H. Lorie. *A Half Century of Returns on Stocks and Bonds.* Chicago: University of Chicago Graduate School of Business, 1977.

Grabbe, J. Orlin. *International Financial Markets.* New York: Elsevier Science Publishing, 1986.

Greshin, Adam M., and Margaret Durasz Hadzima. "International Bond Investing and Portfolio Management." In *The Handbook of Fixed-Income Securities,* 4th ed., edited by Frank J. Fabozzi and T. Dessa Fabozzi. Burr Ridge IL: Irwin Professional Publishing, 1995.

Hamao, Yasushi. "Japanese Stocks, Bonds, Inflation, 1973–1987." *Journal of Portfolio Management* 16, no. 2 (Winter 1989).

Ibbotson, Roger G., and Gary P. Brinson. *Global Investing.* New York: McGraw Hill, 1993.

Lessard, Donald R. "International Diversification." In *The Financial Analyst's Handbook,* 2d ed., edited by Sumner N. Levine. Homewood, IL: Dow Jones-Irwin, 1988.

Murphy, Brian, David Won, and Deepak Gulrajani. "Valuation and Risk Analysis of International Bonds." In *The Handbook of Fixed-Income Securities,* 4th ed., edited by Frank J. Fabozzi and T. Dessa Fabozzi. Burr Ridge, IL: Irwin Professional Publishing, 1995.

Reilly, Frank K., and David J. Wright. "Global Bond Markets: An Analysis of Alternative Benchmarks and Risk–Return Performance." Midwest Finance Association Meeting (March 1995).

Robinson, Anthony W., and Stephen W. Glover. "International Fixed-Income Markets and Securities." In *The Financial Analyst's Handbook,* 2d ed., edited by Sumner N. Levine. Homewood, IL: Dow Jones-Irwin, 1988.

Rosenberg, Michael R. "International Fixed-Income Investing: Theory and Practice." In *The Handbook of Fixed-Income Securities,* 4th ed., edited by Frank J. Fabozzi and T. Dessa Fabozzi. Burr Ridge, IL: Irwin Professional Publishing, 1995.

Siegel, Laurence B., and Paul D. Kaplan. "Stocks, Bonds, Bills, and Inflation Around the World." In *Managing Institutional Assets,* edited by Frank J. Fabozzi. New York: Harper & Row, 1990.

Solnik, Bruno. *International Investments.* 3d ed. Reading, MA: Addison-Wesley Publishing, 1995.

Van der Does, Rein W. "Investing in Foreign Securities." In *The Financial Analyst's Handbook,* 2d ed., edited by Sumner N. Levine. Homewood, IL: Dow Jones-Irwin, 1988.

Viner, Aron. *Inside Japanese Financial Markets.* Homewood, IL: Dow Jones-Irwin, 1988.

Wilson, Richard S. *Corporate Senior Securities.* Chicago: Probus Publishing, 1987.

Wilson, Richard S., and Frank J. Fabozzi. *The New Corporate Bond Market.* Chicago: Probus Publishing, 1990.

Chapter 3
APPENDIX   COVARIANCE AND CORRELATION

COVARIANCE   Because most students have been exposed to the concepts of covariance and correlation, the following discussion is set forth in intuitive terms with examples to help the reader recall the concepts.[1]

Covariance is an absolute measure of the extent to which two sets of numbers move together over time, that is, how often they move up or down together. In this regard, move together means they are generally above their means or below their means at the same time. Covariance between i and j is defined as:

$$COV_{ij} = \frac{\Sigma(i - \bar{i})(j - \bar{j})}{N}$$

If we define $(i - \bar{i})$ as i' and $(j - \bar{j})$ as j', then

$$COV_{ij} = \frac{\Sigma i' j'}{N}$$

Obviously, if both numbers are consistently above or below their individual means at the same time, their products will be positive, and the average will be a large positive value. In contrast, if the i value is below its mean when the j value is above its mean or vice versa, their products will be large negative values, giving negative covariance.

Table 3A.1 should make this clear. In this example, the two series generally moved together, so they showed positive covariance. As noted, this is an *absolute* measure of their

[1] A more detailed, rigorous treatment of the subject can be found in any standard statistics text, including S. Christian Albright, *Statistics for Business and Economics* (New York: Macmillan, 1987), 63–67.

TABLE 3A.1   **CALCULATION OF COVARIANCE**

Observation	i	j	$i - \bar{i}$	$j - \bar{j}$	$\bar{i}'\bar{j}'$
1	3	8	−4	−4	16
2	6	10	−1	−2	2
3	8	14	+1	+2	2
4	5	12	−2	0	0
5	9	13	+2	+1	2
6	11	15	+4	+3	12
Σ	42	72			34
Mean	7	12			
Cov_{ij}	$= \dfrac{34}{6} = +5.67$				

relationship and, therefore, can range from $+\infty$ to $-\infty$. Note that the covariance of a variable with itself is its *variance*.

CORRELATION   To obtain a relative measure of a given relationship, we use the correlation coefficient (r_{ij}), which is a measure of the relationship:

$$r_{ij} = \frac{COV_{ij}}{\sigma_i \sigma_j}$$

You will recall from your introductory statistics course that:

$$\sigma_i = \sqrt{\frac{\Sigma(i - \bar{i})^2}{N}}$$

If the two series move completely together, then the covariance would equal $\sigma_i \sigma_j$ and:

$$\frac{COV_{ij}}{\sigma_i \sigma_j} = 1.0$$

The correlation coefficient would equal unity in this case, and we would say the two series are perfectly correlated. Because we know that:

$$r_{ij} = \frac{COV_{ij}}{\sigma_i \sigma_j}$$

we also know that $COV_{ij} = r_{ij}\sigma_i\sigma_j$. This relationship may be useful when computing the standard deviation of a portfolio, because in many instances the relationship between two securities is stated in terms of the correlation coefficient rather than the covariance.

Continuing the example given in Table 3A.1, the standard deviations are computed in Table 3A.2, as is the correlation between i and j. As shown, the two standard deviations are rather large and similar, but not exactly the same. Finally, when the positive covariance is normalized by the product of the two standard deviations, the results indicate a correlation coefficient of 0.898, which is obviously quite large and close to 1.00. Apparently, these two series are highly related.

| TABLE 3A.2 | CALCULATION OF CORRELATION COEFFICIENT |

Observation	$i - \bar{i}^a$	$(i - \bar{i})^2$	$j - \bar{j}^a$	$(j - \bar{j})^2$
1	−4	16	−4	16
2	−1	1	−2	4
3	+1	1	+2	4
4	−2	4	0	0
5	+2	4	+1	1
6	+4	16	+3	9
		42		34

$$\sigma_i^2 = 42/6 = 7.00 \qquad\qquad \sigma_j^2 = 34/6 = 5.67$$

$$\sigma_i = \sqrt{7.00} = 2.65 \qquad\qquad \sigma_j = \sqrt{5.67} = 2.38$$

$$r_{ij} = Cov_{ij}/\sigma_i\sigma_j = \frac{5.67}{(2.65)(2.38)} = \frac{5.67}{6.31} = 0.898$$

Problems

1. As a new analyst, you have calculated the following annual rates of return for both Lauren Corporation and Kayleigh Industries.

Year	Lauren's Rate of Return	Kayleigh's Rate of Return
1994	5	5
1995	12	15
1996	−11	5
1997	10	7
1998	12	−10

Your manager suggests that because these companies produce similar products, you should continue your analysis by computing their covariance. Show all calculations.

2. You decide to go an extra step by calculating the coefficient of correlation using the data provided in Problem 1 above. Prepare a table showing your calculations and explain how to interpret the results. Would the combination of Lauren and Kayleigh be good for diversification?

Chapter

4

Organization and Functioning of Securities Markets

This chapter answers the following questions:

- What is the purpose and function of a market?
- What are the characteristics that determine the quality of a market?
- What is the difference between a primary and secondary capital market and how do these markets support each other?
- What are the national exchanges and how are the major securities markets around the world becoming linked (what is meant by "passing the book")?
- What are regional stock exchanges and the over-the-counter (OTC) markets?
- What are the alternative market-making arrangements available on the exchanges and the OTC market?
- What are the major types of orders available to investors and market makers?
- What are the major functions of the specialist on the NYSE and how does the specialist differ from the central market maker on other exchanges?
- What are the major factors that have caused significant changes in markets around the world during the past 10 to 15 years?
- What are some of the major changes in world capital markets expected over the next decade?

The stock market, the Dow Jones Industrials, and the bond market are part of our everyday experience. Each evening on the television news broadcasts we find out how stocks and bonds fared; each morning we read in our daily newspapers about expectations for a market rally or decline. Yet how the domestic and world capital markets actually function is imperfectly understood by most. To be a successful investor in a global environment, you must know what financial markets are available around the world and how they operate.

In Chapter 1, we considered why individuals invest and what determines their required rate of return on investments. In Chapter 2, we discussed the life cycle for investors and the alternative asset allocation decisions by investors during different phases. In Chapter 3, we learned about the numerous alternative investments available and why we should diversify with securities from around the world. This chapter takes a broad view of securities markets and then provides a detailed discussion of how major stock markets function. We conclude with a consideration of how global securities markets are changing.

We begin with a discussion of securities markets and the characteristics of a good market. There are two components of the capital markets that are described: primary and secondary. Our main emphasis in this chapter is on the secondary stock market. We consider the national stock exchanges around the world and how these markets that are separated by geography and by time zones are becoming linked into a 24-hour market. We also consider regional stock markets and the over-the-counter market and then provide a detailed analysis of how alternative exchange markets operate. The final section considers numerous historical changes in financial markets since the mid-1970s, the additional current changes, and the significant changes that are expected to occur into the next century. These numerous changes in our securities markets will have a profound effect on what investments are available to you from around the world and how you buy and sell them.

<table>
<tr><td>WHAT IS A
MARKET?</td><td>This section provides the necessary background for understanding different securities markets around the world and the changes that are occurring. The first part considers the general concept of a market and its function. The second part describes the characteristics that determine how well a particular market will fulfill its function. The third part of the section describes primary and secondary capital markets and how they interact and depend on one another.</td></tr>
</table>

A **market** is the means through which buyers and sellers are brought together to aid in the transfer of goods and/or services. Several aspects of this general definition seem worthy of emphasis. First, a market need not have a physical location. It is only necessary that the buyers and sellers can communicate regarding the relevant aspects of the transaction.

Second, the market does not necessarily own the goods or services involved. When we discuss what is required for a good market, you will note that ownership is not involved; the important criterion is the smooth, cheap transfer of goods and services. In most financial markets, those who establish and administer the market do not own the assets. They simply provide a physical location or an electronic system that allows potential buyers and sellers to interact, and they help the market function by providing information and facilities to aid in the transfer of ownership.

Finally, a market can deal in any variety of goods and services. For any commodity or service with a diverse clientele, a market should evolve to aid in the transfer of that commodity or service. Both buyers and sellers will benefit from the existence of a market. Basically, we take markets for granted because they are vital to a smooth-operating economy. Still, it is important to recognize that the quality of alternative markets can differ.

<table>
<tr><td>*CHARACTERISTICS OF A*
GOOD MARKET</td><td>Throughout this book, we will discuss markets for different investments such as stocks, bonds, options, and futures in the United States and throughout the world. We will refer to these markets using various terms of quality such as strong, active, liquid, or illiquid. There are many financial markets, but they are not all equal—some are active and liquid, others are relatively inactive, illiquid, and not very efficient in their operations. To appreciate these discussions, you should be aware of the characteristics that investors look for when evaluating the quality of a market. In this section, we describe those characteristics.</td></tr>
</table>

One enters a market to buy or sell a good or service quickly at a price justified by the prevailing supply and demand. To determine the appropriate price, participants must have timely and accurate information on the volume and prices of past transactions and on all currently outstanding bids and offers. Therefore, one attribute of a good market is *availability of* **information.**

Another prime requirement is **liquidity,** the ability to buy or sell an asset quickly and at a known price; that is, a price not substantially different from the prices for prior transactions, assuming no new information is available. An asset's likelihood of being sold quickly, sometimes referred to as its *marketability,* is a necessary, but not a sufficient, condition for liquidity. The expected price should also be fairly certain, based on the recent history of transaction prices and current bid-ask quotes.[1]

A component of liquidity is **price continuity,** which means that prices do not change much from one transaction to the next unless substantial new information becomes available. Suppose no new information is forthcoming, and the last transaction was at a price of $20; if the next trade were at $20\frac{1}{8}$, the market would be considered reasonably continuous.[2] A continuous market without large price changes between trades is a characteristic of a liquid market.

A market with price continuity requires *depth,* which means that numerous potential buyers and sellers must be willing to trade at prices above and below the current market price. These buyers and sellers enter the market in response to changes in supply and/or demand and thereby prevent drastic price changes. In summary, liquidity requires marketability and price continuity, which, in turn, requires depth.

Another factor contributing to a good market is the **transaction cost.** Lower costs (as a percentage of the value of the trade) make for a more efficient market. An individual comparing the cost of a transaction between markets would choose one that charges 2 percent of the value of the trade compared with a market that charges 5 percent. Most microeconomic textbooks define an efficient market as one in which the cost of the transaction is minimal. This attribute is referred to as *internal efficiency.*

Finally, a buyer or seller wants the prevailing market price to adequately reflect all the information available regarding supply and demand factors in the market. If such conditions change as a result of new information, the price should change accordingly. Therefore, participants want prices to adjust quickly to new information regarding supply or demand, which means that prices reflect all available information about the asset. This attribute is referred to as *external efficiency* or *informational efficiency.* This attribute is discussed extensively in Chapter 7.

In summary, a good market for goods and services has the following characteristics:

1. Timely and accurate information is available on the price and volume of past transactions.
2. It is liquid, meaning an asset can be bought or sold quickly at a price close to the prices for previous transactions (has price continuity), assuming no new information has been received. In turn, price continuity requires depth.
3. Transactions entail low costs, including the cost of reaching the market, the actual brokerage costs, and the cost of transferring the asset.
4. Prices rapidly adjust to new information so the prevailing price reflects all available information regarding the asset.

ORGANIZATION OF THE SECURITIES MARKET

Before discussing the specific operation of the securities market, you need to understand its overall organization. The principal distinction is between **primary markets,** where new securities are sold, and **secondary markets,** where outstanding securities are bought and sold. Each of these markets is further divided based on the economic unit that issued the security. The following discussion considers each of these major segments of the

---

[1] For a more formal discussion of liquidity and the impact of different market systems, see Sanford J. Grossman and Merton H. Miller, "Liquidity and Market Structure," *Journal of Finance* 43, no. 3 (July 1988): 617–633; and Puneet Handa and Robert A. Schwartz, "How Best to Supply Liquidity to a Securities Market," *The Journal of Portfolio Management* 22, no. 2 (Winter 1996): 44–51.

[2] You should be aware that common stocks are sold in increments of eighths of a dollar, or $0.125. Therefore, $20\frac{1}{8}$ means the stock sold at $20.125 per share.

securities market with an emphasis on the individuals involved and the functions they perform.

PRIMARY CAPITAL MARKETS

The primary market is where new issues of bonds, preferred stock, or common stock are sold by government units, municipalities, or companies to acquire new capital.[3]

GOVERNMENT BOND ISSUES

All U.S. government bond issues are subdivided into three segments based on their original maturities. **Treasury bills** are negotiable, non-interest-bearing securities with original maturities of 1 year or less. They are currently issued for 3 months, 6 months, or 1 year. **Treasury notes** have original maturities of 2 to 10 years, and they have generally been issued with 2-, 3-, 4-, 5-, 7-, and 10-year terms. Finally, **Treasury bonds** have original maturities of more than 10 years.

To sell bills, notes, and bonds, the Treasury relies on Federal Reserve System auctions. In an auction held each week, institutions and some individuals submit bids for T-bills at prices below par that imply specific yields. (The bidding process and pricing are discussed in detail in Chapter 15.)

Treasury notes and bonds are likewise sold at auction by the Federal Reserve, but the bids state yields rather than prices. That is, the Treasury specifies how much it wants and when the notes or bonds will mature. After receiving the competitive bid yields and quantity, the Treasury determines the stop-out yield bid (the highest yield it will accept) based on the bids received and how much it wants to borrow. The Fed also receives many noncompetitive bids from investors who are willing to pay the average price of the accepted competitive tenders. All noncompetitive bids are accepted.

MUNICIPAL BOND ISSUES

New municipal bond issues are sold by one of three methods: competitive bid, negotiation, or private placement. Competitive bid sales typically involve sealed bids. The bond issue is sold to the bidding syndicate of underwriters that submits the bid with the lowest interest cost in accordance with the stipulations set forth by the issuer. Negotiated sales involve contractual arrangements between underwriters and issuers wherein the underwriter helps the issuer prepare the bond issue and set the price and has the exclusive right to sell the issue. Private placements involve the sale of a bond issue by the issuer directly to an investor or a small group of investors (usually institutions).

Note that two of the three methods require an *underwriting* function. Specifically, in a competitive bid or a negotiated transaction, the investment banker typically underwrites the issue, which means the firm purchases the entire issue at a specified price, relieving the issuer from the risk and responsibility of selling and distributing the bonds. Subsequently, the underwriter sells the issue to the investing public. For municipal bonds, this underwriting function is performed by both investment banking firms and commercial banks.

The underwriting function can involve three services: origination, risk-bearing, and distribution. Origination involves the design of the bond issue and initial planning. To fulfill the risk-bearing function, the underwriter acquires the total issue at a price dictated by the competitive bid or through negotiation and accepts the responsibility and risk of reselling it for more than the purchase price. Distribution means selling it to investors,

---

[3] For an excellent set of studies related to the primary market, see Michael C. Jensen and Clifford W. Smith, Jr., eds., "Symposium on Investment Banking and the Capital Acquisition Process," *Journal of Financial Economics* 15, no. 1/2 (January–February 1986).

typically with the help of a selling syndicate that includes other investment banking firms or commercial banks.

In a negotiated bid, the underwriter will carry out all three services. In a competitive bid, the issuer specifies the amount, maturities, coupons, and call features of the issue and the competing syndicates submit a bid for the entire issue that reflects the yields they estimate for the bonds. The issuer may have received advice from an investment firm on the desirable characteristics for a forthcoming issue, but this advice would have been on a fee basis and would not necessarily involve the ultimate underwriter who is responsible for risk-bearing and distribution. Finally, a private placement involves no risk-bearing, but an investment banker could assist in locating potential buyers and negotiating the characteristics of the issue.

Municipal bonds are either general obligation (GO) bonds that are backed by the full taxing power of the municipality, or revenue bonds that are dependent on the revenues from a specific project that was funded by an issue such as a toll road, a hospital, or a sewage system. Commercial banks dominate the management of GO bond sales, and investment banking firms dominate revenue bond sales.

The municipal bond market has experienced two major trends during the past decade. First, it has shifted toward negotiated bond issues versus competitive bids. Currently, about 75 percent of issues are negotiated deals. Second, there has been a shift toward revenue bonds, wherein almost 70 percent of the market is revenue issues. These two trends are related because revenue issues tend to be negotiated underwritings. Although many states require that GO bond issues be sold through competitive bidding, they seldom impose such a requirement on revenue issues.[4]

CORPORATE BOND AND STOCK ISSUES

Corporate securities include bond and stock issues. Corporate bond issues are almost always sold through a negotiated arrangement with an investment banking firm that maintains a relationship with the issuing firm. In a global capital market that involves an explosion of new instruments, the origination function is becoming more important because the corporate chief financial officer (CFO) will probably not be completely familiar with the availability and issuing requirements of many new instruments and the alternative capital markets around the world. Investment banking firms compete for underwriting business by creating new instruments that appeal to existing investors and by advising issuers regarding desirable countries and currencies. As a result, the expertise of the investment banker can help reduce the issuer's cost of new capital.

Once a stock or bond issue is specified, the underwriter will put together a syndicate of other major underwriters and a selling group for its distribution. For common stock, **new issues** are typically divided into two groups. The first and largest group is *seasoned* new issues that are offered by companies that have outstanding stock with existing public markets. For example, in 1995 General Motors sold a new issue of common stock. Obviously there was already a large and active market for General Motors common stock, and the company decided to issue new shares, which increased the number of outstanding shares, to acquire new equity capital.

The second major category of new stock issues is referred to as **initial public offerings (IPOs),** wherein a company decides to sell common stock to the public for the first time. At the time of an IPO offering, there is no existing public market for the stock, that is, the

---

[4] For a further discussion, see David S. Kidwell and Eric H. Sorensen, "Investment Banking and the Underwriting of New Municipal Issues," in *The Municipal Bond Handbook,* ed. by F. J. Fabozzi, S. G. Feldstein, I. M. Pollack, and F. G. Zarb (Homewood, IL: Dow Jones-Irwin, 1983).

company has been closely held. An example would be an IPO by Netscape Communications Corp. in August 1995 at $28 a share. The company is a leading provider of open software that enables people and organizations to exchange information and conduct commerce over the Internet and private Internet Protocol networks. The purpose of the offering was to get additional capital to expand its operations.

New issues (seasoned or IPOs) are typically underwritten by investment bankers, who acquire the total issue from the company and sell the securities to interested investors. The underwriter gives advice to the corporation on the general characteristics of the issue, its pricing, and the timing of the offering. The underwriter also accepts the risk of selling the new issue after acquiring it from the corporation.[5]

RELATIONSHIPS WITH INVESTMENT BANKERS   The underwriting of corporate issues typically takes one of three forms: negotiated, competitive bids, or best-efforts arrangements. As noted, negotiated underwritings are the most common, and the procedure is the same as for municipal issues.

A corporation may also specify the type of securities to be offered (common stock, preferred stock, or bonds) and then solicit competitive bids from investment banking firms. This is rare for industrial firms but is typical for utilities, which may be required to sell the issue via a competitive bid by state laws. Although competitive bids typically reduce the cost of an issue, it also brings fewer services from the investment banker. The banker gives less advice but still accepts the risk-bearing function by underwriting the issue and fulfills the distribution function.

Alternatively, an investment banker can agree to support an issue and sell it on a *best-efforts basis*. This is usually done with speculative new issues. In this arrangement, the investment banker does not underwrite the issue because it does not buy any securities. The stock is owned by the company, and the investment banker acts *as a broker* to sell whatever it can at a stipulated price. The investment banker earns a lower commission on such an issue than on an underwritten issue. With any of these arrangements, the lead investment banker will typically form an underwriting syndicate of other investment bankers to spread the risk and also help in the sales. In addition, if the issue is very large, the lead underwriter and underwriting syndicate will form a selling group of smaller firms to help in the distribution.

INTRODUCTION OF RULE 415   The typical practice of negotiated arrangements involving numerous investment banking firms in syndicates and selling groups has changed with the introduction of Rule 415, which allows large firms to register security issues and sell them piecemeal during the following two years. These issues are referred to as *shelf registrations* because after they are registered, the issues lie on the shelf and can be taken down and sold on short notice whenever it suits the issuing firm. As an example, General Electric could register an issue of 5 million shares of common stock during 1997 and sell a million shares in early 1997, another million shares late in 1997, 2 million shares in early 1998, and the rest in late 1998.

Each offering can be made with little notice or paperwork by one underwriter or several. In fact, because there may be relatively few shares involved, the lead underwriter often handles the whole deal without a syndicate or will use only one or two other firms. This arrangement has benefited large corporations because it provides great flexibility, reduces

---

[5] For an extended discussion of the underwriting process, see Richard A. Brealey and Stewart C. Myers, *Principles of Corporate Finance*, 4th ed. (New York: McGraw-Hill, 1991), Chapter 15.

registration fees and expenses, and allows firms issuing securities to request competitive bids from several investment banking firms.

On the other hand, some observers fear that shelf registrations do not allow investors enough time to examine the current status of the firm issuing the securities. Also, the follow-up offerings reduce the participation of small underwriters because the underwriting syndicates are smaller and selling groups are almost nonexistent. Shelf registrations have typically been used for the sale of straight debentures rather than common stock or convertible issues.[6]

PRIVATE PLACEMENTS AND RULE 144A

Rather than a public sale using one of these arrangements, primary offerings can be sold privately. In such an arrangement, referred to as a **private placement,** the firm designs an issue with the assistance of an investment banker and sells it to a small group of institutions. The firm enjoys lower issuing costs because it does not need to prepare the extensive registration statement required for a public offering. The institution that buys the issue typically benefits because the issuing firm passes some of these cost savings on to the investor as a higher return. In fact, the institution should require a higher return because of the absence of any secondary market for these securities, which implies higher liquidity risk.

The private placement market has been changed dramatically by the introduction of Rule 144A by the SEC. This rule allows corporations—including non-U.S. firms—to place securities privately with large, sophisticated institutional investors without extensive registration documents. The SEC intends to provide more financing alternatives for U.S. and non-U.S. firms and possibly increase the number, size, and liquidity of private placements.[7]

SECONDARY FINANCIAL MARKETS

In this section, we consider the purpose and importance of secondary markets and provide an overview of the secondary markets for bonds, financial futures, and stocks. Next, we consider national stock markets around the world. Finally, we will discuss regional and over-the-counter stock markets and provide a detailed presentation on the functioning of stock exchanges.

Secondary markets permit trading in outstanding issues; that is, stocks or bonds already sold to the public are traded between current and potential owners. The proceeds from a sale in the secondary market do not go to the issuing unit (i.e., the government, municipality, or company), but rather to the current owner of the security.

WHY SECONDARY MARKETS ARE IMPORTANT

Before discussing the various segments of the secondary market, we must consider its overall importance. Because the secondary market involves the trading of securities initially sold in the primary market, *it provides liquidity to the individuals who acquired these securities.* After acquiring securities in the primary market, investors want to sell them again to acquire other securities, buy a house, or go on a vacation. The primary market benefits greatly from the liquidity provided by the secondary market because investors

---

[6] For further discussion of Rule 415, see Beth McGoldrick, "Life with Rule 415," *Institutional Investor* 17, no. 2 (February 1983): 129–133; and Robert J. Rogowski and Eric H. Sorensen, "Deregulation in Investment Banking. Shelf Registrations, Structure and Performance," *Financial Management* 14, no. 1 (Spring 1985): 5–15.

[7] For a discussion of the rule and private placements, see Michael Siconolfi and Kevin Salwen, "SEC Ready to Ease Private-Placement Rules," *The Wall Street Journal,* April 13, 1990, C1, C5. For a discussion of some reactions to Rule 144A, see John W. Milligan, "Two Cheers for 144A," *Institutional Investor* 24, no. 9 (July 1990): 117–119; and Sara Hanks, "SEC Ruling Creates a New Market," *The Wall Street Journal,* May 16, 1990, A12.

would hesitate to acquire securities in the primary market if they felt they could not subsequently sell them in the secondary market. That is, without an active secondary market, potential issuers of stocks or bonds would have to provide a much higher rate of return to compensate investors for the substantial liquidity risk.

Secondary markets are also important to issuers because the prevailing market price of the securities is determined by transactions in the secondary market. New issues of outstanding stocks or bonds to be sold in the primary market are based on prices and yields in the secondary market. As a result, capital costs for the government, municipalities, and corporations are determined by investor expectations and actions that are reflected in market prices prevailing in the secondary market.[8] Even nonpublic IPOs are priced based on the prices and values of comparable stocks or bonds in the public secondary market.

SECONDARY BOND MARKETS

The secondary market for bonds distinguishes among those issued by the federal government, municipalities, or corporations.

SECONDARY MARKETS FOR U.S. GOVERNMENT AND MUNICIPAL BONDS   U.S. government bonds are traded by bond dealers that specialize in either Treasury bonds or agency bonds. Treasury issues are bought or sold through a set of 35 primary dealers, including large banks in New York and Chicago and some of the large investment banking firms (e.g., Merrill Lynch, First Boston, Morgan Stanley). These institutions and other firms also make markets for government agency issues, but there is no formal set of dealers for agency securities.[9]

The major market makers in the secondary municipal bond market are banks and investment firms. Banks are active in municipal bond trading because they are involved in the underwriting of general obligation issues and they commit large parts of their investment portfolios to these securities. Also, many large investment firms have municipal bond departments that are active in underwriting and trading these issues.

SECONDARY CORPORATE BOND MARKETS   The secondary market for corporate bonds has two major segments: security exchanges and an over-the-counter (OTC) market. The major exchange for corporate bonds is the New York Stock Exchange Fixed Income Market. By the end of 1995, over 1,100 corporate bond issues were listed on this exchange with a combined par value of about $254 billion and a combined market value of approximately $257 billion.[10] On a typical day, there are about 1,500 trades with a total volume of about $29 million. Notably, most of the trading on the NYSE's bond market is done through its *Automated Bond System (ABS),* which is a fully automated trading and information system that allows subscribing firms to enter and execute bond orders through terminals in their offices. Users receive immediate execution reports and locked-in compared

---

[8] In the literature on market microstructure, it is noted that the secondary markets also have an effect on market efficiency, the volatility of security prices, and the serial correlation in security returns. In this regard, see F. D. Foster and S. Viswanathan, "The Effects of Public Information and Competition on Trading Volume and Price Volatility," *Review of Financial Studies* 6, no. 1 (Spring 1993): 23–56; C. N. Jones, G. Kaul, and M. L. Lipson, "Information, Trading and Volatility," *Journal of Financial Economics* 36, no. 1 (August 1994): 127–154; H. Bessembinder, Kalok Chan, and P. J. Sequin, "An Empirical Examination of Information Differences of Opinion, and Trading Activity," *Journal of Financial Economics* 40, no. 1 (January 1996): 105–134.

[9] For a discussion of non-U.S. bond markets, see European Bond Commission, *The European Bond Markets* (Chicago: Probus Publishing, 1989); and Frank J. Fabozzi, ed., *The Japanese Bond Market* (Chicago: Probus Publishing, 1990).

[10] *NYSE Fact Book* (New York: NYSE, 1995), 82. If you include U.S. government issues and non-U.S. issues of companies, banks, and governments, there are almost 2,100 issues with a par value and market value of over $2,700 billion.

trades. In addition, 232 issues are listed on the American Stock Exchange (AMEX) with par value of over $22 billion, a total market value of almost $17 billion, and typical daily trading volume in excess of $3.4 million.

All corporate bonds not listed on one of the exchanges are traded over-the-counter by dealers who buy and sell for their own accounts. In sharp contrast to what occurs for stocks where most of the trading takes place on the national exchanges such as the NYSE, in the United States *most corporate bond trades occur on the OTC market*. Virtually all large trades are carried out on the OTC market, even for bonds that are listed on an exchange. The fact is, the NYSE bond market is considered the "odd-lot" market for bonds. As such, the prices reported on the exchanges are generally considered to be inexact estimates of prices associated with large transactions.[11]

The major bond dealers are the large investment banking firms that underwrite the issues such as Merrill Lynch, Goldman Sachs, Salomon Brothers, Lehman Brothers, Kidder Peabody, and Morgan Stanley. Because of the limited trading in corporate bonds compared to the fairly active trading in government bonds, corporate bond dealers do not carry extensive inventories of specific issues. Instead, they hold a limited number of bonds desired by their clients, and when someone wants to do a trade, they work more like brokers than dealers.

FINANCIAL FUTURES   In addition to the market for the bonds, recently a market has developed for futures contracts related to these bonds. These contracts allow the holder to buy or sell a specified amount of a given bond issue at a stipulated price. The two major exchanges are located in Chicago: the Chicago Board of Trade (CBOT) and the Chicago Mercantile Exchange (CME). These futures contracts and the futures market are discussed in Chapter 11.

SECONDARY EQUITY MARKETS   The secondary equity market is usually broken down into three major segments: (1) the major national stock exchanges, including the New York, the American, the Tokyo, and the London stock exchanges; (2) regional stock exchanges in such cities as Chicago, San Francisco, Boston, Osaka and Nagoya in Japan, and Dublin in Ireland; and (3) the over-the-counter (OTC) market, which involves trading in stocks not listed on an organized exchange.

The first two segments, referred to as *listed securities exchanges,* differ only in size and geographic emphasis. Both are composed of formal organizations with specific members and specific securities (stocks or bonds) that have qualified for listing. Although the exchanges typically consider similar factors when evaluating firms that apply for listing, the level of requirement differs (the national exchanges have more stringent requirements). Also, the prices of securities listed on alternative stock exchanges are determined using several different trading (pricing) systems that will be discussed in the next section.

SECURITIES EXCHANGES   As indicated, the secondary stock market is composed of three segments: national stock exchanges, regional stock exchanges, and the over-the-counter market. We will discuss each of these separately because they differ in importance within countries and they have different trading systems. As an investor interested in trading global securities, you should be aware of these differences. Following a brief discussion of alternative trading systems and a consideration of call versus continuous markets, we describe the three segments of the equity market. We begin with a discussion

---

[11] For an empirical analysis of the differences, see Arthur D. Warga, "Corporate Bond Price Discrepancies in the Dealer and Exchange Markets," *Journal of Fixed Income* 1, no. 3 (December 1991): 7–16.

of the major national stock exchanges in the world because they typically are the dominant markets within a country. The next section will consider regional stock exchanges, and then we discuss the over-the-counter stock market.

Alternative trading systems   Although stock exchanges are similar in that only qualified stocks can be traded by individuals who are members of the exchange, they can differ in their *trading systems*. There are two major trading systems, and an exchange can use one of these or a combination of them. One is a pure auction market, in which interested buyers and sellers submit bid and ask prices for a given stock to a central location where the orders are matched by a broker who does not own the stock, but who acts as a facilitating agent. Participants refer to this system as one that is *price-driven* because shares of stock are sold to the investor with the highest bid price and bought from the seller with the lowest selling price.

The other major trading system is a dealer market where individual dealers provide liquidity by buying and selling the shares of stock for themselves. Therefore, in such a market, investors wanting to buy or sell shares of a stock must go to a dealer. Ideally, there will be a number of dealers competing against each other to provide the highest bid prices when you are selling and the lowest asking price when you are buying stock. When we discuss the various exchanges, we will indicate the trading system used.

Call versus continuous markets   Beyond the alternative trading systems for equities, the operation of exchanges can differ in terms of when and how the stocks are traded.

There are **call markets** in which trading for individual stocks takes place at specified times. The intent is to gather all the bids and asks for the stock and attempt to arrive at a single price that will possibly clear the market at that time. That is, the goal is to determine a price where the quantity demanded is as close as possible to the quantity supplied. This trading arrangement is generally used during the early stages of development of an exchange when there are few stocks listed or a small number of active investors–traders. If you envision an exchange with only a few stocks listed and a few traders, you would call the roll of stocks and ask for interest in one stock at a time. After determining all the available buy and sell orders, exchange officials attempt to arrive at a single price that will satisfy *most* of the orders, and all orders are transacted at this one price.

Notably, call markets also are used at the opening for stocks on the NYSE if there is a buildup of buy and sell orders overnight, in which case the opening price can differ from the prior day's closing price. Also, this concept is used if trading is suspended during the day because of some significant new information. In either case, the specialist or market maker would attempt to derive a price using a call market approach that would reflect the imbalance and take care of most of the orders. For example, assume a stock had been trading at about $42 a share and some significant, new, positive information was released overnight or during the day. If it was overnight it would affect the opening; if it happened during the day it would affect the price established after trading was suspended. If the buy orders were three or four times as numerous as the sell orders, the price based on the call market might be $44, which is the specialists' estimate of a new equilibrium price that reflects the supply–demand caused by the new information. It is contended that this temporary use of the call market mechanism contributes to a more orderly market and less volatility in such instances because it attempts to avoid the major up and down price swings.

In a **continuous market,** trades occur at any time the market is open. Stocks in this continuous market are priced either by auction or by dealers. If it is a dealer market, it assumes that there are always some dealers who are willing to make a market in the stock, which means that the dealer is willing to buy or sell for his or her own account at a specified bid and ask price. If it is an auction market, it is assumed that there are enough buyers and sellers to allow the market to be continuous, that is, when you come to buy stock, there is another investor available and willing to sell stock. A compromise between a pure dealer market and a pure auction market is a combination wherein the market is basically an auction market, but there exists an intermediary who is willing to act as a dealer if the pure auction market does not have enough activity. These dealers provide temporary liquidity to ensure that the market will be liquid as well as continuous.

The Chapter 4 Appendix contains two tables that list the characteristics of stock exchanges around the world and indicate whether the exchange provides a continuous market, a call market mechanism, or a mixture of the two. Notably, although many exchanges are considered to be continuous, they also employ a call market mechanism on specific occasions such as at the open and during trading suspensions. The NYSE is such a market.

NATIONAL STOCK EXCHANGES   Two U.S. securities exchanges are generally considered national in scope: the New York Stock Exchange (NYSE) and the American Stock Exchange (AMEX). Outside the United States, each country typically has one national exchange, such as the Tokyo Stock Exchange (TSE), the London Exchange, the Frankfurt Stock Exchange, and the Paris Bourse. These exchanges are considered national because of the large number of listed securities, the prestige of the firms listed, the wide geographic dispersion of the listed firms, and the diverse clientele of buyers and sellers who use the market.

New York Stock Exchange (NYSE)   The New York Stock Exchange (NYSE), the largest organized securities market in the United States, was established in 1817 as the New York Stock and Exchange Board. The Exchange dates its founding when the famous Buttonwood Agreement was signed in May 1792 by 24 brokers.[12] The name was changed to the New York Stock Exchange in 1863.

At the end of 1995, 2,570 companies had stock issues listed on the NYSE, for a total of 3,060 stock issues (common and preferred) with a total market value of over $4.5 trillion. The specific listing requirements for the NYSE as of 1995 appear in Table 4.1.

TABLE 4.1   **LISTING REQUIREMENTS FOR STOCKS ON THE NYSE AND THE AMEX**

	NYSE	AMEX
Pretax income last year[a]	$ 2,500,000	$ 750,000 latest year or 2 of last 3 years
Pretax income last 2 years	2,000,000	
Net tangible assets	18,000,000	4,000,000
Shares publicly held	1,100,000	500,000
Market value of publicly held shares[b]	18,000,000	3,000,000[c]
Minimum number of holders of round lots (100 shares or more)	2,000	800

[a]For AMEX, this is *net* income last year.
[b]This minimum required market value varies over time, depending on the value of the NYSE Common Stock Index. For specifics, see the *1995 NYSE Fact Book,* 31–34.
[c]The AMEX only has one minimum.

Sources: *NYSE Fact Book* (New York: NYSE, 1995); and *AMEX Fact Book* (New York: AMEX, 1995). Reprinted by permission.

---

[12] The NYSE considers the signing of this agreement the birth of the Exchange and celebrated its 200th birthday during 1992. For a pictorial history, see *Life,* collector's edition, Spring 1992.

TABLE 4.2	AVERAGE DAILY REPORTED SHARE VOLUME TRADED ON SELECTED STOCK MARKETS (000)				

Year	NYSE	AMEX	NASDAQ	TSE
1955	2,578	912	N.A.	8,000
1960	3,042	1,113	N.A.	90,000
1965	6,176	2,120	N.A.	116,000
1970	11,564	3,319	N.A.	144,000
1975	18,551	2,138	5,500	183,000
1980	44,871	6,427	26,500	359,000
1985	109,169	8,337	82,100	428,000
1986	141,028	11,773	113,600	709,000
1987	188,938	13,858	149,800	962,000
1988	161,461	9,941	122,800	1,035,000
1989	165,470	12,401	133,100	894,000
1990	156,777	13,158	131,900	500,000
1991	178,917	13,309	163,300	380,000
1992	202,266	14,157	190,800	269,000
1993	264,519	18,111	263,000	353,000
1994	291,357	17,945	295,100	342,200
1995	346,101	20,128	401,400	369,600

N.A. = not available.

Sources: *NYSE Fact Book* (New York: NYSE, various issues); *AMEX Fact Book* (New York: AMEX, various issues); *Tokyo Stock Exchange Fact Book* (Tokyo: TSE, various issues). Reprinted with permission.

The average number of shares traded daily on the NYSE has increased steadily and substantially, as shown in Table 4.2. Prior to the 1960s, the daily volume averaged less than 3 million shares, compared with current average daily volume in excess of 346 million shares and record volume of over 600 million shares.

The NYSE has dominated the other exchanges in the United States in trading volume. During the past decade, the NYSE has consistently accounted for about 80 percent of all shares traded on U.S. listed exchanges, as compared with about 10 percent for the American Stock Exchange and about 10 percent for all regional exchanges combined. Because share prices on the NYSE tend to be higher than those on the AMEX, the dollar value of trading on the NYSE has averaged about 85 percent of the total value of U.S. trades, compared with less than 5 percent for the AMEX and a little over 10 percent for the regional exchanges.[13]

The volume of trading and relative stature of the NYSE is reflected in the price of a membership on the exchange (referred to as a seat). As shown in Table 4.3, the price of membership has fluctuated in line with trading volume and other factors that influence the profitability of membership.

American Stock Exchange (AMEX)   The American Stock Exchange (AMEX) was begun by a group who traded unlisted shares at the corner of Wall and Hanover Streets in New York. It was originally called the Outdoor Curb Market. In 1910, it established formal trading rules and its name changed to the New York Curb Market Association. The mem-

---

[13] For a breakdown of shares traded and their value, see Securities and Exchange Commission, *Annual Report* (Washington, DC: U.S. Government Printing Office, annual); and *NYSE Fact Book* (New York: NYSE, annual). For a discussion of trading volume and membership prices, see Anita Rashavan, "Stock Boom Doesn't Spur Bull Market in Seats," *The Wall Street Journal*, March 24, 1993, C1, C25.

| TABLE 4.3 | MEMBERSHIP PRICES ON THE NYSE AND THE AMEX ($000) | | | | | | | | | |

	NYSE		AMEX				NYSE		AMEX	
	High	Low	High	Low			High	Low	High	Low
1925	$150	$ 99	$ 38	$ 9		1986	$ 600	$455	$285	$145
1935	140	65	33	12		1987	1,150	560	420	265
1945	95	49	32	12		1988	820	580	280	180
1955	90	49	22	12		1989	675	420	215	155
1960	162	135	60	51		1990	430	250	170	84
1965	250	190	80	55		1991	440	345	120	80
1970	320	130	185	70		1992	600	410	110	76
1975	138	55	72	34		1993	775	500	163	92
1980	275	175	252	95		1994	830	760	205	155
1985	480	310	160	115		1995	1,050	785	152	105

Sources: *NYSE Fact Book* (New York: NYSE, various issues); *AMEX Fact Book* (New York: AMEX, various issues). Reprinted by permission of the New York Stock Exchange and the American Stock Exchange.

bers moved inside a building in 1921 and continued to trade mainly in unlisted stocks (i.e., stocks not listed on one of the registered exchanges) until 1946, when its volume in listed stocks finally outnumbered that in unlisted stocks. The current name was adopted in 1953.

The AMEX is a national exchange, distinct from the NYSE because, except for a short period in the late 1970s, no stocks have been listed on both the NYSE and AMEX at the same time. The AMEX has emphasized listing foreign securities, listing 85 foreign issues in 1994, with trading in these issues constituting about 13 percent of total volume.[14] Warrants were listed on the AMEX for a number of years before the NYSE listed them.

The AMEX has become a major options exchange since January 1975 when it began listing options on stocks. Since then it has added options on interest rates and stock indexes, which are discussed in Chapter 11.

At the end of 1995, 1,005 stock issues were listed on the AMEX.[15] As shown in Table 4.2, average daily trading volume has fluctuated substantially over time, growing overall from below 500,000 shares to over 20 million shares a day in 1995. Because of the differences between the NYSE and the AMEX, most large brokerage firms are members of both exchanges.

Tokyo Stock Exchange (TSE)   Of the eight stock exchanges in Japan, those in Tokyo, Osaka, and Nagoya are the largest. The TSE dominates its country's market much as the NYSE does. Specifically, about 87 percent of trades in volume and 83 percent of value occur on the TSE. The market value of stocks listed on the TSE surpassed the NYSE during 1987 but fell below it when the Japanese stock market declined following its peak in December 1989.

The Tokyo Stock Exchange Co. Ltd., established in 1878, was replaced in 1943 by the Japan Securities Exchange, a quasi-governmental organization that absorbed all existing exchanges in Japan. The Japan Securities Exchange was dissolved in 1947, and the Tokyo Stock Exchange in its present form was established in 1949. The trading mechanism is a price-driven system wherein an investor submits bid and ask prices for stocks. At the end of 1994, there were about 1,782 companies listed with a total market value of 358.4 trillion yen (this is equal to about 3.6 trillion dollars at an exchange rate of 99.7 yen to the dollar).

[14] *AMEX Fact Book* (New York: AMEX, 1994).

[15] The requirements for listing on the AMEX appear in Table 4.1.

As shown in Table 4.2, average daily share volume has increased by more than 10 times, from 90 million shares per day in 1960 to a peak of over 1 billion shares in 1988 prior to a decline to 369 million shares in 1995. The value of shares traded in U.S. dollars has increased by almost 50 times from 1960 to 1995 because of the substantial increase in the prices of the shares and the rising value of the yen.

Both domestic and foreign stocks are listed on the Tokyo Exchange. The domestic stocks are further divided between the First and Second Sections. The First Section contains about 1,200 stocks while there are about 450 stocks on the Second Section. The 150 most active stocks on the First Section are traded on the trading floor. Trading in all other domestic stocks and all foreign stocks is conducted by computer. From on-line terminals in their offices, member firms enter buy and sell orders that are received at the exchange. A clerk employed by a *Saitori* member, the TSE member firm responsible for this function, matches buy and sell orders for each stock on the electronic book-entry display screen and returns confirmations to the trading parties. The same information is also recorded on the trade-report printer and displayed on all stock-quote screens on the trading floor.

Besides domestic stocks, foreign company stocks are listed and traded on the TSE foreign stock market, which was opened in December 1973. Only a limited number of foreign companies were listed before 1985, but by the end of 1995, there were 77 foreign companies listed on the TSE. The value of daily average trading in foreign stocks has fluctuated dramatically. It was very active in 1987 and 1989 (over 11 billion yen), but has been declining steadily since 1989.

London Stock Exchange (LSE)   The largest established securities market in the United Kingdom, generally referred to as "The Stock Exchange," is the London Stock Exchange. Since 1973, it has served as the stock exchange of Great Britain and Ireland, with operating units in London, Dublin, and six other cities. Both listed securities (bonds and equities) and unlisted securities are traded on the LSE. The listed equity segment involves over 2,600 companies (2,700 security issues) with a market value in excess of 374 billion pounds (approximately $561 billion at an exchange rate of $1.50/pound). Of the 2,600 companies listed on the LSE, about 600 are foreign firms—the largest number on any exchange.

The stocks listed on the LSE are divided into three groups: Alpha, Beta, and Gamma. The Alpha stocks are the 65 most actively traded stocks, and the Betas are the 500 next most active stocks. In Alpha and Beta stocks, market makers are required to offer firm bid–ask quotes to all members of the exchange. For the rest of the stocks (Gamma stocks), market quotations are only indicative and must be confirmed before a trade. All equity trades must be reported to the Stock Exchange Automated Quotation (SEAQ) system within minutes, although only trades in Alpha stocks are reported in full on the trading screen.

The pricing system on the LSE is done by competing dealers who communicate via computers in offices away from the stock exchange. This system is very similar to the NASDAQ system used in the OTC market in the United States, which is described in the next section.

Other national exchanges   Other national exchanges are located in Frankfurt, Toronto, and Paris.[16] In addition, the International Federation of Stock Exchanges was estab-

---

[16] In an attempt to attain global recognition and economies of scale, Germany's three major exchanges proposed a merger in 1995. See Andrew Fisher, "Top Three German Exchanges to Merge," *Financial Times*, May 9, 1995; and Andrew Fisher, "German Stock Market Seeks Ambitious Revamp," *Financial Times*, June 1, 1995. Also, the Paris exchange proposed electronic trading and a continuous market rather than its former call market.

lished in 1961. Members include 35 exchanges or national associations of stock exchanges in 29 countries. Located in Paris, the federation's 29 full members and six associate members meet every autumn to promote closer collaboration among themselves and to promote the development of securities markets.[17]

New exchanges are constantly being established in many emerging countries around the world. Almost all of these countries have exceptionally large needs for capital to finance private growth as well as the necessary infrastructure projects to support growth (e.g., roads, housing, sewage systems). As noted earlier, it is recognized that operational, liquid secondary equity markets are mandatory if a country aims to take advantage of the international sources of capital. For example, stock markets have been established between 1991 and 1993 in Russia and Poland, in China (Shanghai and Shenzchen) in 1986, and in Hungary (Budapest) in 1990. Recent exchanges were created in Peru and Sri Lanka.

As an indication of growth in the area, the International Finance Corporation (IFC), a subsidiary of the World Bank, began creating stock indexes for emerging markets in the early 1980s. By 1995, they had created stock market indexes for 26 major emerging markets with prices beginning in 1975, and subsequent stock indexes for 34 markets. For example, their database during 1994 went from 50 to 60 countries.[18]

The global 24-hour market   Our discussion of the global securities market will tend to emphasize the three markets in New York, London, and Tokyo because of their relative size and importance, and because they represent the major segments of a worldwide 24-hour stock market. You will often hear about a continuous market where investment firms "pass the book" around the world. This means the major active market in securities moves around the globe as trading hours for these three markets begin and end. Consider the individual trading hours for each of the three exchanges, translated into a 24-hour eastern standard time (EST) clock:

	Local Time (24-hr. Notations)	24-Hour EST
New York Stock Exchange	0930–1600	0930–1600
Tokyo Stock Exchange	0900–1100	2300–0100
	1300–1500	0300–0500
London Stock Exchange	0815–1615	0215–1015

Imagine trading starting in New York at 0930 and going until 1600 in the afternoon, being picked up by Tokyo late in the evening and going until 0500 in the morning, and continuing in London (with some overlap) until it begins in New York again (with some overlap) at 0930. Alternatively, it is possible to envision trading as beginning in Tokyo at 2300 hours and continuing until 0500, when it moves to London, then ends the day in New York. This latter model seems the most relevant because the first question a London trader asks in the morning is "What happened in Tokyo?" and the U.S. trader asks

---

[17] For further discussions of equity markets around the world, see Thomas J. Carroll, ed., *International Guide to Security Exchanges* (New York: Peat, Marwick, Mitchell, Co., 1980); David Smyth, *Worldly Wise Investor* (New York: Franklin Watts, 1988); *The Spicer and Oppenheim Guide to Securities Markets around the World* (New York: John Wiley & Sons, 1988); and Bryan de Caires, ed., *The Kidder Peabody Guide to International Capital Markets* (London: Euromoney Publications, 1988). An appendix at the end of this chapter summarizes information about stock exchanges around the world in both developed markets and emerging markets.

[18] The primary source of information and data on these markets is the annual *Emerging Stock Markets Fact Book* (Washington, DC: International Finance Corporation).

"What happened in Tokyo and what *is* happening in London?" The point is, the markets operate almost continuously and are related in their response to economic events. Therefore, as an investor you are not dealing with three separate and distinct exchanges, but with one interrelated world market.[19] Clearly, this interrelationship is growing daily because of numerous multiple listings where stocks are listed on several exchanges around the world (e.g., NYSE and TSE) and the availability of sophisticated telecommunications.

REGIONAL EXCHANGES AND THE OVER-THE-COUNTER MARKET

Within most countries, there are regional stock exchanges that compete with and supplement the national exchanges by providing secondary markets for the stocks of smaller companies. Beyond these exchanges, there is trading off the exchange in what is called the over-the-counter (OTC) market, which includes all stocks that are not listed on one of the formal exchanges. The size and significance of the regional exchanges versus the OTC market and the relative impact of these two sectors to the overall secondary stock markets vary among countries. In the first part of this section, we will discuss the rationale for and operation of regional stock exchanges. The second part of the section describes the OTC market, including heavy emphasis on the OTC market in the United States where it is a large and growing part of the total secondary stock market.

REGIONAL SECURITIES EXCHANGES   Regional exchanges typically have the same operating procedures as the national exchanges in the same countries, but they differ in their listing requirements and the geographic distributions of the listed firms. There are two main reasons for the existence of regional stock exchanges. First, they provide trading facilities for local companies that are not large enough to qualify for listing on one of the national exchanges. Their listing requirements are typically less stringent than are those of the national exchanges, as presented in Table 4.1.

Second, regional exchanges in some countries list firms that are also listed on one of the national exchanges to give local brokers who are not members of a national exchange access to these securities. As an example, American Telephone & Telegraph and General Motors are listed on both the NYSE and several regional exchanges. This dual listing allows a local brokerage firm that is not large enough to purchase a membership on the NYSE to buy and sell shares of a dual-listed stock (e. g., General Motors) without going through the NYSE and giving up part of the commission. Currently, about 90 percent of the volume on regional exchanges is attributable to trading in dual-listed issues. The regional exchanges in the United States are:

- Chicago Stock Exchange
- Pacific Stock Exchange (San Francisco–Los Angeles)
- PBW Exchange (Philadelphia–Baltimore–Washington)
- Boston Stock Exchange
- Spokane Stock Exchange (Spokane, Washington)
- Honolulu Stock Exchange (Honolulu, Hawaii)
- Intermountain Stock Exchange (Salt Lake City, Utah)

---

[19] For an example of global trading, see "How Merrill Lynch Moves Its Stock Deals All Around the World," *The Wall Street Journal,* November 9, 1987, 1, 19; and *Opportunity and Risk in the 24-Hour Global Marketplace* (New York: Coopers & Lybrand, 1987). In response to this trend toward global trading, the International Organization of Securities Commissions (IOSCO) has been established. For a discussion of it, see David Lascelles, "Calls to Bring Watchdogs Into Line," *Financial Times,* August 14, 1989, 10.

The Chicago, Pacific, and PBW exchanges account for about 90 percent of all regional exchange volume. In turn, total regional exchange volume is 9 to 10 percent of total exchange volume in the United States.

In Japan, there are seven regional stock exchanges that supplement the Tokyo Stock Exchange. The exchange in Osaka accounts for about 10 percent and that in Nagoya for about 2.3 percent of the total volume. The remaining exchanges in Kyoto, Hiroshima, Fukuoto, Niigata, and Sapporo together account for less than 1 percent of volume.

The United Kingdom has one stock exchange in London with operating units in seven cities, including Dublin, Belfast, Birmingham, Manchester, Bristol, Liverpool, and Glasgow. Germany has eight stock exchanges, including its national exchange in Frankfurt where approximately 50 percent of the trading occurs. There are regional exchanges in Düsseldorf, Munich, Hamburg, Berlin, Stuttgart, Hanover, and Bremen.[20]

Without belaboring the point, each country typically has one national exchange that accounts for the majority of trading and several regional exchanges that have less stringent listing requirements to allow trading in smaller firms. Recently, several national exchanges have created second-tier markets that are divisions of the national exchanges to allow smaller firms to be traded as part of the national exchanges.[21] In general, the fortunes of the regional exchanges have fluctuated substantially over time, based on interest in small, young firms and/or institutional interest in dual-listed stocks.

OVER-THE-COUNTER (OTC) MARKET   The over-the-counter (OTC) market includes trading in all stocks not listed on one of the exchanges. It can also include trading in listed stocks, which is referred to as the *third market,* and is discussed in the following section. The OTC market is not a formal organization with membership requirements or a specific list of stocks deemed eligible for trading.[22] In theory, any security can be traded on the OTC market as long as a registered dealer is willing to make a market in the security (i.e., willing to buy and sell shares of the stock).

Size of the OTC market   The U.S. OTC market is the largest segment of the U.S. secondary market in terms of the number of issues traded. It is also the most diverse in terms of quality. As noted earlier, about 2,600 issues are traded on the NYSE and about 800 issues on the AMEX. In contrast, almost 3,700 issues are actively traded on the OTC market's NASDAQ National Market System (NMS).[23] Another 1,000 stocks are traded on the NASDAQ system independent of the NMS. Finally, 1,000 OTC stocks are regularly quoted in *The Wall Street Journal* but not in the NASDAQ system. Therefore, a total of almost 6,000 issues are traded on the OTC market—substantially more than on the NYSE and AMEX combined.

Table 4.4 sets forth the growth in the number of companies and issues on NASDAQ. The growth in average daily trading is shown in Table 4.2 relative to some national

---

[20] As noted, the largest three exchanges are merging, which will create an exchange encompassing over 80 percent of total volume.

[21] An example of these second-tier markets is the Second Section on the TSE and the Unlisted Stock Market (USM) on the LSE. In both cases, the exchange is attempting to provide trading facilities for smaller firms without changing their listing requirements for the national exchange. Unfortunately, the LSE eliminated the USM during 1993 due to lack of trading. This is discussed further in a subsequent section.

[22] The requirements of trading on different segments of the OTC trading system will be discussed later in this section.

[23] NASDAQ is an acronym for National Association of Securities Dealers Automated Quotations. The system is discussed in detail in a later section. To be traded on the NMS, a firm must have a certain size and trading activity and at least four market makers. A specification of requirements for various components of the NASDAQ system is contained in Table 4.5.

| TABLE 4.4 | NUMBER OF COMPANIES AND ISSUES TRADING ON NASDAQ: 1980–1995 |

Year	Number of Companies	Number of Issues
1980	2,894	3,050
1981	3,353	3,687
1982	3,264	3,664
1983	3,901	4,467
1984	4,097	4,723
1985	4,136	4,784
1986	4,417	5,189
1987	4,706	5,537
1988	4,451	5,144
1989	4,293	4,963
1990	4,132	4,706
1991	4,094	4,684
1992	4,113	4,764
1993	4,611	5,393
1994	4,902	5,761
1995	5,122	5,955

Source: *NASDAQ Fact Book* (Washington, DC: National Association of Securities Dealers, 1996), 5.

exchanges. As of the end of 1995, 350 issues on NASDAQ were either foreign stocks or American Depository Receipts (ADRs). Trading in foreign stocks and ADRs represented over 5 percent of total NASDAQ share volume in 1995. About 300 of these issues trade on both NASDAQ and a foreign exchange such as Toronto. In March 1988, NASDAQ developed a link with the Singapore Stock Exchange that allows 24-hour trading from NASDAQ in New York to Singapore to a NASDAQ/London link and back to New York.

Although the OTC market has the greatest number of issues, the NYSE has a larger total value of trading. In 1995, the approximate value of equity trading on the NYSE was $3,083 billion, and NASDAQ was $2,398 billion. Notably, the NASDAQ value exceeded what transpired on the LSE ($700 billion) and on the TSE ($873 billion).

There is tremendous diversity in the OTC market because it imposes no minimum requirements. Stocks that trade on the OTC range from those of small, unprofitable companies to large, very profitable firms (e.g., Microsoft, Intel). On the upper end, all U.S. government bonds are traded on the OTC market as are the majority of bank and insurance stocks. Finally, about 100 exchange-listed stocks are traded on the OTC—the third market.

Operation of the OTC   As noted, any stock can be traded on the OTC as long as someone indicates a willingness to make a market whereby the party buys or sells for his or her own account acting as a dealer.[24] This differs from most transactions on the listed exchanges, where some members keep the book and as brokers attempt to match buy and sell orders. Therefore, the OTC market is referred to as a *negotiated market,* in which investors directly negotiate with dealers. Several of the major exchanges are continuous auction markets, with some of the members acting as intermediaries (auctioneers).

Unlisted Securities Market (USM)   The Unlisted Securities Market (USM) was started by the LSE in 1980 to handle smaller companies without the sufficiently long trading records required for full listing. The USM was established and supervised by the

---

[24] Dealer and market maker are synonymous.

LSE. In late 1992, a number of market makers in this market withdrew because the low volume made it unprofitable for them. A resolution to disband the market was passed in 1993. The result is twofold for stocks on this market—either they had to become listed on the main exchange (LSE) or become part of a bulletin board market without market makers.[25]

The NASDAQ System **The National Association of Securities Dealers Automated Quotation (NASDAQ)** system is an automated, electronic quotation system for the vast OTC market. Any number of dealers can elect to make markets in an OTC stock. The actual number depends on the activity in the stock. The average number of market makers for all stocks on the NASDAQ system was 10.2 in 1995 according to the *NASDAQ Fact Book.*

NASDAQ makes all dealer quotes available immediately. The broker can check the quotation machine and call the dealer with the best market, verify that the quote has not changed, and make the sale or purchase. The NASDAQ system has three levels to serve firms with different needs and interests.

Level 1 provides a single median representative quote for the stocks on NASDAQ. This quote system is for firms that want current quotes on OTC stocks but do not consistently buy or sell OTC stocks for their customers and are not market makers. This composite quote changes constantly to adjust for any changes by individual market makers.

Level 2 provides instantaneous current quotations on NASDAQ stocks by all market makers in a stock. This quotation system is for firms that consistently trade OTC stocks. Given an order to buy or sell, brokers check the quotation machine, call the market maker with the best market for their purposes (highest bid if they are selling, lowest offer if buying), and consummate the deal.

Level 3 is for OTC market makers. Such firms want Level 2, but they also need the capability to change their own quotations, which Level 3 provides.

Listing requirements for NASDAQ Quotes and trading volume for the OTC market are reported in two lists: a National Market System (NMS) list and a regular NASDAQ list. As of 1996, there were four sets of listing requirements. The first, for initial listing on any NASDAQ system, is the least stringent. The second is for automatic (mandatory) inclusion on the NASDAQ/NMS system. For stocks on this system, there is up-to-the-minute volume and last-sale information for the competing market makers as well as end-of-the-day information on total volume and high, low, and closing prices. In addition, two sets of criteria govern voluntary participation on the NMS by companies with different characteristics. Alternative 1 accommodates companies with limited assets or net worth but substantial earnings; Alternative 2 is for large companies that are not necessarily as profitable. The four sets of criteria are set forth in Table 4.5.

A sample trade Assume you are considering the purchase of 100 shares of Apple Computer. Although Apple is large enough and profitable enough to be listed on a national exchange, the company has never applied for listing because it enjoys a very active market on the OTC. (It is one of the volume leaders with daily volume typically above 500,000 shares and often in excess of 1 million shares.) When you contact your broker, he or she will consult the NASDAQ electronic quotation machine to determine the current dealer quotations for AAPL, the trading symbol for Apple Computer.[26] The quote machine will

---

[25] The bulletin board would be a broker market.

[26] Trading symbols are one- to four-letter codes used to designate stocks. Whenever a trade is reported on a stock ticker, the trading symbol appears with the figures. Many symbols are obvious, such as GM (General Motors), F (Ford Motors), GE (General Electric), and T (American Telephone & Telegraph).

TABLE 4.5	QUALIFICATION STANDARDS FOR INCLUSION IN NASDAQ AND NMS			
			VOLUNTARY NASDAQ/NMS INCLUSION	
Standard	Initial NASDAQ Inclusion (Domestic Common Stocks)	Mandatory NASDAQ/ NMS Inclusion	Alternative 1	Alternative 2
Total assets	$2 million		$2 million	$2 million
Net tangible assets	—	$2 million	$4 million	$12 million
Capital and surplus	$1 million	$1 million	$1 million	$8 million
Net income	—	—	$400,000 in latest or last 2 of 3 fiscal years	—
Pretax income	—	—	$750,000 in latest or last 2 of 3 fiscal years	—
Operating history	—	—	—	3 years
Public float (shares)	100,000	500,000	500,000	1 million
Market value of float	—	—	$3 million	$15 million
Minimum bid	—	$10 for 5 business days	$5	$3
Trading volume	—	Average 600,000 shares/ month for 6 months	—	—
Shareholders of record	100	300	800	400
Market makers	2	Four for 5 business days	2	2

Source: *NASDAQ Fact Book* (Washington, DC: National Association of Securities Dealers, 1995), 44.

show that there are about 20 dealers making a market in AAPL. An example of differing quotations might be as follows:

Dealer	Bid	Ask
1	55½	55¾
2	55⅜	55⅝
3	55¼	55⅝
4	55⅜	55¾

Assuming these are the best markets available from the total group, your broker would call either Dealer 2 or Dealer 3 because they have the lowest offering prices. After verifying the quote, your broker would give one of these dealers an order to buy 100 shares of AAPL at 55⅝ ($55.625 a share). Because your firm was not a market maker in the stock, the firm would act as a broker and charge you $5,562.50 plus a commission for the trade. If your firm had been a market maker in AAPL, with an asking price of 55⅝, the firm would have sold the stock to you at 55⅝ net (without commission). If you had been interested in selling 100 shares of Apple Computer instead of buying, the broker would have contacted Dealer 1, who made the highest bid.

Changing dealer inventory　Let us consider the price quotations by an OTC dealer who wants to change his or her inventory on a given stock. For example, assume Dealer 4, with a current quote of 55⅜ bid–55¾ ask, decides to increase his or her holdings of AAPL. The NASDAQ quotes indicate that the highest bid is currently 55½. Increasing the bid to 55½ would bring some of the business currently going to Dealer 1. Taking a more aggressive action, the dealer might raise the bid to 55⅝ and buy all the stock offered, including some from Dealers 2 and 3, who are offering it at 55⅝. In this example, the dealer raises the bid price but does not change the asking price, which was above those of Dealers 2 and 3. This dealer will buy stock but probably will not sell any. A dealer that had excess stock would keep the bid below the market (lower than 55½) and reduce the asking price to 55⅝ or less. Dealers constantly change their bid and/or ask prices, depending on their current inventories or changes in the outlook based on new information for the stock.[27]

THIRD MARKET   As mentioned, the term **third market** describes over-the-counter trading of shares listed on an exchange. Although most transactions in listed stocks take place on an exchange, an investment firm that is not a member of an exchange can make a market in a listed stock. Most of the trading on the third market is in well-known stocks such as AT&T, IBM, and Xerox. The success or failure of the third market depends on whether the OTC market in these stocks is as good as the exchange market and whether the relative cost of the OTC transaction compares favorably with the cost on the exchange. This market is very important during the relatively few periods when trading is not available on the NYSE either because trading is suspended or the exchange is closed.[28]

FOURTH MARKET   The term **fourth market** describes direct trading of securities between two parties with no broker intermediary. In almost all cases, both parties involved are institutions. When you think about it, a direct transaction is really not that unusual. If you own 100 shares of AT&T Corp. and decide to sell it, there is nothing wrong with simply offering it to your friends or associates at a mutually agreeable price (e.g., based on exchange transactions) and making the transaction directly.

Investors typically buy or sell stock through brokers because it is faster and easier. Also, you would expect to get a better price for your stock because the broker has a good chance of finding the best buyer. You are willing to pay a commission for these liquidity services. The fourth market evolved because of the substantial fees charged by brokers to institutions with large orders. At some point, it becomes worthwhile for institutions to attempt to deal directly with each other and bypass the brokerage fees. Assume an institution decides to sell 100,000 shares of AT&T, which is selling for about $60 a share, for a total value of $6 million. The average commission on such a transaction prior to the advent of negotiated rates in 1975 was about 1 percent of the value of the trade, or about $60,000. This cost made it attractive for a selling institution to spend some time and effort finding another institution interested in increasing its holdings of AT&T and negotiating a direct sale. Currently, such transactions cost about 5 cents a share, which implies a cost of $5,000 for the 100,000 share transactions. This is lower, but still not trivial. Because of the diverse nature of the fourth market and the lack of reporting requirements, no data are available regarding its specific size or growth.

| DETAILED ANALYSIS OF EXCHANGE MARKETS | Because of the importance of the listed exchange markets, they must be dealt with at some length. In this section, we discuss several types of membership on the exchanges, the major types of orders, and the role and function of exchange market makers—a critical component of a good exchange market. |

EXCHANGE MEMBERSHIP   Listed U.S. securities exchanges typically offer four major categories of membership: (1) specialist, (2) commission broker, (3) floor broker, and (4) registered trader. Specialists

---

[27] A number of studies have examined the determinants of dealers' bid–ask spreads, including H. R. Stoll, "Inferring the Components of the Bid–Ask Spread: Theory and Empirical Tests," *Journal of Finance* 44, no. 1 (March 1989): 115–134.

[28] Craig Torres, "Third Market Trading Crowds Stock Exchanges," *The Wall Street Journal,* March 8, 1990, C1, C9.

(or exchange market makers) who constitute about 25 percent of the total membership on exchanges will be discussed after a description of types of orders.

Commission brokers are employees of a member firm who buy or sell for the customers of the firm. When you place an order to buy or sell stock through a brokerage firm that is a member of the exchange, in many instances the firm contacts its commission broker on the floor of the exchange. That broker goes to the appropriate post on the floor and buys or sells the stock as instructed.

Floor brokers are independent members of an exchange who act as brokers for other members. As an example, when commission brokers for Merrill Lynch become too busy to handle all of their orders, they will ask one of the floor brokers to help them. At one time, these people were referred to as *$2 brokers* because that is what they received for each order. Currently, they receive about $4 per 100-share order.

Registered traders are allowed to use their memberships to buy and sell for their own accounts. They therefore save commissions on their own trading, and observers believe they have an advantage because they are on the trading floor. The exchanges and others are willing to allow these advantages because these traders provide the market with added liquidity, but regulations limit how they trade and how many registered traders can be in a trading crowd around a specialist's booth at any time. In recent years, registered traders have become **registered competitive market makers (RCMMs),** who have specific trading obligations set by the exchange. Their activity is reported as part of the specialist group.[29]

TYPES OF ORDERS   It is important to understand the different types of orders entered by investors and the specialist as a dealer.

MARKET ORDERS   The most frequent type of order is a **market order,** an order to buy or sell a stock at the best current price. An investor who enters a market sell order indicates a willingness to sell immediately at the highest bid available at the time the order reaches the specialist on the exchange or an OTC dealer. A market buy order indicates that the investor is willing to pay the lowest offering price available at the time the order reaches the floor of the exchange or an OTC dealer. Market orders provide immediate liquidity for someone willing to accept the prevailing market price.

Assume you are interested in General Electric (GE) and you call your broker to find out the current "market" on the stock. The quotation machine indicates that the prevailing market is 75 bid–75¼ ask. This means that the highest current bid on the books of the specialist is 75; that is, $75 is the most that anyone has offered to pay for GE. The lowest offer is 75¼; that is, the lowest price anyone is willing to accept to sell the stock. If you placed a market buy order for 100 shares, you would buy 100 shares at $75.25 a share (the lowest ask price) for a total cost of $7,525 plus commission. If you submitted a market sell order for 100 shares, you would sell the shares at $75 each and receive $7,500 less commission.

LIMIT ORDERS   The individual placing a **limit order** specifies the buy or sell price. You might submit a bid to purchase 100 shares of Coca-Cola stock at $65 a share when the current market is 70 bid–70¼ ask, with the expectation that the stock will decline to $65 in the near future.

---

[29] Prior to the late 1970s, there were also odd lot dealers who bought and sold to individuals with orders for less than round lots (usually 100 shares). Currently, this function is handled by either the specialist or some large brokerage firm.

You must also indicate how long the limit order will be outstanding. Alternative time specifications are basically boundless. A limit order can be instantaneous ("fill or kill," meaning fill the order instantly or cancel it). It can also be good for part of a day, a full day, several days, a week, or a month. It can also be open-ended, or good until canceled (GTC).

Rather than wait for a given price on a stock, your broker will give the limit order to the specialist, who will put it in a limit-order book and act as the broker's representative. When and if the market reaches the limit-order price, the specialist will execute the order and inform your broker. The specialist receives a small part of the commission for rendering this service.

SHORT SALES   Most investors purchase stock (i. e., "go long") expecting to derive their return from an increase in value. If you believe that a stock is overpriced, however, and want to take advantage of an expected decline in the price, you can sell the stock short. A **short sale** is the sale of stock that you do not own with the intent of purchasing it back later at a lower price. Specifically, you would borrow the stock from another investor through your broker, sell it in the market, and subsequently replace it at (you hope) a price lower than the price at which you sold it. The investor who lent the stock has the proceeds of the sale as collateral. In turn, this investor can invest these funds in short-term, risk-free securities. Although a short sale has no time limit, the lender of the shares can decide to sell the shares, in which case your broker must find another investor willing to lend the shares.[30]

Three technical points affect short sales. First, a short sale can be made only on an *uptick trade,* meaning the price of the short sale must be higher than the last trade price. This is because the exchanges do not want traders to force a profit on a short sale by pushing the price down through continually selling short. Therefore, the transaction price for a short sale must be an uptick or, without any change in price, the previous price must have been higher than its previous price (a zero uptick). For an example of a zero uptick, consider the following set of transaction prices: 42, 42¼, 42¼. You could sell short at 42¼ even though it is no change from the previous trade at 42¼ because that trade was an uptick trade.

The second technical point concerns dividends. The short seller must pay any dividends due to the investor who lent the stock. The purchaser of the short-sale stock receives the dividend from the corporation, so the short seller must pay a similar dividend to the lender.

A final point is that short sellers must post the same margin as an investor who had acquired stock. This margin can be in any unrestricted securities owned by the short seller.

SPECIAL ORDERS   In addition to these general orders, there are several special types of orders. A *stop loss order* is a conditional market order whereby the investor directs the sale of a stock if it drops to a given price. Assume you buy a stock at 50 and expect it to go up. If you are wrong, you want to limit your losses. To protect yourself, you could put in a stop loss order at 45. In this case, if the stock dropped to 45, your stop loss order would become a market sell order, and the stock would be sold at the prevailing market price. The stop loss order does not guarantee that you will get the $45; you can get a little bit more or a little bit less. Because of the possibility of market disruption caused by a large number of stop loss orders, exchanges have, on occasion, canceled all such orders on certain stocks and not allowed brokers to accept further stop loss orders on those issues.

---

[30] For a discussion of profitable short-selling results, see Gary Putka, "Fortune Smiles on Short Side of Market," *The Wall Street Journal,* October 27, 1987, 5, while negative results are highlighted in William Power, "Short Sellers Take It on the Chin Again," *The Wall Street Journal,* June 29, 1993, C1, C2; and William Power, "Short Sellers Set to Catch Tumbling Overvalued Stocks," *The Wall Street Journal,* December 28, 1993, C1, C2. For a discussion of some recent short-selling events, see Carol J. Loomis, "Short Sellers and the Seamy Side of Wall Street," *Fortune,* July 22, 1996, pp. 66–72; and Gary Weiss, "The Secret World of Short Sellers," *Business Week,* August 5, 1996, pp. 62–68.

A related type of stop loss tactic for short sales is a *stop buy order.* An investor who has sold stock short and wants to minimize any loss if the stock begins to increase in value would enter this conditional buy order at a price above that at which the investor sold the stock short. Assume you sold a stock short at 50, expecting it to decline to 40. To protect yourself from an increase, you could put in a stop buy order to purchase the stock using a market buy order if it reached a price of 55. This conditional buy order would hopefully limit any loss on the short sale to approximately $5 a share.

MARGIN TRANSACTIONS   On any type of order, an investor can pay for the stock with cash or borrow part of the cost, leveraging the transaction. Leverage is accomplished by buying on **margin,** which means the investor pays for the stock with some cash and borrows the rest through the broker, putting up the stock for collateral.

As shown in Figure 4.1, the dollar amount of margin credit extended by members of the NYSE has increased consistently since 1991 and reached record levels in 1995. The interest rate charged on these loans by the investment firms is typically 1.50 percent above the rate charged by the bank making the loan. The bank rate, referred to as the *call money rate,* is generally about 1 percent below the prime rate. For example, in June 1996, the prime rate was 8.25 percent, and the call money rate was 7.0 percent.

Federal Reserve Board Regulations T and U determine the maximum proportion of any transaction that can be borrowed. These regulations were enacted during the 1930s because

---

FIGURE 4.1   **MARGIN DEBT EXTENDED BY THE MEMBERS OF THE NYSE AS OF END OF QUARTERS, 1985–1995**

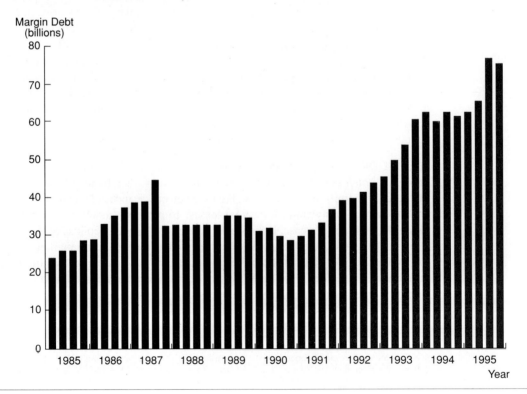

Source: *NYSE Fact Book* (New York: NYSE, 1995).

it was contended that the excessive credit extended for stock acquisition contributed to the stock market collapse of 1929. Since the enactment of the regulations, this *margin requirement* (the proportion of total transaction value that must be paid in cash) has varied from 40 percent (allowing loans of 60 percent of the value) to 100 percent (allowing no borrowing). As of June 1996, the initial margin requirement specified by the Federal Reserve was 50 percent, although individual investment firms can require higher rates.

After the initial purchase, changes in the market price of the stock will cause changes in the *investor's equity,* which is equal to the market value of the collateral stock minus the amount borrowed. Obviously, if the stock price increases, the investor's equity as a proportion of the total market value of the stock increases, that is, the investor's margin will exceed the initial margin requirement.

Assume you acquired 200 shares of a $50 stock for a total cost of $10,000. A 50 percent initial margin requirement allowed you to borrow $5,000, making your initial equity $5,000. If the stock price increases by 20 percent to $60 a share, the total market value of your position is $12,000, and your equity is now $7,000, or 58 percent ($7,000/$12,000). In contrast, if the stock price declines by 20 percent to $40 a share, the total market value would be $8,000, and your investor's equity would be $3,000, or 37.5 percent ($3,000/$8,000).

This example demonstrates that buying on margin provides all the advantages and the disadvantages of leverage. Lower margin requirements allow you to borrow more, increasing the percentage of gain or loss on your investment when the stock price increases or decreases. The leverage factor equals 1/percent margin. Thus, as in this example, if the margin is 50 percent, the leverage factor is 2, that is, 1/.50. Therefore, when the rate of return on the stock is plus or minus 10 percent, the return on your equity is plus or minus 20 percent. If the margin declines to 33 percent, you can borrow more (67 percent), and the leverage factor is 3 (1/.33). When you acquire stock or other investments on margin, you are increasing the financial risk of the investment beyond the risk inherent in the security itself. You should increase your required rate of return accordingly.[31]

The following example shows how borrowing by using margin affects the distribution of your returns before commissions and interest on the loan. When the stock increased by 20 percent, your return on the investment was as follows:

1. The market value of the stock is $12,000, which leaves you with $7,000 after you pay off the loan.
2. The return on your $5,000 investment is:

$$\frac{7,000}{5,000} - 1 = 1.40 - 1$$

$$= 0.40 = 40\%$$

In contrast, if the stock declined by 20 percent to $40 a share, your return would be as follows:

1. The market value of the stock is $8,000, which leaves you with $3,000 after you pay off the loan.

---

[31] For a discussion of margin calls following market declines in 1987 and 1990, see Karen Slater, "Margin Calls Create Dilemma for Investors," *The Wall Street Journal,* October 23, 1987, 21; William Power, "Stocks' Drop Spurs Margin Calls Less Severe than in Earlier Falls," *The Wall Street Journal,* August 15, 1990, C1. For a discussion of the environment in 1993, see Michael Siconolfi, "Does Margin-Loan Binge Signal Stock-Market Top?" *The Wall Street Journal,* April 23, 1993, C1, C16.

2. The return on your $5,000 investment is:

$$\frac{3{,}000}{5{,}000} - 1 = 0.60 - 1$$

$$= -0.40 = -40\%$$

You should also recognize that this symmetrical increase in gains and losses is only true prior to commissions and interest. Obviously, if we assume a 6 percent interest on the borrowed funds (which would be $5,000 × .06 = $300) and a $100 commission on the transaction, the results would indicate a lower increase and a larger negative return as follows:

$$20\% \text{ increase: } \frac{\$12{,}000 - \$5{,}000 - \$300 - \$100}{\$5{,}000} - 1$$

$$= \frac{6{,}600}{5{,}000} - 1$$

$$= 0.32 = 32\%$$

$$20\% \text{ decline: } \frac{\$8{,}000 - \$5{,}000 - \$300 - \$100}{\$5{,}000} - 1$$

$$= \frac{2{,}600}{5{,}000} - 1$$

$$= -0.48 = -48\%$$

In addition to the initial margin requirement, another important concept is the **maintenance margin,** which is the required proportion of your equity to the total value of the stock; the maintenance margin protects the broker if the stock price declines. At present, the minimum maintenance margin specified by the Federal Reserve is 25 percent, but, again, individual brokerage firms can dictate higher margins for their customers. If the stock price declines to the point where your equity drops below 25 percent of the total value of the position, the account is considered undermargined, and you will receive a **margin call** to provide more equity. If you do not respond with the required funds in time, the stock will be sold to pay off the loan. The time allowed to meet a margin call varies between investment firms and is affected by market conditions. Under volatile conditions, the time allowed to respond to a margin call can be shortened drastically.

Given a maintenance margin of 25 percent, when you buy on margin you must consider how far the stock price can fall before you receive a margin call. The computation for our example is as follows: If the price of the stock is P and you own 200 shares, the value of the position is 200P and the equity in the account is 200P − $5,000. The percentage margin is (200P − 5,000)/200P. To determine the price, P, that is equal to 25 percent (0.25), we use the equation:

$$200P - \frac{\$5{,}000}{200P} = 0.25$$

$$200P - 5{,}000 = 50P$$
$$P = \$33.33$$

Therefore, when the stock is at $33.33, the equity value is exactly 25 percent; so if the stock goes below $33.33, the investor will receive a margin call.

To continue the previous example, if the stock declines to $30 a share, its total market value would be $6,000 and your equity would be $1,000, which is only about 17 percent of the total value ($1,000/$6,000). You would receive a margin call for approximately $667, which would give you equity of $1,667, or 25 percent of the total value of the account ($1,667/$6,667).[32]

EXCHANGE MARKET MAKERS

Now that we have discussed the overall structure of the exchange markets and the orders that are used to buy and sell stocks, we can discuss the role and function of the market makers on the exchange. These people and the role they play differ among exchanges. For example, on U.S. exchanges these people are called **specialists**; on the TSE they are a combination of the *Saitori* and regular members. Most exchanges do not have a single market maker but have competing dealers. On exchanges that have central market makers, these individuals are critical to the smooth and efficient functioning of these markets.

As noted, a major requirement for a good market is liquidity, which depends on how the market makers do their job. Our initial discussion centers on the specialist's role in U.S. markets, followed by a consideration of comparable roles on exchanges in other countries.

U.S. MARKETS   The specialist is a member of the exchange who applies to the exchange to be assigned stocks to handle.[33] The typical specialist will handle about 15 stocks. The capital requirement for specialists changed in April 1988 in response to the October 1987 market crash. Specifically, the minimum capital required of each specialist unit was raised to $1 million or the value of 15,000 shares of each stock assigned, whichever is greater.

Functions of the specialist   Specialists have two major functions. First, they serve as *brokers* to match buy and sell orders and to handle special limit orders placed with member brokers. An individual broker who receives a limit order (or stop loss or stop buy order) leaves it with the specialist, who executes it when the specified price occurs. For this service, the specialist receives a portion of the broker's commission on the trade.

The second major function of a specialist is to act as a *dealer* to maintain a fair and orderly market by providing liquidity when the normal flow of orders is not adequate. In this capacity, the specialist must buy and sell for his or her own account (like an OTC dealer) when public supply or demand is insufficient to provide a continuous, liquid market.

Consider the following example. If a stock is currently selling for about $40 per share, the current bid and ask in an auction market (without the intervention of the specialist) might be a 40 bid–41 ask. Under such conditions, random market buy and sell orders might cause the stock price to fluctuate between 40 and 41 constantly—a movement of 2.5 percent between trades. Most investors would probably consider such a price pattern too volatile; the market would not be considered continuous. Under such conditions, the specialist is expected to provide "bridge liquidity" by entering alternative bids and/or asks to narrow the spread and improve the stock's price continuity. In this example, the specialist could enter a bid of 40½ or 40¾ or an ask of 40½ or 40¼ to narrow the spread to one-half or one-quarter point.

Specialists can enter either side of the market, depending on several factors, including the trend of the market. They are expected to buy or sell against the market when prices are

---

[32] For a further discussion, see Georgette Jasen, "Cheap Margin Loans Are Tempting, but Beware," *The Wall Street Journal,* April 23, 1993, C1, C21.

[33] Each stock is assigned to one specialist. Most specialists are part of a unit that can be a formal organization of specialists (a specialist firm) or a set of independent specialists who join together to spread the work load and the risk of the stocks assigned to the unit. At the end of 1995, a total of 446 individual specialists made up 53 specialist units (about 8 specialists per unit).

clearly moving in one direction. Specifically, they are required to buy stock for their own inventories when there is an excess of sell orders and the market is definitely declining. Alternatively, they must sell stock from their inventories or sell it short to accommodate an excess of buy orders when the market is rising. Specialists are not expected to prevent prices from rising or declining, but only to ensure that the prices change in an orderly fashion (i.e., to maintain price continuity). Evidence that they have fulfilled this requirement is that during recent years NYSE stocks traded unchanged from, or within one-eighth point of, the price of the previous trade about 95 percent of the time.

Another factor affecting a specialists' decision on how to narrow the spread is their current inventory position in the stock. For example, if they have large inventories of a given stock, all other factors being equal, they would probably enter on the ask (sell) side to reduce these heavy inventories. In contrast, specialists who have little or no inventory of shares because they had been selling from their inventories, or selling short, would tend toward the bid (buy) side of the market to rebuild their inventories or close out their short positions.

Finally, the position of the limit order book will influence how they act. Numerous limit buy orders (bids) close to the current market and very few limit sell orders (asks) might indicate a tendency toward higher prices because demand is apparently heavy and supply is limited. Under such conditions, a specialist who is not bound by one of the other factors would probably opt to accumulate stock in anticipation of a price increase. The specialists on the NYSE have historically participated as dealers in 10 to 12 percent of all trades.

Specialist income   The specialist derives income from the broker and the dealer functions. The actual breakdown between the two sources depends on the specific stock. In an actively traded stock such as IBM, a specialist has little need to act as a dealer because the substantial public interest in the stock creates a tight market (i.e., a small bid–ask spread). In such a case, the main source of income would come from maintaining the limit orders for the stock. The income derived from acting as a broker for a stock such as IBM can be substantial and it is basically without risk.

In contrast, a stock with low trading volume and substantial price volatility would probably have a fairly wide bid–ask spread, and the specialist would have to be an active dealer. The specialist's income from such a stock would depend on his or her ability to trade it profitably. Specialists have a major advantage when trading because of their limit-order books. Officially, only specialists are supposed to see the limit-order book, which means that they would have a monopoly on very important information regarding the current supply and demand for a stock. The fact is that currently the specialists routinely share the limit-order book with other brokers, so it is not a competitive advantage.[34]

Most specialists attempt to balance their portfolios between strong broker stocks that provide steady, riskless income and stocks that require active dealer roles. Notably, following the October 1987 market crash, specialists were required to increase their capital positions substantially, which would reduce their return on investment.[35]

---

[34] For evidence that the specialists do not fare too badly when they trade against the market, see Frank K. Reilly and Eugene F. Drzycimski, "The Stock Exchange Specialist and the Market Impact of Major World Events," *Financial Analysts Journal* 31, no. 4 (July–August 1975): 27–32. Also, if a major imbalance in trading arises due to new information, the specialist can request a temporary suspension of trading. For an analysis of what occurs during these trading suspensions, see Michael H. Hopewell and Arthur L. Schwartz, Jr., "Temporary Trading Suspensions in Individual NYSE Securities," *Journal of Finance* 33, no. 5 (December 1978): 1355–1373; and Frank J. Fabozzi and Christopher K. Ma, "The Over-the-Counter Market and New York Stock Exchange Trading Halts," *The Financial Review* 23, no. 4 (November 1988): 427–437. An example of a dramatic halt is discussed in Martha Brannigan, "Shares of Policy Management Nose-Dive 43%," *The Wall Street Journal,* April 7, 1993, A4.

[35] For a discussion of the problems facing specialists, see Edward A. Wyatt, "Eye of the Hurricane," *Barron's,* February 19, 1990, 20.

TOKYO STOCK EXCHANGE (TSE)   As of 1995, the TSE has a total of 124 "regular members" (100 Japanese members and 24 foreign members) and 1 *Saitori* member (4 *Saitori* firms merged during 1992). For each membership, the firm is allowed several people on the floor of the exchange, depending on its trading volume and capital position (the average number of employees on the floor is 20 per firm for a regular member and about 300 employees for the *Saitori* member). The employees of a regular member are called *trading clerks,* and the employees of the *Saitori* member are called *intermediary clerks.*

Regular members buy and sell securities on the TSE either as agents or principals (i.e., brokers or dealers). *Saitori* members specialize in acting as intermediaries (brokers) for transactions among regular members, and they maintain the books for limit orders. (Stop loss and stop buy orders as well as short selling are not allowed.) Therefore, *Saitori* members have some of the characteristics of the U.S. exchange specialists, because they match buy and sell orders for customers, handle limit orders, and are not allowed to deal with public customers. They *differ* from the U.S. exchange specialists because they do not act as dealers to maintain an orderly market. Only regular members are allowed to buy and sell for their own accounts. Therefore, the TSE is a two-way, continuous auction, order-driven market where buy and sell orders directly interact with one another with the *Saitori* acting as the auctioneer (intermediary) between firms submitting the orders.

Also, although there are about 1,700 listed domestic stocks and 100 foreign stocks on the First Section, only the largest 150 stocks are traded on the floor of the exchange. Trading on the floor is enhanced by an electronic system called the Floor Order Routing and Execution System (FORES). This system is designed to: (1) automate order routing for small orders, (2) replace manual order books with electronic order books that can execute orders, and (3) computerize the reporting and confirmation process. All other stocks on the TSE are traded through a computer system called CORES, which stands for Computer-assisted Order Routing and Execution System. With CORES, after an order is entered into the central processing unit, it becomes part of an electronic "book," which is monitored by a *Saitori* member who matches all buy and sell orders on the computer in accordance with trading rules. The system also automatically executes all orders for transactions at the last sale price and provides a narrow bid–ask spread within which orders are executed.

TSE membership is available to corporations licensed by the Minister of Finance. Member applicants may request any of four licenses: (1) to trade securities as a dealer, (2) to trade as a broker, (3) to underwrite new securities on secondary offerings, or (4) to handle retail distribution of new or outstanding securities. A firm may have more than one license, but cannot act as a principal and agent in the same transaction. The minimum capital requirements for these licenses vary from 200 million to 3 billion yen ($2 million to $30 million) depending on the type of license.

Although Japan's securities laws allow foreign securities firms to obtain membership on the exchanges, the individual exchanges determine whether membership will be granted. Twenty-four foreign firms have become members of the TSE since 1986.[36]

LONDON STOCK EXCHANGE (LSE)   Historically, members on the LSE were either brokers who could trade shares on behalf of customers, or jobbers who bought and sold shares

---

[36] Some observers have questioned the pure economics of these memberships, but the firms have defended them as a means of becoming a part of the Japanese financial community. In this regard, see Kathryn Graven, "Tokyo Stock Exchange's Broker-Fees Cut Is Seen Trimming Foreign Firms' Profits," *The Wall Street Journal,* October 2, 1987, 17; and Marcus W. Brauchli, "U.S. Brokerage Firms Operating in Japan Have Mixed Results," *The Wall Street Journal,* August 16, 1989, A1, A8.

as principals. Following a major deregulation (the "Big Bang") on October 27, 1986, brokers are allowed to make markets in various equities and gilts (British government bonds) and jobbers can deal with non-stock-exchange members, including the public and institutions.

Membership in the LSE is granted based on experience and competence, and there are no citizenship or residency requirements. Currently, over 5,000 individual memberships are held by 214 broker firms and 22 jobbers. Although individuals gain membership, the operational unit is a firm that pays membership fees based on the number of exchange-approved members it employs during its first year of membership. Subsequently, a member firm pays an annual charge equal to 1 percent of its gross revenues.

CHANGES IN THE SECURITIES MARKETS

Since 1965, there have been numerous changes prompted by the significant growth of trading by large financial institutions such as banks, insurance companies, pension funds, and investment companies because the trading requirements of these institutions differ from those of individual investors. Additional changes have transpired because of capital market globalization. In this section, we point out these changes and discuss why they occurred, consider their impact on the market, and speculate about future changes.

EVIDENCE AND EFFECT OF INSTITUTIONALIZATION

The growing impact of large financial institutions is evidenced by data on block trades (transactions involving at least 10,000 shares) and the size of trades, as seen in Table 4.6.

TABLE 4.6	**BLOCK TRANSACTIONS**[a] **AND AVERAGE SHARES PER SALE ON THE NYSE**			
Year	Total Number of Block Transactions	Total Number of Shares in Block Trades (000)	Percentage of Reported Volume	Average Number of Block Transactions per Day	Average Shares per Sale
1965	2,171	48,262	3.1%	9	224
1970	17,217	450,908	15.4	68	388
1975	34,420	778,540	16.6	136	495
1980	133,597	3,311,132	29.2	528	872
1981	145,564	3,771,442	31.8	575	1,013
1982	254,707	6,742,481	41.0	1,007	1,305
1983	363,415	9,842,080	45.6	1,436	1,434
1984	433,427	11,492,091	49.8	1,713	1,781
1985	539,039	14,222,272	51.7	2,139	1,878
1986	665,587	17,811,335	49.9	2,631	1,881
1987	970,679	24,497,241	51.2	3,639	2,112
1988	768,419	22,270,680	54.5	3,037	2,303
1989	872,811	21,316,132	51.1	3,464	2,123
1990	843,365	19,681,849	49.6	3,333	2,082
1991	981,077	22,474,382	49.6	3,878	1,670
1992	1,134,832	26,069,383	50.7	4,468	1,684
1993	1,477,859	35,959,117	53.7	5,841	1,441
1994	1,654,505	40,757,770	55.5	6,565	1,495
1995	1,963,889	49,736,912	57.0	7,793	1,489

[a]Trades of 10,000 shares or more.

Source: *NYSE Fact Book* (New York: NYSE, various issues). Reprinted by permission.

Financial institutions are the main source of large block trades, and the number of block trades on the NYSE has grown steadily from a daily average of 9 in 1965 to almost 7,800 a day in 1995. On average, such trades constitute over half of all the volume on the exchange. Institutional involvement is also reflected in the average size of trades, which has grown consistently from about 200 shares in 1965 to almost 1,500 shares per trade in 1995.[37]

Several major effects of this institutionalization of the market have been identified:

1. Negotiated (competitive) commission rates
2. The influence of block trades
3. The impact on stock price volatility
4. The development of a National Market System (NMS)

In the following sections, we discuss how each of these effects has impacted the operation of the U.S. securities market.

NEGOTIATED COMMISSION RATES

BACKGROUND   When the NYSE was formally established in 1792, it was agreed that the members would carry out all trades in designated stocks on the exchange, and that they would charge nonmembers on the basis of a *minimum commission schedule* that outlawed price cutting. Because the market was initially used by individual investors, the minimum commission schedule was developed to compensate for handling small orders and made no allowance for the trading of large orders by institutions. As a result, institutional investors had to pay substantially more in commissions than the costs of the transactions justified.

The initial reaction to the excess commissions was give-ups, whereby brokers agreed to pay part of their commissions (sometimes as much as 80 percent) to other brokerage houses or research firms designated by the institution making the trade. These firms provided services to the institution. These commission transfers were referred to as *soft dollars*. Another response was the increased use of the third market, where commissions were not fixed as they were on the NYSE.

The fixed commission structure also fostered the development and use of the fourth market. Finally, some institutions became members of one of the regional exchanges (the NYSE and AMEX would not allow institutional members).

NEGOTIATED COMMISSIONS   In 1970, the SEC began a program of negotiated commissions on large transactions and finally allowed negotiated commissions on all transactions on May 1, 1975 ("May Day").

The effect on commissions charged has been dramatic. Initially, the negotiated commissions were stated in terms of 30 to 50 percent discounts from pre–May Day fixed rates. Currently, commissions for institutions are in the range of 5 to 10 cents per share regardless of the price of the stock, which implies a very large discount on high-priced shares. Although individuals initially enjoyed little discounting, currently there are numerous competing discount brokers who charge a straight transaction fee and do not provide research advice or safekeeping services. These discounts vary depending on the size of the trade. Discount brokerage firms advertise extensively in *The Wall Street Journal* and *Barron's*.

---

[37] Although the influence of institutional trading is greatest on the NYSE, it is also a major factor on the AMEX, where block trades constituted about 43 percent of share volume in 1995, and on the NASDAQ-NMS, where block trades accounted for almost 50 percent of share volume in 1995. Evidence of continued institutional growth is that mutual fund sales in 1995 were a record $128 billion and fund sales were already $99 billion during the first four months of 1996, as discussed in Robert McGough, "Stock Funds' Inflows Total $99 Billion in '96," *The Wall Street Journal,* May 29, 1996, C1, C23.

The reduced commissions caused numerous mergers and liquidations by smaller investment firms after May Day. Also, with fixed minimum commissions, it was cheaper for most institutions to buy research using soft dollars than to do their own research. When competitive rates reduced excess commissions, the institutions switched to large brokerage firms that had good trading and research capabilities. As a result, many independent research firms either disbanded or merged with full-service brokerage firms.

Regional stock exchanges flourished prior to competitive rates because they helped institutions distribute soft dollars and facilitated trading in large blocks. Some observers expected regional exchanges to be adversely affected by competitive rates. Apparently, the unique trading capabilities on these exchanges prevented this because the relative trading on these exchanges has been maintained and increased.[38]

Total commissions paid have shown a significant decline, and the size and structure of the industry have changed as a result. Although independent research firms and the third market have contracted, regional stock exchanges have felt little impact.

THE IMPACT OF BLOCK TRADES   Because the increase in institutional development has caused an increase in the number and size of block trades, it is important to consider how block trades influence the market and understand how they trade.

BLOCK TRADES ON THE EXCHANGES   The increase in block trading by institutions has strained the specialist system, which had three problems with block trading: capital, commitment, and contacts (the "three Cs"). First, specialists did not have the capital needed to acquire blocks of 10,000 or 20,000 shares. Second, even when specialists had the capital, they may have been unwilling to commit the capital because of the large risks involved. Finally, because of Rule 113, specialists were not allowed to directly contact institutions to offer a block brought by another institution. Therefore, they were cut off from the major source of demand for blocks and were reluctant to take large positions in thinly traded stocks.

BLOCK HOUSES   This lack of capital, commitment, and contacts by specialists on the exchange created a vacuum in block trading that resulted in the development of block houses. *Block houses* are investment firms (also referred to as *upstairs traders* because they are away from the exchange floor) that help institutions locate other institutions interested in buying or selling blocks of stock. A good block house has (1) the capital required to position a large block, (2) the willingness to commit this capital to a block transaction, and (3) contacts among institutions.

EXAMPLE OF A BLOCK TRADE   Assume a mutual fund decides to sell 50,000 of its 250,000 shares of Ford Motors. The fund decides to do it through Goldman Sachs & Company (GS&Co.), a large block house and lead underwriter for Ford that knows institutions interested in the stock. After being contacted by the fund, the traders at Goldman Sachs contact several institutions that own Ford to see if any of them want to add to their position and to determine their bids. Assume that the previous sale of Ford on the NYSE

---

[38] For a discussion of trading on regional exchanges and the third market, see J. L. Hamilton, "Off-Board Trading of NYSE-Listed Stocks: The Effects of Deregulation and the National Market System," *Journal of Finance* 42, no. 5 (December 1987); 1331–1346. Three recent papers examine the impact of regional exchanges and the practice of purchasing order flow that would normally go to the NYSE; see Robert H. Battalio, "Third Market Broker-Dealers: Cost Competitors or Cream Skimmers?" *Journal of Finance,* forthcoming; and Robert Battalio, Jason Greene, and Robert Jennings, "Do Competing Specialists and Preferencing Dealers Affect Market Quality?" University of Notre Dame Working Paper (December 1995); and David Easley, Nicholas Kiefer, and Maureen O'Hara, "Cream-Skimming or Profit Sharing? The Curious Role of Purchased Order Flow," *Journal of Finance* 51, no. 3 (July, 1996): 811–833.

was at 36¾ and GS&Co. receives commitments from four different institutions for a total of 40,000 shares at an average price of 36⅝. Goldman Sachs returns to the mutual fund and bids 36½ minus a negotiated commission for the total 50,000 shares. Assuming the fund accepts the bid, Goldman Sachs now owns the block and immediately sells 40,000 shares to the four institutions that made prior commitments. It also "positions" 10,000 shares; that is, it owns the 10,000 shares and must eventually sell them at the best price possible. Because GS&Co. is a member of the NYSE, the block will be processed ("crossed") on the exchange as one transaction of 50,000 shares at 36½. The specialist on the NYSE might take some of the stock to fill limit orders on the book at prices between 36½ and 36¾.

For working on this trade, GS&Co. receives a negotiated commission, but it has committed almost $370,000 to position the 10,000 shares. The major risk to GS&Co. is the possibility of a subsequent price change on the 10,000 shares. If it can sell the 10,000 shares for 36½ or more, it will just about break even on the position and have the commission as income. If the price of the stock weakens, GS&Co. may have to sell the position at 36¼ and take a loss on it of about $2,500, offsetting the income from the commission.

This example indicates the importance of institutional contacts, capital to position a portion of the block, and willingness to commit that capital to the block trade. Without all three, the transaction would not take place.

INSTITUTIONS AND STOCK PRICE VOLATILITY   Some stock market observers speculate there should be a strong positive relationship between institutional trading and stock price volatility because institutions trade in large blocks, and it is contended that they tend to trade together. Empirical studies of the relationship between the proportion of trading by large financial institutions and stock price volatility have never supported the folklore.[39] In a capital market where trading is dominated by institutions, the best environment is one where all institutions are actively involved because they provide liquidity for one another and for noninstitutional investors.

NATIONAL MARKET SYSTEM (NMS)   The development of a National Market System (NMS) has been advocated by financial institutions because it is expected to provide greater efficiency, competition, and lower cost of transactions. Although there is no generally accepted definition of an NMS, four major characteristics are generally expected:

1. Centralized reporting of all transactions
2. Centralized quotation system
3. Centralized limit-order book (CLOB)
4. Competition among all qualified market makers.

CENTRALIZED REPORTING   Centralized reporting requires a composite tape to report all transactions in a stock regardless of where the transactions took place. On the tape you might see a trade in GM on the NYSE, another trade on the Chicago Exchange, and a third on the OTC. The intent is to provide on the tape full information of all completed trades.

As of June 1975, the NYSE began operating a central tape that includes all NYSE stocks traded on other exchanges and on the OTC. The volume of shares reported on the consolidated tape is shown in Table 4.7. The breakdown among the seven exchanges and two OTC markets appears in Table 4.8. Therefore, this component of a National Market System

---

[39] In this regard, see Frank K. Reilly and John M. Wachowicz, "How Institutional Trading Reduces Market Volatility," *Journal of Portfolio Management* 5, no. 2 (Winter 1979): 11–17; Neil Berkman, "Institutional Investors and the Stock Market," *New England Economic Review* (November–December 1977): 60–77; and Frank K. Reilly and David J. Wright, "Block Trades and Aggregate Stock Price Volatility," *Financial Analysts Journal* 40, no. 2 (March–April 1984): 54–60.

TABLE 4.7	**CONSOLIDATED TAPE VOLUME (THOUSANDS OF SHARES)**

1976	6,281,008	1990	48,188,072
1980	12,935,607	1991	55,294,725
1985	32,988,595	1992	63,064,667
1986	42,478,164	1993	81,926,892
1987	55,472,855	1994	88,870,770
1988	47,390,121	1995	106,554,583
1989	49,794,547		

Source: *NYSE Fact Book* (New York: NYSE, 1996): 24.

TABLE 4.8	**EXCHANGES AND MARKETS INVOLVED IN CONSOLIDATED TAPE WITH PERCENTAGE OF TRADES DURING 1995**

	Percentage		Percentage
AMEX	0.00%	NASD	10.77%
Boston	2.51	NYSE	70.22
Chicago	5.13	Pacific	5.32
Cincinnati	3.91	Philadelphia	2.14
Instinet	0.00		

Source: *NYSE Fact Book* (New York: NYSE, 1996): 25.

(NMS) is available for stocks listed on the NYSE. As shown, although the volume of trading is dispersed among the exchanges and the NASD, the NYSE is clearly dominant.[40]

CENTRALIZED QUOTATION SYSTEM   A centralized quotation system would list the quotes for a given stock (e.g., IBM) from all market makers on the national exchanges, the regional exchanges, and the OTC. With such a system, a broker who requested the current market quota for IBM would see all the prevailing quotes and should complete the trade on the market with the best quote.

Intermarket Trading System   A centralized quotation system is currently available—the Intermarket Trading System (ITS), developed by the American, Boston, Midwest, New York, Pacific, and Philadelphia Stock Exchanges and the NASD. ITS consists of a central computer facility with interconnected terminals in the participating market centers. As shown in Table 4.9, the number of issues included, the volume of trading, and the size of trades have all grown substantially. Of the 3,542 issues included on the system in 1995, 3,064 were listed on the NYSE and 478 were listed on the AMEX.

With ITS, brokers and market makers in each market center indicate specific buying and selling commitments through a composite quotation display that shows the current quotes for each stock in every market center. A broker is expected to go to the best market to execute a customer's order by sending a message committing to a buy or sell at the price quoted. When this commitment is accepted, a message reports the transaction. The following example illustrates how ITS works.

---

[40] For a discussion of these changes, see Craig Torres and William Power, "Big Board Is Losing Some of Its Influence Over Stock Trading," *The Wall Street Journal,* April 17, 1990, A1, A6; Janet Bush, "Hoping for a New Broom at the NYSE," *Financial Times,* August 16, 1990, 13; William Power, "Big Board, at Age 200, Scrambles to Protect Grip on Stock Market," *The Wall Street Journal,* May 13, 1992, A1, A8; Pat Widder, "NYSE in 200th Year as 'Way of Doing Business' " *Chicago Tribune,* May 17, 1992, Section 7, pp. 1, 4; and Pat Widder, "NASDAQ Has Its Eyes Set on the Next 100 Years," *Chicago Tribune,* May 17, 1992, Section 7, pp. 1, 4.

| TABLE 4.9 | | INTERMARKET TRADING SYSTEM ACTIVITY | | |

INTERMARKET TRADING SYSTEM ACTIVITY

| | | DAILY AVERAGE | | |
Year	Issues Eligible	Share Volume	Executed Trades	Average Size of Trade
1980	884	1,565,900	2,868	546
1985	1,288	5,669,400	5,867	966
1986	1,278	7,222,100	7,712	987
1987	1,537	8,608,559	8,573	1,004
1988	1,816	7,625,926	7,069	1,079
1989	2,082	9,168,867	8,065	1,137
1990	2,126	9,387,114	8,744	1,075
1991	2,306	10,408,566	9,971	1,044
1992	2,532	10,755,704	10,179	1,057
1993	2,922	11,488,147	10,567	1,087
1994	3,293	11,122,019	10,650	1,045
1995	3,542	12,185,064	10,911	1,117

Source: *NYSE Fact Book* (New York: NYSE, 1996): 26.

A broker on the NYSE has a market order to sell 100 shares of IBM stock. Assuming the quotation display at the NYSE shows that the best current bid for IBM is on the Pacific Stock Exchange (PSE), the broker will enter an order to sell 100 shares at the bid on the PSE. Within seconds, the commitment flashes on the computer screen and is printed out at the PSE specialist's post where it is executed against the PSE bid. The transaction is reported back to New York and on the consolidated tape. Both brokers receive immediate confirmation and the results are transmitted to the appropriate market centers at the end of each day. Thereafter, each broker completes his or her own clearance and settlement procedure.

The ITS system currently provides centralized quotations for stocks listed on the NYSE and specifies whether a bid or ask *away* from the NYSE market is superior to that *on* the NYSE. Note, however, that the system lacks several characteristics. It does not have the capability for automatic execution at the best market. Instead you must contact the market maker and indicate that you want to buy or sell, at which time the bid or ask may be withdrawn. Also, it is not mandatory that a broker go to the best market. Although the best price may be at another market center, a broker might consider it inconvenient to trade on that exchange if the price difference is not substantial. It is almost impossible to audit such actions. Still, even with these shortcomings, there has been substantial technical and operational progress on a central quotation system.

CENTRAL LIMIT-ORDER BOOK (CLOB)   Substantial controversy has surrounded the idea of a central limit-order book (CLOB) that would contain all limit orders from all exchanges. Ideally, the CLOB would be visible to everyone, and all market makers and traders could fill orders on it. Currently, most limit orders are placed with specialists on the NYSE and filled when a transaction on the NYSE reaches the stipulated price. The NYSE specialist receives some part of the commission for rendering this service. The NYSE has opposed a CLOB because its specialists do not want to share this very lucrative business. Although the technology for a CLOB is available, it is difficult to estimate when it will become a reality.

COMPETITION AMONG MARKET MAKERS (RULE 390)   Market makers have always competed on the OTC market, but competition has been opposed by the NYSE. The argument in favor of competition among market makers is that it forces dealers to offer better bids and asks, or they will not do any business. Several studies have indicated that competition among a large number of dealers (as in the OTC market) results in a smaller spread. In contrast, the NYSE argues that a central auction market forces all orders to one central location where the orders are exposed to all interested participants and this central auction results in the best market and execution, including many transactions at prices between the current bid and ask.

To help create a centralized market, the NYSE's Rule 390 requires members to obtain the permission of the exchange before carrying out a transaction in a listed stock off the exchange. This rule is intended to draw all volume to the NYSE so that the exchange can provide the most complete auction market. The exchange contends that Rule 390 is necessary to protect the auction market, arguing that its elimination would fragment the market, tempting members to trade off the exchange and to internalize many orders (i.e., members would match orders from their own customers, which would keep these orders from exposure to the full auction market). Hamilton contends that the adverse effects of fragmentation are more than offset by the benefits of competition.[41] Progress in achieving this final phase of the NMS has been slow because of strong opposition by members of the investment community and caution by the SEC.

NEW TRADING SYSTEMS

As daily trading volume has gone from about 5 million shares to over 340 million shares, it has become necessary to introduce new technology into the trading process. Currently, the NYSE routinely handles days with volume over 400 million and had a record daily high of 652 million in December 1995. The following discussion considers some technological innovations that assist in the trading process.

SUPER DOT   Super Dot is an electronic order-routing system through which member firms transmit market and limit orders in NYSE-listed securities directly to the posts where securities are traded or to the member firm's booth. After the order has been executed, a report of execution is returned directly to the member firm office over the same electronic circuit, and the execution is submitted directly to the comparison systems. Member firms can enter market orders up to 2,099 shares and limit orders in round or odd lots up to 30,099 shares. An estimated 85 percent of all market orders enter the NYSE through the Super Dot system.

DISPLAY BOOK   The Display Book is an electronic workstation that keeps track of all limit orders and incoming market orders. This includes incoming Super Dot limit orders.

OPENING AUTOMATED REPORT SERVICE (OARS)   OARS, the opening feature of the Super Dot system, accepts member firms' preopening market orders up to 30,099 shares. OARS automatically and continuously pairs buy and sell orders and presents the imbalance to the specialist prior to the opening of a stock. This system helps the specialist determine the opening price and the potential need for a preopening call market.

MARKET ORDER PROCESSING   Super Dot's postopening market order system is designed to accept member firms' postopening market orders up to 30,099 shares. The system provides rapid execution and reporting of market orders. During 1994, market orders were executed and reported within 24 seconds on average.

---

[41] James L. Hamilton, "Marketplace Fragmentation Competition and the Efficiency of the Stock Exchange," *Journal of Finance* 34, no. 1 (March 1979): 171–187. For a more recent article on this topic, see Hans R. Stoll, "Organization of the Stock Market: Competition or Fragmentation," *Journal of Applied Corporate Finance* 5, no. 4 (Winter 1993): 89–93.

LIMIT-ORDER PROCESSING   The limit-order processing system electronically files orders to be executed when and if a specific price is reached. The system accepts limit orders up to 99,999 shares and electronically updates the Specialists' Display Book. Good-until-canceled orders that are not executed on the day of submission are automatically stored until executed or canceled.

GLOBAL MARKET CHANGES

NYSE OFF-HOURS TRADING   One of the major concerns of the NYSE is the continuing erosion of its market share for stocks listed on the NYSE due to global trading. Specifically, the share of trading of NYSE-listed stock has declined from about 80 to 85 percent during the early 1980s to about 60 to 65 percent in 1994. This reflects an increase in trading on regional exchanges and the third market, some increase in fourth-market trading, but mainly an increase in trading in foreign markets in London and Tokyo. The NYSE has attempted to respond to this by expanding its trading hours and listing more non-U.S. stocks. The expansion of hours was initiated in May 1991, when the SEC approved a 2-year pilot program of two NYSE crossing sessions.

Crossing Session I (CSI) provides the opportunity to trade individual stocks at the NYSE closing prices after the regular session—from 4:15 P.M. to 5:00 P.M. In 1994, CSI averaged 189,900 shares per day and had a record of 4.3 million shares in April 1994. Crossing Session II (CSII) allows trading a collection of at least 15 NYSE stocks with a market value of at least $1 million. This session is from 4:00 P.M. to 5:15 P.M. During 1995, the average daily share volume during CSII was about 1.5 million shares.

Listing foreign stocks on the NYSE   A major goal/concern for the NYSE is the ability to list foreign stocks on the exchange. The NYSE chairman, Richard A. Grasso, has stated on several occasions that the exchange recognizes that much of the growth in the coming decades will be in foreign countries and their stocks. As a result, the exchange wants to list a number of these stocks. The problem is that current SEC regulations will not allow the NYSE to list these firms because they follow less-stringent foreign accounting and disclosure standards. Specifically, many foreign companies issue financial statements less frequently and with less information than what is required by the SEC. As a result, there are currently about 185 foreign firms that have shares traded on the NYSE (mainly through ADRs), but it is contended that there are 2,000 to 3,000 foreign companies that would qualify for listing on the NYSE except for the accounting rules. The exchange contends that unless the rules are adjusted and the NYSE is allowed to compete with other world exchanges (the LSE lists over 600 foreign stocks), it will eventually become a regional exchange in the global capital market. The view of the SEC is that they have an obligation to ensure that investors receive adequate disclosure. This difference hopefully will be resolved during 1996 in favor of allowing additional foreign listings.[42] Even with the stringent requirements, stocks (ADRs) from over 30 companies were listed during 1995.

LONDON STOCK EXCHANGE   The London Stock Exchange initiated several major changes on October 27, 1986, in an event referred to as the *Big Bang*. As a result of this event, brokers can act as market makers, jobbers can deal with the public and with institutions, and all commissions are fully negotiable.

The gilt market was restructured to resemble the U.S. government securities market. The Bank of England approved a system whereby 27 primary dealers make markets in

---

[42] The NYSE argument is supported in the following articles: William J. Baumol and Burton Malkiel, "Redundant Regulation of Foreign Security Trading and U.S. Competitiveness," *Journal of Applied Corporate Finance* 5, no. 4 (Winter 1993): 19–27; and Franklin Edwards, "Listing of Foreign Securities on U.S. Exchanges," *Journal of Applied Corporate Finance* 5, no. 4 (Winter 1993): 28–36.

U.K. government securities and transact with a limited number of interdealer brokers. This new arrangement has created a more competitive environment.

Trades are reported on a system called *Stock Exchange Automated Quotations (SEAQ) International,* which is an electronic market-price information system similar to NASDAQ. In addition, real-time prices are being shared with the NYSE while the NASD provides certain U.S. OTC prices to the London market. Also, as discussed earlier, 35 U.S. OTC stocks are available for 24-hour trading between New York, Tokyo, Singapore, and London.

There is increased access to membership on the exchange whereby foreign firms are admitted as members, and they can be wholly owned by non-U.K. firms. As a result, some U.S. banks have acquired British stockbrokers, and several major U.S. firms are now members of the exchange.

Effects of the Big Bang　　Probably one of the most visually striking changes caused by the Big Bang occurred on the trading floor of the LSE. Prior to October 1986, the activity on the floor of the LSE was similar to that on the NYSE and the TSE—there were large numbers of people gathered around trading posts and moving between the phones and the posts. Currently, the exchange floor is completely deserted except for some traders in stock options. Once they introduced competitive market makers on the floor of the exchange, it was just as easy to buy and sell listed stocks away from the exchange using the quotes on SEAQ.

The rest of the Big Bang's effects can be summarized by the phrase "more business, less profit." Specifically, there is more activity throughout the system, but profit margins have declined or disappeared due to the intense competition. In the process, many firms have merged or been acquired by firms from the United States, Japan, or Germany that have been willing to accept lower returns to establish market presence.[43]

TOKYO STOCK EXCHANGE (TSE)　　Thus far, changes on the TSE have been minimal because the exchange has resisted competitive pressures through regulation. Trading commissions are still based on fixed-scale rates that vary by the type and value of the transactions. Most transactions require a fixed charge plus a percentage of the value of the trade.

By late 1995, 25 foreign firms were members of the TSE. Four Japanese investment firms dominate the Japanese financial market: Nomura, Daiwa, Nikko, and Yamaichi. The equity bases and market values of these firms exceed those of most U.S. firms and all firms from other countries. The foreign firms were less aggressive between 1992 and 1995 because of the dramatic slowdown in the Japanese economy and its securities market.[44]

PARIS BOURSE　　In 1988, the monopoly on stock trading held by the big brokerage houses was opened up to French and foreign banks, and some investment firms began to merge with banks to acquire the capital needed to trade in a world market. The Bourse also introduced a continuous auction market rather than a call market that had been operating for 2 hours a day.[45]

[43] Craig Forman, "Britain's Deregulation Leaves a Casualty Trail in Securities Industry," *The Wall Street Journal,* October 14, 1987, 1, 18.

[44] For a discussion of the problems in the early 1990s, see Manny Sender, "Why Japan's Financial Crisis Is so Scary," *Institutional Investor* (June 1992): 60–66. The call for reform is discussed in Robert Thomson, "New Plea to Japan to Reform Markets," *Financial Times,* February 5, 1993, 17.

[45] Fiona Gleizes, "Paris Bourse Begins Its Own 'Big Bang' in Effort to Rival London's Exchange," *The Wall Street Journal,* January 4, 1988, 15.

FRANKFURT STOCK EXCHANGE   As noted earlier, the big change for the German stock market is the proposed merger of the three largest stock exchanges to create a large high-technology exchange that could compete with the London Exchange for European business.[46]

FUTURE
DEVELOPMENTS

In addition to the expected effects of the NMS and a global capital market, other changes are anticipated as well. You should understand and contemplate their effects.

MORE SPECIALIZED INVESTMENT COMPANIES   Although more individuals want to own stocks and bonds, they have increasingly acquired this ownership through institutions such as investment companies because most individuals feel that it is too difficult and time-consuming to do their own analysis. This increase in fund sales has caused a proliferation of new funds (discussed in Chapters 3 and 26) that provide numerous opportunities to diversify.

This trend toward specialized funds will continue and could include other investment alternatives such as stamps, coins, and art. Because of the lower liquidity of foreign securities, stamps, coins, and art, many of these new mutual funds will be closed-end and will be traded on an exchange. These closed-end funds and their surge in popularity will be discussed in Chapter 26.

CHANGES IN THE FINANCIAL SERVICES INDUSTRY   The financial services industry is experiencing a major change in makeup and operation. Prior to 1960, the securities industry was composed of specialty firms that concentrated in specific investments such as stocks, bonds, commodities, real estate, or insurance. A trend during the early 1980s focused on creating financial supermarkets that considered all of these investment alternatives around the world. A prime example would be Merrill Lynch, which acquired insurance and real estate subsidiaries. A subset includes firms that are global in coverage, but limit their product line to mainstream investment instruments such as bonds, stock, futures, and options. Firms in this category would include Merrill Lynch, Goldman Sachs, Salomon Brothers, and Morgan Stanley, among others. At the other end of the spectrum, large banks such as Citicorp want to become involved in the investment banking business.

In contrast to financial supermarkets, some firms have decided not to be all things to all people. These firms are going the specialty, or "boutique," route, attempting to provide unique, superior financial products. Examples include discount brokers, investment firms that concentrate on institutional or individual investors, or firms that concentrate on an industry such as banking or a unique sector such as small-cap growth stocks.

It appears we are moving toward a world with two major groups. Specifically, one would be a few large global investment firms that deal in almost all the asset classes available, while the second group would include numerous firms that provide specialized services in unique products.

Beyond these firm changes, the advances in technology continue to accelerate and promise to affect how the secondary market will be organized and operated.[47] Specifically, computerized trading has made tremendous inroads during the last 5 years and promises to

---

[46] Andrew Fisher, "Top Three German Exchanges to Merge," *Financial Times*, May 9, 1995.

[47] This includes the "Market 2000" report, prepared by the SEC, that is concerned with the organization and operation of securities markets in the United States. Notably, many of the new exchanges in emerging markets are able to "leapfrog" the technology of current exchanges and are creating electronic systems initially using the latest technology.

introduce numerous additional changes into the twenty-first century in markets around the world. The 24-hour market will require extensive computerized trading.

Summary

- The securities market is divided into primary and secondary markets. Secondary markets provide the liquidity that is critical for primary markets. The major segments of the secondary markets include listed exchanges (the NYSE, AMEX, TSE, LSE, and regional exchanges), the over-the-counter market, the third market, and the fourth market. Because you will want to invest across these secondary markets within a country as well as among countries, you need to understand how the markets differ and how they are similar.
- Many of the dramatic changes in our securities markets during the last 30 years are due to an increase in institutional trading and to rapidly evolving global markets. It is important to understand what has happened and why it happened because numerous changes have occurred—and many more are yet to come. You need to understand how these changes will affect your investment alternatives and opportunities. You need to look not only for the best investment, but also for the best securities market. This discussion should provide the background to help you make that trading decision.

Questions

1. Define *market* and briefly discuss the characteristics of a good market.
2. You own 100 shares of General Electric stock, and you want to sell it because you need the money to make a down payment on a stereo. Assume there is absolutely no secondary market system in common stocks. How would you go about selling the stock? Discuss what you would have to do to find a buyer, how long it might take, and the price you might receive.
3. Define *liquidity* and discuss the factors that contribute to it. Give examples of a liquid asset and an illiquid asset, and discuss why they are considered liquid and illiquid.
4. Define a primary and secondary market for securities and discuss how they differ. Discuss how the primary market is dependent on the secondary market.
5. Give an example of an initial public offering (IPO) in the primary market. Give an example of a seasoned equity issue in the primary market. Discuss which would involve greater risk to the buyer.
6. Find an advertisement for a recent primary offering in *The Wall Street Journal*. Based on the information in the ad, indicate the characteristics of the security sold and the major underwriters. How much new capital did the firm derive from the offering before paying commissions?
7. Briefly explain the difference between a competitive bid underwriting and a negotiated underwriting.
8. The figures in Table 4.3 reveal a major difference in the price paid for a membership (seat) on the NYSE compared with one on the AMEX. How would you explain this difference?
9. What are the major reasons for the existence of regional stock exchanges? Discuss how they differ from the national exchanges.
10. Which segment of the secondary stock market (listed exchanges or the OTC) is larger in terms of the number of issues? Which is larger in terms of the value of the issues traded?
11. Discuss the three levels of NASDAQ in terms of what each provides and who would subscribe to each.
12. a. Define the third market. Give an example of a third-market stock.
    b. Define the fourth market. Discuss why a financial institution would use the fourth market.
13. Briefly define each of the following terms and give an example:
    a. Market order
    b. Limit order
    c. Short sale
    d. Stop loss order
14. Briefly discuss the two major functions and sources of income for the NYSE specialist.
15. Describe the duties of the *Saitori* member on the TSE. Discuss how these duties differ from those of the NYSE specialist.

16. Discuss why the U.S. equity market has experienced major changes since 1965.
17. What were give-ups? What are "soft dollars"? Discuss why soft dollars and give-ups existed when there were fixed commissions.
18. The discussion of block trades noted that the specialist is hampered by the three Cs. Discuss each of the three Cs as it relates to block trading.
19. Describe block houses and explain why they evolved. Describe what is meant by *positioning* part of a block.
20. a. Describe the major attributes of the National Market System (NMS).
    b. Briefly describe the ITS and what it contributes to the NMS. Discuss the growth of the ITS.
21. In the chapter, there is a discussion of expected changes in world capital markets. Discuss one of the suggested changes in terms of what has been happening or discuss an evolving change that was not mentioned.

Problems

1. The initial margin requirement is 60 percent. You have $40,000 to invest in a stock selling for $80 a share. Ignoring taxes and commissions, show in detail the impact on your rate of return if the stock rises to $100 a share and if it declines to $40 a share assuming: (a) you pay cash for the stock, and (b) you buy it using maximum leverage.
2. Lauren has a margin account and deposits $50,000. Assuming the prevailing margin requirement is 40 percent, commissions are ignored, and The Gentry Shoe Corporation is selling at $35 per share:
   a. How many shares can Lauren purchase using the maximum allowable margin?
   b. What is Lauren's profit (loss) if the price of Gentry's stock
      1. Rises to $45?
      2. Falls to $25?
   c. If the maintenance margin is 30 percent, to what price can Gentry Shoe fall before Lauren will receive a margin call?
3. Suppose you buy a round lot of Maginn Industries stock on 55 percent margin when the stock is selling at $20 a share. The broker charges a 10 percent annual interest rate, and commissions are 3 percent of the total stock value on both the purchase and sale. A year later you receive a $0.50 per share dividend and sell the stock for 27. What is your rate of return on the investment?
4. You decide to sell short 100 shares of Charlotte Horse Farms when it is selling at its yearly high of 56. Your broker tells you that your margin requirement is 45 percent and that the commission on the purchase is $155. While you are short the stock, Charlotte pays a $2.50 per share dividend. At the end of 1 year, you buy 100 shares of Charlotte at 45 to close out your position and are charged a commission of $145 and 8 percent interest on the money borrowed. What is your rate of return on the investment?
5. You own 200 shares of Microsoft that you bought at $25 a share. The stock is now selling for $45 a share.
   a. If you put in a stop loss order at $40, discuss your reasoning for this action.
   b. If the stock eventually declines in price to $30 a share, what would be your rate of return with and without the stop loss order?
6. Two years ago, you bought 300 shares of Kayleigh Milk Co. for $30 a share with a margin of 60 percent. Currently, the Kayleigh stock is selling for $45 a share. Assuming no dividends and ignoring commissions, (a) compute the annualized rate of return on this investment if you had paid cash and (b) your rate of return with the margin purchase.
7. The stock of the Michele Travel Co. is selling for $28 a share. You put in a limit buy order at $24 for one month. During the month, the stock price declines to $20, then jumps to $36. Ignoring commissions, what would have been your rate of return on this investment? What would be your rate of return if you had put in a market order? What if your limit order was at $18?

References

AMEX Fact Book. New York: AMEX, published annually.

Amihad, Y., T. Ho, and Robert Schwartz. *Market Making and the Changing Structure of the Securities Industry.* New York: Lexington-Heath, 1985.

Amihad, Y., and H. Mendelson. "Trading Mechanisms and Stock Returns: An Empirical Investigation." *Journal of Finance* 42, no. 3 (July 1987).

Beidleman, Carl, ed. *The Handbook of International Investing.* Chicago: Probus Publishing, 1987.

Blume, Marshall E., and Jeremy J. Siegel. "The Theory of Security Pricing and Market Structure." *Financial Markets, Institutions and Instruments* 1, no. 3 (1992). New York University Salomon Center.

Cohen, Kalman, Steven Maier, Robert Schwartz, and David Whitcomb. *The Microstructure of Securities Markets.* Englewood Cliffs, NJ: Prentice-Hall, 1986.

Economides, Nicholas, and Robert A. Schwartz. "Electronic Call Market Trading." *Journal of Portfolio Management* 21, no. 3 (Spring 1995).

Fabozzi, Frank J., and Frank G. Zarb, eds. *Handbook of Financial Markets.* 2d ed. Homewood, IL: Dow Jones-Irwin, 1986.

Grabbe, J. Orlin. *International Financial Markets.* New York: Elsevier, 1986.

Grossman, S. J., and Merton H. Miller. "Liquidity and Market Structure." *Journal of Finance* 43, no. 2 (June 1988).

Hasbrouck, Joel. "Assessing the Quality of a Security Market: A New Approach to Transaction-Cost Measurement." *The Review of Financial Studies* 6, no. 1 (1993).

Hasbrouck, Joel, and R. A. Schwartz. "An Assessment of Stock Exchange and Over-the-Counter Markets." *Journal of Portfolio Management* 14, no. 3 (Spring 1988).

Ibbotson, Roger G., and Gary P. Brinson. *Global Investing.* New York: McGraw-Hill, 1993.

Kee, C. "Market Integration and Price Execution for NYSE-Listed Securities." *Journal of Finance* 48, no. 2 (June 1993).

Madhaven, Ananth. "Trading Mechanisms in Securities Markets." *Journal of Finance* 47, no. 2 (June 1992).

McInish, Thomas, and Robert A. Wood." Hidden Limit Orders on the NYSE." *Journal of Portfolio Management* 21, no. 3 (Spring 1995).

NASDAQ Fact Book. Washington, DC: National Association of Securities Dealers, published annually.

NYSE Fact Book. New York: NYSE, published annually.

Pagano, M. "Trading Volume and Asset Liquidity." *Quarterly Journal of Economics* 104, no. 2 (1989).

Petersen, M., and D. Fialkowski. "Posted versus Effective Spreads: Good Prices or Bad Quotes?" *Journal of Financial Economics* 35, no. 3 (June 1994).

Schwartz, Robert A. *Equity Markets: Structure, Trading, and Performance.* New York: Harper & Row, 1988.

Sherrerd, Katrina F., ed. *Trading Strategies and Execution Costs,* Charlottesville, VA: Institute of Chartered Financial Analysts, 1988.

Sherrerd, Katrina F., ed. *Execution Techniques, True Trading Costs, and the Microstructure of Markets,* Charlottesville, VA: Association for Investment Management and Research, 1993.

Sobel, Robert. *N.Y.S.E.: A History of the New York Stock Exchange, 1935–1975.* New York: Weybright and Talley, 1975.

Sobel, Robert. *The Curbstone Brokers. The Origins of the American Stock Exchange.* New York: Macmillan, 1970.

Solnik, Bruno. *International Investments.* 3d ed. Reading, MA: Addison-Wesley, 1995.

Stoll, Hans. *The Stock Exchange Specialist System: An Economic Analysis.* Monograph Series in Financial Economics 1985–2. New York University, 1985.

Stoll, Hans. "Principles of Trading Market Structure." Working Paper 90–31. Vanderbilt University, 1990.

Stoll, Hans, and Robert Whaley. "Stock Market Structure and Volatility." *Review of Financial Studies* 3, no. 1 (1990).

Tokyo Stock Exchange Fact Book. Tokyo: TSE, published annually.

U.S. Congress, Office of Technology Assessment. *Trading Around the Clock: Global Securities Markets and Information Technology—Background Paper,* OTA-BP-CIT-66. Washington, DC: U.S. Government Printing Office, July 1990.

Viner, Aron. *Inside Japanese Financial Markets.* Homewood, IL: Dow Jones-Irwin, 1988.

APPENDIX

CHARACTERISTICS OF DEVELOPED AND DEVELOPING MARKETS AROUND THE WORLD

TABLE 4A   DEVELOPED MARKETS AROUND THE WORLD

Country	Principal Exchange	Other Exchanges	Total Market Capitalization ($ Billions)	Available Market Capitalization ($ Billions)	Trading Volume ($ Billions)	Domestic Issues Listed	Total Issues Listed	Auction Mechanism	Official Specialists	Options/Futures Trading	Price Limits	Principal Market Indexes
Australia	Sydney	5	82.3	53.5	39.3	N. A.	1,496	Continuous	No	Yes	None	All Ordinaries—324 issues
Austria	Vienna	—	18.7	8.3	37.2	125	176	Call	Yes	No	5%	GZ Aktienindex—25 issues
Belgium	Brussels	3	48.5	26.2	6.8	186	337	Mixed	No	Few	10%	Brussels Stock Exchange Index—186 issues
Canada	Toronto	4	186.8	124.5	71.3	N. A.	1,208	Continuous	Yes	Yes	None	TSE 300 Composite Index
Denmark	Copenhagen	—	29.7	22.2	11.1	N. A.	284	Mixed	No	No	None	Copenhagen Stock Exchange Index—38 issues
Finland	Helsinki	—	9.9	1.7	5.2	N. A.	125	Mixed	N. A.	N. A.	N. A.	KOP (Kansallis-Osake-Pannki) Price Index
France	Paris	6	256.5	137.2	129.0	463	663	Mixed	Yes	Yes	4%	CAC General Index—240 issues
Germany	Frankfurt	7	297.7	197.9	1,003.7	N. A.	355	Continuous	Yes	Options	None	DAX; FAZ (Frankfurter Allgemeine Zeitung)
Hong Kong	Hong Kong	—	67.7	37.1	34.6	N. A.	479	Continuous	No	Futures	None	Hang Seng Index—33 issues
Ireland	Dublin	—	8.4	6.4	5.5	N. A.	N. A.	Continuous	No	No	None	J&E Davy Total Market Index
Italy	Milan	9	137.0	73.2	42.6	N. A.	317	Mixed	No	No	10–20%	Banca Commerziale—209 issues
Japan	Tokyo	7	2,754.6	1,483.5	1,602.4	N. A.	1,576	Continuous	Yes	No	10% down	TOPIX—1,097 issues; TSE II—423 issues; Nikkei 225
Luxembourg	Luxembourg	—	1.5	0.9	0.1	61	247	Continuous	N. A.	N. A.	N. A.	Domestic Share Price Index—9 issues
Malaysia	Kuala Lumpur	—	199.3	95.0	126.4	430	478	Continuous	No	No	None	Kuala Lumpur Composite Index—83 issues

DEVELOPED MARKETS AROUND THE WORLD (concluded)

Country	Principal Exchange	Other Exchanges	Total Market Capitalization ($ Billions)	Available Market Capitalization ($ Billions)	Trading Volume ($ Billions)	Domestic Issues Listed	Total Issues Listed	Auction Mechanism	Official Specialists	Options/Futures Trading	Price Limits	Principal Market Indexes
The Netherlands	Amsterdam	—	112.1	92.4	80.4	279	569	Continuous	Yes	Options	Variable	ANP—CBS General Index—51 issues
New Zealand	Wellington	—	6.7	5.3	2.0	295	451	Continuous	No	Futures	None	Barclay's International Price Index—40 issues
Norway	Oslo	9	18.4	7.9	14.1	N. A.	128	Call	No	No	None	Oslo Bors Stock Index—50 issues
Singapore	Singapore	—	28.6	15.6	8.2	N. A.	324	Continuous	No	No	None	Straits Times Index—30 issues; SES—32 issues
South Africa	Johannesburg	—	72.7	N. A.	8.2	N. A.	N. A.	Continuous	No	Options	None	JSE Actuaries Index—141 issues
Spain	Madrid	3	86.6	46.8	41.0	N. A.	368	Mixed	No	No	10%	Madrid Stock Exchange Index—72 issues
Sweden	Stockholm	—	59.0	24.6	15.8	N. A.	151	Mixed	No	Yes	None	Jacobson & Ponsbach—30 issues
Switzerland	Zurich	6	128.5	75.4	376.6	161	380	Mixed	No	Yes	5%	Societe de Banque Suisse—90 issues
United Kingdom	London	5	756.2	671.1	280.7	1,911	2,577	Continuous	No	Yes	None	Financial Times—(FT) Ordinaries—750 issues; FTSE 100; FT 33
United States	New York	6	2,754.3	2,429.2	1,787.1	N. A.	2,234	Continuous	Yes	Yes	None	S&P 500; Dow Jones Industrial Average; Wilshire 5000; Russell 3000

Notes: Market capitalizations (both total and available) are as of December 31, 1990, except for South African market capitalization, which is from 1988. Available differs from total market capitalization by subtracting cross holdings, closely held and government-owned shares, and takes into account restrictions on foreign ownership. Number of issues listed are from 1988 except for Malaysia, which is from 1994. Trading volume data are 1990 except for Switzerland, which are from 1988. Trading institutions data are from 1988. Market capitalizations (both total and available) for all countries except the United States and South Africa are from the Salomon-Russell Global Equity Indices. U.S. market capitalization (both total and available) is from the Frank Russell Company. All trading volume information (except for Switzerland) and Malaysian total issues listed are from the *Emerging Stock Markets Factbook: 1991*, International Finance Corp., 1991. Trading institutions information is from Richard Roll, "The International Crash of 1987," *Financial Analysts Journal*, September/October 1988. South African market capitalization, number of issues listed for all countries (except Malaysia), and Swiss trading volume are reproduced courtesy of Euromoney Books, extracted from *The G.T. Guide to World Equity Markets: 1989, 1988*.

Source: Roger G. Ibbotson and Gary P. Brinson, *Global Investing* (New York: McGraw-Hill, 1993): 109–111. Reproduced with permission of The McGraw-Hill Companies.

TABLE 4B   EMERGING MARKETS AROUND THE WORLD

Country	Principal Exchange	Other Exchanges	Market Capitalization ($ Billions)	Trading Volume ($ Billions)	Total Issues Listed	Auction Mechanism	Principal Market Indexes
Argentina	Buenos Aires	4	36.9	11.4	156	N.A.	Buenos Aires Stock Exchange Index
Brazil	São Paulo	9	189.2	109.5	544	Continuous	BOVESPA Share Price Index—83 issues
Chile	Santiago	—	68.2	5.3	279	Mixed	IGPA Index—180 issues
China	Shanghai	1	43.5	97.5	291	Continuous	Shanghai Composite Index
Colombia	Bogotá	1	14.0	2.2	90	N.A.	Bogotá General Composite Index
Greece	Athens	—	14.9	5.1	216	Continuous	Athens Stock Exchange Industrial Price Index
India	Bombay	14	127.5	27.3	4,413	Continuous	Economic Times Index—72 issues
Indonesia	Jakarta	—	47.2	11.8	216	Mixed	Jakarta Stock Exchange Index
Israel	Tel Aviv	—	10.6	5.5	267	Call	General Share Index—all listed issues
Jordan	Amman	—	4.6	0.6	95	N.A.	Amman Financial Market Index
Mexico	Mexico City	—	130.2	83.0	206	Continuous	Bolsa de Valores Index—49 issues
Nigeria	Lagos	—	2.7	N.A.	177	Call	Nigerian Stock Exchange General Index
Pakistan	Karachi	—	12.2	3.2	724	Continuous	State Bank of Pakistan Index
Philippines	Makati	1	55.5	13.9	189	N.A.	Manila Commercial & Industrial Index—25 issues
Portugal	Lisbon	1	16.2	5.2	195	Call	Banco Totta e Acores Share Index—50 issues
South Korea	Seoul	—	191.8	286.0	699	Continuous	Korea Composite Stock Price Index
Taiwan	Taipei	—	247.3	711.0	313	Continuous	Taiwan Stock Exchange Index
Thailand	Bangkok	—	131.4	80.2	389	Continuous	Securities Exchange of Thailand Price Index
Turkey	Istanbul	—	21.6	21.7	176	Continuous	Istanbul Stock Exchange Index—50 issues
Venezuela	Caracas	1	4.1	0.9	90	Continuous	Indice de Capitalization de la BVC
Zimbabwe	N.A.	—	1.8	0.2	64	N.A.	Zimbabwe S.E. Industrial Index

Notes: Market capitalizations, trading volume, and total issues listed are as of 1994. Market capitalization, trading volume, and total issues listed for Brazil and São Paulo only. Trading volume for the Philippines is for both Manila and Makati. Total issues listed for India is Bombay only. Total issues listed are from the *Emerging Stock Markets Factbook: 1995*, International Finance Corp., 1995. Trading institutions information is from 1987 and 1988. Market capitalizations, trading volume, and total issues listed are from the *Emerging Stock Markets Factbook: 1995*, International Finance Corp., 1995. Trading institutions information is from Richard Roll, "The International Crash of 1987," *Financial Analysts Journal*, September/October 1988.

Source: Roger G. Ibbotson and Gary P. Brinson, *Global Investing* (New York: McGraw-Hill, 1993): 125–126. Reproduced with permission of The McGraw-Hill Companies.

Chapter
5

Security-Market Indicator Series

This chapter answers the following questions:

- What are some major uses of security-market indicator series (indexes)?
- What are the major characteristics that cause alternative indexes to differ?
- What are the major stock-market indexes in the United States and globally, and what are their characteristics?
- What are the major bond-market indexes for the United States and the world?
- What are some of the composite stock–bond market indexes?
- Where can you get historical and current data for all these indexes?
- What is the relationship among many of these indexes in the short run (monthly)?

A fair statement regarding **security-market indicator series**—especially those outside the United States—is that everybody talks about them, but few people understand them. Even those investors familiar with widely publicized stock-market series, such as the Dow Jones Industrial Average (DJIA), usually know very little about indexes for the U.S. bond market or for non-U.S. stock markets such as Tokyo or London.

Although portfolios are obviously composed of many different individual stocks, investors typically ask, "What happened to the market today?" The reason for this question is that if an investor owns more than a few stocks or bonds, it is cumbersome to follow each stock or bond individually to determine the composite performance of the portfolio. Also, there is an intuitive notion that most individual stocks or bonds move with the aggregate market. Therefore, if the overall market rose, an individual's portfolio probably also increased in value. To supply investors with a composite report on market performance, some financial publications or investment firms have developed stock-market and bond-market indexes.[1]

The initial section discusses several ways that investors use market indicator series. An awareness of these significant functions should provide an incentive for becoming familiar with these series and indicates why we present a full chapter on this topic. The second section considers what characteristics cause alternative indexes to differ. In this chapter, we discuss numerous stock-market and bond-market indexes. You should understand their differences and why one of them is preferable for a given task because of its characteristics. The third section presents the most well-known U.S. and global stock market series separated into groups based on the weighting scheme used. The fourth section considers bond-market indexes, which is a relatively new topic, not because the bond market is new, but because the creation and maintenance of total return bond indexes are new. Again, we consider international bond indexes following the domestic indexes. In section five, we

---

[1] Throughout this chapter and the book, we will use indicator series and indexes interchangeably, although indicator series is the more correct specification because it refers to a broad class of series; one popular type of series is an index, but there can be other types and many different indexes.

consider composite stock market–bond market series. Our final section examines how these indexes relate to each other over monthly intervals. This comparison demonstrates the important factors that cause high or low correlation among series. With this background, you should be able to make an intelligent choice of the indicator series that is best for you based upon how you want to use the index.

USES OF SECURITY-MARKET INDEXES

Security-market indexes have at least five specific uses. A primary application is to use the index values to compute total returns for an aggregate market or some component of a market over a specified time period and use the rates of return computed as a *benchmark* to judge the performance of individual portfolios. A basic assumption when evaluating portfolio performance is that any investor should be able to experience a rate of return comparable to the market return by randomly selecting a large number of stocks or bonds from the total market; hence, a superior portfolio manager should consistently do better than the market. Therefore, *an aggregate stock- or bond-market index can be used as a benchmark to judge the performance of professional money managers.* You should recall from our earlier discussion that you should also analyze the differential risk for the portfolios being judged as compared to the market index.

Indicator series are also used to develop an index portfolio. As we will discuss later, it is difficult for most money managers to consistently outperform specified market indexes on a risk-adjusted basis over time. If this is true, an obvious alternative is to invest in a portfolio that will emulate this market portfolio. This notion led to the creation of *index funds,* whose purpose is to track the performance of the specified market series (index) over time, that is, derive similar rates of return.[2] Although the original index fund concept was related to common stocks, the development of comprehensive, well-specified bond-market indexes and similar inferior performance relative to the bond market by most bond portfolio managers has led to a similar phenomenon in the fixed-income area (i.e., the creation of bond index funds).[3]

Securities analysts, portfolio managers, and others use security-market indexes to examine the factors that influence aggregate security price movements (i.e., the indexes are used to measure aggregate market movements). A similar use is to analyze the relationship among stock and bond returns of different countries. An example is the analysis of the relationship among U.S., Japanese, and German stock or bond returns.

Another group interested in an aggregate market series is "technicians," who believe past price changes can be used to predict future price movements. For example, to project future stock price movements, technicians would plot and analyze price and volume changes for a stock market series like the Dow Jones Industrial Average.

Finally, work in portfolio and capital market theory has implied that the relevant risk for an individual risky asset is its *systematic risk,* which is the relationship between the rates of return for a risky asset and the rates of return for a market portfolio of risky assets.[4] Therefore, it is necessary when computing the systematic risk for an individual risky asset

---

[2] For a discussion of developments in indexing, see "New Ways to Play the Indexing Game," *Institutional Investor* 22, no. 13 (November 1988): 92–98; and Edward A. Wyatt, "Avidly Average," *Barron's,* May 22, 1989, 17, 30.

[3] See Fran Hawthorne, "The Battle of the Bond Indexes," *Institutional Investor* 20, no. 4 (April 1986).

[4] This concept and its justification are discussed in Chapters 8 and 9. Subsequently, we will consider the difficulty of finding an index that is an appropriate proxy for the market portfolio of risky assets.

(security) to relate its returns to the returns for an aggregate market index that is used as a proxy for the market portfolio of risky assets.

DIFFERENTIATING FACTORS IN CONSTRUCTING MARKET INDEXES

Because indicator series are intended to reflect the overall movements of a group of securities, it is necessary to consider which factors are important in computing an index that is intended to represent a total population.

THE SAMPLE

The size of the sample, the breadth of the sample, and the source of the sample used to construct a series are all important.

A small percentage of the total population will provide valid indications of the behavior of the total population *if* the sample is properly selected. In fact, at some point the costs of taking a larger sample will almost certainly outweigh any benefits of increased size. The sample should be *representative* of the total population; otherwise, its size will be meaningless. A large biased sample is no better than a small biased sample. The sample can be generated by completely random selection or by a nonrandom selection technique that is designed to incorporate the characteristics desired. Finally, the *source* of the sample becomes important if there are any differences between alternative segments of the population, in which case samples from each segment are required.

WEIGHTING SAMPLE MEMBERS

Our second concern is with the weight given to each member in the sample. Three principal weighting schemes are used: (1) a price-weighted series, (2) a value-weighted series, and (3) an unweighted series, or what would be described as an equally weighted series.

COMPUTATIONAL PROCEDURE

Our final consideration is with the computational procedure used. One alternative is to take a simple arithmetic average of the various members in the series. Another is to compute an index and have all changes, whether in price or value, reported in terms of the basic index. Finally, some prefer using a geometric average of the components rather than an arithmetic average.

STOCK-MARKET INDICATOR SERIES

As mentioned in the introduction to this chapter, we hear a lot about what happens to the Dow Jones Industrial Average (DJIA) each day. In addition, you might also hear about other stock indexes, such as the NYSE Composite, the S&P 500 index, the AMEX index, or even the Nikkei Average. If you listen carefully, you will realize that all of these indexes do not change by the same amount. The reason for some of the differences is obvious, such as the DJIA versus the Nikkei Average, but others are not. The purpose of this section is to briefly review how each of the major series differs in terms of the characteristics discussed in the prior section. As a result, you should come to understand that the movements over time for alternative indexes *should* differ and you will understand why they differ.

The discussion of the indexes is organized by the weighting of the sample of stocks. We begin with the price-weighted series because some of the most popular indexes are in this category. The next group is the value-weighted series, which is the technique currently used for most indexes. Finally, we will examine the unweighted series.

PRICE-WEIGHTED SERIES

A **price-weighted series** is an arithmetic average of current prices, which means that index movements are influenced by the differential prices of the components.

DOW JONES INDUSTRIAL AVERAGE   The best-known price series is also the oldest and certainly the most popular stock-market indicator series, the Dow Jones Industrial Average (DJIA). The DJIA is a price-weighted average of 30 large, well-known industrial stocks that are generally the leaders in their industry (blue chips) and are listed on the NYSE. The DJIA is computed by totaling the current prices of the 30 stocks and dividing the sum by a divisor that has been adjusted to take account of stock splits and changes in the sample over time.[5] The adjustment of the divisor is demonstrated in Table 5.1.

$$DJIA_t = \sum_{i=1}^{30} p_{it}/D_{adj}$$

where:

$DJIA_t$ = the value of the DJIA on day t
p_{it} = the closing price of stock i on day t
D_{adj} = the adjusted divisor on day t

In Table 5.1, three stocks are employed to demonstrate the procedure used to derive a new divisor for the DJIA when a stock splits. When stocks split, the divisor becomes smaller. An idea of the cumulative effect of splits can be derived from the fact that the divisor was originally 30.0, but as of June 1996 it was 0.33840.

The adjusted divisor ensures that the new value for the series is the same as it would have been without the split. In this case, the pre-split index value was 20. Therefore, after the split, given the new sum of prices, the divisor is adjusted downward to maintain this value of 20. The divisor is also changed if there is a change in the sample makeup of the series, which does not happen very often.

Because the series is price weighted, a high-priced stock carries more weight than a low-priced stock, so, as shown in Table 5.2, a 10 percent change in a $100 stock ($10) will cause a larger change in the series than a 10 percent change in a $30 stock ($3). In Case A, when the $100 stock increases by 10 percent, the average rises by 5.5 percent; in Case B, when the $30 stock increases by 10 percent, the average rises by only 1.7 percent.

The DJIA has been criticized over time on several counts. First, the sample used for the series is limited. It is difficult to conceive that 30 nonrandomly selected blue-chip stocks

| TABLE 5.1 | EXAMPLE OF CHANGE IN DJIA DIVISOR WHEN A SAMPLE STOCK SPLITS |

	Before Split	After Three-for-One Split by Stock A	
	Prices	Prices	
A	30	10	
B	20	20	
C	10	10	
	60 ÷ 3 = 20	40 ÷ X = 20	X = 2 (New Divisor)

---

[5] A complete list of all events that have caused a change in the divisor since the DJIA went to 30 stocks on October 1, 1928, is contained in Phyllis S. Pierce, ed., *The Business One Irwin Investor's Handbook* (Burr Ridge, IL: Dow Jones Books, annual). Prior to 1992, it was *The Dow Jones Investor's Handbook*. In May 1996 the DJIA celebrated its 100th birthday, which was acknowledged with two special sections entitled "A Century of Investing" and "100 Years of the DJIA," *The Wall Street Journal*, May 28, 1996.

TABLE 5.2   **DEMONSTRATION OF THE IMPACT OF DIFFERENTLY PRICED SHARES ON A PRICE-WEIGHTED INDICATOR SERIES**

| | | Period T + 1 | |
	Period T	Case A	Case B
A	100	110	100
B	50	50	50
C	30	30	33
Sum	180	190	183
Divisor	3	3	3
Average	60	63.3	61
Percentage change		5.5	1.7

can be representative of the 1,800 stocks listed on the NYSE. Beyond the limited number, the stocks included are, by definition, offerings of the largest and most prestigious companies in various industries. Therefore, it is contended that the DJIA probably reflects price movements for large, mature, blue-chip firms rather than for the typical company listed on the NYSE. Several studies have pointed out that the DJIA has not been as volatile as other market indexes and that the long-run returns on the DJIA are not comparable to the other NYSE stock indexes.

In addition, because the DJIA is price weighted, when companies have a stock split, their prices decline, and therefore their weight in the DJIA is reduced—even though they may be large and important. Therefore, the weighting scheme causes a downward bias in the DJIA, because the stocks that have higher growth rates will have higher prices, and because such stocks tend to split, they will consistently lose weight within the index.[6] Regardless of the several criticisms made of the DJIA, there is a fairly close relationship between the *daily* percentage changes for the DJIA and comparable price changes for other NYSE indexes, as shown in a subsequent section of this chapter. Dow Jones also publishes an average of 20 stocks in the transportation industry and 15 utility stocks. Detailed reports of the averages are contained daily in *The Wall Street Journal* and weekly in *Barron's,* including hourly figures.

NIKKEI-DOW JONES AVERAGE   Also referred to as the Nikkei Stock Average Index, the Nikkei-Dow Jones Average is an arithmetic average of prices for 225 stocks on the First Section of the Tokyo Stock Exchange (TSE). This is the most well-known series in Japan, and it has been used to show stock price trends since the reopening of the TSE. Notably, it was formulated by Dow Jones and Company, and, similar to the DJIA, it is a price-weighted series, so a large dollar change for a small company will have the same impact of a similar price change of a large firm. It is also criticized because the 225 stocks that are included only comprise about 15 percent of all stocks on the First Section. The results for this index are reported daily in *The Wall Street Journal* and *The Financial Times* and weekly in *Barron's.*

[6]For discussions of these problems, see H. L. Butler, Jr., and J. D. Allen, "The Dow Jones Industrial Average Reexamined," *Financial Analysts Journal* 35, no. 6 (November–December 1979): 37–45; and E. E. Carter and K. J. Cohen, "Stock Averages, Stock Splits, and Bias," *Financial Analysts Journal* 23, no. 3 (May–June 1967): 77–81. For several articles that consider the origin and performance of the DJIA during its 100 years, see "100 Years of the DJIA," section in *The Wall Street Journal,* May 28, 1996, R29 R56.

VALUE-WEIGHTED SERIES

A **value-weighted series** is generated by deriving the initial total market value of all stocks used in the series (Market Value = Number of Shares Outstanding × Current Market Price). This figure is typically established as the base and assigned an index value (the most popular beginning index value is 100, but it can vary—e.g., 10, 50). Subsequently, a new market value is computed for all securities in the index, and the current market value is compared to the initial "base" value to determine the percentage of change, which in turn is applied to the beginning index value.

$$\text{Index}_t = \frac{\sum P_t Q_t}{\sum P_b Q_b} \times \text{Beginning Index Value}$$

where:

Index$_t$ = **index value on day t**
 P$_t$ = **ending prices for stocks on day t**
 Q$_t$ = **number of outstanding shares on day t**
 P$_b$ = **ending price for stocks on base day**
 Q$_b$ = **number of outstanding shares on base day**

A simple example for a three-stock index is shown in Table 5.3. As can be seen, there is an *automatic adjustment* for stock splits and other capital changes in a value-weighted index because the decrease in the stock price is offset by an increase in the number of shares outstanding.

In a value-weighted index, the importance of individual stocks in the sample is dependent on the market value of the stocks. Therefore, a specified percentage change in the value of a large company has a greater impact than a comparable percentage change for a

---

TABLE 5.3   **EXAMPLE OF A COMPUTATION OF A VALUE-WEIGHTED INDEX**

Stock	Share Price	Number of Shares	Market Value
December 31, 1996			
A	$10.00	1,000,000	$ 10,000,000
B	15.00	6,000,000	90,000,000
C	20.00	5,000,000	100,000,000
Total			$200,000,000
			Base Value Equal to an Index of 100
December 31, 1997			
A	$12.00	1,000,000	$ 12,000,000
B	10.00	12,000,000[a]	120,000,000
C	20.00	5,500,000[b]	110,000,000
Total			$242,000,000

$$\frac{\text{New}}{\text{Index Value}} = \frac{\text{Current Market Value}}{\text{Base Value}} \times \frac{\text{Beginning}}{\text{Index Value}}$$

$$= \frac{\$242,000,000}{\$200,000,000} \times 100$$

$$= 1.21 \times 100$$

$$= 121$$

[a]Stock split two-for-one during the year.
[b]Company paid a 10 percent stock dividend during the year.

| TABLE 5.4 | DEMONSTRATION OF THE IMPACT OF DIFFERENT VALUES ON A MARKET VALUE-WEIGHTED STOCK INDEX | | | | | | | |

| | | DECEMBER 31, 1996 | | | DECEMBER 31, 1997 | | | |
| | | | | | CASE A | | CASE B | |
Stock	Number of Shares	Price	Value		Price	Value	Price	Value
A	1,000,000	$10.00	$ 10,000,000		$12.00	$ 12,000,000	$10.00	$ 10,000,000
B	6,000,000	15.00	90,000,000		15.00	90,000,000	15.00	90,000,000
C	5,000,000	20.00	100,000,000		20.00	100,000,000	24.00	120,000,000
			$200,000,000			$202,000,000		$220,000,000
Index Value			100.00			101.00		110.00

small company. As shown in Table 5.4, if we assume that the only change is a 20 percent increase in the value of Stock A, which has a beginning value of $10 million, the ending index value would be $202 million, or an index of 101. In contrast, if only Stock C increases by 20 percent from $100 million, the ending value will be $220 million or an index value of 110. The point is, price changes for the large market value stocks in a value-weighted index will dominate changes in the index value over time.

Table 5.5 is a summary of the characteristics of the major price-weighted, market value-weighted, and equal-weighted stock price indexes for the United States and major foreign countries. As shown, the major differences are the number of stocks in the index, but more important, the *source* of the sample (e.g., the NYSE, the OTC, the AMEX, or a foreign country such as the United Kingdom or Japan).

Figure 5.1 shows the "Stock Market Data Bank" from *The Wall Street Journal* of November 3, 1995, which contains values for many of the U.S. stock indexes we have discussed. Figure 5.2 shows a similar table for alternative indexes created and maintained by the *Financial Times*.

UNWEIGHTED PRICE INDICATOR SERIES

In an **unweighted index,** all stocks carry equal weight regardless of their price and/or their market value. A $20 stock is as important as a $40 stock, and the total market value of the company is not important. Such an index can be used by individuals who randomly select stock for their portfolio and invest the same dollar amount in each stock. One way to visualize an unweighted series is to assume that equal dollar amounts are invested in each stock in the portfolio (e.g., an equal $1,000 investment in each stock would work out to 50 shares of a $20 stock, 100 shares of a $10 stock, and 10 shares of a $100 stock). In fact, the actual movements in the index are typically based on *the arithmetic average of the percent price changes for the stocks in the index.* The use of percentage price changes means that the price level or the market value of the stock does not make a difference—each percentage change has equal weight. This arithmetic average of percent changes procedure is used in academic studies when the authors specify equal weighting.

In contrast to computing an arithmetic average of percentage changes, both Value Line and the *Financial Times* Ordinary Share Index compute a *geometric* mean of the holding period returns *and* derive the holding period yield from this calculation. Table 5.6 contains an example of an arithmetic average and a geometric average. This demonstrates the downward bias of the geometric calculation. Specifically, the geometric mean of holding period yields (HPY) shows an average change of only 5.3 percent versus the actual change in wealth of 6 percent.

TABLE 5.5	SUMMARY OF STOCK MARKET INDEXES		
Name of Index	Weighting	Number of Stocks	Source of Stocks
Dow Jones Industrial Average	Price	30	NYSE
Nikkei-Dow Jones Average	Price	225	TSE
S&P 400 Industrial	Market value	400	NYSE, OTC
S&P Transportation	Market value	20	NYSE, OTC
S&P Utilities	Market value	40	NYSE, OTC
S&P Financials	Market value	40	NYSE, OTC
S&P 500 Composite	Market value	500	NYSE, OTC
NYSE			
Industrial	Market value	1,420	NYSE
Utility	Market value	227	NYSE
Transportation	Market value	48	NYSE
Financial	Market value	864	NYSE
Composite	Market value	2,559	NYSE
NASDAQ			
Composite	Market value	4,879	OTC
Industrial	Market value	3,019	OTC
Banks	Market value	320	OTC
Insurance	Market value	107	OTC
Other finance	Market value	646	OTC
Transportation	Market value	91	OTC
Telecommunications	Market value	141	OTC
AMEX Market Value	Market value	900	AMEX
Dow Jones Equity Market Index	Market value	2,300	NYSE, AMEX, OTC
Wilshire 5000 Equity Value	Market value	5,000	NYSE, AMEX, OTC
Russell Indexes			
3,000	Market value	3,000	NYSE, AMEX, OTC
1,000	Market value	1,000 largest	NYSE, AMEX, OTC
2,000	Market value	2,000 smallest	NYSE, AMEX, OTC
Financial Times Actuaries Index			
All Share	Market value	700	LSE
FT100	Market value	100 largest	LSE
Small Cap	Market value	250	LSE
Mid Cap	Market value	250	LSE
Combined	Market value	350	LSE
Tokyo Stock Exchange Price Index (TOPIX)	Market value	1,800	TSE
Value Line Averages			
Industrials	Equal (geometric average)	1,499	NYSE, AMEX, OTC
Utilities	Equal	177	NYSE, AMEX, OTC
Rails	Equal	19	NYSE, AMEX, OTC
Composite	Equal	1,695	NYSE, AMEX, OTC
Financial Times Ordinary Share Index	Equal (geometric average)	30	LSE
FT-Actuaries World Indexes	Market value	2,275 (70%) of value	24 countries, 3 regions (returns in $, £, ¥, DM, and local currency)
Morgan Stanley Capital International (MSCI) Indexes	Market value	1,375	19 countries, 3 international, 38 international industries (returns in $ and local currency)
Dow Jones World Stock Index	Market value	2,200	13 countries, 3 regions, 120 industry groups (returns in $, £, ¥, DM, and local currency)
Euromoney–First Boston Global Stock Index	Market value	—	17 countries (returns in $ and local currency)
Salomon-Russell World Equity Index	Market value	Russell 1000 and S-R PMI of 600 non-U.S. stocks	22 countries (returns in $ and local currency)

FIGURE 5.1   STOCK MARKET DATA BANK

STOCK MARKET DATA BANK   3/21/96

MAJOR INDEXES

	— †365 DAY —			DAILY			NET		†365		FROM	
	HIGH	LOW		HIGH	LOW	CLOSE	CHG	% CHG	DAY CHG	% CHG	12/31	% CHG
DOW JONES AVERAGES												
	5683.60	4087.83	30 Industrials	5668.79	5613.87	x5626.88	− 28.54	− 0.50	+ 1539.05	+ 37.65	+ 509.76	+ 9.96
	2215.21	1574.26	20 Transportation	2203.27	2177.93	2188.90	− 5.60	− 0.26	+ 614.64	+ 39.04	+ 207.90	+ 10.49
	234.00	185.67	15 Utilities	214.43	213.11	214.02	− 0.06	− 0.03	+ 28.35	+ 15.27	− 11.38	− 5.05
	1847.58	1356.99	65 Composite	1843.43	1828.47	x1832.65	− 6.84	− 0.37	+ 475.66	+ 35.05	+ 139.44	+ 8.24
	623.15	467.17	Equity Mkt. Index	616.00	612.86	613.98	− 0.62	− 0.10	+ 146.81	+ 31.43	+ 32.55	+ 5.60
NEW YORK STOCK EXCHANGE												
	351.70	267.92	Composite	348.71	347.64	348.06	− 0.14	− 0.04	+ 80.14	+ 29.91	+ 18.55	+ 5.63
	443.68	340.36	Industrials	442.24	440.97	441.47	unch		+ 101.11	+ 29.71	+ 28.18	+ 6.82
	266.69	203.66	Utilities	247.42	246.56	247.27	+ 0.97	+ 0.39	+ 43.61	+ 21.41	− 5.63	− 2.23
	333.59	243.93	Transportation	328.41	326.19	328.41	− 1.35	− 0.41	+ 84.48	+ 34.63	+ 26.45	+ 8.76
	298.31	212.58	Finance	291.51	290.25	290.25	− 1.32	− 0.45	+ 77.67	+ 36.54	+ 16.00	+ 5.83
STANDARD & POOR'S INDEXES												
	661.45	495.95	500 Index	651.54	648.10	649.19	− 0.79	− 0.12	+ 153.24	+ 30.90	+ 33.26	+ 5.40
	776.23	591.34	Industrials	769.80	765.82	767.19	− 0.65	− 0.08	+ 175.85	+ 29.74	+ 46.00	+ 6.38
	213.83	157.68	Utilities	194.75	193.16	194.11	+ 0.77	+ 0.40	+ 36.43	+ 23.10	− 8.47	− 4.18
	232.53	179.91	400 MidCap	230.67	229.85	229.99	− 0.29	− 0.13	+ 50.08	+ 27.84	+ 12.15	+ 5.58
	126.48	97.02	600 SmallCap	126.55	126.12	126.19	− 0.12	− 0.10	+ 29.17	+ 30.07	+ 5.09	+ 4.20
	142.35	107.56	1500 Index	140.87	140.19	140.39	− 0.17	− 0.12	+ 32.83	+ 30.52	+ 7.15	+ 5.37
NASDAQ												
	1117.79	811.39	Composite	1104.36	1098.58	1099.79	− 2.03	− 0.18	+ 288.40	+ 35.54	+ 47.66	+ 4.53
	1026.46	791.75	Industrials	1021.86	1017.53	1019.66	+ 1.74	+ 0.17	+ 227.70	+ 28.75	+ 54.98	+ 5.70
	1344.70	999.36	Insurance	1308.57	1300.30	1303.70	+ 2.05	+ 0.16	+ 304.34	+ 30.45	+ 11.06	+ 0.86
	1050.72	768.89	Banks	1042.08	1039.80	1040.71	+ 0.51	+ 0.05	+ 271.53	+ 35.30	+ 31.30	+ 3.10
	500.28	362.63	Nat. Mkt. Comp.	494.23	491.56	492.08	− 0.99	− 0.20	+ 129.45	+ 35.70	+ 20.91	+ 4.44
	417.86	321.61	Nat. Mkt. Indus.	415.90	414.12	414.93	+ 0.60	+ 0.14	+ 92.46	+ 28.67	+ 21.63	+ 5.50
OTHERS												
	570.31	458.52	Amex	568.76	566.63	568.32	+ 1.05	+ 0.19	+ 109.80	+ 23.95	+ 20.09	+ 3.66
	351.81	263.52	Russell 1000	347.66	345.98	346.45	− 0.37	− 0.11	+ 82.93	+ 31.47	+ 17.56	+ 5.34
	328.93	257.53	Russell 2000	329.06	328.31	328.67	+ 0.33	+ 0.10	+ 71.14	+ 27.62	+ 12.70	+ 4.02
	374.89	282.46	Russell 3000	371.40	369.80	370.26	− 0.30	− 0.08	+ 87.80	+ 31.08	+ 18.35	+ 5.21
	344.93	286.95	Value-Line(geom.)	344.30	343.48	343.81	− 0.01	− 0.00	+ 56.86	+ 19.82	+ 12.77	+ 3.86
	6449.34	4865.05	Wilshire 5000	...	...	6383.31	− 5.93	− 0.09	+ 1518.26	+ 31.21	+ 326.10	+ 5.38

†-Based on comparable trading day in preceding year.

Source: *The Wall Street Journal,* March 22, 1996, C2.

FIGURE 5.2   *FINANCIAL TIMES* ACTUARIES SHARES INDICES

FT - SE Actuaries Share Indices   The UK Series

	Apr 9	Day's chge%	Apr 4	Apr 3	Apr 2	Year ago	Div. yield%	Net cover	P/E ratio	Xd adj. ytd	Total Return
FT-SE 100	3758.6	+0.1	3755.6	3725.1	3728.5	3190.9	3.94	2.12	14.95	62.20	1527.46
FT-SE Mid 250	4377.1	−0.2	4385.3	4359.9	4348.7	3484.3	3.39	1.71	21.53	63.00	1746.52
FT-SE Mid 250 ex Inv Trusts	4409.2	−0.2	4416.6	4390.1	4376.6	3493.5	3.50	1.76	20.30	66.82	1761.88
FT SE A 360	1891.7	......	1891.3	1877.0	1877.2	1583.8	3.82	2.04	16.04	30.41	1571.37
FT-SE-A 350 Higher Yield	1835.2	−0.1	1837.1	1823.1	1824.2	1595.2	5.04	1.90	13.06	37.66	1273.61
FT-SE-A 350 Lower Yield	1955.7	+0.1	1953.1	1938.3	1937.7	1572.6	2.69	2.29	20.34	23.41	1347.23
FT-SE SmallCap	2109.70	......	2109.64	2102.12	2098.77	1737.34	3.05	1.78	23.06	16.89	1719.59
FT-SE SmallCap ex Inv Trusts	2094.58	......	2093.72	2085.73	2081.50	1714.16	3.26	1.86	20.63	17.01	1716.69
FT-SE-A ALL-SHARE	1869.86	......	1869.53	1855.89	1855.90	1563.24	3.76	2.02	16.42	28.89	1577.23

Source: *The Financial Times,* April 10, 1996, 30. Reprinted with permission.

| TABLE 5.6 | **EXAMPLE OF AN ARITHMETIC AND GEOMETRIC MEAN OF PERCENTAGE CHANGES** |

| | **SHARE PRICE** | | | |
Stock	T	T + 1	HPR	HPY
X	10	12	1.20	0.20
Y	22	20	.91	−0.09
Z	44	47	1.07	0.07

$$\Pi = 1.20 \times .91 \times 1.07 \qquad\qquad \Sigma = 0.18$$
$$= 1.168 \qquad\qquad\qquad\quad 0.18/3 = 0.06$$
$$1.168^{1/3} = 1.0531 \qquad\qquad\qquad = 6\%$$

$$\text{Index Value (T)} \times 1.0531 = \text{Index Value (T + 1)}$$
$$\text{Index Value (T)} \times 1.06 \ \ \ = \text{Index Value (T + 1)}$$

GLOBAL EQUITY
INDEXES

As described in the Chapter 4 Appendix, there are stock-market indexes available for most individual foreign markets similar to those we described for Japan (the Nikkei and TOPIX) and the United Kingdom (the several *Financial Times* indexes) described in Table 5.5. While these local indexes are closely followed within each country, there can be a problem comparing the results implied by these indexes to one another because there is no consistency among them in sample selection, weighting, or computational procedure. To solve these comparability problems, several groups have computed a set of country stock indexes with consistent sample selection, weighting, and computational procedure. As a result, these indexes can be directly compared and combined to create various regional indexes (e.g., Pacific Basin). We will describe the three major sets of global equity indexes.

FT/S&P-ACTUARIES WORLD INDEXES   The FT/S&P-Actuaries World Indexes are jointly compiled by The Financial Times Limited, Goldman Sachs & Company, and Standard & Poor's (the "compilers") in conjunction with the Institute of Actuaries and the Faculty of Actuaries. Approximately 2,275 equity securities in 24 countries are measured, covering at least 70 percent of the total value of all listed companies in each country. Actively traded medium and small capitalization stocks are included along with major international equities. All securities must allow direct holdings of shares by foreign nationals.

The indexes are market value weighted and have a base date of December 31, 1986 = 100. The index results are reported in U.S. dollars, U.K. pound sterling, Japanese yen, German mark, and the local currency of the country. Performance results are calculated after the New York markets close and are published, as shown in Table 5.7, the following day in *The Financial Times*. The 24 countries and the proportion of each in U.S. dollars is as follows (as of June 1995):

Australia	1.48	Hong Kong	1.78	Norway	0.24
Austria	0.18	Ireland	0.17	Singapore	0.59
Belgium	0.73	Italy	1.30	South Africa	1.31
Canada	1.61	Japan	25.54	Spain	1.01
Denmark	0.37	Malaysia	1.10	Sweden	1.13
Finland	0.37	Mexico	0.38	Switzerland	2.75
France	3.58	The Netherlands	2.05	United Kingdom	9.65
Germany	3.74	New Zealand	0.21	United States	38.15

In addition to the individual countries and the world index, there are several geographic subgroups, as shown in Table 5.7

TABLE 5.7   FT/S&P ACTUARIES WORLD INDICES

FT/S&P ACTUARIES WORLD INDICES

The FT/S&P Actuaries World Indices are owned by FT-SE International Limited, Goldman, Sachs & Co. and Standard & Poor's. The Indices are compiled by FT-SE International and Goldman Sachs in conjunction with the Faculty of Actuaries and the Institute of Actuaries. NatWest Securities Ltd. was a co-founder of the Indices.

NATIONAL AND REGIONAL MARKETS Figures in parentheses show number of lines of stock	MONDAY APRIL 8 1996								FRIDAY APRIL 5 1996					DOLLAR INDEX		
	US Dollar Index	Day's Change %	Pound Sterling Index	Yen Index	DM Index	Local Currency Index	Local % chg on day	Gross Div. Yield	US Dollar Index	Pound Sterling Index	Yen Index	DM Index	Local Currency Index	52 week High	52 week Low	Year ago (approx)
Australia (81)	198.95	-0.1	192.70	135.07	152.85	169.11	0.0	4.11	199.19	193.16	135.30	153.53	169.19	202.74	162.68	170.67
Austria (24)	184.05	0.3	178.27	124.96	141.40	141.22	0.0	1.54	183.45	177.90	124.61	141.40	141.22	199.28	168.11	187.66
Belgium (34)	210.72	0.4	204.10	143.06	161.89	157.73	0.0	4.13	209.93	203.59	142.60	161.81	157.73	215.81	184.81	187.75
Brazil (28)	150.19	-2.7	145.47	101.97	115.39	272.88	-2.7	1.61	154.32	149.66	104.83	118.95	280.37	170.25	109.87	116.97
Canada (100)	158.43	-0.3	153.45	107.56	121.72	155.77	-0.2	2.41	158.88	154.07	107.92	122.46	156.09	159.32	133.09	133.09
Denmark (30)	299.07	0.3	289.67	203.04	229.77	232.10	0.0	1.92	298.13	289.11	202.51	229.79	232.10	305.17	255.18	260.45
Finland (24)	175.22	0.4	169.72	118.96	134.62	169.97	0.0	2.90	174.60	169.32	118.60	134.58	169.97	276.11	171.73	188.18
France (98)	196.88	0.3	190.69	133.67	151.26	155.56	0.0	3.01	196.33	190.39	133.36	151.33	155.56	196.88	167.70	185.25
Germany (60)	173.65	0.3	168.19	117.90	133.42	133.42	0.0	1.96	173.09	167.86	117.57	133.42	133.42	174.38	146.95	150.24
Hong Kong (59)	437.68	-0.2	423.93	297.15	336.27	434.50	-0.2	3.25	438.54	425.27	297.88	338.02	435.37	451.19	323.87	339.99
Ireland (16)	267.91	0.1	259.49	181.89	205.83	239.14	0.0	3.40	267.57	259.48	181.75	206.24	239.14	267.91	215.82	218.24
Italy (59)	73.28	0.1	70.98	49.75	56.30	85.41	0.0	2.14	73.19	70.98	49.72	56.42	85.41	82.71	67.21	68.60
Japan (481)	154.70	-0.2	149.84	105.03	118.86	105.03	-0.3	0.72	155.05	150.36	105.32	119.51	105.32	164.82	137.75	151.63
Malaysia (107)	546.08	-1.8	528.92	370.74	419.55	532.39	-1.8	1.64	555.93	539.12	377.63	428.50	542.01	561.96	425.77	486.77
Mexico (18)	1181.93	-2.7	1144.78	802.43	908.06	9771.41	-2.2	1.42	1214.85	1178.11	825.21	936.39	9995.15	1237.14	791.99	949.68
Netherland (13)	291.22	0.3	282.07	197.72	223.74	219.36	0.0	3.19	290.22	281.44	197.14	223.70	219.36	291.22	235.13	238.83
New Zealand (15)	81.85	0.1	79.28	55.57	62.89	63.60	0.0	4.33	81.78	79.31	55.55	63.03	63.60	85.49	76.26	79.94
Norway (33)	239.43	0.2	231.90	162.55	183.95	208.10	0.0	2.51	239.02	231.79	162.36	184.23	208.10	243.79	213.52	216.23
Singapore (44)	433.60	-2.2	419.98	294.38	333.13	280.80	-2.2	1.35	443.39	429.98	301.18	341.76	287.04	465.21	355.81	360.17
South Africa (45)	371.12	-0.8	359.45	251.96	285.13	331.96	-1.0	2.54	370.21	359.02	251.47	285.35	331.96	437.76	338.91	352.62
Spain (37)	172.35	-0.8	166.94	117.02	132.42	161.51	-1.0	3.42	173.72	168.47	118.00	133.90	163.20	175.88	134.05	135.25
Sweden (46)	337.05	-0.1	326.46	228.83	258.95	331.64	0.0	2.50	337.36	327.16	229.16	260.03	331.64	352.28	241.23	243.05
Switzerland (39)	247.99	0.2	240.19	168.36	190.53	183.34	0.0	1.54	247.37	239.88	168.03	190.67	183.34	252.34	181.68	184.91
Thailand (46)	185.57	-0.1	179.74	125.99	142.57	182.00	0.0	1.79	185.72	180.54	126.15	143.15	182.00	193.95	134.53	136.39
United Kingdom (204)	233.15	0.1	225.82	158.29	179.13	225.82	0.0	4.05	232.87	225.82	158.18	179.49	225.82	235.50	206.28	208.93
USA (629)	262.68	-1.8	254.42	178.34	201.81	262.68	-1.8	2.20	267.57	259.48	181.75	206.24	267.57	269.11	206.41	206.89
Americas (775)	239.77	-1.8	232.23	162.78	184.21	201.50	-1.8	2.20	244.14	236.75	165.84	188.18	205.16	245.54	189.06	189.39
Europe (723)	209.03	0.2	202.46	141.92	160.60	180.60	0.0	3.05	208.68	202.03	141.75	160.84	180.67	209.03	178.19	180.99
Nordic (133)	288.94	0.1	279.86	196.17	221.99	248.73	0.0	2.45	288.77	280.04	196.15	222.58	248.73	297.48	231.64	233.46
Pacific Basin (833)	167.82	-0.3	162.55	113.94	128.93	116.52	-0.3	1.15	168.35	163.25	114.35	129.76	116.93	171.87	148.86	159.86
Euro-Pacific (1556)	184.89	-0.1	179.07	125.52	142.05	140.85	-0.2	2.04	185.04	179.45	125.69	142.63	141.13	185.04	166.51	168.57
North America (729)	256.16	-1.8	248.11	173.92	196.81	255.44	-1.8	2.21	260.80	252.91	177.15	201.02	260.06	262.26	202.03	202.32
Europe Ex. UK (519)	190.78	0.2	184.78	129.52	146.57	154.54	-0.1	2.50	190.40	184.64	129.33	146.76	154.63	190.78	159.17	162.04
Pacific Ex. Japan (352)	289.59	-0.7	280.49	196.61	222.49	251.15	-0.6	2.95	291.56	282.74	198.04	224.73	252.78	293.58	237.71	241.00
World Ex. US (1747)	185.95	-0.1	180.10	126.24	142.86	144.98	-0.2	2.06	186.17	180.54	126.46	143.50	145.32	186.17	167.36	169.05
World Ex. UK (2172)	207.08	-0.9	200.57	140.59	159.09	174.15	-1.0	1.92	209.04	202.72	142.00	161.13	175.91	209.04	177.60	177.60
World Ex. Japan (1895)	239.83	-1.0	232.29	162.82	184.25	225.93	-1.1	2.54	242.33	235.00	164.61	186.78	228.44	242.36	196.03	197.35
The World Index (2376)	209.41	-0.8	202.83	142.17	160.89	178.86	-0.9	2.12	211.20	204.81	143.46	162.79	180.50	211.20	180.34	180.34

Source: *The Financial Times*, April 10, 1996, 30. Reprinted with permission.

MORGAN STANLEY CAPITAL INTERNATIONAL (MSCI) INDEXES   The Morgan Stanley Capital International Indexes consist of 3 international, 19 national, and 38 international industry indexes. The indexes consider some 1,375 companies listed on stock exchanges in 19 countries with a combined market capitalization that represents approximately 60 percent of the aggregate market value of the stock exchanges of these countries. All the indexes are market value weighted. Table 5.8 contains the countries included, the number of stocks, and market values for stocks in the various countries and groups.

In addition to reporting the indexes in U.S. dollars and the country's local currency, the following valuation information is available: (1) price-to-book value (P/BV) ratio, (2) price-to-cash earnings (earnings plus depreciation) (P/CE) ratio, (3) price-to-earnings (P/E) ratio, and (4) dividend yield (YLD). These ratios help in analyzing different valuation levels among countries and over time for specific countries.

Notably, the Morgan Stanley group index for Europe, Australia, and the Far East (EAFE) is being used as the basis for futures and options contracts on the Chicago Mercantile Exchange and the Chicago Board Options Exchange. Several of the MSCI country indexes, the EAFE index, and a world index are reported daily in *The Wall Street Journal,* as shown in Figure 5.3.

DOW JONES WORLD STOCK INDEX   In January 1993, Dow Jones introduced its World Stock Index. Composed of over 2,200 companies worldwide and organized into 120 industry groups, the index includes 28 countries representing more than 80 percent of the combined capitalization of these countries. In addition to the 28 countries shown in Figure 5.4, the countries are grouped into three regions: Asia/Pacific, Europe/Africa, and the Americas. Finally, each country's index is calculated in its own currency as well as in the U.S. dollar, British pound, German mark, and Japanese yen. The index is reported daily in *The Wall Street Journal* (domestic), in *The Wall Street Journal Europe,* and in *The Asian Wall Street Journal.* It is published weekly in *Barron's.*[7]

| FIGURE 5.3 | LISTING OF MORGAN STANLEY CAPITAL INTERNATIONAL STOCK INDEX VALUES FOR MARCH 20, 1996 |

Here are price trends on the world's major stock markets, as calculated by Morgan Stanley Capital International Perspective, Geneva. To make them directly comparable, each index, calculated in local currencies, is based on the close of 1969 equaling 100. The percentage change is since year-end.

	Mar. 20	Mar. 19	% This Year
U.S.	615.4	617.1	+ 5.9
Britain	1114.4	1116.7	+ 0.6
Canada	537.2	538.1	+ 5.5
Japan	951.0	951.0	− 0.7
France	635.2	635.0	+ 7.1
Germany	345.7	346.1	+ 8.0
Hong Kong	7322.8	7351.0	+ 9.2
Switzerland	460.0	458.9	+ 9.4
Australia	462.3	463.9	+ 0.9
World Index	754.9	756.3	+ 2.8

Source: *The Wall Street Journal,* March 22, 1996, C12.

---

[7]"Journal Launches Index Tracking World Stocks," *The Wall Street Journal,* January 5, 1993, C1.

| TABLE 5.8 | MARKET COVERAGE OF MORGAN STANLEY CAPITAL INTERNATIONAL INDEXES AS OF APRIL 30, 1996 |

	GDP EAFE	Weights[a] World	COS in Index	U.S. $ Billion	EAFE[b]	World
Austria	1.7	1.1	24	$ 24.1	0.4	0.2
Belgium	1.7	1.1	19	61.8	1.1	0.6
Denmark	1.1	0.7	24	42.2	0.8	0.4
Finland	0.5	0.3	20	26.7	0.5	0.3
Finland (free)	—	—	20	13.6	—	—
France	10.8	6.9	73	361.9	6.5	3.7
Germany	15.4	9.9	69	366.3	6.6	3.8
Ireland	0.4	0.3	11	16.2	0.3	0.2
Italy	8.3	5.3	54	131.4	2.4	1.3
The Netherlands	2.6	1.7	22	223.1	4.0	2.3
Norway	0.9	0.6	22	26.8	0.5	0.3
Norway (free)	—	—	18	10.9	—	—
Spain	3.9	2.5	31	103.2	1.9	1.1
Sweden	1.7	1.1	30	115.5	2.1	1.3
Sweden (free)	—	—	30	115.5	—	—
Switzerland	2.1	1.4	49	321.0	5.6	3.3
United Kingdom	7.5	4.8	142	898.0	16.2	9.2
Europe 14 (free)	—	—	590	2,718.2	—	—
Europe 14	58.8	37.6	594	2,718.2	48.9	27.8
Australia	2.6	1.7	49	148.3	2.7	1.5
Hong Kong	1.0	0.7	30	182.5	3.3	1.9
Japan	36.1	23.1	317	2,280.9	41.1	23.4
Malaysia	0.6	0.4	11	21.3	0.4	1.4
New Zealand	0.4	0.2	76	139.1	2.5	0.6
Singapore	0.5	0.3	32	64.9	1.2	0.2
Singapore (free)	—	—	32	85.3	—	—
Pacific	41.2	26.4	522	2,836.9	51.1	29.1
Pacific (free)	—	—	522	2,857.4	—	—
EAFE (free)	—	—	1,106	5,575.6	—	—
EAFE	100.0	64.0	1,106	5,555.2	100.0	56.9
Canada	—	2.6	84	222.8	—	2.3
United States	—	33.4	376	3,987.6	—	40.8
The World Index (free)	—	—	1,566	9,786.0	—	—
The World Index	—	100.0	1,566	9,765.6	—	100. 0
Nordic countries (free)	—	—	91	—	—	—
Nordic countries	4.3	2.7	96	211.1	3.8	2.2
Europe 14 ex. UK	51.2	32.8	442	1,820.2	32.8	18.6
Far East	38.2	24.5	463	2,667.3	46.6	27.3
Far East (free)	—	—	463	2,667.8	—	—
EASEA (EAFE ex. Japan)	63.9	40.9	789	3,274.2	58.9	35.5
North America	—	36.0	460	4,210.4	—	43.1
Kokusai (World ex. Japan)	—	76.9	1,249	7,484.7	—	76.6

[a]GDP weight figures represent the initial weights applicable for the first month. They are used exclusively in the MSCI "GDP weighted" indexes.

[b]Free indicates that only stocks that can be acquired by foreign investors are included in the index. If the number of companies is the same and the value is different, it indicates that the stocks available to foreigners are priced differently from domestic shares.

Source: Morgan Stanley Capital International (New York: Morgan Stanley & Co., 1996).

FIGURE 5.4   **DOW JONES WORLD STOCK INDEX LISTING**

DOW JONES WORLD INDUSTRY GROUPS

Thursday, March 21, 1996

REGION/ COUNTRY	DJ EQUITY MARKET INDEX, LOCAL CURRENCY	PCT. CHG.	CLOSING INDEX	CHG.	PCT. CHG.	12-MO HIGH	12-MO LOW	12-MO CHG.	PCT. CHG.	FROM 12/31	PCT. CHG.
Americas			151.62	− 0.18	− 0.12	153.90	115.84	+ 35.79	+ 30.89	+ 8.01	+ 5.58
Canada	132.54	− 0.29	112.43	− 0.53	− 0.47	115.26	96.33	+ 15.18	+ 15.61	+ 4.19	+ 3.87
Mexico	212.66	0.00	86.57	0.00	0.00	91.88	57.79	+ 28.78	+ 49.80	+ 8.61	+11.04
U.S.	613.98	− 0.10	613.98	− 0.62	− 0.10	623.15	467.17	+146.81	+ 31.43	+32.55	+ 5.60
Europe/Africa			141.18	− 0.07	− 0.05	141.34	118.05	+ 23.13	+ 19.60	+ 4.16	+ 3.04
Austria	103.77	− 0.04	106.83	− 0.04	− 0.04	113.71	96.56	+ 1.43	+ 1.35	+ 5.54	+ 5.47
Belgium	138.37	+ 0.25	142.78	− 0.30	− 0.21	148.48	117.76	+ 23.81	+ 20.02	+ 0.23	+ 0.16
Denmark	110.14	+ 0.33	114.27	+ 0.08	+ 0.07	118.94	97.96	+ 13.59	+ 13.50	+ 1.85	+ 1.65
Finland	227.53	− 0.58	204.53	− 2.06	− 1.00	303.04	186.32	+ 12.25	+ 6.37	+ 1.65	+ 0.81
France	122.38	+ 0.30	124.87	− 0.37	− 0.30	127.26	111.60	+ 12.58	+ 11.20	+ 4.84	+ 4.03
Germany	143.72	+ 0.81	147.07	+ 0.58	+ 0.40	147.49	121.19	+ 23.62	+ 19.13	+ 8.83	+ 6.39
Ireland	189.16	− 1.19	155.54	− 2.09	− 1.33	157.63	124.70	+ 30.85	+ 24.74	+ 2.71	+ 1.78
Italy	130.11	+ 0.52	102.70	− 0.03	− 0.03	121.02	94.98	+ 5.66	+ 5.83	− 0.80	− 0.78
Netherlands	171.79	− 0.29	174.62	− 1.28	− 0.73	176.06	138.96	+ 34.94	+ 25.01	+ 7.32	+ 4.37
Norway	141.74	− 0.27	132.24	− 0.76	− 0.57	140.54	116.12	+ 15.45	+ 13.23	+ 3.04	+ 2.35
South Africa	203.63	0.00	142.72	+ 0.56	+ 0.39	160.95	122.07	+ 18.99	+ 15.34	+ 0.02	+ 0.01
Spain	151.49	+ 0.56	118.48	+ 0.33	+ 0.28	122.25	84.41	+ 34.07	+ 40.36	+ 4.17	+ 3.65
Sweden	216.25	− 1.06	180.35	− 2.95	− 1.61	183.30	120.08	+ 60.13	+ 50.02	+17.21	+10.55
Switzerland	216.76	+ 0.53	245.52	+ 0.40	+ 0.16	245.52	173.64	+ 71.88	+ 41.39	+12.89	+ 5.54
United Kingdom	152.09	+ 0.26	125.06	+ 0.15	+ 0.12	127.62	111.26	+ 13.81	+ 12.41	+ 0.57	+ 0.46
Europe/Africa (ex. South Africa)			140.92	− 0.11	− 0.08	141.07	118.05	+ 22.87	+ 19.38	+ 4.38	+ 3.21
Europe/Africa (ex. U.K. & S. Africa)			153.05	− 0.28	− 0.18	153.41	123.97	+ 28.89	+ 23.27	+ 6.82	+ 4.67
Asia/Pacific			119.08	+ 0.99	+ 0.84	124.04	108.03	+ 9.66	+ 8.83	− 0.72	− 0.60
Australia	133.12	+ 0.70	136.29	+ 1.30	+ 0.96	136.79	106.89	+ 29.26	+ 27.34	+ 8.38	+ 6.55
Hong Kong	245.05	+ 1.59	246.30	+ 3.88	+ 1.60	260.15	185.19	+ 56.86	+ 30.01	+22.63	+10.12
Indonesia	215.66	0.00	184.06	+ 0.24	+ 0.13	200.27	150.13	+ 27.36	+ 17.46	+11.58	+ 6.71
Japan	94.76	+ 1.15	110.66	+ 0.74	+ 0.67	121.30	102.27	+ 5.50	+ 5.23	− 3.42	− 3.00
Malaysia	235.87	+ 1.92	252.23	+ 4.74	+ 1.92	255.72	198.20	+ 38.21	+ 17.85	+29.15	+13.07
New Zealand	146.26	+ 0.85	185.80	+ 1.78	+ 0.97	189.29	161.30	+ 24.50	+ 15.19	+ 9.63	+ 5.47
Philippines	315.09	+ 0.14	312.49	+ 0.31	+ 0.10	328.15	239.18	+ 67.93	+ 27.78	+31.01	+11.02
Singapore	186.38	+ 2.66	214.20	+ 5.70	+ 2.73	224.73	170.17	+ 41.62	+ 24.12	+18.29	+ 9.34
South Korea	146.67	− 0.26	141.82	− 0.77	− 0.54	167.89	135.98	− 13.47	− 8.68	− 3.76	− 2.58
Thailand	216.25	+ 0.39	201.96	+ 0.70	+ 0.35	227.64	171.02	+ 22.71	+ 12.67	+ 5.20	+ 2.64
Asia/Pacific (ex. Japan)			188.31	+ 2.65	+ 1.43	191.66	152.69	+ 35.62	+ 23.33	+14.85	+ 8.56
World (ex. U.S.)			126.59	+ 0.51	+ 0.41	127.99	110.60	+ 15.25	+ 13.70	+ 1.47	+ 1.17
DJ WORLD STOCK INDEX			137.45	+ 0.26	+ 0.19	138.49	113.98	+ 23.47	+ 20.59	+ 3.99	+ 2.99

Indexes based on 6/30/82=100 for U.S., 12/31/91=100 for World.   ©1996 Dow Jones & Co. Inc., All Rights Reserved.

Source: *The Wall Street Journal,* March 22, 1996, C12.

COMPARISON OF WORLD STOCK INDEXES   Table 5.10 contains the correlations among the three alternative indexes from 1986 to 1995 when available. The correlation between the MS and the FT world indexes for this period was .998. The following correlations between the three series since December 31, 1991, when the DJ series became available, indicate that the results with the alternative series are quite comparable.

	U.S. Dollars
FT—MS:	.998
FT—DJ:	.999
MS—DJ:	.996

BOND-MARKET INDICATOR SERIES[8]

Investors know little about the several bond-market series because these bond series are relatively new and not widely published. Knowledge regarding these bond series is becoming more important because of the growth of fixed-income mutual funds and the consequent need to have a reliable set of benchmarks to use in evaluating performance.[9] Also, because the performance of many fixed-income money managers has not been able to match that of the aggregate bond market, there has been a growing interest in bond index funds, which requires the development of an index to emulate.[10]

Notably, the creation and computation of bond-market indexes is more difficult than a stock-market series for several reasons. First, the universe of bonds is much broader than that of stocks, ranging from U.S. Treasury securities to bonds in default. Second, the universe of bonds is changing constantly because of numerous new issues, bond maturities, calls, and bond sinking funds. Third, the volatility of prices for individual bonds and bond portfolios changes because bond price volatility is affected by duration, which is likewise changing constantly because of changes in maturity, coupon, and market yield (see Chapter 16). Finally, there can be significant problems in correctly pricing the individual bond issues in an index (especially corporate and mortgage bonds) compared to the current and continuous transactions prices available for most stocks used in stock indexes.

The subsequent discussion will be divided into the following three subsections: (1) U.S. investment-grade bond indexes, including Treasuries; (2) U.S. high-yield bond indexes; and (3) global government bond indexes. Notably, all of these indexes indicate total rates of return for the portfolio of bonds, including price change, accrued interest, and coupon income reinvested. Also most of the indexes are market value weighted using current prices and outstanding par values publicly held. Table 5.9 is a summary of the characteristics for the indexes available for these three segments of the bond market.

INVESTMENT-GRADE BOND INDEXES

As shown in Table 5.9, there are four investment firms that have created and maintain indexes for Treasury bonds and other bonds that are considered to be investment grade, that is, the bonds are rated BBB or higher. As demonstrated in Reilly, Kao, and Wright and shown in Chapter 4, the relationship among the returns for these bonds is very strong (i.e., correlations average about 0.95), regardless of the segment of the market. This implies that

---

[8]The discussion in this section draws heavily from Frank K. Reilly, Wenchi Kao, and David J. Wright, "Alternative Bond Market Indexes," *Financial Analysts Journal* 48, no. 3 (May–June 1992): 44–58.

[9]For a discussion of the evaluation of bond portfolios, see Gifford Fong, Charles Pearson, Oldrick Vasicek, and Theresa Conroy, "Fixed-Income Portfolio Performance: Analyzing Sources of Return," in *The Handbook of Fixed-Income Securities,* 3d ed., ed. by Frank J. Fabozzi (Homewood, IL: Business One Irwin, 1991). For a discussion of benchmark selection, see Chris P. Dialynas, "The Active Decisions in the Selection of Passive Management and Performance Bogeys," and Daralyn B. Peifer, "A Sponsor's View of Benchmark Portfolios," in *The Handbook of Fixed-Income Securities,* 4th ed., edited by Frank J. Fabozzi and T. Dessa Fabozzi (Burr Ridge, IL: Irwin Professional Publishing, 1995).

[10]For a discussion of this phenomenon, see Fran Hawthorne, "The Battle of the Bond Indexes," *Institutional Investor* 20, no. 4 (April 1986); and Sharmin Mossavar-Rahmani, *Bond Index Funds* (Chicago: Probus Publishing, 1991).

TABLE 5.9							
			SUMMARY OF BOND MARKET INDEXES				

Name of Index	Number of Issues	Maturity	Size of Issues	Weighting	Pricing	Reinvestment Assumption	Subindexes Available
U.S. Investment-Grade Bond Indexes							
Lehman Brothers	5,000+	Over 1 year	Over $100 million	Market value	Trader priced and model priced	No	Government, gov./corp., corporate, mortgage-backed, asset-backed
Merrill Lynch	5,000+	Over 1 year	Over $50 million	Market value	Trader priced and model priced	In specific bonds	Government, gov./corp., corporate, mortgage
Ryan Treasury	300+	Over 1 year	All Treasury	Market value and equal	Market priced	In specific bonds	Treasury
Salomon Brothers	5,000+	Over 1 year	Over $50 million	Market value	Trader priced	In one-month T-bill	Broad inv. grade, Treas.-agency, corporate, mortgage
U.S. High-Yield Bond Indexes							
Blume-Keim	233	Over 10 years	Over $25 million	Equal	Trader priced	Yes	Only composite
First Boston	423	All maturities	Over $75 million	Market value	Trader priced	Yes	Composite and by rating
Lehman Brothers	624	Over 1 year	Over $100 million	Market value	Trader priced	No	Composite and by rating
Merrill Lynch	735	Over 1 year	Over $25 million	Market value	Trader priced	Yes	Composite and by rating
Salomon Brothers	299	Over 7 years	Over $50 million	Market value	Trader priced	Yes	Composite and by rating
Global Government Bond Indexes (Initial Date of Index)							
Lehman Brothers (January 1987)	800	Over 1 year	Over $200 million	Market value	Trader priced	Yes	Composite and 13 countries, local and U.S. dollars
Merrill Lynch (December 1985)	9,736	Over 1 year	Over $50 million	Market value	Trader priced	Yes	Composite and 9 countries, local and U.S. dollars
J. P. Morgan (12/31/85)	445	Over 1 year	Over $100 million	Market value	Trader priced	Yes in index	Composite and 11 countries, local and U.S. dollars
Salomon Brothers (12/31/84)	400	Over 1 year	Over $250 million	Market value	Trader priced	Yes at local short-term rate	Composite and 14 countries, local and U.S. dollars

Source: Frank K. Reilly, Wenchi Kao, and David J. Wright, "Alternative Bond Market Indexes," *Financial Analysts Journal* 48, no. 3 (May–June, 1992): 14–58; Frank K. Reilly and David J. Wright, "An Analysis of High-Yield Bond Benchmarks," *Journal of Fixed Income* 3, no. 4 (March 1994): 6–24; and Frank K. Reilly and David J. Wright, "Global Bond Markets: An Analysis of Alternative Benchmarks and Risk–Return Performance," mimeo (March 1995).

the returns for all these bonds are being driven by aggregate interest rates—that is, shifts in the government yield curve.

HIGH-YIELD BOND INDEXES

One of the fastest-growing segments of the U.S. bond market during the past 15 years has been the high-yield bond market, which includes bonds that are not investment grade—that is, they are rated BB, B, CCC, CC, and C. Because of this growth, four investment firms and two academicians created indexes related to this market. A summary of the characteristics for these indexes is included in Table 5.9. As shown in a study by Reilly and Wright, the relationship among the alternative indexes is substantially weaker than among the investment-grade indexes, and this is especially true for the bonds rated CCC.[11]

MERRILL LYNCH CONVERTIBLE SECURITIES INDEXES   In March 1988, Merrill Lynch introduced a convertible bond index with data beginning in January 1987. This index includes 600 issues in three major subgroups: U.S. domestic convertible bonds, Eurodollar convertible bonds issued by U.S. corporations, and U.S. domestic convertible preferred stocks. The issues included must be public U.S. corporate issues, have a minimum par value of $25 million, and have a minimum maturity of 1 year.

GLOBAL GOVERNMENT BOND MARKET INDEXES

Similar to the high-yield bond market, the global bond market has experienced significant growth in size and importance during the recent 5-year period. Unlike the high-yield bond market, this global segment is completely dominated by government bonds because most non-U.S. countries do not have a corporate bond market, much less a high-yield corporate bond market. Once again, several major investment firms have responded to the needs of investors and money managers by creating indexes that reflect the performance for the global bond market, a number of individual countries, and several regions. As shown in Table 5.9, the alternative indexes have several similar characteristics such as measuring total rates of return, using market-value weighting, and using trader pricing. At the same time, the total sample sizes differ and there are differences in the number of countries included.

An analysis of the performance in this market by Reilly and Wright, which was shown in Chapter 3, indicates that the differences mentioned have caused some large differences in the long-term risk–return performance by the alternative indexes.[12] Also, the low correlation among the various countries is confirmed to be similar to stocks. Finally, there was a significant exchange rate effect on volatility and correlations.

COMPOSITE STOCK–BOND INDEXES

Beyond separate stock indexes and bond indexes for individual countries, a natural step is the development of a composite series that measures the performance of all securities in a given country. A composite series of stocks and bonds makes it possible to examine the benefits of diversifying with a combination of stocks and bonds in addition to diversifying within the asset classes of stocks or bonds.

[11] Frank K. Reilly and David J. Wright, "An Analysis of High Yield Bond Benchmarks," *Journal of Fixed Income* 3, no. 4 (March 1994): 6–24. The uniqueness of CCC bonds is demonstrated in Frank K. Reilly and David J. Wright, "High-Yield Bonds and Segmentation in the Bond Market," mimeo (August 1995).

[12] Frank K. Reilly and David J. Wright, "Global Bond Markets: An Analysis of Alternative Benchmarks and Risk–Return Performance," mimeo (March 1995).

MERRILL LYNCH–
WILSHIRE U.S.
CAPITAL MARKETS
INDEX (ML–WCMI)

A market-value-weighted index called Merrill Lynch–Wilshire Capital Markets Index (ML–WCMI) measures the total return performance of the combined U.S. taxable fixed-income and equity markets. It is basically a combination of the Merrill Lynch fixed-income indexes and the Wilshire 5000 common stock index. As such, it tracks more than 10,000 stocks and bonds. The makeup of the index is as follows (as of October 1995):

Security	$ in Billions	Percent of Total
Treasury bonds	$1,085	20.89%
Agency bonds	166	3.20
Mortgage bonds	467	8.99
Corporate bonds	453	8.72
OTC stocks	331	6.37
AMEX stocks	105	2.02
NYSE stocks	2,586	49.92
	$5,193	100.00%

BRINSON PARTNERS
GLOBAL SECURITY
MARKET INDEX
(GSMI)

The Brinson Partner GSMI series contains both U.S. stocks and bonds and includes non-U.S. equities and nondollar bonds as well as an allocation to cash. The specific breakdown is as follows (as of November 1995):

	Percent
Equities	
U.S. large capitalization	35
U.S. small and mid-cap	15
Non-U.S.	17
Fixed Income	
U.S. domestic investment grade	18
International dollar bonds	2
Nondollar bonds	8
Cash	5
Total	100

Although related to the relative market values of these asset classes, the weights specified are not constantly adjusted. The construction of the GSMI used optimization techniques to identify the portfolio mix of available global asset classes that matches the risk level of a typical U.S. pension plan. The index is balanced to the policy weights monthly.

Because the GSMI contains both U.S. and international stocks and bonds, it is clearly the most diversified benchmark available with a weighting scheme that approaches market values. As such, it is closest to the theoretically specified "market portfolio of risky assets" referred to in the CAPM literature.[13]

---

[13] This GSMI series is used in a study that examines the effect of alternative benchmarks on the estimate of the security market line and estimates of individual stock betas. See Frank K. Reilly and Rashid A. Akhtar, "The Benchmark Error Problem with Global Capital Markets," *Journal of Portfolio Management* 22, no. 1 (Fall 1995). Brinson Partners has a Multiple Markets Index (MMI) that also contains venture capital and real estate. Because these assets are not actively traded, the value and rate of return estimates tend to be relatively stable, which reduces the standard deviation of the series.

COMPARISON OF INDEXES OVER TIME

This section discusses price movements in the different series for various monthly or annual intervals.

CORRELATIONS AMONG MONTHLY EQUITY PRICE CHANGES

Table 5.10 contains a matrix of the correlation coefficients of the monthly percentage of price changes for a set of U.S. and non-U.S. equity-market indexes during the 23-year period from 1972 to 1995 (288 observations).[14] Most of the correlation differences are attributable to sample differences, that is, differences in the firms listed on the alternative stock exchanges. Most of the major series—except the Nikkei Stock Average—are market-value-weighted indexes that include a large number of stocks. Therefore, the computational procedure is generally similar and the sample sizes are large or all-encompassing. Thus, the major difference between the indexes is that the stocks are from different segments of the U.S. stock market or from different countries.

There is a high positive correlation (0.99) between the alternative NYSE series (the S&P 500 and the NYSE composite). These indexes are also highly correlated with the Wilshire 5000 index that is value weighted, which means it is heavily impacted by the large NYSE stocks in the index.

In contrast, there are lower correlations between these NYSE series and the AMEX series (about 0.80) or the NASDAQ index (about 0.88). Further, the relationship between the Russell 2000 Index and the other U.S. series ranges from 0.80 to 0.97, which reflects the fact that the Russell 2000 series includes a sample of small cap stocks from all exchanges.

The correlations among the U.S. series and those from Canada, the United Kingdom, Germany, and Japan support the case for global investing. The relationships among the two TSE series were correlated about 0.87 even though the sample sizes, weightings, and computations differ. These within-country results attest to the importance of the basic sample. In contrast, the U.S.–Canada and U.S.–U.K. correlations, which averaged about 0.73, and the U.S.–Japan correlations, which were about 0.30, confirm the benefits of global diversification because such low correlations reduce the variance of a portfolio.

CORRELATIONS AMONG MONTHLY BOND INDEXES

The correlations among the monthly bond return series in Table 5.11 consider a variety of bond series, including investment-grade bonds, U.S. high-yield bonds, and government bond indexes for several major non-U.S. countries (GE–Germany, JA–Japan, and UK–the United Kingdom). The correlations among the U.S. investment grade bond series ranged from 0.90 to 0.99, confirming that although the *level* of interest rates differs due to the risk premium, the overriding factors that determine the rates of return for investment-grade bonds over time are *systematic* interest rate variables.

The correlations among investment-grade bonds and HY bonds indicate significantly lower correlations (0.40 to 0.54), which is due to the fact that HY bonds have definite equity characteristics.[15] Finally, the low and diverse relationships among U.S. investment-grade bonds and non-U.S. government bond series (0.17 to 0.35) reflect different interest rate movements and exchange rate effects (these non-U.S. government results are U.S. dollar returns). They also support global diversification.

---

[14] In earlier editions of the text, the correlations examined daily percentage price changes. The shift to monthly percentage price changes made it possible to consider a wider range of non-U.S. equity indexes. Notably, the monthly price change correlation results among U.S. indexes are very similar to the daily results.

[15] For a detailed analysis of this point, see Frank K. Reilly and David J. Wright, "High Yield Bonds and Segmentation in the Bond Market," mimeo (August 1995).

TABLE 5.10   CORRELATION COEFFICIENTS AMONG MONTHLY PERCENTAGE PRICE CHANGES IN ALTERNATIVE EQUITY MARKET INDICATOR SERIES: JANUARY 1972 (WHEN AVAILABLE) TO DECEMBER 1995

	S&P 500	NYSE	AMEX	Nasdaq Industr.	Wilshire 5000	Russell 2000[a]	Toronto SE 300	Tokyo SE	Nikkei	FAZ[b]	FT All-Share[b]	M-S World	FT/S&P World[c]
S&P 500	—												
NYSE	0.994	—											
AMEX	0.789	0.809	—										
Nasdaq Ind.	0.866	0.887	0.831	—									
Wilshire 5000	0.982	0.988	0.823	0.910	—								
Russell 2000	0.862	0.888	0.803	0.969	0.910	—							
Toronto 300	0.745	0.760	0.770	0.739	0.766	0.769	—						
Tokyo SE	0.293	0.299	0.246	0.248	0.283	0.264	0.275	—					
Nikkei	0.333	0.340	0.278	0.299	0.324	0.340	0.292	0.870	—				
FAZ	0.506	0.511	0.382	0.398	0.496	0.465	0.442	0.283	0.321	—			
FT All-Share	0.723	0.729	0.590	0.627	0.706	0.664	0.631	0.277	0.392	0.514	—		
M S World	0.815	0.818	0.660	0.708	0.805	0.684	0.717	0.589	0.627	0.504	0.657	—	
FT/S&P World	0.710	0.714	0.525	0.602	0.679	0.608	0.654	0.694	0.760	0.497	0.643	0.998	—

[a] Russell 2000 series starts in 1979.
[b] FAZ and FT All-Share series start in 1983.
[c] FT/S&P World Index series starts in 1986.

| | | TABLE 5.11 | | **CORRELATIONS AMONG MONTHLY BOND RETURNS FOR U.S. INVESTMENT-GRADE BONDS, U.S. HIGH-YIELD BONDS, AND NON-U.S. GOVERNMENT BONDS: 1985–1995 (132 OBSERVATIONS)** | | | | | |

	LBGC	LBG	LBC	LBM	LBA	MLHYM	SBGE	SBJA	SBUK
LBGC	—								
LBG	0.997	—							
LBC	0.975	0.955	—						
LBM	0.916	0.901	0.926	—					
LBA	0.995	0.990	0.977	0.950	—				
MLHYM	0.451	0.411	0.547	0.447	0.459	—			
SBGE	0.308	0.323	0.258	0.299	0.309	−0.035	—		
SBJA	0.205	0.221	0.156	0.159	0.197	0.005	0.699	—	
SBUK	0.272	0.290	0.215	0.228	0.267	−0.023	0.666	0.568	—

Note: The symbols are as follows: LB—Lehman Brothers; GC—Government/Corporate; G—Government; C—Corporate; M—Mortgage; A—Aggregate; ML—Merrill Lynch; HYM—High-Yield Master; SB—Salomon Brothers; GE—Germany; JA—Japan; UK—United Kingdom.

Source: Modified and updated from Frank K. Reilly, Wenchi Kao, and David J. Wright, "Alternative Bond Market Indexes," *Financial Analysts Journal* 48, no. 3 (May–June 1992); Frank K. Reilly and David J. Wright, "High-Yield Bonds and Segmentation in the Bond Market," mimeo (August 1995); and Frank K. Reilly and David J. Wright, "Global Bond Markets: An Analysis of Alternative Benchmarks and Risk–Return Performance," mimeo (March 1995).

ANNUAL STOCK PRICE CHANGES

The annual percentage of price changes for the major stock indexes is contained in Table 5.12. One would expect differences among the price changes and measures of risk for the various series due to the different samples. For example, the NYSE series should have lower rates of return and risk measures than the AMEX and OTC series. The results generally confirm these expectations. For example, the Russell 2000 reflects the results for the small capitalization segment of the U.S. stock market. This series, which began in 1979, shows higher returns than the large-cap NYSE series during most individual years.

Regarding non-U.S. results, the Canadian results on the Toronto Exchange had higher average returns than the NYSE, and lower risk than the AMEX or the OTC. The United Kingdom (i.e., the FT All-Share) had higher returns than the U.S. indexes, but much larger variability, while Germany (the FAZ) had comparable returns to the U.S., but larger volatility. Finally, the Japanese markets experienced higher returns and much greater volatility than the U.S. markets. Remember, these non-U.S. stock results reflect the domestic price changes and do not consider the exchange-rate effect.

These results for the Japanese market were significantly impacted by poor results during 1990 to 1992. Because the Japanese stock market had relatively low correlation with alternative U.S. stock-market indexes (Table 5.10), it indicates that Japan would have been a prime source of diversification benefits even with the higher volatility.

ANNUAL BOND RATES OF RETURN

Table 5.13 shows the annual total rates of return for the Lehman Brothers bond-market indexes.[16] You cannot directly compare the bond and stock results because the bond results are *total* rates of return versus annual percentage price change results for stocks (most of the stock series do not report dividend data).

[16] Because of the high correlations among the monthly rates of return as shown in Table 5.11, the results for various bond-market segments (government, corporate, mortgages) are very similar regardless of the source (Lehman Brothers, Merrill Lynch, Salomon Brothers, Ryan). Therefore, only the Lehman Brothers results are presented in Table 5.13.

TABLE 5-12 **ANNUAL PERCENTAGE RATES OF RETURN FOR STOCK PRICE INDICATOR SERIES: 1972–1995**

	DJIA	S&P 400	S&P 500	AMEX Value Index	NASDAQ Composite	Russell 2000[1]	Wilshire 5000	Toronto SE 300 Composite	FT All-Share	FAZ	Nikkei	Tokyo SE Index	MS World
1972	14.58	16.10	15.63	10.33	17.18	n/a	14.86	27.38	12.11	15.20	91.91	101.40	19.95
1973	−16.58	−17.38	−17.37	−30.00	−31.06	n/a	−20.96	0.27	−31.36	−27.35	−17.30	−23.71	−17.08
1974	−27.57	−29.93	−29.72	−33.22	−35.11	n/a	−31.49	−25.93	−54.34	1.40	−11.37	−9.01	−27.83
1975	38.44	31.92	31.55	38.40	29.76	n/a	32.83	18.48	136.33	40.18	19.18	15.99	28.92
1976	17.86	18.42	19.15	31.58	26.10	n/a	21.69	11.02	−3.87	−9.63	14.51	18.69	10.31
1977	−17.27	−12.53	−11.50	16.43	7.33	n/a	−6.98	10.71	41.18	9.27	−2.51	−5.16	−2.46
1978	−3.15	2.39	1.06	17.73	12.31	n/a	3.96	29.72	2.70	6.00	23.33	23.48	12.68
1979	4.19	12.88	12.31	64.10	28.11	43.09	19.28	44.77	4.30	−13.62	9.46	2.24	7.21
1980	14.93	27.62	25.77	41.25	33.88	38.58	27.61	30.13	27.07	0.25	3.33	7.50	21.45
1981	−9.23	−11.22	−9.73	−8.13	−3.21	2.03	−8.43	−10.25	7.24	−0.67	7.95	15.42	−7.92
1982	19.60	14.95	14.76	6.23	18.67	24.95	12.86	5.54	22.07	14.43	4.36	4.10	5.82
1983	20.27	18.16	17.27	30.95	19.87	29.13	18.74	35.49	23.10	41.59	23.42	23.26	18.56
1984	−4.33	−0.40	0.81	−9.07	−11.67	−7.30	−1.25	−2.39	26.02	6.43	16.66	24.81	1.77
1985	27.66	25.86	26.33	20.50	31.86	31.05	27.18	25.07	15.18	70.25	13.61	14.89	37.02
1986	22.58	17.30	16.87	7.30	7.51	5.68	12.48	8.95	22.34	4.23	42.61	48.31	39.11
1987	2.26	3.90	0.06	−1.42	−5.40	−8.77	1.49	5.88	4.16	−37.14	21.35	10.89	14.34
1988	11.85	12.38	12.40	17.54	15.41	24.89	13.29	11.08	6.48	29.32	42.54	36.57	21.19
1989	26.96	25.60	27.25	23.53	20.44	16.24	26.69	21.37	30.01	34.75	28.67	22.25	14.75
1990	−4.34	−5.07	−6.56	−18.49	−0.98	−19.51	−10.61	−14.80	−14.37	−18.61	−38.72	−39.83	−18.65
1991	20.32	27.18	26.31	28.22	57.54	46.05	30.28	12.02	15.13	6.18	−3.63	−1.10	16.00
1992	4.17	9.53	4.46	6.06	15.45	18.41	6.15	−1.43	14.81	−5.83	−28.60	−25.95	−7.14
1993	14.94	11.72	8.09	15.58	16.32	18.91	9.30	32.55	23.36	40.57	2.21	10.73	20.39
1994	2.14	−5.54	−1.54	−9.11	−3.20	−1.82	−2.52	−0.18	−9.55	−7.45	13.24	5.78	3.34
1995	33.45	31.71	34.11	26.41	39.91	26.20	33.40	11.86	21.75	6.99	0.73	1.19	18.71
Arithmetic Mean	8.91	9.40	9.07	12.20	12.79	16.93	9.58	11.97	14.24	8.61	11.54	11.78	9.61
Standard Deviation	16.85	16.53	16.47	22.92	21.20	19.11	17.25	17.00	33.28	24.46	25.89	27.32	16.85
Geometric Mean	7.58	8.09	7.79	9.81	10.67	15.38	8.16	10.68	9.94	6.02	8.76	8.78	8.28

[1] Russell 2000 series started in 1979.

TABLE 5.13	**ANNUAL PERCENTAGE RATES OF RETURN: ARITHMETIC AND GEOMETRIC MEAN ANNUAL RATES OF RETURN AND STANDARD DEVIATION OF ANNUAL RATES OF RETURN: 1976–1995**

LEHMAN BROTHERS

	Government/ Corporate	Government	Corporate	Mortgage- Backed	Yankee Bond	Aggregate Bond
1976	15.59	12.35	19.34	16.31	15.08	15.60
1977	2.98	2.81	3.16	1.90	5.23	3.03
1978	1.19	1.80	0.35	2.41	2.91	1.40
1979	2.30	5.40	−2.11	0.13	−0.43	1.93
1980	3.06	5.19	−2.29	0.65	1.93	2.70
1981	7.26	9.36	2.95	0.07	3.48	6.25
1982	31.09	27.74	39.21	43.04	35.82	32.62
1983	8.00	7.39	9.27	10.13	9.43	8.35
1984	15.02	14.50	16.63	15.79	16.38	15.15
1985	21.30	20.43	24.06	25.21	25.99	22.11
1986	15.62	15.31	16.53	13.43	16.27	15.26
1987	2.29	2.20	2.56	4.28	1.89	2.76
1988	7.58	7.03	9.22	8.72	8.81	7.89
1989	14.24	14.23	14.09	15.35	15.42	14.53
1990	8.28	8.72	7.05	10.72	7.05	8.96
1991	16.30	15.32	18.51	15.72	18.68	16.00
1992	7.58	7.23	8.69	6.96	7.90	7.40
1993	11.03	10.66	12.16	6.84	13.44	9.75
1994	−3.51	−3.37	−3.93	−1.61	−4.65	−2.92
1995	19.24	18.33	22.24	16.80	24.96	18.48
Arithmetic Mean	10.32	10.13	10.89	10.64	11.28	10.36
Standard Deviation	8.29	7.33	10.76	10.52	10.05	8.46
Geometric Mean	10.03	10.00	10.41	10.20	10.86	10.06

Source: Adapted from Frank K. Reilly, G. Wenchi Kao, and David J. Wright, "Alternative Bond Market Indexes," *Financial Analysts Journal* 48, no. 3 (May–June 1992). Reprinted by permission of the *Financial Analysts Journal*.

The major comparison for the bond series should be among the average rate of return and the risk measures, because although the monthly rates of return are correlated, we would expect a difference in the level of return due to the differential risk premiums. The results generally confirm our expectations (i.e., there typically are lower returns and risk measures for the government series followed by higher returns and risk for corporate bonds and the highest returns and risk for the mortgage series).

Summary

• Given the several uses of security-market indicator series, you should know how they are constructed and the differences among them. If you want to use one of the many series to learn how the "market" is doing, you should be aware of what market you are dealing with so you can select the appropriate index. As an example, are you only interested in the NYSE or do you also want to consider the AMEX and the OTC? Beyond the U.S. market, are you interested in Japanese or U.K. stocks, or do you want to examine the total world market?[17]

[17] For a readable discussion on this topic, see Anne Merjos, "How's the Market Doing?" *Barron's*, August 20, 1990, 18–20, 27, 28. There will be an extensive discussion of the purpose and construction of benchmarks in Chapter 27, where we consider the evaluation of portfolio performance.

- Indexes are also used as benchmarks to evaluate portfolio performance. In this case, you must be sure the index (benchmark) is consistent with your investing universe. If you are investing world-wide, you should not judge your performance relative to the DJIA, which is limited to 30 U.S. blue-chip stocks. For a bond portfolio, the index should match your investment philosophy. Finally, if your portfolio contains both stocks and bonds, you must evaluate your performance against an appropriate combination of indexes.
- Whenever you invest, you examine numerous market indexes to tell you what has happened and how successful you have been. The selection of the appropriate indexes for information or evaluation will depend on how knowledgeable you are regarding the various series. The purpose of this chapter is to help you understand what to look for and how to make the right decision.

Questions

1. Discuss briefly several uses of security-market indicator series.
2. What major factors must be considered when constructing a market index? Put another way, what characteristics differentiate indexes?
3. Explain how a market indicator series is price weighted. In such a case, would you expect a $100 stock to be more important than a $25 stock? Why?
4. Explain how to compute a value-weighted series.
5. Explain how a price-weighted series and a value-weighted series adjust for stock splits.
6. Describe an unweighted price-indicator series and describe how you would construct such a series. Assume a 20 percent price change in GM ($40/share; 50 million shares outstanding) and Coors Brewing ($25/share and 15 million shares outstanding). Explain which stock's change will have the greater impact on this index.
7. If you correlated percentage changes in the Wilshire 5000 equity index with percentage changes in the NYSE composite, the AMEX index, and the NASDAQ composite index, would you expect a difference in the correlations? Why or why not?
8. There are high correlations among the monthly percentage price changes for the alternative NYSE indexes. Discuss the reason for this similarity: is it size of sample, source of sample, or method of computation?
9. Compare stock price indicator series for the three U.S. equity-market segments (NYSE, AMEX, OTC) for the period 1972 to 1995. Discuss whether the results in terms of average annual price change and risk (variability of price changes) were consistent with economic theory.
10. Discuss the relationship (correlations) between the two stock price indexes for the Tokyo Stock Exchange (TSE). Examine the correlations among the TSE series and two NYSE series. Explain why these relationships differ.
11. You learn that the Wilshire 5000 market value-weighted series increased by 16 percent during a specified period, whereas a Wilshire 5000 equal-weighted series increased by 23 percent during the same period. Discuss what this difference in results implies.
12. Why is it contended that bond-market indexes are more difficult to construct and maintain than stock-market index series?
13. The Wilshire 5000 market value-weighted index increased by 5 percent, whereas the Merrill Lynch–Wilshire Capital Markets Index increased by 15 percent during the same period. What does this difference in results imply?
14. The Russell 1000 increased by 8 percent during the past year, whereas the Russell 2000 increased by 15 percent. Discuss the implication of these results.
15. Based on what you know about the *Financial Times* (FT) World Index, the Morgan Stanley Capital International World Index, and the Dow Jones World Stock Index, what level of correlation would you expect among monthly rates of return? Discuss the reasons for your answer based on the factors that affect indexes.

Problems   1. You are given the following information regarding prices for a sample of stocks:

| | | PRICE | |
Stock	Number of Shares	T	T + 1
A	1,000,000	60	80
B	10,000,000	20	35
C	30,000,000	18	25

    a. Construct a *price-weighted* series for these three stocks, and compute the percentage change in the series for the period from T to T + 1.

    b. Construct a *value-weighted* series for these three stocks, and compute the percentage change in the series for the period from T to T + 1.

    c. Briefly discuss the difference in the results for the two series.

2. a. Given the data in Problem 1, construct an equal-weighted series by assuming $1,000 is invested in each stock. What is the percentage change in wealth for this portfolio?

    b. Compute the percentage of price change for each of the stocks in Problem 1. Compute the arithmetic average of these percentage changes. Discuss how this answer compares to the answer in 2a.

    c. Compute the geometric average of the percentage changes in 2b. Discuss how this result compares to the answer in 2b.

3. For the last five trading days, on the basis of figures in *The Wall Street Journal,* compute the daily percentage price changes for the following stock indexes:

    a. DJIA

    b. S&P 400

    c. AMEX Market Value Series

    d. NASDAQ Industrial Index

    e. FT-100 Share Index

    f. Nikkei Stock Price Average

Discuss the difference in results for a and b, a and c, a and d, a and e, a and f, e and f. What do these differences imply regarding diversifying within the United States versus diversifying between countries?

4.

| | PRICE | | | SHARES | | |
Company	A	B	C	A	B	C
Day 1	12	23	52	500	350	250
Day 2	10	22	55	500	350	250
Day 3	14	46	52	500	175[a]	250
Day 4	13	47	25	500	175	500[b]
Day 5	12	45	26	500	175	500

[a]Split at close of Day 2
[b]Split at close of Day 3

    a. Calculate a Dow Jones Industrial Average for Days 1 through 5.

    b. What effects have the splits had in determining the next day's index? (Hint: Think of the relative weighting of each stock.)

    c. From a copy of *The Wall Street Journal,* find the divisor that is currently being used in calculating the DJIA. (Normally this value can be found on the inside back pages.)

5. Utilizing the price and volume data in Problem 4,
   a. Calculate a Standard & Poor's Index for Days 1 through 5 using a beginning index value of 10.
   b. Identify what effects the splits had in determining the next day's index. (Hint: Think of the relative weighting of each stock.)

6. Using Table 5.12, calculate the average annual percentage change for five of the indexes for the 10-year period 1986 to 1995, using (a) the arithmetic mean and (b) the geometric mean. Discuss what the differences in these two mean values tell you about the relative variability of these indexes.

7. Based on the following stock price and shares outstanding information, compute the beginning and ending values for a price-weighted index and a market-value-weighted index.

| | **DECEMBER 31, 1995** | | **DECEMBER 31, 1996** | |
	Price	Shares Outstanding	Price	Shares Outstanding
Stock K	20	100,000,000	32	100,000,000
Stock M	80	2,000,000	45	4,000,000[a]
Stock R	40	25,000,000	42	25,000,000

[a]Stock split 2-for-1 during the year

   a. Compute the percent change in the value of each index.
   b. Explain the difference in results between the two indexes.
   c. Compute the results for an unweighted index and discuss why these results differ from others.

8. a. Assume a base index value of 100 at the beginning of 1986. Using the returns in Table 5.1, what would be your ending index value if you owned the stocks in the Nikkei Average through 1995?
   b. Given this index value, compute the compound annual rate of return (geometric mean value) experienced by a Japanese investor during this 10-year period.
   c. In addition to knowing this domestic rate of return, you are told that the exchange rate at the beginning of 1986 was ¥250 to the dollar and it was ¥105 to the dollar at the end of 1995. Compute the compound return in U.S. dollars.

References

Fisher, Lawrence, and James H. Lorie. *A Half Century of Returns on Stocks and Bonds.* Chicago: University of Chicago Graduate School of Business, 1977.

Ibbotson Associates. *Stocks, Bonds, Bills and Inflation.* Chicago: Ibbotson Associates, annual.

Lorie, James H., Peter Dodd, and Mary Hamilton Kimpton. *The Stock Market: Theories and Evidence.* 2d ed. Homewood, IL: Richard D. Irwin, 1985.

Reilly, Frank K. and David J. Wright, "Bond Market Indexes," in *Handbook of Fixed Income Securities,* 5th ed., edited by Frank J. Fabozzi. Burr Ridge, IL: Irwin Professional Publishing, 1997.

Chapter 5
APPENDIX   FOREIGN STOCK-MARKET INDEXES

Index Name	Number of Stocks	Weights of Stocks	Calculation Method	History of Index
ATX-index (Vienna)	All stocks listed on the exchange	Market capitalization	Value weighted	Base year 1967, 1991 began including all stocks (Value = 100)
Swiss Market Index	18 stocks	Market capitalization	Value weighted	Base year 1988, stocks selected from the Basle, Geneva, and Zurich Exchanges (Value = 1500)
Stockholm General Index	All stocks (voting) listed on exchange	Market capitalization	Value weighted	Base year 1979, continuously updated (Value = 100)
Copenhagen Stock Exchange Share Price Index	All stocks traded	Market capitalization	Value weighted	Share price is based on average price of the day
Oslo SE Composite Index (Sweden)	25 companies			Base year 1972 (Value = 100)
Johannesburg Stock Exchange Actuaries Index	146 companies	Market capitalization	Value weighted	Base year 1959 (Value = 100)
Mexican Market Index	Variable number, based on capitalization and liquidity		Value weighted (adjustment for value of paid-out dividends)	Base year 1978, high dollar returns in recent years
Milan Stock Exchange MIB	Variable number, based on capitalization and liquidity		Weighted arithmetic average	Change base at beginning of each year (Value = 1000)
Belgium BEL-20 Stock Index	20 companies	Market capitalization	Value weighted	Base year 1991 (Value = 1000)
Madrid General Stock Index	92 stocks	Market capitalization	Value weighted	Change base at beginning of each year
Hang Seng Index (Hong Kong)	33 companies	Market capitalization	Value weighted	Started in 1969, accounts for 75 percent of total market
FT-Actuaries World Indexes	2,212 stocks	Market capitalization	Value weighted	Base year 1986
FT-SE 100 Index (London)	100 companies	Market capitalization	Value weighted	Base year 1983 (Value = 1000)
CAC General Share Index (French)	212 companies	Market capitalization	Value weighted	Base year 1981 (Value = 100)
Morgan Stanley World Index	1,482 stocks	Market capitalization	Value weighted	Base year 1970 (Value = 100)
Singapore Straits Times Industrial Index	30 stocks	Unweighted		
German Stock Market Index (DAX)	30 companies (Blue Chips)	Market capitalization	Value weighted	Base year 1987 (Value = 1000)
Frankfurter Allgemeine Zeitung Index (FAZ) (German)	100 companies (Blue Chips)	Market capitalization	Value weighted	Base year 1958 (Value = 100)
Australian Stock Exchange Share Price Indices	250 stocks (92 percent) of all shares listed	Market capitalization	Price weighted	Introduced in 1979
Dublin ISEQ Index	71 stocks (54 official, 17 unlisted). All stocks traded	Market capitalization	Value weighted	Base year 1988 (Value = 1000)
HEX Index (Helsinki)	Varies with different share price indexes	Market capitalization	Value weighted	Base changes every day
Jakarta Stock Exchange	All listed shares (148 currently)	Market capitalization	Value weighted	Base year 1982 (Value = 100)
Taiwan Stock Exchange Index	All ordinary stocks (listed for at least a month)	Market capitalization	Value weighted	Base year 1966 (Value = 100)
TSE 300 Composite Index (Toronto)	300 stocks (comprised of 14 subindexes)	Market capitalization (adjusted for major shareholders)	Value weighted	Base year 1975 (Value = 1000)
KOSPI (Korean Composite Stock Price Index)	All common stocks listed on exchange	Market capitalization (adjusted for major shareholders)	Value weighted	Base year 1980 (Value = 100)

Chapter 6

Sources of Information on Global Investments

This chapter answers the following questions:

- What are the major sources of information and data for aggregate economic analysis in the United States?
- What are the major sources for non-U.S. economic data, including the principal bibliographies?
- What are the major sources of information and data for those interested in aggregate security market analysis? Which sources are available annually, weekly, and daily?
- What investment firms provide comments and recommendations for global markets?
- What are the major sources of information and data needed for industry analysis?
- What are the major sources of information and data available for individual firm stock and bond analysis?
- What are the major investment magazines, and which ones are available monthly, bi-weekly, and weekly?
- What are some of the major academic journals that publish theoretical and empirical studies related to investments?
- What are the major computerized data sources?
- What are the names and addresses for the major sources of investment information?

In this chapter, we will describe some of the major sources of information needed for global investment analysis. Relevant information is both important and difficult to obtain especially in the current global capital market. The initial discussion considers sources of information related to aggregate economic analysis including data from the government, various bank publications, as well as sources of non-U.S. economic data. The second section considers sources of data for aggregate security market analysis. Again, we will review government publications, commercial publications, and brokerage firm reports. The third section considers sources of information for industry analysis, which generally receives significantly less attention than either the aggregate market or individual securities. As we will discuss, the major sources are industry publications, industry magazines, and information provided through industry trade associations. The fourth section on individual stock analysis considers company-generated information, numerous commercial publications provided to individual and institutional investors, as well as brokerage firm reports. Finally, there are a growing number of investment magazines. The fifth section discusses sources of information for bond investors and again considers what is provided in government publications as well as numerous commercial publications. In many instances, bond information is included in publications with stock data.

Beyond the analysis of individual stocks and bonds, a point made throughout this textbook is that many investors will implement their investment program using mutual funds. Therefore, there is a section dealing with sources of information on funds that considers basic descriptive information, but also sources of portfolio performance evaluation. Notably, this is an area of growing interest and commercial publications are responding with new services and magazines.

Section six shifts from commercial publications and investment magazines for the typical investor to a discussion of academic journals that contain more theoretical and empirical studies expected to have a long-run impact on the investment process. We conclude the chapter with a discussion of a growing list of computerized data sources available to individuals and institutions. This includes very large databases typically available on computer tapes to online databases available through your individual PC.

While it is certainly not necessary to become completely familiar with each of the items mentioned in this chapter, it is important to become aware of what is available so that when you need specific data or information, you will know where to look for the material.

AGGREGATE ECONOMIC ANALYSIS

This section describes the data used to estimate overall economic changes for the United States and other major countries, as contrasted to data regarding the aggregate securities markets (stocks, bonds, etc.).

U.S. Government Sources

It should come as no surprise that the main source of information on the U.S. economy is the federal government, which issues a variety of publications on the topic.

Federal Reserve Bulletin is a monthly publication issued by the Board of Governors of the Federal Reserve System. It is the primary source for almost all monetary data, including monetary aggregates, factors affecting member bank reserves, member bank reserve requirements, Federal Reserve open market transactions, and loans and investments of all commercial banks. In addition, the publication contains figures on financial markets, interest rates, and some stock-market statistics; data for corporate finance, including profits, assets, and liabilities of corporations; extensive nonfinancial statistics on output, the labor force, and the GDP; and a major section on international finance.

Survey of Current Business is a monthly publication issued by the U.S. Department of Commerce that gives details on national income and production figures. It is probably the best source for current, detailed information on all segments of the GDP and national income and contains industrial production data for numerous segments of the economy. The *Survey* is an excellent secondary source for labor statistics (employment and wages), interest rates, and statistics on foreign economic development. It also contains data regarding the leading, coincident, and lagging economic series published by the Department of Commerce.[1] These series are considered important by those who attempt to project peaks and troughs in the business cycle.

Economic Indicators—a monthly publication prepared for the Joint Economic Committee by the Council of Economic Advisers—contains monthly and annual data on output, income, spending, employment, production, prices, money and credit, federal finance, and international economies.

The Quarterly Financial Report (QFR) is prepared by the Federal Trade Commission and contains aggregate statistics on the financial position of U.S. corporations. Based on an extensive quarterly sample survey, the *QFR* presents estimated statements of income and retained earnings, balance sheets, and related financial and operating ratios for all manufacturing corporations. The publication also includes data on mining and trade corporations. The statistical data are classified by industry and, within the manufacturing group, by size.

---

[1] These series are discussed more extensively in Chapter 14 where they are related to stock-market movements.

Business Statistics is a biennial supplement to the *Survey of Current Business* that contains extensive historical data for about 2,500 series contained in the survey. The historical section contains monthly data for the past 4 or 5 years, quarterly data for the previous 10 years, and annual data back to 1947 if available. A notable feature is a section of explanatory notes for each series that describes the series and indicates the original source for the data.

Historical Chart Book is an annual supplement to the *Federal Reserve Bulletin* that includes long-range financial and business series. There is an excellent section on the various series that indicates the source of the data.

Economic Report of the President is published each January wherein the president transmits to Congress what has transpired during the past year, what is the current environment, and what he considers to be the major economic problems that will face the country during the coming year. This publication also contains an extensive document, "The Annual Report of the Council of Economic Advisers," which includes a detailed discussion of developments in the domestic and international economies gathered by the council (the group that advises the president on economic policy). An appendix contains statistical tables relating to income, employment, and production. The tables typically provide annual data from the 1940s, and in some instances from 1929.

Statistical Abstract of the United States, published annually since 1878, is the standard summary of statistics on the social, political, and economic organization of the United States. Prepared by the Bureau of the Census, it is designed to serve as a convenient statistical reference and as a guide to other statistical publications and sources. This large volume includes data from many statistical publications, both government and private.

BANK PUBLICATIONS   In addition to government material, much data on the economy are published by various banks. These generally appear monthly, are free of charge, and can be categorized as publications of the Federal Reserve Banks or commercial banks.

PUBLICATIONS OF FEDERAL RESERVE BANKS   The Federal Reserve System is divided into 12 Federal Reserve Districts with a major Federal Reserve Bank in each location as follows:[2]

1. Boston	7. Chicago
2. New York	8. St. Louis
3. Philadelphia	9. Minneapolis
4. Cleveland	10. Denver
5. Richmond	11. Dallas
6. Atlanta	12. San Francisco

Each of the Federal Reserve district banks has a research department that issues periodic reports. Although the various bank publications differ, monthly reviews—which are available to interested parties—are published by all district banks. These reviews typically contain one or several articles as well as regional economic statistics. A major exception is the St. Louis Federal Reserve Bank, which publishes statistical releases weekly, monthly, and quarterly that contain extensive national and international data in addition to its monthly review.[3]

---

[2] Specific addresses for each of the district banks and names of major personnel are contained in the *Federal Reserve Bulletin,* published monthly by the Federal Reserve Board.

[3] An individual can request to be put on the mailing list for these publications by writing to Federal Reserve Bank of St. Louis, P.O. Box 442, St. Louis, MO 63166. Most of them are free.

PUBLICATIONS OF COMMERCIAL BANKS   A number of large banks prepare monthly letters available to interested individuals. These letters generally include commentary on the current and future outlook of the economy and specific industries or segments of the economy.

Non-U.S. Economic Data

In addition to data on the U.S. economy, data on other countries where you might consider investing are also important to acquire. Some of the available sources follow.[4]

The Economic Intelligence Unit (EIU) publishes 83 separate quarterly reviews and an annual supplement covering the economic and business conditions and outlook for 160 countries. For each country, the reviews consider the economy, trade and finance, trends in investment and consumer spending, along with comments on its political environment. Tables contain data on economic activity and foreign trade.

The EIU also publishes *European Trends,* which discusses the aggregate economic environment for the overall European community and the world.

The Organization for Economic Cooperation and Development (OECD) publishes semiannual surveys showing recent trends and policies and assesses short-term prospects for each country. An annual volume, *Historical Statistics,* contains annual percent change data for the most recent 20 years.

The Economist prepares country reports on more than 100 countries around the world that contain extensive economic and demographic statistics. Of greater importance is a detailed discussion that critically analyzes the current economic and political environment in the country and considers the future outlook. It is possible to subscribe to reports for a selected list of countries or for all of them. The reports are updated twice a year.

Worldwide Economic Indicators is an annual book published by the Business International Corporation that contains data for 131 countries on population, GDP by activity, wages and prices, foreign trade, and a number of specific items for the most recent 4 years.

Demographic Yearbook, published by the United Nations, consists of statistics on population, births, deaths, life expectancy, marriages, and divorces for approximately 240 countries.

International Marketing Data and Statistics, published by Euromonitor Publications Inc. of London, is an annual guide that contains data for 132 non-European countries covering population, employment, production, trade, the economy, and other economic data.

United Nations Statistical Yearbook is a reference book that contains extensive economic statistics on all UN countries (population, construction, industrial production, etc.).

Eurostatistics, a monthly publication by the *Statistical Office of the European Communities (Luxembourg),* contains statistics for short-term economic analysis in 10 European community countries and the United States. There are generally data for 6 years covering industrial production, employment and unemployment, external trade, prices, wages, and finance.

U.S. International Trade Administration, International Economic Indicators, is a quarterly publication of the U.S. Government Printing Office that includes comparative economic indicators and trends in the United States and its seven principal industrial competitors: France, Germany, Italy, The Netherlands, United Kingdom, Japan, and Canada. The data are organized in five parts: general indicators, trade indicators, price indicators, finance indicators, and labor indicators. The sources for the data are contained at the back of the booklet.

---

[4]This discussion draws heavily from P. M. Daniells, *Business Information Sources,* 2nd ed. (Berkeley, CA: University of California Press, 1986).

International Financial Statistics, a monthly publication (with a yearbook issue) of the International Monetary Fund, is an essential source of current financial statistics such as exchange rates, fund position, international liquidity, money and banking statistics, interest rates (including LIBOR), prices, and production.[5]

International Monetary Fund, Balance of Payments Yearbook is a two-part publication. The first part contains detailed balance-of-payments figures for over 110 countries, and the second part contains world totals for balance-of-payments components and aggregates.

United Nations, Yearbook of International Trade Statistics is an annual report on import statistics over a 4-year period for each of 166 countries. The commodity figures for each country are given by commodity code.

United Nations Yearbook of National Accounts Statistics is a comprehensive source of national account data that contains detailed statistics for 155 countries on domestic product and consumption expenditures, national income, and disposable income for a 12-year period.

Some individual countries publish national income studies with detailed breakdowns as well as annual statistical reports that contain the more important statistics and include bibliographical sources for the tables. Brazil, Great Britain, Japan, and Switzerland are a few examples.

Similar to the United States, major banks in various countries publish bulletins or letters that contain statistical reviews for individual countries. Examples include:

- *Bank of Canada Review* (monthly)
- *Bank of England* (quarterly)
- *Bank of Japan* (monthly)
- *National Bank of Belgium* (monthly)
- *Deutsche Bundesbank* (monthly)

In addition to these specific sources of data, you should be aware of the following bibliographies:

- G.R. Dicks, ed. *Sources of World Financial and Banking Information.* Westport, CT: Greenwood Press, 1981. A descriptive list of nearly 5,000 financial and banking sources arranged by country.
- David Hoopes, ed. *Global Guide to International Business.* New York: File Publications, 1983. A descriptive list of source information about individual countries.
- *Index of International Statistics.* Washington, DC: Congressional Information Service. A monthly descriptive guide and index to statistical publications by the world's major international government organizations.

AGGREGATE SECURITY-MARKET ANALYSIS

Several government publications provide useful data on the stock and bond markets, but the bulk of detailed information is provided by private firms. Some of the government publications discussed earlier (e.g., *Federal Reserve Bulletin* and *Survey of Current Business*) contain financial market data such as interest rates and stock prices.

GOVERNMENT PUBLICATIONS

The main source of data in this area is the Securities and Exchange Commission (SEC)—the federal agency that regulates the operation of the securities markets and collects data in this regard. The *Annual Report of the SEC* is published for the fiscal year ending in June. It

---

[5] LIBOR is an acronym for London Interbank Borrowing Rate. It is used as a base rate for many international financial transactions.

contains a detailed discussion of important developments during the year and comments on the SEC's disclosure system and regulation of the securities markets. Finally, it includes a statistics section containing historical data on many security-market series.

COMMERCIAL
PUBLICATIONS

Considering the numerous advisory services in existence, a section dealing with their publications could become voluminous. Therefore, our intent is to list and discuss only *major* services and allow you to develop your own list of other available sources. An excellent source of advertisements for these services is *Barron's.* A publication that lists and briefly describes these publications is the *Fortune Investment Information Directory.*[6] The order of our presentation will be by frequency of publication: annual, weekly, daily.

ANNUAL SECURITY-MARKET PUBLICATIONS   *New York Stock Exchange Fact Book* is an annual publication of the New York Stock Exchange. The book is an outstanding source of current and historical data on stock and bond activity on the NYSE.

AMEX Fact Book is a comparable data book for the American Stock Exchange. It is published annually and contains pertinent information on the exchange, its membership, administration, and trading activities in stocks, bonds, and derivative products.

NASDAQ Fact Book is an annual data book for the OTC market. It contains extensive data on trading volume and information related to the stocks on the NASDAQ system and discusses past growth and future plans for the NASDAQ market system.

Tokyo Stock Exchange Fact Book is an annual publication in English, containing information on the TSE. It is similar to the fact books prepared by U.S. institutions and contains extensive data related to stocks and bond and options trading on the exchange. Copies are available through the New York office of the TSE.

Emerging Stock Markets Factbook is an annual publication of the International Finance Corporation (IFC). The *Factbook* contains five sections:

1. A background on the IFC and its emerging markets database, which contains statistics on stock markets in developing countries.
2. Extensive statistical data related to both developed and developing countries.
3. Stock indexes for 52 developing countries. There is a description of the index methodology and an analysis of performance for many of the countries using the IFC index and a commonly used local stock index.
4. A statistical analysis of 33 emerging markets.
5. A directory of pertinent information for more than 50 stock exchanges in developing countries.

American Banker Yearbook is an annual publication by the publisher of *American Banker,* a daily newspaper serving the financial services industry (this newspaper is described later in this section). The *Yearbook* contains a review of annual events that affect the banking industry plus an extensive statistical section that includes operating and size data on commercial banks, finance companies, mortgage banking, thrifts, and also international banks (the top 100 banks in the world).

The Bond Buyer Yearbook is an annual publication by the publisher of *The Bond Buyer,* a daily newspaper related to the fixed-income market (this newspaper is described later in this section). In addition to a review of the major events of the year, there are extensive

---

[6] This directory contains extensive listings of print material (newspapers, magazines), audiovisual, electronic (software, databases), and interpersonal (seminars). It is published by the Dushkin Publishing Group, Inc., Sluice Dock, Guilford, CT 06437.

statistics related to the municipal bond market such as the volume of long- and short-term issues in total by purpose and by states, the interest rates on alternative issues, the top underwriter, and the top counseling firms. This is the major source of data related to the tax-exempt bond market.

The Business One Irwin Investor's Handbook is an annual publication that covers the complete DJIA results for each year along with earnings and dividends for the series since 1939. It also contains data on other U.S. stock indexes. A recent important addition is data for a number of individual foreign stocks and historical data for a number of non-U.S. stock indexes (e.g., Japan, Hong Kong, Singapore, Australia, Philippines, Thailand). Individual reports on common and preferred stocks and bonds listed on the NYSE and AMEX, including high and low prices, volume, dividends, and the year's most active stocks, are also included.[7]

Business and Investment Almanac, published annually by Irwin Professional Publishing, contains a wide range of information on the economy, various industries, U.S. and foreign securities markets, and individual investments (stocks, bonds, options, futures, real estate, diamonds, and other collectibles). It concludes with a helpful business and information directory.

The Wall Street Waltz is a book that contains 90 charts dealing with financial cycles and trends of historical interest put together by Kenneth Fisher. Examples include "Price-to-Book Value Ratios" from 1921; "Stock Prices Abroad" (stock prices for seven foreign countries); and a chart of the South Seas Bubble from 1719 to 1720. It provides excellent historical and current perspectives.

S&P Trade and Security Statistics is a service of Standard & Poor's that includes historical data on various economic and security price series and a monthly supplement that updates the series for the recent period. There are two major sets of data: (1) business and financial and (2) security price index record. Within the business and finance section are long-term statistics on trade, banking, industry, prices, agriculture, and the financial sector.

The security price index record contains historical data for all of Standard & Poor's indexes. This includes the 500 stocks broken down into 88 individual groups. The four main groups are industrials, rails, utilities, and financial firms. There also are four supplementary group series: capital goods companies, consumer goods, high-grade common stocks, and low-priced common stocks. In addition, there is a quarterly series of earnings and dividends for each of the four main groups from 1946 to the present. The booklet also contains daily stock sales on the NYSE since 1918 and historical yields for a number of corporate and government bond series.

Stocks, Bonds, Bills, and Inflation is published annually by Ibbotson Associates and contains monthly rates of return for seven primary U.S. capital market series and a number of derived series. The primary series are (1) large cap common stocks, (2) small cap common stocks, (3) long-term corporate bonds, (4) long-term government bonds, (5) intermediate-term government bonds, (6) U.S. Treasury bills, and (7) inflation. Besides the extensive data (which are also available on disk), there is a detailed discussion of the results over time and consideration of how the data can be used by portfolio managers and regulators.

WEEKLY SECURITY-MARKET PUBLICATIONS   *Barron's,* a weekly publication of Dow Jones and Company, typically contains approximately six articles on topics of interest to investors. In the middle of the paper is an extensive statistical section, "Market Week,"

---

[7] Prior to 1992, this was titled *The Dow Jones Investor's Handbook,* published by Irwin Professional Publishing.

that contains the most complete weekly listing of prices and quotes for all U.S. financial markets. It provides weekly data on individual stocks and the latest information on earnings and dividends as well as quotes on commodities, stock options, and financial futures. Also included in the publication is an extensive statistical section with detailed information on the U.S. securities market for the past week.[8] There is also a fairly extensive set of world security-market indicator series and interest rates around the world as well as an "International Trader" section that discusses price movements in the major global stock markets.

Asian Wall Street Journal is a weekly publication of *The Wall Street Journal* that concentrates on the Asian region. It includes detailed economic news and stock and bond quotes related to this area of the global market.

Credit Markets is a weekly newspaper by the publishers of *The Bond Buyer.* It provides a longer-term overview of the major news items that affect the aggregate Treasury and corporate bond market and individual bonds. There is an extensive statistical section listing bond calls, redemptions, the long-term future underwriting calendar, along with several security-market series.

Banking World is a weekly newspaper from the publishers of *American Banker.* It summarizes all the major news stories from Washington, the Federal Reserve, and financial services industry sectors. There is news on marketing, technology, federal and state regulations, and specific financial firms.

Financial Services Week is a weekly publication from Fairchild Publications that is billed as "The Financial Planner's Newspaper." It contains articles on the overall stock and bond market, insurance, and special features such as "Planning for Dentists," and "Baby Boomers and Financial Services." There is also consideration of tax changes and other legislation of importance to those involved in personal financial planning.

International Financing Review is a weekly magazine that contains stories and data regarding international investment banking firms and the international securities markets. Emphasis is on fixed-income securities, global economies, and politics. It is published by IFR Publishing Ltd.

Equities International, a weekly magazine that is also produced by IFR Publishing, deals with global markets but concentrates on equity instruments such as common stock, warrants, convertibles, options, and futures. The emphasis is on major trends and events in countries around the world. There is a complete listing of stock-market indexes for major global markets.

Euro Week, billed as "The Euromarket's First Newspaper," includes discussions related to notes, bonds, and stocks throughout Europe as well as longer articles on major news items in individual countries. A capital markets guide provides information on forthcoming securities issues. Finally, there is a listing of market indexes for various countries and a quarterly listing of the top investment banking firms in various categories (Eurobonds, Euro-equities) based on the value of the issues underwritten.

DAILY SECURITY-MARKET PUBLICATIONS   *The Wall Street Journal,* published by Dow Jones and Company, is a daily national business newspaper published five days a week. It contains complete listings for the NYSE, the AMEX, the NASDAQ-OTC market, U.S. bond markets, options markets, and commodities quotations. There also are a limited number of quotes for foreign stocks and a few non-U.S. stock market indicator series. It is

---

[8] For a discussion of the features in *Barron's* and how the series are used by technicians, see Martin E. Zweig, *Understanding Technical Forecasting.* Free copies are available from *The Wall Street Journal,* Educational Service Bureau, P.O. Box 300, Princeton, NJ 08540.

recognized worldwide as a prime source of financial and business information for the United States.[9]

Investor Daily, billed as "America's Business Newspaper," was initiated in 1984 as competition to *The Wall Street Journal.* It provides much of the same information but attempts to provide added information related to stock prices, earnings, and trading volume. An extensive set of U.S. general market indexes, including several unique to it, are included. It contains little information on non-U.S. markets.

The Financial Times is published five times a week in London with issues printed in New York and Los Angeles. Although it could be considered a British version of *The Wall Street Journal,* it is actually much more because it has a true *world* perspective on the financial news. It does an outstanding job of reporting financial news related to England, and discusses the U.S. economy and security markets, including extensive stock and bond quotes and security-market indicator series. It also contains news and data for Japan and other countries. Most important, however, is its global perspective in discussing and interpreting the news, which is critical to those involved in global investing.

The Bond Buyer is a daily newspaper (five days a week) that concentrates on news and quotes related to the overall bond market, with special emphasis on the municipal bond market—its caption reads, "The Authority on Municipal Bonds Since 1891." Besides news stories on events that affect bonds, there are extensive listings of new and forthcoming bond sales, bond calls and redemptions, and information on bond ratings. There also are numerous market indicator series reported with the emphasis on fixed-income series.

The American Banker is referred to as "The Daily Financial Services Newspaper." It contains articles of interest to bankers and others involved in the financial services industry on topics such as legislation and general news of the industry and major banks. There also is a brief summary of the financial markets related to Treasuries, financial futures, and mortgage securities.

BROKERAGE FIRM REPORTS

As a means of competing for investor's business, brokerage firms provide, among other services, information and recommendations on the outlook for securities markets (bonds and stocks). These reports are typically prepared monthly and distributed to customers (or potential customers) of the firm free of charge. In the competition for institutional business, investment firms have generated reports that are quite extensive and sophisticated. Among the brokerage firms issuing these reports are Goldman Sachs & Company; Kidder Peabody & Company; Merrill Lynch, Pierce, Fenner & Smith; Morgan Stanley; and Salomon Brothers.

Beyond these reports on the U.S. securities markets, several investment banking firms publish extensive reviews of the world capital markets. The economic outlook for the major countries is discussed along with import/export and exchange rate considerations that culminate in evaluations of the outlook for particular industries specified as *global industries* and recommendations related to world bond and stock markets. Examples of such publications include:

• Goldman Sachs International Corporation's monthly publication, *World Investment Strategy Highlights,* begins with world investment factors such as economic activity,

[9] For a discussion of many of the features of *The Wall Street Journal,* see "A Future Manager's Guide to *The Wall Street Journal.*" Copies are available from *The Wall Street Journal,* Educational Service Bureau, P.O. Box 300, Princeton, NJ 08540.

monetary conditions, and interest rates and moves to individual country reports for about 12 individual countries and groups. The culmination is a recommended world portfolio strategy that considers individual country expectations and exchange rate forecasts.

- Morgan Stanley Capital International has a monthly publication that provides up-to-date pricing and valuation data on individual stocks and world industries. For example, it is assumed that an analyst or a portfolio manager would evaluate U.S. chemical firms as part of the global chemical industry, not just the U.S. chemical industry. This set of world data allows the analyst or portfolio manager to examine stocks across industries and countries.

  The firm also has a quarterly publication that provides over 20 years of share price information (adjusted for capital changes) for 1,700 of the largest companies in the world, representing over 75 percent of the world's market capitalization. The most recent balance sheet is provided, along with 5 years of operating data.

- The Fixed Income Group of Kidder Peabody & Company publishes "The International Report"—a monthly publication that suggests a global investment strategy for the fixed-income market based on world markets. Specifically, it considers global fixed-income returns, yields, and exchange rates, including specific country analyses for the United States, Japan, Germany, the United Kingdom, and other countries of current interest. It also publishes a weekly "Capital Markets Report" that contains numerous charts on output, demand (consumer spending, personal income), inflation, Federal Reserve data, domestic and international interest rates, and international statistics.

- The Merrill Lynch Capital Markets Group publishes "World Bond Market Monitor," a biweekly analysis of international bond yields, spreads, and yield curves that specifically considers the U.S. dollar bond market, the floating rate note market, U.K. sterling bond market, Japanese yen bond market, Deutschemark (DM) bond market, Dutch guilder bond market, and several other countries along with data on world inflation and yields in currency hedged instruments. It also has a monthly publication, "International Fixed Income Strategy," which considers the global perspective for the dollar; the world climate for bonds; and specific market perspectives for the Japanese yen, the sterling bond market, and Deutschemark (DM) bonds. It concludes with a recommended international fixed-income strategy for the coming six months.

- Salomon Brothers Inc. has three interlocking monthly reports: "Global Fixed-Income Investment Strategy," "Global Equity Investment Strategy," and "Global Economic Outlook and Asset Allocation." Based on the outlook for the U.S. and world economies and markets, it makes a recommendation for a total world portfolio, including a global fixed-income-equity allocation that considers the exchange rate outlook.

- Nomura Research Institute (NRI)[10] publishes *Nomura Investment Review,* a monthly publication that analyzes and projects the general investment climate in Japan and the rest of the world. Although the emphasis is on the Japanese economy and its securities markets, there also is an extensive discussion of the world stock markets as well as various sectors (industries). The result is a world portfolio structure recommendation and suggestions for specific stocks.

- Daiwa Securities Company, Ltd., has a quarterly publication, *Tokyo Stock Market Quarterly Review,* that includes an in-depth analysis of the Japanese economy and securities market and discusses numerous markets around the world.

---

[10] The Nomura Research Institute is an independently managed research company affiliated with the Nomura Securities Company, Ltd.

INDUSTRY
ANALYSIS

There only are a few publications with extensive information on a wide range of industries. The major sources of data on various industries are industry publications and trade association magazines.

INDUSTRY
PUBLICATIONS

Standard & Poor's Industry Survey is a two-volume reference work divided into 34 segments dealing with 69 major domestic industries. Coverage in each area is divided into a basic analysis and a current analysis. The *basic analysis* examines the long-term prospects for a particular industry based on an analysis of historical trends and problems. Major segments of the industry are spotlighted, and a comparative analysis of the principal companies in the industry is included. The *current analysis* discusses recent developments and provides statistics for an industry and specific companies along with appraisals of the industry's investment outlook.

Standard & Poor's Analysts Handbook contains selected income account and balance sheet items along with related financial ratios for the Standard & Poor's industry groups. (It is typically not available until about seven months after year-end.) With these fundamental income and balance sheet series, it is possible to compare the major factors bearing on group stock price movements (e.g., sales, profit margins, earnings, assets, debt). These data are used extensively in the industry analysis chapter. Figure 6.1 is a sample page from the *Handbook*.

Value Line Industry Survey is an integral part of the *Value Line Investment Survey*. The reports for the 1,700 companies included are divided into 91 industries and updated by industry. The industry report contains summary statistics for the industry on assets, earnings, and important ratios similar to what is included for companies. There also is an industry stock price index as well as a table that provides comparative data for all the individual companies in the industry on timeliness rank, safety rank, and financial strength. The discussion considers the major factors affecting the industry and concludes with an investment recommendation for the industry.

INDUSTRY MAGAZINES

The magazines published for various industries are an excellent source of data and general information. Depending on the industry, there can be several publications (e.g., the computer industry has spawned at least five such magazines). Examples of industry publications include:

- *Computers*
- *Real Estate Today*
- *Chemical Week*
- *Modern Plastics*
- *Paper Trade Journal*
- *Automotive News*

TRADE ASSOCIATIONS   Trade associations are organizations set up by those involved in an industry or a general area of business to provide information for such topics as education, advertising, lobbying for legislation, and problem solving. Trade associations typically gather extensive statistics for the industry. Examples of such organizations include:[11]

- Iron and Steel Institute
- American Railroad Association

---

[11] For a more extensive list, see *Encyclopedia of Associations* (Detroit: Gale Research Company, 1977); and *The World Guide to Trade Associations* (New York: R. R. Bowker, 1986).

CHEMICALS

Per Share Data — Adjusted to stock price index level. Average of stock price indexes, 1941-1943=10

	Sales	Oper. Profit	Profit Margin %	Depr.	Income Taxes	Cash Flow	Earnings Per Share	Earnings % of Sales	Dividends Per Share	Dividends % of Earn.	Prices 1941-1943=10 High	Prices Low	Price/Earn. Ratio High	Price/Earn. Ratio Low	Div. Yields High	Div. Yields Low	Book Value Per Share	% Return	Working Capital	Capital Expenditures
1965	34.52	8.59	24.88	2.64	2.55		3.41	9.88	1.89	55.43	76.78	68.78	22.52	20.17	2.75	2.46	21.94	15.54	9.90	4.88
1966	38.18	8.97	23.49	2.88	2.58		3.50	9.17	1.94	55.43	75.38	49.82	21.54	14.23	3.89	2.57	23.51	14.89	9.93	5.41
1967	38.63	8.12	21.02	3.15	1.99		2.84	7.35	1.87	65.85	60.53	50.87	21.31	17.91	3.68	3.09	24.40	11.64	10.21	5.07
1968	43.96	9.37	21.31	3.51	2.56		3.16	7.19	2.00	63.29	61.43	50.20	19.44	15.89	3.98	3.26	26.25	12.04	11.21	4.59
1969	47.18	9.55	20.24	3.70	2.52		3.17	6.72	1.94	61.20	57.95	40.08	18.28	12.64	4.84	3.35	27.17	11.67	11.79	5.40
1970	47.51	8.89	18.71	3.90	1.95		2.70	5.68	1.90	70.37	47.11	36.93	17.45	13.68	5.14	4.03	27.77	9.72	11.75	5.95
1971	49.55	9.36	18.89	3.99	2.07		2.93	5.91	1.90	64.85	58.71	47.56	20.04	16.23	3.99	3.24	29.48	9.94	12.97	5.25
1972	54.18	10.77	19.88	4.15	2.66		3.61	6.66	1.97	54.57	67.13	56.40	18.60	15.62	3.49	2.93	30.64	11.78	14.51	5.00
1973	64.00	13.54	21.16	4.23	3.91		5.10	7.97	2.08	40.78	72.95	55.46	14.30	10.87	3.75	2.85	33.84	15.07	16.39	6.39
1974	85.47	17.01	19.90	4.76	5.10		6.79	7.94	2.21	32.55	68.80	47.20	10.13	6.95	4.68	3.21	38.34	17.71	18.71	10.26
1975	80.33	15.24	18.97	4.92	4.18		5.51	6.86	2.18	39.56	74.63	48.76	13.54	8.85	4.47	2.92	39.26	14.03	17.59	11.95
1976	91.16	17.47	19.17	5.49	4.52		6.59	7.23	2.48	37.63	89.70	67.27	13.61	10.21	3.69	2.76	43.27	15.23	18.93	12.97
1977	101.01	18.44	18.26	6.37	4.31	12.52	6.16	6.10	2.78	45.13	72.45	52.70	11.76	8.56	5.28	3.84	46.55	13.23	19.77	12.10
1978	112.76	20.82	18.46	7.21	5.07	14.36	7.16	6.35	3.10	43.30	59.62	46.05	8.33	6.43	6.73	5.20	50.65	14.14	22.27	12.13
1979	129.30	22.59	17.47	7.51	5.13	16.67	9.17	7.09	3.38	36.86	61.04	51.75	6.66	5.64	6.53	5.54	54.58	16.80	24.87	12.48
1980	140.37	20.86	14.86	7.73	4.03	15.79	8.07	5.75	3.56	44.11	64.88	49.70	8.04	6.16	7.16	5.49	60.53	13.33	25.83	15.11
1981	143.65	21.09	14.68	7.72	4.79	15.42	7.71	5.37	3.37	43.71	73.84	52.81	9.58	6.85	6.38	4.56	65.84	11.71	29.45	15.26
1982	159.01	21.85	13.74	9.56	5.52	14.76	5.21	3.28	3.57	68.52	63.30	45.44	12.15	8.72	7.86	5.64	65.63	7.94	26.03	15.89
1983	161.68	23.41	14.48	10.18	6.66	14.46	4.98	3.08	3.66	73.49	81.75	57.95	16.41	11.64	6.32	4.48	66.32	7.51	22.60	12.06
1984	168.26	26.85	15.96	9.84	7.97	17.39	7.39	4.39	4.00	54.13	75.82	61.58	10.26	8.33	6.50	5.28	68.72	10.75	21.35	13.35
1985	151.04	24.21	16.03	10.47	3.84	13.35	2.34	1.55	3.91	...	91.58	63.14	39.14	26.98	6.19	4.27	60.10	3.89	18.64	13.90
1986	142.01	27.14	19.11	11.64	5.92	19.59	7.95	5.60	6.04	75.97	132.68	87.43	16.69	11.00	6.91	4.55	58.74	13.53	20.02	13.63
1987	171.62	33.40	19.46	12.25	10.21	24.99	12.75	7.43	4.72	37.02	185.85	118.65	14.58	9.31	3.98	2.54	68.96	18.49	25.94	15.02
1988	200.84	44.65	22.23	13.38	11.09	31.10	17.73	8.83	5.19	29.27	151.64	128.15	8.55	7.23	4.05	3.42	84.36	21.02	21.86	21.12
1989	219.60	47.21	21.50	14.44	11.15	32.59	18.15	8.27	6.88	37.91	184.92	146.63	10.19	8.08	4.69	3.72	74.17	24.47	17.12	24.06
1990	245.58	45.20	18.41	16.35	10.16	30.63	14.28	5.81	6.84	47.90	186.89	124.41	13.09	8.71	5.50	3.66	82.40	17.33	23.51	30.16
1991	230.78	38.20	16.55	17.32	6.00	24.80	7.48	3.24	6.98	93.32	190.89	136.71	25.52	18.28	5.11	3.66	83.86	8.92	25.35	25.75
1992	232.50	35.39	15.22	17.90	3.69	22.54	4.64	2.00	7.09	...	213.51	184.11	46.02	39.68	3.85	3.32	61.90	7.50	19.87	23.33
1993	211.25	37.77	17.88	18.74	4.45	25.38	6.64	3.14	7.22	...	214.23	185.65	32.26	27.96	3.89	3.37	60.32	11.01	18.13	20.15
1994	225.07	44.58	19.81	17.48	9.24	33.15	15.67	6.96	7.49	47.80	258.78	212.03	16.51	13.53	3.53	2.89	68.40	22.91	23.65	17.96
1995	267.75	60.24	22.50	18.65	15.41	43.96	25.31	9.45	8.43	33.31	304.70	225.31	12.04	8.90	3.74	2.77	77.66	32.59	21.19	24.01

Source: *Analysts Handbook*, 1995 edition (New York: Standard & Poor's, Inc.). Reprinted by permission of Standard & Poor's Corporation.

- National Consumer Finance Association
- Institute of Life Insurance
- American Bankers Association
- Machine Tool Association

INDIVIDUAL STOCK AND BOND ANALYSIS

The most extensive material is available on individual firms' stocks and bonds. The sources of these publications include individual companies; commercial publishing firms, which produce a vast array of material; reports provided by investment firms; and several investment magazines, which discuss the overall financial markets and provide opinions on individual companies and their stocks or bonds. We will discuss each of these sources and specific publications; however, you should keep in mind that many of the prior sources such as *The Wall Street Journal* and *Barron's* also include discussions of individual stocks or bonds.

COMPANY-GENERATED INFORMATION

An obvious source of information about a company is the company itself. Indeed, for some small firms, it may be the only source of information because trading activity in the firm's stock is not sufficient to justify its inclusion in publications of commercial services or brokerage firms.

ANNUAL REPORTS   Every firm with publicly traded stock must prepare and distribute to its stockholders an annual report of financial operations and current financial position. In addition to basic information, most reports discuss what happened during the year and outline future prospects. Most firms also publish quarterly financial reports that include brief income statements for the interim period and, sometimes, a balance sheet. These reports can be obtained directly from the company. To find an address for a company, you should consult Volume 1 of *Standard & Poor's Register of Corporations, Directors, and Executives,* which contains an alphabetical listing, by business name, of approximately 37,000 corporations.

SECURITY PROSPECTUS   When a firm wants to sell securities (bonds, preferred stock, or common stock) in the primary market to raise new capital, the SEC requires that it file a registration statement describing the securities being offered. It must provide extensive financial information beyond what is required in an annual report as well as nonfinancial information on its operations and personnel. A condensed version of the registration statement, referred to as a *prospectus,* is published by the underwriting firm and contains most of the relevant information. Copies of a prospectus for a current offering can be obtained from the underwriter or from the company. Investment banking firms will often advertise offerings in publications such as *The Wall Street Journal, Barron's,* or *The Financial Times.*

REQUIRED SEC REPORTS   In addition to registration statements, the SEC requires three *periodic* statements from publicly held firms. First, the 8-K form is filed each month, reporting any action that affects debt, equity, amount of capital assets, voting rights, or other changes that might have a significant impact on the stock.

Second, the 9-K form is an unaudited report filed every six months containing revenues, expenses, gross sales, and special items. It typically contains more extensive information than the quarterly statement.

Finally, the 10-K form is an annual version of the 9-K but is even more complete. The SEC requires that firms indicate in their annual reports that a copy of their 10-K is available from the company—on request and without charge.

COMMERCIAL PUBLICATIONS   Numerous advisory services supply information on the aggregate market and individual stocks. A partial list follows.

STANDARD & POOR'S PUBLICATIONS   *Standard & Poor's Corporation Records* is a set of seven volumes. The first six contain basic information on all types of corporations (industrial, financial) and are arranged alphabetically. The volumes are in binders and are updated throughout the year. The seventh volume is a daily news volume that contains recent data on all companies listed in all the volumes.

Standard & Poor's Stock Reports are comprehensive two-page reports on numerous companies with stocks listed on the NYSE and AMEX and traded OTC. They include the near term sales and earnings outlook, recent developments, key income statement and balance sheet items, and a chart of stock price movements. They are in bound volumes by exchange and are revised every three to four months. A sample page is shown in Figure 6.2.

Standard & Poor's Stock Guide is a monthly publication that contains compact, pertinent financial data on more than 5,000 common and preferred stocks. A separate section covers over 400 mutual fund issues. For each stock, the guide provides information on price ranges (historical and recent), dividends, earnings, financial position, institutional holdings, and a ranking for earning and dividend stability. It is a very useful quick reference for almost all actively traded stocks, as is shown by the example in Figure 6.3.

Standard & Poor's Bond Guide is a monthly publication containing the most pertinent comparative financial and statistical information on a broad list of bonds, including domestic and foreign bonds (about 3,900 issues), 200 foreign government bonds, and about 650 convertible bonds.

The Outlook is a weekly publication of Standard & Poor's Corporation that advises investors about the general market environment and specific groups of stocks or industries (e.g., high-dividend stocks, stocks with low price-to-earnings ratios, high-yield bonds, stocks likely to increase their dividends). Weekly stock index figures for 88 industry groups and other market statistics are included.

Daily Stock Price Records is published quarterly by Standard & Poor's, with individual volumes for the NYSE, the AMEX, and the OTC market. Each quarterly book is divided into two parts. Part 1, "Major Technical Indicators of the Stock Market," is devoted to market indicators widely followed as technical guides to the stock market and includes price indicator series, volume series, and data on odd lots and short sales. Part 2, "Daily and Weekly Stock Action," gives daily high, low, close, and volume information as well as monthly data on short interest for individual stocks, insider trading information, a 200-day moving average of prices, and a weekly relative strength series. The books for the NYSE and AMEX are available from 1962 to the present; the OTC books begin in 1968.

MOODY'S PUBLICATIONS   *Moody's Industrial Manual* resembles the Standard & Poor's Corporation records service except this service is organized by type of corporation (i.e., industrial, utility, etc.). The two-volume industrial service is published once a year and covers industrial companies listed on the NYSE, the AMEX, and regional exchanges. One section concentrates on international industrial firms. Like all Moody's manuals, there is a news report volume that covers events that occurred after publication of the basic manual.

STANDARD &POOR'S
STOCK REPORTS

Int'l Business Machines   **1210**

NYSE Symbol **IBM**

In S&P 500

06-MAY-96   **Industry:** Data Processing

Summary: The world's largest technology company, IBM offers a diversified line of computer hardware equipment, application and system software, and related services.

S&P Opinion: Accumulate (★★★★)   Recent Price • 108⅛   Yield • 1.3%
52 Wk Range • 128⅞-83⅛   12-Mo. P/E • 16.6

Quantitative Evaluations

Outlook
(1 Lowest—5 Highest)
• **2⁺**

Fair Value
• **104%**

Risk
• **Low**

Earn./Div. Rank
• **B-**

Technical Eval.
• **Bullish since 12/93**

Rel. Strength Rank
(1 Lowest—99 Highest)
• **23**

Insider Activity
• **Favorable**

Earnings vs. Previous Year
▲=Up ▼=Down ▶=No Change

10 Week Mov. Avg. ----
30 Week Mov. Avg. ·····
Relative Strength ——

DJFMAMJJASOND JFMAMJJASOND JFMAMJJASOND JFMAMJJ
1993   1994   1995   1996

OPTIONS: CBOE

Overview - 03-MAY-96

We have lowered our revenue forecast for 1996 to 6.5% from 9% following the disappointing revenue performance in the first quarter. Growth will be fueled by gains in service revenues (+27%) and software (+6%), offset by slower growth in hardware revenues and slightly negative growth in maintenance and rentals and financing, which account for about 14% of revenues. Hardware growth will be led by RS/6000 workstations and parallel processing systems, while revenue contributions from AS/400 minicomputers and a new line of mainframes are likely to remain uneven. Margins are expected to narrow, reflecting continued price pressures, particularly in the personal computer segment and on sales of older bi-polar mainframes. Operating expenses will grow at a slower rate than revenues, helped by reductions in SG&A expenses under a previously announced staff reduction program targeting 5,000 to 10,000 positions. EPS are expected to reach $12.50 (excluding special charges).

Valuation - 06-MAY-96

We continue to recommend accumulating the shares despite the uneven first quarter results and the related negative market reaction that saw IBM's shares fall almost $10. While we were disappointed in the slightly negative hardware comparisons, the lower gross margins and the likelihood of difficult comparisons over the next two quarters, we are still bullish on IBM's long-term growth prospects as key product lines have been stabilized and its dependence on the mainframe has lessened. More importantly, IBM's cash flow generation abilities and $7 billion cash position should allow it to make strategic acquisitions and institute additional shareholder-oriented actions. As a result, we continue to recommend selective purchases of the shares as they remain undervalued based on our 1996 estimate.

Key Stock Statistics

S&P EPS Est. 1996	11.50	Tang. Bk. Value/Share	38.89
P/E on S&P Est. 1996	9.4	Beta	0.66
S&P EPS Est. 1997	13.75	Shareholders	65,300
Dividend Rate/Share	1.40	Market cap. (B)	$ 58.8
Shs. outstg. (M)	543.8	Inst. holdings	46%
Avg. daily vol. (M)	4.277		

Value of $10,000 invested 5 years ago: $ 11,712

Fiscal Year Ending Dec. 31

	1996	1995	1994	1993	1992	1991
Revenues (Million $)						
1Q	16,559	15,735	13,373	13,058	14,037	13,550
2Q	—	17,531	15,351	15,519	16,224	14,730
3Q	—	16,754	15,431	14,743	14,702	14,430
4Q	—	21,920	19,897	19,396	19,560	22,080
Yr.	—	71,940	64,052	62,716	64,520	64,790
Earnings Per Share ($)						
1Q	1.41	2.12	0.64	-0.50	1.12	0.93
2Q	E3.05	2.97	1.14	-14.10	1.29	0.20
3Q	E2.80	-0.96	1.18	-0.12	-4.87	0.30
4Q	E4.25	3.09	2.06	0.62	-9.57	-2.42
Yr.	E11.50	7.23	5.02	-14.02	-12.03	-0.99

Next earnings report expected: mid July

Dividend Data (Dividends have been paid since 1916.)

Amt. of Div. $	Date Decl.	Ex-Div. Date	Stock of Record	Payment Date
0.250	Jul. 25	Aug. 08	Aug. 10	Sep. 09 '95
0.250	Oct. 30	Nov. 08	Nov. 10	Dec. 09 '95
0.250	Jan. 30	Feb. 07	Feb. 09	Mar. 09 '96
0.350	Apr. 17	May. 08	May. 10	Jun. 10 '96

FIGURE 6.3   EXAMPLE FROM *STANDARD & POOR'S STOCK GUIDE*

122 MAT-MED

Standard & Poor's

Index	Ticker	Name of Issue (Call Price of Pfd. Stocks) / Market	Com. Rank. & Pfd. Rating	Inst. Hold Cos	Inst. Hold Shs (000)	Principal Business
		S&P 500 / MidCap 400 / SmallCap 600 / ◆ Options				
1	MC	✓Matsushita El Ind ADR ... NY,B,Ch,P,Ph	NR	52	913	Japan mfr consumer elec eq
2	MAT	✓Mattel, Inc ... NY,B,Ch,P,Ph	B	630	211317	Design,mfg,market toys
3	MTSN	Mattson Technology	NR	40	3877	Mfr semiconductor mfg equip
4	NUT	Mauna Loa Macadamia'A' ... NY,Ch	B-	9	101	Owns macadamia nut orchards
5	MAXE	✓Max & Erma's Restaurants ... NNM	B-	13	779	Family style restr:Franch'g
6	MAXC	✓Maxco Inc ... NNM	B-	10	234	Auto prod/constr supplies
7	MAXI	✓Maxicare Health Plans ... NNM	NR	109	9290	Multi-state HMO services
8	MXIM	✓Maxim Integrated Prod. ... NNM	NR	243	50449	Mfr,mkt integrated circuits
9	MXIS	✓Maxis Inc. ... NNM	NR	51	3402	Dvlp personal computer softwr
10	MXWL	✓Maxwell Labs ... NNM	B-	22	800	Defense/comm'l electr sys
11	MXM	✓MAXXAM Inc. ... AS,B,Ch,P,Ph	C	70	2753	Alum'n/forest prod:RE mgmt
12	MAM	✓Maxxim Medical ... NY,Ch,Ph	B	62	3552	Mfr medical/therapy products
13	MA	✓May Dept Stores ... NY,B,C,Ch,P,Ph	A+	806	173652	Large department store chain
14	SPEH	✓May & Speh Inc. ... NNM	NR	23	2806	Computer based info mgmt svc
15	MYG	✓Maytag Corp ... NY,B,Ch,P	B-	292	64530	Mrs major home appliances
16	MBI	✓MBIA Inc. ... NY,B,Ch,P	A+	344	35253	Insurance for muni bonds
17	KRB	✓MBNA Corp ... NY,Ch,Ph	A-	556	147438	Bank hldg/credit card svc'g
18	MCX	✓MC Shipping ... AS,Ph	NR		19	Inv/owns 2nd hand cargo ships
19	MCAF	✓McAfee Associates ... NNM	NR	170	28787	Dvlp personal computer softwr
20	MNI	✓McClatchy Newspapers'A' ... NY,Ch,P	A	58	5753	Publish newsp CA,WA,Alaska
21	MCCRK	✓McCormick & Co ... NNM	A	195	39109	Spices, flavoring, tea, mixes
22	MDR	✓McDermott Int'l ... NY,B,C,Ch,P,Ph	B-	227	36532	Offshore oil & gas constr
23	MDEPrA	$2.20cmCvAPfd(31.25:SF)11/2vtg ... NY	BB+	24	495	Steam gen exp:tubular goods
24	JRM	✓McDermott(J.Ray)S.A. ... NY,Ch,Ph	NR	104	7469	Marine constr'n svcs o&g ind
25	MDD	✓McDonald & Co Invest ... NY,B,Ph	B+	46	1412	Invest'm't bank'g/brokerage
26	MCD	✓McDonald's Corp ... NY,To,B,C,Ch,P,Ph	A+	1076	359630	Fast food restaurant:franch'g
27	MCZ	McDonald's Corp 8.35%'QUIDS' ... NY		66 / 31	31	Qlty Income Debt Securities
28	MD	✓McDonnell Douglas ... NY,B,C,Ch,P,Ph	B	474	117519	Aircraft/aerospace/missiles
29	MCFE	✓McFarland Energy ... NNM	B	23	2748	Oil & gas expl & prod'r
30	MGRC	✓McGrath RentCorp ... NNM	B+	47	3594	Rents/sells modular offices
31	MHP	✓McGraw-Hill Companies ... NY,B,Ch,P,Ph	B+	483	64402	Books:educ/info svs:publ:TV
32	MCIC	✓MCI Communications ... NNM	B	804	383798	Telecommun'ns network,svcs
33	MCK	✓McKesson Corp ... NY	B+	231	22546	Dstr drugs, toiletries/hm pd
34	MCLD	McLeod Inc'A' ... NNM	NR	231		Local,L-D telecommun svcs
35	MCN	✓MCN Corp ... NY,Ph	B+	231	30275	Natural gas distr,Michigan
36	MRLA	✓McRae Indus Cv'B' ... AS	B+	4	13	Mfr elect sys/combat boots
37	MRLB	Class 'A' (1/10 vtg) ... AS	B+	10	56	
38	MWT	McWhorter Technologies ... NY	B+	55	5524	Produce ind'l resin products
39	MDQ	MDC Communication Cl'A' ... AS,To	NR	15	3367	Advertising/mktg svcs
40	MDC	✓M.D.C. Hldgs ... NY,B,C,P	B-	52	9843	Home bldg,mtge banking
41	MDLI	✓MDL Information Sys. ... NNM	NR	76	6833	Chemical info mgmt softwr
42	MDTC	MDT Corp ... NNM	B-	26	2161	Mfr sterility assurance sys
43	MDU	✓MDU Resources Group ... NY,B,C,Ch,P	B+	102	5368	Gas & elec utility:coal,o&g
44	MEA	✓Mead Corp ... NY,B,C,Ch,P,Ph	B+	406	34955	Mfr paper,lumber,wood prod
45	MIG	Meadowbrook Insurance Grp. ... NY	NR	40	2208	Alternate Mkt risk mgmt ins
46	MSS	✓Measurement Specialties. ... AS	B-	5	126	Mfr temp,distance,pressure eq
47	MX	✓Measurex Corp ... NY,B,Ch,P,Ph	B-	159	11990	Ind'l process control sys
48	MECN	Mecon Inc ... NNM	NR	46	2448	Hospital indus info/softwr
49	TAXI	Medallion Financial ... NNM	NR			Taxicab medallion finance svcs
50	MEDA	Medaphis Corp ... NNM,Ch	NR	268	36699	Hospital/Dr. acc rec mgmt svcs
51	MDXR	✓Medar Inc. ... NNM	C	28	2726	Quality control equip

Index	Ticker	1971-94 High	1971-94 Low	1995 High	1995 Low	1996 High	1996 Low	Jun Sales 100s	LS High	LS Low	LS Last	%Div Yield	P-E Ratio	EPS 5 Yr Growth	12 Mo	36 Mo	60 Mo
1	MC	219	6¼	172½	15¼	188	157¼	458	188	169¼	186	0.5	73	-16	20.6	17.4	10.1
2	MAT	18⅝	1⅝	24¼	15¼	29¼	23¼	101750	29¾	26¾	28¾	0.8	19	18	35.7	31.6	34.1
3	MTSN	10½	6	31¼	8	17	8⅛	32802	15¼	10¼	10¼		13	-7	-53.1		
4	NUT	11⅛	2⅛	2¾	2	2½	2	1833	2⅛	2	2⅛	7.6	26	32	-2.8	-10.0	-16.0
5	MAXE	9¼	⅞	8⅛	5⅞	8	5⅞	967	8⅛	7¼	7¼		15	Neg	-9.4	-12.3	-20.4
6	MAXC	11¼	⅞	10⅝	7	10½	8½	2205	10½	8⅜	8½		d	Neg	4.5	11.9	31.2
7	MAXI	16½	6⅜	27¼	14	31¾	14¼	122025	34¾	24	27¼		12	69	28.0	22.6	20.3
8	MXIM	17⅞	1⅝	41⅛	14⅛	43¾	24	128227	34¾	24	27¼		16	46	20.0	56.8	49.9
9	MXIS					37½	16	12763	24	18	19¼		35	40	-30.1		
10	MXWL	25¼	5⅝	11	6½	15½	6½	5047	15¼	12½	15¼		d	Neg	87.7	16.1	7.1
11	MXM	67¼	2⅝	67⅞	27¼	50½	35½	1983	39¼	39	39¼		6	NM	14.6	17.0	-3.3
12	MAM	24¼	4	17	12¼	20½	16⅛	4793	19	17	17½		38	-9	12.3	-1.2	10.5
13	MA	46½	1⅞	45	32½	52½	40	116662	48¾	43¼	43¾	2.7	15	8			
14	SPEH	32⅜	4	21	14½	16½	14¼	8657	16	14¼	15¼		14	Neg			
15	MYG	32⅜	4	21⅛	14¼	21⅝	16⅛	44666	22	19	21¼	2.7	14	10	35.7	14.7	10.2
16	MBI	18⅜	10⅛	77½	55⅜	80¾	70	24874	80¾	74¼	77½	1.8	15	12	17.8	8.2	22.4
17	KRB	18¼	5⅝	29⅛	14⅜	32⅜	22	157002	32⅜	26⅜	28⅜	2.2	11	21	27.7	33.3	38.0
18	MCX	15⅛	2⅜	4½	2¾	4½	3⅛	1075	3¾	3⅜	3⅜	4.3	d	Neg	8.8	0.2	-10.2
19	MCAF	30⅜	2⅝	35½	6	54	19	169554	54	49	49		26	16	291	151	
20	MNI	30½	13¼	24½	18⅝	27	20	3608	27	24½	27	1.4	26	5	24.1	11.2	6.5
21	MCCRK	46½	1⅝	26½	18⅝	24¼	20	49746	22	21¼	22	2.5	20	-1	-4.8	1.2	4.1
22	MDR	47⅜	7¼	29½	19⅝	23¼	20⅛	29994	21¼	20	20¼	4.8	17	NM	-13.3	-6.4	6.8
23	MDEPrA	47¼	17⅞	32½	26¼	30½	26¼	297	28⅛	27¾	27¾	7.9	d		3.1	17.9	33.0
24	JRM	22⅝	4⅛	28⅛	15	26¼	20	5989	26	25	25		d		3.1	17.9	33.0
25	MDD	16½	3¼	18⅝	11	20	17½	1139	19½	19	19¼	1.7	9	27	26.7	18.7	25.7
26	MCD	31½	¾	48	28	54	42	383504	49½	45	46¾	0.6	21	12	22.6	24.3	24.3
27	MCZ			27	25¼	26½	25	959	26¼	25	25	8.2					
28	MD	28¼	1¼	46¾	23⅝	52¼	44	81420	52	47¼	48¾	1.0	13	NM	28.8	59.6	44.8
29	MCFE	28⅜	1⅜	8⅝	5½	10½	7⅛	767	10	9	9		13	NM	28.6	12.2	6.7
30	MGRC	18	2⅛	19½	14⅜	22½	17½	1400	22½	19	22½	2.5	13	8	38.0	24.3	9.3
31	MHP	43¾	1⅝	43½	31½	49⅛	42	32627	48	43⅜	45½	2.9	20	19	24.5	19.5	12.9
32	MCIC	29⅜	⅞	27⅜	17½	31½	25	750694	29¼	25	25	0.2	15	-4	24.5	-2.7	13.0
33	MCK	33⅜	30½	53⅛	31½	55⅝	44	14037	49	46	47¾	2.1	15		6.3		
34	MCLD					26½	20	149215	26¾	20	24						
35	MCN	20½	8½	23⅝	16⅞	25⅜	21	17443	24¼	22⅞	24	3.8	15	17	31.1	19.3	24.5
36	MRLA	10½	1⅞	8⅝	5½	8½	8	740	8¾	8	8½B	4.1	12	-4	37.5	13.6	7.0
37	MRLB	10⅛	1⅝	8⅛	5½	8½	7¾		8½	7¾	8⅛		8	-4	37.4	17.9	12.7
38	MWT	19¼	13¼	16¾	14	19⅞	16⅛	2538	19½	16⅛	17¾		16	95	18.8		
39	MDQ	22⅜	⅜	12⅝	4	10½	7⅛	1530	8¼	7	7¾		8	NM	-36.5		
40	MDC	20	⅜	8⅝	4½	7⅜	6⅛	5718	7⅜	6¾	6⅞	1.8	8	NM	9.9	3.9	30.2
41	MDLI	13¼	5¼	26¼	8⅛	32¼	16⅛	8277	30¾	28	29½		22		114		
42	MDTC	15⅛	2⅛	4⅞	3	5	4¼	6950	5	4¼	4½			Neg	-22.9	-20.4	-7.7
43	MDU	22⅛	3⅜	23⅜	17⅜	21½	18⅝	2880	21¼	20⅝	21⅛	5.1	14	4	14.7	8.1	15.4
44	MEA	53¼	3⅜	64½	46⅞	57⅜	49	48586	53¾	50⅜	51¼	2.3	16	62	-9.1	7.6	12.0
45	MIG			9¾	8⅛	10⅞	9¾	1206	10½	9¾	9¾	0.3	17				
46	MSS	6½	1	7	3	5	3	1385	4½	4	4		15	84	-3.0	0.0	7.0
47	MX	35¾	2⅛	36	22⅛	30	25	14925	29¼	27⅞	29¼	1.5	29	NM	-2.7	19.3	9.4
48	MECN			18⅜	13	13⅛	11	7270	13¼	12½	12½			-29			
49	TAXI					13⅜	11	17802	13	12¼	12½		17				
50	MEDA	24	6	38½	20	53¼	34	215776	45¼	34¾	39¼		36	Neg	87.1	59.2	
51	MDXR	16⅛	1⅞	16⅜	6	11¼	9	9808	11¼	9	10		d	9	10.7	14.7	21.0

Uniform Footnote Explanations-See Page 1. Other: ¹ASE:Cycle 1. ²ASE:Cycle 2. ³P:Cycle 3. ⁴CBOE:Cycle 2. ⁵CBOE,NY:Cycle 1. ⁶Ph:Cycle 3. ⁷ASE,CBOE:Cycle 3. ⁸Ph:Cycle 3. ⁹Ch,Ph. ¹⁰CBOE:Cycle 1. ⁵¹Each ADR equal 10 com yen 50 par. ⁵²Approx. ⁵³⑥$0.60,'93. ⁵⁴L.P. Dep Unit. ⁵⁵Excl 1.5M Cl B units. ⁵⁶⑥$1.50,'95. ⁵⁷Stk dstr of Payless ShoeSource Inc. ⁵⁸Excl ESOP Shs. ⁵⁹⑥$2.82,'96. ⁶⁰Non-vtg. ⁶¹SF at $31.25. ⁶²Plus $0.10 in cash. ⁶³Payable upon presentation of ctfs. ⁶⁴68.6% owned by McDermott Int'l. ⁶⁵Fiscal Jul'92 & prior. ⁶⁶Rated AA- by S&P. ⁶⁷⑥$2.41,'95. ⁶⁸S&P is a division of the McGraw-Hill Companies; common not ranked, pfd not rated. ⁶⁹Subsid Pfd in M$. ⁷⁰Cv into 1 Cl'A'. ⁷¹Subordinate vtg shrs. ⁷²Fiscal Nov'94 & prior. ⁷³13 Mo Dec'95. ⁷⁴⑥$0.79,'95. ⁷⁵Getinge Ind AB offer,$4.50 to Jun 28. ⁷⁶To be determined.

Source: *Standard & Poor's Stock Guide* (New York: Standard & Poor's Corp., 1996). Reprinted by permission of Standard & Poor's Corporation.

Moody's OTC Industrial Manual is similar to the *Moody's Industrial Manual* of listed firms but is limited to stocks traded on the OTC market.

Moody's has manuals for various sectors as well. *Moody's Public Utility Manual* provides information on public utilities, including electric and gas, gas transmission, telephone, and water companies. *Moody's Transportation Manual* covers the transportation sector, including railroads, airlines, steamship companies, electric railway, bus and truck lines, oil pipe lines, bridge companies, and automobile and truck leasing companies. *Moody's Bank and Finance Manual* covers the field of financial services represented by banks, savings and loan associations, credit agencies of the U.S. government, all phases of the insurance industry, investment companies, real estate firms, real estate investment trusts, and miscellaneous financial enterprises.

Moody's Municipal and Government Manual contains data on the U.S. government, all the states, state agencies, and over 13,500 municipalities. It also includes some excellent information and data on foreign governments and international organizations.

Moody's International Manual provides financial information on about 3,000 major foreign corporations.

VALUE LINE PUBLICATIONS   *The Value Line Investment Survey* is published in two parts. Volume 1 contains basic historic information on about 1,700 companies, including a number of analytical measures of earnings stability, growth rates, a common stock safety factor, and a timing factor rating. A number of studies have examined the usefulness of the timing factor ratings for investment purposes. The results of these studies will be discussed in the efficient markets chapter.

The *Investment Survey* also includes extensive two-year *projections* for the given firms and three-year *estimates* of performance. As an example, in early 1997, it will include an earnings projection for 1997, 1998, and 1999–2001. The second volume contains a weekly service that provides general investment advice and recommends individual stocks for purchase or sale. An example of a Value Line company report is shown in Figure 6.4.

The Value Line OTC Special Situations Service is published 24 times a year. It serves the experienced investor who is willing to accept high risk in the hope of realizing exceptional capital gains. Each issue discusses past recommendations and presents eight to ten new stocks for consideration.

BROKERAGE FIRM REPORTS

Besides the products of these information firms, many brokerage firms prepare reports on individual companies and their securities. Some of these reports are objective and contain only basic information, but others make specific recommendations (e.g., buy, hold, sell).

INVESTMENT MAGAZINES

Many periodicals cover the securities industry for the benefit of professionals and individual investors. As noted earlier, although many of these publications emphasize individual companies and their stocks, they also discuss the overall financial markets and industries. Again, the order of presentation will be based on frequency of publication: monthly, biweekly, weekly.

MONTHLY MAGAZINES   *Money,* a monthly publication of Time Inc., deals specifically with topics of interest to individual investors, including articles on individual companies and general investment suggestions (e.g., "How to Determine Your Net Worth" and "The Why and How of Investing in Foreign Securities"). Also, each issue presents a financial planning discussion with an individual or couple.

FIGURE 6.4 **SAMPLE LISTING FROM *VALUE LINE***

Institutional Investor is a monthly publication of Institutional Investors Systems aimed at professional investors and portfolio managers. It emphasizes events in the investment industry as they relate to corporate finance, pensions, money management, portfolio strategy, and global stock markets. A popular annual feature is the selection of a group of sell-side equity analysts—an "All-American Analysts Team." This concept has been expanded to involve an "All-American Fixed-Income Team" and an international team.

Financial Planning, a monthly publication billed by its publisher, Financial Services Information Company, as "The Magazine for Financial Service Professionals," is intended for individuals involved in financial planning. It contains feature articles on alternative investment products and procedures, important regulatory information affecting financial planning (e.g., tax legislation), various industries, and specific classes of investments (e.g., mutual funds, real estate, equipment leasing).

OTC Review is a monthly publication devoted to the analysis and discussion of stocks traded on the OTC market. It usually analyzes an industry that is dominated by OTC companies and discusses three or four individual firms. In addition, there are numerous earnings reports on OTC firms, name changes, stock exchange listings, and price and volume statistics on OTC stocks.

Global Finance, a monthly magazine published by Global Information, Inc., contains a number of articles on trends around the world. It is an international version of *Institutional Investor* because it is written for the practicing money manager or investment professional. It also contains regular columns on venture capital, hedging, and investment strategies.

Global Investor is published monthly (but it produces combined issues for July/August and December/January) by Euromoney Publications PLC. Like *Global Finance*, it contains articles on various markets, international instruments, and specific money management firms. It features regular columns on the overall bond and stock markets and an extensive section on international bond and stock indexes.

BIWEEKLY MAGAZINES   *Forbes* is published twice monthly and contains 12 to 14 articles on individual companies, industries, and the market. Several regular columnists discuss the economy, the aggregate money and stock markets, and the commodity markets, and they include specific stock recommendations.

Fortune, published biweekly by Time Inc., provides extensive articles on the economy, politics, individual companies, securities markets, and personal investing. The magazine is well-known for its special annual reports on the Fortune 500 and the Fortune 1000 largest industrial firms in the country. The magazine also publishes a listing of large nonindustrial firms and major foreign companies. The importance of this information on non-U.S. firms is growing with the increase in globalization.

Financial World, published twice a month, generally contains about six articles on companies, industries, and the overall market along with several regular features on taxes and options. A separate section reports market data.

Pension and Investment Age, published by Crain Communications, Inc., is a biweekly newspaper of corporate and institutional investing. It is referred to as "The International Newspaper of Money Management" and is intended for those who invest in pension fund assets as either corporate managers or money managers. The paper emphasizes stories and interviews related to pension fund management such as asset class decisions by pension funds. There is substantial consideration of personnel changes.

WEEKLY MAGAZINES   *Business Week* is published weekly by McGraw-Hill. Although not strictly an investment magazine, it contains numerous articles on companies and industries as well as several features of importance to investors, including a weekly production index and a leading economic index. The magazine also has initiated several special issues compiling lists such as the Top 1000 U.S. firms and the Top 500 global firms.

The Economist is a weekly magazine published in London and New York by The Economist Newspaper, Inc. It is directed to worldwide reporting similar to what *The Financial Times* does on a daily basis. Beyond a set of articles dealing with the major events around the world, the magazine contains two major sections. The first, "World Politics and Current Affairs," is divided into sections on American Survey, Asia, International, Europe, and Britain. The second section, "Business, Finance and Science," has sections on business, finance, and science and technology. There also is an excellent set of economic and financial indicators from around the world. Similar to *The Financial Times,* this magazine is required reading for a global investor.

The Wall Street Transcript is published weekly as a composite of sources of information other than market quotations. It contains texts of speeches made at analysts' meetings, copies of brokerage house reports on companies and industries, and interviews with corporate officials. It includes discussions of forthcoming new stock issues.

The Media General Financial Weekly features a series of articles and columns. Of primary interest is a comprehensive set of financial and statistical information on 3,400 common stocks, including every common stock listed on the NYSE and the AMEX and over 700 OTC issues. It also presents charts on 60 major industry groups.

OBTAINING INFORMATION ON BONDS

As might be expected, the data needs of bond investors are considerably different from those of stockholders. For one thing, there is less emphasis on fundamental analysis because, except for speculative-grade bonds and revenue obligations, most bond investors rely on the rating agencies for credit analysis. An exception is large institutions that employ in-house analysts to confirm assigned agency ratings or to uncover incremental return opportunities. Because of the large investments by these institutions, the total dollar rewards from only a few basis points can be substantial. As you might expect, the institutions enjoy economies of scale in research. Finally, there are a few private research firms that concentrate on the independent appraisal of bonds.

REQUIRED INFORMATION

In addition to information on the risk of default, bond investors need information on (1) market and economic conditions and (2) intrinsic bond features. Market and economic information allows investors to stay abreast of the general tone of the bond market, overall interest rate developments, and yield-spread behavior in different market sectors. Bond investors also require information on bond indenture provisions such as call features and sinking-fund provisions.

Some of this information is readily available in *The Wall Street Journal, Barron's, Business Week, Fortune,* and *Forbes.* In addition, two popular sources of bond data are the *Federal Reserve Bulletin* and the *Survey of Current Business.*

A number of other sources of specific information are important to bond investors. The following are specifically concerned with information and analysis of bonds.

- *Treasury Bulletin* (monthly)
- *Standard & Poor's Bond Guide* (monthly)
- *Moody's Bond Record* (monthly)
- *Moody's Bond Survey* (weekly)
- *Fitch Rating Register* (monthly)
- *Fitch Corporate Credit Analysis* (monthly)
- *Fitch Municipal Credit Analysis* (monthly)
- *Investment Dealers Digest* (weekly)

- *Credit Markets* (weekly)
- *Duff & Phelps Credit Decisions* (weekly)
- *The Bond Buyer* (daily)

SOURCES OF
BOND QUOTES

The listed information sources fill three needs of investors: evaluating the risk of default, staying abreast of bond market and interest rate conditions, and obtaining information on specific bonds. Another important data need is current bond quotes and prices.

Unfortunately, many of the prime sources of bond prices are not widely distributed. For example, *Bank and Quotation Record* is a valuable, though not widely circulated, source that provides monthly price information for government and agency bonds, listed and OTC corporate bonds, municipal bonds, and money market instruments. Current quotes on municipal bonds are available only through a fairly costly publication that is used by many financial institutions—*The Blue List of Current Municipal Offerings.* It contains over 100 pages of price quotes for municipal bonds, municipal notes, and industrial development and pollution-control revenue bonds.

Daily information on all publicly traded Treasury issues, most agency obligations, and numerous corporate issues is published in *The Wall Street Journal.* Similar data are available weekly in *Barron's.* Both publications include corporate bond quotes for bonds listed on the New York and American exchanges that represent a minor portion of the total corporate bond market. You will recall that the majority of corporate bond trading is on the OTC market. Finally, major bond dealers maintain firm quotes on a variety of issues for clients. We will discuss bond quotes in more detail in Chapter 15.

SOURCES OF
INFORMATION ON
MUTUAL FUNDS

Because there is a wide variety of types of funds available, you should examine the performance of various funds over time to derive some understanding of their goals and management philosophies. Daily quotations for numerous open-end funds appear in *The Wall Street Journal.* A description of what is provided is shown in Figure 6.5. *The Wall Street Journal* provides information on a fund's objective, NAV, offer price, load, expense ratio, and historical returns ranked on a 5-point scale.[12]

A comprehensive weekly list of quotations with data on dividend income and capital gain for the previous 12 months is carried in *Barron's.* In addition, *Barron's* publishes quarterly updates on the performance of a number of funds over the previous 10 years. *Barron's* lists closed-end stock and bond funds with their current net asset values, current market quotes, and the percentage of difference between the two figures.

A major source of comprehensive historical information is an annual publication issued by Arthur Wiesenberger Services—*Investment Companies.* This book contains statistics for over 600 mutual funds arranged alphabetically. It describes each major fund, including a brief history, investment objectives and portfolio analysis, statistical history, special services, personnel, advisors and distributors, sales charges, and a chart of the value of a hypothetical $10,000 investment over 10 years. The Wiesenberger book also contains a summary list with annual rates of return and price volatility measures for a number of additional funds.

Wiesenberger has two other services. Every three months, the firm publishes *Management Results,* which updates the long-term performance of more than 400 mutual funds, arranged alphabetically and grouped by investment objective. The firm's monthly publica-

---

[12] NAV is net asset value per share for the fund, which is equal to the market value of all assets in the fund (stocks and/or bonds) minus any liabilities, divided by the number of shares outstanding.

FIGURE 6.5

DESCRIPTION OF DAILY MUTUAL FUND QUOTATIONS IN *THE WALL STREET JOURNAL* FOR ALTERNATIVE DAYS

How to Read These Tables

Data come from two sources. The daily Net Asset Value (NAV) and Net Change calculations are supplied by the National Association of Securities Dealers (NASD). The NASD requires a mutual fund to have at least 1,000 shareholders or net assets of $25 million before being listed. Performance and cost data come from **Lipper Analytical Services Inc.**

Though verified, the data cannot be guaranteed by Lipper or its data sources. Double-check with funds before investing.

Performance calculations assume reinvestment of all distributions, and are after subtracting annual expenses. But figures don't reflect sales charges ("loads") or redemption fees.

These expanded tables appear Fridays. Other days, you'll find net asset value and the daily change and year-to-date performance.

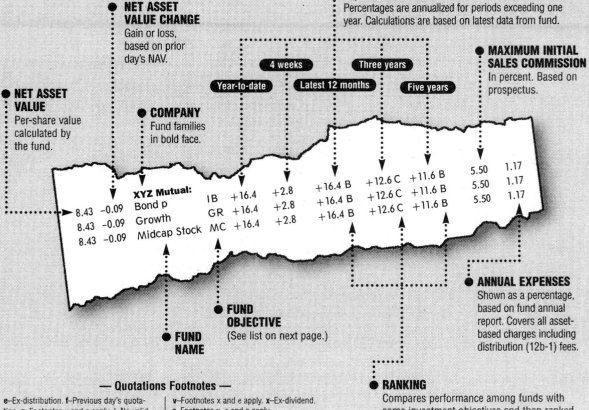

● **NET ASSET VALUE CHANGE**
Gain or loss, based on prior day's NAV.

● **TOTAL RETURN**
NAV change plus accumulated income for the period, in percent. Assumes reinvestment of all distributions. Percentages are annualized for periods exceeding one year. Calculations are based on latest data from fund.

● **MAXIMUM INITIAL SALES COMMISSION**
In percent. Based on prospectus.

● **NET ASSET VALUE**
Per-share value calculated by the fund.

● **COMPANY**
Fund families in bold face.

● **ANNUAL EXPENSES**
Shown as a percentage, based on fund annual report. Covers all asset-based charges including distribution (12b-1) fees.

● **FUND OBJECTIVE**
(See list on next page.)

● **FUND NAME**

XYZ Mutual:

			4 weeks		Latest 12 months	Three years	Five years		
8.43	−0.09	Bond p	IB	+16.4	+2.8	+16.4 B	+12.6 C	+11.6 B	5.50	1.17
8.43	−0.09	Growth	GR	+16.4	+2.8	+16.4 B	+12.6 C	+11.6 B	5.50	1.17
8.43	−0.09	Midcap Stock	MC	+16.4	+2.8	+16.4 B	+12.6 C	+11.6 B	5.50	1.17

— Quotations Footnotes —

e–Ex-distribution. **f**–Previous day's quotation. **g**–Footnotes x and s apply. **i**–No valid comparison with other funds because of expense structure. **j**–Footnotes e and s apply. **k**–Recalculated by Lipper, using updated data. **p**–Distribution costs apply, 12b-1 **r**–Redemption charge may apply. **s**–Stock split or dividend. **t**–Footnotes p and r apply.

v–Footnotes x and e apply. **x**–Ex-dividend. **z**–Footnotes x, e and s apply.

NA–Not available due to incomplete price, performance or cost data. **NE**–Deleted by Lipper editor; data in question. **NL**–No Load (sales commission). **NN**–Fund doesn't wish to be tracked. **NS**–Fund didn't exist at start of period.

● **RANKING**
Compares performance among funds with same investment objectives and then ranked for time periods listed. Performance is measured from either the closest Thursday or month-end for periods of more than three years. **A**=top 20%; **B**=next 20%; **C**=middle 20%; **D**=next 20%; **E**=bottom 20%.

tion, *Current Performance and Dividend Record,* reports the dividend and short-run performance of more than 400 funds.

Another source of analytical historical information on funds is *Forbes.* This biweekly financial publication typically discusses individual companies and their investment potential. In addition, the magazine's August issue contains an annual survey of mutual funds. The survey also provides information regarding each fund's yield, its sales charge, and its annual expense ratio.

Business Week publishes a "Mutual Fund Scoreboard" for open-end, equity, and fixed-income funds. The magazine publishes a comparable one for closed-end, fixed-income funds and equity funds. Besides information on performance (both risk-adjusted performance and total return), sales charges (including those for 12b-1 plans), expenses, and portfolio yield and maturity, an accompanying table contains telephone numbers for all the funds. The *Business Week* fund listings contain information on funds' after-tax returns, 10-year trend analysis, and investment style (e.g., growth versus value, small capitalization-versus large capitalization-oriented).

Morningstar provides a number of services for mutual fund investors. Its basic service is *Morningstar Mutual Funds,* which evaluates the performance of over 1,300 open-end mutual funds and provides a very informative one-page sheet on each fund. This sheet provides up-to-date information on the fund's objective and its risk-adjusted performance relative to the risk-adjusted performance of all other funds in the same class (e.g., equity, hybrid, taxable bond, or tax-free bond). There also is an analysis of performance and a discussion of the fund's investment strategy based on an interview with the fund manager.

In addition, the firm publishes an annual source book that provides a year-end profile of 2,400 open-end funds, a source book for 370 closed-end funds, a monthly performance report (similar to the stock guide) on 2,500 mutual funds, and an annual reference publication of the elite 500 open- and closed-end funds.

The newest service for mutual funds is "The Value Line Mutual Fund Survey." The service, which is modeled after their well-regarded company analysis service, covers 2,000 funds—1,500 established funds and 500 newer, smaller funds. Each fund survey contains performance data, portfolio data, and tax data. Notably, the report considers what happened during the latest bull and bear markets.

THEORETICAL AND EMPIRICAL ANALYSIS

ACADEMIC JOURNALS

The material in academic journals differs from that in investment magazines in timeliness and general orientation. Investment magazines are concerned with the *current* investment environment and with providing advice for current action. The material is generally non-quantitative. In contrast, academic journals contain longer, more theoretical, and more quantitative articles that typically are not intended to be immediately applicable. These journals contain theoretical or empirical studies related to investments that could have long-run implications.

Journal of Finance is a quarterly published by the American Finance Association. The articles are almost all by academicians and are rather theoretical and empirical. The typical issue includes 15 articles, notes and comments, and book reviews.

Journal of Financial Economics is published quarterly by North Holland Publishing Company in collaboration with the Simon Graduate School of Management of the University of Rochester. It publishes academic research in the areas of consumption and investment decisions under uncertainty, portfolio analysis, efficient markets, and the normative theory of financial management.

The Review of Financial Studies is published quarterly by Oxford University Press for the Society for Financial Studies. Its purpose is to publish new research in financial economics balanced between theoretical and empirical research. Although the subject matter appears similar to that of the *Journal of Financial Economics,* it places a stronger emphasis on the theoretical treatment of topics.

Journal of Financial and Quantitative Analysis is a quarterly published by the University of Washington. Almost all of its articles are by academicians and deal with topics in investments and corporate finance.

Financial Analysts Journal is published six times a year by the Association of Investment Management and Research (AIMR). Each issue contains six or seven articles of interest to financial analysts and portfolio managers, a regular feature on securities regulation, and book reviews. The articles are authored by either academicians or practitioners.

Journal of Portfolio Management is published quarterly by Institutional Investors Systems as a forum for academic research of interest to the practicing portfolio manager. Over half the articles are written by academicians, but they are written for the practitioner. Many articles are less technical and mathematical versions of studies previously published in heavily academic journals.

Journal of Fixed Income is published quarterly by Institutional Investor, Inc., as a forum for academic research related to fixed-income securities that can be understood and read by professional analysts and portfolio managers. The topics range from credit analysis and interest rates forecasting to various bond portfolio management strategies.

The Journal of Derivatives is a quarterly publication by Institutional Investor, Inc., as a forum to publish new developments in both derivative theory and practice. It provides a practical analysis of the latest derivative innovations and practical insights.

Real Estate Finance is a quarterly publication of Institutional Investor, Inc., that is intended to provide critical analysis on the latest financing techniques, securitization trends, IRS rulings, and environmental issues related to real estate.

Financial Management, published quarterly by the Financial Management Association, is intended for executives and academicians interested in the financial management of a firm. It contains investment-related articles on such topics as stock splits, dividend policy, mergers, initial public offerings, and stock listings when it is shown that such events are important to the investment and financing decisions of a firm.

The Financial Review is a quarterly journal sponsored by the Eastern Finance Association. About half of its articles are concerned with capital markets, investments, and portfolio management.

Journal of Financial Research is a joint quarterly publication of the Southern Finance Association and the Southwestern Finance Association. It contains articles on financial management, investments, financial institutions, capital market theory, and portfolio theory.

Financial Services Review is a quarterly journal sponsored by the Academy of Financial Services and published by JAI Press, Inc. It is a journal devoted to publishing academic research on individual financial management, which involves examining the application and effect of all facets of finance on the financial planning decisions made by individuals.

The C.F.A. Digest is published quarterly by the Institute of Chartered Financial Analysts (a subsidiary of the Association of Investment Management and Research). Its purpose is to provide, as a service to members of the investment community, about 20 abstracts of published articles from a wide variety of academic and nonacademic journals that are of interest to financial analysts and portfolio managers.

There are a number of general business and economics journals that include articles on finance and some specifically on investments. One of the foremost is the *Journal of Business,* published by the University of Chicago, which has outstanding articles in the area of investments. Other journals to consider include: *Quarterly Review of Economics and Finance* (University of Illinois), *International Review of Economics and Finance* (JAI Press, Inc.), *Review of Business and Economic Research* (University of New Orleans), *Journal of Business Research* (North Holland Publishing), *American Economic Review* (American Economic Association), *Journal of Political Economy* (University of Chicago), *Rand Journal of Economics* (American Telephone and Telegraph), and *The Journal of Applied Corporate Finance* (Bank of America).

COMPUTERIZED DATA SOURCES

In addition to the numerous published sources of data, some financial service firms have developed computerized data sources. The following discussion considers (1) major data banks and (2) the well-known on-line data systems. Space limitations restrict the discussion to major sources.

DATA BANKS

Compustat is a computerized bank of financial data developed by Standard & Poor's and is currently handled by a subsidiary, Investors Management Services. The Compustat tapes contain 20 years of data for approximately 2,220 listed industrial companies, 1,000 OTC companies, 175 utilities, 120 banks, and 500 Canadian firms. Quarterly tapes contain 20 years of quarterly financial data for over 2,000 industrial firms and 12 years of quarterly data for banks and utilities. The financial data on the annual tapes include almost every possible item from each firm's balance sheet and income statement as well as stock-market data (stock prices and trading volume).

Value Line Data Base contains historical annual and quarterly financial and market data for 1,600 industrial and finance companies beginning in 1954. It also provides quarterly data from 1963. In addition to historical data, it gives estimates of dividends and earnings for the coming year and the Value Line opinion regarding stock price stability and investment timing.

Compact Disclosure is a database on a compact disk with information on over 4,000 public companies filing with the SEC. It is available from Disclosure Information Group of Bethesda, Maryland.

University of Chicago Stock Price Tapes is a set of monthly and daily stock price tapes developed by the Center for Research in Security Prices (CRSP) at the University of Chicago Graduate School of Business. The monthly tapes contain month-end prices from January 1926 to the present (updated annually) for every stock listed on the NYSE. Stock prices are adjusted for all stock splits, dividends, and any other capital changes. They added monthly AMEX data beginning from July 1962 to the NYSE monthly file to create the current NYSE/AMEX monthly file with information on approximately 6,100 securities.

The daily stock price tape contains the daily high, low, close, and volume figures since July 1962 for every stock listed on the NYSE and AMEX (approximately 5,600 securities). In 1988, the CRSP developed its NASDAQ historical data file with daily price quotes, volume, and information about capitalization and distributions to shareholders for over 9,600 common stocks traded on the NASDAQ system since December 14, 1972. These tapes are updated at the end of each calendar year and supplied to subscribers each spring.

The *Media General Data Bank,* compiled by Media General Financial Services, Inc., includes current price and volume data plus major corporate financial data on 2,000 major companies. In addition, it contains 10 years of daily price and volume information on over 8,000 issues of approximately 4,000 firms on the NYSE, the AMEX, and the OTC market. Finally, it includes price and volume data on several major market indexes.

ISL Daily Stock Price Tapes are prepared by Interactive Data Corporation. They contain the same information as the *Daily Stock Price Records.*

ONLINE DATABASES

Bi Data includes international statistical data including national accounts, labor statistics, foreign trade, consumption, prices, and production. It is produced by Business International Corp. and sold by General Electric Information Service.

Commodities Market Data Bank provides statistical data on all traded commodities. The producer and vendor are Data Resources Inc. (DRI).

Bloomberg is a data service that also includes very useful analytical programs for the analysis of bonds and stocks. Although the system initially emphasized bonds, it has been expanding its capability in domestic and international equities and derivatives. The firm publishes a monthly magazine that discusses new data and analytical program uses.

Bridge Information System is a comprehensive worldwide securities database. Global stocks, options, bonds, commodities, futures, indexes, currencies, and other derivatives are available on the Bridge system. Numerous, easy-to-read tables and graphs are available through a Microsoft Windows–based system. The firm publishes a monthly magazine that describes new additions to the database.

CompuServe, Inc. provides references, statistical data, and full text retrieval of information on numerous topics, including financial and investment data from Compustat and the Value Line databases. The producer and vendor are CompuServe, Inc.

Quick Quote provides current price quotations, trading volume information, and high–low data for the securities of U.S. public corporations. The producer and vendor are CompuServe, Inc.

Dow Jones News/Retrieval Service supplies texts of articles appearing in major financial publications including *The Wall Street Journal* and *Barron's.* The *StockQuote Reporter* service provides quotes on stocks, bonds, and mutual funds. The producer and vendor of both are Dow Jones & Company.

DRI Capsule/EEI Capsule services provide over 3,700 U.S. social and economic statistical time series on topics such as population, income, money supply, and interest rates. The producer is DRI and the vendor is Business Information Services.

The GTE Financial System One Quotation Service provides current quotations and statistical data on U.S. and Canadian stocks, bonds, options, and commodities along with other market data. The producer and vendor are GTE Information Systems, Inc.

The Information Bank provides extensive information on current affairs based on abstracts from numerous English-language publications. The producer and vendor are the New York Times Information Service.

Quotron 800 provides up-to-the-minute quotations and statistics for a broad range of stocks, bonds, options, and commodities. The producer and vendor are Quotron Systems, Inc.[13]

---

[13] An excellent source for additional computer databases and software as well as general information on business and economics is *The Irwin Business and Investment Almanac,* edited by Sumner W. Levine and Caroline Levine (Burr Ridge, IL: Irwin Professional Publishing, annual).

Summary

As an investor you must be aware of sources of information on the U.S. and world economies, the securities markets around the globe, alternative industries, and individual firms. You should use the information in this chapter as a *starting* point and spend time in a university library examining these and the many other sources available. Six books that will help are:

- Paul Wasserman, ed. *Encyclopedia of Business Information Sources.* 3d ed. Detroit: Gale Research Co., 1976.
- P. M. Daniells. *Business Information Sources.* 2d ed. Berkeley: University of California Press, 1986.
- Sylvia Michanie. *Course Syllabus for Information Sources of Business and Economics.* Brooklyn, NY: Pratt Institute School of Library and Information Science, 1977.
- *Fortune Investment Information Directory.* Guilford, CT: The Dushkin Publishing Group, Inc., 1986. This booklet contains a listing and brief description of numerous newspapers, magazines, investment letters, and books. There also is an excellent listing of software and databases of interest to investors in stocks, bonds, futures, and options.
- *Encyclopedia of Information Systems and Services.* Detroit: Gale Research Co., 1988.
- *Guide to American Directories.* Coral Springs, FL: B. Klein Publications, 1987.

Questions

1. Name at least three sources of information on the gross domestic product for the past 10 years.
2. Name two sources of information on rates of exchange with major foreign countries.
3. Assume you want to compare production in the steel and auto industry to industrial production for the economy. Discuss how you would do it, what data you would use, and where you would get the data.
4. You are told that a relationship exists between the growth rate of the money supply and stock price movements. Where would you obtain the data to test this relationship?
5. You are an analyst for Growth Stock Investment Company. The head of research tells you about a tip on an OTC firm, the Shamrock Corporation. He wants data on the company's sales, earnings, and recent stock price movements. Discuss several sources for this information. (One source is insufficient because the company may not be big enough to be included in some of them.)
6. The head of your research department indicates that the investment committee has decided to become involved in global investing. To get started, the committee wants you to recommend two sources of macroeconomic data for various countries, two sources of industry information, and two sources of company data. Discuss your recommendations.
7. As an individual investor, discuss four publications to which you believe you should subscribe (besides *The Wall Street Journal*). Indicate what each publication can give you and why it is appropriate for you as an individual investor. Be sure that at least two of these sources relate to global investing.
8. As the director of a newly established investment research department at a money management firm, discuss the first four investment services to which you will subscribe, and justify each selection.
9. Select one company each from the NYSE, the AMEX, and the OTC, and look up the name and address of the financial officers you would contact at each firm to obtain recent financial reports.

References

SOURCES OF INVESTMENT INFORMATION

American Banker-Bond Buyer, A division of International Thomson Publishing Corporation, One State Street Plaza, New York, NY 10004.

American Stock Exchange, 86 Trinity Place, New York, NY 10006.

Bloomberg, P.O. Box 888, Princeton, NJ 08542-0888.

Bridge Information Systems, Inc., 717 Office Parkway, St. Louis, MO 63141.

Business One Irwin Investor's Handbook is available from Irwin Professional Publishing, Burr Ridge, IL 60521.

Business Statistics is obtained from Superintendent of Documents, U.S. Government Printing Office, Washington, DC 20402.

Center for Research in Security Prices, Graduate School of Business, University of Chicago, Chicago, IL 60637.

CompuServe, Inc., 5000 Arlington Centre Boulevard, Columbus, OH 43220.

Data Resources, Inc. (DRI), 29 Hartwell Avenue, Lexington, MA 02173.

Dow Jones & Co., 200 Burnett Road, Chicopee, MA 01021.

Economic Indicators is available from Superintendent of Documents, U.S. Government Printing Office, Washington, DC 20402.

Economic Report of the President may be obtained from Superintendent of Documents, U.S. Government Printing Office, Washington, DC 20402.

Euromoney Publications PLC, Nestor House, Playhouse Yard, London ECUV 5EX. The address for North American subscriptions: Reed Business Publishing, 205 East 42nd Street, New York, NY 10017.

Federal Reserve Bulletin is available from the Division of Administrative Services, Board of Governors of the Federal Reserve System, Washington, DC 20551.

Financial Times is available from Bracken House, Cannon Street, London EC4P 4BY England. U.S. office: 44 East 60th Street, New York, NY 10022.

Global Information, Inc., 55 John Street, New York, NY 10038.

GTE Information Systems, Inc., East Park Drive, Mount Laurel, NJ 08054.

Ibbotson Associates, 225 North Michigan Ave., Chicago, IL 60601-7676.

IFR Publishing Ltd., 97 Middlesex Street, London EL 7EZ.

Institutional Investor Systems, Inc., 488 Madison Avenue, New York, NY 10022.

Interactive Data Corporation, 122 E. 42nd Street, New York, NY 10017.

International Finance Corporation, 1818 H Street, N.W., Washington, DC 20433.

Investors Management Services, P. O. Box 239, Denver, CO 80201.

London Stock Exchange, Trogmorton Street, London EG2N 1HP, England.

Media General Financial Services, Inc., P. O. Box 26991, Richmond, VA 23261.

Moody's Investor's Services, Inc., 99 Church Street, New York, NY 10007.

National Association of Securities Dealers, Inc. (NASD), 1735 K Street, N.W., Washington, DC 20006

New York Stock Exchange, 11 Wall Street, New York, NY 10005.

New York Times Information Services, Inc., 1719-A Route 10, Parsippany, NJ 07054.

Quarterly Financial Report is available from Superintendent of Documents, U.S. Government Printing Office, Washington, DC 20402.

Quotron Systems, Inc., 5454 Beethoven Street, Los Angeles, CA 90066.

Securities and Exchange Commission, 450 5th Street, N.W., Washington, DC 20549.

Standard & Poor's Corporation, 345 Hudson Street, New York, NY 10014.

Statistical Abstract of the United States is available from the Superintendent of Documents, U.S. Government Printing Office, Washington, DC 20402.

Statistical Bulletin is available from the Superintendent of Documents, U.S. Government Printing Office, Washington, DC 20402.

Survey of Current Business is available from Superintendent of Documents, U.S. Government Printing Office, Washington, DC 20402.

Tokyo Stock Exchange. The Exchange has an office in New York: TSE, New York Research Office, 45 Broadway, New York, NY 10006.

Value Line Services is available from Arnold Bernhard and Company, Inc., 5 East 44th Street, New York, NY 10017.

Part

2

Developments in Investment Theory

Chapter 7   *Efficient Capital Markets*

Chapter 8   *An Introduction to Portfolio Management*

Chapter 9   *An Introduction to Asset Pricing Models*

Chapter 10   *Extensions and Testing of Asset Pricing Theories*

Chapter 11   *An Introduction to Derivative Markets and Securities*

The chapters in Part I provided background on why individuals invest their funds and what they expect to derive from this activity. We also argued very strongly for a global investment program, described the major instruments and capital markets in a global investment environment, and showed the relationship among these instruments and markets. Finally, we discussed where you can get relevant information on these instruments and markets.

We now are ready to discuss how to analyze and value the various investment instruments available. In turn, valuation requires the estimation of expected returns (cash flows) and a determination of the risk involved in the securities. Before we can begin the analysis, we need to understand several major developments in investment theory that have influenced how we specify and measure risk in the valuation process. The purpose of the five chapters in this part is to provide this background on risk and asset valuation.

Chapter 7 describes the concept of efficient capital markets, which hypothesizes that security prices reflect the effect of all information. This chapter considers why markets should be efficient, discusses how one goes about testing this hypothesis, describes the results of the tests, and discusses the implications of the results for those engaged in technical and fundamental analysis as well as portfolio management.

Chapter 8 provides an introduction to portfolio theory, which was developed by Harry Markowitz. This theory provided the first rigorous measure of risk for investors and showed how one selects alternative assets to diversify and reduce the risk of a portfolio. Markowitz also derived a risk measure for individual securities within the context of an efficient portfolio.

Following the development of the Markowitz portfolio model, William Sharpe and several other academicians extended the Markowitz model into a general equilibrium asset pricing model that included an alternative risk measure for all risky assets. Chapter 9 contains a detailed discussion of these developments and an explanation of the relevant risk measure implied by this valuation model, referred to as the *capital asset pricing model* (CAPM). We introduce the CAPM at this early point in the book because the risk measure implied has been used extensively in various valuation models.

Chapter 9 also contains a discussion of an alternative asset pricing model referred to as the *arbitrage pricing theory* (APT). This theory was developed by Steve Ross in response to criticisms of the CAPM because of its restrictive assumptions and the difficulty in testing it. The fundamental differences between the CAPM and the APT models is that APT requires fewer assumptions and is considered a multivariate risk model compared to the CAPM, which is referred to as a single risk variable model (beta).

In Chapter 10, we return to the asset pricing models and consider the effect of changing some of the assumptions of the models. More important, we review the numerous studies that have empirically tested the CAPM and generated divergent results, including a fairly recent one that casts serious doubt on the basic model. We also revisit the "benchmark problem," which contends that it is not possible to use this model to analyze portfolio performance because the market portfolio typically used is clearly incomplete.

This chapter also includes a review of the APT model and how it differs from the CAPM. This is followed by a discussion of numerous studies that have tested the usefulness of this model compared to the CAPM. Again, the results are mixed in terms of supporting the model, and there are some who question whether it is possible to test this model because the factors cannot be identified.

In addition to the development of asset pricing models, another major development has been the creation and development of new markets and instruments beyond stocks and bonds. The greatest growth and development has been in the area referred to as *derivatives*, which includes options and futures. These instruments create a wider range of risk–return opportunities for investors. Chapter 11 provides an initial description of these instruments, including an understanding of the fundamental principles that determine their prices. Again, these derivative pricing principles can and should be applied to other assets including stocks, and especially bonds.

Chapter

7

Efficient Capital Markets

This chapter answers the following questions:

- What is meant by the concept that capital markets are efficient?
- Why *should* capital markets be efficient?
- What are the specific factors that contribute to an efficient market?
- Given the overall efficient market hypothesis, what are the three subhypotheses and what are the implications of each?
- How do you test the weak-form efficient market hypothesis (EMH) and what are the results of the tests?
- How do you test the semistrong-form EMH and what are the test results?
- How do you test the strong-form EMH and what are the test results?
- For each set of tests, which results support the hypothesis and which results indicate an anomaly related to the hypothesis?
- What are the implications of the results for:
  - technical analysis?
  - fundamental analysis?
  - portfolio managers with superior analysts?
  - portfolio managers with inferior analysts?
- What is the evidence related to the EMH for markets in foreign countries?

An **efficient capital market** is one in which security prices adjust rapidly to the arrival of new information and, therefore, the current prices of securities reflect all information about the security. Some of the most interesting and important academic research over the past 20 years has analyzed whether our capital markets are efficient. This extensive research is important because its results have significant real-world implications for investors and portfolio managers. In addition, the efficiency of capital markets is one of the most controversial areas in investment research because opinions regarding the efficiency of capital markets differ widely.

Because of its importance and the controversy, you need to understand the meaning of the terms *efficient capital markets* and *efficient market hypothesis (EMH)*. You should understand the analysis performed to test the EMH and the results of studies that either support or contradict the hypothesis. Finally, you should be aware of the implications of these results when you analyze alternative investments and work to construct a portfolio.

We consider the topic of efficient capital markets at this point for two reasons. First, the discussions in previous chapters have given you an understanding of how the capital markets function, so now it seems natural to consider the efficiency of the market in terms of how prices react to new information. Second, the overall evidence on capital market efficiency is best described as mixed, some studies support the hypothesis and others do not. The implications of these diverse results are important for you as an investor involved in analyzing securities and working to build a portfolio.

There are four major sections in this chapter. The first discusses why we would expect capital markets to be efficient and the factors that contribute to an efficient market where the prices of securities reflect available information.

The single efficient market hypothesis has been divided into three subhypotheses to facilitate testing. The second section describes these three subhypotheses and the implications of each of them.

Section three contains a discussion of the tests used to examine the three subhypotheses and reviews the results of numerous studies. This review of the research reveals that a large body of evidence supports the EMH, but a growing number of other studies do not support the hypotheses. These results that do not support the EMH indicate that there are a number of **anomalies.**

The final section discusses what these results mean for an investor who uses either technical analysis or fundamental analysis or for a portfolio manager who has access to superior or inferior analysts. This includes a discussion of how an analyst can take advantage of the anomalies noted in our review of the evidence from the tests. We conclude with a brief discussion of the evidence for markets in foreign countries.

As noted, we will discuss numerous empirical studies of efficient markets in this chapter. Because space limitations preclude dealing with them in depth, we encourage you to consult the literature cited in the footnotes and the reference section at the end of this chapter.

WHY SHOULD CAPITAL MARKETS BE EFFICIENT?

As noted earlier, in an efficient capital market, security prices adjust rapidly to the infusion of new information, and, therefore, current security prices fully reflect all available information. To be absolutely correct, this is referred to as an **informationally efficient market.** Although the idea of an efficient capital market is relatively straightforward, we often fail to consider *why* capital markets *should* be efficient. What set of assumptions imply an efficient capital market?

An initial, and very important, premise of an efficient market requires that *a large number of competing profit-maximizing participants analyze and value securities,* each independently of the others.

A second assumption is that *new information regarding securities comes to the market in a random fashion,* and the timing of one announcement is generally independent of others.

The third assumption is especially crucial: *The competing investors attempt to adjust security prices rapidly to reflect the effect of new information.* Although the price adjustment may be imperfect, it is unbiased. This means that sometimes the market will overadjust, and other times it will underadjust, but you cannot predict which will occur at any given time. Security prices adjust rapidly because numerous profit-maximizing investors are competing against one another.

The combined effect of (1) information coming in a random, independent fashion and (2) numerous competing investors analyzing the new information and adjusting stock prices rapidly to reflect this new information means that one would expect price changes to be independent and random. The adjustment process requires a large number of investors following the movements of the security, analyzing the impact of new information on its value, and buying or selling the security until its price adjusts to reflect the new information. This scenario implies that (1) informationally efficient markets require some minimum number of competing investors who analyze new information and trade and (2) more trading by numerous competing investors should cause a faster price adjustment, making the market more efficient. We will return to this need for trading and investor attention when we discuss some anomalies of the EMH.

Finally, because security prices adjust to all new information, these security prices should reflect all information that is publicly available at any point in time. Therefore, the security prices that prevail at any time should be an unbiased reflection of all currently available information, including the risk involved in owning the security. Therefore, in an efficient market, *the expected returns implicit in the current price of the security should reflect its risk.*

ALTERNATIVE EFFICIENT MARKET HYPOTHESES

Most of the early work related to efficient capital markets was based on the *random walk hypothesis,* which contended that changes in stock prices occurred randomly. This early academic work contained extensive empirical analysis without much theory behind it. Fama attempted to formalize the theory and organize the growing empirical evidence.[1] Fama presented the efficient market theory in terms of a *fair game* model.

EXPECTED RETURN OR FAIR GAME MODEL[2]

Unlike work done under the random walk hypothesis, which dealt with price movement over time, the fair game model deals with price at a specified point in time. It assumes that the price of a security fully reflects all available information at that point in time. The model requires that the price-formation process be specified in enough detail so that it is possible to indicate what is meant by "fully reflect." Most of the available models of equilibrium prices formulate prices in terms of rates of return that are dependent on alternative definitions of risk. All such expected return theories of price formation can be described notationally as follows:

$$E(\overline{P}_{j,t+1} \mid \phi_t) = [1 + E(\bar{r}_{j,t+1} \mid \phi_t)]P_{j,t},$$

where

E = expected value operator
$P_{j,t}$ = price of security j at time t
$P_{j,t+1}$ = price of security j at time $t + 1$
$r_{j,t+1}$ = the one period percent rate of return for security j during period $t + 1$
ϕ_t = the set of information that is assumed to be "fully reflected" in the security price at time t

This equation indicates that the expected price of security j, given the full set of information available at time $t(\phi_t)$, is equal to the current price times 1 plus the expected return on security j, given the set of available information. This expected future return should reflect the set of information available at t, which includes the state of the world at time t, including all current and past values of any relevant variables such as inflation, interest rates, earnings, GDP, and so forth. In addition, it is assumed that this information set includes knowledge of *all the relevant relationships among variables*—that is, it considers how alternative economic series relate to each other and how they relate to security prices.

If equilibrium market prices can be stated in terms of expected returns that "fully reflect" the information set ϕ_t, this implies that it is not possible to derive trading systems or investment strategies based on this current very encompassing information set and

---

[1] Eugene F. Fama, "Efficient Capital Markets: A Review of Theory and Empirical Work," *Journal of Finance* 25, no. 2 (May 1970): 383–417.

[2] This section is drawn from Fama, *ibid.*

experience returns beyond what should be expected on the basis of an asset's risk. Thus, let us define $x_{j,t+1}$ as the difference between the actual price in $t + 1$ and the expected price in $t + 1$:

$$x_{j,t+1} = P_{j,t+1} - E(P_{j,t-1}\ \phi_t)$$

The above equation can be described as a definition of *excess market value* for security j because it is the difference between the actual price and the expected price projected at t on the basis of the information set ϕ_t. In an efficient market:

$$E(\bar{x}_{j,t+1}\ \phi_t) = 0$$

This equation indicates that the market reflects a "fair game" with respect to the information set ϕ_t. This means that investors can be confident that *current prices fully reflect all available information and are consistent with the risk involved.*

Beyond articulating the efficient market (EM) theory in terms of a fair game model, in his original article, Fama divided the overall efficient market hypothesis (EMH) and the empirical tests of the hypotheses into three subhypotheses depending on the information set involved: (1) weak-form EMH, (2) semistrong-form EMH, and (3) strong-form EMH.

In a later article Fama again divided the empirical results into three groups, but shifted empirical results between the prior categories.[3] Basically, the weak-form category was broadened to include numerous studies previously considered in the semistrong-form category. Therefore, the following discussion uses the original categories but organizes the presentation of test results using the new categories.

In the remainder of this section, we describe the three hypotheses and the implications of each. In the following section, we describe how researchers have tested each of these hypotheses and briefly discuss the results of numerous studies.

WEAK-FORM EFFICIENT MARKET HYPOTHESIS

The **weak-form EMH** assumes that current stock prices fully reflect all *security-market information*, including the historical sequence of price, rates of return, trading volume data, and other market-generated information, such as odd-lot transactions, block trades, and transactions by exchange specialists or other unique groups. Because it assumes that current market prices already reflect all past returns and any other security-market information, this hypothesis implies that past rates of return and other market data should have no relationship with future rates of return (i.e., rates of return should be independent). Therefore, you should gain little from any trading rule that decides whether to buy or sell a security based on past rates of return or any other past market data.

SEMISTRONG-FORM EFFICIENT MARKET HYPOTHESIS

The **semistrong-form EMH** asserts that security prices adjust rapidly to the release of *all public information*: that is, current security prices fully reflect all public information. The semistrong hypothesis encompasses the weak-form hypothesis because all the market information considered by the weak-form hypothesis—such as stock prices, rates of return, and trading volume—is public. Public information also includes all nonmarket information such as earnings and dividend announcements, price-to-earnings (P/E) ratios, dividend-yield (D/P) ratios, book value–market value (BV/MV) ratios, stock splits, news about the economy, and political news. This hypothesis implies that investors who base their decisions on important new information *after it is public* should not derive above-average

[3] Eugene F. Fama, "Efficient Capital Markets: II," *Journal of Finance* 46, no. 5 (December 1991): 1575–1617.

profits from their transactions because the security price already reflects all such new public information.

The **strong-form EMH** contends that stock prices fully reflect *all information from public and private sources*. This means that no group of investors has monopolistic access to information relevant to the formation of prices. Therefore, no group of investors should be able to consistently derive above-average profits. The strong-form EMH encompasses both the weak-form and the semistrong-form EMH. Further, the strong-form EMH extends the assumption of efficient markets, in which prices adjust rapidly to the release of new public information, to assume perfect markets, in which all information is cost-free and available to everyone at the same time.

Now that you understand the three components of the EMH and what each of them implies regarding the effect on security prices of different sets of information, we can consider how a person doing research in this area tests to see whether the hypotheses are supported by the data. Therefore, in this section we discuss the specific tests used to gauge support for the hypotheses and we summarize the results of these tests.

Like most hypotheses in finance and economics, the evidence on the EMH is mixed. Results from some studies have supported the hypothesis and indicate that capital markets are efficient. Results from some other studies have not been consistent with the hypotheses and have revealed some anomalies related to these hypotheses, raising questions about support for them.

Researchers have formulated two groups of tests of the weak-form EMH. The first category involves statistical tests of independence between rates of return. The second entails a comparison of risk–return results for trading rules that make investment decisions based on past market information versus results from a simple buy-and-hold policy, which assumes that you buy stock at the beginning of a test period and hold it to the end.

STATISTICAL TESTS OF INDEPENDENCE   As discussed earlier, the EMH contends that security returns over time should be independent of one another because new information comes to the market in a random, independent fashion, and security prices adjust rapidly to this new information. Two major statistical tests have been used to verify this independence.

First, **autocorrelation tests** of independence measure the significance of positive or negative correlation in returns over time. Does the rate of return on day t correlate with the rate of return on day $t - 1$, $t - 2$, or $t - 3$?[4] Those who believe that capital markets are efficient would expect insignificant correlations for all such combinations.

Several researchers have examined the serial correlations among stock returns for several relatively short time horizons, including 1 day, 4 days, 9 days, and 16 days.[5] The results typically indicated insignificant correlation in stock returns over time. The typical range of correlation coefficients was from +.10 to −.10, and these were typically not statistically significant. Some recent studies that considered portfolios of stocks with dif-

[4] For a discussion of tests of independence, see S. Christian Albright, *Statistics for Business and Economics* (New York: Macmillan Publishing, 1987), 515–517.

[5] Eugene F. Fama, "The Behavior of Stock Market Prices," *Journal of Business* 38, no. 1 (January 1965): 34–105; and Eugene Fama and James MacBeth, "Risk, Return and Equilibrium: Empirical Tests," *Journal of Political Economy* 81, no. 3 (May–June 1973): 607–636.

ferent market values (size) have indicated that the autocorrelation is stronger for portfolios of small stocks.[6] Therefore, although the older results tend to support the hypothesis, the more recent studies cast doubt on it for portfolios of small firms, although these results could be affected by nonsynchronous trading for small-firm stocks.

The second statistical test of independence is the **runs tests.**[7] Given a series of price changes, each price change is either designated a plus (+) if it is an increase in price or a minus (−) if it is a decrease in price. The result is a set of pluses and minuses as follows: + + + − + − − + + − − + +. A run occurs when two consecutive changes are the same; two or more consecutive positive or negative price changes constitute one run. When the price changes in a different direction, such as when a negative price change is followed by a positive price change, the run ends and a new run may begin. To test for independence, you would compare the number of runs for a given series to the number in a table of expected values for the number of runs that should occur in a random series.

Studies that have examined stock price runs have confirmed the independence of stock price changes over time. The actual number of runs for stock price series consistently fell into the range expected for a random series. Therefore, these statistical tests have confirmed the independence of stock price changes over time. These statistical tests of independence have been repeated for stocks traded on the OTC market, and the results supported the EMH.[8]

Although short horizon stock returns have generally supported the weak-form EMH, several studies that examined price changes for individual *transactions* on the NYSE found significant serial correlations. Notably, none of these studies attempted to show that the dependence of transaction price movements could be used to earn above-average, risk-adjusted returns. Apparently, the significant correlation among individual transactions returns is due to the market-making activities of the specialist, but investors probably cannot use this small imperfection to derive excess profits after considering the trading rule's substantial transactions costs.[9]

TESTS OF TRADING RULES   The second group of tests of the weak-form EMH were developed in response to the assertion that the prior statistical tests of independence were too rigid to identify the intricate price patterns examined by technical analysts. Technical analysts do not accept a set number of positive or negative price changes as a signal of a move to a new equilibrium in the market—they typically look for a general consistency in the price and volume trends over time. Such a trend might include both positive and negative changes. For this reason, technical analysts felt that their **trading rules** were too sophisticated and complicated to be simulated by rigid statistical tests.

In response to this objection, investigators attempted to examine alternative technical trading rules through simulation. Advocates of an efficient market hypothesized that inves-

[6] Jennifer Conrad and Gantam Kaul, "Time Variation in Expected Returns," *Journal of Business* 61, no. 4 (October 1988): 409–425; and Andrew W. Lo and A. Craig MacKinley, "Stock Market Prices Do Not Follow Random Walks: Evidence from a Simple Specifications Test," *Review of Financial Studies* 1, no. 1 (Spring 1988): 41–66.

[7] For the details of a runs test, see Albright, *Statistics for Business and Economics,* 695–699.

[8] Robert L. Hagerman and Richard D. Richmond, "Random Walks, Martingales and the OTC," *Journal of Finance* 28, no. 4 (September 1973): 897–909.

[9] J. Campbell, S. Grossman, and J. Wang, "Trading Volume and Serial Correlation in Stock Returns," *Quarterly Journal of Economics* 108, no. 3 (1993): 905–934; L. Glosten, "Insider Trading, Liquidity, and the Role of the Monopolist Specialist," *Journal of Business* 54, no. 2 (April 1989): 579–596; and L. Harris, "A Transactions Data Study of Weekly and Intradaily Patterns in Stock Returns," *Journal of Financial Economics* 16, no. 1 (May 1986): 99–117.

tors could not derive profits above a buy-and-hold policy, or abnormal profits, using any trading rule that depended solely on any past market information about factors such as price, volume, odd-lot sales, or specialist activity.

The trading rule studies compared the risk–return results derived from such a simulation, including transactions costs, to the results from a simple buy-and-hold policy. Three major pitfalls can negate the results of a trading rule study:

1. The investigator should *use only publicly available data* in the decision rule. For example, the earnings for a firm as of December 31 may not be publicly available until April 1, so you should not factor in an earnings report until then.
2. When computing the returns from a trading rule, you should *include all transactions costs* involved in implementing the trading strategy because most trading rules involve many more transactions than a simple buy-and-hold policy.
3. You must *adjust the results for risk* because a trading rule might simply select a portfolio of high-risk securities that should experience higher returns.

Researchers have encountered two operational problems in carrying out these tests of specific trading rules. First, some trading rules require too much subjective interpretation of data to simulate mechanically. Second, the almost infinite number of potential trading rules makes it impossible to test all of them. As a result, only the better-known technical trading rules have been examined.

Another factor you should recognize is that some studies have been somewhat biased. Specifically, the operational problems noted above have restricted the studies to relatively simple trading rules, which many technicians contend are rather naive.

In addition, these studies typically employ readily available data from the NYSE, which is biased toward well-known, heavily traded stocks that certainly should trade in efficient markets. Because markets should be more efficient with higher numbers of aggressive, profit-maximizing investors attempting to adjust stock prices to reflect new information, market efficiency depends on trading volume. Specifically, *more trading in a security should promote market efficiency.* Alternatively, for securities with relatively few stockholders and little trading activity, the market could be inefficient because fewer investors would be analyzing the effect of new information and this limited interest would result in insufficient trading activity to move the price of the security quickly to a new equilibrium value that would reflect the new information. Therefore, using only active, heavily traded stocks in the trading rule tests could bias the results toward finding efficiency.

RESULTS OF SIMULATIONS OF SPECIFIC TRADING RULES   In the most popular trading technique, **filter rules,** an investor trades a stock when the price change exceeds a filter value set for it. As an example, an investor using a 5 percent filter would envision a positive breakout if the stock were to rise 5 percent from some base, suggesting that the stock price would continue to rise. A technician would acquire the stock to take advantage of the expected continued rise. In contrast, a 5 percent decline from some peak price would be considered a breakout on the downside, and the technician would expect a further price decline and would sell any holdings of the stock, and possibly even sell the stock short.

Studies of this trading rule have used a range of filters from 0.5 percent to 50 percent. The results indicated that small filters would yield above-average profits before taking account of trading commissions. However, small filters generate numerous trades and, therefore, substantial trading costs. When these trading commissions were considered, all the trading profits turned to losses. Alternatively, larger filters did not yield returns above those of a simple buy-and-hold policy.[10]

Researchers have simulated other trading rules that used past market data other than stock prices.[11] Trading rules have been devised that use odd-lot figures, advanced-decline ratios, short sales, short positions, and specialist activities. These simulation tests have generated mixed results. Most of the early studies suggested that these trading rules generally would not outperform a buy-and-hold policy on a risk-adjusted basis after taking account of commissions, while a couple of recent studies have indicated support for specific trading rules.[12] Therefore, most evidence from simulations of specific trading rules indicates that these trading rules have not been able to beat a buy-and-hold policy. These results support the weak-form EMH.

SEMISTRONG-FORM HYPOTHESIS: TESTS AND RESULTS

Recall that the semistrong-form EMH asserts that security prices adjust rapidly to the release of all public information; that is, security prices fully reflect all public information. Using the organization adopted by Fama, studies that have tested the semistrong-form EMH can be divided into the following sets of studies:

1. Studies to predict future rates of return using available public information beyond the pure market information such as prices and trading volume considered in the weak-form tests. These studies can involve either *time-series analysis* of returns or the *cross-section distribution* of returns or other characteristics (e.g., price/earnings ratios or price/book value ratios) for individual stocks. Those who believe in the EMH would contend that it would not be possible to predict *future* returns using past returns or to predict the distribution of future returns using public information.
2. Event studies that examine how fast stock prices adjust to specific significant economic events. A corollary approach would be to test whether it is possible to invest in a security after the public announcement of a significant event and experience significant abnormal rates of return. Again, advocates of the EMH would expect security prices to adjust very rapidly, such that it would not be possible for investors to experience superior risk-adjusted returns by investing after the public announcement of any significant information and paying normal transactions costs.

ADJUSTMENT FOR MARKET EFFECTS   For any of these tests, you need to adjust the security's rates of return for the rates of return of the overall market during the period considered. A 5 percent return in a stock during the period surrounding an announcement is not meaningful until you know what the aggregate stock market did during the same period and how this stock normally acts under such conditions. If the market had experienced a 10 percent return during this period, the 5 percent return for the stock may be lower than expected.

---

[10] Eugene Fama and Marshall Blume, "Filter Rules and Stock Market Trading Profits," *Journal of Business* 39, no. 1 (January 1966 Supplement): 226–241.

[11] Many of these trading rules are discussed in Chapter 21 on technical analysis.

[12] George Pinches, "The Random Walk Hypothesis and Technical Analysis," *Financial Analysts Journal* 26, no. 2 (March–April 1970): 104–110. Two studies have indicated support for some technical trading rules that use a three-part filter or adjust relative strength for the January effect; see John S. Brush, "Eight Relative Strength Models Compared," *Journal of Portfolio Management* 13, no. 1 (Fall 1986): 21–28; and Stephen W. Pruitt and Richard E. White, "Who Says Technical Analysis Can't Beat the Market?" *Journal of Portfolio Management* 14, no. 3 (Spring 1988): 55–58. For a study that casts doubt on the ability to implement such trading rules in the real world, see Ray Ball, S. P. Kothari, and Charles Wasley, "Can We Implement Research on Stock Trading Rules?" *The Journal of Portfolio Management* 21, no. 2 (Winter 1995): 54–63.

Authors of studies prior to 1970 generally recognized the need to make such adjustments for market movements. They typically assumed that the individual stocks should experience returns equal to the aggregate stock market. This assumption meant that the market adjustment process simply entailed subtracting the market return from the return for the individual security to derive its **abnormal rate of return,** as follows:

$$AR_{it} = R_{it} - R_{mt}$$

where

AR_{it} = abnormal rate of return on security i during period t
R_{it} = rate of return on security i during period t
R_{mt} = rate of return on a market index during period t

In the example where the stock experienced a 5 percent increase while the market increased 10 percent, the stock's abnormal return would be minus 5 percent.

Some authors have adjusted the rates of return for securities by an amount different from the market rate of return, recognizing that all stocks do not change by the same amount as the market; that is, some stocks are more volatile than the market, and some are less volatile. These possibilities mean that you must determine an *expected* rate of return for the stock based on the market rate of return *and* the stock's relationship with the market. As an example, suppose a stock is generally 20 percent more volatile than the market. In such a case, if the market experiences a 10 percent rate of return, you would expect this stock to experience a 12 percent rate of return. Therefore, you would determine the abnormal return by computing the difference between the stock's actual rate of return and its **expected rate of return** as follows:

$$AR_{it} = R_{it} - E(R_{it})$$

where

$E(R_{it})$ = the expected rate of return for stock i during period t based on the market rate of return and the stock's normal relationship with the market (its beta)

Continuing with the example, if the stock that was expected to have a 12 percent return (based on a market return of 10 percent and a stock beta of 1.20) had only a 5 percent return, its abnormal rate of return during the period would be minus 7 percent. Over the normal long-run period, you would expect the abnormal returns for a stock to be zero. Specifically, during one period the returns may exceed expectations, and in the next period they may fall short of expectations.

To summarize, there are two sets of tests of the semistrong-form EMH. In the first set, investigators attempt to predict the future rates of return for individual stocks or the aggregate market (i.e., predict the time series) using public information such as the aggregate dividend yield or the risk premium spread for bonds. Alternatively, analysts look for public information regarding individual stocks that will allow them to predict the cross-sectional distribution of risk-adjusted rates of return (i.e, test whether it is possible to use variables such as the earnings-price ratio, market value size, book value/market value ratio, or the dividend yield to predict which stocks will experience above-average or below-average risk-adjusted rates of return). In the second set of tests (event studies), they examine abnormal rates of return for the period immediately after an announcement of a significant economic event to determine whether it is possible for an investor to derive above-average risk-adjusted rates of return by investing after the release of public information.

In both sets of tests, the emphasis is on the analysis of abnormal rates of return that deviate from long-term expectations, or returns that are adjusted for a stock's specific risk characteristics and overall market rates of return during the period.

RESULTS OF RETURN PREDICTION STUDIES   The *time-series tests* assume that in an efficient market the best estimate of *future* rates of return will be the long-run *historical* rates of return. The point of the tests is to determine whether there is any public information that will provide superior estimates of returns for a short-run horizon (1 to 6 months) or a long-run horizon (1 to 5 years).

The results of these studies have indicated that there is limited success in predicting short-horizon returns, but the analysis of long-horizon returns has been quite successful. Rozeff and Shiller postulated that the aggregate dividend yield (D/P) was a proxy for the risk premium on stocks.[13] Their results indicated a positive relationship between the D/P and future stock-market returns. An analysis and explanation of this relationship for long horizons of 2 to 4 years is contained in papers by Fama and French, which show that the predictive power increases with the horizon.[14] A subsequent study by Balvers, Cosimano, and McDonald showed that within an efficient market framework, stock prices do not have to follow a random walk and *long-run* returns on stocks can be predicted as long as you can predict aggregate output.[15]

Several studies have considered dividend yield and two variables related to the term structure of interest rates: (1) a default spread, which is the difference between the yields on lower-grade and Aaa-rated long-term corporate bonds (this spread has been used in earlier chapters of this book as a proxy for a market risk premium); and (2) the *term structure or horizon spread,* which is the difference between the long-term Aaa yield and the yield on 1-month Treasury bills.[16] These studies find that these variables can be used to predict stock returns and bond returns and have even been found to be useful for predicting returns for foreign common stocks.[17]

The reasoning for these empirical results is that when the two most significant variables—the dividend yield (D/P) and the default spread—are high, it implies that investors are expecting or requiring a high return on stocks and bonds, and this occurs when the economic environment has been poor, as reflected in the growth rate of output. Such a poor economic environment indicates a low wealth environment wherein investors perceive

[13] Michael Rozeff, "Dividend Yields as Equity Risk Premiums," *Journal of Portfolio Management* 11, no. 1 (Fall 1984): 68–75; and Robert Shiller, "Stock Prices and Social Dynamics," *Brookings Papers on Economic Activity* 2 (1984): 457–510.

[14] Eugene F. Fama and Kenneth R. French, "Dividend Yields and Expected Stock Returns," *Journal of Financial Economics* 22, no. 1 (October 1988): 3–25; and Eugene F. Fama and Kenneth R. French, "Business Conditions and Expected Returns on Stocks and Bonds," *Journal of Financial Economics* 25, no. 1 (November 1989): 23–49.

[15] Ronald J. Balvers, Thomas F. Cosimano, and Bill McDonald, "Predicting Stock Returns in an Efficient Market," *Journal of Finance* 45, no. 4 (September 1990): 1109–1128.

[16] Donald B. Keim and Robert F. Stambaugh, "Predicting Returns in Stock and Bond Markets," *Journal of Financial Economics* 17, no. 2 (December 1986): 357–390; John Y. Campbell, "Stock Returns and the Term Structure," *Journal of Financial Economics* 18, no. 2 (June 1987): 373–399; and Nai fu Chen, "Financial Investment Opportunities and the Macroeconomy," *Journal of Finance* 46, no. 2 (June 1991): 529–594.

[17] Harvey Campbell, "The World Price of Covariance Risk," *Journal of Finance* 46, no. 1 (March 1991): 111–157.

higher risk for investments, which means that to invest and shift consumption from the present to the future investors will require a high rate of return.

A recent study by Pesaran and Timmermann considered a number of business cycle variables and found that the predictive power of various economic factors related to stock returns changes through time and tends to vary with the volatility of returns.[18] Specifically, the predictability of returns was low during the calm markets of the 1960s, but predictions could have been exploited even considering transactions costs during the volatile markets of the 1970s.

QUARTERLY EARNINGS STUDIES   An important set of studies involves quarterly earnings reports, which can be considered part of the time-series analysis. The question is, is it possible to predict future returns for a stock based on publicly available quarterly earnings reports?

Numerous studies by Latané and associates on the usefulness of quarterly reports consistently have failed to support the semistrong EMH.[19] A study by Joy, Litzenberger, and McEnally (JLM) examined firms that experienced unanticipated changes in quarterly earnings using three categories based on how actual earnings deviated from expectations: (1) any deviation from expectations, (2) a deviation of plus or minus 20 percent, and (3) a deviation of at least 40 percent.[20] They examined abnormal price changes from 13 weeks prior to the announcement to 26 weeks following it. The abnormal price movements for the "any deviation" category for companies with good earnings was about 1 to 2 percent during the period compared to transactions costs of 2 to 3 percent, indicating a lack of profit opportunities. For the 20-percent-above-expectations category, the post-announcement gain was about 4 percent compared to 5 to 6 percent gains when actual earnings were 40-percent-above-expectations. These abnormal returns exceeded transaction costs. The price adjustment to unfavorable earnings performance was more rapid, and there were no abnormal returns for any category.

These results suggest that favorable information contained in quarterly earnings reports (i.e., positive earnings surprises) is not instantaneously reflected in stock prices and that a significant relationship exists between the size of the unexpected earnings performance and the post-announcement stock price change.

In reviewing these studies, Joy and Jones noted problems in several of the earlier studies that they believed were remedied in the more recent ones.[21] Ball reviewed 20 studies of price reaction to earnings announcements and found that the post-announcement risk-adjusted abnormal returns are consistently positive, which is inconsistent with market efficiency.[22] He contended that the abnormal returns are due to problems with the capital asset pricing model (the CAPM is discussed in Chapter 9) used to derive expected returns,

[18] M. Hashem Pesaran and Allann Timmermann, "Predictability of Stock Returns: Robustness and Economic Significance," *Journal of Finance* 50, no. 4 (September 1995): 1201–1228.

[19] Representative studies in the area are H. A. Latané, O. Maurice Joy, and Charles P. Jones, "Quarterly Data, Sort-Rank Routines, and Security Evaluation," *Journal of Business* 43, no. 4 (October 1970): 427–438; and C. Jones and R. Litzenberger, "Quarterly Earnings Reports and Intermediate Stock Price Trends," *Journal of Finance* 25, no. 1 (March 1970): 143–148.

[20] O. Maurice Joy, Robert H. Litzenberger, and Richard W. McEnally, "The Adjustment of Stock Prices to Announcements of Unanticipated Changes in Quarterly Earnings," *Journal of Accounting Research* 15, no. 2 (Autumn 1977): 207–225.

[21] O. Maurice Joy and Charles P. Jones, "Earnings Reports and Market Efficiencies: An Analysis of Contrary Evidence," *Journal of Financial Research* 2, no. 1 (Spring 1979): 51–63.

[22] Ray Ball, "Anomalies in Relationships Between Securities' Yields and Yield-Surrogates," *Journal of Financial Economics* 6, no. 2/3 (June–September 1978): 103–126.

not market inefficiencies. Watts found significant abnormal returns even after making all the adjustments suggested by Ball.[23] He explicitly showed that the abnormal returns were due to market inefficiencies rather than the CAPM, but noted that the abnormal returns were small and not completely consistent over time.

The more recent earnings announcement studies have used the concept of *standardized unexpected earnings (SUE)*.[24] Rather than examine the percentage differences between actual and expected, this technique normalizes the difference between actual and expected earnings for the quarter by the standard error of estimate from the regression used to derive the expected earnings figure. Therefore, the SUE is:

$$\frac{\text{Reported EPS}_t - \text{Predicted EPS}_t}{\substack{\text{Standard Error of Estimate for the} \\ \text{Estimating Regression Equation}}}$$

The predicted earnings are estimated by a time-series model that considers the earnings during the prior 20 quarters and includes quarterly dummy variables that adjust for any seasonal factors. Therefore, the SUE indicates how many standard errors the reported EPS figure is above or below the predicted EPS figure. The typical categories are greater than 4.0, between 4.0 and 3.0, between 3.0 and 2.0, and so on, all the way to less than minus 4.0.

An extensive analysis by Rendleman, Jones, and Latané (RJL) using a very large sample and daily returns provided evidence that large SUEs were accompanied by significant abnormal stock price changes.[25] These results contrasted with the earlier findings by Reinganum that the abnormal returns between high and low SUE portfolios were not statistically different from zero.[26] The RJL results were confirmed for the time period examined by Reinganum (1975–1977), but also from 1971 to 1980. RJL also examined the impact of different risk adjustments and concluded that the results were not sensitive to the risk adjustments. The analysis of daily data from 20 days before a quarterly earnings announcement to 90 days after the announcement indicated that 31 percent of the total response in stock returns came before the announcement, 18 percent on the announcement day, and 51 percent afterwards.

Foster, Olsen, and Shevlin examined several reasons for the return drift following earnings announcements and confirmed the prior results using different earnings expectations models.[27] The unexpected earnings explained over 80 percent of the subsequent stock price drift for the total time period and during several subperiods. Mendenhall and later Bernard and Thomas review the prior studies and attempt to explain this pervasive drift.[28]

---

[23] Ross L. Watts, "Systematic 'Abnormal' Returns After Quarterly Earnings Announcements," *Journal of Financial Economics* 6, no. 2/3 (June–September 1978): 127–150.

[24] These include Henry A. Latané and Charles P. Jones, "Standardized Unexpected Earnings—A Progress Report," *Journal of Finance* 32, no. 5 (December 1977): 1457–1465; and Henry A. Latané and Charles Jones, "Standardized Unexpected Earnings; 1971–1977," *Journal of Finance* 34, no. 3 (June 1979): 717–724.

[25] Richard J. Rendleman, Jr., Charles P. Jones, and Henry A. Latané, "Empirical Anomalies Based on Unexpected Earnings and the Importance of Risk Adjustments," *Journal of Financial Economics* 10, no. 3 (November 1982): 269–287; and C. P. Jones, R. J. Rendleman, Jr., and H. A. Latané, "Earnings Announcements: Pre- and Post-Responses," *Journal of Portfolio Management* 11, no. 3 (Spring 1985): 28–32.

[26] Marc R. Reinganum, "Misspecification of Capital Asset Pricing," *Journal of Financial Economics* 9, no. 1 (March 1981): 19–46.

[27] George Foster, Chris Olsen, and Terry Shevlin, "Earnings Releases, Anomalies, and the Behavior of Security Returns," *Accounting Review* 59, no. 4 (October 1984): 574–603.

[28] Richard R. Mendenhall, "An Investigation of Anomalies Based on Unexpected Earnings" (Ph.D. dissertation, Indiana University, 1986); and Victor L. Bernard and Jacob K. Thomas, "Post-Earnings-Announcement Drift: Delayed Price Response or Risk Premium?" *Journal of Accounting Research* 27, Supplement (1989).

In summary, these results indicate that the market has not adjusted stock prices to reflect the release of quarterly **earnings surprises** as fast as expected by the semistrong EMH. As a result, it appears that earnings surprises can be used to predict returns for individual stocks.[29]

Another set of studies that attempted to predict rates of return are the *calendar studies,* which questioned whether some regularities exist in the rates of return during the calendar year that would allow investors to predict returns on stocks. These include numerous studies on "the January anomaly" and those that consider a variety of other daily and weekly regularities.

The January anomaly   Several years ago, Branch proposed a unique trading rule for taking advantage of tax selling.[30] Investors tend to engage in tax selling at the end of the year to establish losses on stocks that have declined. After the new year, there is a tendency to reacquire these stocks or to buy other stocks that look attractive. This scenario would produce downward pressure on stock prices in late November and December and positive pressure in early January. Those who believe in efficient markets would not expect such a seasonal pattern to persist; it should be eliminated by arbitrageurs who would buy in December and sell in early January.

Dyl supported the tax selling hypothesis when he found that December trading volume was abnormally high for stocks that had declined during the previous year and that volume was abnormally low for stocks that had experienced large gains.[31] He found significant abnormal returns during January for stocks that had experienced losses during the prior year.

Roll confirmed the price pattern on the last day of December and the first four days of January.[32] Stocks with negative returns during the prior year had higher returns around January 1 and 2. The results also indicated that smallness had an effect beyond volatility and tax selling. To examine the impact of transaction costs, Roll assumed a purchase on the second-to-last day of the year and a sale of the fourth day of the new year. This trading rule generated returns of 6.89 percent for the NYSE and 14.2 percent for the AMEX. Applying the 6.77 percent commissions estimated by Stoll and Whaley for small firms, they still had excess returns of 3.94 percent for the NYSE and 10.3 percent for the AMEX. Assuming a purchase at the high price for the second-to-last trading day and sales at the low price on the fourth day of the new year—and adding commissions—there was no profit on the NYSE, but there was an excess return on the AMEX. Roll concluded that because of transaction costs, arbitrageurs must not be eliminating the January tax selling anomaly.

Keim analyzed the relation between abnormal returns and market value during each month of the year. Overall he found a negative relationship between size and abnormal returns, but the strongest relationship was always in January, where nearly 50 percent of the overall size effect occurred.[33] In fact, more than 50 percent of the January effect was concentrated in the first week of trading, particularly on the first day of the year.

---

[29] Academic studies such as these that have indicated the importance of earnings surprises have led *The Wall Street Journal* to publish a section on "earnings surprises" in connection with regular quarterly earnings reports.

[30] Ben Branch, "A Tax Loss Trading Rule," *Journal of Business* 50, no. 2 (April 1977): 198–207. These results were generally confirmed in Ben Branch and Kyun Chun Chang, "Tax-Loss Trading—Is the Game Over or Have the Rules Changed?" *The Financial Review* 20, no. 1 (February 1985): 55–69.

[31] Edward A. Dyl, "Capital Gains Taxation and Year-End Stock Market Behavior," *Journal of Finance* 32, no. 1 (March 1977): 165–175.

[32] Richard Roll, "Vas Ist Das?" *Journal of Portfolio Management* 9, no. 2 (Winter 1983): 18–28.

[33] Donald B. Keim, "Size-Related Anomalies and Stock Return Seasonality," *Journal of Financial Economics* 12, no. 1 (June 1983): 13–32.

Following the earlier work by Rozeff and Kinney,[34] Reinganum found large abnormal returns at the beginning of January, consistent with tax-loss selling.[35] Still, small firms that did very well the prior year also experienced large abnormal returns in early January, which is not consistent with the tax selling hypothesis.

Brown, Keim, Kleidon, and Marsh examined the January effect using Australian data because the year-end for tax purposes in Australia is June 30, making the seasonal tax effect occur in July.[36] The results indicated the largest seasonals in January and July. Although the results for July support the tax selling hypothesis, the January impact cannot be explained. Berges, McConnell, and Schlarbaum document the January effect using Canadian data for the period 1951–1980, but Canada did not introduce the capital gains tax until 1973.[37] Therefore, the tax-loss hypothesis cannot explain the January effect, but they did not find the small-firm effect in January.

Chang and Pinegar indicate support for the tax-loss selling hypothesis based on an analysis of long-term government and corporate bonds, with most of the support coming from lower-rated bonds (BB and B).[38] Because they also derived January gains that could not be explained by tax selling, they felt that tax-loss selling is probably not the only cause of January gains. Tinic and West highlighted the January effect by examining the seasonality of the relationship between expected return and risk.[39] They found that there was no significant risk–return relationship in any single month (except January), nor during the other eleven months combined.

Keim analyzed dividend yields and stock returns overall and found a nonlinear relationship in January.[40] Specifically, the zero dividend securities had the largest return, and for the rest of the groups there was a positive relationship between the dividend yield and the stock returns. He likewise found a strong seasonal pattern because the dividend yield–stock return relationship only existed during January. Lakonishok and Smidt found a year-end effect in trading volume for small firms—the most active day being the last day of the year with above-normal trading activity continuing in January.[41]

The January anomaly is intriguing because it is so pervasive. Its relationship with the small-firm effect is fascinating because of the apparent speed of impact. This seasonal impact also influences the dividend yield effect and trading volume, and a tax-loss explana-

---

[34] Michael S. Rozeff and William R. Kinney, Jr., "Capital Market Seasonality: The Case of Stock Returns," *Journal of Financial Economics* 3, no. 4 (December 1976): 379–402.

[35] Marc R. Reinganum, "The Anomalous Stock Market Behavior of Small Firms in January: Empirical Tests for Tax-Loss Selling Effects," *Journal of Financial Economics* 12, no. 1 (January 1983): 89–104.

[36] Philip Brown, Donald B. Keim, Allan W. Kleidon, and Terry A. Marsh, "Stock Return Seasonalities and the Tax-Loss Selling Hypothesis," *Journal of Financial Economics* 12, no. 1 (June 1983): 105–127.

[37] Angel Berges, John J. McConnell, and Gary G. Schlarbaum, "The Turn-of-the-Year in Canada," *Journal of Finance* 39, no. 1 (March 1984): 185–192.

[38] Eric C. Chang and J. Michael Pinegar, "Return Seasonality and Tax-Loss Selling in the Market for Long-Term Government and Corporate Bonds," *Journal of Financial Economics* 17, no. 2 (December 1986): 391–415.

[39] Seha M. Tinic and Richard R. West, "Risk and Return: January vs. the Rest of the Year," *Journal of Financial Economics* 13, no. 4 (December 1984): 561–574.

[40] Donald B. Keim, "Dividend Yields and Stock Returns: Implications of Abnormal January Returns," *Journal of Financial Economics* 14, no. 3 (September 1985): 473–489; Donald B. Keim, "Dividend Yields and the January Effect," *Journal of Portfolio Management* 12, no. 2 (Winter 1986): 54–60.

[41] Josef Lakonishok and Seymour Smidt, "Volume and Turn-of-the-Year Behavior," *Journal of Financial Economics* 13, no. 3 (September 1984): 435–455; and Josef Lakonishok and Seymour Smidt, "Trading Bargains in Small Firms at Year-End," *Journal of Portfolio Management* 12, no. 3 (Spring 1986): 24–29.

tion of this anomaly has received mixed support. Despite numerous studies, the January anomaly poses as many questions as it answers.[42]

Other calendar effects   Although not as significant as the January anomaly, several other "calendar" effects have been examined, including a monthly effect, a weekend/day-of-the-week effect, and an intraday effect. Ariel found a significant monthly effect wherein all the market's cumulative advance occurred during the first half of trading months.[43]

The weekend effect has been documented by French and by Gibbons and Hess.[44] French found that the mean return for Monday was significantly negative during 5-year subperiods and during the full period. In contrast, the average return for the other 4 days was positive. Gibbons and Hess had results that were consistent with French, and found negative returns on Monday for individual stocks and Treasury bills, Keim and Stambaugh found negative Monday results back to 1928 for individual exchange-listed stocks and for active OTC stocks.[45] The effect was similar for different size firms that were exchange-traded or OTC.

Rogalski decomposed the Monday effect that is typically measured from Friday close to Monday close into a *weekend effect* from Friday close to Monday open and a *Monday trading effect* from Monday open to the Monday close.[46] He showed that the negative Monday effect found in prior studies occurs from the Friday close to the Monday open (i.e., the weekend effect). After adjusting for the weekend effect, the Monday trading effect was positive. When the day-of-the-week returns were segmented into January and the rest of the year, the Monday effect and the nontrading effect were on average positive in January and negative for all other months. Also, the size effect only existed in January.

Two studies have examined this question using intraday observations. Smirlok and Stacks examined hourly observations between 1963 and 1983 for the total period and three subperiods.[47] They found a change in the pattern of returns before and after 1974. The results for the period 1974–1983 were consistent with Rogalski wherein the Monday effect is concentrated in the weekend effect. In contrast, before 1974 the Monday effect occurred during the Monday trading period. These results imply a shift in the timing of the weekend effect wherein recently the negative effect is during the weekend. Notably, the Monday trading effect has turned positive because the negative Monday morning effect is swamped by positive Monday afternoon returns.

Harris examined the NYSE transactions data, which allowed an analysis across firms and over time.[48] The analysis of trading and nontrading returns indicated that for *large firms,* the negative Monday effect occurred before the market opened (it was a weekend effect), whereas for smaller firms most of the negative Monday effect occurred during the

[42] An article that reviews these studies and others is Donald B. Keim, "The CAPM and Equity Return Regularities," *Financial Analysts Journal* 42, no. 3 (May–June 1986): 19–34.

[43] Robert A. Ariel, "A Monthly Effect in Stock Returns," *Journal of Financial Economics* 18, no. 1 (March 1987): 161–174.

[44] Kenneth R. French, "Stock Returns and the Weekend Effect," *Journal of Financial Economics* 8, no. 1 (March 1980): 55–70; and Michael R. Gibbons and Patrick Hess, "Day of the Week Effects and Asset Returns," *Journal of Business* 54, no. 4 (October 1981): 579–596. For a subsequent note, see Josef Lakonishok and Maurice Levi, "Weekend Effects on Stock Returns: A Note," *Journal of Finance* 37, no. 2 (June 1982): 883–889.

[45] Donald B. Keim and Robert F. Stambaugh, "A Further Investigation of the Weekend Effect in Stock Returns," *Journal of Finance* 39, no. 3 (July 1984): 819–835.

[46] Richard J. Rogalski, "New Findings Regarding Day-of-the-Week Returns Over Trading and Non-Trading Periods: A Note," *Journal of Finance* 39, no. 5 (December 1984): 1603–1614.

[47] Michael Smirlock and Laura Stacks, "Day-of-the-Week and Intraday Effects in Stock Returns," *Journal of Financial Economics* 17, no. 1 (September 1986): 197–210.

[48] Lawrence Harris, "A Transaction Data Study of Weekly and Intradaily Patterns in Stock Returns," *Journal of Financial Economics* 16, no. 1 (May 1986): 99–117.

day on Monday (it was a Monday trading effect). An analysis of 15-minute intervals during the day indicated that the only differences occurred during the first 45 minutes of the day— on Monday mornings prices tended to drop; on other weekday mornings, they increased. Price patterns during the day were otherwise similar. Finally, prices tended to rise on the last trade of the day.

PREDICTING CROSS-SECTIONAL RETURNS   Assuming an efficient market, all securities should lie along a security market line that relates the expected rate of return to an appropriate risk measure. That is, *all securities should have equal risk-adjusted returns* because security prices should reflect all public information that would influence the security's risk. Therefore, studies in this category attempt to determine if it is possible to predict the future distribution of risk-adjusted rates of return (i.e., using public information, is it possible to determine what stocks will enjoy above-average, risk-adjusted returns, and which stocks will experience below-average, risk-adjusted returns?).

These studies typically examine the usefulness of alternative measures of size or quality as a tool to rank stocks in terms of risk-adjusted returns. The reader should be forewarned that all of these tests involve *a joint hypothesis* because they consider not only the efficiency of the market, but they also are dependent on the asset pricing model that provides the measure of risk used in the test. Specifically, if the results of a test determine that it is possible to predict future risk-adjusted returns, these results could occur *either* because the market is not efficient, *or* because the measure of risk is faulty and, therefore, the measures of risk-adjusted returns are wrong.

Price-earnings ratios and returns   Basu tested the EMH by examining the relationship between the historical price-earnings (P/E) ratios for stocks and their returns.[49] Some have suggested that low P/E stocks will outperform high P/E stocks because growth companies enjoy high P/E ratios, but the market tends to overestimate the growth potential and thus overvalues these growth companies while undervaluing low-growth firms with low P/E ratios. A relationship between the historical P/E ratios and subsequent risk-adjusted market performance would constitute evidence against the semistrong EMH because it would imply that investors could use publicly available P/E ratios to predict future abnormal returns.

Basu divided the stocks into five P/E classes and determined the risk and return for portfolios of high and low P/E ratio stocks. Risk-adjusted performance measures indicated that low P/E ratio stocks experienced superior results relative to the market, whereas high P/E ratio stocks had significantly inferior results.[50] Although there was some impact of taxes and transaction costs, it was concluded that publicly available P/E ratios possess valuable information. Obviously, these results are not consistent with semistrong efficiency.

Peavy and Goodman examined P/E ratios with adjustments for firm size, industry effects, and infrequent trading.[51] After these adjustments, they found that the risk-adjusted returns for stocks in the lowest P/E ratio quintile were superior to those in the highest P/E ratio quintile.

---

[49] S. Basu, "Investment Performance of Common Stocks in Relation to Their Price-Earnings Ratios: A Test of the Efficient Market Hypothesis," *Journal of Finance* 32, no. 3 (June 1977): 663–682; and S. Basu, "The Information Content of Price-Earnings Ratios," *Financial Management* 4, no. 2 (Summer 1975): 53–64.

[50] Composite performance measures are discussed in Chapter 26.

[51] John W. Peavy III and David A. Goodman, "The Significance of P/Es for Portfolio Returns," *Journal of Portfolio Management* 9, no. 2 (Winter 1983): 43–47.

The size effect Two authors simultaneously examined the impact of size (measured by total market value) on the risk-adjusted rates of return.[52] All stocks of the NYSE (Banz) or on the NYSE and the AMEX (Reinganum) were ranked by market value and divided into ten equally weighted portfolios. The risk-adjusted returns for extended periods (10 to 15 years) indicated that the small firms consistently experienced significantly larger risk-adjusted returns than the larger firms. In addition, they contended that it was really the size—not the P/E ratio—that caused the Basu results. Subsequently, Basu reexamined Reinganum's results using a different sample period and different portfolio creation techniques and found that the highest risk-adjusted returns were in portfolios with small firms and low P/E ratios.[53]

As noted, these studies on market efficiency are dual tests of the EMH *and* the CAPM. Abnormal returns may occur because the markets are not efficient or because the market model does not provide correct estimates of expected returns. Reinganum contended that the abnormal returns were the result of the simple one-period CAPM—an inadequate description of the real-world capital markets.[54]

Roll suggested that the riskiness of the small firms was improperly measured.[55] Because small firms are traded less frequently, this causes an increase in serial correlation of prices over time and a decrease in the variance of returns, which also means that the covariance of returns for the stock with the market portfolio is reduced, so the stock's beta is lower. Earlier, Dimson suggested adding lagged and leading market returns to the market model and summing the coefficients to arrive at the beta for infrequently traded stocks.[56] Reinganum computed betas for the alternative market value portfolios using the standard *ordinary least squares (OLS) model* and using Dimson's *aggregated coefficients model* and found a substantial difference in the estimated betas (e.g., the smallest firm portfolio beta was 0.75 using OLS and 1.69 using the aggregated coefficients method).[57] The difference between betas narrowed with size until the largest firm portfolio beta was 0.98 with OLS and 0.97 with aggregated coefficients. Although the results demonstrated that the risk for small firms was underestimated, these larger betas could not explain the very large differences in rates of return.

Chan, Chen, and Hsich applied a multifactor pricing model with several risk variables and found the difference in returns between the top and bottom groups was only about 1 or 2 percent, compared with about 12 percent before the multifactor adjustment for risk.[58] The authors contend that these results imply that most of the difference in size-related returns can be explained by *complete measures of risk.*

---

[52] R. W. Banz, "The Relationship Between Return and Market Value of Common Stocks," *Journal of Financial Economics* 9, no. 1 (March 1981): 3–18; and Marc R. Reinganum, "Misspecification of Capital Asset Pricing: Empirical Anomalies Based on Earnings Yield and Market Values," *Journal of Financial Economics* 9, no. 1 (March 1981): 19–46.

[53] S. Basu, "The Relationship Between Earnings Yield, Market Value, and Return for NYSE Common Stocks," *Journal of Financial Economics* 12, no. 1 (June 1983): 129–156.

[54] Marc R. Reinganum, "Abnormal Returns in Small Firm Portfolios," *Financial Analysts Journal* 37, no. 2 (March–April 1981): 52–57.

[55] Richard Roll, "A Possible Explanation of the Small Firm Effect," *Journal of Finance* 36, no. 4 (September 1981): 879–888.

[56] Elroy Dimson, "Risk Measurement When Shares Are Subject to Infrequent Trading," *Journal of Financial Economics* 7, no. 2 (June 1979): 197–226.

[57] Marc R. Reinganum, "A Direct Test of Roll's Conjecture on the Firm Size Effect," *Journal of Finance* 37, no. 1 (March 1982): 27–35.

[58] K. C. Chan, Nai-fu Chen, and David A. Hsich, "An Exploratory Investigation of the Firm Size Effect," *Journal of Financial Economics* 14, no. 3 (September 1985): 451–471.

Stoll and Whaley confirmed that total market value varies inversely with risk-adjusted returns but also found a strong positive correlation between average price per share and market value; firms with small market value have low stock prices.[59] Because transaction costs vary inversely with price per share, they must be considered when examining the small-firm effect. Transaction costs include both the dealer's bid–ask spread and the broker's commission, which both vary inversely with price. Specifically, the proportional bid–ask spread varied from 2.93 percent for small-value stocks to 0.69 percent for large-value stocks, and the broker's commission was 3.84 percent for small firms and 2.02 percent for large firms. This indicates a total difference in transaction cost of 4.06 percent between large and small firms, a combined cost of 2.93 plus 3.84 (6.77 percent) for small firms, and 0.69 plus 2.02 (2.71 percent) for large firms. This differential in transaction cost—with frequent trading—can have a significant impact on the results. Assuming daily transactions, the original small-firm effects are reversed, whereas with less trading, the original abnormal returns recur. These results imply that subsequent size effect studies must consider realistic transaction costs and specify holding period assumptions.

Reinganum investigated a buy-and-hold strategy for longer periods of time and had results that were similar to an annual trading strategy.[60] Two holding period strategies were considered: a one-year holding period, with rebalancing every year; and a buy-and-hold strategy from 1963 through 1980. With annual rebalancing, the small-firm portfolio grew from $1 in 1963 to over $46 without commissions, whereas $1 in the largest-firm portfolio grew to about $4. With no rebalancing, a dollar in the small-firm portfolio grew to about $11, whereas $1 in the large-firm portfolio again grew to over $4. Transaction costs with annual rebalancing were not considered because the differential returns were so large that any reasonable transaction costs could not overcome this return superiority. In summary, the small firms outperformed the large firms after considering risk and transaction costs, assuming annual rebalancing.

Most studies on size effect used large databases and long time periods (30 to 50 years) to show that this phenomenon has existed for many years. In contrast, Brown, Kleidon, and Marsh examined the performance over various intervals of time and concluded that *the small firm effect is not stable*.[61] During some periods, they found the negative relationship derived by others, but during others (e.g., 1967 to 1975), large firms outperformed the small firms. Some recent analysis indicates that this positive relationship held during the periods of 1984–1987 and 1989–1990. Reinganum acknowledges this instability, but contends that the small-firm effect is still a long-run phenomenon.[62]

Neglected firms and trading activity   Arbel and Strebel considered an additional influence beyond size—attention or neglect.[63] They measured attention in terms of the number of analysts who regularly follow a stock and divided the stocks into three groups: (1) highly followed, (2) moderately followed, and (3) neglected. They confirmed the small-firm effect

[59] Hans R. Stoll and Robert E. Whaley, "Transactions Costs and the Small Firm Effect," *Journal of Financial Economics* 12, no. 1 (June 1983): 57–80.

[60] Marc R. Reinganum, "Portfolio Strategies Based on Market Capitalization," *Journal of Portfolio Management* 9, no. 2 (Winter 1983): 29–36.

[61] Philip Brown, Allen W. Kleidon, and Terry A. Marsh, "New Evidence on the Nature of Size-Related Anomalies in Stock Prices," *Journal of Financial Economics* 12, no. 1 (June 1983): 33–56.

[62] Marc R. Reinganum, "A Revival of the Small Firm Effect," *The Journal of Portfolio Management* 18, no. 3 (Spring 1992): 55–62.

[63] Avner Arbel and Paul Strebel, "Pay Attention to Neglected Firms!" *Journal of Portfolio Management* 9, no. 2 (Winter 1983): 37–42.

but also found a neglected-firm effect caused by lack of information and limited institutional interest. The neglected-firm concept applied across size classes.

James and Edmister examined the impact of trading volume by considering the relationship between returns, market volume, and trading activity.[64] They confirmed the relationship between size and rates of return and then considered the impact of trading volume as an alternative explanation because of a strong positive correlation between size and trading activity. A relationship between return and trading activity would justify the excess return for small stocks on the basis of a liquidity premium. The results indicated there was not the hypothesized inverse relationship between trading activity and mean daily returns. A test on firms with comparable trading activity confirmed the size effect. In summary, the size effect could not be explained by differential trading activity.

Barry and Brown hypothesized that firms with less information require higher returns.[65] Using the period of listing as a proxy for information, they found a negative relationship between returns and the period of listing after adjusting for firm size and the January effect.

Firm size has emerged as a major predictor of future returns and an anomaly in the efficient markets literature. There have been numerous attempts to explain the anomaly in terms of superior risk measurements, transaction costs, analysts' attention, trading activity, and differential information. In general, no single study has been able to explain these very unusual results. Apparently, the two strongest explanations are risk measurements and higher transaction costs. Depending on the frequency of trading, these two factors may account for much of the differential. Given these results, Dimson and Marsh warn that the size effect must be considered in any event study that uses long intervals and contains sample firms with significantly different market values.[66]

Book value–market value ratio   The ratio that relates the book value (BV) of a firm's equity to the market value (MV) of its equity was initially suggested by Rosenberg, Reid, and Lanstein as a predictor of stock returns.[67] They found a significant positive relationship between the BV/MV ratio and future stock returns and contended that this relationship was evidence against the EMH.

The strongest support for the importance of this ratio was provided by Fama and French, who evaluated the joint effects of market beta, size, E/P ratio, leverage, and the BV/MV ratio on the cross-section average returns on the NYSE, AMEX, and NASDAQ stocks.[68] They analyzed the hypothesized positive relationship between beta and expected returns, and concluded that the positive relationship found in empirical studies before 1969 disappeared between 1963 and 1990. In contrast, the negative relationship between size and average return was significant by itself and after inclusion of other variables.

In addition, Fama and French found a significant positive relationship between the BV/MV ratio and average return that persisted when other variables are included. Most importantly, *both* size and the BV/MV ratio are significant when included together, and they dominate other ratios. Specifically, although leverage and the E/P ratio were signifi-

[64] Christopher James and Robert Edmister, "The Relation Between Common Stock Returns, Trading Activity, and Market Value," *Journal of Finance* 38, no. 4 (September 1983): 1075–1086.

[65] Christopher B. Barry and Stephen J. Brown, "Differential Information and the Small Firm Effect," *Journal of Financial Economics* 13, no. 2 (June 1984): 283–294.

[66] Elroy Dimson and Paul Marsh, "Event Study Methodologies and the Size Effect: The Case of UK Press Recommendations," *Journal of Financial Economics* 17, no. 1 (September 1986): 113–142.

[67] Barr Rosenberg, Kenneth Reid, and Ronald Lanstein, "Persuasive Evidence of Market Inefficiency," *Journal of Portfolio Management* 11, no. 3 (Spring 1985): 9–17.

[68] Eugene F. Fama and Kenneth R. French, "The Cross-Section of Expected Stock Returns," *Journal of Finance* 47, no. 2 (June 1992): 427–465.

cant by themselves or when considered with size, they become insignificant when *both* size and the BV/MV ratio are considered.

A demonstration of the significance of both size and the BV/MV ratio can be seen from the results in Table 7.1, which shows the separate and combined effect of the two variables. As shown, controlling for size, BV/MV captures strong variation in average returns (0.70 to 1.92 percent), whereas controlling for the BV/MV ratio leaves a size effect in average returns (if you have the high BV/MV portfolio, you can increase your return from 1.18 to 1.92 by moving from large ME to small ME). These positive results for the BV/MV ratio were replicated by Chan, Hamao, and Lakonishok for returns on Japanese stocks.[69]

Given the results of the Fama-French study, which casts doubt on the CAPM and the use of beta as well as the significant support for the BV/MV ratio as an indicator of returns, several studies of these results followed. The studies focused on two questions: (1) Is beta really dead whereby no relationship exists between beta and rates of returns? and (2) Why and how does the BV/MV ratio help predict rates of return? In contrast to Fama-French (who measured beta with monthly returns), Kothari, Shanken, and Sloan (KSS) measured

TABLE 7.1

AVERAGE MONTHLY RETURNS ON PORTFOLIOS FORMED ON SIZE AND BOOK-TO-MARKET EQUITY; STOCKS SORTED BY ME (DOWN) AND THEN BE/ME (ACROSS); JULY 1963 TO DECEMBER 1990

In June of each year t, the NYSE, AMEX, and NASDAQ stocks that meet the CRSP-COMPUSTAT data requirements are allocated to 10 size portfolios using the NYSE size (ME) breakpoints. The NYSE, AMEX, and NASDAQ stocks in each size decile are then sorted into 10 BE/ME portfolios using the book-to-market ratios for year $t - 1$. BE/ME is the book value of common equity plus balance-sheet deferred taxes for fiscal year $t - 1$, over market equity for December of year $t - 1$. The equal-weighted monthly portfolio returns are then calculated for July of year t to June of year $t + 1$.

Average monthly return is the time-series average of the monthly equal-weighted portfolio returns (in percent).

The All *column* shows average returns for equal-weighted size decile portfolios. The All *row* shows average returns for equal-weighted portfolios of the stocks in each BE/ME group.

BOOK-TO-MARKET PORTFOLIOS

	All	Low	2	3	4	5	6	7	8	9	High
All	1.23	0.64	0.98	1.06	1.17	1.24	1.26	1.39	1.40	1.50	1.63
Small-ME	1.47	0.70	1.14	1.20	1.43	1.56	1.51	1.70	1.71	1.82	1.92
ME-2	1.22	0.43	1.05	0.96	1.19	1.33	1.19	1.58	1.28	1.43	1.79
ME-3	1.22	0.56	0.88	1.23	0.95	1.36	1.30	1.30	1.40	1.54	1.60
ME-4	1.19	0.39	0.72	1.06	1.36	1.13	1.21	1.34	1.59	1.51	1.47
ME-5	1.24	0.88	0.65	1.08	1.47	1.13	1.43	1.44	1.26	1.52	1.49
ME-6	1.15	0.70	0.98	1.14	1.23	0.94	1.27	1.19	1.19	1.24	1.50
ME-7	1.07	0.95	1.00	0.99	0.83	0.99	1.13	0.99	1.16	1.10	1.47
ME-8	1.08	0.66	1.13	0.91	0.95	0.99	1.01	1.15	1.05	1.29	1.55
ME-9	0.95	0.44	0.89	0.92	1.00	1.05	0.93	0.82	1.11	1.04	1.22
Large-ME	0.89	0.93	0.88	0.84	0.71	0.79	0.83	0.81	0.96	0.97	1.18

Source: Eugene F. Fama and Kenneth French, "The Cross-Section of Expected Stock Returns," *Journal of Finance* 47, no. 2 (June 1992): 446. Reprinted with permission.

[69] Louis K. Chan, Yasushi Hamao, and Josef Lakonishok, "Fundamentals and Stock Returns in Japan," *Journal of Finance* 41, no. 5 (December 1991): 1739–1789

beta with annual returns to avoid some of the trading problems with monthly data.[70] Using annual betas, KSS found substantial compensation for beta risk and suggested that the relationship between returns and the BV/MV ratio may be periodic and was not significant over a longer period. Alternatively, Pettengill, Dundaram, and Matthur note that these studies typically used *realized returns* to test the model when the theory specifies *expected returns*. When adjusting for expectations concerning negative market excess returns, they found a consistent and significant relationship between beta and returns.[71]

A study by Fairfield examined the characteristics and usefulness of the BV/MV ratio (referred to as the P/B ratio). Fairfield's valuation model illustrates (in accounting terms) that the P/B ratio depends on the expected *level* of future profitability, while the P/E ratio depends on the expected *changes* in future profitability.[72] The evidence indicated that the P/B ratio was related to future ROE, while the P/E was related to future growth in earnings. Finally, P/Bs were more stable than P/Es and high P/B–P/E firms generally maintained their classifications.

As a follow-up to their earlier study, Fama and French examined whether the behavior of stock price to size and the BV/MV ratio reflected earnings changes.[73] The analysis centered on the relationship of high and low BV/MV stocks and profitability, which was measured as earnings-to-book-equity (ROE). Notably, low BV/MV stocks (generally referred to as growth stocks) tended to have high ROE in the years prior to forming portfolios, but lower ROE in subsequent years. In contrast, high BV/MV stocks (generally referred to as value stocks) experienced low ROE prior to the portfolio formation, but increases in ROE after the formation. The BV/MV ratios were persistent, which is consistent with Fairfield. Size played a more important role in the small-stock portfolios, while the BV/MV ratio was more important for firms with high BV/MV ratios.

The original Fama-French results were confirmed in a study by Dennis, Perfect, Snow, and Wiles.[74] They not only confirmed that the optimal combination was portfolios of small firms with high BV/MV ratios, but showed that this superiority prevailed after assuming a 1 percent transaction cost and annual rebalancing. It is shown that the best results are derived assuming rebalancing every four years.

In summary, the tests of publicly available ratios that can be used to predict the cross section of expected returns for stocks have provided substantial evidence in conflict with the semistrong-form EMH. Significant results were found for E/P ratios, market value size, neglected firms, leverage, and BV/MV ratios. The latest work has indicated that the optimal combination appears to be size and the BV/MV ratio.

RESULTS OF EVENT STUDIES   The use of event studies to test the EMH has been a major growth sector during the past 20 years. Recall that these studies examine how abnormal

[70] S. P. Kothari, Jay Shanken, and Richard G. Sloan, "Another Look at the Cross Section of Expected Stock Returns," *Journal of Finance* 50, no. 2 (March 1995): 185–224.

[71] Glenn Pettengill, Sridhar Dundaram, and Ike Matthur, "The Conditional Relation Between Beta and Returns," *Journal of Financial and Quantitative Analysis* 30, no. 1 (March 1995): 101–115. For another defense of beta, see K. Grundy and Burton Malkiel, "Reports of Beta's Death Are Greatly Exaggerated," *Journal of Portfolio Management* 22, no. 3 (Spring 1996): 36–45.

[72] Patricia M. Fairfield, "P/E, P/B, and the Present Value of Future Dividends," *Financial Analysts Journal* 50, no. 4 (July–August 1994): 23–31.

[73] Eugene F. Fama and Kenneth French, "Size and Book-to-Market Factors in Earnings and Returns," *Journal of Finance* 50, no. 1 (March 1995): 131–155.

[74] Patrick Dennis, Steven Perfect, Karl Snow, and Kenneth Wiles, "The Effects of Rebalancing on Size and Book-to-Market Ratio Portfolio Returns," *Financial Analysts Journal* 51, no. 3 (May–June 1995): 47–57. For a study that shows CEOs do not acknowledge these results, see H. Shefrin and M. Statman, "Making Sense of Beta, Size and Book-to-Market," *Journal of Portfolio Management* 21, no. 2 (Winter 1995): 26–34.

rates of return react to significant economic information. Those who advocate the EMH would expect returns to adjust very quickly to announcements of new information such as it is not possible for investors to experience positive abnormal rates of return by acting after the announcement. Because of space constraints, it is impossible to consider the many studies, but only to summarize the results for some of the more popular events considered.

Numerous studies have examined the price reaction to specific events such as stock splits, exchange listings, and earnings announcements. Therefore, the discussion of results is organized by event or item of public information. Specifically, we will review the results of **event studies** that examined the price movements and profit potential surrounding stock splits, the sale of initial public offerings, exchange listings, unexpected world or economic events, and the announcement of significant accounting changes. We will see that the results for most of these studies have supported the semistrong-form EMH.

Stock split studies   One of the more popular economic events to examine is stock splits. Some observers believe the prices of stocks that split will increase in value because the shares are priced lower, which increases demand for them. In contrast, advocates of efficient markets would not expect a change in value, reasoning that the firm has simply issued additional stock and nothing fundamentally affecting the value of the firm has occurred.

A well-known test of the semistrong hypothesis is the FFJR study, which asserts that stock splits alone should not cause higher rates of return because they add nothing to the value of a firm.[75] Therefore, there should be no significant price change following a split. Any relevant information (e.g., earnings growth) that caused the split would have already been discounted.[76]

One reason for expecting a price increase is because companies typically raise their dividends when they split their stock. The dividend change has an information effect because it indicates that management is confident that it will have a new, higher level of earnings in the future, which will justify a higher level of dividends. Therefore, it is contended that any price increase that accompanies a dividend increase is not caused by the dividend itself, but by the expected earnings information it transmits.

To adjust for the market effect, FFJR derived unique parameters for each stock relative to the market and computed abnormal returns for the period 20 months before and after the stock split. The analysis was intended to determine whether the positive effects took place before or after the split. The total sample was divided into two groups: stocks that split and increased their dividend rate, and those that split but did not increase their dividend rate.

Both groups experienced positive abnormal price changes prior to the split. Stocks that split but did *not* increase their dividend experienced abnormal price declines following the split and within 12 months lost all their accumulated abnormal gains. In contrast, stocks that split and increased their dividend experienced no abnormal returns after the split.

These results, which indicated that stock splits do not result in higher rates of return for stockholders, support the semistrong EMH because they indicate that investors cannot gain from the information on a split after the public announcement. Hausman, West, and Largay confirmed this conclusion when they examined monthly data.[77] Reilly and Drzycimski also found strong support for the EMH using daily price and volume data for the period sur-

[75] E. F. Fama, L. Fisher, M. Jensen, and R. Roll, "The Adjustment of Stock Prices to New Information," *International Economic Review* 10, no. 1 (February 1969): 1–21.

[76] For a detailed analysis of why firms split their stock, see Josef Lakonishok and Baruch Lev, "Stock Splits and Stock Dividends: Why, Who and When," *Journal of Finance* 42, no. 4 (September 1987): 913–932.

[77] W. H. Hausman, R. R. West, and J. A. Largay, "Stock Splits, Price Changes, and Trading Profits: A Synthesis," *Journal of Business* 44, no. 1 (January 1971): 69–77.

rounding the split announcement.[78] In contrast, Grinblatt, Masulis, and Titman reported positive results on the day of the announcement and subsequent days.[79]

In summary, most studies attribute no short-run or long-run positive impact on security returns because of a stock split, although the results are not unanimous.[80]

Initial public offerings   During the past 20 years, a number of closely held companies have gone public by selling some of their common stock. Determining the appropriate price for an initial public offer (IPO) is a difficult task. Because of uncertainty about price and the risk involved in underwriting such issues, it has been hypothesized that underwriters would tend to underprice these new issues.[81]

Given this general expectation of underpricing, the studies in this area have generally considered three questions: (1) How great is the underpricing on average, does the underpricing vary over time, and if so why? (2) What factors cause different amounts of underpricing for alternative issues? (3) How fast does the market adjust the price for the underpricing?

The answer to the first question seems to be an average underpricing of about 15 percent, but it varies over time as shown by the results in Table 7.2.[82] Numerous factors have been suggested for the differential underpricing of alternative issues, but the major variables seem to be various risk measures, the size of the firm, the prestige of the underwriter, and the status of the firm's accounting firm.[83] Finally, on the question of direct interest to the EMH, the more recent results indicate that the price adjustment takes place within one day after the offering.[84] Therefore, on average there is some underpricing of IPOs when they are offered, but only the few investors who receive allocations of the

[78] Frank K. Reilly and Eugene F. Drzycimski, "Short-Run Profits from Stock Splits," *Financial Management* 10, no. 3 (Summer 1981): 64–74.

[79] Mark S. Grinblatt, Ronald W. Masulis, and Sheridan Titman, "The Valuation Effects of Stock Splits and Stock Dividends," *Journal of Financial Economics* 13, no. 4 (December 1984): 461–490.

[80] Another question of interest related to stock splits is the impact on the liquidity and volatility of the stocks involved. For a study on this question, see Ohlson and Penman, "Volatility Increases Subsequent to Stock Splits," *Journal of Financial Economics* 14, no. 2 (June 1985): 251–266.

[81] For a discussion of these reasons, see Frank K. Reilly and Kenneth Hatfield, "Investor Experience with New Stock Issues," *Financial Analysts Journal* 25, no. 5 (September–October 1969): 73–80.

[82] Example studies that measured these returns include Roger G. Ibbotson, "Price Performance of Common Stock New Issues," *Journal of Financial Economics* 2, no. 3 (September 1975): 235–272; Dennis E. Logue, "On the Pricing of Unseasoned New Issues, 1965–1969," *Journal of Financial and Quantitative Analysis* 8, no. 1 (January 1973): 91–103; Frank K. Reilly, "Further Evidence on Short-Run Results for New Issue Investors," *Journal of Financial and Quantitative Analysis* 8, no. 1 (January 1973): 83–90; Frank K. Reilly, "New Issues Revisited," *Financial Management* 6, no. 4 (Winter 1977): 28–42; and B. M. Neuberger and C. A. Lachapelle, "Unseasoned New Issue Price Performance on Three Tiers: 1975–1980," *Financial Management* 12, no. 3 (Autumn 1983): 23–28.

[83] See Randolph Beatty and Jay Ritter, "Investment Banking, Reputation, and the Underpricing of Initial Public Offerings," *Journal of Financial Economics* 15, no. 1 (March 1986): 213–232; J. R. Ritter, "The 'Hot' Issue Market of 1980," *Journal of Business* 57, no. 2 (April 1984): 215–240; K. Rock, "Why New Issues Are Underpriced," *Journal of Financial Economics* 15, no. 1 (March 1986): 187–212; and R. Michaely and W. H. Shaw, "Does the Choice of Auditor Convey Quality in an Initial Public Offering?" *Financial Management* 24, no. 4 (Winter 1995): 15–30.

[84] See Robert E. Miller and Frank K. Reilly, "An Examination of Mispricing, Returns, and Uncertainty for Initial Public Offerings," *Financial Management* 16, no. 2 (January 1987): 33–38; Andrew J. Chalk and John W. Peavy III, "Initial Public Offerings: Daily Returns, Offering Types, and the Price Effect," *Financial Analysts Journal* 43, no. 5 (September–October 1987): 65–69; and Kathleen Weiss Hanley, "Underpricing of Initial Public Offerings and the Partial Adjustment Phenomenon," *Journal of Financial Economics* 34, no. 2 (October 1993): 231–250. For an excellent review of the research on this topic, see Roger G. Ibbotson, Judy L. Sindelar, and Jay R. Ritter, "The Market Problems with the Pricing of Initial Public Offerings," *Journal of Applied Corporate Finance* 7, no. 1 (Spring 1994): 66–74.

TABLE 7.2

NUMBER OF OFFERINGS, AVERAGE INITIAL RETURN, AND GROSS PROCEEDS OF INITIAL PUBLIC OFFERINGS IN 1960–1992

Year	Number of Offerings[a]	Average Initial Return, %[b]	Gross Proceeds $ Millions[c]
1960	269	17.83	553
1961	435	34.11	1,243
1962	298	−1.61	431
1963	83	3.93	246
1964	97	5.32	380
1965	146	12.75	409
1966	85	7.06	275
1967	100	37.67	641
1968	368	55.86	1,205
1969	780	12.53	2,605
1970	358	−0.67	780
1971	391	21.16	1,655
1972	562	7.51	2,724
1973	105	−17.82	330
1974	9	−6.98	51
1975	14	−1.86	264
1976	34	2.90	237
1977	40	21.02	151
1978	42	25.66	247
1979	103	24.61	429
1980	259	49.36	1,404
1981	438	16.76	3,200
1982	198	20.31	1,334
1983	848	20.79	13,168
1984	516	11.52	3,932
1985	507	12.36	10,450
1986	953	9.99	19,260
1987	630	10.39	16,380
1988	435	5.27	5,750
1989	371	6.47	6,068
1990	276	9.47	4,519
1991	367	11.83	16,420
1992	509	10.90	23,990
1960–69	2,661	21.25	7,988
1970–79	1,658	8.95	6,868
1980–89	5,155	15.18	80,946
1990–92	1,152	10.85	44,929
Total	10,626	15.26	140,731

[a]The number of offerings excludes Regulation A offerings (small issues, raising less than $1.5 million during the 1980s), real estate investment trusts (REITs), and closed-end funds. Data are from Roger G. Ibbotson and Jeffry F. Jaffe, "'Hot Issues' Markets," *Journal of Finance* (September 1975) for 1960–70; Jay R. Ritter, "The 'Hot Issues' Market of 1980," *Journal of Business* (April 1984) for 1971–82; *Going Public: The IPO Reporter* for 1983–84; and Investment Dealer's Digest Information Services and Security Data Company for 1985–92. Returns data for 1988–92 exclude best efforts offerings. If these are included, the average initial returns for these years would presumably be higher.

[b]Initial returns are computed as the percentage return from the offering price to the end-of-the-calendar-month bid price, less the market return, for offerings in 1960–76. For 1977–92, initial returns are computed as the percentage return from the offering price to the end-of-the-first-day bid price, without adjusting for market movements. Data are from Ibbotson and Jaffe (op. cit.) for 1960–70, Ritter (op. cit.) for 1971–82, and prepared by the authors for 1983–92. Initial returns for 1988–92 were prepared with the assistance of Zhewei Ma.

[c]Gross proceeds data come from various issues of the *S.E.C. Monthly Statistical Bulletin* and *Going Public: The IPO Reporter* for 1960–87, and Securities Data Co. for 1988–92. Only the U.S. portion of international equity offerings is included in the gross proceeds figures.

Source: Roger G. Ibbotson, Jody L. Sindelar, and Jay R. Ritter, "The Market Problems with the Pricing of Initial Public Offerings," *Journal of Applied Corporate Finance* Vol. 7, No. 1 (Spring 1994): 69.

original issue will benefit. Further, Hanley and Wilhelm show that institutional investors capture the vast majority (70 percent) of the short-term profits.[85]

The evidence indicates that investors who acquire the stock after the initial adjustment do not experience abnormal returns. This is best documented by Ritter, who shows that a strategy of investing in IPOs at the end of the first day of public trading and holding them for three years would have resulted in a wealth relative to 0.83 compared to a portfolio of matched stocks from the NYSE or AMEX.[86]

Exchange listing   Another significant economic event for a firm and its stock is the decision to become listed on a national exchange, especially the NYSE. Such a listing is expected to increase the market liquidity of the stock and add to its prestige. Two questions are important. First, does an exchange listing increase a stock's liquidity and permanently increase the value of the firm? Second, can an investor derive abnormal returns from investing in the stock when a new listing is announced or around the time of the actual listing? On the first question, the results indicate differences regarding the effect on liquidity and the overall consensus is that listing on a national exchange does not cause a permanent change in the long-run value of a firm.[87] The results about abnormal returns surrounding the listing have been mixed. The studies generally agreed that the stocks' prices increased before any listing announcements and that stock prices consistently declined after the actual listing. The crucial question is, what happens between the listing announcement and the actual listing (a period of 4 to 6 weeks)? Most recent studies point toward profit opportunities immediately after the announcement that a firm is applying for listing, and some suggest the possibility of excess returns from price declines after the actual listing.[88] A recent study by Dharan and Ikenberry confirms that on average there is a decline after listing, but they also show that the results differ by size of firm.[89] The major impact is on small firms that tend to list prior to a decline in performance—in contrast to large firms that do not experience poor performance. Finally, studies that have examined the impact of listing on the risk of the securities found no significant change in systematic risk or the firm's cost of equity.[90]

---

[85] Kathleen Weiss Hanley and William J. Wilhelm, Jr., "Evidence on the Allocation of Initial Public Offerings," *Journal of Financial Economics* 37, no. 2 (February 1995): 239–257.

[86] Jay R. Ritter, "The Long-Run Performance of Initial Public Offerings," *Journal of Finance* 46, no. 1 (March 1991): 3–27. This has been confirmed internationally, as in M. Levis, "The Long-Run Performance of Initial Public Offerings: The U.K. Experience," *Financial Management* 22, no. 1 (Spring 1993): 28–41.

[87] Regarding liquidity effects, see William G. Christie and Roger D. Huang, "Market Structures and Liquidity: A Transactions Data Study of Exchange Listings," *Journal of Financial Intermediation* 3 (1993): 300–326; Gregord Kadlec and J. J. McConnell, "The Effect of Market Segmentation and Illiquidity on Asset Prices: Evidence from Exchange Listings," *Journal of Finance* 49, no. 2 (June 1994): 611–636. Also see James C. VanHorne, "New Listings and Their Price Behavior," *Journal of Finance* 25, no. 4 (September 1970): 783–794; and Waldemar M. Goulet, "Price Changes, Managerial Actions, and Insider Trading at the Time of Listing," *Financial Management* 3, no. 1 (Spring 1974): 30–36.

[88] See Gary Sanger and John McConnell, "Stock Exchange Listings Firm Value and Security Market Efficiency: The Impact of NASDAQ," *Journal of Financial and Quantitative Analysis* 21, no. 1 (March 1986): 1–25; John J. McConnell and Gary Sanger, "The Puzzle in Post-Listing Common Stock Returns," *Journal of Finance* 42, no. 1 (March 1987): 119–140; and John J. McConnell and Gary Sanger, "A Trading Strategy for New Listings on the NYSE," *Financial Analysts Journal* 40, no. 1 (January–February 1989): 38–39.

[89] Bala G. Dharan and David L. Ikenberry, "The Long-Run Negative Drift of Post-Listing Stock Returns," *Journal of Finance* 50, no. 5 (December 1995): 1547–1574.

[90] Frank J. Fabozzi, "Does Listing on the AMEX Increase the Value of Equity?" *Financial Management* 10, no. 1 (Spring 1981): 43–50; and Kent Baker and James Spitzfaden, "The Impact of Exchange Listing on the Cost of Equity Capital," *The Financial Review* 17, no. 3 (September 1982): 128–141.

In summary, these studies on exchange listings indicate no long-run effects on value or risk. They do, however, give some evidence of short-run profit opportunities from public information, which does not support the semistrong-form EMH.

Unexpected world events and economic news   The results of several studies of the response of security prices to world or economic news have supported the semistrong-form EMH. Reilly and Drzycimski examined the reaction of stock prices to unexpected world events and found that prices adjusted to the news before the market opened or before it reopened after the announcement.[91] Pierce and Roley examined the response to announcements about money supply, inflation, real economic activity, and the discount rate and found either no impact or an impact that did not persist beyond the announcement day.[92] When Jain analyzed hourly stock returns and trading volume response to surprise announcements about money supply, prices, industrial production, and the unemployment rate, he found that money supply and prices had an impact that was reflected in about one hour.[93]

Announcements of accounting changes   Numerous studies have analyzed the impact of announcements of accounting changes on stock prices. In efficient markets, security prices should react quickly and predictably to announcements of accounting changes. An announcement of an accounting change that affects the economic value of the firm should cause a rapid change in stock prices. An accounting change that affects reported earnings, but has no economic significance, should not affect stock prices. An analysis of stock price movements surrounding an accounting change in depreciation method from accelerated to straight line, which increases reported earnings, generally supported the EMH because there was no indication of positive price changes following the change. There were some negative effects because it was postulated that firms making such an accounting change are typically performing poorly.[94]

During periods of high inflation, many firms will change their inventory method from first-in, first-out (FIFO) to last-in, first-out (LIFO). Such a change causes a decline in reported earnings but benefits the firm because it reduces its taxable earnings and, therefore, tax expenses. Advocates of efficient markets would expect positive price changes from the tax savings, and study results confirmed this expectation. Although earnings were lower than with FIFO, stock prices generally increased for these firms.[95]

Therefore, these studies indicate that the securities markets react quite rapidly to accounting changes and adjust security prices as one would expect on the basis of the true value (i.e., analysts are able to pierce the accounting veil and value securities on the basis of economic events).[96]

---

[91] Frank K. Reilly and Eugene F. Drzycimski, "Tests of Stock Market Efficiency Following Major World Events," *Journal of Business Research* 1, no. 1 (Summer 1973): 57–72.

[92] Douglas Pierce and Vance Roley, "Stock Prices and Economic News," *Journal of Business* 59, no. 1 (Summer 1985): 49–67.

[93] Prom C. Jain, "Response of Hourly Stock Prices and Trading Volume to Economic News," *Journal of Business* 61, no. 2 (April 1988): 219–231.

[94] Examples of such studies include T. Ross Archibald, "Stock Market Reaction to the Depreciation Switch-Back," *Accounting Review* 47, no. 1 (January 1972): 22–30; and Robert S. Kaplan and Richard Roll, "Investor Evaluation of Accounting Information: Some Empirical Evidence," *Journal of Business* 45, no. 3 (April 1972): 225–257.

[95] For a study that examined this change, see Shyam Sunder, "Stock Price and Risk Related to Accounting Changes in Inventory Valuation," *The Accounting Review* 50, no. 3 (April 1975): 305–315.

[96] For an extensive review of studies directed to this contention, see William H. Beaver, *Financial Reporting: An Accounting Revolution* (Englewood Cliffs, NJ: Prentice-Hall, Inc., 1981), especially Chapter 6. For a recent

Corporate events   An area that has received substantial analysis during the last few years is corporate finance events such as mergers and acquisitions, reorganizations, and various security offerings (common stock, straight bonds, convertible bonds). Again there are two general questions of interest: (1) What is the market impact of these alternative events? (2) How fast does the market react to these events and adjust the security prices?

On the question of the reaction to corporate events, the answer is almost unanimous that prices react as one would expect based on the underlying economic impact of the action. An example would be the reaction to mergers where the stock of the firm being acquired increases in line with the premium offered by the acquiring firm, whereas the stock of the acquiring firm typically declines or experiences no change because of the concern that they overpaid for the firm. On the question of speed of reaction, the evidence indicates fairly rapid adjustment, with the time period shortening as shorter interval data are analyzed (i.e., using daily data, most studies find that the price adjustment is completed in about 3 days). Numerous studies related to financing decisions are reviewed by Smith.[97] The rapidly growing number of studies on corporate control that consider mergers and reorganizations are reviewed by Jensen and Warner.[98]

SUMMARY ON THE SEMISTRONG FORM EMH   Clearly, the evidence from tests of the semistrong EMH is mixed. The hypothesis receives strong and almost unanimous support from the numerous event studies on a range of events including stock splits, initial public offerings, world events and economic news, accounting changes, and a variety of corporate finance events. About the only mixed results come from exchange listing studies.

In sharp contrast, the numerous studies on predicting rates of return over time or for a cross section of stocks presented evidence that indicated markets were not semistrong efficient. This included time-series studies on dividend yields, risk premiums, calendar patterns, and quarterly earnings surprises. Equally pervasive were the anomalous results for cross-sectional predictors such as size, the BV/MV ratio, E/P ratios, and neglected firms.

STRONG-FORM HYPOTHESIS: TESTS AND RESULTS

The strong-form EMH contends that stock prices fully reflect *all information*, public and private. This implies that no group of investors has access to *private information* that will allow them to consistently experience above-average profits. This extremely rigid hypothesis requires not only that stock prices must adjust rapidly to new public information, but also that no group has access to private information.

Tests of the strong-form EMH have analyzed returns over time for different identifiable investment groups to determine whether any group consistently received above-average risk-adjusted returns. To consistently earn positive abnormal returns, the group must have access to important private information or an ability to act on public information before other investors. Such results would indicate that security prices were not adjusting rapidly to *all* new information.

Investigators interested in testing this form of the EMH have analyzed the performance of four major groups of investors. First, several researchers have analyzed the returns experienced by *corporate insiders* from their stock trading. Another group of studies

article that reviews studies of accounting and stock prices, see Michael J. Brennan, "A Perspective on Accounting and Stock Prices," *Journal of Applied Corporate Finance* 8, no. 1 (Spring 1995): 43–52.

[97] Clifford W. Smith, Jr., "Investment Banking and the Capital Acquisition Process," *Journal of Financial Economics* 15, no. 1/2 (January/February 1986): 3–29.

[98] Michael C. Jensen and Jerald B. Warner, "The Distribution of Power Among Corporate Managers, Shareholders, and Directors," *Journal of Financial Economics* 20, no. 1/2 (January/March 1988): 3–24.

analyzed the returns available to *stock exchange specialists*. The third group of tests examined the ability of the group of *security analysts* at Value Line and elsewhere to select stocks that will outperform the market. Finally, a number of studies have examined the overall performance of *professional money managers*. The analysis of money managers' performance emphasized the risk-adjusted returns experienced by mutual funds because of the availability of data. Recently, these tests have been replicated for pension plans and endowment funds.

CORPORATE INSIDER TRADING   Corporate insiders are required to report to the SEC each month their transactions (purchases or sales) in the stock of the firm for which they are insiders. Insiders include major corporate officers, members of the board of directors, and owners of 10 percent or more of any equity class of securities. About 6 weeks after the reporting period, this insider trading information is made public by the SEC. These insider trading data have been used to identify how corporate insiders have traded and determine whether they bought on balance before abnormally good price movements and sold on balance before poor market periods for their stock.[99] The results of these studies have generally indicated that corporate insiders consistently enjoyed above-average profits especially on purchase transactions.

Jaffe found that public investors who consistently traded with the insiders based on announced insider transactions would have enjoyed excess risk-adjusted returns (after commissions).[100] Kerr tested this trading rule and concluded that the market had eliminated this inefficiency.[101] Trivoli contended that you can substantially increase the returns from using insider trading information by combining it with key financial ratios.[102] Nunn, Madden, and Gombola contended that you should consider which group of insiders (board chair, officers, directors versus other insiders) is doing the buying and selling.[103] Seyhun also agreed that the realizable return to investors who attempt to act on insider reports was not positive after considering total transactions costs. Finally, the most recent study by Pettit and Venkatesh has results that show a significant relationship between insider trading and longer-term security performance.[104]

Overall, these results provide mixed support for the EMH. Although several studies indicate the ability for insiders to experience abnormal profits, an almost equal number of studies indicate it is not possible for the noninsider to use this information to receive excess returns. Lee and Solt found it is not possible to use *aggregate* insider trading activity as a

---

[99] The early studies on this topic are James H. Lorie and Victor Niederhoffer, "Predictive and Statistical Properties of Insider Trading," *Journal of Law and Economics* 11 (April 1968): 35–53; Joseph E. Finnerty, "Insiders and Market Efficiency," *Journal of Finance* 31, no. 4 (September 1976): 1141–1148; and Joseph E. Finnerty, "Insiders Activity and Inside Information: A Multivariate Analysis," *Journal of Financial and Quantitative Analysis* 11, no. 2 (June 1976): 205–215.

[100] Jeffrey F. Jaffe, "Special Information and Inside Trading," *Journal of Business* 47, no. 2 (April 1974): 410–428.

[101] Halbert Kerr, "The Battle of Insider Trading and Market Efficiency," *Journal of Portfolio Management* 6, no. 4 (Summer 1980): 47–50. These results are supported by Michael S. Rozeff and Mir A. Zaman, "Market Efficiency and Insider Trading: New Evidence," *Journal of Business* 61, no. 1 (January 1988): 25–44.

[102] George W. Trivoli, "How to Profit from Insider Trading Information," *Journal of Portfolio Management* 6, no. 4 (Summer 1980): 51–56.

[103] Kenneth P. Nunn, Jr., Gerald P. Madden, and Michael J. Gombola, "Are Some Insiders More 'Inside' Than Others?" *Journal of Portfolio Management* 9, no. 3 (Spring 1982): 18–22. This was supported by Seyhun, in H. Nejat Seyhun, "Insiders' Profits, Costs of Trading, and Market Efficiency," *Journal of Financial Economics* 16, no. 2 (June 1986): 189–212.

[104] R. Richardson Pettit and P. C. Venkatesh, "Insider Trading and Long-Run Return Performance," *Financial Management* 24, no. 2 (Summer 1995): 88–103.

guide to market timing.[105] Notably, because of investor interest in these data as a result of academic research, *The Wall Street Journal* currently publishes a monthly column entitled "Inside Track" that discusses the largest insider transactions.

STOCK EXCHANGE SPECIALISTS   Several studies examining the function of stock exchange specialists have determined that specialists have monopolistic access to certain very important information about unfilled limit orders. One would expect specialists to derive above-average returns from this information. This expectation is generally supported by the data. Specialists seem to generally make money because they typically sell shares at higher prices than they purchase shares. Also, they apparently make money when they buy or sell after unexpected announcements and when they trade in large blocks of stock.

An SEC study in the early 1970s examined the rates of return earned on capital by the specialists.[106] The results indicated that these rates of return were substantially above normal, which would not support the strong-form EMH. In fairness to current specialists, the prevailing environment differs substantially from that in the early 1970s. More recent results indicate that specialists are experiencing much lower rates of return following the introduction of competitive rates and other trading practices that have reduced specialists' fees.

SECURITY ANALYSTS   Several tests have considered whether it is possible to identify a set of analysts who have the ability to select stocks that are undervalued. The analysis involves determining whether there are significant abnormal returns available to those who invest after their recommendations are public. These studies and those that follow regarding money managers are more realistic and relevant than those that considered corporate insiders and stock exchange specialists because these analysts and money managers are full-time investment professionals with no obvious advantage except emphasis and training. If anyone should be able to select undervalued stocks, it should be these "pros." The first group of tests examine Value Line rankings, followed by an analysis of recommendations by individual analysts.

The Value Line enigma   Value Line (VL) is a large, well-known advisory service that publishes financial information on approximately 1,700 stocks. Included in its report is a timing rank, which indicates Value Line's expectation regarding a firm's common stock performance over the coming 12 months. A rank of 1 is the most favorable performance and 5 the worst. This ranking system, initiated in April 1965, assigns numbers based on four factors:

1. An earnings and price rank of each security relative to all others
2. A price momentum factor
3. Year-to-year relative changes in quarterly earnings
4. A quarterly earnings "surprise" factor (i.e., actual quarterly earnings compared with VL estimated earnings)

---

[105] Wayne Y. Lee and Michael E. Solt, "Insider Trading: A Poor Guide to Market Timing," *Journal of Portfolio Management* 12, no. 4 (Summer 1986): 65–71. These results are generally confirmed in H. N. Seyhun, "The Information Content of Aggregate Insider Trading," *The Journal of Business* 61, no. 1 (January 1988): 1–24; and M. Chowdhury, J. S. Howe, and J. C. Lin, "The Relation Between Aggregate Insider Transactions and Stock Market Returns," *Journal of Financial and Quantitative Analysis* 28, no. 3 (September 1993): 431–437.

[106] *Report of the Special Study of the Security Markets* (Washington, DC: Securities and Exchange Commission, 1963): Part 2, 54.

The firms are ranked based on a composite score for each firm. The top and bottom 100 are ranked 1 and 5 respectively, the next 300 from the top and bottom are ranked 2 and 4, and the rest (approximately 900) are ranked 3. Rankings are assigned every week based on the latest data. Notably, all the data used to derive the four factors are public information.

The preliminary ranking is made every Wednesday, and the final ranking is sent to the printer on Friday (there are typically five or six changes between Wednesday and Friday due to unusual new information). The new rankings are ready to be distributed on the following Wednesday, and Value Line attempts a staggered mailing so that everyone receives the weekly *Survey* on Friday.

Several years after the ranking was started, Value Line indicated that the performance of the stocks in the various ranks differed substantially. Specifically, it was contended that the stocks rated 1 substantially outperformed the market, and the stocks rated 5 seriously underperformed the market (the performance figures did not include dividend income but also did not charge commissions).

Black tested the Value Line system over the period 1965–1970 by constructing portfolios grouped by rank and revised the portfolios monthly.[107] He concluded that rank-1 firms outperformed rank-5 firms by 20 percent per year on a risk-adjusted basis and that even with round-trip transaction costs of 2 percent, the net rate of return for a long position in rank-1 stocks would have been positive. Holloway examined the top 100 stocks and concluded that if you adjusted your portfolio weekly, the returns would be superior before transaction costs—but not after.[108] Alternatively, assuming annual portfolio revisions, there were abnormal returns after transaction costs.

Copeland and Mayers found that the abnormal returns were consistent with the rankings, but only the returns for rank 5 were significantly negative, implying that VL has the ability to select underperformers.[109] An analysis of a strategy of buying upgraded stocks and selling short those downgraded indicated significant negative abnormal returns for down-ranked stocks, but only limited significance for stocks that were upgraded. Finally, although the negative abnormal returns for the rank-5 portfolios were *statistically* significant, the trading rules were not profitable after transaction costs.

Stickel found that although all rank changes affect stock prices, the most significant impact occurs when stocks go from rank 2 to 1.[110] Other changes in rank were followed by statistically significant changes that were much smaller than for a move from 2 to 1. Stickel contends that the price movements require three days, but he counts Thursday as Day 0 because some people might receive the *Value Line Survey* on Thursday. Clearly, after Monday, there is no significant impact. Also, smaller firms experienced a larger reaction to changes in rank, and the change requires several days. However, acting on the rank change from 2 to 1 for the smallest firms would not be profitable due to the large transaction costs of small firms. Therefore, although evidence shows that there is information content in VL rank changes and that the price adjustment is not instantaneous, some recent evidence

[107] Fischer Black, "Yes, Virginia, There Is Hope: Tests of the Value Line Ranking System," *Financial Analysts Journal* 29, no. 5 (September–October 1973): 10–14.

[108] Clark Holloway, "A Note on Testing an Aggressive Investment Strategy Using Value Line Ranks," *Journal of Finance* 36, no. 3 (June 1981): 711–719.

[109] Thomas E. Copeland and David Mayers, "The Value Line Enigma (1965–1978): A Case Study of Performance Evaluation Issues," *Journal of Financial Economics* 10, no. 3 (November 1982): 289–321.

[110] Scott E. Stickel, "The Effect of Value Line Investment Survey Changes on Common Stock Prices," *Journal of Financial Economics* 14, no. 1 (March 1985): 121–143.

indicates that the absolute price change is possibly *not* large enough to generate excess returns after transaction costs.

To see if the VL record is a result of the firm size phenomenon, Huberman and Kandel examined the relationship between the VL recommendation and firm size.[111] The overall results indicated no relationship between the VL rankings and size. Also, although the VL investment service favors large firms, the system appears to be better at predicting the relative returns on small-firm stocks.

Peterson examined the daily price changes around the release of initial reviews and consequent new rankings of stocks.[112] The analysis considers the day before official release, the release day, and the following day (typically Thursday, Friday, and Monday). The portfolio returns for stocks ranked 1 were significant on Days −1, 0, and +1, individually and combined. In general, there were no significant abnormal returns for stocks assigned any other ranking, which implies that these other rankings contain very little information. Notably, there were no significant price changes after Day +1. It is concluded that there is information in some of the rankings (mainly rank 1), but the market is fairly efficient in adjusting to them.

Finally, as noted previously, one of the four factors considered by VL when ranking firms is quarterly earnings "surprises." Affleck-Graves and Mendenhall contend that the longer-term abnormal returns from the VL ranking is really caused by the quarterly post-earnings announcement drift that follows the earnings' "surprise" as discussed earlier.[113] That is, the authors contend that this VL anomaly is caused by the quarterly earnings anomaly.

The studies on the Value Line enigma indicate that there is information in the VL rankings (especially either rank 1 or 5) and in changes in the rankings (especially going from 2 to 1). Although these changes in rank have a larger effect on smaller firms, there is no direct relationship between the VL rankings and the size anomaly. Further, most of the recent evidence indicates that the market is fairly efficient because the abnormal adjustments appear to be complete by Day +2. An analysis of study results over time indicates a faster adjustment to the rankings during recent years. In fact, a study by Hulbert indicates weaker performance for rank-1 stocks after 1983.[114] Also, although there are statistically significant price changes, there is mounting evidence that it is not possible to derive abnormal returns from these announcements after considering realistic transaction costs. Some of the strongest evidence in this regard is the fact that Value Line's Centurion Fund, which concentrates on rank-1 stocks, has consistently underperformed the market over the past decade.

Analysts' recommendations   Mixed evidence exists regarding analysts who possess private information. Studies by Lloyd-Davies and Canes and by Lin, Smith, and Syed found that the prices of stocks mentioned in *The Wall Street Journal* column "Heard on the Street" experience a significant change on the day the column appears, in contrast to Desai and Jain, who examined the performance of stocks recommended by "superstar" money

---

[111] Gur Huberman and Shmuel Kandel, "Value Line Rank and Firm Size," *Journal of Business* 60, no. 4 (October 1987): 577–589; and Gur Huberman and Shmuel Kandel, "Market Efficiency and Value Line's Record," *Journal of Business* 63, no. 2 (April 1990): 187–216.

[112] David R. Peterson, "Security Price Reactions to Initial Reviews of Common Stock by the Value Line Investment Survey," *Journal of Financial and Quantitative Analysis* 22, no. 4 (December 1987): 483–494.

[113] John Affleck-Graves and Richard R. Mendenhall, "The Relation Between the Value Line Enigma and Post-Earnings-Announcement Drift," *Journal of Financial Economics* 31, no. 1 (February 1992): 75–96.

[114] Mark Hulbert, "Proof of Pudding," *Forbes* (December 10, 1990): 316.

managers at *Barron's* roundtable and found abnormal returns of 1.91 percent from the meeting date to the publication date, but *zero* abnormal returns for all postpublication holding periods.[115] The most recent and comprehensive analysis of analysts' recommendations by Womach finds that analysts appear to have both market timing and stock picking ability, especially in connection with sell recommendations that are relatively rare.[116]

PERFORMANCE OF PROFESSIONAL MONEY MANAGERS   The studies of professional money managers are more realistic and widely applicable than the analysis of insiders and specialists because money managers typically do not have monopolistic access to important new information. Still, they are highly trained professionals who work full time at investment management. Therefore, if any "normal" set of investors should derive above-average profits, it would be this group. Also, if any noninsider should derive inside information, professional money managers would because they conduct extensive management interviews.

Most studies on the performance of money managers have examined mutual funds because performance data are readily available. Only recently have data been available for bank trust departments, insurance companies, and investment advisers. The original mutual fund studies indicated that most funds could not match the performance of a buy-and-hold policy.[117] When risk-adjusted returns were examined *without* considering commission costs, slightly more than half of the money managers did better than the overall market. When commission costs, load fees, and management costs were considered, approximately two-thirds of the mutual funds did *not* match aggregate market performance. Also, Klemkosky and, more recently, Shukla and Trzcinka (ST) found that funds were inconsistent in their performance.[118] In fact, ST found that the only persistence was in inferior performance.

Studies by Henriksson and by Chang and Lewellen provided similar results on performance.[119] In contrast, Ippolito found that funds during the period 1965–1984 beat the market after research and transaction costs.[120] Finally, Elton, Gruber, Davis, and Aklarka use a three-factor model to measure risk and found that during the Ippolito period the

[115] Peter Lloyd-Davies and Michael Canes, "Stock Prices and the Publication of Second-Hand Information," *Journal of Business* 51, no. 1 (January 1987): 43–56; Pu Lin, Stanley D. Smith, and Axmat A. Syed, "Security Price Reaction to the *Wall Street Journal's* Securities Recommendations," *Journal of Financial and Quantitative Analysis* 25, no. 3 (September 1990): 399–410; and Hemang Desai and Prem Jain, "An Analysis of the Recommendations of the 'Superstars' Money Managers at *Barron's* Annual Roundtable," *Journal of Finance* 50, no. 4 (September 1995): 1257–1273.

[116] Kent L. Womack, "Do Brokerage Analysts' Recommendations Have Investment Value?" *The Journal of Finance* 51, no. 1 (March 1996): 137–167.

[117] Notable studies include William F. Sharpe, "Mutual Fund Performance," *Journal of Business* 39, no. 1 (January 1966 Supplement): 119–139; Michael Jensen, "The Performance of Mutual Funds in the Period 1945–1964," *Journal of Finance* 23, no. 2 (May 1968): 389–416; and Jack L. Treynor, "How to Rate Management of Investment Funds," *Harvard Business Review* 43, no. 1 (January–February 1965): 63–75. These studies and others on this topic are reviewed in Chapter 27.

[118] Robert C. Klemkosky, "How Consistently Do Managers Manage?" *Journal of Portfolio Management* 3, no. 2 (Winter 1977): 11–15; and Ravi Shukla and Charles Trzcinka, "Persistent Performance in the Mutual Fund Market: Tests with Funds and Investment Advisers," *Review of Quantitative Finance and Accounting* 4, no. 2 (June 1994): 115–135.

[119] Roy T. Henriksson, "Market Timing and Mutual Fund Performance: An Empirical Investigation," *Journal of Business* 57, no. 1, part 1 (January 1984): 73–96; and Eric C. Chang and Wilber G. Lewellen, "Market Timing and Mutual Fund Investment Performance," *Journal of Business* 57, no. 1, part 1 (January 1984): 57–72.

[120] Richard A. Ippolito, "Efficiency with Costly Information: A Study of Mutual Fund Performance, 1965–84," *Quarterly Journal of Economics* 104, no. 1 (March 1989): 1–23.

abnormal returns using more extensive risk measurement were negative.[121] Therefore, the vast majority of money manager studies support the EMH with results that indicate mutual fund managers generally cannot beat a buy-and-hold policy.

As noted, recently it has been possible to get performance data for pension plans and endowment funds. Given these data, a study by Brinson, Hood, and Beebower as well as several other studies have documented that the performances of pension plans did not match that of the aggregate market.[122] Likewise, Berkowitz, Finney, and Logue documented that the performance of endowment funds was not able to beat a buy-and-hold policy.[123]

The figures in Table 7.3 provide a rough demonstration of these results. These data are collected by Frank Russell Analytical Services as part of its performance evaluation service. Table 7.3 contains the mean rates of return for several investment groups compared to the Standard & Poor's 500 Index.[124]

The first set of universes are banks that generally never experienced returns above the Standard & Poor's 500 during any of the periods. The exception was the equity-oriented separate accounts, which experienced superior rates of return for the 10-year comparisons. The mutual funds never had superior results. Finally, some of the equity style universes did

| TABLE 7.3 | ANNUALIZED RATES OF RETURN DURING ALTERNATIVE PERIODS ENDING DECEMBER 31, 1992 |

	1 Year	2 Years	4 Years	6 Years	8 Years	10 Years
U.S. Equity Broad Universe Medians						
Equity accounts	9.0	20.6	15.8	13.7	16.3	15.7
Equity pooled accounts	7.7	19.5	15.8	13.6	15.9	15.3
Equity-oriented separate accounts	9.7	21.0	15.9	13.9	16.6	16.5
Special equity pooled accounts	15.7	32.4	18.5	15.9	16.3	15.8
Mutual Fund Universe Medians						
Balanced mutual funds	7.9	15.7	12.2	11.2	13.4	13.5
Equity mutual funds	9.3	21.9	14.7	12.7	15.1	14.0
U.S. Equity Style Universe Medians						
Earnings growth accounts	7.5	28.0	22.3	17.0	19.1	16.5
Small capitalization accounts	15.4	32.8	18.2	15.8	16.9	16.2
Price-driven accounts	13.5	20.7	13.6	12.9	15.7	15.9
Market-oriented accounts	8.9	19.8	16.3	14.5	17.0	16.5
S&P 500 Index	7.7	18.6	15.6	14.0	16.6	16.0
Number of Universes with Returns above the S&P 500	9	9	7	4	4	4

Source: Frank Russell Company, Tacoma, WA. Reprinted with permission.

[121] Edwin Elton, Martin J. Gruber, Sanjiv Das, and Matt Aklarka, "Efficiency with Costly Information: A Reinterpretation of Evidence from Managed Portfolios" (New York University Graduate School of Business, 1994).

[122] Gary P. Brinson, Randolph Hood, and Gilbert Beebower, "Determinants of Portfolio Performance," *Financial Analysts Journal* 43, no. 4 (July–August 1986): 39–44; Alicia Munnell, "Who Should Manage the Assets of Collectively Bargained Pension Plans?" *New England Economic Review* (July–August 1983): 18–30; and Richard A. Ippolito and John A. Turner, "Turnover Fees and Pension Plan Performance," *Financial Analysts Journal* 43, no. 6 (November–December 1987): 16–26.

[123] Stephen A. Berkowitz, Louis D. Finney, and Dennis E. Logue, *The Investment Performance of Corporate Pension Plans* (New York: Quorum Books, 1988).

[124] The results for these individual accounts have an upward bias because they consider only accounts retained (e.g. if a firm or bank does a poor job on an account and the client leaves, those results would not be included).

better for the 1-, 8-, and 10-year periods. Notably, these results are *not* adjusted for risk. As noted, these results are generally consistent with the mutual fund results and support the strong-form EMH.

CONCLUSIONS REGARDING THE STRONG-FORM EMH   The tests of the strong-form EMH generated mixed results, but the bulk of relevant evidence supported the hypothesis. The results for two unique groups of investors (corporate insiders and stock exchange specialists) did not support the hypothesis because both groups apparently have monopolistic access to important information and use it to derive above-average returns.

Tests to determine whether there are analysts with private information concentrated on the Value Line rankings and publications of analysts' recommendations. The results for Value Line rankings have changed over time and currently lean toward support for the EMH. Specifically, the adjustment to rankings and ranking changes is fairly rapid, and it appears that trading is not profitable after transactions costs. Also, there is a question whether the Value Line anomaly is really due to the quarterly earnings surprise anomaly. Alternatively, some analysts' recommendations (especially sell recommendations) seem to contain significant information.

Finally, the performance by professional money managers provided support for the strong-form EMH. The vast majority of money manager performance studies have indicated that the investments by these highly trained, full-time investors could not consistently outperform a simple buy-and-hold policy on a risk-adjusted basis. This has been true for mutual funds, pension plans, and endowment funds. Because these money managers are similar to most investors who do not have consistent access to inside information, these results are considered more relevant to the hypothesis. Therefore, there appears to be substantial support for the strong-form EMH as applied to most investors.

IMPLICATIONS OF EFFICIENT CAPITAL MARKETS

Having reviewed numerous studies related to different facets of the EMH, the important question is: what does this mean to individual investors, financial analysts, portfolio managers, and institutional investors? Overall, the results of numerous studies indicate that the capital markets are efficient as related to numerous sets of information. At the same time, a growing number of studies have uncovered a substantial number of instances where the market apparently does not adjust rapidly to public information. Given these mixed results regarding the existence of efficient capital markets, it is very important to consider the implications of this contrasting evidence of market efficiency. The following discussion considers the implications of both sets of evidence. Specifically, given results that support the EMH, we consider what techniques will not work and what you do if you can't beat the market. In contrast, because of the evidence that does not support the EMH, we discuss what information should be considered when attempting to derive superior investment results.

EFFICIENT MARKETS AND TECHNICAL ANALYSIS

The assumptions of technical analysis directly oppose the notion of efficient markets. A basic premise of technical analysis is that stock prices move in trends that persist.[125] Technicians believe that when new information comes to the market, it is not immediately available to everyone but typically is disseminated from the informed professional to the aggressive investing public and then to the great bulk of investors. Also, technicians contend that investors do not analyze information and act immediately. This process takes

---

[125] Chapter 21 contains an extensive discussion of technical analysis.

time. Therefore, they hypothesize that stock prices move to a new equilibrium after the release of new information in a gradual manner, which causes trends in stock price movements that persist for certain periods.

Technical analysts believe that nimble traders can develop systems to detect the beginning of a movement to a new equilibrium (called a "breakout"). Hence, they hope to buy or sell stock immediately after its breakout to take advantage of the subsequent price adjustment. The belief in this pattern of price adjustment directly contradicts advocates of the EMH who believe that security prices rapidly adjust to new information. These EMH advocates do not contend, however, that prices adjust perfectly, which means there can be an overadjustment or underadjustment. Still, because it is not certain whether the market will over- or underadjust at any time, you cannot derive abnormal profits from adjustment errors.

If the capital market is efficient and prices fully reflect all relevant information, no technical trading system that depends only on past trading data can have any value. By the time the information is public, the price adjustment has taken place. Therefore, a purchase or sale using a technical trading rule should not generate abnormal returns after considering risk and transactions costs.

EFFICIENT MARKETS AND FUNDAMENTAL ANALYSIS

As you know from our prior discussion, fundamental analysts believe that, at any time, there is a basic intrinsic value for the aggregate stock market, various industries, or individual securities and that these values depend on underlying economic factors. Therefore, a fundamental analyst would determine the intrinsic value of an investment asset at a point in time by examining the variables that determine value such as current and future earnings, interest rates, and risk variables. If the prevailing market price differs from the intrinsic value by enough to cover transaction costs, an investor should take appropriate action: buy if the market price is substantially below intrinsic value and sell if it is above. Fundamental analysts believe that occasionally market price and intrinsic value differ, but eventually investors recognize the discrepancy and correct it.

If you can do a superior job of *estimating* intrinsic value, you can consistently make superior market timing (asset allocation) decisions or acquire undervalued securities and generate above-average returns. Fundamental analysis involves aggregate market analysis, industry analysis, company analysis, and portfolio management. The EMH has important implications for all of these components of fundamental analysis.

AGGREGATE MARKET ANALYSIS WITH EFFICIENT CAPITAL MARKETS   Chapter 13 makes a strong case that intrinsic value analysis should use a top-down approach and begin with aggregate market analysis. Still, the EMH implies that any analysis that examines only *past* economic events is unlikely to help you outperform a buy-and-hold policy because the market adjusts very rapidly to known economic events. Evidence suggests that the market experiences long-run price movements, but to take advantage of these movements in an efficient market, you must do a superior job of *estimating* the relevant economic variables that cause these long-run movements. That is, if you only use historical data to estimate future values and invest on the basis of these estimates, the EMH contends that you will not experience superior risk-adjusted returns.

INDUSTRY AND COMPANY ANALYSIS WITH EFFICIENT CAPITAL MARKETS   The wide range of returns from different industries and companies during a period of time and over time clearly justifies industry and company analysis. Again, the EMH does not contradict the value of such fundamental analysis, but implies that to be successful you need to

(1) understand the relevant variables that affect rates of return, and (2) do a superior job of *estimating* movements in these valuation variables. To demonstrate this, Malkiel and Cragg developed a model that did an excellent job of explaining past stock price movements using historical data. When this model was used to project *future* stock price changes but continued using *past* company data, the results were consistently inferior to a buy-and-hold policy.[126] This implies that, even with a good valuation model, you cannot be superior in selecting stocks using only past data.

Another study showed that the crucial difference between stocks that enjoyed the best and worst price performance during a given year was the relationship between expected earnings of professional analysts and actual earnings (i.e., earning surprises). Specifically, stock prices increased if actual earnings substantially exceeded expected earnings (i.e., a positive earnings surprise) and fell if earnings did not reach expected levels (i.e, there was a negative earnings surprise).[127] Thus, if you can do a superior job of projecting earnings and your expectations *differ from the consensus,* you will probably have a superior stock selection record.[128]

In the quest to be a superior analyst, there are some good news and some suggestions. The good news is related to the strong-form tests that indicated the likely existence of superior analysts. It was shown that the rankings by Value Line contained information value, even though it might not be possible to profit from it after transactions costs. Also, the short-run and long-term price adjustment to the publication of analyst recommendations indicates that there are superior analysts. The point is, there clearly are some superior analysts, but it is not easy to be one. Most notably, to be a superior analyst you must do a superior job of *estimating* the relevant valuation variables.

The suggestions related to the relevant data to consider in your analysis are based on the studies that considered the cross section of future returns. As noted, these studies indicated that E/P ratios, size, and the BV/MV ratios differentiated future return patterns. Further, it appeared that size and the BV/MV ratio were the optimal combination to consider when selecting a universe of stocks for intensive analysis. In addition, the evidence suggests that neglected firms should be given extra consideration.

HOW TO EVALUATE ANALYSTS OR INVESTORS   If you want to determine if an individual is a superior analyst or investor, you should examine the performance of numerous securities that this analyst or investor recommends over time in relation to the performance of a set of randomly selected stocks of equal risk. The stock selections of a superior analyst or investor should *consistently* outperform the randomly selected stocks. The consistency requirement is crucial because you would expect a portfolio developed by random selection to outperform the market about half the time.

CONCLUSIONS ABOUT FUNDAMENTAL ANALYSIS   A text on investments can indicate the relevant variables that you should analyze and describe the important techniques, but estimating the relevant variables is as much an art and a product of hard work as it is a science. If the estimates could be done on the basis of some formula, you could program a computer to do it, and there would be no need for analysts. Therefore, the superior analyst

---

[126] Burton G. Malkiel and John G. Cragg, "Expectations and the Structure of Share Prices," *American Economic Review* 60, no. 4 (September 1970): 601–617.

[127] Gary A. Benesh and Pamela P. Peterson, "On the Relation Between Earnings Changes, Analysts' Forecasts and Stock Price Fluctuations," *Financial Analysts Journal* 41, no. 6 (November–December 1986).

[128] This is a major point made in H. Russell Fogler, "A Modern Theory of Security Analysis," *Journal of Portfolio Management* 19, no. 3 (Spring 1993): 6–14.

or successful investor must understand what variables are relevant to the valuation process and have the ability to do a superior job of *estimating* these variables. Alternatively, one could be superior if he or she has the ability to interpret the impact or estimate the effect of some public information better than others.

EFFICIENT MARKETS AND PORTFOLIO MANAGEMENT

As noted, a number of studies have indicated that professional money managers cannot beat a buy-and-hold policy on a risk-adjusted basis. One explanation for this generally inferior performance is that there are no superior analysts and the cost of research forces the results of merely adequate analysis into the inferior category. Another explanation, which is favored by the author and has some empirical support from the Value Line and recommendation results, is that money management firms employ both superior and inferior analysts, and the gains from the recommendations by the few superior analysts are offset by the costs of the research department and the poor results due to the recommendations of the inferior analysts.

This raises the question: should a portfolio be managed actively or passively? A portfolio manager with superior analysts or an investor who feels he or she has the time and expertise to be a superior investor can manage a portfolio actively, looking for undervalued securities and attempting to time the market wherein you shift your asset allocation between aggressive and defensive positions, depending on your outlook for the market. In contrast, without superior analysts or the time and ability to be a superior investor, you should manage passively and assume that all securities are properly priced based on their levels of risk. The following subsections consider each of these two alternatives in more detail.

PORTFOLIO MANAGEMENT WITH SUPERIOR ANALYSTS   A portfolio manager with superior analysts who have unique insights and analytical ability should follow their recommendations. The superior analysts should make investment recommendations for a certain proportion of the portfolio, ensuring that the risk preferences of the client are maintained. Also, the superior analysts should concentrate their efforts in mid-cap stocks. These mid-cap stocks possess the liquidity required by institutional portfolio managers, but because they do not receive the substantial attention given to the large cap stocks, the markets for these stocks, which could be considered neglected, may be less efficient than the market for large cap stocks.

Recall that capital markets are expected to be efficient because many investors receive new information and analyze its effect on security values. If the number of analysts following a stock differ, one could conceive of differences in the efficiency of the markets. New information on top-tier stocks is well publicized and rigorously analyzed. As a result, the price of these securities should adjust rapidly to reflect the new information. In contrast, middle-tier firms receive less publicity, fewer analysts follow these firms because there is less institutional interest in them, and prices adjust less rapidly to new information. Therefore, the possibility of finding temporarily undervalued securities among these neglected stocks is greater. Again, in line with the cross-section study results, these superior analysts should pay particular attention to neglected firms and to the BV/MV ratio and the size of stocks being analyzed.[129]

PORTFOLIO MANAGEMENT WITHOUT SUPERIOR ANALYSTS   If you do not have access to superior analysts, your procedure should be as follows. First, you should *measure*

---

[129] The strongest evidence in this regard is contained in Eugene F. Fama and Kenneth French, "The Cross-Section of Expected Stock Returns," *Journal of Finance* 47, no. 2 (June 1992): 427–465. One should also read several of the follow-up studies on the BV/MV ratio (P/B) that were discussed earlier in this chapter.

your risk preferences or those of your clients. You should then build a portfolio to match this risk level by investing a certain proportion of the portfolio in risky assets and the rest in a risk-free asset.

You must *completely diversify* the risky asset portfolio on a global basis so it moves consistently with the world market. In this context, proper diversification means eliminating all unsystematic (unique) variability. In Chapter 3, we discussed studies that estimated the number of securities needed to gain most of the benefits (over 90 percent) of a completely diversified portfolio. The studies generally concluded that it required about 15 to 20 securities, while more than 100 stocks are required for complete diversification. To decide how many securities to actually include in your portfolio, you must balance the added benefits of worldwide diversification against the costs of research for the additional stocks. To diversify globally will require international securities that are probably best added via mutual funds.

Finally, you should *minimize transaction costs.* Assuming that the portfolio is completely diversified and is structured for the desired risk level, excessive transaction costs that do not generate added returns will detract from your expected rate of return. Three factors are involved in minimizing total transaction costs.

1. Minimize taxes. Methods of accomplishing this objective vary, but it should receive prime consideration.
2. Reduce trading turnover. You should trade only to liquidate part of the portfolio or to maintain a given risk level.
3. When you trade, minimize liquidity cost by trading relatively liquid stocks. To accomplish this, you should submit limit orders to buy or sell several stocks at prices that approximate the specialist's quote. That is, you would put in limit orders to buy stock at the bid price or sell at the ask price. The stock that is bought or sold first is the most liquid one; all other orders should be withdrawn.

In summary, if you do not have access to superior analysts, you should do the following:

1. Determine and quantify your risk preferences.
2. Construct the appropriate portfolio by dividing the total portfolio between lending or borrowing risk-free assets and risky assets.
3. Diversify completely on a global basis to eliminate all unsystematic risk.
4. Maintain the specified risk level by rebalancing when necessary.
5. Minimize total transaction costs.

THE RATIONALE AND USE OF INDEX FUNDS   As the prior discussion indicates, efficient capital markets and a lack of superior analysts imply that many portfolios should be managed so that their performance matches that of the aggregate market, minimizing the costs of research and trading. The idea is, if you don't have superior analysts who can beat the market, then simply attempt to *match* the market at the lowest cost. In response to this desire, several institutions have introduced *market funds,* also referred to as *index funds,* which are security portfolios designed to duplicate the composition and therefore the performance of a selected market index series.

Three major investment services started equity index funds in the early 1970s that were intended to match the performance of the S&P 500 index: American National Bank and Trust Company of Chicago; Batterymarch Financial Management Corporation of Boston; and Wells Fargo Investment Advisors, a division of Wells Fargo Bank in San Francisco. Analysis by the author has documented that the correlation of quarterly rates of return for the index fund and the S&P 500 from 1975 to 1994 exceeded .98. This shows that the funds generally fulfill their stated goal of matching market performance.

Although these initial funds were only available to institutional investors, there are currently at least five index mutual funds available to individuals. In addition, this concept has been extended to other areas of investments. Index bond funds attempt to emulate the bond-market indexes discussed in Chapter 5 such as the Lehman Brothers bond indexes. Also, there are indexes that focus on specific segments of the market such as international bond index funds and international stock index funds that target specific countries; there are even index funds that target small capitalization stocks in the United States and Japan.[130] When portfolio managers decide they want a given asset class in their portfolio to aid diversification, they often look for index funds for the asset class. The use of index funds as the best way to get representation may be easier and less costly in terms of research and commissions, and it may provide the same or better performance than what is available from specific security selection.[131]

EFFICIENCY IN
EUROPEAN EQUITY
MARKETS

With rare exception, the discussion in this chapter has been concerned with the efficiency of U.S. markets. The growing importance of world markets raises a natural question about the efficiency of securities markets outside the United States. Numerous studies have dealt with this set of questions, and a discussion of them would substantially lengthen the chapter. Fortunately, a monograph by Hawawini contains a review of numerous studies that examined the behavior of European stock prices and evaluated the efficiency of European equity markets.[132] The monograph lists over 280 studies covering 14 Western European countries from Austria to the United Kingdom classified by country and within each country into five categories:

1. Market model, beta estimation, and diversification
2. Capital asset pricing model and arbitrage pricing model
3. Weak-form tests of market efficiency
4. Semistrong-form tests of market efficiency
5. Strong-form tests of market efficiency

Hawawini offers the following overall conclusion after acknowledging that European markets are smaller and less active than U.S. markets.

> Our review of the literature indicates that despite the peculiarities of European equity markets, the behavior of European stock prices is, with few exceptions, surprisingly similar to that of U.S. common stocks. That is true even for countries with extremely narrow equity markets such as Finland. The view that most European equity markets, particularly those of smaller countries, are informationally inefficient does not seem to be borne out by the data. We will see that most of the results of empirical tests performed on European common stock prices are generally in line with those reported by researchers who used U.S. data.

---

[130] For a discussion of some of these indexes, see James A. White, "The Index Boom: It's No Longer Just the S&P 500 Stock Index," *The Wall Street Journal*, May 19, 1991, C1, C3

[131] Two articles that indicate this trend are Terry Williams, "Sandoz Indexes All Large Cap Stocks," *Pensions and Investments*, January 8, 1996, 1; and Sabine Schramm, "Indexed Assets Leap 39.9% for Year to $600 Billion," *Pensions and Investments*, February 19, 1996, 1.

[132] Gabriel Hawawini, *European Equity Markets: Price Behavior and Efficiency*, Monograph 1984–4/5, Monograph Series in Finance and Economics, Salomon Brothers Center for the Study of Financial Institutions, Graduate School of Business, New York University, 1984.

This implies that when one considers securities markets outside the United States, it is appropriate to assume a level of informational efficiency similar to that for U.S. markets.

Summary

- You must consider the efficiency of capital markets because of the implications of it for your investment analysis and the management of your portfolio. Capital markets should be efficient because numerous rational, profit-maximizing investors react quickly to the release of new information. Assuming prices reflect new information, they are unbiased estimates of the securities' true, intrinsic value, and the relationship between the return on an investment and its risk should be consistent.
- The voluminous research on the EMH has been divided into three segments, which have been tested separately. The weak-form EMH states that stock prices fully reflect all market information, so any trading rule that uses past market data to predict future returns should have no value. The results of most studies consistently supported this hypothesis.
- The semistrong-form EMH asserts that security prices adjust rapidly to the release of all public information. The tests of this hypothesis either examined the opportunities to predict future rates of return (either a time series or a cross section), or they involved event studies in which investigators analyzed whether investors could derive above-average returns from trading on the basis of public information. The test results were clearly mixed. On the one hand, the results for almost all the event studies related to economic events such as stock splits, initial public offerings, and accounting changes consistently support the semistrong hypothesis. In contrast, several studies that examined the ability to predict differential rates of return on the basis of unexpected quarterly earnings, P/E ratios, size, neglected stocks, and the BV/MV ratio, as well as several calendar effects, generally did not support the hypothesis.
- The strong-form EMH states that security prices reflect all information. This implies that nobody has private information so no group should be able to derive above-average returns consistently. Studies that examined the results for corporate insiders and stock exchange specialists do not support the strong-form hypothesis. An analysis of individual analysts as represented by Value Line or by recommendations published in *The Wall Street Journal* gives mixed results. The results indicated that the Value Line rankings have significant information but it may not be possible to profit from it after transaction costs, whereas the recommendations by analysts indicated the existence of private information by some analysts. In contrast, the performance by professional money managers supported the EMH because their risk-adjusted investment performance (whether mutual funds, pension funds, or endowment funds) was typically inferior to results achieved with buy-and-hold policies.

    We conclude the chapter with a very important discussion of what all these empirical results mean for investors, analysts (fundamental or technical), or portfolio managers. The EMH indicates that technical analysis should be of no value. All forms of fundamental analysis are useful, but they are difficult to implement because they require the ability to *estimate future values* for relevant economic variables. Superior analysis is possible but is *very difficult* because it requires superior projections of the relevant variables, i.e., you need to be accurate and different. Those who manage portfolios should constantly evaluate investment advice to determine whether it is superior.
- Without access to superior analytical advice, you should run your portfolio like an index fund. In contrast, those with superior analytical ability should be allowed to make decisions, but they should concentrate their efforts on mid-cap firms and neglected firms, where there is a higher probability of discovering misvalued stocks. In the analysis, there should be particular concern with alternative firms' BV/MV ratio and size.
- This chapter contains some good news and some bad news. The good news is that the practice of investment analysis and portfolio management is not an art that has been lost to the great computer in the sky. Viable professions still await those willing to extend the effort and able to accept the pressures. The bad news is that many bright, hardworking people with extensive resources make the game tough. In fact, those competitors have created a fairly efficient capital market in which it is extremely difficult for most analysts and portfolio managers to achieve superior results.

Questions

1. Discuss the rationale for expecting an efficient capital market. What factor would you look for to differentiate the market for two alternative stocks? Specifically, why should the efficiency of the markets for the stocks differ?

2. Define and discuss the weak-form EMH. Describe the two sets of tests used to examine the weak-form EMH.

3. Define and discuss the semistrong-form EMH. Describe the two sets of tests used to examine the semistrong-form EMH.

4. What is meant by the term *abnormal rate of return*?

5. Describe how you would compute the abnormal rate of return for a stock for a period surrounding an economic event. Give a brief example for a stock with a beta of 1.40.

6. When testing the EMH by comparing alternative trading rules to a buy-and-hold policy, there are three common mistakes that can bias the results against the EMH. Discuss each individually and explain why it would cause a bias.

7. Describe the results of a study that supported the semistrong-form EMH. Discuss the nature of the test and why the results support the hypothesis.

8. Describe the results of a study that did *not* support the semistrong-form EMH. Discuss the nature of the test and why the results reported did not support the hypothesis.

9. For many EMH tests, it is noted that it is really a test of a "joint hypothesis." Discuss this concept and the joint hypotheses being tested.

10. Define and discuss the strong-form EMH. Why do some observers contend that the strong-form hypothesis requires a perfect market in addition to an efficient market? Be specific.

11. Discuss how you would test the strong-form EMH. Why are these tests relevant? Give a brief example.

12. Describe the results of a study that did *not* support the strong-form EMH. Discuss the test involved and why the test results did not support the hypothesis.

13. Describe the results of a study that supported the strong-form EMH. Discuss the test involved and why these test results support the hypothesis.

14. What does the EMH imply for the use of technical analysis?

15. What does the EMH imply for fundamental analysis? Discuss what is does *not* imply.

16. In a world of efficient capital markets, what do you have to do to be a superior analyst? Be specific. How would you test whether an analyst were truly superior?

17. What advice would you give to your superior analysts in terms of the set of firms to analyze and variables that should be considered in the analysis? Discuss your reasoning for this advice.

18. How should a portfolio manager without any superior analysts run his or her portfolio?

19. What are the goals of an index fund? Discuss the contention that index funds are the ultimate answer in a world with efficient capital markets.

20. At a social gathering, you meet the portfolio manager for the trust department of a local bank. He confides to you that he has been following the recommendations of the department's six analysts for an extended period and has found that two are superior, two are average, and two are clearly inferior. What would you recommend that he do to run his portfolio?

21. Discuss whether you were surprised by Hawawini's summary of findings related to the EMH for the European equity markets.

22. Describe a test of the weak-form EMH for the Japanese stock market and indicate where you would get the required data.

23. *CFA Examination I (1992)*
   a. List and briefly define the *three* forms of the Efficient Market Hypothesis. [6 minutes]
   b. Discuss the role of a portfolio manager in a perfectly efficient market. [9 minutes]

24. *CFA Examination II (1993)*
   Tom Max, TMP's quantitative analyst, has developed a portfolio construction model about which he is very excited. To create the model, Max made a list of the stocks currently in the S&P 500 Stock Index and obtained annual operating cash flow, price, and total return data for each issue for the past five years. As of each year-end, this universe was divided into five equal-

weighted portfolios of 100 issues each, with selection based solely on the price/cash flow rankings of the individual stocks. Each portfolio's average annual return was then calculated.

During this five-year period, the linked returns from the portfolios with the lowest price/cash flow ratio generated an annualized total return of 19.0%, or 3.1 percentage points better than the 15.9% return on the S&P 500 Stock Index. Max also noted that the lowest price/cash flow portfolio had a below-market beta of 0.91 over this same time span.

    a. Briefly comment on Max's use of the beta measure as an indicator of portfolio risk in light of recent academic tests of its explanatory power with respect to stock returns. [5 minutes]

    b. You are familiar with the literature on market anomalies/inefficiencies. Against this background, discuss Max's use of a single-factor model (i.e., price/cash flow) in his research. [8 minutes]

    c. Identify and briefly describe *four* specific concerns about Max's test procedures and/or model design. (The issues already discussed in your answers to Parts a and b above may *not* be used in answering Part c.) [12 minutes]

25. *CFA Examination III (1995)*

    a. Briefly explain the concept of the *efficient market hypothesis* (EMH) and each of its three forms—*weak, semistrong, and strong*—and briefly discuss the degree to which existing empirical evidence supports each of the three forms of the EMH. [8 minutes]

    b. Briefly discuss the implications of the efficient market hypothesis for investment policy as it applies to:

     (i) technical analysis in the form of charting, and

     (ii) fundamental analysis. [4 minutes]

    c. Briefly explain *two* major roles or responsibilities of portfolio managers in an efficient market environment. [4 minutes]

    d. Briefly discuss whether active asset allocation among countries could consistently outperform a world market index. Include a discussion of the implications of *integration versus segmentation* of international financial markets as it pertains to portfolio diversification, but ignore the issue of stock selection. [6 minutes]

Problems

1. Compute the abnormal rates of return for the following stocks during period t (ignore differential systematic risk):

Stock	R_{it}	R_{mt}
B	11.5%	4.0%
F	10.0	8.5
T	14.0	9.6
C	12.0	15.3
E	15.9	12.4

R_{it} = return for stock i during period t
R_{mt} = return for the aggregate market during period t

2. Compute the abnormal rates of return for the five stocks in Problem 1, assuming the following systematic risk measures (betas):

Stock	i
B	0.95
F	1.25
T	1.45
C	0.75
E	−0.30

3. Compare the abnormal returns in Problems 1 and 2, and discuss the reason for the difference in each case.

4. You are given the following data regarding the performance of a group of stocks recommended by an analyst and a set of stocks with matching betas.

Stock	Beginning Price	Ending Price	Dividend
C	43	47	1.50
C-match	22	24	1.00
R	75	73	2.00
R-match	42	38	1.00
L	28	34	1.25
L-match	18	16	1.00
H	52	57	2.00
H-match	38	44	1.50
S	63	68	1.75
S-match	32	34	1.00

Based on the individual and composite results for these stocks (assume equal weights), would you judge this individual to be a superior analyst? Discuss your reasoning.

5. Look up the daily trading volume for the following stocks during a recent 5-day period.

- Abbott Labs
- Anheuser Busch
- Chrysler
- McDonald's
- General Electric

Randomly select five stocks from the NYSE and examine their daily trading volume for the same 5 days.

a. What are the average daily volumes for the two samples?

b. Would you expect this difference to have an impact on the efficiency of the markets for the two samples? Why or why not?

References

Ball, Ray. "The Theory of Stock Market Efficiency: Accomplishments and Limitations." *Journal of Applied Corporate Finance* 8, no. 1 (Spring 1995).

Fama, Eugene F. "Efficient Capital Market: II." *Journal of Finance* 46, no. 5 (December 1991).

Haugen, Robert A. *The New Finance.* Englewood Cliffs, NJ: Prentice Hall, 1995.

Hawawini, Gabriel. *European Equity Markets: Price Behavior and Efficiency,* Monograph 1984–4/5. Monograph Series in Finance and Economics, Salomon Brothers Center for the Study of Financial Institutions, Graduate School of Business, New York University, 1984.

Keim, Donald B. "The CAPM and Equity Return Regularities." *Financial Analysts Journal* 41, no. 3 (May–June 1986).

Keim, Donald B. and Robert F. Stambaugh. "Predicting Returns in Stock and Bond Markets." *Journal of Financial Economics* 17, no. 2 (December 1986).

Lorie, James H., Peter Dodd, and Mary Hamilton Kimpton. *The Stock Market: Theories and Evidence.* 2d ed. Homewood, IL: Richard D. Irwin, 1985.

Malkiel, Burton G. *A Random Walk Down Wall Street.* New York: W. W. Norton, 1990.

Chapter
8

An Introduction to Portfolio Management

This chapter answers the following questions:

- What is meant by risk aversion and what evidence is there that investors are generally risk averse?
- What are the basic assumptions behind the Markowitz portfolio theory?
- What is meant by risk and what are some of the alternative measures of risk used in investments?
- How do you compute the expected rate of return for an individual risky asset or a portfolio of assets?
- How do you compute the standard deviation of rates of return for an individual risky asset?
- What is meant by the covariance between rates of return and how do you compute covariance?
- What is the relationship between covariance and correlation?
- What is the formula for the standard deviation for a portfolio of risky assets and how does it differ from the standard deviation of an individual risky asset?
- Given the formula for the standard deviation of a portfolio, why and how do you diversify a portfolio?
- What happens to the standard deviation of a portfolio when you change the correlation between the assets in the portfolio?
- What is the risk-return efficient frontier of risky assets?
- Is it reasonable for alternative investors to select different portfolios from the portfolios on the efficient frontier?
- What determines which portfolio on the efficient frontier is selected by an individual investor?

One of the major advances in the investment field over the past couple of decades has been the recognition that the creation of an optimum investment portfolio is not simply a matter of combining a lot of unique individual securities that have desirable risk–return characteristics. Specifically, it has been shown that you must consider the relationship *among* the investments if you are going to build an optimum portfolio that will meet your investment objectives. The recognition of what is important in creating a portfolio was demonstrated in the derivation of portfolio theory.

This chapter explains portfolio theory step by step. This involves introducing you to the basic portfolio risk formula that you must understand when you are combining different assets. When you understand this formula and its implications, you will increase your understanding of not only why you should diversify your portfolio, but also *how* you should diversify. The subsequent chapter introduces asset pricing models and capital market theory with an emphasis on determining the appropriate risk measure for individual assets.

SOME
BACKGROUND
ASSUMPTIONS

Before presenting portfolio theory, we need to clarify some general assumptions of the theory. This includes not only what is meant by an *optimum portfolio,* but also what is meant by the terms *risk aversion* and *risk.* Therefore, these concepts are considered in this section before the presentation of portfolio theory.

One basic assumption of portfolio theory is that as an investor, you want to maximize the returns from your investments for a given level of risk. To adequately deal with such an assumption, certain ground rules must be laid. First, your portfolio should *include all of your assets and liabilities,* not only your stocks or even your marketable securities, but also such items as your car, house, and less marketable investments such as coins, stamps, art, antiques, and furniture. The full spectrum of investments must be considered because the returns from all these investments interact, and *this relationship between the returns for assets in the portfolio is important.* Hence, a good portfolio is *not* simply a collection of individually good investments.

RISK AVERSION

Portfolio theory also assumes that investors are basically **risk averse,** meaning that, given a choice between two assets with equal rates of return, they will select the asset with the lower level of risk. Evidence that most investors are risk averse is that they purchase various types of insurance, including life insurance, car insurance, and health insurance. Buying insurance basically involves an outlay of a given amount to guard against an uncertain, possibly larger outlay in the future. When you buy insurance, this implies that you are willing to pay the current known cost of the insurance policy to avoid the uncertainty of a potentially large future cost related to a car accident or a major illness. Further evidence of risk aversion is the difference in promised yield (the required rate of return) for different grades of bonds that supposedly have different degrees of credit risk. As you might know from reading about corporate bonds, the promised yield on bonds increases as you go from AAA (the lowest risk class) to AA to A, and so on. This increase in yields means that investors require a higher rate of return to accept higher risk.

This does not imply that everybody is risk averse, or that investors are completely risk averse regarding all financial commitments. The fact is, not everybody buys insurance for everything. Some people have no insurance against anything, either by choice or because they cannot afford it. In addition, some individuals buy insurance related to some risks such as auto accidents and illness, but they also buy lottery tickets and gamble at race tracks or in Las Vegas, where it is known that the expected returns are negative, which means that participants are willing to pay for the excitement of the risk involved. This combination of risk preference and risk aversion can be explained by an attitude toward risk that is not completely risk averse or risk preferring, but is a combination of the two that depends on the amount of money involved. Friedman and Savage speculate that this is the case for people who like to gamble for small amounts (in lotteries or nickel slot machines), but buy insurance to protect themselves against large losses such as fire or accidents.[1]

While recognizing such attitudes, our basic assumption is that most investors committing large sums of money to developing an investment portfolio are risk averse. Therefore, we expect a positive relationship between expected return and expected risk. Notably, this is also what we generally find in terms of historical results—that is, there is a positive relationship between the rates of return on various assets and their measures of risk as shown in Chapter 3.

---

[1] Milton Friedman and Leonard J. Savage, "The Utility Analysis of Choices Involving Risk," *Journal of Political Economy* 56, no. J (August 1948): 279–304.

DEFINITION OF RISK   Although there is a difference in the specific definitions of *risk* and *uncertainty,* for our purposes and in most financial literature the two terms are used interchangeably. In fact, one way to define risk is *the uncertainty of future outcomes.* An alternative definition might be *the probability of an adverse outcome.* Subsequently, in our discussion of portfolio theory, we will consider several measures of risk that are used when developing the theory.

MARKOWITZ PORTFOLIO THEORY

In the 1950s and early 1960s, the investment community talked about risk, but there was no specific measure for the term. To build a portfolio model, however, investors had to quantify their risk variable. The basic portfolio model was developed by Harry Markowitz, who derived the expected rate of return for a portfolio of assets and an expected risk measure.[2] Markowitz showed that the variance of the rate of return was a meaningful measure of portfolio risk under a reasonable set of assumptions, and he derived the formula for computing the variance of a portfolio. This formula for the variance of a portfolio not only indicated the importance of diversifying your investments to reduce the total risk of a portfolio, but also showed *how* to effectively diversify. The Markowitz model is based on several assumptions regarding investor behavior:

1. Investors consider each investment alternative as being represented by a probability distribution of expected returns over some holding period.
2. Investors maximize one-period expected utility, and their utility curves demonstrate diminishing marginal utility of wealth.
3. Investors estimate the risk of the portfolio on the basis of the variability of expected returns.
4. Investors base decisions solely on expected return and risk, so their utility curves are a function of expected return and the expected variance (or standard deviation) of returns only.
5. For a given risk level, investors prefer higher returns to lower returns. Similarly, for a given level of expected return, investors prefer less risk to more risk.

Under these assumptions, *a single asset or portfolio of assets is considered to be efficient if no other asset or portfolio of assets offers higher expected return with the same (or lower) risk, or lower risk with the same (or higher) expected return.*

ALTERNATIVE MEASURES OF RISK   One of the best-known measures of risk is the *variance,* or *standard deviation of expected returns.*[3] It is a statistical measure of the dispersion of returns around the expected value whereby a larger variance or standard deviation indicates greater dispersion, all other factors being equal. The idea is that the more disperse the expected returns, the greater the uncertainty of those returns in any future period.

Another measure of risk is the *range of returns.* In this case, it is assumed that a larger range of expected returns, from the lowest to the highest return, means greater uncertainty and risk regarding future expected returns.

Instead of using measures that analyze all deviations from expectations, some observers believe that when you invest you should be concerned only with *returns below expectations,* which means that you only consider deviations below the mean value. A measure

---

[2] Harry Markowitz, ''Portfolio Selection,'' *Journal of Finance* 7, no. 1 (March 1952): 77–91; and Harry Markowitz, *Portfolio Selection—Efficient Diversification of Investments* (New York: John Wiley & Sons, 1959).

[3] We consider the variance and standard deviation as one measure of risk because the standard deviation is the square root of the variance.

that only considers deviations below the mean is the *semivariance*. Extensions of the semivariance measure only computed expected returns *below zero* (i.e., negative returns), or returns below some specific asset such as T-bills, the rate of inflation, or a benchmark. These measures of risk implicitly assume that investors want to *minimize the damage* from returns less than some target rate. Obviously, it is assumed that investors would welcome positive returns or returns above some target rate, so these returns above expectations are not considered when measuring risk.

Although there are numerous potential measures of risk, we will use the variance or standard deviation of returns because (1) this measure is somewhat intuitive, (2) it is a correct and widely recognized risk measure, and (3) it has been used in most of the theoretical asset pricing models.

EXPECTED RATES OF RETURN

The expected rate of return for *an individual investment* is computed as shown in Table 8.1. The expected return for an individual risky asset with the set of potential returns and an assumption of equal probabilities used in the example would be 11 percent.

The expected rate of return for a *portfolio* of investments is simply the weighted average of the expected rates of return for the individual investments in the portfolio. The weights are the proportion of total value for the investment.

The expected return for a hypothetical portfolio with four risky assets is shown in Table 8.2. The expected return for this portfolio of investments would be 11.5 percent. The effect of adding or dropping any investment from the portfolio would be easy to determine because you would use the new weights based on value and the expected returns for each of the investments. This computation of the expected return for the portfolio [$E(R_{port})$] can be generalized as follows:

$$E(R_{port}) = \sum_{i=1}^{n} W_i R_i$$

where:

W_i = the percent of the portfolio in asset *i*
R_i = the expected rate of return for asset *i*.

VARIANCE (STANDARD DEVIATION) OF RETURNS FOR AN INDIVIDUAL INVESTMENT

As noted, we will be using the variance or the standard deviation of returns as the measure of risk (recall that the standard deviation is the square root of the variance). Therefore, at this point, we will demonstrate how you would compute the standard deviation of returns for an individual investment. Subsequently, after discussing some other statistical concepts, we will consider the determination of the standard deviation for a *portfolio* of investments.

TABLE 8.1	COMPUTATION OF EXPECTED RETURN FOR AN INDIVIDUAL RISKY ASSET

Probability	Possible Rate of Return (Percent)	Expected Return (Percent)
.25	.08	.0200
.25	.10	.0250
.25	.12	.0300
.25	.14	.0350
		$E(R) = .1100$

| TABLE 8.2 | COMPUTATION OF THE EXPECTED RETURN FOR A PORTFOLIO OF RISKY ASSETS |

Weight (W_i) (Percent of Portfolio)	Expected Security Return (R_i)	Expected Portfolio Return ($W_i \times R_i$)
.20	.10	.0200
.30	.11	.0330
.30	.12	.0360
.20	.13	.0260
		$E(R_{port}) = .1150$

The variance, or standard deviation, is a measure of the variation of possible rates of return, R_i, from the expected rate of return [$E(R_i)$], as follows:

$$\text{Variance } (\sigma^2) = \sum_{i=1}^{n} [R_i - E(R_i)]^2 P_i.$$

where P_i is the probability of the possible rate of return, R_i.

$$\text{Standard Deviation } (\sigma) = \sqrt{\sum_{i=1}^{n} [R_i - E(R_i)]^2 P_i}.$$

The computation of the variance and standard deviation of returns for the individual risky asset in Table 8.1 is set forth in Table 8.3.

VARIANCE (STANDARD DEVIATION) OF RETURNS FOR A PORTFOLIO

Two basic concepts in statistics, covariance and correlation, must be understood before we discuss the formula for the variance of the rate of return for a portfolio.

COVARIANCE OF RETURNS   In this section, we discuss what the covariance of returns is intended to measure, give the formula for computing it, and present an example of the computation. **Covariance** is a measure of the degree to which two variables "move together" relative to their individual mean values over time. In portfolio analysis, we usually are concerned with the covariance of *rates of return* rather than prices or some other

| TABLE 8.3 | COMPUTATION OF THE VARIANCE FOR AN INDIVIDUAL RISKY ASSET |

Possible Rate of Return (R_i)	Expected Return $E(R_i)$	$R_i - E(R_i)$	$[R_i - E(R_i)]^2$	P_i	$(R_i - E(R_i))^2 P_i$
.08	.11	.03	.0009	.25	.000225
.10	.11	.01	.0001	.25	.000025
.12	.11	.01	.0001	.25	.000025
.14	.11	.03	.0009	.25	.000225
					.000500

Variance (σ^2) = .00050
Standard Deviation (σ) = .02236

TABLE 8.4	COMPUTATION OF MONTHLY RATES OF RETURN					
	Coca-Cola			**Exxon**		
	Closing Price	Dividend	Rate of Return (Percent)	Closing Price	Dividend	Rate of Return (Percent)
Dec-94	51.500			60.750		
Jan-95	52.500		1.94	62.500		2.88
Feb-95	55.000		4.76	63.875		2.20
Mar-95	56.375	0.22	2.90	66.625	0.75	5.48
Apr-95	58.125		3.10	69.625		4.50
May-95	61.625		6.02	71.375		2.51
Jun-95	64.500	0.22	5.02	70.875	0.75	0.35
Jul-95	65.625		1.74	72.500		2.29
Aug-95	64.250		−2.10	68.750		−5.17
Sep-95	69.000	0.22	7.74	72.250	0.75	6.18
Oct-95	71.875		4.17	76.375		5.71
Nov-95	75.750		5.39	77.375		1.31
Dec-95	74.250	0.22	−1.69	80.500	0.75	5.01
			$E(R_{Coca-Cola}) = 3.25$			$E(R_{Exxon}) = 2.77$

variable.[4] A positive covariance means that the rates of return for two investments tend to move in the same direction relative to their individual means during the same time period. In contrast, a negative covariance indicates that the rates of return for two investments tend to move in different directions relative to their means during specified time intervals over time. The *magnitude* of the covariance depends on the variances of the individual return series, as well as on the relationship between the series.

Table 8.4 contains the monthly closing prices and dividends for Coca-Cola and Exxon. You can use these data to compute monthly rates of return for these two stocks during 1995. Figures 8.1 and 8.2 contain a time-series plot of the monthly rates of return for the two stocks during 1995. Although the rates of return for the two stocks moved together during some months, in other months they moved in opposite directions. The covariance statistic provides an *absolute* measure of how they moved together over time.

For two assets, i and j, the covariance of rates of return is defined as

$$Cov_{ij} = E\{[R_i - E(R_i)][R_j - E(R_j)]\}.$$

When we apply this formula to the monthly rates of return for Coca-Cola and Exxon during 1995, it becomes:

$$\frac{1}{12} \sum_{i=1}^{12} [R_i - E(R_i)][R_j - E(R_j)].$$

As can be seen, if the rates of return for one stock are above (below) its mean rate of return during a given period, and the returns for the other stock are likewise above (below)

---

[4] Returns, of course, can be measured in a variety of ways, depending on the type of asset being considered. You will recall that we defined returns (R_i) in Chapter 1 as:

$$R_i = \frac{EV - BV + CF}{BV}$$

where EV is ending value, BV is beginning value, and CF is the cash flow during the period.

FIGURE 8.1

TIME-SERIES RETURNS FOR COCA-COLA: 1995

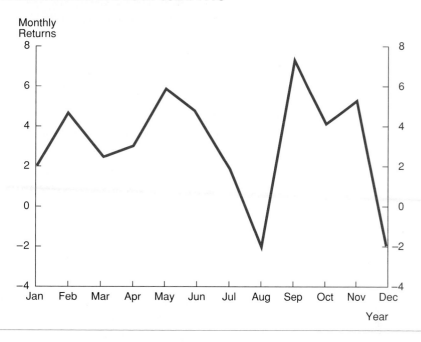

FIGURE 8.2

TIME-SERIES RETURNS FOR EXXON: 1995

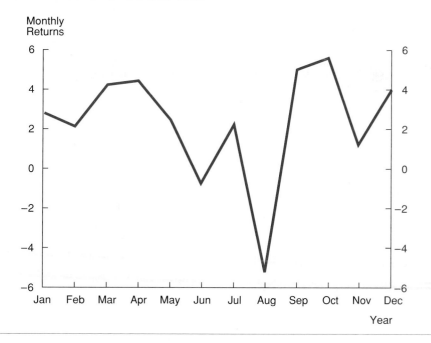

its mean rate of return during this same period, then the *product* of these deviations from the mean is positive. If this happens consistently, the covariance of returns between these two stocks will be some large positive value. If, however, the rate of return for one of the securities is above its mean return while the return on the other security is below its mean return, the product will be negative. If this contrary movement happened consistently, the covariance between the rates of return for the two stocks would be a large negative value.

Table 8.5 contains the monthly rates of return during 1995 for Coca-Cola and Exxon as computed in Table 8.4. One might expect the returns for the two stocks to have reasonably low covariance because of the differences in the products of these firms. The expected returns E(R) were the arithmetic mean of the monthly returns:

$$E(R_i) = \frac{1}{12} \sum_{i=1}^{12} R_{it}$$

and

$$E(R_j) = \frac{1}{12} \sum_{j=1}^{12} R_{jt}$$

All figures (except those in the last column) were rounded to the nearest hundredth of 1 percent. As shown in Table 8.4, the average monthly return was 3.25 percent for Coca-Cola and 2.77 percent for Exxon stock. The results in Table 8.5 show that the covariance between the rates of return for these two stocks was:

$$Cov_{ij} = \frac{1}{12} \times 39.81$$
$$= 3.32$$

TABLE 8.5   COMPUTATION OF COVARIANCE OF RETURNS FOR COCA-COLA AND EXXON: 1995

Date	Coca-Cola (R$_i$)	Exxon (R$_j$)	Coca-Cola R$_i$ − E(R$_i$)	Exxon R$_j$ − E(R$_j$)	[R$_i$ − E (R$_i$)] × [R$_j$ − E (R$_j$)]
	MONTHLY RETURNS (PERCENT)				
Jan-95	1.94	2.88	−1.31	0.11	−0.14
Feb-95	4.76	2.20	1.51	−0.57	−0.86
Mar-95	2.90	5.48	−0.35	2.71	−0.95
Apr-95	3.10	4.50	−0.15	1.73	−0.26
May-95	6.02	2.51	2.77	−0.26	−0.72
Jun-95	5.02	0.35	1.77	−2.42	−4.28
Jul-95	1.74	2.29	−1.51	−0.48	0.72
Aug-95	−2.10	−5.17	−5.35	−7.94	42.48
Sep-95	7.74	6.18	4.49	3.41	15.31
Oct-95	4.17	5.71	0.92	2.94	2.70
Nov-95	5.39	1.31	2.14	−1.46	−3.12
Dec-95	−1.69	5.01	−4.94	2.24	−11.07
	E(R$_i$) = 3.25	E(R$_j$) = 2.77			Sum = 39.81

$$Cov_{i,j} = 39.81 / 12 = 3.32$$

| FIGURE 8.3 | **SCATTER PLOT OF MONTHLY RETURNS FOR COCA-COLA AND EXXON: 1995** |

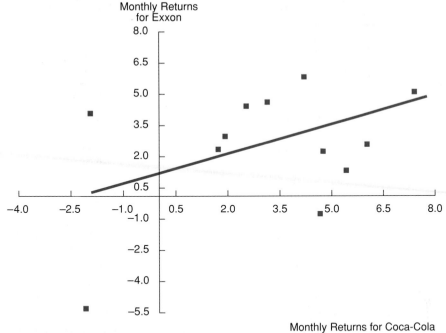

Interpretation of a number like 3.32 is difficult; is it high or low for covariance? We know the relationship between the two stocks is generally positive, but it is not possible to be more specific. Figure 8.3 contains a scatter diagram with paired values of R_{it} and R_{jt} plotted against each other. This plot demonstrates the linear nature and strength of the relationship and shows several instances during 1995 when Coca-Cola experienced negative returns relative to its mean return when Exxon had positive rates of return relative to its mean.

COVARIANCE AND CORRELATION   Covariance is affected by the variability of the two individual return series. Therefore, a number such as the 3.32 in our example might indicate a weak positive relationship if the two individual series were very volatile, but would reflect a strong positive relationship if the two series were very stable. Obviously, you want to "standardize" this covariance measure taking into consideration the variability of the two individual return series, as follows:

$$r_{i,j} = \frac{\text{Cov}_{i,j}}{\sigma_i \sigma_j}$$

where:

$r_{i,j}$ = **the correlation coefficient of returns**
σ_i = **the standard deviation of R_{it}**
σ_j = **the standard deviation of R_{jt}.**

Standardizing the covariance by the individual standard deviations yields the **correlation coefficient** ($r_{i,j}$), which can vary only in the range −1 to +1. A value of +1 would

| TABLE 8.6 | **COMPUTATION OF STANDARD DEVIATION OF RETURNS FOR COCA-COLA AND EXXON: 1995** |

Date	COCA-COLA		EXXON	
	$R_i - E(R_i)$	$[R_i - E(R_i)]^2$	$R_j - E(R_j)$	$[R_j - E(R_j)]^2$
Jan-95	−1.31	1.72	0.11	0.01
Feb-95	1.51	2.28	−0.57	0.32
Mar-95	−0.35	0.12	2.71	7.34
Apr-95	−0.15	0.02	1.73	2.99
May-95	2.77	7.67	−0.26	0.07
Jun-95	1.77	3.13	−2.42	5.86
Jul-95	−1.51	2.28	−0.48	0.23
Aug-95	−5.35	28.62	−7.94	63.04
Sep-95	4.49	20.16	3.41	11.63
Oct-95	0.92	0.85	2.94	8.64
Nov-95	2.14	4.58	−1.46	2.13
Dec-95	−4.94	24.40	2.24	5.02
	Sum =	95.83	Sum =	107.28

$$\sigma^2_{\text{Coca-Cola}} = 95.83 / 12 = 7.99 \qquad \sigma^2_{\text{Exxon}} = 107.28 / 12 = 8.94$$

$$\sigma_{\text{Coca-Cola}} = (7.99)^{1/2} = 2.83 \qquad \sigma_{\text{Exxon}} = (8.94)^{1/2} = 2.99$$

indicate a perfect positive linear relationship between R_i and R_j, meaning the returns for the two stocks move together in a completely linear manner. A value of −1 means that there is a perfect negative relationship between the two return series such that when one stock's rate of return is above its mean, the other stock's rate of return will be below its mean by the comparable amount.

To calculate this standardized measure of the relationship, you need to compute the standard deviation for the two individual return series. We already have the values for $R_{it} - E(R_i)$ and $R_{jt} - E(R_j)$ in Table 8.5. We can square each of these values and sum them as shown in Table 8.6 to calculate the variance of each return series.

$$\sigma_i^2 = \frac{1}{12}(95.83) = 7.99$$

and

$$\sigma_j^2 = \frac{1}{12}(107.28) = 8.94$$

The standard deviation for each series is the square root of the variance for each, as follows:

$$\sigma_i = \sqrt{7.99} = 2.83$$
$$\sigma_j = \sqrt{8.94} = 2.99$$

Thus, based on the covariance between the two series and the individual standard deviations, we can calculate the correlation coefficient between returns for Coca-Cola and Exxon as

$$r_{i,j} = \frac{\text{Cov}_{i,j}}{\sigma_i \sigma_j} = \frac{3.32}{(2.83)(2.99)} = \frac{3.32}{8.46} = 0.392$$

Obviously, this formula also implies that

$$\text{Cov}_{i,j} = r_{i,j}\,\sigma_i\,\sigma_j$$

Standard Deviation of a Portfolio

As noted, a correlation of +1.0 would indicate perfect positive correlation, and a value of −1.0 would mean that the returns moved in a completely opposite direction. A value of zero would mean that the returns had no linear relationship, that is, they were uncorrelated statistically. That does *not* mean that they are independent. The value of $r_{i,j} = 0.392$ is significant but not very high. This relatively low correlation is not unusual for stocks in diverse industries. Correlations between stocks of companies *within* some industries approach 0.85.

PORTFOLIO STANDARD DEVIATION FORMULA   Now that we have discussed the concepts of covariance and correlation, we can consider the formula for computing the standard deviation of returns for a *portfolio* of assets, our measure of risk for a portfolio. As noted, Harry Markowitz derived the formula for computing the standard deviation of a portfolio of assets.[5]

In Table 8.2, we showed that the expected rate of return of the portfolio was the weighted average of the expected returns for the individual assets in the portfolio; the weights were the percentage of value of the portfolio. Under such conditions, we can easily see the impact on the portfolio's expected return of adding or deleting an asset.

One might assume it is possible to derive the standard deviation of the portfolio in the same manner, that is, by computing the weighted average of the standard deviations for the individual assets. This would be a mistake. Markowitz derived the general formula for the standard deviation of a portfolio as follows:[6]

$$\sigma_{\text{port}} = \sqrt{\sum_{i=1}^{n} w_i^2 \sigma_i^2 + \sum_{\substack{i=1 \\ i \neq j}}^{n} \sum_{j=1}^{n} w_i w_j \text{Cov}_{i,j}}$$

where:

σ_{port} = **the standard deviation of the portfolio**
w_i = **the weights of the individual assets in the portfolio, where weights are determined by the proportion of value in the portfolio**
σ_i^2 = **the variance of rates of return for asset** *i*
$\text{Cov}_{i,j}$ = **the covariance between the rates of return for assets** *i* **and** *j*, **where** $\text{Cov}_{i,j} = r_{i,j}\sigma_i\sigma_j$.

This formula indicates that the standard deviation for a portfolio of assets is a function of the weighted average of the individual variances (where the weights are squared), *plus* the weighted covariances between all the assets in the portfolio. The standard deviation for a portfolio of assets encompasses not only the variances of the individual assets, but *also* includes the covariances between pairs of individual assets in the portfolio. Further, it can be shown that, in a portfolio with a large number of securities, this formula reduces to the sum of the weighted covariances.

---

[5] Markowitz, *Portfolio Selection.*

[6] For the detailed derivation of this formula, see Markowitz, *Portfolio Selection.*

Although most of the subsequent demonstration will consider portfolios with only two assets because it is possible to show the effect in two dimensions, we will demonstrate the computations for a three-asset portfolio. Still, it is important at this point to consider what happens in a large portfolio with many assets. Specifically, what happens to the portfolio's standard deviation when you add a new security to such a portfolio? As shown by the formula, there are two effects. The first is the asset's own variance of returns, and the second is the covariance between the returns of this new asset and the returns of *every other asset that is already in the portfolio.* The relative weight of these numerous covariances is substantially greater than the asset's unique variance, and the more assets in the portfolio, the more this is true. This means that the important factor to consider when adding an investment to a portfolio that contains a number of other investments is *not* the investment's own variance, but *its average covariance with all the other investments in the portfolio.*

In the following examples we will consider the simple case of a two-asset portfolio. We do these relatively simple calculations and provide graphs with two assets to demonstrate the impact of different covariances on the total risk (standard deviation) of the portfolio.

DEMONSTRATION OF THE PORTFOLIO STANDARD DEVIATION CALCULATION   Because of the assumptions used in developing the Markowitz portfolio model, any asset or portfolio of assets can be described by two characteristics: the expected rate of return and the expected standard deviation of returns. Therefore, the following demonstrations can be applied to two *individual* assets with the indicated return–standard deviation characteristics and correlation coefficients, two *portfolios* of assets, or two *asset classes* with the indicated return–standard deviation characteristics and correlation coefficients.

Equal risk and return—changing correlations   Consider first the case in which both assets have the same expected return and expected standard deviation of return. As an example, let us assume

$$E(R_1) = .20$$
$$E(\sigma_1) = .10$$
$$E(R_2) = .20$$
$$E(\sigma_2) = .10.$$

To show the effect of different covariances, assume different levels of correlation between the two assets. Consider the following examples where the two assets have equal weights in the portfolio ($W_1 = .50$; $W_2 = .50$). Therefore, the only value that changes in each example is the correlation between the returns for the two assets.

Recall that

$$Cov_{i,j} = r_{i,j}\sigma_i\sigma_j.$$

Consider the following alternative correlation coefficients and the covariances they yield. The covariance will be equal to $r_{1,2}$ (.10)(.10) because both standard deviations are 0.10.

a. $r_{1,2} = 1.00$; $Cov_{1,2} = (1.00)(.10)(.10) = .01$
b. $r_{1,2} = .50$; $Cov_{1,2} = (0.50)(.10)(.10) = .005$
c. $r_{1,2} = .00$; $Cov_{1,2} = .000$
d. $r_{1,2} = -.50$; $Cov_{1,2} = -.005$
e. $r_{1,2} = -1.00$; $Cov_{1,2} = .01$.

Now let us see what happens to the standard deviation of the portfolio under these five conditions. Recall that

$$\sigma_{port} = \sqrt{\sum_{i=1}^{n} w_i^2 \sigma_i^2 + \sum_{i=1}^{n} \sum_{\substack{j=1 \\ i \neq j}}^{n} w_i w_j Cov_{i,j}}$$

When this general formula is applied to a two-asset portfolio, it is

$$\sigma_{port} = \sqrt{w_1^2 \sigma_1^2 + w_2^2 \sigma_2^2 + 2w_1 w_2 r_{1,2} \sigma_1 \sigma_2}$$

or

$$\sigma_{port} = \sqrt{w_1^2 \sigma_1^2 + w_2^2 \sigma_2^2 + 2w_1 w_2 Cov_{1,2}}.$$

Thus, in Case a,

$$\begin{aligned}
\sigma_{port\,(a)} &= \sqrt{(0.5)^2(0.10)^2 + (0.5)^2(0.10)^2 + 2(0.5)(0.5)(0.01)} \\
&= \sqrt{(0.25)(0.01) + (0.25)(0.01) + 2(0.25)(0.01)} \\
&= \sqrt{0.01} \\
&= 0.10.
\end{aligned}$$

In this case, where the returns for the two assets are perfectly positively correlated, the standard deviation for the portfolio is, in fact, the weighted average of the individual standard deviations. The important point is that we get no real benefit from combining two assets that are perfectly correlated; they are like one asset already because their returns move together.

Now consider Case b, where $r_{1,2}$ equals 0.50.

$$\begin{aligned}
\sigma_{port\,(b)} &= \sqrt{(0.5)^2(0.10)^2 + (0.5)^2(0.10)^2 + 2(0.5)(0.5)(0.005)} \\
&= \sqrt{(0.0025) + (0.0025) + 2(0.25)(0.005)} \\
&= \sqrt{0.0075} \\
&= 0.0866
\end{aligned}$$

The only term that changed from Case a is the last term, $Cov_{1,2}$, which changed from 0.01 to 0.005. As a result, the standard deviation of the portfolio declined by about 13 percent, from 0.10 to 0.0866. Note that *the expected return did not change* because it is simply the weighted average of the individual expected returns; it is equal to 0.20 in both cases.

You should be able to confirm through your own calculations that the standard deviations for Portfolios c and d are as follows:

c. .0707
d. .05.

The final case where the correlation between the two assets is −1.00 indicates the ultimate benefits of diversification.

$$\begin{aligned}
\sigma_{port\,(e)} &= \sqrt{(0.5)^2(0.10)^2 + (0.5)^2(0.10)^2 + 2(0.5)(0.5)(-0.01)} \\
&= \sqrt{(0.0050) + (-0.0050)} \\
&= \sqrt{0} \\
&= 0.
\end{aligned}$$

| FIGURE 8.4 | **TIME PATTERNS OF RETURNS FOR TWO ASSETS WITH PERFECT NEGATIVE CORRELATION** |

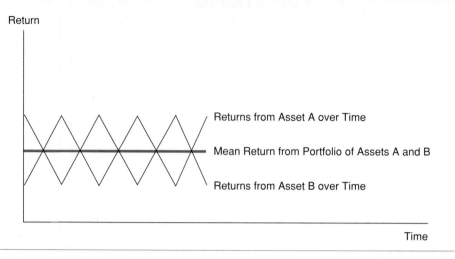

Here, the negative covariance term exactly offsets the individual variance terms, leaving an overall standard deviation of the portfolio of zero. *This would be a risk-free portfolio.*

Figure 8.4 illustrates a graph of such a pattern. Perfect negative correlation gives a mean combined return for the two securities over time equal to the mean for each of them, so the returns for the portfolio show no variability. Any returns above and below the mean for each of the assets are *completely offset* by the return for the other asset, so there is *no variability* in total returns, that is, *no risk,* for the portfolio. This combination of two assets that are completely negatively correlated provides the maximum benefits of diversification—it completely eliminates risk.

The graph in Figure 8.5 shows the difference in the risk–return posture for these five cases. As noted, the only impact of the change in correlation is the change in the standard deviation of this two-asset portfolio. Combining assets that are not perfectly correlated does *not* affect the expected return of the portfolio, but it *does* reduce the risk of the portfolio (as measured by its standard deviation). When we eventually reach the ultimate combination of perfect negative correlation, risk is eliminated.

Combining stocks with different returns and risk   The previous discussion indicated what happens when only the correlation coefficient (covariance) differs between the assets. We now consider two assets (or portfolios) with different expected rates of return and individual standard deviations.[7] We will show what happens when we vary the correlations between them. We will assume two assets with the following characteristics:

Asset	$E(R_i)$	W_i	σ_i^2	σ_i
1	.10	.50	.0049	.07
2	.20	.50	.0100	.10

[7] As noted, these could be two asset classes. For example, asset 1 could be low risk–low return bonds and asset 2 could be higher return, higher risk stocks.

FIGURE 8.5

RISK–RETURN PLOT FOR PORTFOLIOS WITH EQUAL RETURNS AND STANDARD DEVIATIONS BUT DIFFERENT CORRELATIONS

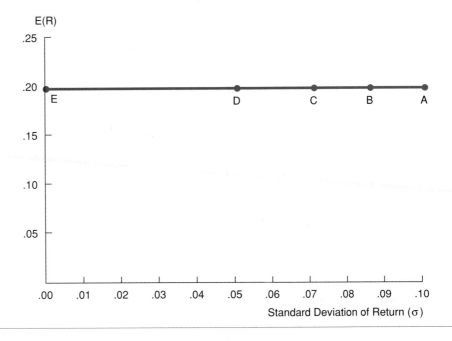

The previous set of correlation coefficients gives a different set of covariances because the standard deviations are different. For example, the covariance in case b would be $(0.50)(.07)(.10) = .0035$.

Case	Correlation Coefficient	Covariance $(r_{ij}\sigma_i\sigma_j)$
a	+1.00	.0070
b	+0.50	.0035
c	0.00	.0000
d	−0.50	−.0035
e	−1.00	−.0070

Because we are assuming the same weights in all cases (.50 − .50), the expected return in every instance will be

$$E(R_{port}) = 0.50(0.10) + 0.50(0.20)$$
$$= 0.15.$$

The standard deviation for Case a will be

$$\sigma_{port\,(a)} = \sqrt{(0.5)^2(0.07)^2 + (0.5)^2(0.10)^2 + 2(0.5)(0.5)(0.0070)}$$
$$= \sqrt{0.007225}$$
$$= 0.085.$$

Again, with perfect positive correlation, the standard deviation of the portfolio is the weighted average of the standard deviations of the individual assets:

$$(0.5)(0.07) + (0.5)(0.10) = 0.085.$$

As you might envision, changing the weights with perfect positive correlation causes the standard deviation for the portfolio to change in a linear fashion. This is an important point to remember when we discuss the capital asset pricing model (CAPM) in the next chapter.

For Cases b, c, d, and e, the standard deviation for the portfolio would be as follows:[8]

$$\sigma_{\text{port (b)}} = \sqrt{(0.001225) + (0.0025) + (0.5)(0.0035)}$$
$$= \sqrt{0.005475}$$
$$= 0.07399$$

$$\sigma_{\text{port (c)}} = \sqrt{(0.001225) + (0.0025) + (0.5)(0.00)}$$
$$= 0.0610$$

$$\sigma_{\text{port (d)}} = \sqrt{(0.001225) + (0.0025) + (0.5)(-0.0035)}$$
$$= 0.0444$$

$$\sigma_{\text{port (e)}} = \sqrt{(0.003725) + 0.5(-0.0070)}$$
$$= 0.015.$$

Note that, in this example, with perfect negative correlation the standard deviation of the portfolio is not zero. This is because the different examples have equal weights, but the individual standard deviations are not equal.[9]

Figure 8.6 shows the results for the two individual assets and the portfolio of the two assets assuming the correlation coefficients vary as set forth in Cases a through e. As before, the expected return does not change because the proportions are always set at .50 − .50, so all the portfolios lie along the horizontal line at the return, R = .15.

Constant correlation with changing weights   If we changed the weights of the two assets while holding the correlation coefficient constant, we would derive a set of combinations that trace an ellipse starting at Asset 2, going through the .50 − .50 point, and ending at Asset 1. We can demonstrate this with Case c, in which the correlation coefficient of zero eases the computations. We begin with 100 percent in Asset 2 (Case f) and change the weights as follows, ending with 100 percent in Asset 1 (Case l):

Case	W_1	W_2	$E(R_i)$
f	.00	1.00	.20
g	.20	.80	.18
h	.40	.60	.16
i	.50	.50	.15
j	.60	.40	.14
k	.80	.20	.12
l	1.00	.00	.10

We already know the standard deviation (σ) for Portfolio i. In Cases f, g, h, j, k, and l, the standard deviations would be[10]

---

[8] In all the following examples we will skip some steps because you are now aware that only the last term changes. You are encouraged to work out the individual steps to ensure understanding of the computational procedure.

[9] The two appendixes to this chapter show proofs for equal weights with equal variances and solve for the appropriate weights to get zero standard deviation when standard deviations are not equal.

[10] Again, you are encouraged to fill in the steps we skipped in the computations.

FIGURE 8.6

RISK–RETURN PLOT FOR PORTFOLIOS WITH DIFFERENT RETURNS, STANDARD DEVIATIONS, AND CORRELATIONS

$$\sigma_{\text{port (g)}} = \sqrt{(0.20)^2(0.07)^2 + (0.80)^2(0.10)^2 + 2(0.20)(0.80)(0.00)}$$
$$= \sqrt{(0.04)(0.0049) + (0.64)(0.01) + (0)}$$
$$= \sqrt{0.006596}$$
$$= 0.0812$$

$$\sigma_{\text{port (h)}} = \sqrt{(0.40)^2(0.07)^2 + (0.60)^2(0.10)^2 + 2(0.40)(0.60)(0.00)}$$
$$= \sqrt{0.004384}$$
$$= 0.0662$$

$$\sigma_{\text{port (j)}} = \sqrt{(0.60)^2(0.07)^2 + (0.40)^2(0.10)^2 + 2(0.60)(0.40)(0.00)}$$
$$= \sqrt{0.003364}$$
$$= 0.0580$$

$$\sigma_{\text{port (k)}} = \sqrt{(0.80)^2(0.07)^2 + (0.20)^2(0.10)^2 + 2(0.80)(0.20)(0.00)}$$
$$= \sqrt{0.003536}$$
$$= 0.0595.$$

These alternative weights with constant correlations would yield the following risk–return combinations:

Case	W_1	W_2	$E(R_i)$	$E(\sigma_{\text{port}})$
f	0.00	1.00	0.20	0.1000
g	0.20	0.80	0.18	0.0812
h	0.40	0.60	0.16	0.0662
i	0.50	0.50	0.15	0.0610
j	0.60	0.40	0.14	0.0580
k	0.80	0.20	0.12	0.0595
l	1.00	0.00	0.10	0.0700

A graph of these combinations appears in Figure 8.7. You could derive a complete curve by simply varying the weighting by smaller increments.

FIGURE 8.7

PORTFOLIO RISK–RETURN PLOTS FOR DIFFERENT WEIGHTS WHEN $r_{i,j}$ = +1.00; +0.50; 0.00; –0.50; –1.00

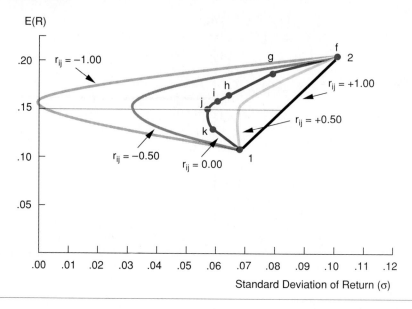

A notable result is that with low, zero, or negative correlations, it is possible to derive portfolios that have *lower risk than either single asset*. In our set of examples where $r_{i,j}$ = 0.00, this occurs in cases h, i, j, and k. This ability to reduce risk is the essence of diversification. In turn, we see that the crucial factors are the correlation between assets and the weighting among them.

As shown in Figure 8.7, the curvature in the graph depends on the correlation between the two assets or portfolios. With $r_{i,j}$ = +1.00, the combinations lie along a straight line between the two assets. When $r_{i,j}$ = 0.50, the curve is to the right of our $r_{i,j}$ = 0.00 curve, while the $r_{i,j}$ = –0.50 is to the left. Finally, when $r_{i,j}$ = –1.00, the graph would be two straight lines that would touch at the vertical line (zero risk) with some combination. As discussed in Appendix B of this chapter, it is possible to solve for the specified set of weights that would give a portfolio with zero risk. In this case, it is W_1 = 0.412 and W_2 = 0.588.

A THREE-ASSET
PORTFOLIO

A demonstration of what occurs with a three-asset class portfolio is useful because it shows the dynamics of the portfolio process when we add additional assets to a portfolio. It also shows the rapid growth in the computations required, which is why we will stop at three assets.

In this example, we will combine three asset classes we have been discussing: stocks, bonds, and cash equivalents.[11] We will assume the following characteristics for these assets:

Asset Classes	$E(R_i)$	$F(\sigma_i)$	W_i
Stocks (S)	.12	.20	.60
Bonds (B)	.08	.10	.30
Cash equivalent (C)	.04	.03	.10

[11] The asset allocation articles regularly contained in *The Wall Street Journal* generally refer to these three asset classes.

The correlations are as follows:

$$r_{S,B} = 0.25; \ r_{S,C} = -0.08; \ r_{B,C} = 0.15$$

Given the weights specified, the $E(R_p)$ is:

$$E(R_p) = (0.60)(0.12) + (0.30)(0.08) + (0.10)(0.04)$$
$$= (.072 + .024 + .004) = .100 = 10.00\%$$

When we apply the generalized formula to the expected standard deviation of a three-asset class, it is as follows:

$$\sigma_p^2 = [W_S^2 \sigma_S^2 + W_B^2 \sigma_B^2 + W_C^2 \sigma_C^2] + [2W_S W_B \sigma_S \sigma_B r_{S,B} + 2W_S W_C \sigma_S \sigma_C r_{S,C} + 2W_B W_C \sigma_B \sigma_C r_{B,C}]$$

Using the characteristics specified, the standard deviation of this three-asset class portfolio (σ_p) would be:

$$\sigma_p^2 = [0.6)^2(.20)^2 + (0.3)^2(.10)^2 + (0.1)^2(.03)^2]$$
$$+ \{[2(0.6)(0.3)(0.20)(0.10)(0.25)] + [2(0.6)(0.1)(0.20)(0.03)(-0.08)]$$
$$+ [2(0.3)(0.1)(0.10)(0.03)(0.15)]\}$$
$$= [.015309] + \{[.0018] + [-.0000576] + [.000027]\}$$
$$= 0.0170784$$
$$\sigma_p = (0.0170784)^{1/2} = .1306 = 13.06\%$$

ESTIMATION ISSUES   It is important to keep in mind that the results of this portfolio asset allocation depend on the accuracy of the statistical inputs. In the current instance, this means that for every asset (or asset class) being considered for inclusion in the portfolio, you must estimate its expected returns and standard deviation. In addition, the correlation coefficient among the entire set of assets must also be estimated. The number of correlation estimates can be significant—for example, for a portfolio of 100 securities, the number is 4,950 (i.e., $99 + 98 + 97 + \ldots$). The potential source of error that arises from these approximations is referred to as *estimation risk.*

It is possible to reduce the number of correlation coefficients that must be estimated by assuming that stock returns can be described by a single index market model as follows:

$$R_i = a_i + b_i R_m + \Sigma_i$$

where:

b_i = the slope coefficient that relates the returns for security *i* to the returns for the aggregate stock market
R_m = the returns for the aggregate stock market

If all the securities are similarly related to the market and a b_i derived for each one, it can be shown that the correlation coefficient between two securities *i* and *j* is given as:

$$r_{i,j} = b_i b_j \frac{\sigma_m^2}{\sigma_i \sigma_j}$$

where σ_m^2 = the variance of returns for the aggregate stock market.

This reduces the number of estimates from 4,950 to 100—i.e., once you have derived a slope estimate (b_i) for each security, the correlation estimates can be computed. Keep in mind that this assumes that the single index market model provides a good estimate of security returns.

THE EFFICIENT
FRONTIER

If we examined different two-asset combinations and derived the curves assuming all the possible weights, we would have a graph like that in Figure 8.8. The envelope curve that contains the best of all these possible combinations is referred to as the **efficient frontier.** Specifically, *the efficient frontier represents that set of portfolios that has the maximum rate of return for every given level of risk, or the minimum risk for every level of return.* An example of such a frontier is shown in Figure 8.9. Every portfolio that lies on the efficient frontier has either a higher rate of return for equal risk or lower risk for an equal rate of return than some portfolio beneath the frontier. Thus, we would say that Portfolio A *dominates* Portfolio C because it has an equal rate of return but substantially less risk. Similarly, Portfolio B dominates Portfolio C because it has equal risk but a higher expected rate of return. Because of the benefits of diversification among imperfectly correlated assets, we would expect the efficient frontier to be made up of *portfolios* of investments rather than individual securities. Two possible exceptions arise at the end points, which represent the asset with the highest return and that asset with the lowest risk.

As an investor, you will target a point along the efficient frontier based on your utility function and your attitude toward risk. No portfolio on the efficient frontier can dominate any other portfolio on the efficient frontier. All of these portfolios have different return and risk measures, with expected rates of return that increase with higher risk.

THE EFFICIENT
FRONTIER AND
INVESTOR UTILITY

The curve in Figure 8.9 shows that the slope of the efficient frontier curve decreases steadily as you move upward. This implies that adding equal increments of risk as you move up the efficient frontier gives you diminishing increments of expected return. To evaluate this slope, we calculate the slope of the efficient frontier as follows:

$$\frac{\Delta E(R_{port})}{\Delta E(\sigma_{port})}$$

FIGURE 8.8 **NUMEROUS PORTFOLIO COMBINATIONS OF AVAILABLE ASSETS**

E(R)

Standard Deviation of Return (σ)

FIGURE 8.9

EFFICIENT FRONTIER FOR ALTERNATIVE PORTFOLIOS

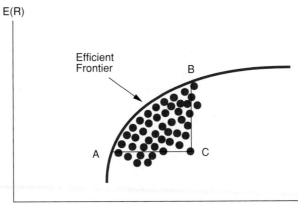

An individual investor's utility curves specify the trade-offs he or she is willing to make between expected return and risk. In conjunction with the efficient frontier, these utility curves determine which *particular* portfolio on the efficient frontier best suits an individual investor. Two investors will choose the same portfolio from the efficient set only if their utility curves are identical.

Figure 8.10 shows two sets of utility curves along with an efficient frontier of investments. The curves labeled U_1 are for a very risk-averse investor (with U_3 U_2 U_1). These

FIGURE 8.10

SELECTING AN OPTIMAL RISKY PORTFOLIO

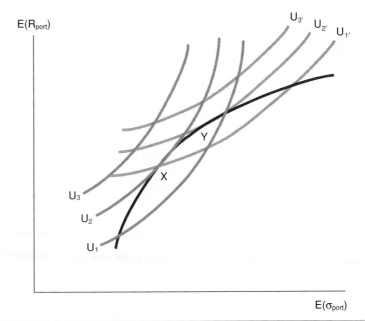

utility curves are quite steep, indicating that the investor will not tolerate much additional risk to obtain additional returns. The investor is equally disposed toward any E(R), E(σ) combinations along a specific utility curve, such as U₁.

The curves labeled U₁′ (U₃′ U₂′ U₁′) characterize a less risk-averse investor. Such an investor is willing to tolerate a bit more risk to get a higher expected return.

The **optimal portfolio** is the efficient portfolio that has the highest utility for a given investor. It lies at *the point of tangency between the efficient frontier and the curve with the highest possible utility.* A conservative investor's highest utility is at point X in Figure 8.10, where the curve U₂ just touches the efficient frontier. A less risk-averse investor's highest utility occurs at point Y, which represents a portfolio with higher expected returns and higher risk than the portfolio at X.

Summary

- The basic Markowitz portfolio model derives the expected rate of return for a portfolio of assets and a measure of expected risk, which is the standard deviation of expected rate of return. Markowitz shows that the expected rate of return of a portfolio is the weighted average of the expected return for the individual investments in the portfolio. The standard deviation of a portfolio is a function not only of the standard deviations for the individual investments, but *also* of the covariance between the rates of return for all the pairs of assets in the portfolio. In a large portfolio, these covariances are the important factors.
- Different weights or amounts of a portfolio held in various assets yield a curve of potential combinations. Correlation coefficients among assets are the critical factor you must consider when selecting investments because you can maintain your rate of return while reducing the risk level of your portfolio by combining assets or portfolios that have low positive or negative correlation.
- Assuming numerous assets and a multitude of combination curves, the efficient frontier is the envelope curve that encompasses all of the best combinations. It defines the set of portfolios that has the highest expected return for each given level of risk, or the minimum risk for each given level of return. From this set of dominant portfolios, you select the one that lies at the point of tangency between the efficient frontier and your highest utility curve. Because risk–return utility functions differ, your point of tangency and, therefore, your portfolio choice will probably differ from those of other investors.
- At this point, we understand that an optimum portfolio is a combination of investments, each having desirable individual risk–return characteristics that also fit together based on their correlations. This deeper understanding of portfolio theory should lead you to reflect back on our earlier discussion of global investing. Because many foreign stock and bond investments provide superior rates of return compared with U.S. securities *and* have very low correlations with portfolios of U.S. stocks and bonds, including these foreign securities will help you to reduce the overall risk of your portfolio while possibly increasing your rate of return.

Questions

1. Why do most investors hold diversified portfolios?
2. What is covariance, and why is it important in portfolio theory?
3. Why do most assets of the same type show positive covariances of returns with each other? Would you expect positive covariances of returns between *different* types of assets such as returns on Treasury bills, General Electric common stock, and commercial real estate? Why or why not?
4. What is the relationship between the covariance and the correlation coefficient?
5. Explain the shape of the efficient frontier.
6. Draw a properly labeled graph of the Markowitz efficient frontier. Describe the efficient frontier in exact terms. Discuss the concept of dominant portfolios and show an example of one on your graph.
7. Assume you want to run a computer program to derive the efficient frontier for your feasible set of stocks. What information must you input to the program?

8. Why are investors' utility curves important in portfolio theory?
9. Explain how a given investor chooses an optimal portfolio. Will this choice always be a diversified portfolio, or could it be a single asset? Explain your answer.
10. Assume that you and a business associate develop an efficient frontier for a set of investments. Why might the two of you select different portfolios on the frontier?
11. Draw a hypothetical graph of an efficient frontier of U.S. common stocks. On the same graph, draw an efficient frontier assuming the inclusion of U.S. bonds as well. Finally, on the same graph, draw an efficient frontier that includes U.S. common stocks, U.S. bonds, and stocks and bonds from around the world. Discuss the differences in these frontiers.

Problems

1. Considering the world economic outlook for the coming year and the estimates of sales and earnings for the pharmaceutical industry, you expect the rate of return for Lauren Labs common stock to fall between −20 percent and +40 percent with the following range of probabilities:

Probability	Possible Returns
.10	−0.20
.15	−0.05
.20	0.10
.25	0.15
.20	0.20
.10	0.40

Compute the expected rate of return $[E(R_i)]$ for Lauren Labs.

2. Given the following market values of stocks in your portfolio and their expected rates of return, what is the expected rate of return for your common stock portfolio?

Stock	Market Value	$E(R_i)$
Phillips Petroleum	$15,000	0.14
Ford Motor	17,000	−0.04
International Paper	32,000	0.18
Apple Computer	23,000	0.16
Walgreens	7,000	0.05

3. The following are the monthly rates of return for Microsoft and for General Electric during a six-month period.

Month	Microsoft	General Electric
1	−.04	.07
2	.06	−.02
3	−.07	−.10
4	.12	.15
5	−.02	−.06
6	.05	.02

Compute the following:
a. Expected monthly rate of return $[E(R_i)]$ for each stock.
b. Standard deviation of returns for each stock.
c. Covariance between the rates of return.
d. The correlation coefficient between the rates of return.

What level of correlation did you expect? How did your expectations compare with the computed correlation? Would these two stocks offer a good chance for diversification? Why or why not?

4. You are considering two assets with the following characteristics:

$$E(R_1) = .15 \qquad E(\sigma_1) = .10 \qquad W_1 = .5$$
$$E(R_2) = .20 \qquad E(\sigma_2) = .20 \qquad W_2 = .5$$

Compute the mean and standard deviation of two portfolios if $r_{1,2} = .40$ and $-.60$, respectively. Plot the two portfolios on a risk–return graph and briefly explain the results.

5. Given: $E(R_1) = .10$
   $\qquad E(R_2) = .15$
   $\qquad E(\sigma_1) = .03$
   $\qquad E(\sigma_2) = .05$

Calculate the expected returns and expected standard deviations of a two-stock portfolio in which Stock 1 has a weight of 60 percent under the following conditions:

a. $r_{1,2} = \ 1.00$
b. $r_{1,2} = \quad .75$
c. $r_{1,2} = \quad .25$
d. $r_{1,2} = \quad .00$
e. $r_{1,2} = \ -.25$
f. $r_{1,2} = \ -.75$
g. $r_{1,2} = -1.00$

6. Given: $E(R_1) = .12$
   $\qquad E(R_2) = .16$
   $\qquad E(\sigma_1) = .04$
   $\qquad E(\sigma_2) = .06$

Calculate the expected returns and expected standard deviations of a two-stock portfolio having a correlation coefficient of .70 under the following conditions:

a. $w_1 = 1.00$
b. $w_1 = \quad .75$
c. $w_1 = \quad .50$
d. $w_1 = \quad .25$
e. $w_1 = \quad .05$

Plot the results on a return–risk graph. Without calculations, draw in what the curve would look like if the correlation coefficient had been 0.00; or if it had been −0.70.

7. The following are monthly percentage price changes for four market indexes:

Month	DJIA	S&P 400	AMEX	NIKKEI
1	.03	.02	.04	.04
2	.07	.06	.10	−.02
3	−.02	−.01	−.04	.07
4	.01	.03	.03	.02
5	.05	.04	.11	.02
6	−.06	−.04	−.08	.06

Compute the following:

a. Expected monthly rate of return for each series.
b. Standard deviation for each series.
c. Covariance between the rates of return for the following indexes:
   DJIA—S&P 400
   S&P 400—AMEX
   S&P 400—NIKKEI
   AMEX—NIKKEI

d. The correlation coefficients for the same four combinations.

e. Using the answers from parts a, b, and d, calculate the expected return and standard deviation of a portfolio consisting of equal parts of (1) the S&P and the AMEX and (2) the S&P and the NIKKEI. Discuss the two portfolios.

References

Elton, Edwin J., and Martin J. Gruber. *Modern Portfolio Theory and Investment Analysis.* 5th ed. New York: John Wiley & Sons, Inc., 1995.

Farrell, James L., Jr. *Guide to Portfolio Management.* New York: McGraw-Hill, 1983.

Harrington, Diana R. *Modern Portfolio Theory, the Capital Asset Pricing Model, and Arbitrage Pricing Theory: A User's Guide.* 2d ed. Englewood Cliffs, NJ: Prentice-Hall, 1987.

Maginn, John L., and Donald L. Tuttle, eds. *Managing Investment Portfolios: A Dynamic Process.* 2d ed. Sponsored by The Institute of Chartered Financial Analysts. Boston: Warren, Gorham and Lamont, 1990.

Markowitz, Harry. "Portfolio Selection." *Journal of Finance* 7, no. 1 (March 1952).

Markowitz, Harry. *Portfolio Selection: Efficient Diversification of Investments.* New York: John Wiley & Sons, 1959.

Chapter 8
APPENDIX

A. PROOF THAT MINIMUM PORTFOLIO VARIANCE OCCURS WITH EQUAL WEIGHTS WHEN SECURITIES HAVE EQUAL VARIANCE

When $E(\sigma_1) = E(\sigma_2)$, we have:

$$E(\sigma_{port}^2) = w_1^2 E(\sigma_1)^2 + (1 - w_1)^2 E(\sigma_1)^2 + 2w_1(1 - w_1)r_{1,2}E(\sigma_1)^2$$
$$= E(\sigma_1)^2[w_1^2 + 1 - 2w_1 + w_1^2 + 2w_1r_{1,2} - 2w_1^2r_{1,2}]$$
$$= E(\sigma_1)^2[2w_1^2 + 1 - 2w_1 + 2w_1r_{1,2} - 2w_1^2r_{1,2}]$$

For this to be a minimum,

$$\frac{\partial E(\sigma_{port}^2)}{\partial w_1} = 0 = E(\sigma_1)^2[4w_1 \times 2 + 2r_{1,2} \times 4w_1r_{1,2}]$$

Assuming $E(\sigma_1)^2 > 0$,

$$4w_1 - 2 + 2r_{1,2} - 4w_1r_{1,2} = 0$$
$$4w_1(1 - r_{1,2}) - 2(1 - r_{1,2}) = 0$$

from which

$$w_1 = \frac{2(1 - r_{1,2})}{4(1 - r_{1,2})} = \frac{1}{2}$$

regardless of $r_{1,2}$. Thus, if $E(\sigma_1) = E(\sigma_2)$, $E(\sigma_{port}^2)$ will *always* be minimized by choosing $w_1 = w_2 = \frac{1}{2}$, regardless of the value of $r_{1,2}$, except when $r_{1,2} = +1$ (in which case $E(\sigma_{port}) = E(\sigma_1) = E(\sigma_2)$. This can be verified by checking the second-order condition

$$\frac{\partial E(\sigma_{port}^2)}{\partial w_1^2} > 0.$$

Problems   The following information applies to Questions 1a and 1b. The general equation for the weight of the first security to achieve minimum variance (in a two-stock portfolio) is given by

$$w_1 = \frac{E(\sigma_2)^2 - r_{1,2}\ E(\sigma_1)E(\sigma_2)}{E(\sigma_1)^2 + E(\sigma_2)^2 - 2r_{1,2}\ E(\sigma_1)E(\sigma_2)}\ .$$

1a. Show that $w_1 = .5$ when $E(\sigma_1) = E(\sigma_2)$.

1b. What is the weight of Security 1 that gives minimum portfolio variance when $r_{1,2} = .5$, $E(\sigma_1) = .04$, and $E(\sigma_2) = .06$?

B. Derivation of Weights That Will Give Zero Variance When Correlation Equals −1.00

$$\begin{aligned}E(\sigma_{port}^2) &= w_1^2 E(\sigma_1)^2 + (1 - w_1)^2 E(\sigma_2)^2 + 2w_1(1 - w_1)r_{1,2}E(\sigma_1)E(\sigma_2)\\ &= w_1^2 E(\sigma_1)^2 + E(\sigma_2)^2 - 2w_1 E(\sigma_2) + w_1^2 E(\sigma_2)^2 + 2w_1 r_{1,2}E(\sigma_1)E(\sigma_2) - 2w_1^2 r_{1,2}E(\sigma_1)E(\sigma_2)\end{aligned}$$

If $r_{1,2} = 1$, this can be rearranged and expressed as

$$\begin{aligned}E(\sigma_{port}^2) &= w_1^2[E(\sigma_1)^2 + 2E(\sigma_1)E(\sigma_2) + E(\sigma_2)^2] - 2w_1[E(\sigma_2)^2 + E(\sigma_1)E(\sigma_2)] + E(\sigma_2)^2\\ &= w_1^2[E(\sigma_1) + E(\sigma_2)]^2 - 2w_1 E(\sigma_2)[E(\sigma_1) + E(\sigma_2)] + E(\sigma_2)^2\\ &= \{w_1[E(\sigma_1) + E(\sigma_2)] - E(\sigma_2)\}^2\end{aligned}$$

We want to find the weight, w_1, which will reduce $E(\sigma_{port}^2)$ to *zero;* therefore,

$$w_1[E(\sigma_1) + E(\sigma_2)] - E(\sigma_2) = 0,$$

which yields

$$w_1 = \frac{E(\sigma_2)}{E(\sigma_1) + E(\sigma_2)}\ ,\ \text{and}\ w_2 = 1 - w_1 = \frac{E(\sigma_1)}{E(\sigma_1) + E(\sigma_2)}\ .$$

Problem   1. Given two assets with the following characteristics:

$$E(R_1) = .12 \qquad E(\sigma_1) = .04$$
$$E(R_2) = .16 \qquad E(\sigma_2) = .06$$

Assume that $r_{1,2} = -1.00$. What is the weight that would yield a zero variance for the portfolio?

Chapter
9
An Introduction to Asset Pricing Models

This chapter answers the following questions:

- What are the assumptions of the capital asset pricing model?
- What is a risk-free asset and what are its risk–return characteristics?
- What is the covariance and correlation between the risk-free asset and a risky asset or portfolio of risky assets?
- What is the expected return when you combine the risk-free asset and a portfolio of risky assets?
- What is the standard deviation when you combine the risk-free asset and a portfolio of risky assets?
- When you combine the risk-free asset and a portfolio of risky assets on the Markowitz efficient frontier, what does the set of possible portfolios look like?
- Given the initial set of portfolio possibilities with a risk-free asset, what happens when you add financial leverage (i.e., borrow)?
- What is the market portfolio, what assets are included in this portfolio, and what are the relative weights for the alternative assets included?
- What is the capital market line (CML)?
- What do we mean by complete diversification?
- How do we measure diversification for an individual portfolio?
- What are systematic and unsystematic risk?
- Given the capital market line (CML), what is the separation theorem?
- Given the CML, what is the relevant risk measure for an individual risky asset?
- What is the security market line (SML), and how does it differ from the CML?
- What is beta and why is it referred to as a standardized measure of systematic risk?
- How can you use the SML to determine the expected (required) rate of return for a risky asset?
- Using the SML, what is meant by an undervalued and overvalued security, and how do you determine whether an asset is undervalued or overvalued?
- What is an asset's characteristic line and how do you compute the characteristic line for an asset?
- What is the impact on the characteristic line when you compute it using different return intervals (e.g., weekly versus monthly) and when you employ different proxies (i.e., benchmarks) for the market portfolio (e.g., the S&P 500 versus a global stock index)?
- What is the arbitrage pricing theory (APT) and how does it differ from the CAPM in terms of assumptions?
- How does the APT differ from the CAPM in terms of risk measures?

Following the development of portfolio theory by Markowitz, there have been two major theories put forth that employ the theory to derive a model for the valuation of risky assets. In this chapter, we introduce these two models. The background on asset pricing models is important at this point in the book because the risk measures implied by these models are a necessary input for our subsequent discussion on the valuation of risky assets. The bulk of the presentation concerns capital market theory and the capital asset pricing model (CAPM) that was developed almost concurrently by three individuals. More recently, an alternative asset valuation model has been proposed, entitled the arbitrage pricing theory (APT). This theory and the implied pricing model are likewise introduced and discussed.

CAPITAL MARKET THEORY: AN OVERVIEW

Because capital market theory builds on portfolio theory, this chapter begins where the discussion of the Markowitz efficient frontier ended. We assume that you have examined the set of risky assets and derived the aggregate efficient frontier. Further, we assume that you and all other investors want to maximize your utility in terms of risk and return, so you will choose portfolios of risky assets on the efficient frontier at points where your utility maps are tangent to the frontier as shown in Figure 8.10. When you make your investment decision in this manner, you are referred to as a *Markowitz efficient investor.*

Capital market theory extends portfolio theory and develops a model for pricing all risky assets. The final product, the *capital asset pricing model (CAPM),* will allow you to determine the required rate of return for any risky asset.

We begin with the background of capital market theory that includes the underlying assumptions of the theory and a discussion of the factors that led to its development following the Markowitz portfolio theory. Principal among these factors was the analysis of the effect of assuming the existence of a risk-free asset. This is the subject of the next section.

We will see that assuming the existence of a risk-free rate has significant implications for the potential return and risk and alternative risk–return combinations. This discussion implies a central portfolio of risky assets on the efficient frontier, which we call the *market portfolio.* We discuss the market portfolio in the third section and what it implies regarding different types of risk.

The fourth section considers which types of risk are relevant to an investor who believes in capital market theory. Having defined a measure of risk, we consider how you determine your required rate of return on an investment. You can then compare this required rate of return to your estimate of the asset's expected rate of return during your investment horizon to determine whether the asset is undervalued or overvalued. The section ends with a demonstration of how to calculate the risk measure implied by capital market theory.

The final section discusses an alternative asset pricing model, the arbitrage pricing theory (APT). This model requires fewer assumptions than the CAPM and contends that the required rate of return for a risky asset is a function of *multiple* factors. This is in contrast to the CAPM, which is a single-factor model, that is, it assumes that the risk of an asset is determined by a single variable, its beta. There is a brief demonstration of how to evaluate the risk of an asset and determine its required rate of return using the APT model.

BACKGROUND FOR CAPITAL MARKET THEORY

When dealing with any theory in science, economics, or finance, it is necessary to articulate a set of assumptions that specify how the world is expected to act. This allows the theoretician to concentrate on developing a theory that explains how some facet of the world will respond to changes in the environment. In the first part of this section, we consider the main assumptions that underlie the development of capital market theory. The second part of the section considers the major assumptions that allowed theoreticians to extend the portfolio model's techniques for combining investments into an optimal portfolio to a model that explains how to determine the value of those investments (or other assets),

ASSUMPTIONS OF CAPITAL MARKET THEORY   Because capital market theory builds on the Markowitz portfolio model, it requires the same assumptions, along with some additional ones:

1. All investors are Markowitz efficient investors who want to target points on the efficient frontier. The exact location on the efficient frontier and, therefore, the specific portfolio selected, will depend on the individual investor's risk–return utility function.
2. Investors can borrow or lend any amount of money at the risk-free rate of return (RFR). Clearly, it is always possible to lend money at the nominal risk-free rate by buying risk-free securities such as government T-bills. It is not always possible to borrow at this risk-free rate, but we will see that assuming a higher borrowing rate does not change the general results.
3. All investors have homogeneous expectations; that is, they estimate identical probability distributions for future rates of return. Again, this assumption can be relaxed. As long as the differences in expectations are not vast, their effects are minor.
4. All investors have the same one-period time horizon such as 1 month, 6 months, or 1 year. The model will be developed for a single hypothetical period, and its results could be affected by a different assumption. A difference in the time horizon would require investors to derive risk measures and risk-free assets that are consistent with their investment horizons.
5. All investments are infinitely divisible, which means that it is possible to buy or sell fractional shares of any asset or portfolio. This assumption allows us to discuss investment alternatives as continuous curves. Changing it would have little impact on the theory.
6. There are no taxes or transaction costs involved in buying or selling assets. This is a reasonable assumption in many instances. Neither pension funds nor religious groups have to pay taxes, and the transaction costs for most financial institutions are less than 1 percent on most financial instruments. Again, relaxing this assumption modifies the results, but it does not change the basic thrust.
7. There is no inflation or any change in interest rates, or inflation is fully anticipated. This is a reasonable initial assumption, and it can be modified.
8. Capital markets are in equilibrium. This means that we begin with all investments properly priced in line with their risk levels.

You may consider some of these assumptions unrealistic and wonder how useful a theory we can derive with these assumptions. In this regard, two points are important. First, as mentioned, relaxing many of these assumptions would have only minor impacts on the model and would not change its main implications or conclusions. Second, a theory should never be judged on the basis of its assumptions, but rather on how well it explains and helps us predict behavior in the real world. If this theory and the model it implies help us explain the rates of return on a wide variety of risky assets, it is very useful, even if some of its assumptions are unrealistic. Such success implies that the questionable assumptions must not be very important to the ultimate objective of the model, which is to explain the pricing and rates of return on assets.

DEVELOPMENT OF CAPITAL MARKET THEORY   The major factor that allowed portfolio theory to develop into capital market theory is the concept of a risk-free asset. Following the development of the Markowitz portfolio model, several authors considered the implications of assuming the existence of a **risk-free asset,** that is, an asset with *zero variance.* As we will show, such an asset would have zero correlation with all other risky assets and would provide the *risk-free rate of return (RFR)*. It would lie on the vertical axis of a portfolio graph.

This assumption allows us to derive a generalized theory of capital asset pricing under conditions of uncertainty from the Markowitz portfolio theory. This achievement is generally attributed to William Sharpe, for which he received the Nobel prize, but Lintner and Mossin derived similar theories independently.[1] Consequently, you may see references to the Sharpe-Lintner-Mossin (SLM) capital asset pricing model.

RISK-FREE ASSET

As noted, the assumption of a risk-free asset in the economy is critical to asset pricing theory. Therefore, this section explains the meaning of a risk-free asset and then shows the effect on the risk and return measures when this risk-free asset is combined with a portfolio on the Markowitz efficient frontier.

We have defined a **risky asset** as one from which future returns are uncertain and we have measured this uncertainty by the variance, or standard deviation of returns. Because the expected return on a risk-free asset is entirely certain, the standard deviation of its return is zero ($\sigma_{RF} = 0$). The rate of return earned on such an asset should be the risk-free rate of return (RFR), which, as we discussed in Chapter 1, should equal the expected long-run growth rate of the economy with an adjustment for short-run liquidity. The next sections show what happens when we introduce this risk-free asset into the risky world of the Markowitz portfolio model.

COVARIANCE WITH A RISK-FREE ASSET   Recall that the covariance between two sets of returns is

$$\text{Cov}_{i,j} = \sum_{i=1}^{n} [R_i - E(R_i)][R_j - E(R_j)]/n.$$

Because the returns for the risk-free asset are certain, $\sigma_{RF} = 0$, which means $R_i = E(R_i)$ during all periods. Thus, $R_i - E(R_i)$ will also equal zero, and the product of this expression with any other expression will equal zero. Consequently, the covariance of the risk-free asset with any risky asset or portfolio of assets will always equal zero. Similarly, the correlation between any risky asset i, and the risk-free asset, RF, would be zero because it is equal to

$$r_{RF,i} = \text{Cov}_{RF,i}/\sigma_{RF}\sigma_j.$$

COMBINING A RISK-FREE ASSET WITH A RISKY PORTFOLIO   What happens to the average rate of return and the standard deviation of returns when you combine a risk-free asset with a portfolio of risky assets such as those that exist on the Markowitz efficient frontier?

Expected return   Like the expected return for a portfolio of two risky assets, the expected rate of return for a portfolio that includes a risk-free asset is the weighted average of the two returns:

$$E(R_{port}) = w_{RF}(RFR) + (1 - w_{RF})E(R_i)$$

---

[1] William F. Sharpe, "Capital Asset Prices: A Theory of Market Equilibrium Under Conditions of Risk," *Journal of Finance* 19, no. 3 (September 1964): 425–442; John Lintner, "Security Prices, Risk and Maximal Gains from Diversification," *Journal of Finance* 20, no. 4 (December 1965); 587–615; and J. Mossin, "Equilibrium in a Capital Asset Market," *Econometrica* 34, no. 4 (October 1966): 768–783.

where:

w_{RF} = the proportion of the portfolio invested in the risk-free asset
$E(R_i)$ = the expected rate of return on risky Portfolio i.

Standard deviation   Recall from Chapter 8 that the expected variance for a two-asset portfolio is

$$E(\sigma_{port}^2) = w_1^2 \sigma_1^2 + w_2^2 \sigma_2^2 + 2w_1 w_2 r_{1,2} \sigma_1 \sigma_2.$$

Substituting the risk-free asset for Security 1, and the risky asset portfolio for Security 2, this formula would become

$$E(\sigma_{port}^2) = w_{RF}^2 \sigma_{RF}^2 + (1 - w_{RF})^2 \sigma_i^2 + 2w_{RF}(1 - w_{RF})r_{RF,i}\sigma_{RF}\sigma_i.$$

We know that the variance of the risk-free asset is zero, that is, $\sigma_{RF}^2 = 0$. Because the correlation between the risk-free asset and any risky asset, i, is also zero, the factor $r_{RF,i}$ in the equation above also equals zero. Therefore, any component of the variance formula that has either of these terms will equal zero. When you make these adjustments, the formula becomes

$$E(\sigma_{port}^2) = (1 - w_{RF})^2 \sigma_i^2$$

The standard deviation is

$$E(\sigma_{port}) = \sqrt{(1 - w_{RF})^2 \sigma_i^2}$$
$$= (1 - w_{RF})\sigma_i$$

Therefore, the standard deviation of a portfolio that combines the risk-free asset with risky assets is *the linear proportion of the standard deviation of the risky asset portfolio.*

The risk–return combination   Because both the expected return *and* the standard deviation of return for such a portfolio are linear combinations, a graph of possible portfolio returns and risks looks like a straight line between the two assets. Figure 9.1 shows a graph depicting portfolio possibilities when a risk-free asset is combined with alternative risky portfolios on the Markowitz efficient frontier.

You can attain any point along the straight line RFR-A by investing some portion of your portfolio in the risk-free asset w_{RF} and the remainder $(1 - w_{RF})$ in the risky asset portfolio at Point A on the efficient frontier. This set of portfolio possibilities dominates all the risky asset portfolios on the efficient frontier below Point A because some portfolio along Line RFR-A has equal variance with a higher rate of return than the portfolio on the original efficient frontier. Likewise, you can attain any point along the Line RFR-B by investing in some combination of the risk-free asset and the risky asset portfolio at Point B. Again, these potential combinations dominate all portfolio possibilities on the original efficient frontier below Point B (including Line RFR-A).

You can draw further lines from the RFR to the efficient frontier at higher and higher points until you reach the point where the line is tangent to the frontier, which occurs in Figure 9.1 at Point M. The set of portfolio possibilities along Line RFR-M dominates *all* portfolios below Point M. For example, you could attain a risk and return combination between the RFR and Point M (Point C) by investing one-half of your portfolio in the risk-

FIGURE 9.1

PORTFOLIO POSSIBILITIES COMBINING THE RISK-FREE ASSET AND RISKY PORTFOLIOS ON THE EFFICIENT FRONTIER

free asset (that is, lending money at the RFR) and the other half in the risky portfolio at Point M.

Risk–return possibilities with leverage   An investor may want to attain a higher expected return than is available at Point M in exchange for accepting higher risk. One alternative would be to invest in one of the risky asset portfolios on the efficient frontier beyond Point M such as the portfolio at Point D. A second alternative is to add *leverage* to the portfolio by *borrowing* money at the risk-free rate and investing the proceeds in the risky asset portfolio at Point M. What effect would this have on the return and risk for your portfolio?

If you borrow an amount equal to 50 percent of your original wealth at the risk-free rate, w_{RF} will not be a positive fraction, but rather a negative 50 percent ($w_{RF} = -.50$). The effect on the expected return for your portfolio is

$$E(R_{port}) = w_{RF}(RFR) + (1 - w_{RF})E(R_M)$$
$$= -0.50(RFR) + [1 - (-0.50)]E(R_M)$$
$$= -0.50(RFR) + 1.50E(R_M).$$

The return will increase in a *linear* fashion along the Line RFR-M because the gross return increases by 50 percent, but you must pay interest at the RFR on the money borrowed. For example, assume that $E(RFR) = .06$ and $E(R_M) = .12$. The return on your leveraged portfolio would be:

$$E(R_{port}) = -0.50(0.06) + 1.5(0.12)$$
$$= -0.03 + 0.18$$
$$= 0.15$$

FIGURE 9.2

DERIVATION OF CAPITAL MARKET LINE ASSUMING LENDING OR BORROWING AT THE RISK-FREE RATE

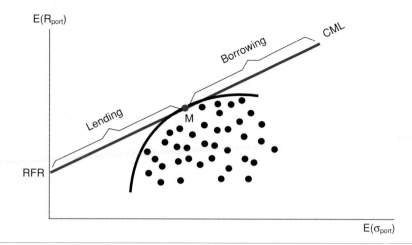

The effect on the standard deviation of the leveraged portfolio is similar.

$$E(\sigma_{port}) = (1 - w_{RF})\sigma_M$$
$$= [1 - (-0.50)]\sigma_M = 1.50\sigma_M$$

where:

σ_M = **the standard deviation of the M portfolio.**

Therefore, *both return and risk increase in a linear fashion along the original Line RFR-M,* and this extension dominates everything below the line on the original efficient frontier. Thus, you have a new efficient frontier: the straight line from the *RFR* tangent to Point M. This line is referred to as the **capital market line (CML)** and is shown in Figure 9.2.

Our discussion of portfolio theory stated that, when two assets are perfectly correlated, the set of portfolio possibilities falls along a straight line. Therefore, because the CML is a straight line, it implies that all the portfolios on the CML are perfectly positively correlated. This positive correlation appeals to our intuition because all these portfolios on the CML combine the risky asset Portfolio M and the risk-free asset. You either invest part of your portfolio in the risk-free asset and the rest in the risky asset portfolio M, or you borrow at the risk-free rate and invest these funds in the risky asset portfolio. In either case, all the variability comes from the risky asset M portfolio. The only difference between the alternative portfolios on the CML is the magnitude of the variability caused by the proportion of the risky asset portfolio in the total portfolio.

THE MARKET PORTFOLIO   Because Portfolio M lies at the point of tangency, it has the highest portfolio possibility line, and everybody will want to invest in Portfolio M and borrow or lend to be somewhere on the CML. This portfolio must, therefore, include *all risky assets*. If a risky asset were not in this portfolio in which everyone wants to invest, there would be no demand for it and therefore no value.

Because the market is in equilibrium, it is also necessary that all assets are included in this portfolio in *proportion to their market value*. If, for example, an asset accounts for a higher proportion of the M portfolio than its market value justifies, excess demand for this asset will increase its price until its relative market value becomes consistent with its proportion in the portfolio.

This portfolio that includes all risky assets is referred to as the **market portfolio**. It includes not only common stocks, but *all* risky assets, such as non-U.S. stocks, U.S. and non-U.S. bonds, options, real estate, coins, stamps, art, or antiques. Because the market portfolio contains all risky assets, it is a **completely diversified portfolio,** which means that all the risk unique to individual assets in the portfolio is diversified away. Specifically, the unique risk of any asset is offset by the unique variability of the other assets in the portfolio.

This unique (diversifiable) risk is also referred to as **unsystematic risk**. This implies that only **systematic risk,** which is defined as the variability in all risky assets caused by macroeconomic variables, remains in the market portfolio. This systematic risk, measured by the standard deviation of returns of the market portfolio, can change over time with changes in the macroeconomic variables that affect the valuation of all risky assets.[2] Examples of such macroeconomic variables would be variability of growth in the money supply, interest rate volatility, and variability in such factors as industrial production, corporate earnings, and cash flow.

HOW TO MEASURE DIVERSIFICATION   All portfolios on the CML are perfectly positively correlated, which means that all portfolios on the CML are perfectly correlated with the completely diversified market Portfolio M. This implies a measure of complete diversification.[3] Specifically, a completely diversified portfolio would have a correlation with the market portfolio of +1.00. This is logical because complete diversification means the elimination of all the unsystematic or unique risk. Once you have eliminated all unsystematic risk, only systematic risk is left, which cannot be diversified away. Therefore, completely diversified portfolios would correlate perfectly with the market portfolio because it has only systematic risk.

DIVERSIFICATION AND THE ELIMINATION OF UNSYSTEMATIC RISK   As discussed in Chapter 8, the purpose of diversification is to reduce the standard deviation of the total portfolio. This assumes imperfect correlations among securities.[4] Ideally, as you add securities, the average covariance for the portfolio declines. An important question is, about how many securities must be included to arrive at a completely diversified portfolio? To discover the answer, you must observe what happens as you increase the sample size of the portfolio by adding securities that have some positive correlation. The typical correlation among U.S. securities is about 0.5 to 0.6.

[2] For an analysis of changes in stock price volatility, see G. William Schwert, "Why Does Stock Market Volatility Change Over Time?" *Journal of Finance* 44, no. 5 (December 1989): 1115–1153; Peter S. Spiro, "The Impact of Interest Rate Changes on Stock Price Volatility," *Journal of Portfolio Management* 16, no. 2 (Winter 1990): 63–68; James M. Poterba and Lawrence H. Summers, "The Persistence of Volatility and Stock Market Fluctuations," *American Economic Review* 76, no. 4 (December 1981): 1142–1151; R. R. Officer, "The Variability of the Market Factor of the New York Stock Exchange," *The Journal of Business* 46, no. 3 (July 1973): 434–453.

[3] James Lorie, "Diversification: Old and New," *Journal of Portfolio Management* 1, no. 2 (Winter 1975): 25–28.

[4] The discussion in Chapter 8 leads one to conclude that securities with negative correlation would be ideal. Although this is true in theory, it is very difficult to find such assets in the real world.

FIGURE 9.3

NUMBER OF STOCKS IN A PORTFOLIO AND THE STANDARD DEVIATION OF PORTFOLIO RETURN

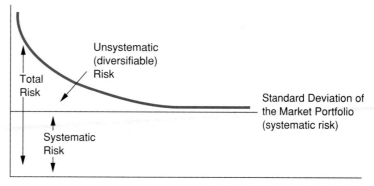

One set of studies examined the average standard deviation for numerous portfolios of randomly selected stocks of different sample sizes.[5] For example, Evans and Archer computed the standard deviation for portfolios of increasing numbers up to 20 stocks. The results indicated a large initial impact wherein the major benefits of diversification were achieved rather quickly. Specifically, about 90 percent of the maximum benefit of diversification was derived from portfolios of 12 to 18 stocks. Figure 9.3 shows a graph of the effect.

A study by Statman compared the benefits of lower risk from diversification to the added transaction costs with more securities. It concluded that a well-diversified stock portfolio must include at least 30 stocks for a borrowing investor and 40 stocks for a lending investor.[6]

By adding stocks to the portfolio that are not perfectly correlated with stocks in the portfolio, you can reduce the overall standard deviation of the portfolio, but you *cannot eliminate variability*. The standard deviation of your portfolio will eventually reach the level of the market portfolio, where you will have diversified away all unsystematic risk, but you still have market or systematic risk. You cannot eliminate the variability and uncertainty of macroeconomic factors that affect all risky assets. At the same time, you will recall from the discussion in Chapter 3 that you can attain a lower level of systematic risk by diversifying globally versus only investing in the United States because some of the systematic risk factors in the U.S. market (e.g., U.S. monetary policy) are not correlated with systematic risk variables in other countries such as Germany and Japan. As a result, if you diversify globally you eventually get down to a world systematic-risk level.

THE CML AND THE SEPARATION THEOREM   The CML leads all investors to invest in the same risky asset portfolio, the M portfolio. Individual investors should only differ regarding their position on the CML, which depends on their risk preferences.

[5] John L. Evans and Stephen H. Archer, "Diversification and the Reduction of Dispersion: An Empirical Analysis," *Journal of Finance* 23, no. 5 (December 1968): 761–767; Thomas M. Tole, "You Can't Diversify without Diversifying," *Journal of Portfolio Management* 8, no. 2 (Winter 1982): 5–11.

[6] Meir Statman, "How Many Stocks Make a Diversified Portfolio?" *Journal of Financial and Quantitative Analysis* 22, no. 3 (September 1987): 353–363.

FIGURE 9.4 **CHOICE OF OPTIMAL PORTFOLIO COMBINATIONS ON THE CML**

In turn, how they get to a point on the CML is based on their *financing decisions*. If you are relatively risk averse, you will lend some part of your portfolio at the RFR by buying some risk-free securities and investing the remainder in the market portfolio. For example, you might invest in the portfolio combination at Point A in Figure 9.4. In contrast, if you prefer more risk, you might borrow funds at the RFR and invest everything (all of your capital plus what you borrowed) in the market portfolio, building the portfolio at Point B. This financing decision provides more risk but greater returns than the market portfolio. As discussed earlier, because portfolios on the CML dominate other portfolio possibilities, the CML becomes the efficient frontier of portfolios, and investors decide where they want to be along this efficient frontier. Tobin called this division of the investment decision from the financing decision the **separation theorem**.[7] Specifically, to be somewhere on the CML efficient frontier, you initially decide to invest in the market portfolio M. This is your *investment* decision. Subsequently, based on your risk preferences, you make a separate *financing* decision either to borrow or to lend to attain your preferred point on the CML.

A RISK MEASURE FOR THE CML   In this section, we show that the relevant risk measure for risky assets is *their covariance with the M portfolio,* which is referred to as their systematic risk. The importance of this covariance is apparent from two points of view.

First, in discussing the Markowitz portfolio model, we noted that the relevant risk to consider when adding a security to a portfolio is *its average covariance with all other assets in the portfolio.* In this chapter, we have shown that *the only relevant portfolio is the M portfolio.* Together, these two findings mean that the only important consideration for any individual risky asset is its average covariance with all the risky assets in the M portfolio, or simply, *the asset's covariance with the market portfolio.* This covariance, then, is the relevant risk measure for an individual risky asset.

[7] James Tobin, "Liquidity Preference as Behavior Towards Risk," *Review of Economic Studies* 25, no. 2 (February 1958): 65–85.

Second, because all individual risky assets are a part of the M portfolio, one can describe their rates of return in relation to the returns for the M portfolio using the following linear model:

$$R_{it} = a_i + b_i R_{Mt} + \epsilon$$

where:

$R_{i,t}$ = **return for asset *i* during period *t***
  a_i = **constant term for asset *i***
  b_i = **slope coefficient for asset *i***
R_{Mt} = **return for the M portfolio during period *t***
  ϵ = **random error term.**

The variance of returns for a risky asset could be described as

$$\begin{aligned} \text{Var}(R_{it}) &= \text{Var}(a_i + b_i R_{Mt} + \epsilon) \\ &= \text{Var}(a_i) + \text{Var}(b_i R_{Mt}) + \text{Var}(\epsilon) \\ &= 0 + \text{Var}(b_i R_{Mt}) + \text{Var}(\epsilon). \end{aligned}$$

Note that $\text{Var}(b_i R_{Mt})$ is the variance of return for an asset related to the variance of the market return, or the *systematic variance or risk*. Also, $\text{Var}(\epsilon)$ is the residual variance of return for the individual asset that is not related to the market portfolio. This residual variance is the variability that we have referred to as the unsystematic or *unique risk or variance* because it arises from the unique features of the asset. Therefore:

$$\text{Var}(R_{i,t}) = \text{Systematic Variance} + \text{Unsystematic Variance.}$$

We know that a completely diversified portfolio such as the market portfolio has had all the unsystematic variance eliminated. Therefore, the unsystematic variance of an asset is not relevant to investors, because they can and do eliminate it when making an asset part of the market portfolio. Therefore, investors should not expect to receive added returns for assuming this unique risk. Only the systematic variance is relevant because it *cannot* be diversified away, because it is caused by macroeconomic factors that affect all risky assets.

THE CAPITAL ASSET PRICING MODEL: EXPECTED RETURN AND RISK

Up to this point, we have considered how investors make their portfolio decisions, including the significant effects of a risk-free asset. The existence of this risk-free asset resulted in the derivation of a capital market line (CML) that became the relevant efficient frontier. Because all investors want to be on the CML, an asset's covariance with the market portfolio of risky assets emerged as the relevant risk measure.

Now that we understand this relevant measure of risk, we can proceed to use it to determine an appropriate expected rate of return on a risky asset. This step takes us into the **capital asset pricing model (CAPM),** which is a model that indicates what should be the expected or required rates of return on risky assets. This transition is important because it helps you to value an asset by providing an appropriate discount rate to use in dividend valuation models. Alternatively, if you have already estimated the rate of return that you think you will earn on an investment, you can compare this *estimated* rate of return to the *required* rate of return implied by the CAPM and determine whether the asset is undervalued, overvalued, or properly valued.

To accomplish the foregoing, we demonstrate the creation of a security market line (SML) that visually represents the relationship between risk and the expected or the required rate of return on an asset. The equation of this SML, together with estimates for the return on a risk-free asset and on the market portfolio, can generate expected or required rates of return for any asset based on its systematic risk. You compare this required rate of return to the rate of return you estimate that you will earn on the investment to determine if the investment is undervalued or overvalued. After demonstrating this procedure, we finish the section with a demonstration of how to calculate the systematic risk variable for a risky asset.

THE SECURITY MARKET LINE (SML)

We know that the relevant risk measure for an individual risky asset is its covariance with the market portfolio ($Cov_{i,M}$). Therefore, we draw the risk–return relationship as shown in Figure 9.5 with the systematic covariance variable ($Cov_{i,M}$) as the risk measure.

The return for the market portfolio (R_M) should be consistent with its own risk, which is the covariance of the market with itself. If you recall the formula for covariance, you will see that the covariance of any asset with itself is its variance, $Cov_{i,i} = \sigma_i^2$. In turn, the covariance of the market with itself is the variance of the market rate of return $Cov_{m,m} = \sigma_M^2$. Therefore, the equation for the risk–return line in Figure 9.5 is

$$E(R_i) = RFR + \frac{R_M - RFR}{\sigma_M^2} (Cov_{i,M})$$

$$= RFR + \frac{Cov_{i,M}}{\sigma_M^2} (R_M - RFR).$$

Defining $Cov_{i,M}/\sigma_M^2$ as beta (β_i), this equation can be stated:

$$E(R_i) = RFR + \beta_i(R_M - RFR).$$

FIGURE 9.5   **GRAPH OF SECURITY MARKET LINE**

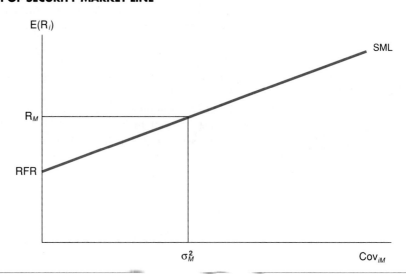

Beta can be viewed as a *standardized* measure of systematic risk. Specifically, we already know that the covariance of any asset i with the market portfolio (Cov_{iM}) is the relevant risk measure. Beta is a standardized measure of risk because it relates this covariance to the variance of the market portfolio. As a result, the market portfolio has a beta of 1. Therefore, if the β_i for an asset is above 1.0, the asset has higher systematic risk than the market, which means that it is more volatile than the overall market portfolio.

Given this standardized measure of systematic risk, the SML graph can be expressed as shown in Figure 9.6. This is the same graph as in Figure 9.5, except there is a different measure of risk. Specifically, the graph in Figure 9.6 replaces the covariance of an asset's returns with the market portfolio as the risk measure with the standardized measure of systematic risk (beta), which is the covariance of an asset with the market portfolio divided by the variance of the market portfolio.

DETERMINING THE EXPECTED RATE OF RETURN FOR A RISKY ASSET   The equation above and the graph in Figure 9.6 tell us that the expected rate of return for a risky asset is determined by the RFR plus a risk premium for the individual asset. In turn, the risk premium is determined by the systematic risk of the asset (β_i), and the prevailing **market risk premium** ($R_M - RFR$). To demonstrate how you would compute the expected or required rates of return, consider the following example stocks assuming you have already computed betas:

Stock	Beta
A	0.70
B	1.00
C	1.15
D	1.40
E	−0.30

FIGURE 9.6

GRAPH OF SML WITH NORMALIZED SYSTEMATIC RISK

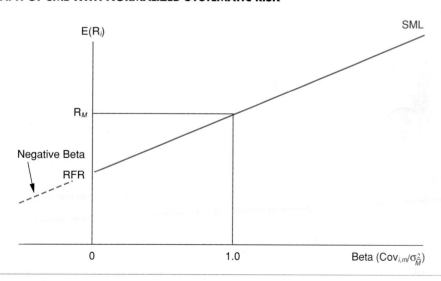

Assume that we expect the economy's RFR to be 8 percent (0.08) and the return on the market portfolio (R_M) to be 14 percent (0.14). This implies a market risk premium of 6 percent (0.06). With these inputs, the SML equation would yield the following expected (required) rates of return for these five stocks:

$$E(R_i) = RFR + \beta_i(R_M - RFR)$$
$$E(R_A) = 0.08 + 0.70\,(0.14 - 0.08)$$
$$= 0.122 = 12.2\%$$
$$E(R_B) = 0.08 + 1.00\,(0.14 - 0.08)$$
$$= 0.14 = 14\%$$
$$E(R_C) = 0.08 + 1.15\,(0.14 - 0.08)$$
$$= 0.149 = 14.9\%$$
$$E(R_D) = 0.08 + 1.40\,(0.14 - 0.08)$$
$$= 0.164 = 16.4\%$$
$$E(R_E) = 0.08 + (-0.30)\,(0.14 - 0.08)$$
$$= 0.08 - 0.018$$
$$= 0.062 = 6.2\%.$$

As stated, these are the expected (required) rates of return that these stocks should provide based on their systematic risks and the prevailing SML.

Stock A has lower risk than the aggregate market, so an investor should not expect (require) its return to be as high as the return on the market portfolio of risky assets. You should expect (require) Stock A to return 12.2 percent. Stock B has systematic risk equal to the market's (beta = 1.00), so its required rate of return should likewise be equal to the expected market return (14 percent). Stocks C and D have systematic risk greater than the market's so they should provide returns consistent with their risk. Finally, Stock E has a *negative* beta (which is quite rare in practice), so its required rate of return, if such a stock could be found, would be below the RFR.

In equilibrium, *all* assets and *all* portfolios of assets should plot on the SML. That is, all assets should be priced so that their **estimated rates of return,** which are the actual holding period rates of return that you anticipate, are consistent with their levels of systematic risk. Any security with an estimated rate of return that plots above the SML would be considered underpriced because it implies that you *estimated* you would receive a rate of return on the security that is above its *required* rate of return based on its systematic risk. In contrast, assets with estimated rates of return that plot below the SML would be considered overpriced. This position relative to the SML implies that your estimated rate of return is below what you should require based on the asset's systematic risk.

In an efficient market in equilibrium, you would not expect any assets to plot off the SML because, in equilibrium, all stocks should provide holding period returns that are equal to their required rates of return. Alternatively, a market that is "fairly efficient" but not completely efficient may misprice certain assets because not everyone will be aware of all the relevant information for an asset.

As we discussed in Chapter 7 on the topic of efficient markets, a superior investor has the ability to derive value estimates for assets that are consistently superior to the consensus market evaluation. As a result, such an investor will earn better rates of return than the average investor on a risk-adjusted basis.

IDENTIFYING UNDERVALUED AND OVERVALUED ASSETS   Now that we understand how to compute the rate of return one should expect or require for a specific risky asset using the SML, we can compare this *required* rate of return to the asset's *estimated* rate of return over a specific investment horizon to determine whether it would be an appropriate

TABLE 9.1

PRICE, DIVIDEND, AND RATE OF RETURN ESTIMATES

Stock	Current Price (P_i)	Expected Price (P_{t+1})	Expected Dividend (D_{t+1})	Estimated Future Rate of Return (Percent)
A	25	27	1.00	12.0%
B	40	42	1.25	8.1
C	33	40	1.00	24.2
D	64	65	2.40	5.3
E	50	55	—	10.0

TABLE 9.2

COMPARISON OF REQUIRED RATE OF RETURN TO ESTIMATED RATE OF RETURN

Stock	Beta	Required Return $E(R_i)$	Estimated Return	Estimated Return Minus $E(R_i)$	Evaluation
A	0.70	12.2	12.0	−0.2	Properly valued
B	1.00	14.0	8.1	−5.9	Overvalued
C	1.15	14.9	24.2	9.3	Undervalued
D	1.40	16.4	5.3	−11.1	Overvlaued
E	−0.30	6.2	10.0	3.8	Undervalued

investment. To make this comparison, you need an independent estimate of the return outlook for the security based on either fundamental or technical analysis techniques that will be discussed in subsequent chapters. Let us continue the example for the five assets discussed in the previous section.

Analysts in a major trust department have been following these five stocks. Based on extensive fundamental analysis, the analysts provide the price and dividend outlooks contained in Table 9.1. Given these projections, you can compute the estimated rates of return the analysts would anticipate during this holding period.

Table 9.2 summarizes the relationship between the required rate of return for each stock based on its systematic risk as computed earlier and its estimated rate of return (from Table 9.1) based on the current and future prices, and its dividend outlook.

Plotting these estimated rates of return and stock betas on the SML we specified earlier gives the graph shown in Figure 9.7. Stock A is almost exactly on the line, so it is considered properly valued because its estimated rate of return is almost equal to its required rate of return. Stocks B and D are considered overvalued because their estimated rates of return during the coming period are below what an investor should expect (require) for the risk involved. As a result, they plot below the SML. In contrast, Stocks C and E are expected to provide rates of return greater than we would require based on their systematic risk. Therefore, both stocks plot above the SML, indicating that they are undervalued stocks.

Assuming that you trusted your analyst to forecast estimated returns, you would take no action regarding Stock A, but you would buy Stocks C and E and sell Stocks B and D. You might even sell Stocks B and D short if you favored such aggressive tactics.

CALCULATING SYSTEMATIC RISK: THE CHARACTERISTIC LINE   The systematic risk input for an individual asset is derived from a regression model, referred to as the asset's **characteristic line** with the market portfolio:

$$R_{i,t} = \alpha_i + \beta_i R_{M,t} + \epsilon$$

FIGURE 9.7   **PLOT OF ESTIMATED RETURNS ON SML GRAPH**

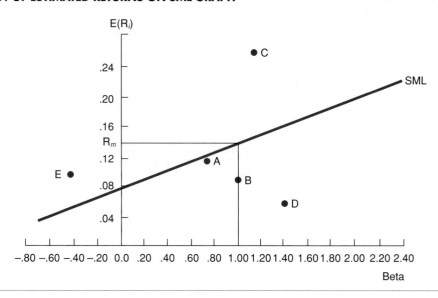

where:

> $R_{i,t}$ = the rate of return for asset i during period t
> $R_{M,t}$ = the rate of return for the market portfolio M during period t
> α_i = the constant term, or intercept, of the regression, which equals $R_i - \beta_i R_m$
> β_i = the systematic risk (beta) of asset i equal to $\text{Cov}_{i,M}/\sigma_M^2$
> ϵ = the random error term.

The characteristic line is the regression line of best fit through a scatter plot of rates of return for the individual risky asset and for the market portfolio of risky assets over some designated past period, as shown in Figure 9.8.

The impact of the time interval   In practice the number of observations and the time interval used in the regression vary. Value Line Investment Services derives characteristic lines for common stocks using weekly rates of return for the most recent five years (i.e., 260 weekly observations). Merrill Lynch, Pierce, Fenner & Smith uses monthly rates of return for the most recent five years (60 monthly observations). Because there is no theoretically correct time interval for analysis, we must make a trade-off between enough observations to eliminate the impact of random rates of return and an excessive length of time such as 15 or 20 years over which the subject company may have changed dramatically. Remember that what you really want is the *expected* systematic risk for the potential investment. In this analysis, you are analyzing historical data to help you derive a reasonable expectation of systematic risk.

A couple of studies have considered the impact of the time interval used to compute betas (weekly versus monthly) Statman examined the relationship between Value Line (VL) betas and Merrill Lynch (ML) betas and found a relatively weak relationship.[8] Reilly and Wright examined a larger sample and analyzed the differential effects of return compu-

---

[8] Meir Statman, "Betas Compared: Merrill Lynch vs. Value Line," *Journal of Portfolio Management* 7, no. 2 (Winter 1981). 11 11.

FIGURE 9.8   **SCATTER PLOT OF RATES OF RETURN**

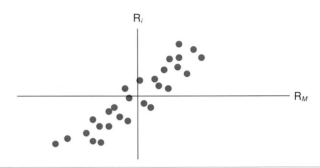

tation, market index, and the time interval and likewise found a weak relationship between VL and ML betas.[9] They showed that the major cause of the significant differences in beta was the use of monthly versus weekly intervals.

They also found that the interval effect depended on the sizes of the firms. The shorter weekly interval caused a larger beta for large firms and a smaller beta for small firms. For example, from 1975 to 1979, the average beta for the smallest decile of firms using monthly data was 1.682, but the average beta for these small firms using weekly data was only 1.080. The authors concluded that the return time interval makes a difference, and the impact of the interval increases as the size of the firm declines.

The effect of the market proxy   Another significant decision when computing an asset's characteristic line is which indicator series to use as a proxy for the market portfolio of all risky assets. Most investigators use the Standard & Poor's 500 Composite Index as a proxy for the market portfolio, because the stocks in this index encompass a large proportion of the total market value of U.S. stocks. Also, it is a value-weighted series, which is consistent with the theoretical market series. Still, this series only contains U.S. stocks, most of them listed on the NYSE. You will recall our earlier discussion where it was noted that the theoretically correct market portfolio of all risky assets should include U.S. stocks and bonds, non-U.S. stocks and bonds, real estate, coins, stamps, art, antiques, and any other marketable risky asset from around the world.[10]

EXAMPLE COMPUTATIONS OF A CHARACTERISTIC LINE   The following examples show how you would compute characteristic lines for Coca-Cola based on the monthly rates of return during 1995.[11] Twelve is not enough observations for statistical purposes, but it should provide a good example. We demonstrate the computations using three

[9] Frank K. Reilly and David J. Wright, "A Comparison of Published Betas," *Journal of Portfolio Management* 14, no. 3 (Spring 1988): 64–69.

[10] There has been substantial discussion of the market index used and its impact on the empirical results and usefulness of the CAPM. This concern is discussed further and demonstrated in the subsequent section on computing an asset's characteristic line. The effect of the market proxy is also considered when we discuss the arbitrage pricing theory (APT) in this chapter and in Chapter 27 when we discuss the evaluation of portfolio performance.

[11] These betas are computed using only monthly price changes for Coca-Cola, the S&P 500, the MS World Index, and the GSMI (i.e., dividends are not included). This is done for simplicity but is also based on a study indicating that betas derived with and without dividends are correlated 0.99: William Sharpe and Guy M. Cooper, "Risk–Return Classes of New York Stock Exchange Common Stocks," *Financial Analysts Journal* 28, no. 2 (March–April 1972): 35–43.

different proxies for the market portfolio. The first is the typical analysis where the S&P 500 is used as the market proxy. The second example uses the Morgan Stanley (M-S) World Equity Index as the market proxy. This analysis allows us to demonstrate the effect of a more complete proxy of stocks. Finally, we use the Brinson Partners Global Security Market Index (GSMI), which contains U.S. stocks and bonds and international stocks and bonds.

The monthly price changes are computed using the closing prices for the last day of each month. These data for Coca-Cola, the S&P 500, the M-S World Index, and the Brinson GSMI are contained in Table 9.3. Figure 9.9 contains the scatter plot of the percentage price changes for Coca-Cola and the S&P 500. During this 12-month period, Coca-Cola had returns that varied when compared with the aggregate market returns as proxied by the S&P 500. As a result, the covariance between Coca-Cola and the S&P 500 series was positive, but it was not a very large positive value (2.30). The covariance divided by the variance of the S&P 500 market portfolio (2.19) indicates that Coca-Cola's beta relative to the S&P 500 was equal to 1.05. This analysis indicates that during this limited time period Coca-Cola was riskier than the aggregate market proxied by the S&P 500.

When we draw this characteristic line on Figure 9.9, the scatter plots are not very close to the characteristic line, which is consistent with the correlation coefficient of 0.55.

The computation of the characteristic line for Coca-Cola using the M-S World Index and the Brinson GSMI as the proxy for the market is contained in Table 9.3, and the scatter plots are in Figures 9.10 and 9.11. At this point, it is important to consider what one might expect

---

FIGURE 9.9　**SCATTER PLOT OF COCA-COLA AND THE S&P 500 WITH CHARACTERISTIC LINE FOR COCA-COLA: 1995**

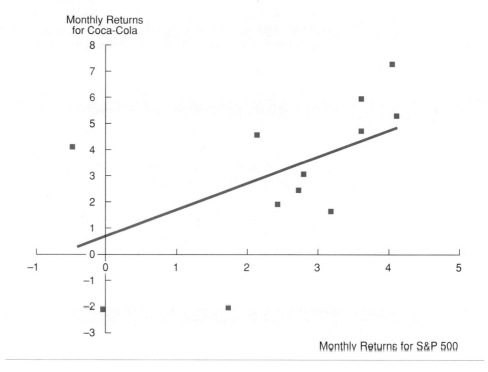

TABLE 9.3 — COMPUTATION OF BETA OF COCA-COLA WITH SELECTED INDEXES

Date	Index S&P 500	Index M-S World	Index Brinson GSMI	Return S&P 500	Return M-S World	Return Brinson GSMI	Return Coca Cola	S&P 500 $R_{S\&P} - E(R_{S\&P})$ (1)	M-S World $R_{M\text{-}S} - E(R_{M\text{-}S})$ (2)	Brinson GSMI $R_{GSMI} - E(R_{GSMI})$ (3)	Coca-Cola $R_{KO} - E(R_{KO})$ (4)	(5)[a]	(6)[b]	(7)[c]
Dec–94	459.27	618.59	1400.72											
Jan–95	470.42	608.26	1414.94	2.43	-1.67	1.02	1.94	-0.06	-3.24	-0.89	-1.19	0.07	3.86	1.06
Feb–95	487.39	616.07	1453.03	3.61	1.28	2.69	4.76	1.12	-0.29	0.78	1.63	1.83	-0.47	1.27
Mar–95	500.71	644.67	1499.85	2.73	4.64	3.22	2.50	0.24	3.07	1.31	-0.63	-0.15	-1.93	-0.83
Apr–95	514.71	666.04	1534.90	2.80	3.31	2.34	3.10	0.31	1.74	0.43	-0.03	-0.01	-0.05	-0.01
May–95	533.40	670.64	1573.42	3.63	0.69	2.51	6.02	1.14	-0.88	0.60	2.89	3.29	-2.54	1.73
Jun–95	544.75	669.32	1597.43	2.13	-0.20	1.53	4.67	-0.36	-1.77	-0.38	1.54	-0.55	-2.73	-0.59
Jul–95	562.06	701.69	1647.19	3.18	4.84	3.12	1.74	0.69	3.27	1.21	-1.39	-0.96	-4.55	-1.68
Aug–95	561.88	684.96	1641.44	-0.03	-2.38	-0.35	-2.10	-2.52	-3.95	-2.26	-5.23	13.18	20.66	11.82
Sep–95	584.41	699.07	1685.37	4.01	2.06	2.68	7.39	1.52	0.49	0.77	4.26	6.48	2.09	3.28
Oct–95	581.50	689.90	1674.79	-0.50	-1.31	-0.63	4.17	-2.99	-2.88	-2.54	1.04	-3.11	-3.00	-2.64
Nov–95	605.37	714.20	1724.92	4.10	3.52	2.99	5.39	1.61	1.95	1.08	2.26	3.64	4.41	2.44
Dec–95	615.93	743.30	1756.77	1.74	4.07	1.85	-1.98	-0.75	2.50	-0.06	-5.11	3.83	-12.78	0.31
Average				2.49	1.57	1.91	3.13					Total = 27.54	2.97	16.16
Standard Deviation				1.48	2.56	1.30	2.81							

$\text{Cov}_{KO,S\&P} = 27.54 / 12 = 2.30$

$\text{Cov}_{KO,M\text{-}S} = 2.97 / 12 = 0.25$

$\text{Cov}_{KO,GSMI} = 16.16 / 12 = 1.35$

$\text{Var}_{S\&P} = \text{St.Dev}_{S\&P}^2 = 1.48^2 = 2.19$

$\text{Var}_{S\&P} = \text{St.Dev}_{M\text{-}S}^2 = 2.56^2 = 6.55$

$\text{Var}_{GSMI} = \text{St.Dev}_{GSMI}^2 = 1.30^2 = 1.69$

$\text{Beta}_{KO,S\&P} = 2.30 / 2.19 = 1.05$

$\text{Beta}_{KO,M\text{-}S} = 0.25 / 6.55 = 0.04$

$\text{Beta}_{KO,GSMI} = 1.35 / 1.69 = 0.80$

$\text{Alpha}_{KO,S\&P} = 3.13 - (1.05 \times 2.49) = 0.52$

$\text{Alpha}_{KO,M\text{-}S} = 3.13 - (0.04 \times 1.57) = 3.07$

$\text{Alpha}_{KO,GSMI} = 3.13 - (0.80 \times 1.91) = 1.60$

Correlation coef.$_{KO,S\&P}$ = 2.30 / (1.48 × 2.81) = 0.55

Correlation coef.$_{KO,M\text{-}S}$ = 0.25 / (2.56 × 2.81) = 0.03

Correlation coef.$_{KO,GSMI}$ = 1.35 / (1.30 × 2.81) = 0.37

[a] Column (5) is equal to column (1) multiplied by column (4).
[b] Column (6) is equal to column (2) multiplied by column (4).
[c] Column (7) is equal to column (3) multiplied by column (4).

FIGURE 9.10   **SCATTER PLOT OF COCA-COLA AND THE M.S. WORLD INDEX WITH CHARACTERISTIC LINE FOR COCA-COLA: 1995**

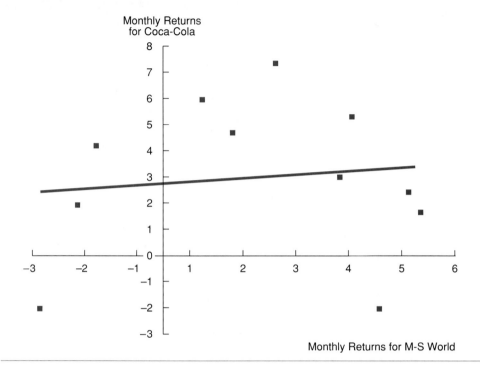

to be the relationship between the beta relative to the S&P 500 versus the betas with the M.S. World Index and the Brinson series. This requires a consideration of the two components in the computation of beta: (1) the covariance between the stock and the benchmark and (2) the variance of returns for the benchmark series. Notably, there is no obvious answer regarding what will happen for either series because one would typically expect both components to change. Specifically, the covariance of Coca-Cola with the S&P 500 will probably be higher than with either of the other series because you are matching a U.S. stock with a U.S. market index rather than a world index. Thus, the covariance with the other indexes will generally be smaller. At the same time, the variance of returns for the world stock index should typically also be smaller than the variance for the S&P 500 because it is a more diversified stock portfolio. The variance for the Brinson GSMI Series should be *much* lower because it is diversified with U.S. stocks *and* bonds as well as international stocks and bonds.

Therefore, the direction of change for the beta will depend on the relative change in the two components. An empirical observation is that generally the beta is smaller with the world stock index because the covariance is definitely lower, but the variance is only slightly smaller. In contrast, the beta is almost always larger when using the Brinson GSMI series because, although the covariance is lower, the variance of the Brinson series is typically substantially smaller.[12] The results of this example were not completely consistent with expectations. The beta with the world stock index was very small (0.04) because the

[12] For a demonstration of this effect for a large sample that confirms these expectations, see Frank K. Reilly and Rashid A. Akhtar, "The Benchmark Error Problem with Global Capital Markets," *Journal of Portfolio Management* 22, no. 1 (Fall 1995): 33–52.

FIGURE 9.11

SCATTER PLOT OF COCA-COLA AND THE BRINSON GSMI WITH CHARACTERISTIC LINE FOR COCA-COLA: 1995

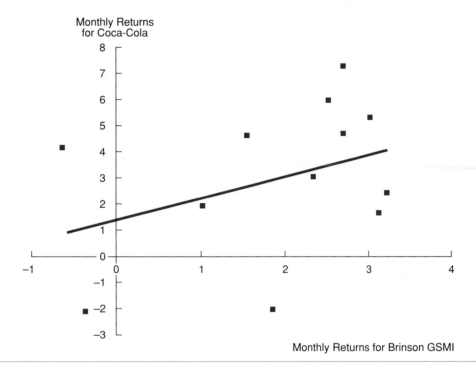

covariance was lower, but the variance of the market was much larger. In turn, the beta with Brinson was also smaller (0.80) because the covariance was much lower, while the variance was smaller, but not as small as usual (it was 1.69 vs. 2.19 for the S&P 500).

The differences in beta were not consistent with expectations. The fact that they differed is significant and reflects the potential problem that can occur in a global environment where it becomes difficult to select the appropriate proxy for the market portfolio.

ARBITRAGE PRICING THEORY (APT)

At this point, we have discussed the basic theory of the CAPM, the impact of changing some of its major assumptions, and its dependence on a market portfolio of all risky assets. In addition, the model assumes that investors have quadratic utility functions and that the distribution of security prices is normal—that is, symmetrically distributed, with a variance term that can be estimated.

Some tests of the CAPM indicate that the beta coefficients for individual securities are not stable, but the beta of portfolios generally were stable assuming long enough sample periods and adequate trading volume. Some studies have also supported a positive linear relationship between rates of return and systematic risk for portfolios of stock. In contrast, a set of papers by Roll criticized the usefulness of the model because of its dependence on a market portfolio of risky assets and Roll contends that such a portfolio is not currently available.[13] Roll points out that when the CAPM is used to evaluate portfolio performance,

---

[13] Richard Roll, "A Critique of the Asset Pricing Theory's Tests," *Journal of Financial Economics* 4, no. 4 (March 1977); 129–176; Richard Roll, "Ambiguity When Performance Is Measured by the Securities Market

it is necessary to select a proxy for the market portfolio as a benchmark for performance. It has been shown in the Reilly–Akhtar paper that the performance results can be changed substantially because of the market proxy used.

Given these questions, the academic community has considered an alternative asset pricing theory that is reasonably intuitive and requires only limited assumptions. This **arbitrage pricing theory (APT),** developed by Ross in the early 1970s and initially published in 1976, has three major assumptions:[14]

1. Capital markets are perfectly competitive.
2. Investors always prefer more wealth to less wealth with certainty.
3. The stochastic process generating asset returns can be represented as a K factor model (to be described).

Equally important, the following major assumptions are *not* required: (1) quadratic utility function, (2) normally distributed security returns, and (3) a market portfolio that contains all risky assets and is mean-variance efficient. Obviously, if a theory without these assumptions is able to explain differential security prices, it would be considered a superior theory because it is simpler (i.e., it requires fewer assumptions).

As noted, the theory assumes that the stochastic process generating asset returns can be represented as a K factor model of the form

$$R_i = E_i + b_{i1}\delta_1 + b_{i2}\delta_2 + \ldots + b_{ik}\delta_k + \epsilon_i \quad \text{for } i = 1 \text{ to } N$$

where:

R_i = **return on asset i during a specified time period**
E_i = **expected return for asset i**
b_{ik} = **reaction in asset i's returns to movements in a common factor**
δ_k = **a common factor with a zero mean that influences the returns on all assets**
ϵ_i = **a unique effect on asset i's return that, by assumption, is completely diversifiable in large portfolios and has a mean of zero**
N = **number of assets.**

Two terms require elaboration: δ_k and b. As indicated, the δ_k terms are the *multiple* factors expected to have an impact on the returns of *all* assets. Examples of such factors might include inflation, growth in GNP, major political upheavals, or changes in interest rates. The APT contends there are many such factors, in contrast to the CAPM, where it is contended that the only relevant variable is the covariance of the asset with the market portfolio, that is, its beta coefficient.

Given these common factors, the b_{ik} terms determine how each asset reacts to this common factor. To extend the earlier example, although all assets may be affected by growth in GNP, the impact will differ across assets. For example, stocks of cyclical firms that produce autos, steel, or heavy machinery will have larger b_{ik} terms for this common factor than noncyclical firms, such as grocery chains. Likewise, you will hear discussions about interest-sensitive stocks: all stocks are affected by changes in interest rates, but some stocks experience larger impacts. It is possible to envision other examples of common factors such as inflation, exchange rates, interest rate spreads, and so on. Still, in the

---

Line," *Journal of Finance* 33, no. 4 (September 1978): 1051–1069; and Richard Roll, "Performance Evaluation and Benchmark Error II," *Journal of Portfolio Management* 7, no. 2 (Winter 1981): 17–22.

[14] Stephen Ross, "The Arbitrage Theory of Capital Asset Pricing," *Journal of Economic Theory* 13, no. 2 (December 1976): 341–360; Stephen Ross, "Return, Risk, and Arbitrage," in *Risk and Return in Finance*, edited by I. Friend and J. Bicksler (Cambridge: Ballinger, 1977), 189–218.

application of the theory, *the factors are not identified*. That is, when we discuss the empirical studies, three, four, or five factors that affect security returns will be identified, but *there is no indication of what these factors represent*.

Similar to the CAPM model, it is assumed that the unique effects (ϵ_i) are independent and will be diversified away in a large portfolio. The APT assumes that, in equilibrium, the return on a zero-investment, zero-systematic-risk portfolio is zero when the unique effects are diversified away. This assumption and some theory from linear algebra imply that the expected return on any asset i (E_i) can be expressed as

$$E_i = \lambda_0 + \lambda_1 b_{i1}, + \lambda_2 b_{i2} + \ldots + \lambda_k b_{ik}$$

where:

λ_0 = the expected return on an asset with zero systematic risk where $\lambda_0 = E_0$
λ_i = the risk premium related to each of the common factors—for example, the risk premium related to interest rate risk ($\lambda_i = E_i = E_0$)
b_i = the pricing relationship between the risk premium and asset i—that is, how responsive asset i is to this common factor K.

Consider the following example of two stocks and a two-factor model:

λ_1 = changes in the rate of inflation. The risk premium related to this factor is 1 percent for every 1 percent change in the rate ($\lambda_1 = .01$)
λ_2 = percent growth in real GNP. The average risk premium related to this factor is 2 percent for every 1 percent change in the rate ($\lambda_2 = .02$).
λ_0 = the rate of return on a zero-systematic-risk asset (zero beta: $b_{0j} = 0$) is 3 percent ($\lambda_0 = .03$).

The two assets (X, Y) have the following response coefficients to these factors:

b_{x1} = the response of asset X to changes in the rate of inflation is 0.50 ($b_{x1} = .50$). This asset is not very responsive to changes in the rate of inflation
b_{y1} = the response of asset Y to changes in the rate of inflation is 2.00 ($b_{y1} = 2.00$)
b_{x2} = the response of asset X to changes in the growth rate of real GNP is 1.50 ($b_{x2} = 1.50$)
b_{y2} = the response of asset Y to changes in the growth rate of real GNP is 1.75 ($b_{y2} = 1.75$)

These response coefficients indicate that if these are the major factors influencing asset returns, asset Y is a higher-risk asset, and therefore its expected (required) return should be greater, as shown below:

$$E_i = \lambda_0 + \lambda_1 b_{i1} + \lambda_2 b_{i2}$$
$$= .03 + (.01)b_{i1} + (.02)b_{i2}.$$

Therefore:

$$E_x = .03 + (.01)(0.50) + (.02)(1.50)$$
$$= .065 = 6.5\%$$
$$E_y = .03 + (.01)(2.00) + (.02)(1.75)$$
$$= .085 = 8.5\%.$$

If the prices of the assets do not reflect these returns, we would expect investors to enter into arbitrage arrangements whereby they would sell overpriced assets short and use the proceeds to purchase the underpriced assets until the relevant prices were corrected. Given these linear relationships, it should be possible to find an asset or a combination of assets with equal risk to the mispriced asset, yet a higher return.

EMPIRICAL TESTS
OF THE APT

Studies by Roll and Ross and by Chen have provided results that support the APT because the model was able to explain different rates of return, in some cases with results that were superior to those of the CAPM.[15] In contrast, results of Reinganum's study do not support the model because it did not explain small-firm results.[16] Finally, Dhrymes and Shanken both questioned the usefulness of the model because it was not possible to identify the factors. Under these conditions, they question whether the theory is testable.[17]

At this time, the theory is relatively new and will be subject to continued testing. The important points to remember are that the model requires fewer assumptions and considers multiple factors to explain the risk of an asset, in contrast to the single-factor CAPM.[18]

Summary

- The assumptions of capital market theory expand on those of the Markowitz portfolio model and include consideration of the risk-free rate of return. The correlation and covariance of any asset with a risk-free asset is zero, so that any combination of an asset or portfolio with the risk-free asset generates a linear return and risk function. Therefore, when you combine the risk-free asset with any risky asset on the Markowitz efficient frontier, you derive a set of straight-line portfolio possibilities.
- The dominant line is the one that is tangent to the efficient frontier. This dominant line is referred to as the *capital market line (CML),* and all investors should target points along this line depending on their risk preferences.
- Because all investors want to invest in the risky portfolio at the point of tangency, this portfolio—referred to as the market portfolio—must contain all risky assets in proportion to their relative market values. Moreover, the investment decision and the financing decision can be separated because, although everyone will want to invest in the market portfolio, investors will make different financing decisions about whether to lend or borrow based on their individual risk preferences.
- Given the CML and the dominance of the market portfolio, the relevant risk measure for an individual risky asset is its covariance with the market portfolio, that is, its *systematic risk.* When this covariance is standardized by the covariance for the market portfolio, we derive the well-known beta measure of systematic risk and a security market line (SML) that relates the expected or required rate of return for an asset to its beta. Because all individual securities and portfolios should plot on this SML, you can determine the expected (required) return on a security based on its systematic risk (its beta).
- Alternatively, assuming security markets are not always completely efficient, you can identify undervalued and overvalued securities by comparing your estimate of the rate of return to be earned on an investment to its expected (required) rate of return. The systematic risk variable (beta) for an individual risky asset is computed using a regression model that generates an equation referred to as the asset's *characteristic line.*
- We conclude the chapter with a discussion of an alternative asset pricing model—the arbitrage pricing theory (APT) model. This includes a discussion of the necessary assumptions and the

[15] Richard Roll and Stephen A. Ross, "An Empirical Investigation of the Arbitrage Pricing Theory," *Journal of Finance* 35, no. 5 (December 1980): 1073–1103; and Nai-fu Chen, "Some Empirical Tests of Theory of Arbitrage Pricing," *Journal of Finance* 18, no. 5 (December 1983): 1393–1414.

[16] Marc R. Reinganum, "The Arbitrage Pricing Theory: Some Empirical Results," *Journal of Finance* 36, no. 2 (May 1981): 313–321.

[17] Phoebus J. Dhrymes, "The Empirical Relevance of Arbitrage Pricing Models," *Journal of Portfolio Management* 10, no. 4 (Summer 1984): 35 –44; Jay Shanken, "The Arbitrage Pricing Theory: Is It Testable?" *Journal of Finance* 37, no. 5 (December 1982): 1129–1140.

[18] For a discussion of how these models relate to each other, see William F. Sharpe, "Factor Models, CAPMs and the APT," *Journal of Portfolio Management* 11, no. 1 (Fall 1984): 21–25. For a set of papers on the topic, see *The CAPM Controversy: Policy and Strategy Implications for Investment Management,* edited by Diana R. Harrington and Robert A. Konajczyk (Charlottesville, VA: Association of Investment Management and Research, March 1993).

basics of the model as well as an example of its use. We also consider some of the tests of the model that have generated mixed results. Because of the mixed results and the importance of the topic, it is likely that testing of this model will continue.

Questions

1. Explain why the set of points between the risk-free asset and a portfolio on the Markowitz efficient frontier is a straight line.
2. Draw a graph that shows what happens to the Markowitz efficient frontier when you combine a risk-free asset with alternative risky asset portfolios on the Markowitz efficient frontier. Explain this graph.
3. Draw and explain why the line from the RFR that is tangent to the efficient frontier defines the dominant set of portfolio possibilities.
4. Discuss what risky assets are in Portfolio M and why they are in it.
5. Discuss leverage and its effect on the CML.
6. Discuss and justify a measure of diversification for a portfolio in terms of capital market theory.
7. What changes would you expect in the standard deviation for a portfolio of stocks between 4 and 10 stocks, between 10 and 20 stocks, and between 50 and 100 stocks?
8. Discuss why the investment and financing decisions are separate when you have a CML.
9. Given the CML, discuss and justify the relevant measure of risk for an individual security.
10. Capital market theory divides the variance of returns for a security into systematic variance and unsystematic or unique variance. Describe each of these terms.
11. The capital asset pricing model (CAPM) contends that there is systematic and unsystematic risk for an individual security. Which is the relevant risk variable and why is it relevant? Why is the other risk variable not relevant?
12. How does the SML differ from the CML?

13. *CFA Examination I (1993)*
    Identify and briefly discuss *three* criticisms of beta as used in the Capital Asset Pricing Model (CAPM). [6 minutes]

14. *CFA Examination I (1993)*
    Briefly explain whether investors should expect a higher return from holding Portfolio A versus Portfolio B under Capital Asset Pricing Theory (CAPM). Assume that both portfolios are fully diversified. [6 minutes]

	Portfolio A	Portfolio B
Systematic risk (beta)	1.0	1.0
Specific risk for each individual security	High	Low

15. *CFA Examination II (1994)*
    You have been recently appointed chief investment officer of a major charitable foundation. Its large endowment fund is currently invested in a broadly-diversified portfolio of stocks (60 percent) and bonds (40 percent). The foundation's board of trustees is a group of prominent individuals whose knowledge of modern investment theory and practice is superficial. You decide a discussion of basic investment principles would be helpful.
    a. Explain the concepts of *specific risk, systematic risk, variance, covariance, standard deviation,* and *beta* as they relate to investment management. [12 minutes]
       You believe that the addition of other asset classes to the endowment portfolio would improve the portfolio by reducing risk and enhancing return. You are aware that depressed conditions in U.S. real estate markets are providing opportunities for property acquisition at levels of expected return that are unusually high by historical standards. You believe that an investment in U.S. real estate would be both appropriate and timely, and have decided to recommend a 20 percent position be established with funds taken equally from stocks and bonds.

Preliminary discussions revealed that several trustees believe real estate is too risky to include in the portfolio. The Board Chairman, however, has scheduled a special meeting for further discussion of the matter and has asked you to provide background information that will clarify the risk issue.

To assist you, the following expectational data have been developed:

			CORRELATION MATRIX			
Asset Class	Return	Standard Deviation	U.S. Stocks	U.S. Bonds	U.S. Real Estate	U.S. T-Bills
U.S. Stocks	12.0%	21.0%	1.00			
U.S. Bonds	8.0	10.5	0.14	1.00		
U.S. Real Estate	12.0	9.0	−0.04	−0.03	1.00	
U.S. Treasury Bills	4.0	0.0	−0.05	−0.03	0.25	1.00

b. Explain the effect on *both* portfolio risk *and* return that would result from the addition of U.S. real estate. Include in your answer *two* reasons for any change you expect in portfolio risk. (Note: It is *not* necessary to compute expected risk and return.) [8 minutes]

c. Your understanding of capital market theory causes you to doubt the validity of the expected return and risk for U.S. real estate. Justify your skepticism. [5 minutes]

Problems

1. Assume that you expect the economy's rate of inflation to be 3 percent, giving an RFR of 6 percent and a market return (R_M) of 12 percent.
   a. Draw the SML under these assumptions.
   b. Subsequently, you expect the rate of inflation to increase from 3 percent to 6 percent. What effect would this have on the RFR and the R_M? Draw another SML on the graph from Part a.
   c. Draw an SML on the same graph to reflect an RFR of 9 percent and an R_M of 17 percent. How does this SML differ from that derived in Part b? Explain what has transpired.

2. You expect an RFR of 10 percent and the market return (R_M) of 14 percent. Compute the expected (required) return for the following stocks, and plot them on an SML graph.

Stock	Beta	$E(R_i)$
U	0.85	
N	1.25	
D	−0.20	

3. You ask a stockbroker what the firm's research department expects for these three stocks. The broker responds with the following information:

Stock	Current Price	Expected Price	Expected Dividend
U	22	24	0.75
N	48	51	2.00
D	37	40	1.25

Plot your estimated returns on the graph from Problem 2 and indicate what actions you would take with regard to these stocks. Discuss your decisions.

4. Select a stock from the NYSE and collect its month-end prices for the latest 13 months to compute 12 monthly percentage of price changes ignoring dividends. Do the same for the S&P 500 series. Prepare a scatter plot of these series on a graph and draw a visual characteristic line of

best fit (the line that minimizes the deviations from the line). Compute the slope of this line from the graph.

5. Given the returns derived in Problem 4, compute the beta coefficient using the formula and techniques employed in Table 9.3. How many negative products did you have for the covariance? How does this computed beta compare to the visual beta derived in Problem 4?

6. Look up the index values and compute the monthly rates of return for either the FT World Index or the Morgan Stanley World Index.
   a. Compute the beta for your NYSE stock from Problem 4 using one of these world stock indexes as the proxy for the market portfolio.
   b. How does this world beta compare to your S&P 500 beta? Discuss the difference.

7. Look up this stock in *Value Line* and record the beta derived by *VL*. How does this *VL* beta compare to the beta you computed using the S&P 500? Discuss reasons why the betas might differ.

8. Select a stock that is listed on the AMEX and plot the returns during the last 12 months relative to the S&P 500. Compute the beta coefficient. Did you expect this stock to have a higher or lower beta than the NYSE stock? Explain your answer.

9. Given the returns for the AMEX stock in Problem 8, plot the stock returns relative to monthly rates of return for the AMEX Market Value Index and compute the beta coefficient. Does this beta differ from that derived in Problem 8? If so, how can you explain this? (Hint: Analyze the specific components of the formula for the beta coefficient. How did the components differ between Problems 8 and 9?)

10. Using the data from the prior questions, compute the beta coefficient for the AMEX Index relative to the S&P 500 Index. A priori, would you expect a beta less than or greater than 1.00? Discuss your expectations and the actual results.

11. Based on 5 years of monthly data, you derive the following information for the companies listed.

Company	a_i (Intercept)	σ_i	r_{iM}
Apple Computer	0.22	12.10%	0.72
Chrysler	0.10	14.60	0.33
Anheuser Busch	0.17	7.60	0.55
Monsanto	0.05	10.20	0.60
S&P 500	0.00	5.50	1.00

   a. Compute the beta coefficient for each stock.
   b. Assuming a risk-free rate of 8 percent and an expected return for the market portfolio of 15 percent, compute the expected (required) return for all the stocks and plot them on the SML.
   c. Plot the following estimated returns for the next year on the SML and indicate which stocks are undervalued or overvalued.
      • Apple Computer—20%
      • Chrysler—15%
      • Anheuser Busch—19%
      • Monsanto—10%

12. Calculate the expected (required) return for each of the following stocks when the risk-free rate is .08 and you expect the market return to be .15.

Stock	Beta
A	1.72
B	1.14
C	0.76
D	0.44
E	0.03
F	−0.79

13. The following are the historic returns for the Golden Computer Company:

Year	Golden Computer	General Index
1	37	15
2	9	13
3	−11	14
4	8	−9
5	11	12
6	4	9

Based on this information, compute the following:
a. The correlation coefficient between Golden Computer and the General Index.
b. The standard deviation for the company and the index.
c. The beta for the Golden Computer Company.

14. *CFA Examination II (1995)*
The following information describes the expected return and risk relationship for the stocks of two of WAH's competitors.

	Expected Return	Standard Deviation	Beta
Stock X	12.0%	20%	1.3
Stock Y	9.0	15	0.7
Market Index	10.0	12	1.0
Risk free rate	5.0		

Using only the data shown above:
a. Draw and label a graph showing the Security Market Line and position stocks X and Y relative to it using the template provided in the answer book. [5 minutes]
b. Compute the alphas *both* for stock X *and* for stock Y. Show your work. [4 minutes]
c. Assume that the risk free rate increases to 7% with the other data in the matrix above remaining unchanged. Select the stock providing the higher expected risk-adjusted return and justify your selection. Show your calculations.

References

Brinson, Gary P., Jeffrey J. Diermeier, and Gary Schlarbaum. "A Composite Portfolio Benchmark for Pension Plans." *Financial Analysts Journal* 42, no. 2 (March–April 1986).

Chen, F. N., Richard Roll, and Steve Ross. "Economic Forces and the Stock Market." *Journal of Business* (July 1986).

Hagin, Robert. *Modern Portfolio Theory*. Homewood, IL: Dow Jones-Irwin, 1979.

Handa, Puneet, S. P. Kothari, and Charles Wasley. "The Relation between the Return Interval and Betas: Implications of the Size Effect." *Journal of Financial Economics* 23, no. 1 (June 1989).

Hawawini, Gabriel A. "Why Beta Shifts as the Return Interval Changes." *Financial Analysts Journal* 39, no. 3 (May–June 1983).

Reilly, Frank K., and Rashid A. Akhtar. "The Benchmark Error Problem with Global Capital Markets." *Journal of Portfolio Management* 22, no. 1 (Fall 1995),

Chapter
10

Extensions and Testing of Asset Pricing Theories

This chapter answers the following questions:

- What happens to the capital market line (CML) when you assume there are differences in the risk-free borrowing and lending rates?
- What is a zero–beta asset and how does its use impact the CML?
- What happens to the security market line (SML) when you assume transactions costs, heterogeneous expectations, different planning periods, and taxes?
- What are the major questions considered when empirically testing the CAPM?
- What are the empirical results from tests that examine the stability of beta?
- How do alternative published estimates of beta compare?
- What are the empirical test results of studies that examine the relationship between systematic risk and return?
- What other variables besides beta have had a significant impact on returns?
- What is the theory and practice regarding the "market portfolio"? How does this difference between theory and the market proxy relate to the benchmark problem?
- Assuming there is a benchmark problem, what variables are affected by it?
- What are the major assumptions *not* required by the APT model compared to the CAPM?
- How do you test the APT by examining anomalies found with the CAPM?
- What are the empirical test results related to the APT?
- Why do some authors contend that the APT model is untestable?
- What are the concerns related to the multiple factors of the APT model?

Chapters 8 and 9 introduced in detail the Markowitz portfolio theory and the capital asset pricing model (CAPM). This chapter considers several extensions of the CAPM, relaxes some of the assumptions, and examines the impact of these changes on the model. More important, we discuss the empirical tests of the theory. As we will discuss, some of the early results supported the predictive ability of the CAPM, but also raised some questions, including a contention by Roll that it is not possible to test the model. We also discuss in some detail the recent study by Fama and French that raises serious questions about the relationship between beta and rates of return. This is followed by a discussion of the results of several studies that have responded to the Fama-French contentions.

In Chapter 9, we discussed a well-regarded alternative asset pricing model—the arbitrage pricing theory (APT)—developed by Stephen Ross. Again, we will discuss the empirical tests of the APT. The empirical tests of this alternative theory yield mixed results, including a suggestion that the APT is likewise untestable.

RELAXING THE ASSUMPTIONS

In Chapter 9, several assumptions were set forth related to the CAPM. In this section, we discuss the impact on the capital market line (CML) and the security market line (SML) when we relax several of these assumptions.

DIFFERENTIAL BORROWING AND LENDING RATES

One of the first assumptions of the CAPM was that investors could borrow and lend any amount of money at the risk-free rate. It is reasonable to assume that investors can *lend* unlimited amounts at the risk-free rate by buying government securities (e.g., T-bills). In contrast, one may question the ability of investors to borrow unlimited amounts at the T-bill rate because it is usually lower than the prime rate, and most investors must pay a premium relative to the prime rate when borrowing money. For example, when T-bills are yielding 5 percent, the prime rate will probably be about 7 percent, and most individuals would have to pay about 8 percent to borrow at the bank.

The effect of this differential is that there will be two different lines going to the Markowitz efficient frontier, as shown in Figure 10.1. The segment *RFR–F* indicates the investment opportunities available when an investor combines risk-free assets (i.e., lending at the RFR) and Portfolio F on the Markowitz efficient frontier. It is not possible to extend this line any further if it is assumed that you cannot borrow at this risk-free rate to acquire further units of Portfolio F. If it is assumed that you can borrow at R_b, the point of tangency from this rate would be on the curve at point *K*. This indicates that you could borrow at R_b and use the proceeds to invest in Portfolio K to extend the CML along the line segment *K–G*. Therefore, the CML is made up of *RFR–F–K–G;* that is, a line segment (*RFR–F*), a curve segment (*F–K*), and another line segment (*K–G*). This implies that you can either lend or borrow, but the borrowing portfolios are not as profitable as when it was assumed that you could borrow at the RFR. In this instance, because you must pay a borrowing rate that is higher than the RFR, your net return is less—that is, the slope of the borrowing line (*K–G*) is below that for *RFR–F*.[1]

FIGURE 10.1

INVESTMENT ALTERNATIVES WHEN THE COST OF BORROWING IS HIGHER THAN THE COST OF LENDING

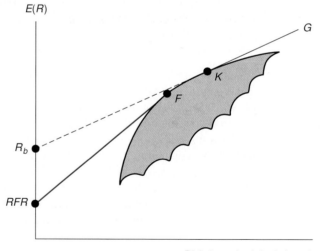

---

[1] For a detailed discussion, see Michael Brennan, "Capital Market Equilibrium with Divergent Borrowing and Lending Rates," *Journal of Financial and Quantitative Analysis* 4, no. 1 (March 1969): 4–14.

ZERO–BETA MODEL   If the market portfolio (*M*) is mean-variance efficient (i.e., it has the lowest risk for a given level of return among the attainable set of portfolios), an alternative model, derived by Black, does not require a risk-free asset.[2] Specifically, within the set of feasible alternative portfolios, several portfolios exist where the returns are completely uncorrelated with the market portfolio; the beta of these portfolios with the market portfolio is zero. From among the several zero–beta portfolios, you would select the one with minimum variance. Although this portfolio does not have any systematic risk, it does have some unsystematic risk. The availability of this zero–beta portfolio will not affect the CML, but it will allow construction of a linear SML, as shown in Figure 10.2. In the model, the intercept is the expected return for the zero–beta portfolio. Similar to the proof in Chapter 9, the combinations of this zero–beta portfolio and the market portfolio will be a linear relationship in return and risk because the covariance between the zero–beta portfolio (*R*$_z$) and the market portfolio likewise is similar to the risk-free asset. Assuming the return for the zero–beta portfolio is greater than that for a risk-free asset, the slope of the line through the market portfolio would not be as steep. The equation for this zero–beta CAPM line would be

$$E(R_i) = E(R_z) + B_i[E(R_m) - E(R_z)]$$

Obviously, the risk premiums for individual assets would be a function of the beta for the individual security and the market risk premium:

$$[E(R_m) - E(R_z)]$$

Some of the empirical results discussed in the next section support this model with its higher intercept and flatter slope. Alternatively, several studies have specifically tested this

FIGURE 10.2   **SECURITY MARKET LINE WITH A ZERO–BETA PORTFOLIO**

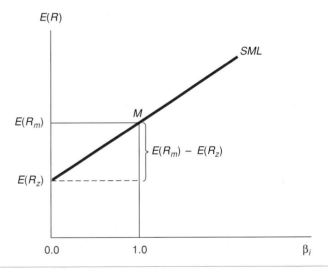

[2] Fischer Black, "Capital Market Equilibrium with Restricted Borrowing," *Journal of Business* 45, no. 3 (July 1972): 444–445.

model and had conflicting results. Specifically, studies by Gibbons and Shanken rejected the model.[3] In contrast, the results of a study by Stambaugh supported the zero–beta CAPM.[4]

TRANSACTION COSTS The basic assumption is that there are no transaction costs, so investors will buy or sell mispriced securities until they again plot on the SML. For example, if a stock plots above the SML, it is underpriced (its $E(R)$ is greater than justified by its risk level). As a result, investors should buy it and bid up its price until its $E(R)$ is in line with its risk—that is, until it plots on the SML. With transaction costs, investors will not correct all mispricing because in some instances the cost of buying and selling the mispriced security will offset any potential excess return. Therefore, securities will plot very close to the SML—but not exactly on it. Thus, the SML will be a band of securities, as shown in Figure 10.3, rather than a single line. Obviously, the width of the band is a function of the amount of the transaction costs. In a world with a large proportion of purchases and sales by institutions at pennies per share and with numerous discount brokers available for individual investors, the band should be quite narrow.

FIGURE 10.3   **SECURITY MARKET LINE WITH TRANSACTION COSTS**

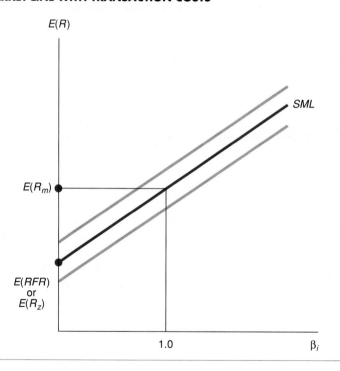

---

[3] Michael Gibbons, "Multivariate Tests of Financial Models: A New Approach," *Journal of Financial Economics* 10, no. 1 (March 1982): 3–28; and Jay Shanken, "Multivariate Tests of the Zero Beta CAPM," *Journal of Financial Economics* 14, no. 3 (September 1985): 327–348.

[4] Robert Stambaugh, "On the Exclusion of Assets from Tests of the Two-Parameter Model: A Sensitivity Analysis," *Journal of Financial Economics* 10, no. 4 (November 1982): 237–268.

The existence of transaction costs also will affect the extent of diversification by investors. In Chapter 9, we discussed the relationship between the number of stocks in a portfolio and the variance of the portfolio (see Figure 9.3). Initially, the variance declined rapidly, approaching about 90 percent of complete diversification with about 15 to 18 securities. An important question is, how many securities must be added to derive the last 10 percent. Clearly, the existence of transaction costs indicates that at some point the additional cost of diversification relative to its benefit would be excessive for most investors, especially when considering the costs of monitoring and analyzing the added securities.

HETEROGENEOUS EXPECTATIONS AND PLANNING PERIODS

If all investors have different expectations about risk and return, each would have a unique CML and/or SML, and the composite graph would be a set (band) of lines with a breadth determined by the divergence of expectations. If all investors had similar information and background, the band would be reasonably narrow.

The impact of *planning periods* is similar. Recall that the CAPM is a one-period model, and the period employed should be the planning period for the individual investor. Thus, if you are using a one-year planning period, your CML and SML could differ from mine, which assumes a one-month planning period.

TAXES

The rates of return that we normally record and that were used throughout the model were pretax returns. In fact, the actual returns for most investors are affected as follows:

$$E(R_i)(AT) = \frac{(P_e - P_b) \times (1 - T_{cg}) + (Div) \times (1 - T_i)}{P_b}$$

where

$R_i(AT)$ = **after-tax rate of return**
P_e = **ending price**
P_b = **beginning price**
T_{cg} = **tax on capital gain or loss**
Div = **dividend paid during period**
T_i = **tax on ordinary income**

Clearly, tax rates differ between individuals and institutions. Hence, for many institutions that do not pay taxes, the original pretax model is correctly specified—that is, T_{cg} and T_i take on values of zero. Alternatively, if investors have heavy tax burdens, this could cause major differences in the CML and SML among investors, depending on their marginal tax rates.[5] Several recent studies have examined the effect of the differential taxes on dividends versus capital gains. Although most of the studies have indicated that this tax difference has had an impact, the evidence is not unanimous.[6] Obviously, the tax legislation in 1986 that equated the taxes on capital gains and losses and on dividends could affect future results.

[5] For a detailed consideration of this, see Fischer Black and Myron Scholes, "The Effects of Dividend Yield and Dividend Policy on Common Stock Prices and Returns," *Journal of Financial Economics* 1, no. 1 (March 1979): 1–22; and Robert Litzenberger and K. Ramaswamy, "The Effect of Personal Taxes and Dividends on Capital Asset Prices: Theory and Empirical Evidence," *Journal of Financial Economics* 7, no. 2 (June 1979): 163–196.

[6] Edwin Elton, Martin Gruber, and Joel Rentzler, "A Single Examination of the Empirical Relationship Between Dividend Yields and Deviations from the CAPM," *Journal of Banking and Finance* 7, no. 1 (March 1983): 135–146; Roger Gordon and David Bradford, "Taxation and the Stock Market Valuation of Capital Gains and Dividends: Theory and Empirical Results," *Journal of Public Economics* 14, no. 4 (October 1980): 109–136; Merton Miller and Myron Scholes, "Dividends and Taxes: Some Empirical Evidence," *Journal of Political Economy* 90, no. 4 (December 1982): 1118–1141; and William Christie, "Dividend Yield and Expected Returns," *Journal of Financial Economics* 28, no. 1 (November–December 1990): 95–125.

EMPIRICAL TESTS
OF THE CAPM

When we discussed the assumptions of capital market theory, we pointed out that a theory should not be judged on the basis of its assumptions, but on *how well it explains the relationships that exist in the real world.* When testing the CAPM, two major questions should concern us. The first is, *how stable is the measure of systematic risk (beta)?* Because beta is our principal risk measure, it is important to know whether past betas can be used as estimates of future betas. Also, what do we know about the alternative published estimates of beta? The second question is basic to the theory: *Is there a positive linear relationship as hypothesized between beta and the rate of return on risky assets?* More specifically, how well do returns conform to the following SML equation:

$$E(R_i) = RFR + \beta_i(R_m - RFR)$$

Some specific questions might include:

- Does the intercept approximate the RFR that prevailed during the period?
- Was the slope of the line positive? Was it consistent with the slope implied by the risk premium $(R_m - RFR)$ that prevailed during the test period?

We consider these two major questions in the following section.

STABILITY OF BETA

Numerous studies have examined the stability of beta and generally reached similar conclusions. Levy examined weekly rates of return for 500 NYSE stocks on the NYSE and concluded that the risk measure was *not* stable for individual stocks over fairly short periods (52 weeks).[7] Alternatively, the stability of the beta for *portfolios* of stocks increased dramatically. Further, the larger the portfolio of stocks (e.g., 25 or 50 stocks) and the longer the period (over 26 weeks), the more stable the beta of the portfolio. Specifically, the correlation of the betas for 50-stock portfolios over 26-week periods averaged above 0.91. Also, the betas tended to regress toward the mean. Specifically, high-beta portfolios tended to decline over time toward unity (1.00), whereas low-beta portfolios tended to increase over time toward unity. A study by Blume for the period 1926 to 1962 provided very similar results.[8]

Fielitz examined the impact of the number of randomly selected securities on the systematic risk of the portfolio and found substantial stability of risk with eight securities.[9] Porter and Ezzell examined the correlation of average betas over contingent periods and found no increase in the correlations as the average size of the portfolio increased.[10] Tole examined the standard deviation of the betas for portfolios of different sizes and agreed with Fielitz that there was substantially greater stability in beta as the portfolio size increased.[11] He also contended that the benefit of larger portfolios extends beyond 100 stocks in the portfolio.

Another factor that affects the stability of beta is how many months are used to estimate the original beta and the test beta. Baesel found that the stability of the individual betas

[7] Robert A. Levy, "On the Short-Term Stationarity of Beta Coefficients," *Financial Analysts Journal* 27, no. 6 (November–December 1971): 55–62.

[8] Marshall E. Blume, "On the Assessment of Risk," *Journal of Finance* 26, no. 1 (March 1971): 1–10.

[9] Bruce Fielitz, "Indirect versus Direct Diversification," *Financial Management* 3, no. 4 (Winter 1974): 54–62.

[10] R. Burr Porter and John R. Ezzell, "A Note on the Predictive Ability of Beta Coefficients," *Journal of Business Research* 3, no. 4 (October 1975): 365–372.

[11] Thomas M. Tole, "How to Maximize Stationarity of Beta," *Journal of Portfolio Management* 7, no. 2 (Winter 1981): 45–49.

increased as the length of the estimation period increased.[12] Altman, Jacquillat, and Levasseur found similar results using French data.[13] Roenfeldt, Griepentrog, and Pflamm (RGP) examined the relationship between the length of the base period and the test period.[14] RGP compared betas derived from 48 months of data to subsequent betas for 12, 24, 36, and 48 months. The 48-month betas were not good for estimating subsequent 12-month betas, but were quite good for estimating 24-, 36-, and 48-month betas.

Theobald derived a set of analytical expressions that explained the Baesel empirical results and partially explained the findings of Roenfeldt, Griepentrog, and Pflamm regarding the improved stability as the period was lengthened.[15] Theobald contended that the optimal length could be over 120 months, assuming the beta did not shift during the period. Chen concluded that the *ordinary least square (OLS)* estimate of portfolio betas would be biased if individual betas were unstable, so he suggested a Bayesian approach to estimating these time-varying betas.[16]

Carpenter and Upton considered the influence of the trading volume on beta stability and found small differences in the betas derived.[17] They contended that the predictions of betas were slightly better using the volume-adjusted betas. This impact of volume on beta estimates is related to the discussion in Chapter 7 on the small-firm effect where it was noted that the estimated beta for low-volume securities was biased downward.

To summarize, individual betas were generally volatile over time whereas portfolio betas were stable. Also, it is important to use at least 36 months of data to estimate beta. Finally, the analyst should be conscious of the stock's trading volume.

COMPARABILITY OF PUBLISHED ESTIMATES OF BETA

In contrast to deriving your own estimate of beta for a stock, you may want to use a published source for speed or convenience such as Merrill Lynch's *Security Risk Evaluation Report* (published monthly) and the weekly *Value Line Investment Survey*. Although the methods of computation differ for these two estimates, both services use the following market model equation:

$$R_i = RFR + \beta_i R_m + E_t$$

Notably, they differ in the data used. Specifically, Merrill Lynch estimates the beta using *60 monthly observations* and the S&P 500 as the market proxy, whereas the *Value Line* estimates beta using *260 weekly observations* and uses the NYSE composite series as the market proxy. They both use an adjustment process because of the regression tendencies, and their adjustment equations differ slightly.

---

[12] Jerome B. Baesel, "On the Assessment of Risk: Some Further Considerations," *Journal of Finance* 29, no. 5 (December 1974): 1491–1494.

[13] Edward Altman, B. Jacquillat, and M. Levasseur, "Comparative Analysis of Risk Measures: France and the United States," *Journal of Finance* 29, no. 5 (December 1974): 1495–1511.

[14] Rodney L. Roenfeldt, Gary L. Griepentrog, and Christopher C. Pflamm, "Further Evidence on the Stationarity of Beta Coefficients," *Journal of Financial and Quantitative Analysis* 13, no. 1 (March 1978): 117–121.

[15] Michael Theobald, "Beta Stationarity and Estimation Period: Some Analytical Results," *Journal of Financial and Quantitative Analysis* 16, no. 5 (December 1981): 747–757.

[16] Son-Nan Chen, "Beta Nonstationarity, Portfolio Residual Risk, and Diversification," *Journal of Financial and Quantitative Analysis* 16, no. 1 (March 1981): 95–111.

[17] Michael D. Carpenter and David E. Upton, "Trading Volume and Beta Stability," *Journal of Portfolio Management* 7, no. 2 (Winter 1981): 60–64.

Given these relatively minor differences, one would probably expect the published betas to be quite comparable. Statman examined the betas for 195 firms for a comparable five-year period and found the following relationship between the adjusted betas:[18]

Merrill Lynch Adjusted Beta = 0.127 + 0.879 Value Line Adjusted Beta

These results are not consistent with equality. Notably, the R^2 was only .55 and did not indicate any systematic bias in the differences. When he examined 19 portfolios of 10 stocks each, the coefficient of determination was almost the same as for individual stocks (.54 versus .55). These results imply a small but significant difference in beta estimates.

Reilly and Wright examined over 1,100 securities for three nonoverlapping periods and confirmed the difference in beta found by Statman.[19] They also indicated that the reason for the difference was the alternative time intervals (i.e., weekly versus monthly observations). Also, they found that the security's market value affected both the size and the direction of the interval effect. Therefore, when estimating beta or using a published source, you must consider the interval used and the firm's relative size.

RELATIONSHIP BETWEEN SYSTEMATIC RISK AND RETURN

The ultimate question regarding the CAPM is whether it is useful in explaining the return on risky assets. Specifically, is there a positive linear relationship between the systematic risk and the rates of return on these risky assets? Sharpe and Cooper found a positive relationship between return and risk, although it was not completely linear (i.e., they found that the returns increased with risk class except for the highest risk classes, where the returns leveled off and declined slightly).[20]

Douglas examined the relationship by analyzing a systematic risk variable and a variance of return measure relative to return.[21] The results indicated intercepts that were larger than the prevailing risk-free rates. Further, although the coefficient for the total risk variable (variance) was generally significant, the coefficients for the systematic risk variables were typically *not* significant.

Miller and Scholes noted that the Douglas results could be caused by errors in measuring stock betas.[22] Unsystematic risk and betas are highly correlated, and the distribution of returns for the stocks was very skewed. These problems were not able to fully explain the Douglas results.

Because of the statistical problems with individual stocks, Black, Jensen, and Scholes examined the risk and return for portfolios of stocks and found a positive linear relationship between monthly excess return and portfolio beta, although the intercept was higher

[18] Meir Statman, "Betas Compared: Merrill Lynch vs. Value Line," *Journal of Portfolio Management* 7, no. 2 (Winter 1981): 41–44.

[19] Frank K. Reilly and David J. Wright, "A Comparison of Published Betas," *Journal of Portfolio Management* 14, no. 3 (Spring 1988): 64–69.

[20] William F. Sharpe and Guy M. Cooper, "Risk–Return Classes of New York Stock Exchange Common Stocks: 1931–1967," *Financial Analysts Journal* 28, no. 2 (March–April 1972): 46–54. A subsequent study that considered yield tilting portfolios confirmed many of these results. See William F. Sharpe and Howard B. Sosin, "Risk, Return, and Yield: New York Stock Exchange Common Stocks: 1928–1969," *Financial Analysts Journal* 32, no. 2 (March–April 1976): 33–42.

[21] G. W. Douglas, "Risk in the Equity Markets: An Empirical Appraisal of Market Efficiency," *Yale Economic Essays* 9, no. 1 (1969): 3–48.

[22] Merton H. Miller and Myron Scholes, "Rates of Return in Relation to Risk: A Re-Examination of Some Recent Findings," in *Studies in the Theory of Capital Markets*, edited by Michael Jensen (New York: Praeger, 1972).

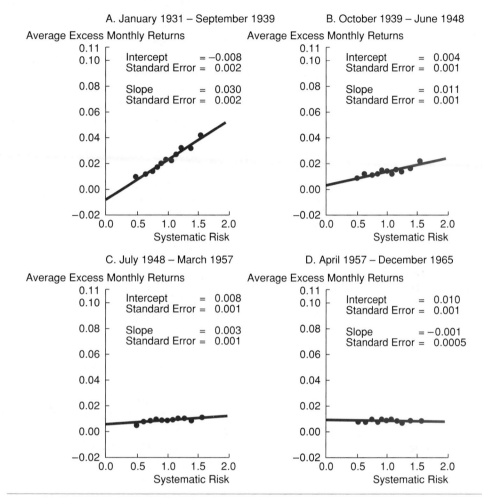

FIGURE 10.4

AVERAGE EXCESS MONTHLY RATES OF RETURN COMPARED TO SYSTEMATIC RISK DURING ALTERNATIVE TIME PERIODS

Source: Michael C. Jensen, ed., *Studies in the Theory of Capital Markets* (New York: Praeger Publishers, 1972): 96–97. Reprinted with permission.

than the zero value expected.[23] Figure 10.4 contains charts from this study, which show that (1) most of the measured SMLs had a positive slope, (2) the slopes change between periods, (3) the intercepts are not zero, and (4) the intercepts likewise change between periods.

Fama and MacBeth examined the relationship between the rates of return during a given month and betas, a beta-squared variable (to test for linearity), and a measure of unsystematic risk during the prior month.[24] Although the monthly results varied over time, the overall results supported the CAPM. The intercept was about equal to that implied by the

[23] Fischer Black, Michael Jensen, and Myron Scholes, "The Capital Asset Pricing Model: Some Empirical Tests" in *Studies in the Theory of Capital Markets,* edited by Michael Jensen (New York: Praeger, 1972).

[24] Eugene Fama and R. MacBeth, "Risk, Return and Equilibrium: Empirical Tests," *Journal of Political Economy* 81, no. 2 (May–June 1973): 453–474.

RFR, the systematic risk coefficient was positive and significant, and neither of the coefficients for beta squared or for unsystematic risk were significant.

EFFECT OF SKEWNESS
ON THE RELATIONSHIP

Beyond the analysis of return and beta, several authors also have considered the impact of skewness on expected returns. You will recall from your statistics course that skewness reflects the presence of too many large positive or negative observations in a distribution. A normal distribution is referred to as symmetric, which means that balance exists between positive and negative observations. In contrast, if a return distribution has positive skewness, it means there is an abnormal number of large positive price changes.

Investigators considered skewness as a means to possibly explain the prior results wherein the model appeared to underprice low-beta stocks (so investors received returns above expectations) and overprice high-beta stocks (so investors received returns lower than expected). McEnally found results such as these, but also found that high-beta stocks had high positive skewness.[25] These results could be explained by investors who prefer stocks with high risk and high positive skewness that provide an opportunity for very large returns.

Kraus and Litzenberger examined this relationship more formally by testing a CAPM with a skewness term and found results that confirmed that investors are willing to pay for positive skewness.[26] They concluded that their three-moment CAPM corrects for the apparent mispricing of high- and low-risk stocks encountered with the standard CAPM. Subsequent testing of the model by Friend and Westerfield derived mixed results, but the importance of skewness was supported in studies by Sears and Wei and most recently by Lim.[27]

EFFECT OF SIZE, P/E,
AND LEVERAGE

We know from our discussion in Chapter 7 dealing with the efficient markets hypothesis (EMH) that there has been extensive analysis of the size effect (the small-firm anomaly) and the P/E effect. Both of these variables were shown to have an inverse impact on returns after considering the CAPM. One could interpret these results as implying that these variables (size and P/E) are additional risk factors that need to be considered along with beta (similar to the skewness argument). Specifically, expected returns are a positive function of beta and a negative function of relative size, wherein investors require higher returns from relatively small firms even after allowing for beta. Investors would have a similar additional return requirement for stocks with relatively low P/E ratios.

An analysis by Bhandari finds that financial leverage (measured by the debt/equity ratio) also helps explain the cross section of average returns after both beta and size are considered.[28] This would imply a multivariate CAPM with three risk variables: beta, size, and financial leverage.

[25] Richard McEnally, "A Note on the Return Behavior of High Risk Common Stocks," *Journal of Finance* 29, no. 2 (May 1974): 199–202.

[26] Alan Kraus and Robert Litzenberger, "Skewness Preference and the Valuation of Risky Assets," *Journal of Finance* 31, no. 4 (September 1976): 1085–1094.

[27] Irwin Friend and Randolph Westerfield, "Co-Skewness and Capital Asset Pricing," *Journal of Finance* 35, no. 4 (September 1980): 897–914; R. Stephen Sears and John Wei, "The Structure of Skewness Preferences in Asset Pricing Models with Higher Moments," *Financial Review* 23, no. 1 (February 1988): 25–38; and Kian-Guan Lim, "A New Test of the Three-Moment Capital Asset Pricing Model," *Journal of Financial and Quantitative Analysis* 24, no. 2 (June 1989): 205–216.

[28] Laxims Chand Bhandari, "Debt/Equity Ratio and Expected Common Stock Returns: Empirical Evidence," *Journal of Finance* 43, no. 2 (June 1988): 507–528.

EFFECT OF BOOK-TO-MARKET VALUE: THE FAMA-FRENCH STUDY

A recent study that examined the viability and usefulness of the CAPM is quite damaging not only because of the depth of the analysis, but also because one of the authors, Eugene Fama, has been a great supporter of the CAPM. The purpose of the study by Fama and French was to evaluate the joint roles of market beta, size, E/P, financial leverage, and the book-to-market equity ratio in the cross section of average returns on the NYSE, AMEX, and NASDAQ stocks.[29] Some of the earlier studies (including Fama-MacBeth) found a significant positive relationship between returns and beta. In contrast, this study finds that the relationship between beta and the average rate of return disappears during the more recent period 1963 to 1990, even when beta is used alone to explain average returns. In contrast, univariate tests between average returns and size, leverage, E/P, and book-to-market equity (BE/ME) indicate that all of these variables are significant and have the expected sign.

In the multivariate tests, the results contained in Table 10.1 show that the negative relationship between size [ln (ME)] and average returns is robust to the inclusion of other variables. Further, the positive relation between BE/ME and average returns also persists when the other variables are included. Interestingly, when both of these variables are included, the book-to-market value ratio (BE/ME) has the consistently stronger role in explaining average returns. The joint effect of size and BE/ME are shown in Table 7.1. The top row shows the univariate results and confirms the positive relationship between return versus the book-to-market ratio—i.e., as the book-to-market ratio increases, the returns go from 0.64 to 1.63. The left-hand column shows the negative relationship between return and size—i.e., as the size declines, the returns increase from 0.89 to 1.47. The body of the table shows that even within a size class, the returns increase with the BE/ME ratio. Similarly, within a BE/ME decile, there is generally a negative relationship for size. Hence, it is not surprising that the single highest average return is in the upper, right-hand corner (1.92), which is the portfolio with the smallest size and highest BE/ME stocks.

The authors conclude that between 1963 and 1990, size and book-to-market equity capture the cross-sectional variation in average stock returns associated with size, E/P, book-to-market equity, and leverage. Moreover, of the two variables, the book-to-market equity ratio seems to be more powerful and appears to subsume E/P and leverage.[30] Following these results, Fama-French suggested the use of a three-factor CAPM model and used this model in a subsequent study to explain a number of the anomalies from prior studies.[31]

SUMMARY OF CAPM RISK–RETURN EMPIRICAL RESULTS

Most of the early evidence regarding the relationship between rates of return and systematic risk of portfolios indicated support for the CAPM. Still, the evidence was not without question because it was found that the intercepts were generally higher than implied by the

---

[29] Eugene F. Fama and Kenneth French, "The Cross Section of Expected Stock Returns," *Journal of Finance* 47, no. 2 (June 1992): 427–465.

[30] A prior study that documented the importance of the BE/ME ratio was Barr Rosenberg, Kenneth Reid, and Ronald Lanstein, "Persuasive Evidence of Market Inefficiency," *Journal of Portfolio Management* 11, no. 3 (Spring 1985): 9–17. The relationship was confirmed in the Japanese market in Louis K. Chan, Yasusho Hamao, and Josef Lakonishok, "Fundamentals and Stock Returns in Japan," *Journal of Finance* 46, no. 5 (December 1991): 1739–1764.

[31] The three-factor model was suggested in Eugene F. Fama and Kenneth French, "Common Risk Factors in the Returns on Stocks and Bonds," *Journal of Financial Economics* 33, no. 1 (February 1993): 3–56. The model was used in Eugene F. Fama and Kenneth French, "Multifactor Explanations of Asset Pricing Anomalies," *Journal of Finance* 51, no. 1 (March 1996): 55–84.

TABLE 10.1

AVERAGE SLOPES (*t*-STATISTICS) FROM MONTH-BY-MONTH REGRESSIONS OF STOCK RETURNS ON β, SIZE, BOOK-TO-MARKET EQUITY, LEVERAGE, AND E/P: JULY 1963 TO DECEMBER 1990

Stocks are assigned the post-ranking β of the size-β portfolio they are in at the end of June of year *t*. BE is the book value of common equity plus balance-sheet deferred taxes, A is total book assets, and E is earnings (income before extraordinary items, plus income-statement deferred taxes, minus preferred dividends). BE, A, and E are for each firm's latest fiscal year ending in calendar year *t* − 1. The accounting ratios are measured using market equity ME in December of year *t* − 1. Firm size ln(ME) is measured in June of year *t*. In the regressions, these values of the explanatory variables for individual stocks are matched with returns for the CRSP tapes from the University of Chicago for the months from July of year *t* to June of year *t* + 1. The gap between the accounting data and the returns ensures that the accounting data are available prior to the returns. If earnings are positive, E(+)/P is the ratio of total earnings to market equity and E/P dummy is 0. If earnings are negative, E(+)/P is 0 and E/P dummy is 1.

The average slope is the time-series average of the monthly regression slopes for July 1963 to December 1990, and the *t*-statistic is the average slope divided by its time-series standard error.

On average, there are 2,267 stocks in the monthly regressions. To avoid giving extreme observations heavy weight in the regressions, the smallest and largest 0.5% of the observations of E(+)/P, BE/ME, A/ME, and A/BE are set equal to the next largest or smallest values of the ratios (the 0.005 and 0.995 fractiles). This has no effect on inferences.

β	ln(ME)	ln(BE/ME)	ln(A/ME)	ln(A/BE)	E/P Dummy	E(+)/P
0.15 (0.46)						
	−0.15 (−2.58)					
−0.37 (−1.21)	−0.17 (−3.41)					
		0.50 (5.71)				
			0.50 (5.69)	−0.57 (−5.34)		
					0.57 (2.28)	4.72 (4.57)
	−0.11 (−1.99)	0.35 (4.44)				
	−0.11 (−2.06)		0.35 (4.32)	−0.50 (−4.56)		
	−0.16 (−3.06)				0.06 (0.38)	2.99 (3.04)
	−0.13 (−2.47)	0.33 (4.46)			−0.14 (−0.90)	0.87 (1.23)
	−0.13 (−2.47)		0.32 (4.28)	−0.46 (−4.45)	−0.08 (−0.56)	1.15 (1.57)

Source: Eugene F. Fama and Kenneth French, "The Cross Section of Expected Stock Returns," *Journal of Finance* 47, no. 2 (June 1992): 439. Reprinted by permission.

RFR that prevailed, which is either consistent with a zero–beta model or the existence of higher borrowing rates. In a search for other variables that could explain the above-expected return for low-beta stocks and the below-expected returns for high-beta stocks, additional variables were considered. Several studies indicated support for including the third moment of the distribution (skewness) as a variable, assuming that investors preferred positive skewness and were willing to accept lower average rates of return for the opportunity for very large returns. The results indicated that positive skewness and high betas were correlated.

The efficient markets literature has provided extensive evidence that both size and the P/E ratio were variables that could help explain cross-sectional returns in addition to beta. Recent studies also have found that financial leverage and the book-to-market value of equity ratio (i.e., B/P ratio) have explanatory power regarding returns beyond beta.

The Fama-French study considered most of the other variables suggested and concluded that between 1963 and 1990, beta was not related to average returns on stocks when included with other variables, or when considered alone. Moreover, the two dominant variables were size and the book value to market value ratio, which was even stronger than size although both variables were significant.

Given the significance of the Fama-French study, several studies followed that considered these results. First, a study by Dennis, Perfect, Snow, and Wiles confirmed the Fama-French results.[32] They not only confirmed the optimal combination involved portfolios of small firms with high BV/MV ratios, but showed that this superiority prevailed after assuming 1 percent transaction costs and annual rebalancing. They subsequently showed that the optimal results were derived if one assumes rebalancing every four years. Alternatively, two studies came out with contrary results related to the importance of beta. In contrast to Fama-French who measure beta with monthly returns, Kothari, Shanken, and Sloan (KSS) measure beta with annual returns to avoid trading problems involved with using monthly data.[33] Using annual betas, KSS found that there was substantial compensation for beta risk. They suggested that the relationship between rates of return and the BV/MV ratio may have been periodic to this time frame and might not be significant over a longer period. A study by Pettengill, Dundaram, and Matthur noted that empirical studies typically use realized returns to test the CAPM model when theory specifies expected returns.[34] When the authors adjust for expectations concerning negative market excess returns, they find a consistent and significant relationship between beta and rates of return. Jagannathan and Wang also employ a conditional CAPM that allows for changes in betas and the market risk premium.[35] It is shown that this specification of the model performs well in explaining the cross section of returns. Grundy and Malkiel also contend that beta is a very useful measure of risk during declining markets, which is when it is important.[36]

THE MARKET PORTFOLIO: THEORY VERSUS PRACTICE

Throughout our presentation of the CAPM, we noted that the market portfolio included *all* the risky assets in the economy. Further, in equilibrium, the various assets would be included in the portfolio in proportion of their market value. Therefore, this market portfolio should contain not only U.S. stocks and bonds, but also real estate, options, art, stamps, coins, foreign stocks and bonds, and so on, with weights equal to their relative market value.

Although this concept of a market portfolio is reasonable in theory, it is difficult—if not impossible—to implement when testing or using the CAPM. The easy part is getting a

[32] Patrick Dennis, Steven Perfect, Karl Snow, and Kenneth Wiles, "The Effects of Rebalancing on Size and Book-to-Market Ratio Portfolio Returns," *Financial Analysts Journal* 51, no. 3 (May–June 1995): 47–57.

[33] S. P. Kothari, Jay Shanken, and Richard G. Sloan, "Another Look at the Cross Section of Expected Stock Returns," *Journal of Finance* 50, no. 2 (March 1995): 185–224.

[34] Glenn Pettengill, Sridhar Dundaram, and Ike Matthur, "The Conditional Relation Between Beta and Returns," *Journal of Financial and Quantitative Analysis* 30, no. 1 (March 1995): 101–115.

[35] Ravi Jagannathan and Zhenyu Wang, "The Conditional CAPM and the Cross Section of Expected Returns," *Journal of Finance* 51, no. 1 (March 1996): 3–53.

[36] Kevin Grundy and Burton Malkiel, "Reports of Beta's Death Have Been Greatly Exaggerated," *Journal of Portfolio Management* 22, no. 3 (Spring 1996): 36–44.

stock series for the NYSE, the AMEX, and major world stock exchanges such as Tokyo, London, and Germany. There are stock series for the OTC market, too, but these series generally are incomplete. Also, as noted in Chapter 5, there is a growing number of world stock indexes. There also are some well-regarded U.S. bond series available (e.g., from Lehman Brothers, Merrill Lynch, Ryan Labs, and Salomon Brothers) and several world bond series (e.g., from J.P. Morgan, Salomon Brothers, and Merrill Lynch). Because of the difficulty in deriving series that are available monthly in a timely fashion for the numerous other assets mentioned, most studies have limited themselves to using a stock or bond series alone. In fact, the vast majority of studies have chosen the S&P 500 series or some other NYSE stock series that is obviously limited to only U.S. stocks, which constitutes *less than 20 percent* of a truly global risky asset portfolio (see Figure 2.1). At best, it was assumed that the particular series used as a proxy for the market portfolio was highly correlated with the true market portfolio.

Most academicians recognize this potential problem but assume that the deficiency is not serious. Several articles by Roll, however, concluded that, on the contrary, the use of these indexes as a proxy for the market portfolio had very serious implications for tests of the model and especially for using the model when evaluating portfolio performance.[37] Roll referred to it as a **benchmark error** because the practice is to compare the performance of a portfolio manager to the return of an unmanaged portfolio of equal risk—that is, the market portfolio adjusted for risk would be the benchmark. Roll's point is that if the benchmark is mistakenly specified, you cannot measure the performance of a portfolio manager properly. A mistakenly specified market portfolio can have two effects. First, the beta computed for alternative portfolios would be wrong because the market portfolio used to compute the portfolio's systematic risk is inappropriate. Second, the SML derived would be wrong because it goes from the RFR through the improperly specified M portfolio. Figure 10.5 shows an example where the true portfolio risk (β_T) is underestimated (β_e) possibly because of the proxy market portfolio used in computing the estimated beta. As shown, the portfolio being evaluated may appear to be above the SML using β_e, which would imply superior management. If, in fact, the true risk (β_T) is greater, the portfolio will shift to the right and be below the SML, which would indicate inferior performance.

Figure 10.6 indicates that the intercept and slope will differ if (1) there is an error in selecting a proper risk-free asset and (2) if the market portfolio selected is not the correct mean-variance efficient portfolio. Obviously, it is very possible that under these conditions, a portfolio judged to be superior relative to the first SML (i.e., the portfolio plotted above the measured SML) could be inferior relative to the true SML (i.e., the portfolio would plot below the true SML).

Roll contends that a test of the CAPM requires an analysis of whether the proxy used to represent the market portfolio is mean-variance efficient (on the Markowitz efficient frontier) and whether it is the true optimum market portfolio. Roll showed that if the proxy market portfolio (e.g., the S&P 500 index) is mean-variance efficient, it is mathematically possible to show a linear relationship between returns and betas derived with this portfolio. Unfortunately, this is not a true test of the CAPM because you are not working with the true SML (see Figure 10.7).

[37]Richard Roll, "A Critique of the Asset Pricing Theory's Tests," *Journal of Financial Economics* 4, no. 4 (March 1977): 129–176; Richard Roll, "Ambiguity when Performance Is Measured by the Securities Market Line," *Journal of Finance* 33, no. 4 (September 1978): 1051–1069; Richard Roll, "Performance Evaluation and Benchmark Error I," *Journal of Portfolio Management* 6, no. 4 (Summer 1980): 5–12; and Richard Roll, "Performance Evaluation and Benchmark Error II," *Journal of Portfolio Management* 7, no. 2 (Winter 1981): 17–22. This discussion draws heavily from these articles.

FIGURE 10.5

DIFFERENTIAL PERFORMANCE BASED ON AN ERROR IN ESTIMATING SYSTEMATIC RISK

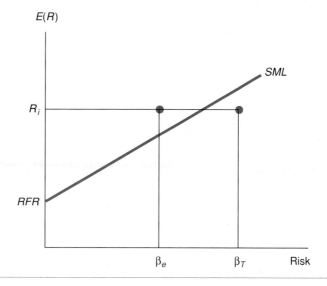

FIGURE 10.6

DIFFERENTIAL SML BASED ON MEASURED RISK-FREE ASSET AND PROXY MARKET PORTFOLIO

FIGURE 10.7   **DIFFERENTIAL SML USING MARKET PROXY THAT IS MEAN-VARIANCE EFFICIENT**

A demonstration of the impact of the benchmark problem is provided in a study by Reilly and Akhtar.[38] Table 10.2 shows the substantial difference in average beta for the 30 stocks in the DJIA during three alternative periods using three different proxies for the market portfolio: (1) the S&P 500 Index, (2) the Morgan Stanley World Stock Index, and (3) the Brinson Partners Global Security Market Index (GSMI). The GSMI includes not only U.S. and international stocks, but also U.S. and international bonds. The results in Table 10.2 are as one would expect because, as we know from Chapter 9, beta is equal to:

$$\text{Beta} = \frac{\text{Cov}_{i,m}}{\sigma_m^2}$$

where

$\text{Cov}_{i,m}$ = the covariance between asset i and the m portfolio
σ_m^2 = the variance of the m portfolio

As we change from an all U.S. stock index to a world stock index (M-S World) or a world stock and bond index (GSMI), we would expect the covariance with U.S. stocks to decline. The other component is the standard deviation for the market portfolio. As shown in the table, typically the M-S World Stock Index has a smaller variance than the S&P 500 because it is more diversified with international stocks. Therefore, while both covariance and market variance decline, the covariance effect dominates, so the beta is smaller with the M-S World Stock Index. In contrast, although the covariance between the U.S. stocks

[38] Frank K. Reilly and Rashid A. Akhtar, "The Benchmark Error Problem with Global Capital Markets," *Journal of Portfolio Management* 22, no. 1 (Fall 1995): 33–52.

| TABLE 10.2 | **AVERAGE BETA FOR THE 30 STOCKS IN THE DOW JONES INDUSTRIAL AVERAGE DURING ALTERNATIVE TIME PERIODS USING DIFFERENT PROXIES FOR THE MARKET PORTFOLIOS** |

	ALTERNATIVE MARKET PROXIES		
Time Period	S&P 500	M-S World	Brinson GSMI
1983–1988			
Average beta	0.820	0.565	1.215
Mean index return	0.014	0.017	0.014
Standard deviation of index returns	0.049	0.043	0.031
1989–1994			
Average beta	0.991	0.581	1.264
Mean index return	0.010	0.004	0.008
Standard deviation of index returns	0.036	0.043	0.026
1983–1994			
Average beta	0.880	0.606	1.223
Mean index return	0.012	0.011	0.011
Standard deviation of index returns	0.043	0.043	0.029

Source: Frank K. Reilly and Rashid A. Akhtar, "The Benchmark Error Problem with Global Capital Markets," *Journal of Portfolio Management* 22, no. 1 (Fall 1995): 33–52.

and the GSMI also is lower, the variance of the highly diversified GSMI market portfolio is substantially lower (about 25–33 percent). As a result, the beta is substantially larger (about 27 percent to 48 percent larger) when the Brinson Partners Index is used rather than the S&P 500 Index. Notably, the Brinson Index has a composition of assets that is substantially closer to the "true" M portfolio than either of the other proxies that only contain U.S. stocks or global stocks.

There also was a difference in the SMLs implied by each of the market proxies that only contain U.S. stocks or global stocks. Table 10.3 contains the average RFR, the market returns, and the slope of the SML during the three time periods for the three indexes and for market series from Japan (Nikkei), Germany (FAZ), and the United Kingdom (FT All-Share). Clearly, the slopes differ dramatically among the alternative indexes and over time. Needless to say, the benchmark used does make a difference.

Finally, it is necessary to combine the estimate of systematic risk (beta) with the estimated SML to determine the combined effect on the required rate of return for an asset. Table 10.4 shows that during specific time periods the difference between the highest and the lowest expected return ranges from about 4 percent to 7.5 percent, with the highest expected returns when the market proxy was the Brinson GSMI because of the high betas. The differences for individual stocks were similar (i.e., a range of about 4–5 percent), which can have a substantial impact on valuation.

In summary, the concern is that an incorrect market proxy will affect the beta risk measures as well as the position and slope of the SML that is used to evaluate portfolio performance. In general, the errors will tend to overestimate the performance of portfolio managers because the proxy used for the market portfolio is probably not as efficient as the true market portfolio, so the slope of the SML will be underestimated. Also, the beta generally will be underestimated because the true market portfolio will have a lower variance due to greater diversification.

TABLE 10.3	COMPONENTS OF SECURITY MARKET LINES USING ALTERNATIVE MARKET PROXIES								
	1983–1988			**1989–1994**			**1983–1994**		
	R_m	RFR	$(R_m - RFR)$	R_m	RFR	$(R_m - RFR)$	R_m	RFR	$(R_m - RFR)$
S&P 500	18.20	8.31	9.90	13.07	5.71	7.36	15.61	7.01	8.60
Nikkei	26.05	5.35	20.70	−3.62	4.70	−8.32	10.30	5.02	5.28
FAZ	16.36	5.01	11.35	7.97	7.83	0.14	12.09	6.42	5.67
FT AllShare	18.01	10.00	8.01	10.09	10.07	0.02	13.99	10.03	3.95
M-S World	22.64	8.31	14.33	5.18	5.71	−0.52	13.60	7.01	6.60
Brinson GSMI	18.53	8.31	10.22	10.18	5.71	4.48	14.28	7.01	7.28

RFR = risk-free return.

Source: Frank K. Reilly and Rashid Akhtar, "The Benchmark Error Problem with Global Capital Markets," *Journal of Portfolio Management* 22, no. 1 (Fall 1995): 33–52.

TABLE 10.4	THE AVERAGE EXPECTED RETURNS FOR STOCKS IN THE DJIA BASED ON DIFFERENT BETAS AND SECURITY MARKET LINES DERIVED WITH ALTERNATIVE BENCHMARKS

	MEAN EXPECTED RATE OF RETURN		
Time Period	S&P 500	M-S World	Brinson GSMI
1983–1988	16.41	17.72	20.75
1989–1994	13.00	5.40	11.36

Source: Frank K. Reilly and Rashid A. Akhtar, "The Benchmark Error Problem with Global Capital Markets," *Journal of Portfolio Management* 22, no. 1 (Fall 1995): 33–52.

Roll's benchmark problems, however, do not invalidate the value of the CAPM as *a normative model of asset pricing;* they only indicate a problem in *measurement* when attempting to test the theory and when using this model for evaluating portfolio performance. Therefore, it is necessary to develop a better market portfolio proxy similar to the Brinson GSMI and/or adjust the portfolio performance measures to reflect this measurement problem.

ARBITRAGE PRICING THEORY (APT)

At this point, we have discussed the basic theory of the CAPM, the impact of changing some of its major assumptions, the empirical evidence that does and does not support the theory, and its dependence on a market portfolio of all risky assets. In addition, the model assumes that investors have quadratic utility functions and that the distribution of security prices is normal (symmetrically distributed), with a variance term that can be estimated.

The tests of the CAPM indicated that the beta coefficients for individual securities were not stable, but the portfolio betas generally were stable assuming long enough sample periods and adequate trading volume. There was mixed support for a positive linear relationship between rates of return and systematic risk for portfolios of stock, with some recent evidence indicating the need to consider additional risk variables or a need for different risk proxies. In addition, several papers by Roll criticized the tests of the model and the usefulness of the model in portfolio evaluation because of its dependence on a market portfolio of risky assets that is not currently available.

Consequently, the academic community has considered an alternative asset pricing theory that is reasonably intuitive and that requires only limited assumptions. This *arbi-*

trage pricing theory (APT), developed by Ross in the early 1970s and initially published in 1976, has three major assumptions:[39]

1. Capital markets are perfectly competitive.
2. Investors always prefer more wealth to less wealth with certainty.
3. The stochastic process generating asset returns can be expressed as a linear function of a set of K factors or indexes (to be described).

Equally important, the following major assumptions are *not* required: (1) quadratic utility function, (2) normally distributed security returns, and (3) a market portfolio that contains all risky assets and is mean-variance efficient. Obviously, if such a theory can explain differential security prices, it would be considered a superior theory to the CAPM because it is simpler (i.e., it requires fewer assumptions). Prior to discussing the empirical tests of the model, we provide a brief review of the basics of the model. The following review of the APT model is very similar to the discussion in Chapter 9. It is repeated here for the reader's convenience.

As noted, the theory assumes that the stochastic process generating asset returns can be represented as a K factor model of the form

$$R_i = E_i + b_{i1}\delta_1 + b_{i2}\delta_2 + \ldots + b_{ik}\delta_k + \epsilon_i \quad \text{for } i = 1 \text{ to } N$$

where

R_i = **return on asset i during a specified time period, i = 1, 2, 3, . . . m**
E_i = **expected return for asset i if all of the factors or indexes have zero changes**
b_{ik} = **reaction in asset i's returns to movements in a common factor K or index K**
δ_k = **a set of common factors or indexes with a zero mean that influences the returns on all assets**
ϵ_i = **a unique effect on asset i's return (i.e., a random error term that, by assumption, is completely diversifiable in large portfolios and has a mean of zero)**
N = **number of assets**

Two terms require elaboration: δ_k and b_{ik}. As indicated, δ terms are the *multiple* factors expected to have an impact on the returns of *all* assets. Examples of these factors might include inflation, growth in GDP, major political upheavals, or changes in interest rates. The APT contends that there are many such factors that affect returns, in contrast to the CAPM, where the only relevant risk variable is the covariance of the asset with the market portfolio (i.e., the asset's beta).

Given these common factors, the b_{ik} terms determine how each asset reacts to a particular common factor. To extend the earlier example, although all assets may be affected by growth in GDP, the impact (i.e., reaction) to a factor will differ. For example, stocks of cyclical firms will have larger b_{ik} terms for the "growth in GDP" factor than noncyclical firms such as grocery chains. Likewise, you will hear discussions about interest-sensitive stocks. All stocks are affected by changes in interest rates; however, some experience larger impacts. For example, an interest-sensitive stock would have a b_k for interest of 2.0 or more, whereas a stock that is relatively insensitive to interest rates would have a b_k of 0.5. Other examples of common factors include inflation, exchange rates, and interest rate spreads. Notably, when we apply the theory, *the factors are not identified.* That is, when we discuss the empirical studies, the investigators will note that they found three, four, or five

---

[39] Stephen Ross, "The Arbitrage Theory of Capital Asset Pricing," *Journal of Economic Theory* 13, no. 2 (December 1976): 341–360; and Stephen Ross, "Return, Risk, and Arbitrage," in *Risk and Return in Finance,* edited by I. Friend and J. Bicksler (Cambridge: Ballinger, 1977), 189–218.

factors that affect security returns, but *they will give no indication of what these factors represent.*

Similar to the CAPM model, it is assumed that the unique effects (ϵ_i) are independent and will be diversified away in a large portfolio. The APT assumes that in equilibrium the return on a zero-investment, zero-systematic-risk portfolio is zero when the unique effects are diversified away. This assumption and some theory from linear algebra imply that the expected return on any asset i (E_i) can be expressed as

$$E_0 = \lambda_0 + \lambda_1 b_{i1} + \lambda_2 b_{i2} + \ldots + \lambda_k b_{ik},$$

where

λ_0 = the expected return on an asset with zero systematic risk where $\lambda_0 = E_0$

λ_i = the risk premium related to each of the common factors—for example, the risk premium related to the interest rate risk factor ($\lambda_i = E_i - E_0$).

b_i = the pricing relationship between the risk premium and asset i—that is, how responsive asset i is to this common factor K

For example, if we assume that the risk premium related to interest rate sensitivity is .02 and a stock that is sensitive to interest rates has a β_k (where K is interest rate sensitivity) of 2.0, this means that this factor would cause the stock's expected return to increase by 4 percent ($K = 2.0 \times .02$). Consider the following example of two stocks and a two-factor model.

K_1 = changes in the rate of inflation. The risk premium related to this factor is 1 percent for every 1 percent change in the rate ($\lambda_1 = .01$).

K_2 = percent growth in real GDP. The average risk premium related to this factor is 2 percent for every 1 percent change in the rate of growth ($\lambda_2 = 0.02$).

λ_0 = the rate of return on a zero-systematic risk asset (zero beta: $b_{0j} = 0$) is 3 percent ($\lambda_0 = .03$)

The two assets (X, Y) have the following response coefficients to these factors:

b_{x1} = the response of asset X to changes in the rate of inflation is 0.50 ($b_{x1} = .50$). This asset is not very responsive to changes in the rate of inflation.

b_{y1} = the response of asset Y to changes in the rate of inflation is 2.00 ($b_{y1} = 2.00$)

b_{x2} = the response of asset X to changes in the growth rate of real GDP is 1.50 ($b_{x2} = 1.50$)

b_{y2} = the response of asset Y to changes in the growth rate of real GDP is 1.75 ($b_{y2} = 1.75$)

These response coefficients indicate that if these are the major factors influencing asset returns, asset Y is a higher risk asset, and therefore, its expected return should be greater. The overall expected return equation will be

$$E_i = \lambda_0 + \lambda_1 b_{i1} + \lambda_2 b_{i2}$$
$$= .03 + (.01)b_{i1} + (.02)b_{i2}$$

Therefore:

$$E_x = .03 + (.01)(0.50) + (.02)(1.50)$$
$$= .065 = 6.5\%$$
$$E_y = .03 + (.01)(2.00) + (.02)(1.75)$$
$$= .085 = 8.5\%$$

If the prices of the assets do not reflect these expected returns, we would expect investors to enter into arbitrage arrangements whereby they would sell overpriced assets short and use the proceeds to purchase the underpriced assets until the relevant prices were corrected. Given these linear relationships, it should be possible to find an asset or a combination of assets with equal risk to the mispriced asset, yet provide a higher expected return.

EMPIRICAL TESTS OF THE APT

Although the APT is relatively new, it has undergone numerous empirical studies. Before we begin discussing the empirical tests, remember the earlier caveat that when applying the theory, we do not know what the factors generated by the statistical model represent. This becomes a major point in some discussions of test results.

ROLL-ROSS STUDY

The Roll and Ross test followed a two-step procedure:[40]

1. Estimate the expected returns and the factor coefficients from time-series data on individual asset returns.
2. Use these estimates to test the basic cross-sectional pricing conclusion implied by the APT. Specifically, are the expected returns for these assets consistent with the common factors derived in Step 1?

Roll and Ross tested the following pricing relationship:

H_0: There exist nonzero constants $(E_0, \lambda_i, \ldots, \lambda_k)$ such that
$$E_1 - E_0 = \lambda_1 b_{i1} + \lambda_2 b_{i2} + \ldots + \lambda_k b_{ik}.$$

The specific b_i coefficients were estimated using factor analysis. The authors pointed out that the estimation procedure was generally appropriate for the model involved, but there is very little known about the small sample properties of the results. Therefore, they emphasized the tentative nature of the conclusions.

The data file was daily returns for the period July 1962 through December 1972. Stocks were put into 42 portfolios of 30 stocks each (1,260 stocks) by alphabetical order. The estimation of the factor model indicated that the maximum reasonable number of factors was five. The factors derived were applied to all 42 portfolios, with the understanding that the importance of the various factors might differ among portfolios (e.g., the first factor in Portfolio A might not be first in Portfolio B).

Assuming a risk-free rate of 6 percent ($\lambda_0 = .06$), the subsequent analysis indicated at least three important pricing factors, but probably not more than four. Further, the weight on the first two factors was quite heavy with changes in relative weights for the remaining three factors. When they allowed the model to estimate the risk-free rate (λ_0), only two factors were consistently significant, which indicates that the earlier estimate of three factors may have been an overestimate.

A subsequent test related returns to a security's own standard deviation, which should not affect expected return if the APT is valid because a security's diversifiable component would be eliminated by diversification, and the nondiversifiable components should be explained by the factor loadings. The test analyzed returns against the five factors plus the security's own standard deviation. The initial results indicated that the security's own standard deviation was statistically significant, which was evidence against the APT. Subsequently, they adjusted the results for skewness and found that the security's own standard deviation was insignificant, which supports the APT.

---

[40] Richard Roll and Stephen A. Ross, "An Empirical Investigation of the Aribtrate Pricing Theory," *Journal of Finance* 35, no. 5 (December 1980): 1073–1103.

Finally, they tested whether the three or four factors that affect Group A were the same as the factors that affect Group B. The analysis involved testing for cross-sectional consistency by examining whether the λ_0 terms for the 42 groups are similar. The results yielded no evidence that the intercept terms were different, although the test was admittedly weak. The authors concluded that the evidence generally supported the APT, but acknowledged that these initial tests were weak.

EXTENSIONS OF THE ROLL-ROSS TESTS

Cho, Elton, and Gruber tested the model by examining the number of factors in the return-generating process that were priced.[41] Because the APT model contends that more factors affect stock returns than are implied by the CAPM, they examined different sets of data to determine what happened to the number of factors priced in the model compared to prior studies that found between three and five significant factors. They simulated returns using the zero–beta CAPM with betas derived from Wilshire's fundamental betas and with betas derived from historical data. They found that five factors were required using the Roll-Ross procedures. The results using historical betas implied six factors were necessary, whereas the Wilshire fundamental betas indicated a need for three factors.

The authors concluded that even when returns are generated by a two-factor model, two or three factors are required to explain the returns. These results support the APT model because it allows for the consideration of these additional factors, which is not possible with the classical CAPM.

Dhrymes, Friend, and Gultekin (DFG) reexamined the techniques used in prior studies and contended that these techniques have several major limitations.[42] Although the division of the total sample of stocks into numerous portfolios of 30 stocks was necessary because of computer limitations, this practical constraint produced results that differed from large sample results, especially for the total sample of over 1,000 stocks. Specifically, they found *no* relationship between the "factor loading" for groups of 30 stocks and for a group of 240 stocks.

Also, DFG could not identify the actual number of factors that characterize the return-generating process. When they applied the model to portfolios of different size, the number of factors changed. For example, for 15 securities, it is a two-factor model; for 30 securities, a three-factor model; for 45, a four-factor model; for 60, a six-factor model; and for 90, a nine-factor model. Also, with multiple factors it was difficult to know which of them were significant in explaining the returns.

Roll and Ross acknowledged that the factors differ with 30 stocks versus 240, but contended that the important consideration is whether the resulting estimates are *consistent* because it is not feasible to consider all of the stocks together.[43] When they tested for consistency, the model was generally supported. They point out that the number of factors is a secondary issue compared to how well the model explains the return-generating process compared to alternative models. Also, one would *expect* the number of factors to increase with the sample size because more potential relationships would arise (e.g., you would introduce industry effects). The relevant question is, how many of these factors are significant in a diversified portfolio?

[41] D. Chinhyung Cho, Edwin J. Elton, and Martin J. Gruber, "On the Robustness of the Roll and Ross Arbitrage Pricing Theory," *Journal of Financial and Quantitative Analysis* 19, no. 1 (March 1984): 1–10.

[42] Phoebus J. Dhrymes, Irwin Friend, and N. Bulent Gultekin, "A Critical Re-Examination of the Empirical Evidence on the Arbitrage Pricing Theory," *Journal of Finance* 39, no. 2 (June 1984): 323–346.

[43] Richard Roll and Stephen Ross, "A Critical Re-Examination of the Empirical Evidence on the Arbitrage Pricing Theory: A Reply," *Journal of Finance* 39, no. 2 (June 1984): 347–350.

Dhrymes, Friend, Gultekin, and Gultekin repeated the prior tests for larger groups of securities.[44] When they increased the number of securities in each group (30, 60, and 90 securities), both the number of factors that entered the model and the number of significant ("priced") factors increased, although most factors are not "priced." These results confirmed the DFG results. In addition, they found that the unique or total standard deviation for a period was as good at predicting subsequent returns as the factor loadings. Also, the number of time-series observations affected the number of factors discovered, and the group size of securities affected the model's intercept. These findings are not favorable to the empirical relevance of APT because they indicate extreme instability in the relationships and suggest that the risk-free rate implied by the model depends on group size and the number of observations. Also the fact that the total standard deviation is significant is discouraging.

THE APT AND ANOMALIES

An alternative set of tests of the APT considers how well it explains anomalies that are not explained by a competing model. Two anomalies considered are the small-firm effect and the January anomaly.

Reinganum addressed the APT's ability to account for the differences in average returns between small firms and large firms.[45] Reinganum contended that this anomaly, which could not be explained by the CAPM, should be explained by the APT if the APT was to be considered a superior theory or an empirical replacement for the CAPM. Reinganum's test is conducted in two stages:

1. During Year Y−1, factor loadings are estimated for all securities, and securities with similar factor loadings are put into common control portfolios that should have similar risk characteristics. (The author tests models with three, four, and five factors.) During Year Y, excess security returns are derived for each control portfolio from the daily returns of the individual stocks in the portfolio. Assuming that all stocks within a control portfolio have equal risk according to the APT, they should have similar average returns and the average excess returns should be zero.
2. Given the excess returns during Year Y, all the stocks were ranked on the basis of their market value at the end of Year Y−1, and the excess returns of the firms in the bottom 10 percent of the size distribution were combined (equal weights) to form the average excess returns for Portfolio MV1. Similarly, nine other portfolios were formed, with MV10 containing excess returns for the largest firms.

Under the null hypothesis, the ten portfolios should possess identical average excess returns, which should be insignificantly different from zero. If the ten portfolios do not have identical average excess returns, this evidence would be inconsistent with the APT.

The ranking procedure described in Step 2 was done annually because the market values change, and firms are added and deleted. As stated, the APT would be supported if the average excess returns for the ten portfolios equaled zero.

The test results were *clearly inconsistent with the APT*. Specifically, the average excess returns of the ten portfolios were not equal to zero for either a three-, four-, or five-factor model. The small-firm portfolio, MV1, experienced a positive and statistically significant average excess return, whereas Portfolio MV10 had a statistically significant negative

---

[44] Phoebus J. Dhrymes, Irwin Friend, Mustofa N. Gultekin, and N. Bulent Gultekin, "New Tests of the APT and Their Implications," *Journal of Finance* 40, no. 3 (July 1985): 659–674.

[45] Mark R. Reinganum, "The Arbitrage Pricing Theory: Some Empirical Results," *Journal of Finance* 36, no. 2 (May 1981): 313–321.

average excess return. The mean difference in excess returns between the small and large firms was about 25 percent a year. Also, the mean excess returns of MV1 through MV10 were perfectly inversely ordered with firm size.

Reinganum also tested for significant differences between individual portfolio returns and the difference between the high and low portfolio each year. Both tests confirmed that the low-market-value portfolios outperformed the high-market-value portfolios regardless of whether excess returns were derived from the three-, four-, or five-factor model. The author concluded that these results did not support the APT, but he acknowledged that the analysis involved a joint test of several hypotheses implicit in the theory and that it was impossible to pinpoint the error.

A subsequent study by Chen supported the APT model compared to the CAPM and provided evidence related to the small-firm effect that was contrary to Reinganum.[46] Prior to discussing the tests, the author contended that problems caused by the need for a limited sample and the existence of multiple factors were related to the *testing* of the theory and should not reflect on the theory itself. The analysis employed 180 stocks and five factors. The cross-sectional results indicated that the first factor was highly correlated with beta. Chen's test of the two models for performance measurement was based on the contention that if the CAPM does not capture all the information related to returns, this remaining information will be in the residual series. In turn, if the APT can provide factors to explain these residual returns, it would be superior. He concluded that the CAPM was misspecified and that the missing price information was picked up by the APT.

The final tests examined whether some major variables have explanatory power after the factor loadings from the APT model. If so, it would cause one to reject the APT. The two variables considered based on prior CAPM studies were a stock's own variance and firm size. The results supported the APT because neither a stock's own variance nor a firm's size had explanatory power after adjusting for risk based on factor loadings. Again, these results are in contrast to the earlier results by Reinganum.

APT AND THE JANUARY EFFECT   Given the January anomaly where returns in January are significantly larger than in any other month, Gultekin and Gultekin tested the ability of the APT model to adjust for this anomaly.[47] The APT model was estimated for each month and risk premia were *always* significant in January, but rarely priced in other months. It was concluded that the APT model, like the CAPM, can explain the risk–return relation only in January, which indicates that the APT model does not explain this anomaly any better than the CAPM.

Burmeister and McElroy estimated a linear factor model (LFM), the APT, and a CAPM.[48] They found a significant January effect that was not captured by any of the models. When they went beyond the January effect, however, they rejected the CAPM in favor of the APT.

THE APT AND INFLATION   Elton, Gruber, and Rentzler extended the APT to consider the impact of inflation on asset returns.[49] After deriving an equilibrium model of real returns,

---

[46] Nai-fu Chen, "Some Empirical Tests of the Theory of Arbitrage Pricing," *Journal of Finance* 38, no. 5 (December 1983): 1393–1414.

[47] Mustofa N. Gultekin and N. Bulent Gultekin, "Stock Return Anomalies and the Tests of APT," *Journal of Finance* 42, no. 5 (December 1987): 1213–1224.

[48] Edwin Burmeister and Marjorie B. McElroy, "Joint Estimation of Factor Sensitivities and Risk Premia for the Arbitrage Pricing Theory," *Journal of Finance* 43, no. 3 (July 1988): 721–733.

[49] Edwin Elton, Martin Gruber, and Joel Rentzler, "The Arbitrage Pricing Model and Returns on Assets under Uncertain Inflation," *Journal of Finance* 38, no. 2 (May 1983): 323–337.

they assumed the inflation factor was not priced, so they employed the APT model and compared the results to prior inflation-adjusted CAPM models. They contended that it was important to develop APT models with statistically identifiable factors that had economic meaning such as inflation and growth in real GDP.

The Shanken Challenge to Testability of the APT   Similar to Roll's critique of the CAPM, a set of papers by Shanken challenged whether the APT can be empirically verified.[50] Rather than question specific tests or methods, Shanken questioned whether the APT is more susceptible to testing than the CAPM based on the usual empirical test that determines whether asset returns conform to a K factor model. One problem is that if returns are not explained by such a model, it is not considered a rejection of the model; however, if the factors do explain returns, it is considered support. Also, it is contended that APT has no advantage because the factors need not be observable, which means that equivalent sets of securities may conform to different factor structures. Therefore, the empirical formulation of the APT may yield different implications regarding the expected returns for a given set of securities. Unfortunately, this implies that the theory cannot explain differential returns between securities because it cannot identify the relevant factor structure that explains the differential returns. This need to identify the relevant factor structure that affects asset returns is similar to the CAPM benchmark problem. In summary, each of the models has a problem with testing. Specifically, before you can test the CAPM, you must identify and use the true market portfolio, whereas before you can test the APT, you must identify the relevant factor structure that affects security returns.

Dybvig and Ross replied by suggesting that the APT is testable as an equality rather than the "empirical APT" proposed by Shanken.[51] Shanken responded that what has developed is a set of equilibrium APT pricing models that are testable, but the original arbitrage based models ("APT") are not testable as originally specified.[52]

ALTERNATIVE TESTING TECHNIQUES   Beyond those that were concerned with prior tests, several other articles have proposed alternative statistical techniques for testing the APT model. Jobson proposes that the APT be tested using a multivariate linear regression model.[53] Brown and Weinstein propose an approach to estimating and testing asset pricing models using a bilinear paradigm.[54] A number of subsequent papers have proposed new methodologies for testing the APT.[55]

---

[50] Jay Shanken, "The Arbitrage Pricing Theory: Is It Testable?" *Journal of Finance* 37, no. 5 (December 1982): 1129–1140.

[51] Philip H. Dybvig and Stephen A. Ross, "Yes, the APT Is Testable," *Journal of Finance* 40, no. 4 (September 1985): 1173–1188.

[52] Jay Shanken, "Multi-Beta CAPM or Equilibrium APT?: A Reply," *Journal of Finance* 40, no. 4 (September 1985): 1189–1196.

[53] J. D. Jobson, "A Multivariate Linear Regression Test for the Arbitrage Pricing Theory," *Journal of Finance* 37, no. 4 (September 1982): 1037–1042.

[54] Stephen J. Brown and Mark I. Weinstein, "A New Approach to Testing Asset Pricing Models: The Bilinear Paradigm," *Journal of Finance* 38, no. 3 (June 1983): 711–743.

[55] Among the papers are Chinhyang Cho, "On Testing the Arbitrage Pricing Theory: Inter-Battery Factor Analysis," *Journal of Finance* 39, no. 5 (December 1984): 1485–1502; Gregory Connor and Robert Korajczyk, "Risk and Return in an Equilibrium APT: Applications of a New Test Methodology," *Journal of Financial Economics* 21, no. 2 (September 1988): 255–290; Robert McCulloch and Peter Rossi, "Posterior, Predictive, and Utility-Based Approaches to Testing the Arbitrage Pricing Theory," *Journal of Financial Economics* 28, no. 1 and 2 (November–December 1990): 7–38; Ravi Shakla and Charles Trzcinka, "Sequential Tests of the Arbitrage Pricing Theory: A Comparison of Principle Components and Maximum Likelihood Factors," *Journal of Finance* 45, no. 5 (December 1990): 1542–1564; and Punect Handa and Scott C. Linn, "Arbitrage Pricing with Estimation Risk," *Journal of Financial and Quantitative Analysis* 28, no. 1 (March 1993): 81–100.

Summary

- When we relax several of the major assumptions of the CAPM, the required modifications are reasonably minor and do not change the overall concept of the model. Empirical studies have indicated stable portfolio betas, especially when enough observations were used to derive the betas and there was adequate volume. Although most of the early tests confirmed the expected relationship between returns and systematic risk (with allowance for the zero–beta model), several more recent studies have indicated that the univariate beta model needed to be supplemented with additional variables that considered skewness, size, P/E, leverage, and the book value/market value ratio. A study by Fama and French contended that during the period 1963 to 1990, beta was not relevant by itself or when supplemented. In their study, the most significant variables were book-to-market value (BE/ME) and size. Subsequent studies both supported their findings and differed with them because some authors found a significant relationship between beta and rates of return on stocks.
- Another problem has been raised by Roll, who contends that it is not possible to empirically derive a true market portfolio, so it is not possible to test the CAPM model properly or to use the model to evaluate portfolio performance. A study by Reilly and Akhtar provided empirical support for this contention by demonstrating significant differences in betas, SMLs, and expected returns with alternative benchmarks.
- Ross subsequently devised an alternative asset pricing model (the APT) with fewer assumptions that does not require a market portfolio. The results from the empirical tests of the APT have thus far been mixed. Also, Shanken contends that the nature of many of the tests are such that it is impossible to reject the theory.
- In conclusion, it is probably safe to assume that both the CAPM and APT will continue to be used to price capital assets. Coincident with their use will be further empirical tests of both theories, the ultimate goal being to determine which theory does the best job of explaining current and future returns. Notably, the APT model requires fewer assumptions and considers multiple factors to explain the risk of an asset.[56] At the same time, several authors (including Fama-French) have proposed either multifactor CAPMs or conditional CAPMs that allow for changing betas and market risk premiums over time.

Questions

1. In the empirical testing of the CAPM, what are two major concerns? Why are they important?
2. Briefly discuss why it is important for beta coefficients to be stationary over time.
3. Discuss the empirical results relative to beta stability for individual stocks and portfolios of stocks.
4. In the tests of the relationship between systematic risk (beta) and return, what are you looking for?
5. Draw an ideal SML. Based on the early empirical results, what did the actual risk–return relationship look like relative to the ideal relationship implied by the CAPM?
6. According to the CAPM, what assets are included in the market portfolio, and what are the relative weightings? In empirical studies of the CAPM, what are the typical proxies used for the market portfolio?
7. Assuming that the empirical proxy for the market portfolio is not a good proxy, what factors related to the CAPM will be affected?
8. Some studies related to the efficient market hypothesis generated results that implied additional factors beyond beta should be considered to estimate expected returns. What are these other variables and why should they be considered?
9. According to the Fama-French study, discuss what variables you should consider when selecting a cross section of stocks.
10. What are the major assumptions required by the APT? What critical assumptions of the CAPM are *not* required by the APT?

---

[56] For a discussion of how these models relate to each other, see William F. Sharpe, "Factor Models, CAPMs, and the APT," *Journal of Portfolio Management* 11, no. 1 (Fall 1984): 21–25.

11. Briefly discuss one study that does not support the APT. Briefly discuss a study that supports the APT.

12. Briefly discuss why Shanken contends that the APT is not testable.

13. *CFA Examination III (1986)*

Multifactor models of security returns have received increased attention. The arbitrage pricing theory (APT) probably has drawn the most attention and has been proposed as a replacement for the capital asset pricing model (CAPM).

a. Briefly explain the primary differences between APT and CAPM. [5 minutes]

b. Identify the *four* systematic factors suggested by Roll and Ross that determine an asset's riskiness. Explain how these factors affect an asset's expected rate of return. [10 minutes]

Problems

1. Given the following results, indicate what will happen to the beta for Stock E, relative to the market proxy, compared to the beta relative to the true market portfolio:

YEARLY RATES OF RETURN

Year	Stock (percent)	Market Proxy (percent)	True Market (percent)
1	10	8	6
2	20	14	11
3	−14	−10	−7
4	−20	−18	−12
5	15	12	10

Discuss the reason for the differences in measured beta. Does the suggested relationship appear reasonable? Why or why not?

2. Draw the implied SMLs for the following two sets of conditions:

a. $RFR = .07$; $R_m(S + P500) = .16$

b. $R_z = .09$; $R_m(True) = .18$

Under which set of conditions would it be more difficult for a portfolio manager to be superior?

3. Using the graph and equations from Problem 2, which of the following portfolios would be superior?

a. $R_a = 11\%$; $\beta = .09$

b. $R_b = 14\%$; $\beta = 1.00$

c. $R_c = 12\%$; $\beta = -.40$

d. $R_d = 20\%$; $\beta = 1.10$

Does it matter which SML you use?

4. Draw the security market line for each of the following conditions:

a. (1) $RFR = .08$ $R_m(proxy) = .12$

   (2) $R_z = .06$ $R_m(true) = .15$

b. Radius Tire has the following results for the last six periods. Calculate and compare the betas using each index.

Period	Return of Radius (percent)	Proxy Specific Index (percent)	True General Index (percent)
1	29	12	15
2	12	10	13
3	−12	−9	−8
4	17	14	18
5	20	25	28
6	−5	−10	0

c. If the current period return for the market is 12 percent and for Radius is 11 percent, are superior results being obtained?

5. Under the following conditions, what are the expected returns for Stocks J and L?

$\lambda_0 = .05$ $b_{J1} = 0.80$
$K_1 = .02$ $b_{J2} = 1.40$
$K_2 = .04$ $b_{L1} = 1.60$
$b_{L2} = 2.25$

References

Black, Fischer. "Capital Market Equilibrium with Restricted Borrowing." *Journal of Business* 45, no. 3 (July 1972).

Campbell, John Y. and John Ammer. "What Moves the Stock and Bond Markets? A Variance Decomposition for Long-Term Asset Returns." *Journal of Finance* 48, no. 1 (March 1993).

Chen, Nai-fu, Richard Roll, and Stephen A. Ross. "Economic Forces and the Stock Market." *Journal of Business* 56, no. 3 (July 1986).

Chen, Nai-Fu. "Some Empirical Tests of the Theory of Arbitrage Pricing." *Journal of Finance* 38, no. 5 (December 1983).

Handa, Punect and Scott C. Linn. "Arbitrage Pricing with Estimation Risk." *Journal of Financial and Quantitative Analysis* 28, no. 1 (March 1993).

Lehmann, B. N. and D. M. Modest. "The Empirical Foundations of the Arbitrage Pricing Theory." *Journal of Financial Economics* 21, no. 3 (September 1988).

Roll, Richard and Stephen A. Ross. "An Empirical Investigation of the Arbitrage Pricing Theory." *Journal of Finance* 35, no. 5 (December 1980).

Ross, Stephen A. "The Arbitrage Theory of Capital Asset Pricing." *Journal of Economic Theory* 13, no. 2 (December 1976).

Ross, Stephen A. "Risk, Return and Arbitrage." In *Risk and Return in Finance,* edited by I. Friend and J. Bicksler. Cambridge: Ballinger, 1977.

Shanken, Jay. "Multivariate Proxies and Asset Pricing Relations." *Journal of Financial Economics* 18, no. 1 (March 1987).

Chapter
11

An Introduction to Derivative Markets and Securities

This chapter answers the following questions:

- What distinguishes a derivative security, such as a forward, futures, or option contract, from more fundamental securities such as stocks and bonds?
- What are the important characteristics of forward, futures, and option contracts, and in what sense can they be interpreted as insurance policies?
- How are the markets for derivative securities organized and how do they differ from other security markets?
- What terminology is used to describe transactions that involve forward, futures, and option contracts?
- What are the similarities and differences between forward and futures contracts?
- What do the payoff diagrams look like for investments in forward and futures contracts?
- What do the payoff diagrams look like for investments in put and call option contracts?
- How are forward contracts, put options, and call options related to one another?
- How can derivatives be used in conjunction with stock and Treasury bills to replicate the payoffs to other securities and create arbitrage opportunities for an investor?
- How can derivative contracts be used to restructure cash flow patterns and modify the risks in existing investment portfolios?
- What are the challenges involved in measuring the risk of an investment portfolio that contains derivative securities?

So far, we have seen several ways in which individuals and institutions can design their investments to take advantage of future market conditions. We have also seen how investors can control the volatility associated with their positions—at least in part—by forming well-diversified portfolios of securities around a common investment theme, thereby reducing or eliminating the unsystematic component of a stock's risk.

In this chapter, we begin our formal investigation of the role played by **derivative securities** in modern investment portfolios. A derivative instrument is one for which the ultimate payoff to the investor depends directly on the value of another security or commodity. Earlier, we briefly described two basic types of derivatives: (1) forward and futures contracts and (2) option contracts. A call option, for example, gives its **owner** the right to purchase an underlying security, such as a stock or a bond, at a fixed price within a certain amount of time. Naturally, this right to purchase would most certainly be exercised only if the value of the underlying asset at the call's expiration date was greater than the contractual purchase price. In this manner, the option's ultimate value can be said to depend on—and thus derive from—that of the other (underlying) asset. Similarly, a forward contract to sell a specific bond for a fixed price at a future date will see its value to the investor rise or fall with decreases or increases in the market price of the underlying bond.

The growth of the markets in which derivative securities are created and exchanged has been nothing short of phenomenal. The last few decades have seen the emergence of forward, futures, and option contracts to trade such fundamental products as agricultural commodities, energy, precious metals, currencies, common stock, and bonds. There are even derivatives to trade hypothetical underlying assets (e.g., options and futures contracts on the Standard & Poor's stock indexes) as well as "combination" derivatives, such as option contracts that allow the investor to decide at a later date to enter into a futures contract involving another security or commodity. Interest rate swaps, which will be shown in Chapter 25 to be forward contracts on a short-term borrowing or lending rate, are a good example of the prodigious growth of these markets. Starting with the first swap in 1981, the volume of swap market activity had grown in size to the tens of trillions of dollars by the mid-1990s. Although this sort of rapid expansion is not typical of all new derivative products, these instruments represent one of the true legacies of the financial markets in the latter part of the twentieth century.

As we will see, derivative securities can be used by investors in the same way and for the same reasons as the underlying assets; an investor believing that a certain common stock will increase in value will likely benefit from either a purchase of the stock directly or through the acquisition of an option to purchase that stock at a predetermined price. The exact returns will not be equal for these two alternatives, but both will benefit from an upward movement in the stock's price. Ultimately, however, the real key to understanding how and why derivatives are used in practice lies in their ability to modify the risk and expected return characteristics of existing investment portfolios. That is, options and futures allow investors to **hedge** (or even increase) the risk of a collection of stocks in ways that go far beyond the diversification results presented in the preceding chapters. In addition, we will see that derivative securities also allow for the convenient duplication of cash flow patterns that already exist in other forms, thereby creating the possibility of **arbitrage** if two otherwise identical series of cash flows do not carry the same current price.

The balance of this chapter describes the fundamental nature and uses of forward, futures, and option contracts on common stock and bonds. (Subsequent chapters deal with more advanced forms of these products and valuation issues.) In the next section, we describe the basic terminology associated with the forward, futures, and option markets while the second section explains the similarities and differences in the payoff structures created by each of these instruments. Section three is devoted to developing the formal relationship between forwards and options, the result of which will be a series of conditions collectively known as **put-call parity.** In the final section, we consider three of the more popular ways in which derivatives have been used in managing stock and bond portfolios, with a particular emphasis on how derivatives can adjust risk to better suit the needs of the investor.

OVERVIEW OF DERIVATIVE MARKETS

As with any financial product, derivative transactions have a specific terminology that must be understood in order to use these instruments effectively. Unlike many other securities, however, the language used to describe forward, futures, and option contracts is often a confusing blend of jargon drawn from the equity, debt, and insurance markets with some unique expressions thrown in for good measure. Thus, we begin by summarizing the most important aspects of these products and the markets in which they trade.

THE LANGUAGE AND STRUCTURE OF FORWARD AND FUTURES MARKETS

To most investors, the **forward contract** is the most basic derivative product available. Generally, a forward contract gives its holder both the *right and full obligation* to conduct a transaction involving another security or commodity—the underlying asset—at a predetermined future date and at a predetermined price. The future date on which the transaction is to be consummated is called the contract's *maturity* (or expiration) *date,* while the prede-termined price at which the trade takes place is the forward **contract price.** Notice there must always be two parties (sometimes called **counterparties**) to a forward transaction: the eventual buyer (or **long position**), who pays the contract price and receives the underly-ing security, and the eventual seller (or **short position**), who delivers the security for the fixed price.

Forward contracts are not securities in the traditional sense; they are more appropriately viewed as *trade agreements* negotiated directly between two parties for a transaction that is scheduled to take place in the future. Suppose, for example, that two investors agree at date 0 (the present) to transfer a bond from one party to the other at the future date T. To specify the full terms of this agreement, the two parties must agree on which bond and how much of it is to be exchanged, the date and location at which this exchange will take place, and the price at which the bond will be bought and sold. Consequently, the terms that must be considered in forming a forward contract are the same as those that would be necessary for a bond transaction that settled immediately (i.e., a *spot market* transaction), but with two exceptions. First, the settlement date agreed to in the contract is purposefully set to be in the future. Second, the contract price—which we will represent as $F_{0,T}$, meaning a forward price set at date 0 for a contract that matures at date T—is usually different from the prevailing spot price (S_0) because of the different time frames involved. Typically, $F_{0,T}$ is chosen so that neither party needs to make an upfront payment to the other.

One important way in which spot and forward market transactions are similar is the conditions under which the long and short positions will profit. To illustrate this idea, suppose that at date T, the long position in a bond forward contract is obligated to pay $1,000 (= $F_{0,T}$) for a bond that is worth $S_T = \$1,050$ (i.e., the spot price at date T). Since $F_{0,T} < S_T$, this will result in a profitable settlement for the long position in the contract since he will be able to acquire the bond for $50 less than its current market value. On the other hand, the short position must deliver the bond at date T and will lose $50 on her forward position; she would have profited if S_T had been below the contract price of $1,000. Thus, just as if the bond had been purchased at date 0, the long position benefits when bond prices rise, at least relative to the contract price $F_{0,T}$. Conversely, the short position to the forward contract will gain from falling bond prices, just as if she had short sold the bond at date 0. Even though the timing of the trade's settlement has shifted, "buy low, sell high" is still the way to make a profit in the forward market.

Forward contracts are negotiated in the over-the-counter market. This means that for-ward contracts are agreements between two private parties—one of which is often a deriva-tives intermediary such as a commercial or investment bank—rather than traded through a formal security or commodity exchange. One advantage of this private arrangement is that the terms of the contract are completely flexible; they can be whatever any two mutually consenting counterparties agree to. Another desirable feature to many counterparties is that these arrangements may not require *collateral*; instead, the long and short positions trust each other to honor their respective commitments at date T. This lack of collateral means that forward contracts involve *credit* (or default) *risk,* which is one reason why commercial banks are often market makers in these instruments.

One disadvantage of a forward contract is that it is quite often *illiquid,* meaning that it might be difficult or costly for a counterparty to exit the contract before it matures. Illiquid-ity is really a by-product of the contract's flexibility because the more specifically tailored an agreement is to the needs of a particular individual, the less marketable it will be to someone else. **Futures contracts** solve this problem by standardizing the terms of the agreement (e.g., expiration date, identity and amount of the underlying asset) to the extent that it can be exchange traded. In contrast to the forward market, both parties in a futures contract trade through a centralized market, called a *futures exchange*. Although the standardization of contracts reduces the ability of the ultimate end-users to select the most desirable terms, it does create contract *homogeneity,* whereby the counterparties can always *unwind* a previous commitment prior to expiration by simply trading their existing position back to the exchange at the prevailing market price.

The *futures price* is analogous to the forward contract price and, at any time during the life of a contract, is set at a level such that a brand new long or short position would not have to pay a premium to enter the agreement. However, the futures exchange will require both counterparties to post collateral, or *margin,* to protect itself against the possibility of default. (A futures exchange is not a credit-granting institution.) These margin accounts are held by the exchange's *clearinghouse* and are *marked-to-market* (i.e., adjusted for contract price movements) on a daily basis to ensure that both end-users always maintain sufficient collateral to guarantee their eventual participation. A list of some of the more popular futures contracts, along with the markets where they trade, is shown in Table 11.1. Although generally quite diverse, all of these underlying assets have two things in common: *volatile price movements* and *strong interest* from both buyers and sellers.

THE LANGUAGE AND STRUCTURE OF OPTION MARKETS

An **option contract** gives its holder the right—but not the obligation—to conduct a transaction involving an underlying security or commodity at a predetermined future date and at a predetermined price. Unlike the forward contract, the option gives the long position the right to decide whether or not the trade will eventually take place. On the other hand, the seller (or *writer*) of the option must perform on his side of the agreement if the buyer

TABLE 11.1	POPULAR FUTURES CONTRACTS AND EXCHANGES	
Underlying Asset		Exchange
A. Physical Commodities		
Corn, soybeans, soybean meal, soybean oil, wheat		Chicago Board of Trade
Cattle—feeder, cattle—live, hogs, pork bellies Lumber Heating oil		Chicago Mercantile Exchange
Cocoa, coffee, sugar—world, sugar—domestic		Cocoa, Sugar, and Coffee Exchange
Copper, gold, silver		New York Commodity Exchange
Crude oil, heating oil, gasoline, natural gas Platinum		New York Mercantile Exchange
B. Financial Securities		
Yen, Deutschemark, Canadian dollar, Swiss franc, British pound, Mexican peso, Australian dollar Treasury bills, Eurodollar (LIBOR) S&P 500 Index, Nikkei 225 Index, Russell 2000 Index		International Monetary Market (Chicago Mercantile Exchange)
Treasury bonds, Treasury notes, Municipal bond index, federal funds Major Market Index		Chicago Board of Trade
Eurodollar, British gilt, German bunds Euromarks, Eurofrancs, Eurolira FTSE 100 Index		London International Financial Futures Exchange

chooses to exercise the option. Thus, the obligation in the option market is inherently one-sided; buyers can do as they please, but sellers are obligated to the buyers under the terms of the agreement. As a consequence, two different types of options are needed to cover all potential transactions: a **call option**—the right to buy the underlying security, and a **put option**—the right to sell that same asset.

There are two prices that are important in evaluating an option position. The **exercise,** or striking, **price** is the price the call buyer will pay to—or the put buyer will receive from—the seller if the option is exercised. The exercise price (represented here as X) is to an option what the contract price (i.e., $F_{0,T}$) is to a forward agreement. The second price of interest is the price that the option buyer must pay to the seller at date 0 to acquire the contract itself. To avoid confusion, this second price is typically referred to as the **option premium.** A basic difference between options and forwards is that an option requires this up-front premium payment from buyer to seller while the forward ordinarily does not. This is because the forward contract allowed both the long and short positions to "win" at date T (depending on where S_T settled, relative to $F_{0,T}$), but the option agreement will only be exercised in the buyer's favor; hence the seller must be compensated at date 0, or he would never agree to the deal. Notice also that although a premium payment will be required for both puts and calls, it is quite likely that these two prices will differ. In the analysis that follows, we will define the date 0 premium to acquire an option expiring at date T as $C_{0,T}$ for a call and $P_{0,T}$ for a put. For example, in lieu of a long position in a bond forward contract, the investor in the previous example could have paid $20 (= $C_{0,T}$) at date 0 for a call option that would have given him the right to buy the bond for $1,000 (= X) at date T, but not required him to do so if S_T < $1,000.

Options can be designed to provide a choice of when the contract can be exercised. **European** options can only be exercised at maturity (date T) while **American** contracts can be executed any time up to expiration. For a European-style call option, the buyer will only exercise when the expiration date market value of the underlying asset that could be purchased is greater than the exercise price. Conversely, a European-style put option will only be rationally exercised when the date T price of the asset that could be sold is lower than X. (The decision to exercise an American-style contract is more complex and will be discussed in a later chapter.)

Given these parameters, the date 0 premium for an option can be divided into two components: **intrinsic value** and **time premium.** Intrinsic value represents the value that the buyer could extract from the option if she exercised it immediately. For a call, this is the greater of either zero or the difference between the price of the underlying asset and the exercise price (i.e., $\max[0, S_0 - X]$). For a put, intrinsic value would be $\max[0, X - S_0]$ as X would now represent the proceeds generated from the asset's sale. An option with positive intrinsic value is said to be **in-the-money,** while one with zero intrinsic value is **out-of-the-money.** For the special case where $S_0 = X$, the option is **at-the-money.** The time premium component is then simply the difference between the whole option premium and the intrinsic component: ($C_{0,T} - \max[0, S_0 - X]$) for a call and ($P_{0,T} - \max[0, X - S_0]$) for a put. The buyer is willing to pay this amount in excess of the option's immediate exercise value because of her ability to complete the transaction at a price of X that will remain in force until date T. Thus, the time premium is connected to the likelihood that the underlying asset's price will move in the anticipated direction by the contract's maturity.

Like forwards and futures, options trade both in over-the-counter markets and on exchanges. When exchange-traded, just the seller of the contract is required to post a margin account because he is the only one obligated to perform on the contract at a later date. Also, options can be based on a wide variety of underlying securities, including futures contracts

TABLE 11.2	POPULAR OPTION CONTRACTS AND EXCHANGES	
	Underlying Asset	Exchange

A. Financial Securities

Individual Equities S&P 100 Index	Chicago Board Options Exchange

Yen, Deutschemark, Canadian dollar, Swiss franc, British pound,
    Australian dollar
    S&P 500 Index
	International Monetary Market
	(Chicago Mercantile Exchange)

B. Futures Options

Cattle—feeder, cattle—live, hogs, pork bellies	Chicago Mercantile Exchange

Yen, Deutschemark, Canadian dollar, Swiss franc, British pound
    Eurodollar (LIBOR), 2 year Eurodollar
    S&P 500 Index
	International Monetary Market
	(Chicago Mercantile Exchange)

Corn, soybeans, soybean meal, soybean oil, wheat
    Treasury bonds, Treasury notes
    Major Market Index
	Chicago Board of Trade

British gilt, German bunds
    Euromark
    FT-SE 100 Index
	London International Financial
	Futures Exchange

Crude oil, heating oil, gasoline, natural gas	New York Mercantile Exchange
Copper, gold, silver	New York Commodity Exchange

or other options. Table 11.2 lists the underlying assets and exchanges where a number of the most popular option contracts trade.

INVESTING WITH DERIVATIVE SECURITIES

Although the preceding section highlighted many of the differences between forward and option agreements, the two types of derivatives are quite similar in terms of the benefits they produce for investors. The ultimate difference between forwards and options lies in the way the investor must pay to acquire those benefits. This concept, along with an examination of the basic payoff structures that exist in these markets, is described below.

THE BASIC NATURE OF DERIVATIVE INVESTING

Consider an investor who has decided to purchase a share of stock in SAS Corporation six months from now, a time frame that coincides with an anticipated receipt of funds. We will assume that both SAS stock forward contracts and call options are available with the market prices of $F_{0,T}$ and $C_{0,T}$ (where $T = 0.50$ year) and that the exercise price of the call option, X, is equal to $F_{0,T}$. Thus, if the investor wants to secure the price now at which the stock purchase will eventually take place, he has two alternatives: a long position in the forward or the purchase of the call option. Figure 11.1 compares the date 0 and date T cash flow exchanges for both possibilities.

The clear difference between these strategies at the time of origination is that the forward position requires no payment or receipt by either party to the transaction whereas the investor must pay a cash premium to the seller of the call option. As noted earlier, this front-end option payment releases the investor from the obligation to purchase SAS stock at date T if the terms of the contract turn out to be unfavorable (i.e., $S_T < X$). This is shown in the lower panel of Figure 11.1 When the expiration date price of SAS stock exceeds the exercise price, the investor will exercise the call and purchase the share of stock. Notice,

FIGURE 11.1   **EXCHANGES FOR LONG FORWARD AND LONG CALL TRANSACTIONS**

A. Exchange at Origination (i.e., Date 0)

Forward:

Investor (i.e., Long) — Short

Initial Cost: 0

Call Option:

Investor (i.e., Long) — Premium → Seller

Initial Cost: Premium > 0

B. Exchange at Contract Expiration (i.e., Date T)

Forward:

Call Option:

(i) If $S_T > X (= F_{0,T})$:

Investor (i.e., Long) ← Stock — Short — $F_{0,T}$ →

Net Contract Receipt: $[S_T - F_{0,T}] > 0$

Investor (i.e., Long) ← Stock — Seller — X →

Net Contract Receipt: $[S_T - X] > 0$

(ii) If $S_T \leq X (= F_{0,T})$:

Investor (i.e., Long) ← Stock — Short — $F_{0,T}$ →

Net Contract Receipt: $[S_T - F_{0,T}] < 0$

Investor (i.e., Long)   Seller

Net Contract Receipt: 0

however, that this leads to exactly the same exchange as did the long forward contract. It is only when the stock price falls below X (and $F_{0,T}$) on date T that there is a difference between the two positions; under this condition, the right provided by the option *not* to purchase SAS stock is valuable since the investor will be required to execute his forward contract at a loss. In this sense, the call option can be viewed as the "good half" of the long forward position because it allows for the future acquisition of SAS stock at a fixed price but doesn't require the transaction to take place.

This is the critical distinction between forward and option contracts. Both the long forward and the long call positions have been structured to provide the investor with exactly the same amount of "insurance" against the price of SAS stock rising over the next six months. That is, both contracts provide a payoff of $[S_T - X]$ ($= [S_T - F_{0,T}]$) whenever S_T exceeds X, which reduces the effective purchase price for the stock back down to X. The difference in contract design can then be viewed in terms of how the investor is required to pay for that price insurance. With a forward contract, no money is paid up-front, but the investor will have to make a payment at the expiration date even if the stock price falls below $F_{0,T}$. Conversely, the call option will never require a future settlement payment, but the investor will have to pay the premium at origination. Thus, for the same date T benefit, the investor's decision between these two "insurance policies" comes down to choosing the certainty of a present premium payment (i.e., long call) versus the possibility of a future payment (i.e., long forward) that could potentially be much larger.

To see this distinction more clearly, suppose that an investor plans to buy SAS stock in six months when some of the bonds in his portfolio mature. He is concerned that share values could rise substantially between now and the time he receives his investment funds and so to hedge that risk he considers two "insurance" strategies to lock in the eventual purchase price: (1) pay nothing now to take the long position in a six-month SAS stock forward contract with a contract price of $F_{0,T} = \$45$, or (2) pay a premium of $C_{0,T} = \$3.24$ for a six-month, European-style call option with an exercise price of $X = \$45$. Assuming that at the time of his decision the price of SAS stock is $S_0 = \$40$, the call option is out of the money meaning that its intrinsic value is zero and the entire $3.24 is time premium. As mentioned earlier, an obvious difference between these two strategies is that the option entails a front-end expense while the forward position does not. The other difference occurs at the expiration date, depending on whether the SAS stock price is above or below $45. If, for instance, $S_T = \$51$, both the long forward position and the call option will be worth $6 (i.e., $51 - 45$) to the investor, reducing his net purchase price for SAS shares to $45 (= $51 - 6$). That is, when the stock settled above $45 (i.e., the common value for $F_{0,T}$ and X), both the long forward and long call positions provided the same protection against rising prices. On the other hand, if $S_T = \$41.75$, the forward contract would have required that the investor pay $4.25 (= $41.75 - 45$) to his counterparty, which would have once again raised the net cost of his shares to $45. With the call option, however, he could have let the contract expire without exercising it and purchased his SAS shares in the market for only $41.75. Thus, in exchange for the option's front-end expense of $3.24, the investor retains the possibility of paying less than $45 for his eventual stock purchase.

The connection between forward contracts and put options can be made in a similar fashion. Suppose a different investor has decided to liquidate a share of SAS stock from her portfolio in six months' time. Rather than risk a falling stock price over that period, she could arrange now to sell the share at that future date for a predetermined fixed price in one of two ways: a short forward position or the purchase of a put option. Figure 11.2 illustrates the exchanges for these alternatives. Once again, for the same insurance against SAS stock price declines, the choice comes down to the certainty of paying the put option premium versus the possibility of making a potentially larger payment with the forward contract by having to sell her stock for $X (= F_{0,T})$ when that value is considerably less than the stock's date T market price. Importantly, notice once again that the put option allows the investor to walk away from her obligation under the short forward position to sell her stock on the expiration date under disadvantageous conditions. Thus, in exchange for a front-end premium payment, the put option enables the investor to acquire the "good half" of the short position in a forward contract.

BASIC PAYOFF DIAGRAMS FOR FORWARD CONTRACTS

Figures 11.1 and 11.2 show that the respective expiration date payoffs for long and short positions in a forward contract are $[S_T - F_{0,T}]$ and $[F_{0,T} - S_T]$ and that these values could be either positive or negative depending on the spot price prevailing at date T. These terminal payoffs are plotted against the possible expiration date values of the underlying security price in Figure 11.3. There are two interesting items in this display.

First, the payoffs to both long and short positions in the forward contract are *symmetric*, or two-sided, around the contract price. This, of course, is a direct result of the terms of the contract that fully obligate each party to complete the agreed-upon transaction—even at a financial loss. For instance, in the last example the investor holding a long position in a SAS stock forward contract with a contract price of $45 lost $4.25 when the date T price of SAS stock was $41.75, but gained $6 when $S_T = \$51$.

FIGURE 11.2	**EXCHANGES FOR SHORT FORWARD AND LONG PUT TRANSACTIONS**

A. Exchange at Origination (i.e., Date 0)

Forward:

Investor (i.e., Short)	Long

Initial Cost: 0

Put Option:

Investor (i.e., Long)	→ Premium →	Seller

Initial Cost: Premium > 0

B. Exchange at Contract Expiration (i.e., Date T)

Forward:

Put Option:

(i) If $S_T > X (= F_{0,T})$:

Investor (i.e., Short)	← Stock → ← $F_{0,T}$	Long

Net Contract Receipt: $[F_{0,T} - S_T] < 0$

Investor (i.e., Long)		Seller

Net Contract Receipt: 0

(ii) If $S_T \le X (= F_{0,T})$:

Investor (i.e., Short	← Stock → ← $F_{0,T}$	Long

Net Contract Receipt: $[F_{0,T} - S_T] > 0$

Investor (i.e., Long)	Stock → ← X	Seller

Net Contract Receipt: $[X - S_T] > 0$

Second, the date T payoffs to the short and long positions are mirror images of each other; in market jargon, forward contracts are *zero-sum games* because the long position gains must be paid by the short position and vice versa. This illustration shows that when the date T spot price is lower than the contract price (i.e., S_1), the short position will receive the net payoff of $[F_{0,T} - S_1]$ from the long position while the settlement is reversed at S_2, where the security price is above $F_{0,T}$. Thus, forward markets reinforce the fundamental financial tenet that long positions benefit from rising prices while short positions benefit from falling prices. Finally, notice that these gains and losses can be quite large. In fact, the short forward position has the potential for unlimited loss while the long forward position has the potential for unlimited gain since there is no theoretical limit on how high the price for the underlying security can rise. Conversely, the loss potential for the long position (and the gain potential for the short position) is limited because the price of the underlying security cannot fall below zero.

BASIC PAYOFF DIAGRAMS FOR CALL AND PUT OPTIONS

Figures 11.1 and 11.2 clearly show that options differ from forward contracts in two fundamental ways. Most directly, the expense of purchasing either a put or a call represents a sunk cost to the investor reducing her upside return relative to the comparable forward position. In exchange for this initial fee, the investor receives expiration date payoffs that are decidedly *asymmetric,* or one-sided. Figure 11.4 shows the net effect these differences have on the terminal payoffs to both long and short positions in call options, while Figure

FIGURE 11.3   **EXPIRATION DATE PAYOFFS TO LONG AND SHORT FORWARD POSITIONS**

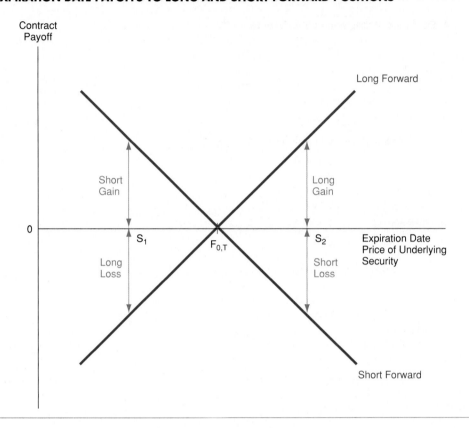

11.5 provides a similar illustration for put option traders. This analysis assumes that both options are European-style, and so they actually reach expiration without having been exercised prematurely.

For call option positions, notice again that the buyer of the contract still benefits whenever the terminal security price (i.e., S_T) exceeds the contract purchase (i.e., exercise) price of X. However, given that the holder had to pay an initial premium of $C_{0,T}$, the position doesn't generate a positive payoff until S_T is greater than X by the amount of the premium paid. Put another way, although the call option is in-the-money (and hence will be exercised) when $S_T > X$, it will not produce a capital gain for the buyer until $S_T > (X + C_{0,T})$.[1] When $X < S_T < (X + C_{0,T})$, the option is exercised at a loss, but this loss will be less than the full cost of the option, which is what the long position would incur if the call is not exercised. In fact, when $S_T < X$, the option is out-of-the-money and the buyer who makes the rational decision to let the contract expire will lose $C_{0,T}$.

Notice, then, that the buyer of the call option has unlimited gain potential as the security price could rise indefinitely with losses limited to the option premium no matter how far prices fall. Conversely, the short position benefits from a terminal price for the underlying

---

[1] The expiration date payoffs shown in Figures 11.4 and 11.5 are somewhat inaccurate in that they show the net of the date T value of the option and its initial cost, which was paid at date 0. Thus, although this is an accurate way of portraying capital gains and losses from an accounting standpoint, it ignores the value differential in the timing of the two payments.

FIGURE 11.4

EXPIRATION DATE PAYOFFS TO LONG AND SHORT CALL POSITIONS

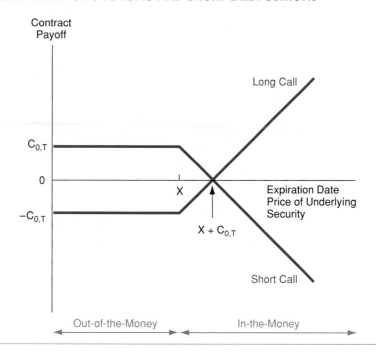

FIGURE 11.5

EXPIRATION DATE PAYOFFS TO LONG AND SHORT PUT POSITIONS

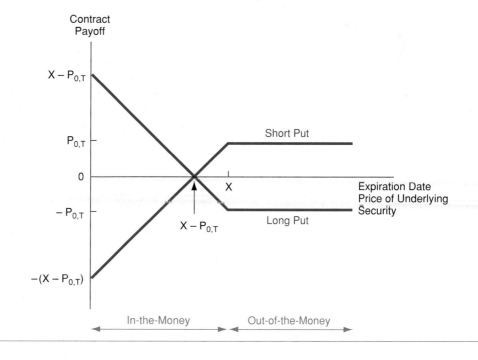

asset beneath X, but only to the extent that he gets to keep the full amount of the option premium. When $S_T > X$, the seller of the call has unlimited liability. Like forward contracts, the call option is a zero-sum game between the long and short positions.

For the put option positions shown in Figure 11.5, the buyer benefits whenever $X > S_T$, and receives a positive payoff when the date T price of the underlying security falls below the contractual selling price, less the cost of the option. In this case, the put buyer's maximum capital gain is limited to $X - P_{0,T}$ as the underlying security itself is limited to a minimum price of zero; the best the put holder can hope for is to force the seller of the contract to buy worthless stock for X at the expiration date. On the other hand, as with the call option, the owner of an out-of-the-money put can only lose his initial investment of $P_{0,T}$, which will occur when $S_T > X$. Not surprisingly, the profit and loss opportunities for the put seller are exactly opposite of those for the put buyer. The contract seller will gain when $S_T > (X - P_{0,T})$, but this gain is limited to the amount of the option premium. A short position in a put also has limited loss potential, but at a maximum of $X - P_{0,T}$, this can still be a large amount.

In summary, when they are held as investments, options are *directional views* on movements in the price of the underlying security. Call buyers and put sellers count on S_T to rise (or remain) above X, while put buyers and call sellers hope for S_T to fall (or remain) below the exercise price at the expiration date. However, the exact payoffs to each of these positions vary greatly for any given terminal security value. Importantly, option buyers—whether a put or a call—always have limited liability since they do not have to exercise an out-of-the-money position. This limited liability feature for option holders also means that the gain potential for the seller is limited as the two positions are mirror images of each other. For adverse price movements, though, option sellers face large potential losses, with the liability of the call writer being theoretically infinite just as if she had sold short the underlying security.

OPTION PAYOFF DIAGRAMS: AN EXAMPLE

Although there will only be one value of $F_{0,T}$ that allows the present value of a forward contract to be zero (i.e., does not require an initial payment from either the long or the short position), option contracts can be designed with several different values for the exercise price. It is interesting, therefore, to consider how the choice of the exercise price affects the instrument's expiration date payoff. Extending the last example, suppose that a share of SAS stock currently sells for $40, and six different SAS options—three calls and three puts—are available to investors. The options all expire on the same date in the future and have exercise prices of either $35, $40, or $45. Current market prices for these contracts, which are assumed to be European-style, are shown in Table 11.3 where they are broken down into their intrinsic value and time premium components.

TABLE 11.3   **HYPOTHETICAL STOCK AND OPTION PRICES**

Instrument	Exercise Price	Market Price	Intrinsic Value	Time Premium
SAS Stock	—	$40.00	—	—
Call: #1	$35.00	8.07	$5.00	$3.07
#2	40.00	5.24	0.00	5.24
#3	45.00	3.24	0.00	3.24
Put: #1	35.00	1.70	0.00	1.70
#2	40.00	3.67	0.00	3.67
#3	45.00	6.47	5.00	1.47

Given that $S_0 = \$40$, call #1 (with $X = 35$) and put #3 (with $X = 45$) are both $5 in the money, which leaves $3.07 and $1.47, respectively, of their value in the form of time premium. Call #3 and put #1 are both currently $5 out of the money and so their market prices are purely time premium; someone buying either of these two contracts anticipates that stock prices will move in the desired direction by at least the option price *plus* $5. Notice that neither of the two at-the-money options, call #2 and put #2, have any intrinsic value, but they still sell in the market for different prices. Specifically, the call with $X = \$40$ is more valuable than the comparable put option. This is generally true for stock options because the underlying share should always be priced to yield a positive expected return, most of which comes from price appreciation. (This result need not be true for bond or currency options, where the underlying interest or exchange rates could be expected to change in either direction.) Finally, the last column of Table 11.3 shows that the time premium is largest for the at-the-money options because, at this point, the greatest amount of uncertainty exists as to whether the option will be in or out of the money (and hence valuable) at expiration.

It is instructive to compare the expiration date payoff diagrams for options on the same security with varying exercise prices but similar in every other respect. This is done for both call and put options in Figure 11.6. For simplicity, only the payoffs for the long positions in these contracts are shown. The call option payoffs portrayed in the first panel of the figure indicate that although it is the most expensive, the deepest in-the-money contract (call #1) becomes profitable the quickest, requiring only that S_T rise to $43.07 ($= 35 + 8.07$). Call #3, on the other hand, is the least expensive to purchase, but requires the greatest movement in the price of the underlying stock—to $48.24 in this example—before it provides a positive payoff to the investor. The put options illustrated in the second panel tell the same story, with put #1 (the out-of-the-money contract) costing the least but needing the largest price decline to be profitable at expiration. In general, by varying the exercise price on a series of options with otherwise identical contract terms, an investor can

FIGURE 11.6   **TERMINAL PAYOFFS TO OPTIONS WITH DIFFERENT EXERCISE PRICES**

TABLE 11.4	STOCK AND OPTION INVESTMENT RETURNS

A. Long Stock versus Long Call

Terminal Stock Price	Long Stock	Long Call
30	$\frac{30}{40} - 1 = -25.0\%$	$\frac{0}{5.24} - 1 = -100.0\%$
40	$\frac{40}{40} - 1 = 0.0\%$	$\frac{0}{5.24} - 1 = -100.0\%$
50	$\frac{50}{40} - 1 = 25.0\%$	$\frac{10}{5.24} - 1 = 90.8\%$

B. Short Stock versus Long Put

Terminal Stock Price	Short Stock	Long Put
30	$1 - \frac{30}{40} = 25.0\%$	$\frac{10}{3.67} - 1 = 172.5\%$
40	$1 - \frac{40}{40} = 0.0\%$	$\frac{0}{3.67} - 1 = -100.0\%$
50	$1 - \frac{50}{40} = -25.0\%$	$\frac{0}{3.67} - 1 = -100.0\%$

create just as many different risk–reward trade-offs for herself. This is one of several examples of how derivatives can be used to modify investment risk and to "customize" a desired payoff structure.

As a final extension of this example, let us compare the returns to an investment in either a put or a call option with an investment (or short sale) in a share of the underlying SAS stock. To focus on the important issues, we will limit the analysis to call #2 and put #2, the two at-the-money contracts. Table 11.4 summarizes the holding period returns for various positions assuming three different expiration date stock prices: $30, $40, and $50. Two different comparisons are made: (1) long stock versus long call and (2) short stock versus long put. In calculating the returns to the stock positions, we have measured the change in value of the SAS share as a percentage of the initial price of $40. For the option positions, the terminal payoffs of max$[0, S_T - 40]$ for the call and max$[0, 40 - S_T]$ for the put are listed relative to the contract's purchase price.

The most important thing to realize about these calculations is that both put and call options magnify the possible positive and negative returns of investing in the underlying security. In the case of the long call option position, for an initial cost of $5.24 the investor can retain the right to access the price appreciation of a share of SAS stock without spending $40 to own the share outright. This degree of financial *leverage* manifests itself in a 100 percent loss when the stock price falls by a quarter of that amount and a 91 percent gain when SAS shares increase in value from $40 to $50. Notably, if the stock price remains at $40, the owner of the share would not have lost anything while the call holder would have lost his entire investment, which was pure time premium at origination for the at-the-money contract. This suggests that in addition to anticipating the *direction* of the subsequent underlying stock price movement, the option investor also is taking a view on the *timing* of that movement. If the price of SAS stock had stayed at $40 through date T and then rose to $50 on the following day, the stockholder would have experienced a 25 percent gain while the buyer of the call option would have seen the instrument expire worthless.

THE
RELATIONSHIP
BETWEEN
FORWARD AND
OPTION
CONTRACTS

The preceding discussion highlighted the fact that positions in forward and option contracts can lead to similar investment payoffs if the price of the underlying security moves in the anticipated direction. As we saw, the difference in the payoffs to these derivatives came when the security's price changed adversely. This similarity in payoff structures suggests that there is a tractable set of relationships between these instruments. In fact, we will see that the values of five different securities can be linked: a risk-free bond, an underlying asset, a forward contract for the future purchase or sale of that asset, a call option, and a put option. These relationships, known as **put-call parity,** specify how the put and call premiums should be set relative to one another. Further, these conditions can be expressed in terms of the connection between these two option types and either the spot or forward market price for the underlying asset. They depend on the assumption that financial markets are free from arbitrage opportunities, meaning that securities (or portfolios of securities) offering identical payoffs with identical risks must sell for the same current price. As such, put-call parity represents an important first step in understanding how derivatives are valued in an efficient capital market.[2]

PUT-CALL-SPOT
PARITY

Suppose that at date 0 (the present) an investor forms the following portfolio involving three securities related to Company WYZ:

- Long in a share of WYZ common stock at a purchase price of S_0;
- Long in a put option to deliver one share of WYZ stock at an exercise price of X on the expiration date T. This put could be purchased for the price of $P_{0,T}$;
- Short in a call option allowing the purchase of one share of WYZ stock at an exercise price of X on the expiration date T. This call could be sold for the price $C_{0,T}$.

In this example, both of the WYZ options are European-style and have the same expiration date and exercise price. However, the specific values of the expiration date and exercise price do not affect the conclusion of the analysis that follows. Further, we will assume initially that WYZ stock does not pay a dividend during the life of the options.

With these definitions, notice in the top panel of Table 11.5 that the date 0 investment necessary to acquire this portfolio is $(S_0 + P_{0,T} - C_{0,T})$, which is the cost of the long positions in the stock and the put option less the proceeds generated by the sale of the call option.[3] A more interesting thing to consider is the value that this portfolio will have at the expiration date of the two options. Given that the stock's value at date T (i.e., S_T) is unknown when the investment is made at period 0, two general outcomes are possible: (1) $S_T \leq X$ and (2) $S_T > X$. The bottom panel of Table 11.5 shows the value of each position as well as the net value of the whole portfolio at date T.

Notice that whenever the date T value of WYZ stock is less than the exercise price common to the put and call options, it is best for the investor to exercise the long position in

[2] The development of the relationships linking put and call option prices is commonly attributed to Hans R. Stoll, "The Relationship Between Put and Call Option Prices," *Journal of Finance* 24, no. 5 (December 1969): 801–824. It has been embellished in many interesting ways, including Robert C. Merton, "The Relationship Between Put and Call Option Prices: Comment," *Journal of Finance* 28, no. 1 (March 1973): 183–184; Joel S. Sternberg, "A Reexamination of Put-Call Parity on Index Futures," *Journal of Futures Markets* 14, no. 1 (Spring 1994): 79–105; and Avraham Kamara and Thomas W. Miller, Jr., "Daily and Intradaily Tests for European Put-Call Parity," *Journal of Financial and Quantitative Analysis* 30, no. 4 (December 1995): 519–539.

[3] In the "arithmetic" of engineering financial portfolios, a plus ("+") sign can be interpreted as a long position and a minus ("−") sign represents a short position. Thus the portfolio investment represented by $(S_0 + P_{0,T} - C_{0,T})$ can also be expressed as (long stock) + (long put) + (short call). Donald J. Smith, "The Arithmetic of Financial Engineering," *Journal of Applied Corporate Finance* 1, no. 4 (Winter 1989): 49–58, explains this approach in more detail.

| TABLE 11.5 | PUT-CALL-SPOT PARITY |

A. Net Portfolio Investment at Initiation (Date 0)

Portfolio

Long 1 WYZ Stock	S_0
Long 1 Put Option	$P_{0,T}$
Short 1 Call Option	$-C_{0,T}$
Net Investment:	$S_0 + P_{0,T} - C_{0,T}$

B. Portfolio Value at Option Expiration (Date T)

Portfolio	(1) If $S_T \leq X$:	(2) If $S_T > X$:
Long 1 WYZ Stock	S_T	S_T
Long 1 Put Option	$(X - S_T)$	0
Short 1 Call Option	0	$-(S_T - X)$
Net Position:	X	X

the put and sell the WYZ share for X instead of its lower market value. Under the same condition, it will not be rational for the holder of the call to pay X for a share that is worth less. Therefore, the call will expire out of the money. On the other hand, when S_T exceeds X, the holder of the call will exercise the option to purchase WYZ stock for X from the investor while the put would be out of the money. In either case, the net expiration date value of the position is X because the combination of options contained in the portfolio guarantees that the investor will sell the share of WYZ stock at date T for the fixed price X. That is, at stock prices lower than X, the investor will choose to sell the share at a profit, although he will be forced to sell at a loss when WYZ trades on the market at a price higher than X. The investor has, in effect, a guaranteed contract to sell the share of stock when the long put and short call positions are considered jointly.

The consequence of this result is that when the investor commits $(S_0 + P_{0,T} - C_{0,T})$ to acquire the position at date 0, he knows that it will be worth X at date T. Thus, this particular portfolio has a comparable payoff structure to a U.S. Treasury bill, another risk-free, zero-coupon security that can be designed to have a face value of X and a maturity date T. In an arbitrage-free (i.e., efficient) capital market, this means that the date 0 value of the portfolio must be equal to that of the T-bill, which is just the face value X discounted to the present using the risk-free rate. This "no arbitrage" condition can be formalized as follows:

$$S_0 + P_{0,T} - C_{0,T} = \frac{X}{(1 + RFR)^T}$$

where:

RFR = the annualized risk-free rate
T = the time to maturity (expressed in years)

Defining $[X(1 + RFR)^{-T}]$ as the present value of a T-bill this equation can be expressed in "financial arithmetic" terms as:

(long stock) + (long put) + (short call) = (long T-bill).

In either form, this condition—known as the *put-call-spot* parity condition—indicates the efficient market linkages between prices for stock, T-bills, put options, and call options.

PUT-CALL PARITY:
AN EXAMPLE

As an example of how put-call parity might be used, suppose that WYZ stock is currently valued at $53 and that call and put options on WYZ stock with an exercise price of $50 sell for $6.74 and $2.51, respectively. Assuming that both options can only be exercised on their shared expiration date in exactly six months, the above equation suggests that we can "make" a synthetic T-bill by purchasing the stock, purchasing the put, and selling the call for a net price of $48.77 (= 53.00 + 2.51 − 6.74). At the options' expiration date, this portfolio would have a terminal value of $50. Thus, the risk-free rate implied by this investment can be established by solving the following equation for RFR:

$$48.77 = 50 \, (1 + RFR)^{-0.5}$$

or

$$RFR = [(50 \div 48.77)^2 - 1] = 5.11\%.$$

The practical application of this finding is that if the rate of return on an actual six-month T-bill with a face value of $50 is not 5.11%, then an investor could exploit the difference. Suppose, for instance, that the actual T-bill rate is 6.25% and that there are no restrictions against using the proceeds from the short sale of any security. In such a situation, an investor wanting a risk-free investment would clearly choose the actual T-bill to lock in the higher return, while someone seeking a loan might attempt to secure a 5.11% borrowing rate by short-selling the synthetic T-bill. With an arithmetic rearrangement of the parity condition in the previous equation, such an artificial short position can be obtained as (short stock) + (short put) + (long call) = (short T-bill).

With no transaction costs, a financial arbitrage could be constructed by combining a long position in the actual T-bill with a short sale of the synthetic portfolio. Given that the current value of the actual T-bill is $48.51 (= $50 $(1.0625)^{-0.5}$), this set of transactions would generate the cash flows shown in Table 11.6 and produce only a $0.26 profit per each T-bill pair created. However, as the arbitrage trade did not require the investor to bear

---

TABLE 11.6   **A PUT-CALL PARITY ARBITRAGE EXAMPLE**

A. Net Initial Investment (Date 0)

Transaction	
1. Long actual T-bill at 6.25%	−48.51
2. Short synthetic T-bill at 5.11%:	
Short WYZ stock	53.00
Short put option	2.51
Long call option	−6.74
Net receipt:	0.26

B. Position Value at Option Expiration (Date T)

Transaction	(1) If $S_T \leq 50$:	(2) If $S_T > 50$:
1. Long actual T-bill at 6.25%	50	50
2. Short synthetic T-bill at 5.11%:		
Short WYZ stock	$-S_T$	$-S_T$
Short put option	$-(50 - S_T)$	0
Long call option	0	$(S_T - 50)$
Net position:	0	0

any risk (i.e., both the date 0 and date T values of the net position were known at inception) nor commit any capital, there is nothing in this example to prevent the investor from expanding the size of the trade to increasingly larger levels. Unfortunately, as additional transactions take place, the price discrepancy will disappear. In this case, the purchase of the actual T-bill and sale of the synthetic (short stock, short put, and long call) will continue until rates are equalized. This is how the markets remain efficient through arbitrage trading.

Another way of seeing this trade is

$$C_{0,T} - P_{0,T} = S_0 - X(1 + RFR)^{-T}.$$

That is, the "no arbitrage" difference between the call and put prices should equal the difference between the stock price and the present value of the joint exercise price. The market-determined risk-free rate of 6.25% implies that the correct difference between the two derivatives should be $4.49 (= 53 − 48.51), which is $0.26 greater than the $4.23 (= 6.74 − 2.51) actual difference. This discrepancy suggests that if you assume the actual T-bill is priced correctly, the call price is undervalued relative to the put option. Notice that the arbitrage transaction requires the purchase of the call option while shorting the put option.

CREATING SYNTHETIC SECURITIES USING PUT-CALL PARITY

The preceding example demonstrates that a risk-free portfolio could be created by combining three risky securities: stock, a put option, and a call option. The parity condition developed above can be expressed in other useful ways as well. In particular, one of the four assets represented in the first equation is always *redundant* because it can be defined in terms of the others. Three additional ways of manipulating this result are:

$$P_{0,T} = \frac{X}{(1 + RFR)^T} - S_0 + C_{0,T}$$

$$C_{0,T} = S_0 + P_{0,T} - \frac{X}{(1 + RFR)^T}$$

$$S_0 = \frac{X}{(1 + RFR)^T} - P_{0,T} + C_{0,T}$$

The first two of these equations indicate, respectively, that (1) a long position in a put option can be replicated by a portfolio consisting of a long position in a T-bill, a short stock position, and the purchase of a call option; and (2) a synthetic call option can be mimicked by a portfolio that is long in the stock and the put option and short in the T-bill. The final equation indicates that the payoff to the stock itself can be expressed by its derivative securities and the T-bill.

These results are useful in two ways. First, if there are not markets in either put or call options, the relationships summarized by these equations outline how investors can create the desired, but unavailable, pattern of cash flows through the appropriate "packaging" of the other three interrelated assets. Suppose, for example, that a put option on WYZ stock did not exist, but a call option does. Table 11.7 shows the date 0 and date T cash flows associated with the portfolio replicating the terminal payoff. Combining both panels of the display, an initial investment of $[X(1 + RFR)^{-T} - S_0 + C_{0,T}]$ leads to a final cash flow that is no less than zero and as large as $X - S_T$ whenever $X > S_T$. Expressed in a more traditional manner, the expiration date payoff to the synthetic put is $\max[0, X - S_T]$.

Another way the alternative expressions for the put-call parity model (summarized by the three above equations) are used in practice is the identification of arbitrage opportunities. Even when a particular derivative instrument trades actively in the market, if its cash

TABLE 11.7	REPLICATING A PUT OPTION

A. Net Portfolio Investment at Initiation (Date 0)

Portfolio	
Long 1 T-bill	$X(1 + RFR)^{-T}$
Short 1 WYZ stock	$-S_0$
Long 1 call option	$C_{0,T}$
Net investment:	$X(1 + RFR)^{-T} - S_0 + C_{0,T}$

B. Portfolio Value at Option Expiration (Date T)

Portfolio	(1) If $S_T \leq X$:	(2) If $S_T > X$:
Long 1 T-bill	X	X
Short 1 WYZ stock	$-S_T$	$-S_T$
Long 1 call option	0	$(S_T - X)$
Net position:	$X - S_T$	0

flows and risks can be duplicated, this leads to the possibility that the price of the actual instrument and the net cost of the replicating portfolio will differ. Using the numbers from the previous example, the date T distribution of max$[0, 50 - S_T]$ could be acquired through the synthetic strategy at a cost of $2.25 (= 48.51 - 53 + 6.74) or through the purchase of the actual put for $2.51.

This is the same $0.26 price differential we saw earlier when designing an arbitrage transaction involving the actual and synthetic T-bill. The put option arbitrage would be to short the actual put while buying the replicating portfolio (i.e., long T-bill, short stock, and long call), which is the same set of transactions we used in the T-bill arbitrage. This result underscores the important point that the put-call parity model only allows us to make *relative*—rather than absolute—statements about security values. Although we can change our perspective in identifying the misvalued instrument (e.g., T-bill versus put option), the real source of the market inefficiency came from examining the *difference* between the put and call prices in relation to the stock and T-bill prices. Consequently, all four securities need to be included in the arbitrage trade.

ADJUSTING PUT-CALL-SPOT PARITY FOR DIVIDENDS

A second extension of the put-call-spot parity model involves the payment of dividends to the shareholders of WYZ stock. Suppose for simplicity that in the basic portfolio listed in Table 11.5, WYZ stock pays a dividend of D_T immediately prior to the expiration of the options at date T. Assume further that the amount of this distribution is known when the investment is initiated, a condition that is almost certainly met for values of $T \leq 0.25$ year because U.S.-based companies typically pay quarterly dividends. The result of these modifications is that the terminal value of the long stock position will be $(S_T + D_T)$. On the other hand, the terminal payoffs to the put and call options remain max$[0, X - S_T]$ and max$[0, S_T - X]$, respectively, as the holders of the two derivative contracts will not participate directly in the payment of dividend to the stockholder.[4] Thus, the net date T value of the portfolio acquired originally for $(S_0 + P_{0,T} - C_{0,T})$ is $(X + D_T)$.

---

[4] The fact that the expiration date payoff to a call option on both a dividend- and nondividend-paying stock can be expressed as max$[0, S_T - X]$ does not mean that the two will generate the same dollar amount of cash flow. This is because the stock's value will be reduced by the payment of the dividend in the former case but not in the latter. Thus with the lower terminal payout, the call on the dividend-paying stock will be less valuable than an otherwise comparable contract on a nondividend-paying equity. We will explore this topic more fully in Chapter 24.

With the critical assumption that the dividend payment is known at date 0, the portfolio long in WYZ stock, long in the put, and short in the call once again can be viewed as equivalent to a T-bill, now having a face value of $(X + D_T)$. This allows the first equation to be adapted as follows:

$$S_0 + P_{0,T} - C_{0,T} = \frac{X + D_T}{(1 + RFR)^T} = \frac{X}{(1 + RFR)^T} + \frac{D_T}{(1 + RFR)^T}$$

which can be interpreted as:

(long stock) + (long put) + (short call) = (long T-bill) + (long present value of dividends).

Alternatively, it is often more useful to rearrange this equation as follows:

$$\left\{ S_0 - \frac{D_T}{(1 + RFR)^T} \right\} + P_{0,T} - C_{0,T} = \frac{X}{(1 + RFR)^T}.$$

In this form, the equation can be compared directly with the no-dividend put-call-spot parity result and shows that the current stock price must be *adjusted downward* by the present value of the dividend. With an initial stock price of $53 and an annualized risk-free rate on a six-month T-bill of 6.25%, a $1 dividend paid just before the expiration of a call and a put option with an exercise price of $50 would result in a theoretical price differential of:

$$C_{0,0.5} - P_{0,0.5} = \left\{ 53 - \frac{1}{(1 + .0625)^{0.5}} \right\} - \frac{50}{(1 + .0625)^{0.5}} = \$3.52.$$

This value differs from the parity differential for options on the nondividend-paying stock, which was shown earlier to be $4.49. Thus the payment of the dividend has reduced the price of the call relative to the put by $0.97, which is the discounted amount of the $1 distribution.

Put-Call-Forward Parity

At this point in our analysis of the structural relationships between derivative instruments and their underlying securities, we have not explicitly included forward or futures contracts. Suppose that instead of buying the stock in the spot market at date 0, we took a long position in a forward contract allowing us to purchase one share of WYZ stock at date T. The price of this acquisition, $F_{0,T}$, would be established by the forward agreement at date 0. As before, we will assume that this transaction is supplemented by the purchase of a put option and the sale of a call option, each having the same exercise price and expiration date. Table 11.8 summarizes both the initial and terminal cash flows to this position.

The bottom panel of the table reveals that this is once again a risk-free portfolio. There are, however, two important differences in its cash flow patterns. First, the net initial investment of $(P_{0,T} - C_{0,T})$ is substantially smaller than when the stock was purchased in the spot market. Second, the riskless terminal payoff of $(X - F_{0,T})$ also is smaller than before as the stock now must be purchased at date T rather than at date 0. This intuition leads directly to the *put-call-forward* parity condition:

$$P_{0,T} - C_{0,T} = \frac{X - F_{0,T}}{(1 + RFR)^T} = \frac{X}{(1 + RFR)^T} - \frac{F_{0,T}}{(1 + RFR)^T}$$

TABLE 11.8	**PUT-CALL-FORWARD PARITY**

A. Net Portfolio Investment at Initiation (Date 0)

Portfolio	
Long 1 forward contract	0
Long 1 put option	$P_{0,T}$
Short 1 call option	$-C_{0,T}$
Net investment:	$P_{0,T} - C_{0,T}$

B. Portfolio Value at Option Expiration (Date T)

Portfolio	(1) If $S_T \leq X$:	(2) If $S_T > X$:
Long 1 forward contract	$(S_T - F_{0,T})$	$(S_T - F_{0,T})$
Long 1 put option	$(X - S_T)$	0
Short 1 call option	0	$-(S_T - X)$
Net position:	$(X - F_{0,T})$	$(X - F_{0,T})$

which says that for markets to be free from arbitrage, the difference between put and call prices must equal the discounted difference between the shared exercise price and the contract price of the forward agreement. Just as $F_{0,T}$ did not appear in the spot market version of the parity condition, the current stock price does not appear in this equation.

This result implies that the only time that put and call prices should be equal to one another in an efficient market is when $X = F_{0,T}$. That is, although the put-call parity result holds for any common exercise price, there is only one value of X for which there would be no net cost to the option combination and that is the prevailing forward price. Recall, for example, that when WYZ stock did not pay a dividend, the theoretical difference between $C_{0,0.5}$ and $P_{0,0.5}$ was $4.49 (= 53 − 48.51). This meant that an investor long in the call and short in the put with a shared $50 exercise price would have what amounted to a forward contract to buy WYZ stock in six months at a price of $50.[5] However, she would have to pay $4.49 for this arrangement, suggesting that $50 is a below-market forward price. How much below the prevailing forward contract price is $50? By the future value of $4.49, invested at the prevailing risk-free rate of 6.25%. Thus the no-arbitrage forward price under these circumstances should be $54.63 [= 50 + 4.49(1 + .0625)^{0.5}].

Another way to see this result comes from combining the put-call-forward parity condition with the put-call-spot condition. Specifically, inserting the expression for $(P_{0,T} - C_{0,T})$ from the put-call-forward parity condition into the put-call-spot condition leaves:

$$S_0 + \left\{ \frac{X}{(1 + RFR)^T} - \frac{F_{0,T}}{(1 + RFR)^T} \right\} = \frac{X}{(1 + RFR)^T}$$

which simplifies to:

$$S_0 = \frac{F_{0,T}}{(1 + RFR)^T}.$$

---

[5] This interpretation follows by noting that the long call position will be exercised when $S_T \geq 50$ and the short put will be exercised against the investor when $S_T < 50$. Therefore, the investor's net option position produces an identical result to holding a long position in a forward contract with a contract price of $50. Generalizing this result, any time we have a call and a put option on the same underlying stock with a common exercise price and expiration date, the following is true: (long call at X) + (short put at X) = (long forward at X). Similarly, shorting the call and buying the put produces a short forward position.

This equation indicates that, in the absence of dividend payments, the spot price for the share of stock should simply be the discounted value of purchasing the same security in the forward market. Equivalently, this equation can be rewritten so that $F_{0,T} = S_0(1 + RFR)^T$. In the above example, this means that the market-clearing (i.e., no net initial cost) contract price for a WYZ stock forward agreement should be $F_{0,0.5} = (53)(1 + .0625)^{0.5} = \$54.63$. Finally, in the case where dividends are paid, the equation for the put-call-forward parity condition can be inserted into the dividend-adjusted spot parity condition to produce the more general relationship between spot and forward prices:

$$\left\{ S_0 - \frac{D_T}{(1 + RFR)^T} \right\} = \frac{F_{0,T}}{(1 + RFR)^T} \, .$$

Thus, if a $1 dollar dividend were paid on WYZ stock just prior to the maturity of the contract in six months, the forward price would be adjusted down to $F_{0,0.5} = (53)(1 + .0625)^{0.5} - 1 = \$53.63$ to account for the cash distribution that would benefit the actual shareholders but not the derivative holder.

APPLICATIONS OF DERIVATIVES IN PORTFOLIO MANAGEMENT

Beyond the unique risk–reward profiles they offer as stand-alone investments, derivatives also are used widely in investment management to restructure the fundamental nature of an existing portfolio of assets. Although the typical intent of this sort of restructuring is to modify the portfolio's risk, derivatives also can create opportunities to enhance the short-term income generated by a portfolio. In this section, we review three prominent derivative applications in the management of equity positions: shorting forward contracts, purchasing **protective puts,** and writing **covered calls.**

RESTRUCTURING ASSET PORTFOLIOS WITH FORWARD CONTRACTS

Suppose the manager of a small corporate pension fund currently has all of her investable funds committed to a well-diversified portfolio of equity securities designed to reflect the movements of a broad indicator of the stock market's performance, such as Standard & Poor's 500 index. Implicit in this investment approach is the manager's belief that she cannot "add value" by trying to select superior individual securities. She does, however, feel that it is possible to take advantage of perceived trends at a macroeconomic level by switching her funds between her current equity holding and any of several other portfolios mimicking different asset classes (e.g., fixed-income, cash equivalents), depending on her forecast of future events. Switching a portfolio's composition in an attempt to time general market movements instead of company-specific trends is known as *tactical asset allocation.*

The stock market has increased steadily over the past several months, and the pension fund has a present market value of $100 million. At this time, though, the manager has become concerned about the possibility that inflationary pressures will dampen corporate earnings and drive stock prices down. Although it is unclear now whether this concern will be realized, she feels confident that the uncertainty will be resolved in the coming quarter. Accordingly, she would like to shift her allocation from 100 percent equity to 100 percent T-bills for the next three months. There are two ways she can make this change. The most direct method would be to sell her stock portfolio and buy $100 million (less the transaction costs) of 90-day T-bills. When the T-bills mature in three months, she could then repurchase her original equity holdings.

The second approach would be to maintain her current stock holdings, but convert them into a synthetic risk-free position with a three-month forward contract specifying $100 million of the stock index as the underlying asset. This is a classic example of a hedge position, wherein the price risk of the underlying asset is offset (rather than eliminated) by a supplementary derivative transaction. The following table captures the dynamics of this hedge at a basic level.

Economic Event	Actual Stock Exposure	Desired Forward Exposure
Stock prices fall	Loss	Gain
Stock prices rise	Gain	Loss

To neutralize the risk of falling stock prices, the fund manager will need to adopt a forward position that benefits from that potential movement. Said differently, the manager requires a hedge position with payoffs that are *negatively correlated* with those of the existing exposure. As we saw in Figure 11.3, this requires committing to the short side of the contract. This hedging argument is identical to the point we made in the portfolio formation analysis of Chapter 8 that it is always possible to combine two perfectly negatively correlated assets to create a risk-free position.

The primary benefit of converting the pension fund's asset allocation using this approach is that it is far more cost-effective than the physical transformations demanded by the first solution. Hill has shown that when all the costs of trading are considered, the average expense of the actual conversion is about ten times greater than the synthetic one in many markets throughout the world.[6] These statistics are summarized in Table 11.9 and include the *transaction costs* of acquiring or divesting the positions, the *market impact*

TABLE 11.9

ESTIMATED TRANSACTION COSTS AS A PERCENTAGE OF INVESTMENT (AS OF NOVEMBER 1992)

Cost	United States (S&P 500)	Japan (Nikkei 225)	United Kingdom (FT-SE 100)	France (CAC 40)	Germany (DAX)
A. Stocks					
Commissions	0.14%	0.20%	0.20%	0.10%	0.10%
Market impact	0.55	0.70	0.90	0.55	0.50
Taxes	0.00	0.30	0.50	0.00	0.00
Total	0.69%	1.20%	1.60%	0.65%	0.60%
Average share price (in U.S. dollars)	$39.10	$27.30	$7.73	$158.60	$385.65
B. Futures					
Commissions	0.01%	0.06%	0.02%	0.04%	0.03%
Market impact	0.05	0.05	0.10	0.10	0.05
Taxes	0.00	0.00	0.00	0.00	0.00
Total	0.06%	0.11%	0.12%	0.14%	0.08%

Source: Joanne M. Hill, "Adding Value with Equity Derivatives," in *Derivative Strategies for Managing Portfolio Risk,* edited by K. Brown (Charlottesville, VA: Association for Investment Management and Research, 1993): 62–71.

---

[6] See Joanne M. Hill, "Adding Value with Equity Derivatives," in *Derivative Strategies for Managing Portfolio Risk,* edited by K. Brown (Charlottesville, VA: Association for Investment Management and Research, 1993): 62–71.

(i.e., price displacement caused by the trade itself) costs, and *tax obligations*. In the United States, the total round-trip expense associated with a stock trade is 69 basis points of the asset's value, while the same trade with an index futures contract would cost just six basis points.[7] Trading costs in other countries, though different in absolute level, reflect this same general trend.

A possible disadvantage of modifying portfolio risk with the short forward position is that the contract's underlying asset will not match exactly the actual equity holding. The danger in such a situation is that prices for the stock portfolio and the contract may not change in precisely the same fashion, which could leave the manager exposed to a larger drop in the value of the fund than would be offset by an increase in the value of the short forward position. The mismatch level in these two price movements is called the *tracking error* of the derivative. Hill documented that this tracking error is between 1 percent and 4 percent for most of the world's index futures contracts. In terms of our previous notation, assume that the date T value of the stock portfolio is S_T while the settlement of the forward contract is $[F_{0,T} - S_T^*]$, with S_T^* reflecting a slightly different composition of the contract's underlying security portfolio relative to the actual equity holding. At the origination of the hedge, the date T value for the converted stock portfolio is then $[F_{0,T} + (S_T - S_T^*)]$, which is only risk-free if S_T and S_T^* are equal. The tracking error can therefore be seen as the degree to which movements in S_T and S_T^* are not perfectly correlated.

A final way of seeing this synthetic restructuring is through the effect that it has had on the systematic risk—or beta— of the portfolio. By its original construction, we will assume that the original stock holding had a beta of one, matching the volatility of a proxy for the market portfolio. Further assuming that the stock index forward contract has no tracking error (i.e., $S_T = S_T^*$), the combination of being long $100 million of stock and short a forward covering $100 million of a stock index converts the systematic portion of the portfolio into a synthetic T-bill, which by definition has a beta of zero. Once the contract matures in three months, however, the position will revert to its original risk profile. This is illustrated in Figure 11.7. More generally, the short forward position can be designed to allow for intermediate combinations of stock and T-bills as well. To see this, let w_S be the stock allocation so that $(1 - w_S)$ is the allocation to the risk-free asset created synthetically. The net beta for the converted portfolio is simply a weighted average of the systematic risks of its equity and T-bill portions or:

$$\beta_P = (w_S)\beta_S + (1 - w_S)\beta_{RFR}.$$

Thus, if the manager had wished to change the original allocation from 100 percent stock to a "60–40" mix of stock and T-bills, she would have shorted only $40 million of the index forward to leave her with an unhedged equity position totaling $60 million (i.e., $w_S = 0.60$ and $(1 - w_S) = 0.40$). By the above equation, this in turn would leave her with an adjusted portfolio beta of $[(0.6)(1) + (0.4)(0)] = 0.6$.

PROTECTING PORTFOLIO VALUE WITH PUT OPTIONS

Although the manager's concern in the previous example was to protect her stock portfolio against possible share price declines over the next three months, by shorting the stock index forward contract, she has effectively committed to "selling" her equity position— even if stock prices rise. That is, by using a derivative with a symmetric payoff structure to hedge her risk, the manager also has surrendered the upside potential of her original

---

[7] A *basis point* is 1/100 of one percent, or 0.01%. Thus, the reported United States stock transaction cost of 0.69% can be expressed as 69 basis points.

FIGURE 11.7   **ALTERING THE SYSTEMATIC RISK OF A STOCK PORTFOLIO SYNTHETICALLY**

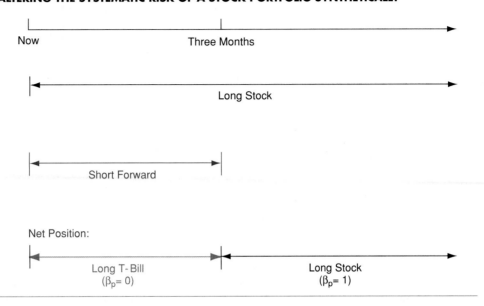

holding. Recognizing this, suppose instead that she attempted to design a hedge position correlated to her stock portfolio as shown in the following table.

Economic Event	Actual Stock Exposure	Desired Hedge Exposure
Stock prices fall	Loss	Gain
Stock prices rise	Gain	*No loss*

In seeking an asymmetric hedge, this manager wants a derivative contract that allows her to sell stock when prices fall but keep her shares when prices rise. As we have seen, she must purchase a put option to obtain this exposure.

The purchase of a put option to hedge the downside risk of an underlying security holding is called a *protective put* position and is the most straightforward example of a more general set of derivative-based strategies known as *portfolio insurance*.[8] To see this insurance interpretation, suppose that in lieu of the short forward position, the manager purchased a three-month, at-the-money put option on her $100 million stock portfolio. Under the prevailing market conditions, let us also assume that this put cost the manager an up-front premium of $1.324 million. The value of the protective put position (net of the initial cost of the hedge) is calculated in Table 11.10 for several different expiration date prices for the underlying stock portfolio. In particular, notice that with the exercise price set equal to the current portfolio value of $100 million, the put contract exactly offsets any

[8] The concept and use of portfolio insurance has received a great deal of scrutiny in research literature. See, for example, the studies by Mark Rubinstein, "Alternative Paths to Portfolio Insurance," *Financial Analysts Journal* 41, no. 4 (July–August 1985): 42–52; Mark Kritzman, "What's Wrong with Portfolio Insurance?" *Journal of Portfolio Management* 13, no. 1 (Fall 1986): 13–17; and Harry M. Kat, "Portfolio Insurance: A Comparison of Alternative Strategies," *Journal of Financial Engineering* 1, no. 4 (1993): 415–442.

| TABLE 11.10 | **EXPIRATION DATE VALUE OF A PROTECTIVE PUT POSITION** |

Potential Portfolio Value	Value of Put Option	Cost of Put Option	Net Protective Put Position
60	(100 − 60) = 40	−1.324	(60 + 40) − 1.324 = 98.676
70	(100 − 70) = 30	−1.324	(70 + 30) − 1.324 = 98.676
80	(100 − 80) = 20	−1.324	(80 + 20) − 1.324 = 98.676
90	(100 − 90) = 10	−1.324	(90 + 10) − 1.324 = 98.676
100	0	−1.324	(100 + 0) − 1.324 = 98.676
110	0	−1.324	(110 + 0) − 1.324 = 108.676
120	0	−1.324	(120 + 0) − 1.324 = 118.676
130	0	−1.324	(130 + 0) − 1.324 = 128.676
140	0	−1.324	(140 + 0) − 1.324 = 138.676

expiration date share price decline while allowing the position to increase in value as stock prices increase. Thus the put provides the manager with insurance against falling prices with no *deductible*.[9]

An intriguing aspect of the terminal value of the combined stock and put option portfolio shown in the last column of Table 11.10 is that it resembles the payoff diagram of the long call option position illustrated earlier in Figure 11.4. A different way of seeing this is shown in Figure 11.8, which indicates that being long in the stock and long in the put generates the same net payoff as an at-the-money long call option holding "elevated" by $100 million. Given the put-call-spot parity results of the previous section, however, this should come as no surprise. Indeed, the no-arbitrage equation can be rewritten:

$$S_0 + P_{0,T} = C_{0,T} + \frac{X}{(1 + RFR)^T}.$$

This expression says that the protective put method of providing portfolio insurance generates an equivalent expiration date payoff as a long position in a call option with the same characteristics as the put and a long position in a T-bill with a face value equal to the options' common exercise price. It is this final term that provides the "elevation" to the call payoff diagram in Figure 11.8. Thus the manager has two ways of providing price insurance for her current stock holding: (1) continue to hold her shares and purchase a put option, or (2) sell her shares and buy both a T-bill and a call option. Her choice between them will undoubtedly come down to specific logistic considerations such as relative option prices and transaction costs.

Finally, it is interesting to consider the effect that the purchase of a protective put option has on the measured risk of the hedged portfolio. In past chapters, we have seen that the standard deviation of a security's return distribution is a useful way to capture the dispersion of the potential payoffs from that expected by the capital market. By its construction, though, the standard deviation is a symmetric measure of dispersion; it does not distinguish a potential return that is two percent below the mean from one that is two percent above

---

[9] In general, the deductible portion of the portfolio insurance contract can be defined as $[S_0 − X]$. For instance, with an exercise price of only 95, the manager would not receive compensation from the hedge until the portfolio value fell below $95 million; she would effectively be "self-insuring" the first $5 million of losses. Naturally, the larger this deductible amount, the lower the cost of the put option. For a more complete discussion of "insured stocks," see Keith C. Brown and Meir Statman, "The Benefits of Insured Stocks for Corporate Cash Management," *Advances in Futures and Options Research* 2 (1987): 243–261.

FIGURE 11.8   **TERMINAL PAYOFF TO AN "INSURED" STOCK POSITION**

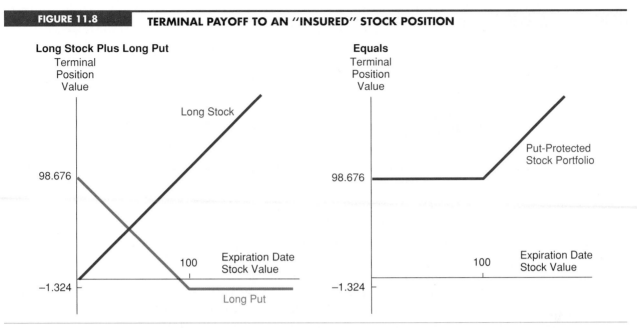

Implicit in this choice of risk measure, then, is the assumption that the distribution of future returns is also symmetric, thereby making the distinction between downside and upside risk a moot point. As we have just seen, however, adding a put option to a stock portfolio that otherwise might have had symmetric returns truncates the combined distribution by eliminating losses beneath the level of the option premium plus the deductible. Consequently, depending on the degree of "optionality" in a portfolio, standard deviation might not be an effective measure of risk because it does not discriminate between potential losses and potential gains.[10]

In this example, a convenient tool for understanding the effect that adding an at-the-money put option will have on the manager's distribution of potential portfolio values is a *Monte Carlo simulation*. This statistical method attempts to recreate a frequency distribution of potential outcomes by repeatedly choosing random values based on the underlying risk and return characteristics of the securities themselves.[11] For example, suppose that the manager's portfolio has an expected annual return of 12 percent and a standard deviation of 10 percent. Under these circumstances, she can expect her portfolio to increase in value by $3 million after three months. However, assuming that returns to the stock portfolio are normally distributed (i.e., bell-shaped), $103 million is just the midpoint of the possible outcomes three months in the future. For a random sampling of 10,000 observations, this

---

[10] Many authors have studied the effect that adding options to an underlying security position has on the risk of the combined portfolio. In particular, see Robert C. Merton, Myron S. Scholes, and Mathew L. Gladstein, "A Simulation of the Returns and Risk of Alternative Option Portfolio Investment Strategies," *Journal of Business* 51, no. 2 (April 1978): 183–242, and Richard M. Bookstaber and Roger G. Clarke, "Options Can Alter Portfolio Return Distributions," *Journal of Portfolio Management* 7, no. 3 (Spring 1981): 63–70. Also, Roger G. Clarke, "Stochastic Dominance Properties of Option Strategies," *Advances in Futures and Options Research* 2 (1987): 1–18, discusses how a *stochastic dominance* approach can overcome some of the limitations of traditional mean-variance analysis when options are included in a portfolio.

[11] An explanation of this forecasting technique in the fixed-income security management context can be found in Frank J. Fabozzi, *Bond Markets, Analysis and Strategies*, 3d ed. (Upper Saddle River, NJ: Prentice Hall, 1996).

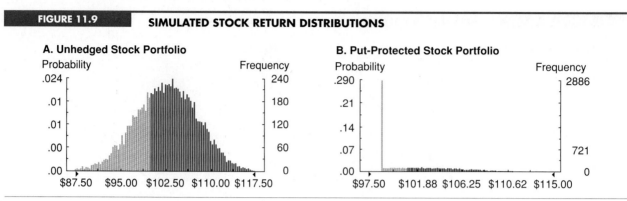

FIGURE 11.9   **SIMULATED STOCK RETURN DISTRIBUTIONS**

distribution of potential values for the unhedged stock portfolio is shown on the left-hand side of Figure 11.9.

The situation changes dramatically when the put option is added to the original portfolio. From the second panel of the figure, notice that the new return distribution is truncated at a value of $98.676 million, once again indicating that the manager can lose no more than the premium she paid for the protective put. On the other hand, the standard deviation for this insured portfolio is 7.65 percent, suggesting an investment with more than a negligible amount of risk. However, even with the expected return reduced to 10.20 percent, the majority of the variability in the insured distribution lies *above* the current portfolio value of $100 million. Consequently, investors who define risk simply in terms of whether they make or lose money would be far more attracted to the second distribution in Figure 11.9 than to the first. Clearly, the put option has not only altered the stock portfolio's risk–return trade-off in a desirable (if costly) way, but has made the measurement of that risk a challenging proposition as well.

ALTERING PORTFOLIO PAYOFFS WITH CALL OPTIONS

A final popular way in which derivatives are used to alter the payoff structure of an asset portfolio involves the sale of call options. When investors sell call options based on their underlying position, they are writing *covered calls*. Usually, the purpose of this strategy is to generate additional income for a portfolio that is not expected to change in value much over the near term. By selling a call in such a situation, an investor receives the premium from the option contract to bolster an otherwise small (or negative) return. The danger, of course, is that the value of the stock position rises above the exercise price by the end of the contract's life, causing the shares to be called away at the lower price.[12]

Extending the preceding example, suppose now that our pension fund manager thinks that over the next three months the value of her stock portfolio will neither rise nor fall by an appreciable amount. Accordingly, she decides not to insure her position against losses, but instead to increase the cash flow of the investment by selling an at-the-money call option. In exchange for granting the contract buyer the right to purchase her stock for $100 million in three months, assume that market conditions dictate that she receive an immediate payment of $2.813 million. Using the same potential stock prices as before, the expiration date values for the covered call position are listed in Table 11.11. The construction of the payoff diagram for net position is shown in Figure 11.10.

_____

[12] For more analysis of the covered call strategy, see James W. Yates, Jr. and Robert W. Kopprasch, Jr., "Writing Covered Call Options: Profits and Risks," *Journal of Portfolio Management* 7, no. 1 (Fall 1980): 74–79.

| TABLE 11.11 | **EXPIRATION DATE VALUE OF A COVERED POSITION** |

Potential Portfolio Value	Value of Call Option	Proceeds from Call Option	Net Protective Put Position
60	0	2.813	$(60 + 0) + 2.813 =\ \ 62.813$
70	0	2.813	$(70 + 0) + 2.813 =\ \ 72.813$
80	0	2.813	$(80 + 0) + 2.813 =\ \ 82.813$
90	0	2.813	$(90 + 0) + 2.813 =\ \ 92.813$
100	0	2.813	$(100 + 0) + 2.813 = 102.813$
110	$-(110 - 100) = -10$	2.813	$(110 - 10) + 2.813 = 102.813$
120	$-(120 - 100) = -20$	2.813	$(120 - 20) + 2.813 = 102.813$
130	$-(130 - 100) = -30$	2.813	$(130 - 30) + 2.813 = 102.813$
140	$-(140 - 100) = -40$	2.813	$(140 - 40) + 2.813 = 102.813$

| FIGURE 11.10 | **TERMINAL PAYOFF TO A COVERED STOCK POSITION** |

Long Stock Plus Short Call

Terminal Position Value

Long Stock

2.813

100

Expiration Date Stock Value

Short Call

Equals

Terminal Position Value

102.813

Covered Call Portfolio

2.813

100

Expiration Date Stock Value

The numbers and the pictures from these displays indicate that the value of the covered call position is comparable to the short put option payoff diagram illustrated earlier in Figure 11.5. Once again, this can be seen directly by adjusting the put-call-spot parity condition:

$$S_0 - C_{0,i} = \frac{X}{(1 + RFR)^i} - P_{0,T}$$

That is, a portfolio long stock and short a call option generates terminal payoffs equivalent to buying a T-bill with a face value equal to the joint exercise price and selling the put. As before, the purpose of the T-bill position is to raise the overall investment to a scale similar to the original position. Notice from Figure 11.10 that there are two dimensions to the price risk inherent in this strategy. First, if the portfolio's date T value rises above $100 million, the manager will be forced to sell her shares for less than they are actually worth. Second, if the portfolio experiences a decline in value, her potential loss is not hedged beyond the $2.813 million in premium income that she received for selling the call; after prices fall beyond $95.863 million (= 100 − 2.813 − 1.324), she would have been better off purchasing the protective put option. To be profitable, the covered call strategy requires that the manager anticipate correctly that share values will remain in a fairly narrow band around their present levels.

Summary

- As their popularity in financial markets has increased over the past two decades, derivative securities have become an indispensable part of the investment manager's toolkit. Although forward, futures, and option contracts play important roles as stand-alone investments, the real advantage of derivatives is their ability to modify the risk–return characteristics of a collection of existing securities in a cost-effective manner. This use of forwards and options to restructure a portfolio synthetically has two dimensions. First, we saw that it is possible to combine derivatives with the underlying position in a way that replicates the cash flow patterns of another traded instrument. For instance, a well-diversified stock portfolio could be converted into the equivalent of a T-bill by shorting an appropriate amount of a stock index futures contract. Second, derivatives can also be used with the original portfolio to create a payoff structure that is otherwise unavailable. The use of a protective put to eliminate the downside risk of an equity holding while maintaining its upside profit potential is an example.
- At a fundamental level, forward and option contracts can be viewed as insurance policies that an investor can hold against adverse price movements in his underlying position. As forwards and options can be structured to provide exactly the same degree of "coverage," the basic difference between these contracts lies in how the investor must pay for the desired insurance. Forwards, with symmetrical terminal payoffs, typically do not require any initial payment but do obligate the investor to the possibility of an unfavorable transaction at a future date. Conversely, with options, which provide asymmetrical terminal payoffs, the investor must pay an up-front premium, but then has no further obligation to his counterparty.
- Given these similarities, it is not surprising that there are well-defined relationships that must exist in an efficient capital market between the prices of forward and option contracts. In particular, the put-call parity conditions delineated the linkages between five different securities: the underlying asset (e.g., stock), T-bills, forward contracts, call options, and put options. An important consequence of these relationships is that one of these securities is always redundant because its cash flow patterns can be replicated by the remaining instruments. This realization leads to another important use for derivatives: arbitrage investing. Through their ability to help create synthetic replicas of existing securities, derivatives provide investors with the possibility of riskless excess returns when the synthetic and actual instruments sell for different prices.

Although this chapter provides a broad overview of the dynamics of these important financial contracts, there are several issues related to the use and management of derivative securities that remain to be addressed. Chief among these are ways in which individual positions in forwards, futures, and options are valued and the adjustments that investors need to make when designing derivatives on an underlying asset other than common stock. These topics will be considered in subsequent chapters after we have explored the valuation and investment applications of a more basic set of securities (i.e., stocks and bonds). For now, though, it is important to appreciate these instruments for their ability to assist investors in repackaging the risks and cash flows of their portfolios.

Questions

1. Explain why the difference between put and call prices depends on whether or not the underlying security pays a dividend during the life of the contracts.
2. When comparing futures and forward contracts, it has been said that futures are more liquid but forwards are more flexible. Explain what this statement means and comment on how differences

in contract liquidity and design flexibility might influence an investor's preference in choosing one instrument over the other.

3. Compare and contrast the gain and loss potential for investors holding the following positions: long forward, short forward, long call, short call, long put, and short put. Indicate what the terms *symmetric* and *asymmetric* mean in this context.

4. *CFA Examination III (June 1993)*

   The Franklin Medical Research Foundation is to be established with a gift from Mr. John Franklin in memory of his deceased wife. The foundation's grant-making and investment policy issues have been finalized. Receipt of the expected $45 million Franklin cash gift will not occur for 90 days, yet the committee believes current stock and bond prices are unusually attractive and wishes to take advantage of this perceived opportunity.

   a. Briefly describe two strategies which utilize derivative financial instruments and could be implemented to take advantage of the committee's market expectations.

   b. Evaluate whether or not it is appropriate for the foundation to undertake a derivatives-based hedge to bridge the expected 90-day time gap, considering both positive and negative factors.

5. *CFA Examination II (June 1991)*

   Robert Chen, CFA, is reviewing the characteristics of derivative securities and their use in portfolios. Chen is considering the addition of either a short position in stock index futures or a long position in stock index options to an existing well-diversified portfolio of equity securities. Contrast the way in which each of these two alternatives would affect the risk and return of the resulting combined portfolios.

6. *CFA Examination III (June 1986)*

   Futures contracts and options on futures contracts can be used to modify risk.

   a. Identify the fundamental distinction between a futures contract and an option on a futures contract, and briefly explain the difference in the manner that futures and options modify portfolio risk.

   b. The risk or volatility of an individual asset can be reduced either by writing a covered call option against the asset or by purchasing a put option on the asset. Explain the difference in the extent to which each of these two option strategies modifies an individual asset's risk. In your answer, describe the effect of each strategy on the potential upside and downside performance of the asset.

7. Explain how call and put options can represent a leveraged way of investing in the stock market and also enable investors to hedge their risk completely. Specifically, under what circumstances will the addition of an option increase the risk of an existing portfolio and under what circumstances will it decrease portfolio risk?

8. It has been said that from an investor's perspective a long position in a call option represents the "good half" of a long position in a forward contract. Explain what is meant by this statement. Also, describe what the "bad half" of the long forward position would have to be for this statement to be true.

9. Discuss the difficulties that having options in a security portfolio create for the measurement of portfolio risk. Specifically, explain why standard deviation is a deficient statistic for capturing the essence of risk in a put-protected portfolio. How could the standard deviation statistic be modified to account for this concern?

10. If the current price of a nondividend-paying stock is $32 and a one-year futures contract on that stock has a contract price of $35, explain how an investor could create an "off-market" long position in a forward contract at an exercise price of $25. Would this synthetic contract require a cash payment from either the long or short position? If so, explain which party would have to make the payment and how that payment should be calculated.

Problems

1. The common stock of Tando Enterprises serves as the underlying asset for the following derivative securities: (1) forward contracts, (2) European-style call options, and (3) European-style put options.

a. Assuming that all Tando derivatives expire at the same date in the future, complete a table similar to that shown below for each of the following contract positions:
   i. a long position in a forward with a contract price of $50;
   ii. a long position in a call option with an exercise price of $50 and a front-end premium expense of $5.20;
   iii. a short position in a call option with an exercise price of $50 and a front-end premium receipt of $5.20.

Expiration Date Tando Stock Price	Expiration Date Derivative Payoff	Initial Derivative Premium	Net Profit
25	_____	_____	_____
30	_____	_____	_____
35	_____	_____	_____
40	_____	_____	_____
45	_____	_____	_____
50	_____	_____	_____
55	_____	_____	_____
60	_____	_____	_____
65	_____	_____	_____
70	_____	_____	_____
75	_____	_____	_____

In calculating net profit, ignore the time differential between the initial derivative expense or receipt and the terminal payoff.

b. Graph the net profit for each of the three derivative positions, using net profit on the vertical axis and Tando's expiration date stock price on the horizontal axis. Label the breakeven (i.e., zero profit) point(s) on each graph.

c. Briefly describe the belief about the expiration date price of Tando stock that an investor using each of these three positions implicitly holds.

2. Refer once again to the derivative securities using Tando common stock as an underyling asset discussed in Problem 1.

a. Assuming that all Tando derivatives expire at the same date in the future, complete a table similar to that shown below for each of the following contract positions:
   i. a short position in a forward with a contract price of $50;
   ii. a long position in a put option with an exercise price of $50 and a front-end premium expense of $3.23;
   iii. a short position in a put option with an exercise price of $50 and a front-end premium receipt of $3.23.

Expiration Date Tando Stock Price	Expiration Date Derivative Payoff	Initial Derivative Premium	Net Profit
25	_____	_____	_____
30	_____	_____	_____
35	_____	_____	_____
40	_____	_____	_____
45	_____	_____	_____
50	_____	_____	_____
55	_____	_____	_____
60	_____	_____	_____
65	_____	_____	_____
70	_____	_____	_____
75	_____	_____	_____

In calculating net profit, ignore the time differential between the initial derivative expense or receipt and the terminal payoff.

   b. Graph the net profit for each of the three derivative positions, using net profit on the vertical axis and Tando's expiration date stock price on the horizontal axis. Label the breakeven (i.e., zero profit) point(s) on each graph.

   c. Briefly describe the belief about the expiration date price of Tando stock that an investor using each of these three positions implicitly holds.

3. Suppose that an investor holds a share of Tando common stock, currently valued at $50. He is concerned that over the next few months the value of his holding might decline and he would like to hedge that risk by supplementing his holding with one of three different derivative positions, all of which expire at the same point in the future:

   i. a short position in a forward with a contract price of $50;

   ii. a long position in a put option with an exercise price of $50 and a front-end premium expense of $3.23;

   iii. a short position in a call option with an exercise price of $50 and a front-end premium receipt of $5.20.

   a. Using a table similar to the one shown below, calculate the expiration date value of the investor's combined (i.e., stock and derivative) position. In calculating net portfolio value, ignore the time differential between the initial derivative expense or receipt and the terminal payoff.

Expiration Date Tando Stock Value	Expiration Date Derivative Payoff	Initial Derivative Premium	Combined Terminal Position Value
25	_____	_____	_____
30	_____	_____	_____
35	_____	_____	_____
40	_____	_____	_____
45	_____	_____	_____
50	_____	_____	_____
55	_____	_____	_____
60	_____	_____	_____
65	_____	_____	_____
70	_____	_____	_____
75	_____	_____	_____

   b. For each of the three hedge portfolios, graph the expiration date value of his combined position on the vertical axis, with potential expiration date share prices of Tando stock on the horizontal axis.

   c. Assuming that the options are priced fairly, use the concept of put-call parity to calculate the zero-value contract price (i.e., $F_{0,T}$) for a forward agreement on Tando stock. Explain why this value differs from the $50 contract price used in parts a and b.

4. *CFA Examination III (June 1985)*

You have been asked to provide information concerning the use of the following option/futures strategies to modify portfolio risk–return relationships:

- Writing covered calls
- Purchasing protective puts (the long stock, long put strategy)
- Selling stock market futures

   a. Briefly describe each of these three strategies.

   b. Draw a graph for each strategy that shows the manner in which the risk–return relationship is modified. Briefly explain the manner in which the use of each of these three strategies would modify a portfolio's risk–return relationship.

5. The common stock of Company XYZ is currently trading at a price of $42. Both a put and a call option are available for XYZ stock, each having an exercise price of $40 and an expiration date in exactly six months. The current market prices for the put and call are $1.45 and $3.90, respectively. The risk-free holding period return for the next six months is 4%, which corresponds to an 8% annual rate.

   a. For each possible stock price in the following sequence, calculate the expiration date payoffs (net of the initial purchase price) for the following positions: (1) buy one XYZ call option, and (2) short one XYZ call option:

   20, 25, 30, 35, 40, 45, 50, 55, 60

   Draw a graph of these payoff relationships, using net profit on the vertical axis and potential expiration date stock price on the horizontal axis. Be sure to specify the prices at which these respective positions will break even (i.e., produce a net profit of zero).

   b. Using the same potential stock prices as in Part a, calculate the expiration date payoffs (net of the initial purchase price) for the following positions: (1) buy one XYZ put option, and (2) short one XYZ put option. Draw a graph of these payoff relationships, labeling the prices at which these investments will break even.

   c. Determine whether the $2.45 difference in the market prices between the call and put options is consistent with the put–call parity relationship for European-style contracts.

6. *CFA Examination III (June 1987)*

   On June 1, 1987, an institutional portfolio manager is managing a $1 million portfolio consisting of U.S. government bonds. Currently, the portfolio is fully invested in one bond issue—Government 8% Bonds due June 1, 2002, selling at a market price of 100.

   The manager is concerned about the outlook for interest rates over the next six months. The manager believes interest rates will move significantly with probabilities favoring a strong rise in rates, but a strong decline is also possible. For the next six-month holding period, the manager's goal is to structure a portfolio which will be substantially protected from a rate rise, but which will also participate in any market advances.

   Other available investment instruments are the following:

   (1) Futures Contract on Government 8% Bonds, due 6/1/02

Futures Expiration	12/1/87
Futures Current Price	$101
Contract Size	$100,000

   (2) Option Contracts on Government 8% Bonds, due 6/1/02 expiring 12/1/87

Option	Strike Price	Market Price	Contract Size
Calls	100	4.00	$100,000
Puts	100	2.00	$100,000

   (3) Treasury Bills maturing 12/1/87, yielding 3% for six months.

   a. Assume that the manager wishes to maintain the current bond holding. Design an option strategy that will achieve the manager's goal of protecting against an interest rate rise while also participating in any market advances.

   b. Assume that the manager is willing to maintain or sell the current bond holding. With the available instruments listed above, design two alternative portfolio structures which accomplish the same goal.

   c. Based on the put–call parity relationship shown below, calculate which of the two strategies designed in Part b should be implemented:

   Put Price = Call Price − Bond Price + (Present Value of Exercise Price)

7. Consider Commodity Z that has both exchange-traded futures and option contracts associated with it. As you look in today's paper, you find the following put and call prices for options that expire exactly six months from now:

Exercise Price	Put Price	Call Price
40	$0.59	$8.73
45	1.93	—
50	—	2.47

a. Assuming that the futures price of a six-month contract on Commodity Z is $48, what must be the price of a put with an exercise price of $50 in order to avoid arbitrage across markets? Similarly, calculate the "no arbitrage" price of a call with an exercise price of $45. In both calculations, assume that the yield curve is flat and the annual risk-free rate is 6%.

b. What is the "no arbitrage" price differential that should exist between the put and call options having an exercise price of $40? Is this differential satisfied by current market prices? If not, demonstrate an arbitrage trade to take advantage of the mispricing.

8. *CFA Examination III (June 1988)*

Frederick Selbst, a self-employed mechanical engineer, recently sold the patent rights for an industrial process that he developed. Selbst had been fairly successful in managing his personal savings and Keogh plans over the years. Because he is a "hands on," "do it myself" individual, he decided to retire from engineering and to manage his personal wealth since the money he received was more than enough to support him in early retirement. He also plans to take extended trips to remote areas, often leaving on very short notice.

Selbst often meets with you to seek advice on investment policy or to discuss new investment concepts. However, he has not given you discretionary authority over his portfolio and continues to select his own individual securities and execute his own trades.

Selbst has scheduled a meeting with you to discuss ways to control risk in his $10 million portfolio, now invested 90% in common stocks and 10% in cash equivalents. The portfolio of common stocks is broadly diversified but is not an index fund. He plans to use a risk-control strategy for the foreseeable future. In addition, Selbst has told you that he may need to withdraw $3 million from his $10 million portfolio to fund a commitment he has made to a limited partnership investment.

Selbst is at your office to discuss two possible ways to reduce risk: (1) buy stock index put options and (2) sell a fixed number of stock index futures. For the purpose of discussion, Selbst has given you two possible portfolios:

Portfolio 1:	Broadly diversified common stocks	$9,000,000
	Cash equivalents	950,000
	Hold stock index put options to sell $1,000,000 of stocks, at-the-money, expiring in three months	50,000
	Total	$10,000,000
Portfolio 2:	Broadly diversified common stocks	$9,000,000
	Cash equivalents (including futures margin)	1,000,000
	Sell $2,000,000 stock index futures, expiring in three months	0
	Total	$10,000,000

a. Compare and contrast Portfolio 1 and Portfolio 2 with respect to the distribution of returns and the systematic and specific risk.

b. Discuss for each portfolio the ease of constructing and revising the portfolio and the ability to withdraw $3 million, given the fact that Selbst has retained discretionary authority but is often unavailable. Based on your discussion, justify your choice of one of these portfolios for Selbst.

Portfolio 1 specifies the purchase of index puts. Alternatively, one of your staff recommends purchasing puts on each of the individual stocks in Selbst's portfolio. To compare the costs of these two approaches, you assume the portfolio to be protected has only 100 shares each of two stocks: X and Y. The index, called XY, is 50% invested in X and 50% invested in Y. Both individual stocks and the index have put options as indicated:

Stock/Index	Standard Deviation	Current Stock Price	Put Strike Price	Put Option Price (Per Share)
X (only)	35%	$60	$60	$6.3750
Y (only)	20	40	40	3.2500
XY	15	50	50	1.9375

All puts expire in three months and the T-bill rate for that period is 6% per annum.

Approach 1: Buy a put on X and a put on Y (covering 100 shares each). The cost of protecting the portfolio's current market value with puts (in-the-money) is (100 × $6.375) + (100 × $3.25) = $962.50. Note that the portfolio has 200 shares and puts covering 200 shares.

Approach 2: Buy puts on the XY index. The cost of two index puts is 200 × $1.9375 = $387.50.

c. Demonstrate numerically that, excluding the cost of the puts, the downside protection is the same for both Approach 1 and Approach 2.
d. Compare the costs and benefits of Approach 1 relative to Approach 2.

9. *CFA Examination III (June 1990)*
Industrial Products Corp. (IPC), a publicly held company, is considering going private. It is extremely important to IPC's management that the pension fund's present surplus level be preserved pending completion of buyout financing. For the next three months (until September 1, 1990), management's goal is to sustain no loss of value in the pension fund portfolio. Today (June 1, 1990), this value is $300 million. Of this total, $150 million is invested in equities in the form of an S&P 500 Index fund, producing an annual dividend yield of 4%; the balance is invested in a single U.S. government bond issue, having a coupon of 8% and a maturity of 6/01/2005. Since the "no-loss strategy" has only a three-month time horizon, management does not wish to sell any of the present security holdings.

Assume that sufficient cash is available to satisfy margin requirements, transaction costs, etc., and that the following market conditions exist as of June 1, 1990:

- the S&P 500 Index is at the 350 level, with a yield of 4.0%
- the U.S. government 8.0% bonds due 6/1/2005 are selling at 100; and
- U.S. Treasury Bills due on 9/1/90 are priced to yield 1.5% for the three-month period (i.e., 6% annually)

Available investment instruments are the following:

Contract	Expiration	Current Contract Price	Strike Price	Contract Size
S&P 500 Index future	9/1/90	$355.00	—	$175,000
Future on U.S. government 8% bonds due 6/1/2005	9/1/90	101.00		100,000
S&P 500 call option	9/1/90	8.00	350	35,000
S&P 500 put option	9/1/90	7.00	350	35,000
U.S. government 8% due 6/1/2005 call option	9/1/90	2.50	100	100,000
U.S. government 8% due 6/1/2005 put option	9/1/90	1.50	100	100,000

a. Assume that the management wishes to protect the portfolio against any losses (ignoring the costs of purchasing options or futures contracts), but wishes also to participate in any stock or bond market advances over the next three months. Using the above instruments, design two strategies to accomplish this goal, and calculate the number of contracts needed to implement each strategy.

b. Using the put–call parity relationship and the fair value formula for futures (both shown below), recommend which one of the two strategies designed in Part a should be implemented. Justify your choice.

> Put Price = Call price minus Security Price plus Present Value of (Exercise Price plus Income on the Underlying Security)
>
> Futures Price = Underlying Security Price plus (Treasury Bill Income minus Income on the Underlying Security)

10. a. Use combinations of payoff diagrams similar to those shown in Figures 11.3–11.5 to demonstrate why the "synthetic put" version of the put-call-spot parity condition must hold in an arbitrage-free capital market.

b. Once again using the appropriate payoff diagrams, provide an explanation for the put-call-forward parity relationship of the following equation:

$$S_0 = \frac{F_{0,T}}{(1 + RFR)^T}$$

11. As an option trader, you are constantly looking for opportunities to make an arbitrage transaction (i.e., a trade in which you do not need to commit your own capital or take any risk, but still make a profit). Suppose you observe the following prices for options on DRKC Co. stock: $3.18 for a call with an exercise price of $60 and $3.38 for a put with an exercise price of $60. Both options expire in exactly six months and the price of a six-month T-bill is $97.00 (for face value of $100).

a. Using the put-call-spot parity condition, demonstrate graphically how you could synthetically recreate the payoff structure of a share of DRKC stock in six months using a combination of puts, calls, and T-bills transacted today.

b. Given the current market prices for the two options and the T-bill, calculate the no-arbitrage price of a share of DRKC stock.

c. If the actual market price of DRKC stock is $60, demonstrate the arbitrage transaction you could create to take advantage of the discrepancy. Be specific as to the positions you would need to take in each security and the dollar amount of your profit.

12. You are currently managing a stock portfolio worth $55 million and you are concerned that over the next four months equity values will be flat and may even fall. Consequently, you are considering two different strategies for hedging against possible stock declines: (1) a protective put, and (2) a covered call. An over-the-counter derivatives dealer has expressed interest in your business and has quoted the following bid and offer prices (in millions) for at-the-money call and put options that expire in four months and match the characteristics of your portfolio:

	Bid	Ask
Call	$2.553	$2.573
Put	1.297	1.317

a. For each of the expiration date values for the unhedged equity position listed below, calculate the terminal values for a protective put strategy.

35, 40, 45, 50, 55, 60, 65, 70, 75

    b. Draw a graph of the protective put payoff structure in Part a and demonstrate how this position could have been constructed by using call options and T-bills, assuming a risk-free rate of 7%.

    c. For each of these same expiration date stock values, calculate the terminal values for a covered call strategy.

    d. Draw a graph of the covered call payoff structure in Part c and demonstrate how this position could have been constructed by using put options and T-bills, again assuming a risk-free rate of 7%.

13. You are a market maker in derivative instruments linked to KemCo stock. In addition to acting as a dealer in KemCo call options, put options, and forward contracts, you also spend part of your time surveying other dealers in the industry looking for arbitrage profit opportunities. Currently, the market-clearing (i.e., zero-value) contract price for a KemCo forward contract with nine months to maturity is $45. Also, an average of the last few trades involving nine-month KemCo puts with a $45 exercise price revealed a contract price of $3.22.

    a. If the nine-month T-bill is priced to yield an annual return of 6.5%, what bid–ask spread would you quote for a nine-month KemCo call option struck at a price of $45? In establishing this spread, first calculate the theoretical no-arbitrage price for the contract and then round this price up (or down) to the nearest one-eighth of a dollar for your ask (or bid) quote.

    b. Given the prevailing market prices for the forward and put option contracts, what should be the fair market value of KemCo stock at the present time?

    c. Assuming the actual market price of KemCo stock is $41, create an arbitrage portfolio that will allow you to profit from the discrepancy. Be specific as to the positions you would need to take in each security and the dollar amount of your profit.

    d. Suppose that KemCo's management has just announced that it will pay a cash dividend in exactly nine months (i.e., just before the derivative contract expiration date). To make the existing stock and forward prices arbitrage-free, what would the amount of this dividend have to be?

References

Brown, Keith C., ed. *Derivative Strategies for Managing Portfolio Risk.* Charlottesville, VA: Association for Investment Management and Research, 1993.

Chance, Don M. *An Introduction to Options and Futures.* 3d ed. Fort Worth, TX: The Dryden Press, 1995.

Clarke, Roger G. *Options and Futures: A Tutorial.* Charlottesville, VA: The Research Foundation of the Institute of Chartered Financial Analysts, 1992.

Dubofsky, David A. *Options and Financial Futures: Valuation and Uses.* New York: McGraw-Hill, 1992.

Garcia, C. B. and F. J. Gould. "An Empirical Study of Portfolio Insurance." *Financial Analysts Journal* 43, no. 4 (July–August 1987).

Gastineau, Gary L. *The Options Manual.* 3d ed. New York, NY: McGraw Hill, 1988.

Fabozzi, Frank J. and Gregory M. Kipnis, eds. *The Handbook of Stock Index Futures and Options.* Homewood, IL: Dow Jones-Irwin, 1989.

Hull, John. *Options, Futures, and Other Derivative Instruments.* 2d ed. Englewood Cliffs, NJ: Prentice-Hall, 1993.

Klemkosky, Robert C. and Bruce G. Resnick. "Put-Call Parity and Market Efficiency." *Journal of Finance* 34, no. 5 (December 1979).

Merton, Robert C., Myron S. Scholes, and Mathew L. Gladstein. "The Returns and Risks of Alternative Put–Option Portfolio Investment Strategies." *Journal of Business* 55, no. 1 (January 1982).

Moriarty, Eugene, Susan Phillips, and Paula Tosini. "A Comparison of Options and Futures in the Management of Portfolio Risk." *Financial Analysts Journal* 37, no. 1 (January–February 1981).

Rubinstein, Mark. "Portfolio Insurance and the Market Crash." *Financial Analysts Journal* 44, no. 1 (January–February 1988).

Part
3

VALUATION PRINCIPLES AND PRACTICES

Chapter 12   *Analysis of Financial Statements*

Chapter 13   *An Introduction to Security Valuation*

Chapter 14   *The Analysis of Alternative Economics and Security Markets: The Global Asset Allocation Decision*

*B*ased on the chapters in the first two parts, you know the purpose of investing and the importance of an appropriate asset allocation decision. You also know about the numerous investment instruments available on a global basis, and you have the background regarding the institutional characteristics of the capital markets. In addition, you are aware of the major developments in investment theory as they relate to efficient capital markets, portfolio theory, capital asset pricing, and derivative securities. Therefore, at this point you are in a position to consider the theory and practice of estimating the value of various securities, which is the heart of investing and leads to the construction of a portfolio that is consistent with your risk–return objectives. You will recall that the investment decision is based on a comparison of an asset's intrinsic value and its market price.

The major source of information regarding a stock or bond is the corporation's financial statements. Chapter 12 considers what financial statements are available and what information they provide, followed by a discussion of the financial ratios used to answer several important questions about a firm's liquidity, its operating performance, its risk profile, and its growth potential.

Chapter 13 considers the basic principles of valuation and applies those principles to the valuation of bonds, preferred stock, and common stock under several alternative operating scenarios. We conclude by reviewing the basic factors that determine the required rate of return for an investment and the growth rate of earnings and dividends for domestic and international firms.

Chapter 14 deals with a major question for the global investor that was introduced in Chapter 2—how to allocate assets across countries based on the state of their economies and the security markets. We examine some specific tools used in this macroeconomic analysis. Additionally, within each country it is necessary to make a further allocation among available asset classes including stocks, bonds, and cash.

Chapter
12

Analysis of Financial Statements

This chapter answers the following questions:

- What are the major financial statements that are provided by firms and what is the specific information contained in each of them?
- Why do we use financial ratios to examine the performance of a firm and why is it important to examine performance relative to the economy and a firm's industry?
- What are the major categories for financial ratios and what questions are being answered by the ratios in these categories?
- What specific ratios are useful to determine a firm's internal liquidity, operating performance, risk profile, growth potential, and external liquidity?
- How can the DuPont analysis help evaluate a firm's return on equity over time?
- What are some of the major differences between U.S. and non-U.S. financial statements and how do these differences impact the financial ratios?
- What is a "quality" balance sheet or income statement?
- Why is financial statement analysis done if markets are efficient and forward-looking?
- What are the major financial ratios that have been used to help analysts in the following areas: stock valuation, estimating and evaluating systematic risk, predicting the credit ratings on bonds, and predicting bankruptcy?

Financial statements are the main source of information for major investment decisions, including whether to lend money to a firm (invest in its bonds), to acquire an ownership stake in a firm (buy its preferred or common stock), or to buy warrants or options on a firm's stock. In this chapter, we first introduce a corporation's major financial statements and discuss why and how financial ratios are useful. In subsequent sections, we provide example computations of ratios that reflect internal liquidity, operating performance, risk analysis, growth analysis, and external liquidity. Because analysts deal with foreign stocks and bonds, we also discuss factors that affect the analysis of foreign financial statements. In the final section, we address four major areas in investments where financial ratios have been effectively employed.

Our example company in this chapter is Quaker Oats, a worldwide marketer of consumer grocery products, including cereals, mixes, grain-based snacks, syrup, corn products, edible oils, and pet food.

MAJOR FINANCIAL STATEMENTS

Financial statements are intended to provide information on the resources available to management, how these resources were financed, and what the firm accomplished with them. Corporate shareholder annual and quarterly reports include three required financial statements: the balance sheet, the income statement, and the statement of cash flows. In addition, reports that must be filed with the Securities and Exchange Commission (SEC), for example, the 10-K and 10-Q reports, carry very detailed information about the firm such as information on loan agreements and data on product line and subsidiary performance. Information from the basic financial statements can be used to calculate financial ratios and to analyze the operations of the firm to determine what influences a firm's earnings and cash flows.

GENERALLY ACCEPTED ACCOUNTING PRINCIPLES

Among the input used to construct the financial statements are **generally accepted accounting principles (GAAP),** which are formulated by the Financial Accounting Standards Board (FASB). FASB recognizes it would be improper for all companies to use identical and restrictive accounting principles. Some flexibility and choice are needed because industries and firms within industries differ in their operating environments. Therefore, the FASB allows companies some flexibility to choose among appropriate GAAP for their use. This flexibility allows the firm's managers to choose accounting standards that best reflect company practice. On the negative side, this flexibility can allow firms to appear healthier than they really are; it is the task of the financial analyst to rigorously analyze the available financial information to separate those firms that appear attractive from those that really are in good financial shape.

Fortunately, the FASB requires that financial statements include footnotes that inform analysts regarding which accounting principles were used by the firm. Because accounting principles frequently differ among firms, the footnote information assists the financial analyst in adjusting the financial statements of companies so the analyst can better compare "apples with apples." Table 12.1 contains a partial list of generally accepted accounting principles, which shows that businesses have a number of options when choosing among accounting principles.

BALANCE SHEET

The **balance sheet** shows what resources (assets) the firm controls and how it has financed these assets. Specifically, it indicates the current and fixed assets available to the firm *at a point in time* (the end of the fiscal year or the end of a quarter). In most cases, the firm owns these assets, but some firms lease assets on a long-term basis. How the firm has financed the acquisition of these assets is indicated by its mixture of current liabilities (accounts payable or short-term borrowing), long-term liabilities (fixed debt), and owners' equity (preferred stock, common stock, and retained earnings).

The balance sheet for Quaker Oats in Table 12.2 represents the *stock* of assets and its financing mix as of the end of Quaker Oats' fiscal year, June 30, 1993, 1994, and 1995. Notably, during fiscal 1995, the firm split its stock but did not reduce its par value. Thus $420 million of retained earnings was transferred to the common stock account.

INCOME STATEMENT

The **income statement** contains information on the profitability of the firm during some *period of time* (a quarter or a year). In contrast to the balance sheet, which indicates the firm's financial position at a fixed point in time, the income statement indicates the *flow* of sales, expenses, and earnings during a period of time. The income statement for Quaker Oats for the years 1993, 1994, and 1995 appears in Table 12.3. Notably, these data differ from the reports by the firm. Specifically, the authors have adjusted the net income figures to recognize the several adjustments for accounting changes, income taxes, and gains or losses on divestitures. These changes were very large in 1995 and without adjustments would seriously distort the firm's performance. We concentrate on earnings from operations after tax as the relevant net earnings figure. As shown, while reported earnings per share was $6.00, the operating income after taxes was only $1.41—the rest was a gain on

TABLE 12.1	GAAP—GENERALLY ACCEPTED ACCOUNTING PRINCIPLES

Revenue Recognition

1. Recognized at time goods sold (accrual)
2. As cash is collected (installment or cost-recovery-first)
3. As production progresses (percentage of completion method)

Uncollectible Accounts

1. Recognize when revenue is recognized (allowance method)
2. When accounts are found to be uncollectible (direct write-off)

Inventories

Cash Flow Assumption:
1. LIFO
2. FIFO
3. Weighted average

Cost Assumption:
1. Acquisition cost
2. Lower of acquisition cost or market
3. Standard cost
4. Net realizable value

Investments in Securities

1. Lower of cost or market
2. Equity method
3. Consolidation method

Depreciation

1. Straight line
2. Double declining balance
3. Sum of the years' digits
4. Units of production
5. MACRS (modified accelerated cost recovery system)

divestiture. This adjustment shows that operating earnings declined substantially from $2.48 in 1994. We will generally use the operating income after taxes in our analysis.

STATEMENT OF CASH FLOWS   Financial analysis should examine cash inflows and outflows. From accounting classes, you know that unless the firm operates on a 100 percent cash sale basis, recognizing revenue does not mean a cash inflow has occurred; cash may not flow into the firm until some time in the future. Similarly, matching expenses to revenue distorts the perception of cash outflows. The matched expenses include raw materials costs, production costs, and labor expenses. These expenses were likely paid (and cash outflows occurred) some time prior to the sale of goods.

Another example of an income statement expense item that does not reflect a cash outflow is depreciation expense. Depreciation expense is computed by using one of a number of accounting principles, as shown in Table 12.1; it is a concept that reflects the fact that assets are "used up" over time. No actual cash outflow is associated with depreciation expense (actual cash outflows reflecting repair and maintenance will be reflected elsewhere in the income statement expense items).

The **statement of cash flows** integrates the information on the balance sheet and income statement. For a given period, it shows the effects on the firm's cash flow of income flows (based on the most recent year's income statement) and changes in various items on the balance sheet (based on the two most recent annual balance sheets). The result is a set of cash flow values that you can use to evaluate the risk and return of the firm's bonds and stock.

The statement of cash flows has three sections: cash flows from operating activities, cash flows from investing activities, and cash flows from financing activities. The sum total of the cash flows from the three sections is the net change in the cash position of the firm; this bottom-line number should equal the difference in the cash balance between the ending and beginning balance sheet. The statement of cash flows for Quaker Oats for 1993, 1994,

TABLE 12.2

THE QUAKER OATS COMPANY AND SUBSIDIARIES CONSOLIDATED BALANCE SHEET ($ MILLIONS)—YEARS ENDED JUNE 30, 1993, 1994, AND 1995

	1995	1994	1993
Assets			
Current assets			
Cash and cash equivalents	$ 101.8	$ 140.4	$ 61.0
Trade accounts receivable—net of allowances	546.8	509.4	478.9
Inventories:			
Finished goods	267.4	266.5	241.5
Grains and raw materials	94.4	78.8	73.1
Packaging materials and supplies	44.2	40.2	39.4
Total Inventories	406.0	385.5	354.0
Other current assets	262.0	218.3	173.7
Total current assets	1,316.6	1,253.6	1,067.6
Other assets	85.8	82.1	88.8
Property, plant, and equipment,	1,843.7	2,125.9	2,059.2
less accumulated depreciation	730.3	911.7	831.0
Property—net	1,113.4	1,214.2	1,228.2
Intangible assets—net of amortization	2,311.1	493.4	431.3
Total assets	$4,826.9	$3,043.3	$2,815.9
Liabilities and Shareholders' Equity			
Current liabilities			
Short-term debt	$ 510.1	$ 211.3	$ 128.0
Current portion of long-term debt	38.8	45.4	48.9
Trade accounts payable	423.8	406.3	391.6
Accrued payrolls, pensions, and bonuses	123.8	158.9	161.3
Accrued advertising and merchandising	165.0	149.6	130.6
Income taxes payable	180.1	40.6	33.7
Other accrued liabilities	371.3	247.0	211.0
Total current liabilities	1,812.9	1,259.1	1,105.1
Long-term debt	1,103.1	759.5	632.6
Other liabilities	530.0	481.4	426.2
Deferred income taxes	233.3	82.2	89.5
Preferred stock, Series B, no par value, authorized 1,750,000 shares; issued 1,282,051 of $5.46 cumulative convertible shares (liquidating preference of $78 per share)	100.0	100.0	100.0
Deferred compensation	(74.9)	(80.8)	(85.9)
Treasury preferred stock, at cost, 81,194 shares, 47,817 shares, and 34,447 shares, respectively	(6.3)	(3.9)	(2.7)
Common shareholders' equity			
Common stock, $5 par value, authorized 400 million, 200 million, and 200 million, respectively	840.0	420.0	420.0
Reinvested earnings	1,499.3	1,273.6	1,190.1
Cumulative exchange adjustment	(61.4)	(75.4)	(65.4)
Deferred compensation	(132.2)	(143.5)	(154.0)
Treasury common stock, at cost	(1,016.9)	(1,028.9)	(839.6)
Total common shareholders' equity	1,128.8	445.8	551.1
Total liabilities and common shareholders' equity	4,826.9	$3,043.3	$2,815.9

Source: Quaker Oats annual reports.

TABLE 12.3

THE QUAKER OATS COMPANY AND SUBSIDIARIES CONSOLIDATED STATEMENT OF INCOME ($ MILLIONS, EXCEPT PER SHARE DATA)—YEARS ENDED JUNE 30, 1993, 1994, AND 1995

	1995	1994	1993
Net sales	$ 6,365.2	$ 5,955.0	$ 5,730.6
Cost of goods sold	3,381.5	2,926.2	2,870.0
Gross profit	2,983.7	3,028.8	2,860.6
Selling, general, and administrative expenses	2,603.2	2,425.6	2,302.3
Operating profit	380.5	603.2	558.3
Interest expense—net of $6.3, $8.9, and $10.5 interest income[a]	110.7	89.7	55.1
Foreign exchange loss—net	4.2	26.2	15.1
Operating income before income taxes	265.6	487.3	488.1
Provision for income taxes	77.6	147.2	180.8
Operating income after taxes	188.0	340.1	307.3
Adjustment for cumulative effect of accounting changes, income taxes, and gains on divestitures and restructuring charges	614.0	(108.6)	(136.0)
Reported net income	802.0	231.5	171.3
Preferred dividends—net of tax	4.0	4.0	4.2
Operating income after taxes available for common	184.0	336.1	303.1
Reported net income available for common	798.0	227.5	167.1
Per common share			
Operating income after taxes	$ 1.41	$ 2.48	$ 2.11
Adjustment for cumulative effect of accounting changes, income taxes, and gains on divestitures and restructuring charges	$ 4.59	$ (0.80)	$ (0.94)
Reported net income	$ 6.00	$ 1.68	$ 1.17
Dividends declared	$ 1.14	$ 1.06	$ 0.96
Average number of common shares outstanding (000)	133,763	135,236	143,948

[a]Gross interest expense for 1995, 1994, and 1993 was $117.0, $98.6, and $65.6 million, respectively.

Source: Quaker Oats annual reports.

and 1995 appears in Table 12.4. Note that it is possible to begin with the reported net income figure for 1995 because this inflated income value is subsequently partially offset by a negative "gain on divestiture after taxes." Therefore, the cash flow from operations value is appropriate.

CASH FLOWS FROM OPERATING ACTIVITIES   This section lists the fund sources and uses that arise from the normal operations of a firm. In general, the net cash flow from operations is computed as the net income reported on the income statement including changes in net working capital items (i.e., receivables, inventories, etc.) plus adjustments for noncash revenues and expenses, or:

$$\text{Cash Flow from Operating Activities} = \text{Net Income} + \text{Depreciation} + \text{Changes in Net Working Capital Items}$$

Consistent with our discussion above, the cash account is not included in the calculations of cash flow from operations. Notably, Quaker Oats has been able to generate consistently

| TABLE 12.4 | THE QUAKER OATS COMPANY AND SUBSIDIARIES CONSOLIDATED STATEMENT OF CASH FLOWS ($ MILLIONS)—YEARS ENDED JUNE 30, 1993, 1994, AND 1995 |

	1995	1994	1993
Cash Flows from Operating Activities			
Net income	$ 802.0	$ 231.5	$ 171.3
Adjustments to reconcile net income to net cash provided by operating activities:			
Cumulative effect of accounting changes	4.1	—	115.5
Depreciation and amortization	191.4	171.2	156.9
Deferred income taxes and other items	17.8	(7.7)	(46.4)
Gains on divestitures—net of tax	(694.6)	(9.8)	(27.8)
Restructuring charges	76.5	118.4	48.3
Loss on disposition of property and equipment	22.0	15.0	23.8
Changes in operating assets and liabilities (used in) provided from continuing operations:			
(Increase) decrease in trade accounts receivable	(70.8)	(77.7)	59.1
(Increase) decrease in inventories	(56.5)	(67.6)	41.9
(Increase) decrease in other current assets	(53.4)	(56.3)	(25.8)
Increase (decrease) in trade accounts payable	83.9	44.1	(7.6)
Increase (decrease) in other current liabilities	52.1	6.6	(6.4)
Change in deferred compensation	17.2	15.6	11.0
Other items	83.8	67.5	44.4
Net cash provided by operating activities	$ 475.5	$ 450.8	$ 558.2
Cash Flows from Investing Activities			
Additions to property, plant, and equipment	$ (275.5)	$(175.1)	$(172.3)
Business acquisitions	(1,876.5)	(96.3)	(40.4)
Business divestitures—net of tax	1,253.4	1.2	41.6
Change in other assets	(4.0)	(6.4)	(25.6)
Net cash used in investing activities	$ (902.6)	$(263.6)	$(196.7)
Cash Flows from Financing Activities			
Cash dividends	$ (154.8)	$(144.6)	$(140.3)
Change in short-term debt	216.4	83.3	67.0
Proceeds from long-term debt	213.3	222.2	0.5
Reduction of long-term debt	(89.3)	(100.6)	(59.0)
Proceeds from short-term debt to be refinanced	188.0	—	—
Issuance of common treasury stock	23.0	11.8	23.3
Repurchases of common stock	(22.5)	(214.9)	(323.1)
Repurchases of preferred stock	(2.4)	(1.2)	(1.1)
Net cash used in financing activities	$ 371.7	$(144.0)	$(432.7)
Effect of exchange rate changes of cash and cash equivalents	16.8	36.2	37.0
Net increase (decrease) in cash and cash equivalents	(38.6)	79.4	(34.2)
Cash and cash equivalents—beginning of year	140.4	61.0	95.2
Cash and cash equivalents—end of year	$ 101.8	$ 140.4	$ 61.0

Source: Quaker Oats annual reports.

large cash flows from operations after accounting for consistent increases in receivables and inventory.

CASH FLOWS FROM INVESTMENT ACTIVITIES   A firm makes investments in both its own noncurrent and fixed assets and the equity of other firms (which may be subsidiaries or joint ventures of the parent firm; they are listed in the "investment" account of the balance sheet). Increases and decreases in these accounts are considered investment activities. The cash flow from investment activities is the change in gross plant and equipment plus the change in the investment account. The changes are added if they represent a source of funds; otherwise they are subtracted. The dollar changes in these accounts are computed using the firm's two most recent balance sheets. Most firms experience negative cash flows from investments due to capital expenditures. Quaker Oats results likewise reflect large negative values due to significant acquisitions—even after the substantial cash inflow from the sale of subsidiaries (i.e., the divestitures).

CASH FLOWS FROM FINANCING ACTIVITIES   Cash flow from financing activities is computed as financing sources minus financing uses. Inflows are created by actions increasing notes payable and long-term liability and equity accounts, such as bond and stock issues. Financing uses (outflows) include decreases in such accounts (i.e., the pay down of liability accounts or the repurchase of common shares, which Quaker Oats did heavily in 1993 and 1994). Dividend payments to equityholders are likewise a cash outflow.

The sum total of the cash flows from operating, investing, and financing activities is the net increase or decrease in the firm's cash. The statement of cash flows provides some of the cash flow detail that is lacking in the balance sheet and income statement.

ALTERNATIVE MEASURES OF CASH FLOW   There are several cash flow measures an analyst can use to determine the underlying health of the corporation.

CASH FLOW FROM OPERATIONS   This includes the traditional measure of cash flow, which is equal to net income plus depreciation expense and deferred taxes. But as we have just seen, it is also necessary to adjust for changes in operating (current) assets and liabilities that either use or provide cash. For example, an increase in accounts receivable implies that either the firm is using cash to support this increase or the firm did not collect all the sales reported. In contrast, an increase in a current liability account such as accounts payable means that the firm acquired some assets but has not paid for them, which is a source (increase) of cash flow (i.e., the firm's suppliers are implicitly providing financing to the firm). These changes in operating assets or liabilities can add to or subtract from the cash flow estimated from the traditional measure of cash flow: net income plus noncash expenses. The table below compares the cash flow from operations figures (Table 12.4) to the traditional cash flow figures for Quaker Oats from 1993 to 1995:

	Traditional Cash Flow Equals Net Income + Depreciation		Cash Flow from Operations from Statement of Cash Flows
1995	993.4	(298.8*)	475.5
1994	402.7		450.8
1993	328.2		558.2

*This is the traditional cash flow after adjusting for the $694.6 million gain from the sale of subsidiaries.

In all three years the cash flow from operations (after adjusting for the gain for divestitures) was larger than the traditional cash flow estimate because of the several adjustments needed to arrive at cash flows. Therefore, using this more exact measure of cash flow, the Quaker Oats ratios would have been stronger. For many firms this would not be true because the effect of working capital changes is often a large negative cash flow due to increases in receivables or inventory (especially for high growth companies).

FREE CASH FLOW **Free cash flow** further modifies cash flow from operations to recognize that some investing and financing activities are critical to the ongoing success of the firm. It is assumed that these expenditures must be made before a firm can feel free to use its cash flow for other purposes such as reducing debt outstanding or repurchasing common stock. The two additional expenditures considered are: (1) capital expenditures (an investing expenditure) and (2) dividends (a financing activity). These two items are subtracted from cash flow from operations as follows:

	Cash Flow from Operations	− Capital Expenditures	− Dividends	= Free Cash Flow
1995	475.5	275.5	154.8	45.2
1994	450.8	175.1	144.6	131.1
1993	558.2	172.3	140.3	245.6

For firms involved in leveraged buyouts, this free cash flow number is critical because the new owners typically want to use the free cash flow as funds available for retiring outstanding debt. It is not unusual for a firm's free cash flow to be a negative value. The free cash flow for Quaker Oats has been positive, even assuming fairly heavy capital expenditures and larger dividends. Still, it has declined during each of the past two years.

PURPOSE OF FINANCIAL STATEMENT ANALYSIS

Financial statement analysis seeks to evaluate management performance in several important areas, including profitability, efficiency, and risk. Although we will necessarily analyze historical data, the ultimate goal is to provide insights that will help you to *project* future management performance, including pro forma balance sheets, income statements, cash flows, and risk. It is the firm's expected future performance that determines whether you should lend money to a firm or invest in it.

ANALYSIS OF FINANCIAL RATIOS

Analysts use financial ratios because numbers in isolation are typically not very meaningful. Knowing that a firm earned a net income of $100,000 is less informative than also knowing the sales figure that generated this income ($1 million or $10 million) and the assets or capital committed to the enterprise. Thus, ratios are intended to provide meaningful *relationships* between individual values in the financial statements.

Because the major financial statements report numerous individual items, it is possible to produce numerous potential ratios, many of which will have very little value. Therefore, you want to limit your examination to the most relevant ratios and categorize them into groups that provide information on important economic characteristics of the firm. It is also important to recognize the need for relative analysis.

IMPORTANCE OF RELATIVE FINANCIAL RATIOS

Just as a single number from a financial statement is not very useful, an individual financial ratio has little value except in relation to other ratios. That is, *only relative financial ratios are relevant*. The important comparisons examine a firm's performance relative to:

• The aggregate economy
• Its industry or industries
• Its major competitors within the industry (cross-sectional analysis)
• Its past performance (time-series analysis)

The comparison to the aggregate economy is important because almost all firms are influenced by the economy's expansions and contractions (recessions) in the business cycle. It is not reasonable to expect an increase in the profit margin for a firm during a recession; a stable margin might be very encouraging under such conditions. In contrast, a small increase in a firm's profit margin during a major business expansion may be a sign of weakness. Comparing a firm's financial ratios relative to a similar set of ratios for the economy will help you to understand how a firm reacts to the business cycle and will help you project the future performance of the firm during subsequent business cycles.

Probably the most popular comparison relates a firm's performance to that of its industry. Different industries affect the firms within them differently, but this relationship is always significant. The industry effect is strongest for industries with homogenous products such as steel, rubber, glass, and wood products, since all firms within these industries experience coincidental shifts in demand. In addition, these firms employ fairly similar technology and production processes. For example, even the best-managed steel firm experiences a decline in sales and profit margins during a recession. In such a case, the relevant question might be, how did the firm perform relative to other steel firms? As part of this, you should examine an industry's performance relative to aggregate economic activity to understand how the industry responds to the business cycle.

Data for industry average and median financial ratios are published by a number of organizations such as Dun & Bradstreet (*Industry Norms and Key Business Ratios*); Robert Morris Associates (*Annual Statement Studies*); Standard and Poor's (*Analysts Handbook*); and the Federal Trade Commission (*Quarterly Financial Report for Manufacturing, Mining and Trade Corporations*). These sources are available at most libraries.

When comparing a firm's financial ratios to industry ratios, you may not feel comfortable using the average (mean) industry value when there is wide nonsymmetric dispersion of individual firm ratios within the industry. This specific problem can be addressed by using industry median ratios (one-half of firms in the industry have ratios above the median value; one-half have ratios below it). An inter-quartile range for the ratio may also be helpful.

Alternatively, you may believe that the firm being analyzed is not typical—i.e., it has a unique component. Under these conditions, a **cross-sectional analysis** may be appropriate, in which you compare the firm to a subset of firms within the industry that are comparable in size or characteristics. As an example, within the computer industry, you might want to compare IBM to firms such as Digital or Apple rather than industry average data, which include numerous small firms that produce unique products or services.

Another practical problem with comparing a firm's ratios to an industry average is that many large firms are multi-product and multi-industry in nature. Inappropriate comparisons can arise when a multi-industry firm is evaluated against the ratios from a single industry. Two approaches can help mitigate this problem. The first method is to use cross-sectional analysis by comparing the firm against a rival that operates in many of the same markets. The second method is to construct composite industry average ratios for the firm. To do this, the firm's annual report or 10-K filing is used to identify each industry in which the firm operates and the proportion of total firm sales derived from each industry. Composite industry average ratios are constructed by computing weighted average ratios based on the proportion of firm sales derived from each industry.

You also should examine a firm's relative performance over time to determine whether it is progressing or declining. This **time-series analysis** is helpful when estimating future performance. For example, some may want to calculate the average of a ratio for a 5- or 10-year period without considering the trend. This can result in misleading conclusions. For example, an average rate of return of 10 percent can be based on rates of return that have increased from 5 percent to 15 percent over time, or it can be based on a series that begins at 15 percent and declines to 5 percent. Obviously, the difference in the trend for these series would have a major impact on your estimate for the future.

COMPUTATION OF FINANCIAL RATIOS

We divide ratios into six major categories that will help us understand the important economic characteristics of a firm. In this section, we focus on describing the various ratios and computing them using Quaker Oats' data. Comparative analysis of Quaker Oats' ratios with the economy and industry will be discussed in a later section. The six categories are:

1. Common size statements
2. Internal liquidity (solvency)
3. Operating performance
   a. Operating efficiency
   b. Operating profitability
4. Risk analysis
   a. Business risk
   b. Financial risk
5. Growth analysis
6. External liquidity (marketability)

COMMON SIZE STATEMENTS

Common size statements "normalize" balance sheet and income statement items to allow easier comparison of different-size firms. A common size balance sheet expresses all balance sheet accounts as a percentage of total assets. A common size income statement expresses all income statement items as a percentage of sales. Table 12.5 is the common size balance sheet for Quaker Oats, and Table 12.6 contains the common size income statement. Common size ratios are useful to quickly compare two different-size firms and to examine trends over time within a single firm. Common size statements also give an analyst insight into the structure of a firm's financial statements, that is, the percentage of sales consumed by production costs or interest expense, the proportion of assets that are liquid, or the proportion of liabilities that are short-term obligations. For example, for Quaker Oats the common size balance sheet shows a significant decline in the ratio of all current and fixed assets and a major increase in the proportion of intangible assets (i.e., goodwill). Alternatively, the common size income statement in Table 12.6 shows Quaker's cost of goods sold increased substantially from 1993 to 1995 in proportion to sales. This resulted in a major decline in the firm's operating profit margin and in its proportion of operating income after taxes.

EVALUATING INTERNAL LIQUIDITY

Internal liquidity (solvency) ratios indicate the ability of the firm to meet future short-term financial obligations. They compare near-term financial obligations such as accounts payable or notes payable with current assets or cash flows that will be available to meet these obligations.

INTERNAL LIQUIDITY RATIOS

CURRENT RATIO   Clearly the best-known liquidity measure is the current ratio, which examines the relationship between current assets and current liabilities as follows:

$$\text{Current Ratio} = \frac{\text{Current Assets}}{\text{Current Liabilities}}$$

TABLE 12.5

THE QUAKER OATS COMPANY AND SUBSIDIARIES COMMON SIZE BALANCE SHEET*— YEARS ENDED JUNE 30, 1993, 1994, AND 1995

	1995	1994	1993
Assets			
Current assets			
Cash and cash equivalents	2.1%	4.6%	2.2%
Trade accounts receivable—net of allowances	11.3	16.7	17.0
Inventories			
Finished goods	5.5	8.8	8.6
Grains and raw materials	2.0	2.6	2.6
Packaging materials and supplies	0.9	1.3	1.4
Total inventories	8.4	12.7	12.6
Other current assets	5.4	7.2	6.2
Total current assets	27.3	41.2	37.9
Other assets	1.8	2.7	3.2
Property, plant, and equipment	38.2	69.9	73.1
Less accumulated depreciation	15.1	30.0	29.5
Property—net	23.1	39.9	43.6
Intangible assets—net of amortization	47.9	16.2	15.3
Total assets	100.0%	100.0%	100.0%
Liabilities and Shareholders' Equity			
Current liabilities			
Short-term debt	10.6%	6.9%	4.5%
Current portion of long-term debt	0.8	1.5	1.7
Trade accounts payable	8.8	13.4	13.9
Accrued payrolls, pensions, and bonuses	2.6	5.2	5.7
Accrued advertising and merchandising	3.4	4.9	4.6
Income taxes payable	3.7	1.3	1.2
Other accrued liabilities	7.7	8.1	7.5
Total current liabilities	37.6	41.4	39.2
Long-term debt	22.9	25.0	22.5
Other liabilities	11.0	15.8	15.1
Deferred income taxes	4.8	2.7	3.2
Preferred stock, Series B, no par value, authorized 1,750,000 shares; issued 1,282,051 of $5.46 cumulative convertible shares (liquidating preference of $78 per share)	2.1	3.3	3.6
Deferred compensation	(1.6)	(2.7)	(3.1)
Treasury preferred stock, at cost, 81,194 shares, 47,817 shares, and 34,447 shares, respectively	(0.1)	(0.1)	(0.1)
Common shareholders' equity			
Common stock, $5 par value, authorized 400 million, 200 million, and 200 million, respectively	17.4	13.8	14.9
Reinvested earnings	31.1	41.8	42.3
Cumulative exchange adjustment	(1.3)	(2.5)	(2.3)
Deferred compensation	(2.7)	(4.7)	(5.5)
Treasury common stock, at cost	(21.1)	(33.8)	(29.8)
Total common shareholders' equity	23.4	14.6	19.6
Total liabilities and common shareholders' equity	100.0%	100.0%	100.0%

*Percentages may not add up to 100.0%, due to rounding.

TABLE 12.6	THE QUAKER OATS COMPANY AND SUBSIDIARIES COMMON SIZE INCOME STATEMENT*—YEARS ENDED JUNE 30, 1993, 1994, AND 1995					
	1995	%	1994	%	1993	%
Net sales	6,365.2	100.0	5,955.0	100.0	5,730.6	100.0
Cost of goods sold	3,381.5	53.1	2,926.2	49.1	2,870.0	50.1
Gross profit	2,983.7	46.9	3,028.8	50.9	2,860.6	49.9
Selling, general and administrative expenses	2,603.2	40.9	2,425.6	40.7	2,302.3	40.2
Operating profit	380.5	6.0	603.2	10.1	558.3	9.7
Interest expense—net of $6.3, $8.9, and $10.5 interest income	110.7	1.7	89.7	1.5	55.1	1.0
Foreign exchange loss—net	4.2	0.1	26.2	0.4	15.1	0.3
Operating income before income taxes	265.6	4.2	487.3	8.2	488.1	8.5
Provision for income taxes	77.6	1.2	147.2	2.5	180.8	3.2
Operating income after taxes	188.0	3.0	340.1	5.7	307.3	5.4
Adjustment for cumulative effect of accounting changes, income taxes, and gains on divestitures and restructuring charges	614.0	9.6	(108.6)	(1.8)	(136.0)	(2.4)
Reported net income	802.0	12.6	231.5	3.9	171.3	3.0
Preferred dividends—net of tax	4.0	0.1	4.0	0.1	4.2	0.1
Operating income after taxes available for common	$184.0	2.9	$336.1	5.6	$303.1	5.3
Reported net income available for common	$798.0	12.5	$227.5	3.8	$167.1	2.9

*Percentages may not add up to 100.0%, due to rounding.

For Quaker Oats, the current ratios were (all ratios are in thousands of dollars):

$$1995: \frac{1,316.6}{1,812.9} = 0.73$$

$$1994: \frac{1,253.6}{1,259.1} = 0.99$$

$$1993: \frac{1,067.6}{1,105.1} = 0.97$$

These current ratios experienced an overall decline during the 3 years and are definitely low relative to the "typical" current ratio. Given these ratios below 1.00, which indicates *negative* working capital, it is important to compare these values with similar figures for the firm's industry and the aggregate market. If the ratios differ from the industry results, it is necessary to determine what causes the difference and what might explain it. This comparative analysis is considered in a subsequent section.

QUICK RATIO   Some observers believe you should not consider total current assets when gauging the ability of the firm to meet current obligations because inventories and some other assets included in current assets might not be very liquid. As an alternative, they prefer the quick ratio, which relates current liabilities to only relatively liquid current assets (cash items and accounts receivable) as follows:

$$\text{Quick Ratio} = \frac{\text{Cash} + \text{Marketable Securities} + \text{Receivables}}{\text{Current Liabilities}}$$

This ratio is intended to indicate the amount of very liquid assets available to pay near-term liabilities. Quaker Oats' quick ratios were

$$1995: \frac{648.6}{1,812.9} = 0.36$$

$$1994: \frac{649.8}{1,259.1} = 0.52$$

$$1993: \frac{539.9}{1,105.1} = 0.49$$

These quick ratios for Quaker Oats were below the norm and declined over the 3 years. As before, you should compare these values relative to what happened in the industry and the economy. When possible, you would want to question management regarding the reason for these relatively low liquidity ratios.

CASH RATIO   The most conservative liquidity ratio is the cash ratio, which relates the cash and short-term marketable securities to current liabilities as follows:

$$\text{Cash Ratio} = \frac{\text{Cash and Marketable Securities}}{\text{Current Liabilities}}$$

Quaker Oats' cash ratios were:

$$1995: \frac{101.8}{1,812.9} = 0.06$$

$$1994: \frac{140.4}{1,259.1} = 0.11$$

$$1993: \frac{61.0}{1,105.1} = 0.06$$

The cash ratios during these 3 years have been quite low and would be cause for concern except that the firm has strong lines of credit at various banks. Still, as an investor you would want to know the reason for these low levels.

RECEIVABLES TURNOVER   In addition to examining liquid assets relative to near-term liabilities, it is useful to analyze the quality (liquidity) of the accounts receivable. One way to do this is to calculate how often they turn over, which implies an average collection period. The faster these accounts are paid, the sooner the firm gets the funds that can be used to pay off its own current liabilities. Receivables turnover is computed as follows:

$$\text{Receivables Turnover} = \frac{\text{Net Annual Sales}}{\text{Average Receivables}}$$

Analysts typically derive the average receivables figure from the beginning figure plus the ending value divided by 2. Quaker Oats' receivables turnover ratios were

$$1995: \frac{6,365.2}{(509.4 + 546.8)/2} = 12.05$$

$$1994: \frac{5,955.0}{(478.9 + 509.4)/2} = 12.05$$

It is not possible to compute a turnover value for 1993 because the tables used do not include a beginning receivables figure for 1993 (i.e., we do not have the ending receivables figure for 1992).

Given these annual receivables turnover figures, you can compute an average collection period as follows:

$$\text{Average Receivables Collection Period} = \frac{365}{\text{Annual Turnover}}$$

$$1995: \frac{365}{12.05} = 30.3 \text{ days}$$

$$1994: \frac{365}{12.05} = 30.3 \text{ days}$$

These results indicate that Quaker Oats currently collects its accounts receivable in about 30 days, on average, and this collection record is fairly stable. To determine whether these account collection numbers are good or bad, they should be related to the firm's credit policy and to comparable numbers for other firms in the industry.

The receivables turnover is one of the ratios where you do not want to deviate too much from the norm. In an industry where the norm is 40 days, a collection period of 80 days would indicate slow-paying customers, which increases the capital tied up in receivables and the possibility of bad debts. You would want the firm to be somewhat below the norm (e.g., 35 days versus 40 days), but a figure *substantially below* the norm (e.g., 20 days) might indicate overly stringent credit terms relative to your competition, which could be detrimental to sales.

INVENTORY TURNOVER   Another current asset that should be examined in terms of its liquidity is inventory—i.e., the firm's inventory turnover and the implied processing time. Inventory turnover can be calculated relative to sales or cost of goods sold. The preferred turnover ratio is relative to cost of goods sold (CGS) because CGS does not include the profit implied in sales as follows:

$$1995: \frac{3,381.5}{(406.0 + 385.5)/2} = 8.54$$

$$1994: \frac{2,926.2}{(385.5 + 354.0)/2} = 7.91$$

Given the turnover values, you can compute the average inventory processing time as follows:

$$\text{Average Inventory Processing Period} = \frac{365}{\text{Inventory Turnover}}$$

$$1995: \frac{365}{8.54} = 42.7 \text{ days}$$

$$1994: \frac{365}{7.91} = 46.1 \text{ days}$$

It is encouraging that the inventory processing period is declining, but it is always essential to examine this figure relative to an industry norm.

As with receivables, you don't want an extremely low turnover value and long processing time because this implies that capital is being tied up in inventory and could signal obsolete inventory. Alternatively, a very high inventory turnover and a very short processing time could mean inadequate inventory that could lead to outages and slow delivery to customers, which would adversely affect sales.

CASH CONVERSION CYCLE   An alternative measure of internal liquidity is the cash conversion cycle, which makes use of the receivables turnover, the inventory turnover, and the accounts payable turnover. The point is, cash is tied up in assets for a certain number of days. Specifically, cash is committed to receivables for the collection period and is tied up for a number of days in inventory—i.e., the inventory process period. At the same time, the firm receives an offset to this capital commitment from its own suppliers who provide interest-free loans to the firm by carrying the firm's payables (i.e., the payables' payment period, which is equal to 365/the payables' turnover ratio). In turn, the payables turnover ratio is equal to:

$$\text{Payables Turnover Ratio} = \frac{\text{Cost of Goods Sold}}{\text{Average Trade Payables}}$$

$$1995: \frac{3,381.5}{(423.8 + 406.3)/2} = 8.15 \text{ times}$$

$$1994: \frac{2,926.2}{(406.3 + 391.6)/2} = 7.33 \text{ times}$$

$$\text{Payables Payment Period} = \frac{365}{\text{Payables Turnover}}$$

$$1995: \frac{365}{8.15} = 44.8 \text{ days}$$

$$1994: \frac{365}{7.33} = 49.8 \text{ days}$$

Therefore the cash conversion cycle equals:

Year	Receivables Days	+	Inventory Processing Days	−	Payables Payment Period	=	Cash Conversion Cycle
1995	30.3		42.7		44.8		28.2 days
1994	30.3		46.1		49.8		26.6 days

Quaker Oats has improved (reduced) its inventory processing days, but also appears to be paying its bills faster, which has caused a small increase in its cash conversion cycle. Although the overall cash conversion cycle appears to be quite good (about 28 days), as always you should examine the firm's long-term trend and compare it to its industry.

EVALUATING OPERATING PERFORMANCE   The ratios that indicate how well the management is operating the business can be divided into two subcategories: (1) operating efficiency ratios and (2) operating profitability ratios. Efficiency ratios examine how the management uses its assets and capital, measured in terms of the dollars of sales generated by various asset or capital categories. Profitability ratios analyze the profits as a percentage of sales and as a percentage of the assets and capital employed.

OPERATING
EFFICIENCY RATIOS

TOTAL ASSET TURNOVER   The total asset turnover ratio indicates the effectiveness of the firm's use of its total asset base (net assets equals gross assets minus depreciation on fixed assets). It is computed as follows:

$$\text{Total Asset Turnover} = \frac{\text{Net Sales}}{\text{Average Total Net Assets}}$$

Quaker Oats' asset turnover values were

$$1995: \frac{6,365.2}{(3,043.3 + 4,826.9)/2} = 1.62$$

$$1994: \frac{5,955.0}{(2,815.9 + 3,043.3)/2} = 2.03$$

You must compare this ratio to that of other firms in an industry because it varies substantially between industries. Total asset turnover ratios range from about 1 for large capital-intensive industries (e.g., steel, autos, and other heavy manufacturing companies) to over 10 for some retailing operations. It also can be affected by the use of leased facilities.

Again, you should consider a *range* of turnover values. It is poor management to have an exceedingly high asset turnover relative to your industry because this might imply too few assets for the potential business (sales) or the use of outdated, fully depreciated assets. It is equally poor management to have a very low relative asset turnover because this implies tying up capital in an excess of assets relative to the needs of the firm.

Beyond the analysis of the total asset base, it is insightful to examine the utilization of some specific assets such as inventories and fixed assets. Since we have already examined the receivables and inventory turnover as part of our liquidity analysis, we will examine the fixed asset ratio.

NET FIXED ASSET TURNOVER   The net fixed asset turnover ratio reflects the firm's utilization of fixed assets. It is computed as follows:

$$\text{Fixed Asset Turnover} = \frac{\text{Net Sales}}{\text{Average Net Fixed Assets}}$$

Quaker Oats' fixed asset turnover ratios were

$$1995: \frac{6,365.2}{(1,214.2 + 1,113.4)/2} = 5.47 \text{ times}$$

$$1994: \frac{5,955.0}{(1,228.2 + 1,214.2)/2} = 4.88 \text{ times}$$

These turnover ratios must be compared with those of firms in the same industry and should consider the impact of leased assets. Also remember that an abnormally low turnover implies capital tied up in excessive fixed assets, while an abnormally high asset turnover ratio can indicate the use of old, fully depreciated equipment that may be obsolete.

EQUITY TURNOVER   In addition to specific asset turnover ratios, it is useful to examine the turnover for alternative capital components. An important one, equity turnover, is computed as follows:

$$\text{Equity Turnover} = \frac{\text{Net Sales}}{\text{Average Equity}}$$

Equity includes preferred and common stock, paid-in capital, and total retained earnings.[1] The difference between this ratio and total asset turnover is that it excludes current liabilities and long-term debt. Therefore, when examining this series, you must consider the firm's capital ratios because the firm can increase its equity turnover ratio by increasing its proportion of debt capital (i.e., a higher debt/equity ratio).

Quaker Oats' equity turnover ratios were

$$1995: \frac{6,365.2}{(445.8 + 1,128.8)/2} = 8.08$$

$$1994: \frac{5,955.0}{(551.1 + 445.8)/2} = 11.95$$

Quaker has experienced a fairly consistent increase in this ratio during the past several years. There was a reversal of the increase in 1995 because of an increase in equity due to the significant gains from divestitures (see Table 12.3). In our later analysis of sustainable growth, we examine the variables that affect the equity turnover ratio to understand what caused the long-term increase and subsequent decline in 1995.

Given some understanding of the firm's record of operating efficiency, as shown by its ability to generate sales from its assets and capital, the next step is to examine its profitability in relation to sales and capital.

OPERATING PROFITABILITY RATIOS   The ratios in this category indicate two facets of profitability: (1) the rate of profit on sales (profit margin) and (2) the percentage return on capital employed.

GROSS PROFIT MARGIN   Gross profit equals net sales minus the cost of goods sold. The gross profit margin is computed as

$$\text{Gross Profit Margin} = \frac{\text{Gross Profit}}{\text{Net Sales}}$$

The gross profit margins for Quaker Oats were

$$1995: \frac{2,983.7}{6,365.2} = 46.88\%$$

$$1994: \frac{3,028.8}{5,955.0} = 50.86\%$$

$$1993: \frac{2,860.6}{5,730.6} = 49.92\%$$

This ratio indicates the basic cost structure of the firm. An analysis over time relative to a comparable industry figure shows the firm's relative cost–price position. Quaker Oats experienced a definite decline in this margin during 1995. You would certainly want to question management about the reason for this decline. As always, it is important to compare these margins with industry statistics.

---

[1] Some investors prefer to only consider owner's equity, which would not include preferred stock.

OPERATING PROFIT MARGIN   Operating profit is gross profit minus sales, general, and administrative (SG + A) expenses. The operating profit margin equals

$$\text{Operating Profit Margin} = \frac{\text{Operating Profit}}{\text{Net Sales}}$$

For Quaker Oats, the operating profit margins were

$$1995: \frac{380.5}{6,365.2} = 5.98\%$$

$$1994: \frac{603.2}{5,955.0} = 10.13\%$$

$$1993: \frac{558.3}{5,730.6} = 9.74\%$$

The variability of the operating profit margin over time is a prime indicator of the business risk for a firm. For Quaker Oats, this margin declined during 1995, but the drop was mainly caused by the decline in gross margin—i.e., as shown in Table 12.6, the SG + A expense relative to sales ratio was quite stable over the three-year period.

There are two additional deductions from operating profit—interest expense and net foreign exchange loss. This indicates operating income before income taxes.

In some instances, investors add back depreciation expense and compute a profit margin that consists of earnings before depreciation, interest, and taxes (EBDIT). This alternative operating profit margin reflects all controllable expenses. It can provide great insights regarding the profit performance of heavy manufacturing firms with large depreciation charges. It also can indicate earnings available to pay fixed financing costs. This latter use will be discussed in the section on financial risk.

NET PROFIT MARGIN   This margin relates net income to sales. In the case of Quaker Oats, it is appropriate to use operating income after taxes but before the several significant nonoperating adjustments, including the cumulative effect of accounting changes, but more important (especially for 1995), the gains or losses on divestitures and restructuring charges. The net income used is operating earnings after taxes but before dividends on preferred and common stock. For most firms this margin is equal to

$$\text{Net Profit Margin} = \frac{\text{Net Income}}{\text{Net Sales}}$$

As noted, Quaker Oats' net profit margin is based on operating income after taxes as follows:

$$1995: \frac{188.0}{6,365.2} = 2.95\%$$

$$1994: \frac{340.1}{5,955.0} = 5.71\%$$

$$1993: \frac{307.3}{5,730.6} = 5.00\%$$

This ratio is computed based on sales and operating earnings from *continuing* operations because our analysis seeks to derive insights about *future* expectations. Therefore, results for continuing operations are relevant rather than the profit or loss that considers earnings from discontinued operations or the gain or loss from the sale of these operations.

This focus on continuing operations was important in 1995 when the firm sold several divisions. The change in the net profit margin during 1995 is important because it reflects the effect of the acquisition of Snapple beverages.

COMMON SIZE INCOME STATEMENT   Beyond these ratios, an additional technique for analyzing operating profitability is a common size income statement, which lists all expense and income items as a percentage of sales. Analyzing this statement for several years (five at least) will provide useful insights regarding the trends in cost figures and profit margins.

Table 12.6 shows a common size statement for Quaker Oats for the last three years. These statements were discussed earlier where the significant increase in the percentage of cost of goods was highlighted that ultimately had a major impact on the net margin.

Beyond the analysis of earnings on sales, the ultimate measure of the success of management is the profits earned on the assets or the capital committed to the enterprise. Several ratios help us evaluate this important relationship.

RETURN ON TOTAL CAPITAL   The return on total capital ratio relates the firm's earnings to all the capital involved in the enterprise (debt, preferred stock, and common stock). Therefore, the earnings figure used is the net income from continuing operations (before any dividends) *plus* the interest paid on debt.

$$\text{Return on Total Capital} = \frac{\text{Net Income} + \text{Interest Expense}}{\text{Average Total Capital}}$$

Quaker Oats incurred interest expense for long- and short-term debt. The gross interest expense value used in this ratio differs from the "net" interest expense item in the income statement, which is measured as gross interest expense minus interest income.

Quaker Oats' rate of return on total capital was

$$1995: \frac{188.0 + 117.0}{(3{,}043.3 + 4{,}826.9)/2} = 7.75\%$$

$$1994: \frac{340.1 + 98.6}{(2{,}815.9 + 3{,}043.3)/2} = 14.97\%$$

This ratio indicates the firm's return on all the capital it employed. It should be compared with the ratio for other firms in the industry and the economy. If this rate of return does not match the perceived risk of the firm, one might question if the entity should continue to exist because the capital involved in the enterprise could be used more productively elsewhere in the economy. For Quaker Oats, the results indicate a significant decline in 1995 because of the reduced operating income.

RETURN ON OWNER'S EQUITY   The return on owner's equity (ROE) ratio is extremely important to the owner of the enterprise (the common stockholder) because it indicates the rate of return that management has earned on the capital provided by the owner after accounting for payments to all other capital suppliers. If you consider all equity (including preferred stock), this return would equal

$$\text{Return on Total Equity} = \frac{\text{Net Income}}{\text{Average Total Equity}}$$

If an investor is concerned only with owner's equity (i.e., the common shareholder's equity), the ratio would be calculated

$$\text{Return on Owner's Equity} = \frac{\text{Net Income} - \text{Preferred Dividend}}{\text{Average Common Equity}}$$

Quaker Oats generated return on owner's equity of

$$1995: \frac{188.0 - 4.0}{(445.8 + 1{,}128.8)/2} = 23.37\%$$

$$1994: \frac{340.1 - 4.0}{(551.1 + 445.8)/2} = 67.43\%$$

The ROE in 1995 of 23.37 percent is a very respectable value compared to all industrial firms, which averaged about 18 percent in 1994–1995. At the same time, it was a significant decline from the 67.43 percent earned in 1994. The reasons for the changes in Quaker Oats' ROE will be discussed in the following section.

This ratio reflects the rate of return on the equity capital provided by the owners. It should correspond to the firm's overall business risk, but it also should reflect the financial risk assumed by the common stockholder because of the prior claims of the firm's bondholders.

THE DUPONT SYSTEM   The importance of ROE as an indicator of performance makes it desirable to divide the ratio into several components that provide insights into the causes of a firm's ROE or any changes in it. This breakdown of ROE into component ratios is generally referred to as the **DuPont System.** To begin, the return on equity (ROE) ratio can be broken down into two ratios that we have discussed—net profit margin and equity turnover.

$$\text{ROE} = \frac{\text{Net Income}}{\text{Common Equity}} = \frac{\text{Net Income}}{\text{Net Sales}} \times \frac{\text{Net Sales}}{\text{Common Equity}}$$

This breakdown is an identity because we have both multiplied and divided by net sales. To maintain the identity, the common equity value used is the year-end figure rather than the average of the beginning and ending value. This identity reveals that ROE equals the net profit margin times the equity turnover, which implies that a firm can improve its return on equity by *either* using its equity more efficiently (i.e., increasing its equity turnover) or by becoming more profitable (i.e., increasing its net profit margin).

As noted previously, a firm's equity turnover is affected by its capital structure. Specifically, a firm can increase its equity turnover by employing a higher proportion of debt capital. We can see this effect by considering the following relationship.

$$\frac{\text{Sales}}{\text{Equity}} = \frac{\text{Sales}}{\text{Total Assets}} \times \frac{\text{Total Assets}}{\text{Equity}}$$

Similar to the prior breakdown, this is an identity because we have both multiplied and divided the equity turnover ratio by total assets. This equation indicates that the equity turnover ratio equals the firm's *total asset turnover* (a measure of efficiency) times the ratio of total assets to equity, which is a measure of financial leverage. Specifically, this latter ratio of total assets to equity indicates the proportion of total assets financed with debt. *All assets have to be financed by either equity or some form of debt* (either current liabilities or long-term debt). Therefore, the higher the ratio of assets to equity, the higher the proportion of debt to equity. A total asset/equity ratio of 2, for example, indicates that for every 2 dollars of assets there is a dollar of equity, which means the firm financed one-half of its assets with equity. This implies that it financed the other half with debt. A total asset/equity ratio of 3 indicates that only one-third of total assets was financed with equity, so two-thirds must have been financed with debt. This breakdown of the equity turnover ratio implies that a firm can increase its equity turnover either by increasing its total asset turnover (i.e., becoming more efficient) or by increasing its financial leverage ratio (i.e., financing assets with a higher proportion of debt capital).

Combining these two breakdowns, we see that a firm's ROE is composed of three ratios as follows:[2]

$$\frac{\text{Net Income}}{\text{Common Equity}} = \frac{\text{Net Income}}{\text{Sales}} \times \frac{\text{Sales}}{\text{Total Assets}} \times \frac{\text{Total Assets}}{\text{Common Equity}}$$

$$= \frac{\text{Profit}}{\text{Margin}} \times \frac{\text{Total Asset}}{\text{Turnover}} \times \frac{\text{Financial}}{\text{Leverage}}$$

As an example of this important set of relationships, the figures in Table 12.7 indicate what has happened to the ROE for Quaker Oats and the components of its ROE during the 18-year period from 1978 to 1995. As noted, these ratio values employ year-end balance sheet figures (assets and equity) rather than the average of beginning and ending data.

The DuPont results in Table 12.7 indicate several significant trends: the overall ROE experienced (1) an increase from 1978 to 1986; (2) a softening during the period 1986–1989; (3) an explosive growth from 1989–1994; and (4) a precipitous decline in 1995. Most of the increase before 1991 was due to a steady increase in the total asset/equity ratio and reflected increases in financial leverage. Notably, the explosive increases in ROE during the period 1990–1994 (i.e., from 22.39% to 76.29%) was caused by increases in all three ratios. Specifically, total asset turnover (TAT) went from 1.51 to 1.96; total assets/equity increased from 3.26 to 6.83; and the net profit margin (NPM) grew from 4.55% to 5.71%. Although the changes in both TAT and the NPM are impressive operating performance changes, the total asset/equity ratio that reflects financial leverage could be of concern. Specifically, a 3.26 ratio implies a total debt to total asset ratio of about 69% debt and a 6.83 ratio implies that about 85% of the firm's assets are financed by debt. In the next section, we analyze additional measures of financial risk.

The significant decline in the ROE for 1995 also was caused by declines in all the component ratios. The first two ratios (TAT and TA/EQ) were impacted by the increases in equity due to gains on divestiture and the increases in intangible assets. As a result, the TAT went from 1.96 to 1.32 and the TA/EQ ratio went from 6.83 to 4.28, even though the firm's total debt increased by over $800 million. Finally, the NPM declined from the firm's highest margin during the 18 years of 5.71% to its lowest of 2.95%.

Based on all of this, an analyst would be deeply concerned about what has occurred and would want to find out what caused these changes and what management will do to turn this around in the future.

---

[2] In contrast to this discussion that considered profit margin and equity turnover, some analysts group the three ratios differently. Specifically, they combine the profit margin times total asset turnover to get return on total assets and multiply this times the leverage ratio to get ROE. Obviously, the final ROE values will be the same since the three ratios are the same and the only change is how they are arranged.

TABLE 12.7

THE DUPONT ANALYSIS OF ROE FOR QUAKER OATS COMPANY[a]

Year	(1) Sales/Total Assets	(2) Total Assets/ Equity	(3)[b] Sales/ Equity	(4) Net Profit Margin (%)	(5)[c] Return on Equity (%)
1978	1.49	1.97	2.94	4.87	14.32
1979	1.56	2.01	3.14	4.65	14.60
1980	1.63	2.11	3.44	4.36	15.00
1981	1.62	2.21	3.58	4.37	15.64
1982	1.68	2.14	3.60	4.55	16.38
1983	1.71	2.15	3.68	4.57	16.82
1984	1.80	2.38	4.28	4.19	17.93
1985	1.82	2.23	4.06	4.48	18.19
1986	1.70	2.45	4.17	4.83	20.14
1987	1.36	2.99	4.07	4.20	17.09
1988	1.56	2.31	3.60	4.36	15.70
1989	1.56	2.75	4.29	3.05	13.08
1990	1.51	3.26	4.92	4.55	22.39
1991	1.82	3.35	6.10	4.29	26.17
1992	1.83	3.61	6.61	4.44	29.35
1993[d]	2.04	5.11	10.42	5.36	55.88
1994[d]	1.96	6.83	13.36	5.71	76.29
1995[d]	1.32	4.28	5.64	2.95	16.66

[a]Ratios use year-end data for total assets and common equity rather than averages of the year.
[b]Column (3) is equal to column (1) times column (2).
[c]Column (5) is equal to column (3) times column (4).
[d]ROE is calculated using operating income after taxes.

AN EXTENDED DUPONT SYSTEM[3]   Beyond the original DuPont System, some analysts have suggested using an extended DuPont System, which provides additional insights into the effect of financial leverage on the firm and also pinpoints the effect of income taxes on the firm's ROE. Because both financial leverage and tax rates have changed dramatically over the last decade, these additional insights are important.

In the prior presentation, we started with the ROE and divided it into components. In contrast, we now begin with the operating profit margin (EBIT divided by sales) and introduce additional ratios to derive an ROE value. Combining the operating profit margin and the total asset turnover ratio yields the following:

$$\frac{EBIT}{Sales} \times \frac{Sales}{Total\ Assets} = \frac{EBIT}{Total\ Assets}$$

This ratio is the operating profit return on total assets. To consider the negative effects of financial leverage, we examine the effect of interest expense as a percentage of total assets:

$$\frac{EBIT}{Total\ Assets} - \frac{Interest\ Expense}{Total\ Assets} = \frac{Net\ Before\ Tax}{Total\ Assets}$$

[3]The original DuPont System was the three-component breakdown discussed in the prior section. Because this analysis also involves the components of ROE, some still refer to it as the DuPont System. In our presentation, we refer to it as the extended DuPont System to differentiate it from the original system.

We consider the positive effect of financial leverage with the leverage multiplier as follows:

$$\frac{\text{Net Before Tax (NBT)}}{\text{Total Assets}} \times \frac{\text{Total Assets}}{\text{Common Equity}} = \frac{\text{Net Before Tax (NBT)}}{\text{Common Equity}}$$

This indicates the pretax return on equity. To arrive at ROE, we must consider the tax rate effect. We do this by multiplying the pretax ROE by a tax retention rate as follows:

$$\frac{\text{Net Before Tax}}{\text{Common Equity}} \times \left(100\% - \frac{\text{Income Taxes}}{\text{Net Before Tax}} \right) = \frac{\text{Net Income}}{\text{Common Equity}}$$

In summary, we have the following five components:

1. $\dfrac{\text{EBIT}}{\text{Sales}}$ = Operating Profit Margin

2. $\dfrac{\text{Sales}}{\text{Total Assets}}$ = Total Asset Turnover

3. $\dfrac{\text{Interest Expense}}{\text{Total Assets}}$ = Interest Expense Rate

4. $\dfrac{\text{Total Assets}}{\text{Common Equity}}$ = Financial Leverage Multiplier

5. $\left(100\% - \dfrac{\text{Income Tax}}{\text{Net Before Tax}} \right)$ = Tax Retention Rate

To demonstrate the use of this extended DuPont System, Table 12.8 contains the calculations using the five components for the years 1982 through 1995. The first column indicates that the firm's operating profit margin peaked in 1983 and has subsequently generally declined prior to the major drop in 1995. We know from the prior discussion that the firm's total asset turnover (column 2) has tended to increase and reached a peak in 1993 and a low in 1995. As a result, operating return on assets looked good between 1993–1994 prior to the decline in 1995. The negative impact of leverage in column 4 shows that the relative importance of interest expense as a percent of total assets was greatest in the early 1980s.

Column 5 reflects the firm's operating performance before the positive impact of financing (the leverage multiplier) and any impact of taxes. These results show strong performance by the firm during 1983–1986, with a peak between 1993–1994 before a collapse in 1995. Column 6 reflects the significant change in financial leverage and this effect shows up in column 7, where the pretax return on equity is greatest during 1993–1994. Column 8 shows the effect of much lower tax rates and thus a higher overall tax retention rate during 1988–1990 and 1993–1995. In summary, this breakdown should likewise help you to understand *what* happened to a firm's ROE as well as *why* it happened. The intent is to determine what happened to the firm's internal operating results, its financial leverage, and what was the effect of external government tax policy.

RISK ANALYSIS   Risk analysis examines the uncertainty of income flows for the total firm and for the individual sources of capital (i.e., debt, preferred stock, and common stock). The typical approach examines the major factors that cause a firm's income flows to vary. More volatile income flows mean greater risk (uncertainty) facing the investor.

TABLE 12.8   EXTENDED DUPONT SYSTEM ANALYSIS FOR QUAKER OATS: 1982–1995[a]

Year	(1) EBIT/Sales (Percent)	(2) Sales/Total Assets (Times)	(3) EBIT/Total Assets (Percent)[b]	(4) Interest Expense/Total Assets (Percent)	(5) Net Before Tax/Total Assets (Percent)[c]	(6) Total Assets/Common Equity (Times)	(7) Net Before Tax/Common Equity (Percent)[d]	(8) Tax Retention Rate	(9) Return on Equity (Percent)[e]
1982	10.5	1.68	17.6	4.6	13.0	2.14	27.8	0.57	15.85
1983	10.7	1.71	18.3	3.7	14.6	2.15	31.4	0.54	16.96
1984	10.0	1.80	18.0	4.1	13.9	2.38	33.1	0.53	17.54
1985	10.4	1.82	18.9	3.7	15.2	2.23	33.9	0.54	18.31
1986	10.1	1.70	17.2	2.3	14.9	2.45	36.5	0.56	20.44
1987	9.4	1.36	12.8	2.0	10.8	2.99	32.3	0.52	16.80
1988	8.4	1.56	13.1	2.4	10.7	2.31	24.7	0.62	15.31
1989	6.3	1.56	9.8	3.6	6.2	2.75	17.1	0.62	10.60
1990	9.6	1.51	14.5	2.6	11.9	3.32	39.5	0.60	23.70
1991	9.1	1.82	16.6	3.4	13.2	3.40	44.8	0.57	25.54
1992	8.8	1.83	16.1	2.5	13.6	3.61	49.1	0.59	28.97
1993f	9.5	2.04	19.3	2.3	17.0	5.11	86.7	0.63	54.58
1994f	9.7	1.96	19.0	3.2	15.7	6.83	107.3	0.70	74.89
1995f	5.9	1.32	7.8	2.4	5.4	4.28	23.0	0.71	16.28

[a] The percents in this table may not be the same as in Table 12.7 due to rounding of the numerous ratios.
[b] Column (3) is equal to column (1) times column (2).
[c] Column (5) is equal to column (3) minus column (4).
[d] Column (7) is equal to column (5) times column (6).
[e] Column (9) is equal to column (7) times column (8).
[f] ROE is calculated using operating income after taxes.

The total risk of the firm has two components: business risk and financial risk. The next section discusses the concept of business risk: how you measure it, what causes it, and how you measure its individual causes. The following section discusses financial risk and describes the ratios by which you measure it.

BUSINESS RISK[4]   Recall that business risk is the uncertainty of income that is caused by the firm's industry. In turn, this uncertainty is due to the firm's variability of sales due to its products, customers, and the way it produces its products. Specifically, a firm's earnings vary over time because its sales and production costs vary. As an example, the earnings for a steel firm will probably vary more than those of a grocery chain because (1) over the business cycle, steel sales are more volatile than grocery sales and (2) the steel firm's large fixed production costs make its earnings vary more than its sales.

Business risk is generally measured by the variability of the firm's operating income over time. In turn, the earnings variability is measured by the standard deviation of the historical operating earnings series. You will recall from Chapter 1 that the standard deviation is influenced by the size of the numbers, so investors standardize this measure of volatility by dividing it by the mean value for the series (i.e., the average operating earnings). The resulting ratio of the standard deviation of operating earnings divided by the average operating earnings is the familiar coefficient of variation (CV):

$$\text{Business Risk} = f(\text{Coefficient of Variation of Operating Earnings})$$

$$= \frac{\text{Standard Deviation of Operating Earnings (OE)}}{\text{Mean Operating Earnings}}$$

$$= \frac{\sqrt{\sum_{i=1}^{n} (OE_i - \overline{OE})^2/N}}{\sum_{i=1}^{n} OE_i/N}$$

The CV of operating earnings allows comparisons between standardized measures of business risk for firms of different sizes. To compute the CV of operating earnings, you need a minimum of 5 years up to about 10 years. Less than 5 years is not very meaningful, and data more than 10 years old are typically out of date. We cannot compute the CV of operating earnings for Quaker Oats because we have data for only 3 years.

Besides measuring overall business risk, we can examine the two factors that contribute to the variability of operating earnings: sales variability and operating leverage.

SALES VARIABILITY   Sales variability is the prime determinant of earnings variability. Operating earnings must be as volatile as sales. Notably, the variability of sales is largely outside the control of management. Specifically, although the variability of sales is affected by a firm's advertising and pricing policy, the major cause is its industry. For example, sales for a firm in a cyclical industry, such as automobiles or steel, will be volatile over the business cycle compared to sales of a firm in a noncyclical industry, such as retail food or hospital supplies. Like operating earnings, the variability of a firm's sales is typically measured by the CV of sales during the most recent 5 to 10 years. The CV of sales equals the standard deviation of sales divided by the mean sales for the period.

$$\text{Sales Volatility} = f(\text{Coefficient of Variation of Sales})$$

$$= \frac{\sqrt{\sum_{i=1}^{n} (S_i - \overline{S})^2/N}}{\sum_{i=1}^{n} S_i/N}$$

---

[4]For a further discussion on this general topic, see Eugene Brigham and Louis C. Gapenski, *Financial Management: Theory and Practice*, 8th ed. (Fort Worth, TX: The Dryden Press, 1997), Chapters 6 and 10.

OPERATING LEVERAGE   The variability of a firm's operating earnings also depends on its mixture of production costs. Total production costs of a firm with no *fixed* production costs would vary directly with sales, and operating profits would be a constant proportion of sales. The firm's operating profit margin would be constant and its operating profits would have the same relative volatility as its sales. Realistically, firms always have some fixed production costs (e.g., buildings, machinery, or relatively permanent personnel). Fixed production costs cause operating profits to vary more than sales over the business cycle. During slow periods, profits decline by a larger percentage than sales. In contrast, during an economic expansion, profits will increase by a larger percentage than sales.

The employment of fixed production costs is referred to as **operating leverage.** Clearly, greater operating leverage makes the operating earnings series more volatile relative to the sales series.[5] This basic relationship between operating profit and sales leads us to measure operating leverage as the percentage change in operating earnings relative to the percentage change in sales during a specified period as follows:

$$\text{Operating Leverage} = \frac{\sum_{i=1}^{n} \left| \frac{\%\Delta OE}{\%\Delta S} \right|}{N}$$

We take the absolute value of the percentage changes because the two series can move in opposite directions. The direction of the change is not important, but the relative size of the change is relevant. The more volatile the operating earnings as compared to sales, the greater the firm's operating leverage.

FINANCIAL RISK   Financial risk, you will recall, is the additional uncertainty of returns to equity holders due to a firm's use of fixed obligation debt securities. This financial uncertainty is in addition to the firm's business risk. When a firm sells bonds to raise capital, the interest payments on this capital precede the computation of common stock earnings, and these interest payments are fixed obligations. As with operating leverage, during good times the earnings available for common stock will experience a larger percentage increase than operating earnings, whereas during a business decline the earnings available to stockholders will decline by a larger percentage than operating earnings because of these fixed financial costs. Also, as a firm increases its debt financing with fixed contractual obligations, it increases its financial risk and the possibility of default and bankruptcy.

Two sets of financial ratios help measure financial risk. The first set are balance sheet ratios that indicate the proportion of capital derived from debt securities compared to equity capital (preferred and common stock). The second set of ratios considers the flow of earnings or cash available to pay fixed financial charges.

PROPORTION OF DEBT (BALANCE SHEET) RATIOS   The proportion of debt ratios indicate what proportion of the firm's capital is derived from debt compared to other sources of capital such as preferred stock, common stock, and retained earnings. A higher proportion of debt capital compared to equity capital makes earnings more volatile and increases the probability that a firm will not be able to meet the required interest payments and will default on the debt. Therefore, higher proportion of debt ratios indicate greater financial risk.

The acceptable level of financial risk for a firm depends on its business risk. If the firm has low business risk, investors are willing to accept higher financial risk. For example,

[5] For a further treatment of this area, see James C. Van Horne, *Financial Management and Policy,* 9th ed. (Englewood Cliffs, NJ: Prentice-Hall, 1993), Chapter 27.

retail food companies typically have rather stable operating earnings over time and therefore relatively low business risk, which means that they can have higher financial risk.

Debt/equity ratio   The debt/equity ratio is equal to

$$\text{Debt/Equity Ratio} = \frac{\text{Total Long-Term Debt}}{\text{Total Equity}}$$

The debt figure includes all long-term fixed obligations, including subordinated convertible bonds. The equity typically is the book value of equity and includes preferred stock, common stock, and retained earnings. Some analysts prefer to exclude preferred stock and consider only common equity. Total equity is preferable if some of the firms being analyzed have preferred stock. Alternatively, if the preferred stock dividend is considered an interest payment, you might want to compute a ratio of debt plus preferred stock relative to common equity.

Two sets of debt ratios are computed: *with and without deferred taxes*. Most balance sheets include an accumulated deferred tax figure, which comes just below long-term debt and other liabilities on the balance sheet. There is some controversy regarding whether you should treat these deferred taxes as a liability or as part of permanent capital. Some argue that if the deferred tax has accumulated because of the difference in accelerated and straight-line depreciation, this liability may never be paid. That is, as long as the firm continues to grow and add new assets, this total deferred tax account continues to grow and is never paid off. Alternatively, if the deferred tax account is because of differences in the recognition of income on long-term contracts such as government contracts, there will be a reversal, and this liability must eventually be paid. To resolve this question, you must determine the reason for the deferred tax account and examine its long-term trend.[6]

Quaker Oats' deferred tax account arose because of a depreciation difference, and it has typically grown over time. Several of the following ratios are computed with and without deferred taxes as a long-term liability. This dual treatment demonstrates that the impact of this difference can be substantial. The two sets of debt/equity ratios for Quaker Oats were

A. Including Deferred
Taxes as Long-Term Debt

$$1995: \frac{1,866.4}{1,128.8} = 165.34\%$$

$$1994: \frac{1,323.1}{445.8} = 296.79\%$$

$$1993: \frac{1,148.3}{551.1} = 208.37\%$$

B. Excluding Deferred
Taxes as Long-Term Debt

$$1995: \frac{1,631.1}{1,128.8} = 103.04\%$$

$$1994: \frac{1,240.9}{445.8} = 278.33\%$$

$$1993: \frac{1,058.8}{551.1} = 192.12\%$$

[6]For a further discussion of this, see Gerald I. White, Ashwinpaul C. Sondhi, and Dov Fried, *The Analysis and Use of Financial Statements* (New York: John Wiley & Sons, 1994), 1017–1018.

These ratios indicate an increase and a decline in the firm's debt burden over the three-year period. Notably, the decline in 1995 was due to the very large increase in equity, which caused the decline even though there was about a $400 million increase in debt.

Long-term debt/total capital ratio   The debt/total capital ratio indicates the proportion of long-term capital derived from long-term debt capital. It is computed as

$$\text{L.T. Debt/Total Capital Ratio} = \frac{\text{Total Long-Term Debt}}{\text{Total Long-Term Capital}}$$

The long-term capital would include all long-term debt, any preferred stock, and total equity. Again, the ratios are computed including and excluding deferred taxes from long-term debt and long-term capital. The two sets of debt/total capital ratios for Quaker Oats were

A. Including Deferred Taxes as Long-Term Debt

$$1995: \frac{1,866.4}{3,095.2} = 60.30\%$$

$$1994: \frac{1,323.1}{1,868.9} = 70.80\%$$

$$1993: \frac{1,148.3}{1,799.4} = 63.82\%$$

B. Excluding Deferred Taxes from Long-Term Debt and Long-Term Capital

$$1995: \frac{1,633.1}{2,861.9} = 57.06\%$$

$$1994: \frac{1,240.9}{1,786.7} = 69.45\%$$

$$1993: \frac{1,058.8}{1,709.9} = 61.92\%$$

Again, this ratio indicates an increase followed by a decrease in the firm's financial risk for the same reason as before (a large increase in equity capital). It also shows the effect of including deferred taxes as both debt and long-term capital.

Total debt ratios   In some cases, it is useful to compare total debt (current liabilities plus long-term liabilities) to total capital (total debt plus total equity). This is especially revealing for a firm that derives substantial capital from short-term borrowing, which Quaker Oats does. The two sets of total debt/total capital ratios for Quaker Oats were

A. Including Deferred Taxes as Long-Term Debt

$$1995: \frac{3,679.3}{4,826.9} = 76.22\%$$

$$1994: \frac{2,582.2}{3,043.3} = 84.85\%$$

$$1993: \frac{2,253.4}{2,815.9} = 80.02\%$$

B. Excluding Deferred
Taxes from Long-Term
Debt and Long-Term
Capital

$$1995: \frac{3,446.0}{4,593.6} = 75.02\%$$

$$1994: \frac{2,500.0}{2,961.1} = 84.43\%$$

$$1993: \frac{2,163.9}{2,726.4} = 79.37\%$$

This ratio indicates that about three-fourths of Quaker Oats' assets are currently financed with debt, which corresponds to the total asset/equity ratio (the financial leverage multiplier) of about 4.0. Notably, this is down from about 85% in 1994 because of the large increase in equity in 1995. These ratios should be compared with those of other companies in the industry to evaluate their consistency with the business risk of this industry. Such a comparison also would indicate how much higher this total debt ratio can go. This is important because Quaker Oats has an ROE target of 25 percent, and investors need to know the impact of financial leverage on it as shown earlier in Tables 12.7 and 12.8.

EARNINGS OR CASH FLOW RATIOS   In addition to ratios that indicate the proportion of debt on the balance sheet, investors use ratios that relate the *flow* of earnings or cash that is available to meet the required interest and lease payments. A higher ratio of earnings or cash flow relative to fixed financial charges indicates lower financial risk.

Interest coverage   Interest coverage is computed as follows:

$$\text{Interest Coverage} = \frac{\text{Income Before Interest and Taxes (EBIT)}}{\text{Debt Interest Charges}}$$

$$= \frac{\text{Net Income + Income Taxes + Interest Expense}}{\text{Interest Expense}}$$

This ratio indicates how many times the fixed interest charges are earned, based on the earnings available to pay these expenses.[7] Alternatively, 1 minus the reciprocal of the coverage ratio indicates how far earnings could decline before it would be impossible to pay the interest charges from current earnings. For example, a coverage ratio of 5 means that earnings could decline by 80 percent (1 minus $\frac{1}{5}$), and the firm could still pay its fixed financial charges. Quaker Oats' interest coverage ratios (using the gross interest expense) were

$$1995: \frac{188.0 + 77.6 + 117.0}{117.0} = 3.27 \text{ times}$$

$$1994: \frac{340.1 + 147.2 + 98.6}{98.6} = 5.94 \text{ times}$$

$$1993: \frac{307.3 + 180.8 + 65.6}{65.6} = 8.44 \text{ times}$$

The good news is that all the coverage ratios were in excess of 3. The bad news is that these coverage ratios have declined steadily over the three-year period by over 50 percent. Notably,

---

[7] The net income figure used in the analysis is the operating income after taxes because, once again, it is important to exclude earnings and cash flows that are considered nonrecurring and only consider those that should be available in the future (i.e., those from ongoing operations).

the trend of Quaker Oats' coverage ratios has been consistent with the overall trend in the proportion of debt ratios. The proportion of debt ratios and the cash flow ratios do not always give consistent results because the proportion of debt ratios are not sensitive to changes in earnings and cash flow or to changes in the interest rates on the debt. For example, if there is an increase in interest rates or if the firm replaced old debt with new debt that had a higher interest rate, there would be no change in the proportion of debt ratios, but the interest coverage ratio would decline. Also, the interest coverage ratio is sensitive to an increase or decrease in earnings. Therefore, although the results using balance sheet ratios and coverage ratios can differ, they were consistent for Quaker Oats during 1993–1995.

Notably, the experience of Quaker Oats during the period prior to 1993 was a dramatic example of a positive difference. Specifically, although the proportion of debt ratios generally indicated that Quaker Oats had increased its debt and financial risk, the firm's flow ratios indicated *lower* financial risk because earnings had increased and finance charges had declined due to lower interest rates during this period. As a result, the firm's coverage ratios increased during the period 1990–1993.

Total fixed charge coverages You might want to determine how well earnings cover *total* fixed financial charges including any noncancellable lease payments and any preferred dividends paid out of earnings *after* taxes. If you want to consider preferred dividends, you need to determine the pretax earnings needed to meet these dividend payments, as follows:

$$\frac{\text{Fixed}}{\text{Charge Coverage}} = \frac{\text{Income Before Interest, Taxes, and Lease Payments}}{\text{Debt Interest} + \text{Lease Payments} + (\text{Preferred Dividend}/(1 - \text{Tax Rate})}$$

CASH FLOW RATIOS As an alternative to these earnings coverage ratios, analysts employ several cash flow ratios that relate the cash flow available from operations to either interest expense, total fixed charges, or the face value of outstanding debt. The first set of cash flow to interest expense or total fixed charges are an extension of the earnings coverage ratios. The second set of cash flow ratios are unique because they relate the *flow* of earnings and noncash expenses against the *stock* of outstanding debt. These cash flow to debt ratios have been significant variables in numerous studies concerned with predicting bankruptcies and bond ratings.[8]

Cash flow/interest expense These ratios are an alternative to the earnings coverage return. The motivation is that a firm's earnings and cash flow typically will differ substantially (these differences have been noted and will be considered in a subsequent section). To have ratios that can be compared to similar values for the industry and the aggregate market, the cash flow value used is the "traditional" measure of cash flow, which is equal to net income plus depreciation expense plus deferred taxes (if there was an increase in deferred taxes) for the period (the depreciation expense and deferred tax values are typically given in footnotes).

Quaker Oats' cash flow/interest expense ratios were

$$1995: \frac{188.0 + 191.4 + 17.8}{117.0} = 3.39 \text{ times}$$

$$1994: \frac{340.1 + 171.2 - 1.7}{98.6} = 5.11 \text{ times}$$

$$1993: \frac{307.3 + 156.9 - 46.4}{65.6} = 6.37 \text{ times}$$

---

[8] A list of studies where ratios or cash flow variables are used to predict bankruptcies or bond ratings is included in the reference section.

These ratios are similar to the earnings coverage ratios. Unfortunately they likewise indicate a decline in the coverage for Quaker Oats. Also, as we will see, the decline in 1994 was not consistent with the industry or the market series.

Cash flow coverage ratio To compute a cash flow coverage ratio that is comparable to the earnings coverage ratio, it is necessary to add back the interest charges to this cash flow value because interest expense was deducted to arrive at net income. The cash flow coverage ratios are:

$$1995: \frac{397.2 + 117.0}{117.0} = 4.39 \text{ times}$$

$$1994: \frac{503.6 + 98.6}{98.6} = 6.11 \text{ times}$$

$$1993: \frac{417.8 + 65.6}{65.6} = 7.37 \text{ times}$$

Cash flow/long-term debt ratio Beyond relating cash flow to the required interest expense, several studies have used a ratio that relates cash flow to a firm's outstanding debt as a predictor of bankruptcy and found that this ratio was very good as an explanatory variable in these studies (as noted, they are listed in the references). The cash flow figure used in most studies is the traditional measure used in the prior cash flow coverage ratios. Therefore, the ratios would be computed as

$$\text{Cash Flow/LT Debt} = \frac{\text{Net Income} + \text{Depreciation Expense} + \text{Deferred Tax}}{\text{Book Value of Long-Term Debt}}$$

For Quaker Oats, these ratios were computed based on operating earnings after taxes plus the depreciation expense and deferred taxes reported in the footnotes. Again, we computed these ratios with and without deferred taxes as follows:

A. Including Deferred
Taxes as Long-Term Debt

$$1995: \frac{397.2}{1,866.4} = 21.28\%$$

$$1994: \frac{503.6}{1,323.1} = 38.06\%$$

$$1993: \frac{417.8}{1,148.3} = 36.38\%$$

B. Excluding Deferred
Taxes from Long-Term
Debt

$$1995: \frac{397.2}{1,633.1} = 24.32\%$$

$$1994: \frac{503.6}{1,240.9} = 40.58\%$$

$$1993: \frac{417.8}{1,058.8} = 39.46\%$$

The values were relatively stable during 1993–1994, but declined substantially in 1995. Subsequently, we will see that these ratios were comparable to the industry between 1993–1994, but were below the industry in 1995.

Cash flow/total debt ratio Investors also should consider the relationship of cash flow to total debt to check that a firm has not had a significant increase in its short-term borrowing. For Quaker Oats, these ratios were

A. Including Deferred Taxes as Long-Term Debt

1995: $\dfrac{397.2}{3,679.3} = 10.80\%$

1994: $\dfrac{503.6}{2,582.2} = 19.50\%$

1993: $\dfrac{417.8}{2,253.4} = 18.54\%$

B. Excluding Deferred Taxes from Long-Term Debt

1995: $\dfrac{397.2}{3,446.0} = 11.53\%$

1994: $\dfrac{503.6}{2,500.0} = 20.14\%$

1993: $\dfrac{417.8}{2,163.9} = 19.31\%$

When you compare these ratios to those with only long-term debt, they reflect a high proportion of short-term debt for Quaker Oats due to short-term borrowing and trade accounts payable. As before, it is important to compare these flow ratios with similar ratios for other companies in the industry and with the overall economy to gauge the firm's relative performance.

Alternative measures of cash flow As noted, these cash flow ratios used the traditional measure of cash flow. The requirement that companies must prepare and report the statement of cash flows to stockholders has raised interest in other, more exact measures of cash flow. The first is the *cash flow from operations,* which is taken directly from the statement of cash flows. A second measure is *free cash flow,* which is a modification of the cash flow from operations discussed earlier on page 381. The table below summarizes the values derived earlier in the chapter.

Year	Traditional Cash Flow		Cash Flow from Operations	Free Cash Flow
1995	993.4	(298.8*)	475.5	45.2
1994	402.7		450.8	131.1
1993	328.2		558.2	245.6

*This cash flow value uses the net earnings from operations after adjusting for the $694.6 million gain from the sale of subsidiaries.

ANALYSIS OF GROWTH POTENTIAL

IMPORTANCE OF GROWTH ANALYSIS

The analysis of **sustainable growth potential** examines ratios that indicate how fast a firm should grow. Analysis of a firm's growth potential is important for both lenders and owners. Owners know that the value of the firm depends on its future growth in earnings and dividends. In the following chapter, we discuss the dividend discount model, which determines the value of the firm based on its current dividends, your required rate of return for the stock, and the firm's expected growth rate of dividends.

Creditors also are interested in a firm's growth potential because the firm's future success is the major determinant of its ability to pay an obligation, and the firm's future success is influenced by its growth. Some financial ratios used in credit analysis measure the book value of a firm's assets relative to its financial obligations. The rationale for this ratio is that it is assumed that the firm can sell these assets and use the proceeds to pay off the loan in case of default. Selling assets in a forced liquidation will typically yield only about 10 to 15 cents on the dollar. Currently, most analysts recognize that the more relevant analysis measures the ability of the firm to pay off its obligations as an ongoing enterprise, and its growth potential indicates its future status as an ongoing enterprise.

DETERMINANTS OF GROWTH

The growth of a business, like the growth of any economic entity including the aggregate economy, depends on

1. The amount of resources retained and reinvested in the entity
2. The rate of return earned on the resources retained

The more a firm reinvests, the greater its potential for growth. Alternatively, for a given level of reinvestment, a firm will grow faster if it earns a higher rate of return on the resources reinvested. Therefore, the growth of equity earnings is a function of two variables: (1) the percentage of net earnings retained (i.e., the firm's retention rate) and (2) the rate of return earned on the firm's equity capital (i.e., the firm's ROE).

$$g = \text{Percentage of Earnings Retained} \times \text{Return on Equity}$$
$$= \text{RR} \times \text{ROE}$$

where:

g = potential growth rate
RR = the retention rate of earnings
ROE = the firm's return on equity

The retention rate is a decision by the board of directors based on the investment opportunities available to the firm. Theory suggests that the firm should retain earnings and reinvest them as long as the expected rate of return on the investment exceeds the firm's cost of capital.

As discussed earlier in the chapter, the firm's ROE is a function of three components:

• Net profit margin
• Total asset turnover
• Financial leverage (total assets/equity)

Therefore, a firm can increase its ROE by increasing its profit margin, by becoming more efficient (increasing its total asset turnover), or by increasing its financial leverage and financial risk. As discussed, you should examine and estimate each of the components when estimating the ROE for a firm.

The growth potential analysis for Quaker Oats begins with the retention rate (RR):

$$\text{Retention Rate} = 1 - \frac{\text{Dividends Declared}}{\text{Operating Income after Taxes}}$$

Quaker Oats' RR figures were

$$1995: 1 - \frac{1.14}{1.41} = 1 - 0.81 = 0.19$$

$$1994: 1 - \frac{1.06}{2.48} = 1 - 0.43 = 0.57$$

$$1993: 1 - \frac{0.96}{2.11} = 1 - 0.45 = 0.55$$

These results indicate that even before 1995 the retention rate for Quaker Oats was lower than it was during the 1980s and experienced a substantial decline during 1995.

Table 12.7 contains the three components of ROE for the period 1978–1995. Table 12.9 contains the two factors that determine a firm's growth potential and the implied growth rate during the last 18 years. Overall, prior to 1995 Quaker Oats experienced an increase in its growth potential, although there were declines in 1988 and 1989 because of a lower ROE and a decline in the RR. This was followed by a strong recovery during 1990–1994, prior to the dramatic decline in 1995 because of a much lower ROE and RR.

TABLE 12.9

QUAKER OATS COMPANY COMPONENTS OF GROWTH AND THE IMPLIED SUSTAINABLE GROWTH RATE

Year	(1) Retention Rate	(2) Return on Equity[a]	(3)[b] Sustainable Growth Rate
1978	0.69	14.32	9.88
1979	0.69	14.60	10.07
1980	0.69	15.00	10.35
1981	0.67	15.64	10.48
1982	0.68	16.38	11.14
1983	0.64	16.82	10.76
1984	0.66	17.93	11.83
1985	0.66	18.19	12.01
1986	0.66	20.14	13.29
1987	0.66	17.09	11.28
1988	0.59	15.70	9.26
1989	0.36	13.08	4.71
1990	0.52	22.39	11.64
1991	0.49	26.17	12.82
1992	0.47	29.35	13.79
1993[c]	0.55	55.88	30.46
1994[c]	0.57	76.29	43.68
1995[c]	0.19	16.66	3.17

[a]From Table 12.7.
[b]Column (3) is equal to column (1) times column (2).
[c]Operating income after taxes is used to calculate retention rate.

This table reinforces our understanding of the importance of the firm's ROE. Quaker Oats' retention rate was quite stable prior to 1988, implying that the firm's ROE determined its growth rate. This analysis indicates that the important consideration is the long-run outlook for the components of sustainable growth. As an investor, you need to *project* changes in each of the components of ROE and employ these projections to estimate an ROE to use in the growth model along with an estimate of the firm's long-run retention rate. We will come back to these concepts on numerous occasions when valuing the market, industries, and individual firms, especially growth companies where the ROEs are very high and vulnerable to competition.

EXTERNAL MARKET LIQUIDITY

MARKET LIQUIDITY DEFINED

In Chapter 1, we discussed market liquidity as the ability to buy or sell an asset quickly with little price change from a prior transaction assuming no new information. AT&T and IBM are examples of liquid common stocks because you can sell them very quickly with little price change from the prior trade. You might be able to sell an illiquid stock quickly, but the price would be significantly different from the prior price. Alternatively, the broker might be able to get a specified price, but it could take several days.

DETERMINANTS OF MARKET LIQUIDITY

Investors should know the liquidity characteristics of securities they currently own or may buy because it can be important if they want to change the composition of their portfolios. Although the major determinants of market liquidity are reflected in market trading data, several internal corporate variables are good proxies for these market variables. The most important determinant of external market liquidity is the number of or the dollar value of shares traded (the dollar value adjusts for different price levels). More trading activity indicates a greater probability that you can find someone to take the other side of a desired transaction. Another measure of market liquidity is the bid–ask spread (a smaller spread indicates greater liquidity). Fortunately, certain internal corporate variables correlate highly with these market trading variables:

1. Total market value of outstanding securities (number of common shares outstanding times the market price per share)
2. Number of security owners

Numerous studies have shown that the main determinant of the bid–ask spread (besides price) is the dollar value of trading.[9] In turn, the value of trading is highly correlated with the market value of the outstanding securities and the number of security holders. This relationship holds because with more shares outstanding, there will be more stockholders to buy or sell at any time for a variety of purposes. Numerous buyers and sellers provide liquidity.

You can estimate the market value of outstanding Quaker Oats' stock as the average number of shares outstanding during the year (adjusted for stock splits) times the average market price for the year (equal to the high price plus the low price divided by two) as follows:[10]

$$1995: 133,763,000 \times [(42 + 30)/2] = \$4.82 \text{ billion}$$
$$1994: 135,236,000 \times [(41 + 31)/2] = \$4.87 \text{ billion}$$
$$1993: 143,948,000 \times [(39 + 28)/2] = \$4.82 \text{ billion}$$

---

[9] Studies on this topic were discussed in Chapter 4.

[10] To be consistent with financial statement data, these values are for the Quaker Oats fiscal year ending June 30. The stock prices are rounded to the nearest whole dollar.

These market values would place Quaker Oats in the large capitalization category, which usually begins at about $5 billion. The number of Quaker Oats' stockholders is 29,148, including over 350 institutions that own approximately 50 percent of the outstanding stock.

A final measure, **trading turnover** (the percentage of outstanding shares traded during a period of time), also indicates trading activity. During calendar year 1995, there were about 153 million shares of Quaker Oats traded, which indicates turnover of approximately 114 percent (153 mil/134 mil). This compares with the average turnover for the NYSE of about 48 percent. These large values for market value, the number of stockholders and institutional holders, and the high trading turnover indicate that there is a very liquid market in the common stock of Quaker Oats, i.e., Quaker Oats has very low external liquidity risk.

COMPARATIVE ANALYSIS OF RATIOS

We have discussed the importance of comparative analysis, but so far we have concentrated on the selection and computation of specific ratios. Table 12.10 contains most of the ratios discussed for Quaker Oats, the Food Industry (as derived from the S&P *Analysts Handbook*), and the S&P 400 Index. The 3-year comparison should provide some insights, although you typically would want to examine data for a 5- to 10-year period. It is necessary to do the comparison for the period 1992–1994 because industry and market data from Standard and Poor's were not available for 1995 until very late in 1996.

INTERNAL LIQUIDITY

The three basic ratios (current ratio, quick ratio, and cash ratio) all show reduced liquidity for Quaker Oats relative to the industry and market, including negative working capital. The firm's receivables turnover has increased and collection period has declined such that the collection period is substantially less than the S&P 400 and slightly less than the food industry (30 days versus 45 in 1995). Because it has declined steadily, the difference is probably because of its basic credit policy. The working capital/sales ratio is lower than the industry and both the company and industry are much lower than the market series. As noted, the firm currently has negative working capital.

Overall, the comparisons indicate very weak internal liquidity. A positive factor is the firm's ability to sell high-grade commercial paper and the existence of several major bank credit lines.

OPERATING PERFORMANCE

This segment of the analysis considers efficiency ratios (turnovers) and profitability ratios. Given the nature of the analysis, the major comparison is relative to the industry. Quaker Oats' turnover ratios were fairly consistent relative to the food industry. Specifically, during 1992–1994, all the turnover ratios for Quaker Oats (except for working capital turnover) were higher than the comparable industry turnovers.

Profitability from sales is best described as adequate. Operating profit margins were consistently below the aggregate market and industry, including the net profit margin in 1994.

The profit performance related to invested capital was historically strong. The food industry return on total capital was consistently above the S&P 400, and Quaker Oats was above the food industry in 1993 and 1994. The food industry experienced ROEs that were substantially above the market, and Quaker Oats attained substantially higher ROEs than its industry in 1993 and 1994. As noted, this changed dramatically in 1995.

FINANCIAL RISK

Quaker Oats' financial risk ratios measured in terms of proportion of debt were consistently above those of the industry and the market, indicating a riskier posture. In contrast,

TABLE 12.10									
SUMMARY OF FINANCIAL RATIOS FOR QUAKER OATS, S&P FOOD INDUSTRY, AND S&P 400 INDEX: 1992–1994									

	1994			**1993**			**1992**		
	Quaker Oats	Food Industry	S&P 400	Quaker Oats	Food Industry	S&P 400	Quaker Oats	Food Industry	S&P 400
Internal Liquidity									
Current ratio	0.99	1.20	1.38	0.97	1.20	1.24	1.19	1.20	1.25
Quick ratio	0.52	0.70	0.96	0.49	0.60	0.85	0.64	0.70	0.85
Cash ratio	0.11	0.17	0.18	0.06	0.15	0.16	0.09	0.16	0.16
Receivables turnover	12.05	9.00	4.07	10.87	11.94	4.23	9.08	11.89	4.07
Average collection period	30.30	40.56	89.60	33.57	30.56	86.26	40.20	30.70	89.79
Working capital/sales	−0.09	0.05	12.26	−0.65	0.04	8.43	3.62	0.04	8.45
Operation Performance									
Total asset turnover	2.03	1.39	0.90	1.96	1.49	0.90	1.83	1.48	0.90
Inventory turnover (sales)[a]	7.91	6.74	9.50	7.27	8.82	9.60	6.57	9.13	9.30
Working capital turnover	−11.11	18.59	8.16	−1.54	27.00	11.86	0.28	25.77	11.83
Net fixed asset turnover	4.88	3.00	2.78	4.58	3.96	2.77	4.45	4.02	2.69
Equity turnover	11.95	3.61	3.33	8.23	4.67	3.29	6.40	4.38	3.13
Profitability									
Gross profit margin	50.86	—	—	49.92	—	—	49.47	—	—
Operating profit margin	10.13	14.56	14.86	9.74	12.68	13.61	9.79	12.66	13.08
Net profit margin[b]	3.89	5.13	5.35	5.00	4.96	3.73	4.44	4.99	3.24
Return on total capital[b]	10.96	7.72	6.96	11.68	9.80	5.76	10.50	10.20	5.61
Return on equity[b]	45.64	18.53	17.80	40.57	23.20	12.28	27.50	21.82	10.14
Financial Risk									
Debt/equity ratio[c]	296.79	84.79	130.20	208.37	107.23	136.30	134.82	91.15	122.62
Long-term debt/long-term capital[c]	70.80	44.95	56.56	63.82	50.50	57.68	54.65	46.80	55.08
Total debt/total capital[c]	84.85	60.72	69.96	80.02	64.93	72.00	72.04	63.19	70.30
Interest coverage[b]	5.22	6.41	4.70	9.49	6.17	3.40	6.47	5.97	2.90
Cash flow/long-term debt[b, c]	29.85	39.87	25.07	34.60	36.22	21.48	33.52	37.33	22.52
Cash flow/total debt[b, c]	15.30	19.15	14.01	17.63	18.15	11.39	17.38	18.42	11.67
Growth Analysis[d]									
Retention rate[b]	0.57	0.56	0.61	0.55	0.56	0.42	0.47	0.56	0.33
Return on equity[b]	76.29	20.78	17.14	52.10	24.31	12.86	29.35	21.54	9.79
Total asset turnover	1.96	1.39	0.91	2.04	1.49	0.92	1.83	1.48	0.94
Total assets/equity	6.83	2.91	3.51	5.11	3.30	3.76	3.61	2.92	3.50
Net profit margin[b]	5.71	5.13	5.35	5.00	4.96	3.73	4.44	4.99	3.24
Sustainable growth rate[b]	43.68	11.58	10.47	28.66	13.66	5.40	13.79	11.98	3.23

[a]Computed using sales since cost of sales is not available for the industry and the S&P 400.
[b]Calculated using net income from continuing operations.
[c]Ratios include deferred taxes and long-term debt.
[d]Calculated using year-end data.

the financial risk flow ratios for Quaker Oats were above the market but lower than its industry. These comparisons confirm that Quaker Oats has increased its financial risk position during the last several years. Note that the financial risk ratios in Table 12.10 assume that deferred taxes are long-term debt, which is a very conservative assumption for a firm with a strong growth pattern like Quaker Oats.

GROWTH ANALYSIS

Except for 1988 and 1989, Quaker Oats has generally maintained a sustainable growth rate similar to its industry, and both Quaker Oats and the industry have outperformed the aggregate market. The major factor causing a difference in growth for the firm and its industry is ROE. Quaker Oats' ROE was 76.29 percent in 1994, which caused the potential growth rate to be much higher than its industry.

In sum, Quaker Oats has weak liquidity and a good operating record (prior to 1995, which could not be compared due to nonavailable data). Concern arises due to the added debt and a profit margin that has lagged its industry. As an investor, you would monitor the firm's future ability to service its debt and the trend in its profit margin. Your success as an investor depends on how well you use these historical numbers to derive meaningful *estimates* of future performance.

ANALYSIS OF NON-U.S. FINANCIAL STATEMENTS

As noted previously, your portfolio should encompass other economies and markets, numerous global industries, and many foreign firms in these global industries. You should recognize, however, that non-U.S. financial statements will be very different from those in this chapter and a typical accounting course. Accounting conventions differ substantially among countries. Although it is not possible to discuss alternative accounting conventions in detail, we will consider some of the major differences in format and principle.

ACCOUNTING STATEMENT FORMAT DIFFERENCES

Table 12.11 contains examples of balance sheet formats for several countries and indicates some major differences in accounts and the order of presentation. As an example, in the United Kingdom fixed assets are presented above current assets, and current liabilities are automatically subtracted from current assets. In Australia, capital accounts are presented initially, and the current assets are placed below long-term assets. The balance sheet items are similar to those in the United States, but almost exactly opposite in presentation. Clearly, the accounts and presentation in Canada are very similar to those in the United States. Germany's accounts also are similar except that they have numerous reserve accounts on the liability side. Besides finding similarities to the U.S. firms, you need to consider the techniques used to derive individual items.

The comparative income statement formats in Table 12.12 show that the U.K. statements have much less detail than U.S. statements. This limits your ability to analyze trends in expense items. Although Japanese statements are fairly similar to those of the United States, you should be aware of nonoperating income and expense items. These can be substantial because Japanese firms typically have heavy investments in the common stock of suppliers and customers as a sign of goodwill. The income and gains (or losses) from these equity holdings can be a substantial permanent component of a firm's net income.

The Australian statements, like the British, combine numerous expense items and include several items concerned with the distribution of the net income. Finally, income statements from Germany are very detailed and contain many unusual income and expense items. These details provide numerous opportunities to control the profit or loss for the period.

DIFFERENCES IN ACCOUNTING PRINCIPLES

Beyond the differences in the presentation format, there are numerous differences in the accounting principles used to arrive at the income, expense, and balance sheet items. Choi and Bavishi compared accounting standards for ten countries and highlighted the differ-

| TABLE 12.11 | COMPARATIVE BALANCE SHEET FORMATS |

United Kingdom

Net assets employed
    Fixed assets
    Subsidiaries
    Associated companies
    Current assets
    Less: current liabilities
    Less: deferred liabilities
Assets represented by:
    Share capital
    Reserves

Canada

Assets
    Current assets
    Investments
    Fixed assets
    Other assets
Liabilities and shareholders' equity
    Current liabilities
    Long-term debt
    Deferred income taxes
    Shareholders' equity

Australia

Share capital and reserves and liabilities
    Share capital and reserves
    Long-term debt and deferred income taxes
    Current liabilities
Assets
    Fixed assets
    Investments
    Current assets

Germany

Assets
    Outstanding payments on subscribed share capital
    Fixed assets and investments
    Revolving assets
    Deferred charges and prepaid expenses
    Accumulated net loss (of period)
Liabilities and shareholders' equity
    Share capital
    Open reserves
    Adjustments to assets
    Reserves for estimated liabilities and accrued expenses
    Liabilities, contractually payable beyond 4 years
    Deferred income
    Accumulated net profit (of period)

Source: *Professional Accounting in 30 Countries,* pp. 51, 125–126, 169, 629, 746–749. Copyright © 1975 by the American Institute of Certified Public Accountants, Inc. Reprinted by permission of the AICPA.

ences.[11] Table 12.13 synthesizes the differences in 32 specific items. Following a discussion of several major areas, the authors conclude:

> Perhaps the major conclusion drawn from analyzing the annual reports of the world's leading industrial firms is that fundamental differences in accounting practices between each of ten countries examined are not as extensive as was initially feared. Major differences observed relate to accounting for goodwill, deferred taxes, long-term leases, discretionary reserves, and foreign-currency translation. Having observed this comforting fact, the user must be cautioned against assuming that consistency and harmonization exist among the annual reports of all foreign companies.[12]

INTERNATIONAL RATIO ANALYSIS

The tendency is to analyze accounting statements using financial ratios similar to those discussed in this chapter. Although this is certainly legitimate, it is important to recognize that the representative ratio values and trends may differ among countries because of local accounting practices and business norms. Choi et al. compared a common set of ratios for a

[11] Frederick D. S. Choi and Vinod B. Bavishi, "Diversity in Multinational Accounting," *Financial Executive* 50, no. 7 (August 1982): 36–39. This table also is presented and discussed in Frederick D. S. Choi and Gerhard G. Mueller, *International Accounting* (Englewood Cliffs, NJ: Prentice-Hall, 1984), 72–76.

[12] Choi and Bavishi, "Diversity in Multinational Accounting," 39. Another comparison of accounting standards for the United States, the United Kingdom, the European Economic Community, and Canada is contained in Thomas G. Evans, Martin E. Taylor, and Oscar Holzmann, *International Accounting and Reporting* (New York: Macmillan, 1985), 106–113.

| TABLE 12.12 | **COMPARATIVE INCOME STATEMENT FORMATS** |

United Kingdom

Group turnover
Profit before taxation and extraordinary items
   Less: Taxation based on profit for the year
Profit after taxation and before extraordinary
   items
   Less: Extraordinary items
Profits attributable to shareholders of parent
   company

Japan

Sales
   Less: Cost of goods sold
Gross profit on sales
   Less: Selling and administrative expenses
Operating income
   Add: Nonoperating revenue
Gross profit for the period
   Less: Nonoperating expenses
Net income for the period

Australia

Sales and revenue
   Less: Cost of sales
Operating profit
   Add: Income from investments
   Less: Interest to other persons
Pretax profit
   Less: Provision for income tax
Net profit before extraordinary items
   Less: Extraordinary items
Net profit after extraordinary items
Unappropriated profits, previous year
Prior year adjustments
Transfer from general reserve
Available for appropriation
Dividends
Transfer to general reserve
Transfer to capital profits reserve
Unappropriated profits, end of year

Germany

Net sales
Increase or decrease of finished and unfinished
   products
Other manufacturing costs for fixed assets
Total output
Raw materials and supplies, purchased goods
   consumed in sale
Gross profit
Income from profit transfer agreements
Income from trade investments
Income from other long-term investments
Other interest and similar income
Income from retirement and appraisal of fixed
   assets
Income from the cancellation of lump
   allowances
Income from the cancellation of overstated
   reserves
Other income, including extraordinary in the
   sum of DM
Income from loss transfer agreements
Total income
Wages and salaries
Social taxes
Expenses for pension plans and relief
Depreciation and amortization of fixed assets
   and investments
Depreciation and amortization of finance
   investments
Losses by deduction or on retirement of current
   assets
Losses on retirement of fixed assets and
   investments
Interest and similar expenses
Taxes on income and net assets
Other expenses
Profits transferable to parent company under
   profit transfer agreement
Profit or loss for the period
Profit or loss brought forward from preceding
   year
Release of reserves
Amounts appropriated to reserves out of profit
   of period
Accumulated net profit or loss

Source: *Professional Accounting in 30 Countries,* pp. 52, 350, 351, 630, 750, 753. Copyright © 1975 by the American Institute of Certified Public Accountants, Inc. Reprinted by permission of the AICPA.

TABLE 12.13   SYNTHESIS OF ACCOUNTING DIFFERENCES

Accounting Principles	United States	Australia	Canada	France	Germany	Japan	The Netherlands	Sweden	Switzerland	United Kingdom
1. Marketable securities recorded at the lower of cost or market?	Yes	Yes	Yes	Yes	Yes	Yes	Yes	Yes	Yes	Yes
2. Provision for uncollectible accounts made?	Yes	Yes	Yes	No	Yes	Yes	Yes	Yes	Yes	Yes
3. Inventory costed using FIFO?	Mixed	Yes	Mixed	Mixed	Yes	Mixed	Mixed	Yes	Yes	Yes
4. Manufacturing overhead allocated to year-end inventory?	Yes	Yes	Yes	Yes	Yes	Yes	Yes	Yes	No	Yes
5. Inventory valued at the lower of cost or market?	Yes	Yes	Yes	Yes	Yes	Yes	Yes	Yes	Yes	Yes
6. Accounting for long-term investments: less than 20 percent ownership: cost method?	Yes	Yes	Yes	Yes*	Yes	Yes	No(K)	Yes	Yes	Yes
7. Accounting for long-term investments: 21–50 percent ownership: equity method?	Yes	No(G)	Yes	Yes*	No(B)	No(B)	Yes	No(B)	No(B)	Yes
8. Accounting for long-term investments: more than 50 percent ownership: full consolidation?	Yes	Yes	Yes	Yes*	Yes	Yes	Yes	Yes	Yes	Yes
9. Both domestic and foreign subsidiaries consolidated?	Yes	Yes	Yes	Yes	No**	Yes	Yes	Yes	Yes	Yes
10. Acquisitions accounted for under the pooling of interest method?	Yes	No(C)	No(C)	No(C)	No(C)	No(C)	No(C)	No(C)	No(C)	No(C)
11. Intangible assets: goodwill amortized?	Yes	Yes	Yes	Yes	No	Yes	Mixed	Yes	No**	No**
12. Intangible assets: other than goodwill amortized?	Yes	Yes	Yes	Yes	Yes	Yes	Yes	Yes	No**	No**
13. Long-term debt includes maturities longer than 1 year?	Yes	Yes	Yes	Yes	Yes	Yes	Yes	Yes	Yes	Yes
14. Discount/premium on long-term debt amortized?	Yes	Yes	Yes	No	No(D)	Yes	Yes	No	No	No
15. Deferred taxes recorded when accounting income is not equal to taxable income?	Yes	Yes	Yes	Yes	Yes	Yes	Yes	No	No	Yes
16. Financial leases (long-term) capitalized?	Yes	No	Yes	No	No	No	No	No	No	No
17. Company pens on fund contribution provided regularly?	Yes	Yes	Yes	Yes	Yes	Yes	Yes	Yes	Yes	Yes
18. Total pension fund assets and liabilities excluded from company's financial statement?	Yes	Yes	Yes	Yes	No	Yes	Yes	Yes	Yes	Yes
19. Research and development expensed?	Yes	Yes	Yes	Yes	Yes	Yes	Yes	Yes	Yes	Yes
20. Treasury stock deducted from owner's equity?	Yes	NF	Yes	Yes	No	Yes	Mixed	NF	NF	NF
21. Gains or losses on treasury stock taken to owner's equity?	Yes	NF	Yes	Yes	No	No**	Mixed	NF	NF	NF

(continued)

TABLE 12.13 (concluded)

Accounting Principles	United States	Australia	Canada	France	Germany	Japan	The Netherlands	Sweden	Switzerland	United Kingdom
22. No general purpose (purely discretionary) reserves allowed?	Yes	Yes	Yes	No	No	No	No	No	No	Yes
23. Dismissal indemnities accounted for on a pay-as-you-go basis?	Yes	Yes	Yes	Yes	Yes	Yes	NF	Yes	NF	Yes
24. Minority interest excluded from consolidated income?	Yes	Yes	Yes	Yes	No	Yes	Yes	Yes	Yes	Yes
25. Minority interest excluded from consolidated owner's equity?	Yes	Yes	Yes	Yes	No	Yes	Yes	Yes	Yes	Yes
26. Are intercompany sales/profits eliminated on consolidation?	Yes	Yes	Yes	Yes	Yes	Yes	Yes	Yes	Yes	Yes
27. Basic financial statements reflect a historical cost valuation (no price level adjustment)?	Yes	No	Yes	No	Yes	Yes	No**	No	No	No
28. Supplementary inflation-adjusted financial statements provided?	Yes	No**	No**	No	No	No	No**	No	No**	Yes
29. Straight-line depreciation adhered to?	Yes	Yes	Yes	Mixed	Mixed	Mixed	Yes	Yes	Yes	Yes
30. No expense depreciation permitted?	Yes	No	Yes	No	Yes	Yes	No	No	No	No
31. Temporal method of foreign currency translation employed?	Yes	Mixed	Yes	No(E)	No(E)	Mixed	No(E)	No(L)	No(E)	No(E)
32. Currency translation gains or losses reflected in current income?	Yes	Mixed	Yes	Mixed	Mixed	Mixed	No(J)	Mixed	No(H)	No

Key
Yes—Predominant practice.
Yes*—Minor modifications, but still predominant practice.
No**—Minority practice.
No—Accounting principle in question is not adhered to.
NF—Not found.
Mixed—Alternative practices followed with no majority.
B—Cost method is used.
C—Purchase method is used.
D—Long-term debt includes maturities longer than 4 years.

E—Current rate method of foreign currency translation.
F—Weighted average is used.
G—Cost or equity.
H—Translation gains and losses are deferred.
I—Market is used.
J—Owner's equity.
K—Equity.
L—Monetary/Nonmonetary.

Source: "Diversity in Multinational Accounting" by Frederick D. S. Choi and Vinod B. Bavishi. Reprinted with permission from *Financial Executive*, August 1982, copyright © 1982 by Financial Executives Institute, 10 Madison Avenue, P.O. Box 1938, Morristown, NJ 07962-1938.

TABLE 12.14

MEAN DIFFERENCES IN AGGREGATE FINANCIAL RATIOS: UNITED STATES, JAPAN, KOREA (UNADJUSTED)

Enterprise Category	Current Ratio	Quick Ratio	Debt Ratio	Times Interest Earned	Inventory Turnover
All Manufacturing					
Japan (976)	1.15	0.80	0.84	1.60	5.00
Korea (354)	1.13	0.46	0.78	1.80	6.60
United States (902)	1.94	1.10	0.47	6.50	6.80
Difference (U.S.–Japan)	40%	26%	(77%)	75%	26%
Difference (U.S.–Korea)	42%	58%	(66%)	73%	2%
Chemicals					
Japan (129)	1.30	0.99	0.79	1.80	7.10
Korea (54)	1.40	0.70	0.59	2.40	7.10
United States (n.a.)	2.20	1.30	0.45	6.50	6.50
Difference (U.S.–Japan)	42%	22%	(74%)	72%	(8%)
Difference (U.S.–Korea)	36%	45%	(31%)	62%	(9%)
Textiles					
Japan (81)	1.00	0.77	0.81	1.10	6.20
Korea (34)	1.00	0.37	0.83	1.30	4.90
United States (n.a.)	2.30	1.20	0.48	4.30	6.50
Difference (U.S.–Japan)	55%	38%	(70%)	74%	5%
Difference (U.S.–Korea)	55%	70%	(74%)	70%	24%
Transportation					
Japan (85)	1.20	0.86	0.83	1.90	3.90
Korea (14)	0.95	0.40	0.91	1.90	18.60
United States (n.a.)	1.60	0.74	0.52	8.70	5.60
Difference (U.S.–Japan)	21%	(16%)	(61%)	78%	28%
Difference (U.S.–Korea)	40%	46%	(75%)	77%	(234%)

sample of companies in the United States, Japan, and Korea.[13] Table 12.14 compares the mean values for these ratios and the differences among them. These ratios differ substantially for all manufacturing as well as for specific important industries (chemical, textiles, and transportation). Following an extensive discussion of the ratios, the authors conclude:

> On the basis of these findings, institutional, cultural, political and tax considerations in Japan and Korea do indeed cause their accounting ratios to differ from U.S. norms without necessarily reflecting better or worse financial risk and return characteristics being measured. . . .
>
> A major conclusion of our study is that accounting measurements reflected in corporate financial reports represent, in one sense, merely "numbers" that have limited meaning and significance in and of themselves. Meaning and significance come from and depend upon an understanding of the environmental context from which the numbers are drawn as well as the relationship between the numbers and the underlying economic phenomena that are the real items of interest.[14]

[13]Frederick D. S. Choi, Hisaaki Hino, Sang Kee Min, Sang Oh Nam, Junichi Ujiie, and Arthur J. Stonehill, "Analyzing Foreign Financial Statements: The Use and Misuse of International Ratio Analysis," *Journal of International Business Studies* (Spring–Summer 1983): 113–131, reprinted in Frederick D. S. Choi and Gerhard G. Mueller, *Frontiers of International Accounting: An Anthology* (Ann Arbor, MI: UMI Research Press, 1985).

[14]Choi et al., "Analyzing Foreign Financial Statements," 131.

TABLE 12.14	(concluded)					
Enterprise Category	Average Collection Period	Fixed Asset Turnover	Total Asset Turnover	Profit Margin	Return on Total Assets	Return on Net Worth
All Manufacturing						
Japan (976)	86	3.10	0.93	.013	.012	.071
Korea (354)	33	2.80	1.20	.023	.028	.131
United States (902)	43	3.90	1.40	.054	.074	.139
Difference (U.S.–Japan)	(102%)	22%	32%	26%	84%	49%
Difference (U.S.–Korea)	24%	29%	9%	57%	62%	6%
Chemicals						
Japan (129)	88	2.80	0.90	.015	.014	.065
Korea (54)	33	1.60	0.90	.044	.040	.100
United States (n.a.)	50	2.80	1.10	.073	.081	.148
Difference (U.S.–Japan)	(75%)	0%	19%	79%	83%	52%
Difference (U.S.–Korea)	34%	44%	19%	39%	50%	32%
Textiles						
Japan (81)	66	3.50	0.92	.003	.003	.017
Korea (34)	30	2.20	1.00	.010	.011	.064
United States (n.a.)	48	5.80	1.80	.027	.049	.094
Difference (U.S.–Japan)	(39%)	40%	50%	87%	93%	82%
Difference (U.S.–Korea)	36%	63%	44%	62%	78%	32%
Transportation						
Japan (85)	116	4.50	0.90	.017	.015	.092
Korea (14)	18	1.10	0.80	.026	.021	.221
United Sates (n.a.)	31	6.50	1.60	.049	.078	.161
Difference (U.S.–Japan)	278%	30%	44%	65%	80%	43%
Difference (U.S.–Korea)	40%	84%	50%	47%	73%	(37%)

Note: Parentheses indicate foreign ratios greater than U.S. ratios.

Source: Frederick D. S. Choi, Hisaaki Hino, Sang Kee Min, Sang Oh Nam, Junichi Ujiie, and Arthur J. Stonehill, "Analyzing Foreign Financial Statements: The Use and Misuse of International Ratio Analysis," *Journal of International Business Studies* (Spring–Summer 1983): 113–131.

THE QUALITY OF FINANCIAL STATEMENTS

Analysts sometimes speak of the quality of a firm's earnings, or the quality of a firm's balance sheet. In general, quality financial statements are a good reflection of reality; accounting tricks and one-time changes are not used to make the firm appear stronger than it really is. Some factors that lead to lower-quality financial statements were mentioned previously when we discussed ratio analysis. Other quality influences are discussed below.

BALANCE SHEET

A high-quality balance sheet typically has a conservative use of debt or leverage. Therefore, the potential of financial distress resulting from the need to service debt is quite low. Little use of debt also implies the firm has unused borrowing capacity; should an attractive investment opportunity arise, the firm can draw on that unused capacity to invest wisely for the shareholders' benefit.

A quality balance sheet contains assets with a market value greater than their book value. The capability of management and the existence of intangible assets such as goodwill, trademarks, or patents will make the market value of the firm's assets exceed their book values. In general, as a result of inflation and historical cost accounting, we might expect the market value of assets to exceed their book values. Some situations in which the opposite may occur include the use of outdated, technologically inferior assets; unwanted or out-of-fashion inventory; and the presence of nonperforming assets on the firm's books (an example would be a bank that has not written off nonperforming loans).

The presence of off-balance-sheet liabilities also harms the quality of a balance sheet. Such liabilities may include joint ventures and loan commitments or guarantees to subsidiaries.

INCOME STATEMENT

High-quality earnings are *repeatable* earnings. For example, they arise from sales among customers who are expected to do repeat business with the firm and from costs that are not artificially low as a result of unusual and short-lived input price reductions. One-time and nonrecurring items, such as accounting changes, mergers, and asset sales, should be ignored when examining earnings. Unexpected exchange rate fluctuations that work in the firm's favor to raise revenues or reduce costs should also be viewed as nonrecurring.

High-quality earnings result from the use of conservative accounting principles that do not result in overstated revenues and understated costs. The closer the earnings are to cash, the higher the quality of the income statement. Suppose a firm sells furniture "on time" by allowing customers to make monthly payments. A higher-quality income statement will recognize revenue using the "installment" principle; that is, as the cash is collected each month, in turn, annual sales will reflect only the cash collected from sales during the year. A lower-quality income statement will recognize 100 percent of the revenue from a sale at the time of sale, even though payments may stretch well into next year.

THE VALUE OF FINANCIAL STATEMENT ANALYSIS

Financial statements, by their nature, are backward-looking. They report the firm's assets, liabilities, and equity as of a certain (past) date; they report a firm's revenues, expenses, or cash flows over some (past) time period. An efficient capital market will have already incorporated this past information into security prices; so it may seem, at first glance, that analysis of a firm's financial statements and ratios is a waste of the analyst's time.

The fact is, the opposite is true. Analysis of financial statements allows the analyst to gain knowledge of a firm's operating and financial structure. This, in turn, assists the analyst in determining the effects of *future* events on the firm's cash flows. Likely future scenarios can be analyzed and a knowledge of the firm's operating and financial leverage can help the analyst gauge the risk and expected cash flows of the firm. Combining knowledge of the firm's strategy, operating, and financial leverage and possible macro- and microeconomic scenarios is necessary to determine an appropriate market price for the firm's stock. Combining what is known about the firm, based on the analysis of historical data, with potential future scenarios allows analysts to evaluate the risks facing the firm and then to develop an expected return forecast based on these risks. The final outcome of the process, as future chapters will detail, is the market's determination of the firm's current security price.

USES OF FINANCIAL RATIOS

We have discussed the role of financial ratios in credit analysis and security valuation. There are four major areas in investments where financial ratios have been used: (1) stock valuation, (2) the identification of internal corporate variables that affect a stock's system atic risk (beta), (3) assigning credit quality ratings on bonds, and (4) predicting insolvency (bankruptcy) of firms. In this section, we discuss how ratios have been used in each of these four areas and the specific ratios found to be most useful.

STOCK VALUATION MODELS

Most valuation models attempt to derive an appropriate price/earnings ratio for a stock. As we will discuss in Chapter 13, the earnings multiple is influenced by the expected growth rate of earnings and dividends and the required rate of return on the stock. Clearly, financial ratios can help in making both estimates. The estimate of the growth rate employs the ratios discussed in the potential growth rate section—the retention rate and the return on equity.

When estimating the required rate of return on an investment (k), you will recall from Chapter 1 that it depends on the risk premium for the security, which is a function of business risk, financial risk, and liquidity risk. Business risk typically is measured in terms of earnings variability, financial risk is identified by either the debt proportion ratios or the flow ratios (i.e., the interest coverage ratios or the cash flow ratios), and insights regarding a stock's liquidity risk can be derived from the external liquidity measures discussed.

The typical empirical valuation model has examined a cross section of companies and used a multiple regression model that relates the price/earnings ratios for the sample firms to some of the following corporate variables (the averages generally consider the last 5 or 10 years):[15]

Financial Ratios

1. Average debt/equity
2. Average interest coverage
3. Average dividend payout
4. Average return on equity
5. Average market price to book value

Variability Measures

1. Coefficient of variation of operating earnings
2. Systematic risk (beta)

Nonratio Variables

1. Average growth rate of earnings

FINANCIAL RATIOS AND SYSTEMATIC RISK

As discussed in Chapter 9, the capital asset pricing model (CAPM) asserts that the relevant risk variable for an asset should be its systematic risk, which is its beta coefficient related to the market portfolio of all risky assets. In efficient markets, a relationship should exist between internal corporate risk variables and market-determined risk variables such as beta. Numerous studies have tested this relationship by examining internal corporate variables intended to reflect business risk and financial risk.[16] Some of the significant variables (usually 5-year averages) included were

---

[15] A list of studies in this area appears in the reference section at the end of the chapter.

[16] A list of studies in this area appears in the reference section at the end of the chapter.

Financial Ratios

1. Dividend payout
2. Total debt/total assets
3. Cash flow/total debt
4. Interest coverage
5. Working capital/total assets
6. Current ratio

Variability Measures

1. Variance of operating earnings
2. Coefficient of variation of operating earnings
3. Coefficient of variation of operating profit margins
4. Operating earnings beta (company earnings related to aggregate earnings)

Nonratio Variables

1. Asset size
2. Market value of trading in stock

FINANCIAL RATIOS AND BOND RATINGS

As discussed in Chapter 15, there are four financial services that assign quality ratings to bonds on the basis of the issuing company's ability to meet all its obligations related to the bond. An AAA or Aaa rating indicates very high quality and almost no chance of default, whereas a C rating indicates the bond is already in default. A number of studies have used financial ratios to predict the rating to be assigned to a bond.[17] The major financial ratios considered (again, typically 5-year averages) were as follows:

Financial Ratios

1. Long-term debt/total assets
2. Total debt/total capital
3. Net income plus depreciation (cash flow)/long-term senior debt
4. Cash flow/total debt
5. Net income plus interest/interest expense (fixed charge coverage)
6. Market value of stock/par value of bonds
7. Net operating profit/sales
8. Net income/total assets
9. Working capital/sales
10. Sales/net worth (equity turnover)

Variability Measures

1. Coefficient of variation (CV) of net earnings
2. Coefficient of variation of return on assets

Nonratio Variables

1. Subordination of the issue
2. Size of the firm (total assets)
3. Issue size
4. Par value of all publicly traded bonds of the firm

---

[17] A list of studies in this area appears in the reference section at the end of the chapter.

FINANCIAL RATIOS AND INSOLVENCY (BANKRUPTCY)

Analysts have always been interested in using financial ratios to identify which firms might default on a loan or declare bankruptcy. Several studies have attempted to identify a set of ratios for this purpose.[18] The typical study examines a sample of firms that have declared bankruptcy against a matched sample of firms in the same industry and of comparable size that have not failed. The analysis involves examining a number of financial ratios expected to reflect declining liquidity for several years (usually 5 years) prior to the declaration of bankruptcy. The goal is to determine which ratios or set of ratios provide the best predictions of bankruptcy. Some of the models have been able to properly classify over 80 percent of the firms 1 year prior to failure, and some achieve high classification results 3 to 5 years before failure. The financial ratios typically included in successful models were:[19]

Financial Ratios

1. Cash flow/total debt
2. Cash flow/long-term debt
3. Sales/total assets*
4. Net income/total assets
5. EBIT/total assets*
6. Total debt/total assets
7. Market value of stock/book value of debt*
8. Working capital/total assets*
9. Retained earnings/total assets*
10. Current ratio
11. Cash/current liabilities
12. Working capital/sales

LIMITATIONS OF FINANCIAL RATIOS

We must reinforce the earlier point that you should always consider *relative* financial ratios. In addition, you should be aware of other limitations of financial ratios:

1. Are alternative firms' accounting treatment comparable? As you know from prior accounting courses, there are several generally accepted methods for treating various accounting items, and the alternatives can cause a difference in results for the same event. Therefore, you should check on the accounting treatment of significant items and adjust the values for major differences. This becomes a critical consideration when dealing with non-U.S. firms.
2. How homogeneous is the firm? Many companies have several divisions that operate in different industries. This may make it difficult to derive comparable industry ratios.
3. Are the implied results consistent? It is important to develop a total profile of the firm and not depend on only one set of ratios (e.g., internal liquidity ratios). As an example, a firm may be having short-term liquidity problems but be very profitable, and the profitability will eventually alleviate the short-run liquidity problems.

---

[18] A list of studies on this topic appears in the reference section at the end of the chapter. The five ratios designated by an asterisk (*) are the ratios used in the well-known Altman Z-score model as follows. Edward I. Altman, "Financial Ratios, Discriminant Analysis and the Prediction of Corporate Bankruptcy," *Journal of Finance* 23, no. 4 (September 1968): 589–609.

[19] In addition to the several studies that have used financial ratios to predict bond ratings and failures, a number of studies have also used cash flow variables or a combination of financial ratios and cash flow variables for these predictions, and the results have been quite successful. These studies are listed in the reference section at the end of the chapter.

4. Is the ratio within a reasonable range for the industry? As noted on several occasions, you typically want a *range* of values for the ratio because a value that is either too high or too low for the industry can be a cause for concern.

Summary

- The overall purpose of financial statement analysis is to help you make decisions on investing in a firm's bonds or stocks. Financial ratios should be examined relative to the economy, the firm's industry, the firm's main competitors, and the firm's past relative ratios.
- The specific ratios can be divided into five categories, depending on the purpose of the analysis: internal liquidity, operating performance, risk analysis, growth analysis, and external market liquidity. When analyzing the financial statements for non-U.S. firms, you must consider differences in format and in accounting principles. These differences will cause different values for specific ratios in alternative countries. Four major uses of financial ratios are (1) stock valuation, (2) the identification of internal corporate variables affecting a stock's systematic risk (beta), (3) assigning credit quality ratings on bonds, and (4) predicting insolvency (bankruptcy).
- A final caveat: you can envision a very large number of potential financial ratios through which to examine almost every possible relationship. The trick is not to come up with more ratios, but to attempt to limit the number of ratios so you can examine them in a meaningful way. This entails an analysis of the ratios over time relative to the economy, the industry, or the past. Any additional effort should be spent on deriving better comparisons for a limited number of ratios that provide insights into the questions of interest to you (e.g., the firm's future operating performance or its financial risk).

Questions

1. Discuss briefly two decisions that require the analysis of financial statements.
2. Why do analysts use financial ratios rather than the absolute numbers? Give an example.
3. The Murphy Company, which produces polish sausage, earned 12 percent on its equity last year. What does this indicate about the firm's management? What other information do you want and why do you want it?
4. Besides comparing a company's performance to its total industry, discuss what other comparisons should be considered *within* the industry.
5. How might a jewelry store and a grocery store differ in terms of asset turnover and profit margin? Would you expect their return on total assets to differ assuming equal business risk? Discuss.
6. Describe the components of business risk, and discuss how the components affect the variability of operating earnings.
7. Would you expect a steel company or a retail food chain to have greater business risk? Discuss this expectation in terms of the components of business risk.
8. When examining a firm's financial structure, would you be concerned with the firm's business risk? Why or why not?
9. How does the fixed charge coverage ratio differ from the total debt/total asset ratio? If they gave conflicting signals regarding financial risk, which would you prefer and why?
10. Give an example of how a cash flow ratio might differ from a proportion of debt ratio. Assuming these ratios differ for a firm (e.g., the cash flow ratios indicate high financial risk, while the proportion of debt ratio indicates low risk), which ratios would you follow? Justify your choice.
11. Why is the analysis of growth potential important to the common stockholder? Why is it important to the debt-investor?
12. Discuss the general factors that determine the rate of growth of *any* economic unit.
13. A firm is earning 24 percent on equity and has low risk. Discuss why you would expect it to have a high or low retention rate.
14. The Orange Company earned 18 percent on equity, whereas the Blue Company earned only 14 percent on equity. Does this mean that Orange will grow faster than Blue? Explain.
15. In terms of the factors that determine market liquidity, why do investors consider real estate to be a relatively illiquid asset?
16. Discuss some internal company factors that would indicate a firm's market liquidity.
17. Select one of the limitations of ratio analysis and indicate why you believe it is the major limitation.

Problems

1. The Shamrock Vegetable Company has the following results:

Net sales	$6,000,000
Net total assets	4,000,000
Depreciation	160,000
Net income	400,000
Long-term debt	2,000,000
Equity	1,160,000
Dividends	160,000

   a. Compute Shamrock's ROE directly. Confirm this using the three components.

   b. Using the ROE computed in Part a, what is the expected sustainable growth rate for Shamrock?

   c. Assuming the firm's net profit margin went to .04, what would happen to Shamrock's ROE?

   d. Using the ROE in Part c, what is the expected sustainable growth rate? What if dividends were only $40,000?

2. Three companies have the following results during the recent period.

	A	B	C
Net profit margin	.04	.06	.10
Total assets turnover	2.20	2.00	1.40
Total assets/equity	2.40	2.20	1.50

   a. Derive for each its return on equity based on the three components.

   b. Given the following earnings and dividends, compute the sustainable growth rate for each firm.

Earnings/share	2.75	3.00	4.50
Dividends/share	1.25	1.00	1.00

3. Given the following balance sheet, fill in the ratio values for 1997 and discuss how these results compare with both the industry average and Eddies' past performance.

EDDIES ENTERPRISES
CONSOLIDATED BALANCE SHEET
YEARS ENDED DECEMBER 31, 1996 AND 1997

ASSETS (DOLLARS IN THOUSANDS)

	1997	1996
Cash	$ 100	$ 90
Receivables	220	170
Inventories	330	230
Total current assets	650	490
Property, plant, and equipment	1,850	1,650
Depreciation	350	225
Net properties	1,500	1,425
Intangibles	150	150
Total assets	2,300	2,065

LIABILITIES AND SHAREHOLDERS' EQUITY

	1997	1996
Accounts payable	$ 85	$ 105
Short-term bank note	125	110
Current portion of long-term debt	75	—
Accruals	65	85
Total current liabilities	350	300
Long-term debt	625	540
Deferred taxes	100	80
Preferred stock (10%, $100 par)	150	150
Common stock ($2 par, 100,000 issued)	200	200
Additional paid-in capital	325	325
Retained earnings	550	470
Common shareholders' equity	1,075	995
Total liabilities and shareholders' equity	2,300	2,065

EDDIES ENTERPRISES
CONSOLIDATED STATEMENT OF INCOME
YEARS ENDED DECEMBER 31, 1996 AND 1997
(DOLLARS IN THOUSANDS)

	1997	1996
Net sales	$3,500.7	$2,990.6
Cost of goods sold	2,135.2	1,823.0
Selling, general, and administrative expenses	1,107.3	974.6
Operating profit	258.2	193.0
Net interest expense	62.5	54.0
Income from operations	195.7	139.0
Income taxes	66.5	47.3
Net income	129.2	91.7
Preferred dividends	15.0	15.0
Net income available for common shares	114.2	76.7
Dividends declared	40.0	30.0

	Eddies (1997)	Eddies' Average	Industry Average
Current ratio	_____	2.000	2.200
Quick ratio	_____	1.000	1.100
Receivables turnover	_____	18.000	18.000
Average collection period	_____	20.000	21.000
Total asset turnover	_____	1.500	1.400
Inventory turnover	_____	11.000	12.500
Fixed asset turnover	_____	2.500	2.400
Equity turnover	_____	3.200	3.000
Gross profit margin	_____	.400	.350
Operating profit margin	_____	8.000	7.500
Return on capital	_____	.107	.120
Return on equity	_____	.118	.126
Return on common equity	_____	.128	.135
Debt/equity ratio	_____	.600	.500
Debt/total capital ratio	_____	.400	.370
Interest coverage	_____	4.000	4.500
Fixed charge coverage	_____	3.000	4.000
Cash flow/long-term debt	_____	.400	.450
Cash flow/total debt	_____	.250	.300
Retention rate	_____	.350	.400

4. *CFA Examination I (1990)*

(Question 4 is composed of two parts, for a total of 20 minutes.)

The duPont formula defines the net return on shareholders' equity as a function of the following components:

- operating margin
- asset turnover
- interest burden
- financial leverage
- income tax rate

Using *only* the data in the table shown below:

a. Calculate *each* of the *five* components listed above for 1985 *and* 1989, and calculate the return on equity (ROE) for 1985 *and* 1989, using all of the *five* components. Show calculations. [15 minutes]

b. Briefly discuss the impact of the changes in asset turnover *and* financial leverage on the change in ROE from 1985 to 1989. [5 minutes]

	1985	1989
Income Statement Data		
Revenues	$542	$979
Operating income	38	76
Depreciation and amortization	3	9
Interest expense	3	0
Pretax income	32	67
Income taxes	13	37
Net income after tax	19	30
Balance Sheet Data		
Fixed assets	$ 41	$ 70
Total assets	245	291
Working capital	123	157
Total debt	16	0
Total shareholders' equity	159	220

References

GENERAL

Beaver, William H. *Financial Reporting: An Accounting Revolution.* Englewood Cliffs, NJ: Prentice-Hall, 1989.

Bernstein, Leopold A. *Financial Statement Analysis: Theory, Application, and Interpretation.* 4th ed. Homewood, IL: Richard D. Irwin, 1989.

Chen, Kung H. and Thomas A. Shimerda. "An Empirical Analysis of Useful Financial Ratios." *Financial Management* 10, no. 1 (Spring 1981).

Foster, George. *Financial Statement Analysis.* 2d ed. Englewood Cliffs, NJ: Prentice-Hall, 1978.

Frecka, Thomas J. and Cheng F. Lee. "Generalized Financial Ratio Adjustment Processes and Their Implications." *Journal of Accounting Research* 27, no. 1 (Spring 1983).

Gombola, Michael J. and Edward Ketz. "Financial Ratio Patterns in Retail and Manufacturing Organizations." *Financial Management* 12, no. 2 (Summer 1983).

Heckel, Kenneth S. and Joshua Livnat. *Cash Flow and Security Analysis.* 2d ed. Burr Ridge, IL: Business One Irwin, 1996.

Helfert, Erich A. *Techniques of Financial Analysis.* 6th ed. Homewood, IL: Richard D. Irwin, 1987.

Johnson, W. Bruce. "The Cross-Sectional Stability of Financial Ratio Patterns." *Journal of Financial and Quantitative Analysis* 14, no. 5 (December 1979).

Lev, Baruch and S. Ramu Thiagarajan. "Fundamental Information Analysis." *Journal of Accounting Research* 37, no. 2 (Autumn 1993).

Page, John R. and Paul Hooper. "Financial Statements for Security Analysts." *Financial Analysts Journal* 35, no. 5 (September–October 1979).

White, Gerald I., Ashwinpaul Sondhi, and Dov Fried. *The Analysis and Use of Financial Statements.* New York: John Wiley & Sons, Inc., 1994.

ANALYSIS OF INTERNATIONAL FINANCIAL STATEMENTS

Arpan, Jeffrey S. and Lee H. Rodebaugh. *International Accounting and Multinational Enterprises.* New York: John Wiley & Co., 1981.

Choi, Frederick D. S., ed. *Multinational Accounting: A Research Framework for the Eighties.* Ann Arbor, MI: UMI Research Press, 1981.

Choi, Frederick D. S. and Vinod B. Bavishi. "Diversity in Multinational Accounting." *Financial Executive* 50, no. 7 (August 1982).

Choi, Frederick D. S., H. Hino, S. K. Min, S. O. Nam, J. Ujiie, and A. I. Stonehill. "Analyzing Foreign Financial Statements: The Use and Misuse of International Ratio Analysis." *Journal of International Business Studies* (Spring–Summer 1983).

Choi, Frederick D. S. and Gerhard G. Mueller. *International Accounting.* Englewood Cliffs, NJ: Prentice-Hall, 1984.

Choi, Frederick D. S. and Gerhard G. Mueller. *Frontiers of International Accounting: An Anthology.* Ann Arbor, MI: UMI Research Press, 1985.

Davidson, Sidney and John M. Kohlmeier. "A Measure of the Impact of Some Foreign Accounting Principles." *International Journal of Accounting* (Fall 1967).

Drury, D. H. "Effects of Accounting Practice Divergence: Canada and the U.S.A." *Journal of International Business Studies* 10 (Fall 1979).

Evans, Thomas G., Martin E. Taylor, and Oscar Holzmann. *International Accounting and Reporting.* New York: Macmillan, 1985.

Fitzgerald, R., A. Stickler, and T. Watts. *International Survey of Accounting Principles and Practices.* Scarborough, Ontario: Price Waterhouse International, 1979.

Gray, S. J., J. C. Shaw, and L. B. McSweeney. "Accounting Standards and Multinational Corporations." *Journal of International Business Studies* 12, no. 1 (Spring–Summer 1981).

Hatfield, H. R. "Some Variations in Accounting Practice in England, France, Germany and the United States." *Journal of Accounting Research* 4, no. 2 (Autumn 1966).

Nair, R. D. and Werner G. Frank. "The Impact of Disclosure and Measurement Practices in International Accounting Classifications." *Accounting Review* 55, no. 3 (July 1980).

FINANCIAL RATIOS AND STOCK VALUATION MODELS

Babcock, Guilford. "The Concept of Sustainable Growth." *Financial Analysts Journal* 26, no. 3 (May–June 1970).

Beaver, William and Dale Morse. "What Determines Price–Earnings Ratios?" *Financial Analysts Journal* 34, no. 4 (July–August 1978).

Estep, Tony. "Security Analysis and Stock Selection: Turning Financial Information into Return Forecasts." *Financial Analysts Journal* 43, no. 4 (July–August 1987).

Fairfield, Patricia M. "P/E, P/B and the Present Value of Future Dividends." *Financial Analysts Journal* 50, no. 4 (July–August 1994).

Farrell, James L. "The Dividend Discount Model: A Primer." *Financial Analysts Journal* 41, no. 6 (November–December 1985).

Malkiel, Burton G. and John G. Cragg. "Expectations and the Structure of Share Prices." *American Economic Review* 60, no. 4 (September 1970).

Wilcox, Jarrod W. "The P/B-ROE Valuation Model." *Financial Analysts Journal* 40, no. 1 (January–February 1984).

FINANCIAL RATIOS AND SYSTEMATIC RISK (BETA)

Beaver, William H., Paul Kettler, and Myron Scholes. "The Association Between Market-Determined and Accounting-Determined Risk Measures." *Accounting Review* 45, no. 4 (October 1970).

Gahlon, James M. and James A. Gentry. "On the Relationship Between Systematic Risk and the Degrees of Operating and Financial Leverage." *Financial Management* 11, no. 2 (Summer 1982).

Mandelker, Gershon M. and S. Ghon Rhee. "The Impact of the Degrees of Operating and Financial Leverage on the Systematic Risk of Common Stock." *Journal of Financial and Quantitative Analysis* 19, no. 1 (March 1984).

Rosenberg, Barr. "Prediction of Common Stock Investment Risk." *Journal of Portfolio Management* 11, no. 1 (Fall 1984).

Rosenberg, Barr. "Prediction of Common Stock Betas." *Journal of Portfolio Management* 11, no. 2 (Winter 1985).

Thompson, Donald J., II. "Sources of Systematic Risk in Common Stocks." *Journal of Business* 49, no. 2 (April 1976).

FINANCIAL RATIOS AND BOND RATINGS

Ang, James S. and A. Kiritkumar. "Bond Rating Methods: Comparison and Validation." *Journal of Finance* 30, no. 2 (May 1975).

Fisher, Lawrence. "Determinants of Risk Premiums on Corporate Bonds." *Journal of Political Economy* 67, no. 3 (June 1959).

Gentry, James A., David T. Whitford, and Paul Newbold. "Predicting Industrial Bond Ratings with a Probit Model and Funds Flow Components." *The Financial Review* 23, no. 3 (August 1988).

Kaplan, Robert S. and Gabriel Urwitz. "Statistical Models of Bond Ratings: A Methodological Inquiry." *Journal of Business* 52, no. 2 (April 1979).

Pinches, George E. and Kent A. Mingo. "The Role of Subordination and Industrial Bond Ratings." *Journal of Finance* 30, no. 1 (March 1975).

Standard and Poor's Corporation. "Corporation Bond Ratings: An Overview." 1978.

FINANCIAL RATIOS AND CORPORATE BANKRUPTCY

Altman, Edward I. "Financial Ratios, Discriminant Analysis, and the Prediction of Corporate Bankruptcy." *Journal of Finance* 23, no. 4 (September 1968).

Altman, Edward I. *Corporate Financial Distress and Bankruptcy.* 2d ed. New York: John Wiley & Sons, 1993.

Altman, Edward I., Robert G. Haldeman, and P. Narayanan. "Zeta Analysis: A New Model to Identify Bankruptcy Risk of Corporations." *Journal of Banking and Finance* 1, no. 2 (June 1977).

Aziz, A. and G. H. Lawson. "Cash Flow Reporting and Financial Distress Models: Testing of Hypothesis." *Financial Management* 18, no. 1 (Spring 1989).

Beaver, William H. "Financial Ratios as Predictors of Failure." *Empirical Research in Accounting: Selected Studies,* 1966, supplement to vol. 4 *Journal of Accounting Research.*

Beaver, William H. "Market Prices, Financial Ratios, and the Prediction of Failure." *Journal of Accounting Research* 6, no. 2 (Autumn 1968).

Beaver, William H. "Alternative Accounting Measures as Predictors of Failure." *The Accounting Review* 43, no. 1 (January 1968).

Casey, Cornelius and Norman Bartczak. "Using Operating Cash Flow Data to Predict Financial Distress: Some Extensions." *Journal of Accounting Research* 23, no. 1 (Spring 1985).

Collins, R. B. "An Empirical Comparison of Bankruptcy Prediction Models." *Financial Management* 9, no. 2 (Summer 1980).

Dumbolena, I. G. and J. M. Shulman. "A Primary Rule for Detecting Bankruptcy: Watch the Cash." *Financial Analysts Journal* 44, no. 5 (September–October 1988).

Gentry, James A., Paul Newbold, and David T. Whitford. "Classifying Bankrupt Firms with Funds Flow Components." *Journal of Accounting Research* 23, no. 1 (Spring 1985).

Gentry, James A., Paul Newbold, and David T. Whitford. "Predicting Bankruptcy: If Cash Flow's Not the Bottom Line, What Is?" *Financial Analysts Journal* 41, no. 5 (September–October 1985).

Gombola, M. F., M. E. Haskins, J. E. Katz, and D. D. Williams. "Cash Flow in Bankruptcy Prediction." *Financial Management* 16, no. 4 (Winter 1987).

Largay, J. A. and C. P. Stickney. "Cash Flows Ratio Analysis and the W. T. Grant Company Bankruptcy." *Financial Analysts Journal* 36, no. 4 (July–August 1980).

Menash, Yaw M. "The Differential Bankruptcy Predictive Ability of Specific Price Level Adjustments: Some Empirical Evidence." *The Accounting Review* 58, no. 2 (April 1983).

Ohlson, J. A. "Financial Ratios and the Probabalistic Prediction of Bankruptcy." *Journal of Accounting Research* 18, no. 2 (Spring 1980).

Reilly, Frank K. "Using Cash Flows and Financial Ratios to Predict Bankruptcies." In *Analyzing Investment Opportunities in Distressed and Bankrupt Companies.* Charlottesville, VA: The Institute of Chartered Financial Analysts, 1991.

Scott, J. "The Probability of Bankruptcy: A Comparison of Empirical Predictions and Theoretical Models." *Journal of Banking and Finance* 5 (1981).

Wilcox, Jarrod W. "A Prediction of Business Failure Using Accounting Data." *Empirical Research in Accounting: Selected Studies,* 1973, supplement to vol. 11 *Journal of Accounting Research.*

Chapter
13

An Introduction to Security Valuation

This chapter answers the following questions:

- What are the two major approaches to the investment process?
- What are the specifics of the top-down (three-step) approach, what is the logic behind it, and what is the empirical evidence related to its viability?
- When valuing an asset, what are the required inputs?
- Once you have derived a value for an asset, what is the investment decision process?
- How do you determine the value of bonds?
- How do you determine the value of preferred stock?
- What are the alternative techniques available to derive a value for common stock?
- What is the dividend discount model (DDM) and what is its logic?
- How do you apply the DDM assuming a one-period investment horizon and a multiple-year holding period?
- What is the effect of the assumptions of the DDM when valuing a growth company?
- How do you apply the DDM to the valuation of a firm that is expected to experience temporary supernormal growth?
- How can you use the DDM to develop an earnings multiplier model?
- What does the DDM model imply are the factors that determine a stock's P/E ratio?
- How do you estimate the major inputs to the stock valuation models: (1) the required rate of return and (2) the expected growth rate of earnings and dividends?
- What additional factors must be considered when estimating the required rate of return and growth rate for a foreign security?

At the start of this book, we defined an investment as a commitment of funds for a period of time to derive a rate of return that would compensate the investor for the time during which the funds are invested, for the expected rate of inflation during the investment horizon, and for the uncertainty involved. From this definition, we know that the first step in making an investment is determining your required rate of return.

Once you have determined this rate, some investment alternatives such as savings accounts and T-bills are fairly easy to evaluate because they provide stated cash flows. Most investments have expected cash flows and a stated market price (e.g., common stock), and you must evaluate the investment to determine if its market price is consistent with your required return. To do this, you must estimate the value of the security based on its expected cash flows and your required rate of return. This is the process of estimating the value of an asset. After you have completed estimating a security's value, you compare this estimated value to the prevailing market price to decide whether you want to buy the security.

This **investment decision process** is similar to what you do when shopping for a suit or dress, a stereo, or a car. In each case, you examine the item and decide how much you think it is worth to you (i.e., its value). If the price is equal to its estimated value or less, you would buy it. The same technique applies to securities, except that the determination of value is more formal.

We start our investigation of security valuation by discussing the **valuation process.** There are two general approaches to the valuation process: (1) the top-down, three-step approach or (2) the bottom-up, stock valuation, stockpicking approach. Both of these approaches can be implemented by either fundamentalists or technicians. The difference between the two approaches is the perceived importance of the economic and industry influence on individual firms and stocks.

Advocates of the top-down, three-step approach believe that both the economy/market and the industry effect have a significant impact on the total returns for individual stocks. In contrast, those who employ the bottom-up, stockpicking approach contend that it is possible to find stocks that are undervalued relative to their market price, and these stocks will provide superior returns *regardless* of the market and industry outlook.

Both of these approaches have numerous supporters, and advocates of both approaches have been quite successful.[1] In this book, we advocate and present the top-down, three-step approach because of its logic and empirical support. Although we believe that a portfolio manager or an investor can be successful using the bottom-up approach, we believe that it is more difficult to be successful because these stockpickers are ignoring substantial information from the market and the firms' industry.

Although we know that the value of a security is determined by its quality and profit potential, we also believe that the economic environment and the performance of a firm's industry influence the value of a security and its rate of return. Because of the importance of these economic and industry factors, we present an overview of the valuation process that describes these influences and explains how they can be incorporated into the analysis of security value. Subsequently, we describe the theory of value and emphasize the factors that affect the value of securities.

Next, we apply these valuation concepts to the valuation of different assets—bonds, preferred stock, and common stock. In this section, we show how the valuation models help investors calculate how much they should pay for these assets. In the final section, we emphasize the estimation of the variables that affect value (the required rate of return and the expected rate of growth). We conclude with a discussion of additional factors that must be considered when we extend our analysis to the valuation of international securities.

AN OVERVIEW OF THE VALUATION PROCESS

Psychologists suggest that the success or failure of an individual can be caused as much by environment as by genetic gifts. Extending this idea to the valuation of securities means we should consider the economic environment during the valuation process. Regardless of the qualities or capabilities of a firm and its management, the economic environment will have a major influence on the success of a firm and the realized rate of return on the investment.

As an example, assume you own shares of the strongest and most successful firm producing home furnishings. If you own the shares during a strong economic expansion, the sales and earnings of the firm will increase and your rate of return on the stock should be quite high. In contrast, if you own the same stock during a major economic recession, the sales and earnings of this firm would probably experience a decline and the price of its stock would be stable or decline. Therefore, when assessing the future value of a security, it is necessary to analyze the outlook for the aggregate economy, the security markets, and the firm's specific industry.

The valuation process is like the chicken-and-egg dilemma. Do you start by analyzing the macroeconomy and various industries before individual stocks, or do you begin with

---

[1] For the history and selection process of a legendary stockpicker, see Robert G. Hagstrom, Jr., *The Warren Buffett Way* (New York: John Wiley & Sons, 1995).

| FIGURE 13.1 | OVERVIEW OF THE INVESTMENT PROCESS |

Analysis of Alternative Economies and Security Markets

Objective: Decide how to allocate investment funds among countries and within countries to Bonds, Stocks, and Cash.

Analysis of Alternative Industries

Objective: Based upon the Economic and Market Analysis, determine which industries will prosper and which industries will suffer on a global basis and within countries.

Analysis of Individual Companies and Stocks

Objective: Following the selection of the best industries, determine which companies within these industries will prosper and which stocks are undervalued.

individual securities and gradually combine these firms into industries and the industries into the entire economy? For the reasons discussed in the next section, we contend that the discussion should begin with an analysis of aggregate economies and overall securities markets and progress to different industries with a global perspective. Only after a thorough industry analysis are you in a position to properly evaluate the securities issued by individual firms within the better industries. Thus, we recommend a three-step, top-down valuation process in which you first examine the influence of the general economy on all firms and the security markets, then analyze the prospects for various industries in this economic environment, and finally turn to the analysis of individual firms in the industries and to the common stock of these firms. Figure 13.1 indicates the procedure recommended.

WHY A THREE-STEP VALUATION PROCESS?

GENERAL ECONOMIC INFLUENCES

Monetary and fiscal policy measures enacted by various agencies of national governments influence the aggregate economies of those countries. The resulting economic conditions influence all industries and companies within the economies.

Fiscal policy initiatives such as tax credits or tax cuts can encourage spending, whereas additional taxes on income, gasoline, cigarettes, and liquor can discourage spending. Increases or decreases in government spending on defense, on unemployment insurance or retraining programs, or on highways also influence the general economy. All such policies influence the business environment for firms that rely directly on those expenditures. In addition, we know that government spending has a strong *multiplier effect*. For example, increases in road building increases the demand for earthmoving equipment and concrete materials. As a result, in addition to construction workers, the employees in those industries that supply the equipment and materials have more to spend on consumer goods, which raises the demand for consumer goods, which affects another set of suppliers.

Monetary policy produces similar economic changes. A restrictive monetary policy that reduces the growth rate of the money supply reduces the supply of funds for working capital and expansion for all businesses. Alternatively, a restrictive monetary policy that targets interest rates would raise market interest rates and therefore firms' costs, and make it more expensive for individuals to finance home mortgages and the purchase of other durable goods such as autos and appliances. Monetary policy therefore affects all segments of an economy and that economy's relationship with other economies.

Any economic analysis requires the consideration of inflation. As we have discussed, inflation causes differences between real and nominal interest rates and changes the spending and savings behavior of consumers and corporations. In addition, unexpected changes in the rate of inflation make it difficult for firms to plan, which inhibits growth and innovation. Beyond the impact on the domestic economy, differential inflation and interest rates influence the trade balance between countries and the exchange rate for currencies.

In addition to monetary and fiscal policy actions, events such as war, political upheavals in foreign countries, or international monetary devaluations produce changes in the business environment that add to the uncertainty of sales and earnings expectations and therefore the risk premium required by investors. For example, the political uncertainty in Russia during 1993–1995 caused a significant increase in the risk premium for investors in Russia and a subsequent reduction in investment and spending in Russia. In contrast, the end of apartheid in South Africa and its open election in 1994 were viewed as a very positive event and led to a significant increase in economic activity in the country. Similarly, the peace accord in Northern Ireland caused a major influx of investment dollars.

In short, it is difficult to conceive of any industry or company that can avoid the impact of macroeconomic developments that affect the total economy. Because aggregate economic events have a profound effect on all industries and companies within these industries, these macroeconomic factors should be considered before industries are analyzed.

Taking a global portfolio perspective, the asset allocation for a country within a global portfolio will be affected by its economic outlook. If a recession is imminent in a country, you would expect a negative impact on its security prices. Because of these economic expectations, investors would be apprehensive about investing in most industries in the country. Given these expectations, the best investment decision would probably be a smaller allocation to the country. Specifically, the country will be **underweighted** in portfolios relative to its weight based on its market value. Further, given these pessimistic expectations, any funds invested in the country would be directed to low-risk sectors of the economy.

In contrast, optimistic economic and stock market outlooks for a given country should lead an investor to increase the overall allocation to this country (**overweight** the country compared to its weights determined by its relative market value). After allocating funds among countries, the investor looks for outstanding industries in each country. This search for the best industries is enhanced by the economic analysis because the future performance of an industry depends on the country's economic outlook *and* the industry's expected relationship to the economy.

INDUSTRY INFLUENCES

The second step in the valuation process is to identify those industries that will prosper or suffer during the expected aggregate economic environment. Examples of conditions that affect specific industries are strikes within a major producing country, import or export quotas or taxes, a worldwide shortage or an excess supply of a resource, or government-imposed regulations on an industry.

You should remember that alternative industries react to economic changes at different points in the business cycle. For example, firms typically increase capital expenditures when they are operating at full capacity at the peak of the economic cycle. Therefore, industries that provide plant and equipment will typically be affected toward the end of a cycle. In addition, alternative industries have different responses to the business cycle. As an example, cyclical industries such as steel or autos typically do much better than the aggregate economy during expansions, but they suffer more during contractions. In contrast, noncyclical industries such as retail food would not experience a significant decline during a recession, but also would not experience a strong increase during an economic expansion.

Firms that sell in international markets can benefit or suffer as foreign economies shift. An industry with a substantial worldwide market might experience low demand in its domestic market, but benefit from growing demand in its international market. As an example, much of the growth for Coca-Cola and Pepsi and the fast-food chains like McDonald's and Burger King has come from international expansion in Europe and the Far East.

In general, an industry's prospects within the global business environment determine how well or poorly an individual firm will fare, so industry analysis should precede company analysis. Few companies perform well in a poor industry, so even the best company in a poor industry is a bad prospect for investment. For example, poor sales and earnings in the farm equipment industry during the late 1980s had a negative impact on Deere and Co., a very well-managed firm and probably the best firm in its industry. Though Deere performed better than other firms in the industry (some went bankrupt), its earnings and stock performance still fell far short of its past performance, and the company did poorly compared to firms in most other industries.

COMPANY ANALYSIS   After determining that an industry's outlook is good, an investor can analyze and compare individual firms' performance within the entire industry using financial ratios and cash flow values. As we discussed in Chapter 12, many ratios for firms are valid only when they are compared to the performance of their industries.

You undertake company analysis to identify the best company in a promising industry. This involves examining a firm's past performance, but more important, its future prospects. After you understand the firm and its outlook, you can determine its value. In the final step, you compare this estimated value to the firm's market price and decide whether its stock or bonds are good investments.

Your final goal is to select the best stock or bonds within a desirable industry and include it in your portfolio based on its relationship (correlation) with all other assets in your portfolio. As we will discuss in more detail in Chapter 20, the best stock for investment purposes may not necessarily be issued by the best company because the stock of the finest company in an industry may be overpriced, which would cause it to be a poor investment. You cannot know whether a security is undervalued or overvalued until you have analyzed the company, estimated its value, and compared your estimated value to the market price of the stock.

DOES THE THREE-STEP PROCESS WORK?   Although you might agree with the logic of the three-step investment process, you might wonder how well this process works in selecting investments. Several academic studies have supported this technique. First, studies indicated that most changes in an individual firm's *earnings* could be attributed to changes in aggregate corporate earnings and changes in the firm's industry, with the aggregate earnings changes being more important. Although the relative influence of the general economy and the industry on firm earnings varied among individual firms, the results consistently demonstrated that the economic environment had a significant effect on firm earnings.

Second, several studies have found a relationship between aggregate stock prices and various economic series such as employment, income, or production. These results supported the view that there is a relationship between stock prices and economic expansions and contractions.[2]

Third, an analysis of the relationship between *rates of return* for the aggregate stock market, alternative industries, and individual stocks showed that most of the changes in rates of return for individual stocks could be explained by changes in the rates of return for the aggregate stock market and the stock's industry. Although the importance of the market effect tended to decline over time and the significance of the industry effect varied among industries, the combined market–industry effect on the individual firm's rate of return was still important.[3]

These results from academic studies support the use of the three-step investment process. This investment decision approach is consistent with the discussion in Chapter 2, which contended that the most important decision is the asset allocation decision.[4] The asset allocation specifies: (1) what proportion of your portfolio will be invested in various nations' economies; (2) within each country, how you will divide your assets among stocks, bonds, or other assets; and (3) your industry selections, based on which industries are expected to prosper or suffer in the projected economic environment. We provide an example of global asset allocation in Chapter 14.

Now that we have described and justified the three-step process in which we evaluate the overall economy and market, alternative industries, and individual companies and stocks, we need to consider the theory of valuation. The application of this theory allows us to compute a value for the market, for alternative industries, and for individual firms and stocks. Finally, we compare these estimated values to current market prices and decide whether we want to make particular investments.

THEORY OF VALUATION

You may recall from your studies in accounting, economics, or corporate finance that the value of an asset is the present value of its expected returns. Specifically, you expect an asset to provide a stream of returns during the period of time you own it. To convert this estimated stream of returns to a value for the security, you must discount this stream at your required rate of return. This process of valuation requires estimates of (1) the stream of expected returns and (2) the required rate of return on the investment.

STREAM OF EXPECTED RETURNS

An estimate of the expected returns from an investment encompasses not only the size but also the form, time pattern, and the uncertainty of returns, which affect the required rate of return.

FORM OF RETURNS   The returns from an investment can take many forms, including earnings, dividends, interest payments, or capital gains (i.e., increases in value) during a

---

[2] For a further discussion of this and empirical support, see Geoffrey Moore and John P. Cullity, "Security Markets and Business Cycles" in *The Financial Analysts Handbook,* 2d ed., edited by Sumner N. Levine (Homewood, IL: Dow Jones-Irwin, 1988).

[3] For an analysis, see Stephen L. Meyers, "A Re-Examination of Market and Industry Factors in Stock Price Behavior," *Journal of Finance* 28, no. 3 (June 1973): 695–705.

[4] Authors who examine this question generally refer to it as market timing. Studies on this topic include Robert F. Vandell and Jerry L. Stevens, "Evidence of Superior Performance from Timing," *Journal of Portfolio Management* 15, no. 3 (Spring 1989): 38–42; and Jerry Wagner, Steve Shellans, and Richard Paul, "Market Timing Works Where It Matters Most . . . in the Real World," *Journal of Portfolio Management* 18, no. 4 (Summer 1992): 86–90.

period. Alternative valuation techniques use different forms of returns. As an example, one common stock valuation model applies a multiplier to a firm's earnings, whereas another valuation model computes the present value of dividend payments. Returns or cash flows can come in many forms, and you must consider all of them to evaluate an investment accurately.

TIME PATTERN OF RETURNS   You cannot calculate an accurate value for a security unless you can estimate when you will receive the returns. Because money has a time value, you must know the time pattern of returns from an investment. This knowledge will make it possible to properly value the stream of returns relative to alternative investments with a different time pattern of returns.

REQUIRED RATE OF RETURN

UNCERTAINTY OF RETURNS   You will recall from Chapter 1 that the required rate of return on an investment is determined by (1) the economy's real risk-free rate of return, plus (2) the expected rate of inflation during the holding period, plus (3) a risk premium that is determined by the uncertainty of returns. All investments are affected by the risk-free rate and the expected rate of inflation because these two variables determine the nominal risk-free rate. Therefore, the factor that causes a difference in required rates of return is the risk premium for alternative investments. In turn, this risk premium depends on the uncertainty of returns on the assets.

We can identify the sources of the uncertainty of returns by the internal characteristics of assets or by market-determined factors. Earlier, we subdivided the internal characteristics into business risk (BR), financial risk (FR), liquidity risk (LR), exchange rate risk (ERR), and country risk (CR). The market-determined risk measures are the systematic risk of the asset, its beta, or its multiple APT factors.

INVESTMENT DECISION PROCESS: A COMPARISON OF ESTIMATED VALUES AND MARKET PRICES

To ensure that you receive your required return on an investment, you must estimate the value of the investment at your required rate of return, and then compare this estimated investment value to the prevailing market price. You should not buy an investment if its market price exceeds your estimated value because the difference will prevent you from receiving your required rate of return on the investment. In contrast, if the estimated value of the investment exceeds the market price, you should buy the investment. In summary:

- If Estimated Value > Market Price, Buy
- If Estimated Value < Market Price, Don't Buy

For example, assume you read about a firm that produces athletic shoes and that its stock is listed on the NYSE. Using one of the valuation models we will discuss, and making estimates of earnings and growth based on the company's annual report and other information, you estimate the company's stock value using your required rate of return as $20 a share. After estimating this value, you look in the paper and see that the stock is currently being traded at $15 a share. You would want to buy this stock because you think it is worth $20 a share and you can buy it for $15 a share. In contrast, if the current market price were $25 a share, you would not consider buying the stock.

The theory of value provides a common framework for the valuation of all investments. Different applications of this theory generate different estimated values for alternative investments because of the different payment streams and characteristics of the securities. The interest and principal payments on a bond differ substantially from the expected dividends and future selling price for a common stock. The initial discussion that follows applies the discounted cash flow method to bonds, preferred stock, and common stock.

This presentation demonstrates that the same basic model is useful across a range of investments. Subsequently, because of the difficulty in estimating the value of common stock, we consider several additional techniques for evaluating this class of security.

VALUATION OF ALTERNATIVE INVESTMENTS

Valuation of Bonds

Calculating the value of bonds is relatively easy because the size and time pattern of cash flows from the bond over its life are known. A bond typically promises

1. Interest payments every 6 months equal to one-half the coupon rate times the face value of the bond.
2. The payment of the principal on the bond's maturity date.

As an example, in 1997 a $10,000 bond due in 2012 with a 10 percent coupon will pay $500 every six months for its 15-year life. In addition, the bond issuer promises to pay the $10,000 principal at maturity in 2012. Therefore, assuming the bond issuer does not default, the investor knows what payments (cash flows) will be made and when they will be made.

Applying the valuation theory, which states that the value of any asset is the present value of its returns, the value of the bond is the present value of the interest payments, which we can think of as an annuity of $500 every 6 months for 15 years, and the present value of the principal payment, which in this case is the present value of $10,000 in 15 years. The only unknown for this asset (assuming the borrower does not default) is the rate of return you should use to discount the expected stream of payments (cash flows). If the prevailing nominal risk-free rate is 9 percent, and the investor requires a 1 percent risk premium on this bond because there is some probability of default, the required rate of return would be 10 percent.

The present value of the interest payments is an annuity for 30 periods (15 years every 6 months) at one-half the required return (5 percent):[5]

$$\$500 \times 15.3725 = \$7,686$$
(present value of interest payments at 10 percent)

The present value of the principal is likewise discounted at 5 percent for 30 periods:[6]

$$\$10,000 \times .2314 = \$2,314$$
(present value of the principal payment at 10 percent)

This can be summarized as follows:

Present value of interest payments	$500 × 15.3725	= $ 7,686
Present value of principal payment	$10,000 × .2314	= 2,314
Total value of bond at 10 percent		= $10,000

This is the amount that an investor should be willing to pay for this bond, assuming that the required rate of return on a bond of this risk class is 10 percent. If the market price of the

---

[5] The annuity factors and present value factors are contained in Appendix C at the end of the book.

[6] If we used annual compounding, this would be 0.239 rather than 0.2314. We use semiannual compounding because it is consistent with the interest payments and is used in practice.

bond is above this value, the investor should not buy it because the promised yield to maturity will be less than the investor's required rate of return.

Alternatively, assuming an investor requires a 12 percent return on this bond, its value would be:

$$\$500 \times 13.7648 = \$6,882$$
$$\$10,000 \times .1741 = \underline{1,741}$$
$$\text{Total value of bond at 12 percent} = \$8,623$$

This example shows that if you want a higher rate of return, you will not pay as much for an asset; that is, a given stream of returns has a lower value to you. As before, you would compare this computed value to the market price of the bond to determine whether you should invest in it.[7]

VALUATION OF PREFERRED STOCK The owner of a preferred stock receives a promise to pay a stated dividend, usually each quarter, for an infinite period. Preferred stock is a **perpetuity** because there is no maturity. As was true with a bond, stated payments are to be made on specified dates although the issuer of this stock does not have the same legal obligation to pay investors as bonds do. Payments are made only after the firm meets its bond interest payments. This increases the uncertainty of returns so investors should require a higher rate of return on a firm's preferred stock than on its bonds. Although this differential in required return should exist in theory, it generally does not exist in practice because of the tax treatment accorded dividends paid to corporations. As described in Chapter 3, 80 percent of intercompany preferred dividends are tax-exempt, making the effective tax rate on them about 6.8 percent, assuming a corporate tax rate of 34 percent. This tax advantage stimulates the demand for preferred stocks and, because of it, the yield on them has generally been below that on the highest-grade corporate bonds.

Because preferred stock is a perpetuity, its value is simply the stated annual dividend divided by the required rate of return on preferred stock (k_p) as follows:

$$V = \frac{\text{Dividend}}{k_p}$$

Assume a preferred stock has a $100 par value and a dividend of $8 a year. Because of the expected rate of inflation, the uncertainty of the dividend payment, and the tax advantage to you as a corporate investor, your required rate of return on this stock is 9 percent. Therefore, the value of this preferred stock to you is

$$V = \frac{\$8}{.09}$$

$$= \$88.89.$$

Given this estimated value, you would inquire about the current market price to decide whether you would want to buy this preferred stock. If the current market price is $95, you would decide against a purchase, whereas if it is $80, you would buy the stock. Also, given

---

[7] To test your mastery of bond valuation, check that if the required rate of return were 8 percent, the value of this bond would be $11,729.

the market price of preferred stock, you can derive its promised yield. Assuming a current market price of $85, the promised yield would be

$$k_p = \frac{\text{Dividend}}{\text{Price}} = \frac{\$8}{\$85.00} = .0941.$$

VALUATION OF
COMMON STOCK

The valuation of common stocks is more difficult than bonds or preferred stock because an investor is uncertain about the size of the returns, the time pattern of returns, and the required rate of return (k_e). In contrast, the only unknown for a bond is the required rate of return, which is the prevailing nominal RFR plus a risk premium. For preferred stock the only unknown is the required rate of return on the stock (k_p). Nevertheless, we can find common stock values using the same theory that we applied to bonds and preferred stock.

We can use either dividends or earnings as the stream of returns to be discounted. Some investors prefer to use earnings because they are the source of dividends. Others feel that investors should discount the cash flows they will receive—dividends. Although we present models that use both streams, we introduce the dividend discount model (DDM) first because it is intuitively appealing (dividends *are* the cash flow received). Also, because the DDM has been used extensively by others, you may be familiar with its reduced form.

THE DIVIDEND DISCOUNT MODEL (DDM)   The **dividend discount model** assumes that the value of a share of common stock is the present value of all future dividends as follows:[8]

$$V_j = \frac{D_1}{(1 + k)} + \frac{D_2}{(1 + k)^2} + \frac{D_3}{(1 + k)^3}$$

$$+ \ldots + \frac{D_\infty}{(1 + k)^\infty}$$

$$= \sum_{t=1}^{n} \frac{D_t}{(1 + k)^t}$$

where:

V_j = **value of common stock** j
D_t = **dividend during period** t
k = **required rate of return on stock** j.

An obvious question is, what happens when the stock is not held for an infinite period? A sale of the stock at the end of Year 2 would imply the following formula:

$$V_j = \frac{D_1}{(1 + k)} + \frac{D_2}{(1 + k)^2} + \frac{SP_{j2}}{(1 + k)^2}.$$

The value is equal to the two dividend payments during Years 1 and 2 plus the sale price (SP) for stock j at the end of Year 2. The expected selling price of stock j at the end of Year 2 (SP_{j2}) is simply the value of all remaining dividend payments.

---

[8] This model was initially set forth in J. B. Williams, *The Theory of Investment Value* (Cambridge, MA: Harvard, 1938). It was subsequently reintroduced and expanded by Myron J. Gordon, *The Investment, Financing, and Valuation of the Corporation* (Homewood, IL: Richard D. Irwin, 1962).

$$SP_{j2} = \frac{D_3}{(1 + k)} + \frac{D_4}{(1 + k)^2} + \ldots + \frac{D_\infty}{(1 + k)^\infty}.$$

If SP_{j2} is discounted back to the present by $1/(1 + k)^2$, this equation becomes

$$PV(SP_{j2}) = \frac{\dfrac{D_3}{(1 + k)} + \dfrac{D_4}{(1 + k)^2} + \ldots + \dfrac{D_\infty}{(1 + k)^\infty}}{(1 + k)^2}$$

$$= \frac{D_3}{(1 + k)^3} + \frac{D_4}{(1 + k)^4} + \ldots + \frac{D_\infty}{(1 + k)^\infty},$$

which is simply an extension of the original equation. Whenever the stock is sold, its value (i.e., the sale price at that time) will be the present value of all future dividends. When this ending value is discounted back to the present, you are back to the original dividend discount model.

What about stocks that do not pay dividends? Again, the concept is the same, except that some of the early dividend payments are zero. Notably, there are expectations that *at some point* the firm will start paying dividends. If investors did not have such an expectation, nobody would be willing to buy the security. It would have zero value. A firm with a nondividend-paying stock is reinvesting its capital rather than paying current dividends so that its earnings and dividend stream will be larger and grow faster in the future. In this case, we would apply the DDM as:

$$V_j = \frac{D_1}{(1 + k)} + \frac{D_2}{(1 + k)^2} + \frac{D_3}{(1 + k)^3}$$

$$+ \ldots + \frac{D_\infty}{(1 + k)^\infty}.$$

where:

$D_1 = 0$
$D_2 = 0.$

The investor expects that when the firm starts paying dividends in Period 3, it will be a large initial amount and dividends will grow faster than those of a comparable stock that had paid out dividends. The stock has value because of these *future* dividends. We will apply this model with several cases having different holding periods that will show you how it works.

One-year holding period   Assume an investor wants to buy the stock, hold it for one year, and then sell it. To determine the value of the stock—that is, how much the investor should pay for it—using the DDM, we must estimate the dividend to be received during the period, the expected sale price at the end of the holding period, and the investor's required rate of return.

To estimate the dividend for the coming year, adjust the current dividend for expectations regarding the change in the dividend during the year. Assume the company we are analyzing earned $2.50 a share last year and paid a dividend of $1 a share. Assume further the firm has been fairly consistent in maintaining this 40 percent payout over time. The consensus of financial analysts is that the firm will earn about $2.75 during the coming year and will raise its dividend to $1.10 per share.

A crucial estimate is the expected selling price for the stock a year from now. You can estimate this expected selling price by either of two alternative procedures. In the first, you can apply the dividend discount model where you estimate the specific dividend payments for a number of years into the future and calculate the value from these estimates. In the second, the earnings multiplier model, you multiply the future expected earnings for the stock by an earnings multiple, which you likewise estimate, to find an expected sale price. We will discuss this model in a later section of the chapter. For now, assume you prefer the DDM. Applying this model, you project the sales price of this stock a year from now to be $22.

Finally, you must determine the required rate of return. As discussed before, the nominal risk-free rate is determined by the real risk-free rate and the expected rate of inflation. A good proxy for this rate is the promised yield on 1-year government bonds because your investment horizon (expected holding period) is 1 year. You estimate the stock's risk premium by comparing its risk level to the risk of other potential investments. In later chapters, we discuss how you can estimate this risk. For the moment, assume that 1-year government bonds are yielding 10 percent, and you believe that a 4 percent risk premium over the yield of these bonds is appropriate for this stock. Thus, you specify a required rate of return of 14 percent.

In summary, you have estimated the dividend at $1.10 (payable at year-end), an ending sale price of $22, and a required rate of return at 14 percent. Given these inputs, you would estimate the value of this stock as follows:

$$
\begin{aligned}
V_1 &= \frac{\$1.10}{(1 + .14)} + \frac{\$22.00}{(1 + .14)} \\
&= \frac{1.10}{1.14} + \frac{22.00}{1.14} \\
&= .96 + 19.30 \\
&= \$20.26.
\end{aligned}
$$

Note that we have not mentioned the current market price of the stock. This is because the market price is not relevant to you as an investor except as a comparison to the independently derived value based on your estimates of the relevant variables. Once we have calculated the stock's value as $20.26, we can compare it to the market price and apply the investment decision rule: If the stock's market price is more than $20.26, do not buy; if it is equal to or less than $20.26, buy.

Multiple-year holding period   If you anticipate holding the stock for several years and then selling it, the valuation estimate is harder because it is necessary to forecast several future dividend payments and to estimate the sale price of the stock several years in the future.

The difficulty with estimating future dividend payments is that the future stream can have numerous forms. The exact estimate of the future dividends depends on two projections. The first is your outlook for earnings growth because earnings are the source of dividends. The second projection is the firm's dividend policy, which can take several forms. A firm can have a constant percent payout of earnings each year, which implies a change in dividend each year, or the firm could follow a step pattern in which it increases the dividend rate by a constant dollar amount each year or every 2 or 3 years. The easiest dividend policy to analyze is one where the firm enjoys a constant growth rate in earnings and maintains a constant dividend payout. This set of assumptions implies that the dividend stream will experience a constant growth rate that is equal to the earnings growth rate.

Assume the expected holding period is 3 years, and you estimate the following dividend payments at the end of each year:

Year 1	$1.10/share
Year 2	$1.20/share
Year 3	$1.35/share

The next estimate is the expected sale price (*SP*) for the stock 3 years in the future. Again, if we use the DDM for this estimate, you would need to project the dividend growth pattern for this stock beginning 3 years from now. Assume an estimated sale price of $34.

The final estimate is the required rate of return on this stock during this period. Assuming the 14 percent required rate is still appropriate, the value of this stock is

$$V = \frac{1.10}{(1 + .14)^1} + \frac{1.20}{(1 + .14)^2} + \frac{1.35}{(1 + .14)^3}$$
$$+ \frac{34.00}{(1 + .14)^3}$$
$$= \frac{1.10}{(1.14)} + \frac{1.20}{(1.30)} + \frac{1.35}{(1.4815)} + \frac{34.00}{(1.4815)}$$
$$= .96 + .92 + .91 + 22.95$$
$$= \$25.74.$$

Again, to make an investment decision you would compare this estimated value for the stock to its current market price to determine whether you should buy.

At this point, you should recognize that the valuation procedure discussed here is similar to that used in corporate finance when making investment decisions, except that the cash flows are from dividends instead of returns to an investment project. Also, rather than estimating the scrap value or salvage value of a corporate asset, we are estimating the ending sale price for the stock. Finally, rather than discounting cash flows using the firm's cost of capital, we use the individual's required rate of return. In both cases, we are looking for excess present value, which means that the present value of expected cash inflows—that is, the estimated value of the asset—exceeds the present value of cash outflows, which is the market price of the asset.

Infinite period model   We can extend the multi-period model by extending our estimates of dividends 5, 10, or 15 years into the future. The benefits derived from these extensions would be minimal, however, and you would quickly become bored with this exercise. Instead, we will move to the infinite period dividend valuation model, which assumes investors estimate future dividend payments for an infinite number of periods.

Needless to say, this is a formidable task! We must make some simplifying assumptions about this future stream of dividends to make the task viable. The easiest assumption is that *the future dividend stream will grow at a constant rate for an infinite period.* This is a rather heroic assumption in many instances, but where it does hold, it allows us to derive a model with which we can value individual stocks as well as the aggregate market and alternative industries. This model is generalized as follows:

$$V_j = \frac{D_0(1 + g)}{(1 + k)} + \frac{D_0(1 + g)^2}{(1 + k)^2} + \dots + \frac{D_0(1 + g)^n}{(1 + k)^n}$$

where:

V_j = the value of stock j
D_0 = the dividend payment in the current period
g = the constant growth rate of dividends
k = the required rate of return on stock j
n = the number of periods, which we assume to be infinite.

In the appendix to this chapter, we show that with certain assumptions, this infinite period model can be simplified to the following expression:

$$V_j = \frac{D_1}{k - g}.$$

You will probably recognize this formula as one that is widely used in corporate finance to estimate the cost of equity capital for the firm.

To use this model, you must estimate (1) the required rate of return (k) and (2) the expected growth rate of dividends (g). After estimating g, it is a simple matter to estimate D_1 because it is the current dividend (D_0) times $(1 + g)$.

Consider the example of a stock with a current dividend of $1 a share, which you expect to rise to $1.09 next year. You believe that, over the long run, this company's earnings and dividends will continue to grow at 9 percent; therefore, your estimate of g is 0.09. For the long run, you expect the rate of inflation to decline, so you set your long-run required rate of return on this stock at 13 percent; your estimate of k is 0.13. To summarize the relevant estimates:

$$g = .09$$
$$k = .13$$
$$D_1 = 1.09 \ (\$1.00 \times 1.09)$$
$$V = \frac{1.09}{.13 - .09}$$
$$= \frac{1.09}{.04}$$
$$= \$27.25.$$

A small change in any of the original estimates will have a large impact on V as shown by the following examples:

1. $g = .09$; $k = .14$; $D_1 = \$1.09$. (We assume an increase in k.)

$$V = \frac{\$1.09}{.14 - .09}$$
$$= \frac{\$1.09}{.05}$$
$$= \$21.80$$

2. $g = .10$; $k = .13$; $D_1 = \$1.10$. (We assume an increase in g.)

$$V = \frac{\$1.10}{.13 - .10}$$
$$= \frac{\$1.10}{.03}$$
$$= \$36.67$$

These examples show that as small a change as 1 percent in either *g* or *k* produces a large difference in the estimated value of the stock. The crucial relationship that determines the value of the stock is the *spread between the required rate of return (k) and the expected growth rate of dividends (g)*. Anything that causes a decline in the spread will cause an increase in the computed value, whereas any increase in the spread will decrease the computed value.

INFINITE PERIOD DDM AND GROWTH COMPANIES

As noted in the appendix, the infinite period DDM had the following assumptions:

1. Dividends grow at a constant rate.
2. The constant growth rate will continue for an infinite period.
3. The required rate of return *(k) is greater than the infinite growth rate (g)*. If it is not, the model gives meaningless results because the denominator becomes negative.

What is the effect of these assumptions if you want to use this model to value the stock of growth companies such as Intel, Merck, Microsoft, McDonald's, and Motorola? **Growth companies** are firms that have the opportunities and abilities to earn rates of return on investments that are consistently above their required rates of return.[9] To exploit these outstanding opportunities, these firms generally retain a high percentage of earnings for reinvestment, and their earnings grow faster than those of the typical firm. You will recall from the discussion in Chapter 12 that a firm's substainable growth is a function of its retention rate and its return on equity (ROE). Notably, as discussed below, the earnings growth pattern for these growth companies is inconsistent with the assumptions of the infinite period DDM.

First, the infinite period DDM assumes dividends will grow at a constant rate for an infinite period. This assumption seldom holds for companies currently growing at above average rates. As an example, Intel and Wal-Mart have both grown at rates in excess of 30 percent a year for several years. It is unlikely that they can maintain such extreme rates of growth and the ROEs implied by this growth for an infinite period in an economy where other firms will compete with them for these high rates of return.

Second, when these firms are experiencing abnormally high rates of growth, their rate of growth will probably exceed their required rates of return. There is *no* automatic relationship between growth and risk; a high-growth company is not necessarily a high-risk company. In fact, a firm growing at a high but fairly constant rate would have lower risk (less uncertainty) than a low-growth firm with an unstable earnings pattern.

In summary, some firms experience periods of abnormally high rates of growth for some periods of time. The infinite period DDM cannot be used to value these true growth firms because of these temporary high-growth conditions, which are inconsistent with the assumptions of the model. In the following section we discuss how to supplement the DDM to value a firm with temporary supernormal growth. In Chapter 20 we will discuss additional models that can be used to estimate the stock values of growth companies.

VALUATION WITH TEMPORARY SUPERNORMAL GROWTH

Thus far, we have considered how to value a firm with different growth rates for short periods of time (1 to 3 years) and how to value a stock with a model that assumes a constant growth rate for an infinite period. We also noted that it is not possible to use the model to value true growth companies because of the assumptions of the model. It was recognized

---

[9] Growth companies are discussed in Ezra Salomon, *The Theory of Financial Management* (New York: Columbia University Press, 1963), and Merton Miller and Franco Modigliani, "Dividend Policy, Growth, and the Valuation of Shares," *Journal of Business* 34, no. 4 (October 1961): 411–433. Models to value growth companies are discussed in Chapter 20.

that a company cannot permanently maintain a growth rate higher than its required rate of return, but certain firms may experience temporary supernormal growth. A firm cannot grow at a supernormal rate for a very long period because competition will enter this apparently lucrative business, which will reduce the firm's profit margins and therefore its ROE and growth rate. Therefore, after a few years of exceptional growth, a firm's growth rate is expected to decline and eventually it will stabilize at a level consistent with the assumptions of the infinite period DDM.

To determine the value of a temporary supernormal growth company, you need to combine the previous models. During the initial years of exceptional growth, you need to examine each year individually. If there are two or three stages of supernormal growth, then you must examine each year during these stages of growth. When the firm's growth rate stabilizes at a rate below the required rate of return, you can compute the remaining value of the firm under constant growth using the DDM and discount this lump-sum constant growth value back to the present. The technique should become clear as you work through the following example.

The Bourke Company has a current dividend (D_0) of $2.00 a share. The following are the expected annual growth rates for dividends.

Year	Dividend Growth Rate
1–3:	25%
4–6:	20
7–9:	15
10 on:	9

The required rate of return for the stock is 14 percent. Therefore, the value equation becomes

$$V_i = \frac{2.00\ (1.25)}{1.14} + \frac{2.00\ (1.25)^2}{(1.14)^2} + \frac{2.00\ (1.25)^3}{(1.14)^3}$$

$$+ \frac{2.00\ (1.25)^3\ (1.20)}{(1.14)^4} + \frac{2.00\ (1.25)^3\ (1.20)^2}{(1.14)^5}$$

$$+ \frac{2.00\ (1.25)^3\ (1.20)^3}{(1.14)^6} + \frac{2.00\ (1.25)^3\ (1.20)^3\ (1.15)}{(1.14)^7}$$

$$+ \frac{2.00\ (1.25)^3\ (1.20)^3\ (1.15)^2}{(1.14)^8} + \frac{2.00\ (1.25)^3\ (1.20)^3\ (1.15)^3}{(1.14)^9}$$

$$+ \frac{\dfrac{2.00\ (1.25)^3\ (1.20)^3\ (1.15)^3\ (1.09)}{(.14 - .09)}}{(1.14)^9}$$

The computations in Table 13.1 indicate that the total value of the stock is $94.36. The difficult part of the valuation is estimating the supernormal growth rates and determining *how long they will last.*

This part of the chapter has demonstrated the application of the valuation model to bonds, preferred stock, and common stock. The valuation of bonds and preferred stock was fairly straightforward, because we knew the amount and timing of the returns and our only estimate was the required rate of return. The bulk of the section dealt with the valuation of common stock, which is more difficult because you do not know the amount of flows, the

TABLE 13.1	COMPUTATION OF VALUE FOR STOCK OF COMPANY WITH TEMPORARY SUPERNORMAL GROWTH

Year	Dividend	Discount Factor (14 percent)	Present Value
1	$ 2.50	0.8772	$ 2.193
2	3.12	0.7695	2.401
3	3.91	0.6750	2.639
4	4.69	0.5921	2.777
5	5.63	0.5194	2.924
6	6.76	0.4556	3.080
7	7.77	0.3996	3.105
8	8.94	0.3506	3.134
9	10.28	0.3075[b]	3.161
10	11.21		
	$224.20[a]	0.3075[b]	68.941
		Total value =	$94.355

[a]Value of dividend stream for Year 10 and all future dividends
(i.e., $11.21/(0.14 − 0.09) = $224.20).
[b]The discount factor is the ninth-year factor because the
valuation of the remaining stream is made at the end of Year 9
to reflect the dividend in Year 10 and all future dividends.

timing of flows, and the required rate of return. The common stock valuation model considered in this section was the dividend discount model (DDM). We noted that the infinite period DDM cannot be applied to the valuation of stock for growth companies because the flow of earnings for the growth company is inconsistent with the assumptions of the DDM model. We were able to modify the DDM model to evaluate companies with temporary supernormal growth.

EARNINGS MULTIPLIER MODEL

Rather than concentrate on dividends alone, many investors prefer to estimate the value of common stock using an **earnings multiplier model.** The reasoning for this approach recalls the basic concept that the value of any investment is the present value of future returns. In the case of common stocks, the returns that investors are entitled to receive are the net earnings of the firm. Therefore, one way investors can derive value is by determining how many dollars they are willing to pay for a dollar of expected earnings (typically represented by the estimated earnings during the following 12-month period). For example, if investors are willing to pay 10 times expected earnings, they would value a stock they expect to earn $2 a share during the following year at $20. You can compute the prevailing earnings multiplier, also referred to as the **price/earnings (P/E) ratio,** as follows:

$$\text{Earnings Multiplier} = \text{Price/Earnings Ratio}$$

$$= \frac{\text{Current Market Price}}{\text{Expected 12 Month Earnings}}$$

This computation of the current earnings multiplier (P/E ratio) indicates the prevailing attitude of investors toward a stock's value. Investors must decide if they agree with the prevailing P/E ratio (i.e., is the earnings multiplier too high or too low?).

To answer this question, we must consider what influences the earnings multiplier (P/E ratio) over time. In Chapter 18 where we will discuss market valuation, it will be shown that the aggregate stock market P/E ratio, as represented by the S&P 400 Index, has varied from about 6 times earnings to about 23 times earnings.[10] The infinite period dividend discount model can be used to indicate the variables that should determine the value of the P/E ratio as follows:[11]

$$P_i = \frac{D_1}{k - g}$$

If we divide both sides of the equation by E_1 (expected earnings during the next 12 months), the result is

$$\frac{P_i}{E_1} = \frac{D_1/E_1}{k - g}$$

Thus, the P/E ratio is determined by

1. The expected *dividend payout ratio* (dividends divided by earnings).
2. The required rate of return on the stock (k).
3. The expected growth rate of dividends for the stock (g).

As an example, if we assume a stock has an expected dividend payout of 50 percent, a required rate of return of 13 percent, and an expected growth rate for dividends of 9 percent, we would have the following:

$$D/E = .50; \, k = .13; \, g = .09$$
$$P/E = \frac{.50}{.13 - .09}$$
$$= .50/.04$$
$$= 12.5.$$

Again, a small change in either k or g will have a large impact on the multiplier, as shown in the following two examples.

1. $D/E = .50; \, k = .14; \, g = .09$. (In this example, we assume an increase in k.)

$$P/E = \frac{.50}{.14 - .09}$$
$$= \frac{.50}{.05}$$
$$= 10$$

2. $D/E = .50; \, k = .13; \, g = .10$. (In this example, we assume an increase in g and the original k.)

---

[10] When computing historical P/E ratios, the practice is to use earnings for the *last* 12 months rather than expected earnings. Although this will influence the level, it demonstrates the changes over time.

[11] In this formulation of the model we use P rather than V (i.e., the value is stated as the estimated price of the stock).

$$P/E = \frac{.50}{.13 - .10}$$

$$= \frac{.50}{.03}$$

$$= 16.7$$

As before, the spread between k and g is *the main determinant of the size of the P/E ratio.* Although the dividend payout ratio has an impact, we are generally referring to a firm's long-run target payout, which is typically rather stable with little effect on year-to-year changes in the P/E ratio (earnings multiplier).

After estimating the earnings multiple, you would apply it to your estimate of earnings for the next year (E_1) to arrive at an estimated value. In turn, E_1 is based on the earnings for the current year (E_0) and your expected growth rate of earnings. Using these two estimates, you would compute an estimated value of the stock and compare this to its market price.

Consider the following estimates for an example firm:

$$D/E = .50$$
$$k = .14$$
$$g = .10$$
$$E_0 = \$2.00$$

Using these estimates, you would compute an earnings multiple of:

$$P/E = \frac{.50}{.14 - .10} = \frac{.50}{.04} = 12.5\times$$

Given current earnings (E_0) of $2.00 and a g of 10 percent, you would expect E_1 to be $2.20. Therefore, you would estimate the value (price) of the stock as

$$V = 12.5 \times \$2.20$$
$$= \$27.50$$

As before, you would compare this estimated value of the stock to its market price to decide whether you should invest in it.

ESTIMATING THE INPUTS: THE REQUIRED RATE OF RETURN AND THE EXPECTED GROWTH RATE OF DIVIDENDS

This section deals with estimating two inputs that are critical to the valuation model process: the required rate of return (k) and the expected growth rate of dividends (g).

We will review these factors and discuss how the estimation of these variables differs for domestic versus foreign securities. Although the valuation procedure is the same for securities around the world, k and g differ among countries. Therefore, we will review the components of the required rate of return for U.S. securities and then consider the components for foreign securities. Following this, we will turn to the estimation of the growth rate of earnings and dividends for domestic stocks and then discuss estimating growth for foreign stocks.

REQUIRED RATE OF RETURN (k)

This discussion reviews the determinants of the nominal required rate of return on an investment including a consideration of factors for non-U.S. markets. Recall that three factors influence an investor's required rate of return:

1. The economy's real risk-free rate (RFR)
2. The expected rate of inflation (I)
3. A risk premium (RP)

THE ECONOMY'S REAL RISK-FREE RATE   This is the absolute minimum rate that an investor should require. It depends on the real growth rate of the economy because capital invested should grow at least as fast as the economy. It is recognized that the rate can be impacted for short periods of time by temporary tightness or ease in the capital markets.

THE EXPECTED RATE OF INFLATION   Investors are interested in real rates of return that will allow them to increase their rate of consumption. Therefore, if investors expect a given rate of inflation, they should increase their nominal required risk-free rates of return to reflect any expected inflation as follows:

$$\text{Nominal RFR} = [1 + \text{Real RFR}][1 + E(I)] - 1$$

where:

$E(I)$ = expected rate of inflation

The two factors that determine the nominal RFR affect all investments, from U.S. government securities to highly speculative land deals. Investors who hope to calculate security values accurately must carefully estimate the expected rate of inflation. Not only does it affect all investments, but its extreme volatility makes its estimation difficult.

THE RISK PREMIUM   The risk premium causes differences in the required rates of return among alternative investments that range from government bonds to corporate bonds to common stocks. This premium also explains the difference in the expected return among securities of the same type. For example, this is the reason corporate bonds with different ratings of Aaa, Aa, or A have different yields, and why different common stocks have widely varying earnings multipliers despite similar growth expectations.

In Chapter 1, we noted that investors demand a risk premium because of the uncertainty of returns expected from an investment. A measure of this uncertainty of returns was the dispersion of expected returns. We suggested several internal factors that influence the variability of returns, so you can derive some understanding of the risk of an investment by analyzing internal factors such as its business risk, financial risk, and liquidity risk. We noted that foreign investments bring additional risk factors, including exchange rate risk and country risk. All of these risk factors will be considered in the following section.

Changes in the risk premium   Because different securities have different patterns of returns and different guarantees to investors, we expect their risk premiums to differ. In addition, the risk premiums for the same securities can *change over time*. For example, Figure 13.2 shows the spread between the yields to maturity for Aaa-rated corporate bonds and Baa-rated corporate bonds from 1966 to 1995. This yield spread, or difference in yield, is a measure of the risk premium for investing in higher-risk bonds (Baa) compared to low-risk bonds (Aaa). As shown, the yield spread varied from about .40 percent to 2.69 percent (from less than one-half of 1 percent to almost 3 percent).

Figure 13.3 contains a plot of the *ratio* of the yields for the same period, which indicates the percentage risk premium of Baa bonds compared to Aaa bonds. You might expect a larger difference in yield between Baa and Aaa bonds if Aaa bonds are yielding 12 percent rather than 6 percent. The ratio in Figure 13.3 adjusts for this size difference. This shows

FIGURE 13.2

TIME-SERIES PLOT OF MOODY'S CORPORATE BOND YIELD SPREADS (Baa–Aaa): MONTHLY 1966–1995

Source: Reprinted by permission of Moody's Investor's Services.

that even adjusting for the yield level difference, the risk premium varies from about 1.07 to 1.23—a 7 percent premium to a 23 percent premium over the base yield on Aaa bonds. This change in risk premium over time occurs because either investors perceive a change in the level of risk of Baa bonds compared to Aaa bonds, or there is a change in the amount of return that investors require to accept the same level of risk. In either case, this change in the risk premium for a set of assets implies a change in the slope of the security market line (SML). This change in the slope of the SML was demonstrated in Chapter 1.

ESTIMATING THE REQUIRED RETURN FOR FOREIGN SECURITIES

Our discussion of the required rate of return for investments has been limited to the domestic market. Although the basic valuation model and its variables are the same around the world, there are significant differences in the specific variables. This section points out where these differences occur.

FOREIGN REAL RFR   Because the real RFR in other countries should be determined by the real growth rate within the particular economy, the estimated rate can vary substantially among countries due to differences in the three variables that affect an economy's real growth rate: (1) growth rate of the labor force, (2) growth rate of the average number of hours worked, and (3) growth rate of labor productivity. An example of differences in the real growth rate of gross domestic product (GDP) can be seen in Table 13.2. There is a range of estimates for 1997 of 1.7 percent (i.e., 1.6 percent for Japan compared with 3.2

| FIGURE 13.3 | PLOT OF THE RATIO OF MOODY'S CORPORATE BOND YIELDS (Baa YIELD ÷ Aaa YIELD): MONTHLY 1966–1996 |

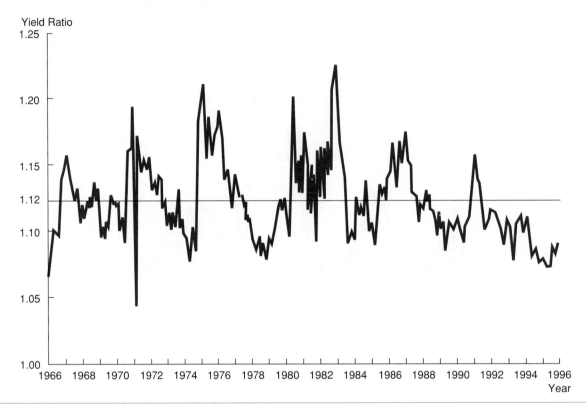

Source: Reprinted by permission of Moody's Investor's Services.

percent for the United Kingdom). This difference in the growth rates of real GDP implies a substantial difference in the real RFR for these countries. To estimate the real rates of growth for alternative countries, you must examine the historical values for the three variables that affect each country's real growth.

INFLATION RATE   To estimate the nominal RFR for a country, you must also estimate its expected rate of inflation and adjust the real RFR for this expectation. Again, this rate of inflation typically varies substantially among countries. The price change data in Table 13.3 show that the expected rate of inflation during 1997 varied from 1.0 percent in Japan to 3.9 percent in Italy. Assuming equal growth, this implies a difference in the nominal required rate of return between these two countries of 2.9 percent. Such a difference in k can have a substantial impact on estimated values as demonstrated earlier. Again, you must make a separate estimate for each individual country in which you are evaluating securities.

To demonstrate the combined impact of differences in real growth and expected inflation, Table 13.4 shows the results of the following computation for the six countries based on the 1997 estimates:

$$\text{Nominal RFR} = (1 + \text{Real Growth}) \times (1 + \text{Expected Inflation}) - 1$$

| TABLE 13.2 | **REAL GDP (PERCENTAGE CHANGES FROM PREVIOUS YEAR)** |

Period	United States	Japan	Germany	France	United Kingdom	Italy
1987	3.7%	4.6%	1.7%	1.9%	4.5%	3.0%
1988	4.4	5.8	3.6	3.4	4.6	4.2
1989	2.5	4.8	4.0	3.6	1.9	3.2
1990	0.8	5.6	4.6	2.5	1.0	1.9
1991	0.1	3.6	3.3	1.2	−1.2	1.5
1992	2.1	1.5	1.5	1.2	−0.5	1.0
1993	3.0	0.1	−1.9	−0.7	1.9	−0.4
1994	3.5	0.5	2.9	2.8	4.0	2.1
1995	2.0	0.9	1.9	2.2	2.5	3.0
1996[(e)]	2.5	2.8	0.5	1.3	1.9	1.1
1997[(e)]	2.9	1.6	2.2	2.8	3.2	2.0

[(e)]estimate.

Source: "World Investment Strategy Highlights" (London: Goldman, Sachs International Ltd., June/July 1996). Reprinted by permission of Goldman, Sachs & Co.

| TABLE 13.3 | **CONSUMER OR RETAIL PRICE (PERCENTAGE CHANGES FROM PREVIOUS YEAR)** |

Period	United States	Japan	Germany	France	United Kingdom	Italy
1987	3.7%	0.1%	0.3%	3.3%	4.1%	4.6%
1988	4.1	0.7	1.3	2.7	4.9	5.0
1989	4.8	2.3	2.8	3.4	7.8	6.6
1990	5.4	3.0	2.7	3.4	9.5	6.1
1991	4.7	3.2	3.5	3.1	6.0	6.0
1992	3.0	1.7	4.0	2.8	3.7	5.2
1993	3.0	1.3	4.2	2.1	1.6	4.2
1994	2.6	0.7	2.7	2.1	2.4	3.9
1995	2.8	0.0	1.8	1.6	2.8	5.4
1996[(e)]	3.1	0.0	1.8	1.8	2.9	4.3
1997[(e)]	3.4	1.0	2.6	1.7	2.5	3.9

[(e)]estimate.

Source: "World Investment Strategy Highlights" (London: Goldman, Sachs International Ltd., June/July 1996). Reprinted by permission of Goldman, Sachs & Co.

| TABLE 13.4 | **ESTIMATES OF 1997 NOMINAL RFR FOR MAJOR COUNTRIES** |

Country	Real Growth in GDP[a]	Expected Inflation[b]	Nominal RFR
United States	2.9%	3.4%	6.4%
Japan	1.6	1.0	2.6
Germany	2.2	2.6	4.9
France	2.8	1.7	4.5
United Kingdom	3.2	2.5	5.8
Italy	2.0	3.9	6.0

[a]Taken from Table 13.2.
[b]Taken from Table 13.3.

Source: Reprinted by permission of Goldman, Sachs & Co.

Given the differences between countries in the two components, the range in the nominal RFR of 3.8 percent is not surprising (6.4 percent for the United States versus 2.6 percent for Japan). As demonstrated earlier, such a difference in k for an investment will have a significant impact on its value.

RISK PREMIUM   You must also derive a risk premium for the investments in each country. Again, the five risk components differ substantially between countries: business risk, financial risk, liquidity risk, exchange rate risk, and country risk. *Business risk* can vary because it is a function of the variability of economic activity within a country and of the operating leverage used by firms within the country. Firms in different countries assume significantly different *financial risk* as well. For example, Japanese firms use substantially more financial leverage than U.S. or U.K. firms. Regarding *liquidity risk,* the U.S. capital markets are acknowledged to be the most liquid in the world, with Japan and London being close behind. In contrast, some small, inactive capital markets (e.g., emerging markets) are quite illiquid and investors should add a significant liquidity risk premium.

When investing globally, you also must estimate exchange rate risk. *Exchange rate risk* is the additional uncertainty of returns caused by changes in the exchange rates for the currency of another country. This uncertainty can range from very small for a U.S. investor in a country such as Hong Kong because the currency is pegged to the U.S. dollar. As a result, there is a negligible effect for a U.S. investor from changes in the exchange rate. In this case, the domestic return of a stock in Hong Kong and the return in U.S. dollars are almost identical. In contrast, there are some countries where there is substantial volatility in the exchange rate over time, which means that there can be significant differences in the domestic return for the country and the return in U.S. dollars.[12] The level of volatility for the exchange rate differs between countries, where the volatility is measured as *the average monthly absolute percentage change in the exchange rate*. The higher the average absolute percentage change, the greater the uncertainty regarding future changes in the exchange rate and the larger the exchange rate risk for the country.

The difference in the exchange rate between countries occurs because of specific trade relations between individual countries. As an example of exchange rate risk, consider the trade imbalances between the United States and Japan during 1985 to 1996 that caused significant fluctuations in the exchange rates between the U.S. dollar and Japanese yen— the exchange rate of yen per dollar went from 250 down to 90, back up to 160, and then down to 97 in early 1996. When the U.S. dollar weakened relative to the yen during 1986, 1987, and 1993, Japanese investors in U.S. stocks and bonds suffered a significant exchange rate loss. Subsequently, when the U.S. dollar strengthened in 1988 and 1989, U.S. investors in Japanese securities suffered. In contrast, during 1995, the Japanese stock market experienced a rally *and* the yen strengthened against the dollar. Because of this, U.S. investors in Japanese stocks experienced high rates of return during this period.

Beyond the difference in the *level* of exchange rate risk (ERR), investors must be aware of *changes* in the level of ERR caused by changes in exchange rate volatility. These changes in ERR are caused by internal changes in the non-U.S. economy, the political conditions in a country, and by changes in the relationship of a country with the United States. Specifically, a country's economy may become more or less stable, or the country

---

[12] Although we generally refer to these as domestic and U.S. dollar returns, you will also see references to *hedged* returns (e.g., domestic) and *unhedged* returns (returns in U.S. dollars). In some cases, the hedged returns will adjust for the cost of hedging. For an example of differences in domestic versus U.S. dollar returns for some major countries, see Table 14.11 in the following chapter.

can develop a different relationship to the U.S. economy that will influence the volatility of its exchange rate with the United States.[13]

Recall that country risk arises from unexpected events in a country such as upheavals in its political or economic environment. For example, many investors expect country risk to rise in Hong Kong in 1997 when it changes from a territory of the United Kingdom to a province of China. A past example of country risk would be the violent confrontation between students and the army in Beijing in 1989—it signaled a major change in the political and economic environment in China. Such political unrest or a change in the economic environment creates uncertainties that increase the risk of investments in these countries. Before investing in such countries, investors must evaluate the additional returns they should require to accept this increased uncertainty.

Thus, when estimating required rates of return on foreign investments, you must evaluate these differences in fundamental risk factors and assign a unique risk premium for each country.

EXPECTED GROWTH RATE OF DIVIDENDS

After arriving at a required rate of return, the investor must estimate the growth rate of earnings and dividends because the valuation models for common stock depend heavily on good estimates of growth (g). The procedure we describe here is similar to the presentation in Chapter 12, where we used financial ratios to measure a firm's growth potential.

The growth rate of dividends is determined by the growth rate of earnings and the proportion of earnings paid out in dividends (the payout ratio). Over the short run, dividends can grow faster or slower than earnings if the firm changes its payout ratio. Specifically, if a firm's earnings grow at 6 percent a year and it pays out exactly 50 percent of earnings in dividends, then the firm's dividends will likewise grow at 6 percent a year. Alternatively, if a firm's earnings grow at 6 percent a year and the firm increases its payout, then during the period when the payout ratio increases, dividends will grow faster than earnings. In contrast, if the firm reduces its payout ratio, dividends will grow slower than earnings for a period of time. Because there is a limit to how long this difference in growth rates can continue, most investors make the assumption that the long-run dividend payout ratio is fairly stable. Therefore, analysis of the growth rate of dividends typically concentrates on an analysis of the growth rate of equity earnings.

When a firm retains earnings and acquires additional assets, if it earns some positive rate of return on these additional assets, the total earnings of the firm will increase because its asset base is larger. How rapidly earnings increase depends on (1) the proportion of earnings it retains and reinvests in new assets and (2) the rate of return it earns on these new assets. Specifically, the growth rate (g) of equity earnings (i.e., earnings per share) without any external financing is equal to the percentage of net earnings retained (the retention rate, which equals 1 − the payout ratio) times the rate of return on equity capital.

$$g = \text{(Retention Rate)} \times \text{(Return on Equity)}$$
$$= \text{RR} \times \text{ROE}$$

Therefore, a firm can increase its growth rate by increasing its retention rate (reducing its payout ratio) and investing these added funds at its historic ROE. Alternatively, the firm can maintain its retention rate but increase its ROE. For example, if a firm retains 50

---

[13] For a thorough analysis of exchange rate determination and forecasting models, see Michael Rosenberg, *Currency Forecasting* (Burr Ridge, IL: Irwin Professional Publishing, 1996).

percent of net earnings and consistently has an ROE of 10 percent, its net earnings will grow at the rate of 5 percent a year, as follows:

$$g = RR \times ROE$$
$$= .50 \times .10$$
$$= .05.$$

If, however, the firm increases its retention rate to 75 percent and invests these additional funds in internal projects that earn 10 percent, its growth rate will increase to 7.5 percent, as follows:

$$g = .75 \times .10$$
$$= .075.$$

If, instead, the firm continues to reinvest 50 percent of its earnings, but derives a higher rate of return on these investments, say 15 percent, it can likewise increase its growth rate, as follows:

$$g = .50 \times .15$$
$$= .075.$$

BREAKDOWN OF ROE   Although the retention rate is a management decision, changes in the firm's ROE result from changes in its operating performance or its financial leverage. As discussed in Chapter 12, we can divide the ROE ratio into three components:

$$ROE = \frac{\text{Net Income}}{\text{Sales}} \times \frac{\text{Sales}}{\text{Total Assets}} \times \frac{\text{Total Assets}}{\text{Equity}}$$
$$= \frac{\text{Profit}}{\text{Margin}} \times \frac{\text{Total}}{\text{Asset Turnover}} \times \frac{\text{Financial}}{\text{Leverage}}$$

This breakdown allows us to consider the three factors that determine a firm's ROE.[14] Because it is a multiplicative relationship, an increase in any of the three ratios will cause an increase in ROE. Two of the three ratios reflect operating performance and one indicates a firm's financing decision.

The first operating ratio, net profit margin, indicates the firm's profitability on sales. This ratio changes over time for some companies and is very sensitive to the business cycle. For growth companies, this is one of the first ratios to decline as increased competition forces price cutting, thus reducing profit margins. Also, during recessions profit margins decline because of price cutting or because of higher percentages of fixed costs due to lower sales.

The second component, total asset turnover, is the ultimate indicator of operating efficiency and reflects the asset and capital requirements of the business. Although this ratio varies dramatically by industry, within an industry it is an excellent indicator of management's operating efficiency.

The final component, total assets/equity, does not measure operating performance, but rather financial leverage. Specifically, it indicates how management has decided to finance

---

[14] You will recall from Chapter 12 (Table 12.8) that it is possible to employ an extended DuPont system that involves eight ratios. For purposes of this discussion, the three ratios indicate the significant differences among countries.

the firm. This management decision regarding the financing of assets has financial risk implications for the stockholder.

Knowing this breakdown of ROE, you must examine past results and expectations for a firm and develop *estimates* of the three components and therefore an estimate of a firm's ROE. This estimate of ROE combined with the firm's retention rate will indicate its growth potential. This breakdown of ROE will be employed extensively in the market-industry-company analysis chapters.

ESTIMATING DIVIDEND GROWTH FOR FOREIGN STOCKS

The underlying factors that determine the growth rates for foreign stocks are similar to those for U.S. stocks, but the value of the equation's components may differ substantially from what is common in the United States. The differences in the retention rate or the components of ROE result from differences in accounting practices as well as alternative management performance or philosophy.

RETENTION RATES   The retention rates for foreign corporations differ within countries, but there are also differences among countries due to differences in the country's investment opportunities. As an example, firms in Japan have a higher retention rate than firms in the United States, whereas the rate of retention in France is much lower. Therefore, you need to examine the retention rates for a number of firms in a country as a background for estimating the standard rate within a country.

NET PROFIT MARGIN   The net profit margin of foreign firms can differ because of different accounting conventions between countries. Foreign accounting rules may allow firms to recognize revenue and allocate expenses differently from U.S. firms. For example, German firms are allowed to build up large reserves for various reasons. As a result, they report very low earnings for tax purposes. Also, different foreign depreciation practices require adjustment of earnings and cash flows.

TOTAL ASSET TURNOVER   Total asset turnover can likewise differ among countries because of different accounting conventions on the reporting of asset value at cost or market values. For example, in Japan a large part of the market values for some firms comes from their real estate holdings and their common stock investments in other firms. These assets are reported at cost, which typically has substantially understated their true value. This also means that the total asset turnover ratio for these firms is substantially overstated.

TOTAL ASSET/EQUITY RATIO   This ratio, a measure of financial leverage, differs among countries because of differences in economic environments, tax laws, management philosophies regarding corporate debt, and accounting conventions. In several countries, the attitude toward debt is much more liberal than in the United States. A prime example is Japan, where debt as a percentage of total assets is almost 50 percent higher than a similar ratio in the United States. Notably, most corporate debt in Japan entails borrowing from banks at fairly low rates of interest. Balance sheet debt ratios may be higher in Japan than in the United States or other countries, but because of the lower interest rates in Japan, the fixed-charge coverage ratios such as the times interest earned ratio might be similar to those in other countries. The point is, it is important to consider the several cash flow financial risk ratios along with the balance sheet debt ratios.

Consequently, when analyzing a foreign stock market or an individual foreign stock, when you estimate the growth rate for earnings and dividends you must consider the three components of the ROE just as you would for a U.S. stock. You must recognize that the financial ratios for foreign firms can differ from those of U.S. firms, as discussed in Chapter 12. Subsequent chapters on stock valuation applied to the aggregate market, various industries, and companies contain examples of these differences.

Summary

- As an investor, you want to select investments that will provide a rate of return that compensates you for your time, the expected rate of inflation, and the risk involved. To help you find these investments, this chapter considers the theory of valuation by which you derive the value of an investment using your required rate of return. We consider the two investment decision processes, which are the top-down, three-step approach or the bottom-up, stockpicking approach. We argue that a preferable approach is the top-down, three-step approach in which you initially consider the aggregate economy and market, then examine alternative industries, and finally analyze individual firms and their stocks.
- We apply the valuation theory to a range of investments including bonds, preferred stock, and common stock. In all instances where we use several different valuation models, the investment decision rule is always the same: if the estimated value of the investment is greater than the market price, you should buy the investment; if the estimated value of an investment is less than its market price, you should not invest in it.
- We conclude with a review of factors that you consider when estimating your required rate of return on an investment and the growth rate of earnings and dividends. Finally, we consider some unique factors that affect the estimation and application of these valuation models to foreign stocks.

Questions

1. Discuss the difference between the top-down and bottom-up approaches. What is the major assumption that causes the difference in these two approaches?
2. What is the benefit of analyzing the market and alternative industries before individual securities?
3. Discuss why you would not expect all industries to have a similar relationship to the economy. Give an example of two industries that have different relationships to the economy.
4. Discuss why estimating the value for a bond is easier than estimating the value for common stock.
5. Would you expect the required rate of return for a U.S. investor in U.S. common stocks to be the same as the required rate of return on Japanese common stocks? What factors would determine the required rate of return for stocks in these countries?
6. Would you expect the nominal RFR in the United States to be the same as in Germany? Discuss your reasoning.
7. Would you expect the risk premium for an investment in an Indonesian stock to be the same as a stock from the United Kingdom? Discuss your reasoning.
8. Would you expect the risk premium for an investment in a stock from Singapore to be the same as a stock from the United States? Discuss your reasoning.

Problems

1. What is the value to you of a 14 percent coupon bond with a par value of $10,000 that matures in 10 years if you want a 12 percent return? Use semiannual compounding.
2. What would the value of the bond in Problem 1 be if you wanted a 16 percent rate of return?
3. The preferred stock of the Clarence Biotechnology Company has a par value of $100 and a $9 dividend rate. You require an 11 percent rate of return on this stock. What is the maximum price you would pay for it? Would you buy it at a market price of $96?
4. The Baron Basketball Company (BBC) earned $10 a share last year and paid a dividend of $6 a share. Next year, you expect BBC to earn $11 and continue its payout ratio. Assume that you expect to be able to sell the stock for $132 a year from now. If you require 14 percent on this stock, how much would you be willing to pay for it?
5. Given the expected earnings and dividend payments in Problem 4, if you expected a selling price of $110 and required a 10 percent return on this investment, how much would you pay for the BBC stock?

6. Over the very long run, you expect dividends for BBC to grow at 8 percent and you require 12 percent on the stock. Using the infinite period DDM, how much would you pay for this stock?

7. Based on new information regarding the popularity of basketball, you revise your growth estimate for BBC to 10 percent. What is the maximum P/E ratio you will apply to BBC, and what is the maximum price you will pay for the stock?

8. The Shamrock Dogfood Company (SDC) has consistently paid out 40 percent of its earnings in dividends. The company's return on equity is 16 percent. What would you estimate as its dividend growth rate?

9. Given the low risk in dog food, your required rate of return on SDC is 13 percent. What P/E ratio would you apply to the firm's earnings?

10. What P/E ratio would you apply if you learned that SDC had decided to increase its payout to 50 percent?

11. Discuss three ways a firm can increase its ROE. Make up an example to illustrate your discussion.

12. It is widely known that grocery chains have very low profit margins—on average they earn about 1 percent on sales. How would you explain the fact that their ROE is about 12 percent? Does this seem logical?

13. Compute a recent 5-year average of the following ratios for three companies of your choice (attempt to select diverse firms):
   a. Retention rate
   b. Net profit margin
   c. Equity turnover
   d. Total asset turnover
   e. Total assets/equity.
   Based on these ratios, explain which firm should have the highest growth rate of earnings.

14. You have been reading about the Pear Computer Company (PCC), which currently retains 90 percent of its earnings ($5 a share this year). It earns an ROE of almost 40 percent. Assuming a required rate of return of 16 percent, how much would you pay for PCC on the basis of the earnings multiplier model? Discuss your answer. What would you pay for Pear Computer if its retention rate was 60 percent and its ROE was 19 percent? Show your work.

15. Gentry Can Company's (GCC) latest annual dividend of $1.25 a share was paid yesterday and maintained its historic 7 percent annual rate of growth. You plan to purchase the stock today because you believe that the dividend growth rate will increase to 8 percent for the next three years and the selling price of the stock will be $40 per share at the end of that time.
   a. How much should you be willing to pay for the GCC stock if you require a 14 percent return?
   b. What is the maximum price you should be willing to pay for the GCC stock if you feel that the 8 percent growth rate can be maintained indefinitely and you require a 14 percent return?
   c. If the 8 percent rate of growth is achieved, what will the price be at the end of Year 3, assuming the conditions in Problem 15b?

16. In the *Federal Reserve Bulletin,* find the average yield of AAA and BBB bonds for a recent month. Compute the risk premium (in basis points) and the percentage risk premium on BBB bonds relative to AAA bonds. Discuss how these values compare to those shown in Figures 13.2 and 13.3.

References

Benesh, Gary A. and Pamela P. Peterson. "On the Relation Between Earnings Changes, Analysts' Forecasts and Stock Price Fluctuations." *Financial Analysts Journal* 42, no. 6 (November–December 1986).

Bhatia, Sanjiv, ed. *Global Equity Investing.* Proceedings of a seminar by the Association of Investment Management and Research. Charlottesville, VA: AIMR, December 1, 1995.

Billingsley, Randall, ed. *Corporate Financial Decision Making and Equity Analysis.* Proceedings of a seminar by the Association of Investment Management and Research. Charlottesville, VA: AIMR, January 18, 1995.

Farrell, James L. "The Dividend Discount Model: A Primer." *Financial Analysts Journal* 41, no. 6 (November–December 1985).

Fogler, H. Russell, ed. *Blending Quantitative and Traditional Equity Analysis.* Proceedings of a seminar by the Association of Investment Management and Research. Charlottesville, VA: AIMR, March 31, 1994.

Gastineau, Gary L. and Sanjiv Bhatia, eds. *Risk Management.* Proceedings of a seminar by the Association of Investment Management and Research. Charlottesville, VA: AIMR, October 10, 1995.

Levine, Sumner N., ed. *The Financial Analysts Handbook.* 2d ed. Homewood, IL: Dow Jones-Irwin, 1988.

Nagorniak, John J. "Thoughts on Using Dividend Discount Models." *Financial Analysts Journal* 41, no. 6 (November–December 1985).

Sharpe, William and Katrina Shernard, eds. *Quantifying the Market Risk Premium Phenomenon for Investment Decision Making.* Proceedings of a seminar by the Association of Investment Management and Research. Charlottesville, VA: AIMR, September 26, 1989.

Shaked, Israel. "International Equity Markets and the Investment Horizon." *Journal of Portfolio Management* 11, no. 2 (Winter 1985).

Squires, Jan, ed. *Value and Growth Styles in Equity Investing.* Proceedings of a seminar by the Association of Investment Management and Research. Charlottesville, VA: AIMR, February 15, 1995.

Vandell, Robert F. and Jerry L. Stevens. "Evidence of Superior Performance from Timing." *Journal of Portfolio Management* 15, no. 3 (Spring 1989).

Wagner, Jerry, Steven Shellans, and Richard Paul. "Market Timing Works Where It Matters Most . . . in the Real World." *Journal of Portfolio Management* 18, no. 4 (Summer 1992).

Chapter 13
APPENDIX

Derivation of Constant Growth Dividend Discount Model (DDM)

The basic model is

$$P_0 = \frac{D_1}{(1 + k)^1} + \frac{D_2}{(1 + k)^2} + \frac{D_3}{(1 + k)^3} + \cdots + \frac{D_n}{(1 + k)^n}$$

where

P_0 = current price
D_i = expected dividend in period i
k = required rate of return on asset j.

If growth rate (g) is constant,

$$P_0 = \frac{D_0(1 + g)^1}{(1 + k)^1} + \frac{D_0(1 + g)^2}{(1 + k)^2} + \cdots + \frac{D_0(1 + g)^n}{(1 + k)^n} \, .$$

This can be written

$$P_0 = D_0 \left[\frac{(1 + g)}{(1 + k)} + \frac{(1 + g)^2}{(1 + k)^2} + \frac{(1 + g)^3}{(1 + k)^3} + \cdots + \frac{(1 + g)^n}{(1 + k)^n} \right] .$$

Multiply both sides of the equation by $\dfrac{1+k}{1+g}$:

$$\left[\dfrac{(1+k)}{(1+g)}\right] P_0 = D_0 \left[1 + \dfrac{(1+g)}{(1+k)} + \dfrac{(1+g)^2}{(1+k)^2} + \ldots + \dfrac{(1+g)^{n-1}}{(1+k)^{n-1}} \right].$$

Subtract the previous equation from this equation:

$$\left[\dfrac{(1+k)}{(1+g)} - 1\right] P_0 = D_0 \left[1 - \dfrac{(1+g)^n}{(1+k)^n} \right]$$

$$\left[\dfrac{(1+k)-(1+g)}{(1+g)}\right] P_0 = D_0 \left[1 - \dfrac{(1+g)^n}{(1+k)^n} \right].$$

Assuming $k > g$, as $N \to \infty$, the term in brackets on the right side of the equation goes to 1, leaving:

$$\left[\dfrac{(1+k)-(1+g)}{(1+g)}\right] P_0 = D_0.$$

This simplifies to

$$\left[\dfrac{(1+k)-(1-g)}{(1+g)}\right] P_0 = D_0.$$

which equals

$$\left[\dfrac{k-g}{(1+g)}\right] P_0 = D_0.$$

This equals

$$(k-g)P_0 = D_0(1+g)$$
$$D_0(1+g) = D_1$$

so:

$$(k-g)P_0 = D_1$$
$$P_0 = \dfrac{D_1}{k-g}.$$

Remember, this model assumes

- A constant growth rate
- An infinite time period
- The required return on the investment (k) is greater than the expected growth rate (g).

Chapter
14

The Analysis of Alternative Economies and Security Markets: The Global Asset Allocation Decision

This chapter answers the following questions:

- What are the expected and the empirical relationships between economic activity and security markets?
- What is the macroeconomic approach to estimating future market returns?
- What are the major macroeconomic techniques used to project the securities market?
- What is the leading economic indicator approach? What are its uses and shortcomings, and can it be used to predict stock prices?
- What are the expected and the empirical relationships between the growth of the money supply and stock prices?
- What is meant by excess liquidity, how is it measured, and what is its relationship to stock prices in the United States and around the world?
- What are the expected and the empirical relationships between inflation, interest rates, and bond prices?
- What are the expected and the empirical relationships between inflation and stock prices?
- When analyzing world security markets, what is the relationship between inflation and interest rates in alternative countries? What is the effect of inflation and interest rates on exchange rates?
- How do the basic valuation variables differ among countries?
- How do stock price returns among countries correlate when considering domestic returns and returns in U.S. dollars?
- What factors should be considered when analyzing the outlook for a foreign economy and its stock and bond market?
- What is the asset allocation procedure for a global portfolio?
- For a world asset allocation, what is meant by normal weighting, underweighting, and overweighting?

In Chapter 13, we introduced the three-step investment process and found that, although we are ultimately interested in securities markets, we analyze economies because of the strong link between the overall economic environment and the performance of security markets. *Security markets reflect what is going on in an economy* because the value of an investment is determined by its expected cash flows and its required rate of return, and both of these factors are influenced by the aggregate economic environment. Therefore, if you want to estimate cash flows, interest rates, and risk premiums for securities, you need to consider aggregate economic analysis.

From this interrelated economic–security market perspective, we initiate discussion of the investment process in this chapter by examining various techniques that relate economic variables to security markets. The first section discusses in detail the expected relationship between economic activity and the security markets and provides empirical evidence of this relationship. Given this documented empirical relationship, we discuss several techniques that are part of this approach, including the use of leading economic indicators, the analysis of money supply growth, and other measures of monetary conditions. Following from the analysis of monetary liquidity, we consider the effect of inflation on interest rates, bond prices, and stock returns.

Although most of the discussion focuses on the U.S. economy, we recognize the need to apply these techniques to other countries. To provide insights into this global investment process, we discuss an example of global investment analysis by an investment firm. The culmination of this analysis is a global asset allocation of investment funds among countries and further allocation within countries to specific asset classes: bonds, stocks, and cash equivalents.

In Chapter 13, we also discussed the importance of analyzing the general economy as part of arriving at an estimate of future aggregate market values that imply future returns from investing in common stocks and/or bonds. Three major techniques are available for analyzing securities markets. First is the *macroeconomic approach,* which attempts to project the outlook for securities markets based on an understanding of the underlying relationship between the aggregate economy and the securities markets. Second is the *microanalysis approach,* which involves using the dividend discount model discussed in Chapter 13 to estimate a value for the aggregate stock market. Finally, the *technical analysis approach* assumes that the best way to determine future changes in security market values is to examine past movements in interest rates, security prices, and other market variables.

This chapter discusses the macroeconomic approach to security market analysis and considers the asset allocation decision that flows from this analysis. Chapter 18 presents the microanalysis of the security markets, and technical analysis techniques are discussed and demonstrated in Chapter 21.

ECONOMIC ACTIVITY AND SECURITY MARKETS

Fluctuations in security markets are related to changes in the aggregate economy. The price of most bonds is determined by the level of interest rates, which are influenced by overall economic activity and Federal Reserve policy. The price of a firm's stock reflects investor expectations about an issuing firm's performance in terms of earnings, cash flow, and the investor's required rate of return. This performance is likewise affected by the overall performance of the economy.

In its monitoring of business cycles, the National Bureau of Economic Research (NBER) has amassed substantial evidence that supports the relationship between security prices and economic behavior. Based on the relationship of alternative economic series to the behavior of the entire economy, the NBER has classified numerous economic series into three groups: leading, coincident, and lagging indicator series. Further, extensive analysis of the relationship between the economy and the stock market has shown that the consistency of this relationship makes stock prices one of the better leading indicator series.

The evidence indicates a strong relationship between stock prices and the economy, and shows that stock prices consistently turn *before* the economy does.[1] The data in Table 14.1 document this relationship, beginning in the 1950s. Although this overall leading relation-

---

[1] A detailed analysis of this relationship is contained in Geoffrey H. Moore and John P. Cullity, "Security Markets and Business Cycles," *The Financial Analysts Handbook,* 2d ed., edited by Sumner N. Levine (Homewood, IL: Dow Jones-Irwin, 1988). Also see Jeremy J. Siegel, "Does It Pay Stock Investors to Forecast the Business Cycle?" *Journal of Portfolio Management* 18, no. 1 (Fall, 1991).

| TABLE 14.1 | TIMING RELATIONSHIPS BETWEEN STOCK MARKET AND BUSINESS CYCLE PEAKS AND TROUGHS |

I. Stock Market Declines Associated with a Subsequent Recession

STOCK MARKET CYCLES[a]				BUSINESS CYCLES				LEAD OF STOCK MARKET OVER BUSINESS CYCLE[a]	
Peak		Trough		Peak		Trough		Peak	Trough
Jan.	1953	Sep.	1953	Jul.	1953	May	1954	6.0	8.0
Aug.	1956	Oct.	1957	Aug.	1957	Apr.	1958	11.0	6.0
Aug.	1959	Oct.	1960	Apr.	1960	Feb.	1961	8.0	4.0
Nov.	1968	May	1970	Dec.	1969	Nov.	1970	12.0	6.0
Jan.	1973	Oct.	1974	Nov.	1973	Mar.	1975	10.0	5.0
Feb.	1980	Aug.	1982	Jan.	1980	Nov.	1982	(1.0)	3.0
							Average	7.7	5.3

II. False Signals

Dec.	1961	Jan.	1962
Apr.	1971	Nov.	1971
Sep.	1976	Mar.	1978

III. Stock Market Declines Associated with a Subsequent Growth Recession

Feb.	1966	Mar.	1968

[a]Defined as market declines of approximately 15 percent or more.

Source: Jason Benderly and Edward McKelvey, "The Pocket Chartbook" (*Economic Research,* Goldman, Sachs & Co.) December 1987. Reprinted by permission of Goldman, Sachs & Co.

ship appears to hold, the data also show several instances of false signals given by the stock market.

There are two possible reasons why stock prices lead the economy. One is that stock prices reflect *expectations* of earnings, dividends, and interest rates. As investors attempt to estimate these future variables, their stock price decisions reflect expectations for *future* economic activity, not current activity. A second possible reason is that the stock market is known to react to various leading indicator series, the most important being corporate earnings, corporate profit margins, interest rates, and changes in the growth rate of the money supply. Because these series tend to lead the economy, when investors adjust stock prices to reflect these leading economic series, it makes stock prices a leading series as well.

Because stock prices lead the aggregate economy, our macroeconomic approach to market analysis concentrates on economic series that lead the economy by more than stock prices do. First, we discuss cyclical indicator approaches developed by various research groups. These include the cyclical indicator approach of the NBER and the *Business Week* leading indicator series, along with several leading series developed by the Center for International Business Cycle Research (CIBCR) at Columbia University. Next, we consider a very popular leading series, the money supply, as well as other measures of monetary liquidity. Finally, we discuss the research related to a number of economic series expected to affect security returns (e.g., production, inflation, and risk premiums).

CYCLICAL INDICATOR APPROACH TO FORECASTING THE ECONOMY

The *cyclical indicator approach* to forecasting the economy is based on the belief that the aggregate economy expands and contracts in discernible periods. This view of the economy has been investigated by the NBER, a nonprofit organization that attempts to interpret important economic facts scientifically and impartially. The NBER explains the business cycle as follows:

TABLE 14.2	ECONOMIC SERIES IN THE NBER LEADING INDICATOR GROUP			
		Median Lead (−) or Lag (+) (in months)		
		Peaks	Troughs	All Turns
	1. Average weekly hours of production workers (manufacturing)	−2	−3	−3
	2. Average weekly initial claims for unemployment insurance (inverted)	−5	−1	−3
	3. Manufacturers' new orders in 1982 dollars, consumer goods, and materials	−2	−2	−2
	4. Contracts and orders for plant and equipment in 1982 dollars	−5	+1	−2½
	5. Index of raw private housing units authorized by local building permits	−9	−6	−7
	6. Index of stock prices, 500 common stocks	−4	−4	−4
	7. M2 money supply in 1982 dollars	−5	−4	−5
	8. Vendor performance (percentage of firms receiving slower deliveries)	−3	−4	−3
	9. Change in sensitive materials, prices smoothed	−4	−8	−5½
	10. Changes in business and consumer credit outstanding	−4	−6	−5
	11. Changes in manufacturing and trade inventories on hand and on order in 1982 dollars	−2	0	−1½

Source: Geoffrey H. Moore, "The Leading Indicator Approach—Value, Limitations, and Future," presented at Annual Western Economic Association Meeting (June 1984), revised June 1986; and Marie P. Hertzberg and Barry A. Beckman, "Business Cycle Indicators: Revised Composite Indexes," *Business Conditions Digest* 17, no. 1 (January 1989).

> The business cycle concept has been developed from the sequence of events discerned in the historical study of the movements of economic activity. Though there are many cross-currents and variations in the pace of business activity, periods of business expansion appear to cumulate to peaks. As they cumulate, contrary forces tend to gain strength, bringing about a reversal in business activity and the onset of a recession. As a recession continues, forces for an expansion gradually emerge until they become dominant and a recovery begins.[2]

The NBER examined the behavior of hundreds of economic time series in relation to past business cycles. (Recall that a time series reports the values for an economic variable over time, such as the monthly industrial production value for the period 1980–1996.) Based on this analysis, the NBER grouped various economic series into three major categories based on their relationship to the business cycle. The initial list of economic series that could predict turns in the economy was compiled in 1938, and it has undergone numerous revisions over the years. The most recent major revision occurred in 1983 with modifications in 1987 and 1993.[3]

CYCLICAL INDICATOR CATEGORIES   The first category, **leading indicators** of the business cycle, includes economic series that usually reach peaks or troughs before corresponding peaks or troughs in aggregate economic activity. The group currently includes the 11 series shown in Table 14.2, which indicates the median lead or lag for each series relative to business cycle peaks or troughs. One of the 11 leading economic series is common stock prices, which has a median lead of

---

[2] Julius Shiskin, "Business Cycle Indicators: The Known and the Unknown," *Review of the International Statistical Institute* 31, no. 3 (1963): 361–383.

[3] For a discussion of these changes, see Marie P. Hertzberg and Barry A. Beckman, "Business Cycle Indicators: Revised Composite Indexes," *Business Conditions Digest* (January 1989): 291–296; and David Wassel, "Leading Index to Be Prepared by New Method," *The Wall Street Journal*, November 23, 1993, A3.

4 months at peaks and troughs. Another leading series, the money supply in constant (1982) dollars, has a median lead of 5 months at peaks and 4 months at troughs.

The second category, **coincident indicators,** includes economic time series that have peaks and troughs that roughly coincide with the peaks and troughs in the business cycle. The bureau uses many of these economic time series to help define the different phases of the cycle.

The third category, **lagging indicators,** includes series that experience their peaks and troughs after those of the aggregate economy. A listing and the average timing relationships for the coincident and lagging series are listed in Table 14.3.

A final category, *selected series,* includes economic series that are expected to influence aggregate economic activity but do not fall neatly into one of the three main groups. This includes U.S. balance of payments, federal surplus or deficit, and military contract awards.

COMPOSITE SERIES AND RATIO OF SERIES   In addition to the individual economic series in each category, a composite time series combines these economic series—the *composite leading indicator index.* This composite leading indicator series is widely reported in the press each month as an indicator of the current and future state of the economy. There also are composite coincident and lagging indicator series.

Some analysts have used a *ratio* of these composite series, contending that the ratio of the composite coincident series divided by the composite lagging series acts like a leading series, in some instances even leading the composite leading series. The rationale for expecting this leading relationship for the ratio is that the coincident series should turn before the lagging series, and the ratio of the two series will be quite sensitive to such changes. As a result, this ratio series is expected to lead both of the individual component series, especially at turning points.

Although movements for this ratio series tend to be parallel to those of the leading series, its real value comes when it diverges from the pure leading indicator series

TABLE 14.3

ECONOMIC SERIES IN THE NBER COINCIDENT AND LAGGING INDICATOR SERIES

	MEDIAN LEAD (−) OR LAG (+) (IN MONTHS)		
	Peaks	Troughs	All Turns
A. Coincident Indicator Series			
1. Employees on nonagricultural payrolls	−2	0	0
2. Personal income less transfer payments in 1982 dollars	0	− 1	− ½
3. Index of industrial production	−3	0	− ½
4. Manufacturing and trade sales in 1982 dollars	−3	0	− ½
B. Lagging Indicator Series			
1. Average duration of unemployment in weeks (inverted)	+1	+ 8	+ 3½
2. Ratio of manufacturing and trade inventories to sales in 1982 dollars	+2	+ 3	+ 3
3. Average prime rate charged by banks	+4	+14	+ 5
4. Commercial and industrial loans outstanding in 1982 dollars	+2	+ 5	+ 4
5. Ratio of consumer installment credit outstanding to personal income	+6	+ 7	+ 7
6. Labor cost per unit of output in manufacturing, actual data as percentage of trend	+8½	+11	+10

Source: Moore, "The Leading Indicator Approach"; and Hertzberg and Beckman, "Business Cycle Indicators."

because this signals a change in the normal relationship between the indicator series. For example, if the leading indicator series has been rising for a period of time, you would expect both the coincident and lagging series also to be rising, but the coincident series should be rising faster than the lagging series, so the ratio of the coincident to the lagging series should likewise be rising. In contrast, assume the leading indicator series is rising, but the ratio of coincident to lagging series is flattening out or declining. This change in trend in the ratio series could occur because the coincident series is not rising as fast as the lagging indicator series, or because the coincident series has turned down. Either scenario would indicate a possible end to an economic expansion or at least a less robust expansion.

An example of such a divergence appears in Figure 14.1. The pattern indicates that between 1991 and mid-1994, the ratio series increased at a faster rate than the leading series because the coincident series was rising while the lagging series declined. It appears that both the ratio series and the leading series experienced softness during 1995.

FIGURE 14.1   **INDICATOR SERIES PERFORMANCE**

Source: "Investment Strategy Highlights" (New York: Goldman, Sachs & Co., May 1996). Reprinted by permission of Goldman, Sachs & Co.

ANALYTICAL MEASURES OF PERFORMANCE

When predicting the future based on an economic series, it is important to consider more than the behavior of the series alone. The NBER has devised certain analytical measures for examining behavior within an alternative economic series.

DIFFUSION INDEXES   As the name implies, *diffusion indexes* indicate how pervasive a given movement is in a series. Diffusion index values are measured by computing the percentage of reporting units in a series that indicate a given result. For example, if 100 companies constitute the sample reporting new orders for equipment, the diffusion index for this series would indicate what proportion of the 100 companies was reporting higher orders during an expansion. In addition to knowing that aggregate new orders are increasing, it is helpful to know whether 55 percent or 95 percent of the companies in the sample are reporting higher orders. This information on the pervasiveness of the increase in new orders would help you project the future length and strength of an expansion.

You also would want to know past diffusion index values to determine the prevailing *trend* for this index. The diffusion index for a series almost always reaches its peak or trough before the peak or trough in the corresponding aggregate series. Therefore, you can use the diffusion index for a series to predict the behavior of the series itself. Assume that you are interested in the leading series, Manufacturers New Orders in 1982 dollars—Consumer Goods. If the diffusion index for this series drops from 85 percent to 75 percent and then to 70 percent, it indicates a widespread receipt of new orders, but it also indicates a diminishing breadth to the increase and possibly an impending decline in the series itself.

Besides creating diffusion indexes for individual series, the NBER has derived a diffusion index that shows the percentage of the 11 leading indicators rising or falling during a given period. This particular diffusion index is widely reported each month as an indicator of the future state of the economy.

RATES OF CHANGE   Knowing whether a series is increasing is useful, but more helpful is knowing that a 7 percent increase one month followed a 10 percent increase the previous month. The point is, the series is growing, but at a declining rate. Similar to the diffusion index, the rate of change values for a series reaches peaks or troughs prior to the peak or trough in the aggregate series.

DIRECTION OF CHANGE   Direction of change tables show which series rose or fell (indicated by plus or minus signs) during the most recent period and how long the movement in this direction has persisted.

COMPARISON WITH PREVIOUS CYCLES   A set of tables and charts shows the movements of individual series during the current business cycle and compares these movements to previous cycles for the same economic series. This comparison reveals whether a given series is moving slower or faster, or more strongly or weakly, than during prior cycles. This information can be useful because, typically, movements in the initial months of an expansion or contraction indicate their ultimate length and strength.[4]

LIMITATIONS OF THE CYCLICAL INDICATOR APPROACH

The NBER consistently has attempted to improve the usefulness of the cyclical indicators while acknowledging some limitations. The most obvious limitation is false signals. Past patterns might suggest that current indicator values signal a contraction, but then the indicator series turns up again and nullifies previous signals. A similar problem occurs

---

[4] Monthly presentations of all the series and analytical measures previously appeared in the U.S. Department of Commerce publication *Business Conditions Digest*. The government stopped publishing the *Digest* in 1990. The data now appear in the *Survey of Current Business*.

when the indicators show hesitancy that is difficult to interpret. Some economic series may exhibit *high variability,* diminishing confidence in short-run signals as compared to projecting longer-term trends.

Another limitation is *the currency of the data* and *revisions.* The problem is that you might not get the original data very soon and then you have to be aware of subsequent revisions that may actually change the sign or direction of a series. Many of the series are seasonally adjusted, so you also must watch for changes in the seasonal adjustment factors.

Also, no series adequately reflects the service sector, which has grown to be a major factor in our economy. Further, no series represents the very important global economy or world securities markets. Similarly, the whole import–export sector is represented only in the "other series" group when, in fact, the export sector has been the fastest-growing sector of our economy in the 1990s. Finally, as the NBER points out, there are numerous political or international developments that significantly influence the economy, but these factors cannot be incorporated into a statistical system.[5]

LEADING INDICATORS AND STOCK PRICES

We now know that stock prices are part of a composite set of leading indicators. An interesting question is whether we can use the composite leading series without stock prices to predict stock prices. A study that considered this question specified the decision rule in terms of percentage changes in the composite series.[6] Comparing the results of this decision rule to those of a buy-and-hold policy indicated that as long as the analysts had perfect foresight regarding the correct percentage change to use, they beat a buy-and-hold policy. When they used the trading rule without foresight as to the best percentage change (merely using the percentage change that would have worked during the prior market cycle), they were not able to beat a buy-and-hold policy after subtracting commissions. Therefore, although these leading economic indicator series tend to lead the economy and can be used to predict aggregate economic activity, the composite leading indicator series does not consistently lead its own stock price component in a way that is useful for investment decisions.

OTHER LEADING INDICATOR SERIES

The NBER leading indicator series employs monthly data. The CIBCR at the Columbia Graduate School of Business has developed several additional leading indicator series.

BUSINESS WEEK LEADING INDICATOR SERIES   Developed by the CIBCR and published weekly in *Business Week,* the *Business Week Leading Indicator Series* includes seven individual series as shown in Figure 14.2 along with a chart for the leading indicator series and a weekly production series along with other weekly data on foreign exchange, prices, and interest rates. This composite weekly leading indicator index is meant to help you gauge upswings and declines in general economic activity. Downturns in the index have preceded every recession since 1948, but some downturns in the leading series have been followed only by slowdowns in the economy rather than recessions.

LONG-LEADING INDEX   The CIBCR also has developed its *Long-Leading Index* to provide earlier signals of major turning points in the economy than other leading indexes. It includes the following four series: (1) Dow Jones bond prices (20 bonds by percentage of

[5] Discussions of these problems are in Evan Koenig and Kenneth Emery, "Misleading Indicators? Using the Composite Leading Indicators to Predict Cyclical Turning Points," Federal Reserve Bank of Dallas *Economic Review* (July 1991): 1–14.

[6] Bryan Heathcotte and Vincent P. Apilado, "The Predictive Content of Some Leading Economic Indicators for Future Stock Prices," *Journal of Financial and Quantitative Analysis* 9, no. 2 (March 1974): 247–258.

FIGURE 14.2   **BUSINESS WEEK INDEX**

Business Week Index

PRODUCTION AND LEADING INDEXES

Change from last week: 0.4%
Change from last year: 1.4%

Change from last week: 0.0%
Change from last year: 2.5%

PRODUCTION INDEX
Feb. 24=125.2
1992=100

LEADING INDEX
Feb. 24=257.8
1967=100

Indexes are 4-week moving averages

The production index increased during the week ended Feb. 24. Before calculation of the four-week moving average, the index also rose, to 127.1, from 125.8. Seasonally adjusted output of autos, trucks, and rail-freight traffic posted gains for the latest week. **The leading index** was unchanged in the latest week. The unaveraged index was down a bit, to 257.1, from 258.2. A retrenchment in the stock market and higher bond yields suggest slower economic growth ahead.

BW production index copyright 1996 by The McGraw-Hill Companies   BW leading index copyright 1996 by CIBCR

PRODUCTION INDICATORS

	LATEST WEEK	WEEK AGO	YEARLY % CHG
STEEL (3/2) thous. of net tons	2,085	2,105r#	4.0
AUTOS (3/2) units	122,932	136,086r#	–16.3
TRUCKS (3/2) units	125,639	123,347r#	6.0
ELECTRIC POWER (3/2) millions of kilowatt-hrs.	60,553	59,905#	–0.3
CRUDE-OIL REFINING (3/2) thous. of bbl./day	13,794	13,533#	1.1
COAL (2/24) thous. of net tons	21,246#	21,641	–4.8
PAPERBOARD (2/24) thous. of tons	NA#	NA	NA
PAPER (2/24) thous. of tons	NA#	NA	NA
LUMBER (2/24) millions of ft.	450.2#	435.5	4.1
RAIL FREIGHT (2/24) billions of ton-miles	25.2#	25.2	2.0

Sources: American Iron & Steel Institute, *Ward's Automotive Reports*, Edison Electric Institute, American Petroleum Institute, Energy Dept., American Forest & Paper Association, WWPA[1], SFPA[2], Association of American Railroads

LEADING INDICATORS

	LATEST WEEK	WEEK AGO	YEARLY % CHG
STOCK PRICES (3/1) S&P 500	645.45	651.67	33.0
CORPORATE BOND YIELD, Aaa (3/1)	7.20%	7.13%	–11.7
INDUSTRIAL MATERIALS PRICES (3/1)	110.6	110.8	–2.2
BUSINESS FAILURES (2/23)	191	324	–43.8
REAL ESTATE LOANS (2/21) billions	$504.4	$507.3	8.0
MONEY SUPPLY, M2 (2/19) billions	$3,665.0	$3,657.0r	2.2
INITIAL CLAIMS, UNEMPLOYMENT (2/17) thous.	382	381r	11.0

Sources: Center for International Business Cycle Research (CIBCR), Standard & Poor's, *Journal of Commerce* (index: 1990=100), Dun & Bradstreet (failures of large companies), Federal Reserve, Labor Dept. CIBCR seasonally adjusts data on business failures and real estate loans.

PRICES

	LATEST WEEK	WEEK AGO	YEARLY % CHG
GOLD (3/6) $/troy oz.	393.600	397.550	4.0
STEEL SCRAP (3/5) #1 heavy, $/ton	144.50	144.50	2.1
COPPER (3/2) ¢/lb.	120.0	120.4	–12.1
ALUMINUM (3/2) ¢/lb.	74.3	76.0	–15.1
COTTON (3/2) strict low middling 1-1/16 in., ¢/lb.	80.28	81.33	–20.8
OIL (3/5) $/bbl.	19.54	19.63	4.9

Sources: London Wednesday final setting, Chicago market, *Metals Week*, Memphis market, NYMEX

INTEREST RATES

	LATEST WEEK	WEEK AGO	YEAR AGO
FEDERAL FUNDS (3/5)	5.13%	5.20%	5.93%
COMMERCIAL PAPER (3/6) 3-month	5.19	5.16	6.19
CERTIFICATES OF DEPOSIT (3/6) 3-month	5.17	5.16	6.20
FIXED MORTGAGE (3/1) 30-year	7.69	7.49r	8.72
ADJUSTABLE MORTGAGE (3/1) one-year	5.50	5.39	6.51
PRIME (3/6)	8.25	8.25	9.00

Sources: Federal Reserve, HSH Associates, Reuters Holdings PLC

FOREIGN EXCHANGE

	LATEST WEEK	WEEK AGO	YEAR AGO
JAPANESE YEN (3/6)	105.32	104.44	91.10
GERMAN MARK (3/6)	1.48	1.47	1.40
BRITISH POUND (3/6)	1.53	1.53	1.60
FRENCH FRANC (3/6)	5.05	5.02	4.99
ITALIAN LIRA (3/6)	1557.1	1547.5	1667.5
CANADIAN DOLLAR (3/6)	1.37	1.37	1.41
MEXICAN PESO (3/6)[3]	7.593	7.545	7.150

Sources: Major New York banks. Currencies expressed in units per U.S. dollar, except for British pound in dollars

#Raw data in the production indicators are seasonally adjusted in computing the BW index (chart); other components (estimated and not listed) include machinery and defense equipment.   1=Western Wood Products Assn.   2=Southern Forest Products Assn.   3=Free market value   NA=Not available   r=revised   NM=Not meaningful

Source: Reprinted from December 5, 1995, issue of *Business Week* by special permission, copyright © 1995 by The McGraw-Hill Companies.

face value); (2) the ratio of price to unit labor cost in manufacturing (1982 = 100); (3) M2 money supply, deflated (billion 1982 dollars); and (4) new housing building permits (1967 = 100). This index has anticipated recessions by 14 months, on average, and always by at least 7 months.

Monthly data for these series developed and maintained by the CIBCR are available in "The Leading Indicator Press Release." This release is published about the tenth day of each month with data as of 6 weeks prior to its release.

LEADING EMPLOYMENT INDEX The purpose of the CIBCR's *Leading Employment Index* (1967 = 100) is to forecast future changes in U.S. employment. It includes the following six component series:

1. Average workweek in manufacturing
2. Overtime hours in manufacturing
3. Percentage layoff rate (inverted)
4. Voluntary/involuntary part-time employment
5. Percentage short duration unemployment rate (inverted)
6. Initial claims for unemployment insurance (inverted)

LEADING INFLATION INDEX The CIBCR *Leading Inflation Index* is intended as a tool for forecasting inflation in the United States. It includes five variables:

1. The percentage employed of the working-age population
2. The growth rate of total debt (including business, consumer, and federal government debt)
3. The growth rate of industrial material prices
4. The growth rate of an index of import prices
5. The percentage of businesspeople anticipating an increase in their selling prices, as determined by a Dun and Bradstreet survey

The leads for this series during the period 1950 to 1995 averaged 7 months at troughs, 4 months at peaks, and 5 months at all turns.

ANALYSIS OF ALTERNATIVE LEADING INFLATION INDICATORS A study by Garner examined the usefulness of the CIBCR series and four other series that have been suggested as leading indicators of inflation, including the price of gold and other composite series.[7] The results indicate that the composite indicators provide useful early indications of inflation turning points. Unfortunately, none of the series provide accurate estimates of the magnitude of inflation.

INTERNATIONAL LEADING INDICATOR SERIES In addition to developing leading indicators for the U.S. economy, the CIBCR also has developed a set of composite leading indicators for eight other major industrial countries: Canada, Germany, France, the United Kingdom, Italy, Japan, Australia, and Taiwan (Republic of China). These International Leading Indicator Series are part of an ongoing project to develop an international economic indicator (IEI) system. The series are comparable in data and analysis to the leading series for the United States.[8]

SURVEYS OF SENTIMENT AND EXPECTATIONS Consumer expectations seem to play a role as the economy approaches turning points in the business cycle. Two surveys of consumer expectations are reported monthly in the financial media. The University of

[7]C. Alan Garner, "How Useful Are Leading Indicators of Inflation?" Federal Reserve Bank of Kansas City *Economic Review* 80, no. 2 (Second Quarter 1995): 5–18.

[8]For an extended discussion, see Geoffrey H. Moore, "An Introduction to International Economic Indicators," *Business Cycles, Inflation, and Forecasting*, 2d ed. (New York: National Bureau of Economic Research, Studies in Business Cycles, No. 24, 1983).

Michigan Consumer Sentiment Index and the Conference Board Consumer Confidence Index both query a sample of households on their expectations over the next six months (Conference Board) or over the next year (Michigan). Although their indexes sometimes deviate from each other month to month, over longer time periods they track each other fairly closely. Both indexes act as a leading indicator by rising and falling before the general level of economic activity does.

Other surveys of consumer and business expectations focus on the overall economy and some focus on areas such as firms' capital spending or inventory investment plans. By subscribing to proprietary services or closely following the financial media, investment analysts can monitor how consumers and the business community feel about the economy and their spending plans. In general, the more optimistic they are, the better the prospects for increases in spending and economic growth. The more pessimistic they are, the worse the prospects for spending and growth. The problem with survey data is that individuals' and firms' reported plans may not come to fruition. Just because a survey reports that manufacturing firms expect to increase capital spending by a certain percentage does not mean they will actually do so.

Economic statistics released by the government are another source of helpful information about current economic trends, particularly concerning various economic sectors. Every Monday, *The Wall Street Journal* publishes a short commentary, "Tracking the Economy." The feature reports statistics that will be released during the coming week (for example, housing starts, agricultural production, GDP), their previous values, and their consensus forecasts. As you would expect from our discussion of efficient markets, investors react to economic "surprises" wherein the actual results deviate from the consensus forecasts (expectations).

MONETARY VARIABLES, THE ECONOMY, AND STOCK PRICES

Many academic and professional observers hypothesize a close relationship between stock prices and various monetary variables that are influenced by monetary policy. The best-known monetary variable in this regard is the *money supply*. You will recall from your economics course that the money supply can be measured in several ways, including currency plus demand deposits (referred to as the M1 money supply), and the M1 money supply plus time deposits (referred to as the M2 money supply). The government publishes other measures of the money supply, but these are the best known.[9] The Federal Reserve controls the money supply through various tools, the most useful of which is open market operations.

MONEY SUPPLY AND THE ECONOMY

In their classic work on the monetary history of the United States, Friedman and Schwartz thoroughly documented the relationship between changes in the growth rate of the money supply and subsequent changes in the economy.[10] Specifically, they demonstrated that declines in the rate of growth of the money supply have preceded business contractions by an average of 20 months, while increases in the growth rate of the money supply have preceded economic expansions by about 8 months.

Friedman suggests a transmission mechanism through which changes in the growth rate of the money supply affect the aggregate economy. He hypothesizes that, to implement

[9] For a discussion of alternative monetary series, see John R. Walter, "Monetary Aggregates: A User's Guide," Federal Reserve Bank of Richmond *Economic Review* (January/February 1989): 53–61.

[10] Milton Friedman and Anna J. Schwartz, "Money and Business Cycles," *Review of Economics and Statistics* 45, no. 1, part 2, supplement (February 1963): 32–78, reprinted in Milton Friedman, *The Optimum Quantity of Money and Other Essays* (Chicago: Aldine Publishing, 1969), 189–235.

planned changes in monetary policy, the Federal Reserve engages in open market operations, buying or selling Treasury bonds to adjust bank reserves and, eventually, the money supply. Because the Fed deals in government bonds, the initial liquidity impact affects the government bond market creating excess liquidity for those who sold bonds to the Fed when the Federal Reserve was buying bonds, or there would be insufficient liquidity when the Federal Reserve sells bonds. Rising or falling government bond prices subsequently filter over to corporate bonds, and this change in liquidity eventually affects common stocks, and then the real goods market. The impact of money supply growth on stock prices is really part of the transmission process whereby money supply affects the aggregate economy. This liquidity transmission scenario implies that the initial effect of a change in monetary policy appears in financial markets (bonds and stocks) and only later in the aggregate economy.

Money Supply and Stock Prices

Numerous studies have tested the relationship suggested by this transmission mechanism. Specifically, do changes in the growth rate of the money supply precede changes in stock prices? The results of these studies have tended to change over time. The initial studies done in the 1960s and early 1970s generally indicated a strong *leading* relationship between money supply changes and stock prices.[11] Such results implied that changes in the growth rate of the money supply could serve as a leading indicator of stock price changes.

Subsequent studies have questioned these findings.[12] Although these studies have likewise typically found a relationship between the money supply and stock prices, the timing of the relationship differs. These more recent studies found that changes in the growth rate of the money supply did not lead stock prices but consistently *lagged* stock returns by about 1 to 3 months.

More recent studies examined the relationship of stock returns to anticipated and unanticipated money supply growth using weekly money supply data.[13] The results indicate that money changes affect stock prices, but the securities markets adjust stock prices very quickly to any unexpected changes in money supply growth. Therefore, to enjoy superior returns, it is necessary to *forecast unanticipated changes* in money supply growth.

EXCESS LIQUIDITY AND STOCK PRICES   Some analysts have looked beyond the growth rate of the money supply. Steven Einhorn of Goldman, Sachs & Co. contends that *excess liquidity* is the relevant monetary variable that influences stock prices.[14] Excess liquidity is defined as the year-to-year percentage change in the M2 money supply adjusted for small time deposits less the year-to-year percentage change in nominal GDP. It is reasoned that the growth rate of nominal GDP indicates the need for liquidity in the economy. If the

---

[11] Studies that generally support this view include Beryl W. Sprinkel, *Money and Markets: A Monetarist View* (Homewood, IL: Richard D. Irwin, 1971); Michael W. Keran, "Expectations, Money, and the Stock Market," Federal Reserve Bank of St. Louis *Review* 53, no. 1 (January 1971): 16–31; and Kenneth Homa and Dwight Jaffee, "The Study of Money and Stock Prices," *Journal of Finance* 26, no. 5 (December 1971): 1015–1066.

[12] These studies include Richard V. L. Cooper, "Efficient Capital Markets and the Quantity Theory of Money," *Journal of Finance* 29, no. 3 (June 1974): 887–908; and M. S. Rozeff, "Money and Stock Prices: Market Efficiency and the Lag Effect of Monetary Policy," *Journal of Financial Economics* 1, no. 3 (September 1974): 245–302.

[13] These studies are found in Lawrence S. Davidson and Richard T. Froyen, "Monetary Policy and Stock Returns: Are Stock Markets Efficient?" Federal Reserve Bank of St. Louis *Review* 64, no. 3 (March 1982): 3–12; and R. W. Hafer, "The Response of Stock Prices to Changes in Weekly Money and the Discount Rate," Federal Reserve Bank of St. Louis *Review* 64, no. 3 (March 1985): 5–14.

[14] Excess liquidity charts are contained in "Investment Strategy Chartbook," edited by Abby Joseph Cohen and Gabrielle Napolitano (New York: Goldman, Sachs & Co., quarterly).

| FIGURE 14.3 | TIME SERIES PLOT OF "EXCESS LIQUIDITY" IN THE UNITED STATES: 1985–1995 |

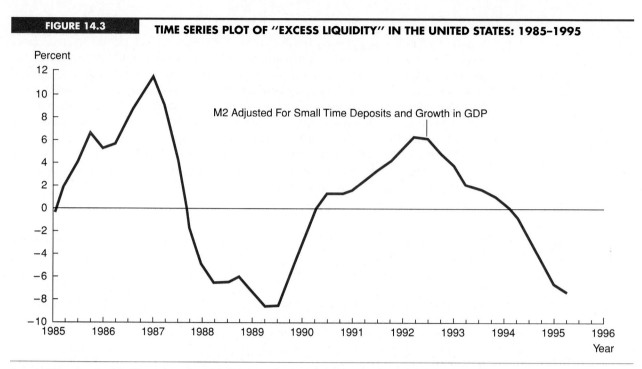

Source: Chart contained in "Investment Strategy Chartbook," Abby Joseph Cohen and Gabrielle Napolitano (New York: Goldman, Sachs & Co., October 1995).

money supply growth rate exceeds the GDP growth rate, this indicates there is excess money (liquidity) in the economy that is available for buying securities. Therefore, it is reasoned that positive excess liquidity should lead to higher security prices.

Figure 14.3 contains the time series plot of excess liquidity in the United States since 1985. As shown, it has been negative since early 1994, although stock prices have risen throughout 1995. This inconsistency could be caused by positive non-U.S. excess liquidity as shown in Figure 14.4. These figures reveal positive excess liquidity for Japan with negative excess liquidity in the United Kingdom and Germany both positive and negative. This non-U.S. liquidity helped the U.S. stock market continue to rise in 1995.

OTHER ECONOMIC VARIABLES AND STOCK PRICES

Chen, Roll, and Ross examined equity returns relative to a set of macroeconomic variables.[15] They found the following variables to be significant in explaining stock returns:

• Growth in industrial production
• Changes in the risk premium
• Twists in the yield curve
• Measures of unanticipated inflation
• Changes in expected inflation during periods of volatile inflation

The authors did not attempt to predict market returns, but suggested that these variables were important in explaining past returns.

---

[15] Nai-Fu Chen, Richard Roll, and Stephen A. Ross, "Economic Forces and the Stock Market," *Journal of Business* 59, no. 3 (July 1986).

FIGURE 14.4

TIME SERIES PLOT OF "EXCESS LIQUIDITY" IN GERMANY, JAPAN, AND THE UNITED KINGDOM: 1985–1995.

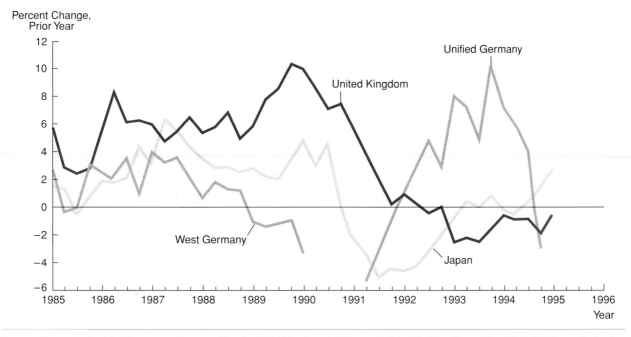

Source: Chart contained in "Investment Strategy Chartbook," Abby Joseph Cohen and Gabrielle Napolitano (New York: Goldman, Sachs & Co., October 1995).

INFLATION, INTEREST RATES, AND SECURITY PRICES   Because this chapter is concerned with the macroeconomic analysis of security markets, we should examine the macroeconomic impact of inflation and interest rates. We have noted throughout the book the critical role of expected inflation and nominal interest rates in determining the required rate of return used to derive the value of all investments. We would expect these variables that are very important in microeconomic valuation to also affect changes in the aggregate markets.

INFLATION AND INTEREST RATES   Figure 14.5 contains a plot of long-term interest rates and the year-to-year percentage change in the consumer price index (CPI, a measure of inflation). This graph demonstrates the strong relationship between inflation and interest rates. We contended in our earlier discussion that when investors anticipated an increase in the rate of inflation, they would increase their required rates of return by a similar amount to derive constant real rates of return. The time-series graph of the promised yield of Aaa corporate bonds and the annual rate of inflation in Figure 14.5 confirm the expected relationship, but also indicate an imperfect relationship between interest rates and inflation. If the relationship was perfect and investors were accurate in their predictions of future inflation, the difference between the interest rate and the inflation rate (the spread between them) would be fairly constant, reflecting the real return on corporate bonds. As shown, the spread between these two curves changes over time.

Figure 14.6 plots this spread and demonstrates the following results. Although the two curves generally move together, in some periods (1975, 1979 to 1980) the inflation rate

FIGURE 14.5

TIME-SERIES PLOT OF THE PROMISED YIELD OF MOODY'S Aaa CORPORATE BONDS AND INFLATION: MONTHLY 1974–1995

Data Source: Moody's Investor's Service.

exceeded the yield on the bonds, which implies that during these periods investors received *negative* real returns on corporate bonds. In contrast, during 1983 to 1985 the real rates of return on these bonds was in the 8 to 10 percent range, which clearly exceeds what most investors would expect on very low risk bonds.

This change in spread does not mean that there is not a relationship between inflation and interest rates; it only shows that *investors are not very good at predicting inflation.* Recall that the theoretical relationship is between *expected* inflation and interest rates, in contrast to these data that reflect actual inflation. Apparently, investors underestimated what the rate of inflation would be during the periods of negative real returns, and overestimated what the rate of inflation would be during periods when there were abnormally high real rates of return.

INTEREST RATES AND BOND PRICES   The relationship between interest rates and bond prices is clearly negative because the only variable that changes in the valuation model is the discount factor. The expected cash flows from a straight noncallable bond would not change. Therefore, an increase in interest rates will cause a decline in bond prices and a decline in interest rates will boost bond prices. For example, if you own a 10-year bond with a coupon of 10 percent, when interest rates go from 10 percent to 12 percent, the price of this bond will go from $1,000 (par) to $885. In contrast, if rates go from 10 percent to 8 percent, the price of the bond will go from $1,000 to $1,136.

FIGURE 14.6

SPREAD BETWEEN PROMISED YIELD OF MOODY'S Aaa CORPORATE BONDS AND INFLATION: MONTHLY 1974–1995

Data Source: Moody's Investor's Service.

The size of the price change will depend on the characteristics of the bond. A longer-term bond will experience a larger price change for a change in interest rates.[16] Therefore, we can anticipate a negative relationship between inflation and the rates of return on bonds because inflation generally has a direct effect on interest rates, and in turn interest rates have an inverse effect on bond prices and rates of return. One example of empirical verification for this negative relationship is provided in Table 3.9, which shows a correlation of −0.647 between inflation and returns on long-term investment-grade bonds.

INTEREST RATES AND STOCK PRICES   The relationship between interest rates and stock prices is not direct and consistent. The reason is that the cash flows from stocks can change along with interest rates, and we cannot be certain whether this change in cash flows will augment or offset the change in interest rates. To demonstrate this, consider the following potential scenarios following an increase in the rate of inflation:

1. Interest rates rise due to an increase in the rate of inflation and corporate earnings likewise increase because firms are able to increase prices in line with cost increases. In this case, stock prices might be fairly stable because the negative effect of an increase in the required rate of return is partially or wholly offset by the increase in the growth rate of earnings and dividends.
2. Interest rates increase, but expected cash flows change very little because firms are not able to increase prices in response to higher costs. This would cause a decline in stock prices similar to what happens with a bond. The required rate of return (k) would increase, but the growth rate of dividends (g) would be constant, that is, the k–g spread discussed in Chapter 13 will widen.

---

[16] Chapter 16 contains a detailed discussion of the specific variables that influence bond price volatility.

3. Interest rates increase while cash flows decline because the factors that cause the rise in interest rates have a negative impact on earnings. For example, during 1981 to 1982, interest rates increased and remained high during a period of economic decline, which caused sales and earnings to decline. Alternatively, one can envision a period of inflation wherein the costs of production increase, but many firms are not able to increase prices, which causes a decline in profit margins. The impact of this set of events can be disastrous. Given this scenario, stock prices will decline significantly because k will increase as g declines, causing a large increase in the k–g spread.

In contrast to these scenarios, you can envision a comparable set of scenarios when inflation and interest rates decline. The relationship between inflation, interest rates, and stock prices is not as direct or consistent as the relationship between interest rates and bonds. The effect of interest rate changes on stock prices will depend on what caused the change in interest rates and the effect of this event on the expected cash flows on common stock.

Notably, the actual relationship between inflation, interest rates, and stock prices is an empirical question and the effect varies over time. Therefore, although there has generally been a significant *negative* relationship between inflation, interest rates, and the returns on stocks, as shown in Chapter 3 (Table 3.9), this is not always true.[17] In addition, even when it is true for the overall market, certain industries or segments of the economy may have earnings and dividends that react positively to inflation and interest rate changes. In such an instance, their stock prices would be positively correlated with inflation and interest rates.[18]

SUMMARY OF MACROECONOMIC ANALYSIS

There is ample evidence of a strong and consistent relationship between economic activity and the stock market, although stock prices consistently seem to turn from 4 to 9 months before the economy does. Therefore, to project the future direction of the stock market using the macroeconomic approach, you must either forecast economic activity about 12 months ahead or examine economic indicator series that lead the economy by more than stock prices do.

The results with the leading indicator series indicated that only with perfect foresight regarding the appropriate change to use with a diffusion index of the leading indicator series could an investor improve on a buy-and-hold policy. The results from studies of the relationship between the money supply and stock prices have indicated a significant relationship, but recent research indicates that stock prices generally turn before the money supply does. Therefore, you *cannot* use the money supply series to develop a mechanical trading rule that will outperform a buy-and-hold policy.

Alternative measures of the monetary environment were also considered, including U.S. and global excess liquidity. Although the historical results with U.S. excess liquidity were interesting, recent results are not as consistent. Some cite global liquidity that has been

---

[17] A sample of studies on the topic of inflation and common stocks includes Frank K. Reilly, Glenn L. Johnson, and Ralph E. Smith, "Inflation, Inflation Hedges and Common Stocks," *Financial Analysts Journal* 26, no. 1 (January–February 1970): 104–110; Frank K. Reilly, "Companies and Common Stocks as Inflation Hedges," New York University, Center for the Study of Financial Institutions, *Bulletin* (April 1975); Jeffrey F. Jaffe and Gershon Mandelker, "The 'Fisher Effect' for Risky Assets: An Empirical Analysis," *Journal of Finance* 31, no. 2 (May 1976): 447–458; Eugene F. Fama, "Stock Returns, Real Activity, Inflation and Money," *American Economic Review* 71, no. 4 (September 1981).

[18] Studies that examined alternative industries as inflation hedges include Stephen P. Ferris and Anil K. Makhija, "A Search for Common Stock Inflation Hedges," *Review of Business and Economic Research* 22, no. 2 (Spring 1987): 27–36; and Frank K. Reilly, "Alternative Industries as Inflation Hedges," Financial Management Association Meeting (October 1987). Both studies found very few industries with positive correlations.

positive, and this global liquidity has had an impact on the U.S. capital markets. Such a global monetary effect is not surprising and emphasizes the need to consider global macroeconomic variables.

ANALYSIS OF WORLD SECURITY MARKETS

Although we have focused on the U.S. market to demonstrate the macroeconomic approach to forecasting movements in the securities markets, you must also consider a similar analysis for numerous foreign markets including those in Japan, Canada, the United Kingdom, and Germany. Although it is not feasible to analyze each of these markets in detail, we can provide an example of such an analysis by reviewing the extensive analysis done by Goldman, Sachs & Co. This analysis is contained in a monthly Goldman, Sachs publication, "World Investment Strategy Highlights," as part of the firm's international research effort. This publication draws on a number of other Goldman, Sachs publications to provide a world portfolio strategy as well as strategies for several individual countries.[19]

Goldman, Sachs uses a version of the three-step process (also referred to as the *top-down approach*) initially examining a country's aggregate economy and its components that relate to the valuation of securities—GDP, inflation, and interest rates. Table 14.4 contains the firm's forecast of GDP for several major countries. Note the fairly substantial differences in outlook for real GDP growth during 1997 (e.g., 1.6 percent for Japan versus 7.5 percent for Singapore).

INFLATION AND EXCHANGE RATES

An analysis of historical and expected price changes in Table 14.5 also reveals major differences in the outlook for inflation, ranging from 0.1 percent for Japan to 8.0 percent for Hong Kong. These inflation estimates feed into an interest rate forecast for the end of 1996 in Table 14.6. This combination of forecasts indicates the expected trend in interest rates. The forecast for interest rates were clearly mixed. The overall range for expected long-term rates at the end of 1996 was from 3.4 percent (Japan) to 12.5 percent (Italy).

Given these differences in inflation and interest rate levels and trends, you can expect major differences in the exchange rates. Table 14.7 presents the firm's forecast for several

---

TABLE 14.4 **FORECASTS FOR WORLD ECONOMIC ACTIVITY—REAL GDP GROWTH**

Country	1994	1995E	1996E	1997E	10-Year Trend
		(percent per annum)			
United States	3.5	2.0	2.5	2.9	2.6
Japan	0.5	0.9	2.8	1.6	3.3
Germany	2.9	1.9	0.5	2.2	2.8
United Kingdom	4.0	2.5	1.9	3.2	2.4
France	2.8	2.2	1.3	2.8	2.1
Italy	2.1	3.0	1.1	2.0	2.1
Canada	4.3	2.0	2.6	3.1	2.5
Hong Kong	5.1	4.6	4.5	5.0	5.5
Singapore	10.2	8.9	8.0	7.5	6.0

Source: Adapted from *World Investment Strategy Highlights* (London: Goldman, Sachs International Corp.) June/July 1996. Reprinted by permission of Goldman, Sachs & Co.

---

[19] The other Goldman, Sachs publications used include *The International Economics Analyst, Financial Markets Perspectives, Investment Strategy Highlights, Japan Investment Strategy Highlights,* and *The U.K. Economics Analyst.*

TABLE 14.5	CONSUMER OR RETAIL PRICE CHANGES (PERCENTAGE CHANGES ON PREVIOUS YEAR)							
Period	United States	Japan	Germany	France	United Kingdom	Italy	Hong Kong	Singapore
1988	4.1%	0.7%	1.3%	2.7%	4.9%	5.0%	NA	NA
1989	4.8	2.3	2.8	3.4	7.8	6.6	NA	NA
1990	4.4	3.0	2.7	3.5	9.5	6.1	NA	NA
1991	4.0	2.8	3.8	3.5	7.0	6.0	NA	NA
1992	3.0	1.7	4.0	2.8	3.7	5.2	NA	NA
1993	3.2	1.2	3.7	2.3	1.8	4.5	NA	NA
1994	2.6	0.7	2.7	2.1	2.4	3.9	8.1	3.1
1995(e)	2.8	0.0	1.8	1.6	2.8	5.4	8.7	1.7
1996(e)	3.1	0.0	1.8	1.8	2.9	4.3	7.0	2.0
1997(e)	3.4	1.0	2.6	1.7	2.5	3.9	7.2	2.5
10-year trend	3.6	1.6	2.4	3.1	5.0	5.7	8.5	2.8

(e)estimate

Source: *World Investment Strategy Highlights* (London: Goldman, Sachs International Ltd.) June/July 1996. Reprinted by permission of Goldman, Sachs & Co.

TABLE 14.6	INTEREST RATE FORECASTS (PERCENT PER ANNUM)		
Country	Current Rate[1]	Short Term (3 Months)	Long Term (12 Months)
United States			
3 month	5.8	5.6	6.1
10 year	5.9	5.9	6.6
Germany			
3 month	4.1	3.7	4.5
10 year	6.4	6.2	6.7
Japan			
3 month	0.6	0.4	0.8
10 year	2.8	2.8	3.4
France			
3 month	6.2	5.7	5.7
10 year	7.3	6.8	7.2
United Kingdom			
3 month	6.7	6.5	6.5
10 year	7.9	7.4	8.0
Canada			
3 month	7.1	6.0	6.3
10 year	7.5	7.6	7.6
Italy			
3 month	10.5	10.2	11.0
10 year	11.7	11.2	12.5

[1]3 November 1995

Source: *World Investment Strategy Highlights* (London: Goldman, Sachs International Ltd.) November/ December 1995. Reprinted by permission of Goldman, Sachs & Co.

currencies. The forecasts for 6 months and 12 months imply trends during the year. These figures indicate that Goldman, Sachs expects the U.S. dollar to become weaker against all the currencies except the Canadian dollar during 1996.

Based on this analysis of the underlying economics, Table 14.8 contains estimates of corporate earnings growth rates for various countries. It also gives estimates of other stock

TABLE 14.7

FORECAST OF EXCHANGE RATES AGAINST THE U.S. DOLLAR

	Canadian Dollar	Japanese Yen	British Pound	German Mark	French Franc	Swiss Franc
Current Rate	1.35	102	0.63	1.41	4.89	1.14
6 month	1.33	106	0.65	1.47	5.06	1.21
12 month	1.33	100	0.61	1.35	4.70	1.08

Source: Adapted from *World Investment Strategy Highlights* (London: Goldman, Sachs International Ltd.) November/December 1995. Reprinted by permission of Goldman, Sachs & Co.

TABLE 14.8

COMPARATIVE STOCK MARKET STATISTICS

	United States	Japan	Hong Kong	United Kingdom	Germany	France	Italy
Earnings Growth							
1995	18	34	13	12	30	15	75
1996(e)	6	32	14	9	25	35	17
1997(e)	11	7	15	11	28	10	25
Dividend Growth							
1995	5	6	14	10	9	8	20
1996(e)	7	9	14	9	10	10	20
1997(e)	8	6	13	9	15	20	20
P/E							
1995	17.3	564.4	14.1	15.1	18.4	48.5	23.3
1996(e)	15.7	63.2	12.4	14.2	17.8	22.2	19.5
1997(e)	14.2	49.4	10.8	13.2	14.3	16.5	14.5
D/Y							
1995	2.1	0.7	3.2	4.0	3.2	3.8	2.3
1996(e)	2.2	0.8	3.6	4.2	3.0	4.1	2.6
1997(e)	2.4	0.9	4.1	4.5	3.5	4.9	3.1

Aggregates and multiples for earnings and dividend are based on a sample of all companies in each country. Note: Figures for the United States refer to the S&P Industrials Index and pertain to operating earnings.

Source: *World Investment Strategy Highlights* (London: Goldman, Sachs International Ltd.), June/July 1996. Reprinted by permission of Goldman, Sachs & Co.

market variables, including dividend growth, price/earnings ratios, and dividend yields. Again, all series show major differences among countries. The estimated earnings growth rates for 1997 vary from 7 percent expected growth for Japan to 28 percent for Germany. Likewise, the price/earnings ratio is expected to continue its historical variation ranging in 1997 from less than 11 times for Hong Kong to 49 times for Japan.

CORRELATIONS AMONG RETURNS These substantial differences in economic performance and major changes in the underlying valuation variables indicate that there should be fairly low correlations among stock market returns for alternative countries. The correlation matrix of price changes in local currencies in Table 14.9 shows a fairly high correlation between the United States with the United Kingdom and Canada, and low correlations between the United States with Italy and Japan. Notably, the U.S.–Japan correlation has increased in recent years as our economies have become more interdependent.

| TABLE 14.9 | CORRELATION OF PRICE RETURNS IN LOCAL CURRENCY: 1986–1995 |

	United States	Japan	Germany	United Kingdom	Canada	France
United States	—					
Japan	0.34	—				
Germany	0.46	0.26	—			
United Kingdom	0.76	0.34	0.55	—		
Canada	0.74	0.38	0.48	0.67	—	
France	0.54	0.40	0.70	0.60	0.51	—
Italy	0.27	0.40	0.51	0.39	0.34	0.54

Source: Prepared by the authors using data provided by Goldman, Sachs International Ltd. Reprinted by permission of Goldman, Sachs & Co.

| TABLE 14.10 | CORRELATION OF PRICE RETURNS IN U.S. DOLLARS: 1986–1995 |

	United States	Japan	Germany	United Kingdom	Canada	France
United States	—					
Japan	0.24	—				
Germany	0.37	0.30	—			
United Kingdom	0.64	0.46	0.55	—		
Canada	0.71	0.29	0.34	0.57	—	
France	0.47	0.47	0.73	0.60	0.41	—
Italy	0.21	0.43	0.49	0.34	0.29	0.49

Source: Prepared by the authors using data provided by Goldman, Sachs International Ltd. Reprinted by permission of Goldman, Sachs & Co.

Table 14.10, a similar matrix in U.S. dollars, shows that all the correlations of returns with the United States decline when one considers the exchange rate effect. Comparisons such as these justify and encourage worldwide diversification of investments.

INDIVIDUAL COUNTRY STOCK PRICE CHANGES

The stock market impact of exchange rates is shown in Table 14.11, which shows the percentage changes in stock prices in the local currency and adjusted for the U.S. dollar. The annual averages for local currency from 1991 to 1995 range from 0.4 percent for Japan to 13.9 percent for the United States. The percentage changes of stock prices in U.S. dollars ranged from 0.9 percent (Italy) to 13.9 percent (United States).

The significant impact of changes in exchange rates can be seen in a couple of examples. Although the rate of change in Japan stock prices during 1994 was 8.0 percent, the change experienced by a U.S. citizen who invested in Japan during 1994 would have been 20.1 percent because of the significant strength of the yen. This increase in the rate of return (or decline in the negative price change) due to exchange rate changes relative to the U.S. dollar was fairly widespread during 1994. In contrast, during 1992 the U.S. dollar was quite strong, and all percentage stock price changes when converted to U.S. dollars were lower. For example, the change in the United Kingdom during 1992 was over 15 percent in local currency but a decline of almost 7 percent in U.S. dollars.

INDIVIDUAL COUNTRY ANALYSIS

Goldman, Sachs provides a detailed analysis of major countries that includes the country's economy and equity market, and culminates in a portfolio recommendation for investors in

TABLE 14.11

WORLD STOCK-MARKET PERFORMANCE: 1991–1995 (IN LOCAL CURRENCY AND U.S. DOLLARS)

Country	1991 Local Currency	1991 U.S. Dollars	1992 Local Currency	1992 U.S. Dollars	1993 Local Currency	1993 U.S. Dollars	1994 Local Currency	1994 U.S. Dollars	1995 Local Currency	1995 U.S. Dollars	Average 1991–1995 Local Currency	Average 1991–1995 U.S. Dollars
United States	25.8	25.8	5.2	5.2	8.2	8.2	−1.1	−1.1	31.1	31.1	13.9	13.9
Japan	2.0	9.9	−23.4	−24.0	11.8	23.3	8.0	20.1	3.9	1.4	0.4	6.1
Germany	7.5	6.5	−5.6	−11.7	40.6	32.4	−9.0	2.2	6.9	14.6	8.1	8.8
United Kingdom	15.2	12.5	15.7	−6.9	21.1	19.1	−10.3	−4.7	18.8	18.1	12.1	7.6
France	16.0	14.5	4.5	−1.8	26.3	19.6	−16.3	−6.7	2.6	10.8	6.6	7.3
Italy	0.0	−0.9	−6.8	−28.8	41.0	24.1	4.2	9.6	−1.6	0.6	7.4	0.9
World	14.4	16.5	−3.7	−7.7	17.6	19.8	−2.1	3.5	15.9	16.9	8.4	9.8

Source: *World Investment Strategy Highlights* (London: Goldman, Sachs International Ltd.), June/July 1996. Reprinted by permission of Goldman, Sachs & Co.

TABLE 14.12

ECONOMIC OUTLOOK FOR THE UNITED KINGDOM

	Current Value	Historical Average
GDP Growth		
1994	3.9	2.4
1995(e)	2.7	
1996(e)	2.5	
Earnings Growth		
1994	14.0	7.0
1995(e)	13.0	
1996(e)	10.0	
Dividend Growth		
1994	11.0	5.0
1995(e)	10.0	
1996(e)	10.0	
Inflation (Consumer Price Index) (Percent)		
1994	2.4	5.0
1995(e)	2.9	
1996(e)	3.1	

Interest Rate Outlook

	Current Rate	3 Months	12 Months
3-month CDs	6.7	6.5	6.5
10-year bond	7.9	7.4	8.0

Source: *World Investment Strategy Highlights* (November/December 1995). Copyright London: Goldman, Sachs International Ltd. Reprinted by permission of Goldman, Sachs & Co.

that country. Table 14.12 shows the major economic indicators for the United Kingdom reflecting a continuation of the economic expansion.

There is an analysis of the U.K. in Table 14.13 equity market following the economic projections. Goldman, Sachs feels that the overall economic outlook for the United Kingdom is moderate but the firm still expects U.K. equities to outperform bonds and short-term bonds (cash) during the next 12 months.

| TABLE 14.13 | | RECENT STOCK MARKET PERFORMANCE FOR UNITED KINGDOM RELATIVE TO WORLD MARKET AND EXPECTED RATES OF RETURN OVER NEXT 3 AND 12 MONTHS | | | | | | |

		PERFORMANCE (PERCENT CHANGE)		52-WEEK RANGE		RELATIVE TO WORLD		
	Current Price	Last 3 Months	12 Months	High	Low	Last Month	YTD	12 Months
FT–SE 100	3523	0.7	14.3	3613	2959	−0.5	2.0	2.5

Expected Return (percent)

	3 Months	12 Months
Equities	−0.1	14.3
Bonds	3.1	−2.5
Cash	1.4	5.5

Source: Adapted from *World Investment Strategy Highlights* (London: Goldman, Sachs International Ltd.) November/December 1995. Reprinted by permission of Goldman, Sachs & Co.

WORLD ASSET ALLOCATION

The final product of this analysis is a recommendation for an investor's world asset allocation. Table 14.14 begins with a division among bonds, equities, and cash. As of early 1996, Goldman, Sachs recommended that an investor should be at the upper end of the range for equity, toward the middle of the cash range, and at the low end of the bond range with a midrange exposure to commodities.

For the equity segment of the portfolio, the firm specified a neutral weighting for each country based on its relative market value. The relative market value of a country's equities is their value as a percentage of the total value of all world equities. For example, as shown in Table 14.14 the market value of U.S. equities is 43.4 percent of the total value of all equities in the world, whereas Japanese equities account for 23.8 percent of the total. A completely neutral portfolio regarding all equity markets would invest a proportion in each country equal to the relative market values of that country's equities. For example, if the value of stocks in a country constituted 10 percent of the value of all stocks in the world, a neutral outlook would lead you to invest 10 percent of your equity portfolio in this country. If you were bullish toward this country relative to other markets, you would *overweight* it, investing more than 10 percent of your equity portfolio there. As of the publication date of this report (July 1996), Goldman, Sachs was slightly bearish on the U.S. stock market because the market was close to fair value and expected returns were below those expected in Asia and Latin America. Therefore, they recommended *underweighting* it (you should invest 40.5 percent of your equity portfolio in the United States versus a 43.4 percent market weighting). The firm was somewhat bullish regarding Japan and recommended that you slightly *overweight* Japanese stocks (the recommended weight is 26 percent versus a market weight of 23.8 percent). Alternatively, they are recommending that you underweight the United Kingdom and overweight Germany (i.e., invest only 6.5 percent in the United Kingdom versus a 9.1 percent market weight, and invest 5.4 percent in Germany versus a 3.6 percent neutral weighting).

After completing the global market analysis, the next step is to analyze alternative industries worldwide within specified countries. Finally, you should consider alternative firms and their stocks in the preferred industries. This analysis is the subject of Chapters 19 and 20.

TABLE 14.14   **ASSET ALLOCATION—WORLD PORTFOLIOS**

	Normal Range (Percent)	Weighting (Percent of Index)	Current Suggested Weighting* (Percent)
Bonds	**20–40**		**23.0**
Equities	**45–65**		**57.0**
United States		43.4	40.5
Japan		23.8	26.0
Hong Kong		2.1	1.7
United Kingdom		9.1	6.5
Germany		3.6	5.4
France		3.4	3.3
Italy		1.1	1.6
The Netherlands		2.0	1.8
Switzerland		2.9	1.7
Spain		1.0	0.9
Belgium		0.7	0.6
Sweden		1.2	2.1
Finland		0.2	0.8
Norway		0.2	0.3
Other Europe		0.9	1.0
Latin America		1.5	5.3
		100.0	**100.0**
Commodities	**0–20**		**13**
Cash	**0–10**		**7**

*It may not add up to 100 due to rounding.

Source: *World Investment Strategy Highlights* (London: Goldman, Sachs International Ltd.) June/July 1996. Reprinted by permission of Goldman, Sachs & Co.

Summary

In earlier chapters, we emphasized the importance of analyzing the aggregate markets before beginning any industry or company analysis. You must assess the economic and security-market outlooks and their implications regarding the bond, stock, and cash components of your portfolio. Then you proceed to consider the best industry or company.

- Three techniques are used to make the market decision: (1) the macroeconomic technique, which is based on the relationship between the aggregate economy and the stock market; (2) the microeconomic technique, which determines future market values by applying the dividend discount model to the aggregate stock market; and (3) technical analysis, which estimates future returns based on recent past returns. This chapter concentrates on the macroeconomic approach. The microeconomic analysis of equity markets will be considered in Chapter 18 as a prelude to industry analysis in Chapter 19 followed by company and stock analysis in Chapter 20. Technical analysis is covered in Chapter 21.
- The economy and the stock market have a strong, consistent relationship, but the stock market generally turns before the economy does. Therefore, the best macroeconomic projection techniques use economic series that likewise lead the economy, and possibly the stock market. The NBER leading indicator series (which includes stock prices) is one possibility, but the evidence does not support its use as a mechanical predictor of stock prices. Leading series for inflation and for other countries exist, along with a weekly leading indicator series, but none of these series has been examined relative to stock prices.
- The money supply has been suggested as a predictor of aggregate market behavior based on its relationship to the economy. Some early studies indicated a strong relationship between the money

supply and stock prices, and suggested that money supply changes turned before stock prices. Subsequent studies confirmed the link between money supply and stock prices, but they indicated that stock prices turn with or before money supply changes. These recent results imply that, although money supply changes have an important impact on stock price movements, it is not possible to use historical money supply data in a mechanical way to predict stock price changes.

- The analysis of excess liquidity indicates an impact on stock prices, but also shows that global liquidity has become important and has weakened the relationship of U.S. markets with U.S. liquidity alone. There also is a problem with the appropriate measure of money supply, which appears to change over time.

- Although we emphasize the analysis of U.S. markets, we know it is also important to analyze numerous foreign markets. Such an analysis is demonstrated by a Goldman, Sachs' application of the three-step, or top-down approach to major countries. This includes an economic analysis and market analysis for each country. The analysis culminates with a recommendation for a world portfolio allocation among bonds, stocks, and cash. It also recommends an allocation of equity investments among countries in comparison to the country's normal weighting based on its relative market value.

This aggregate market analysis should lead you to a decision as to how much of your portfolio should be committed to bonds, stocks, and cash during the forthcoming investment period. The following three chapters deal with the fixed-income portion of your portfolio. Chapter 15 discusses bond fundamentals, Chapter 16 considers the analysis and valuation of individual bonds, and Chapter 17 presents alternative portfolio strategies for bond investors.

Questions

1. Why would you expect a relationship between economic activity and stock price movements?
2. At a lunch with some business associates, you discuss the reason for the relationship between the economy and the stock market. One of your associates contends that she has heard that stock prices typically turn before the economy does. How would you explain this phenomenon?
3. Could a diffusion index of a leading indicator series help you predict stock market movements? Why or why not?
4. Explain the following statements: (a) There is a strong, consistent relationship between money supply changes and stock prices; (b) Money supply changes cannot be used to predict stock price movements.
5. Discuss the rationale for the relationship of excess liquidity and security prices.
6. You are informed of the following estimates: nominal money supply is expected to grow at a rate of 7 percent, and GDP is estimated to grow at 4 percent. Explain what you think will happen to stock prices during this period and why.
7. The current rate of inflation is 3 percent and long-term Treasury bonds are yielding 7 percent. You estimate that the rate of inflation will increase to 6 percent. What do you expect to happen to long-term bond yields? Compute the effect of this change in inflation on the price of a 15-year, 10 percent coupon bond, with a current yield to maturity of 8 percent.
8. Some observers contend that it is harder to estimate the effect of a change in interest rates on common stocks than on bonds. Discuss this contention.
9. Based on the economic projections in Tables 14.5 through 14.8, would you expect the stock prices for the various countries to be highly correlated? Justify your answer with specific examples.
10. You are informed that a well-respected investment firm projects that the rate of return next year for the U.S. equity market will be 10 percent, and returns for German stocks will be 13 percent. Assume that all risks except exchange rate risk are equal and you expect the DM/U.S. dollar exchange rate to go from 1.50 to 1.30 during the year. Given this information, discuss where you would invest and why. Compute the effect if the exchange rate went from 1.50 to 1.90.

Problems

1. Prepare a table showing the percentage change for each of the last 10 years in (a) the Consumer Price Index (all items), (b) nominal GDP, (c) real GDP (in constant dollars), and (d) the GDP deflator. Discuss how much of nominal growth was due to real growth and how much was due to inflation.

2. *CFA Examination I (June 1983)*

There has been considerable growth in recent years in the use of economic analysis in investment management. Further significant expansion may lie ahead as financial analysts develop greater skills in economic analysis and these analyses are integrated more into the investment decision-making process. The following questions address the use of economic analysis in the investment decision-making process.

   a. 1. Differentiate among leading, lagging, and coincident indicators of economic activity, and give an example of each.
      2. Indicate whether the leading indicators are one of the best tools for achieving above-average investment results. Briefly justify your conclusion. (8 minutes)
   b. Interest rate projections are used in investment management for a variety of purposes. Identify three significant reasons why interest rate forecasts may be important in reaching investment conclusions. (6 minutes)
   c. Assume you are a fundamental research analyst following the automobile industry for a large brokerage firm. Identify and briefly explain the relevance of *three* major economic time series, economic indicators, or economic data items that would be significant to automotive industry and company research. (6 minutes)

3. *CFA Examination III (June 1985)*

A U.S. pension plan hired two offshore firms to manage the non-U.S. equity portion of its total portfolio. Each firm was free to own stocks in any country market included in Capital International's Europe, Australia, and Far East Index (EAFE) and free to use any form of dollar and/or nondollar cash or bonds as an equity substitute or reserve. After 3 years had elapsed, the records of the managers and the EAFE Index were as shown below:

SUMMARY: CONTRIBUTIONS TO RETURN

	Currency	Country Selection	Stock Selection	Cash/Bond Allocation	Total Return Recorded
Manager A	(9.0%)	19.7%	3.1%	0.6%	14.4%
Manager B	(7.4)	14.2	6.0	2.8	15.6
Composite of A&B	(8.2)	16.9	4.5	1.7	15.0
EAFE Index	(12.9)	19.9	—	—	7.0

You are a member of the plan sponsor's pension committee, which will soon meet with the plan's consultant to review manager performance. In preparation for this meeting, you go through the following analysis:

   a. Briefly describe the strengths and weaknesses of each manager, relative to the EAFE Index data. (5 minutes)
   b. Briefly explain the meaning of the data in the Currency column. (5 minutes)

4. Each week in *Barron's* in the data section entitled "Market Week" there is a table in the pages for the "International Trader" for Global Stock Markets. Consult the latest available issue of this publication and the issue one year earlier to find the following information.

   a. Show the closing value for five country indexes of your choice on each date relative to the yearly high for each year.
   b. Which countries have markets in downtrends? Which countries are in uptrends?
   c. Based on the percent range for the 52-week period [H − L/(H + L)2], which is the most volatile market?
   d. For the five countries, calculate the percentage change over the one-year period in local currency and in U.S. dollars. Discuss how each country did relative to the World Index.

5. Using a source of financial data such as *Barron's* or *The Wall Street Journal*:

   a. Plot the weekly percentage changes in the S&P 400 index (y-axis) versus comparable weekly percentage changes in the M2 money supply figures (x-axis) for the past 10 weeks. Do you see a positive, negative, or zero correlation? (Monetary aggregates will lag the stock market aggregates.)

    b. Examine the trend in money rates (e.g., federal funds, 90-day T-bills, etc.) over the past 10 weeks. Is there a correlation between these money rates? Estimate the correlation between the individual money rates and percentage changes in M2.

6. For the past 10 weeks, examine the relationship between the weekly percentage changes in the S&P 400 Index and the DJIA. Plot the weekly percentage changes in each index using S&P as the x-axis and DJIA as the y-axis. Discuss your results as they relate to diversification. Do a similar comparison for the S&P 400 and the Nikkei Index and discuss these results as they relate to diversification.

References

Baker, H. Kent, ed. *Improving the Investment Decision Process—Better Use of Economic Inputs in Security Analysis and Portfolio Management.* Charlottesville, VA: Association for Investment Management and Research, 1992.

Belfer, Nathan. "Economic Indicators and Their Significance." In *The Financial Analysts Handbook,* 2d ed., edited by Sumner N. Levine. Homewood, IL: Dow Jones-Irwin, 1988.

Diermeier, Jeffrey J. "Capital Market Expectations: The Macro Factors." In *Managing Investment Portfolios: A Dynamic Process,* 2d ed., edited by John L. Maginn and Donald L. Tuttle. Boston: Warren Gorham and Lamont, 1990.

Droms, William G., ed. *Initiating and Managing a Global Investment Program,* Charlottesville, VA: Association for Investment Management and Research, 1991.

Fogler, H. Russell and Darwin M. Bayston, eds. *Improving the Investment Decision Process: Quantitative Assistance for the Practitioner and for the Firm.* Charlottesville, VA: The Institute of Chartered Financial Analysts, January 1984.

Investing Worldwide. An annual conference (started in 1990) sponsored by the Association of Investment Management and Research, Charlottesville, VA.

Solnik, Bruno. *Predictable Time-Varying Components of International Asset Returns.* Charlottesville, VA: Association of Investment Management and Research, 1993.

Vertin, James R., ed. *Improving the Investment Decision Process: Applying Economic Analysis to Portfolio Management.* Charlottesville, VA: The Institute of Chartered Financial Analysts, September 1984.

Part

4

ANALYSIS AND MANAGEMENT OF BONDS

Chapter 15   *Bond Fundamentals*

Chapter 16   *The Analysis and Valuation of Bonds*

Chapter 17   *Bond Portfolio Management Strategies*

For most investors, bonds are like Rodney Danger-field—"They get no respect!" This is surprising when one considers that the total market value of the bond market in the United States and in most other countries is substantially larger than the market value of the stock market. For example, by the end of 1995, the U.S. market value of all publicly issued bonds was more than $7 trillion, while the market value of all stocks was about $5 trillion. On a global basis, the values are about $18 trillion for bonds versus $12.5 trillion for stocks. Beyond the size factor, bonds have a reputation for low, unexciting rates of return. Although this may have been true 50 or 60 years ago, it certainly has not been true during the past 15 to 20 years. Specifically, the average annual compound rate of return on government/corporate bonds for the period 1978–1995 was slightly over 10 percent versus about 14 percent for common stocks. These rates of return along with corresponding standard deviations (8 percent for bonds versus 13 percent for stocks) and the relatively low correlations between stocks and bonds (about 0.35) indicate that there are substantial opportunities in bonds for individual and institutional investors to enhance their risk–return performance.

The chapters in this section are intended to provide: (a) a basic understanding of bonds and the bond markets around the world, (b) background on analyzing returns and risks in the bond market, and the valuation of bonds, including the numerous new fixed-income securities with very unusual cash flow characteristics, and (c) an understanding of what is involved in either active or passive bond portfolio management.

Chapter 15 describes the global bond market in terms of country participation and the makeup of the bond market in the largest countries. Also, the characteristics of bonds in alternative categories such as government, corporate, and municipal are discussed. We also discuss the many new corporate bond instruments developed in the United States, such as asset-backed securities, zero-coupon bonds, and high-yield bonds. While the use of these securities has generally been limited to a few of the large developed markets, it is certain that they will eventually be used around the world. Finally, we consider the price information needed by bond investors and where to get it.

Chapter 16 is concerned with the analysis and valuation of bonds, including a detailed discussion of how one values a bond using a single discount rate and using spot rates from the theoretical spot rate curve, as well as the alternative rate of return measures for bonds. Subsequently we consider what factors affect yields on bonds, and what influences the volatility of bond returns. This latter discussion considers the very important concept of bond duration, which helps explain and measure bond price volatility and is important in active and passive bond portfolio management. We also consider a related concept of bond convexity and the impact of convexity on bond price volatility. Notably, these concepts are examined as they apply to option-free securities and securities with embedded options (which is becoming very common).

Chapter 17 considers how to use the background provided in Chapters 15 and 16 to create and manage a bond portfolio. There are three major categories of portfolio strategies that we consider in detail. The first is passive portfolio management strategies, which include either a simple buy-and-hold strategy or involve indexing to one of the major benchmarks. The second category includes active management strategies that can involve one of five alternatives: interest rate anticipation, valuation analysis, credit analysis, yield spread analysis, or bond swaps. The third category includes matched funding strategies, which include constructing dedicated portfolios, classical or contingent immunization portfolios, or horizon matching.

The fact there are three chapters devoted to the study of bonds and the length of the chapters attest to the importance of the topic and the extensive research done in this area. During the past 20 years, there have been more developments related to the valuation and portfolio management of bonds than of stocks. This growth of the fixed-income sector does not detract from the importance of equities, but certainly enhances the significance of fixed-income securities. There is a final point that readers of this book should keep in mind. Specifically, this growth in the size, sophistication, and specialization of the bond market means that there are and will be numerous and varied career opportunities in the bond area ranging from trading these securities, valuation, credit analysis, and portfolio management—both domestically and globally.

Chapter
15

Bond Fundamentals

This chapter answers the following questions:

- What are some of the basic features of bonds that affect their risk, return, and value?
- What is the current country structure of the world bond market and how has the makeup of the bond market changed in recent years?
- What are the major components of the world bond market and the international bond market?
- What are bond ratings and what is their purpose? What is the difference between investment-grade bonds and high-yield (junk) bonds?
- What are the characteristics of bonds in the major bond categories such as governments, agencies, municipalities, and corporates?
- How do major countries such as the United States, Japan, the United Kingdom, and Germany differ in their makeup of the major bond categories?
- What are the important characteristics of corporate bond issues developed in the United States during the past decade such as mortgage-backed securities, other asset-backed securities, zero-coupon and deep discount bonds, high-yield bonds, and structured notes?
- How do you read the quotes available for the alternative bonds categories (e.g., governments, municipalities, corporates)?

The global bond market is large and diverse and represents an important investment opportunity. This chapter is concerned with publicly issued, long-term, nonconvertible debt obligations of public and private issuers in the United States and major global markets. In later chapters, we consider preferred stock and convertible bonds. An understanding of bonds is helpful in an efficient market because U.S. and foreign bonds increase the universe of investments available for the creation of a diversified portfolio.[1]

In this chapter, we review some basic features of bonds and examine the structure of the world bond market. The bulk of the chapter involves an in-depth discussion of the major fixed-income investments. The chapter ends with a brief review of the price information sources for bond investors. Chapter 16 discusses the valuation of bonds and considers several factors that influence bond value and bond price volatility.

BASIC FEATURES OF A BOND

Public **bonds** are long-term, fixed-obligation debt securities packaged in convenient, affordable denominations for sale to individuals and financial institutions. They differ from

---

Material on bonds and world bond markets in this chapter is based on information from "How Big Is the World Bond Market," 1995 update by Rosario Benavides of Salomon Brothers Inc. Copyright © 1995 by Salomon Brothers Inc., and "Size and Structure of the World Bond Market: 1995," edited by Eric A. Schatz, International Fixed Income Research, Merrill Lynch & Co., September 1995. Reprinted by permission.

[1] Meir Statman and Neal L. Ushman, "Bonds versus Stocks: Another Look," Journal of Portfolio Management 13, no. 3 (Winter 1987): 33–38.

other debt, such as individual mortgages and privately placed debt obligations, because they are sold to the public rather than channeled directly to a single lender. Bond issues are considered fixed-income securities because they impose fixed financial obligations on the issuers. Specifically, the issuer agrees to

1. Pay a fixed amount of *interest periodically* to the holder of record.
2. Repay a fixed amount of *principal* at the date of maturity.

Normally, interest on bonds is paid every 6 months, although some bond issues pay in intervals as short as a month or as long as a year. The principal is due at maturity; this *par value* of the issue is rarely less than $1,000. A bond has a specified term to maturity, which defines the life of the issue. The public debt market typically is divided into three segments based on an issue's original maturity:

1. Short-term issues with maturities of 1 year or less. The market for these instruments is commonly known as the **money market.**
2. Intermediate-term issues with maturities in excess of 1 year, but less than 10 years. These instruments are known as **notes.**
3. Long-term obligations with maturities in excess of 10 years, called *bonds.*

The lives of debt obligations change constantly as the issues progress toward maturity. Thus, issues that have been outstanding in the secondary market for any period of time eventually move from long-term to intermediate to short-term. This movement is important because a major determinant of the price volatility of bonds is the remaining life (maturity) of the issue.

BOND CHARACTERISTICS   A bond can be characterized based on (1) its intrinsic features, (2) its type, (3) its indenture provisions, or (4) the features that affect its cash flows and/or its maturity.

INTRINSIC FEATURES   The coupon, maturity, principal value, and the type of ownership are important intrinsic features of a bond. The **coupon** of a bond indicates the income that the bond investor will receive over the life (or holding period) of the issue. This is known as *interest income, coupon income,* or *nominal yield.*

The **term to maturity** specifies the date or the number of years before a bond matures (or expires). There are two different types of maturity. The most common is a **term bond,** which has a single maturity date. Alternatively, a **serial obligation bond** issue has a series of maturity dates, perhaps 20 or 25. Each maturity, although a subset of the total issue, is really a small bond issue with generally a different coupon. Municipalities issue most serial bonds.

The **principal,** or **par value,** of an issue represents the original value of the obligation. This is generally stated in $1,000 increments from $1,000 to $25,000 or more. Principal value is *not* the same as the bond's market value. The market prices of many issues rise above or fall below their principal values because of differences between their coupons and the prevailing market rate of interest. If the market interest rate is above the coupon rate, the bond will sell at a discount to par. If the market rate is below the bond's coupon, it will sell at a premium above par. If the coupon is comparable to the prevailing market interest rate, the market value of the bond will be close to its original principal value.

Finally, bonds differ in their terms of ownership. With a **bearer bond,** the holder, or bearer, is the owner, so the issuer keeps no record of ownership. Interest from a bearer bond is obtained by clipping coupons attached to the bonds and sending them to the issuer for payment. In contrast, the issuers of **registered bonds** maintain records of owners and pay the interest directly to them.

TYPES OF ISSUES   In contrast to common stock, companies can have many different bond issues outstanding at the same time. Bonds can have different types of collateral and be either senior, unsecured, or subordinated (junior) securities. **Secured (senior) bonds** are backed by a legal claim on some specified property of the issuer in the case of default. For example, mortgage bonds are secured by real estate assets; equipment trust certificates, which are used by railroads and airlines, provide a senior claim on the firm's equipment.

Unsecured bonds (debentures) are backed only by the promise of the issuer to pay interest and principal on a timely basis. As such, they are secured by the general credit of the issuer. **Subordinated (junior) debentures** possess a claim on income and assets that is subordinated to other debentures. Income issues are the most junior type because interest on them is only paid if it is earned. Although income bonds are unusual in the corporate sector, they are very popular municipal issues, referred to as **revenue bonds.** Finally, **refunding issues** provide funds to prematurely retire another issue.

The type of issue has only a marginal effect on comparative yield because it is the credibility of the issuer that determines bond quality. A study of corporate bond price behavior found that whether the issuer pledged collateral did not become important until the bond issue approached default.[2] The collateral and security characteristics of a bond influence yield differentials only when these factors affect the bond's quality ratings.

INDENTURE PROVISIONS   The indenture is the contract between the issuer and the bond-holder specifying the issuer's legal requirements. A trustee (usually a bank) acting on behalf of the bondholders ensures that all the indenture provisions are met, including the timely payment of interest and principal. All of the factors that dictate a bond's features, its type, and its maturity are set forth in the indenture.

FEATURES AFFECTING BOND'S MATURITY   Investors should be aware of the three alternative call features that can affect the life (maturity) of a bond. One extreme is a *freely callable* provision that allows the issuer to retire the bond at any time with a typical notification period of 30 to 60 days. The other extreme is a *noncallable* provision wherein the issuer cannot retire the bond prior to its maturity.[3] Intermediate between these is a *deferred call* provision, which means the issue cannot be called for a certain period of time after the date of issue (e.g., 5 to 10 years). At the end of the deferred call period, the issue becomes freely callable. Callable bonds have a **call premium,** which is the amount above maturity value that the issuer must pay to the bondholder for prematurely retiring the bond.

A *nonrefunding provision* prohibits a call and premature retirement of an issue from the proceeds of a lower-coupon refunding bond. This is meant to protect the bondholder from a typical refunding, but it is not foolproof. An issue with a nonrefunding provision can be called and retired prior to maturity using other sources of funds such as excess cash from operations, the sale of assets, or proceeds from a sale of common stock. This occurred on several occasions during the 1980s and 1990s when many issuers retired nonrefundable high-coupon issues early because they could get the cash from one of these other sources and felt that this was a good financing decision.

Another important indenture provision that can affect a bond's maturity is the **sinking fund,** which specifies that a bond must be paid off systematically over its life rather than

---

[2] W. Braddock Hickman, *Corporate Bond Quality and Investor Experience* (Princeton, NJ: Princeton University Press, 1958).

[3] The main issuer of noncallable bonds between 1985 and 1995 was the U.S. Treasury. Corporate long-term bonds typically have contained some form of call provision, except during periods of relatively low interest rates (e.g., 1994–1996) when the probability of exercising the option was very low. We discuss this notion in more detail in Chapter 16 in connection with the analysis of embedded options.

only at maturity. There are numerous sinking-fund arrangements, and the bondholder should recognize this as a feature that can change the stated maturity of a bond. The size of the sinking fund can be a percentage of a given issue or a percentage of the total debt outstanding, or it can be a fixed or variable sum stated on a dollar or percentage basis. Similar to a call feature, sinking fund payments may commence at the end of the first year or may be deferred for 5 or 10 years from date of the issue. The amount of the issue that must be repaid before maturity from a sinking fund can range from a nominal sum to 100 percent. Like a call, the sinking-fund feature typically carries a nominal premium, but is generally smaller than the straight call premium (e.g., 1 percent). For example, a bond issue with a 20-year maturity might have a sinking fund that requires that 5 percent of the issue be retired every year beginning in year 10. By year 20, half of the issue has been retired and the rest is paid off at maturity. Sinking-fund provisions have a small effect on comparative yields at the time of issue, but have little subsequent impact on price behavior.

A sinking-fund provision is an obligation and must be carried out regardless of market conditions. Although a sinking-fund allows the issuer to call bonds on a random basis, most of them are retired for sinking-fund purposes through direct negotiations with institutional holders. Essentially, the trustee negotiates with an institution to buy back the necessary amount of bonds at a price slightly above the current market price.

RATES OF RETURN ON BONDS
The rate of return on a bond is computed in the same way as the rate of return on stock or any asset. It is determined by the beginning and ending price and the cash flows during the holding period. The major difference between stocks and bonds is that the interim cash flow on bonds (i.e., the interest) is contractual and accrues over time as discussed below, whereas the dividends on stock may vary. Therefore, the holding period return (HPR) for a bond will be

$$HPR_{i,t} = \frac{P_{i,t+1} + Int_{i,t}}{P_{i,t}}$$

where

$HPR_{i,t}$ = the holding period return for bond i during period t
$P_{i,t+1}$ = the market price of bond i at the end of period t
$P_{i,t}$ = the market price of bond i at the beginning of period t
$Int_{i,t}$ = the interest paid or accrued on bond i during period t. Because the interest payment is contractual, it accrues over time and if a bond owner sells the bond between interest payments, the sale price includes accrued interest.[4]

The holding period yield (HPY) is:

$$HPY = HPR - 1$$

Note that the only contractual factor is the amount of interest payments. The beginning and ending bond prices are determined by market forces, as discussed in Chapter 13. Notably, the ending price is determined by market forces unless the bond is held to maturity, in which case the investor will receive the par value. These price variations in bonds means that investors in bonds can experience capital gains or losses. Interest rate volatility has increased substantially since the 1960s, and this has caused large price fluctuations in

---

[4]The concept of accrued interest will be discussed further in Chapter 16 when we consider the valuation of bonds.

bonds.[5] As a result, capital gains or losses have become a major component of the rates of return on bonds.

THE GLOBAL BOND-MARKET STRUCTURE[6]

The market for fixed-income securities is substantially larger than the listed equity exchanges (NYSE, TSE, LSE) because corporations tend to issue bonds rather than common stock. Federal Reserve figures indicate that in the United States during 1994, 20 percent of all new security issues were equity, which included preferred as well as common stock. Corporations issue less common or preferred stock because firms derive most of their equity financing from internally generated funds (i.e., retained earnings). Also, although the equity market is strictly corporations, the bond market in most countries has four noncorporate sectors: the pure government sector (e.g., the Treasury in the United States), government agencies (e.g., FNMA), state and local government bonds (municipals), and international bonds (e.g., Yankees and Eurobonds in the United States).

The size of the global bond market and the distribution among countries can be gleaned from Table 15.1, which lists the dollar value of debt outstanding and the percentage distribution for the major bond markets for the years 1990, 1992, and 1994. There has been substantial overall growth including a 47 percent increase in the total in 1994 compared with 1990. Also, the country trends are significant. Specifically, the U.S. market went from

TABLE 15.1

TOTAL DEBT OUTSTANDING IN THE 13 MAJOR[a] BOND MARKETS, BY YEAR (U.S. DOLLAR TERMS)

	1994		1992		1990	
	Total Value ($ billions)	Percentage of Total	Total Value ($ billions)	Percentage of Total	Total Value ($ billions)	Percentage of Total
U.S. dollar	$ 8,592	43.1	$ 7,350	46.5	$ 6,150	46.0
Japanese yen	4,533	22.8	3,134	19.8	2,605	19.5
Deutschemark	2,598	13.0	1,919	12.1	1,603	12.0
Italian lira	981	4.9	758	4.8	751	5.6
U.K. sterling	523	2.6	362	2.3	370	2.8
French franc	792	4.0	603	3.8	499	3.7
Canadian dollar	467	2.3	431	2.7	391	2.9
Swedish krona	203	1.0	189	1.2	183	1.4
Danish krone	232	1.2	203	1.3	201	1.5
Swiss franc	217	1.1	178	1.1	170	1.3
Dutch guilder	327	1.6	292	1.8	285	2.1
Belgian franc	335	1.7	296	1.9	259	1.9
Australian dollar	124	0.6	85	0.5	77	0.6
Total	**$19,924**	**100.0%**	**$15,800**	**100.0%**	**$13,374**	**100.0%**

[a]Only includes bonds with maturities over 1 year. (Floating rates are excluded.)

Source: "Size and Structure of the World Bond Market: 1995," Merrill Lynch International Fixed Income Research, September 1995.

---

[5]The analysis of bond price volatility is discussed in detail in Chapter 16.

[6]For a further discussion of global bond markets and specific national bond markets, see *International Bond Handbook,* International Bond Research Unit, James Capel & Co., London, 1987; and Adam Greshin and Margaret Darasz Hadzima, "International Bond Investing and Portfolio Management," and Michael R. Rosenberg, "International Fixed Income Investing: Theory and Practice," both in *The Handbook of Fixed Income Securities,* 4th ed., edited by Frank J. Fabozzi and T. Dessa Fabozzi (Burr Ridge, IL: Irwin Professional Publishing, 1995).

about 46 percent of the total world market in 1990 to about 43 percent in 1994. In contrast, Japan went from about 20 percent to almost 23 percent in 1994. The German market increased as a percentage of the global bond market during the last several years, whereas Italian and Canadian markets experienced an overall decline.

PARTICIPATING ISSUERS   There are generally five different issuers in a country: (1) federal governments (e.g., the U.S. Treasury), (2) agencies of the federal government, (3) various state and local political subdivisions (known as municipalities), (4) corporations, and (5) international issues. The division of bonds among these five types for the three largest markets and the United Kingdom during 1990, 1992, and 1994 is contained in Table 15.2.

| TABLE 15.2 | MAKEUP OF BONDS OUTSTANDING IN UNITED STATES, JAPAN, GERMANY, UNITED KINGDOM: 1990–1994 | | | | | |

	1994		1992		1990	
	Total Value	Percentage of Total	Total Value	Percentage of Total	Total Value	Percentage of Total
A. United States (U.S. dollars in billions)						
Government	2,392	27.8	2,096	28.5	1,668	27.1
Federal agency	2,176	25.3	1,734	23.6	1,446	23.5
Municipal	921	10.7	926	12.6	815	13.3
Corporate	2,247	26.1	1,879	25.6	1,581	25.7
International[a]	856	10.0	714	9.7	640	10.4
Total	8,592	100.0	7,350	100.0	6,150	100.0
B. Japan (yen in trillions)						
Government	195.5	43.2	168.7	43.1	158.1	45.2
Government-associated organization	71.3	15.8	61.7	15.8	54.1	15.5
Municipal	30.1	6.7	21.1	5.4	19.2	5.5
Bank debentures	78.7	17.4	76.6	19.6	67.7	19.3
Corporate	43.1	9.5	37.3	9.5	29.5	8.4
International[a]	33.4	7.4	25.6	6.5	21.6	6.2
Total	452.1	100.0	391.0	100.0	350.1	100.0
C. Germany (deutschemarks in billions)						
Government	1,078.4	26.8	762.4	24.6	560.4	23.4
Agency	198.3	4.9	128.3	4.1	91.7	3.8
State and local	636.9	15.8	532.1	17.2	447.3	18.7
Bank	1,432.7	35.6	1,156.2	37.3	901.0	37.6
Corporate	3.1	0.1	3.0	0.1	2.6	0.1
International[a]	674.2	16.8	515.1	16.6	392.6	16.4
Total	4,023.6	100.0	3,097.0	100.0	2,395.5	100.0
D. United Kingdom (pounds in billions)						
Government	211.9	63.4	144.2	60.3	115.1	60.0
Agency	—	—			—	—
Municipal	—	—	—	—	—	—
Corporate	18.3	5.5	14.9	6.2	14.5	7.6
International[a]	104.2	31.2	80.1	33.5	62.4	32.5
Total	334.4	100.0	239.2	100.0	191.9	100.0

[a]Includes foreign and Eurobonds.

Source: "Size and Structure of the World Bond Market: 1995," Merrill Lynch International Fixed Income Research, September 1995.

GOVERNMENT   The market for government securities is the largest sector in the United States, Japan, and the United Kingdom. It involves a variety of debt instruments issued to meet the growing needs of these governments. In Germany, the government sector is smaller, but is growing in size due to deficits related to reunification of the country.

GOVERNMENT AGENCIES   Agency issues have attained and maintained a major position in the U.S. market (about 25 percent), but are a smaller proportion in other countries (e.g., about 16 percent in Japan, below 5 percent in Germany, and nonexistent in the United Kingdom). These agencies represent political subdivisions of the government, although the securities are *not* typically direct obligations of the government. The U.S. agency market has two types of issuers: government-sponsored enterprises and federal agencies. The proceeds of agency bond issues are used to finance many legislative programs. In the United States, many of these obligations carry government guarantees, although they are not direct obligations of the government. In other countries, the relationship of an agency issue to the government varies. In most countries, the market yields of agency obligations generally exceed those from pure government bonds. Thus, they represent a way for investors to increase returns with only marginally higher risk.

MUNICIPALITIES   Municipal debt includes issues of states, school districts, cities, or other political subdivisions. Unlike government and agency issues, the interest income on municipal bonds in the United States is not subject to federal income tax, although capital gains are taxable. Moreover, these bonds are exempt from state and local taxes when they are issued by the investors' home state. That is, the interest income on a California issue would not be taxed to a California resident, but would be taxable to a New York resident. The interest income of Puerto Rican issues enjoys total immunity from federal, state, and local taxes.

As shown in Table 15.2, the municipal bond market in most other countries is typically smaller than in the United States (6 percent in Japan, about 16 percent in Germany, and nonexistent in the United Kingdom). Also, although each country has unique tax laws, the income from a non-U.S. municipal bond typically would not be exempt for a U.S. investor.

CORPORATIONS   The major nongovernmental issuer of debt is the corporate sector. The importance of this sector differs dramatically among countries. It is a significant but declining factor in the United States; a small sector in Japan where it is supplemented by bank debentures; and a small, declining proportion of the U.K. market. Finally, it is a minuscule part of the German market because most German firms get their financing through bank loans, which explains the very large percentage of bank debt in Germany.

The market for corporate bonds is commonly subdivided into several segments: industrials, public utilities, transportation, and financial issues. The specific makeup varies between countries. Most U.S. issues are industrials and utilities. Most foreign corporations do not issue public debt but borrow from the banks.

The corporate sector provides the most diverse issues in terms of type and quality. In effect, the issuer can range from the highest investment-grade firm, such as American Telephone and Telegraph or IBM, to a relatively new, high-risk firm that defaulted on previous debt securities.[7]

INTERNATIONAL   The international sector has two components: (1) foreign bonds such as Yankee bonds and Samurai bonds, and (2) Eurobonds including Eurodollar, Euroyen,

---

[7] It is possible to distinguish another sector that exists in the United States but not in other countries—institutional bonds. These are corporate bonds issued by a variety of *private, nonprofit institutions* such as schools, hospitals, and churches. They are not broken out because they are only a minute part of the U.S. market and do not exist elsewhere.

Eurodeutschemark, and Eurosterling bonds.[8] Although the relative importance of the international bond sector varies by country (from a low of 7 percent in Japan to a high of over 30 percent in the United Kingdom), it has grown in both absolute and relative terms in all these countries. Although Eurodollar bonds have historically made up over 50 percent of the Eurobond market, the proportion has declined as investors have attempted to diversify their Eurobond portfolios. Specifically, the Eurodollar was about 85 percent of the market in 1984, but only 40 percent in 1994. Clearly, the desire for diversification changes with the swings in the value of the U.S. dollar.

PARTICIPATING INVESTORS

Numerous individual and institutional investors with diverse investment objectives participate in the bond market. Individual investors are a minor portion because of the market's complexity and the high minimum denominations of most issues. Institutional investors typically account for 90 to 95 percent of the trading, although different segments of the market are more institutionalized than others. For example, institutions are involved heavily in the agency market, whereas they are much less active in the corporate sector.

A variety of institutions invest in the bond market. Life insurance companies invest in corporate bonds and, to a lesser extent, in Treasury and agency securities. Commercial banks invest in municipal bonds and government and agency issues. Property and liability insurance companies concentrate on municipal bonds and Treasuries. Private and government pension funds are heavily committed to corporates and invest in Treasuries and agencies. Finally, fixed-income mutual funds have grown substantially in size and their demand spans the full spectrum of the market as they develop bond funds that meet the needs of a variety of investors. As we will discuss in Chapter 26, significant growth has been experienced by municipal bond funds and corporate bond funds (including high-yield bonds).

Alternative institutions tend to favor different sectors of the bond market based on two factors: (1) the tax code applicable to the institution and (2) the nature of the institution's liability structure. For example, because commercial banks are subject to normal taxation and have fairly short-term liability structures, they favor short- to intermediate-term municipals. Pension funds are virtually tax-free institutions with long-term commitments, so they prefer high-yielding, long-term government or corporate bonds. Such institutional investment preferences can affect the short-run supply and demand of loanable funds and impact interest rate changes.

BOND RATINGS

Agency ratings are an integral part of the bond market because most corporate and municipal bonds are rated by one or more of the rating agencies. The exceptions are very small issues and bonds from certain industries such as bank issues. These are known as *nonrated bonds*. There are four major rating agencies: (1) Duff and Phelps, (2) Fitch Investors Service, (3) Moody's, and (4) Standard & Poor's.

Bond ratings provide the fundamental analysis for thousands of issues. The rating agencies analyze the issuing organization and the specific issue to determine the probability of default and inform the market of their analyses through their ratings.[9]

---

[8] These bonds will be discussed in more detail later in this chapter.

[9] For a detailed listing of rating classes and a listing of factors considered in assigning ratings, see "Bond Ratings" and "Bond Rating Outlines," in *The Financial Analysts Handbook,* 2d ed., edited by Sumner N. Levine (Homewood, IL: Dow Jones-Irwin, 1988), 1102–1138. For a study that examines the value of two bond ratings, see L. Paul Hsueh and David S. Kidwell, "Bond Ratings: Are Two Better Than One?" *Financial Management* 17, no. 1 (Spring 1988): 46–53. A very thorough discussion and analysis of the bond rating industry is contained in Richard Cantor and Frank Packer, "The Credit Rating Industry," *Journal of Fixed Income* 5, no. 3 (December 1995): 10–34.

The primary question in bond credit analysis is whether the firm can service its debt in a timely manner over the life of a given issue. Consequently, the rating agencies consider expectations over the life of the issue, along with the historical and current financial position of the company. Although the agencies have done an admirable job, mistakes happen.[10] A study indicated that the rating services have tended to overestimate the risk of default, which has resulted in unnecessarily high risk premiums given the default probabilities.[11] We consider default estimation further when we discuss high-yield (junk) bonds.

Several studies have examined the relationship between bond ratings and issue quality as indicated by financial variables. The results clearly demonstrated that bond ratings were positively related to profitability, size, and cash flow coverage, and they were inversely related to financial leverage and earnings instability.[12]

The original ratings assigned to bonds have an impact on their marketability and effective interest rate. Generally, the four agencies' ratings agree. When they do not, the issue is said to have a *split rating*. Seasoned issues are regularly reviewed to ensure that the assigned rating is still valid. If not, revisions are made either upward or downward. Revisions are usually done in increments of one rating grade.[13] The ratings are based on both the company and the issue. After an evaluation of the creditworthiness of the total company is completed, a company rating is assigned to the firm's most senior unsecured issue. All junior bonds receive lower ratings based on indenture specifications. Also, an issue could receive a higher rating than justified because of credit-enhancement devices such as the attachment of bank letters of credit, surety, or indemnification bonds from insurance companies.

The agencies assign letter ratings depicting what they view as the risk of default of an obligation. The letter ratings range from AAA (Aaa) to D. Table 15.3 describes the various ratings assigned by the major services. Except for slight variations in designations, the meaning and interpretation is basically the same. The agencies modify the ratings with + and − signs for Duff & Phelps, Fitch, and S&P, or with numbers (1-2-3) for Moody's. As an example, an A + bond is at the top of the A-rated group.

The top four ratings—AAA (or Aaa), AA (or Aa), A, and BBB (or Baa)—are generally considered to be *investment-grade securities*. The next level of securities is known as *speculative bonds* and include the BB- and B-rated obligations. The C categories are generally either income obligations or revenue bonds, many of which are trading flat. (Flat bonds are in arrears on their interest payments.) In the case of D-rated obligations, the issues are in outright default, and the ratings indicate the bonds' relative salvage values.[14]

---

[10] W. Braddock Hickman, *Corporate Bond Quality and Investor Experience* (Princeton, NJ: Princeton University Press, 1958).

[11] Gordon Pye, "Gauging the Default Premium," *Financial Analysts Journal* 30, no. 1 (January–February 1974): 49–52.

[12] See, for example, Robert S. Kaplan and Gabrial Urwitz, "Statistical Models of Bond Ratings: A Methodological Inquiry," *Journal of Business* 52, no. 2 (April 1979): 231–262; Ahmed Belkaoui, "Industrial Bond Ratings: A New Look," *Financial Management* 9, no. 3 (Autumn 1980): 44–52; and James A. Gentry, David T. Whitford, and Paul Newbold, "Predicting Industrial Bond Ratings with a Probit Model and Funds Flow Components," *The Financial Review* 23, no. 3 (August 1988): 269–286.

[13] Bond rating changes and bond-market efficiency are discussed in Chapter 16. Split ratings are discussed in R. Billingsley, R. Lamy, M. Marr, and T. Thompson, "Split Ratings and Bond Reoffering Yields," *Financial Management* 14, no. 2 (Summer 1985): 59–65; L. H. Ederington, "Why Split Ratings Occur," *Financial Management* 14, no. 1 (Spring 1985): 37–47; and P. Liu and W. T. Moore, "The Impact of Split Bond Rating on Risk Premia," *The Financial Review* 22, no. 1 (February 1987).

[14] These high yield bonds will be discussed in more detail in the subsequent section on corporate bonds.

TABLE 15.3	**DESCRIPTION OF BOND RATINGS**				
	Duff and Phelps	Fitch	Moody's	Standard & Poor's	Definition
High Grade	AAA	AAA	Aaa	AAA	The highest rating assigned to a debt instrument, indicating an extremely strong capacity to pay principal and interest. Bonds in this category are often referred to as *gilt edge securities.*
	AA	AA	Aa	AA	High-quality bonds by all standards with strong capacity to pay principal and interest. These bonds are rated lower primarily because the margins of protection are less strong than those for Aaa and AAA bonds.
Medium Grade	A	A	A	A	These bonds possess many favorable investment attributes, but elements may suggest a susceptibility to impairment given adverse economic changes.
	BBB	BBB	Baa	BBB	Bonds are regarded as having adequate capacity to pay principal and interest, but certain protective elements may be lacking in the event of adverse economic conditions that could lead to a weakened capacity for payment.
Speculative	BB	BB	Ba	BB	Bonds regarded as having only moderate protection of principal and interest payments during both good and bad times.
	B	B	B	B	Bonds that generally lack characteristics of other desirable investments. Assurance of interest and principal payments over any long period of time may be small.
Default	CCC	CCC	Caa	CCC	Poor-quality issues that may be in default or in danger of default.
	CC	CC	Ca	CC	Highly speculative issues that are often in default or possess other marked shortcomings.
	C	C			The lowest-rated class of bonds. These issues can be regarded as extremely poor in investment quality.
		C		C	Rating given to income bonds on which no interest is being paid.
		DDD, DD, D		D	Issues in default with principal or interest payments in arrears. Such bonds are extremely speculative and should be valued only on the basis of their value in liquidation or reorganization.

Source: *Bond Guide* (New York: Standard & Poor's Corporation, monthly); *Bond Record* (New York: Moody's Investors Services, Inc., monthly); *Rating Register* (New York. Fitch Investors Service, Inc., monthly).

ALTERNATIVE
BOND ISSUES

We have described the basic features available for all bonds and the overall structure of the global bond market in terms of the issuers of bonds and investors in bonds. In this section, we provide a detailed discussion of the bonds available from the major issuers of bonds. The presentation is longer than you would normally expect because when we discuss each issuing unit such as governments, municipalities, or corporations, we consider the bonds available in several of the major world financial centers such as Japan, Germany, and the United Kingdom.

DOMESTIC
GOVERNMENT BONDS

UNITED STATES   As shown in Table 15.2, the U.S. fixed-income market is dominated by U.S. Treasury obligations. The U.S. government with the full faith and credit of the U.S. Treasury issues Treasury bills (T-bills), which mature in less than 1 year, and two forms of long-term obligations: government notes, which have maturities of 10 years or less, and Treasury bonds, with maturities of 10 to 30 years. Current Treasury obligations come in denominations of $1,000 and $10,000. The interest income from the U.S. government securities is subject to federal income tax but exempt from state and local levies. These bonds are popular because of their high credit quality, substantial liquidity, and noncall feature.

Short-term T-bills differ from notes and bonds because they are sold at a discount from par to provide the desired yield. The return is the difference between the purchase price and the par at maturity. In contrast, government notes and bonds carry semiannual coupons that specify the nominal yield of the obligations.

Government notes and bonds have some unusual features. First, the period specified for the deferred call feature on Treasury issues is very long and is generally measured relative to the maturity date rather than from date of issue. They generally cannot be called until 5 years prior to their maturity date. Notably, *all* issues since 1989 have been noncallable.

Certain government issues provide a tax break to investors because they can be redeemed at par to pay federal estate taxes. Therefore, an investor can acquire a Treasury bond at a substantial discount, with which his or her estate can pay estate taxes. Such bonds are called *flower bonds*. No new flower bonds have been authorized for issuance since the early 1980s so there is only one such issue still available in the market. It carries a 3½ percent coupon and matures in November 1998. The lower coupon typically caused a substantial price discount and more assurance of price appreciation at "time of departure."

Recent estate tax law changes increased the portion of an estate exempt from taxes, thereby reducing the demand for such issues. Also as noted, the available supply has declined because when these flower bonds are used to pay estate taxes, they are retired by the government. Therefore, prices have been maintained, and the yields on flower bonds are consistently below those of other Treasury issues of comparable maturity. As an example, during early 1996 when most 2-year Treasury bonds were yielding about 5.3 percent, the remaining flower bond was yielding about 3.5 percent.

JAPAN[15]   The second largest government bond market in the world is Japan's. It is controlled by the Japanese government and the Bank of Japan (Japanese Central Bank). Japanese government bonds are an attractive investment vehicle for those favoring the Japanese

[15]For additional discussion, see "International Bond Handbook" (London: James Capel & Co., 1987); Nicholas Surgun, Kermit L. Schoenhotz, Steven Blitz, and Sahar Elhahashi, "Trading Patterns in the Japanese Government Bond Market" (New York: Salomon Brothers, 1986); Aron Viner, *Inside Japanese Financial Markets* (Homewood, IL: Dow Jones-Irwin, 1988); Edwin J. Elton and Martin J. Gruber, eds. *Japanese Capital Markets* (New York: Harper & Row, 1990); and Frank J. Fabozzi, ed., *The Japanese Bond Markets* (Chicago: Probus Publishing, 1990).

yen because their quality is equal to that of U.S. Treasury securities (they are guaranteed by the government of Japan) and they are very liquid. There are three maturity segments: medium-term (2, 3, or 4 years), long-term (10 years), and super-long (private placements for 15 and 20 years). Bonds are issued in both registered and bearer form, although registered bonds can be converted to bearer bonds through the registrar at the Bank of Japan.

Medium-term bonds are issued monthly through a competitive auction system similar to that of U.S. Treasury bonds. Long-term bonds are authorized by the Ministry of Finance and issued monthly by the Bank of Japan through an underwriting syndicate consisting of major financial institutions. Most super-long bonds are sold through private placement to a few financial institutions. Federal government bonds, which are the most liquid of all Japanese bonds, account for over 40 percent of the Japanese bonds outstanding and over 80 percent of total bond trading volume in Japan.

At least 50 percent of the trading in Japanese government bonds will be in the so-called *benchmark issue* of the time. The selection of the benchmark issue is made from among 10-year coupon bonds. (As of early 1996, the benchmark issue was #174, a 4.60 percent coupon bond maturing in 2004.) The designation of a benchmark issue is intended to assist smaller financial institutions in their trading of government bonds by ensuring these institutions that they would have a liquid market in this particular security. Compared to the benchmark issue, which accounts for about 50 percent of total trading in all Japanese government bonds, the comparable most active U.S. bond within a class accounts for only about 10 percent of the volume.

The yield on this benchmark bond is typically about 30 basis points below other comparable Japanese government bonds, reflecting its superior marketability. In the U.S. market, the most liquid bond sells at a yield differential of only 10 basis points. The benchmark issue changes when a designated issue matures or because of a decision by the Bank of Japan. Because of the difference in yield and liquidity, institutions that are interested in buying and holding (versus trading) acquire the nonbenchmark issues because of their higher yields. Notably, by taking these nonbenchmark issues out of circulation, these institutions ensure that they will not be traded, which confirms assumptions about their lack of liquidity.

GERMANY[16]   The third largest bond market in the world is the German market, although the government segment of this market is relatively small. Table 15.2 showed that approximately 40 percent of domestic deutschemark bonds are issued by the major commercial banks, whereas the Federal government issues about 25 percent through the German Central Bank.

The German capital market is dominated by commercial banks because in Germany there is no formal distinction between investment, merchant, or commercial banks as there is in the United States and the United Kingdom. As a result, firms arrange their financing primarily through bank loans, and these banks in turn raise their capital through public bond issues. Therefore, corporate domestic bonds are substantially less than 1 percent of the total.

Bonds issued by the Federal Republic of Germany, referred to as *bund* bonds, are issued in amounts up to DM 4 billion (4 billion deutschemarks) with a minimum denomination of

[16]For additional information on the German bond market, see Graham Bishop, "Deutschemark" in *Salomon Brothers International Bond Manual,* 2d ed. (New York: Salomon Brothers, 1987); and *The European Bond Markets,* edited by The European Bond Commission (Chicago: Probus Publishing, 1989).

DM 100. Original maturities are normally 10 or 12 years although 30-year bonds have been issued.

Although bonds are issued as bearer bonds, individual bonds do not exist. A global bond is issued and held in safekeeping within the German Securities Clearing System (the *Kassenverein*). Contract notes confirming the terms and ownership of each issue are then distributed to individual investors. Sales are based on these contract notes. Bonds are issued through a fixed quota system by the Federal Bond Syndicate, made up of the Bundesbank and 17 banks including certain resident branches of foreign banks. These government bunds are very liquid because the Bundesbank makes a market at all times. They also are the highest credit quality because they are guaranteed by the German government.

Bunds are quoted and traded on the German Stock Exchanges. Daily prices are determined by the Bundesbank and market makers use this benchmark level as the basis for trading. Although listed on the exchanges, government bonds are primarily traded over the counter and interest is paid annually.

UNITED KINGDOM[17]   The U.K. government bond market changed dramatically on October 17, 1986 (the day of the Big Bang when the trading rules and organizations in the securities business in the United Kingdom were changed). The roles of jobbers and brokers changed so that broker-dealers could act as principals or agents with negotiated commission structures. In addition, the number of primary dealers in the "gilt" market was expanded from 7 gilt jobbers to 27 primary dealers.

Maturities in this market range from short gilts (maturities of less than 5 years) to medium gilts (5 to 15 years) to long gilts (15 years and longer). Government bonds either have a fixed redemption date or a range of dates with redemption at the option of the government after giving appropriate notice. Alternatively, some bonds are redeemable on a given date or at any time afterwards at the option of the government. Government bonds are normally registered, although bearer delivery is available.

Gilts are issued through the Bank of England (the British central bank) using the tender method, whereby prospective purchasers tender offering prices at which they hope to be allotted bonds. The price cannot be less than the minimum tender price stated in the prospectus. If the issue is oversubscribed, allotments are made first to those submitting the highest tenders and continue until a price is reached where only a partial allotment is required to fully subscribe the issue. All successful allottees pay the lowest allotment prices.

These issues are extremely liquid and are highly rated because they are guaranteed by the British government. All gilts are quoted and traded on the London Stock Exchange and pay interest semiannually.

GOVERNMENT AGENCY ISSUES   In addition to pure government bonds, the federal government in each country can establish agencies that have the authority to issue their own bonds. The size and importance of these agencies differ among countries. They are a large and growing sector of the U.S. bond market, a much smaller component of the bond markets in Japan and Germany, and nonexistent in the United Kingdom.

UNITED STATES   Agency securities are obligations issued by the U.S. government through various political subdivisions such as a government agency or a government-

---

[17]For further discussion, see Ian C. Collier, "An Introduction to the Gilt-Edged Market" (London: James Capel & Co., 1987); and *The European Bond Markets*.

| TABLE 15.4 | AGENCY ISSUES: SELECTED CHARACTERISTICS |

Type of Security	Minimum Denomination	Form	Life of Issue	Tax Status		How Interest Is Earned
Government-Sponsored						
Banks for cooperatives (co-ops)	$ 5,000	B, BE	No longer issued Longest issue due 1/02/86	Federal: State: Local:	Taxable Exempt Exempt	Semiannual interest, 360-day year
Federal farm credit banks Consolidated systemwide notes	50,000	BE	5 to 365 days	Federal: State: Local:	Taxable Exempt Exempt	Discount actual, 360-day year
Consolidated systemwide bonds	5,000	BE	6 and 9 months	Federal: State: Local:	Taxable Exempt Exempt	Interest payable at maturity, 360-day year
	1,000	BE	13 months to 15 years	Federal: State: Local:	Taxable Exempt Exempt	Semiannual interest
Federal Home Loan Bank						
Consolidated discount notes	100,000	BE	30 to 360 days	Federal: State: Local:	Taxable Exempt Exempt	Discount actual, 360-day year
Consolidated bonds	10,000[a]	B, BE	1 to 20 years	Federal: State: Local:	Taxable Exempt Exempt	Semiannual interest, 360-day year
Federal Home Loan Mortgage						
Corporation debentures	10,000[a]	BE	18 to 30 years	Federal: State: Local:	Taxable Taxable Taxable	Semiannual interest, 360-day year
Participation certificates	100,000	R	30 years (12-year average life)	Federal: State: Local:	Taxable Taxable Taxable	Monthly interest and principal payments
Federal interstate credit banks	5,000	B, BE	No longer issued Longest issue date 1/05/87	Federal: State: Local:	Taxable Exempt Exempt	Semiannual interest, 360-day year
Federal National Mortgage Association discount notes	50,000[a]	B	30 to 360 days	Federal: State: Local:	Taxable Taxable Taxable	Discount actual, 360-day year
Debentures	10,000[a]	B, BE	1 to 30 years	Federal: State: Local:	Taxable Taxable Taxable	Semiannual interest, 360-day year

(continued)

sponsored corporation. Six government-sponsored enterprises and over two dozen federal agencies issue these bonds. Table 15.4 lists selected characteristics of the more popular government-sponsored and federal agency obligations, including market size, typical denominations, tax features, and the availability of bond quotes.[18] The issues in the table are representative of the wide variety of available obligations.

Agency issues usually pay interest semiannually, and the minimum denominations vary between $1,000 and $10,000. These obligations are not direct Treasury issues, yet they

---

[18] We will no longer distinguish between federal agency and government-sponsored obligations; instead, the term *agency* shall apply to either type of issue.

TABLE 15.4			(concluded)			
Type of Security	Minimum Denomination	Form	Life of Issue	Tax Status		How Interest Is Earned

Government National Mortgage Association

Type of Security	Minimum Denomination	Form	Life of Issue	Tax Status		How Interest Is Earned
Mortgage-backed bonds	25,000	B, R	1 to 25 years	Federal: State: Local:	Taxable Taxable Taxable	Semiannual interest, 360-day year
Modified pass-throughs	25,000[a]	R	12 to 40 years (12-year average)	Federal: State: Local:	Taxable Taxable Taxable	Monthly interest and principal payments
Student Loan Marketing Association discount notes	100,000	B	Out to 1 year	Federal: State: Local:	Taxable Exempt Exempt	Discount actual, 360-day year
Notes	10,000	R	3 to 10 years	Federal: State: Local:	Taxable Exempt Exempt	Semiannual interest, 360-day year
Floating rate notes	10,000[a]	R	6 months to 10 years	Federal: State: Local:	Taxable Exempt Exempt	Interest rate adjusted weekly to an increment over the average auction rate on 91-day Treasury bills and payable quarterly
Tennessee Valley Authority (TVA)	1,000	R, B	5 to 25 years	Federal: State: Local:	Taxable Exempt Exempt	Semiannual interest, 360-day year
U.S. Postal Service	10,000	R, B	25 years	Federal: State: Local:	Taxable Exempt Exempt	Semiannual interest, 360-day year

Notes: Form B = Bearer; R = Registered; BE = Book entry form. Debt issues sold subsequent to December 31, 1982, must be in registered form.
[a]Minimum purchase with increments in $5,000.

Source: *United States Government Securities* (New York: Merrill Lynch Government Securities, Inc., 1985); *Handbook of Securities of the United States Government and Federal Agencies* 31st ed. (New York: First Boston Corporation, 1984).

carry the full faith and credit of the U.S. government. Moreover, unlike government obligations, some of the issues are subject to state and local income tax, whereas others are exempt.[19]

One agency issue offers particularly attractive investment opportunities: GNMA (*Ginnie Mae*) pass-through certificates, which are obligations of the Government National Mortgage Association.[20] These bonds represent an undivided interest in a pool of federally insured mortgages. The bondholders receive monthly payments from Ginnie Mae that

[19] Federal National Mortgage Association (Fannie Mae) debentures, for example, are subject to state and local income tax, whereas the interest income from Federal Home Loan Bank bonds is exempt. In fact, a few issues are exempt from federal income tax as well (e.g., public housing bonds).

[20] For a further discussion of mortgage-backed securities, see Frank J. Fabozzi and Lynn Edens, "Mortgages"; Lakhbir S. Hayne, Cyrus Mohebbi, and Thomas A. Zimmerman, "Mortgage Pass-Through Securities"; and Andrew S. Carron, "Collateralized Mortgage Obligations." All of these chapters are in *The Handbook of Fixed Income Securities*, 4th ed., edited by Frank J. Fabozzi and T. Dessa Fabozzi (Burr Ridge, IL: Irwin Professional Publishing, 1995).

include both principal and interest because the agency "passes through" mortgage payments made by the original borrower (the mortgagee) to Ginnie Mae.

The coupons on these pass-through securities are related to the interest charged on the pool of mortgages. The portion of the cash flow that represents the repayment of the principal is tax-free, but the interest income is subject to federal, state, and local taxes. The issues have minimum denominations of $25,000 with maturities of 25 to 30 years but an average life of only 12 years because as mortgages in the pool are paid off, payments and prepayments are passed through to the investor. Therefore, unlike most bond issues, the monthly payment is not fixed. In fact, the monthly payment is *very uncertain* because of the prepayment schedule that can vary dramatically over time when interest rates change.

The point that will be made in Chapter 16 in connection with the valuation of bonds with embedded options is that mortgages generally have a call option whereby the homeowner has the option to prepay the mortgage (i.e., call the mortgage loan) when it is advantageous because of interest rates or if it is necessary due to the sale of the house. Therefore, there are prepayments on these securities for two reasons. The first is when homeowners pay off their mortgages when they sell their homes. The second occurs because owners refinance their homes when mortgage interest rates decline as they did in 1992 and 1995. A major disadvantage of GNMA issues is that they can be seriously depleted by prepayments, which means that their *maturities are very uncertain.*

The rates of return on these pass-throughs are relatively attractive compared to corporates. Also, most of the return is tax-free in later years because the tax-free part of the payment (the return of principal) is large.

JAPAN   The agencies in Japan, referred to as *government associate organizations,* account for about 15 percent of the total Japanese bond market. This agency market includes a substantial amount of public debt, but almost twice as much is privately placed with major financial institutions. Public agency debt is issued like government debt.

GERMANY   The agency market in Germany finances about 5 percent of the public debt. The major agencies are the Federal Railway, which issues *Bahn* or *Bundesbahn* bonds, and the Federal Post Office, which issues *Post* or *Bundespost* bonds. These Bahns and Posts are issued up to DM 2 billion. The issue procedure is similar to that used for regular government bonds. Bahns and Posts are relatively liquid, although less liquid than government bunds. These agency issues are implicitly guaranteed by the government.

UNITED KINGDOM   As shown in Table 15.2, there are no agency bond issues in the United Kingdom.

MUNICIPAL BONDS

Municipal bonds are issued by states, counties, cities, and other political subdivisions. Again, the size of the municipal bond market (referred to as *local authority* in the United Kingdom) varies substantially among countries. It is about 11 percent of the total U.S. market, compared to about 7 percent in Japan, 16 percent in Germany, and basically nonexistent in the United Kingdom. Because of the size and popularity of this market in the United States, we will discuss only the U.S. municipal bond market.

Municipalities in the United States issue two distinct types of bonds: general obligation bonds and revenue issues. **General obligation bonds** (GOs) are essentially backed by the full faith and credit of the issuer and its entire taxing power. **Revenue bonds,** in turn, are serviced by the income generated from specific revenue-producing projects of the municipality, for example, bridges, toll roads, hospitals, municipal coliseums, and waterworks. Revenue bonds generally provide higher returns than GOs because of their higher default risk. Should a municipality fail to generate sufficient income from a project designated to service a revenue bond, it has no legal debt service obligation until the income becomes sufficient.

GO municipal bonds tend to be issued on a serial basis so that the issuer's cash flow requirements will be steady over the life of the obligation. Therefore, the principal portion of the total debt service requirement generally begins at a fairly low level and builds up over the life of the obligation. In contrast, most municipal revenue bonds are term issues, so the principal value is not due until the final maturity date or the last few payment dates.[21]

The most important feature of municipal obligations is that the interest payments are exempt from federal income tax as well as from taxes in the locality and state in which the obligation was issued. This means that their attractiveness varies with the investor's tax brackets.

You can convert the tax-free yield of a municipal to an equivalent taxable yield (ETY) using the following equation:

$$ETY = \frac{i}{(1-t)}$$

where

ETY = equivalent taxable yield
i = coupon rate of the municipal obligations
t = marginal tax rate of the investor

An investor in the 35 percent marginal tax bracket would find that a 7 percent yield on a municipal bond selling close to its par value is equivalent to a 10.77 percent fully taxable yield according to the following calculation:

$$ETY = \frac{.07}{(1-.35)} = .1077$$

Because the tax-free yield is the major benefit of municipal bonds, an investor's marginal tax rate is a primary concern in evaluating them. As a rough rule of thumb, using the tax rates expected in 1996, an investor must be in the 28 to 30 percent tax bracket before the lower yields available in municipal bonds are competitive with those from fully taxable bonds. However, although the interest payment on municipals is tax-free, any capital gains are not (which is why the ETY formula is only correct for a bond selling close to its par value).

MUNICIPAL BOND INSURANCE   A growing feature of the U.S. municipal bond market is *municipal bond insurance*, which provides that an insurance company will guarantee to make principal and interest payments in the event that the issuer of the bonds defaults. The insurance is placed on the bond at date of issue and is *irrevocable* over the life of the issue. The issuer purchases the insurance for the benefit of the investor, and the municipality

[21] For a more detailed discussion of the overall municipal bond market, see Sylvan G. Feldstein, Frank J. Fabozzi, and T. Dessa Fabozzi, "Municipal Bonds." For an excellent discussion of the credit analysis of these bonds, see Sylvan G. Feldstein, "Guidelines in the Credit Analysis of General Obligation and Revenue Municipal Bonds." Both chapters are in *The Handbook of Fixed Income Securities,* 4th ed., edited by Frank J. Fabozzi and T. Dessa Fabozzi (Burr Ridge, IL: Irwin Professional Publishing, 1995).

benefits from lower interest costs due to lower default risk, which causes an increase in the rating on the bond and increased marketability. Others who would benefit from the insurance are small government units not widely known and bonds with a complex security structure.

As of 1995, approximately 40 percent of all new municipal bond issues were insured. There are six private bond insurance firms: a consortium of four large insurance companies entitled the Municipal Bond Investors Assurance (MBIA), American Municipal Bond Assurance Corporation (AMBAC), the Financial Security Assurance (FSA), the Financial Guaranty Insurance Company (FGIC), Capital Guaranty Insurance Company (CGIC), and Connie Lee Insurance Company. These firms will insure either general obligation or revenue bonds. To qualify for private bond insurance, the issue must initially carry an S&P rating of BBB or better. Currently, the rating agencies will give an AAA (Aaa) rating to bonds insured by these firms because all of the insurance firms have AAA ratings. Issues with these private guarantees have enjoyed a more active secondary market and lower required yields.[22]

CORPORATE BONDS   Again, the importance of corporate bonds varies across countries. The absolute dollar value of corporate bonds in the United States is substantial and has grown overall and as a percentage of U.S. long-term capital. At the same time, corporate debt as a percentage of total U.S. debt has declined from 18 percent to 12 percent because of the faster increase in government debt caused by large government deficits and the growth of agency debt. The pure corporate sector in Japan is small and declining, whereas bank debentures comprise a significant segment (over 20 percent). The pure corporate sector in Germany is almost nonexistent, whereas bank debentures that are used to finance loans to nonbank corporations are the largest segment. The proportion of corporate debt in the United Kingdom is in the 5 to 6 percent range.

U.S. CORPORATE BOND MARKET   Utilities dominate the U.S. corporate bond market. The other important segments include industrials (which rank second to utilities), rail and transportation issues, and financial issues. This market includes debentures, first-mortgage issues, convertible obligations, bonds with warrants, subordinated debentures, income bonds (similar to municipal revenue bonds), collateral trust bonds backed by financial assets, equipment trust certificates, and asset-backed securities (ABS) including mortgage-backed bonds.

If we ignore convertible bonds and bonds with warrants, the preceding list of obligations varies by the type of collateral behind the bond. Most bonds have semiannual interest payments, sinking funds, and a single maturity date. Maturities range from 25 to 40 years, with public utilities generally on the longer end and industrials preferring the 25- to 30-year range. Nearly all corporate bonds provide for deferred calls after 5 to 10 years. The deferment period varies directly with the level of the interest rates. Specifically, during periods of higher interest rates bond issues typically will carry a 7- to 10-year deferment, while during periods of lower interest rates, the deferment periods will be much shorter.

---

[22] For a discussion of municipal bond insurance, see Sylvan Feldstein, Frank J. Fabozzi, and T. Dessa Fabozzi, "Municipal Bonds," in *The Handbook of Fixed-Income Securities,* 4th ed., edited by Frank J. Fabozzi and T. Dessa Fabozzi (Burr Ridge, IL: Irwin Professional Publishing, 1995); and D. S. Kidwell, E. H. Sorenson, and J. M. Wachowicz, "Estimating the Signaling Benefits of Debt Insurance: The Case of Municipal Bonds," *Journal of Financial and Quantitative Analysis* 22, no. 3 (September 1987): 299–313. For a discussion of a problem due to the popularity of insurance, see Constance Mitchell, "Bond Insurers Nearing Their Capacity for Backing Some Municipalities' Debt," *The Wall Street Journal,* June 1, 1992, C1, C7.

On the other hand, corporate notes—with maturities of 5 to 7 years—are generally noncallable. Notes become popular when interest rates are high because issuing firms prefer to avoid long-term obligations during such periods. In contrast, during periods of low interest rates such as 1991–1993 and 1995, most corporate issues did not include a call provision because corporations did not believe that they would be able to exercise the call option and did not want to pay the higher yield required to include them.

Generally, the average yields for industrial bonds will be the lowest of the three major sectors, followed by utility returns, with yields on transportation bonds generally being the highest. The difference in yield between utilities and industrials is because utilities have the largest supply of bonds, so yields on their bonds must be higher to increase the demand for these bonds.

Some corporate bonds have unique features or security arrangements that will be discussed in the following subsections.[23]

Mortgage bonds   The issuer of a mortgage bond has granted to the bondholder a first-mortgage lien on some piece of property or possibly all of the firm's property. Such a lien provides greater security to the bondholder and a lower interest rate for the issuing firm. Additional mortgage bonds can be issued, assuming certain protective covenants related to earnings or assets are met by the issuer.

Collateral trust bonds   As an alternative to pledging fixed assets or property, a borrower can pledge stocks, bonds, or notes as collateral. The bonds secured by these assets are termed *collateral trust bonds*. These pledged assets are held by a trustee for the benefit of the bondholder.

Equipment trust certificates   Equipment trust certificates are issued by railroads (the biggest issuers), airlines, and other transportation firms with the proceeds used to purchase equipment (freight cars, railroad engines, and airplanes), which serves as the collateral for the debt. Maturities range from 1 to about 15 years. The fairly short maturities reflect the nature of the collateral, which is subject to substantial wear and tear and tends to deteriorate rapidly.

Equipment trust certificates are appealing to investors because of their attractive yields and low default record. Although they lack the visibility of other corporate bonds, they typically are fairly liquid.

Collateralized mortgage obligations (CMOs)[24]   Earlier we discussed mortgage bonds backed by pools of mortgages that pay bondholders proportionate shares of principal and interest paid on the mortgages in the pool. You will recall that the pass-through monthly payments are necessarily both interest and principal and that the bondholder is subject to early retirement if the mortgagees prepay because the house is sold or the mortgage refinanced. As a result, when you acquire the typical mortgage pass-through bonds, you receive monthly payments (which may not be ideal), and you would be uncertain about the size and timing of the payments.

Collateralized mortgage obligations (CMOs) were developed to offset some of the problems with the traditional mortgage pass-throughs. The first CMO was issued in June 1983, and the current total issuance exceeds $750 billion. The main innovation of the CMO

[23] For a further discussion, see Frank J. Fabozzi, Harry Sauvain, Richard Wilson, and John Ritchie, "Corporate Bonds," in *The Handbook of Fixed-Income Securities,* 4th ed., edited by Frank J. Fabozzi and T. Dessa Fabozzi (Burr Ridge, IL: Irwin Professional Publishing, 1995).

[24] For a detailed discussion, see Andrew S. Carron, "Collateralized Mortgage Obligations," in *The Handbook of Fixed-Income Securities,* 4th ed., edited by Frank Fabozzi and T. Dessa Fabozzi (Burr Ridge, IL: Irwin Professional Publishing, 1995).

instrument is the segmentation of irregular mortgage cash flows to create securities that are high-quality, short-, medium-, and long-term collateralized bonds. Specifically, CMO investors own bonds that are collateralized by a pool of mortgages or by a portfolio of mortgage-backed securities. The bonds are serviced with the cash flows from these mortgages, but rather than the straight pass-through arrangement, the CMO substitutes a *sequential distribution process* that creates a series of bonds with varying maturities to appeal to a wider range of investors.

The prioritized distribution process is as follows:

- Several classes of bonds (these are referred to as *tranches*) are issued against a pool of mortgages, which are the collateral. As an example, let us assume a CMO issue with four classes (tranches) of bonds. In such a case, the first three (e.g., Classes A, B, C) would pay interest at their stated rates, beginning at their issue date, and the fourth class would be an accrual bond (referred to as a *Z bond*).[25]
- The cash flows received from the underlying mortgages are applied first to pay the interest on the first three classes of bonds, and then to retire these bonds.
- The classes of bonds are retired sequentially. All principal payments are directed first to the shortest-maturity class A bonds until they are completely retired. Then all principal payments are directed to the next shortest-maturity bonds (i.e., the class B bonds). The process continues until all the classes have been paid off.
- During the early periods, the accrual bonds (the class Z bonds) pay no interest, but the interest accrues as additional principle, and the cash flow from the mortgages that collateralize these bonds is used to pay interest on and retire the bonds in the other classes. Subsequently, all remaining cash flows are used to pay off the accrued interest, pay any current interest, and then to retire the Z bonds.

This prioritized sequential pattern means that the A-class bonds are fairly short-term and each subsequent class is a little longer term until the Z-class bond, which is a long-term bond. It also functions like a zero coupon or PIK bond for the initial years.

Besides creating bonds that pay interest in a more normal pattern (quarterly or semiannually) and that have more predictable maturities, these bonds are considered very high-quality securities (AAA) because of the structure and quality of the collateral. To obtain a AAA rating, CMOs are structured to ensure that the underlying mortgages will always generate enough cash to support the bonds issued, even under the most conservative prepayment and reinvestment rates. In fact, most CMOs are overcollateralized.

Further, the credit risk of the collateral is minimal because most are backed by mortgages guaranteed by a federal agency (GNMA, FNMA) or by the FHLMC. Those mortgages that are not backed by agencies carry private insurance for principal and interest and mortgage insurance. Notably, even with this AAA rating, the yield on these CMOs typically has been higher than the yields on AA industrials. This premium yield has, of course, contributed to their popularity and growth.

---

[25] The four-class CMO was the typical configuration during the 1980s and is used here for demonstration purposes. By 1992, CMOs were issued with 18 to 20 classes. More advanced CMOs are referred to as REMICs, which are intended to provide greater certainty regarding the cash flow patterns for various components of the pool or some of those investing in the pool. Discussions of these REMICs include Robert A. Kulason and Michael Waldman, "Understanding TAC and PAC CMO Structures" (New York: Salomon Brothers, 1988); Mark J. Latimer, "Regarding REMICs," *Secondary Mortgage Markets* (McLean, VA: Freddie Mac, 1991); Andrew S. Carron, "Understanding CMOs, REMICs, and Other Mortgage Derivatives," *Fixed Income Research* (New York: The First Boston Corp., 1992).

Asset-backed securities (ABSs)[26]   A rapidly expanding segment of the securities market is that of *asset-backed securities (ABSs)*, which involve *securitizing debt*. This is an important concept because it substantially increases the liquidity of these individual debt instruments, whether they be individual mortgages, car loans, or credit card debt. This general class of securities was introduced in 1983. Since then, more than $300 billion in asset-backed securities have been issued. Beyond the mortgage securities, this market is dominated by securities backed by automobile loans and credit card receivables.

Certificates for automobile receivables (CARs) are securities collateralized by loans made to individuals to finance the purchase of cars. Auto loans are self-amortizing, with monthly payments and relatively short maturities (i.e., 2 to 5 years). These auto loans can either be direct loans from a lending institution or indirect loans that are originated by an auto dealer and sold to the ultimate lender. CARs typically have monthly or quarterly fixed interest and principal payments, and expected weighted average lives of 1 to 3 years with specified maturities of 3 to 5 years. The expected actual life of the instrument typically is shorter than the specified maturity because of early payoffs when cars are sold or traded in. The cash flows of CARs are comparable to short-term corporate debt. They provide a significant yield premium over General Motors Acceptance Corporation (GMAC) commercial paper, which is the most liquid short-term corporate alternative. The popularity of these collateralized securities makes them important not only by themselves, but also as an indication of the potential for issuing additional collateralized securities backed by other assets and/or other debt instruments.

Credit card receivables   Since 1992, the fastest-growing segment of the ABS market has been securities supported by credit card loans. Credit card receivables are considered to be a revolving credit ABS, in contrast to auto loan receivables that are referred to as an installment contract ABS—because of the nature of the loan. Specifically, whereas the mortgaged-backed and auto loan securities amortize principal, the principal payments from credit card receivables are not paid to the investor but are retained by the trustee to reinvest in additional receivables. This allows the issuer to specify a maturity for the security that is consistent with the needs of the issuer and the demands of the investors.

When buying a credit card ABS, the indenture specifies (1) the intended maturity for the security; (2) the "lock-out period" during which no principal will be paid; and (3) the structure for repaying the principal, which can be accomplished through a single-bullet payment such as a bond, or distributed monthly with the interest payment over a specified amortization period. For example, a five-year ABS could have a lockout period of four years followed by a 12-month amortization of the principal.

Beyond this standard arrangement, revolving credit securities are protected by early amortization events that can force early repayment if specific payout events occur that are detrimental to the investor (e.g., an increase in the loss rate or if the issuer goes into bankruptcy or receivership). Although this early amortization feature protects the investor from credit problems, it causes an early payment that may not be desirable.

Variable-rate notes   Introduced in the United States in the mid-1970s, variable-rate notes became popular during periods of high interest rates. The typical **variable-rate note** possesses two unique features:

1. After the first 6 to 18 months of the issue's life, during which a minimum rate is often guaranteed, the coupon rate floats, so that every 6 months it changes to follow some

---

[26]For further discussion, see Tracy Hudson van Eck, "Asset-Backed Securities," in *The Handbook of Fixed Income Securities*, 4th ed., edited by Frank J. Fabozzi and T. Dessa Fabozzi (Burr Ridge, IL: Irwin Professional Publishing, 1995).

standard. Usually it is pegged 1 percent above a stipulated short-term rate. For example, the rate might be the preceding 3 weeks' average 90-day T-bill rate.

2. After the first year or two, the notes are redeemable at par, at the *holder's* option, usually at 6-month intervals.

Such notes represent a long-term commitment on the part of the borrower, yet provide the lender with all the characteristics of a short-term obligation. They typically are available to investors in minimum denominations of $1,000. However, although the 6-month redemption feature provides liquidity, the variable rates can cause the issues to experience wide swings in semiannual coupons.[27]

Zero coupon and deep discount bonds   The typical corporate bond has a coupon and maturity. In turn, the value of the bond is the present value of the stream of cash flows (interest and principal) discounted at the required yield to maturity (YTM). Alternatively, some bonds do not have any coupons or have coupons that are below the market rate at the time of issue. Such securities are referred to as *zero coupon or minicoupon bonds* or *original-issue discount (OID) bonds*. A zero coupon discount bond promises to pay a stipulated principal amount at a future maturity date, but it does not promise to make any interim interest payments. Therefore, the price of the bond is the present value of the principal payment at the maturity date using the required discount rate for this bond. The return on the bond is the difference between what the investor pays for the bond at the time of purchase and the principal payment at maturity.

Consider a zero coupon, $10,000 par value bond with a 20-year maturity. If the required rate of return on bonds of equal maturity and quality is 8 percent and we assume semiannual discounting, the initial selling price would be $2,082.89 because the present value factor at 8 percent compounded semiannually for 20 years is 0.208289. From the time of purchase to the point of maturity, the investor would not receive any cash flow from the firm. The investor must pay taxes, however, on the implied interest on the bond, although no cash is received. Because an investor subject to taxes would experience severe negative cash flows during the life of these bonds, they are primarily of interest to investment accounts not subject to taxes, such as pensions, IRAs, or Keogh accounts.[28]

A modified form of zero coupon bond is the OID bond where the coupon is set substantially below the prevailing market rate, for example, a 5 percent coupon on a bond when market rates are 12 percent. As a result, the bond is issued at a deep discount from par value. Again, taxes must be paid on the implied 12 percent return rather than the nominal 5 percent, so the cash flow disadvantage of zero coupon bonds, though lessened, remains.

High-yield bonds   A segment of the corporate bond market that has grown in size, importance, and controversy is **high-yield bonds,** also referred to as *speculative-grade bonds* and *junk bonds*. These are corporate bonds that have been assigned a bond rating as noninvestment grade, that is, a rating below BBB or Baa. The title of speculative-grade bonds is probably the most objective because bonds that are not rated investment grade are speculative grade. The designation of *high-yield bonds* was by Drexel Burnham Lambert (DBL) as an indication of the returns available for these bonds relative to Treasury bonds

---

[27] For an extended discussion, see Richard S. Wilson, "Domestic Floating-Rate and Adjustable-Rate Debt Securities," in *The Handbook of Fixed-Income Securities,* 4th ed., edited by Frank J. Fabozzi and T. Dessa Fabozzi (Burr Ridge, IL: Irwin Professional Publishing, 1995). Adjustable-rate preferred stocks also are discussed in Richard S. Wilson, *Corporate Senior Securities* (Chicago: Probus Publishing, 1987), Chapter 6.

[28] These bonds will be discussed further in Chapter 16 in the section on volatility and duration and in Chapter 17 when we consider immunization.

and investment-grade corporate bonds. The *junk bond* designation is obviously somewhat derogatory and refers to the quality of the issues.

Brief history of the high-yield bond market   Based on a specification that bonds rated below BBB make up the high-yield market, this segment has been in existence for as long as there have been rating agencies. Prior to 1980, most of the high-yield bonds were referred to as *fallen angels*. These were bonds that were originally issued as investment-grade securities but because of changes in the firm over time, the bonds were downgraded into the high-yield sector (BB and below).

The market changed in the early 1980s when DBL began aggressively underwriting high-yield bonds for two groups of clients: (1) small firms that did not have the financial strength to receive an investment-grade rating by the rating agencies and (2) large and small firms that issued high-yield bonds in connection with leveraged buyouts (LBOs). The high-yield bond market went from a residual market that included fallen angels to a new-issue market where bonds were underwritten with below-investment grade ratings.

The individual who is credited with leading the development of this new-issue, high-yield market is Michael Milken, a bond trader/salesman at DBL. Milken examined the returns and risks related to speculative-grade securities pre-1975 and became convinced that the promised and realized rates of return on these speculative-grade bonds were higher than justified by their default experience. He convinced a number of institutional investors of the superior risk-adjusted returns available on these bonds, which helped create a demand for them. At the same time, Milken and DBL became active in underwriting a large number of these high-yield bond issues for small firms and LBOs.[29] As a result, the high-yield bond market exploded in size and activity beginning in 1983. As shown in Table 15.5, there were a limited number of new high-yield issues in the late 1970s, and they were not very large issues (the average size was less than $30 million). Therefore, they accounted for only about 4 to 7 percent of all public straight debt issues. Beginning in 1983, more large issues became common (the average size of an issue currently is almost $200 million), and high-yield issues became a significant percentage of the total new-issue bond market (approaching 20 percent). As of 1995, the total amount of high-yield debt constituted about 12 percent of all public debt in the United States.

An important point bears repeating: Although the high-yield debt market has existed for many years, its real emergence as a significant factor and a major component of the U.S. capital market did not occur until 1983. This is relevant when considering the liquidity and default experience for these securities.

Distribution of ratings   Table 15.6 contains the distribution of ratings for all outstanding high-yield issues as of December 31, 1993–1995. As shown, the heavy concentration by both issues and par amount is in the B class, which contains almost half of all issues. A notable change during the period was a shift toward higher quality issues—i.e., the propor-

---

[29] After the growth and development of the high-yield bond market, Michael Milken and DBL were indicted for securities law violations. DBL settled with the SEC and paid a fine without admitting guilt. In early 1990, Milken agreed to plea bargain with the SEC that involved a fine and a prison term. It is the author's opinion that observers should separate the development of the high-yield bond market and the securities law violations. Although not condoning the securities law violations, almost everyone would acknowledge that the development of the high-yield debt market has had a positive impact on the capital-raising ability of the economy. For an analysis of this impact, see Glenn Yago, *Junk Bonds* (New York: Oxford University Press, 1991); and Kevin J. Perry and Robert A. Taggart, Jr., "The Growing Role of Junk Bonds in Corporate Finance," *Journal of Applied Corporate Finance* 1, no. 1 (Spring 1988): 37–45. An update on its characteristics and a discussion of the importance of high-yield bonds to midcap companies is contained in Martin S. Fridson, "The State of the High Yield Bond Market: Overshooting or Return to Normalcy," *Journal of Applied Corporate Finance* 7, no. 1 (Spring 1994): 85–97.

TABLE 15.5

HIGH-YIELD BOND ISSUES: ANNUAL DOLLAR VALUE, NUMBER, AVERAGE SIZE, AND PERCENTAGE OF ALL PUBLIC DEBT ISSUES ($ MILLIONS)

| | TOTAL PAR VALUE: NEW HIGH-YIELD DEBT ISSUES | | | PAR VALUE OF TOTAL CORPORATE ISSUES | |
	Amount	Number	Average Size	Total Value	High Yield as Percentage of Total
1977	1,040	61	17.0	26,314	3.95
1978	1,578	82	19.2	21,557	7.32
1979	1,400	56	25.0	25,831	5.42
1980	1,429	45	31.8	36,905	3.87
1981	1,536	34	45.2	40,784	3.77
1982	2,692	52	51.8	47.209	5.70
1983	7,765	95	81.7	38,373	20.24
1984	15,239	131	116.3	82,492	18.47
1985	15,685	175	89.6	80,477	19.49
1986	33,262	226	147.2	156,051	21.31
1987	30,522	190	160.6	126,134	24.20
1988	31,095	160	194.3	134,792	23.07
1989	28.753	130	221.2	142,791	20.14
1990	1,397	10	139.7	109,284	1.28
1991	9,967	48	207.6	207,301	4.81
1992	39,755	245	162.3	317,606	12.52
1993	57,164	341	167.6	313,898	18.21
1994	34,599	191	181.1	173,402	19.95
1995	30,139	152	198.3	253,496	11.89

Source: Securities Data Company and Martin S. Fridson, "This Year in High Yield," *Extra Credit* (New York: Merrill Lynch & Co., January/February 1996).

TABLE 15.6

DISTRIBUTION OF RATINGS FOR HIGH-YIELD BONDS: DECEMBER 31, 1993–DECEMBER 31, 1995

	BY PAR AMOUNT			BY NUMBER OF ISSUES		
Average S&P Rating	1995	1994	1993	1995	1994	1993
BB	49.2	45.8	43.4	45.2	42.5	42.9
B	45.6	49.9	48.4	48.9	52.8	49.5
CCC/CC/C	5.2	4.3	8.2	5.9	4.7	7.6

Source: Martin S. Fridson, "This Year in High Yield," *Extra Credit* (New York: Merrill Lynch & Co., January/February 1994–1996).

tion of BB issues (par value) went from about 43 percent to over 49 percent, while the CCC/CC/C component went from about 8 to 5 percent.

Ownership of high-yield bonds   The major owners of high-yield bonds have been mutual funds, insurance companies, and pension funds. As of the end of 1995, there were almost 100 mutual funds that were either exclusively directed to invest in high-yield bonds or included such bonds in their portfolio. Most observers agree that there has been a shift away from insurance companies and savings and loans toward mutual funds. A great deal of the shift occurred during the dark days of 1989–1990 when regulators "encouraged" the insurance companies and S&Ls to reduce or eliminate high-yield bonds from their port-folios.

The purpose of this discussion has been to introduce you to high-yield bonds because of the growth in size and importance of this segment of the market for individual and institutional investors. We revisit this topic in Chapter 17 on bond portfolio management, where we review the historical rates of return and alternative risk factors, including the default experience for these bonds. All of this must be considered by potential investors in these securities.[30]

 JAPANESE CORPORATE BOND MARKET   The corporate bond market in Japan is made up of two components: (1) bonds issued by industrial firms or utilities and (2) bonds issued by banks to finance loans to corporations. As noted in connection with Table 15.2, the pure corporate bond sector has declined in relative size over time to less than 10 percent of the total. In contrast, the dollar amount of bank debentures is over 17 percent of the total.

Japanese corporate bonds are regulated by the *Kisaikai,* a council composed of 22 bond-related banks and seven major securities companies. It operates under the authority of the Ministry of Finance (MOF) and the Bank of Japan (BOJ) to determine bond-issuing procedures. Specifically, the Kisaikai fixes the coupons on corporate bonds in relation to coupons on long-term government bonds to prevent any competition with the government bond market.

Because of numerous bankruptcies during the 1930s depression, the government mandated that all corporate debt be secured. During the 1970s and 1980s, there was pressure to relax these requirements. Before this was allowed, domestic Japanese firms began issuing convertible bonds because they were not bound by the collateral rule. Also, foreign firms began issuing unrestricted Euroyen bonds, and domestic firms began selling straight debt in the Euroyen market. Finally, the requirement was abolished during 1988.

The issuance of unsecured debt has led to the birth of bond-rating agencies, which were not needed with completely secured debt. The Japan Bond Research Institute was established in 1979, followed by Mikuni's Credit Rating Company in 1981 and by the following firms in 1985 and 1986: Japan Credit Rating Agency, Ltd.; Nippon Investors Service, Inc.; and Moody's Japan K.K. (a subsidiary of Moody's Investor's Service, Inc.).

Corporate bond segments   The corporate industrial debt market in Japan is divided into two major segments: bonds issued by electric power supply companies and bonds issued by all other corporations. The nine electric power supply firms receive preferential treatment because they are regulated public utilities. As a result, about 75 percent of all corporate bond issues are public utility bonds. Corporate bonds for other industrial firms are sold in the domestic market and in the Eurobond market.

The Ministry of Finance specifies minimum corporate requirements and issuing requirements. Also, the ministry controls the issuance system that specifies who can issue bonds and when they can be issued. In addition, lead-underwriting managers are predetermined in accordance with a lead manager rotating system that ensures balance among the big-four securities firms in Japan (Nomura, Nikko, Daiwa, and Yamaichi Capital Management).

---

[30] For additional discussion of these bonds, see Robert Solof, "Historical Perspectives on the Use of High Yield Securities in Corporate Creation: A Hundred Years of 'Junk'" (New York: Drexel Burnham Lambert, February 1989); Edward I. Altman, ed., *The High Yield Debt Market* (Homewood, IL: Dow Jones-Irwin, 1990); Frank J. Fabozzi, ed., *The New High Yield Debt Market* (New York: Harper Business, 1990); Martin S. Fridson, *High Yield Bonds* (Chicago: Probus Publishing, 1989); Frank K. Reilly, ed., *High Yield Bonds: Analysis and Risk Assessment* (Charlottesville, VA: Institute of Chartered Financial Analysts, 1990); and Jane Tripp Howe, *Junk Bonds: Analysis and Portfolio Strategies* (Chicago: Probus Publishing Co., 1988).

Bank bonds   The substantial issuance of bank bonds is because of the banking system in Japan, which is segmented into the following components:

- Commercial banks (13 big-city banks and 64 regional banks)
- Long-term credit banks (3)
- Mutual loan and savings banks (6)
- Specialized financial institutions

During the post–World War II reconstruction, several banks were permitted to obtain funding by issuing medium- and long-term debentures at rates above yields on government bonds. These funds were used to make mortgage loans to firms in the industrial sector to rebuild plant and equipment. Currently, these financial institutions sell 5-year coupon debentures and 1-year discount debentures directly to individual and institutional investors. The long-term credit banks are not allowed to take deposits and thus depend on the debentures to obtain funds. These bonds are traded in the OTC market.[31]

GERMAN CORPORATE BOND MARKET   Germany likewise has a combination sector in corporates that includes pure corporate bonds and bank bonds. Here the contrast is even larger because nonbank corporate bonds are almost nonexistent, whereas bank bonds make up over 35 percent of the total bond market.

Bank bonds may be issued in collateralized or uncollateralized form. For the collateralized bonds, the largest categories are mortgage bonds and commercial bonds.

German mortgage bonds are collateralized bonds of the issuing bank backed by mortgage loans. Due to the supervision of these bonds and the mortgage collateral, these bonds are considered to be very high quality. They are issued in bearer or registered form. Most registered bonds are sold to domestic institutions and cannot be listed on a stock exchange because they are not considered securities. Alternatively, the bearer bonds, which are transferred by book-entry, are sold in small denominations, traded on the exchanges, and enjoy an active secondary market.

German commercial bonds are subject to the same regulation and collateralization as mortgage bonds. The difference is that the collateral consists of loans to or guarantees by a German public-sector entity rather than a first mortgage. Possible borrowers include the federal government, its agencies (the federal railway or the post office), federal states, and agencies of the European Economic Community (EEC). The credit quality of these loans is excellent. Mortgage and commercial bonds have identical credit standing and trade at very narrow spreads.

Schuldscheindarlehen are private loan agreements between borrowers and large investors (usually a bank) who make the loan but who can (with the borrower's permission) sell them or divide the loans among several investors. These instruments are like a negotiable loan participation. All participants receive a copy of the loan agreement, and a letter of assignment gives the participant title to a share of principle and interest, although the bank acts as the agent. These loan agreements, which come in various sizes, account for a substantial proportion of all funds raised in Germany. A large volume of these private loan agreements exist, but because the market is not very liquid they typically are used for the investment of large sums to maturity.

---

[31] For further discussion of this market, see Aron Viner, *Inside Japanese Financial Markets* (Homewood, IL: Dow Jones-Irwin, 1988), Chapters 5 and 6; and Frank J. Fabozzi, ed., *The Japanese Bond Markets* (Chicago: Probus Publishing, 1990).

U.K. CORPORATE BOND MARKET   Corporate bonds in the United Kingdom are available in three forms: debentures, unsecured loans, and convertible bonds. The values of securities in each class are about equal. The maturity structure of the corporate bond market is fairly wide because during the 1980s, the preference of investors shifted toward long maturity bonds. The coupon structure of corporate bonds also is broad with high-coupon bonds issued during the 1980s. The higher end of the coupon range, which goes from 10 to 14 percent, is due to the unsecured segment of this market. In contrast, convertible bonds have the low coupons. Almost all U.K. corporate bonds are callable term bonds.

Corporate bonds in the United Kingdom have been issued through both public offerings and private placements. Early in the 1980s, the market tended toward private placements. Since the Big Bang in October 1986, there have been more public offerings. Prior to the Big Bang, corporate bonds were traded on the stock exchange. Subsequently primary dealers have begun trading corporate bonds directly with each other. All corporate bonds are issued in registered form.

INTERNATIONAL BONDS

Each country's international bond market has two components. The first, *foreign bonds,* are issues sold primarily in one country and currency by a borrower of a different nationality. An example would be U.S. dollar–denominated bonds sold in the United States by a Japanese firm. (These are referred to as *Yankee bonds.*) Second are *Eurobonds,* which are bonds underwritten by international bond syndicates and sold in several national markets. An example would be Eurodollar bonds that are securities denominated in U.S. dollars, underwritten by an international syndicate, and sold to non-U.S. investors outside the United States. The relative size of these two markets (foreign bonds versus Eurobonds) varies by country.

UNITED STATES   The Eurodollar bond market has been much larger than the Yankee bond market (about $635 billion versus $220 billion). However, because the Eurodollar bond market is heavily affected by changes in the value of the U.S. dollar, it has experienced slower growth during periods when the dollar was weak. Such periods have created a desire for diversification by investors.

Yankee bonds are issued by foreign firms who register with the SEC and borrow U.S. dollars, using issues underwritten by a U.S. syndicate for delivery in the United States. These bonds are traded in the United States and pay interest semiannually. Over 60 percent of Yankee bonds are issued by Canadian corporations and typically have shorter maturities and longer call protection than U.S. domestic issues, which increase their appeal.

The Eurodollar bond market is dominated by foreign investors, and the center of trading is in London. Eurodollar bonds pay interest annually, so it is necessary to adjust the standard yield calculation that assumes semiannual compounding. The Eurodollar bond market currently comprises almost 40 percent of the total Eurobond market.

JAPAN   Before 1985, the Japanese international bond market was dominated (over 90 percent) by foreign bonds (Samurai bonds) with the balance in Euroyen bonds. After the issuance requirements for Euroyen bonds were liberalized in 1985, the ratio of issuance swung heavily in favor of Euroyen bonds.

Samurai bonds are yen-denominated bonds sold by non-Japanese issuers and mainly sold in Japan. The market is fairly small and has limited liquidity. The market has experienced very little growth in terms of yen, but substantial growth in U.S. dollar terms because of changes in the exchange rate.

Euroyen bonds are yen-denominated bonds sold in markets outside Japan by international syndicates. As indicated, this market has grown substantially since 1985 because of the liberal issue requirements and favorable exchange rate movements that make yen-denominated securities desirable.

GERMANY   All deutschemark bonds of foreign issuers can be considered Eurobonds. This is because the stability of German currency reduces the importance of the distinction between foreign bonds (DM-denominated bonds sold in Germany by non-German firms) and Euro-DM bonds (DM bonds sold outside Germany). Both types of bonds share the same primary and secondary market procedures, are free of German taxes, and have similar yields, and the amount outstanding is almost equal.

UNITED KINGDOM   U.K. foreign bonds, referred to as *bulldog bonds,* are sterling-denominated bonds issued by non-English firms and sold in London. Eurosterling bonds are sold in markets outside London by international syndicates.

Similar to other countries, the U.K. international bond market has become dominated by the Eurosterling bonds. As of 1994, the ratio of Eurobonds versus foreign bonds had grown to 25-to-one. The procedure for issuing and trading Eurosterling bonds is similar to that of other Eurobonds.

OBTAINING INFORMATION ON BOND PRICES

As might be expected, the price information needs of bond investors are considerably different from those of stockholders. We know that there is substantial up-to-the-minute information on numerous listed and OTC stocks based on recent transactions. In sharp contrast, almost all bond trading (in dollar volume) is done on the OTC market and these transactions are not reported. As a result, almost all prices reported are based upon self-reporting of yield estimates by bond dealers who trade government, corporate, or munici-pal bonds. There was some discussion of this in Chapter 5 when we considered the creation and maintenance of bond indexes. Given this background, the following discussion considers how investors read and interpret bond price information reported in newspapers and quote sheets.

INTERPRETING BOND QUOTES

Essentially, all bonds are quoted on the basis of either yield or price. Price quotes are always interpreted as a *percentage of par.* For example, a quote of 98½ is not interpreted as $98.50, but 98½ percent of par. The dollar price is derived from the quote, given the par value. If the par value is $5,000 on a municipal bond, then the price of an issue quoted at 98½ would be $4,925. Actually, the market follows three systems of bond pricing: one system for corporates, another for governments (both Treasury and agency obligations), and a third for municipals.

CORPORATE BOND QUOTES   Figure 15.1 is a listing of NYSE corporate bond quotes that appeared in *The Wall Street Journal* on February 7, 1996. The data pertain to trading activity on February 6. Several quotes have been designated for illustrative purposes. The first issue designated in column one is a Pacific Bell issue and is representative of most corporate prices. In particular, the 7¼ 02 indicates the coupon and maturity of the obliga-tion; in this case, the Pac Bell issue carries a 7.25 percent coupon and matures in 2002. The next column provides the *current* yield of the obligation and is found by comparing the coupon to the current market price. For example, a bond with a 7.25 percent coupon selling for 107.50 would have a 6.7 percent current yield. This is *not* the YTM or even necessarily a good approximation to it. Both of these yields will be discussed in Chapter 16.

The next column gives the volume of $1,000 par value bonds traded that day (in this case, 300 bonds were traded). The next column indicates closing quotes, followed by the

FIGURE 15.1   **SAMPLE CORPORATE BOND QUOTATIONS**

NEW YORK EXCHANGE BONDS

Quotations as of 4 p.m. Eastern Time
Tuesday, February 6, 1996

Volume $29,929,000

	Domestic		All Issues	
	Tue.	Mon.	Tue.	Mon.
Issues traded	323	346	331	354
Advances	152	145	154	148
Declines	112	140	114	145
Unchanged	59	61	63	61
New highs	31	33	31	35
New lows	2	2	2	2

SALES SINCE JANUARY 1
(000 omitted)

1996	1995	1994
$655,470	$740,833	$936,474

Dow Jones Bond Averages

–1995–		–1996–			Close	Chg.	%Yld	Close	Chg.
High	Low	High	Low		---1996---			--1995--	
105.34	93.63	105.91	105.21	20 Bonds	105.86	+ 0.05	6.74	95.53	+ 0.02
102.30	89.08	102.43	101.86	10 Utilities	102.40	+ 0.19	6.94	90.80	– 0.10
108.96	98.08	109.58	108.53	10 Industrials	109.33	– 0.07	6.54	100.26	+ 0.14

Bonds	Cur Yld	Vol	Close	Net Chg		Bonds	Cur Yld	Vol	Close	Net Chg
Novacr 5½2000	cv	145	86	+ ⅞		Roadmst 8s03	cv	253	80	– ½
OcciP 9⅝99	9.5	40	101⅞			Rohr 7s12	cv	41	88¾	+ 1⅛
OcciP 11¾cld	...	15	104²⁷/₃₂	...		Rowan 11⅞01	10.9	115	109	+ ½
OffDep zr08	...	9	57	– 1		Safwy 9.35s99	8.7	7	107½	– ¼
OhBIT 7½11	7.4	6	101¾	– 1		Safwy 10s01	8.7	79	114¾	+ ¼
OldRep 5¾02	cv	12	136	+ 4		Safwy 9.65s04	8.4	205	114½	
Olsten 4⅞03	4.0	4	123¼	+ ¼		Safwy 9⅞07	8.4	8	117	...
Orient 10¼98	10.1	74	101	– ⅛		SallM zr22	...	5	17	– ⅜
Oryx 7½14	cv	7	90½			Salmln 03	...	20	86½	
Ownlll 10¼99	10.0	16	102⅞	...		Seagte 6¾12	cv	76	139¾	– 1¼
Ownlll 10½02	9.8	5	106¾	+ ¾		Sequa 9⅜03	9.4	5	99½	+ ½
Ownlll 10s02	9.4	65	106	...		SvcMer 8⅜01	8.8	20	95¼	+ ¼
Owlll 11s03	9.7	45	113½	...		SvcMer 9s04	10.6	509	84⅝	+ ⅛
Ownlll 9¾04	9.1	170	106¾	+ ¾		ShellO 7¼02	7.1	4	101½	– 1
Ownlll 9.95s04	9.0	30	110½			Shoney zr04	...	9	39	+ 1
①→ PacBell 7¼02	6.7	300	107½	– ¼		Showboat 9¼08	9.0	260	102½	– ⅛
PacBell 6⅞23	7.0	40	98¼	+ ⅛		Sizeler 03	...	100	83	...
PacBell 7⅛26	6.8	78	104¾	– ¼		Snyder 7s01	cv	57	92	+ ¾
PacBell 7½33	7.3	112	102¼	+ ⅝		SouBell 7⅞10	7.2	33	103	+ 1
PacSci 7¾03	cv	41	119	– 1		SptRec 4½00	cv	40	57⅛	– 1⅞
②→ PacTT 7¼08	7.1	10	102	– ⅜		StdCmcl 07	cv	10	68¼	...
Pathmk zr03	...	51	59⅞	+ ¾		StdPac 10½00	10.2	22	103⅛	...
Paten 8¼12	cv	32	92	+ 1		StoneC 10¾97	10.5	19	102⅝	– ⅜
PaylCsh 9⅛03	11.0	523	83¼	– ⅜		StoneCn 11⅞98	11.2	224	105⅞	– ⅝
PennTr 9⅝05	11.3	670	85½	+ 3¼		StoneC 11½99	11.4	172	100⅝	+ ⅛
Pennzl 6½03	5.3	36	123¼	...		StoneCn 11s99	11.2	1192	98½	...
Pennzl 4¾03	4.6	34	102½	+ ½		StoneC 9⅞01	10.2	4034	97⅜	+ ⅜
PhilEl 7⅜01	7.3	13	101⅝	...		StoneC 10¾02A	11.2	687	96¼	+ ⅛
PhilEl 7⅛23	7.3	6	98	+ 1¼		StoneC 10¾02O	10.4	189	103	...
PhilEl 7¼24	7.3	6	99⅜	+ ½		StoneC 11½04	11.6	216	99½	– ¼
③→ PhilP 8.49s23	7.9	10	107⅛	– 1⅛		StoneCn 6¾07	cv	10	88¾	
Pier1 6⅞02	cv	40	115½	+ ½		StrTch 7s08	5.6	241	124½	+ 2½
PierOn dc11½203	11.1	9	104	...		StrTch 8s15	cv	253	103¾	+ 1½
PogoP 5½04	cv	5	140	+ 9		SwiftEn 6½03	cv	10	109	+ 2
PogoP 8s05	cv	14	102¼	– ¾		TVA 7⅞99	7.6	64	101	+ ⁵/₁₆
PofEl 7s18	cv	8	103½	+ 1		TVA 7⅞01	7.6	38	103¼	– 1½
Primark 8¾00	8.4	4	104¼	+ 1		TVA 6⅞02	6.7	7	102⅜	– ⅝
PrmHsp 9¼06	9.1	45	101⅛	– 1⅛		TVA 6⅛03	6.1	26	100⅜	+ ⅝
PSEG 7⅞00	7.1	10	107	+ 1⅞		TVA 7⅝22	7.4	61	103¼	...
PSEG 8¼22	8.2	15	107	+ ⅛		TVA 7¼22	7.0	42	104	...
PSEG 7½23	7.5	13	100⅛	– ⅞		TVA 8.05s24	7.8	7	103¼	+ ¼
Quanx 6.88s07	cv	51	97	+ ⅞		TVA 8⅝29	7.8	15	110½	+ ¼
RJR Nb 8⅝02	8.3	53	104⅜	– ⅞		TVA 8¼34	7.8	58	105⅝	+ 1⅜
RJR Nb 7⅝03	7.7	990	98⅞			TVA 7.85s44	7.4	6	105⅜	+ 1⅛
RJR Nb 8¾05	8.4	250	104⅛	+ ¼		Teledy 10s04A	9.9	20	101⅜	+ ⅜
RJR Nb 8⅞07	8.6	280	103¾	+ ⅝		Teledy 10s04C	10.0	219	100⅜	– 1⅛
RJR Nb 9¼13	8.9	158	104½	+ ½		Tenet 9⅝02	8.6	50	111⅜	– ⅜
RJR Nb 8¾04	8.4	55	104	– ⅛		Tenet 05	cv	5	114¼	+ 1¼
Rallys 9⅞00	14.9	154	66¼	– 5⅛		Tenco 10s08	7.9	114	127	+ 1⅜
RalsP 9½16	9.1	1	104¾	...		TennGas dc6s11	6.7	80	89¼	– ¾
RalsP 9⅜16	9.1	6	103⅝	...		Tesor 13s00	12.6	10	103½	+ ¼
RalsP 8⅝22	7.7	4	111½	– 1		Texco 9s97	8.5	10	106¼	+ ¼
RelGrp 9s00	8.7	123	103½	– ⅛		Texco 8.95s00†	8.8	5	102¼	...
RelGrp 9¾03	9.4	60	104⅛	...		TmeWar 7.45s98	7.2	71	103⅛	+ ¼
Revl 9½99	9.1	276	104⅛	+ ⅛		TmeWar 7.95s00	7.5	50	106	+ ¾
Revl 10⅞10	10.6	129	102⅜	– 1⅜		TmeWar 7.98s04	7.6	7	105⅜	+ ¾
Rexene 11¾04	11.0	35	106½	+ ⅝						
RiteA zr06	cv	10	53	– ¾						
Rvrwd 6¾03	cv	1	110	+ 2						

Source: *The Wall Street Journal*, February 7, 1996.

column for the net change in the closing price from the last day the issue was traded. In this case, Pac Bell closed at 107.50 which was down ¼ from the prior day ($25).

The second bond in Column 1 is Pathmk zr 03 which refers to a Pathmark Corp. zero coupon bond ("zr") due in 2003. As discussed, zero coupon securities do not pay interest but are redeemed at par at maturity. Because there is no coupon, they sell at a deep discount, which implies a yield. Again, since there are no coupon payments, they do not report a current yield.

Finally, the third bond in Column 1 is a convertible ("cv") bond from Pier 1 Corp. that has a 6.875 coupon and is due in 2002. The conversion feature means that the bond is convertible into the common stock of the company. If you see a bond with a "dc" before the coupon, it means "deep discount," indicating that the original coupon was set below the going rate at the time of issue. An example of such a bond would be a 5 percent coupon bond issued when market rates were 9 or 10 percent. Alternatively, if there is "vj" in front of a bond issue, it means that the firm is in receivership or bankruptcy. The small letter "f" that will usually follow the maturity date of such a bond means that the issue is trading *flat,* which means the issuer is not meeting its interest payments. Therefore, the coupon of the obligation is inconsequential and there is a dash in the current yield column because there are no coupon payments.

All fixed-income obligations, with the exception of preferred stock, are traded on an *accrued interest basis.* The prices pertain to the value of all *future* cash flows from the bond and exclude interest that has accrued to the holder since the last interest payment date. The actual price of the bond will exceed the quote listed because accrued interest must be added. Assume a bond with a 7⅛ percent coupon. If two months have elapsed since interest was paid, the current holder of the bond is entitled to ⅔ or one-third of the bond's semiannual interest payment that will be paid in 4 months. More specifically, the 7⅛ percent coupon provides semiannual interest income of $35.625. The investor who held the obligation for two months beyond the last interest payment date is entitled to one-third (⅓) of that $35.625 in the form of accrued interest. Therefore, whatever the current price of the bond, an accrued interest value of $11.87 will be added.

TREASURY AND AGENCY BOND QUOTES   Figure 15.2 illustrates the quote system for Treasury and agency issues. These quotes resemble those used for OTC securities because they contain both bid and ask prices, rather than high, low, and close. For U.S. Treasury bond quotes, a small "*n*" behind the maturity date indicates that the obligation is a Treasury *note.* A small "*p*" indicates it is a Treasury note on which nonresident aliens are exempt from withholding taxes on the interest.

All other obligations in this section are Treasury bonds. The security identification is different because it is not necessary to list the issuer. Instead, the usual listing indicates the coupon, the month and year of maturity, and information on a call feature of the obligation. For example, quote 1 is an 8¼ percent issue that carries a maturity of 2000–2005. This means that the issue has a deferred call feature until 2000 (and is thereafter freely callable) and a (final) maturity date of 2005. The bid–ask figures provided are stated as a percentage of par. The yield figure provided is yield to maturity, or *promised* yield based on the asking price. This system is used for Treasuries, agencies, and municipals.

Quote 2 is a 5⅞ percent obligation of 2005 that demonstrates the basic difference in the price system of government bonds (i.e., Treasuries and agencies). The bid quote is 101:18, and the ask is 101:20. Governments are traded in thirty-seconds of a point (rather than eighths), and the figures to the right of the colons indicate the number of thirty-seconds in the fractional bid or ask. In this case, the bid price is actually 101.5625 percent of par.

FIGURE 15.2   **SAMPLE QUOTES FOR TREASURY BONDS, NOTES, AND BILLS**

TREASURY BONDS, NOTES & BILLS

Tuesday, February 6, 1996

Representative Over-the-Counter quotations based on transactions of $1 million or more.

Treasury bond, note and bill quotes are as of mid-afternoon. Colons in bid-and-asked quotes represent 32nds; 101:01 means 101 1/32. Net changes in 32nds. n-Treasury note. Treasury bill quotes in hundredths, quoted on terms of a rate of discount. Days to maturity calculated from settlement date. All yields are to maturity and based on the asked quote. Latest 13-week and 26-week bills are boldfaced. For bonds callable prior to maturity, yields are computed to the earliest call date for issues quoted above par and to the maturity date for issues below par. *-When issued.

Source: Federal Reserve Bank of New York.

U.S. Treasury strips as of 3 p.m. Eastern time, also based on transactions of $1 million or more. Colons in bid-and-asked quotes represent 32nds; 99:01 means 99 1/32. Net changes in 32nds. Yields calculated on the asked quotation. ci-stripped coupon interest. bp-Treasury bond, stripped principal. np-Treasury note, stripped principal. For bonds callable prior to maturity, yields are computed to the earliest call date for issues quoted above par and to the maturity date for issues below par.

Source: Bear, Stearns & Co. via Street Software Technology Inc.

GOVT. BONDS & NOTES

Rate	Maturity Mo/Yr	Bid	Asked	Chg.	Ask Yld.
4⅝	Feb 96n	99:31	100:01	....	2.92
7⅞	Feb 96n	100:02	100:04	....	1.25
8⅞	Feb 96n	100:02	100:04	....	2.21
4⅝	Feb 96n	99:30	100:00	....	4.53
7½	Feb 96n	100:04	100:06	....	4.11
5⅛	Mar 96n	99:31	100:01	....	4.82
7¾	Mar 96n	100:11	100:13	....	4.74
9⅜	Apr 96n	100:25	100:27	....	4.59
5½	Apr 96n	100:03	100:05	....	4.73
7⅝	Apr 96n	100:18	100:20	....	4.72
4¼	May 96n	99:25	99:27	....	4.80
7⅜	May 96n	100:19	100:21	....	4.80
5⅞	May 96n	100:08	100:10	+ 1	4.79
7⅝	May 96n	100:24	100:26	....	4.88
6	Jun 96n	100:11	100:13	....	4.91
7⅞	Jun 96n	101:03	101:05	....	4.84
7⅞	Jul 96n	101:07	101:09	....	4.84
6⅛	Jul 96n	100:16	100:18	....	4.91
7⅞	Jul 96n	101:11	101:13	....	4.86
4⅜	Aug 96n	99:21	99:23	....	4.93
6¼	Aug 96n	100:20	100:22	....	4.99
7¼	Aug 96n	101:05	101:07	....	5.01
6½	Sep 96n	100:30	101:00	....	4.90
7	Sep 96n	101:08	101:10	+ 1	4.90
8	Oct 96n	101:31	102:01	....	4.95
6⅞	Oct 96n	101:10	101:12	....	4.93
4⅜	Nov 96n	99:18	99:20	+ 1	4.88
7¼	Nov 96n	101:22	101:24	....	4.90
6½	Nov 96n	101:06	101:08	....	4.91
7¼	Nov 96n	101:24	101:26	....	4.94
6⅛	Dec 96n	101:03	101:05	+ 1	4.79
7½	Dec 96n	102:07	102:09	....	4.86
8	Jan 97n	102:24	102:26	....	4.89
6⅛	Jan 97n	101:08	101:10	....	4.86
7½	Jan 97n	102:14	102:16	+ 1	4.85
4¾	Feb 97n	99:26	99:28	+ 1	4.88
6¾	Feb 97n	101:27	101:29	....	4.88
6⅞	Feb 97n	101:31	102:01	....	4.88

Rate	Maturity Mo/Yr	Bid	Asked	Chg.	Ask Yld.	
8	Aug 96-01	101:13	101:17	+ 1	4.98	
13⅜	Aug 01	138:02	138:06	+ 7	5.30	
7½	Nov 01n	110:14	110:16	+ 6	5.36	
15¾	Nov 01	150:30	151:02	+ 5	5.35	
14¼	Feb 02	145:04	145:08	+ 3	5.36	
7½	May 02n	111:02	111:04	+ 6	5.39	
6⅜	Aug 02n	105:01	105:03	+ 6	5.44	
11⅝	Nov 02	134:13	134:17	+ 7	5.45	
6¼	Feb 03n	104:09	104:11	+ 7	5.50	
10¾	Feb 03	130:03	130:07	+ 6	5.50	
10¾	May 03	130:25	130:29	+ 4	5.53	
5¾	Aug 03n	101:07	101:09	+ 7	5.54	
11⅛	Aug 03	133:25	133:29	+ 4	5.55	
11⅞	Nov 03	139:07	139:11	+ 9	5.57	
5⅞	Feb 04n	101:25	101:27	+ 6	5.59	
7¼	May 04n	110:20	110:22	+ 7	5.62	
12⅜	May 04	144:04	144:08	+ 10	5.61	
7¼	Aug 04n	110:24	110:26	+ 7	5.63	
13¾	Aug 04	154:09	154:13	+ 14	5.62	
7⅞	Nov 04n	115:04	115:06	+ 8	5.65	
11⅝	Nov 04	140:24	140:28	+ 10	5.65	
7½	Feb 05n	112:23	112:25	+ 8	5.67	
6½	May 05n	105:23	105:25	+ 7	5.69	
8½	May 00-05	110:13	110:17	+ 2	5.45	← ①
12	May 05	144:31	145:03	+ 10	5.68	
6½	Aug 05n	105:27	105:29	+ 7	5.69	
10¾	Aug 05	136:20	136:24	+ 10	5.70	
5⅞	Nov 05n	101:18	101:20	+ 5	5.66	← ②
9⅜	Feb 06	127:28	128:00	+ 5	5.67	
7⅝	Feb 02-07	109:24	109:28	....	5.67	
7⅞	Nov 02-07	112:14	112:18	+ 2	5.62	
8⅜	Aug 03-08	116:14	116:18	....	5.64	
8¾	Nov 03-08	118:18	118:22	+ 5	5.74	
9⅛	May 04-09	121:28	122:00	+ 2	5.75	
10¾	Nov 04-09	131:10	131:14	+ 4	5.76	
11¾	Feb 05-10	141:21	141:25	+ 7	5.75	
10	May 05-10	129:25	129:29	+ 5	5.79	
12¾	Nov 05-10	151:08	151:12	+ 6	5.79	
13⅞	May 06-11	161:19	161:23	+ 7	5.81	

U.S. TREASURY STRIPS

Mat.	Type	Bid	Asked	Chg.	Ask Yld.	
Feb 96	ci	99:29	99:29	....	5.05	
Feb 96	np	99:29	99:29	....	5.35	
May 96	ci	98:22	98:22	+ 1	5.02	
May 96	np	98:22	98:22	....	4.99	
Aug 96	ci	97:18	97:18	+ 3	4.81	
Nov 96	ci	96:10	96:11	....	4.93	
Nov 96	np	96:10	96:11	+ 1	4.94	
Feb 97	ci	95:08	95:09	+ 1	4.81	
May 97	ci	94:01	94:02	+ 1	4.89	
May 97	np	94:02	94:03	+ 1	4.87	
Aug 97	ci	92:29	92:30	+ 1	4.88	
Aug 97	np	92:29	92:30	+ 1	4.88	
Nov 97	ci	91:23	91:25	+ 1	4.92	
Nov 97	np	91:23	91:25	+ 1	4.92	
Feb 98	ci	90:18	90:20	+ 1	4.94	
Feb 98	np	90:18	90:20	+ 1	4.93	
May 98	ci	89:13	89:14	+ 1	4.98	
May 98	np	89:14	89:16	+ 1	4.95	
Aug 98	ci	88:08	88:10	+ 1	5.00	
Aug 98	np	88:07	88:09	+ 1	5.01	
Nov 98	ci	87:04	87:06	+ 1	5.02	
Nov 98	np	87:02	87:04	+ 1	5.04	
Feb 99	ci	85:29	85:31	+ 1	5.07	③ →
Feb 99	np	85:30	86:00	+ 1	5.05	
May 99	ci	84:25	84:28	+ 1	5.09	
May 99	np	84:24	84:27	+ 2	5.10	
Aug 99	ci	83:20	83:22	+ 2	5.12	
Aug 99	np	83:17	83:20	+ 3	5.15	
Nov 99	ci	82:16	82:19	+ 2	5.15	
Nov 99	np	82:13	82:16	+ 2	5.18	
Feb 00	ci	81:12	81:15	+ 2	5.17	
Feb 00	np	81:08	81:11	+ 2	5.20	
May 00	ci	80:09	80:13	+ 3	5.18	
May 00	np	80:06	80:09	+ 2	5.21	
Aug 00	ci	79:05	79:08	+ 2	5.21	
Aug 00	np	78:29	79:01	+ 2	5.28	

TREASURY BILLS

Maturity	Days to Mat.	Bid	Asked	Chg.	Ask Yld.
Feb 08 '96	0	5.08	4.98	+0.01	0.00
Feb 15 '96	7	5.01	4.91	−0.02	5.00
Feb 22 '96	14	4.81	4.71	−0.19	4.80
Feb 29 '96	21	4.71	4.61	−0.03	4.70
Mar 07 '96	28	4.80	4.76	−0.06	4.86
Mar 14 '96	35	4.75	4.71	−0.07	4.81
Mar 21 '96	42	4.60	4.56	−0.02	4.66
Mar 28 '96	49	4.67	4.63	−0.04	4.74
Apr 04 '96	56	4.82	4.78	−0.03	4.90
Apr 11 '96	63	4.81	4.79	−0.03	4.91
Apr 18 '96	70	4.68	4.66	−0.04	4.78
Apr 25 '96	77	4.76	4.74	+0.01	4.87
May 02 '96	84	4.85	4.83	−0.01	4.97
May 09 '96	**91**	**4.84**	**4.82**	**−0.02**	**4.96**
May 16 '96	98	4.83	4.81	−0.01	4.96
May 23 '96	105	4.82	4.80	−0.02	4.95
May 30 '96	112	4.82	4.80	−0.01	4.95
Jun 06 '96	119	4.80	4.78	−0.01	4.94
Jun 13 '96	126	4.75	4.74	−0.01	4.91
Jun 20 '96	133	4.78	4.76	−0.01	4.93
Jun 27 '96	140	4.77	4.75	−0.01	4.92
Jul 05 '96	148	4.78	4.76	....	4.94
Jul 11 '96	154	4.77	4.75	−0.02	4.93
Jul 18 '96	161	4.76	4.74	−0.01	4.92
Jul 25 '96	168	4.77	4.75	−0.01	4.94
Aug 01 '96	175	4.77	4.73	−0.01	4.94
Aug 08 '96	**182**	**4.77**	**4.75**	**−0.02**	**4.95**
Aug 22 '96	196	4.76	4.74	−0.01	4.94
Sep 19 '96	224	4.71	4.69	−0.01	4.89
Oct 17 '96	252	4.70	4.68	−0.02	4.89
Nov 14 '96	280	4.69	4.67	−0.02	4.89
Dec 12 '96	308	4.63	4.61	−0.02	4.83
Jan 09 '97	336	4.64	4.62	−0.01	4.85
Feb 06 '97	364	4.62	4.60	−0.01	4.85

Source: *The Wall Street Journal*, February 7, 1996.

These quotes also are notable in terms of the bid–ask spread, which typically is 2 or 3 thirty-seconds, or about one-half the size of the smallest possible spread for most stocks, which is ⅛. This small spread reflects the outstanding liquidity and low transaction costs for Treasury securities.

The lower section of the first column contains quotes for U.S. Treasury securities that have been "stripped." Specifically, the typical bond that promises a series of coupon payments and its principal at maturity is divided into separate units whereby each coupon payment and the principal payment are treated like a zero coupon bond that matures on that date. The security labeled ③ was originally a coupon that was to be paid in February 1999. The asking yield (5.07) is referred to as the spot rate for this maturity (spot rate will be discussed in Chapter 16). The coupon interest payments with no principal is designated as "ci" (stripped coupon interest), while the other strip for February 1999 contains only the principal payment is designated "np" (Treasury note, stripped principal).

The securities listed in the Treasury bond section are for U.S. Treasury bills. Notice that only dates are reported and no coupons. This is because these are pure discount securities, that is, the return is the difference between the price you pay and par at maturity.[32]

MUNICIPAL BOND QUOTES   Figure 15.3 contains municipal bond quotes from *The Blue List of Current Municipal Offerings*. These are ordered according to states and then alphabetically within states. Each issue gives the amount of bonds being offered (in thousands of dollars), the name of the security, the purpose or description of the issue, the coupon rate, the maturity (which includes month, day, and year), the yield or price, and the dealer offering the bonds. Bond quote 1 is for $200,000 of Indiana State Office Building bonds. The MBIA indicates that the bonds are guaranteed by the Municipal Bond Insurance Association (MBIA). These are zero (0.000) coupon bonds due July 1, 2005. In this instance, the yield to maturity is given (5.60 percent). To determine the price, compute the discount value or look up in a yield book the price of a zero coupon bond, due in about 8 years to yield 5.60 percent. The dealer offering the bonds is Bearster. A list in the back of the publication gives the name and phone number of the firm.

The second bond is for $115,000 of Indiana State Toll Road bonds with a 9 percent coupon. These bonds have a M/S/F (mandatory sinking fund) that becomes effective in 2011, although the bond matures in 2015. The ETM means that the sinking fund is put into "escrow till maturity." The market yield on these bonds is 6.30 percent, which means the bond would be selling at a premium.

Bond quote 3 refers to $10,000 of Indianapolis, Indiana, Airport Authority revenue bonds that are backed by a contract with US Air. Although the bonds mature in 2009, they are callable beginning in 1997 (C97) at 102 of par. The coupon is 7.50 percent and in this case, the price of the bond is listed (100), which means its market yield also is 7.50 percent. Such bonds are called *dollar bonds*.

The " +" in the far left column indicates a new item since the prior issue of *The Blue List*. A "#" in the column prior to the yield to maturity or the price indicates that the price or yield has changed since the last issue. It is always necessary to call the dealer to determine the current yield/price because these quotes are at least one day old when they are published.

---

[32] For a discussion on calculating yields, see Bruce D. Fielitz, "Calculating the Bond Equivalent Yield for T-Bills," *Journal of Portfolio Management* 9, no. 3 (Spring 1983): 58–60.

FIGURE 15.3	**QUOTES FOR MUNICIPALS**

Indiana

No. of Bonds Offered	Municipal Issuer	Special Characteristics	Coupon	Maturity	Price/YTM	Broker	
100	INDIANA BD BK REV (HOOSIER EQUIP)	*B/E*	4.300	01/01/96N/C	100	NORWESMN	
550	INDIANA HEALTH FAC FING AUTH	METHODIST	5.625	09/01/02N/C	101	PRUBACG	
45	INDIANA HEALTH FAC FING AUTH	P/R @ 102	7.750	08/15/20C00	5.25	EQUITSEC	
200	INDIANA PORT COMMN PORT REV		6.750	07/01/10	99 3/4	NOYESDAV	
3115	INDIANA ST OFFICE BLDG COMMN	P/R @ 102	8.200	07/01/01C97	4.60	MORGANNT	
200	INDIANA ST OFFICE BLDG COMMN	MBIA	0.000	07/01/05	5.60	BEARSTER	←①
335	INDIANA ST RECREATIONAL DEV		6.050	07/01/14	6.45	SMITHBCH	
115	INDIANA ST TOLL RD COMMN TOLL	M/S/F 11	9.000	01/01/15ETM	6.30	DRIZOS	←②
95	INDIANA ST TOLL RD COMMN TOLL		9.000	01/01/15ETM	6.30	EMMET	
1000	INDIANA ST TOLL RD COMMN TOLL	N/C S/F 11	9.000	01/01/15ETM	6.00	WILLIAMA	
100	ELKHART CNTY IND HOSP AUTH REV (ELKHART GEN HOSP)	*B/E* RFDG	6.200	07/01/01N/C	5.40	BLAIRWM	
45	FORT WAYNE IND HOSP AUTH HOSP	S/F 97	6.875	01/01/02ETM	5.85	EMMET	
100	FORT WAYNE IND HOSP AUTH HOSP	P/R @ 102	9.125	07/01/15C95	3.80	GABRIELE	
55	GOSHEN IND CMNTY SCHS		6.600	07/01/97	4.75	NBDBKIND	
10	INDIANAPOLIS IND ARPT AUTH REV (CA @ 102.01 @ 100)	US AIR	7.500	07/01/09C97	100	HSH	←③
15	INDIANAPOLIS IND ARPT AUTH REV	US AIR	7.500	07/01/19	8.25	STERLING	
500	INDIANAPOLIS IND GAS UTIL REV		4.300	06/01/98	5.00	CITYSEC	
60	INDIANAPOLIS IND LOC PUB IMPT		0.000	08/01/07N/C	8.10	SAPNY	
25	INDIANAPOLIS IND LOC PUB IMPT		6.750	02/01/20	100	COUGHLIN	
200	LAKE CENTRAL IND MULTI-		6.000	01/15/02ETM	5.25	CREWASSC	
300	MICHIGAN CITY IND SEW WKS REV		5.200	08/01/07	5.70	NOYESDAV	
	Thursday May 28, 1994				PAGE	15.A	

Source: *The Blue List of Current Municipal Offerings,* May 26, 1994, p. 15A. The Blue List Division of Standard & Poor's Corp., New York. Reprinted by permission of Standard & Poor's Corp.

Summary

- We consider the basic features of bonds: interest, principal, and maturity. Certain key relationships affect price behavior. Price is essentially a function of coupon, maturity, and prevailing market interest rates. Bond price volatility depends on coupon and maturity. As will be demonstrated in Chapter 16, bonds with longer maturities and/or lower coupons respond most vigorously to a given change in market rates.

- Each bond has unique intrinsic characteristics and can be differentiated by type of issue and indenture provisions. Major benefits to bond investors include high returns for nominal risk, the potential for capital gains, certain tax advantages, and possibly additional returns from active trading of bonds. Aggressive bond investors must consider market liquidity, investment risks, and interest rate behavior. We introduced high-yield (junk) bonds because of the growth in size and status of this segment of the bond market.

- The global bond market includes numerous countries. The non-U.S. markets have experienced strong relative growth, whereas the U.S. market has been stable, but constitutes less than half the world bond market. The four major bond markets (the United States, Japan, Germany, and the United Kingdom) have a different makeup in terms of the proportion of governments, agencies, municipals, corporates, and international issues. The various market sectors also are unique in terms of liquidity, yield spreads, tax implications, and operating features.

- To gauge default risk, most bond investors rely on agency ratings. For additional information on the bond market, prevailing economic conditions, and intrinsic bond features, individual and

institutional investors rely on a host of readily available publications discussed in Chapter 6. Although there are extensive up-to-date quotes available on Treasury bonds and notes, trading and price information for corporates and municipals is relatively difficult to find and is expensive.
- The world bond market is large, and continuing to grow at a strong rate due to government deficits around the world and the need for capital by corporations. It is also very diverse in terms of country alternatives and issuers within countries. This chapter provides the fundamentals that will allow us to consider the valuation of individual bonds in Chapter 16, and the alternative bond portfolio techniques in Chapter 17.

Questions

1. Explain the difference between calling a bond and a bond refunding.
2. Identify the three most important determinants of the price of a bond. Describe the effect of each.
3. Given a change in the level of interest rates, discuss how two major factors will influence the relative change in price for individual bonds.
4. Briefly describe two indenture provisions that can affect the maturity of a bond.
5. Explain the differences in taxation of income from municipal bonds and income from U.S. Treasury bonds and corporate bonds.
6. For several institutional participants in the bond market, explain what type of bond each is likely to purchase and why.
7. Why should investors be aware of the trading volume for bonds in their portfolio?
8. What is the purpose of bond ratings?
9. Based on the data in Table 15.1, which is the fastest-growing bond market in the world? Which markets are losing market share?
10. Based on the data in Table 15.2, discuss the makeup of the German bond market and how and why it differs from the U.S. market.
11. Discuss the positives and negatives of investing in a government agency issue rather than a straight Treasury bond.
12. Discuss the difference between a foreign bond (e.g., a Samurai) and a Eurobond (e.g., a Euroyen issue).
13. *CFA Examination I (1993)*
    List *three* differences between Eurodollar and Yankee bonds.

Problems

1. An investor in the 28 percent tax bracket is trying to decide which of two bonds to purchase. One is a corporate bond carrying an 8 percent coupon and selling at par. The other is a municipal bond with a 5½ percent coupon, and it, too, sells at par. Assuming all other relevant factors are equal, which bond should the investor select?
2. What would be the initial offering price for the following bonds (assume semiannual compounding):
   a. A 15-year zero coupon bond with a yield to maturity (YTM) of 12 percent.
   b. A 20-year zero coupon bond with a YTM of 10 percent.
3. An 8.4 percent coupon bond issued by the state of Indiana sells for $1,000. What coupon rate on a corporate bond selling at its $1,000 par value would produce the same after-tax return to the investor as the municipal bond if the investor is in
   a. The 15 percent marginal tax bracket?
   b. The 25 percent marginal tax bracket?
   c. The 35 percent marginal tax bracket?
4. The Shamrock Corporation has just issued a $1,000 par value zero coupon bond with an 8 percent yield to maturity, due to mature 15 years from today (assume semiannual compounding).
   a. What is the market price of the bond?
   b. If interest rates remain constant, what will be the price of the bond in 3 years?
   c. If interest rates rise to 10 percent, what will be the price of the bond in 3 years?

5. Complete the information requested for each of the following $1,000 face value, zero coupon bonds, assuming semiannual compounding.

Bond	Maturity (Years)	Yield (Percent)	Price ($)
A	20	12	?
B	?	8	601
C	9	?	350

References

Altman, Edward I., ed. *The High Yield Debt Market.* Homewood, IL: Dow Jones-Irwin, 1990.

Altman, Edward I. and Scott A. Nammacher. *Investing in Junk Bonds.* New York: John Wiley & Sons, 1987.

Beidleman, Carl, ed. *The Handbook of International Investing.* Chicago: Probus Publishing, 1987.

Douglas, Livingston G. *The Fixed Income Almanac.* Chicago: Probus Publishing Co., 1993.

Elton, Edwin J. and Martin J. Gruber, eds. *Japanese Capital Markets.* New York: Harper & Row, 1990.

European Bond Commission. *European Bond Markets.* Chicago: Probus Publishing, 1989.

Fabozzi, Frank J., ed. *Advances and Innovations in the Bond and Mortgage Markets.* Chicago: Probus Publishing, 1989.

Fabozzi, Frank J., ed. *The Japanese Bond Market,* Chicago: Probus Publishing, 1990.

Fabozzi, Frank J., ed. *The New High Yield Debt Market.* New York: Harper Business, 1990.

Fridson, Martin S. *High Yield Bonds.* Chicago: Probus Publishing, 1989.

Grabbe, J. Orlin. *International Financial Markets.* New York: Elsevier, 1986.

Howe, Jane Tripp. *Junk Bonds: Analysis and Portfolio Strategies.* Chicago: Probus Publishing, 1988.

Norton, Joseph and Paul Spellman, eds. *Asset Securitization.* Cambridge, MA: Basil Blackwell, Inc., 1991.

Van Horne, James C. *Financial Market Rates and Flows.* 3d ed. Englewood Cliffs, NJ: Prentice-Hall, 1988.

Viner, Aron. *Inside Japanese Financial Markets.* Homewood, IL: Dow Jones-Irwin, 1988.

Wilson, Richard S. *Corporate Senior Securities.* Chicago: Probus Publishing, 1987.

Wilson, Richard S. and Frank J. Fabozzi. *The New Corporate Bond Market.* Chicago: Probus Publishing, 1990.

Yago, Glenn. *Junk Bonds.* New York: Oxford University Press, 1991.

Chapter

16

The Analysis and Valuation of Bonds

This chapter answers the following questions:

- How do you determine the value of a bond based on the present value formula?
- What are the alternative bond yields that are important to investors?
- How do you compute the following major yields on bonds: current yield, yield to maturity, yield to call, and compound realized (horizon) yield?
- What are spot rates and forward rates and how do you calculate these rates from a yield to maturity curve?
- What is the spot rate yield curve and forward rate curve?
- How and why do you use the spot rate curve to determine the value of a bond?
- What are the alternative theories that attempt to explain the shape of the term structure of interest rates?
- What factors affect the level of bond yields at a point in time?
- What economic forces cause changes in bond yields over time?
- When yields change, what characteristics of a bond cause differential price changes for individual bonds?
- What is meant by the duration of a bond, how do you compute it, and what factors affect it?
- What is modified duration and what is the relationship between a bond's modified duration and its volatility?
- What is effective duration and when is it useful?
- What is the convexity for a bond, how do you compute it, and what factors affect it?
- Under what conditions is it necessary to consider both modified duration and convexity when estimating a bond's price volatility?
- What happens to the duration and convexity of bonds that have embedded call options?

In this chapter, we apply the valuation principles that were introduced in Chapter 13 to the valuation of bonds. This chapter is concerned with how one goes about finding the value of bonds using the traditional single yield to maturity rate and using multiple spot rates. We will also come to understand the several measures of yields for bonds. It also is important to understand why these bond values and yields change over time. To do this, we begin with a review of value estimation for bonds using the present value model introduced in Chapter 13. This background on valuation allows us to understand and compute the expected rates of return on bonds, which are their yields. We need to understand how to measure alternative yields on bonds because they are very important to bond investors.

After mastering the measurement of bond yields, we consider what factors influence the level of bond yields and what economic forces cause changes in yields over time. This is followed by a consideration of the alternative shapes of the yield curve and the alternative theories that explain changes in its shape. We discuss the effects of various characteristics and indenture provisions that affect the required returns and, therefore, the value of specific bond issues. This includes factors such as time to maturity, coupon, callability, and sinking funds.

We return to the consideration of bond value and examine the characteristics that cause different changes in a bond's price. When yields change, all bond prices do not change in the same way. An understanding of the factors that affect the price changes for bonds has become more important during the past several decades because the price volatility of bonds has increased substantially. Before 1950, the yields on bonds were fairly low and both yields and prices were stable. In this environment, bonds were considered a very safe investment and most investors in bonds intended to hold them to maturity. During the last several decades, however, the level of interest rates has increased substantially because of inflation, and interest rates have also become more volatile because of changes in the rate of inflation and monetary policy. As a result, bond prices and rates of return on bonds have been much more volatile and the rates of return on bond investments have increased. Although this increase in interest rate volatility has affected all bonds, the impact is more significant on bonds with embedded options such as call features.

THE FUNDAMENTALS OF BOND VALUATION

The value of bonds can be described in terms of dollar values or the rates of return they promise under some set of assumptions. In this section, we describe both the present value model, which computes a specific value for the bond using a single discount value, and the yield model, which computes the promised rate of return based on the bond's current price.

THE PRESENT VALUE MODEL

In our introduction to valuation theory in Chapter 13, we saw that the value of a bond (or any asset) equals the present value of its expected cash flows. The cash flows from a bond are the periodic interest payments to the bondholder and the repayment of principal at the maturity of the bond. Therefore, the value of a bond is the present value of the semiannual interest payments plus the present value of the principal payment. Notably, the standard technique is to use a single interest rate discount factor, which is the required rate of return on the bond. We can express this in the following present value formula that assumes semiannual compounding:[1]

$$P_m = \sum_{t=1}^{2n} \frac{C_i/2}{(1 + i/2)^t} + \frac{P_p}{(1 + i/2)^{2n}}$$

where

P_m = the current market price of the bond
n = the number of years to maturity
C_i = the annual coupon payment for bond i
i = the prevailing yield to maturity for this bond issue
P_p = the par value of the bond

The value computed indicates what an investor would be willing to pay for this bond to realize a rate of return that takes into account expectations regarding the RFR, the expected rate of inflation, and the risk of the bond. The standard valuation technique assumes

---

[1] Almost all U.S. bonds pay interest semiannually so it is appropriate to use semiannual compounding wherein you cut the annual coupon rate in half and double the number of periods. To be consistent, you should also use semiannual compounding for the principal payment of a coupon bond or even a zero coupon bond. All our present value calculations assume semiannual compounding.

holding the bond to the maturity of the obligation. In this case, the number of periods would be the number of years to the maturity of the bond (referred to as its *term to maturity*). In such a case, the cash flows would include all the periodic interest payments and the payment of the bond's par value at the maturity of the bond.

We can demonstrate this formula using an 8 percent coupon bond that matures in 20 years with a par value of $1,000. This calculation implies that an investor who holds this bond to maturity will receive $40 every six months (one half of the $80 coupon) for 20 years (40 periods) and $1,000 at the maturity of the bond in 20 years. If we assume a prevailing yield to maturity for this bond of 10 percent (the market's required rate-of-return on the bond), the value for the bond using the above equation would be:

$$P_m = \sum_{t=1}^{40} \frac{80/2}{(1 + .10/2)^t} + \frac{\$1,000}{(1 + .10/2)^{40}}$$

We know that the first term is the present value of an annuity of $40 every six months for 40 periods at 5 percent, while the second term is the present value of $1,000 to be received in 40 periods at 5 percent. This can be summarized as follows:

Present value of interest payments:		
$40 × 17.1591	=	$686.36
Present value of principal payment		
$1,000 × .1420	=	142.00
Total value of bond at 10%		$828.36

As expected, the bond will be priced at a discount to its par value because the market's required rate of return of 10 percent is greater than the bond's coupon rate, i.e., $828.36 or 82.836 percent of par.

Alternatively, if the market's required rate was 6 percent, the value would be computed the same way except we would compute the present value of the annuity at 3 percent for 40 periods and the present value of the principal at 3 percent for 40 periods as follows:

Present value of interest payments:		
$40 × 23.1148	=	$924.59
Present value of principal payment		
$1,000 × .3066	=	306.60
Total value of bond at 6%		$1,231.19

Because the bond's discount rate is lower than its coupon, the bond would sell at a premium above par value—i.e., $1,231.19 or 123.119 of par.

THE PRICE-YIELD CURVE   When you know the basic characteristics of a bond in terms of its coupon, maturity, and par value, the only factor that determines its value (price) is the market discount rate—its required rate of return. As shown above, as we increase the required rate, the price declines. It is possible to demonstrate the specific relationship between the price of a bond and its yield by computing the bond's price at a range of yields as shown in Table 16.1.

| TABLE 16.1 | PRICE-YIELD RELATIONSHIP FOR A 20-YEAR, 8 PERCENT COUPON BOND ($1,000 PAR VALUE) |

Required Yield	Price of Bond
2	$1,985.09
4	1,547.12
6	1,231.19
8	1,000.00
10	828.36
12	699.05
14	600.07
16	522.98

| FIGURE 16.1 | THE PRICE-YIELD CURVE FOR A 20-YEAR, 8 PERCENT COUPON BOND |

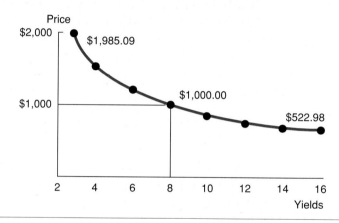

A graph of this relationship between the required return (yield) on the bond and its price is referred to as the price-yield curve as shown in Figure 16.1. Besides demonstrating that price moves inverse to yield, it shows three other important points:

1. When the yield is below the coupon rate, the bond will be priced at a **premium** to its par value.
2. When the yield is above the coupon rate, the bond will be priced at a **discount** to its par value.
3. The price-yield relationship is not a straight line; rather, it is *convex*. As yields decline, the price increases at an increasing rate, and as the yield increases, the price declines at a declining rate. This concept of a convex price-yield curve is referred to as *convexity* and will be discussed further in a later section.

THE YIELD MODEL   Instead of determining the value of a bond in dollar terms, investors often price bonds in terms of **yields**—the promised rates of return on bonds under certain assumptions. Thus far, we have used cash flows and our required rate of return to compute an estimated value for the bond. To compute an expected yield, we use the current market price (P_m) and the expected cash flows to *compute the expected yield on the bond*. We can express this approach using the same present value model. The difference is that in the equation on page 526, it was assumed that we knew the appropriate discount rate (the required rate of return), and we computed the estimated value (price) of the bond. In this case, it is assumed that we know the price of the bond and we compute the discount rate (yield) that will give us the current market price (P_m).

$$P_m = \sum_{t=1}^{2n} \frac{C_i/2}{(1 + i/2)^t} + \frac{P_p}{(1 + i/2)^{2n}}$$

where the variables are the same as previously, except

i = the discount rate that will discount the expected cash flows to equal the current market price of the bond

This i value gives the expected ("promised") yield of the bond under various assumptions to be noted, assuming you pay the price P_m. We will discuss several types of bond yields that arise from the assumptions of the valuation model in the next section.

Approaching the investment decision stating the bond's value as a yield figure rather than a dollar amount, you consider the relationship of the computed bond yield to your required rate of return on this bond. If the computed bond yield is equal to or greater than your required rate of return, you should buy the bond; if the computed yield is less than your required rate of return, you should not buy the bond.

These approaches to pricing bonds and making investment decisions are similar to the two alternative approaches by which firms make investment decisions. We referred to one approach, the net present value (NPV) method, in Chapter 13. With the NPV approach, you compute the present value of the net cash flows from the proposed investment at your cost of capital and subtract the present value cost of the investment to get the net present value (NPV) of the project. If this NPV is positive, you consider accepting the investment; if it is negative, you reject it. This is basically the way we compared the value of an investment to its market price.

The second approach is to compute the **internal rate of return (IRR)** on a proposed investment project. The IRR is the discount rate that equates the present value of cash outflows for an investment with the present value of its cash inflows. You compare this discount rate, or IRR (which is also the expected rate of return on the project), to your cost of capital, and accept any investment proposal with an IRR equal to or greater than your cost of capital. We do the same thing when we price bonds on the basis of yield. If the expected yield on the bond (yield to maturity, yield to call, or horizon yield) is equal to or exceeds your required rate of return on the bond, you should invest in it; if the expected yield is less than your required rate of return on the bond, you should not invest in it.

COMPUTING BOND YIELDS

Bond investors traditionally have used five yield measures for the following purposes:

Yield Measure	Purpose
Nominal yield	Measures the coupon rate.
Current yield	Measures the current income rate.
Promised yield to maturity	Measures the expected rate of return for bond held to maturity.
Promised yield to call	Measures the expected rate of return for bond held to first call date.
Realized (horizon) yield	Measures the expected rate of return for a bond likely to be sold prior to maturity. It considers specific reinvestment assumptions and an estimated sales price. It also can measure the actual rate of return on a bond during some past period of time.

Nominal and current yields are mainly descriptive and contribute little to investment decision making. The last three yields are all derived from the present value model as described in the equation on page 529.

When we present the last three yields based on the present value model, we consider two calculation techniques. First, we consider a fairly simple calculation for the approximate values for each of these yields to provide reasonable estimates. Second, we use the present value model to get accurate values. We provide both techniques because an exact answer with the present value model requires several calculations. In some cases, the approximate yield value is adequate.

To measure an expected realized yield (also referred to as the horizon yield), a bond investor must estimate a bond's future selling price. Following our presentation of bond yields, we present the procedure for finding these prices. We conclude the section by examining the yields on tax-free bonds.

NOMINAL YIELD

Nominal yield is the coupon rate of a particular issue. A bond with an 8 percent coupon has an 8 percent nominal yield. This provides a convenient way of describing the coupon characteristics of an issue.

CURRENT YIELD

Current yield is to bonds what dividend yield is to stocks. It is computed as

$$CY = C_i/P_m$$

where

> CY = **the current yield on a bond**
> C_i = **the annual coupon payment of bond i**
> P_m = **the current market price of the bond**

Because this yield measures the current income from the bond as a percentage of its price, it is important to income-oriented investors who want current cash flow from their investment portfolios. An example of such an investor would be a retired person who lives on this investment income. Current yield has little use for most other investors who are interested in total return because it excludes the important capital gain or loss component.

PROMISED YIELD TO MATURITY

Promised yield to maturity is the most widely used bond yield figure because it indicates the fully compounded rate of return promised to an investor who buys the bond at prevailing prices, *if two assumptions hold true*. Specifically, the *promised* yield to maturity will be equal to the investor's *realized* yield *if* these assumptions are met. The first assumption is that the investor holds the bond to maturity. This assumption gives this value its shortened name, *yield to maturity* (YTM). The second assumption is implicit in the present value method of computation. Referring back to the equation on page 529, recall that it related the current market price of the bond to the present value of all cash flows as follows:

$$P_m = \sum_{t=1}^{2n} \frac{C_i/2}{(1 + i/2)^t} + \frac{P_p}{(1 + i/2)^{2n}}$$

To compute the YTM for a bond, we solve for the rate i that will equate the current price (P_m) to all cash flows from the bond to maturity. As noted, this resembles the computation of the internal rate of return (IRR) on an investment project. Because it is a present value–

based computation, it implies a reinvestment rate assumption because it discounts the cash flows. That is, the equation assumes that *all interim cash flows (interest payments) are reinvested at the computed YTM*. That is why this is referred to as a *promised* YTM because the bond will provide this computed YTM *only if* you meet its conditions:

1. You hold the bond to maturity.
2. You reinvest all the interim cash flows at the computed YTM rate.

If a bond promises an 8 percent YTM, you must reinvest coupon income at 8 percent to realize that promised return. If you spend (do not reinvest) the coupon payments or if you cannot find opportunities to reinvest these coupon payments at rates as high as its promised YTM, then the actual realized yield you earn will be less than the promised yield to maturity. As will be demonstrated in the section on realized return, if you can reinvest at rates above the YTM, your realized (horizon) return will be greater than the promised YTM. The income earned on this reinvestment of the interim interest payments is referred to as **interest-on-interest**.[2]

The impact of the reinvestment assumption (i.e., the interest-on-interest earnings) on the actual return from a bond varies directly with the bond's coupon and maturity. A higher coupon and/or a longer term to maturity will increase the loss in value from failure to reinvest at the YTM. Therefore, a higher coupon or a longer maturity makes the reinvestment assumption more important.

Figure 16.2 illustrates the impact of interest-on-interest for an 8 percent, 25-year bond bought at par to yield 8 percent. If you invested $1,000 today at 8 percent for 25 years and reinvested all the coupon payments at 8 percent, you would have approximately $7,100 at the end of 25 years. We will refer to this money that you have at the end of your investment horizon as your **ending-wealth value**. To prove that you would have an ending-wealth value of $7,100 look up the compound interest factor for 8 percent for 25 years (6.8493) or 4 percent for 50 periods (which assumes semiannual compounding and is 7.1073). In the case of U.S. bonds, the semiannual compounding is the appropriate procedure because almost all bonds pay interest every six months.

Figure 16.2 shows that this $7,100 is made up of $1,000 principal return, $2,000 of coupon payments over the 25 years ($80 a year for 25 years), and $4,100 in interest earned on the semiannual coupon payments reinvested at 4 percent semiannually. If you had never reinvested any of the coupon payments, you would have an ending-wealth value of only $3,000. This ending-wealth value of $3,000 derived from the beginning investment of $1,000 gives you an actual (realized) yield to maturity of only 4.5 percent. That is, the rate that will discount $3,000 back to $1,000 in 25 years is 4.5 percent. Reinvesting the coupon payments at some rate between 0 and 8 percent would cause your ending-wealth position to be above $3,000 and below $7,100; therefore, your actual rate of return would be somewhere between 4.5 percent and 8 percent. Alternatively, if you managed to reinvest the coupon payments at rates consistently above 8 percent, your ending-wealth position would be above $7,100, and your realized (horizon) rate of return would be above 8 percent.

Interestingly, during periods of very high interest rates, you often hear investors talk about "locking in" high yields. Many of these people are subject to **yield illusion** because they do not realize that attaining the high promised yield requires that they reinvest all the coupon payments at the very high promised yields. For example, if you buy a 20-year bond with a promised yield to maturity of 15 percent, you will actually realize the promised

---

[2] This concept is developed in Sidney Homer and Martin L. Leibowitz, *Inside the Yield Book* (Englewood Cliffs, NJ: Prentice-Hall, 1972), Chapter 1.

FIGURE 16.2

THE EFFECT OF INTEREST-ON-INTEREST ON TOTAL REALIZED RETURN

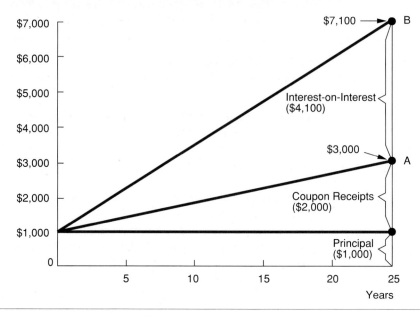

Promised yield at time of purchase: 8.00%
Realized yield over the 25-year investment horizon with no coupon reinvestment (A): 4.50%
Realized yield over the 25-year horizon with coupons reinvested at 8% (B): 8.00%

15 percent yield *only* if you are able to reinvest all the coupon payments at 15 percent over the next 20 years.

COMPUTING THE PROMISED YIELD TO MATURITY   The promised yield to maturity can be computed in two ways: finding an approximate annual yield, or using the present value model with semiannual compounding. The present value model gives an investor a more accurate result, and is the technique used by investment professionals.

The approximate promised yield (APY) measure is easy to calculate:

$$\text{APY} = \frac{C_i + \dfrac{P_p - P_m}{n}}{\dfrac{P_p + P_m}{2}}$$

$$= \frac{\text{Coupon} + \text{Annual Straight-Line Amortization of Capital Gain or Loss}}{\text{Average Investment}}$$

where variables are as defined earlier. This approximate value for the promised yield to maturity assumes interest is compounded annually, and it does not require the multiple computations of the present value model. An 8 percent bond with 20 years remaining to maturity and a current price of $900 has an approximate yield of 8.95 percent:

$$\text{APY} = \frac{80 + \dfrac{1000 - 900}{20}}{\dfrac{1000 + 900}{2}} = \frac{80 + 5}{950}$$

$$= 8.95\%.$$

The present value model provides a more accurate yield to maturity value. Again, the equation on page 529 shows the promised yield valuation model:

$$P_m = \sum_{t=1}^{2n} \frac{C_i/2}{(1 + i/2)^t} + \frac{P_p}{(1 + i/2)^{2n}}$$

All variables are as described previously. This model is more accurate than the approximate promised yield model, but also is more complex because the solution requires iteration. The present value equation is a variation of the internal rate of return (IRR) calculation where we want to find the discount rate, i, that will equate the present value of the stream of coupon receipts (C_i) and principal value (P_p) with the current market price of the bond (P_m). Using the prior example of an 8 percent, 20-year bond, priced at \$900, the equation gives us a semiannual promised yield to maturity of 4.545 percent, which implies an annual promised YTM of 9.09 percent.[3]

$$900 = 40 \sum_{t=1}^{40} \left(\frac{1}{(1.04545)^t} \right) + 1000 \left(\frac{1}{(1.04545)^{40}} \right)$$

$$= 40(18.2574) + 1000(.1702)$$
$$= 900.$$

The values for $1/(1 + i)$ were taken from the present value interest factor tables in the appendix at the back of the book using interpolation.

Comparing the results of this equation with those of the approximate promised yield computation, you find a variation of 14 basis points (8.95 percent vs. 9.09 percent). As a rule, the approximate promised yield tends to understate the present value promised yield for issues selling below par value (i.e., trading at a discount) and to overstate the promised yield for a bond selling at a premium. The size of the differential varies directly with the length of the holding period. Although the estimated yield value differs, the rankings of yields estimated using the APY formula will generally be identical to those determined by the present value method.

YTM FOR A ZERO COUPON BOND   In several instances we have discussed the existence of zero coupon bonds that only have the one cash inflow at maturity. This single cash flow means that the calculation of YTM is substantially easier as shown by the following example:

Assume a zero coupon bond, maturing in 10 years with a maturity value of \$1,000 selling for \$311.80. Because you are dealing with a zero coupon bond, there is only the one cash flow from the principal payment at maturity. Therefore, you simply need to determine what is the discount rate that will discount \$1,000 to equal the current market price of \$311.80 in 20 periods (10 years of semiannual payments). The equation is as follows:

$$\$311.80 = \frac{\$1000}{(1 + i)^{20}}$$

---

[3] You will recall from your corporate finance course that you start with one rate (e.g., 9 percent or 4.5 percent semiannual) and compute the value of the stream. In this example, the value would exceed \$900, so you would select a higher rate until you had a present value for the stream of cash flows of less than \$900. Given the discount rates above and below the true rate, you would do further calculations or interpolate between the two rates to arrive at the correct discount rate that would give you a value of \$900.

You will see that $i = 6$ percent, which implies an annual rate of 12 percent. For future reference, this yield also is referred to as the 10-year spot rate, which is the discount rate for a single cash flow to be received in 10 years.

PROMISED YIELD
TO CALL

Although investors use promised YTM to value most bonds, they must estimate the return on certain callable bonds with a different measure—the **promised yield to call (YTC)**. Whenever a bond with a call feature is selling for a price above par (i.e., at a premium) equal to or greater than its par value plus one year's interest, a bond investor should consider valuing the bond in terms of YTC rather than YTM. This is because the marketplace uses the lowest, most conservative yield measure in pricing a bond. When bonds are trading at or above a specified **crossover price,** which is approximately the bond's call price plus a small premium that increases with time to call, the yield to call will provide the lowest yield measure.[4] The crossover price is important because at this price the YTM and the YTC are equal—this is the *crossover yield*. When the bond rises to this price above par, the computed YTM becomes low enough that it would be profitable for the issuer to call the bond and finance the call by selling a new bond at this prevailing market interest rate.[5] Therefore, the YTC measures the promised rate of return the investor will receive from holding this bond until it is retired at the first available call date, that is, at the end of the deferred call period. Note that if an issue has multiple call dates at different prices (the call price will decline for later call dates), it will be necessary to compute which of these scenarios provides the lowest yield—this is referred to as *yield to worst*. Investors must consider computing the YTC for their bonds after a period when numerous high-yielding, high-coupon bonds have been issued. Following such a period, interest rates will decline, bond prices will rise, and the high coupon bonds will subsequently have a high probability of being called.

COMPUTING PROMISED YIELD TO CALL   Again, there are two methods for computing the promised yield to call: the approximate method and the present value method. Both methods assume that you hold the bond until the first call date. The present value method also assumes that you reinvest all coupon payments at the YTC rate.

Yield to call is calculated using variations of the equations on pages 532 and 533. The approximate yield to call (AYC) is computed as follows:

$$AYC = \frac{C_t + \dfrac{P_c - P_m}{nc}}{\dfrac{P_c + P_m}{2}}$$

where

> AYC = the approximate yield to call (YTC)
> P_c = the call price of the bond (generally equal to par value plus one year's interest)
> P_m = the market price of the bond
> C_i = the annual coupon payment of bond i
> nc = the number of years to first call date

---

[4] For a discussion of the crossover point, see Homer and Leibowitz, *Inside the Yield Book,* Chapter 4

[5] Extensive literature exists on the refunding of bond issues, including W. M. Boyce and A. J. Kalotay, "Optimum Bond Calling and Refunding," *Interfaces* (November 1979): 36–49; R. S. Harris, "The Refunding of Discounted Debt: An Adjusted Present Value Analysis," *Financial Management* 9, no. 4 (Winter 1980): 7–12; A. J. Kalotay, "On the Structure and Valuation of Debt Refundings," *Financial Management* 11, no. 1 (Spring 1982): 41–42; and John D. Finnerty, "Evaluating the Economics of Refunding High-Coupon Sinking-Fund Debt," *Financial Management* 12, no. 1 (Spring 1983): 5–10

This equation is comparable to APY, except that P_c has replaced P_p in the equation and nc has replaced n.

To find the AYC of a 12 percent, 20-year bond that is trading at 115 ($1,150) with 5 years remaining to first call and a call price of 112 ($1,120), we substitute these values into the above equation.

$$\text{AYC} = \frac{120 + \dfrac{1120 - 1150}{5}}{\dfrac{1120 + 1150}{2}} = 10.04\%.$$

This bond's approximate YTC is 10.04 percent, assuming that the issue will be called after 5 years at the call price of 112. To confirm that yield to call is the more conservative and more accurate value for a bond callable in 5 years, you can compute the approximate promised YTM. Using the equation on page 533 indicates a promised YTM of 10.47 percent.

To compute the YTC by the present value method, we would adjust the semiannual present value equation to give

$$P_m = \sum_{t=1}^{2nc} \frac{C_i/2}{(1 + i/2)^t} + \frac{P_c}{(1 + i/2)^{2nc}}$$

where

P_m = the current market price of the bond
C_i = the annual coupon payment of bond i
nc = the number of years to first call date
P_c = the call price of the bond

Following the present value method, we solve for i, which typically requires several computations or extrapolation to get the exact yield.

REALIZED (HORIZON) YIELD

The final measure of bond yield, **realized yield** or **horizon yield,** measures the expected rate of return of a bond that you expect to sell prior to its maturity. In terms of the equation, the investor has a holding period (hp) or investment horizon that is less than n. Realized (horizon) yield can be used to estimate rates of return attainable from various trading strategies. Although it is a very useful measure, it requires several additional estimates not required by the other yield measures. Specifically, the investor must estimate the expected future selling price of the bond at the end of the holding period. Also, this measure requires a specific estimate of the reinvestment rate for the coupon flows prior to the liquidation of the bond. This technique also can be used by investors to measure their actual yields after selling bonds.

COMPUTING REALIZED (HORIZON) YIELD   The realized yields are variations on the promised yield equations. The approximate realized yield (ARY) is calculated as follows:

$$\text{ARY} = \frac{C_i + \dfrac{P_f - P_m}{hp}}{\dfrac{P_f + P_m}{2}}$$

where

ARY = the approximate realized (horizon) yield
C_i = the annual coupon payment of the bond i
P_f = the future selling price of the bond
P_m = the current market price of the bond
hp = the holding period of the bond (in years)

Again, the same two variables change: the holding period (hp) replaces n, and P_f replaces P_p. Keep in mind that P_f is not a contractual value but is *calculated* by defining the years remaining to maturity as $n - hp$ and by estimating a future market interest rate, i. We describe the computation of the future selling price (P_f) in the next section.

Once we determine hp and P_f, we can calculate the approximate realized yield. Assume you acquired an 8 percent, 20-year bond for $750. Over the next two years, you expect interest rates to decline. As you know, when interest rates decline, bond prices increase. Suppose you anticipate that, when interest rates decline, the bond price will rise to $900. The approximate realized yield in this case for the two years would be:

$$\text{ARY} = \frac{80 + \dfrac{900 - 750}{2}}{\dfrac{900 + 750}{2}} = 18.79\%.$$

The estimated high realized (horizon) yield reflects your expectation of substantial capital gains in a fairly short period of time. Similarly, the substitution of P_f and hp into the present value model provides the following realized yield model:

$$P_m = \sum_{t=1}^{2hp} \frac{C_t/2}{(1 + i/2)^t} + \frac{P_f}{(1 + i/2)^{2hp}}$$

Again, this present value model requires you to solve for the i that equates the expected cash flows from coupon payments and the estimated selling price to the current market price. Because of the small number of periods in hp, the added accuracy of this measure is somewhat marginal. It has been suggested that because realized yield measures are based on an uncertain future selling price, the approximate realized (horizon) yield method is appropriate under many circumstances. In contrast, if you are going to use this technique to measure historical performance, you should use the more accurate present value model.

You will note from the present value realized yield formula in the above equation that the coupon flows are implicitly discounted at the computed realized (horizon) yield. In many cases, this is an inappropriate assumption because available market rates might be very different from the computed realized (horizon) yield. Therefore, to derive a realistic estimate of the expected realized yield, you also should estimate your expected reinvestment rate during the investment horizon.

Therefore, to complete your understanding of computing expected realized yield for alternative investment strategies, the next section considers the calculation of future bond prices. This is followed by a section on calculating a realized (horizon) return with different reinvestment rates.

CALCULATING FUTURE BOND PRICES

Dollar bond prices need to be calculated in two instances: (1) when computing realized (horizon) yield, you must determine the future selling price (P_f) of a bond if it is to be sold before maturity or first call, and (2) when issues are quoted on a promised yield basis, as with municipals. You can easily convert a yield-based quote to a dollar price by using the equation on page 535, which does not require iteration. (You need only solve for P_m.) The coupon (C_i) is given, as is par value (P_p), and the promised YTM, which is used as the discount rate.

Consider a 10 percent, 25-year bond with a promised YTM of 12 percent. You would compute the price of this issue as

$$P_m = 100/2 \sum_{t=1}^{50} \frac{1}{\left(1 + \frac{.120}{2}\right)^t} + 1000 \frac{1}{\left(1 + \frac{.120}{2}\right)^{50}}$$

$$= 50(15.7619) + 1000(.0543)$$
$$= \$842.40.$$

In this instance, we are determining the prevailing market price of the bond based on the current market YTM. These market figures indicate the consensus of all investors regarding the value of this bond. An investor with a required rate of return on this bond that differs from the market YTM would estimate a different value for the bond.

In contrast to the current market price, you will need to compute a future price (P_f) when estimating the expected realized (horizon) yield performance of alternative bonds. Investors or portfolio managers who consistently trade bonds for capital gains need to compute expected realized yield rather than promised yield. They would compute P_f through the following variation of the realized yield equation:

$$P_f = \sum_{t=1}^{2n - 2hp} \frac{C_i/2}{(1 + i/2)^t} + \frac{P_p}{(1 + i/2)^{2n - 2hp}}$$

where

    P_f = the future selling price of the bond
    P_p = the par value of the bond
    n = the number of years to maturity
   hp = the holding period of the bond (in years)
    C_i = the annual coupon payment of bond i
    i = the expected market YTM at the end of the holding period

This equation is a version of the present value model that calculates the expected price of the bond at the end of the holding period (hp). The term $2n - 2hp$ equals the bond's remaining term to maturity at the end of the investor's holding period, that is, the number of 6-month periods remaining after the bond is sold. Therefore, the determination of P_f is based on four variables: two that are known and two that must be estimated by the investor.

Specifically, the coupon (C_i) and the par value (P_p) are given. The investor must forecast the length of the holding period, and therefore the number of years remaining to maturity at the time the bond is sold ($n - hp$). The investor also must forecast the expected market YTM at the time of sale (i). With this information, you can calculate the future price of the bond. The real difficulty (and the potential source of error) in estimating P_f lies in predicting hp and i.

Assume you bought the 10 percent, 25-year bond just discussed at $842, giving it a promised YTM of 12 percent. Based on an analysis of the economy and the capital market, you expect this bond's market YTM to decline to 8 percent in 5 years. Therefore, you want to compute its future price (P_f) at the end of year 5 to estimate your expected rate of return, assuming you are correct in your assessment of the decline in overall market interest rates.

As noted, you estimate the holding period (5 years), which implies a remaining life of 20 years, and the market YTM of 8 percent. A semiannual model gives a future price:

$$P_f = 50 \sum_{t=1}^{40} \frac{1}{(1.04)^t} + 1000 \frac{1}{(1.04)^{40}}$$

$$= 50(19.7928) + 1000(.2083)$$
$$= 989.64 + 208.30$$
$$= \$1,197.94.$$

Based on this estimate of the selling price, you would estimate the approximate realized (horizon) yield on this investment on an annual basis as

$$\text{APY} = \frac{100 + \dfrac{1198 - 842}{5}}{\dfrac{1198 + 842}{2}}$$

$$= \frac{100 + 71.20}{1020}$$

$$= .1678$$
$$= 16.78\%$$

REALIZED (HORIZON)
YIELD WITH
DIFFERENTIAL
REINVESTMENT RATES

The realized yield equation on page 537 is the standard present value formula with the changes in holding period and ending price. As such, it includes the implicit reinvestment rate assumption that all cash flows are reinvested at the computed i rate. There may be instances where such an implicit assumption is not appropriate, given your expectations for future interest rates. Assume that current market interest rates are very high and you invest in a long-term bond (e.g., a 20-year, 14 percent coupon) to take advantage of an expected decline in rates from 14 percent to 10 percent over a 2-year period. Computing the future price (equal to $1,330.95) and using the realized yield equation to estimate the realized (horizon) yield, we will get the following fairly high realized rate of return:

$$P_m = \$1,000$$
$$hp = 2 \text{ years}$$

$$P_f = \sum_{t=1}^{36} 70/(1 + .05)^t + \$1,000/(1.05)^{36}$$

$$= \$1,158.30 + \$172.65$$
$$= \$1,330.95$$

$$\$1,000 = \sum_{t=1}^{4} \frac{70}{(1 + i/2)^t} + \frac{1330.95}{(1 + i/2)^4}$$

$$i = 27.5\%.$$

As noted, this calculation assumes that all cash flows are reinvested at the computed i (27.5 percent). However, it is unlikely that during a period when market rates are going from 14 percent to 10 percent you could reinvest the coupon flows at 27.5 percent. It is more appropriate and realistic to explicitly estimate the reinvestment rates and calculate the realized yields based on your *ending-wealth position*. This procedure is more precise and realistic, and it is easier because it does not require iteration.

The basic technique calculates the value of all cash flows at the end of the holding period, which is the investor's ending wealth value. We compare this value to our *begin-*

ning-wealth value to determine the *compound rate of return that equalizes these two values*. Adding to our prior example, assume we have the following cash flows:

$$P_m = \$1,000$$
$$i = \text{interest payments of } \$70 \text{ in } 6, 12, 18, \text{ and } 24 \text{ months}$$
$$P_f = \$1,330.95 \text{ (the ending market value of the bond)}.$$

The ending value of the four interest payments is determined by our assumptions regarding specific reinvestment rates. Assume each payment is reinvested at a different declining rate that holds for its time period (i.e., the first three interest payments are reinvested at progressively lower rates and the fourth interest payment is received at the end of the holding period).

$$
\begin{aligned}
i_1 \text{ at } 13\% \text{ for } 18 \text{ months} &= \$70 \times (1 + .065)^3 = \$\ 84.55 \\
i_2 \text{ at } 12\% \text{ for } 12 \text{ months} &= \$70 \times (1 + .06)^2 = \ \ 78.65 \\
i_3 \text{ at } 11\% \text{ for } \ \ 6 \text{ months} &= \$70 \times (1 + .055) = \ \ 73.85 \\
i_4 \text{ not reinvested} &= \$70 \times (1.0) \ \ \ \ \ \ = \ \ \underline{70.00} \\
\end{aligned}
$$

Future Value of Interest Payments = $307.05

Therefore, our total ending-wealth value is

$$\$1,330.95 + \$307.05 = \$1,638.00.$$

The compound realized (horizon) rate of return is calculated by comparing our ending-wealth value ($1,638) to our beginning-wealth value ($1,000) and determining what interest rate would equalize these two values over a 2-year holding period. To find this, compute the ratio of ending wealth to beginning wealth (1.638). Find this ratio in a compound value table for 4 periods (assuming semiannual compounding). Table A.3 at the end of the book indicates that the realized rate is somewhere between 12 percent (1.5735) and 14 percent (1.6890). Interpolation gives an estimated semiannual rate of 13.16 percent, which indicates an annual rate of 26.32 percent. Using a calculator or computer it is equal to $(1.638)^{\frac{1}{4}} - 1$. This compares to an estimate of 27.5 percent when we assume an implicit reinvestment rate of 27.5 percent.

This realized (horizon) yield computation specifically states the expected reinvestment rates as contrasted to assuming the reinvestment rate is equal to the computed realized yield. The actual assumption regarding the reinvestment rate can be very important.

A summary of the steps to calculate an expected realized (horizon) yield is as follows:

1. Calculate the future value at the horizon date of all coupon payments reinvested at estimated rates.
2. Calculate the expected sales price of the bond at your expected horizon date based on your estimate of the required yield to maturity at that time.
3. Sum the values in (1) and (2) to arrive at the total ending-wealth value.
4. Calculate the ratio of the ending wealth value to the beginning value (the purchase price of the bond). Given this ratio and the time horizon, compute the compound rate of interest that will grow to this ratio over this time horizon.

$$\left(\frac{\text{Ending-wealth value}}{\text{Beginning value}}\right)^{1/2n} - 1$$

5. If all calculations assume semiannual compounding, double the interest rate derived from (4).

PRICE AND YIELD DETERMINATION ON NONINTEREST DATES

So far, we have assumed that the investor buys (or sells) a bond precisely on the date that interest is due, so the measures are accurate only when the issues are traded on coupon payment dates. If the approximate yield method is used, sufficient accuracy normally is obtained by extrapolating for transactions on noninterest payment dates. You already are dealing with an approximation, and a bit more is probably acceptable.

However, when the semiannual model is used, and when more accuracy is necessary, another version of the price and yield model must be used for transactions on noninterest payment dates. Fortunately, the basic models need be extended only one more step because the value of an issue that trades X years, Y months, and so many days from maturity is found by extrapolating the bond value (price or yield) for the month before and the month after the day of transaction. Thus, the valuation process involves full months to maturity rather than years or semiannual periods.[6]

Having computed a value for the bond at a noninterest payment date, it is also necessary to consider the notion of *accrued interest*. Because the interest payment on a bond, which is paid every six months, is a contractual promise by the issuer, the bond investor has the right to receive a portion of the semiannual interest payment if he/she held the bond for some part of the six-month period. For example, assume an 8 percent, $1,000 par value bond that pays $40 every six months. If you sold the bond two months after the prior interest payment, you have held it for one-third of the six-month period and would have the right to one-third of the $40 ($13.33). This is referred to as the accrued interest on the bond. Therefore, when you sell the bond, there will be a calculation of the bond's remaining value until maturity, i.e., its price. What you receive is this price *plus* the accrued interest ($13.33).

YIELD ADJUSTMENTS FOR TAX-EXEMPT BONDS

Municipal bonds, Treasury issues, and many agency obligations possess one common characteristic: Their interest income is partially or fully tax-exempt. This tax-exempt status affects the valuation of taxable versus nontaxable bonds. Although you could adjust each present value equation for the tax effects, it is not necessary for our purposes. We can envision the approximate impact of such an adjustment, however, by computing the fully taxable equivalent yield, which is one of the most often cited measures of performance for municipal bonds.

The **fully taxable equivalent yield (FTEY)** adjusts the promised yield computation for the bond's tax-exempt status. To compute the FTEY, we determine the promised yield on a tax-exempt bond using one of the yield formulas and then adjust the computed yield to reflect the rate of return that must be earned on a fully taxable issue. It is measured as

$$\text{FTEY} = \frac{i}{1 - T}$$

where

    i = **the promised yield on the tax-exempt bond**
    T = **the amount and type of tax exemption. (i.e., the investor's marginal tax rate)**

For example, if the promised yield on the tax-exempt bond is 6 percent and the investor's marginal tax rate is 30 percent, the taxable equivalent yield would be:

---

[6]For a detailed discussion of these calculations, see Chapter 4 in Frank J. Fabozzi and T. Dessa Fabozzi, eds., *The Handbook of Fixed-Income Securities*, 4th ed. (Burr Ridge, IL: Irwin Professional Publishing, 1995).

$$FTEY = \frac{.06}{1 - .30} = \frac{.06}{.70} = .0857$$
$$= 8.57\%$$

The FTEY equation has some limitations. It is applicable only to par bonds or current coupon obligations such as new issues because the measure considers only interest income, ignoring capital gains, which are not tax-exempt. Therefore, we cannot use it for issues trading at a significant variation from par value (premium or discount).

BOND YIELD BOOKS   Bond value tables, commonly known as *bond books* or *yield books,* can eliminate most of the calculations for bond valuation. A bond yield table is like a present value interest factor table in that it provides a matrix of bond prices for a stated coupon rate, various terms to maturity (on the horizontal axis), and promised yields (on the vertical axis). Such a table allows you to determine either the promised yield or the price of a bond.

As might be expected, access to sophisticated calculators or computers has substantially reduced the need for and use of yield books. In addition, to truly understand the meaning of alternative yield measures, you must master the present value model and its variations that generate values for promised YTM, promised YTC, realized (horizon) yield, and bond prices.

BOND VALUATION USING SPOT RATES   Thus far, we have used the valuation model, which assumes that we discount all cash flows by one common yield, reflecting the overall required rate of return for the bond. Similarly, we compute the yield on the bond (YTM, YTC, horizon yield) as the single interest rate that would discount all the flows from the bond to equal the current market price of the bond. It was noted in the YTM calculations that this was a "promised" yield that depended on two assumptions: holding the bond to maturity and reinvesting all cash flows at the computed YTM (the IRR assumption). Notably, this second assumption often is very unrealistic because it requires a flat, constant yield curve. We know that it is extremely rare for the yield curve to be flat, much less remain constant for any period of time. The yield curve typically is upward sloping for several reasons, which we discuss in a later section. Investors at any point in time require *a different rate of return for flows at different times.* For example, if investors are buying alternative zero-coupon bonds (promising a single cash flow at maturity), they will almost always require different rates of return if they are offered a bond that matures in two years, five years, or ten years.

As mentioned earlier, the rates used to discount a flow at a point in time are called spot rates. It is possible to demonstrate the desire for different rates by examining the rates on government discount notes with different maturities (i.e., spot rates) as of early 1996 as shown in Table 16.2. These rates indicate that investors require 5.72 percent for a two-year flow, 6.08 percent for the cash flow in five years, and 6.50 percent for the cash flow in ten years. Although these differences in required rates for alternative maturities are noticeable, they are not nearly as large as they were during 1993–1994. The difference in yield between the one-year bond (5.41 percent) and the 30-year bond (6.50 percent) (referred to as the *maturity spread*) was 109 basis points in early 1996; however, it was over 250 basis points in mid-1993.

Because of these differences in spot rates across maturities, bond analysts and bond portfolio managers recognize that it is inappropriate to discount all the flows for a bond at one single rate where the rate used is often based on the yield to maturity for a government bond with that maturity. For example, when asked about the value of a particular 20-year

| TABLE 16.2 | YIELDS ON U.S. TREASURY STRIPS WITH ALTERNATIVE MATURITIES |

Maturity	Yield
1 Year	5.41
2 Years	5.72
3 Years	5.86
4 Years	6.01
5 Years	6.08
6 Years	6.16
7 Years	6.32
8 Years	6.40
9 Years	6.50
10 Years	6.60
12 Years	6.74
14 Years	6.87
16 Years	6.95
18 Years	7.02
20 Years	7.06
25 Years	7.06
30 Years	6.50

Source: *The Wall Street Journal*,
March 15, 1996.

bond rated AA, a bond trader typically will respond that the bond should trade a certain number of basis points higher than comparable maturity Treasury bonds (e.g., "plus 70 basis points"). This means that if 20-year Treasury bonds are currently yielding 7.06 percent, this bond should trade at about a 7.76 percent yield. Notably, this rate would determine the price for the bond with no consideration given to the specific cash flows of this security (i.e., high or low coupon). Therefore, there is a growing awareness that the valuation formula should be specified such that all cash flows should be discounted at spot rates consistent with the timing of the flows as follows:

$$P_m = \sum_{t=1}^{2n} \frac{C_t}{(1 + i_t/2)^t}$$

where

P_m = the market price for the bond
C_t = the cash flow at time t
n = the number of years
i_t = the spot rate for Treasury securities at time t.

Note that this valuation model requires a different discount rate for each flow so it is not possible to use the annuity concept. Also, the principal payment at the end of the year n is no different from the interest coupon flow.

To demonstrate the effect of this procedure, consider the following hypothetical spot-rate curve for the next five years (in Table 16.3) and three example bonds with equal maturities of five years, but with very different cash flows.

Beyond the differences in value because of the differences in cash flows and the rising spot-rate curve, a significant comparison is the value that would be derived using a single

TABLE 16.3			**DEMONSTRATION OF DIFFERENT VALUATION OF ALTERNATIVE FIVE-YEAR MATURITY BONDS WITH UNIQUE CASH FLOWS, DISCOUNTED USING THE SPOT RATE CURVE**					

| | | | CASH FLOWS | | | | | |
| | | | BOND A | | BOND B | | BOND C | |
Maturity (Years)	Spot Rate	Discount Factor	$	PV	$	PV	$	PV
0.5	5.00	0.9756	60	$ 58.536	30	$ 29.268	—	—
1.0	5.20	0.9499	60	56.994	30	28.497	—	—
1.5	5.50	0.9218	60	55.308	30	27.654	—	—
2.0	5.70	0.8937	60	53.622	30	26.811	—	—
2.5	5.80	0.8668	60	52.008	30	26.004	—	—
3.0	5.90	0.8399	60	50.394	30	25.197	—	—
3.5	6.10	0.8103	60	48.618	30	24.309	—	—
4.0	6.30	0.7803	60	46.818	30	23.409	—	—
4.5	6.40	0.7532	60	45.192	30	22.596	—	—
5.0	6.50	0.7263	1,060	769.878	1,030	748.089	1,000	726.300
Total Present Value				$1,237.368		$981.834		$726.300

discount rate based on the five-year maturity of all three bonds. If we assume yield to maturity of 6 percent and 6.5 percent for five-year bonds, the values for the three bonds are:

	6%			6.5%		
Bond A	$ 60 × 8.5302	=	$ 511.81	$ 60 × 8.6350	=	$ 518.10
	$1,000 × .7441	=	744.10	$1,000 × 727.00	=	727.00
	Total Value	=	$1,255.91		=	$1,245.10
Bond B	$ 30 × 8.5302	=	$ 255.90	$ 30 × 8.6350	=	$ 259.05
	$1,000 × .7441	=	744.10	$1,000 × .7270	=	727.00
	Total Value	=	$1,000.00		=	$ 986.05
Bond C	$1,000 × .7441	=	$ 744.10	$1,000 × .7270	=	$ 727.00
	Total Value	=	$ 744.10		=	$ 727.00

Because there is a rising spot-yield curve, we know the YTM would be somewhere between these two values. The point is, valuing the bonds with either of these single rates generates a value that is greater than that derived from the spot-rate curve. This implies that the single-rate valuation technique would overvalue these bonds relative to the more appropriate technique that considers each flow as a single bond discounted by its own spot rate.

WHAT DETERMINES INTEREST RATES? Now that we have learned to calculate various yields on bonds and to determine the value of bonds using yields and spot rates, the question arises as to what causes differences and changes in yields over time. Market interest rates cause these effects because the interest rates reported in the media are simply the prevailing YTMs for the bonds being discussed. For example, when you hear that the interest rate on long-term government bonds declined from 8.40 percent to 8.32 percent, this means that the price of this particular bond increased such that the computed YTM at the former price was 8.40 percent, but the computed YTM at the new, higher price is 8.32 percent. Yields and interest rates are the same. They are different terms for the same concept.

We have discussed the inverse relationship between bond prices and interest rates. When interest rates decline, the prices of bonds increase; when interest rates rise, there is a decline in bond prices. It is natural to ask which of these is the driving force—bond prices or bond interest rates? It is a simultaneous change, and you can envision either factor causing it. Most practitioners probably envision the changes in interest rates as causes because they constantly use interest rates to describe changes. They use interest rates because they are comparable across bonds, whereas the price of a bond depends not only on the interest rate, but also on its specific characteristics including its coupon and maturity. The point is, as demonstrated in Table 16.1 and Figure 16.1, when you change the interest rate (yield) on a bond, you simultaneously change its price in the opposite direction. Later in the chapter we will have a further discussion of the specific price-yield relationship for individual bonds and demonstrate that this price-yield relationship differs among bonds based on their particular coupon and maturity.

Understanding interest rates and what makes them change is necessary for an investor who hopes to maximize returns from investing in bonds. Therefore, in this section we review our prior discussion of the following topics: what causes overall market interest rates to rise and fall, why alternative bonds have different interest rates, and why the difference in rates (i.e., the yield spread) between alternative bonds changes over time. To accomplish this, we begin with a general discussion of what influences interest rates and then consider the **term structure of interest rates** (shown by yield curves), which relates the interest rates on a set of comparable bonds to their terms to maturity. The term structure is important because it implies a set of spot rates that can be used in the valuation of bonds and it reflects what investors expect to happen to interest rates in the future; it also dictates their current risk attitude. In this section, we specifically consider the calculation of spot rates and forward rates from the reported yield curve. Finally, we turn to the concept of *yield spreads*, which measure the differences in yields between alternative bonds. We describe various yield spreads and explore changes in them over time.

FORECASTING INTEREST RATES   As discussed, the ability to forecast interest rates and changes in these rates is critical to successful bond investing. Later, we consider the major determinants of interest rates, but for now you should keep in mind that interest rates *are the price for loanable funds*. Like any price, they are determined by the supply and demand for these funds. On the one side, investors are willing to provide funds (the supply) at prices based on their required rates of return for a particular borrower. On the other side, borrowers need funds (the demand) to support budget deficits (government), to invest in capital projects (corporations), or to acquire durable goods (cars, appliances) or homes (individuals).

Although lenders and borrowers have some fundamental factors that determine supply and demand curves, the prices for these funds (interest rates) also are affected for short time periods by events that shift the curves. Examples include major government bond issues that affect demand, or significant changes in Federal Reserve monetary policy that affect the supply of money.

Our treatment of interest rate forecasting recognizes that you must be aware of the basic determinants of interest rates and monitor these factors. We also recognize that detailed forecasting of interest rates is a very complex task that is best left to professional economists. Therefore, our goal as bond investors and bond portfolio managers is to monitor current and expected interest rate behavior. We should attempt to continuously assess the major factors that affect interest rate behavior but also rely on others—such as economic

FIGURE 16.3

YIELDS OF INTERNATIONAL LONG-TERM GOVERNMENT BONDS: MONTHLY 1986–1995

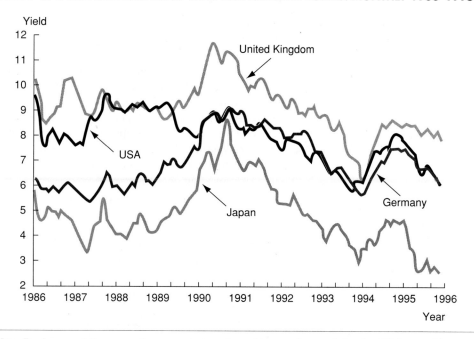

Note: For Japan and Germany, rates on newly issued securities are given until October 1986; secondary market yields are quoted thereafter.

Sources: Federal Reserve Bank, Telerate.

FUNDAMENTAL DETERMINANTS OF INTEREST RATES

consulting firms, banks, or investment banking firms—for detailed insights on such topics as the real RFR and the expected rate of inflation.[7] This is precisely the way most bond portfolio managers operate.

As shown in Figure 16.3, average interest rates for long-term (10-year) U.S. government bonds during the period from late 1990 through 1995 went from 9 percent to 6 percent. These results were midway between the United Kingdom and Japan. UK bonds went from about 12 percent to 8 percent, while the rate on Japanese government bonds declined from 8.7 percent to about 2.7 percent. As a bond investor, you should understand *why* these differences exist and *why* interest rates changed.

As you know from your knowledge of bond pricing, bond prices increased dramatically during periods when market interest rates dropped, and some bond investors experienced very attractive returns. In contrast, some investors experienced substantial losses during periods when interest rates increased. A casual analysis of this chart, which covers about 9 years, indicates the need for monitoring interest rates. Essentially, the factors causing interest rates (*i*) to rise or fall are described by the following model:

$$i = \text{RFR} + I + \text{RP}$$

[7] Sources of information on the bond market and interest rate forecasts would include Merrill-Lynch's *Fixed Income Weekly* and *World Bond Market Monitor*; Goldman, Sach's *Financial Market Perspectives*; Kidder, Peabody's *Economic Outlook and Chartbook*; and the Federal Reserve Bank of St. Louis, *Monetary Trends*.

where

RFR = the real risk-free rate of interest
  I = the expected rate of inflation
RP = the risk premium.

The relationship shown in this equation should be familiar from our presentations in Chapters 1 and 13. It is a simple but complete statement of interest rate behavior. The more difficult task is estimating the *future* behavior of such variables as real growth, expected inflation, and economic uncertainty. In this regard, interest rates, like stock prices, are extremely difficult to forecast with any degree of accuracy.[8] Alternatively, we can visualize the source of changes in interest rates in terms of the economic conditions and issue characteristics that determine the rate of return on a bond:

$$i = f(\text{Economic Forces} + \text{Issue Characteristics})$$
$$= (\text{RFR} + I) + \text{RP}.$$

This rearranged version of the previous equation helps isolate the determinants of interest rates.[9]

EFFECT OF ECONOMIC FACTORS   The real risk-free rate of interest (RFR) is the economic cost of money, that is, the opportunity cost necessary to compensate individuals for forgoing consumption. As discussed previously, it is determined by the real growth rate of the economy with short-run effects due to ease or tightness in the capital market.

The expected rate of inflation is the other economic influence on interest rates. We add the expected level of inflation (I) to the real risk-free rate (RFR) to specify the nominal RFR, which is a market rate like the current rate on government T-bills. Given the stability of the real RFR, it is clear that the wide swings in nominal risk-free interest rates during the years covered by Figure 16.3 occurred because of expected inflation.[10] Besides the unique country and exchange rate risk that we discuss in the section on risk premiums, differences in the rates of inflation between countries have a major impact on their level of interest rates.

To sum up, one way to estimate the nominal RFR is to begin with the real growth rate of the economy, adjust for short-run ease or tightness in the capital market, and then adjust this real rate of interest for the expected rate of inflation.

Another approach to estimating the nominal rate or changes in the rate is the macroeconomic view, where the supply and demand for loanable funds are the fundamental economic determinants of i. As the supply of loanable funds increases, the level of interest rates declines, other things being equal. Several factors influence the supply of funds. Government monetary policies imposed by the Federal Reserve have a significant impact on the supply of money. The savings patterns of U.S. and non-U.S. investors also affect the

---

[8] For an overview of interest rate forecasting, see Frank J. Jones and Benjamin Wolkowitz, "The Determinants of Interest Rates," and W. David Woolford, "Forecasting Interest Rates," in *The Handbook of Fixed-Income Securities*, 4th ed., edited by Frank J. Fabozzi and T. Dessa Fabozzi (Burr Ridge, IL: Irwin Professional Publishing, 1993).

[9] For an extensive exploration of interest rates and interest rate behavior, see James C. Van Horne, *Financial Market Rates and Flows*, 4th ed. (Englewood Cliffs, NJ: Prentice-Hall, 1993).

[10] In this regard, see R. W. Hafer, "Inflation: Assessing Its Recent Behavior and Future Prospects," Federal Reserve Bank of St. Louis *Review* 65, no. 7 (August–September 1983): 36–41; and C. Alan Garner, "How Useful Are Leading Indicators of Inflation?" Federal Reserve Bank of Kansas City *Economic Review* 80, no. 2 (Second Quarter 1995): 5–18.

supply of funds. Non-U.S. investors have become a stronger influence on the U.S. supply of loanable funds during recent years, as shown by the significant purchases of U.S. securities by non-U.S. investors, most notably the Japanese prior to a pullback in 1992. It is widely acknowledged that this foreign addition to the supply of funds has been very beneficial to the United States since it has helped reduce interest rates and cost of capital.

Interest rates increase when the demand for loanable funds increases. The demand for loanable funds is affected by the capital and operating needs of the U.S. government, federal agencies, state and local governments, corporations, institutions, and individuals. Federal budget deficits increase the Treasury's demand for loanable funds. Likewise, the level of consumer demand for funds to buy houses, autos, and appliances affects rates, as does corporate demand for funds to pursue investment opportunities. The total of all groups determines the aggregate demand and supply of loanable funds and the level of the nominal RFR.[11]

THE IMPACT OF BOND CHARACTERISTICS   The interest rate of a specific bond issue is influenced not only by all the factors that affect the nominal RFR, but also by its unique issue characteristics. These issue characteristics influence the bond's risk premium (RP). The economic forces that determine the nominal RFR affect all securities, whereas issue characteristics are unique to individual securities, market sectors, or countries. Thus, the differences in the yields of corporate and Treasury bonds are not caused by economic forces, but rather by different issue characteristics that cause differences in the risk premiums.

Bond investors separate the risk premium into four components:

1. The quality of the issue as determined by its risk of default relative to other bonds
2. The term to maturity of the issue, which can affect yield and price volatility
3. Indenture provisions, including collateral, call features, and sinking-fund provisions
4. Foreign bond risk, including exchange rate risk and country risk

Of the four factors, quality and maturity have the greatest impact on the risk premium for domestic bonds, while exchange rate risk and country risk are important components of risk for non-U.S. bonds.

The credit quality of a bond reflects the ability of the issuer to service outstanding debt obligations. This information is largely captured in the ratings issued by the bond rating firms. As a result, bonds with different ratings have different yields. For example, AAA-rated obligations possess lower risk of default than BBB obligations, so they can provide lower yield.

Notably, the risk premium differences between bonds of different quality levels have changed dramatically over time, depending on prevailing economic conditions. When the economy experiences a recession or a period of economic uncertainty, the desire for quality increases, and investors bid up prices of higher-rated bonds, which reduces their yields. This difference in yield is referred to as the quality spread. It also has been suggested by Dialynas and Edington that this yield spread is influenced by the volatility of interest rates.[12] This variability in the risk premium over time was demonstrated and discussed in Chapters 1 and 13.

---

[11] For an example of an estimate of the supply and demand for funds in the economy, see *Prospects for Financial Markets in 1996* (New York: Salomon Bros., 1995). This is an annual publication of Salomon Brothers that gives an estimate of the flow of funds in the economy and discusses its effect on various currencies and interest rates, making recommendations for portfolio strategy on the basis of these expectations.

[12] Chris P. Dialynas and David H. Edington, "Bond Yield Spreads: A Postmodern View," *Journal of Portfolio Management* 19, no. 1 (Fall 1992): 68–75.

Term to maturity also influences the risk premium because it affects an investor's level of uncertainty as well as the price volatility of the bond. In the section on the term structure of interest rates, we will discuss the typical positive relationship between the term to maturity of a bond issue and its interest rate.

As discussed in Chapter 15, indenture provisions indicate the collateral pledged for a bond, its callability, and its sinking-fund provisions. Collateral gives protection to the investor if the issuer defaults on the bond because the investor has a specific claim on some assets in case of liquidation.

Call features indicate when an issuer can buy back the bond prior to its maturity. A bond is called by an issuer when interest rates have declined so typically it is not to the advantage of the investor who must reinvest the proceeds at a lower interest rate. Obviously, an investor will charge the issuer for including the call option, and the cost of the option (which is a higher yield) will increase with the level of interest rates. Therefore, more protection against having the bond called reduces the risk premium. The significance of call protection increases during periods of high interest rates. When you buy a bond with a high coupon, you want protection from having it called away when rates decline.[13]

A sinking fund reduces the investor's risk and causes a lower yield for several reasons. First, a sinking fund reduces default risk because it requires the issuer to reduce the outstanding issue systematically. Second, purchases of the bond by the issuer to satisfy sinking-fund requirements provide price support for the bond because of the added demand. These purchases by the issuer also contribute to a more liquid secondary market for the bond because of the increased trading. Finally, sinking-fund provisions require that the issuer retire a bond before its stated maturity, which causes a reduction in the issue's average maturity. The decline in average maturity tends to reduce the risk premium of the bond much as a shorter maturity would reduce yield.[14]

We know that foreign currency exchange rates change over time and that this increases the risk of global investing. Differences in the variability of exchange rates among countries arise because the trade balances and rates of inflation differ among countries. More volatile trade balances and inflation rates in a country make its exchange rates more volatile, which will add to the uncertainty of future exchange rates. These factors increase the exchange rate risk premium.

In addition to the ongoing changes in exchange rates, investors always are concerned with the political and economic stability of a country. If investors are unsure about the political environment or the economic system in a country, they will increase the risk premium they require to reflect this country risk.[15]

TERM STRUCTURE OF INTEREST RATES

The term structure of interest rates (or the *yield curve,* as it is more popularly known) is a static function that relates the term to maturity to the yield to maturity for a sample of

[13] William Marshall and Jess B. Yawitz, "Optimal Terms of the Call Provision on a Corporate Bond," *Journal of Financial Research* 3, no. 3 (Fall 1980): 203–211; and Michael G. Ferri, "Systematic Return Risk and the Call Risk of Corporate Debt Instruments," *Journal of Financial Research* 1, no. 1 (Winter 1978): 1–13.

[14] For a further discussion of sinking funds, see Edward A. Dyl and Michael D. Joehnk, "Sinking Funds and the Cost of Corporate Debt," *Journal of Finance* 34, no. 4 (September 1979): 887–893; A. J. Kalotay, "On the Management of Sinking Funds," *Financial Management* 10, no. 2 (Summer 1981): 34–40; and A. J. Kalotay, "Sinking Funds and the Realized Cost of Debt," *Financial Management* 11, no. 1 (Spring 1982): 43–54.

[15] In this regard, see Martin Fridson, "Sovereign Risk from a Corporate Bond Analyst Perspective," and Brian Murphy, David Won, and Deepak Gulrajani, "Valuation and Risk Analysis of International Bonds." Both are in *The Handbook of Fixed Income Securities,* 4th ed., edited by Frank J. Fabozzi and T. Dessa Fabozzi (Burr Ridge, IL: Irwin Professional Publishing, 1995).

FIGURE 16.4 **TREASURY YIELD CURVES**

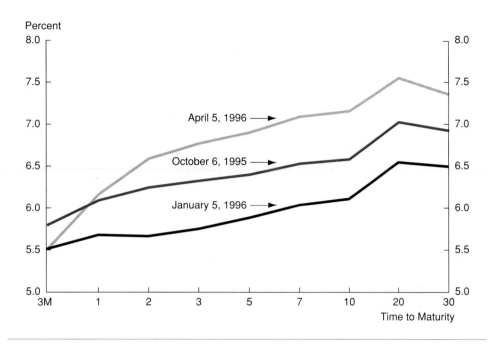

Source: Curves by authors using data from *Federal Reserve Bulletin* (Washington, D.C., various issues.)

bonds at *a given point in time.*[16] Thus, it represents a cross section of yields for a category of bonds that are comparable in all respects but maturity. Specifically, the quality of the issues should be constant, and ideally you should have issues with similar coupons and call features within a single industry category. You can construct different yield curves for Treasuries, government agencies, prime-grade municipals, AAA utilities, and so on. The accuracy of the yield curve will depend on the comparability of the bonds in the sample.

As an example, Figure 16.4 shows yield curves for a sample of U.S. Treasury obligations. It is based on the yield to maturity information for a set of comparable Treasury issues from a publication such as the *Federal Reserve Bulletin* or *The Wall Street Journal*. These promised yields were plotted on the graph, and a yield curve was drawn that represents the general configuration of rates. These data represent yield curves at three different points in time to demonstrate the changes in yield levels and in the shape of the yield curve over time.

All yield curves, of course, do not have the same shape as those in Figure 16.4. Although individual yield curves are static, their behavior over time is quite fluid. As shown, the level of the curve decreased from October, 1995 to January, 1996 and then the slope increased to April 1, 1996. Also, the shape of the yield curve can undergo dramatic alterations, following one of the four patterns shown in Figure 16.5. The rising yield curve is the most common and tends to prevail when interest rates are at low or modest levels.

---

[16] For a discussion of the theory and empirical evidence, see Richard W. McEnally and James V. Jordan, "The Term Structure of Interest Rates," in *The Handbook of Fixed Income Securities*, 4th ed., edited by Frank J. Fabozzi and T. Dessa Fabozzi (Burr Ridge, IL: Irwin Professional Publishing, 1995).

| FIGURE 16.5 | TYPES OF YIELD CURVES |

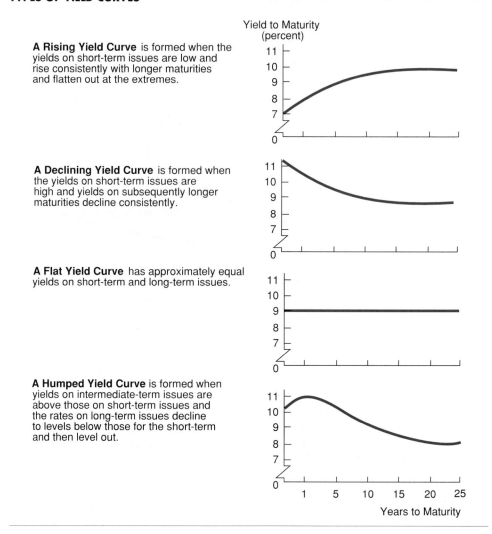

A Rising Yield Curve is formed when the yields on short-term issues are low and rise consistently with longer maturities and flatten out at the extremes.

A Declining Yield Curve is formed when the yields on short-term issues are high and yields on subsequently longer maturities decline consistently.

A Flat Yield Curve has approximately equal yields on short-term and long-term issues.

A Humped Yield Curve is formed when yields on intermediate-term issues are above those on short-term issues and the rates on long-term issues decline to levels below those for the short-term and then level out.

The declining yield curve tends to occur when rates are relatively high. The flat yield curve rarely exists for any period of time. The humped yield curve prevails when extremely high rates are expected to decline to more normal levels. Note that the slope of the curve tends to level off after 15 years.

Why does the term structure assume different shapes? Three major theories attempt to explain this: the expectations hypothesis, the liquidity preference hypothesis, and the segmented market hypothesis.

Before we discuss these three alternative hypotheses, we must first discuss two previously noted rates that not only are an integral part of the term structure, but important in the valuation of bonds. The next two subsections will deal with the specification and computation of *spot rates* and *forward rates*. Earlier, we discussed and used spot rates to value bonds with the idea that any coupon bond can be viewed as a collection of zero coupon securities.

TABLE 16.4	**MATURITY AND YIELD TO MATURITY FOR HYPOTHETICAL TREASURY SECURITIES**

Maturity (Years)	Coupon Rate	Price	Yield-to-Maturity
0.50	0.0000	96.15	0.0800
1.00	0.0000	92.19	0.0830
1.50	0.0850	99.45	0.0890
2.00	0.0900	99.64	0.0920
2.50	0.1100	103.49	0.0940
3.00	0.0950	99.49	0.0970

Source: *Federal Reserve Bulletin,* Moody's *Bond Guide.*

CREATING THE THEORETICAL SPOT-RATE CURVE[17]   Earlier in the chapter, we discussed the notion that the yield on a zero coupon bond for a given maturity is the spot rate for the maturity. Specifically, the spot rate is defined as the discount rate for a cash flow at a specific maturity. At that time, we used the rates on a series of zero coupon government bonds created by stripping coupon government bonds.

In this case, we will construct a theoretical spot-rate curve from the observable yield curve that is based on the existing yields of Treasury bills and the most recent Treasury coupon securities (referred to as *on-the-run* Treasury issues). One might expect the theoretical spot-rate curve and the spot-rate curve derived from the stripped zero-coupon bonds used earlier to be the same. The fact is, while they are close, they will not be exactly the same because the stripped zero-coupon bonds will not be as liquid as the on-the-run issues. In addition, there are instances where institutions will have a strong desire for a particular spot maturity and this preference will distort the term structure relationship. Therefore, while it is possible to use the stripped zero-coupon curve for a general indication, if you are going to use the spot rates for significant valuation, you would want to use the theoretical spot-rate curve.

The process of creating a theoretical spot-rate curve from coupon securities is called *bootstrapping* wherein it is assumed that the value of the Treasury coupon security should be equal to the value of the package of zero-coupon securities that duplicates the coupon bond's cash flow. Table 16.4 lists the maturity and YTM for six hypothetical Treasury bonds that will be used to calculate the initial spot rates.

Consider the six-month Treasury bill in Table 16.4. As discussed earlier, a Treasury bill is a zero-coupon instrument so its annualized yield of 8 percent is equal to the spot rate. Similarly, for the one-year Treasury, the cited yield of 8.3 percent is equal to the one-year spot rate. Given these two spot rates, we can compute the spot rate for a theoretical 1.5-year zero-coupon Treasury. The price should equal the present value of three cash flows from an actual 1.5-year coupon Treasury, where the yield used for discounting is the spot rate corresponding to the cash flow.

Using $100 as par, *the cash flow* for the 1.5-year coupon Treasury is as follows:

0.5 years	$.085 \times \$100 \times .5$	=	$ 4.25
1.0 years	$.085 \times \$100 \times .5$	=	$ 4.25
1.5 years	$.085 \times \$100 \times .5 + \$100$	=	$104.25

[17]This discussion of the theoretical spot-rate cuve and the subsequent presentation on calculating forward rates draws heavily from Frank J. Fabozzi, "The Structure of Interest Rates," in *The Handbook of Fixed Income Securities* 4th ed., edited by Frank J. Fabozzi and T. Dessa Fabozzi (Burr Ridge, IL: Irwin Professional Publishing, 1995).

The present value of the cash flows discounted as the appropriate spot rates is then

$$\frac{4.25}{(1 + z_1)^1} + \frac{4.25}{(1 + z_2)^2} + \frac{104.25}{(1 + z_3)^3}$$

where

z_1 = **One-half the annualized six-month theoretical spot rate**
z_2 = **One-half the one-year theoretical spot rate**
z_3 = **One-half the 1.5-year theoretical spot rate**

Because the six-month spot rate and one-year spot rate are 8.0 percent and 8.3 percent, respectively, we know that

$$z_1 = .04 \quad and \quad z_2 = .0415.$$

We can compute the present value of the 1.5-year coupon Treasury security as

$$\frac{4.25}{(1.0400)^1} + \frac{4.25}{(1.0415)^2} + \frac{104.25}{(1 + z_3)^3}$$

Because the price of the 1.5-year coupon Treasury security (from Table 16.4) is $99.45, the following relationship must hold:

$$99.45 = \frac{4.25}{(1.0400)^1} + \frac{4.25}{(1.0415)^2} + \frac{104.25}{(1 + z_3)^3}$$

We can solve for the theoretical 1.5 year spot rate as follows:

$$99.45 = 4.08654 + 3.91805 + \frac{104.25}{(1 + z_3)^3}$$

$$91.44541 = \frac{104.25}{(1 + z_3)^3}$$

$$\frac{104.25}{91.44541} = (1 + z_3)^3$$

$$(1 + z_3)^3 = 1.140024$$

$$z_3 = .04465$$

Doubling this yield, we obtain the bond-equivalent yield of .0893 or 8.93 percent, which is the theoretical 1.5-year spot rate. That rate is the rate that the market would apply to a 1.5-year zero-coupon Treasury, if such a security existed.

Given the theoretical 1.5-year spot rate, we can obtain the theoretical two-year spot rate. The cash flow for the two-year coupon Treasury in Table 16.4 is

0.5 years	$.090 \times \$100 \times .5$	=	$ 4.50
1.0 years	$.090 \times \$100 \times .5$	=	$ 4.50
1.5 years	$.090 \times \$100 \times .5$	=	$ 4.50
2.0 years	$.090 \times \$100 \times .5 + 100$	=	$104.50

The present value of the cash flow is then

$$\frac{4.50}{(1 + z_1)^1} + \frac{4.50}{(1 + z_2)^2} + \frac{4.50}{(1 + z_3)^3} + \frac{104.50}{(1 + z_4)^4}$$

where

z_4 = One-half the two-year theoretical spot rate

Because the six-month spot rate, one-year spot rate, and 1.5-year spot rate are 8 percent, 8.3 percent, and 8.93 percent respectively, then

$$z_1 = .04 \quad z_2 = .0415 \quad and \quad z_3 = .04465$$

Therefore, the present value of the two-year coupon Treasury security is

$$\frac{4.50}{(1.0400)^1} + \frac{4.50}{(1.0415)^2} + \frac{4.50}{(1.04465)^3} + \frac{104.50}{(1 + z_4)^4}$$

Because the price of the two-year coupon Treasury security is $99.64, the following relationship must hold:

$$99.64 = \frac{4.50}{(1.0400)^1} + \frac{4.50}{(1.0415)^2} + \frac{4.50}{(1.04465)^3} + \frac{104.50}{(1 + z_4)^4}$$

We can solve for the theoretical two-year spot rate as follows:

$$99.64 = 4.32692 + 4.14853 + 3.94730 + \frac{104.50}{(1 + z_4)^4}$$

$$87.21725 = \frac{104.50}{(1 + z_4)^4}$$

$$(1 + z_4)^4 = 1.198158$$

$$z_4 = .046235$$

Doubling this yield, we obtain the theoretical two-year spot rate bond-equivalent yield of 9.247 percent.

One can follow this approach sequentially to derive the theoretical 2.5-year spot rate from the calculated values of z_1, z_2, z_3, z_4 (the six-month, one-year, 1.5-year, and two-year rates), and the price and the coupon of the bond with a maturity of 2.5 years. Further, one could derive the theoretical spot rate for three years. The spot rates thus obtained are shown in Table 16.5. They represent the term structure of interest rates for maturities up to three years, based upon the prevailing bond price quotations.

As shown, with a rising YTM curve, the theoretical spot rate will increase at a faster rate such that the difference increases with maturity (i.e., the theoretical spot-rate curve will be above a positively sloped YTM curve).

| TABLE 16.5 | THEORETICAL SPOT RATES |

Maturity (Years)	Yield-to-Maturity	Theoretical Spot Rate
0.50	0.0800	0.08000
1.00	0.0830	0.08300
1.50	0.0890	0.08930
2.00	0.0920	0.09247
2.50	0.0940	0.09468
3.00	0.0970	0.09787

CALCULATING FORWARD RATES FROM THE SPOT-RATE CURVE

Now that we have derived the theoretical spot-rate curve, it is possible to determine what this curve implies regarding the market's expectation of *future* short-term rates, which are referred to as *forward rates*. The following illustrates the process of extrapolating this information about expected future interest rates.

Consider an investor who has a one-year investment horizon and is faced with the following two alternatives:

Alternative 1: Buy a one-year Treasury bill.

Alternative 2: Buy a six-month Treasury bill and when it matures in six months, buy another six-month Treasury bill.

The investor will be indifferent between the two alternatives if they produce the same return on the one-year investment horizon. The investor knows the spot rate on the six-month Treasury bill and the one-year Treasury bill. However, she does not know what yield will be available on a six-month Treasury bill six months from now. The yield on a six-month Treasury bill six months from now is called a **forward rate.** Given the spot rate for the six-month Treasury bill and the one-year bill, we can determine the forward rate on a six-month Treasury bill *that will make the investor indifferent between the two alternatives.*

At this point, however, we need to digress briefly and recall several present value and investment relationships. First, if you invested in a one-year Treasury bill, you would receive $100 at the end of one year. The price of the one-year Treasury bill would be

$$\frac{100}{(1 + z_2)^2}$$

where

z_2 is one-half the bond-equivalent yield of the theoretical one-year spot rate

Second, suppose you purchased a six-month Treasury bill for $X. At the end of six months, the value of this investment would be

$$X(1 + z_1)$$

where

z_1 is one-half the bond-equivalent yield of the theoretical six-month spot rate

Let $_t s r_s$ represent one-half the forward rate (expressed as a bond equivalent yield) on a six-month Treasury bill (.5) available six months from now ($t + .5$). If the investor were to renew her investment by purchasing that bill at that time, then the future dollars available at the end of the year from the $X investment would be

$$X(1 + z_1) (1 + {}_{t+.5}r_{.5}) = 100$$

Third, it is easy to use that formula to find out how many dollars the investor must invest in order to get $100 one year from now. This can be found as follows:

$$(1 + z_1) (1 + {}_{t+.5}r_{.5}) = 100$$

which gives us

$$X = \frac{100}{(1 + z_1) (1 + {}_{t+.5}r_{.5})}$$

We are now prepared to return to the investor's choices and analyze what that situation says about forward rates. The investor will be indifferent between the two alternatives confronting her if she makes the same dollar investment and receives $100 from both alternatives at the end of one year. That is, the investor will be indifferent if

$$\frac{100}{(1 + z_2)^2} = \frac{100}{(1 + z_1) (1 + {}_{t+.5}r_{.5})}$$

Solving for ${}_{t+.5}r_{.5}$ we get

$${}_{t+.5}r_{.5} = \frac{(1 + z_2)^2}{(1 + z_1)} - 1$$

Doubling r gives the bond-equivalent yield for the six-month forward rate six months from now.

We can illustrate the use of this formula with the theoretical spot rates shown in Table 16.5. From that table, we know that

Six-month bill spot rate = .080   so $z_1 = .0400$
One-year bill spot rate = .083   so $z_2 = .0415$

Substituting into the formula, we have

$${}_{t+.5}r_{.5} = \frac{(1.0415)^2}{1.0400} - 1$$
$$= .043$$

Therefore, the forward rate six months from now ($t + .5$) on a six-month Treasury security, quoted annually, is 8.6 percent (.043 × 2). Let us confirm our results. The price of a one-year Treasury bill with $100 maturity is

$$\frac{100}{(1.0415)^2} = 92.19$$

If $92.19 is invested for six months at the six-month spot rate of 8 percent, the amount at the end of six months would be

$$92.19(1.0400) = 95.8776$$

If $95.8776 is reinvested for another six months in a six-month Treasury bill offering 4.3 percent for six months (8.6 percent annually), the amount at the end of one year would be

$$95.8876(1.043) = 100$$

Both alternatives will have the same $100 payoff if the six-month Treasury bill yield six months from now is 4.3 percent (8.6 percent on a bond-equivalent basis). This means that, if an investor is guaranteed a 4.3 percent yield on a six-month Treasury bill six months from now, she will be indifferent between the two alternatives.

We used the theoretical spot rates to compute the forward rate. The resulting forward rate is called the *implied forward rate*.

It is possible to use the yield curve to calculate the implied forward rate for any time in the future for any investment horizon. This would include six-month or one-year forward rates for each year in the future. The one-year forward rates would be designated as follows:

$_{t+1}r_1$ = **the one-year forward rate, one year from now ($t + 1$)**
$_{t+2}r_1$ = **the one-year forward rate, two years from now ($t + 2$)**
$_{t+3}r_1$ = **the one-year forward rate, three years from now ($t + 3$)**

Given the calculations, it is clear that with a rising spot-rate curve, the forward-rate curve would be above the spot-rate curve. From Table 16.5, we have the following one-year spot rates, which imply the following one-year forward rates:

Maturity (Years)	Spot Rates	One-Year Forward Rates
1.0	.08300	
2.0	.09247	.1020
3.0	.09787	.1087

Therefore:

$$_{t+1}r_1 = \frac{(1.09247)^2}{(1.08300)} - 1 = \frac{1.19349}{1.08300} - 1 = .1020$$

$$_{t+2}r_1 = \frac{(1.09787)^3}{(1.09247)^2} - 1 = \frac{1.32328}{1.19349} - 1 = .1087$$

TERM-STRUCTURE THEORIES

EXPECTATIONS HYPOTHESIS   According to the expectations hypothesis, the shape of the yield curve results from the interest rate expectations of market participants. More specifically, it holds that *any long-term interest rate simply represents the geometric mean of current and future 1-year interest rates expected to prevail over the maturity of the issue*. In essence, the term structure involves a series of intermediate and long-term interest rates, each of which is a reflection of the geometric average of current and expected 1-year interest rates. Under such conditions, the equilibrium long-term rate is the rate the long-term bond investor would expect to earn through successive investments in short-term bonds over the term to maturity of the long-term bond.

Generally, this relationship can be formalized as follows:

$$(1 + _tR_n) = [(1 + _tR_1)(1 + _{t+1}r_1) \ldots (1 + _{t+n-1}r_1)]^{1/N}$$

where

> R_n = the actual long-term rate
> N = the term to maturity (in years) of long issue
> R = the current 1-year rate
> $_{t+i}r_1$ = the expected 1-year yield during some future period, $t + i$ (these future 1-year rates are referred to as *forward rates*).

Given the relationship set forth in this equation, the formula for computing the one-period forward rate beginning at time $t + n$ and implied in the term structure at time t is:

$$1 + _{t+n}r_{1t} = \frac{(1 + _tR_{1t})\,(1 + _{t+1}r_{1t})\,(1 + _{t+2}r_{1t}) \ldots (1 + _{t+n-1}r_{1t})\,(1 + _{t+n}r_{1t})}{(1 + _tR_{1t})\,(1 + _{t+1}r_{1t}) \ldots (1 + _{t+n-1}r_{1t})}$$

$$= \frac{(1 + _tR_{n+1})^{n+1}}{(1 + _tR_n)^n}$$

$$_{t+n}r_{1t} = \frac{(1 + _tR_{n+1})^{n+1}}{(1 + _tR_n)^n} - 1$$

where $_{t+n}r_{1t}$ is the 1-year forward rate prevailing at $t + n$, using the term structure at time t.

Assume that the 5-year spot rate is 10 percent ($_tR_5 = .10$) and the 4-year spot rate is 9 percent ($_tR_4 = .09$). The forward 1-year rate 4 years from now implied by these spot rates can be calculated as follows:

$$_{t+4}r_{1t} = \frac{(1 + _tR_5)^5}{(1 + _tR_4)^4} - 1$$

$$= \frac{(1 + .10)^5}{(1 + .09)^4} - 1$$

$$= \frac{1.6105}{1.4116} - 1$$

$$= 1.1409 - 1 = .1409 = 14.09\%$$

The term structure at time t implies that the 1-year spot rate 4 years from now (during Year 5) will be 14.09 percent. This concept and formula can be used to derive future rates for multiple years. Thus, the 2-year spot rate that will prevail 3 years from now could be calculated using the 3-year spot rate and the 5-year spot rate. The general formula for computing the j-period forward rate beginning at time $t + n$ as of time t is

$$_{t+n}r_{jt} = \sqrt[j]{\frac{(1 + _tR_{n+j})^{n+j}}{(1 + _tR_n)^n}} - 1$$

As a practical approximation of the equation at the top of this page, it is possible to use the *arithmetic* average of 1-year rates to generate long-term yields.

The expectations theory can explain any shape of yield curve. Expectations for rising short-term rates in the future cause a rising yield curve; expectations for falling short-term rates in the future will cause long-term rates to lie below current short-term rates, and the yield curve will decline. Similar explanations account for flat and humped yield curves.

Consider the following explanation by the expectations hypothesis of the shape of the term structure of interest rates using arithmetic averages:

$_tR_1 = 5\frac{1}{2}\%$ the 1-year rate of interest prevailing now (period t)
$_{t+1}r_1 = 6\%$ the 1-year rate of interest expected to prevail next year (period $t + 1$)
$_{t+2}r_1 = 7\frac{1}{2}\%$ the 1-year rate of interest expected to prevail 2 years from now (period $t + 2$)
$_{t+3}r_1 = 8\frac{1}{2}\%$ the 1-year rate of interest expected to prevail 3 years from now (period $t + 3$)

Using these values, and the known rate on a 1-year bond, we compute rates on 2-, 3-, or 4-year bonds (designated R_2, R_3, and R_4) as follows:

$_tR_1 = 5\frac{1}{2}$ percent
$_tR_2 = (0.055 + 0.06)/2 = 5.75$ percent
$_tR_3 = (0.055 + 0.06 + 0.075)/3 = 6.33$ percent
$_tR_4 = (0.055 + 0.06 + 0.075 + 0.085)/4 = 6.88$ percent

In this illustration (which uses the arithmetic average as an approximation of the geometric mean), the yield curve is upward-sloping because, at present, investors expect future short-term rates to be above current short-term rates. This is not the formal method for constructing the yield curve. Rather, it is constructed on the basis of the prevailing promised yields for bonds with different maturities.

The expectations hypothesis attempts to explain *why* the yield curve is upward-sloping, downward-sloping, humped, or flat by explaining the expectations implicit in yield curves with different shapes. The evidence is fairly substantial and convincing that the expectations hypothesis is a workable explanation of the term structure. Because of the supporting evidence, its relative simplicity, and the intuitive appeal of the theory, the expectations hypothesis of the term structure of interest rates is rather widely accepted.

Besides the theory and empirical support, it is also possible to present a scenario wherein investor actions will cause the yield curve postulated by the theory. The expectations hypothesis predicts a declining yield curve when interest rates are expected to fall in the future rather than rise. In such a case, long-term bonds would be considered attractive investments because investors would want to lock in prevailing higher yields (which are not expected to be as high in the future) or they would want to capture the increase in bond prices (as capital gains) that will accompany a decline in rates. By the same reasoning, investors will avoid short-term bonds or sell them and reinvest the funds in long-term bonds. The point is, investor expectations will reinforce the declining shape of the yield curve as they bid up the prices of long-maturity bonds (forcing yields to decline) and short-term bond issues are avoided or sold (so prices decline and yields rise). At the same time, there is confirming action by suppliers of bonds. Specifically, government or corporate issuers will avoid selling long bonds at the current high rates, waiting until the rates decline. In the meantime, they will issue short-term bonds, if needed, while waiting for lower rates. Therefore, in the long-term market you will have an increase in demand and a decline in the supply and vice versa in the short-term market. These shifts between long- and short-term maturities will continue until equilibrium occurs or expectations change.

LIQUIDITY PREFERENCE HYPOTHESIS   The theory of liquidity preference holds that long-term securities should provide higher returns than short-term obligations because investors are willing to sacrifice some yields to invest in short-maturity obligations to avoid the higher price volatility of long-maturity bonds. Another way to interpret the liquidity preference hypothesis is to say that lenders prefer short-term loans, and, to induce them to lend long term, it is necessary to offer higher yields.

The liquidity preference theory contends that uncertainty causes investors to favor short-term issues over bonds with longer maturities because short-term bonds can easily be converted into predictable amounts of cash should unforeseen events occur. This theory argues that the yield curve should slope upward and that any other shape should be viewed as a temporary aberration.

This theory can be considered an extension of the expectations hypothesis because the formal liquidity preference position contends that the liquidity premium inherent in the yields for longer maturity bonds should be added to the expected future rate in arriving at long-term yields. Specifically, the liquidity premium (L) compensates the investor in long-term bonds for the added uncertainty because of less stable prices. Because the liquidity premium (L) is provided to compensate the long-term investor, it is simply a variation of the equation on page 557 as follows:

$$(1 + {_tR_N}) = [(1 + {_tR_1})\ (1 + {_{t+1}r_1} + L_2) \ldots (1 + {_{t+N-1}r_1} + L_n)]^{1/N}$$

In this specification, the Ls are not the same, but would be expected to increase with time. The liquidity preference theory has been found to possess some strong empirical support.[18]

To see how the liquidity preference theory predicts future yields and how it compares with the pure expectations hypothesis, let us predict future long-term rates from a single set of 1-year rates: 6 percent, 7.5 percent, and 8.5 percent. The liquidity preference theory suggests that investors add increasing liquidity premiums to successive rates to derive actual market rates. As an example, they might arrive at rates of 6.3 percent, 7.9 percent, and 9.0 percent.

As a matter of historical fact, the yield curve shows a definite upward bias, which implies that some combination of the expectations theory and the liquidity preference theory will more accurately explain the shape of the yield curve than either of them alone. Specifically, actual long-term rates consistently tend to be above what is envisioned from the price expectations hypothesis, which implies the existence of a liquidity premium.

SEGMENTED MARKET HYPOTHESIS Despite meager empirical support, a third theory for the shape of the yield curve is the segmented market hypothesis, which enjoys wide acceptance among market practitioners. Also known as the *preferred habitat,* the *institutional theory,* or the *hedging pressure theory,* it asserts that different institutional investors have different maturity needs that lead them to confine their security selections to specific maturity segments. That is, investors supposedly focus on short-, intermediate-, or long-term securities. This theory contends that the shape of the yield curve ultimately is a function of these investment policies of major financial institutions.

Financial institutions tend to structure their investment policies in line with factors such as their tax liabilities, the types and maturity structure of their liabilities, and the level of earnings demanded by depositors. For example, because commercial banks are subject to normal corporate tax rates and their liabilities are generally short- to intermediate-term time and demand deposits, they consistently invest in short- to intermediate-term municipal bonds.

---

[18] See Reuben A. Kessel, "The Cyclical Behavior of the Term Structure of Interest Rates," Occasional Paper 91, National Bureau of Economic Research, 1965; Phillip Cagan, *Essays on Interest Rates* (New York: Columbia University Press for the National Bureau of Economic Research, 1969); and J. Huston McCulloch, "An Estimate of the Liquidity Premium," *Journal of Political Economy* 83, no. 1 (January–February 1975): 95–119.

The segmented market theory contends that the business environment, along with legal and regulatory limitations, tends to direct each type of financial institution to allocate its resources to particular types of bonds with specific maturity characteristics. In its strongest form, the segmented market theory holds that the maturity preferences of investors and borrowers are so strong that investors never purchase securities outside their preferred maturity range to take advantage of yield differentials. As a result, the short- and long-maturity portions of the bond market are effectively segmented, and yields for a segment depend on the supply and demand *within* that maturity segment.

TRADING IMPLICATIONS OF THE TERM STRUCTURE   Information on maturities can help you formulate yield expectations by simply observing the shape of the yield curve. If the yield curve is declining sharply, historical evidence suggests that interest rates will probably decline. Expectations theorists would suggest that you need to examine only the prevailing yield curve to predict the direction of interest rates in the future.

Based on these theories, bond investors use the prevailing yield curve to predict the shapes of future yield curves. Using this prediction and knowledge of current interest rates, investors can determine expected yield volatility by maturity sector. In turn, the maturity segments that experience the greatest yield changes give the investor the largest potential price appreciation.[19]

YIELD SPREADS   Another technique that helps make good bond investments or profitable trades is the analysis of *yield spreads*—the differences in promised yields between bond issues or segments of the market at any point in time. Such differences are specific to the particular issues or segments of the bond market. Thus they add to the rates determined by the basic economic forces (RFR + *I*).

There are four major yield spreads:

1. Different *segments* of the bond market may have different yields. For example, pure government bonds will have lower yields than government agency bonds, and government bonds have much lower yields than corporate bonds.
2. Bonds in different *sectors* of the same market segment may have different yields. For example, prime-grade municipal bonds will have lower yields than good-grade municipal bonds; you will find spreads between AA utilities and BBB utilities, or between AAA industrial bonds and AAA public utility bonds.
3. Different *coupons* or *seasoning* within a given market segment or sector may cause yield spreads. Examples include current coupon government bonds versus deep-discount governments or recently issued AA industrials versus seasoned AA industrials.
4. Different *maturities* within a given market segment or sector also cause differences in yields. You will see yield spreads between short-term agency issues and long-term agency issues, or between 3-year prime municipals and 25-year prime municipals.

The differences among these bonds cause yield spreads that may be either positive or negative. More important, *the magnitude or the direction of a spread can change over time.* These changes in size or direction of yield spreads offer profit opportunities. We say that the spread narrows whenever the differences in yield become smaller; it widens as the differences increase. Table 16.6 contains data on a variety of past yield spreads.

---

[19] Gikas A. Hourdouvelis, "The Predictive Power of the Term Structure During Recent Monetary Regimes," *Journal of Finance* 43, no. 2 (June 1988): 339–356.

TABLE 16.6	SELECTED MEAN YIELD SPREADS (REPORTED IN BASIS POINTS)								
Comparisons	1984	1985	1986	1987	1988	1989	1990	1991	1992
1. Short Governments— Long Governments[a]	+10	+111	+108	+96	+72	+3	+48	+127	+210
2. Long Governments— Long Aaa Corporates[b]	+72	+62	+88	+74	+73	+68	+58	+61	+62
3. Long Municipals— Long Aaa Corporates[c]	+272	+226	+170	+175	+203	+203	+220	+199	+185
4. Long Aaa Municipals— Long Baa Municipals[d]	+77	+98	+81	+103	+47	+40	+104	+103	+84
5. AA Utilities—BBB Utilities[e]	+88	+90	+70	+76	+74	+42	+41	+46	+31
6. AA Utilities—AA Industrials[e]	−51	−11	+33	+19	−65	−20	−20	−9	−18

[a]Median yield to maturity of a varying number of bonds with 2 to 5 years' maturity and more than 10 years, respectively.
[b]Long Aaa corporates based on yields to maturity on selected long-term bonds.
[c]Long-term municipal issues based on Bond Buyer Series, a representative list of high-quality municipal bonds with a 20-year period to maturity being maintained.
[d]General obligation municipal bonds only.
[e]Based on a changing list of representative issues.

Source: *Federal Reserve Bulletin,* Moody's *Bond Guide.*

As a bond investor, you should evaluate yield spread changes because these changes influence bond price behavior and comparative return performance. You should attempt to identify (1) any normal yield spread that is expected to become abnormally wide or narrow in response to an anticipated swing in market interest rates, or (2) an abnormally wide or narrow yield spread that is expected to become normal.

Economic and market analysis help develop these expectations of potential for yield spreads to change. Taking advantage of these changes requires a knowledge of historical spreads and an ability to *predict* not only future total market changes, but also why and when specific spreads will change.[20]

WHAT DETERMINES THE PRICE VOLATILITY FOR BONDS?

In this chapter, we have learned about alternative bond yields, how to calculate them, what determines bond yields (interest rates), and what causes them to change. Now that we understand why yields change, we can logically ask, what is the effect of these yield changes on the prices and rates of return for different bonds? We have discussed the inverse relationship between changes in yields and the price of bonds, so we can now discuss *the specific factors that affect the amount of price change for a yield change* in different bonds. This can also be referred to as the *interest rate sensitivity* of a bond. This section lists the specific factors that affect bond price changes for a given change in interest rates (i.e., the interest rate sensitivity of a bond) and demonstrates the effect for different bonds.

A given change in interest rates can cause vastly different percentage price changes for alternative bonds, which implies different interest rate sensitivity. This section will help

---

[20] An article that identifies four determinants of relative market spreads and suggests scenarios when they will change is Chris P. Dialynas and David H. Edington, "Bond Yield Spreads: A Postmodern View," *Journal of Portfolio Management* 19, no. 1 (Fall 1992): 68–75.

you understand what causes these differences in interest rate sensitivity. To maximize your rate of return from your knowledge of a decline in interest rates, for example, you need to know which bonds will benefit the most from the yield change. This section helps you make this bond selection decision.

Throughout this section, we talk about bond price changes or bond price volatility interchangeably. A bond price change is measured as the percentage change in the price of the bond, computed as follows:

$$\frac{EPB}{BPB} - 1$$

where

EPB = the ending price of the bond
BPB = the beginning price of the bond.

Bond price volatility also is measured in terms of percentage changes in bond prices. A bond with high price volatility or high interest rate sensitivity is one that experiences large percentage price changes for a given change in yields.

Bond price volatility is influenced by more than yield behavior alone. Malkiel used the bond valuation model to demonstrate that the market price of a bond is a function of four factors: (1) its par value, (2) its coupon, (3) the number of years to its maturity, and (4) the prevailing market interest rate.[21] Malkiel's mathematical proofs showed the following relationships between yield (interest rate) changes and bond price behavior:

1. Bond prices move inversely to bond yields (interest rates).
2. For a given change in yields (interest rates), longer-maturity bonds post larger price changes; thus, bond price volatility is *directly* related to term to maturity.
3. Price volatility (percentage of price change) increases at a diminishing rate as term to maturity increases.
4. Price movements resulting from equal absolute increases or decreases in yield are *not* symmetrical. A decrease in yield raises bond prices by more than an increase in yield of the same amount lowers prices.
5. Higher coupon issues show smaller percentage price fluctuation for a given change in yield; thus, bond price volatility is *inversely* related to coupon.

Homer and Leibowitz showed that the absolute level of market yields also affects bond price volatility.[22] As the level of prevailing yields rises, the price volatility of bonds increases, *assuming a constant percentage change in market yields*. It is important to note that if you assume a constant percentage change in yield, the basis-point change will be greater when rates are high. For example, a 25 percent change in interest rates when rates are at 4 percent will be 100 basis points; the same 25 percent change when rates are at 8 percent will be a 200 basis-point change. In the discussion of bond duration, we will see that this difference in basis point change is important.

Tables 16.7, 16.8, and 16.9 demonstrate these relationships assuming semiannual compounding. Table 16.7 demonstrates the effect of maturity on price volatility. In all four maturity classes, we assume a bond with an 8 percent coupon and assume that the discount

---

[21] Burton G. Malkiel, "Expectations, Bond Prices, and the Term Structure of Interest Rates," *Quarterly Journal of Economics* 76, no. 2 (May 1962): 197–218.

[22] Sidney Homer and Martin L. Leibowitz, *Inside the Yield Book* (Englewood Cliffs, NJ: Prentice-Hall, 1972).

TABLE 16.7   **EFFECT OF MATURITY ON BOND PRICE VOLATILITY**

PRESENT VALUE OF AN 8 PERCENT BOND ($1,000 PAR VALUE)

Term to Maturity	1 Year		10 Years		20 Years		30 Years	
Discount rate (YTM)	7%	10%	7%	10%	7%	10%	7%	10%
Present value of interest	$ 75	$ 73	$ 569	$498	$ 858	$686	$1,005	$757
Present value of principal	934	907	505	377	257	142	132	54
Total value of bond	$1,009	$980	$1,074	$875	$1,115	$828	$1,137	$811
Percentage change in total value	−2.9		−18.5		−25.7		−28.7	

rate (YTM) changes from 7 percent to 10 percent. The only difference among the four cases is the maturities of the bonds. The demonstration involves computing the value of each bond at a 7 percent yield and at a 10 percent yield and noting the percentage change in price. As shown, this change in yield caused the price of the 1-year bond to decline by only 2.9 percent; the 30-year bond declined by almost 29 percent. Clearly, the longer-maturity bond experienced the greater price volatility.

Also, price volatility increased at a decreasing rate with maturity. When maturity doubled from 10 years to 20 years, the price increased by less than 50 percent (from 18.5 percent to 25.7 percent). A similar change occurred when going from 20 years to 30 years. Therefore, this table demonstrates the first three of our price–yield relationships: Bond price is inversely related to yields, bond price volatility is positively related to term to maturity, and bond price volatility increases at a decreasing rate with maturity.

It also is possible to demonstrate the fourth relationship with this table. Using the 20-year bond, if you computed the percentage change in price related to an *increase* in rates (e.g., from 7 percent to 10 percent), you would get the answer reported—a 25.7 percent decrease. In contrast, if you computed the effect on price of a *decrease* in yields from 10 percent to 7 percent, you would get a 34.7 percent increase in price ($1,115 vs. $828). This demonstrates that prices change more in response to a decrease in rates (from 10 percent to 7 percent) than to a comparable increase in rates (from 7 percent to 10 percent).

Table 16.8 demonstrates the coupon effect. In this set of examples, all the bonds have equal maturity (20 years) and experience the same change in YTM (from 7 percent to 10 percent). The table shows the inverse relationship between coupon rate and price volatility: The smallest coupon bond (the zero) experienced the largest percentage price change (almost 45 percent), versus a 24 percent change for the 12 percent coupon bond.

TABLE 16.8   **EFFECT OF COUPON ON BOND PRICE VOLATILITY**

PRESENT VALUE OF 20-YEAR BOND ($1,000 PAR VALUE)

	0 Percent Coupon		3 Percent Coupon		8 Percent Coupon		12 Percent Coupon	
Discount rate (YTM)	7%	10%	7%	10%	7%	10%	7%	10%
Present value of interest	$ 0	$ 0	$322	$257	$ 858	$686	$1,287	$1,030
Present value of principal	257	142	257	142	257	142	257	142
Total value of bond	$257	$142	$579	$399	$1,115	$828	$1,544	$1,172
Percentage change in total value	44.7		−31.1		−25.7		−24.1	

TABLE 16.9	EFFECT OF YIELD LEVEL ON BOND PRICE VOLATILITY							

PRESENT VALUE OF A 20-YEAR, 4 PERCENT BOND ($1,000 PAR VALUE)

	(1) Low Yields		(2) Intermediate Yields		(3) High Yields		(4) 100 Basis Point Change at High Yields	
Discount rate (YTM)	3%	4%	6%	8%	9%	12%	9%	10%
Present value of interest	$ 602	$ 547	$462	$396	$370	$301	$370	$343
Present value of principal	562	453	307	208	175	97	175	142
Total value of bond	$1,164	$1,000	$769	$604	$545	$398	$545	$485
Percentage change in total value	−14.1		−21.5		−27.0		−11.0	

Table 16.9 demonstrates the yield level effect. In these examples, all the bonds have the same 20-year maturity and the same 4 percent coupon. In the first three cases, the YTM changed by a constant 33.3 percent (i.e., from 3 percent to 4 percent, from 6 percent to 8 percent, and from 9 percent to 12 percent). Note that the first change is 100 basis points, the second is 200 basis points, and the third is 300 basis points. The results in the first three columns confirm the statement that when higher rates change by a *constant percentage,* the change in the bond price is larger when the rates are at a higher level.

The fourth column shows that if you assume a *constant basis-point change in yields,* you get the opposite results. Specifically, a 100 basis point change in yields from 3 percent to 4 percent provides a price change of 14.1 percent, while the same 100 basis point change from 9 percent to 10 percent results in a price change of only 11 percent. Therefore, the yield level effect can differ, depending on whether the yield change is a constant percentage change or a constant basis-point change.

Thus, the price volatility of a bond for a given change in yield (i.e., its interest rate sensitivity) is affected by the bond's coupon, its term to maturity, the level of yields (depending on what kind of change in yield), and the direction of the yield change. However, although both the level and direction of change in yields affect price volatility, they cannot be used for trading strategies. When yields change, the two variables that have a dramatic effect on a bond's interest rate sensitivity are coupon and maturity.

TRADING STRATEGIES   Knowing that coupon and maturity are the major variables that influence a bond's interest rate sensitivity, we can develop some strategies for maximizing rates of return when interest rates change. Specifically, if you expect a major *decline* in interest rates, you know that bond prices will increase, so you want a portfolio of bonds with the *maximum interest rate sensitivity* so that you will enjoy maximum price changes (capital gains) from the change in interest rates. In this situation, the previous discussion regarding the effect of maturity and coupon indicates that you should attempt to build a portfolio of long-maturity bonds with low coupons (ideally a long-term zero coupon bond). A portfolio of such bonds should experience the maximum price appreciation for a given decline in market interest rates.

In contrast, if you expect an *increase* in market interest rates, you know that bond prices will decline, and you want a portfolio with *minimum interest rate sensitivity* to minimize the capital losses caused by the increase in rates. Therefore, you would want to change your portfolio to short-maturity bonds with high coupons. This combination should provide minimal price volatility for a change in market interest rates.

DURATION MEASURES Because the price volatility (interest rate sensitivity) of a bond varies inversely with its coupon and directly with its term to maturity, it is necessary to determine the best combination of these two variables to achieve your objective. This effort would benefit from a composite measure that considered both coupon and maturity.

A measure of the interest-rate sensitivity of a bond is referred to as **duration**. This concept and its development as a tool in bond analysis and portfolio management has existed for over 50 years. Notably, several specifications of duration have been derived. First, *Macaulay duration*, developed almost 60 years ago by Frederick Macaulay, is a measure of the time flow of cash from a bond.[23] A modified version of Macaulay duration can be used under certain conditions to indicate the price volatility of a bond in response to interest rate changes. Second, **modified duration** is derived by making a small adjustment (modification) to the Macaulay duration value. As noted above, under certain restrictive conditions (most important, there are no embedded options) modified duration can provide an approximation to the interest-rate sensitivity of a bond (or any financial asset). Finally, **effective duration** is a direct measure of the interest rate sensitivity of a bond (or any financial instrument). Because of the development of many new financial instruments, which have very unique cash flows *that change with interest rates*, effective duration has become widely used because of its flexibility and ability to provide a useful measure of interest rate sensitivity—the primary goal of duration. Therefore, in this section we discuss and demonstrate these three duration measures, including their limitations.

MACAULAY DURATION   Macaulay showed that the duration of a bond was a more appropriate measure of time characteristics than the term to maturity of the bond because duration considers both the repayment of capital at maturity and the size and timing of coupon payments prior to final maturity. Using annual compounding, duration (D) is

$$D = \frac{\displaystyle\sum_{t=1}^{n} \frac{C_t(t)}{(1+i)^t}}{\displaystyle\sum_{t=1}^{n} \frac{C_t}{(1+i)^t}}$$

where

    t = the time period in which the coupon or principal payment occurs
    C_t = the interest or principal payment that occurs in period t
    i = the yield to maturity on the bond.

The denominator in this equation is the price of a bond as determined by the present value model. The numerator is the present value of all cash flows *weighted according to the time to cash receipt*. The following example, which demonstrates the specific computations for two bonds, shows the procedure and highlights some of the properties of duration. Consider the following two sample bonds:

	Bond A	Bond B
Face Value	$1,000	$1,000
Maturity	10 years	10 years
Coupon	4%	8%

---

[23] Frederick R. Macaulay, *Some Theoretical Problems Suggested by the Movements of Interest Rates, Bond Yields, and Stock Prices in the United States Since 1856* (New York: National Bureau of Economic Research, 1938).

| TABLE 16.10 | COMPUTATION OF MACAULAY DURATION (ASSUMING 8 PERCENT MARKET YIELD) |

BOND A

(1) Year	(2) Cash Flow	(3) PV at 8%	(4) PV of Flow	(5) PV as % of Price	(6) (1) × (5)
1	$ 40	.9259	$ 37.04	.0506	.0506
2	40	.8573	34.29	.0469	.0938
3	40	.7938	31.75	.0434	.1302
4	40	.7350	29.40	.0402	.1608
5	40	.6806	27.22	.0372	.1860
6	40	.6302	25.21	.0345	.2070
7	40	.5835	23.34	.0319	.2233
8	40	.5403	21.61	.0295	.2360
9	40	.5002	20.01	.0274	.2466
10	1,040	.4632	481.73	.6585	6.5850
Sum			$ 731.58	1.0000	8.1193

Duration = 8.12 Years

BOND B

1	$ 80	.9259	$ 74.07	.0741	.0741
2	80	.8573	68.59	.0686	.1372
3	80	.7938	63.50	.0635	.1906
4	80	.7350	58.80	.0588	.1906
5	80	.6806	54.44	.0544	.2720
6	80	.6302	50.42	.0504	.3024
7	80	.5835	46.68	.0467	.3269
8	80	.5403	43.22	.0432	.3456
9	80	.5002	40.02	.0400	.3600
10	1,080	.4632	500.26	.5003	5.0030
Sum			$1,000.00	1.0000	7.2470

Duration = 7.25 Years

Assuming annual interest payments and an 8 percent yield to maturity on the bonds, duration is computed as shown in Table 16.10. If duration is computed by discounting flows using the yield to maturity of the bond, it is called *Macaulay duration*.

Characteristics of Macaulay duration   This example illustrates several characteristics of Macaulay duration. First, the Macaulay duration of a bond with coupon payments always will be less than its term to maturity because duration gives weight to these interim payments.

Second, there is *an inverse relationship between coupon and duration*. A bond with a larger coupon will have a shorter duration because more of the total cash flows come earlier in the form of interest payments. As shown in Table 16.10, the 8 percent coupon bond has a shorter duration than the 4 percent coupon bond.

A zero coupon bond or a pure discount bond such as a Treasury bill will have *duration equal to its term to maturity*. In Table 16.10, if you assume a single payment at maturity, duration will equal term to maturity because the only cash flow comes in the final (maturity) year.

Third, there is *generally a positive relationship between term to maturity and Macaulay duration,* but duration increases at a decreasing rate with maturity. Therefore, a bond with longer term to maturity almost always will have a higher duration. The relationship is not direct because as maturity increases the present value of the principal declines in value.

FIGURE 16.6

DURATION VS. MATURITY

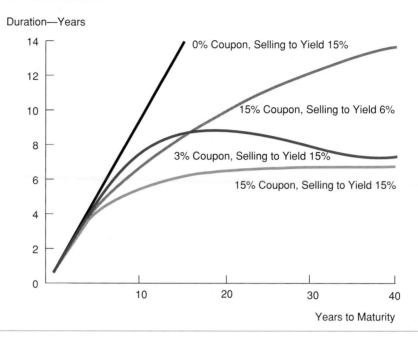

As shown in Figure 16.6, the shape of the duration-maturity curve depends on the coupon and the yield to maturity. The curve for a zero coupon bond is a straight line, indicating that duration equals term to maturity. In contrast, the curve for a low coupon bond selling at a deep discount (due to a high YTM) will turn down at long maturities, which means that under these conditions the longer-maturity bond will have lower duration.

Fourth, all else the same, there is an *inverse relationship between YTM and duration*. A higher yield to maturity of a bond reduces its duration. As an example, in Table 16.10, if the yield to maturity had been 12 percent rather than 8 percent, the duration for the 4 percent bond would have gone from 8.12 to 7.75, and the duration of the 8 percent bond would have gone from 7.25 to 6.80.[24]

Finally, sinking funds and call provisions can have a dramatic effect on a bond's duration. They can change the total cash flows for a bond and, therefore, significantly change its duration. Between these two factors, the characteristic that causes the greatest uncertainty is the call feature because it is difficult to estimate when it will be exercised since it is a function of changes in interest rates. We consider this further when we discuss the effect of the call feature on the convexity of a bond.

A summary of Macaulay duration characteristics is as follows:

- The duration of a zero coupon bond will *equal* its term to maturity.
- The duration of a coupon bond always will be less than its term to maturity.
- There is an *inverse* relationship between coupon and duration.

---

[24] These properties are discussed and demonstrated in Frank K. Reilly and Rupinder Sidhu, "The Many Uses of Bond Duration," *Financial Analysts Journal* 36, no. 4 (July–August 1980): 58–72; and Frank J. Fabozzi, Mark Pitts, and Ravi E. Dattatreya, "Price Volatility Characteristics of Fixed Income Securities," in *The Handbook of Fixed-Income Securities*, 4th ed., edited by Frank J. Fabozzi and T. Dessa Fabozzi (Burr Ridge, IL: Irwin Professional Publishing, 1995).

- There is generally a *positive* relationship between term to maturity and duration. Note that duration increases at a decreasing rate with maturity. Also, the duration of a deep discount bond will decline at very long maturities (over 20 years).
- There is an *inverse* relationship between yield to maturity and duration.
- Sinking funds and call provisions can cause a dramatic change in the duration of a bond. The effect of the call feature is discussed in a subsequent section.

MODIFIED DURATION AND BOND PRICE VOLATILITY

An adjusted measure of duration called *modified duration* can be used to approximate the interest rate sensitivity of a noncallable bond. Modified duration equals Macaulay duration (computed in Table 16.10) divided by 1 plus the current yield to maturity divided by the number of payments in a year. As an example, a bond with a Macaulay duration of 10 years, a yield to maturity (i) of 8 percent, and semiannual payments would have a modified duration of

$$D_{mod} = 10/\left(1 + \frac{.08}{2}\right)$$
$$= 10/(1.04) = 9.62$$

It has been shown, both theoretically and empirically, that price movements of option-free bonds *will vary proportionally* with modified duration for *small changes in yields*.[25] Specifically, as shown in the equation below, an estimate of the percentage change in bond price equals the change in yield times modified duration:

$$\frac{\Delta P}{P} \times 100 = -D_{mod} \times \Delta i$$

where

ΔP = **the change in price for the bond**
P = **the beginning price for the bond**
$-D_{mod}$ = **the modified duration of the bond**
Δi = **the yield change in basis points divided by 100. For example, if interest rates go from 8.00 to 8.50 percent, Δi = 50/100 = 0.50.**

Consider a bond with Macaulay D = 8 years and i = 0.10. Assume that you expect the bond's YTM to decline by 75 basis points (e.g., from 10 percent to 9.25 percent). The first step is to compute the bond's modified duration as follows:

$$D_{mod} = 8/\left(1 + \frac{.10}{2}\right)$$
$$= 8/(1.05) = 7.62$$

The estimated percentage change in the price of the bond is as follows:

$$\% \Delta P = -(7.62) \times \frac{-75}{100}$$
$$= (-7.62) \times (-.75)$$
$$= 5.72$$

---

[25] A generalized proof of this is contained in Michael H. Hopewell and George Kaufman, "Bond Price Volatility and Term to Maturity: A Generalized Respecification," *American Economic Review* 63, no. 4 (September 1973): 749–753. The importance of the specification, "for small changes in yields," will become clear when we discuss convexity in the next section. Because modified duration is an approximate measure of interest rate sensitivity the *years* label is not appropriate.

| TABLE 16.11 | BOND DURATION IN YEARS FOR BOND YIELDING 6 PERCENT UNDER DIFFERENT TERMS |

	COUPON RATES			
Years to Maturity	0.02	0.04	0.06	0.08
1	0.995	0.990	0.985	0.981
5	4.756	4.558	4.393	4.254
10	8.891	8.169	7.662	7.286
20	14.981	12.980	11.904	11.232
50	19.452	17.129	16.273	15.829
100	17.567	17.232	17.120	17.064
∞	17.167	17.167	17.167	17.167

Source: L. Fisher and R. L. Weil, "Coping with the Risk of Interest Rate Fluctuations: Returns to Bondholders from Naive and Optimal Strategies," *Journal of Business* 44, no. 4 (October 1971): 418. Copyright © 1971 by The University of Chicago Press. Reprinted by permission of The University of Chicago Press.

This indicates that the bond price should increase by approximately 5.72 percent in response to the 75 basis point decline in YTM. If the price of the bond before the decline in interest rates was $900, the price after the decline in interest rates should be approximately $900 × 1.0572 = $951.48.

The modified duration is always a negative value for a noncallable bond because of the inverse relationship between yield changes and bond price changes. Also, remember that this formulation provides an *estimate* or *approximation* of the percent change in the price of the bond. The following section on convexity shows that this formula that uses modified duration provides an exact estimate of the percentage price change only for very small changes in yields of option-free securities.

TRADING STRATEGIES USING MODIFIED DURATION   We know that the longest duration security provides the maximum price variation. Table 16.11 demonstrates that numerous ways exist to achieve a given level of duration. The following discussion indicates that an active bond investor can use this measure of interest rate sensitivity to structure a portfolio to take advantage of changes in market yields.

If you expect a *decline* in interest rates, you should *increase* the average modified duration of your bond portfolio to experience maximum price volatility. If you expect an *increase* in interest rates, you should *reduce* the average modified duration of your portfolio to minimize your price decline. Note that the modified duration of your portfolio is the market value weighted average of the modified durations of the individual bonds in the portfolio.

BOND CONVEXITY   Modified duration allows us to estimate bond price changes for a change in interest rates. However, the equation we used to make this calculation (on page 568) is accurate only for *very small changes* in market yields. We will see that the accuracy of the estimate of the price change deteriorates with larger changes in yields because the modified duration calculation is a *linear* approximation of a bond price change that follows a *curvilinear* (convex) function. To understand the effect of this **convexity**, we must consider the price–yield relationship for alternative bonds.[26]

---

[26] For a further discussion of this topic, see Mark L. Dunetz and James M. Mahoney, "Using Duration and Convexity in the Analysis of Callable Bonds," *Financial Analysts Journal* 44, no. 3 (May–June 1988). 53–73.

TABLE 16.12	PRICE–YIELD RELATIONSHIPS FOR ALTERNATIVE BONDS				
A. 12 Percent, 20-Year		**B. 12 Percent, 3-Year**		**C. Zero Coupon, 30-Year**	
Yield	**Price**	**Yield**	**Price**	**Yield**	**Price**
1.0%	$2,989.47	1.0%	$1,324.30	1.0%	$741.37
2.0	2,641.73	2.0	1,289.77	2.0	550.45
3.0	2,346.21	3.0	1,256.37	3.0	409.30
4.0	2,094.22	4.0	1,224.06	4.0	304.78
5.0	1,878.60	5.0	1,192.78	5.0	227.28
6.0	1,693.44	6.0	1,162.52	6.0	169.73
7.0	1,533.88	7.0	1,133.21	7.0	126.93
8.0	1,395.86	8.0	1,104.84	8.0	95.06
9.0	1,276.02	9.0	1,077.37	9.0	71.29
10.0	1,171.59	10.0	1,050.76	10.0	53.54
11.0	1,080.23	11.0	1,024.98	11.0	40.26
12.0	1,000.00	12.0	1,000.00	12.0	30.31

THE PRICE–YIELD RELATIONSHIP FOR BONDS   Because the price of a bond is the present value of its cash flows at a particular discount rate, if you are given the coupon, maturity, and a yield for a bond, you can calculate its price at a point in time. The price–yield curve provides a set of prices for a specific maturity-coupon bond at a point in time using a range of yields to maturity (discount rates). As an example, Table 16.12 lists the computed prices for a 12 percent, 20-year bond assuming yields from 1 percent to 12 percent. The table shows that if you discount the flows from this bond at a yield of 1 percent, you would get a price of $2,989.47; discounting these same flows at 10 percent gives a price of $1,171.59. The graph of these prices relative to the yields that produced them in Figure 16.7 indicates that the price–yield relationship for this bond is not a straight line but a curvilinear relationship. That is, it is convex.

Two points are important about the price–yield relationship:

1. This relationship can be applied to a single bond, a portfolio of bonds, or any stream of future cash flows.
2. The convex price–yield relationship will differ among bonds or other streams, depending on the nature of the cash flow stream, that is, its coupon and maturity. For example, the price–yield relationship for a high-coupon, short-term security will be almost a straight line because the price does not change as much for a change in yields (e.g., the 12 percent, 3-year bond in Table 16.12). In contrast, the price–yield relationship for a low-coupon, long-term bond will curve radically (i.e., be very convex), as shown by the zero coupon, 30-year bond in Table 16.12. These differences in convexity are shown graphically in Figure 16.8. The curved nature of the price–yield relationship is referred to as the bond's *convexity*.

As shown by the graph in Figure 16.8, because of the convexity of the relationship, as yield increases, the rate at which the price of the bond declines becomes slower. Similarly, when yields decline, the rate at which the price of the bond increases becomes faster. Therefore, convexity is considered a desirable trait.

FIGURE 16.7 **PRICE–YIELD RELATIONSHIP AND MODIFIED DURATION AT 4 PERCENT YIELD**

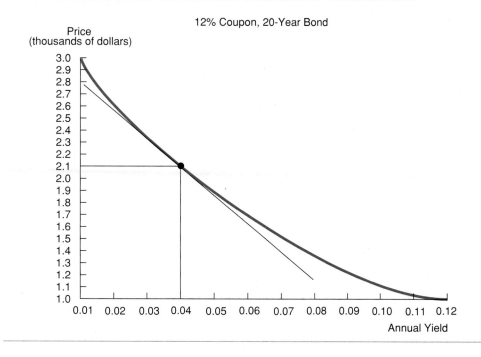

12% Coupon, 20-Year Bond

FIGURE 16.8 **PRICE–YIELD CURVES FOR ALTERNATIVE BONDS**

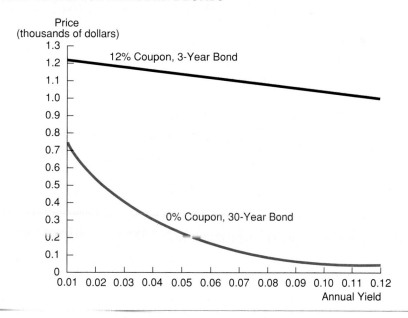

| FIGURE 16.9 | **PRICE APPROXIMATION USING MODIFIED DURATION** |

Source: Frank J. Fabozzi, Mark Pitts, and Ravi E. Dattatreya, "Price Volatility Characteristics of Fixed-Income Securities," in *The Handbook of Fixed-Income Securities*, 4th ed. (Richard D. Irwin, Inc., © 1995) p. 99.

Given this price–yield curve, modified duration is the percentage change in price for a nominal change in yield as follows:[27]

$$D_{mod} = \frac{\dfrac{dP}{di}}{P}$$

Notice that the *dP/di* line is tangent to the price–yield curve *at a given yield* as shown in Figure 16.9. For *small* changes in yields (i.e., from y^* to either y_1 or y_2), this tangent straight line gives a good estimate of the actual price changes. In contrast, for larger changes in yields (i.e., from y^* to either y_3 or y_4), the straight line will estimate the new price of the bond at less than the actual price shown by the price–yield curve. This misestimate arises because the modified-duration line is a linear estimate of a curvilinear relationship. Specifically, the estimate using only modified duration will *underestimate* the actual price *increase* caused by a yield decline and *overestimate* the actual price *decline* caused by an increase in yields. This graph, which demonstrates the convexity effect, also shows that price changes are *not* symmetric when yields increase or decrease. As shown, when rates decline, there is a larger price error than when rates increase

---

[27] In mathematical terms, modified duration is the first differential of this price–yield relationship with respect to yield.

because when yields decline prices rise at an *increasing* rate, while prices decline at a *decreasing* rate when yields rise.

DETERMINANTS OF CONVEXITY   Convexity is a measure of the curvature of the price–yield relationship. In turn, because modified duration is the slope of the curve at a given yield, convexity indicates changes in duration. Mathematically, convexity is the second derivative of price with respect to yield (d^2P/di^2) divided by price. Specifically, convexity is the percentage change in dP/di for a given change in yield:

$$\text{Convexity} = \frac{\frac{d^2P}{di^2}}{P}$$

Convexity is a measure of how much a bond's price–yield curve deviates from the linear approximation of that curve. As indicated by Figures 16.7 and 16.9 for *noncallable* bonds, convexity always is a positive number, implying that the price–yield curve lies above the modified duration (tangent) line. Figure 16.8 illustrates the price–yield relationship for two bonds with very different coupons and maturities. (The yields and prices are contained in Table 16.9.)

These graphs demonstrate the following relationship between these factors and the convexity of a bond.

- There is an *inverse* relationship between coupon and convexity (yield and maturity constant).
- There is a *direct* relationship between maturity and convexity (yield and coupon constant).
- There is an *inverse* relationship between yield and convexity (coupon and maturity constant). This means that the price–yield curve is more convex at its lower-yield (upper left) segment.

Therefore, a short-term, high-coupon bond, such as the 12 percent coupon, 3-year bond in Figure 16.8, has very low convexity—it is almost a straight line. In contrast, the zero coupon, 30-year bond has high convexity.

THE MODIFIED DURATION–CONVEXITY EFFECTS   In summary, the change in a bond's price resulting from a change in yield can be attributed to two sources: the bond's modified duration and its convexity. The relative effect of these two factors on the price change will depend on the characteristics of the bond (i.e., its convexity) and the size of the yield change. For example, if you are estimating the price change for a 300 basis point change in yield for a zero coupon, 30-year bond, the convexity effect would be fairly large because this bond would have high convexity, and a 300 basis point change in yield is relatively large. In contrast, if you are dealing with only a 10 basis point change in yields, the convexity effect would be minimal because it is a small change in yield. Similarly, the convexity effect would be small for a larger yield change if you are concerned with a bond with small convexity (i.e., a high coupon, short maturity bond) because its price–yield curve is almost a straight line.

In conclusion, modified duration can help you derive an *approximate* percentage bond price change for a given change in interest rates, but you must remember that it only is a good estimate when you are considering small yield changes. You must also consider the convexity effect on price change when you are dealing with large yield changes or when the securities or cash flows have high convexity.

COMPUTATION OF CONVEXITY   Again, the formula for computing the convexity of a stream of cash flows looks fairly complex, but it can be broken down into manageable steps. You will recall from our convexity equation above that

$$\text{Convexity} = \frac{\dfrac{d^2P}{di^2}}{P}$$

In turn,

$$\frac{d^2P}{di^2} = \frac{1}{(1 + i)^2}\left[\sum_{t=1}^{n} \frac{CF_t}{(1 + i)^t}(t^2 + t)\right]$$

Table 16.13 contains the computations related to this calculation for a 3-year bond with a 12 percent coupon and 9 percent YTM assuming annual flows.

The convexity for this bond is very low because it has a short maturity, high coupon, and high yield. Note that *the convexity of a security will vary along the price–yield curve*. You will get a different convexity at a 3 percent yield than at a 12 percent yield. In terms of the computation, the maturity and coupon will be the same, but you will use a different discount rate that reflects where you are on the curve. This is similar to the earlier observation that *you will get a different modified duration at different points on the price–yield curve* because the slope varies along the curve. You also can see this mathematically because, depending on where you are on the curve, you will be using a different market yield, and the Macaulay and modified durations are inverse to the discount rate.

TABLE 16.13   **COMPUTATION OF CONVEXITY**

$$\text{Convexity} = \frac{d^2P/di^2}{PV \text{ of Cash Flows}} = \frac{d^2P/di^2}{\text{Price}}$$

$$\frac{d^2P}{di^2} = \frac{1}{(1 + i)^2}\left[\sum_{t=1}^{n} (t^2 + t)\frac{CF_t}{(1 + i)^t}\right]$$

$$\text{Convexity} = \frac{d^2P/di^2}{\text{Price}}$$

Example: 3-Year Bond, 12% Coupon, 9% YTM

(1) Year	(2) CF_t	(3) PV @ 9%	(4) PV CF	(5) $t^2 + t$	(4) × (5)
1	120	.9174	$ 110.09	2	$ 220.18
2	120	.8417	101.00	6	606.00
3	120	.7722	92.66	12	1,111.92
3	1000	.7722	772.20	12	9,266.40
			$1,075.95		$11,204.50

$$\frac{1}{(1 + i)^2} = \frac{1}{(1.09)^2} = \frac{1}{1.19} = .84$$

$$\$11,204.50 \times .84 = \$9,411.78$$

$$\frac{9411.78}{1075.95} = 8.75$$

To compute the price change attributable to the convexity effect after you know the bond's convexity, use this equation:

$$\text{Price Change Due to Convexity} = \tfrac{1}{2} \times \text{Price} \times \text{Convexity} \times (\Delta \text{ in yield})^2$$

Table 16.14 shows the change in bond price considering the duration effect and the convexity effect for an 18-year bond with a 12 percent coupon and 9 percent YTM. For demonstration purposes, we assumed a decline of 100 and 300 basis points (BP) in rates (i.e., 9 percent to 8 percent and 9 percent to 6 percent).

With the 300 BP change, if you considered only the modified-duration effect, you would have *estimated* that the bond went from 126.50 to 158.30 (a 25.14 percent increase), when, in fact, the actual price is closer to 164.41, which is about a *30 percent increase*.

TABLE 16.14 **ANALYSIS OF BOND PRICE CHANGE CONSIDERING DURATION AND CONVEXITY**

Example: 18-Year Bond, 12% Coupon, 9% YTM
Price: 126.50
Modified Duration: 8.38 (D^*)
Convexity: 107.70
Estimate of Price Change Using Duration:
  Percent Δ Price = $-D^*$ (Δ in YLD/100)
Estimate of Price Change from Convexity:
  Price Change = $\tfrac{1}{2} \times$ Price $\times$ Convexity $\times$ (Δ in YLD)^2

A. Change in Yield: -100 BP

    Duration Change: $-8.38 \times \left(\dfrac{-100}{100}\right) = +8.38\%$

                     $+8.38\% \times 126.50 = +10.60$

    Convexity Change: $\dfrac{1}{2} \times (126.50) \times 107.70 \times (.01)^2$

                     $= 63.25 \times 107.70 \times .0001$
                     $= 6,812.03 \times .0001 = .68$
    Combined Effect: 126.50
                  + 10.60 (Duration)
                   137.10
                   +.68 (Convexity)
                   137.78

B. Change in Yield: -300 BP

    Duration Change: $-8.38 \times \left(\dfrac{-300}{100}\right) = +25.14\%$

                     $126.50 \times 1.2514 = 158.30 (+31.80)$

    Convexity Effect: $\dfrac{1}{2} \times (126.50) \times 107.70 \times (.03)^2$

                     $6,812.03 \times .0009 = 6.11$
    Combined Effect: 126.50
                  + 31.80 (Duration)
                   158.30
                   +6.11 (Convexity)
                   164.41

DURATION AND CONVEXITY FOR CALLABLE BONDS
The discussion and presentation thus far regarding Macaulay and modified durations and convexity have been concerned with noncallable bonds. A callable bond is different because it provides the issuer with an option to call the bond under certain conditions and pay it off with funds from a new issue sold at a lower yield. Observers will refer to this as a bond with an *embedded option*. We noted earlier that the duration of a bond can be seriously affected by an embedded call option if interest rates decline substantially below a bond's coupon rate. In such a case, the issuer will likely call the bond, which will dramatically change the maturity and the duration of the bond. For example, assume a firm issues a 30-year bond with a 9 percent coupon with a deferred call provision whereby the bond can be called in 6 years at 109 percent of par. If the bond is issued at par, its original *duration to maturity* will be about 11 years. A year later, if rates decline to about 7 percent, its duration to maturity will still be over *10 years* because duration is inversely related to yield and yields have declined. Notably, at a yield of 7 percent, this bond will probably trade at *yield to call* because at a 7 percent yield the firm will likely exercise its option and call the bond in 5 years. Notably, the bond's *duration to first call* would be about *4 years*. Clearly, there is a significant difference between duration to maturity and duration to first call.

To understand the impact of the call feature on the duration and convexity of a bond, it is important to consider what determines the price of a callable bond. A callable bond is a combination of a noncallable bond plus a *call option* that was *sold to the issuer,* which allows the issuer to call the bond under the conditions discussed earlier. Because the call option is owned by the issuer, it has negative value for the investor in the bond. Thus the bondholder's position is:

Long a Callable Bond = Long a Noncallable Bond + A Short Position in a Call Option

Therefore, the value (price) of a callable bond is equal to:

Callable Bond Price = Noncallable Bond Price − Call Option Price

Given this valuation, anything that increases the value of the call option will reduce the value of the callable bond.[28]

OPTION-ADJUSTED DURATION[29]   Given these two extreme values of duration to maturity and duration to first call, the investment community derives a duration estimate that is referred to as an option-adjusted or call-adjusted duration based on *the probability that the issuing firm will exercise its call option* for the bond when the bond becomes freely callable. This option-adjusted duration will be somewhere between these two extreme values. Specifically, when interest rates are substantially above the coupon rate, the probability of the bond being called is very small (i.e., the call option has very little value) and the option-adjusted duration will approach the duration to maturity. In contrast, if interest

---

[28] For a further discussion of the effect of these embedded options, see Frank J. Fabozzi, Mark Pitts, and Ravi E. Dattatreya, "Price Volatility Characteristics of Fixed Income Securities," and Frank J. Fabozzi, Andrew J. Kalotay, and George O. Williams, "Valuation of Bonds with Embedded Options." Both are in Frank J. Fabozzi and T. Dessa Fabozzi, eds., *The Handbook of Fixed-Income Securities*, 4th ed. (Burr Ridge, IL: Irwin Professional Publishing, 1995). Also see Kurt Winkelmann, "Uses and Abuses of Duration and Convexity," *Financial Analysts Journal* 45, no. 5 (September–October 1989), 72–75, and Chapter 14 in Frank J. Fabozzi, *Bond Markets, Analysis and Strategies,* 3rd ed. (Upper Saddle River, NJ: Prentice Hall, 1996).

[29] The discussion in this subsection will consider the option-adjusted duration on a conceptual and intuitive basis. For a detailed mathematical treatment, see Dunetz and Mahoney, "Using Duration and Convexity in the Analysis of Callable Bonds."

rates decline to levels substantially below the coupon rate, the probability of the bond being called at the first opportunity is very high (i.e., the call option is very valuable and will probably be exercised) and the option-adjusted duration will approach the duration to first call. The bond's option-adjusted duration will be somewhere between these two extremes with the exact option-adjusted duration depending on the level of interest rates relative to the bond's coupon rate.

CONVEXITY OF CALLABLE BONDS   Figure 16.10 shows what happens to the price of a callable bond versus the value of a noncallable bond when interest rates increase or decline. Starting from yield y^* (which is close to the par value yield), if interest rates *increase,* the value of the call option declines because at market interest rates that are substantially above the coupon rate, it is unlikely the issuer will want to call the issue. Therefore, the call option has very little value and the price of the callable bond will be similar to the price of a noncallable bond. In contrast, when interest rates *decline* below y^*, there is an increase in the probability that the issuer will want to use the call option—i.e., the value of the call option increases. As a result, the value of the callable bond will deviate from the value of the noncallable bond—i.e., the price of the callable bond will initially not increase as fast as the noncallable bond price and eventually will not increase at all. This is what is shown in curves a–b.

In the case of the noncallable bond, we indicated that it had *positive convexity* because as yields declined, the price of the bond increased at a *faster* rate. With the callable bond, when rates declined, the price increased at a *slower* rate and eventually does not change at all. This pattern of price–yield change for a callable bond is referred to as *negative convexity*.

Needless to say, this price pattern (negative convexity) is one of the risks of a callable bond versus a noncallable bond, especially if there is a chance of declining interest rates.

FIGURE 16.10

NONCALLABLE AND CALLABLE BOND PRICE–YIELD RELATIONSHIP

Source: Frank J. Fabozzi, Mark Pitts, and Ravi E. Dattatreya, "Price Volatility Characteristics of Fixed Income Securities," in *The Handbook of Fixed-Income Securities*, 4th ed., edited by Frank J. Fabozzi and T. Dessa Fabozzi (Burr Ridge, IL: Irwin Professional Publishing, 1995). Reprinted by permission of the publisher.

LIMITATIONS OF
MACAULAY AND
MODIFIED DURATION

It is important to understand Macaulay and modified duration because of the perspective they provide regarding factors that affect the volatility and interest rate sensitivity of bonds. However, it also is important for bond analysts and portfolio managers to recognize the serious limitations of these measures in the real world. The major limitations are as follows:

First, as noted in the discussion of convexity, the percent change estimates using modified duration only are good for small-yield changes. This was demonstrated in Figure 16.9. As a result, two bonds with equal duration may experience different price changes for large-yield changes—depending on *differences in the convexity* of the bonds.

Second, it is difficult to determine the interest-rate sensitivity of a portfolio of bonds when there is a change in interest rates and the yield curve experiences *a nonparallel shift*. It was noted earlier that the duration of a portfolio is the weighted average of the durations of the bonds in the portfolio. Everything works well as long as all yields change by the same amount—i.e., there is a parallel shift of the yield curve. The problem is, when yields change, the yield curve *seldom* experiences a parallel shift. Assuming a nonparallel shift, which yield do you use to describe the change—the short-, intermediate-, or long-maturity yield? Two portfolios that begin the period with the same duration can have different ending durations and perform very differently, depending on how the yield curve changed (i.e., did it steepen or flatten?) and the composition of the portfolio (i.e., relative to its duration, was it a bullet or a barbell?). Consider the following simple example for two portfolios that have a duration of 4.50 years:

Bond	Coupon	Maturity (Years)	Yield	Modified Duration	Weights
Portfolio A					
A	7.00	4	7.00	2.70	0.555
B	9.00	20	9.00	6.75	0.445
Portfolio B					
C	8.00	10	8.00	4.50	1.000

As shown, the modified durations are equal at the initiation of the portfolio. Assume a nonparallel change in yields where the *yield curve steepens*. Specifically, 4-year yields decline to 6 percent, 10-year yields do not change, and 20-year yields rise to 10 percent. Portfolio B would experience a very small change in value because of stability in yield for 10-year bonds. In contrast, the price for 4-year bonds will experience a small increase (because of small duration) and the value of 20-year bonds will experience a large decline. Overall, the value of portfolio A will decline because of the weight of bond B in the portfolio and its large decline in value due to its large modified duration. Obviously, if the yield curve had flattened or inverted, the barbell portfolio would have benefited from the change. This differential performance because of the change in the shape of the yield curve (i.e., it did not experience a parallel shift) is referred to as *yield curve risk*, which cannot be captured by the traditional duration–convexity presentation.

The third limitation of Macaulay and modified durations involves our initial calculation. We assumed that cash flows from the bond *were not affected by yield changes*—i.e., we assumed option-free bonds. Later, we saw the effect on the computed duration and convexity when we considered the effect of an embedded call option in Figure 16.10. Specifically, we saw that the option-adjusted duration would be some value between the duration to maturity and duration to first call and the specific value would depend on the current market yield relative to the bond's coupon. Further, we saw that when interest rates declined with an embedded option, the convexity of the bond went from some positive value to *negative* convexity because the price of the callable bond increased at a slower rate or it did not change when the yields declined (i.e., there is *price compression*).

Because of these limitations, practitioners have developed a way to approximate the duration of a bond or any security that will be impacted by a change in interest rates. This is referred to as *effective duration,* which is discussed in the following section.

EFFECTIVE DURATION   As noted previously, the purpose of duration is to indicate the price change of an asset to a change in yield—i.e., it is *a measure of the interest-rate sensitivity of an asset.* Because modified duration is based on Macaulay duration, it can provide a reasonable approximation of the interest-rate sensitivity of a bond that experiences a small-yield change and one that is option free—i.e., if yield changes do not change the cash flows for the bond. Unfortunately, the Macaulay and modified duration measures cannot be used for large-yield changes, for assets with embedded options, or for other assets that are affected by variables other than interest rates such as common stocks or real estate.

To overcome these limitations, practitioners use *effective duration*, a direct measure of the interest-rate sensitivity of a bond or any asset where it is possible to observe the market prices surrounding a change in interest rates. As we will demonstrate, using this measure we can derive negative durations (which is not mathematically possible with Macaulay), or durations that are longer than the maturity of the asset (not possible with Macaulay). The concept is best described by recalling the formula to determine the percentage price change for a bond using modified duration as follows:

$$\%\Delta \text{Price} = -D^* \times (\Delta R)$$

where

D^* = the modified Macaulay duration
ΔR = the change in interest rates in basis points divided by 100.

The typical assumption is that we know D^* and ΔR and can solve for the approximate percent price change. Given this relationship, we can solve for D^* as follows:

$$-D^* = \frac{\%\Delta \text{Price}}{\Delta R}$$

When we solve for it this way, it is no longer D^* (modified duration), but D_E—effective duration. Given this formulation, if you observe a change in interest rates (ΔR) and the change in the price of an asset during the same time period, you can solve for the effective duration of the asset. Consider the following simple example.

- Interest rates decline by 200 b.p.
- The price of a bond increases by 10 percent

$$D_E - \frac{10}{-200/100} = -\frac{10}{-2}$$
$$= 5$$

Therefore, the change in price coincident with a change in interest rates indicates that this bond has an effective duration (D_E) of 5. This is a direct measure of the bond's interest-rate sensitivity. Notably, thinking of duration in this way, it is not appropriate to describe it as a measure of time (i.e., in years). As noted, it is a measure of interest rate sensitivity and you should think of it as *the approximate percentage change in price for a 100-basis-point change in interest rates.*

EFFECTIVE DURATION GREATER THAN MATURITY   Because effective duration is simply interest-rate sensitivity, it is possible to have an asset that is highly levered such that its interest-rate sensitivity exceeds its maturity. For example, there are 5-year, collateralized mortgage obligations (CMOs) that are highly levered and their prices will change by 15 percent to 20 percent when interest rates change by 100 basis points. Using the formula discussed, this would imply an effective duration of 15 or 20 for a 5-year maturity security.

NEGATIVE EFFECTIVE DURATION   We know from the formula for Macaulay duration that it is not possible to compute a negative duration. Further, in the calculation for price volatility where we use modified duration, we use $-D^*$ to reflect the negative relationship between price changes and interest rate changes for *option-free bonds*. At the same time, we know that when we leave the world of option-free bonds and consider bonds with embedded options, it is possible to envision cases where bond prices move in the same direction as yields, which implies negative duration. A prime example would be mortgage-backed securities where a significant decline in interest rates will cause a substantial increase in refinancing prepayments by homeowners, which will reduce the value of these bonds to holders. Therefore, you would see a decline in interest rates *and* a decline in the price of these mortgage-backed bonds, which implies *negative duration.*

EFFECTIVE DURATION FOR COMMON STOCK   If one considers the Macaulay duration of common stock, it is possible to envision a fairly high number because you are dealing with a perpetuity, and some growth stocks pay low dividends for many years. The values derived by Reilly and Sidhu, using various assumptions of price and growth, ranged from 10 years to 20 years.[30] In contrast, using effective duration one gets very different results.

Because we are dealing with the interest-rate sensitivity of an asset, it is possible to compute an effective duration for common stock that is much lower than implied by Macaulay duration and it is more variable. Observing a change in interest rates and the accompanying change in stock prices would indicate the interest-rate sensitivity of stocks. Leibowitz conducted such an analysis and derived a rolling, one-year effective duration for the S&P 500 that ranged *from about zero to almost 7.*[31] Because we are measuring interest-rate sensitivity over time, you would expect changes in the interest-rate sensitivity of common stocks over time because the correlation between stocks and bonds varies. In addition you might anticipate significant differences in the effective duration for alternative stocks. For example, you would expect a large difference in the interest-rate sensitivity (effective duration) of a banking or utility stock (which is very interest rate sensitive) compared to the effective duration of a technology growth stock where its value is based more on changes in its growth expectations than interest rates.

[30] Frank K. Reilly and Rupinder Sidhu, "The Many Uses of Bond Duration," *Financial Analysts Journal* 36, no. 4 (July–August 1980): 58–72.

[31] Martin L. Leibowitz, *New Perspective on Asset Allocation* (Charlottesville, VA: The Research Foundation of the Institute of Chartered Financial Analysts, 1987).

Summary

- The value of a bond equals the present value of all future cash flows accruing to the investor. Cash flows for the conservative bond investor include periodic interest payments and principal return; cash flows for the aggressive investor include periodic interest payments and the capital gain or loss when the bond is sold prior to its maturity. Bond investors can maximize their yields by accurately estimating the level of interest rates, and more importantly, by estimating changes in interest rates and yield spreads. Similarly, they must compare coupon rates, maturities, and call features of alternative bonds.
- There are five bond yield measures: nominal yield, current yield, promised yield to maturity, promised yield to call, and realized (horizon) yield. The promised YTM and promised YTC equations include the interest-on-interest (or coupon reinvestment) assumption. For the realized (horizon) yield computation, the investor estimates the reinvestment rate and may need to estimate the future selling price for the bond. The fundamental determinants of interest rates are a real risk-free rate, the expected rate of inflation, and a risk premium.
- The yield curve (or the term structure of interest rates) shows the relationship between the yields on a set of comparable bonds and the term to maturity. Based upon this yield curve it is possible to derive a theoretical spot rate curve. In turn, these spot rates can be used to value bonds using an individual spot rate for each cash flow. In addition, these spot rates imply investor expectations about future rates referred to as forward rates. Yield curves exhibit four basic patterns. Three theories attempt to explain the shape of the yield curve: the expectations hypothesis, the liquidity preference hypothesis, and the segmented market hypothesis.
- It is important to understand what causes changes in interest rates and how these changes in rates affect the prices of bonds. Differences in bond price volatility are mainly a function of differences in yield, coupon, and term to maturity. There are three duration measures that have been used as measures of bond price volatility or interest-rate sensitivity. The Macaulay duration measure incorporates coupon, maturity, and yield in one measure and an adaptation of it (modified duration) provides an estimate of the response of bond prices to changes in interest rates under certain assumptions. Because modified duration provides a straight-line estimate of the curvilinear price–yield function, you must consider modified duration together with the convexity of a bond for large changes in yields and/or when dealing with securities that have high convexity. It is shown that the call feature on a bond can have a significant impact on its modified duration (the call feature can shorten it dramatically) and on its convexity (the call feature can change the convexity from a positive value to a negative value). Following a discussion of some of the limitations of Macaulay and modified durations as measures of interest-rate sensitivity, we present the concept of effective duration, which is a direct measure of interest-rate sensitivity—i.e., it is the approximate percentage change in price for a 100-basis-point change in interest rates. Notably, effective duration allows for durations longer than maturity, negative duration, and duration estimates for common stock.

Given the background in bond valuation and the factors that influence bond value and bond return volatility, we are ready to consider how to build a bond portfolio that is consistent with our goals and objectives. Bond portfolio analysis is the topic for Chapter 17.

Questions

1. Why does the present value equation appear to be more useful for the bond investor than for the common stock investor?
2. What are the important assumptions made when you calculate the promised yield to maturity? What are the assumptions when calculating promised YTC?
3. a. Define the variables included in the following model:

$$i - (RFR, I, RP)$$

   b. Assume that the firm whose bonds you are considering is not expected to break even this year. Discuss which factor will be affected by this information.
4. We discussed three alternative hypotheses to explain the term structure of interest rates. Briefly discuss the three hypotheses and indicate which one you think best explains the alternative shapes of a yield curve.

5. *CFA Examination I (June 1982)*
   a. Explain what is meant by *structure of interest rates*. Explain the theoretical basis of an upward-sloping yield curve. [8 minutes]
   b. Explain the economic circumstances under which you would expect to see the inverted yield curve prevail. [7 minutes]
   c. Define "real" rate of interest. [2 minutes]
   d. Discuss the characteristics of the market for U.S. Treasury securities. Compare it to the market for AAA corporate bonds. Discuss the opportunities that may exist in bond markets that are less than efficient. [8 minutes]
   e. Over the past several years, fairly wide yield spreads between AAA corporates and Treasuries have occasionally prevailed. Discuss the possible reasons for this. [5 minutes]

6. *CFA Examination III (June 1982)*
   As the portfolio manager for a large pension fund, you are offered the following bonds:

	Coupon	Maturity	Price	Call Price	Yield to Maturity
Edgar Corp. (new issue)	14.00%	2002	$101.3/4	$114	13.75%
Edgar Corp. (new issue)	6.00	2002	48.1/8	103	13.60
Edgar Corp. (1972 issue)	6.00	2002	48.7/8	103	13.40

   Assuming that you expect a decline in interest rates over the next 3 years, identify and justify which of these bonds you would select. [10 minutes]

7. You expect interest rates to decline over the next six months.
   a. Given your interest rate outlook, state what kinds of bonds you want in your portfolio in terms of duration and explain your reasoning for this choice.
   b. You must make a choice between the following three sets of noncallable bonds. In each case, select the bond that would be best for your portfolio given your interest rate outlook and the consequent strategy set forth in Part a. In each case briefly discuss why you selected the bond.

	Maturity	Coupon	Yield to Maturity
Case 1: Bond A	15 years	10%	10%
Bond B	15 years	6%	8%
Case 2: Bond C	15 years	6%	10%
Bond D	10 years	8%	10%
Case 3: Bond E	12 years	12%	12%
Bond F	15 years	12%	8%

8. At the present time, you expect a decline in interest rates and must choose between two portfolios of bonds with the following characteristics:

	Portfolio A	Portfolio B
Average maturity	10.5 years	10.0 years
Average YTM	7%	10%
Modified duration	5.7 years	4.9 years
Modified convexity	125.18	40.30
Call features	Noncallable	Deferred call features that range from 1 to 3 years

Select one of the portfolios and discuss three factors that would justify your selection.

9. The Chartered Finance Corporation has issued a bond with the following characteristics:

> Maturity—25 years
> Coupon—9%
> Yield to maturity—9%
> Callable—after 3 years @ 109
> Duration to maturity—8.2 years
> Duration to first call—2.1 years

    a. Discuss the concept of call-adjusted duration and indicate the approximate value (range) for it at the present time.

    b. Assuming interest rates increase substantially (i.e., to 13 percent), discuss what will happen to the call-adjusted duration and the reason for the change.

    c. Assuming interest rates decline substantially (i.e., they decline to 4 percent), discuss what will happen to the bond's call-adjusted duration and the reason for the change.

    d. Discuss the concept of negative convexity as it relates to this bond.

10. *CFA Examination I (1990)*

Duration may be calculated by *two* widely used methods. Identify these *two* methods, and briefly discuss the primary differences between them. [5 minutes]

11. *CFA Examination II (1995)*

Option-adjusted duration and *effective duration* are alternative measures used by analysts to evaluate fixed-income securities with embedded options.

    Briefly describe *each* measure and how to apply *each* to the evaluation of fixed-income securities with embedded options. [8 minutes]

12. *CFA Examination II (1995)*

As a portfolio manager, during a discussion with a client, you explain that historical return and risk premia of the type presented in the following Table are frequently used in forming estimates of future returns for various types of financial assets. While such historical data are helpful in forecasting returns, most users know that history is an imperfect guide to the future. Thus, they recognize that there are reasons why these data should be adjusted if they are to be employed in the forecasting process.

U.S. HISTORICAL RETURN AND RISK PREMIA (1926–94)

	Per Year
Inflation rate	3.0%
Real interest rate on Treasury bills	0.5%
Maturity premium of long Treasury bonds over Treasury bills	0.8%
Default premium of long corporate bonds over long Treasury bonds	0.6%
Risk premium on stock over long Treasury bonds	5.6%
Return on Treasury bills	3.5%
Return on long corporate bonds	4.9%
Return on large-capitalization stocks	9.9%

    a. As shown in the Table the historical real interest rate for Treasury bills was 0.5% per year and the maturity premium on Treasury bonds over Treasury bills was 0.8%. Briefly describe and justify *one* adjustment to *each* of these two data items that should be made before they can be used to form expectations about future real interest rates and Treasury bond maturity premia. [6 minutes]

    b. You recognize that even adjusted historical economic and capital markets data may be of limited use when estimating future returns. Independent of your Part A response, briefly describe *three* key circumstances that should be considered when forming expectations about future returns. [8 minutes]

13. *CFA Examination I (1992)*

A portfolio manager at Superior Trust Company is structuring a fixed-income portfolio to meet the objectives of a client. This client plans on retiring in 15 years and wants a substantial lump sum at that time. The client has specified the use of AAA-rated securities.

The portfolio manager compares coupon U.S. Treasuries with zero coupon stripped U.S. Treasuries and observes a significant yield advantage for the stripped bonds.

Maturity	Coupon U.S. Treasuries	Zero Coupon Stripped U.S. Treasuries
3 year	5.50%	5.80%
5 year	6.00%	6.60%
7 year	6.75%	7.25%
10 year	7.25%	7.60%
15 year	7.40%	8.80%
30 year	7.75%	7.75%

Briefly discuss *two* reasons why zero coupon stripped U.S. Treasuries could yield more than coupon U.S. Treasuries with the same final maturity. [5 minutes]

14. *CFA Examination II (1993)*

a. In terms of option theory, explain the impact on the offering yield of adding a call feature to a proposed bond issue. [5 minutes]

b. Explain the impact on *both* bond duration and convexity of adding a call feature to a proposed bond issue. [10 minutes]

Assume that a portfolio of corporate bonds is managed to maintain targets for modified duration and convexity.

c. Explain how the portfolio could include *both* callable and non-callable bonds while maintaining the targets. [5 minutes]

d. Describe *one* advantage and *one* disadvantage of including callable bonds in this portfolio. [5 minutes]

Problems

1. Four years ago, your firm issued $1,000 par, 25-year bonds, with a 7 percent coupon rate and a 10 percent call premium.
   a. If these bonds are now called, what is the *approximate* yield to call for the investors who originally purchased them?
   b. If these bonds are now called, what is the *actual* yield to call for the investors who originally purchased them at par?
   c. If the current interest rate is 5 percent and the bonds were not callable, at what price would each bond sell?

2. Assume that you purchased an 8 percent, 20-year, $1,000 par, semiannual payment bond priced at $1,012.50 when it has 12 years remaining until maturity. Compute:
   a. Its approximate yield to maturity
   b. Its actual yield to maturity
   c. Its yield to call if the bond is callable in 3 years with an 8 percent premium

3. Calculate the duration of an 8 percent, $1,000 par bond that matures in 3 years if the bond's YTM is 10 percent and interest is paid semiannually.
   a. Calculate this bond's modified duration.
   b. Assuming the bond's YTM goes from 10 percent to 9.5 percent, calculate an estimate of the price change.

4. Two years ago, you acquired a 10-year zero coupon, $1,000 par value bond at a 12 percent YTM. Recently you sold this bond at an 8 percent YTM. Using semiannual compounding, compute the annualized horizon return for this investment.

5. A bond for the Webster Corporation has the following characteristics:

> Maturity—12 years
> Coupon—10%
> Yield to maturity—9.50%
> Macaulay duration—5.7 years
> Convexity—48
> Noncallable

a. Calculate the approximate price change for this bond using only its duration assuming its yield to maturity increased by 150 basis points. Discuss the impact of the calculation, including the convexity effect.
b. Calculate the approximate price change for this bond (using only its duration) if its yield to maturity declined by 300 basis points. Discuss (without calculations) what would happen to your estimate of the price change if this was a callable bond.

6. *CFA Examination I (1992)*
The table below shows selected data on a German government bond (payable in Deutschemarks) and a U.S. government bond. Identify the components of return and calculate the total return in U.S. dollars for both of these bonds for the year 1991. Show the calculations for *each* component. (Ignore interest on interest in view of the short time period.) [8 minutes]

| | | **MARKET YIELD** | | Modified | **EXCHANGE RATE (DM/$U.S.)** | |
	Coupon	1/1/91	1/1/92	Duration	1/1/91	1/1/92
German Government Bond	8.50%	8.50%	8.00%	7.0	1.55	1.50
U.S. Government Bond	8.00%	8.00%	6.75%	6.5	—	—

7. *CFA Examination I (1993)*
Philip Morris has issued bonds that pay semi-annually with the following characteristics:

Coupon	Yield-to-Maturity	Maturity	Macaulay Duration
8%	8%	15 years	10 years

a. Calculate modified duration using the information above. [5 minutes]
b. Explain why modified duration is a better measure than maturity when calculating the bond's sensitivity to changes in interest rates. [5 minutes]
c. Identify the direction of change in modified duration if:
   (i) the coupon of the bond were 4%, not 8%
   (ii) the maturity of the bond were 7 years, not 15 years [5 minutes]
d. Define convexity and explain how modified duration *and* convexity are used to approximate the bond's percentage change in price, given a change in interest rates. [5 minutes]

8. *CFA Examination I (1993)*
You are a U.S. investor considering purchase of one of the following securities. Assume that the currency risk of the German government bond will be hedged, and the six-month discount on Deutschemark forward contracts is −0.75% versus the U.S. dollar.

Bond	Maturity	Coupon	Price
U.S. government	June 1, 2003	6.50%	100.00
German government	June 1, 2003	7.50%	100.00

Calculate the expected price change required in the German government bond which would result in the two bonds having equal total returns in U.S. dollars over a six-month horizon. [8 minutes]

9. *CFA Examination II (1990)*

The following are the average yields on U.S. Treasury bonds at two different points in time:

	YIELD-TO-MATURITY	
Term to Maturity	January 15, 19XX	May 15, 19XX
1 year	7.25%	8.05%
2 years	7.50%	7.90%
5 years	7.90%	7.70%
10 years	8.30%	7.45%
15 years	8.45%	7.30%
20 years	8.55%	7.20%
25 years	8.60%	7.10%

a. Assuming a pure expectations hypothesis, define a forward rate. Describe how you would calculate the forward rate for a three-year U.S. Treasury bond two years from May 15, 19XX using the actual term structure above. [3 minutes]

b. Discuss how *each* of the *three* major term structure hypotheses could explain the January 15, 19XX term structures shown above. [6 minutes]

c. Discuss what happened to the term structure over the time period and the effect of this change on U.S. Treasury bonds of 2 years *and* 10 years. [5 minutes]

d. Assume that you invest solely on the basis of yield spreads, and in January 19XX acted upon the expectation that the yield spread between 1-year and 25-year U.S. Treasuries would return to a more typical spread of 170 basis points. Explain what you would have done on January 15, 19XX, and describe the result of this action based upon what happened between January 15, 19XX and May 15, 19XX. [7 minutes]

10. *CFA Examination II (1992)*

a. Using the information in the table below calculate the projected price change for Bond B if the yield-to-maturity for this bond falls by 75 basis points. [7 minutes]

b. Describe the shortcoming of analyzing Bond A strictly to call or to maturity. Explain an approach to remedy this shortcoming. [6 minutes]

MONTICELLO CORPORATION BOND INFORMATION

	Bond A (Callable)	Bond B (Non-Callable)
Maturity	2002	2002
Coupon	11.50%	7.25%
Current price	125.75	100.00
Yield-to-maturity	7.70%	7.25%
Modified duration to maturity	6.20	6.80
Convexity to maturity	.50	.60
Call date	1996	—
Call price	105	—
Yield to call	5.10%	—
Modified duration to call	3.10	—
Convexity to call	.10	—

11. *CFA Examination II (1992)*

U.S. Treasuries represent a significant holding in Monticello's pension portfolio. You decide to analyze the yield curve for U.S. Treasury Notes.

a. Using the data in the table below, calculate the five-year spot and forward rates assuming annual compounding. Show calculations. [8 minutes]

U.S. TREASURY NOTE YIELD CURVE DATA

Years to Maturity	Par Coupon Yield-to-Maturity	Calculated Spot Rates	Calculated Forward Rates
1	5.00	5.00	5.00
2	5.20	5.21	5.42
3	6.00	6.05	7.75
4	7.00	7.16	10.56
5	7.00	☐	☐

b. Define and describe *each* of the following *three* concepts:
   • Yield-to-maturity
   • Spot rate
   • Forward rate.
   Explain how these *three* concepts are related. [9 minutes]

You are considering the purchase of a zero-coupon U.S. Treasury Note with four years to maturity.

c. Based on the above yield curve analysis, calculate *both* the expected yield-to-maturity and the price for the security. Show calculations. [8 minutes]

12. *CFA Examination III (1992)*

Emily Maguire, manager of the actively managed non-government bond portion of PTC's pension portfolio, has received a fact sheet containing data on a new security offering. It will be a bond issued by a U.S. corporation but denominated in Australian dollars (A$), with both principal and interest payable in that currency.

The terms of the offering made in June, 1992 are as follows:

• Issuer—Student Loan Marketing Association (SLMA—a U.S. Government Sponsored Corporation)
• Rating—AAA
• Coupon Rate—8.5% payable quarterly
• Price—Par
• Maturity—June 30, 1997 (non-callable)
• Principal and interest payable in Australian dollars (A$)

As an alternative, Maguire finds that five-year U.S.$-pay notes issued by SLMA yield 6.75%.

She prepares an analysis directed at several specific questions, beginning with the following table of economic data for Australia and the United States.

Major Economic Indicators	UNITED STATES			AUSTRALIA		
	1990	1991	1992(E)	1990	1991	1992(E)
Real GNP (annual change)	1.1%	−0.5%	2.2%	1.6%	−0.5%	3.0%
Consumer expenditures (annual change)	0.9%	0.0%	1.0%	1.1%	−0.2%	2.0%
Inflation (annual change)	5.4%	4.2%	3.4%	7.3%	3.2%	3.9%
Long-bond yield (end-of-year)	8.1%	7.2%	7.0%	9.8%	10.0%	10.2%
Trade balance (U.S. $ billions)	−100	−83	−80	−30	−20	−25

Assuming that interest rates fall 100 basis points in both the U.S. and Australian markets over the next year, identify which of these two bonds will increase the most in value, and justify your answer. [7 minutes]

13. *CFA Examination II (1993)*

The following table shows yields to maturity on U.S. Treasury securities as of January 1, 1993:

Term to Maturity	Yield to Maturity
1 year	3.50%
2 years	4.50%
3 years	5.00%
4 years	5.50%
5 years	6.00%
10 years	6.60%

a. Based on the data in the table, calculate the implied forward one-year rate of interest at January 1, 1996. [5 minutes]

b. Describe the conditions under which the calculated forward rate would be an unbiased estimate of the one-year spot rate of interest at January 1, 1996. [5 minutes]

Assume that one year earlier, at January 1, 1992, the prevailing term structure for U.S. Treasury securities was such that the implied forward one-year rate of interest at January 1, 1996, was significantly higher than the corresponding rate implied by the term structure at January 1, 1993.

c. On the basis of the pure expectations theory of the term structure, briefly discuss two factors that could account for such a decline in the implied forward rate. [8 minutes]

Multiple scenario forecasting frequently makes use of information from the term structure of interest rates.

d. Briefly describe how the information conveyed by this observed decrease in the implied forward rate for 1996 could be used in making a multiple scenario forecast. [5 minutes]

14. *CFA Examination III (1993)*

TMP is working with the officer responsible for the defined-benefit pension plan of a U.S. company. She has come to the firm for advice on what she calls "the key elements of non-U.S. dollar fixed-income investing."

The following information, based on TMP's assessment of the Italian market, has been developed to illustrate the process by which market and currency expectations are integrated.

ITALIAN GOVERNMENT SECURITIES DATA

Security	Modified Duration	Current Price	Current Yield to Maturity	Expected Yield to Maturity in 3 Months
Bill	0.25	100.00	12.50%	12.50%
Note	6.00	100.00	10.00%	9.00%

LIRA/$(US) EXCHANGE RATE

Current Rate	Expected Rate in 3 Months
L1500/$1.00 (US)	L1526/$1.00 (US)

Based on the information provided above, calculate the expected return (in U.S. dollars) on *each* security over the three month period. [9 minutes]

15. *CFA Examination I (1994)*

    Bonds of Zello Corporation with a par value of $1,000 sell for $960, mature in five years, and have a 7% annual coupon rate paid semiannually.

    a. Calculate the:
       (i) current yield;
       (ii) yield-to-maturity (to the nearest whole percent, i.e., 3%, 4%, 5%, etc.); *and*
       (iii) horizon yield (also called total return) for an investor with a three year holding period and a reinvestment rate of 6% over the period. At the end of three years the 7% coupon bonds with two years remaining will sell to yield 7%.

       Show your work. [9 minutes]

    b. Cite *one* major shortcoming for *each* of the following fixed-income yield measures:
       (i) current yield;
       (ii) yield to maturity; *and*
       (iii) horizon yield (also called total return). [6 minutes]

16. *CFA Examination I (1994)*

    During 1990, Disney issued $2.3 billion face value of zero-coupon subordinated notes which resulted in gross proceeds of $965 million. The notes:

    • mature in 2005;
    • can be exchanged for cash by the note holder at any time for the U.S. dollar equivalent of the current market value of 19.651 common shares of Euro Disney per $1,000 face value of notes; and
    • are callable at any time at their issuance price plus accrued interest.

    On March 11, 1993 Disney called the notes at a price of $483.50 which is equivalent to a yield to maturity of 6%. On the call date, Euro Disney common stock traded at a price of 86.80 French francs per share and the currency exchange rate for U.S. dollars ($US) to French francs (Ffr) was:

	$US/Ffr	Ffr/$US
Exchange rate:	.1761	5.6786

    a. Calculate, as of the call date:
       (i) the price of a share of Euro Disney expressed in U.S. dollars; *and*
       (ii) the exchange value (conversion value) of a $1,000 face value note in U.S. dollars. [6 minutes]

    b. On July 21, 1993, Disney issued, at par, $300 million of 100-year bonds with a coupon rate of 7.55%. The bonds are callable in 30 years at 103.02. From Disney's point of view, state *three* disadvantages of calling the zero-coupon notes and effectively replacing part of that debt capital with the issue of 100-year bonds. [8 minutes]

17. *CFA Examination II (1994)*

Table 1 below shows the characteristics of two annual pay bonds from the same issuer with the same priority in the event of default, and Table 2 below displays spot interest rates. Neither bond's price is consistent with the spot rates.

Using the information in Tables 1 and 2, recommend *either* Bond A *or* Bond B for purchase. Justify your choice. [10 minutes]

TABLE 1   BOND CHARACTERISTICS

	Bond A	Bond B
Coupons	Annual	Annual
Maturity	3 years	3 years
Coupon Rate	10%	6%
Yield-to-maturity	10.65%	10.75%
Price	98.40	88.34

TABLE 2   SPOT INTEREST RATES

Term	Spot Rates (Zero Coupon)
1 year	5%
2 year	8%
3 year	11%

References

Fabozzi, Frank J. *Fixed Income Mathematics.* Chicago: Probus Publishing, 1988.

Fabozzi, Frank J. *Bond Markets, Analysis and Strategies.* 3d ed. Upper Saddle River, NJ: Prentice-Hall, 1996.

Fama, Eugene F. "Forward Rates as Predictors of Future Spot Rates." *Journal of Financial Economics* 3, no. 4 (October 1976).

Tuckman, Bruce. *Fixed Income Securities.* New York: John Wiley & Sons, 1995.

Van Horne, James C. *Financial Market Rates and Flows.* 4th ed. Englewood Cliffs, NJ: Prentice-Hall, 1993.

Chapter
17
Bond Portfolio Management Strategies

This chapter answers the following questions:

- What are the four major alternative bond portfolio management strategies available?
- What are the two specific strategies available within the passive portfolio management category?
- What are the five alternative strategies available within the active bond portfolio management category?
- What is meant by matched-funding techniques and what are the four specific strategies available in this category?
- What are the major contingent procedure strategies that are also referred to as structured active management strategies?
- What are the implications of capital market theory for those involved in bond portfolio management?
- What is the evidence on the efficient market hypothesis as it relates to bond markets?
- What are the implications of efficient market studies for those involved in bond portfolio management?

In this chapter, we shift attention from bond valuation and analysis to the equally important bond portfolio management strategies. In the first section, we discuss the alternative portfolio management strategies. This includes a detailed consideration of the four major strategies: passive management, active management, matched funding techniques, and structured active management. Next, we consider the implications of capital market theory and bond market efficiency on bond portfolio management.

ALTERNATIVE BOND PORTFOLIO STRATEGIES

Bond portfolio management strategies can be divided into four groups:[1]

1. Passive portfolio strategies
   a. Buy and hold
   b. Indexing
2. Active management strategies
   a. Interest rate anticipation
   b. Valuation analysis
   c. Credit analysis
   d. Yield spread analysis
   e. Bond swaps

---

[1] This breakdown benefitted from the discussion in Martin L. Leibowitz, "The Dedicated Bond Portfolio in Pension Funds—Part I: Motivations and Basics," *Financial Analysts Journal* 42, no. 1 (January–February 1986): 61–75.

3. Matched-funding techniques
   a. Dedicated portfolio, exact cash match
   b. Dedicated portfolio, optimal cash match and reinvestment
   c. Classical ("pure") immunization
   d. Horizon matching
4. Contingent procedure (structured active management)
   a. Contingent immunization
   b. Other contingent procedures

We discuss each of these alternatives because they are all viable for certain portfolios with different needs and risk profiles. Prior to the 1960s, only the first two groups were available, and most bond portfolios were managed on the basis of buy and hold. The 1960s and early 1970s saw growing interest in alternative active bond portfolio management strategies. The investment environment during the late 1970s–early 1980s was characterized by record-breaking inflation and interest rates, extremely volatile rates of return in bond markets, and the introduction of many new financial instruments in response to the increase in return volatility. Since the mid-1980s, we have seen matched-funding techniques or contingent portfolio management techniques to meet the emerging needs of institutional clients.

PASSIVE MANAGEMENT STRATEGIES

Two specific passive portfolio strategies exist. First is a **buy-and-hold strategy** in which a manager selects a portfolio of bonds based on the objectives and constraints of the client with the intent of holding these bonds to maturity. In the second passive strategy—**indexing**—the objective is to construct a portfolio of bonds that will equal the performance of a specified bond index such as the Lehman Brothers Corporate/Government Bond Index.

BUY-AND-HOLD STRATEGY   The simplest portfolio management strategy is to buy and hold. Obviously not unique to bond investors, it involves finding issues with desired quality, coupon levels, term to maturity, and important indenture provisions, such as call features. Buy-and-hold investors do not consider active trading to achieve attractive returns, but rather look for vehicles whose maturities (or duration) approximate their stipulated investment horizon to reduce price and reinvestment risk. Many successful bond investors and institutional portfolio managers follow a modified buy-and-hold strategy wherein an investment is made in an issue with the intention of holding it until the end of the investment horizon. However, they still actively look for opportunities to trade into more desirable positions.[2]

Whether the investor follows a strict or modified buy-and-hold approach, the key ingredient is finding investment vehicles that possess attractive maturity and yield features. The strategy does not restrict the investor to accept whatever the market has to offer, nor does it imply that selectivity is unimportant. Attractive high-yielding issues with desirable features and quality standards are actively sought. For example, these investors recognize that agency issues generally provide incremental returns relative to Treasuries with little sacrifice in quality, that utilities provide higher returns than comparably rated industrials, and that various call features affect the risk and realized yield of an issue. Thus, successful buy-and-hold investors use their knowledge of markets and issue characteristics to seek out attractive realized yields. Aggressive buy-and-hold investors also incorporate timing considerations into their investment decisions by using their knowledge of market rates and expectations.

---

[2] Obviously, if the strategy becomes too modified, it would become one of the active strategies.

INDEXING STRATEGY   As discussed in the chapter on efficient capital markets, numerous empirical studies have demonstrated that the majority of money managers have not been able to match the risk–return performance of common stock or bond indexes. As a result, many clients have opted to index some part of their bond portfolios, which means that the portfolio manager builds a portfolio that will match the performance of a selected bond-market index such as the Lehman Brothers Index, Merrill Lynch Index, or Salomon Brothers Index. In such a case, the portfolio manager is not judged on the basis of risk and return compared to an index, but by how closely the portfolio *tracks* the index. Specifically, the analysis of performance involves examining the **tracking error**, which equals the difference between the rate of return for the portfolio and the rate of return for the bond-market index. For example, if the portfolio experienced an annual rate of return of 8.2 percent during a period when the index had a rate of return of 8.3 percent, the tracking error would be 10 basis points.

When initiating an indexing strategy, the selection of the appropriate market index is very important because it directly determines the client's risk–return results. As such, it is necessary to be very familiar with all the characteristics of the index.[3] For bond indexes, it also is important to be aware of how the aggregate market and the indexes change over time.[4] Reilly, Kao, and Wright demonstrated that the market has experienced significant changes in composition, maturity, and duration since 1975. After the appropriate bond index is selected, several techniques are available to accomplish the actual tracking.[5]

ACTIVE MANAGEMENT STRATEGIES[6]   Five active management strategies are available, including interest rate anticipation, which involves economic forecasting, as well as valuation analysis and credit analysis, which require detailed bond and company analysis. Alternatively, yield spread analysis and bond swaps, which require economic and market analysis, are also available.

INTEREST RATE ANTICIPATION   **Interest rate anticipation** is perhaps the riskiest active management strategy because it involves relying on uncertain forecasts of future interest rates. The idea is to preserve capital when an increase in interest rates is anticipated and achieve attractive capital gains when interest rates are expected to decline. Such objectives usually are attained by altering the maturity (duration) structure of the portfolio (i.e.,

---

[3] An article that briefly discusses the indexes is F. Hawthorne, "The Battle of the Bond Indexes," *Institutional Investor* (April 1986). Two articles that discuss how the characteristics of indexes affect their performance in different interest rate environments are Chris P. Dialynas, "The Active Decisions in the Selection of Passive Management and Performance Bogeys," and Daralyn B. Peifer, "A Sponsor's View of Benchmark Portfolios." Both are in *The Handbook of Fixed-Income Securities*, 4th ed., edited by Frank J. Fabozzi and T. Dessa Fabozzi (Burr Ridge, IL: Irwin Professional Publishing, 1995).

[4] An article that describes the major investment grade indexes, analyzes the relationship among them, and examines how the aggregate bond market has changed is Frank K. Reilly, Wenchi Kao, and David J. Wright, "Alternative Bond Market Indexes," *Financial Analysts Journal* 48, no. 3 (May–June 1992): 44–58. A similar study for high-yield indexes is Frank K. Reilly and David J. Wright, "An Analysis of High Yield Bond Benchmarks," *Journal of Fixed Income* 3, no. 4 (March 1994): 6–25.

[5] For a detailed discussion of the alternative tracking techniques available, see Sharmin Mossavar-Rahmoni, "Indexing Fixed-Income Assets," in *The Handbook of Fixed-Income Securities*, 4th ed., edited by Frank J. Fabozzi and T. Dessa Fabozzi (Burr Ridge, IL: Irwin Professional Publishing, 1995); Sharmin Mossavar-Rahmoni, *Bond Index Funds* (Chicago: Probus Publishing, 1991); and Frank J. Fabozzi, *Bond Markets, Analysis and Strategies*, 3d ed. (Upper Saddle River, NJ: Prentice-Hall, 1996), Chapter 18.

[6] For further discussion on this topic, see H. Gifford Fong, "Active Strategies for Managing Bond Portfolios," in *The Revolution in Techniques for Managing Bond Portfolios*, edited by Donald Tuttle (Charlottesville, VA: The Institute of Chartered Financial Analysts, 1983), 21–38; and Thomas Vock, "Managing Global Fixed-Income Portfolios," in *Global Portfolio Management*, edited by Jan R. Squires (Charlottesville, VA: Association for Investment Management and Research, 1996).

reducing portfolio duration when interest rates are expected to increase and increasing the portfolio duration when a decline in yields is anticipated). Thus, the risk in such portfolio restructuring is largely a function of these duration (maturity) alterations. When maturities are shortened to preserve capital, substantial income could be sacrificed and the opportunity for capital gains could be lost if interest rates decline rather than rise. Similarly, the portfolio shifts prompted by anticipation of a decline in rates are very risky. Specifically, if we assume that we are at a peak in interest rates, it is likely that the yield curve is downward-sloping, which means that bond coupons will decline with maturity. Therefore, the investor is sacrificing current income by shifting from high-coupon short bonds to longer-duration bonds. At the same time, the portfolio is purposely exposed to greater price volatility that could work against the portfolio if an unexpected increase in yields occurs. Note that the portfolio adjustments prompted by anticipation of an increase in rates involves less risk of an absolute capital loss. When you reduce the maturity, the worst that can happen is that interest income is reduced and/or capital gains are forgone (opportunity cost).

Once future (expected) interest rates have been determined, the procedure relies largely on technical matters. Assume that you expect an increase in interest rates and want to preserve your capital by reducing the duration of your portfolio. A popular choice would be high-yielding, short-term obligations such as Treasury bills. Although your primary concern is to preserve capital, you would nevertheless look for the best return possible given the maturity constraint. Liquidity also is important because, after interest rates increase, yields may experience a period of stability before they decline, and you would want to shift positions quickly to benefit from the higher income and/or capital gains.

One way to shorten maturities is to use a *cushion bond*—a high-yielding, long-term obligation that carries a coupon substantially above the current market rate and that, due to its current call feature and call price, has a market price lower than what it should be given current market yields. As a result, its yield is higher than normal. An example would be a 10-year bond with a 12 percent coupon, currently callable at 110. If current market rates are 8 percent, this bond (if it were noncallable) would have a price of about 127; because of its call price, however, it will stay close to 110, and its yield will be about 10 percent rather than 8 percent. Bond portfolio managers look for cushion bonds when they expect a modest increase in rates because such issues provide attractive current income *and* protection against capital loss. Because these bonds are trading at an abnormally high yield, market rates would have to rise to that abnormal level before their price would react.

The portfolio manager who anticipates higher interest rates, therefore, has two simple strategies available: shorten the duration of the portfolio and/or look for an attractive cushion bond.[7] In either case, you would want very liquid issues.

A totally different posture is assumed by investors who anticipate a decline in interest rates. The significant risks involved in restructuring a portfolio to take advantage of a decline in interest rates are balanced by the potential for substantial capital gains and holding period returns. When you expect lower interest rates, you will recall that you should increase the duration of the portfolio because the longer the duration, the greater the price volatility. Also, liquidity is important because you want to be able to close out the position quickly when the drop in rates has been completed.

Notably, because interest-rate sensitivity is critical, it is important to recall that the higher the quality of an obligation, the more sensitive it is to interest rate changes. Therefore, high-grade securities should be used such as Treasuries, agencies, or corporates rated

---

[7] For an extended discussion of cushion bonds, see Sidney Homer and Martin L. Leibowitz, *Inside the Yield Book* (Englewood Cliffs, NJ: Prentice-Hall, 1972), Chapter 5.

AAA through BAA. Finally, you want to concentrate on noncallable issues or those with strong call protection because of the substantial call risk discussed in Chapter 16 in connection with the analysis of duration and convexity.

VALUATION ANALYSIS   With **valuation analysis,** the portfolio manager attempts to select bonds based on their intrinsic value. In turn, the bond's value is determined based on its characteristics and the average value of these characteristics in the marketplace. As an example, a bond's rating will dictate a certain spread relative to comparable Treasury bonds: long maturity might be worth an added 60 basis points relative to short maturity (i.e., the maturity spread); a given deferred call feature might require a higher or lower yield; a specified sinking fund would likewise mean higher or lower required yields. Given all the characteristics of the bond and the normal cost of the characteristics in terms of yield, you would determine the required yield and, therefore, the bond's implied intrinsic value. After you have done this for a number of bonds, you would compare these derived bond values to the prevailing market prices to determine which bonds are undervalued or overvalued. Based on your confidence in the characteristic costs, you would buy the undervalued issues and ignore or sell the overvalued issues.

Success in valuation analysis is based on understanding the characteristics that are important in valuation and being able to accurately *estimate* the yield cost of these characteristics over time.

CREDIT ANALYSIS   A **credit analysis** strategy involves detailed analysis of the bond issuer to determine expected changes in its default risk. This involves attempting to project changes in the quality ratings assigned to bonds by the four rating agencies discussed in Chapter 15.[8] These rating changes are affected by internal changes in the entity (e.g., changes in important financial ratios) and by changes in the external environment (i.e., changes in the firm's industry and the economy). During periods of strong economic expansion, even financially weak firms may survive and prosper. In contrast, during severe economic contractions, normally strong firms may find it very difficult to meet financial obligations. Therefore, historically there has been a strong cyclical pattern to rating changes: typically, downgradings increase during economic contractions and decline during economic expansions.

To use credit analysis as a portfolio management strategy, it is necessary to project rating changes prior to the announcement by the rating agencies. As the subsequent discussion on bond-market efficiency notes, the market adjusts rather quickly to bond rating changes—especially downgradings. Therefore, you want to acquire bond issues expected to experience upgradings and sell or avoid those expected to be downgraded.

Credit analysis of high-yield (junk) bonds   One of the most obvious opportunities for credit analysis is the analysis of high-yield (junk) bonds. As demonstrated by several studies, the yield differential between junk bonds that are rated below BBB and Treasury securities ranges from about 200 basis points to over 1,000 basis points. Notably, these yield differentials vary substantially over time as shown by a time-series plot in Figure 17.1. Specifically, the average yield spread ranged from a low of about 200 basis points in late 1984 to a high of almost 1,000 basis points during early 1991, and ended in 1995 at about 400 basis points.

---

[8] For a discussion of changes in the aggregate financial risk of U.S. corporations and the opportunities this has created, see Frank K. Reilly, "The Growing Importance of Credit Analysis," Working paper, University of Notre Dame (April 1995). For a presentation on credit analysis that emphasizes changes in credit ratings, see Jane Tripp Howe, "Credit Analysis for Corporate Bonds," in *The Handbook of Fixed-Income Securities,* 4th ed., edited by Frank J. Fabozzi and T. Dessa Fabozzi (Burr Ridge, IL: Irwin Professional Publishing, 1995).

| FIGURE 17.1 | YIELD SPREAD (BASIS POINTS) BETWEEN THE AVERAGE YIELD ON THE MERRILL LYNCH HIGH-YIELD MASTER INDEX AND THE TEN-YEAR TREASURY INDEX: DECEMBER 1984– DECEMBER 1995 |

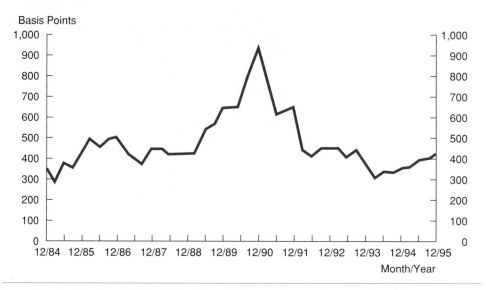

Source: Martin S. Fridson, Chief High Yield Strategist, Merrill Lynch and M. Christopher Garman, Analyst, High Yield Strategy, Merrill Lynch, "This Year in High Yield—1995." Reprinted by permission. Copyright © 1996 Merrill Lynch, Pierce, Fenner & Smith Incorporated.

Although the spreads have changed, a study indicated that the average credit quality of high-yield bonds also changed over time.[9] As an example, interest coverage tends to fluctuate with the business cycle. In addition, the credit quality of bonds *within* rating categories also has declined over time.[10]

These changes in credit quality will make credit analysis of high-yield bonds not only more important, but also more difficult. This means that bond analysts–portfolio managers need to engage in detailed credit analysis to select bonds that will survive. Given the spread in promised yields, if a portfolio manager can—through rigorous credit analysis—avoid bonds with a high probability of default, high-yield bonds will provide substantial rates of return for the investor.[11]

In summary, substantial rates of return can be derived by investing in high-yield bonds if you do the credit analysis required to avoid defaults, which occur with these bonds at substantially higher rates than the overall market. Several recent studies have shown that the average cumulative default rate for high-yield bonds after 10 years is between 30 percent and 35 percent. Of the high-yield bonds sold in 1985, about 38 percent had defaulted by 1995.[12]

---

[9] Roger Lowenstein, "Junk Gets Junkier and That May Explain Bonds' Current Ills," *The Wall Street Journal*, November 3, 1989, C1, C2. This article discussed an early draft of Barrie A. Wigmore, "The Decline in Credit Quality of New Issue Junk Bonds," *Financial Analysts Journal* 46, no. 5 (September–October 1990): 53–62.

[10] These changes are demonstrated in Reilly, "The Growing Importance of Credit Analysis."

[11] For a presentation of the unique factors that must be considered when analyzing high-yield bonds, see Jane Tripp Howe, "Credit Considerations in Evaluating High-Yield Debt," in *The Handbook of Fixed-Income Securities*, 4th ed. edited by Frank J. Fabozzi and T. Dessa Fabozzi (Burr Ridge, IL: Irwin Professional Publishing, 1995).

[12] Although the details of the analysis differ, the overall results for cumulative defaults are quite consistent. See Edward I. Altman, "Measuring Corporate Bond Mortality and Performance," *Journal of Finance* 44, no. 4

TABLE 17.1

AVERAGE CUMULATIVE DEFAULT RATES FOR CORPORATE BONDS: 1971–1994

	YEARS SINCE ISSUE	
Ratings	5	10
AAA	0.08%	0.08%
AA	1.20	1.30
A	0.53	0.98
BBB	2.39	3.66
BB	10.79	15.21
B	23.71	35.91
CCC	45.63	57.39

Source: K. Scott Douglass and Douglas J. Lucas, "Historical Default Rates of Corporate Bond Issuers, 1971–1994" (New York: Moody's Investors Service, July 1989). © Moody's Investors Service.

Table 17.1 lists the results for a study that considers the full spectrum of bonds. It shows substantial differences in cumulative default rates for bonds with different ratings for the periods 5 and 10 years after issue. Over 10 years—the holding period that is widely discussed—the default rate for BBB investment grade bonds is only 3.66 percent, but the default rate increases to over 15 percent for BB-rated, to almost 36 percent for B-rated bonds, and to over 57 percent for CCC-rated bonds.

These default rates do not mean that investors should avoid high-yield bonds, but they do indicate that extensive credit analysis is a critical component for success within this sector. Given the substantial yield spreads over Treasuries, you may experience high returns *if* you can avoid owning bonds that default or are downgraded. The route to avoiding such bond issues is through rigorous, enlightened credit analysis.

Investing in defaulted debt   Beyond high-yield bonds that have high credit risk and high default rates, a new set of investment opportunities has evolved—investing in defaulted debt. While this sector requires an understanding of legal procedures surrounding bankruptcy as well as economic analysis, the returns have generally been consistent with the risk—i.e., between high-yield debt and common stock.[13]

(September 1989): 909–922; Paul Asquith, David W. Mullins, Jr., and Eric D. Wolff, "Original Issue High Yield Bonds: Aging Analysis of Defaults, Exchanges and Calls," *Journal of Finance* 44, no. 4 (September 1989): 929–952; K. Scott Douglass and Douglas J. Lucas, "Historical Default Rates of Corporate Bond Issuers, 1970–1988" (New York: Moody's Investors Services, July 1989). The Altman and Douglass-Lucas studies are updated and discussed in Frank K. Reilly, ed., *High Yield Bonds: Analysis and Risk Assessment* (Charlottesville, VA: Institute of Chartered Financial Analysts, 1990). Another Review of these studies is Edward I. Altman, "Setting the Record Straight on Junk Bonds: A Review of the Research on Default Rates and Returns," *Journal of Applied Corporate Finance* 3, no. 2 (Summer 1990): 82–95, and Edward I. Altman, "Revisiting the High-Yield Bond Market," *Financial Management* 21, no. 2 (Summer 1992): 78–92.

[13] For a discussion of the legal and economic analysis, see Edward I. Altman, *Corporate Financial Distress and Bankruptcy*, 2d ed. (New York: John Wiley & Sons, 1993), and Jane Tripp Howe, "Investing in Chapter 11 and Other Distressed Companies," in *The Handbook of Fixed-Income Securities*, 4th ed., edited by Frank J. Fabozzi and T. Dessa Fabozzi (Burr Ridge, IL: Irwin Professional Publishing, 1995). For an analysis of the investment performance, see Edward I. Altman, "Defaulted Bonds: Demand, Supply and Performance, 1987–1992," *Financial Analysts Journal* 49, no. 3 (May–June 1993): 55–60, 17; Edward I. Altman and Babe E. Simon, "The Investment Performance of Defaulted Bonds for 1994 and 1987–1994," New York University, Salomon Center (February 1995); G. Hradsky and Robert Long, "High Yield Losses and the Return Performance of Bankrupt Debt Issues, 1978–1988," *Financial Analysts Journal* 45, no. 4 (July–August 1989): 38–49; David J. Ward and Gary L. Griepentrog, "Risk and Return in Defaulted Bonds," *Financial Analysts Journal* 49, no. 3 (May–June 1993): 61–65.

Credit analysis models The credit analysis of these bonds can use a statistical model or basic fundamental analysis that recognizes some of the unique characteristics of these bonds. The Altman-Nammacher book suggests that the *Z-score model* used to predict bankruptcy can also be used to predict default for these high-yield bonds or as a gauge of changes in credit quality. The Z-score model combines traditional financial measures with a multivariate technique known as *multiple discriminant analysis* to derive a set of weights for the specified variables. The result is an overall credit score (zeta score) for each firm.[14] The model is of the form.

$$\text{Zeta} = a_0 + a_1X_1 + a_2X_2 + a_3X_3 + \ldots + a_nX_n$$

where

>   **Zeta = the overall credit score**
> $X_1 \ldots X_n$ = **the explanatory variables (ratios and market measures)**
> $a_0 \ldots a_n$ = **the weightings or coefficients**

The final model used in this analysis included the following seven financial measures:

> X_1 = **profitability: earnings before interest and taxes (EBIT)/total assets**
> X_2 = **stability of profitability measure: the standard error of estimate of EBIT/TA (normalized for 10 years)**
> X_3 = **debt service capabilities: EBIT/interest charges**
> X_4 = **cumulative profitability: retained earnings/total assets**
> X_5 = **liquidity: current assets/current liabilities**
> X_6 = **capitalization levels: market value of equity/total capital (5-year average)**
> X_7 = **size: total tangible assets (normalized)**

The weightings, or coefficients, for the variables were not reported.

In contrast to using a model that provides a composite credit score, most analysts simply adapt their basic corporate bond analysis techniques to the unique needs of high-yield bonds, which have characteristics of common stock.[15] Howe claims that the analysis of high-yield bonds is the same as with any bond except that five areas of analysis should be expanded.[16]

1. What is the firm's *competitive position* in terms of cost and pricing? This can be critical to a small firm.
2. What is the firm's *cash flow* relative to cash requirements for interest, research, growth, and periods of economic decline? Also, what is the firm's *borrowing capacity* that can serve as a safety net and provide flexibility?
3. What is the *liquidity value of the firm's assets*? Are these assets available for liquidation (are there any claims against them)? In many cases, asset sales are a critical part of the strategy for a leveraged buyout.
4. How good is the *total management team*? Is the team committed to and capable of operating in the high-risk environment of this firm?

[14] Edward I. Altman and Scott A. Nammacher, *Investing in Junk Bonds* (New York: John Wiley & Sons, 1987).

[15] For an analysis that shows the relationship of high-yield bonds to investment-grade bonds and common stock, see Frank K. Reilly and David J. Wright, "An Analysis of High Yield Bond Benchmarks," *Journal of Fixed Income* 3, no. 4 (March 1994): 6–25.

[16] Jane Tripp Howe, "Credit Considerations in Evaluating High-Yield Bonds," in *The Handbook of Fixed-Income Securities*, 4th ed., edited by Frank J. Fabozzi and T. Dessa Fabozzi (Burr Ridge, IL: Irwin Professional Publishing 1995); and Jane Tripp Howe, *Junk Bonds: Analysis and Portfolio Strategies* (Chicago: Probus Publishing, 1988).

5. What is the firm's *financial leverage* on an absolute basis and on a market-adjusted basis (using market value for equity and debt)?

Hynes suggests that the following areas require additional analysis as part of the process of evaluating cash flows when analyzing a leveraged buyout (which typically involves the issuance of high-yield debt).[17]

- Inherent business risk
- Earnings growth potential
- Asset redevelopment potential
- Refinancing capability

In addition to the potentially higher financial risk, an increase in business risk may exist if the firm sells off some operations that have favorable risk characteristics with the remaining operations—that is, business risk would increase if the firm sells a division or a company that has low correlation of earnings with other units of the firm. Further, a change in management operating philosophy could have a negative impact on operating earnings. The managements of leveraged buyout (LBO) firms are known for making optimistic growth estimates related to sales and earnings, so the analyst should evaluate these estimates very critically. Asset divestiture plans often are a major element of an LBO because they provide necessary capital that is used to reduce the substantial debt taken on as part of the buyout. Therefore, it is important to examine the liquidity of the assets, their estimated selling values, and the timing of these programs. You must ascertain whether the estimated sale prices for the assets are reasonable and whether the timing is realistic. In contrast, if the divestiture program is successful wherein the prices received are above normal expectations and the assets are sold ahead of schedule, this can be grounds for upgrading the debt. Finally, it is necessary to constantly monitor the firm's refinancing flexibility. Specifically, what refinancing will be necessary, what does the schedule look like, and will the capital suppliers be receptive to the refinancing?[18]

High-yield bond research Because of the growth of high-yield bonds, several investment houses have developed specialized high-yield groups that examine high-yield bond issues and monitor yield spreads in the aggregate junk bond market. Kidder, Peabody & Company's weekly publication, *High Yield Sector Report*, typically features commentary on the high-yield market and a review of changes in the spreads for bonds in alternative rating groups (e.g., BB, 10-year issues) and industry sectors that issued high-yield debt (e.g., airlines, energy, transportation). A new-issue section discusses recent issues and previews forthcoming issues, and a specific high-yield issue, its firm, and its overall outlook are discussed in detail.

Merrill Lynch's monthly publication, *High Yield*, provides an overview of the market and reviews several individual industries and firms within these main industries (e.g., retail, steel, building products, and textile). It also contains reports of research done by the firm on general questions about the high-yield market. The firm initiated a high-yield master bond return index in October 1984, and it tracks the yield spreads for high-yield bonds relative to Treasury issues.

---

[17] Joseph Hynes, "Key Risk Factors for LBOs," *Speculative Grade Debt Credit Review* (New York: Standard & Poor's Corporation, June 15, 1987).

[18] For a set of presentations on credit analysis including distressed securities, see *Credit Analysis of Nontraditional Debt Securities,* edited by Ashwinpaul C. Sondhi (Charlottesville, VA: Association for Investment Management and Research, 1995).

Merrill Lynch's weekly publication, *This Week in High Yield*, discusses current events in the high-yield market. This includes weekly yields and yield spreads for the various sectors of the market and news highlights for specific companies and issues.

High Yield Market Update, a Salomon Brothers monthly publication, presents monthly and cumulative long-term returns for its high-yield indexes (long-term and intermediate-term corporates, long-term utilities), as well as spreads between rating categories relative to appropriate Treasuries. The publication also features commentary on timely topics within the high-yield market.

The high-yield research group at First Boston publishes *Monthly Market Review*, which contains an extensive performance review of the HY bond market that examines returns by sectors and industries as well as considering yield spreads and changing volatility for these bonds. First Boston also publishes an annual *High Yield Handbook*, which reviews annual events and considers every aspect of risk, return, and correlation of high-yield bonds with other asset classes. There also is a very helpful listing of new issues, retirements, and defaults.

Lehman Brothers publishes a weekly review, *High Yield Portfolio Advisor*, which analyzes the performance of the firm's high-yield bond indexes and has detailed comments on news events that affect prominent industries in the high-yield market. The firm also publishes a monthly *High Yield Bond Market Report* that briefly discusses the returns and new issues for the month, contains extensive data on returns for all components of the HY market (BB, B, CCC, CC-D, nonrated, default), and contains descriptive statistics regarding bonds in the composite index and various subindexes such as average coupon, maturity, duration to worst, modified adjusted duration, price, and yield.

In addition, several bond-rating firms conduct research on these industries and firms. Standard & Poor's publication, *Speculative Grade Debt Credit Review*, discusses the credit analysis of high-yield bonds. The publication also includes a review of several major industries and specific comments on outstanding issues.

Duff & Phelps has three regular publications related to the high-yield bond market. *Credit Comments* is a weekly publication that discusses developments and changes in default rankings or buy/sell/hold recommendations. *Recommendations* is a monthly summary of current recommendations for over 400 bond issues, including month-end prices, default risk rankings, and yield spreads. Finally, *Profiles* is a quarterly bulletin that contains an updated financial profile for the companies in the high-yield service, including financial ratios, income statement items, and a cash flow summary.

The substantial increase in junk bonds issued and outstanding has been matched by an increase in research and credit analysis. The credit analysis of these bonds is similar to that of investment-grade bonds with an emphasis on the following factors: (1) *the use of cash flows* compared to debt obligations under very conservative assumptions and (2) the detailed analysis of *potential asset sales*, including a conservative estimate of sales prices, the asset's true liquidity, the availability of the assets, and a consideration of the timing of the sales. An in-depth analysis of junk bonds is critical because of the number of issues, the wide diversity of quality within the junk bond universe, and the growing complexity of these issues.

YIELD SPREAD ANALYSIS   As discussed in Chapter 16, spread analysis assumes normal relationships exist between the yields for bonds in alternative sectors (e.g., the spread between high-grade versus low-grade industrial or between industrial versus utility bonds). Therefore, a bond portfolio manager would monitor these relationships, and, when an abnormal relationship occurs, execute various sector swaps. The crucial factor is developing the background to know the normal yield relationship and to evaluate the liquidity necessary to buy or sell the required issues quickly enough to take advantage of the temporary abnormality.

The analysis of yield spreads has been enhanced by a paper by Dialynas and Edington that considers several specific factors that affect the aggregate spread.[19] It is acknowledged that the generally accepted explanation of changes in the yield spread is that it is related to the economic environment. Specifically, the spread widens during periods of economic uncertainty and recession because investors require larger risk premiums (i.e., larger spreads). In contrast, the spread will decline during periods of economic confidence and expansion. Although not denying the existence of such a relationship, the authors contend that a more encompassing factor is the impact of interest rate (yield) volatility. They contend that yield volatility will affect the spread via three effects: (1) yield volatility and the behavior of embedded options, (2) yield volatility and transactional liquidity, and (3) the effect of yield volatility on the business cycle.

Recall that the value of callable bonds is equal to the value of a noncallable bond minus the value of the call option. Obviously, if the value of the option goes up, the value of the callable bond will decline and its yield will increase. When yield volatility increases, the value of the call option increases, which causes a rise in the bond's yield and its yield spread relative to Treasury bonds. Similarly, an increase in yield volatility will raise the uncertainty facing bond dealers and cause them to increase their bid–ask spreads that reflect the transactional liquidity for these bonds. This liquidity will have a bigger effect on nongovernment bonds, so their yield spread relative to Treasury bonds will increase. Finally, interest rate volatility causes uncertainty for business executives and consumers regarding their costs of funds. This typically will precede an economic decline that will, in turn, lead to an increase in the yield spread. It is demonstrated that it is possible to have a change in yield spread for reasons other than economic uncertainty. If there is a period of greater yield volatility, that is not a period of economic uncertainty, the yield spread will increase due to the embedded option effect and the transactional liquidity effect. Therefore, when examining yield spreads, you should pay particular attention to interest rate (yield) volatility.

BOND SWAPS   **Bond swaps** involve liquidating a current position and simultaneously buying a different issue in its place with similar attributes—but a chance for improved return. Swaps can be executed to increase current yield, to increase yield to maturity, to take advantage of shifts in interest rates or the realignment of yield spreads, to improve the quality of a portfolio, or for tax purposes. Some swaps are highly sophisticated and require a computer for calculation. However, most are fairly simple transactions with obvious goals and risk. They go by such names as *profit takeouts, substitution swaps, intermarket spread swaps,* or *tax swaps.* Although many of these swaps involve low risk (such as the pure yield pickup swap), others entail substantial risk (the rate anticipation swap). Regardless of the risk involved, all swaps have one basic purpose: portfolio improvement.

Most swaps involve several different types of risk. One obvious risk is that the market will move against you while the swap is outstanding. Interest rates may move up over the holding period and cause you to incur a loss. Alternatively, yield spreads may fail to respond as anticipated. Possibly the new bond may not be a true substitute and so, even if your expectations and interest rate formulations are correct, the swap may be unsatisfac-

---

[19] Chris P. Dialynas and David H. Edington, "Bond Yield Spreads—A Postmodern View," *Journal of Portfolio Management* 19, no. 1 (Fall 1992): 60–75.

tory because the wrong issue was selected. Finally, if the work-out time is longer than anticipated, the realized yield might be less than expected. You must be willing to accept such risks to improve your portfolio. The following subsections consider three of the more popular bond swaps.[20]

Pure yield pickup swap The pure yield pickup involves swapping out of a low-coupon bond into a comparable higher-coupon bond to realize an automatic and instantaneous increase in current yield and yield to maturity. Your risks are (1) that the market will move against you and (2) that the new issue may not be a viable swap candidate. Also, because you are moving to a higher coupon obligation, there could be greater call risk.

An example of a pure yield pickup swap would be an investor who currently holds a 30-year, Aa-rated 10 percent issue that is trading at an 11.50 percent yield. Assume that a comparable 30-year, Aa-rated obligation bearing a 12 percent coupon priced to yield 12 percent becomes available. The investor would report (and realize) some book loss if the original issue was bought at par but is able to improve current yield and yield to maturity simultaneously if the new obligation is held to maturity as shown in Table 17.2.

The investor need not predict rate changes, and the swap is not based on any imbalance in yield spread. The object simply is to seek higher yields. Quality and maturity stay the same as do all other factors *except coupon*. The major risk is that future reinvestment rates may not be as high as expected, and therefore, the total terminal value of the investment (capital recovery, coupon receipts, and interest-on-interest) may not be as high as expected or comparable to the original obligation. This reinvestment risk can be evaluated by analyzing the results with a number of reinvestment rates to determine the minimum reinvestment rate that would make the swap viable.

Substitution swap The substitution swap generally is short term and relies heavily on interest rate expectations. Therefore, it is subject to considerably more risk than the pure yield pickup swaps. The procedure assumes a short-term imbalance in yield spreads between issues that are perfect substitutes. The imbalance in yield spread is expected to be corrected in the near future. For example, the investor might hold a 30-year, 12 percent issue that is yielding 12 percent and be offered a comparable 30-year, 12 percent bond that is yielding 12.20 percent. Because the issue offered will trade at a price less than $1,000 for every issue sold, the investor can buy more than one of the offered obligations.

You would expect the yield spread imbalance to be corrected by having the yield on the offering bond decline to the level of your current issue. Thus, you would realize capital gains by switching out of your current position into the higher-yielding obligation. This swap is described in Table 17.3

Although a modest increase in current income occurs as the yield imbalance is corrected, attractive capital gains are possible, causing a differential in *realized yield*. The work-out time will have an important effect on the differential realized return. Even if the yield is not corrected until maturity, 30 years later, you will still experience a small increase in realized yield (about 10 basis points). In contrast, if the correction takes place in 1 year, the differential realized return is much greater, as shown in Table 17.3.

After the correction has occurred, you would have additional capital for a subsequent swap or other investment. Several risks are involved in this swap. In addition to the pressure of the work-out time, market interest rates could move against you, the yield

---

[20] For additional information on these and other types of bond swaps, see Sidney Homer and Martin L. Leibowitz, *Inside the Yield Book* (Englewood Cliffs, NJ: Prentice-Hall, 1972); Anand K. Bhattasharya and Frank J. Fabozzi, "Interest Rate Swaps," in *The Handbook of Fixed-Income Securities*, 4th ed., edited by Frank J. Fabozzi and T. Dessa Fabozzi (Burr Ridge, IL: Irwin Professional Publishing, 1995).

TABLE 17.2	**A PURE YIELD PICKUP SWAP**

Pure Yield Pickup Swap: A bond swap involving a switch—from a low-coupon bond to a higher-coupon bond of similar quality and maturity—in order to pick up higher current yield and a better yield to maturity.

Example: Currently hold: 30-yr., 10.0% coupon priced at 874.12 to yield 11.5%.
          Swap candidate: 30-yr., Aa 12% coupon priced at $1,000 to yield 12.0%.

	Current Bond	Candidate Bond
Dollar investment	$874.12	$1,000.00[a]
Coupon	100.00	120.00
i on one coupon (12.0% for 6 months)	3.000	3.600
Principal value at year end	874.66	1,000.00
Total accrued	977.66	1,123.60
Realized compound yield	11.514%	12.0%

Value of swap: 48.6 basis points in one year (assuming a 12.0% reinvestment rate).

The rewards for a pure yield pickup swap are automatic and instantaneous in that both a higher-coupon yield and a higher yield to maturity are realized from the swap.

Other advantages include:

1. No specific work-out period needed because the investor is assumed to hold the new bond to maturity
2. No need for interest rate speculation
3. No need to analyze prices for overvaluation or undervaluation

A major disadvantage of the pure yield pickup swap is the book loss involved in the swap. In this example, if the current bond were bought at par, the book loss would be $125.88 ($1,000 − 874.12).

Other risks involved in the pure yield pickup swap include:

1. Increased risk of call in the event interest rates decline
2. Reinvestment risk is greater with higher-coupon bonds.

[a]Obviously, the investor can invest $874.12—the amount obtained from the sale of the bond currently held—and still obtain a realized compound yield of 12.0%.

Swap evaluation procedure is patterned after a technique suggested by Sidney Homer and Martin L. Leibowitz. Source: Adapted from the book *Inside the Yield Book* by Sidney Homer and Martin L. Leibowitz, Ph.D., © 1972, used by permission of the publisher, Prentice-Hall Inc., Englewood Cliffs, NJ, and New York Institute of Finance, New York, NY.

spread may not be temporary, and the issue may not be a viable swap candidate (i.e., the spread may be due to the issue's lower quality).

Tax swap   The tax swap is popular with individual investors because it is a relatively simple procedure that involves no interest rate projections and few risks. Investors enter into tax swaps due to tax laws and realized capital gains in their portfolios. Assume you acquired $100,000 worth of corporate bonds and after 2 years sold the securities for $150,000, implying a capital gain of $50,000. One way to eliminate the tax liability of that capital gain is to sell an issue that has a comparable long-term capital loss.[21] If you had a long-term investment of $100,000 with a current market value of $50,000, you could execute a tax swap to establish the $50,000 capital loss. By offsetting this capital loss and the comparable capital gain, you would reduce your income taxes.

[21] Although this discussion deals with bond tax swaps, comparable strategies could be used with other types of investments.

| TABLE 17.3 | A SUBSTITUTION SWAP |

Substitution Swap: A swap executed to take advantage of temporary market anomalies in yield spreads between issues that are equivalent with respect to coupon, quality, and maturity.

Example: Currently hold: 30-yr., Aa 12.0% coupon priced at $1,000 to yield 12.0%.
   Swap candidate: 30-yr., Aa 12% coupon priced at $984.08 to yield 12.2%.
   Assumed work-out period: 1 year
   Reinvested at 12.0%

	Current Bond	Candidate Bond
Dollar investment	$1,000.00	$984.08
Coupon	120.00	120.00
i on one coupon (12.0% for 6 months)	3.60	3.60
Principal value at year end (12.0% YTM)	1,000.00	1,000.00
Total accrued	1,123.60	1,123.60
Total gain	123.60	139.52
Gain per invested dollar	.1236	.1418
Realized compound yield	12.00%	13.71%

Value of swap: 171 basis points in one year.

The rewards for the substitution swap are additional basis point pickups for YTM, additional realized compound yield, and capital gains that accrue when the anomaly in yield corrects itself.

In the substitution swap, any basis point pickup (171 points in this example) will be realized only during the work-out period. Thus, in our example, to obtain the 171 basis point increase in realized compound yield, you must swap an average of once each year and pick up an average of 20 basis points in yield to maturity on each swap.

Potential risks associated with the substitution swap include:
1. A yield spread thought to be temporary may, in fact, be permanent, thus reducing capital gains advantages.
2. The market rate may change adversely.

Swap evaluation procedure is patterned after a technique suggested by Sidney Homer and Martin L. Leibowitz. Source: Adapted from the book *Inside the Yield Book* by Sidney Homer and Martin L. Leibowitz, Ph.D., © 1972, used by permission of the publisher, Prentice-Hall Inc., Englewood Cliffs, NJ, and New York Institute of Finance, New York, NY.

Municipal bonds are considered particularly attractive tax swap candidates because you can increase your tax-free income and use the capital loss (subject to normal federal and state taxation) to reduce capital gains tax liability. To continue our illustration, assume you own $100,000 worth of New York City, 20-year, 7 percent bonds that you bought at par, but they have a current market value of $50,000. Given this tax loss, you need a comparable bond swap candidate. Suppose you find a 20-year New York City bond with a 7.1 percent coupon and a market value of 50. By selling your New York 7s and instantaneously reinvesting in the New York 7.1s, you would eliminate the capital gains tax from the corporate bond transaction. In effect, you have $50,000 of tax-free capital gains, and you have increased your current tax-free yield. The money saved by avoiding the tax liability can then be used to increase the portfolio's yield, as shown in Table 17.4.

An important caveat is that *you cannot swap identical issues* (such as selling the New York 7s to establish a loss and then buying back the same New York 7s). If it is not a different issue, the IRS considers the transaction a *wash sale* and does not allow the loss. It is easier to avoid wash sales in the bond market than it is in the stock market because every bond issue, even with identical coupons and maturities, is considered distinct. Likewise, it is easier to find comparable bond issues with only modest differences in coupon, maturity,

TABLE 17.4	A TAX SWAP

Tax Swap: A swap undertaken when you wish to offset capital gains in other securities through the sale of a bond currently held and selling at a discount from the price paid at purchase. By swapping into a bond with as nearly identical features as possible, you can use the capital loss on the sale of the bond for tax purposes and still maintain your current position in the market.

Example: Currently hold: $100,000 worth of corporate bonds with current market value of $150,000 *and* $100,000 in N.Y., 20-year, 7% bonds with current market value of $50,000.
Swap candidate: $50,000 in N.Y., 20-year, 7.1% bonds.

A. Corporate bonds sold and long-term capital gains profit established $50,000

Capital gains tax liability (assume you have 20% capital gains tax rate) ($50,000 × .20) $10,000

B. N.Y. 7s sold and long-term capital *loss* established $50,000

Reduction in capital gains tax liability ($50,000 × .20)   ($10,000)

Net capital gains tax liability   0

Tax *savings* realized $10,000

C. Complete tax swap by buying N.Y. 7.1s from proceeds of N.Y. 7s sale (therefore, amount invested remains largely the *same*)[a]

Annual tax-free interest income—N.Y. 7s $ 7,000

Annual tax-free interest income—N.Y. 7.1s $ 7,100

Net *increase* in *annual* tax-free interest income $ 100

[a]N.Y. 7.1s will result in substantial capital gains when liquidated at maturity (because they were bought at deep discounts) and, therefore, will be subject to future capital gains tax liability. The swap is designed to use the capital loss resulting from the swap to offset capital gains from other investments. At the same time, your funds remain in a security almost identical to your previous holding while you receive a slight increase in both current income and YTM.

Because the tax swap involved no projections in terms of work-out period, interest rate changes, etc., the risks involved are minimal. Your major concern should be to avoid potential wash sales.

and quality. Tax swaps are common at year end as investors establish capital losses because the capital loss must occur in the same taxable year as the capital gain. This procedure differs from other bond swap transactions because it exists due to tax statutes rather than temporary market anomalies.

A GLOBAL FIXED-INCOME INVESTMENT STRATEGY

An active management strategy that considers one or several of the techniques discussed thus far should apply these techniques to a global portfolio. The optimum global fixed-income asset allocation must consider three interrelated factors: (1) the local economy in each country that includes the effect of domestic and international demand, (2) the impact of this total demand and domestic monetary policy on inflation and interest rates, and (3) the effect of the economy, inflation, and interest rates on the exchange rates among countries.[22] Based on the evaluation of these factors, a portfolio manager must decide the

[22] For a detailed discussion of the benefits of international bond investing as well as what is involved in the analysis, see Adam M. Greshin and Margaret Darasz Hadzima, "International Bond Investing and Portfolio Management," and Michael R. Rosenberg, "International Fixed Income Investing: Theory and Practice." Both are included in *The Handbook of Fixed-Income Securities*, 4th ed., edited by Frank J. Fabozzi and T. Dessa Fabozzi (Burr Ridge, IL: Irwin Professional Publishing, 1995). For a discussion of global portfolio management including bonds, see William G. Droms, ed., *Initiating and Managing a Global Investment Program* (Charlottesville, VA: Association of Investment Management and Research, 1991); Dwight D. Churchill, ed., *Fixed-Income Management: Techniques and Practices* (Charlottesville, VA: Association of Investment Management and Research, 1994); and Jan R. Squires, ed., *Global Portfolio Management* (Charlottesville, VA: Association of Investment Management and Research, 1996).

relative weight for each country. In addition, one might consider an allocation within each country among government, municipal, and corporate bonds. In the examples that follow, most portfolio recommendations concentrate on the country allocation and do not become more specific except in the case of the United States.

Table 17.5 is from the 1995 *Investment Review* by Brinson Partners, Inc., a global institutional asset manager. The table's "normal policy" column indicates what the asset allocation would be if Brinson had no opinion regarding the expected bond market performance in the alternative countries. In most cases, this normal allocation is based on the country's relative market value. Here, the normal allocation is 34.3 percent for the United States, 19.9 percent for Japan, and the remaining 45.8 percent for the other countries. Clearly, Brinson *does* have an opinion regarding these countries (as shown in its market allocation) because it has underweighted the U.S. bond market with an allocation of 28.3 percent (versus 34.3 percent) and underweighted the Japan bond market with an allocation of only 7.4 percent (versus 19.9 percent). In turn, several of the other countries are heavily overweighted: Canada (6.6 percent market versus 2.9 percent normal), Denmark (6.4 percent market versus 1.7 percent normal), France (11.3 percent market versus 7.2 percent normal), and Germany (15.2 percent market versus 10.6 percent normal). In addition, Brinson does a specific currency allocation among countries that would likewise be based on the normal policy weight unless the firm had an opinion on currencies. Again, Brinson has a definite opinion: it heavily overweighted the U.S. dollar, had no allocation to the Japanese yen, and was generally underweighted in all other currencies except Australia, Canada, Italy, and Spain.

In making your own allocations based on these specific expectations, you would look for U.S. securities in which yields were expected to decline relative to Treasury securities and for bond markets in foreign countries that likewise had bullish interest rate expectations. Finally, you would look for countries in which the currency was expected to be strong relative to the United States.

TABLE 17.5   **BRINSON PARTNERS GLOBAL BOND PORTFOLIO COMPOSITION: 12/31/95**

	Normal Policy	Market Allocation	Currency Allocation
U.S.	**34.3%**	**28.3%**	**67.9%**
Japan	**19.9%**	**7.4%**	**0.0%**
All Others	**45.8%**	**64.3%**	**32.1%**
Australia	1.0	0.0	3.2
Austria	0.9	0.0	0.0
Belgium	2.7	3.1	0.0
Canada	2.9	6.6	11.5
Denmark	1.7	6.4	0.0
France	7.2	11.3	0.0
Germany	10.6	15.2	0.0
Italy	5.9	3.7	8.5
The Netherlands	3.5	8.5	0.0
Spain	2.3	3.6	3.6
Sweden	1.8	0.0	0.0
U.K.	5.3	5.9	5.3
	100.0%	**100.0%**	**100.0%**

Totals may not add up to 100% due to rounding.
Source: Brinson Partners, Inc., *1995 Investment Review* (Chicago, IL: Brinson Partners, 1995).

In summary, assuming you want to actively manage a bond portfolio, this example shows an approach to the asset allocation decision on a global scale. Similar to our discussion on equity securities, global asset allocation requires substantially more research because you must evaluate each country—individually and relative to every other country. Finally, your global recommendation also must consider exchange rate changes—i.e., you must make a currency decision for each country.

MATCHED-FUNDING TECHNIQUES[23]   As discussed previously, because of an increase in interest rate volatility and the needs of many institutional investors, there has been a growth of the use of matched-funding techniques ranging from pure cash-matched dedicated portfolios to portfolios involved in contingent immunization.

DEDICATED PORTFOLIOS   **Dedication** refers to bond portfolio management techniques that are used to service a prescribed set of liabilities. The idea is that a pension fund has a set of future liabilities, and those responsible for administering these liabilities want a money manager to construct a portfolio of assets with cash flows that will match this liability stream. Such a "dedicated" portfolio can be created in several ways. We will discuss two alternatives.

A **pure cash-matched dedicated portfolio** is the most conservative strategy. Specifically, the objective of pure cash-matching is to develop a portfolio of bonds that will provide a stream of payments from coupons, sinking funds, and maturing principal payments that will exactly match the specified liability schedules. An example of a typical liability stream for a retired-lives component of a pension system is shown in Figure 17.2.

FIGURE 17.2	**A PRESCRIBED SCHEDULE OF LIABILITIES**

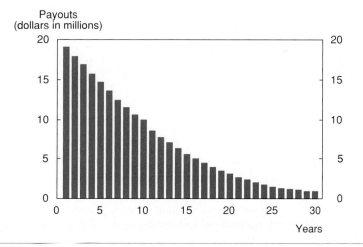

Source: Martin L. Leibowitz, "The Dedicated Bond Portfolio in Pension Funds—Part I: Motivations and Basics," *Financial Analysts Journal* 42, no. 1 (January–February 1986). Reprinted by permission of *Financial Analysts Journal.*

---

[23]An overview of these alternative strategies is contained in Martin L. Leibowitz, "The Dedicated Bond Portfolio in Pension Funds—Part I: Motivation and Basics," *Financial Analysts Journal* 42, no. 1 (January–February 1986): 68–75; and Martin L. Leibowitz, "The Dedicated Bond Portfolio in Pension Funds—Part II: Immunization, Horizon Matching, and Contingent Procedures," *Financial Analysts Journal* 42, no. 2 (March–April 1986): 47–57.

The goal is to build a portfolio that will generate sufficient funds in advance of each scheduled payment to ensure that the payment will be met. One alternative is to find a number of zero coupon Treasury securities that will exactly cash-match each liability. Such an exact cash-match is referred to as a *total passive* portfolio because it is designed so that any prior receipts would not be reinvested (i.e., it assumes a zero reinvestment rate).

Dedication with reinvestment is the same as the pure cash-matched technique except it is assumed that the bonds and other cash flows do not have to exactly match the liability stream. Specifically, any inflows that precede liability claims can be reinvested at some reasonably conservative rate. This assumption allows the portfolio manager to consider a substantially wider set of bonds that may have higher return characteristics. In addition, the assumption of reinvestment within each period and between periods also will generate a higher return for the asset portfolio. As a result, the net cost of the portfolio will be lower, with almost equal safety, assuming the reinvestment rate assumption is conservative. An example would be to assume a reinvestment rate of 6 percent in an environment where market interest rates are currently ranging from 7 percent to 10 percent.

Potential problems exist with both of these approaches to a dedicated portfolio. For example, when selecting potential bonds for these portfolios, it is critical to be aware of call/prepayment possibilities (refundings, calls, sinking funds) with specific bonds or mortgage-backed securities. These prepayment possibilities become very important following periods of historically high rates. A prime example was the period 1982 to 1986, when interest rates went from over 18 percent to under 8 percent. Because of this substantial change in rates, many dedicated portfolios constructed without adequate concern for complete call protection were negatively affected when numerous bonds were called that were not expected to be called "under normal conditions." For example, bonds selling at deep discounts (which typically provide implicit call protection), when rates were 16 percent to 18 percent, went to par and above when rates declined to under 10 percent—and they were called. Obviously, the reinvestment of these proceeds at the lower rates caused many dedicated portfolios to be underfunded. Therefore, it is necessary to find bonds with complete call protection or to consider deep discount bonds under conservative interest rate conditions.

Although quality also is a legitimate concern, it is probably not necessary to invest only in Treasury bonds if the portfolio manager diversifies across industries and sectors. A diversified portfolio of AA or A industrial bonds can provide a current and total annual return of 40 to 60 basis points above Treasuries. This differential over a 30-year period can have a significant impact on the net cost of funding a liability stream.[24]

IMMUNIZATION STRATEGIES   Instead of using a passive strategy, an active strategy, or a dedicated portfolio technique, a portfolio manager (after client consultation) may decide that the optimal strategy is to immunize the portfolio from interest rate changes. The immunization techniques attempt to derive a specified rate of return (generally quite close to the current market rate) during a given investment horizon regardless of what happens to market interest rates.

Components of interest rate risk   A major problem encountered in bond portfolio management is deriving a given rate of return to satisfy an ending-wealth requirement at a future specific date—that is, the **investment horizon.** If the term structure of interest rates were flat and market rates never changed between the time of purchase and the horizon date when

[24] For additional discussion of this strategy, see Peter E. Christensen and Frank J. Fabozzi, "Dedicated Bond Portfolios," and T. Dessa Fabozzi, Tom Wong, and Yu Zhu, "Beyond Cash Matching," both in *The Handbook of Fixed-Income Securities*, 4th ed., edited by Frank J. Fabozzi and T. Dessa Fabozzi (Burr Ridge, IL: Irwin Professional Publishing, 1995).

funds were required, you could acquire a bond with a term to maturity equal to the desired investment horizon, and the ending wealth from the bond would equal the promised wealth position implied by the promised yield to maturity. Specifically, the ending-wealth position would be the beginning wealth times the compound value of a dollar at the promised yield to maturity. For example, assume you acquired a 10-year, $1 million bond with an 8 percent coupon at its par value (8 percent YTM). If conditions were as specified (there was a flat yield curve and there were no changes in the curve), your wealth position at the end of your 10-year investment horizon (assuming semiannual compounding) would be

$$\$1,000,000 \times (1.04)^{20} = \$1,000,000 \times 2.1911 = \$2,191,100$$

You can get the same answer by taking the $40,000 interest payment every 6 months and compounding it semi-annually to the end of the period at 4 percent and adding the $1,000,000 principal at maturity. Unfortunately, in the real world, the term structure of interest rates typically is not flat and the level of interest rates is constantly changing. Consequently, the bond portfolio manager faces **interest rate risk** between the time of investment and the future target date. Interest rate risk is the uncertainty regarding the ending-wealth value of the portfolio due to changes in market interest rates between the time of purchase and the investor's horizon date. It involves two component risks: **price risk** and **coupon reinvestment risk.**

The price risk occurs because if interest rates change before the horizon date and the bond is sold before maturity, the realized market price for the bond will differ from the *expected* price, assuming there had been no change in rates. If rates increased after the time of purchase, the realized price for the bond in the secondary market would be below expectations, whereas if rates declined, the realized price would be above expectations. Because you do not know whether interest rates will increase or decrease, you are uncertain about the bond's future price.

The coupon reinvestment risk arises because the yield to maturity computation implicitly assumes that all coupon cash flows will be reinvested at the promised yield to maturity.[25] If, after the purchase of the bond, interest rates decline, the coupon cash flows will be reinvested at rates below the promised YTM, and the ending wealth will be below expectations. In contrast, if interest rates increase, the coupon cash flows will be reinvested at rates above expectations, and the ending wealth will be above expectations. Again, because you are uncertain about future rates, you are uncertain about these reinvestment rates.

Classical immunization and interest rate risk   The price risk and the reinvestment risk caused by a change in interest rates have opposite effects on the ending-wealth position. An increase in interest rates will cause an ending price below expectations, but the reinvestment rate for interim cash flows will be above expectations. A decline in market interest rates will cause the reverse situation. Clearly, a bond portfolio manager with a specific target date (investment horizon) will attempt to eliminate these two interest rate risks. The process intended to eliminate interest rate risk is referred to as **immunization** and was discussed by Redington in the early 1950s.[26] It has been specified by Fisher and Weil as follows:

> A portfolio of investments in bonds is *immunized* for a holding period if its value at the end of the holding period, regardless of the course of interest rates during the holding period, must be

---

[25] This point was discussed in detail in Chapter 16 and in Homer and Leibowitz, *Inside the Yield Book,* Chapter 1.

[26] F. M. Redington, "Review of the Principles of Life—Office Valuations," *Journal of the Institute of Actuaries* 78 (1952): 286–340.

at least as large as it would have been had the interest-rate function been constant throughout the holding period.

If the realized return on an investment in bonds is sure to be at least as large as the appropriately computed yield to the horizon, then that investment is immunized.[27]

Fisher and Weil found a significant difference between the *promised* yields and the *realized* returns on bonds for the period 1925 to 1968, indicating the importance of immunizing a bond portfolio. They showed that it is possible to immunize a bond portfolio if you can assume that any change in interest rates will be the same for all, that is, if forward interest rates change, all rates will change by the same amount (there is a parallel shift of the yield curve). Given this assumption, Fisher and Weil proved that *a portfolio of bonds is immunized from interest rate risk if the duration of the portfolio is always equal to the desired investment horizon.* For example, if the investment horizon of a bond portfolio is 8 years, the *duration* of the bond portfolio should equal 8 years to immunize the portfolio. To attain a given duration, the weighted average duration (with weights equal to the proportion of value) is set at the desired length following an interest payment, and all subsequent cash flows are invested in securities to keep the portfolio duration equal to the remaining investment horizon.

Fisher and Weil showed that price risk and reinvestment rate risk are affected in opposite directions by a change in market rates and that duration is the time period when these two risks are of equal magnitude but opposite in direction.[28]

Application of the immunization principle   Fisher and Weil simulated the effects of applying the immunization concept (a duration-matched strategy) compared to a naive portfolio strategy where the portfolio's maturity was equal to the investment horizon. They compared the ending-wealth ratio for the duration matched and for the naive strategy portfolios to a wealth ratio that assumed no change in the interest rate structure. In a perfectly immunized portfolio, the actual ending wealth should equal the expected ending wealth implied by the promised yield, so these comparisons should indicate which portfolio strategy does a superior job of immunization. The duration-matched strategy results were consistently closer to the promised yield results; however, the results were not perfect. The duration portfolio was not perfectly immunized because the basic assumption did not always hold; that is, when interest rates changed, all interest rates did not change by the same amount.

Bierwag and Kaufman pointed out several specifications of the duration measure.[29] The Macaulay duration measure, one of the duration measures discussed in Chapter 16, discounts all flows by the prevailing yield to maturity on the bond being measured.[30] Alternatively, Fisher and Weil defined duration using future one-period interest rates (forward rates) to discount the future flows.[31] Depending on the shape of the yield curve, the two definitions could give different answers. If the yield curve is flat, the two definitions will compute equal durations. Bierwag and Kaufman computed alternative measures of duration and found that, except at high coupons and long maturities, the duration values of the

---

[27] Lawrence Fisher and Roman L. Weil, "Coping with the Risk of Interest-Rate Fluctuations: Returns to Bondholders from Naive and Optimal Strategies," *Journal of Business* 44, no. 4 (October 1971): 408–431.

[28] This also is noted and discussed in G. O. Bierwag and George G. Kaufman, "Coping with the Risk of Interest Rate Fluctuations: A Note," *Journal of Business* 50, no. 3 (July 1977): 364–370; and G. O. Bierwag, "Immunization, Duration, and the Term Structure of Interest Rates," *Journal of Financial and Quantitative Analysis* 12, no. 5 (December 1977): 725–742.

[29] Bierwag and Kaufman, "Coping with the Risk of Interest Rate Fluctuations," 364–370.

[30] Frederick R. Macaulay, *Some Theoretical Problems Suggested by the Movements of Interest Rates, Bond Yields, and Stock Prices in the United States Since 1856* (New York: National Bureau of Economic Research, 1938).

[31] Fisher and Weil, "Coping with the Risk of Interest Rate Fluctuations," 408–431.

| TABLE 17.6 | AN EXAMPLE OF THE EFFECT OF A CHANGE IN MARKET RATES ON A BOND (PORTFOLIO) THAT USES THE MATURITY STRATEGY VERSUS THE DURATION STRATEGY |

	RESULTS WITH MATURITY STRATEGY			RESULTS WITH DURATION STRATEGY		
Year	Cash Flow	Reinvestment Rate	End Value	Cash Flow	Reinvestment Rate	End Value
1	$ 80	.08	$ 80.00	$ 80	.08	$ 80.00
2	80	.08	166.40	80	.08	166.40
3	80	.08	259.71	80	.08	259.71
4	80	.08	360.49	80	.08	360.49
5	80	.06	462.12	80	.06	462.12
6	80	.06	596.85	80	.06	596.85
7	80	.06	684.04	80	.06	684.04
8	$1,080	.06	$1,805.08	$1,120.64[a]	.06	$1,845.72

Expected Wealth Ratio = 1.8509 or $1,850.90.

[a]The bond could be sold at its market value of $1,040.64, which is the value for an 8 percent bond with 2 years to maturity priced to yield 6 percent.

alternative definitions were similar, and the Macaulay definition is preferable because it is a function of the yield to maturity of the bond. This means you do not need a forecast of one-period forward rates over the maturity of the bond.[32]

Example of classical immunization   Table 17.6 shows the effect of attempting to immunize a portfolio by matching the investment horizon and the duration of a bond portfolio using a single bond. The portfolio manager's investment horizon is 8 years, and the current yield to maturity for 8-year bonds is 8 percent. Therefore, if we assumed no change in yields, the ending-wealth ratio for an investor should be 1.8509 (1.08^8) with annual compounding.[33] As noted, this also should be the ending-wealth ratio for a completely immunized portfolio.

The example considers two portfolio strategies: (1) the maturity strategy, where the portfolio manager would acquire a bond with a term to maturity of 8 years, and (2) the duration strategy, where the portfolio manager sets the duration of the portfolio at 8 years. For the **maturity strategy,** the portfolio manager acquires an 8-year, 8 percent bond; for the **duration strategy,** the manager acquires a 10-year, 8 percent bond that has approximately an 8-year duration (8.12 years), assuming an 8 percent YTM (see Table 16.2). We assume a single shock to the interest rate structure at the end of Year 4, when rates go from 8 percent to 6 percent and stay there through Year 8.

As shown, due to the interest rate change, the ending wealth ratio for the maturity strategy bond is *below* the desired wealth ratio because of the shortfall in the reinvestment cash flow after Year 4 when the interim coupon cash flow was reinvested at 6 percent rather than 8 percent. Note that *the maturity strategy eliminated the price risk* because the bond matured at the end of Year 8. Alternatively, the duration strategy portfolio likewise suffered a shortfall in reinvestment cash flow because of the change in market rates. Notably, this shortfall due to the reinvestment risk was partially offset by an *increase* in the ending value for the bond because of the decline in market rates. This second bond is sold at the end of Year 8 at 104.06 of par because it is an 8 percent coupon bond with 2 years to maturity selling to yield 6 percent. Because of this partial offset due to the price increase, the

[33] We use annual compounding to compute the ending-wealth ratio because the example uses annual observations.

duration strategy had an ending-wealth value (1845.72) that was much closer to the expected wealth ratio (1850.90) than the maturity strategy (1805.08). The point is, the reinvestment rate shortfall was almost completely offset by the positive price effect.

If market interest rates had increased during this period, the maturity strategy portfolio would have experienced an *excess* of reinvestment income compared to the expected cash flow, and the ending-wealth ratio for this strategy would have been above expectations. In contrast, in the duration portfolio, the excess cash flow from reinvestment under this assumption would have been partially offset by a *decline* in the ending price for the bond (i.e., it would have sold at a small discount to par value). Although the ending-wealth ratio for the duration strategy would have been lower than the maturity strategy, it would have been closer to the expected-wealth ratio. Although the maturity strategy would have provided a higher than expected ending value for this scenario, the whole purpose of immunization is to *eliminate uncertainty* due to interest rate changes by having the realized-wealth position equal the expected-wealth position. As shown, this is what is accomplished with the duration-matched strategy.

Another view of immunization   The prior example assumed that both bonds were acquired and held to the end of the investment horizon. An alternative way to envision what is expected to happen with an immunized portfolio is to concentrate on the specific growth path from the beginning-wealth position to the ending-wealth position and examine what happens when interest rates change.

Assume that the initial-wealth position is $1 million, your investment horizon is 10 years, and the coupon and current YTM are 8 percent. We know from an earlier computation that this implies that the expected ending-wealth value is $2,191,100 (with semiannual compounding). Figure 17.3A shows the compound growth rate path from $1 million to the expected ending value at $2,191,100. In Figure 17.3B, it is assumed that at the end of Year 2, interest rates increase 200 basis points from 8 percent to 10 percent. We know that with no prior rate changes, at the end of Year 2 the value of the portfolio would have grown at an 8 percent compound rate to $1,169,900 [$1.04^4 = 1.1699$]. Given the rate change, we know there will be two changes for this portfolio: (1) the price (value of the portfolio) will decline to reflect the higher interest rate, and (2) the reinvestment rate, which is the growth rate, will increase to 10 percent. An important question is, how much will the portfolio value decline? The answer depends on the modified duration of the portfolio when rates change. Fisher and Weil showed that *if the modified duration is equal to the remaining horizon, the price change will be such that at the new growth rate (10 percent), the new portfolio value will grow to the expected-wealth position.* You can approximate the change in portfolio value using the modified duration and the change in market rates. (Recall that this will not give an exact estimate because of the convexity of the portfolio.) The approximate change in price is 16 percent based on a modified duration of 8 years and a 200-basis-point change. This would imply an approximate portfolio value of $982,716 ($1,169,900 × 0.84). In fact, the actual value would be $1,003,743. (Recall that the estimated value based on using modified duration always is below the value implied by the price–yield curve.) If this new wealth grows at 10 percent a year for 8 years, the ending-wealth value will be

$$\$1,003,743 \times 2.1829 \ (5\% \text{ for } 16 \text{ periods}) = \$2,191,070$$

The difference between the expected value and projected value is due to rounding. This example shows that the price decline is almost exactly offset by the higher reinvestment rate—assuming that the modified duration of the portfolio at the time of the rate change was equal to the remaining investment horizon.

| FIGURE 17.3 | THE GROWTH PATH TO THE EXPECTED ENDING-WEALTH VALUE AND THE EFFECT OF IMMUNIZATION |

A. Constant 8% Growth Rate

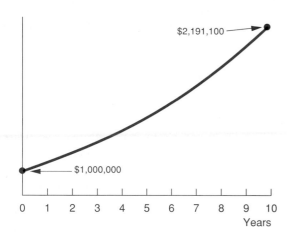

B. Effect of Interest Rate Increase after Two Years with Duration Equal to Investment Horizon

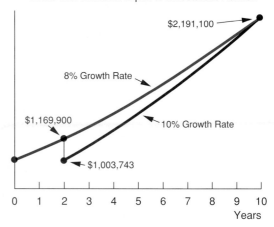

C. Effect of Interest Rate Increase with Duration Greater than Investment Horizon

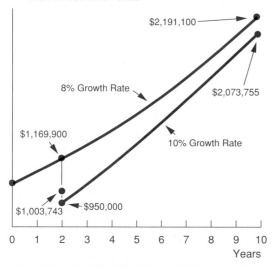

D. Effect of Interest Rate Decline with Duration Greater than Investment Horizon

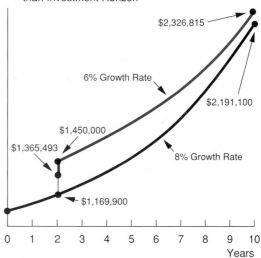

What happens if the portfolio is not properly matched? If the modified duration is greater than the remaining horizon, the price change will be greater. Thus, if interest rates increase, the value of the portfolio after the rate change will be less than $1,003,743. In this case, even if the new value of the portfolio grew at 10 percent a year, it would not reach the expected ending-wealth value. This scenario is shown in Figure 17.3C where it is assumed that the portfolio value declined to $950,000. If this new value grew at 10 percent a year for the remaining 8 years, its ending value would be

$$\$950,000 \times 2.1829 \ (5\% \text{ for } 16 \text{ periods}) = \$2,073,755$$

Therefore, the shortfall of $118,000 between the expected-wealth value and the realized-wealth value is because the portfolio was not properly duration matched (immunized) when interest rates changed.

Alternatively, if interest rates had declined, and the modified duration had been longer than 8 years, the portfolio value would have increased such that the new portfolio value would have been greater than the required value. Figure 17.3D shows what can happen if the portfolio is not properly matched and interest rates decline by 200 basis points to 6 percent. First, if the portfolio *is* properly matched, the value will increase to $1,365,493. If this new portfolio value grows at 6 percent for 8 years, its ending value will be

$$\$1,365,493 \times 1.6047 \text{ (3\% for 16 periods)} = \$2,191,207.$$

Again, this deviates slightly from the expected ending-wealth value ($2,191,100) due to rounding. Alternatively, if the modified duration had been above 8 years, the new portfolio value would have been greater than the required current value of $1,365,493. Assume that because the duration of the portfolio exceeded the remaining horizon, the portfolio value increased to $1,450,000. If so, the ending value would be

$$\$1,450,000 \times 1.6047 \text{ (3\% for 16 periods)} = \$2,326,815$$

In this example, the ending-wealth value would have been greater than the expected-wealth value because you were mismatched and interest rates went in the right direction. When you are not duration matched, you are speculating on interest rate changes, and the result can be very good or very bad. The purpose of immunization is to avoid these uncertainties and to ensure the expected ending-wealth value ($2,191,100), regardless of interest rate changes.

Application of classical immunization   Once you understand the reasoning behind immunization (i.e., it is meant to offset the components of interest rate risk) and the general principle (you need to match modified duration and the investment horizon), you might conclude that this strategy is fairly simple to apply. You might even consider it a passive strategy; simply match modified duration and the investment horizon, and you can ignore the portfolio until the end of the horizon period. The following discussion will show that *immunization is neither a simple nor a passive strategy.*

Except for the case of a zero coupon bond, *an immunized portfolio requires frequent rebalancing* because the modified duration of the portfolio always should be equal to the remaining time horizon. The zero coupon bond is unique because it is a pure discount bond. As such, because there is no cash flow, there is *no reinvestment risk* because the discounting assumes that the value of the bond will grow at the discount rate. For example, if you discount a future value at 10 percent, the present value factor assumes that the value will grow at a compound rate of 10 percent to maturity. Also, there is *no price risk* if you set the duration at your time horizon because you will receive the face value of the bond at maturity. Also, recall that the duration of a zero coupon bond always is equal to its term to maturity. In summary, if you immunize by matching your horizon with a zero coupon bond of equal duration, you do not have to rebalance.

In contrast, if you immunize a portfolio using coupon bonds, several characteristics of duration make it impossible to set a duration equal to the remaining horizon at the initiation of the portfolio and ignore it thereafter. First, *duration declines more slowly than term to maturity, assuming no change in market interest rates.* For example, assume you have a security with a computed duration of 5 years at a 10 percent market yield. A year later, if you compute the duration of the security at 10 percent, you will find that it has a duration of approximately 4.2 years; that is, although the term to maturity has declined by a year, the duration has declined by only 0.8 year. This means that, assuming no change in market rates, the portfolio manager must rebalance the portfolio to reduce its duration to 4 years. Typically, this is not difficult because cash flows from the portfolio can be invested in short-term T-bills if necessary.

Second, *duration changes with a change in market interest rates.* In Chapter 16, we discussed the inverse relationship between market rates and duration—with higher market rates, there will be lower duration and vice versa. Therefore, a portfolio that has the appropriate modified duration at a point in time can have its duration changed immediately if market rates change. If this occurs, a portfolio manager would have to rebalance the portfolio if the deviation from the required duration becomes too large.

Third, you will recall from our initial discussion of immunization that one of the assumptions is that when market rates change, they will change by the same amount and in the same direction (i.e., there will be a parallel shift of the yield curve). Clearly, if this does not happen, it will affect the performance of a portfolio of diffuse bonds. For example, assume you own a portfolio of long- and short-term bonds with a weighted average 6-year duration (e.g., 2-year duration bonds and 10-year duration bonds). Assume the term structure curve changes such that short-term rates decline and long-term rates *rise* (there is an increase in the slope of the yield curve). In such a case, you would experience a major price decline in the long-term bonds, but would be penalized on reinvestment, assuming you generally reinvest the cash flow in short-term securities. This potential problem (caused by a change in the shape of the yield curve) suggests that you should attempt to bunch your portfolio selections close to the desired duration (i.e., use a bullet approach). For example, an 8-year duration portfolio should be made up of 7- to 9-year duration securities to avoid this yield curve reshaping problem.

Finally, there always can be a problem acquiring the bonds you select as optimum for your portfolio. For instance, can you buy long-duration bonds at the price you consider acceptable? In summary, it is important to recognize that classical immunization is *not a passive strategy* because it is subject to all of these potential problems.[34]

HORIZON MATCHING   Horizon matching is a combination of two of the techniques discussed: cash-matching dedication and immunization. As shown in Figure 17.4, the liability stream is divided into two segments. In the first segment, the portfolio is constructed to provide a cash match for the liabilities during this horizon period (e.g., the first 5 years). The second segment is the remaining liability stream following the end of the horizon period—in the example, it is the 25 years after the horizon period. During this second time period, the liabilities are covered by a duration-matched strategy based on immunization principles. As a result, the client receives the certainty of cash matching during the early years and the cost saving and flexibility of duration-matched flows thereafter.

The combination technique also helps alleviate one of the problems with classical immunization: the potential for nonparallel shifts in the yield curve. Most of the problems related to nonparallel shifts are concentrated in the short end of the yield curve because this

---

[34] Several of these problems are discussed in William L. Nemerever, "Managing Bond Portfolios through Immunization Strategies," *The Revolution in Techniques for Managing Bond Portfolios* (Charlottesville, VA: The Institute of Chartered Financial Analysts, 1983), 39–65. Also, see Peter Christensen, Frank J. Fabozzi, and Anthony Lofaso, "Bond Immunization: An Asset/Liability Optimization Strategy," in *The Handbook of Fixed-Income Securities*, 4th ed., edited by Frank J. Fabozzi and T. Dessa Fabozzi (Burr Ridge, Il.: Irwin Professional Publishing, 1995).

FIGURE 17.4   **THE CONCEPT OF HORIZON MATCHING**

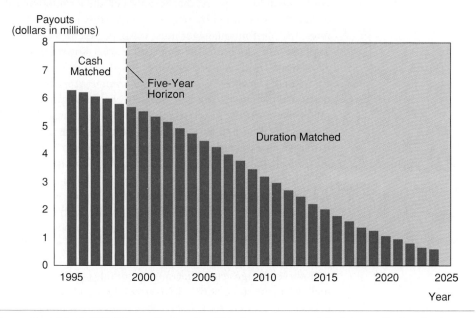

Source: Copyright © 1983 Salomon Brothers Inc. This chart was prepared for Salomon Brothers Inc. by Martin Leibowitz, a former Managing Director, Thomas E. Klaffky, Managing Director, Steven Mandel, Managing Director, and Alfred Weinberger, a former Director. Although the information in this chart has been obtained from sources that Salomon Brothers Inc. believes to be reliable, Salomon does not guarantee its accuracy, and such information may be incomplete or condensed. All figures included in this chart constitute our judgment as of the original publication date.

is where the most severe curve reshaping occurs. Because the short end is taken care of by the cash matching, these are not of concern and we know that the long end of the yield curve tends toward parallel shifts.

An important decision when using horizon matching is the length of the horizon period. The trade-off when making this decision is between the safety and certainty of cash matching and the cost and flexibility of duration-based immunization. The portfolio manager should provide to the client a set of horizon alternatives and the costs and benefits of each of them and allow the client to make the decision.

It also is possible to consider *rolling out* the cash-matched segment over time. Specifically, after the first year the portfolio manager would restructure the portfolio to provide a cash match during the original Year 6, which means that you would still have a 5-year horizon. The ability and cost of rolling out depends on movements in interest rates (ideally, you would want parallel shifts in the yield curve).[35]

CONTINGENT   Contingent procedures are a form of structured active management. The procedure we
PROCEDURES   discuss here is contingent immunization, which entails allowing the portfolio manager some opportunity to actively manage the portfolio with a structure that constrains the portfolio manager if he or she is unsuccessful.

---

[35] For a further discussion on this topic, see Martin L. Leibowitz, Thomas E. Klaffky, Steven Mandel, and Alfred Weinberger, *Horizon Matching: A New Generalized Approach for Developing Minimum-Cost Dedicated Portfolios* (New York: Salomon Brothers, 1983).

CONTINGENT IMMUNIZATION   Subsequent to the development and application of class-ical immunization, Leibowitz and Weinberger developed a portfolio strategy called *contin-gent immunization*.[36] Basically, it allows a bond portfolio manager to pursue the highest returns available through active strategies, while relying on classical bond immunization techniques to ensure a given minimal return over the investment horizon—that is, it allows active portfolio management with a safety net provided by classical immunization.

To understand contingent immunization, it is necessary to recall our discussion of classical immunization. Remember that when the portfolio duration is equal to the investment horizon, a change in interest rates will cause a change in the dollar value of the portfolio such that when the new asset value is compounded at the new market rate, it will equal the desired ending value. This required change in value occurs *only* when the dura-tion of the portfolio is equal to the remaining time horizon, which is why the duration of the portfolio must be maintained at the horizon value.

Consider the following example of this process. Assume that our desired ending-wealth value is $206.3 million. (Figure 17.5 shows an example of the required assets with a 5-year horizon and current market rates of 15 percent.) Specifically, with five years left—assum-ing you can invest funds at 15 percent—you need an initial portfolio worth $100 million to reach $206.3 million ($100 million × 2.063, which is the compound value factor for 10 periods at 7.5 percent). If market rates were lower, you would need more assets; if market rates were higher, you would need less assets. To extend the example, if rates were 12

FIGURE 17.5   **CLASSICAL IMMUNIZATION**

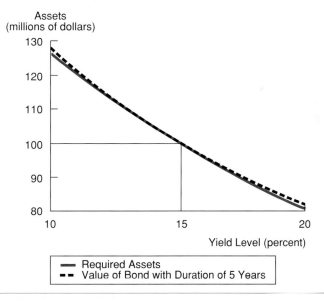

Source: Martin L. Leibowitz and Alfred Weinberger, "Contingent Immunization—Part I: Risk Control Procedures," *Financial Analysts Journal* 30, no. 6 (November–December 1982): 17–32. Reprinted by permission of *Financial Analysts Journal*.

---

[36] Martin L. Leibowitz and Alfred Weinberger, "Contingent Immunization—Part I: Risk Control Procedures," *Financial Analysts Journal* 38, no. 6 (November–December 1982): 17–32; and Martin L. Leibowitz and Alfred Weinberger, "Contingent Immunization—Part II: Problem Areas," *Financial Analysts Journal* 39, no. 1 (January–February 1983): 35–50. This section draws heavily from these articles.

percent, you would need beginning assets of $115.2 million; if rates were at 18 percent, you would need beginning assets of only $87.14 million.[37] The dotted line in Figure 17.5 indicates that the price sensitivity of a portfolio with a modified duration of 5 years will have almost exactly the price sensitivity required.

Contingent immunization requires that the client be willing to accept a potential return below the current market return, referred to as a *cushion spread*—the difference between the current market return and some floor rate. This cushion spread in required yield provides flexibility for the portfolio manager to engage in active portfolio strategies. For example, if current market rates are 15 percent, the client might be willing to accept a floor rate of 14 percent. If we assume the client initiated the fund with $100 million, the acceptance of this lower rate will mean that the portfolio manager does not have the same ending-asset requirements. Specifically, at 14 percent the required ending-wealth value would be $196.72 million (7 percent for 10 periods) compared to the $206.3 million at 15 percent. Because of this lower floor rate (and lower ending-wealth value), it is possible to experience some declines in the value of the portfolio while attempting to do better than the market through active management strategies.

Figure 17.6 shows the value of assets that are required at the beginning assuming a 14 percent required return and the implied ending-wealth value of $196.72 million. Notably, assuming market rates of 15 percent, the required value of assets at the beginning would be $95.56 million, which is the present value of $196.72 million at 15 percent for 5 years. The difference between the client's initial fund of $100 million and the required assets of $95.56 million is the dollar cushion available to the portfolio manager. As noted, this dollar cushion arises because the client has agreed to a lower investment rate, and therefore a lower ending-wealth value.

At this point, the portfolio manager can engage in various active portfolio management strategies to increase the ending-wealth value of the portfolio above that required at 14 percent. As an example, assume that the portfolio manager believes that market rates will decline. Under such conditions, the portfolio manager might consider acquiring a 30-year bond that has a duration greater than the investment horizon of 5 years and, therefore, has greater price sensitivity to changes in market rates. Hence, if rates decline as expected, the value of the long-duration portfolio will rise above the initial value. In contrast, if rates increase, the value of the portfolio will decline rapidly. In this case, depending on how high rates go, the value of the portfolio could decline to a value below that needed to reach the desired ending-wealth value of $196.72 million.

Figure 17.7 shows what happens to the value of this portfolio if we assume an instantaneous change in interest rates when the fund is established. Specifically, if rates decline from 15 percent, the portfolio of long duration, 30-year bonds would experience a large increase in value and develop a *safety margin*—a portfolio value above the required value. In contrast, if rates increase, the value of the portfolio will decline until you reach the asset value required at 14 percent. When the value of the portfolio reaches this point of minimum return (referred to as a *trigger point*), it is necessary to stop active portfolio management and use classical immunization with the remaining assets to ensure that you attain the desired ending-wealth value (i.e., $196.72 million).

---

[37] You derive these required amounts by knowing the desired ending-wealth position (which is $206.3 million in this example) and computing the present value of this amount for the specified time period at the appropriate interest rate (assuming semiannual compounding). Therefore, in these examples we used the present value factor for 6 percent for 10 periods (.5584) and for 9 percent for 10 periods (.4224). Given these present values ($115.2 million and $87.14 million) we know that if we compound them at these rates, we will arrive at our desired ending-wealth value ($206.3 million).

FIGURE 17.6   **PRICE BEHAVIOR REQUIRED FOR FLOOR RETURN**

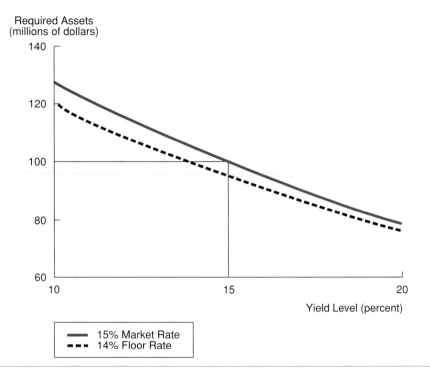

Source: Martin L. Leibowitz and Alfred Weinberger, "Contingent Immunization—Part I: Risk Control Procedures," *Financial Analysts Journal* 38, no. 6 (November–December 1982): 17–32. Reprinted by permission of *Financial Analysts Journal.*

Potential return   The concept of *potential return* is helpful in understanding the objective of contingent immunization. This is the return the portfolio would achieve over the entire investment horizon if, at any point, the assets in hand were immunized at the prevailing market rate. Figure 17.8 contains the various potential rates of return based on dollar asset values shown in Figure 17.7. If the portfolio were immediately immunized when market rates were 15 percent, it would naturally earn the 15 percent market rate; that is, its potential return would be 15 percent. Alternatively, if yields declined instantaneously to 10 percent, the portfolio's asset value would increase to $147 million (see Figure 17.7). If this $147 million portfolio were immunized at the market rate of 10 percent over the remaining 5-year period, the portfolio would compound at 10 percent to a total value of $239 million ($147 million × 1.6289, which is the compound growth factor for 5 percent and 10 periods). This ending value of $239.45 million represents an 18.25 percent realized (horizon) rate of return on the original $100 million portfolio. Consequently, as shown in Figure 17.8, the portfolio's potential return would be 18.25 percent. That is, if rates decline by 5 percent, the potential return for this portfolio at this point in time is 18.25 percent.

In contrast, if interest rates increased, the value of the portfolio will decline substantially and the potential return will decline. For example, if market rates rise to 17 percent (i.e., a yield change of 2 percent), the asset value of the 30-year bond portfolio will decline to $88 million (see Figure 17.7). If this portfolio of $88 million were immunized for the remaining

FIGURE 17.7   **SAFETY MARGIN FOR A PORTFOLIO OF 30-YEAR BONDS**

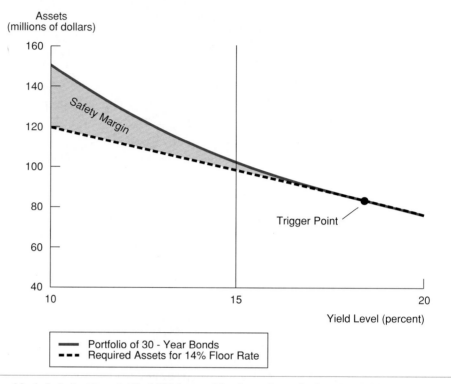

Portfolio of 30 - Year Bonds
Required Assets for 14% Floor Rate

Source: Martin L. Leibowitz and Alfred Weinberger, "Contingent Immunization—Part I: Risk Control Procedures," *Financial Analysts Journal* 38, no. 6 (November–December 1982): 17–32. Reprinted by permission of *Financial Analysts Journal*.

5 years at the prevailing market rate of 17 percent, the ending value would be $199 million. This ending value implies a potential return of 14.32 percent for the total period.

As Figure 17.7 shows, if interest rates rose to 18.50 percent, the 30-year bonds would decline to a value of $81.16 million (the trigger point) and the portfolio would have to be immunized. At this point, if the remaining assets of $81.16 million were immunized at this current market rate of 18.50 percent, the value of the portfolio would grow to $196.73 million ($81.16 × 2.424, which is the compound value factor for 9.25 percent for 10 periods). This ending value implies that the potential return for the portfolio would be exactly 14 percent as shown in Figure 17.8. Regardless of what happens to subsequent market rates, the portfolio has been immunized at the floor rate of 14 percent. That is a major characteristic of the contingent immunized portfolio; if there is proper monitoring, you will always know your trigger point and can be assured of a return no less than the minimum return specified.

Monitoring the immunized portfolio   Clearly, a crucial factor in managing a contingent immunized portfolio is monitoring it to ensure that if the asset value falls to the trigger point, it will be detected and the appropriate action taken to ensure that the portfolio is immunized at the floor-level rate. This can be done using a chart as in Figure 17.9. The top line is the current market value of the portfolio over time. The bottom line is the required value of the immunized floor portfolio. Specifically, the bottom line is *the required value of the portfolio* if we were to immunize at *today's rates* to attain the necessary ending-wealth

FIGURE 17.8   **THE POTENTIAL RETURN CONCEPT**

Source: Martin L. Leibowitz and Alfred Weinberger, "Contingent Immunization—Part I: Risk Control Procedures," *Financial Analysts Journal* 38, no. 6 (November–December 1982): pp. 17–32. Reprinted by permission of *Financial Analysts Journal.*

FIGURE 17.9   **CONTINGENT IMMUNIZATION FLOOR PORTFOLIO OVER TIME**

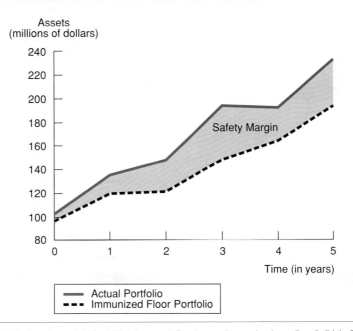

Source: Martin L. Leibowitz and Alfred Weinberger, "Contingent Immunization—Part I: Risk Control Procedures," *Financial Analysts Journal* 38, no. 6 (November–December 1982): 17–32. Reprinted by permission of *Financial Analysts Journal.*

value. This required value for the portfolio is calculated by computing the present value of the promised ending-wealth value at the prevailing market rate.

To demonstrate how this floor portfolio would be constructed, consider our example where we derived a promised ending-wealth value in 5 years of $196.72 million based on an initial investment of $100 million and an acceptable floor rate of 14 percent. If 1 year after the initiation of the portfolio, market rates were 10 percent, you would need a minimum portfolio value of approximately $133.14 million to get to $196.72 million in 4 years. To compute this minimum required value, you multiply the $196.72 million (promised ending-wealth value) times the present value factor for 10 percent for 4 years, assuming semiannual compounding (.6761). The logic is that $133.14 million invested (immunized) at 10 percent for 4 years will equal $196.72 million.

If the active manager had predicted correctly that market rates would decline and had a long-duration portfolio under these conditions, the *actual* value of the portfolio would be much higher than this *minimum required* value, and there would be a safety margin. A year later (after year two), you would determine the assets needed at the rate prevailing at that point in time. Assuming interest rates had increased to 12 percent, you could determine that you would need a floor portfolio of about $138.69 million. Specifically, this is the present value of the $196.72 million for three years at 12 percent, assuming semiannual compounding (.7050). Again, you would expect the actual value of the portfolio to be greater than this required floor portfolio, so you still have a safety margin. If you ever reached the point where the actual value of the portfolio was equal to the required floor value, you would stop the active management and immunize what was left *at the current market rate* to ensure that the ending value would be $196.72 million.

In summary, the contingent immunization strategy encompasses the opportunity for a bond portfolio manager to engage in various active portfolio strategies if the client is willing to accept a floor return (and ending-wealth value) that is below what is currently available. The graph in Figure 17.10 describes the trade-offs involved in contingent immunization. Specifically, by allowing for a slightly lower minimum target rate, the client is making it possible to experience a much higher potential return from active management by the portfolio manager.

| FIGURE 17.10 | **COMPARISON OF RETURN DISTRIBUTIONS** |

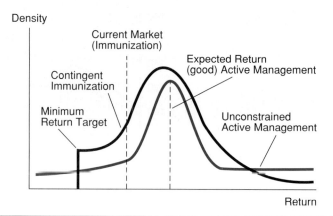

Source: Martin L. Leibowitz and Alfred Weinberger, "Contingent Immunization—Part II: Problem Areas," *Financial Analysis Journal* 39, no. 1 (January–February 1983): 35–50. Reprinted by permission of *Financial Analysts Journal.*

IMPLICATIONS OF CAPITAL MARKET THEORY AND THE EMH ON BOND PORTFOLIO MANAGEMENT

The high level of interest rates that has prevailed since the latter part of the 1960s has provided increasingly attractive returns to bond investors, and the wide swings in interest rates that have accompanied these high market yields have provided numerous capital gains opportunities for bond portfolio managers. As a result, the average compound rates of return on bonds during the 1980s was the highest of any 10-year period in this century, and this performance has continued into the 1990s. Specifically, the results contained in Table 17.7 indicate that the annual returns on the aggregate of high-grade bonds during the period 1980–1995 ranged from −2.92 percent (the only negative annual return) to 32.62 percent, and the average returns of about 11.58 percent were only moderately lower than the average returns on common stocks of 16.61 percent. When these are compared to the longer-term results, it appears that it will be difficult to continue such performance. Still, these results indicate that there are some wonderful opportunities available in bonds. An important consideration for portfolio managers, therefore, is the proper role of fixed-income securities when considering the implications of portfolio theory, capital market theory, and research related to efficient capital markets.

Bonds and Total Portfolio Theory

The performance of bonds has improved even more than indicated by returns alone be-cause bonds offer substantial diversification benefits. In an efficient market, neither stocks nor bonds should dominate a portfolio, but some combination of them should provide a superior risk-adjusted return compared to either one taken alone (assuming low correlation between stocks and bonds). In the study by Reilly, Kao, and Wright, which showed that stock returns were superior to bond yields, they also showed that, due to the low correlation

| TABLE 17.7 | ANNUAL PERCENTAGE RATES OF RETURN AND STANDARD DEVIATIONS FOR LEHMAN BROTHERS BOND INDEXES AND S&P 500 TOTAL RETURN INDEX: 1980–1995 |

	LEHMAN BROTHERS						
Year	Gov't/Corp.	Government	Corporate	Mortgages	Yankee	Aggregate	S&P 500
1980	3.06	5.19	−0.29	0.65	1.92	2.71	32.42
1981	7.26	9.36	2.95	0.07	3.48	6.25	−4.91
1982	31.10	27.75	39.20	43.04	35.82	32.62	21.41
1983	7.99	7.39	9.27	10.13	9.43	8.35	22.51
1984	15.02	14.50	16.62	15.75	16.38	15.15	6.27
1985	21.30	20.43	24.06	25.21	26.00	22.10	32.16
1986	15.62	15.31	16.53	13.43	16.27	15.26	18.47
1987	2.29	2.20	2.56	4.29	1.89	2.76	5.23
1988	7.58	7.03	9.22	8.72	8.81	7.89	16.81
1989	14.24	14.23	14.09	15.35	15.42	14.53	31.49
1990	8.28	8.72	7.05	10.72	7.05	8.96	−3.15
1991	16.13	15.32	18.51	15.72	18.68	16.00	30.55
1992	7.58	7.23	8.69	6.97	7.89	7.40	7.67
1993	11.06	10.64	12.18	6.85	13.42	9.75	9.99
1994	−3.51	−3.38	−3.92	−1.61	−4.63	−2.92	1.31
1995	19.24	18.34	22.25	16.80	23.44	18.47	37.57
Arithmetic mean	11.51	11.27	12.44	12.01	12.58	11.58	16.61
Geometric mean	11.22	11.03	11.98	11.54	12.15	11.28	15.84
Standard deviation	8.37	7.53	10.65	10.91	10.31	8.57	13.80

Source: Frank K. Reilly, G. Wenchi Kao, and David J. Wright, "Alternative Bond Market Indexes," *Financial Analysts Journal* 48, no. 3 (May–June 1992): 48 (updated).

between bonds and equities (about 0.30), the combination of the securities in a portfolio vastly improved the return per unit of risk.[38]

BONDS AND CAPITAL MARKET THEORY

Capital market theory contends that there should be an upward-sloping market line, meaning that greater return should be accompanied by greater risk. Compared to other market vehicles, fixed-income securities have traditionally been viewed as low risk, and their rates of return have typically been modest until the late 1970s. At that time, the inflation rate and bond yields increased. Also, during periods of high economic uncertainty, such as the recessions of 1981–1982 and 1990–1991, the risk premiums on bonds increased substantially because the risk of default for low-rated obligations increased.[39] As demonstrated earlier in the chapter (Figure 17.1), the risk premium on junk bonds has fluctuated dramatically over time.

Capital market theory also relates the risk–return behavior of fixed-income securities to other financial assets. Because fixed-income securities are considered to be relatively conservative investments, we would expect them to be on the lower end of the capital market line. A study by Soldofsky examined the comparative risk–return characteristics of 28 classes of long-term securities.[40] Figure 17.11 shows the basic findings of the study and confirms the a priori expectations. Specifically, government and high-grade corporate bonds were at the low end of the curve, and it progressed to regular preferred stocks, high-quality common stocks, convertible securities, and finally to lower-quality stocks and deep discount bonds. An annual analysis of capital market returns by Ibbotson Associates comparing corporate and government bonds (long- and intermediate-term) to common stocks (total NYSE and small-firm) and Treasury bill obligations indicated similar results. As Figure 17.12 shows, Treasury bills have the least risk and return, followed by government bonds, corporate bonds, total common stocks, and finally small capitalization common stocks.

BOND PRICE BEHAVIOR IN A CAPM FRAMEWORK

The capital asset pricing model (CAPM) is expected to provide a framework for explaining realized security returns as a function of nondiversifiable market risk. Bond returns should be linked directly to risk of default and interest rate risk. Although interest rate risk for investment-quality bonds should be nondiversifiable, some evidence exists that default risk also is largely nondiversifiable because default experience is closely related to the business cycle.[41] Therefore, because the major bond risks are largely nondiversifiable, this implies that we should be able to define bond returns in the context of the CAPM. Still, few studies have attempted it because of data-collection problems. Percival found only a modest effect of a computed beta on bond returns.[42] An analysis of beta and its relationship to the bond

---

[38] Frank K. Reilly, Wenchi Kao, and David J. Wright, "Alternative Bond Market Indexes," *Financial Analysts Journal* 48, no. 3 (May–June 1992): 44–58.

[39] For a detailed discussion on this topic that considers several studies on the subject, see James C. Van Horne, *Financial Market Rates and Flows*, 4th ed. (Englewood Cliffs, NJ: Prentice-Hall, 1993), Chapter 6.

[40] Robert M. Soldofsky, "Risk and Return for Long-Term Securities, 1971–1982," *Journal of Portfolio Management* 11, no. 1 (Fall 1984): 57–64.

[41] W. Braddock Hickman, *Corporate Bond Quality and Investor Experience* (New York: National Bureau of Economic Research, 1958); Thomas R. Atkinson, *Trends in Corporate Bond Quality* (New York: National Bureau of Economic Research, 1967); Dwight M. Jaffee, "Cyclical Variations in the Risk Structure of Interest Rates," *Journal of Monetary Economics* 1, no. 2 (July 1975): 309–325; and Douglas J. Lucas and John G. Lonski, "Changes in Corporate Credit Quality 1970–1990," *Journal of Fixed Income* 1, no. 4 (March 1992): 7–14.

[42] John Percival, "Corporate Bonds in a Market Model Context," *Journal of Business Research* 2, no. 4 (October 1974): 461–467.

FIGURE 17.11   **RISK–RETURN GRAPH FOR LONG-TERM SECURITIES: 1971–1982***

*Minimum term to maturity on bonds is 15 years.

Source: Robert M. Soldofsky, "Risk and Return for Long-Term Securities, 1971–1982." *Journal of Portfolio Management* 11, no. 1 (Fall 1984), p. 60. Reprinted by permission.

and issuer characteristics indicated that bond betas were more responsive to the intrinsic characteristics of the bond *issue* (i.e., coupon, maturity, duration, and call features) than of the issuer.

Reilly and Joehnk found that average bond betas had no significant or consistent relationships with agency ratings.[43] It was contended that, because the study involved only investment-grade securities, the major factor affecting bond prices was market interest rate movements. Evidence that high-grade bond risk is almost all systematic risk is found in the Reilly, Kao, Wright study, which shows that the returns among these bonds, regardless of sector (government, corporate, mortgages) or ratings, were correlated .90 to .99.[44] This

[43] Frank K. Reilly and Michael D. Joehnk, "The Association between Market-Determined Risk Measures for Bonds and Bond Ratings," *Journal of Finance* 31, no. 5 (December 1976): 1387–1403.

[44] Frank K. Reilly, Wenchi Kao, and David J. Wright, "Alternative Bond Market Indexes," *Financial Analysts Journal* 48, no. 3 (May–June 1992): 44–58.

| FIGURE 17.12 | **MEAN RATE OF RETURN AND STANDARD DEVIATION OF RETURNS FOR COMMON STOCKS, GOVERNMENT AND CORPORATE BONDS, T-BILLS, AND INFLATION: 1926–1995** |

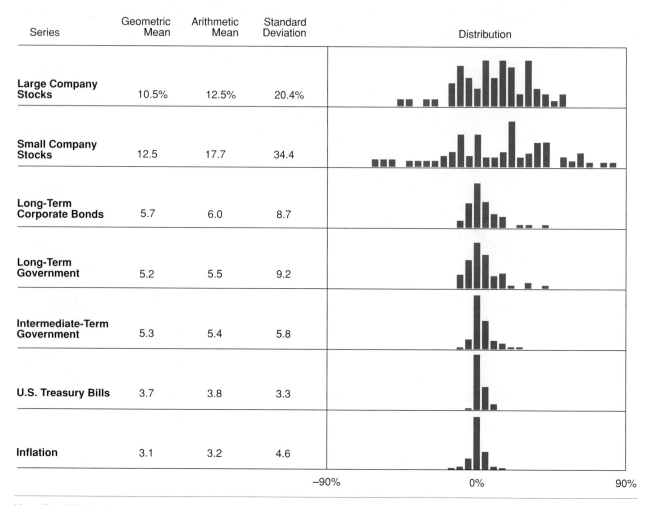

Series	Geometric Mean	Arithmetic Mean	Standard Deviation	Distribution
Large Company Stocks	10.5%	12.5%	20.4%	
Small Company Stocks	12.5	17.7	34.4	
Long-Term Corporate Bonds	5.7	6.0	8.7	
Long-Term Government	5.2	5.5	9.2	
Intermediate-Term Government	5.3	5.4	5.8	
U.S. Treasury Bills	3.7	3.8	3.3	
Inflation	3.1	3.2	4.6	

−90%   0%   90%

Note: The 1933 Small Company Stock Total Return was 142.9 percent.

Source: From *Stocks, Bonds, Bills, and Inflation 1995 Yearbook*™, Ibbotson Associates, Chicago (this book annually updates work by Roger G. Ibbotson and Rex A. Sinquefield). Used with permission. All Rights Reserved.

interest rate risk, which is a market-related, systematic risk factor, has an overpowering effect on price performance and largely negated the effects of differential default risk (a company-specific unique risk factor). It is this unique default risk that is reflected in comparative agency ratings. Notably, the overpowering effect of systematic interest rate risk does *not* prevail when one considers high-yield (junk) bonds. As shown by Reilly and Wright, the correlation between high-yield bonds and investment grade bonds is *lower* than the correlation between high-yield bonds and common stock.[45] This stronger correlation

---

[45] Frank K. Reilly and David J. Wright, "An Analysis of High Yield Bond Benchmarks," *Journal of Fixed Income* 3, no. 4 (March 1994): 6–25.

with stocks is because both high-yield bonds and common stocks have substantial unsystematic risk.

Alexander examined some of the assumptions of the market model as related to bonds and found two major problems.[46] First, the bond beta results were sensitive to the market index used.[47] Specifically, there were major differences with a pure stock index, a pure bond index, or a composite stock-bond index, and the pure bond index had the biggest problems. Second, the results were sensitive to the time period used; the bond betas increased during periods of high bond yields.

Weinstein computed betas for bonds using several market series and related the betas to term to maturity, coupon, and bond ratings.[48] The results for beta using alternative market indexes (pure stock, pure bond, combined) revealed a very strong correlation between the betas from the stock and the combined indexes, a fairly strong relationship between the betas from the bond and the combined indexes, and a weak relationship between the betas from pure stock and bond indexes. No significant relationship existed between the betas and bond ratings for the top four classes of ratings (similar to the findings of Reilly and Joehnk), but there was a weak relationship using the top six ratings. The author postulated a nonlinear relationship where the risk of default becomes significant only for low ratings.

In a subsequent study, Weinstein computed bond betas and examined their stability over time.[49] He used a model that allowed the systematic risk to vary consistently with the Black-Scholes-Merton options pricing model. The results indicated that a model that assumes bond betas change over time has more explanatory power than a constant risk model. Also, he found that a bond's beta was related to firm characteristics (e.g., debt/equity ratios, variance of rate of return on assets) and to bond characteristics (coupon, term to maturity).

Thus, evidence on the usefulness of the CAPM as related to the bond market is mixed. Specifically, there are obvious problems regarding the appropriate market index to use, the systematic risk measure is unstable, and the risk–return relationship did not hold for the higher-quality bonds. Finally, there appears to be a relationship between the systematic risk measure and some characteristics of the firm. However, it also is impacted by the characteristics of the bond such as coupon and maturity that affect the bond's duration and convexity. This is not surprising because we know from Chapter 16 that modified duration is a measure of relative bond price volatility for a given change in market interest rates.

BOND-MARKET EFFICIENCY

Two versions of the efficient market hypothesis (EMH) are examined in the context of fixed-income securities: the weak and the semistrong theories. The weak-form hypothesis contends that security price movements are independent events so historical price information is useless in predicting future price behavior. Studies of weak-form efficiency have examined the ability of investors to forecast interest rates because if you can forecast interest rates you can forecast bond price behavior. Also, interest rate expectations are important for bond portfolio management.

[46] Gordon J. Alexander, "Applying the Market Model to Long-Term Corporate Bonds," *Journal of Financial and Quantitative Analysis* 15, no. 5 (December 1980): 1063–1080.

[47] This is similar to the well-known work by Roll on market series.

[48] Mark I. Weinstein, "The Systematic Risk of Corporate Bonds," *Journal of Financial and Quantitative Analysis* 16, no. 3 (September 1981): 157–278.

[49] Mark I. Weinstein, "Bond Systematic Risk and the Option Pricing Model," *Journal of Finance* 38, no. 5 (December 1983): 1415–1429.

Several studies[50] reached the same conclusion: interest rate behavior cannot be consistently and accurately forecast! In fact, one study suggests that the best forecast is no forecast at all. The models developed ranged from a naive approach to fairly sophisticated techniques. Some models used historical information, some ignored it, and one study used the expectations of acknowledged experts. In all cases, the most naive model, or no forecast at all, provided the best measure of future interest rate behavior. Clearly, if interest rates cannot be forecast, then neither can bond prices using historical prices, all of which supports the weak-form EMH.

The semistrong EMH asserts that current prices fully reflect all public knowledge and that efforts to act on such information are largely unproductive. Several studies have examined the informational value of bond rating changes. Katz examined monthly changes in bond yields surrounding ratings changes and found a significant impact of the change.[51] Weinstein examined monthly bond returns surrounding the announcement of rating changes and found an effect 18 months to 7 months before the announcement, but no effect from 6 months before the announcement to 6 months after the announcement.[52]

In contrast, several studies have examined the impact of bond rating changes on stock prices and returns. Pinches and Singleton found very little impact on stock prices due to the ratings change.[53] Griffin and Sanvicente found a significant stock price impact following bond downgradings.[54] Alternatively, they found no impact on stock prices during the month when an upgrading was announced, but there was an impact during the prior 11 months. Holthausen and Leftwich examined daily stock return data surrounding the announcement of bond rating changes and likewise found negative abnormal returns when bonds were downgraded.[55] However, there was little evidence of abnormal price changes surrounding the announcement of an upgrading.

Summary

• During the past decade, there has been a significant increase in the number and range of bond portfolio management strategies available. Bond portfolio management strategies include the relatively straightforward buy-and-hold and bond indexing strategies, several alternative active portfolio strategies, dedicated cash matching, classical immunization, horizon matching, and contingent immunization. Although you should understand the alternatives available and how to implement them, you also should recognize that the choice of a specific strategy is based on the needs and desires of the client. In turn, the success of any strategy will depend on the background and talents of the portfolio manager.

---

[50] See, for example, William A. Bomberger and W. J. Frazer, "Interest Rates, Uncertainty, and the Livingston Data," *Journal of Finance* 36, no. 3 (June 1981): 661–675; Stephen K. McNees, "The Recent Record of Thirteen Forecasters," *New England Economic Review*, Federal Reserve Bank of Boston (September–October 1981): 3–10; and Adrian W. Throop, "Interest Rate Forecasts and Market Efficiency," Federal Reserve Bank of San Francisco *Economic Review* (Spring 1981): 29–43.

[51] Steven Katz, "The Price Adjustment Process of Bonds to Rating Reclassifications: A Test of Bond Market Efficiency," *Journal of Finance* 29, no. 2 (May 1974): 551–559.

[52] Mark I. Weinstein, "The Effect of a Rating Change Announcement on Bond Price," *Journal of Financial Economics* 5, no. 3 (December 1977): 329–350.

[53] George E. Pinches and Clay Singleton, "The Adjustment of Stock Prices to Bond Rating Changes," *Journal of Finance* 33, no. 1 (March 1978): 29–44.

[54] Paul A. Griffin and Antonio Z. Sanvicente, "Common Stock Returns and Rating Changes: A Methodological Comparison," *Journal of Finance* 37, no. 1 (March 1982): 103–119.

[55] Robert W. Holthausen and Richard W. Leftwich, "The Effect of Bond Rating Changes on Common Stock Prices," *Journal of Financial Economics* 17, no. 1 (September 1986): 57–89.

- The risk–return performance of bonds as a unique asset class has been consistent with expectations. In addition, their inclusion has generally enhanced overall portfolio performance because of their low covariance with other financial assets. The application of CAPM concepts to bonds has been mixed because it has been difficult to derive acceptable measures of systematic risk, and the risk measures derived have been unstable.
- Studies in the bond market have supported the theory of weak-form efficiency. The evidence for semistrong efficiency has been mixed. The results that indicate a lack of efficiency could be due to the relatively inactive secondary markets for most corporate bonds, which causes pricing and adjustment problems compared to the active markets for equities.

Questions

1. What is meant by an indexing portfolio strategy and why is it used?
2. Briefly define the following bond swaps: pure yield pickup swap, substitution swap, and tax swap.
3. Briefly describe three active bond portfolio management strategies.
4. Discuss two variables you would examine very carefully if you were analyzing a junk bond, and indicate why they are important.
5. What are the advantages and difficulties of a cash-matched dedicated portfolio?
6. What are the two components of interest rate risk? Describe each of these components.
7. What is meant by bond portfolio immunization?
8. If the yield curve were flat and did not change, how would you immunize your portfolio?
9. You begin with an investment horizon of 4 years and a portfolio with a duration of 4 years with a market interest rate of 10 percent. A year later, what is your investment horizon? Assuming no change in interest rates, what is the duration of your portfolio relative to your investment horizon? What does this imply about your ability to immunize your portfolio?
10. It has been contended that a zero coupon bond is the ideal financial instrument to use for immunizing a portfolio. Discuss the reasoning for this statement.
11. During a conference with a client, the subject of classical immunization is introduced. The client questions the fee charged for developing and managing an immunized portfolio. The client believes it is basically a passive investment strategy, so the management fee should be substantially lower. What would you tell the client to show that it is not a passive policy?
12. With contingent immunization, what do you give up and what do you gain?

13. *CFA Examination III (June 1983)*

    The ability to *immunize* a bond portfolio is very desirable for bond portfolio managers in some instances.

    a. Discuss the components of interest rate risk. Assuming a change in interest rates over time, explain the two risks faced by the holder of a bond.
    b. Define immunization and discuss why a bond manager would immunize a portfolio.
    c. Explain why a duration-matching strategy is a superior technique to a maturity-matching strategy for the minimization of interest rate risk.
    d. Explain in specific terms how you would use a zero coupon bond to immunize a bond portfolio. Discuss why a zero coupon bond is an ideal instrument in this regard.
    e. Explain how *contingent immunization*, another bond portfolio management technique, differs from *classical immunization*. Discuss why a bond portfolio manager would engage in contingent immunization. [35 minutes]

14. *CFA Examination III (June 1986)*

    During the past several years, there has been substantial growth in the dollar amount of portfolios managed using *immunization* and *dedication* techniques. Assume a client wants to know the basic differences between (1) classical immunization, (2) contingent immunization, (3) cash-matched dedication, and (4) duration-matched dedication.

    a. Briefly describe each of these four techniques.
    b. Briefly discuss the ongoing investment action you would have to carry out if managing an *immunized portfolio*.

c. Briefly discuss three of the major considerations involved with creating a *cash-matched dedicated* portfolio.

d. Describe two parameters that should be specified when using *contingent immunization*.

e. Select one of the four alternative techniques that you believe requires the least degree of active management and justify your selection. [20 minutes]

15. *CFA Examination III (June 1988)*

After you have constructed a structured fixed-income portfolio (i.e., one that is dedicated, indexed, or immunized), it may be possible over time to improve on the initial optimal portfolio while continuing to meet the primary goal. Discuss three conditions that would be considered favorable for a restructuring—assuming no change in objectives for the investor—and cite an example of each condition. [10 minutes]

16. *CFA Examination III (June 1988)*

The use of bond index funds has grown dramatically in recent years.

a. Discuss the reasons you would expect it to be easier or more difficult to construct a bond-market index than a stock-market index.

b. It is contended that the *operational process* of managing a corporate bond index fund is more difficult than managing an equity index fund. Discuss three examples that support this contention. [15 minutes]

17. *CFA Examination III (June 1988)*

Hans Kaufmann is a global fixed-income portfolio manager based in Switzerland. His clients are primarily U.S.-based pension funds. He allocates investments in the United States, Japan, Germany, and the United Kingdom. His approach is to make investment allocation decisions among these four countries based on his global economic outlook. To develop this economic outlook, Kaufmann analyzes the following five factors for each country: real economic growth, inflation, monetary policy, interest rates, and exchange rates.

When Kaufmann believes that the four economies are equally attractive for investment purposes, he equally weights investments in the four countries. When the economies are not equally attractive, he overweights the country or countries where he sees the largest potential returns.

Tables 1 through 5 present relevant economic data and forecasts.

a. Indicate, before taking into account currency hedging, whether Kaufmann should overweight or underweight investments in each country. Justify your position. [15 minutes]

b. Briefly describe how your answer to Part a might change with the use of currency hedging techniques. [5 minutes]

| TABLE 1 | **REAL GNP/GDP (ANNUAL CHANGES)** |

	1985	1986	1987	1988E
United States	3.0%	2.9%	2.4%	2.7%
Japan	4.7	2.4	3.2	3.4
West Germany	2.0	2.5	1.5	2.1
United Kingdom	3.4	3.0	3.4	2.3

| TABLE 2 | **GNP/GDP DEFLATOR (ANNUAL CHANGES)** |

	1985	1986	1987	1988E
United States	3.2%	2.6%	3.3%	3.8%
Japan	1.5	2.8	3.0	3.0
West Germany	2.2	3.1	2.5	2.2
United Kingdom	6.0	3.5	4.5	4.8

TABLE 3

NARROW MONEY (MI) (ANNUAL CHANGES)

	1985	1986	1987	1988E
United States	9.2%	13.4%	5.5%	7.0%
Japan	5.0	6.9	9.9	10.0
West Germany	4.3	8.5	7.5	8.5
United Kingdom	17.8	25.6	16.5	12.0

TABLE 4

LONG-TERM INTEREST RATES (ANNUAL RATES)

	1985	1986	1987	1988E
United States	10.6%	7.7%	8.8%	9.0%
Japan	6.5	5.2	6.1	6.1
West Germany	6.9	5.9	6.1	7.0
United Kingdom	10.6	9.9	9.8	9.5

TABLE 5

EXCHANGE RATES (CURRENCY PER U.S. $)

	1985	1986	1987	1988E
United States (dollars)	1.00	1.00	1.00	1.00
Japan (yen)	228.08	163.87	141.22	140.09
West German (marks)	2.80	2.08	1.74	1.67
United Kingdom (pounds)	0.74	0.67	0.58	0.59

Sources: *World Economic Outlook*, October 1987, and Kaufmann's estimates.

18. *CFA Examination I (1990)*

Robert Devlin and Neil Parish are portfolio managers at the Broward Investment Group. At their regular Monday strategy meeting, the topic of adding international bonds to one of their portfolios came up. The portfolio, an ERISA-qualified pension account for a U.S. client, was currently 90% invested in U.S. Treasury bonds, and 10% invested in 10-year Canadian government bonds.

Devlin suggested buying a position in 10-year German government bonds, while Parish argued for a position in 10-year Australian government bonds.

a. Briefly discuss the *three* major issues that Devlin and Parish should address in their analysis of the return prospects for German and Australian bonds relative to those of U.S. bonds. [6 minutes]

Having made no changes to the original portfolio, Devlin and Parish hold a subsequent strategy meeting and decide to add positions in the government bonds of Japan, United Kingdom, France, Germany and Australia.

b. Identify and discuss *two* reasons for adding a broader mix of international bonds to the pension portfolio. [9 minutes]

19. *CFA Examination III (1990)*

The investment committee of the money management firm of Gentry, Inc. has typically been very conservative and has avoided investing in high-yield (junk) bonds, although they have had major positions in investment-grade corporate bonds. Recently, Pete Squire, a member of the committee, suggested that they should review their policy regarding junk bonds because they currently constitute over 25% of the total corporate bond market.

As a part of this policy review, you are asked to respond to the following questions.

a. Briefly discuss the liquidity *and* pricing characteristics of junk bonds relative to *each* of the following types of fixed income securities:

- Treasuries;
- high-grade corporate bonds;
- corporate loans; and
- private placements.

Briefly discuss the implications of these differences for Gentry's bond portfolio managers. The committee has learned that the correlation of rates of return between Treasuries and high-grade corporate bonds is approximately 0.98, while the correlation between Treasury/high-grade corporate bonds and junk bonds is approximately 0.45.

b. Briefly explain the reason for this difference in correlations, and briefly discuss its implications for bond portfolios.

The committee has also heard that durations at the times of issue for junk bonds are typically much shorter than for newly issued high-grade corporate bonds.

c. Briefly explain the reason for this difference in duration, and briefly discuss its implication for the volatility of bond portfolios. [15 minutes]

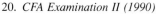 20. *CFA Examination II (1990)*

Greg Kemp, CFA, Chief Investment Officer of Anchor Advisors, has received the following recommendation from his bond management group.

"We believe the current environment has focused excessive pessimism on high-grade corporate bonds. Fears of 'event risk' and weakness in the junk bond market have widened yield spreads to attractive levels.

"It is recommended that our employee benefit bond accounts reduce their current U.S. Treasury weightings from 75% to 25%, with this money to be invested in callable Single-A and AA utility bonds with coupon rates between 9% and 11%. The durations of the bonds purchased will be equal to those sold."

Kemp accepts the idea that yield spreads are wider than normal between U.S. Treasury bonds and corporate issues. Interest rates on long-term U.S. Treasury issues are currently 9%. He expects a significant (more than 100 basis points) drop in interest rates.

a. Kemp has some concerns about the volatility implications of the proposed trade in light of his understanding of the concepts of duration, convexity, and option-adjusted spreads. Given his interest rate expectations, identify and explain *two* key questions that Kemp should raise about the proposed trade. [10 minutes]

b. Recommend *two* modifications to the proposed trade that would address Kemp's concerns mentioned in Part A. [5 minutes]

21. *CFA Examination II (1994)*

Bond analysis often requires more than traditional credit ratio analysis. Discuss *each* of the following *three* considerations as they relate to evaluating a specific fixed-income security:

(i)   Competition within the Industry
(ii) Liquidation Value of Net Assets
(iii) Management [6 minutes]

Problems

1. You have a portfolio with a market value of $50 million and a Macaulay duration of 7 years (assuming a market interest rate of 10 percent). If interest rates jump to 12 percent, what would be the estimated value of your portfolio using modified duration? Show all your computations.

2. Answer the following questions assuming that at the initiation of an investment account, the market value of your portfolio is $200 million, and you immunize the portfolio at 12 percent for 6 years. During the first year, interest rates are constant at 12 percent.

   a. What is the market value of the portfolio at the end of Year 1?

   b. Immediately after the end of the year, interest rates *decline* to 10 percent. Estimate the new value of the portfolio, assuming you did the required rebalancing (use only modified duration).

3. Compute the Macaulay duration under the following conditions:
    a. A bond with a 5-year term to maturity, a 12 percent coupon (annual payments), and a market yield of 10 percent
    b. A bond with a 4-year term to maturity, a 12 percent coupon (annual payments), and a market yield of 10 percent
    c. Compare your answers to Parts a and b, and discuss the implications of this for classical immunization.
4. Compute the Macaulay duration under the following conditions:
    a. A bond with a 4-year term to maturity, a 10 percent coupon (annual payments), and a market yield of 8 percent
    b. A bond with a 4-year term to maturity, a 10 percent coupon (annual payments), and a market yield of 12 percent
    c. Compare your answers to Parts a and b. Assuming it was an immediate shift in yields, discuss the implications of this for classical immunization.
5. A major requirement in running a contingent immunization portfolio policy is monitoring the relationship between the current market value of the portfolio and the required value of the floor portfolio. In this regard, assume a $300 million portfolio with a horizon of 5 years. The available market rate at the initiation of the portfolio is 14 percent, but the client is willing to accept 12 percent as a floor rate to allow you to use active management strategies. The current market values and current market rates at the end of Years 1, 2, and 3 are as follows:

End of Year	Market Value	Market Yield	Required Floor Portfolio	Safety Margin (deficiency)
1	340.00	.12		
2	375.00	.10		
3	360.20	.14		

    a. What is the required ending-wealth value for this portfolio?
    b. What is the value of the required floor portfolio at the end of Years 1, 2, and 3?
    c. Compute the safety margin or deficiency at the end of Years 1, 2, and 3.
6. Evaluate the following pure yield pickup swap: You currently hold a 20-year, Aa-rated, 9.0 percent coupon bond priced to yield 11.0 percent. As a swap candidate, you are considering a 20-year, Aa-rated, 11 percent coupon bond priced to yield 11.5 percent. (Assume reinvestment at 11.5 percent.)

	Current Bond	Candidate Bond
Dollar investment		
Coupon		
i on one coupon		
Principal value at year end		
Total accrued		
Realized compound yield		
Value of swap: _____ basis points in one year		

7. Evaluate the following substitution swap: You currently hold a 25-year, 9.0 percent coupon bond priced to yield 10.5 percent. As a swap candidate, you are considering a 25-year, Aa-rated, 9.0 percent coupon bond priced to yield 10.75 percent. (Assume a 1-year work-out period and reinvestment at 10.5 percent.)

	Current Bond	Candidate Bond
Dollar investment	_____	_____
Coupon	_____	_____
i on one coupon	_____	_____
Principal value at year end	_____	_____
Total accrued	_____	_____
Realized compound yield	_____	_____
Value of swap: _____ basis points in one year		

8. *CFA Examination III (June 1984)*

   Reinvestment risk is a major factor for bond managers to consider when determining the most appropriate or optimal strategy for a fixed-income portfolio. Briefly describe each of the following bond portfolio management strategies, and explain how each deals with reinvestment risk:
   a. Active management
   b. Classical immunization
   c. Dedicated portfolio
   d. Contingent immunization [20 minutes]

9. *CFA Examination III (June 1985)*

   A major requirement in managing a fixed-income portfolio using a contingent immunization policy is monitoring the relationship between the current market value of the portfolio and the required value of the floor portfolio. This difference is defined as the *margin of error*. In this regard, assume a $300 million portfolio with a time horizon of 5 years. The available market rate at the initiation of the portfolio is 12 percent, but the client is willing to accept 10 percent as a floor rate to allow use of active management strategies. The current market values and current market rates at the end of Years 1, 2, and 3 are as follows:

End of Year	Market Value ($Mil)	Market Yield	Required Floor Portfolio ($Mil)	Margin of Error ($Mil)
1	$340.9	10%		
2	405.5	8		
3	395.2	12		

   Table 1
   Present Value (use tables in back of book)

   Table 2
   Compound Value (use tables in back of book)

   Assuming semiannual compounding:
   a. Calculate the required ending-wealth value for this portfolio.
   b. Calculate the value of the required floor portfolios at the end of Years 1, 2, and 3.
   c. Compute the margin of error at the end of Years 1, 2, and 3.
   d. Indicate the action that a portfolio manager utilizing a *contingent immunization* policy would take if the margin of error at the end of any year had been zero or negative.

10. *CFA Examination II (1990)*

    PTC's Investment Committee has decided to allocate 50 percent of the pension plan portfolio's fixed-income investment to non-U.S. government bonds (i.e., bonds representing non-U.S. sovereign credits). For a number of reasons, BAG—the Committee's consultant—has recommended against using a pure dedication approach to management of the bonds. Instead, it has presented the Committee with three alternative strategies for consideration, accompanied by the 15-year historical performance data for each strategy shown in Table 2.

TABLE 2

15-YEAR HISTORICAL UNIVERSE PERFORMANCE

	Average Returns Annualized	Average Top Decile Returns (a) Annualized	Average Bottom Decile Returns (b) Annualized	Standard Deviation of Returns
Strategy Characteristics				
Active management	12.9%	15.6%	6.8%	18.6%
Duration shifts + or −40% of Salomon WGB Index (c)				
Deviations from country allocation benchmarks in Index are unrestricted				
Transactions permitted for any management purpose				
Fee: 35 basis points/year				
Passive management	11.8%	12.8%	10.7%	16.0%
Duration shifts + or −5% of Salomon WGB Index (c)				
Country allocation deviations limited relative to index proportions				
Transactions permitted only for replacement of deteriorating credits				
Fee: 15 basis points/year				
Indexed management	11.3%	12.0%	11.0%	14.9%
Match return of Salomon WGB Index (c)				
No duration shifts permitted				
Transactions allowed only for portfolio rebalancing				
Fee: 6 basis points/year				

(a) Top decile returns are a simple average of the ten best manager records in BAG's 100-manager universe.

(b) Bottom decile returns are a simple average of the ten worst manager records in BAG's 100-manager universe.

(c) Salomon Brothers World Government Bond Index (WGB)

a. Based on the management strategy characteristics set forth in Table 2, as well as your general knowledge, identify and explain *three* advantages of *each* strategy as an alternative for the Investment Committee to consider. In developing your response, regard yourself as a strong advocate as you explain the advantages of *each* of the three alternatives. [15 minutes]

b. Identify and explain *one* key *disadvantage* of *each* of the three strategies. [5 minutes]

PTC has now decided to index the segment of the fixed income portfolio to be invested in non-U.S. government bonds, using the Salomon Brothers World Government Bond Index as the benchmark portfolio. Assume this index includes the sovereign credits of nine major countries in the proportions shown below:

Country	Weighting
Australia	2%
Canada	8%
Denmark	2%
France	11%
Germany	19%
Japan	37%
Netherlands	8%
Switzerland	2%
United Kingdom	11%

Several members of the Investment Committee favor use of the full replication approach to indexing the non-U.S. government bonds, while the chairman favors use of the stratified sampling approach. As the BAG representative assigned to the PTC account, you have been asked to assist the Committee in choosing between the two indexing methods.

c. Describe and evaluate *each* of these two indexing alternatives for the purpose of creating and managing a bond portfolio intended to represent the Salomon Brothers World Government Bond Index benchmark. [10 minutes]

d. Evaluate the appropriateness of using the Salomon Brothers World Government Bond Index as a benchmark for purposes of monitoring PTC's non-U.S. portfolio exposures in relation to its pension benefit liability exposures. [5 minutes]

References

Altman, Edward I., ed. *The High Yield Debt Market.* Homewood, IL: Dow Jones-Irwin, 1990.

Beckers, Stan. "Stocks, Bonds, and Inflation in the World Markets: Implications for Pension Fund Investment." *The Journal of Fixed Income* 1, no. 3 (December 1991).

Bierwag, G. O., George G. Kaufman, and Alden Toevs, eds. *Innovations in Bond Portfolio Management: Duration Analysis and Immunization.* Greenwich, CT: JAI Press, 1983.

Cheung, Rayner, Joseph C. Bencivenga, and Frank J. Fabozzi. "Original Issue High-Yield Bonds: Historical Return and Default Experiences, 1977–1989." *The Journal of Fixed Income* 2, no. 2 (September 1992).

Choie, Kenneth S. "A Simplified Approach to Bond Portfolio Management: DDS." *Journal of Portfolio Management* 16, no. 3 (Spring 1990).

Churchill, Dwight D., ed. *Fixed Income Management: Techniques and Practices.* Charlottesville, VA: Association for Investment Management and Research, 1994.

Dattatreya, Ravi E. and Frank J. Fabozzi. *Active Total Return Management of Fixed Income Portfolios.* Revised edition. Burr Ridge, IL: Irwin Professional Publishing, 1995.

Droms, William G., ed. *Initiating and Managing a Global Investment Program,* Charlottesville, VA: Association for Investment Management and Research, 1991.

Fabozzi, Frank J. *Bond Markets, Analysis and Strategies.* 3d ed. Upper Saddle River, NJ: Prentice-Hall, 1996.

Fabozzi, Frank J., ed. *The New High-Yield Debt Market.* New York: Harper Business, 1990.

Fabozzi, Frank J. and T. Dessa Fabozzi, eds. *The Handbook of Fixed-Income Securities.* 4th ed. Burr Ridge, IL: Irwin Professional Publishing, 1995.

Fridson, Martin. *High Yield Bonds: Assessing Risk and Identifying Value in Speculative Grade Securities.* Chicago: Probus Publishing, 1989.

Howe, Jane Tripp. *Junk Bonds: Analysis and Portfolio Strategies.* Chicago: Probus Publishing, 1988.

Leibowitz, Martin L., William S. Krasker, and Ardavan Nozari. "Spread Duration: A New Tool for Bond Portfolio Management." *Journal of Portfolio Management* 16, no. 3 (Spring 1990)

Reilly, Frank K., ed. *High Yield Bonds: Analysis and Risk Assessment.* Charlottesville, VA: Institute of Chartered Financial Analysts, 1990.

Rosenberg, Michael R. *Currency Forecasting.* Burr Ridge, IL: Irwin Professional Publishing, 1996.

Squires, Jan R., ed. *Global Portfolio Management,* Charlottesville, VA: Association for Investment Management and Research, 1996.

Tuttle, Donald., ed. *The Revolution in Techniques for Managing Bond Portfolios.* Charlottesville, VA: The Institute of Chartered Financial Analysts, 1983.

Wilson, Richard S., and Frank J. Fabozzi. *The New Corporate Bond Market.* Chicago: Probus Publishing, 1990.

Part
5

ANALYSIS OF COMMON STOCKS

Chapter 18   Stock-Market Analysis

Chapter 19   Industry Analysis

Chapter 20   Company Analysis and Stock Selection

Chapter 21   Technical Analysis

Chapter 22   Equity Portfolio Management Strategies

*P*art 3 considered the basic valuation principles and practices applied to all securities and how this was applied to the global asset allocation decision and, in Part 4, we applied these principles to the analysis and management of bonds. In Part 5, we apply these same valuation principles and practices to the analysis of common stocks. The objective is to be in a position to make the critical risk–return decision at the market-industry-company stock level.

You will recall from Chapter 11 that successful investing requires several steps beginning with a valuation of the aggregate economy and market, the examination of various industries, and the analysis of individual companies and their securities. Globalization of the capital markets has definitely complicated this process wherein it is now necessary to consider markets on a worldwide basis followed by the analysis of *world* industries in numerous, complex foreign companies.

In Chapter 18 we begin the three-step, top-down approach and discuss how to analyze the aggregate stock market using the basic dividend discount model. In Chapter 19 we discuss the specific steps in industry analysis using the same dividend discount model that was used in the market analysis.

Chapter 20 on company analysis begins with a discussion of the difference between a company and its stock. In many instances, the common stock of a very fine company may not be a good investment, which is why we emphasize that company analysis and stock selection are two separate but dependent activities. Once again, the analysis procedure is built on the dividend discount model. In addition, other relative valuation factors are considered because of the extensive research indicating the importance and usefulness of factors such as corporate size, book value/market value ratio, and price/cash flow ratio when making cross-sectional decisions on stocks. We also consider other techniques such as economic value added (EVA) that provide insights regarding the economic success of a firm and its management. The overall goal of this procedure is to select one of the best companies in a superior industry during a favorable market environment.

It was noted in Chapter 13 that it is not feasible to use the standard dividend discount model to value true growth companies. Therefore, there is a separate discussion in Chapter 20 in which we discuss several valuation models that have been specifically developed for the analysis of growth companies.

Throughout this section, we refer to the semistrong efficient market hypothesis. You will recall that, although many studies support this hypothesis, there is growing literature dealing with anomalies related to this hypothesis. The presentation in this section provides a consistent and justifiable valuation technique that can be used to find undervalued securities. You should never forget that the output of alternative valuation models is only as good as the estimated inputs and *the superior analyst is the one who provides the best estimates.*

Chapter 21 deals with technical analysis, an alternative or supplement to the fundamental approach discussed in the prior chapters. Rather than estimating value based on external variables, the technical analyst believes that it is possible to project future stock price movements based on past stock price changes or other stock market data. Various techniques used by technical analysts for U.S. and world markets are discussed and demonstrated.

Chapter 22 deals with equity portfolio management strategies. We begin with a general discussion of passive versus active management styles. This is followed by a specific discussion of indexing, including the selection of an appropriate benchmark index, and a consideration of how one selects stocks to include in an indexed portfolio.

The overview of active equity portfolio management strategies includes a discussion of how one constructs an appropriate normalized benchmark portfolio that reflects the client's risk–return objectives and constraints. We consider how a manager implements one of the three major active management approaches: market-timing, sector or style rotation (e.g., growth versus value), or stockpicking. Notably, all of these approaches can and should consider global opportunities.

We conclude this chapter with a discussion of how equity portfolio managers can use derivatives from the following objectives: change the risk–return characteristics of a portfolio; make specific asset allocation decisions (including international allocations); and hedge portfolio inflows and outflows.

Chapter
18

Stock-Market Analysis

This chapter answers the following questions:

- How do we apply the basic dividend discount model (DDM) to the valuation of the aggregate stock market?
- What are the two components involved in the two-part valuation procedure?
- Given the two components in the valuation procedure, which is more volatile?
- What steps are involved in estimating the earnings per share for an aggregate market series?
- What variables affect the aggregate operating profit margin and how do they affect it?
- What are the variables that determine the level and changes in the market earnings multiplier?
- How do you arrive at an expected market value and an expected rate of return for the stock market?
- What additional factors must be considered when you apply this microanalysis approach to the valuation of stock markets around the world?
- What are some differences between stock market statistics for the U.S. versus other countries?

Interest in stock-market movements has grown during the past decade. More individuals own stock than ever before, and significant mergers are increasingly frequent. In earlier chapters, we emphasized the importance of analyzing the aggregate economy and alternative security markets before an industry or a company analysis. As discussed in Chapter 14, it is very important to use the economic and market outlook to make the asset allocation decision between stocks, bonds, or cash before you consider which is the best industry or company.

There are two techniques for making the security-market decision. The first is a macroanalysis approach, which is based on the strong relationship between the aggregate economy and alternative security markets. The second technique involves microanalysis, which applies basic valuation models to the bond or equity markets. Chapter 14 was concerned with the macro techniques and discussed world asset allocation. Chapter 16 discussed the micro valuation of bonds.

This chapter explains the microanalysis of a country's stock market. Your estimate of the future value for the stock market in a country implies an estimate of the rate of return you expect as an equity investor in the country during the holding period.

This chapter begins the three-step valuation process introduced in Chapter 13. We initiate the fundamental analysis of stocks, which determines the future value of the aggregate stock market on the basis of sales, earnings, and risk factors. In this chapter, we estimate the aggregate market outlook based on the outlook for the economy. This will be followed in Chapter 19 by a discussion of how one analyzes alternative industries. Finally, in Chapter 20 we consider how to estimate the value of an individual firm and its stock.

The presentation of how we apply basic valuation theory to the aggregate stock market is presented in five sections. The first presents the theoretical background for the two-step multiplier approach. The second section considers the estimation of earnings per share, and the third section deals with estimating the earnings multiplier or the price/earnings ratio. In section four, we combine the estimates of earnings per share and the price/earnings ratio to derive a future value for the market. In turn, this future value can be used to estimate the expected rate of return on stocks during the holding period. The final section discusses how to apply this approach to foreign markets.

APPLYING THE VALUATION MODEL TO THE MARKET

In Chapter 13, we worked with a valuation model that equated the value of an investment to

1. The stream of expected returns
2. The time pattern of expected returns
3. The required rate of return on the investment

Using this information, we employed the dividend discount model (DDM), which estimated the value of the stock (V_j) assuming a constant growth rate of dividends for an infinite period.

$$V_j = \frac{D_0(1 + g)}{(1 + k)} + \frac{D_0(1 + g)^2}{(1 + k)^2} + \ldots + \frac{D_0(1 + g)^n}{(1 + k)^n}$$

where

V_j = the value of stock j
D_0 = the dividend payment in the current period
g = the constant growth rate of dividends
k = the required rate of return on stock j
n = the number of periods, which is assumed to be infinite

We used this model as the basis for the fundamental analysis of common stock. We also can use it to value a stock-market series. In the appendix to Chapter 13, it was shown that this model can be simplified to the following expression:

$$V_j = P_j = \frac{D_1}{k - g}$$

where

P_j = the price of stock j
D_1 = dividend in period 1, which is equal to: $D_0(1 + g)$
k = the required rate of return for stock j
g = the constant growth rate of dividends

This model suggests that the parameters to be estimated are (1) the required rate of return (k) and (2) the expected growth rate of dividends (g). After estimating g, it is simple to estimate D_1 because it is the known current dividend (D_0) times $(1 + g)$.

Recall too that we can transform the dividend discount model into an earnings multiplier model by dividing both sides of the equation by E:

$$\frac{P_j}{E_1} = \frac{\dfrac{D_1}{E_1}}{k - g}$$

We call this P/E ratio the **earnings multiplier** or the *price/earnings ratio*. It is determined by

1. The expected dividend payout ratio (D_1/E_1),
2. The required rate of return on the stock (k)
3. The expected growth rate of dividends for the stock (g)

We will see that the estimation of this earnings multiplier is important because it varies between stocks and industries. Also the multiplier for the aggregate stock market varies widely over time and has a big impact on changes in the value of the market.

We showed previously that the difficult parameters to estimate are k and g, or more specifically, the *spread* between k and g. Recall that very small changes in either k or g without an offset by the other variable can affect the spread and change the value of the earnings multiplier substantially.

Two-Part Valuation Procedure

To find a value for the stock market, we use the earnings multiplier version of the dividend discount model because it is a theoretically correct model of value assuming a constant growth of dividends for an infinite time period. These are reasonable assumptions for the aggregate stock market.[1] Also this technique of market valuation or a slight modification of it is consistently used in practice.

Recall that k and g are independent variables because k depends heavily on risk, whereas g is a function of the retention rate and the ROE. Therefore, this spread between k and g can and does change over time. The following equations show that you can derive an estimate of this spread at a point in time by examining the prevailing dividend yield:

$$P_j = \frac{D_1}{k - g}$$

$$P_j/D_1 = 1/k - g$$
$$D_1/P_j = k - g$$

Although the dividend yield gives an estimate of the size of the prevailing spread, it does not indicate the values for the two individual components (k and g). More important, it says nothing about the future spread, which is the critical value that must be estimated.

Importance of Both Components of Value

The ultimate objective of this microanalysis is to estimate the future market value for a major stock-market series, such as the S&P 400. This estimation process has two equally important steps:

1. Estimating the future earnings per share for the stock-market series
2. Estimating a future earnings multiplier for the stock-market series[2]

Some analysts have concentrated on estimating the earnings for a market series with little consideration of changes in the earnings multiplier for the series. An investor who considers only the earnings for the series and ignores the earnings multiplier assumes that the earnings multiplier will be relatively constant over time. If this were correct, stock prices would generally move in line with earnings. The fallacy of this assumption is

---

[1] Recall that these assumptions may be unrealistic for many stocks, especially for stocks of growth companies. We will consider these problems and discuss alternative valuation models that consider such conditions in Chapter 20.

[2] Our emphasis will be on estimating *future value*. We will show the relevant variables and provide a procedural framework, but the final estimate depends on the ability of the analyst.

| TABLE 18.1 | ANNUAL CHANGES IN STOCK PRICES, CORPORATE EARNINGS, AND THE EARNINGS MULTIPLIER FOR S&P 400: 1975–1995 | | | | | | | |

Year	Year-End Stock Prices	Percentage Change	Earnings per Share	Percentage Change	Year-End Earnings Multiple (t)	Percentage Change	Earnings Multiple ($t + 1$)	Percentage Change
1975	100.88	31.9	8.58	−10.7	11.76	47.8	9.44	5.9
1976	119.46	18.4	10.69	24.6	11.17	−5.0	10.43	10.6
1977	104.71	−12.3	11.45	7.1	9.14	−18.2	8.03	−23.0
1978	107.21	2.4	13.04	13.9	8.22	−10.1	6.58	−18.0
1979	121.02	12.9	16.29	24.9	7.43	−9.6	7.51	14.1
1980	154.45	27.6	16.12	−1.0	9.58	29.0	9.23	22.9
1981	137.12	−11.2	16.74	3.8	8.19	−14.5	10.39	12.6
1982	157.62	15.0	13.20	−21.1	11.94	45.8	10.67	2.7
1983	186.17	18.1	14.77	11.9	12.60	5.6	10.28	−3.7
1984	186.36	0.1	18.11	22.6	10.29	−18.4	12.20	18.6
1985	234.56	25.9	15.28	−15.6	15.35	49.2	16.14	32.4
1986	269.93	15.1	14.53	−4.9	18.58	21.0	13.31	−17.5
1987	285.85	5.9	20.28	39.6	14.10	−24.1	10.75	−19.2
1988	321.26	12.4	26.59	31.1	12.08	−14.3	11.97	11.4
1989	403.49	25.6	26.83	0.9	15.04	24.5	16.29	36.0
1990	387.42	−4.0	24.77	−7.7	15.64	4.0	22.91	40.6
1991	492.72	27.2	16.91	−31.7	29.14	86.3	25.86	12.9
1992	507.46	3.0	19.05	12.7	26.64	−8.6	23.14	−10.5
1993	540.19	6.4	21.93	15.1	24.63	−7.5	16.32	−29.5
1994	547.51	1.4	33.10	50.9	16.54	−32.8	14.27	−12.6
1995[e]	721.19	31.7	38.37	15.9	18.80	13.6	NA	NA
With Signs								
Mean		8.1		7.5	15.16	3.8	14.01	1.2
Standard deviation		15.5		18.1		27.8		18.4
Coefficient of variation		1.9		2.4		7.4		15.8
Without Signs								
Mean		14.5		15.4		20.9		15.2
Standard deviation		9.6		11.9		18.3		10.1
Coefficient of variation		0.7		0.8		0.9		0.7

[e] estimate
NA—not available

Source: *Standard & Poor's Analysts Handbook* (New York: Standard & Poor's Corporation, 1995). Reprinted by permission of Standard & Poor's Corp.

obvious when one examines data for the two components during the period from 1975 to 1995, as shown in Table 18.1.

The year-end stock price is the closing value for the S&P 400 series on the last trading day of the year. The next column is the percent change in price for the year. The earnings figure is the earnings per share during the year for the S&P 400 series, and the next column shows the percentage change from the prior year. The fifth column is the historical earnings multiplier at the end of the year, which is equal to the year-end value for the S&P 400 series divided by the *historical* earnings for that year. As an example, at the end of 1975, the S&P 400 price series was equal to 100.88 and the earnings per share for the firms that made up the series was 8.58 for the 12 months ending 12/31/75. This implies an earnings multiplier of 11.76 (100.88/8.58). Although this may not be the ideal measure of the multiplier, it is consistent in its measurement and shows the changes in the relationship between stock prices and earnings over time. An alternative measure is to compute the multiplier using *next* year's earnings (i.e., stock price as of 12/31/75 versus earnings for the 12 months ending 12/31/76). This series likewise reflects substantial annual changes that are not quite as large as with historical earnings.

There are numerous striking examples where stock price movements for the S&P 400 series were opposite to earnings changes during the same year:

- 1975 profit *declined* by 10 percent; stock prices *increased* by 32 percent.
- 1977 profits *increased* by 7 percent; stock prices *declined* by 12 percent.
- 1980 profits *decreased* by 1 percent; stock prices *increased* by over 27 percent.
- 1982 profit *decreased* by 21 percent; stock prices *increased* by 15 percent.
- 1984 profits *increased* by almost 23 percent; stock prices were basically *unchanged.*
- 1985 profits *decreased* by 15 percent; stock prices *increased* by about 26 percent.
- 1989 profits were almost *unchanged*; stock prices *increased* by over 25 percent.
- 1991 profits *decreased* by almost 32 percent; stock prices *increased* by over 27 percent.
- 1994 profits *increased* by almost 52 percent; stock prices were basically *unchanged.*

During each of these years, the major influences on stock price movements came from changes in the earnings multiplier. The greater volatility of the multiplier series compared to the earnings per share series can be seen from the summary figures at the bottom of Table 18.1 and from the graph of the earnings multiplier in Figure 18.1. The standard deviation of annual changes for the earnings multiplier series is much larger than the standard deviation of earnings changes (28.2 versus 18.3). The same is true for the relative volatility measures

FIGURE 18.1   **YEAR-END EARNINGS MULTIPLE FOR S&P 400, BASED ON HISTORICAL EARNINGS**

of the coefficient of variability (8.2 versus 2.6). Also, if you consider the mean annual percentage change of the two series without sign, the earnings multiplier series has a larger mean annual percent change value (21.2 versus 14.1) and a larger standard deviation of annual percentage change (18.9 versus 10.4). Therefore, these figures show that, of the two estimates required for market valuation, the earnings multiplier is the more volatile component.

This calculation of future market value requires two separate estimates and *both* are important and necessary. Therefore, we will begin by considering a procedure for estimating aggregate earnings. Later, we discuss the factors that should be analyzed when estimating the aggregate market earnings multiplier.

ESTIMATING EXPECTED EARNINGS PER SHARE

The estimate of expected earnings per share for the market series will consider the outlook for the aggregate economy and for the corporate sector. This requires the following steps:

1. Estimate sales per share for a stock-market series such as the S&P 400. This estimate of sales involves a prior estimate of gross national product (GNP) because of the relationship between the sales of major industrial firms and this measure of aggregate economic activity. Therefore, prior to estimating sales per share, we will consider sources for an estimate of GNP.
2. Estimate the operating profit margin for the series, which equals operating profit divided by sales. Given the data available from Standard & Poor's, we will define operating profit as earnings before depreciation, interest, and taxes (EBDIT).
3. Estimate depreciation per share for the next year.
4. Estimate interest expense per share for the next year.
5. Estimate the corporate tax rate for the next year.

These steps will lead to an estimate of earnings per share that will be combined with an estimate of the earnings multiplier to arrive at an estimate of the ending price for the stock-market series.

ESTIMATING GROSS NATIONAL PRODUCT

GNP is a measure of aggregate economic output or activity. Therefore, one would expect aggregate corporate sales to be related to GNP. We begin our estimate of sales for a stock-market series with a prediction of nominal GNP from one of several banks or financial service firms that regularly publish such estimates.[3] Using this estimate of nominal GNP, we can estimate corporate sales based on the historical relationship between S&P 400 sales per share and aggregate economic activity (GNP).

ESTIMATING SALES PER SHARE FOR A MARKET SERIES

As noted, we will use a sales figure for an existing stock-market series—the S&P 400 Industrial Index.[4] The plot in Figure 18.2 shows the relationship between the annual percentage changes in GNP and S&P 400 sales per share contained in Table 18.2. Generally,

---

[3] This would include projections by Standard & Poor's appearing late in the year in *The Outlook*, projections by several of the large investment firms such as Goldman, Sachs & Company ("The Pocket Chartbook"), Merrill Lynch, as well as by banks. *The Wall Street Journal* publishes a survey of over 50 economists every six months that includes estimates of various interest rates, GDP, inflation, and the value of the dollar versus the Japanese yen. For a recent survey, see Fred R. Bleakley, "Economy's Strength Is Seen Cooling in Second Half," *The Wall Street Journal* (July 1, 1996): A2.

[4] Sales per share figures are available from 1945 in Standard & Poor's *Analysts Handbook* (New York: Standard & Poor's Corporation). Because the composite series include numerous companies of different sizes, all data are on a per share basis. The book is updated annually, and some series are updated quarterly in a monthly supplement.

FIGURE 18.2

SCATTER PLOT OF ANNUAL PERCENTAGE CHANGES IN S&P 400 SALES AND GNP

there is a strong relationship between the two series whereby a large proportion of the percentage changes in S&P 400 sales per share can be explained by percentage changes in nominal GNP. The reason the relationship is not stronger is that the S&P 400 sales series is more volatile than the GNP series including the fact that the GNP series never experienced a decline. The equation for the least-squares regression line relating annual percentage changes (% Δ) in the two series for the period 1975–1995 is

$$\% \ \Delta \ \text{S\&P 400 Sales}_t = -3.60 + 1.38 \ (\% \ \Delta \text{ in Nominal GNP}_t)$$
$$(-0.85) \ (4.06)$$
$$\text{Adj. } R^2 = 0.40 \quad F(1,29) = 16.48$$

These results indicate that about 40 percent of the variance in percentage changes in S&P 400 sales can be explained by percentage changes in the nominal GNP. Notably, the −3.60 intercept value is statistically insignificant and can be ignored when using this regression for estimating sales per share. Thus, given an estimate of the expected percentage change in nominal GNP for next year, we can estimate the percentage change in sales for the S&P 400 series and therefore the amount of sales per share. For example, assume the consensus estimate by economists is that nominal GNP next year will increase by approximately 6 percent (a 3 percent increase in real GNP plus 3 percent inflation). This estimate combined with the regression results implies the following estimated increase in S&P 400 sales:

$$\% \ \Delta \ \text{S\&P 400 Sales} = +1.38(.06)$$
$$= 0.003$$

| TABLE 18.2 | NOMINAL GNP AND STANDARD & POOR'S INDUSTRIAL SALES PER SHARE: 1975–1995 |

Year	Nominal GNP (Billions of Dollars)	Percentage Change	S&P 400 Sales (Dollar Value of Sales per Share)	Percentage Change
1975	1598.4	8.53	185.16	1.68
1976	1728.8	8.16	202.66	9.45
1977	1990.5	15.14	224.24	10.65
1978	2249.7	13.02	251.32	12.08
1979	2508.2	11.49	292.38	16.34
1980	2732.9	8.96	327.36	11.96
1981	3052.6	11.70	344.31	5.18
1982	3166.0	3.71	333.86	−3.04
1983	3405.7	7.57	334.07	0.06
1984	3772.2	10.76	379.70	13.66
1985	4010.3	6.31	398.42	4.93
1986	4235.0	5.60	387.76	−2.68
1987	4539.9	7.20	430.35	10.98
1988	4900.4	7.94	486.92	13.15
1989	5250.8	7.15	541.38	11.18
1990	5546.1	5.62	594.55	9.82
1991	5724.8	3.22	586.86	−1.29
1992	6020.3	5.16	601.39	2.48
1993	6343.3	5.37	603.62	0.37
1994	6738.4	6.23	631.51	4.62
1995[e]	7088.8	5.20	655.51	3.80
Average		8.10		7.50

[e] estimate

Source: *Standard & Poor's Analysts Handbook* (New York: Standard & Poor's Corporation, 1995). Reprinted by permission of Standard & Poor's Corp.

Notably, this is referred to as a *point estimate of sales* because it is based on a point estimate of GNP. Although we know there is actually a *distribution* of estimates for GNP, we have used the mean value, or expected value, as our point estimate. In actual practice, you would probably consider several estimates and assign probabilities to each of them.

ALTERNATIVE ESTIMATES OF CORPORATE NET PROFITS

Once sales per share for the market series have been estimated, the difficult estimate is the net profit margin. Three alternative procedures are possible depending on the desired level of aggregation.

The first is a direct estimate of the *net* profit margin based on recent trends. As shown in Table 18.3, the net profit margin series is quite volatile because of changes in depreciation, interest, and the tax rate over time. As such, it is the most difficult series to estimate.

The second procedure would attempt to estimate the *net before tax* (NBT) profit margin. Once the NBT margin is derived, a separate estimate of the tax rate is obtained based on recent tax rates and current government tax pronouncements. Examples of critical tax rate estimates were during 1987 and 1988 following the 1986 Tax Reform Act and in 1993–1994 following the Clinton deficit reduction program.

The third method estimates an *operating* profit margin, defined as earnings before depreciation, interest, and taxes as a percentage of sales (EBDIT). Because this measure of operating earnings as a percentage of sales is not influenced by changes in depreciation allowances, interest expense, or tax rates, it should be a stable series compared to either the

| TABLE 18.3 | **S&P 400 SALES PER SHARE AND COMPONENTS OF OPERATING PROFIT MARGIN: 1977–1995** |

		EBDIT		DEPRECIATION		INTEREST		INCOME TAX		NET INCOME	
Year	Sales per Share	Per Share	Percent of Sales	Per Share	Percent of Sales	Per Share	Percent of Sales	Per Share	Tax Rate	Per Share	Percent of Sales
1977	224.24	34.34	15.31	8.53	3.80	3.22	1.44	11.14	49.31	11.45	5.11
1978	251.32	38.63	15.37	9.64	3.84	3.81	1.52	12.14	48.21	13.04	5.19
1979	292.38	45.71	15.63	10.82	3.70	4.58	1.57	14.02	46.26	16.29	5.57
1980	327.36	48.11	14.70	12.37	3.78	5.95	1.82	13.67	45.89	16.12	4.92
1981	344.31	51.00	14.81	13.82	4.01	7.49	2.18	12.95	43.62	16.74	4.86
1982	333.86	47.68	14.28	15.30	4.58	8.23	2.47	10.95	45.34	13.20	3.95
1983	334.07	50.18	15.02	15.67	4.69	7.62	2.28	12.12	45.07	14.77	4.42
1984	379.70	57.11	15.04	16.31	4.30	8.54	2.25	14.15	43.86	18.11	4.77
1985	398.42	56.39	14.15	18.19	4.57	9.24	2.32	13.68	47.24	15.28	3.84
1986	387.76	54.70	14.11	19.41	5.01	9.75	2.51	11.01	43.11	14.53	3.75
1987	430.35	64.59	15.01	20.21	4.70	10.14	2.36	13.96	40.77	20.28	4.71
1988	486.92	80.02	16.43	23.59	4.84	14.84	3.05	15.00	36.07	26.59	5.46
1989	541.38	85.56	15.80	24.21	4.47	18.79	3.47	15.73	36.96	26.83	4.96
1990	594.55	87.52	14.72	26.31	4.43	20.17	3.39	16.27	39.64	24.77	4.17
1991	586.86	75.35	12.84	27.50	4.69	18.74	3.19	12.20	41.91	16.91	2.88
1992	601.39	76.74	12.76	29.48	4.90	16.20	2.69	12.01	38.67	19.05	3.17
1993	603.62	78.67	13.03	28.72	4.76	14.66	2.43	13.36	37.86	21.93	3.63
1994	631.51	95.64	15.14	29.92	4.74	13.55	2.15	19.07	36.55	33.10	5.24
1995[e]	655.51	103.57	15.80	31.60	4.82	12.50	1.91	21.10	35.48	38.37	5.85

[e]This is used as an estimate of operating earnings.

Source: *Standard & Poor's Analysts Handbook* (New York: Standard & Poor's Corporation, 1995). Reprinted by permission of Standard & Poor's Corp.

net profit margin or net before tax margin series. Our analysis will begin with estimating this operating profit series.

After we estimate this operating profit margin, we will multiply it by the sales estimate to derive a dollar estimate of operating EBDIT. Subsequently, we will derive separate estimates of depreciation and interest expenses, which are subtracted from the EBDIT to arrive at earnings before taxes (EBT). Finally, we estimate the expected tax rate (T) and multiply EBT times $(1 - T)$ to get our estimate of net income. The following sections discuss the details of estimating earnings per share beginning with the operating profit margin.

ESTIMATING AGGREGATE OPERATING PROFIT MARGIN   Finkel and Tuttle hypothesized that the following four variables affected the aggregate profit margin.[5]

1. Capacity utilization rate
2. Unit labor costs
3. Rate of inflation
4. Foreign competition

CAPACITY UTILIZATION RATE   One would expect a positive relationship between the capacity utilization rate and the profit margin because if production increases as a propor-

---

[5] Sidney R. Finkel and Donald L. Tuttle, "Determinants of the Aggregate Profit Margin," *Journal of Finance* 26, no. 5 (December 1971): 1067–1075.

TABLE 18.4

VARIABLES THAT AFFECT THE AGGREGATE PROFIT MARGIN: CAPACITY UTILIZATION RATE, PERCENTAGE CHANGE IN COMPENSATION, PRODUCTIVITY, UNIT LABOR COST, AND CONSUMER PRICE INDEX: 1975–1995

Year	Utilization Rate (Mfg.)	COMPENSATION/ WORK HOURS[a] Percentage Rate	OUTPUT/ WORK HOURS[b] Percentage Change	UNIT LABOR COST[a] Percentage Change	Rate of Inflation[b]
1975	74.6	10.1	2.7	7.3	7.0
1976	79.3	8.7	3.7	4.7	4.8
1977	83.3	8.0	1.5	6.4	6.8
1978	85.5	9.1	1.3	7.7	9.0
1979	86.2	9.5	−0.7	10.3	13.3
1980	82.1	10.8	−0.4	11.2	12.4
1981	80.9	9.7	1.2	8.4	8.9
1982	75.0	7.4	−0.9	8.3	3.9
1983	75.8	4.2	4.2	0.0	3.8
1984	81.1	4.3	1.8	2.4	4.0
1985	80.3	4.6	1.0	3.6	3.8
1986	79.2	5.2	2.7	2.5	1.1
1987	81.5	3.7	−0.2	4.0	4.4
1988	83.7	4.3	0.6	3.7	4.4
1989	83.7	2.7	0.5	2.1	4.6
1990	82.1	5.5	0.5	5.0	6.1
1991	79.2	4.9	0.7	4.3	3.1
1992	80.3	5.2	3.2	1.9	3.0
1993	81.4	2.3	0.2	2.1	2.7
1994	83.9	2.2	0.5	1.6	2.7
1995[c]	84.1	2.0	0.5	1.5	2.5

[a]Private nonfarm business, 1992 = 100. Source: Department of Labor, Bureau of Labor Statistics.
[b]Percentage Change (December to December) Consumer Price Index, All Items (1982–1984 = 100).
[c]1995 figures are preliminary or estimates.

Source: Federal Reserve Board Series, "Total Manufacturing," in *Economic Report of the President, 1996* (Washington DC: U.S. Government Printing Office, 1996).

tion of total capacity, there is a decrease in per-unit fixed production costs and fixed financial costs. The relationship may not be completely linear at very high rates of capacity utilization because operating diseconomies are introduced as firms are forced to use marginal labor and/or older plant and equipment to reach the higher capacity. The figures in Table 18.4 indicate that capacity utilization ranged from a peak of over 86 percent in 1979 to a trough of less than 75 percent during the recession of 1975.

UNIT LABOR COST   The change in unit labor cost is a compound effect of two individual factors: (1) changes in wages per hour and (2) changes in worker productivity. Wage costs per hour typically increase every year by varying amounts depending on the economic environment. As shown in Table 18.4, the annual percentage increase in wages varied from 2.2 percent to about 10.8 percent. If workers did not become more productive, this increase in per-hour wage costs would be the increase in per-unit labor cost. Fortunately, because of advances in technology and greater mechanization, the worker units of output per hour (labor productivity) have increased over time—the laborer has become *more productive*. If wages per hour increase by 5 percent and labor productivity increases by 5 percent, there would be no increase in unit labor costs because the workers would offset wage increases by producing more. Therefore, the increase in *per-unit labor cost* is a function of the percentage change in hourly wages minus the increase in productivity during the period. The actual relationship typically is not this exact due to measurement problems, but it is quite close as indicated by the figures in Table 18.4. For example, during 1983 productivity increased by as much as the hourly compensation did, so there was no change in unit labor cost. In contrast, during 1980, wage rates increased by 10.8 percent, productivity *declined* by 0.4 percent because of the recession, and, therefore, unit labor costs increased by 11.2 percent. Because unit labor is the major variable cost of a firm, one would expect a *negative* relationship between the operating profit margin and percentage changes in unit labor cost—i.e., a small (below average) change in unit labor cost should correspond to an above average operating profit margin.

RATE OF INFLATION   The precise effect of inflation on the aggregate profit margin is unresolved. Finkel and Tuttle hypothesized a positive relationship between inflation and the profit margin for several reasons. First, it was contended that a higher level of inflation increases the ability of firms to pass higher costs on to the consumer and thereby raise their profit margin. Second, assuming the classical demand-pull inflation, the increase in prices would indicate an increase in general economic activity, which typically is accompanied by higher margins. Finally, an increase in the rate of inflation might stimulate consumption as individuals attempt to shift their holdings from financial assets to real assets, which would contribute to an expansion.

In contrast, many observers doubt that most businesses can consistently increase prices in line with rising costs. Assume a 5 percent rate of inflation that impacts labor and material costs. The question is whether all firms can *completely* pass these cost increases along to their customers. If a firm increases prices at the same rate as cost increases, the result will be a *constant* profit margin, *not* an increase. Only if a firm can raise prices by *more than* cost increases can it increase its margin. Many firms are not able to raise prices in line with increased costs because of the elasticity of demand for their products.[6] Such an environment will cause the profit margin to decline. Given the three alternative scenarios, it is contended that most firms will not be able to increase their profit margins or even hold them constant. Because many firms will experience lower profit margins during periods of inflation, it is expected that the aggregate profit margin will probably decline when there is an increase in the rate of inflation.

Given the contrasting expectations, one would need to consider the empirical evidence to determine how inflation has affected the operating profit margin.

FOREIGN COMPETITION   Finkel and Tuttle contend that export markets are more competitive than domestic markets so export sales are made at a lower margin. This implies that lower exports by U.S. firms would increase profit margins. In contrast, Gray believed that only exports made by two independent firms should be considered, and they should be examined relative to total output exported.[7] Further, he felt that imports could have an important negative impact on the operating profit margin because they influence the selling price of all competing domestic products. This impact of imports has been a major factor

---

[6] An extreme example of this inability is regulated industries that may not be able to raise prices at all until after lengthy hearings before regulatory agencies. Even then, the increase in rates may not match the cost increases.

[7] H. Peter Gray, "Determinants of the Aggregate Profit Margin: A Comment," *Journal of Finance* 31, no. 1 (March 1976): 163–165.

since the early 1980s when the U.S. trade balance became very negative. Therefore, there is a divergence of expectations regarding the ultimate effect of foreign trade on the operating profit margin, so it is likewise an empirical question.

The results of the empirical tests by Finkel and Tuttle can be summarized as follows:

- Utilization rate—positive and significant at 0.01 level
- Unit labor cost—negative and significant at 0.01 level
- Inflation—positive and significant at 0.05 level
- Trade surplus—negative and significant at 0.01 level

Analysis of the annual data for the period 1977 to 1994 confirmed that the relationship between the operating profit margin and the capacity utilization rate was always significant and positive, whereas the relationship between the unit labor cost and the operating profit margin was always negative and significant. Alternatively, the rate of inflation and foreign trade variables were never significant in the multiple regression. Finally, the simple correlation between the profit margin and inflation was consistently *negative*.

Therefore, when estimating the operating profit margin, you should concentrate on the capacity utilization rate for the economy and the rate of change in unit labor cost. As an example, consider what will happen at two extremes of the business cycle. At the end of an economic recession, the capacity utilization rate will be very low. Therefore, during the early stages of an economic recovery, a large increase in capacity utilization exists as firms increase production and sales. At the same time, workers will not be asking for very large wage increases and as production increases, there will be large increases in labor productivity. As a result, unit labor costs will increase very slowly (or could decline). Therefore, as a result of an increase in capacity utilization and a very small increase (or a decline) in unit labor cost, there should be a large increase in the operating profit margin.

In contrast, at the peak of the business cycle, firms will be operating at full capacity, so there will be very small increases or possibly declines in capacity utilization. Also, one would expect a higher rate of inflation, which will prompt demands for large wage increases during a time when you would expect small increases in labor productivity because firms are using marginal labor and production facilities. The effect will be large increases in unit labor cost. Therefore, as a result of very small increases or possibly decreases in capacity utilization and large increases in unit labor cost, there should be a major decline in the operating profit margin at the peak of a business cycle.

How do you use this information to estimate an operating profit margin? The most important estimate is *the direction of the change from current levels.* Assuming that you know the recent operating profit margin, your primary analysis should be concerned with deciding whether the profit margin will increase, decrease, or stay about the same based on your expectation regarding capacity utilization and changes in unit labor cost. The size of the estimated change in the operating profit margin will depend on where the economy is in the business cycle and the direction and size of the expected changes in capacity utilization and unit labor cost.

After estimating the operating profit margin, you can calculate the dollar value of the EBDIT by applying this operating profit margin estimate to the previously estimated sales per share figure. The next step is to estimate depreciation per share, which we subtract from operating profits to get EBIT. Table 18.3 contains data on the operating earnings components for the period since 1977, which is when S&P began providing this detailed breakdown of the earnings statement.

FIGURE 18.3   TIME SERIES PLOT OF S&P 400 DEPRECIATION (PER SHARE DATA, ADJUSTED TO STOCK PRICE INDEX LEVEL)

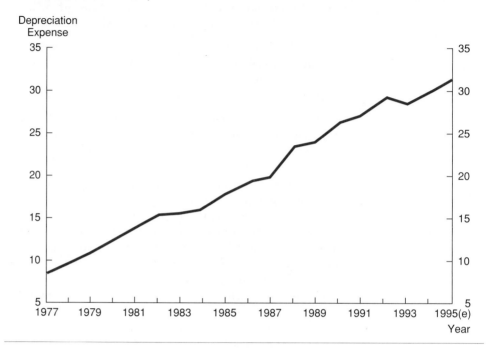

ESTIMATING DEPRECIATION EXPENSE

As shown in Figure 18.3, the depreciation expense per share series has declined only once since 1977 (in 1993). This is not surprising because depreciation expense is an estimate of the fixed cost expense related to the total fixed assets held by the S&P 400 industrial firms. Naturally, this fixed asset base increases over time. Therefore, the relevant question when estimating depreciation expense is generally *not* whether it will increase or decrease, but by *how much will it increase*.

You can use time series analysis, which involves using the recent trend as a guide to the future increase. Probably the biggest external factor that could influence the rate of growth of the depreciation expense series is recent capital expenditures. If capital expenditures have been above normal, you would expect subsequent depreciation expense to grow at an above average rate. Recently, the average annual percentage increase in depreciation expense has been in the range of 5 to 8 percent. Because a column in the figure indicates that depreciation is a percent of sales, you might consider this as an estimating approach—this would be a *mistake*. Depreciation is clearly a *fixed* expense, which means generally it is independent of sales and so should not be expected to vary with sales. As shown, depreciation as a percent of sales has varied from 3.70 percent to over 5 percent, which is consistent with its fixed nature. Based on these factors, you would estimate what you expect for this year. After you have estimated the depreciation expense, you subtract it from the operating profit estimate to get an EBIT estimate.

ESTIMATING INTEREST EXPENSE

As shown in Table 18.3, interest expense of the companies in the S&P 400 series generally increased in absolute value until 1991 and increased as a percentage of sales from 1.44 percent in 1977 to a peak of 3.47 percent in 1989. This growth is consistent with our prior discussions, which alluded to the overall increase in debt financing and financial risk assumed by U.S. firms—especially during the 1980s. This strong growth of interest expense was reversed after the 1989–1990 recession because (1) corporations reduced their debt levels and (2) interest rates declined. The estimate of interest expense should be based on an estimate of debt outstanding (will it grow and by how much?) and the level of interest rates (do you expect interest rates to rise or decline in the future?). Similar to depreciation, this generally is a fixed expense that is impacted by corporate financing decisions and the cost of debt (i.e., interest rates). Therefore, interest expense as a percent of sales is a very unstable value and should *not* be used when estimating this value.

After you have estimated the interest expense figure, this value is subtracted from the EBIT per share value to estimate EBT.

ESTIMATING THE
TAX RATE

This is the final step in estimating the earnings per share for the S&P 400 series. As shown in Table 18.3 and Figure 18.4, the average tax rate for the firms in the S&P 400 series during the late 1970s was in the 45 to 50 percent range. During the 1980s, it declined to almost 35 percent (in 1988) following the 1986 Tax Reform Act, then reversed and increased during the period 1989–1991, followed by declines in 1992–1994. Subsequently, we speculate on what will happen in 1996.

Estimating the future tax rate is difficult because it depends on political action. You must evaluate the current tax rate and recent tax legislation that affects business firms (e.g., tax credits). Once you have estimated the tax rate (T), you multiply one minus this tax rate ($1 - T$) times the EBT per-share figure to derive an estimate of the net income per share for the S&P 400 series.

FIGURE 18.4   **TIME SERIES PLOT OF S&P 400 TAX RATE**

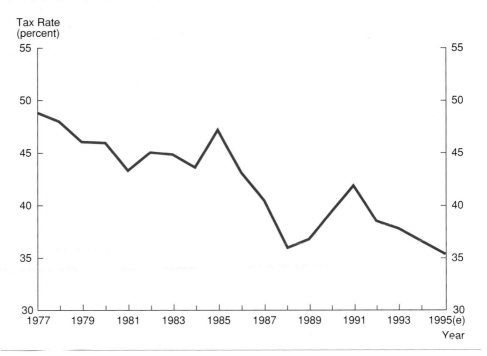

At this point, we have derived an estimate of sales per share for an aggregate stock-market series and discussed how to estimate an operating profit margin and several specific expense items to estimate earnings per share. In the next section, we demonstrate this procedure by estimating earnings per share for 1996.

CALCULATING
EARNINGS PER SHARE:
AN EXAMPLE

The following demonstration for estimating earnings per share emphasizes the procedure rather than the actual numbers. An analyst engaged in this exercise would take much longer and be involved in a very detailed analysis. In this example, we estimate earnings per share for the S&P 400 during 1996 using 1995 data.

STEP 1   Nominal GNP for 1996 is based on an estimate for 1995 of approximately $7,089 billion. In 1995, the economy was in the fifth year of expansion following a recession in 1989–1990. The consensus is that the United States experienced a "soft landing" in 1995 engineered by the Federal Reserve. During this sixth year of expansion, real GNP is expected to increase by about 2.5 percent and inflation will be approximately 3 percent. Therefore, nominal GNP in 1996 should increase by about 5.5 percent to $7,479 billion.

STEP 2   Corporate sales have had a strong relationship with nominal GNP as shown in Figure 18.2. During 1995, when nominal GNP increased by about 5 percent, S&P sales were expected to grow by about 4 percent to $655 per share. In 1996, with GNP rising 5.5 percent, this model indicates that sales should increase by about 4.5 percent to $684 per share.

STEP 3   The operating profit margin increased to about 15.80 percent in 1995, compared to 15.14 percent in 1994. This increase was a function of a higher utilization rate (84.1 percent in 1995 compared to 83.9 percent during 1994), and a lower rate of increase in unit labor cost (1.5 percent in 1995 versus 1.6 percent during 1994). For 1996, the outlook is for a small decrease in the operating profit margin because of little if any increase in the capacity utilization rate, and, if it does increase, we would be at the point of diseconomies. We also expect a larger increase in unit labor cost. Specifically, compensation per hour will likely experience a relatively small increase, but there will be limited gains in productivity during 1996 since we are in the sixth year of expansion. Therefore, the outlook is for a 3 percent increase in unit labor cost. In summary, the outlook is for a decline in the operating profit margin from 15.80 percent in 1995 to 15.40 percent in 1996. Applying this operating profit margin to the sales per share figure ($684) indicates an operating profit (EBDIT) of $105.34 (.1540 × $684).

STEP 4   The depreciation expense during 1995 was approximately $31.60 per share. Because the utilization rate is relatively high, the expectation is for an increase in capital expenditures of about 7 percent during 1996 and, therefore, an increase in depreciation expense of about 5.5 percent to $33.34 per share. Thus the estimated EBIT is $72.00 ($105.34 − $33.34).

STEP 5   The interest expense declined in 1995 because of a constant debt level and the steady decline in interest rates during the year. Interest expense will be slightly lower in 1996 because rates are beginning at a low level and are not expected to increase very much during the year. Based on this interest rate scenario and no major change in leverage, interest expense is estimated at $12.00.

When we subtract this interest expense from the EBIT estimate of $72.00, we have an EBT of $60.00.

STEP 6   The corporate tax rate during 1995 was expected to be slightly lower than during 1994. The tax rate is expected to remain fairly constant during 1996. Applying a 64.5 percent after tax rate $(1 - .355)$ to the NBT figure of \$60.00 indicates that the net income per share for 1996 will be approximately \$38.70. Therefore, the 1996 earnings per share estimate used in future discussions is \$38.70 a share.

This per share estimate can be summarized as follows:

Sales	\$684.00
EBDIT	105.34 (.1540)
Depreciation	33.34
EBIT	72.00
Interest Expense	12.00
EBT	60.00
Taxes	21.30 (.355)
Net Income (EPS)	\$ 38.70

ESTIMATING THE EARNINGS MULTIPLIER FOR A STOCK-MARKET SERIES

Given our estimate of earnings per share, the next step is to estimate an earnings multiplier. A combination of the earnings per share estimate times the estimated earnings multiplier provides an estimate of the future value for the stock-market series. This estimated value for the stock-market series and an estimate of the dividend during the year are used to compute the expected rate of return for investors who own a portfolio of stocks during this holding period.

Our prior discussion related to Table 18.1 indicated that the earnings multiplier (i.e., P/E ratio) over time has been more volatile than the earnings per share series because the multiplier is very sensitive to changes in the spread between k and g. Earlier we discussed several instances where the changes in the earnings multiplier (P/E ratio) was the dominant factor in stock price changes. Because of the significance of the earnings multiplier, we will examine each of the variables in the P/E ratio equation to determine what determines the value for them and why they change. Given this understanding, we can consider the whole P/E ratio equation and demonstrate how an investor would estimate a value for the earnings multiplier.

DETERMINANTS OF THE EARNINGS MULTIPLIER

Recall the variables that influence the earnings multiplier or the P/E ratio by using the equation generated from the dividend discount model:

$$P/E = \frac{D_1/E_1}{k - g}$$

where

> D_1 = dividends expected in period 1, which is equal to $D_0(1 + g)$
> E_1 = earnings expected in period 1
> D_1/E_1 = the dividend-payout ratio expected in period 1
> k = the required rate of return on the stock
> g = the expected growth rate of dividends for the stock

Therefore, the major variables that affect the earnings multiplier for common stocks in a country are

- The dividend-payout ratio.
- The required rate of return on common stock in the country being analyzed.
- The expected growth rate of dividends for the stocks in the country being analyzed.

Because this equation is derived from the dividend discount model, it assumes constant growth for an infinite period. Also, the required rate of return is the long-term estimate. Therefore, the k and g projections are *long-term estimates*. Thus, although these variables can be impacted by near-term events, they should not experience major changes on a year-to-year basis.

It is easier to discuss the dividend-payout ratio after we have considered both k and g. Therefore, the order of discussion will be

- Estimating k, the required rate of return
- Estimating g, the growth rate of dividends
- Estimating D_1/E_1, the dividend-payout ratio

ESTIMATING THE REQUIRED RATE OF RETURN (k)   The multiplier equation indicates that the earnings multiplier is inversely related to the required rate of return; the higher an investor's required rate of return, the less he or she will pay for a future earnings stream. Our prior discussions indicated that the required rate of return (k) is determined by (1) the economy's risk-free rate (RFR); (2) the expected rate of inflation during the period of investment (I): and (3) the risk premium (RP) for the specific investment.

The nominal risk-free rate   We combined the first two factors (the RFR and I) into a nominal risk-free rate that affects *all* investments. We saw that the major factor causing changes in the nominal RFR is changes in the expected rate of inflation. Specifically, if the expected rate of inflation changes, investors should increase their nominal required rate of return as follows:

$$\text{Nominal RFR} = (1 + \text{Real RFR})(1 + I) - 1.$$

For example, if the real RFR were 3 percent and you expected the rate of inflation during your period of investment to be 4 percent, your nominal risk-free required rate of return would be 7.12 percent [(1.03)(1.04) − 1]. A good proxy for the nominal RFR rate is the current promised yield to maturity of a government bond that has a maturity equal to your investment horizon. For example, if you had a short horizon, you could use the rate on Treasury bills, whereas you would use intermediate or long-term government bond rates if your horizon extended over several years. The tendency during the recent past has been to use the intermediate bond rate (i.e., about 5 years) because it reflects the attitude of most investors who feel that one year is too short and 15–20 years is too long.

The equity risk premium   The attitude toward the estimation of the equity risk premium has undergone significant changes during the 1990s. The initial rigorous empirical estimate of an equity risk premium was provided by the pioneering work of Ibbotson and Sinquefield. In their monograph for the Financial Analysts Research Foundation, they estimated the risk premium on common stock as a mean of the difference in the annual rates of return from common stocks and Treasury Bills,[8] Although the original estimate

---

[8] Roger G. Ibbotson and Rex A. Sinquefield, *Stocks, Bonds, Bills and Inflation: The Past and Future* (Charlottesville, VA: Financial Analysts Research Foundation, 1982).

was for 1926–1981, this estimated risk premium has been updated annually in a yearbook provided by Ibbotson Associates.[9] For example, the equity risk premium as of 1996 for 1926–1995 was 8.4 percent using the arithmetic mean of the annual values, and was 6.8 percent using the geometric mean of the annual values. The geometric mean is appropriate for long-run asset class comparisons, whereas the arithmetic mean is what you would use to estimate the premium for a given year (e.g., the *expected* performance next year). Because our application is to the long-term DDM model, the geometric mean value would probably be more appropriate, which implies using the 6.8 percent risk premium value.

An additional adjustment is suggested to reflect the belief that the typical investment horizon is longer than that implied by the T-bill rate. Assuming that most investors consider the intermediate time frame (five years) a more appropriate investment horizon, the risk premium should be computed as the stock return less the return on intermediate government bonds. Given the typical upward sloping yield curve, it is not surprising that this measure of the risk premium is about 1 percent less than the T-bill premium—i.e., the arithmetic mean of the annual risk premiums relative to intermediate government bonds was 7.4 percent during 1926–1995, and the geometric mean of the annual risk premiums was 5.9 percent. Therefore, the risk premium to use should be about *6 percent*, if you are interested in the long-term historical estimate.

Several authors have contended that there are problems with this estimate in a dynamic real-world environment. The major criticism is that it is *too long term* and assumes that the *market-risk premium is almost a constant value*.[10] Given that we are dealing with an average value that encompasses about 70 years, this technique will not reflect any changes over time. There are ways to adjust for this constant value problem and there are estimation suggestions.

The first suggestion to adjust for the constant value is to use a constant period moving average for the Ibbotson-Sinquefield technique—e.g., rather than a single mean value for the total period since 1926, employ a 20- or 10-year moving average of the series. This would indicate any trends in the series over time, with the 10-year moving average being more sensitive to changes. Figures 18.5 and 18.6 show the impact of employing a moving average and using the intermediate bond return as the risk-free asset. These time series plots also suggest that the risk premium series is not very stable since the 20-year moving average values vary from about 1 percent to 16 percent.

Beyond the historical equity risk premium approach, three other approaches have been suggested. These include (1) the dividend yield estimate, (2) the credit risk series, and (3) an estimate based on the relative volatility of stocks versus bonds.

A paper by Rozeff reviews the equity risk premium (RP) concept similar to what is discussed in this book.[11] This is followed by a review of alternative measures of the RP, including the Ibbotson-Sinquefield series, an estimate using the CAPM, and a brief consideration of the default risk premium (referred to as the credit risk series). Rozeff shows that, given some economic assumptions, the risk premium on equity is equal to the dividend yield. He further contends that when the dividend yield exceeds 6 percent, it is an excellent time to buy stocks; and when the yield is below 3 percent, it is generally a poor time to buy stocks. Some relatively casual empirical results were provided to support these

---

[9] *Stocks, Bonds, Bills and Inflation* (Chicago, IL: Ibbotson Associates, annual).

[10] This is the contention contained in, Michael Rozeff, "Dividend Yields Are Equity Risk Premiums," *Journal of Portfolio Management* 11, no. 1 (Fall, 1984): 68–75.

[11] Michael Rozeff, "Dividend Yields Are Equity Risk Premiums," *Journal of Portfolio Management* 11, no. 1 (Fall 1984): 68–75.

FIGURE 18.5

INTERMEDIATE-TERM EQUITY RISK PREMIUM: 10-YEAR MOVING ARITHMETIC AND GEOMETRIC AVERAGES

contentions. This decision rule has not worked during the period 1991–1995 and especially 1995 because during 1995 the dividend yield was typically about 2.5 percent and yet, stocks experienced a rate of return that exceeded 30 percent.

The credit risk premium is a concept that has been referred to on several occasions in this book when discussing changes in the capital market risk premium. The notion is that changes in the absolute or percentage spread between the yield on BAA and AAA bonds indicates a change in the required rate of return by the investors for accepting credit risk. Further, this change in the credit risk premium implies a change in the slope of the security market line (SML). The percent yield spread is considered a preferable measure because it adjusts for the level of yields. An advantage of the credit risk measure is that it is based on current market results and reflects the investors' attitudes.

An alternative estimate of the equity risk premium is suggested by Reichenstein and Rich—namely the Value Line forecast of dividends and capital gain.[12] This total market

---

[12] William Reichenstein and Steven P. Rich, "The Market Risk Premium and Long-Term Stock Returns," *Journal of Portfolio Management* 19, no. 4 (Summer 1993): 63–72.

FIGURE 18.6

INTERMEDIATE-TERM EQUITY RISK PREMIUM: 20-YEAR MOVING ARITHMETIC AND GEOMETRIC AVERAGES

return less short-term government bond yield is shown to provide better and more consistent results than an earnings price value or dividend yield.

A comparison used by Woolridge to justify a change in the equity risk premium is the relative volatility of stocks versus bonds.[13] Woolridge argues that the risk premium for equity has declined from the 6 percent estimate based on the Ibbotson-Sinquefield data to about 2.5 percent because of the *increase* in bond market volatility relative to stock volatility.[14] Specifically, the risk premium spread has declined, not because stocks have become less volatile, but because bonds have become more volatile. Thus, the difference in risk between the two asset classes is less than before, so the spread has declined.

In summary, if you use the current intermediate government bond rate as your estimate of the minimal RFR, these studies indicate that the equity risk premium should be some-

---

[13] Randall Woolridge, "Do Stock Prices Reflect Fundamental Values?" *Journal of Applied Corporate Finance* 8, no. 1 (Spring 1995): 64–69.

[14] For an analysis of relative volatility of bonds versus stocks, see Frank K. Reilly and David J. Wright, "An Analysis of Changes in Bond Market Volatility," Working Paper, University of Notre Dame College of Business Administration (February 1996).

where between 2.5 percent and 6.0 percent, depending on the current environment. In turn, you can derive an indicator of the current environment by examining the dividend yield, the prevailing credit risk spread, or the relative volatility of bonds versus stocks.

Once you have estimated the required rate of return for the current period, you must determine whether the expected rate of inflation or the risk premium on common stock will change during your investment horizon. We know that the fundamental factors that influence the risk premium are business risk (BR), financial risk (FR), liquidity risk (LR), exchange rate risk (ERR), and country risk (CR). These latter two risk components become important when investing in non-U.S. equity.

To incorporate these factors into the estimate of k, the required return on common stocks can be expressed as:

$$k_e = f(\text{RFR}, I, \text{BR}, \text{FR}, \text{LR}, \text{ERR}, \text{CR})$$

where

> k_e = the required return on equity
> RFR = the economy's risk-free rate of return
> I = the expected rate of inflation
> BR = aggregate corporate business risk
> FR = aggregate corporate financial risk
> LR = aggregate stock-market liquidity risk
> ERR = exchange rate risk
> CR = country risk

ESTIMATING THE GROWTH RATE OF DIVIDENDS (g)   The earnings multiple that is applied to next year's earnings must take into account the expected growth rate (g) for common dividends.[15] There is a positive relationship between the earnings multiplier and the growth rate of earnings and dividends; the higher the expected growth rate, the higher the multiple.[16] When estimating g, you should consider the current expected rate of growth and estimate any *changes* in the growth rate. Such changes in expectations indicate a change in the relationship between k and g and will have a profound effect on the earnings multiplier.

As discussed in Chapters 12 and 13, a firm's growth rate is equal to (1) the proportion of earnings retained and reinvested by the firm, that is, its retention rate (b), times (2) the rate of return earned on investments (ROE). An increase in either or both of these variables causes an increase in the expected growth rate (g) and an increase in the earnings multiplier. Therefore, the growth rate can be stated as

$$g = f(b, \text{ROE})$$

where

> g = expected growth rate
> b = the expected retention rate equal to $1 - \dfrac{D}{E}$
> ROE = the expected return on equity investments

---

[15] You know that the g in the valuation model is the expected growth rate for dividends. In our discussion, we assume a relatively constant dividend-payout ratio (dividend/earnings), so the growth of dividends is dependent on the growth in earnings, and the growth rates are approximately equal.

[16] A paper that specifically examines this relationship is Patricia M. Fairfield, "P/E, P/B, and the Present Value of Future Dividends," *Financial Analysts Journal* 50, no. 4 (July/August 1994): 23–31.

FIGURE 18.7

TIME SERIES PLOT OF S&P 400 RETENTION RATE

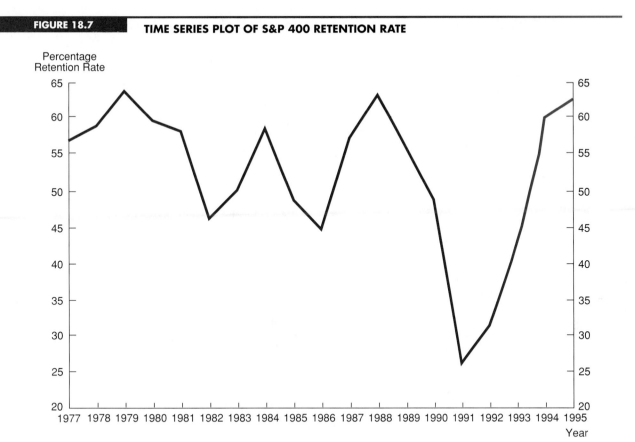

Therefore, to estimate the growth rate, you need to estimate changes in the retention rate (*b*) and the return on equity (ROE). The plot in Figure 18.7 shows that the retention rate was relatively high (56 to 63 percent) during the 1970s, declined to the 50 percent range during the early 1980s, increased back to 60 percent in 1988, declined in 1991 when earnings declined but many firms did not cut their dividends, and returned to over 50 percent during 1992–94. Because the valuation model is a long-run model, you should estimate only relatively permanent changes, although short-run changes can affect expectations. Specifically, you should recognize that the annual retention rate which has been quite volatile (between 45 and 60 percent) is heavily impacted by annual earnings changes (as will be discussed in the dividend payout section).

The second variable is changes in the return on equity (ROE) defined as

$$\text{ROE} = \frac{\text{Net Income}}{\text{Equity}}$$

You will recall from the discussion in Chapter 12 that ROE can be broken down as follows:

$$\frac{\text{Net Income}}{\text{Equity}} = \frac{\text{Net Income}}{\text{Sales}} \times \frac{\text{Sales}}{\text{Total Assets}} \times \frac{\text{Total Assets}}{\text{Equity}}$$

$$= \frac{\text{Net Profit}}{\text{Margin}} \times \frac{\text{Total Asset}}{\text{Turnover}} \times \frac{\text{Financial}}{\text{Leverage}}$$

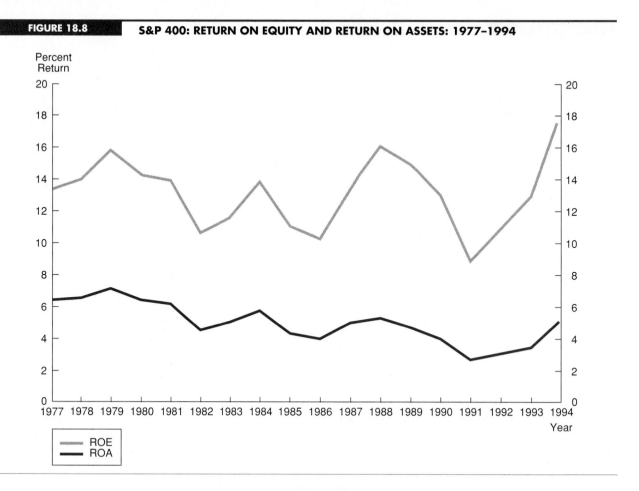

| FIGURE 18.8 | S&P 400: RETURN ON EQUITY AND RETURN ON ASSETS: 1977–1994 |

This equation shows that the ROE increases if either the equity turnover or the profit margin increases. In turn, you can increase the equity turnover by increasing either total asset turnover or financial leverage. Because the S&P 400 series includes historical information on total assets only since 1977, we examine this three-component breakdown of ROE for this 18-year period.

As shown in Figure 18.8, the ROE for the S&P 400 series experienced very little change over the 15-year period prior to the decline in 1991 and strong recovery in 1993–1994. An analysis of the three components of ROE indicate what contributed to the overall change (or lack of change) over time. First, the profit margin (Figure 18.9) ended about where it began during this period. The second component, total asset turnover (Figure 18.10) increased in 1980 and 1981, but declined subsequently and overall was much lower in 1994. Therefore, we know by process of elimination that the major variable that caused no significant change in ROE was the financial leverage ratio (Figure 18.11) that increased from about 2.00 to 3.50 in 1994.

All of this shows a need for an investor to estimate the long-term outlook for ROE, which in turn requires a long-term estimate for each of the three component ratios. Once established, multiply this long-term estimate of ROE by your estimate of b, the retention rate, to calculate an estimate of g. As an example, if you estimate the long-run retention rate

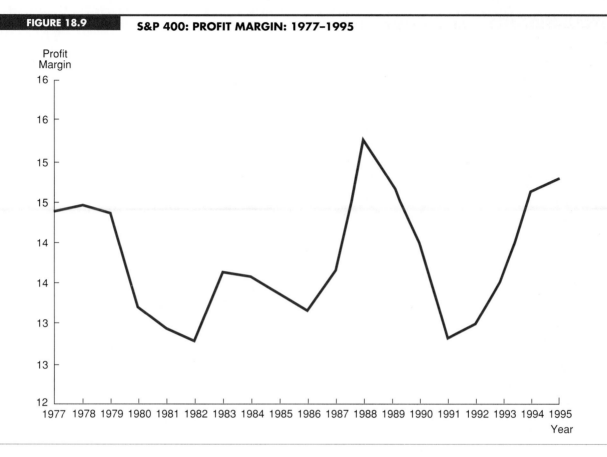

FIGURE 18.9   **S&P 400: PROFIT MARGIN: 1977–1995**

of firms will be 60 percent and their ROE at 12 percent, this means you would expect the long-run growth rate of

$$g = b \times \text{ROE}$$
$$= .60 \times .12$$
$$= .072 = 7.2\%$$

ESTIMATING THE DIVIDEND-PAYOUT RATIO (D_1/E_1)   Based on the P/E equation, there is a positive relationship between payout ratio and the P/E ratio. Therefore, if the k–g spread is constant and this dividend-payout ratio increases, there will be an increase in the earnings multiplier. At the same time, you should recognize that the dividend-payout ratio is equal to one minus the earnings retention rate (b). Therefore, if the dividend payout *increases*, there will be a *decline* in the earnings retention rate (b), which will cause a *decline* in the growth rate (g). Thus, there is a partial offset between changes in the dividend-payout rate and the expected growth rate (g).

In the discussion of the growth rate, we indicated that the retention rate was high in the 1970s, declined in the early 1980s, and increased again during the late 1980s. This implies that the payout ratio has declined recently.

DIVIDEND PAYOUT—ACTIVE OR RESIDUAL DECISION?   When examining or attempting to estimate the dividend payout for the aggregate market or an individual firm, it is

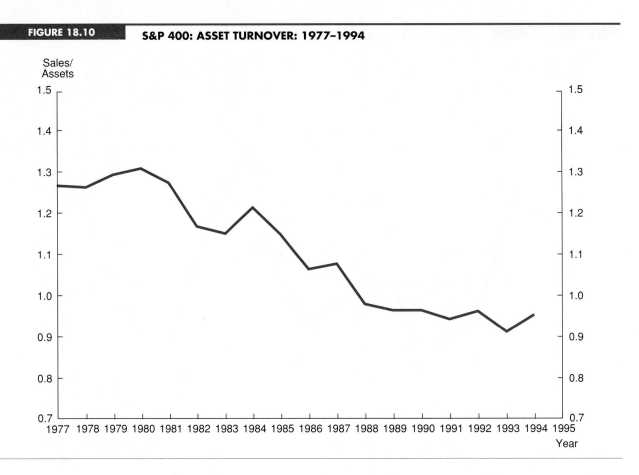

FIGURE 18.10   **S&P 400: ASSET TURNOVER: 1977–1994**

important to consider whether the payout is (1) an active decision of management (and the Board of Directors) or (2) a residual outcome because the active decision is the dividend payment. Obviously, if payout is the active decision, the dividend payment would vary over time in line with earnings. In contrast, if the dividend payout is a residual decision, then the dividend payments would be reasonably stable and show fairly steady increases while the payout ratio would be very volatile because it would be dictated by the earnings. That is, the dividend payout would increase dramatically during periods of low earnings and decline significantly during periods of abnormally high earnings.

The time series plots in Figures 18.12 and 18.13 support the residual payout theory because they show fairly constant changes in dividend payments (Figure 18.12) but high volatility for the dividend payout ratio in Figure 18.13 (the dividend payout was high during the recession in 1991 and quite low during the expansion in 1993–1994). This discussion can be summarized as follows: the annual dividend payout is inversely related to earnings changes. Put another way, there is a positive relationship between the earnings retention rate and earnings changes. Therefore, when estimating the dividend payout ratio, it is necessary to estimate the dividend payment using time series analysis and then relate this dividend to the earnings estimate. Because of its volatility, it is important *not* to emphasize annual dividend payout changes, but use a long-run perspective regarding the dividend payout ratio.

FIGURE 18.11   **S&P 400: ASSETS/EQUITY: 1977–1994**

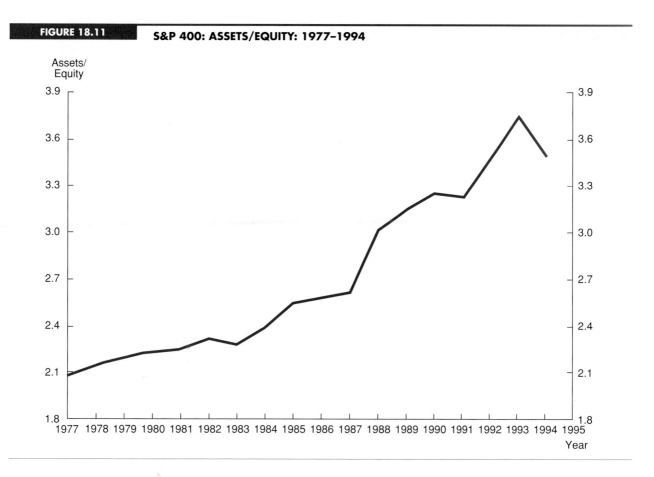

ESTIMATING AN EARNINGS MULTIPLIER: AN EXAMPLE

There are two ways to estimate the earnings multiplier based on our discussion of the multiplier variables. The first approach begins with the current earnings multiplier and attempts to estimate the direction and amount of any change based on your expectations for changes in the three major components. We will call this approach the *direction of change approach.*

In the second approach, you estimate a specific value for the earnings multiplier by deriving specific estimates for each of the three components in the P/E ratio equation. When using this approach, most analysts derive several estimates based on alternative optimistic or pessimistic scenarios. We will call this the *specific estimate approach.*

THE DIRECTION OF CHANGE APPROACH   Begin with the current earnings multiplier and estimate the direction and extent of change for the dividend payout and the variables that influence *k* and *g*. The direction of the change is more important than its size.

The variables that must be estimated are

1. Changes in the dividend-payout ratio
2. Changes in the real RFR
3. Changes in the rate of inflation   } Changes in *k*
4. Changes in the risk premium for common stock
5. Changes in the earnings retention rate   } Changes in *g*
6. Changes in the return on equity (ROE)

FIGURE 18.12   **EARNINGS PER SHARE AND DIVIDENDS PER SHARE FOR S&P 400: 1977–1995**

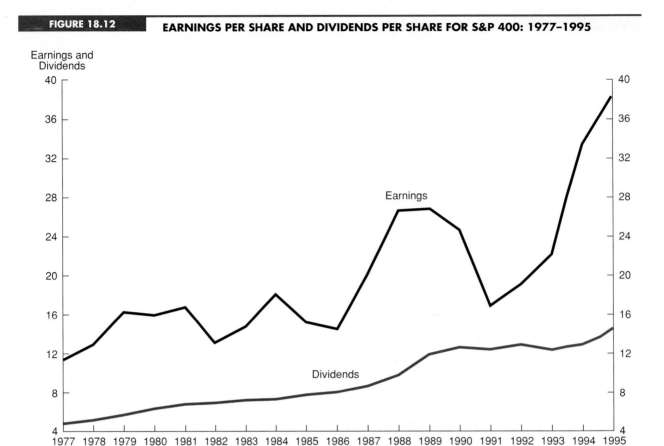

The dividend-payout ratio is expected to increase slightly in the near term because recent payout values have been lower than the historical average because of the strong earnings growth which has lead to an increase in the retention rate.

Given the three variables that affect the required rate of return on common stocks (k), there will probably be very little change in the real RFR in 1996 because there will be almost no change in the rate of real growth caused by higher productivity. The rate of inflation is likewise expected to experience very little change in 1996. Finally, the risk premium is expected to experience a small increase for two reasons. First, we are in the sixth year of a business expansion wherein there could be more uncertainty. Second, although there was a decrease in stock price volatility during the early 1990s, at the current point in the market cycle, it could increase. Therefore, given the trends in the components, overall one would expect a small increase in k during 1996.

The last two factors in the earnings multiplier estimate relate to the growth rate. We expect a small increase in the payout rate, which implies a decline in the retention rate. The outlook is for a small decrease in the aggregate ROE during 1996 because the profit margin in 1996 is expected to decline relative to the margin in 1995. Also, there should be very little change in the total asset turnover at this time in the economic expansion. Finally, there should be a small decline in the financial leverage ratio during 1996 as firms continue to

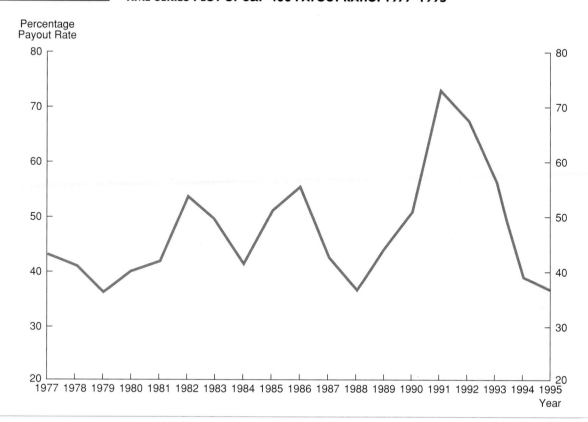

FIGURE 18.13

TIME SERIES PLOT OF S&P 400 PAYOUT RATIO: 1977–1995

reduce their financial leverage. The result of a lower profit margin, no change in asset turnover, and a decline in financial leverage should be a decrease in the ROE during 1996. Therefore, with a small decrease in the retention rate and in ROE, you would estimate a small decline in the expected growth rate.[17] In summary, we expect

- An increase in the payout ratio
- A small increase in the required rate of return
- A small decline in the growth rate

Overall, this would imply a *small decline* in the earnings multiple. The earnings multiplier early in 1996 is about 18.5 times. This discussion would indicate that the multiplier could decline to about 17.5 times during 1996.

SPECIFIC ESTIMATE APPROACH   This approach derives specific estimates for the earnings multiplier based on a range of estimates for the three variables: dividend payout (D/E), required rate of return (*k*), and growth (*g*). As indicated earlier, the retention rate has

---

[17]This is the most reasonable scenario given the economic environment. At the same time, there have been changes in the value of common equity caused by asset write-offs and share repurchases. Both of these events can cause a significant decline in the equity account but have little impact on operating earnings. As a result, there has been a higher ROE simply because of a lower equity value.

fluctuated between 45 and 60 percent during the past 10 years. Therefore, a reasonable dividend-payout ratio (D/E) would be 53 percent.

The required return (k) can be estimated using the interest rate on government bonds plus an estimate of the risk premium for common stocks. An appropriate risk premium could range from 3 percent to 6 percent, depending on the government security used to estimate a nominal risk-free rate. The 6 percent is based on the long-term geometric average risk premium as indicated by the Ibbotson-Sinquefield studies for the period 1926 to 1995 using T-bills as the risk-free investment. Notably, during the recent period (1975 to 1995), the risk premium has been in the range of 2.5 to 3.5 percent. In early 1996, the rate on T-bills was about 5 percent, the rate on 5-year government bonds was about 5.5 percent, and the rate on long-term bonds was 6 percent. Notably, these interest rates are the lowest in over a decade and most observers expect a small increase by the end of the year. If there is an adjustment to reflect this, you could conceive of the following possibilities:

	Expected at Year-End
A. 5-year government bonds	6.0%
Historical risk premium	6.0
Estimated k	12.0%
B. 5-year government bonds	6.0%
Low risk premium	2.5
Estimated k	8.5%
C. 5-year government bonds	6.0%
Medium risk premium	4.0
Estimated k	10.0%

Therefore, the required return (k) could be in the range of 8 to 12 percent.

The estimate of growth should be based on the current and expected return on equity (ROE) and the rate of retention. The graph in Figure 18.8 shows that the ROE for the S&P 400 was in the 8 to 18 percent range during the period 1981 to 1994. Assuming that 1996 is toward the end of an economic expansion that officially started in October 1991, a range of 13 to 15 percent for the ROE seems appropriate. As indicated earlier, the retention rate has been between 40 and 55 percent. Therefore, a conservative estimate of the growth rate would combine the 40 percent retention rate and an ROE of 13 percent: $.40 \times .13 = .052$. An optimistic growth rate estimate would combine the 55 percent retention rate and a 15 percent ROE: $.55 \times .15 = .082$. To summarize,

Dividend/earnings	.400–.550
Government securities	.05–.06
Equity risk premium	.025–.060
Required return (k)	.080–.120
ROE	.130–.160
Sustainable growth	.052–.082

By combining the most optimistic figures, we can derive a reasonably generous estimate. Or, by using the pessimistic estimates, we can derive a very conservative estimate. The dividend-payout (D/E) figure should be consistent with the retention rate.

High estimate: D/E = .45
$$k = .10$$
$$g = .082 \ (.55 \times .15)$$

$$P/E = \frac{.45}{.100 - .082} = \frac{.45}{.018} = 25.0 \times$$

Low estimate: D/E = .55
$$k = .12$$
$$g = .059$$

$$P/E = \frac{.55}{.120 - .059} = \frac{.55}{.061} = 9.02 \times$$

Therefore, these data imply a range of earnings multipliers from about 9 times to 24 times with a midrange of about 16X. The midrange is consistent with the expectation of a P/E ratio of 17.5 derived from the direction of change approach.

CALCULATING AN ESTIMATE OF THE VALUE FOR THE MARKET SERIES

Previously, we estimated the earnings per share for Standard & Poor's 400 of $38.70. Clearly, it would have been possible to derive additional earnings estimates.

In our work with the P/E, we developed several estimates for the price-earnings multiple that varied from about 9 to 24. At this point, we can combine these estimates of an earnings per share of $38.70 and the several earnings multipliers and calculate the following estimates of value for Standard & Poor's 400 market series:

$$9.0 \times 38.70 = 348.30$$
$$12.0 \times 38.70 = 464.40$$
$$15.0 \times 38.70 = 580.50$$
$$18.0 \times 38.70 = 696.60$$
$$21.0 \times 38.70 = 812.70$$
$$24.0 \times 38.70 = 928.80$$

This example is intended to help you understand the estimation procedure. The estimation of values for D/E, k, and g was fairly complex, but it was not as extensive as the process used by professional analysts. In addition, we used a point estimate for earnings per share rather than a range of estimates (pessimistic, optimistic, most likely), which would have been preferable. Our discussion has provided the skeleton of the process that includes the theoretical background that forms the foundation for the fundamental analysis of stocks. It is important to understand *the relevant variables and how they relate to the critical estimates of earnings per share and the earnings multiplier.*

CALCULATING THE EXPECTED RATE OF RETURN ON COMMON STOCKS

Having estimated the expected value for the stock-market series, we can estimate the expected rate of return that this ending value implies by using the following equation.

$$E(R_t) = \frac{EV - BV + Div}{BV}$$

where

$E(R_t)$ = the expected rate of return during period t (We will assume a 1-year period.)

EV = the ending value for the stock-market series (We will use the several estimates of the ending value of the S&P 400 series derived in this section.)

BV = the beginning value for the stock-market series (You would typically use the current value for the stock-market series assuming you would be investing at this time.)

Div = the expected dividend payment on the stock-market series during the investment horizon

We will compute six rate of return estimates based on the six value estimates for the S&P 400 series. We will always assume the same beginning value for the S&P 400 that prevailed in early 1996 (720.00) and an estimate of the dividend per share during the next 12 months (20.51).[18] Therefore, the six estimates of expected rate of return are

1. $\dfrac{348.30 - 720.00 + 20.51}{720.00} = -48.78\%$

2. $\dfrac{464.40 - 720.00 + 20.51}{720.00} = -32.65\%$

3. $\dfrac{580.50 - 720.00 + 20.51}{720.00} = -16.53\%$

4. $\dfrac{696.60 - 720.00 + 20.51}{720.00} = -0.40\%$

5. $\dfrac{812.70 - 720.00 + 20.51}{720.00} = 15.72\%$

6. $\dfrac{928.80 - 720.00 + 20.51}{720.00} = 31.85\%$

As you would expect, there is a wide range of expected rates of return because of the range of ending values for the S&P 400. At this point, you either select the most reasonable estimate and use this value and the implied rate of return to make the investment decision, or you can assign probabilities to each of the estimates and derive an expected value estimate. In either case, you would compare this *expected* rate of return on common stocks to your *required* rate of return on common stocks. If we use the required k used in calculating the earnings multiplier, we know it is somewhere between 10 and 12 percent. Assuming that it is 11 percent, our investment decision would depend on whether the expected return calculated was equal to or greater than 11 percent as follows:

Estimate	Estimated Rate of Return	Required Rate of Return	Investment Decision
1	−48.78%	11%	Significant underweight
2	−32.65	11	Significant underweight
3	−16.53	11	Underweight
4	−0.40	11	Underweight
5	15.72	11	Overweight
6	31.85	11	Significant overweight

Based on the discussion in Chapter 14, we know that this would cause us to underweight or overweight the U.S. market relative to either U.S. bonds or stocks in other markets depending on the positive or negative excess returns.

One might want to compute the market value that would provide the desired return as follows:

$$\frac{x + 20.51}{720.00} = 1.11$$
$$x = 778.70$$

---

[18] This is an approximate estimate based on the expected earnings of $38.70 and a payout ratio of 53 percent.

The question then becomes, what combinations of reasonable earnings and P/E would provide such a market value?

ANALYSIS OF WORLD MARKETS

Although we have worked with the U.S. market to demonstrate the procedure for analyzing a country's stock market, investors should perform a similar analysis for non-U.S. markets, especially the major world markets—Japan, Canada, the United Kingdom, and Germany. We do not have the space to carry out a detailed analysis of each of these markets, but we can provide an example of the extensive analysis by a major investment firm. Specifically, Goldman, Sachs & Company provides a monthly publication entitled "World Investment Strategy Highlights" that contains a world portfolio strategy as well as a strategy for investors in several individual countries.

Overall, it is a top-down approach in which Goldman, Sachs initially examines the components of a country's economy that relate to the valuation of securities (i.e., GDP, capital investments, industrial production, inflation, and interest rates). In Chapter 14, we discussed the substantial difference in outlook for GDP growth during 1996. Likewise, there are major differences in the outlook for inflation, which leads to major differences in expectations for exchange rates during 1997.

Given this approach, Table 18.5 contains forecasts for real GDP growth and inflation for seven major countries. These data provide insights regarding individual countries in two areas. First is the status of their expansion that started for most of the countries (except Japan) in 1993. Goldman, Sachs expected most countries, including Japan, to experience a continuation of their economic expansion in 1996 and 1997.

TABLE 18.5

FORECASTS FOR COUNTRY REAL GDP GROWTH AND INFLATION (% PER ANNUM)

Country	1994	1995E	1996E	1997E
United States				
GDP	3.5	2.0	2.5	2.9
Inflation	2.6	2.8	3.1	3.4
Japan				
GDP	0.5	0.9	2.8	1.6
Inflation	0.7	0.0	0.0	1.0
Germany				
GDP	2.9	1.9	0.5	2.2
Inflation	2.7	1.8	1.8	2.6
United Kingdom				
GDP	4.0	2.5	1.9	3.2
Inflation	2.4	2.8	2.9	2.5
France				
GDP	2.8	2.2	1.3	2.8
Inflation	2.1	1.6	1.8	1.7
Italy				
GDP	2.1	3.0	1.1	2.0
Inflation	3.9	5.4	4.3	3.9
Canada				
GDP	4.6	2.3	2.8	3.1
Inflation	2.7	2.6	2.9	3.2

Source: Adapted from *World Investment Strategy Highlights* (London: Goldman, Sachs International Ltd.) November/December 1995. Reprinted by permission of Goldman, Sachs & Co.

TABLE 18.6	COMPARATIVE CORPORATE GROWTH STATISTICS					
	United States	Japan	United Kingdom	Germany	France	Italy
Earnings Growth						
1995	18	34	12	30	15	75
1996F	6	32	9	25	35	17
1997F	11	7	11	28	10	25
Dividend Growth						
1995	5	6	10	9	8	20
1996F	7	9	9	10	10	20
1997F	8	6	9	15	20	20

Aggregates for earnings and dividend are based on an industrial sample of all the companies in each country.
F = forecast.
Note: Figures for the United States refer to the S&P Industrials Index and pertain to operating earnings.

Source: Adapted from *World Investment Strategy Highlights* (London: Goldman, Sachs International Ltd.), November/December 1995. Reprinted by permission of Goldman, Sachs & Co.

Going from the economy to results for corporations, Table 18.6 contains comparative results for firms in numerous countries regarding earnings growth and dividend growth. The range in results is substantial. For example, expected earnings growth in 1997 varies from 7 percent (Japan) to 28 percent (Germany).

Because of the importance of interest rates in the valuation process, Table 18.7 contains interest rate forecasts for seven countries for the short term (3 months) and the long term (12 months). As one might expect, the range of current short-term rates was greater (0.4 percent to 10.2 percent) than the range of long-term rates (2.8 percent to 11.2 percent).

Putting the earnings growth estimate and interest rates together brings us to market valuation variables including P/E ratios and dividend yields. The prevailing values for various countries contained in Table 18.8 indicate a wide range between countries (e.g., an estimated 1997 P/E of about 13 for the United Kingdom versus 49 in Japan). The expected 1997 dividend yields range from less than 1.0 percent (Japan) to 4.9 percent for France.

INDIVIDUAL COUNTRY ANALYSIS Following the summary of market statistics for the major equity markets, Goldman, Sachs provides a detailed analysis of each of the major countries. This begins with a discussion of the country's economy as part of an analysis of the country's equity market. Table 18.9 contains estimates of the major economic indicators for Germany. These projections reflect an economy in the middle of an economic expansion. Currently, government authorities are concerned about the future competitiveness of German firms in the European economic community.

Following the discussion of the economy and the projections, we analyze the country's equity market. A summary for Germany is set forth in Table 18.10. Goldman, Sachs feels that the overall investment outlook for Germany is fairly strong because of the positive earnings outlook. Therefore, they recommend an overweighting of German equities in a global portfolio.

TABLE 18.7   **INTEREST RATE FORECASTS (% PER ANNUM)**

Country	Current Rate[a]	Short Term (3 months)	Long Term (12 months)
United States			
3 month	5.8	5.6	6.1
10 year	5.9	5.9	6.6
Germany			
3 month	4.1	3.7	4.5
10 year	6.4	6.2	6.7
Japan			
3 month	0.6	0.4	0.8
10 year	2.8	2.8	3.4
France			
3 month	6.2	5.7	5.7
10 year	7.3	6.8	7.2
United Kingdom			
3 month	6.7	6.5	6.5
10 year	7.9	7.4	8.0
Canada			
3 month	7.1	6.0	6.3
10 year	7.5	7.6	7.6
Italy			
3 month	10.5	10.2	11.0
10 year	11.7	11.2	12.5

[a]3 November 1995.

Source: Adapted from *World Investment Strategy Highlights* (London: Goldman, Sachs International Ltd.) November/December 1995. Reprinted by permission of Goldman, Sachs & Co.

TABLE 18.8   **WORLD MARKET VALUATION MATRIX**

	United States	Japan	United Kingdom	Germany	France	Italy
P/E						
1995	17.3	564.4	15.1	18.4	48.5	23.3
1996(e)	15.7	63.2	14.2	17.8	22.2	19.5
1997(e)	14.2	49.4	13.2	14.3	16.5	14.5
Div. Yield						
1995	2.1	0.7	4.0	3.2	3.8	2.3
1996(e)	2.2	0.8	4.2	3.0	4.1	2.6
1997(e)	2.4	0.9	4.5	3.5	4.9	3.1

Based on Datastream market indices.

(e) = estimate.

U.S. figures refer to S&P Composite Index and pertain to operating earnings. U.K. figures refer to FT-500 Index.

Source: Adapted from *World Investment Strategy Highlights* (London: Goldman, Sachs International Ltd.), November/December 1995. Reprinted by permission of Goldman, Sachs & Co.

TABLE 18.9   **MAJOR GERMAN ECONOMIC VARIABLES**

	Current Value	Historical Average
GDP Growth		
1994	2.9	2.8
1995	2.4	
1996F	2.6	
Earnings Growth (Industrials)		
1994	33	8.0
1995	36	
1996F	32	
Dividend Growth (Industrials)		
1994	5	4.0
1995	4	
1996F	14	
Inflation (Consumer Price Index) (%)		
1994	2.7	2.4
1995	1.8	
1996F	2.2	

Interest Rate Outlook

	Current Rate	3 Months	12 Months
3 month	4.1	3.7	4.5
10 year	6.4	6.2	6.7

Source: Adapted from *World Investment Strategy Highlights* (London: Goldman, Sachs International Ltd.) November/December 1995. Reprinted by permission of Goldman, Sachs & Co.

TABLE 18.10   **STOCK INDEXES FOR THE GERMAN EQUITY MARKET AND EXPECTED RATES OF RETURN**

	Current Price	PERFORMANCE (% CHANGE)		
		Last Month	YTD	12 Months
DAX	2600	−1.7	−7.4	6.9

Expected Returns (%)	3 Months	12 Months
Equities	5.8	20.9
Bonds	8.8	3.0
Cash	2.2	4.5

Source: Adapted from *World Investment Strategy Highlights* (London: Goldman, Sachs International Ltd.) November/December 1995. Reprinted by permission of Goldman, Sachs & Co.

Summary

- We consistently emphasize the importance of analyzing the economies and security markets before analyzing alternative industries or companies. You should determine whether the economic and market outlook indicates an underweighting or overweighting related to investing in stocks, bonds, or cash before you consider which is the best industry or company.
- There are two techniques available to help you make the market decision. The first are macro techniques, which are based on the strong relationship between the economy and security markets. These models base their market projections on their outlook for the aggregate economy and certain components. The second are micro techniques, which estimate future market values by applying

basic valuation models to equity markets. In Chapter 14, we examined the macro techniques and discussed a world asset allocation. This chapter has been devoted to the microanalysis of equity markets in the United States and other countries.

- We apply the dividend discount model discussed in Chapter 13 to a stock-market series (the S&P 400) that reflects the U.S. equity market. We estimate earnings per share for this series and generate a set of estimates for the earnings multiplier. Given these two components, we compute an estimate of the future value for the market and use that estimate to derive an expected return for common stocks during the future holding period. It is important to recognize that it is appropriate to make several estimates that reflect various possible conditions.

   This micro technique is best summarized by listing its steps:

   I. Estimate expected earnings.
      A. Estimate nominal GDP for the year.
      B. Estimate corporate sales based on the relationship of sales to GDP.
      C. Estimate the aggregate operating profit margin (NBDIT/sales) based on an analysis of:
         1. Capacity utilization rate
         2. Unit labor cost
            a. Wage/hour increases
            b. Productivity changes
         3. Inflation
         4. Foreign competition
      D. Estimate net profits (earnings per share).
         1. Compute operating profits (operating profit margin times sales).
         2. Subtract estimated depreciation expense.
         3. Subtract estimated interest expense.
         4. Estimate the tax rate (T).
         5. Multiply earnings before taxes (EBT) by $(1 - T)$.
   II. Estimate the expected earnings multiplier.
      A. Estimate changes in the required rate of return (k).
         1. Changes in the risk-free rate (ΔRFR)
         2. Changes in the expected rate of inflation (ΔI)
         3. Changes in the equity risk premium (ΔRP).
            a. Changes in fundamental risk variables (BR, FR, LR, ERR, CR)
            b. Changes in the moving average of the LR historical risk premium
            c. Changes in the aggregate dividend yield
            d. Changes in the credit risk spread
            e. Changes in the volatility of the equity market compared to the volatility of the bond market
      B. Estimate changes in the expected growth rate of dividends (earnings) (g).
         1. Changes in the aggregate earnings retention rate
         2. Changes in the return on equity (ROE)
            a. Changes in profit margin
            b. Changes in total asset turnover
            c. Changes in financial leverage
      C. Estimate changes in the spread between k and g.
   III. Estimate the future value of a stock-market series.
      A. Estimated earnings per share times the estimated earnings multiplier.

- Finally, although we apply this two-step estimation procedure to the stock market in the United States, we know it is necessary to do a similar analysis for non-U.S. markets. An example of such an analysis by Goldman, Sachs shows how it applied the top-down approach to several major countries.

Following this aggregate market analysis, the next step is industry analysis, which is considered in the following chapter.

Questions

1. An investor believes the stock market will experience a substantial increase next year because corporate earnings are expected to rise by at least 12 percent. Do you agree or disagree? Why or why not?

2. In the library, find at least three sources of historical information on nominal and real GDP. Find two sources that generally provide an estimate of nominal GDP each year.

3. To arrive at an estimate of the *net profit margin*, why would you spend time estimating the operating profit margin and working down?

4. You are convinced that capacity utilization next year will decline from 82 percent to about 79 percent. Explain what effect this change will have on the operating profit margin.

5. You see an estimate that hourly wage rates will increase by 6 percent next year. How does this affect your estimate of the operating profit margin? What other information do you need to use this estimate of a wage rate increase and why do you need it?

6. You see an estimate that next year hourly wage rates will increase by 7 percent and productivity will increase by 5 percent. What would you expect to happen to unit labor cost? Discuss how this unit labor cost estimate would influence your estimate of the operating profit margin.

7. Assume that each of the following changes is independent (i.e., except for this change, all other factors remain unchanged). In each case, indicate what will happen to the earnings multiplier and why.
   a. The return on equity increases.
   b. The aggregate debt/equity ratio declines.
   c. Overall productivity of capital increases.
   d. The dividend-payout ratio declines.

Problems

1. You are told that nominal GDP will increase by about 10 percent next year. Using Figure 18.1 and the regression equation, what increase would you expect in corporate sales? How would this estimate change if you gave more weight to the recent observations?

2. Currently, the dividend-payout ratio (D/E) for the aggregate market is 60 percent, the required return (k) is 13 percent, and the expected growth rate for dividends (g) is 7 percent.
   a. Compute the current earnings multiplier.
   b. You expect the D/E ratio to decline to 50 percent, but you assume there will be no other changes. What will be the P/E?
   c. Starting with the initial conditions, you expect the dividend-payout ratio to be constant, the rate of inflation to increase by 3 percent, and the growth rate to increase by 2 percent. Compute the expected P/E.
   d. Starting with the initial conditions, you expect the dividend-payout ratio to be constant, the rate of inflation to decline by 3 percent, and the growth rate to decline by 1 percent. Compute the expected P/E.

3. *CFA Examination III (1985)*
   A U.S. pension plan hired two offshore firms to manage the non-U.S. equity portion of its total portfolio. Each firm was free to own stocks in any country market included in Capital International's Europe, Australia, and Far East Index (EAFE), and to use any form of dollar and/or nondollar cash or bonds as an equity substitute or reserve. After three years had elapsed, the records of the managers and the EAFE Index were as shown below:

SUMMARY: CONTRIBUTIONS TO RETURN

	Currency	Country Selection	Stock Selection	Cash/Bond Allocation	Total Return Recorded
Manager A	(9.0%)	19.7%	3.1%	0.6%	14.4%
Manager B	(7.4)	14.2	6.0	2.8	15.6
Composite of A&B	(8.2)	16.9	4.5	1.7	15.0
EAFE Index	(12.9)	19.9	—	—	7.0

You are a member of the plan sponsor's pension committee, which will soon meet with the plan's consultant to review manager performance. In preparation for this meeting, you go through the following analysis:

   a. Briefly describe the strengths and weaknesses of each manager, relative to the EAFE Index data. (5 minutes)

   b. Briefly explain the meaning of the data in the "Currency" column. (5 minutes)

4. As an analyst for Middle, Diddle, and O'Leary, you are forecasting the market P/E ratio using the dividend discount model. Because the economy has been expanding for 4 years, you expect the dividend-payout ratio will be at its high of 60 percent and that long-term government bond rates will rise to 8 percent. Because investors are becoming less risk-averse, the equity risk premium will decline to 3 percent. As a result, investors will require an 11 percent return, and the return on equity will be 9 percent.

   a. What is the expected growth rate?

   b. What is your expectation of the market P/E ratio?

   c. What will be the value for the market index if the expectation is for earnings per share of $39.00?

   d. What will be your rate of return if you acquired the index at a value of 700, you sold the index at the value computed in (c), and dividends during the year were $22.00?

5. You are given the following estimated per share date related to the S&P 400 for the year 1998:

Sales	$850.00
Depreciation	38.00
Interest expense	16.00

You also are informed that the estimated operating profit margin is 0.152 and the tax rate is 32 percent.

   a. Compute the estimated EPS for 1998.

   b. Assume that a member of the research committee for your firm feels that it is important to consider a range of operating profit margin (OPM) estimates. Therefore, you are asked to derive both optimistic and pessimistic EPS estimates using 0.149 and 0.155 for the OPM and holding everything else constant.

6. Given the three EPS estimates in Problem 5, you are also given the following estimates related to the market earnings multiple.

	Pessimistic	Consensus	Optimistic
D/E	.65	.55	.45
Nominal RFR	.10	.09	.08
Risk premium	.05	.04	.03
ROE	.10	.13	.16

   a. Based on the three EPS and P/E estimates, compute the high, low, and consensus market value for the S&P 400 in 1998.

   b. Assuming that the S&P 400 at the beginning of the year was priced at 750, compute your expected rate of return under the three scenarios from Part a. Assuming your required rate of return is equal to the consensus, how would you weight the S&P 400 in your global portfolio?

References

Copeland, Basil L., Jr. "Inflation, Interest Rates and Equity Risk Premia." *Financial Analysts Journal* 38, no. 3 (May–June 1982).

Fama, Eugene F. and Kenneth French. "Business Conditions and Expected Returns on Stocks and Bonds." *Journal of Financial Economics* 25, no. 1 (November 1989).

Fama, Eugene F. and Kenneth R. French, "Common Risk Factors in the Returns on Stocks and Bonds," *Journal of Financial Economics* 33, no. 1 (February 1993).

Finnerty, John D. and Dean Leistikow. "The Behavior of Equity and Debt Risk Premiums." *The Journal of Portfolio Management* 19, no. 4 (Summer 1993).

Gray, William S., III. "The Anatomy of a Stock Market Forecast." *Journal of Portfolio Management* 16, no. 1 (Fall 1989).

Haugen, Robert A. and Nardin L. Baker, "Commonality in the Determinants of Expected Stock Returns," *Journal of Financial Economics* 41, no. 3 (July 1996).

Reichenstein, William and Steven P. Rich. "The Market Risk Premium and Long-Term Stock Returns." *The Journal of Portfolio Management* 19, no. 4 (Summer 1993).

Reilly, Frank K., Frank T. Griggs, and Wenchi Wong. "Determinants of the Aggregate Stock Market Earnings Multiple." *Journal of Portfolio Management* 10, no. 1 (Fall 1983).

Shiller, Robert J. and John Campbell. "Stock Prices, Earnings, and Expected Dividends." *Journal of Finance* 43, no. 3 (July 1988).

Vandell, Robert F. and George W. Keuter. *A History of Risk-Premia Estimates for Equities: 1944–1978.* Charlottesville, VA: The Financial Analysts Research Foundation, 1989.

Chapter

19

Industry Analysis

This chapter answers the following questions:

- Is there a difference between the returns for alternative industries during specific time periods? What is the implication of these results?
- Is there consistency in the returns for industries over time? What do these results imply regarding industry analysis?
- Is the performance for firms within an industry consistent? What is the implication of these results for industry and company analysis?
- Is there a difference in risk among industries? What are the implications of these results for industry analysis?
- What happens to risk for individual industries over time? What does this imply for industry analysis?
- What are the steps involved in estimating earnings per share for an industry?
- What are the stages in the industrial life cycle and how does the life cycle stage affect the sales estimate for an industry?
- What are the five basic competitive forces that determine the intensity of competition in an industry and, thus, its rate of return on capital?
- How does the estimating procedure for the operating profit margin differ for the aggregate market versus an industry?
- What are the two alternative procedures for estimating an industry earnings multiplier?
- What is involved in a macroanalysis of the industry earnings multiplier?
- What are the steps in the microanalysis of an industry earnings multiplier?
- After you estimate an industry earnings multiplier, how do you determine if the industry's multiplier is relatively high or low?
- How do industries differ in terms of what dictates their return on assets?
- What are some of the unique factors that must be considered in global industry analysis?

When asked about his or her job, a securities analyst typically will reply that he or she is an oil analyst, a retail analyst, or a computer analyst. A widely read trade publication, *The Institutional Investor,* selects an All-American analyst team each year based on industry groups. Investment managers talk about being in or out of the metals, the autos, or the utilities. This constant reference to industry groups is because most professional investors are extremely conscious of differences among alternative industries and organize their analyses and portfolio decisions according to industry groups. Recently, the Association for Investment Management and Research (AIMR) has responded to this interest by sponsoring a number of conferences that are specifically concerned with the techniques and topics relevant for specific industries.[1]

---

[1] Examples of industries include health care, oil and gas, automotive, telecommunications, and the retail industry. Detailed references are contained at the end of the chapter.

We share this appreciation of the importance of industry analysis as a component of the three-step fundamental analysis procedure initiated in Chapter 13. Industry analysis is the second step as we progress toward selecting specific firms and stocks for our investment portfolio. As the first step, in Chapter 14 we discussed the macroanalysis of the stock market to decide whether the expected rate of return from investing in common stocks was equal to or greater than our required rate of return. Based on this comparison, we would decide to be overweighted, market-weighted, or underweighted in stocks. We also discussed the microanalysis of the market in Chapter 18 to support the macroanalysis. Following this economic/market decision, we take the second step in this chapter when we analyze different industries to make a similar industry decision. The decision criteria are the same: Is the expected rate of return for an industry equal to or greater than our required rate of return for this industry? Based on this relationship, we decide how to weight the industry in our stock portfolio. We will take the final step in Chapter 20 when we analyze the individual companies and stocks within the alternative industries.

In the first section, we discuss the results of several studies that will help us identify the benefits and uses of industry analysis. Following that, we present a technique for analyzing industries that resembles the process used in Chapter 18 for analyzing the aggregate stock market. Specifically, we discuss how to estimate earnings per share and an earnings multiplier for an industry, then we combine these two factors to estimate the industry's expected value and its expected rate of return. Another section raises questions that are unique to industry analysis: What is the impact of the competitive environment within an industry and the effect of the intensity of competition on potential industry returns? We conclude the chapter with a demonstration of global industry analysis that recognizes that many industries transcend U.S. borders and compete on a worldwide basis.

WHY DO INDUSTRY ANALYSIS?

Investment practitioners perform industry analysis because they believe it helps them isolate investment opportunities that have favorable return–risk characteristics. We likewise have recommended it as part of our three-step, top-down plan for valuing individual companies and selecting stocks for inclusion in our portfolio. What exactly do we learn from an industry analysis? Can we spot trends in industries that make them good investments? Studies of these questions indicate unique patterns in the rates of return and risk measures over time in different industries. In this section, we survey the results of studies that addressed these questions.

In the research we describe, investigators asked a set of questions designed to pinpoint the benefits and limitations of industry analysis. In particular, they wanted answers to the following questions:

- Is there a difference between the returns for alternative industries during specific time periods?
- Will an industry that performs well in one period continue to perform well in the future? That is, can we use past relationships between the market and an industry to predict future trends for the industry?
- Is the performance of firms within an industry consistent over time?

Several studies also considered questions related to risk:

- Is there a difference in the risk for alternative industries?
- Does the risk for individual industries vary, or does it remain relatively constant over time?

We consider the results of these studies and come to some general conclusions about the value of industry analysis. This assessment helps us interpret the results of our industry valuation in the next section.

CROSS-SECTIONAL *INDUSTRY* *PERFORMANCE*

To find out if the rates of return among different industries varied during a given time period (e.g., 1998), researchers compared the performance of alternative industries during a specific time period. Consistent performance during specific time periods for different industries would indicate that industry analysis is not necessary. For example, assume that during 1998, the aggregate stock market experienced a rate of return of 10 percent and the returns for *all* industries were bunched between 9 percent and 11 percent. If this was the result and this consistency in performance persisted for future periods, you might question whether it was worthwhile to conduct an industry analysis to find an industry that would return 11 percent when random selection would provide a return of about 10 percent (the average return).

Studies of the annual industry performance have found that different industries have consistently shown wide dispersion in their rates of return (e.g., a typical range during a year will be from minus 30 percent to plus 50 percent). A specific example is the year 1995. As shown in Figure 19.1, although the aggregate stock market experienced a total return of

---

FIGURE 19.1   **HOW THE DOW JONES INDUSTRY GROUPS FARED**

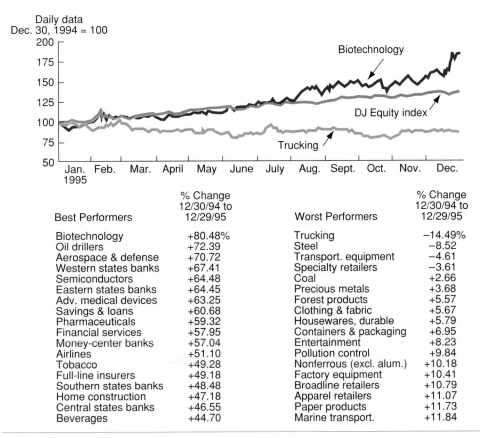

Daily data
Dec. 30, 1994 = 100

Best Performers	% Change 12/30/94 to 12/29/95	Worst Performers	% Change 12/30/94 to 12/29/95
Biotechnology	+80.48%	Trucking	−14.49%
Oil drillers	+72.39	Steel	−8.52
Aerospace & defense	+70.72	Transport. equipment	−4.61
Western states banks	+67.41	Specialty retailers	−3.61
Semiconductors	+64.48	Coal	+2.66
Eastern states banks	+64.45	Precious metals	+3.68
Adv. medical devices	+63.25	Forest products	+5.57
Savings & loans	+60.68	Clothing & fabric	+5.67
Pharmaceuticals	+59.32	Housewares, durable	+5.79
Financial services	+57.95	Containers & packaging	+6.95
Money-center banks	+57.04	Entertainment	+8.23
Airlines	+51.10	Pollution control	+9.84
Tobacco	+49.28	Nonferrous (excl. alum.)	+10.18
Full-line insurers	+49.18	Factory equipment	+10.41
Southern states banks	+48.48	Broadline retailers	+10.79
Home construction	+47.18	Apparel retailers	+11.07
Central states banks	+46.55	Paper products	+11.73
Beverages	+44.70	Marine transport.	+11.84

Source: *The Wall Street Journal,* January 2, 1996, R3.

37.57 percent (the S&P 500), the industry performance ranged from −14.49 percent (trucking) to 80.48 percent (biotechnology). These results imply that *industry analysis is important and necessary* to uncover performance differences that will help identify both unprofitable and profitable opportunities.

INDUSTRY PERFORMANCE OVER TIME

In another group of investigations, researchers tried to determine whether industries that perform well in one time period would continue to perform well in subsequent time periods or at least outperform the aggregate market in the later time period. In this case, investigators found *almost no association* in individual industry performance year to year or over sequential rising or falling markets.

These studies imply that past performance alone does not help project future industry performance. The results do *not*, however, negate the usefulness of industry analysis. They simply confirm that variables that affect industry performance change over time and investors must project future industry performance on the basis of future estimates of these relevant variables.

PERFORMANCE OF THE COMPANIES WITHIN AN INDUSTRY

Other studies were designed to determine whether there is consistency in the performance of companies *within* an industry. If all the firms within an industry performed consistently during a specified time period, investors would not need company analysis. In such a case, industry analysis alone would be enough because once you selected a profitable industry, you would know that all the stocks in that industry would do well.

These studies typically have found *wide dispersion* in the performance among companies in most industries. An alternative way to measure this same impact is to examine the industry influence on the returns for individual stocks. Studies that have done such an analysis have shown evidence of an industry effect in specific industries such as oil or autos, but most stocks showed small industry effects. In addition, the results indicated that the industry impact has been declining over time.[2]

IMPLICATIONS OF DISPERSION WITHIN INDUSTRIES   Citing studies such as these, some theorists have contended that industry analysis is useless because all firms in an industry do not move together. Obviously, consistent firm performance in an industry would be ideal because you would not need to do company analysis. For industries that have a strong, consistent industry influence such as oil, gold, steel, autos, and railroads, you can reduce the extent of your company analysis after your industry analysis.

Most analysts do not expect such a strong industry influence, which means that a thorough *company* analysis is still necessary. Even for industries that do not have a strong industry influence, industry analysis is valuable because it is much easier to select a superior company from a good industry than to find a good company in an unhealthy industry. By selecting the best stocks within an industry with good expectations, you avoid the risk that your analysis and selection of a good company will be offset by poor industry performance.

DIFFERENCES IN INDUSTRY RISK

Although a number of studies have focused on industry rates of return, few studies have examined industry risk measures. A study by Reilly and Drzycimski investigated two questions: (1) Did risk differ among industries during a given time period? (2) Were

---

[2]For example, see Stephen L. Meyers, "A Re-Examination of Market and Industry Factors in Stock Price Behavior," *Journal of Finance* 28, no. 3 (June 1973): 695–705; and Miles Livingston, "Industry Movements of Common Stocks," *Journal of Finance* 32, no. 2 (June 1977): 861–874.

industry risk measures stable over time?[3] The study found *a wide range of risk* among different industries and the spreads between risk levels typically widened during rising and falling markets. On a positive note, an analysis of the risk measures over time indicated that they were *reasonably stable over time.*

We can interpret these findings as follows: although risk measures for different industries showed substantial dispersion during a period of time, individual industries' risk measures are stable over time. This means that the analysis of past industry risk is necessary, but this historical analysis is of value when you attempt to estimate the future risk for an industry.

SUMMARY OF RESEARCH ON INDUSTRY ANALYSIS

Earlier we noted that a number of academic studies have sought answers to questions dealing with industry analysis. The conclusions of the studies are:

- During any time period, the returns for different industries vary within a wide range, which means that industry analysis can be useful in the process of targeting investments.
- The rates of return for individual industries vary over time, so we cannot simply extrapolate past industry performance into the future.
- The rates of return of firms within industries also vary, so company analysis is a necessary follow-up to industry analysis.
- During any time period, different industries' risk levels vary within wide ranges, so we must examine and estimate the risk factors for alternative industries as well as returns.
- Risk measures for different industries remain fairly constant over time, so the historical risk analysis can be useful when estimating future risk.

The results imply that industry analysis is necessary, both to avoid losses and to find better industries. It is also important when you examine individual stocks to identify superior risk–return opportunities for investors.

ESTIMATING INDUSTRY RATES OF RETURN

Having determined that industry analysis helps an investor select profitable investment opportunities, how do we go about valuing an industry and estimating the expected rate of return that an investment will provide? The procedure for estimating the expected value of an industry is a two-step process, similar to the microanalysis of the stock market. First, you estimate the expected earnings per share for the industry and then you estimate the expected industry P/E ratio (earnings multiplier). As before, multiplying the expected earnings per share by the expected earnings multiplier gives the expected ending value for the industry index.

We compute an expected rate of return for the industry by comparing the ending value plus its expected dividend to its beginning value. Comparing this expected rate of return to your required rate of return for this industry allows you to apply the investment decision rule. You would overweight your investment in this industry if the expected rate of return was greater than your required rate of return.

To demonstrate industry analysis, we use Standard & Poor's Retail Store-Drug (RSD) index to represent industrywide data and this industry. This retail store-drug index contains three companies as follows: (1) Longs Drug Stores, (2) Rite Aid, and (3) Walgreen Company. This industry was selected because it should be reasonably familiar to most observ-

[3] Frank K. Reilly and Eugene Drzycimski, "Alternative Industry Performance and Risk," *Journal of Financial and Quantitative Analysis* 9, no. 3 (June 1974). 423–446.

ers, and because it is consistent and useful for the subsequent company analysis that uses Walgreen as the example company.

ESTIMATING EARNINGS PER SHARE

To estimate earnings per share, you must start by estimating sales per share. The first part of this section describes three techniques that provide help and insights for the sales estimate. Next, we derive an estimate of earnings per share, which implies a net profit margin for the industry. As in Chapter 18 where we estimated earnings per share for a stock market series, we begin with the operating profit margin because it is less volatile and easier to estimate than the net profit margin. Then we subtract estimates of depreciation and interest expenses and apply a tax rate to find the earnings per share.

FORECASTING SALES PER SHARE

Three techniques can be useful when deriving a sales forecast for an industry:

1. Industrial life cycle
2. Input–output analysis
3. Industry–aggregate economy relationship

Notably, these techniques are *not* competing alternatives, but are complementary and supplementary. Together they will help you develop a complete picture of the current position and outlook of the industry under a variety of scenarios.

SALES FORECASTING AND THE INDUSTRIAL LIFE CYCLE   An insightful analysis when predicting industry sales is to view the industry over time and divide its development into stages, similar to those that humans progress through as they move from birth to adolescence to adulthood to middle age to old age. The number of stages in this **industry life cycle analysis** can vary based on how much detail you want. A five-stage model would include:

1. Pioneering development
2. Rapid accelerating growth
3. Mature growth
4. Stabilization and market maturity
5. Deceleration of growth and decline

Figure 19.2 shows the growth path of sales during each stage. The vertical scale in logs reflects *rates* of growth, whereas the arithmetic horizontal scale has different widths representing different, unequal time periods. To estimate industry sales, you must predict the length of time for each stage. This requires answers to such questions as: How long will an industry grow at an accelerating rate (Stage 2)? How long will it be in a mature growth phase (Stage 3) before its sales growth stabilizes (Stage 4) and then declines (Stage 5)?

Besides being useful when estimating sales, this analysis of an industry's life cycle also can provide some insights into profit margins and earnings growth, although these profit measures do not necessarily parallel the sales growth. The profit margin series typically peaks very early in the total cycle and then levels off and declines as competition is attracted by the early success of the industry.

To illustrate the contribution of life cycle stages to sales estimates, we briefly describe these stages and their effects on sales growth and profits:

1. *Pioneering development.* During this start up stage, the industry experiences modest sales growth and very small or negative profit margins and profits. The market for the industry's product or service during this time is small, and firms incur major development costs.

| FIGURE 19.2 | LIFE CYCLE FOR AN INDUSTRY |

Net Sales
Log Scale

	Stage 1	Stage 2	Stage 3	Stage 4	Stage 5
	Pioneering Development	**Rapid Accelerating Growth**	**Mature Growth**	**Stabilization and Market Maturity**	**Deceleration of Growth and Decline**

2. *Rapid accelerating growth.* During this rapid growth stage, a market develops for the product or service and demand becomes substantial. The limited number of firms in the industry face little competition and individual firms can experience substantial backlogs. The profit margins are very high. The industry builds its productive capacity as sales grow at an increasing rate as the industry attempts to meet excess demand. High sales growth and high profit margins that increase as firms become more efficient cause industry and firm profits to explode. During this phase, profits can grow at over 100 percent a year as a result of the low earnings base and because of the rapid growth of sales and net profit margins.

3. *Mature growth.* The success in Stage 2 has satisfied most of the demand for the industry goods or service. The large sales base may keep future sales growth above normal, but it no longer accelerates. For example, if the overall economy is growing at 8 percent, sales for this industry might grow at a stabilizing rate of 15 percent to 20 percent a year. Also, the rapid growth of sales and the high historical profit margins attract competitors to the industry, which causes an increase in supply and lower prices such that the profit margins stabilize and begin to decline to normal levels.

4. *Stabilization and market maturity.* During this stage, which is probably the longest phase, the industry growth rate matches the growth rate of the aggregate economy or the segment of the economy of which the industry is a part. During this stage, investors can estimate growth easily because sales correlate highly with an economic series. Although sales grow in line with the economy, profit growth varies by industry and by individual firms within the industry because management ability to control costs differs among companies. Competition produces tight profit margins and the rates of return on

capital (e.g., return on assets, return on equity) eventually become equal to or slightly below the competitive level.

5. *Deceleration of growth and decline.* At this stage of maturity, the industry's sales growth declines because of shifts in demand or growth of substitutes. Profit margins continue to be squeezed, and some firms experience low profits or even losses. Firms that remain profitable may show very low rates of return on capital and investors begin thinking about alternative uses for the capital tied up in this industry.

Although these are general descriptions of the alternative life cycle stages, they should help you identify the stage your industry is in, which should help you estimate its potential sales growth. Obviously, everyone is looking for an industry in the early phases of Stage 2 and hopes to avoid industries in Stages 4 or 5. Comparing the sales and earnings growth of an industry to activity in the economy should help you identify the industry's stage within the industrial life cycle.

SALES FORECASTING AND INPUT–OUTPUT ANALYSIS   Input–output analysis is another way to gain insights regarding the outlook for an industry by separating industries that supply the input for a specific industry from those that get its output. In other words, we want to identify an industry's suppliers and customers. This will help us identify (1) the future demand from customers and (2) the ability of suppliers to provide the goods and services required by the industry. The goal is to determine the long-run sales outlook for both the industry's suppliers and its major customers.[4] To extend this analysis to global industries, we must include worldwide suppliers and customers.

SALES FORECASTING AND THE INDUSTRY–ECONOMY RELATIONSHIP   A third technique that is used extensively to help forecast industry sales is to compare sales for the industry with one or several aggregate economic series that are related to the goods and services produced by the industry. That is, we try to find a relationship between the industry and the economy. In the following example, we will demonstrate this industry–economy technique for the retail stores-drug industry.

DEMONSTRATING A SALES FORECAST   The retail stores-drug (RSD) industry includes retailers of basic necessities including medicine and many nonmedical products such as cosmetics, snacks, pop, and liquor. Therefore, we want a series that (1) reflects broad consumption expenditures and (2) gives weight to the impact of medical expenditures. The economic series we consider are personal consumption expenditures (PCE) and PCE-medical care. Table 19.1 contains the aggregate and per capita values for the two series.

A casual analysis of these time series indicates that although personal consumption expenditures (PCE) have experienced reasonably steady growth of over 8 percent a year during this period, PCE-medical care has grown at a faster rate of over 11 percent. As a result, as shown in the table's last column, medical care as a percentage of all PCE has grown from 9.6 percent in 1977 to 15.7 percent in 1994. Obviously, as an analyst, you would be pleased that apparently retail drugstore sales had benefited from this growth in medical expenditures, as shown by the annual growth of drugstore sales of almost 14 percent.

The scatter plot in Figure 19.3 indicates a strong linear relationship between retail store-drug sales per share and PCE-medical care. Although not shown, there also is a good

---

[4]For an explanation of input–output analysis, see Howard B. Bonham, Jr., "The Use of Input–Output Economics In Common Stock Analysis," *Financial Analysis Journal* 23, no. 1 (January–February 1967). 27–31.

| TABLE 19.1 | S&P RETAIL STORE-DRUG SALES AND VARIOUS ECONOMIC SERIES: 1977–1994 | | | | | |

| | | | | PER CAPITA | | |
Year	Retail Store-Drug Sales ($/Share)	Personal Consumption Expenditures ($ Billions)	PCE-Medical Care ($ Billions)	Personal Consumption Expenditures (Dollars)	PCE-Medical Care (Dollars)	Medical Care as a Percentage of PCE
1977	43.99	1,271.5	122,4	5,773.3	555.8	9.6
1978	49.87	1,421.2	139.7	6,400.2	629.1	9.8
1979	73.39	1,583.7	157.8	7,036.9	701.2	10.0
1980	84.82	1,748.1	181.3	7,676.3	796.1	10.4
1981	95.50	1,926.2	213.6	8,376.0	928.8	11.1
1982	109.22	2,059.2	240.5	8,868.7	1,035.8	11.7
1983	118.85	2,257.5	265.7	9,634.8	1,134.0	11.8
1984	135.15	2,460.3	290.6	10,409.7	1,229.5	11.8
1985	153.30	2,667.4	319.3	11,185.7	1,339.0	12.0
1986	157.74	2,850.6	346.4	11,854.5	1,440.5	12.2
1987	191.72	3,052.2	384.7	12,570.6	1,584.4	12.6
1988	217.80	3,296.1	427.7	13,452.3	1,745.6	13.0
1989	239.68	3,523.1	471.9	14,243.8	1,907.9	13.4
1990	265.77	3,761.2	526.2	15,050.2	2,105.5	14.0
1991	283.50	3,902.4	571.9	15,446.3	2,263.7	14.7
1992	309.78	4,136.9	628.3	16,197.3	2,460.0	15.2
1993	329.20	4,378.2	680.5	16,961.9	2,636.4	15.5
1994	363.71	4,627.0	727.1	17,751.7	2,789.6	15.7
Mean Annual Growth	13.97%	8.10%	11.31%	7.03%	10.21%	

Source: *Standard & Poor's Analysts Handbook* (New York: Standard & Poor's Corporation, 1995). Reprinted by permission of Standard & Poor's Corp. *Economic Report of the President* (Washington, DC: U.S. Government Printing Office, 1995).

relationship with PCE. Therefore, if you can accurately estimate changes in these economic series, you should derive a good estimate of expected sales for the retail drug store industry.

As the industry being analyzed becomes more specialized, you need a more individualized economic series that reflects the demand for the industry's product. There also can be instances where industry sales are dependent on several components of the economy, in which case you would consider a multivariate model that would include two or more economic series. For example, if you were dealing with the tire industry, you might want to consider new-car production, new-truck production, and a series that would reflect the replacement tire demand.

You also should consider *per capita* personal consumption expenditures–medical care. Although aggregate PCE-medical care increases each year, there also is an increase in the aggregate population, so the increase in the PCE-medical care per capita (the average PCE-medical care for each adult and child) will be less than the increase in the aggregate series. As an example, during 1994 aggregate PCE-medical care increased about 6.8 percent, but per capita PCE-medical care increased only 5.8 percent. Finally, an analysis of the relationship between changes in the economic variable and changes in industry sales will indicate how the two series move together and highlight any changes in the relationship. Using annual percentage changes provides the following regression model:

$$\% \, \Delta \text{ Industry Sales} = \alpha + \beta_i(\% \, \Delta \text{ in Economic Series})$$

FIGURE 19.3   **SCATTER PLOT OF RSD SALES PER SHARE AND PCE-MEDICAL CARE**

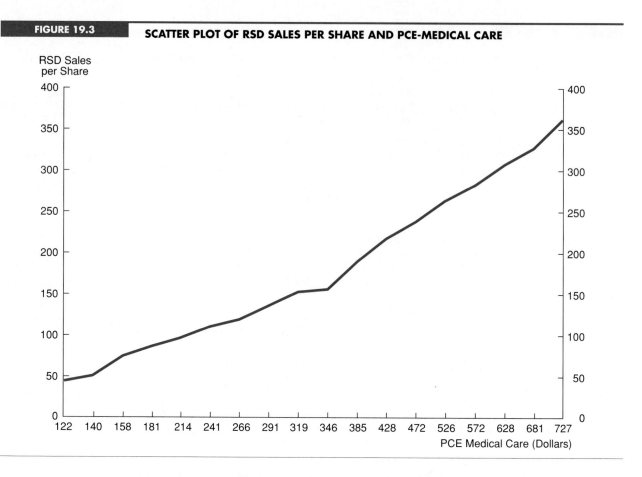

The size of the β_i coefficient should indicate how closely the two series move together. Assuming the intercept (α_i) is close to zero, a slope (β_i) value of 1.00 would indicate relatively equal percentages of change (e.g., this would indicate that a 10 percent increase in PCE typically is associated with a 10 percent increase in industry sales). A β_i of less than unity would imply that industry sales are not as volatile annually as the economy is. This analysis and the levels of relationship reflected in Figure 19.3 would help you find an economic series that closely reflects the demand for the industry's products; it also would indicate the form of the relationship.

As indicated in this analysis, the best relationship was between retail stores-drug and PCE-medical care. The specific regression result was

$$\% \, \Delta \text{ Retail Stores-Drug Sales } = \quad 1.746 \quad + \quad 0.92 \; (\% \, \Delta \text{ PCE-Medical Care})$$
$$\text{(}t\text{-values)} \qquad\qquad (0.42) \quad (2.57)$$
$$R^2 = 0.31 \qquad\qquad F = 6.62$$

The specific sales estimate procedure would begin with an estimate of aggregate PCE for the coming year. Given the importance of the PCE series, it should be relatively easy to find one or several estimates. The next step would be to estimate the increase in the proportion of PCE spent on medical care. As noted, this proportion has grown steadily from 7.7 percent to 13.7 percent. Once you estimate this percentage, you apply it to the PCE estimate to arrive at an estimate of PCE-medical care. Finally, you would use this PCE-medical care estimate in a regression equation to derive a sales estimate for the industry. This procedure will be demonstrated in a subsequent section.

FORECASTING
EARNINGS PER
SHARE

EARNINGS FORECASTING AND THE ANALYSIS OF INDUSTRY COMPETITION   Similar to the sales forecast that can be enhanced by the analysis of the industrial life cycle, an industry earnings forecast should be preceded by the analyses of the competitive structure for the industry. Specifically, a critical factor affecting the profit potential of an industry is the intensity of competition in the industry, as Porter has discussed in a series of books and articles.[5]

COMPETITION
AND EXPECTED
INDUSTRY
RETURNS

Porter's concept of **competitive strategy** is described as the search by a firm for a favorable competitive position in an industry. To create a profitable competitive strategy, a firm must first examine the basic competitive structure of its industry because the potential profitability of a firm is heavily influenced by the profitability of its industry. After determining the competitive structure of the industry, you examine the factors that determine the relative competitive position of a firm within its industry. In this section, we consider the competitive forces that determine the competitive structure of the industry. In the next chapter, our discussion of company analysis will cover the factors that determine the relative competitive position of a firm within its industry.

*BASIC COMPETITIVE
FORCES*

Porter believes that the **competitive environment** of an industry (the intensity of competition among the firms in that industry) determines the ability of the firms to sustain above-average rates of return on invested capital. As shown in Figure 19.4, he suggests that five competitive forces determine the intensity of competition, and that the relative effect of each of these five factors can vary dramatically among industries.

1. *Rivalry among the existing competitors.* For each industry analyzed, you must judge if the rivalry among firms is currently intense and growing, or if it is polite and stable. Rivalry increases when many firms of relatively equal size compete in an industry. When estimating the number and size of firms, be sure to include foreign competitors. Further, *slow growth* causes competitors to fight for market share and increases competition. *High fixed costs* stimulate the desire to sell at the full capacity, which can lead to price cutting and greater competition. Finally, look for *exit barriers,* such as specialized facilities or labor agreements. These can keep firms in the industry despite below-average or negative rates of return.

2. *Threat of new entrants.* Although an industry may have few competitors, you must determine the likelihood of firms entering the industry and increasing competition. *High barriers to entry,* such as low current prices relative to costs, keep the threat of new entrants low. Other barriers to entry include the need to invest large financial resources to compete and the availability of capital. Also, substantial economies of scale give a current industry member an advantage over a new firm. Further entrants might be discouraged if success in the industry requires extensive distribution channels that are

---

[5] Michael E. Porter, *Competitive Strategy: Techniques for Analyzing Industries and Competitors* (New York: Free Press, 1980); Michael Porter, "Industry Structure and Competitive Strategy: Keys to Profitability," *Financial Analysts Journal* 36, no. 4 (July–August 1980); and Michael Porter, *Competitive Advantage: Creating and Sustaining Superior Performance* (New York: Free Press, 1985), Chapter 1.

FIGURE 19.4   **FORCES DRIVING INDUSTRY COMPETITION**

Source: Adapted/reprinted with the permission of The Free Press, a division of Simon and Schuster, from *Competitive Strategy: Techniques for Analyzing Industries and Competitors,* by Michael E. Porter. Copyright © 1980 by The Free Press.

hard to build because of exclusive distribution contracts. Similarly, high costs of switching products or brands such as those required to change a computer or telephone system keep competition low. Finally, government policy can restrict entry by imposing licensing requirements or limiting access to materials (lumber, coal). Without some of these barriers, it might be very easy for competitors to enter an industry, increasing the competition and driving down potential rates of return.

3. *Threat of substitute products.* Substitute products limit the profit potential of an industry because they limit the prices firms in an industry can charge. Although almost everything has a substitute, you must determine how close the substitute is in price and function to the product in your industry. As an example, the threat of substitute glass containers hurt the metal container industry. Glass containers kept declining in price, forcing metal container prices and profits down. In the food industry, consumers constantly substitute between beef, pork, chicken, and fish. The more commoditylike the product, the greater the competition and the lower the profit margins.

4. *Bargaining power of buyers.* Buyers can influence the profitability of an industry because they can bid down prices or demand higher quality or more services by bargaining among competitors. Buyers become powerful when they purchase a large volume relative to the sales of a supplier. The most vulnerable firm is a one-customer firm that supplies a single large manufacturer, as is common for auto parts manufacturers or software developers. Buyers will be more conscious of the costs of items that represent a significant percentage of the firm's total costs. This consciousness increases if the buying firm is feeling cost pressure from its customers. Also, buyers who know a lot

about the costs of supplying an industry will bargain more intensely; for example, when the buying firm supplies some of its own needs and buys from the outside.

5. *Bargaining power of suppliers.* Suppliers can alter future industry returns if they increase prices or reduce the quality of the product or the services they provide. The suppliers are more powerful if they are few and if they are more concentrated than the industry to which they sell, and if they supply critical inputs to several industries, for which few, if any, substitutes exist. In this instance, the suppliers are free to change prices and services they supply to the firms in an industry. When analyzing supplier bargaining power, be sure to consider labor's power within each industry.

An investor can analyze these competitive forces to determine the intensity of the competition in an industry and assess its long-run profit potential. You should examine each of these factors for every industry and develop a relative competitive profile. You need to update this analysis of an industry's competitive environment over time because an industry's competitive structure can and will change over time.

INDUSTRY PROFIT MARGIN FORECAST   Similar to the aggregate market, the net profit margin is the most volatile and the hardest margin to estimate directly. Alternatively, it is suggested that you begin with the operating profit margin (EBDIT/Sales) and then estimate depreciation expense, interest expense, and the tax rate.

INDUSTRY'S GROSS PROFIT MARGIN   Recall that in the market analysis we analyzed the factors that should influence the economy's operating profit margin, including capacity utilization, unit labor cost, inflation, and net exports. The most important variables were capacity utilization and unit labor cost. We cannot do such an analysis for most industries because the relevant variables typically are not available for individual industries. As an alternative, we can assume that movements in these industry profit margin variables are related to movements in similar economic variables. For example, when an increase in capacity utilization for the aggregate economy exists, there is probably a comparable increase in utilization for the auto industry or the chemical industry. The same could be true for unit labor cost and exports. If there is a stable relationship between these variables for the industry and the economy, you would expect a relationship to exist between the profit margins for the industry and the economy. Although it is not necessary that the relationship be completely linear, it is important for the relationship (whatever it is) to be generally stable.

The operating profit margin (OPM) for the S&P 400 industrial index and the retail store-drug (RSD) index is presented in Table 19.2. The time series plot in Figure 19.5 indicates that the S&P 400 OPM experienced a decline during the 1980s and early 1990s, but ended the period with a margin slightly higher than in 1977. In contrast, the RSD OPM experienced a fairly steady decline. The analysis of the relationship between the OPM for the market and industry using regression analysis was not useful, so is not discussed. It appears that the best estimate can be derived from the OPM time series plot using what we know about the changing competitive environment and profit trends in the retail drugstore business. It is a matter of judgment for each specific industry whether you use regression analysis or the time-series analysis. In any case, any such mathematical analysis should be considered a supplement to the economic analysis of the competitive environment for the industry.

Either regression analysis or time-series techniques can be useful tools, but *neither technique should be applied mechanically.* You should be aware of any unique factors

| TABLE 19.2 | PROFIT MARGINS AND COMPONENT EXPENSES FOR THE S&P 400 AND THE RSD INDUSTRY INDEX: 1977–1994 |

Year	OPERATING PROFIT ($)		OPERATING PROFIT MARGIN (%)		DEPRECIATION EXPENSE ($)		INTEREST EXPENSE ($)		TAX RATE (%)		NET PROFIT MARGIN (%)	
	S&P 400	RSD	S&P 400	RSD	S&P 400	RSD	S&P 400	RSD	S&P 400	RSD	S&P 400	RSD
1977	32.20	3.94	14.36	8.96	8.53	0.41	3.22	0.13	48.90	48.60	5.20	4.07
1978	36.19	4.38	14.40	8.78	9.64	0.49	3.81	0.13	48.00	47.90	5.23	4.03
1979	42.01	5.31	14.37	7.24	10.82	0.71	4.58	0.23	46.00	45.70	5.63	3.47
1980	43.08	6.00	13.16	7.07	12.37	0.83	5.95	0.28	45.60	44.70	4.98	3.47
1981	44.50	6.85	12.92	7.17	13.82	1.02	7.49	0.39	43.30	44.20	4.92	3.45
1982	42.67	7.97	12.78	7.30	15.30	1.21	8.23	0.41	45.00	44.60	4.02	3.44
1983	45.57	9.48	13.64	7.98	15.67	1.40	7.62	0.43	44.60	45.00	4.51	3.79
1984	51.50	9.72	13.56	7.19	16.31	1.71	8.54	0.78	42.70	45.10	5.86	3.04
1985	53.23	10.73	13.36	7.00	18.19	2.02	9.24	0.73	46.70	45.90	3.92	2.96
1986	51.02	11.62	13.16	7.37	19.41	2.08	9.75	0.77	42.70	45.10	3.81	3.11
1987	58.89	13.57	13.68	7.08	20.21	2.63	10.14	1.17	40.50	43.90	4.77	2.88
1988	74.31	14.60	15.26	6.70	23.59	3.09	14.84	1.42	35.30	38.60	5.33	2.90
1989	79.52	16.08	14.69	6.71	24.21	3.39	18.79	1.65	37.00	37.80	4.96	2.79
1990	82.47	17.84	13.87	6.71	26.31	4.15	20.17	1.63	39.60	38.30	4.26	2.89
1991	75.10	18.49	12.80	6.52	27.50	4.03	18.74	1.32	41.19	36.70	2.97	2.91
1992	78.17	19.68	13.00	6.35	29.48	4.39	16.20	1.08	37.91	36.95	3.27	2.89
1993	82.16	20.56	13.61	6.25	28.72	4.75	14.66	0.80	37.27	38.29	3.73	2.15
1994	92.52	23.36	14.65	6.42	29.92	5.32	13.55	1.01	36.10	38.29	5.35	2.89

Source: *Standard & Poor's Analysts Handbook* (New York: Standard & Poor's Corporation, 1995). Reprinted by permission of Standard & Poor's Corp.

affecting the specific industry such as price wars, contract negotiations, building plans, or foreign competition. An analysis of these unique events is critical when estimating the final gross profit margin or when estimating a range of industry profit margins (optimistic, pessimistic, most likely).

Beyond this discussion, which is primarily concerned with an estimate of the near-term OPM, it also is important to consider the long-term profitability of the industry based on the competitive structure of the industry as discussed in an earlier section.

INDUSTRY DEPRECIATION   The next step is estimating industry depreciation, which typically is easier because the series generally is increasing; the only question is by how much. As shown in Table 19.2, except for 1991, the depreciation series for RSD increased every year since 1977. The results in Table 19.2 and the time series plots in Figure 19.6 relate depreciation for the S&P 400 and the RSD industry. There is not a strong relationship between levels or growth rates. Depreciation expense for the RSD industry has been growing at the rate of about 8 percent to 10 percent annually in recent years. Therefore, rather than relating it to S&P 400 depreciation, it would probably be best to estimate depreciation based on a time-series analysis of the industry series with some consideration of recent capital expenditures. Subtracting an estimate of depreciation expense from the operating profit figure indicates the industry's net before interest and taxes (EBIT).

INDUSTRY INTEREST EXPENSE   An industry's interest expense will be a function of its financial leverage and interest rates. As shown in Figure 19.7, interest expense for the RSD industry always has been relatively low when compared to the S&P 400 and did not

FIGURE 19.5   **TIME SERIES PLOT OF OPERATING PROFIT MARGINS FOR S&P 400 AND RSD INDUSTRY: 1977–1994**

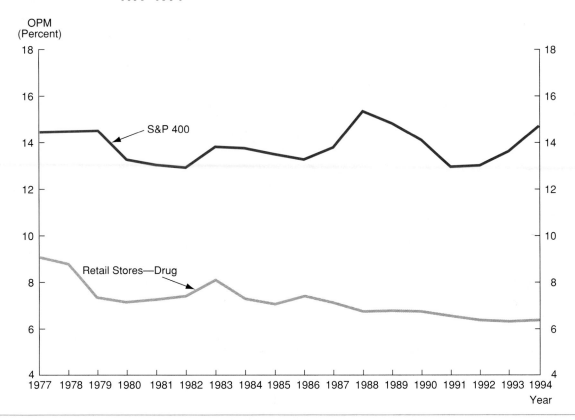

increase at the same rate during the 1980s. Therefore, looking for a relationship between the two interest expense series would not be fruitful. Examining the interest expense series in Table 19.2, it shows steady growth until 1989, a flattening in 1990, followed by a decline to 1993 and a small increase in 1994. Your estimate for the future would be based on two separate estimates: (1) changes in the amount of debt outstanding for this industry during the year, and (2) an estimate of the level of interest rates (will they increase or decline?)

INDUSTRY TAX RATE   As you might expect, tax rates differ between industries. An extreme example would be the oil industry where heavy depletion allowances cause lower taxes. In some instances, however, you can assume that tax law changes have similar impacts on all industries. To see if this is valid, you need to examine the relationship of tax rates over time for your industry and the aggregate market to determine if you can use regression analysis or a time series plot. In either case, it is important to be aware of unique tax factors for the industry.

As shown in Figure 19.8, the RSD tax rate historically has moved with the economy's tax rate. Therefore, the time series plot in this figure is fairly informative, although you still need to consider impending national legislation and specific industry factors. Once you have estimated the tax rate, you multiply the EBT per share value by (1 − tax rate) to get your estimate of earnings per share.

| FIGURE 19.6 | TIME SERIES PLOT OF DEPRECIATION FOR S&P 400 AND RSD INDUSTRY: 1977–1994 |

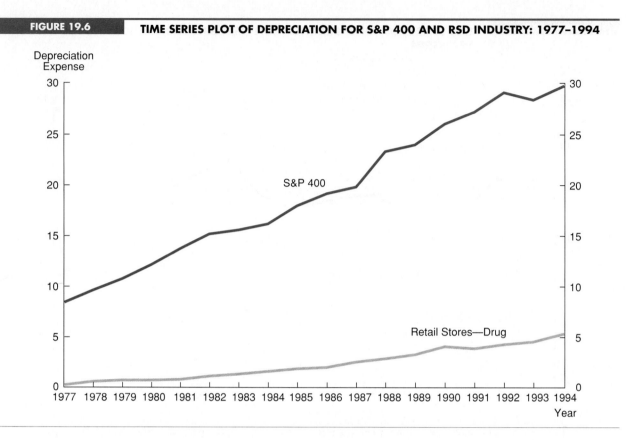

In addition to an estimate of earnings per share, you also should derive an estimate of the industry's net profit margin as a check on your EPS estimate. A time series plot of the profit margin series for the industry and the S&P 400 is contained in Figure 19.9. Two important characteristics are notable. First, the S&P 400 net profit margin series is much more volatile than that for retail drugstores. Second, although both profit margin series appear to show an overall decline, the S&P 400 experienced a strong recovery during 1993–1994 back to a margin over 5 percent. In contrast, while the RSD margin started at about 4 percent, even with the increase in 1994, it is currently not back to 3 percent.

AN INDUSTRY EARNINGS ESTIMATE EXAMPLE

Now that we have described how to estimate each variable in the equation to help you understand the procedure, the following is an estimate of earnings per share for the retail drugstore industry using the economic forecasts from Chapter 18 and the relationship between the RSD industry and the market derived in this chapter. Our results are not as exact as those of a practicing analyst who would use this example as an *initial* estimate that would be modified based on industry knowledge, current events, and expectations of future unique factors.

The regressions and the plots in Figure 19.3 indicated that the best relationship was between retail drugstore sales and PCE-medical care. The outlook for PCE is for an increase of 5.5 percent in 1995 (to $4,881.5 billion) and a 5 percent increase in 1996 to $5,125.6 billion. It is further assumed that medical care expenditures will be 15.9 percent of PCE in 1995 and 16.1 percent in 1996. This implies that PCE-medical care will be about

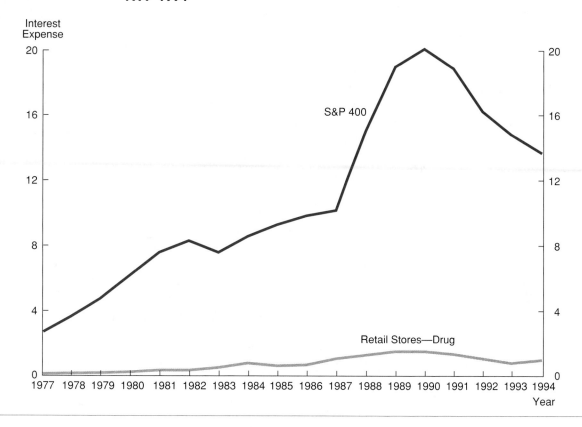

FIGURE 19.7

TIME SERIES PLOT OF INTEREST EXPENSE FOR S&P 400 AND RSD INDUSTRY: 1977–1994

$776 billion in 1995 and $825 billion in 1996. Using these results in the earlier equation indicates that retail drugstore sales in 1996 should be about $425, which implies a 17 percent increase over the two years from 1994.

The OPM for retail drugstores was 6.42 in 1994. During 1995 the OPM for the S&P 400 was expected to increase, and retail drugstore margins probably experienced a similar increase to about 6.50. The aggregate OPM was expected to experience a small decline during 1996. Based on the time series plot in Figure 19.4, this would indicate that retail drugstore margins should also decline to about 6.45 percent, which implies an operating profit per share for the retail drugstore industry of $27.41 (0.0645 × $425).

Aggregate depreciation for the S&P 400 series during 1995 was estimated to be $31.60 and expected to grow to $33.34 in 1996. Assuming the retail drugstore industry will experience similar growth, the depreciation expense is estimated at $5.75 in 1995 and $6.10 in 1996. Therefore, earnings before interest and taxes would be $21.31 (27.41 – 6.10).

As noted, the industry's interest expense did not decline in 1994 along with the aggregate market. Given the continued decline in yields during 1995 and overall stability in rates during 1996 along with no major debt financing, we would estimate interest expense of $0.95 for 1995 and no change in 1996. Thus, EBT would be $20.36 (21.31 – 0.95).

| FIGURE 19.8 | TIME SERIES PLOT OF TAX RATE FOR S&P 400 AND RSD INDUSTRY: 1977–1994 |

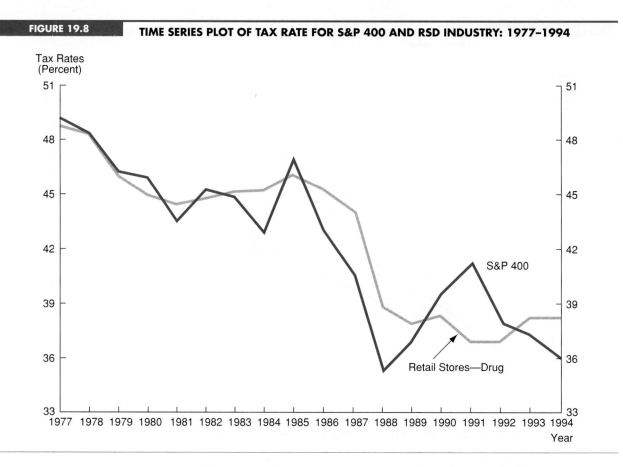

The tax rate for the retail drugstore industry has been higher than the aggregate during the last 2 years when the aggregate tax rate declined. The aggregate tax rate was expected to be relatively stable in 1995 and in 1996. Therefore, a rate of about 38 percent seems appropriate for the retail drugstore industry. This implies taxes of $7.74 (20.36 × .38) and net income (earnings per share) of $12.62 (20.36 − 7.74). This indicates a net profit margin for the RSD industry of 2.97 percent (12.62/425), which is slightly above the recent experience.

Given an estimate of the industry's net income per share, your next step is to estimate the likely earnings multiplier for this industry. Together, the earnings per share and the earnings multiplier provide an estimate of the expected value for the industry index. Given this expected value and an estimate of dividends per share during the holding period, you can compute an expected rate of return from investing in this industry.

ESTIMATING AN
INDUSTRY
EARNINGS
MULTIPLIER

This section discusses how to estimate an industry earnings multiplier using two alternative techniques: macroanalysis and microanalysis. In macroanalysis, you examine the relationship between the multiplier for the industry and the market. In microanalysis, you estimate the industry earnings multiplier by examining the specific variables that influence it—the dividend-payout ratio, the required rate of return for the industry (k), and the expected growth rate of earnings and dividends for the industry (g).

FIGURE 19.9

TIME SERIES PLOT OF NET PROFIT MARGINS FOR S&P 400 AND RSD INDUSTRY: 1977–1994

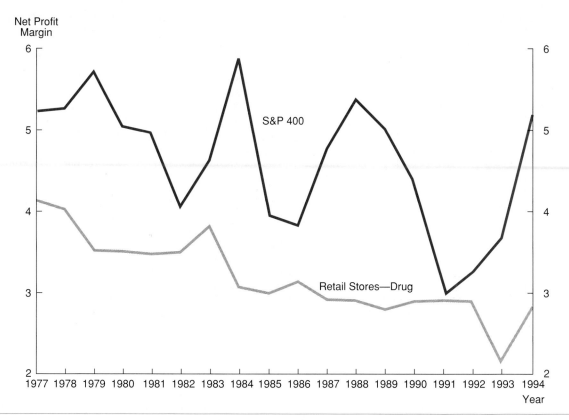

MACROANALYSIS OF AN INDUSTRY MULTIPLIER

Macroanalysis assumes a relationship between changes in k and g for specific industries and for the aggregate market. A similar pattern of changes for these variables (even though they are not the same values) would imply a relationship between changes in the industry P/E ratio and changes in the P/E ratio for the stock market.

An examination of the relationship between the P/E ratios for 71 S&P industries and the S&P 400 index during four partially overlapping 21-year periods indicated a significant positive relationship between percentage changes in P/E ratios for most industries examined.[6] Notably, there was a difference in the quality of the relationship between industries, that is, the relationship was not always significant. Therefore, it is necessary to evaluate the quality of the relationship between the P/E ratios for a specific industry and the market before using this technique.

The results in Table 19.3 and Figure 19.10 for the retail drugstore industry during the period 1977 to 1994 indicate a relatively close relationship between the market and the RSD industry. The P/E ratio for drugstores was generally above the market P/E ratio until 1991 when the market P/E increased while the P/E for drugstores was relatively stable. The P/Es were very similar in 1993 and 1994. Also, the industry P/E ratios are less volatile than

---

[6] Frank K. Reilly and Thomas Zeller, "An Analysis of Relative Industry Price–Earnings Ratios," *The Financial Review* (1974): 17–33.

TABLE 19.3		EARNINGS MULTIPLIER FOR THE S&P 400 AND THE RSD INDUSTRY, AND INFLUENTIAL VARIABLES: 1977–1994												

	EARNINGS MULTIPLIER		RETENTION RATE		NET PROFIT MARGIN		TOTAL ASSET TURNOVER		RETURN ON TOTAL ASSETS		TOTAL ASSETS/ EQUITY		RETURN ON EQUITY	
Year	S&P 400	RSD	S&P 400	RSD	S&P 400	RSD	S&P 400	RSD	S&P 400	RSD	S&P 400	RSD	S&P 400	RSD
1977	9.55	10.58	56.80	79.90	5.15	4.07	1.27	2.84	6.54	11.56	2.08	1.53	13.60	17.68
1978	8.21	11.05	58.80	76.10	5.19	4.03	1.27	2.81	6.59	11.32	2.15	1.52	14.17	17.21
1979	7.11	8.78	63.70	72.60	5.57	3.47	1.30	3.00	7.24	10.41	2.20	1.65	15.93	17.18
1980	8.44	8.36	59.70	70.80	4.92	3.47	1.31	3.04	6.45	10.55	2.23	1.66	14.37	17.51
1981	8.45	10.52	58.10	69.00	4.86	3.45	1.28	3.03	6.22	10.45	2.25	1.65	14.00	17.25
1982	10.37	11.06	46.00	68.90	3.95	3.44	1.17	2.97	4.62	10.22	2.31	1.66	10.68	16.96
1983	11.84	12.60	50.40	70.70	4.42	3.79	1.15	2.86	5.08	10.84	2.28	1.88	11.59	20.38
1984	9.92	14.22	58.50	62.40	4.77	3.04	1.22	2.65	5.82	8.06	2.39	1.93	13.91	15.55
1985	13.68	16.18	48.50	59.20	3.84	2.96	1.15	2.68	4.42	7.93	2.54	1.88	11.22	14.91
1986	17.48	17.10	44.00	67.10	3.75	3.11	1.07	2.71	4.01	8.43	2.58	1.94	10.35	16.35
1987	16.00	17.89	57.00	68.40	4.77	2.88	1.08	2.80	5.15	8.06	2.62	2.04	13.50	16.45
1988	11.38	14.77	63.10	69.40	5.51	2.90	0.98	2.82	5.40	8.18	3.03	2.07	16.36	16.93
1989	13.59	16.07	55.97	67.71	5.01	2.79	0.97	2.82	4.86	7.87	3.16	2.03	15.36	15.97
1990	15.83	14.94	49.80	68.32	4.26	2.89	0.97	2.82	4.13	8.13	3.27	2.00	13.50	16.26
1991	25.36	16.91	28.19	67.19	2.97	2.91	0.94	2.85	2.80	8.31	3.24	1.83	9.09	15.25
1992	25.74	17.82	33.86	66.41	3.27	2.89	0.96	2.83	3.13	8.19	3.50	1.82	10.95	14.89
1993	23.72	22.88	41.96	53.17	3.73	2.15	0.92	2.79	3.42	6.00	3.76	1.88	12.86	11.27
1994	16.21	15.48	61.06	66.22	5.35	2.89	0.91	2.63	4.89	7.60	3.51	2.00	17.14	15.17
Mean	14.05	14.29	51.97	67.97	4.52	3.17	1.11	2.83	5.04	9.01	2.73	1.83	13.25	16.29

Source: *Standard & Poor's Analysts Handbook* (New York: Standard and Poor's Corp., 1995). Reprinted by permission of Standard and Poor's Corp.

the market P/E ratios. These results imply that the macroanalysis technique could be useful for this industry, but you also should use the microanalysis approach.

MICROANALYSIS OF AN INDUSTRY MULTIPLIER

In Chapter 18, we estimated the future earnings multiplier for the stock-market series in two ways. In the first, the direction of change approach, we estimated the changes for the three variables that determine the earnings multiplier—the dividend-payout ratio, the required rate of return, and the expected growth rate of earnings and dividends. Based on the consensus of changes, we estimated a direction of change for the multiplier from its current value. In the second approach, the specific multiplier estimate, we estimated a range of values for the three variables that determine the multiplier and derived a range of P/E ratio estimates. These two approaches provided five multiplier estimates that were used with our EPS estimate to compute a range of expected values for the market index that, in turn, provided expected rates of return on common stocks.

Our microanalysis of the industry multiplier could use the same two approaches for each industry. Although this would certainly be reasonable, it would not take advantage of the prior work on the stock-market multiplier. Because the variables that affect the stock-market multiplier also determine the industry multiplier, it should be possible to compare the two sets of variables.

Therefore, in our microanalysis, we estimate the three variables that determine the industry earnings multiplier and compare them to the comparable values for the market P/E. This allows us to determine whether the industry earnings multiplier should be above, below, or equal to the market multiplier. Once we feel confident about this relationship, it is

where

% Δ RSD_t = **the percentage price change in the retail drugstore (RSD) index during month** *t*
α_i = **the regression intercept for the RSD industry**
β_i = **the systematic risk measure for the RSD industry equal to** $Cov_{i,m}/\sigma^2_m$

To derive an estimate for the RSD industry, the model specified was run with monthly data for the 5-year period 1991 to 1995. The results for this regression are as follows:

α_i = 0.004	R^2 = 0.70
β_i = 0.50	DW = 1.78
t-value = 8.70	F = 70.52

The systematic risk (β = 0.50) for the retail drugstore industry is clearly below unity indicating a low-risk industry (i.e., risk less than the market). These results are quite consistent with the prior analysis of fundamental risk factors (BR, FR, LR, ERR, CR).

Translating this systematic risk into a required return figure (k) calls for using the security market line model as follows:

$$k_i = \text{RFR} + \beta_i(R_m - \text{RFR})$$

Assuming a nominal risk-free rate during this period of 7 percent (.07), a market return (R_m) of 11 percent, and a beta for the industry of 0.50 indicates the following:

$$k_i = .07 + 0.50(.11 - .07)$$
$$= .09$$
$$= 9 \text{ percent}$$

A micro estimate of fundamental risk below average and a risk estimate using the CAPM likewise below average implies an industry earnings multiple above the market multiple, all other factors being equal.

ESTIMATING THE EXPECTED GROWTH RATE (g)   You will recall that earnings and dividend growth are determined by the retention rate and the return on equity.

$$g = f(\text{Retention Rate and Return on Equity})$$

We have consistently broken down return on equity into the following three components:

$$\frac{\text{Net Profit}}{\text{Equity}} = \frac{\text{Net Income}}{\text{Sales}} \times \frac{\text{Sales}}{\text{Total Assets}} \times \frac{\text{Total Assets}}{\text{Equity}}$$

$$= \frac{\text{Profit}}{\text{Margin}} \times \frac{\text{Total Asset}}{\text{Turnover}} \times \frac{\text{Financial}}{\text{Leverage}}$$

Therefore, we need to examine each of these variables in Table 19.3 to determine if they imply a difference in the expected growth rate for RSD as compared to the aggregate market (S&P 400).

Earnings retention rate   As noted earlier, the retention rate data in Table 19.3 indicated that the RSD industry had a higher retention rate (68 percent versus 52 percent). This means that the RSD industry would have a potentially higher growth rate, all else being the same (i.e., equal ROE).

Return on equity   Because the return on equity is a function of the net profit margin, total asset turnover, and a measure of financial leverage, these three variables are examined individually.

Historically, the net profit margin for the S&P 400 series has been consistently higher than the margin for the RSD industry. This is not surprising because retail firms typically have lower profit margins but higher turnover. This difference in profit margin increased in 1994 because the S&P 400 margin experienced a larger increase than the RSD industry.

As noted, one would normally expect the total asset turnover (TAT) for a retail firm to be higher than the average company. This expectation was confirmed because the average TAT for the S&P 400 was 1.11 versus 2.83 for the RSD industry. Beyond the overall difference, the spread between the two series increased over the period—in the early years, the turnovers were about 1.30 versus 2.80, and in the final years, they were about 0.91 versus 2.63. Obviously, this change occurred because the TAT for the S&P 400 series declined steadily over the period as shown in Figure 19.11. Multiplying these two ratios indicates the industry's return on total assets (ROTA).

$$\frac{\text{Net Income}}{\text{Sales}} \times \frac{\text{Sales}}{\text{Total Assets}} = \frac{\text{Net Income}}{\text{Total Assets}}$$

FIGURE 19.11   **TIME SERIES PLOT OF TOTAL ASSET TURNOVER FOR S&P 400 AND RSD INDUSTRY: 1977–1994**

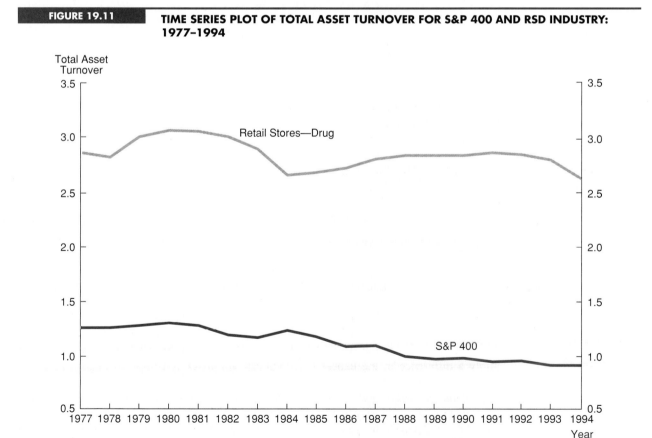

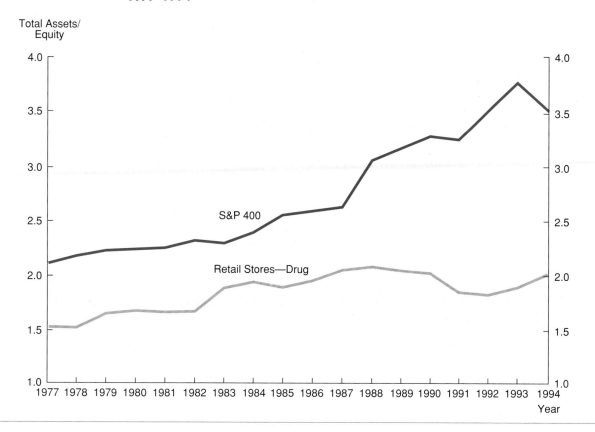

FIGURE 19.12

TIME SERIES PLOT OF FINANCIAL LEVERAGE FOR S&P 400 AND RSD INDUSTRY: 1977–1994

When we do this for the two series, the results in Table 19.3 indicate that the return on total assets (ROTA) for the S&P 400 series went from 6.54 percent to 4.89 percent and averaged 5.04 percent, whereas the ROTA for the RSD industry went from 11.56 percent to 7.60 percent and averaged 9.01 percent. Clearly the industry ROTA results were superior.

The final component is the financial leverage multiplier (total assets/equity). As shown in Table 19.3 and Figure 19.12, the leverage multiplier for the S&P 400 increased fairly steadily from 2.08 to 3.51, whereas the leverage multiplier for the RSD industry went from 1.53 to 2.00. Although this higher financial leverage multiplier implies greater financial risk for both the S&P 400 series and the RSD industry, it also will contribute to a higher ROE, all else being the same.

This brings us to the final value of ROE, which is the product of the three ratios (profit margin, total asset turnover, and financial leverage); one also can use the product of return on total asset and the financial leverage multiplier. The figures in Table 19.3 and the plot in Figure 19.13 indicate that the ROE for the RSD industry was higher than the market throughout the period until 1993. The average annual ROE was 16.29 percent for the RSD industry versus 13.25 percent for the S&P 400 series. These average percentages are quite consistent with what would be derived from multiplying the averages of the components from Table 19.3 as follows:

	Profit Margin		Total Asset Turnover		Total Assets/ Equity		ROE
S&P 400	4.52	×	1.11	×	2.73	=	13.70
RSD Industry	3.17	×	2.83	×	1.83	=	16.42

Although examining the historical trends and the averages for each of the components is important, you should never lose sight of the fact that expectations of *future* performance will determine value. In the current case, this analysis of expectations is very important because of the change in relative ROE in 1993 and 1994. As an analyst, it is necessary to determine whether this is a temporary or permanent change in the relative performance of this industry versus the market. Ideally, you should estimate each of the three components and use these to arrive at an estimate of ROE.

Estimating growth   The growth rate is a function of the retention rate times the return on equity. As noted, the RSD industry has consistently had a higher retention rate (all years: 68 versus 52) and has experienced a higher average return on equity (all years: 16.29 versus 13.25). When these are combined, the estimated long-run growth rates would be

FIGURE 19.13   **TIME SERIES PLOT OF RETURN ON EQUITY FOR S&P 400 AND RSD INDUSTRY: 1977–1994**

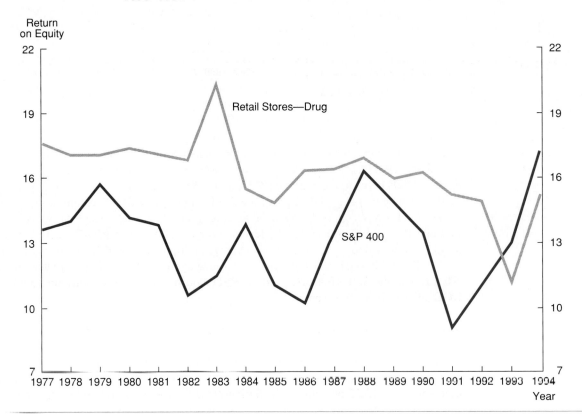

S&P 400	.52 × 13.25 =	6.89%
RSD	.68 × 16.29 =	11.08%

Clearly, if you were comfortable with the ROE estimate used, the fairly large difference in sustainable growth would favor the RSD series and would indicate that the industry earnings multiplier should be higher, all else being the same. As indicated, the critical question that must be answered is whether the reversal in ROE that occurred in 1993–1994 because of the increase in the profit margin for the S&P 400 is temporary or permanent.

WHY THE DIFFERENCE?   Because the earnings multiplier is a function of the dividend-payout ratio, the required rate of return, and the expected growth rate, any differences in P/E ratios would be explained by differences in these variables.

Our initial analysis indicated that the earnings multiplier for the RSD industry was historically higher than the market multiplier, but in 1990 they were almost equal and in 1991 the industry multiple was clearly smaller. The question then becomes: Why has the RSD industry lost this premium? There was a small difference in the payout ratio that favored the S&P 400 series. In contrast, the analysis of risk in terms of fundamental characteristics and a market measure of risk indicates that risk for the RSD industry was lower than the aggregate market risk, which implies a higher industry multiplier.

Finally, an analysis of the growth characteristics of the two series indicated long-term average differences in the profit margin, the total asset turnover, and the financial leverage multiplier that resulted in a higher ROE for the RSD industry pre-1993–1994. When the return on equity figures were combined with higher RSD retention rates, the implied growth rates clearly favored the RSD industry.

In summary, the payout ratio favored the market multiplier, the risk factor strongly favored the RSD industry, and the growth comparison indicated that pre-1993–1994 the multiplier for the RSD industry should be higher than for the market. This would imply that unless investors expected this recent change in the long-run growth relationship to be permanent, *the RSD industry earnings multiplier should be higher than the market multiplier.*

ESTIMATING THE FUTURE   Our purpose has been to demonstrate a technique and to indicate the relationships that should exist between an industry and the market so that you will be aware of the important variables. Still, you should remember that *the past alone is of limited value when projecting the future*. This is because past relationships may not hold in the future. As an analyst, you need to determine the future values for the relevant variables based on your unique knowledge of the industry.

EXAMPLE OF MULTIPLE ESTIMATE   Ideally, you should apply both techniques (macro and micro) to derive fairly consistent estimates of the earnings multiple. In the current case, there was some support for using a macroanalysis approach. The results indicate that the retail drugstore P/E is less volatile than the market P/E. In Chapter 18, it was estimated that the market multiplier would decline slightly during 1996. This would imply almost no change in the multiple for the retail drugstore industry.

The analysis of individual components indicated that the earnings multiplier for the RSD industry should be higher than for the market because it is assumed (expected) that eventually the long-run growth superiority of the RSD industry will prevail. This would imply a multiplier of about 19 for the RSD industry. In summary, the industry macro P/E estimate is about 18, whereas the microanalysis indicates a multiple of about 19. For our example, we will use the higher value of these two estimates (19).

THE TOTAL ESTIMATE   The net earnings estimate was for $12.62 a share during 1996. This, coupled with a multiple estimate of 19, implied an index value estimate of 239.78 at the end of 1996. Given this index value, you can derive your expected return—$E(R)$—based on the current value of the index and the expected dividend as follows:

$$E(R_{rsd}) = \frac{239.78 - \text{Index (Current)} + \text{Dividend}}{\text{Index (Current)}}$$

The RSD industry value as of early 1996 was 225.50. If we use this value and assume a dividend payout of about 30 percent of the $12.62 earnings, it implies a dividend of about $3.80. Plugging these values in the equation, we get:

$$E(R_{rsd}) = \frac{239.78 - 225.50 + 3.80}{225.50} - 1$$
$$= 8$$

We would then compare this expected rate of return to our required rate of return of about 9 percent, which was based on the industry's beta of 0.50. This comparison would imply a small underweighting of this industry.

GLOBAL INDUSTRY ANALYSIS

Because so many firms are active in foreign markets and because the proportion of foreign sales is growing for so many firms, we must expand industry analysis to include the effects of foreign firms on global trade and industry returns. To see why this is so, consider the auto industry. Besides Chrysler, Ford, and General Motors, the auto industry for a global investor includes numerous firms from Japan, Germany, Italy, and Korea, among others. Thus we must extend the analysis described earlier to include additional global factors. This section presents an example of such an analysis for the European chemical industry performed by industry analysts at Goldman, Sachs & Company.[7] Although the report discusses individual firms in the industry, we emphasize the overall chemical industry.

THE EUROPEAN CHEMICAL INDUSTRY

Table 19.4 contains the expected economic outlook for the major European countries during the period 1995 to 1997. The economic outlook clearly varied depending upon the country. Specifically, Germany, the United Kingdom and the United States reflected increasing growth over the three years, in contrast to Italy and Japan where the outlook was for slower growth each year (France was a mixture).

PROFIT PERFORMANCE   Table 19.5 shows EPS, ROE, the debt/equity ratio, and several measures of relative value (P/E, P/CF, P/B) for eight major companies, which reflects what happened to most other firms in this industry. These data indicate that most firms in the industry were expected to experience an increase in profit results during 1997 versus 1996. Also, the ROEs for 1995 were quite respectable with the exception of Schering and Rhone-Poulenc. Similar to the past, the expected P/E ratios were wide ranging, as were the P/CF

[7] Charles K. Brown, Mark Tracey, and Paul Krikler, "The Major European Chemicals/Pharma Groups—Share Price Surge" (London: Goldman, Sachs International Ltd., April 1996).

TABLE 19.4

ECONOMIC SCENARIO 1995E–1997E (ANNUAL PERCENTAGE CHANGES)[a]

	GDP		
	1995E	1996E	1997E
Germany	1.0	1.3	2.1
France	0.7	3.0	1.3
UK	2.0	2.1	3.3
Italy	2.4	2.1	1.8
US	1.4	2.2	2.7
Japan	2.5	2.2	1.5

[a]Goldman, Sachs & Co. estimates.

Source: Charles K. Brown, Mark Tracey, and Paul Krinkler, "The Major European Chemical/Pharma Groups—Share Price Surge," (London: Goldman, Sachs International Ltd., April 1996). Reprinted by permission of Goldman, Sachs & Co.

TABLE 19.5

KEY EARNINGS AND FINANCIAL STATISTICS FOR MAJOR CHEMICAL FIRMS[a]

Firm	Currency	EPS		1995(%)		P/E	P/CF	P/B
		1996E	1997E	ROE	ND/Eq	1996E	1996	1995
BASF	DM	40.0	46.0	15	−19	10.8	4.3	1.5
Bayer	DM	38.0	44.0	14	6	13.7	6.7	2.0
Hoechst	DM	34.0	47.5	14	93	15.5	6.3	2.5
Schering	DM	5.0	5.8	8	−61	23.2	8.9	2.7
AKZO	DFL	19.0	22.5	20	55	9.9	5.1	2.0
DSM	DFL	24.3	29.5	23	0	6.5	3.5	1.1
L'Air Liquide	FFr	45.0	51.6	12	16	20.4	10.0	2.6
Rhone-Poulenc	Ffr	8.6	12.4	5	153	15.6	4.8	1.2

[a]Goldman, Sachs & Co. estimates.

Source: Charles K. Brown, Mark Tracey, and Paul Krikler, "The Major European Chemicals/Pharma Groups—Share Price Surge" (London: Goldman, Sachs International Ltd., April 1996). Reprinted by permission of Goldman, Sachs & Co..

and P/B ratios. As noted in the financial statement analysis chapter, because of the differences among countries in accounting treatments, it is typically not possible to compare such ratios across countries, but only to examine them over time within a country.

The final segment of the analysis examined the currency factors involved in forecasting production for each country, and the export–import possibilities based on the exchange rate outlook. Table 19.6 lists exchange rate trends for each of the major countries relative to the U.S. dollar and on a trade-weighted basis to all currencies. The main point that comes across from looking at these results for the period 1994–1996E is the cyclical changes—periods of strength followed by periods of weakness, then strength again. It emphasizes the importance of these exchange rate changes and the need to forecast them.

Overall, the prospects for the latter part of 1996 and into 1997 were considered relatively optimistic. The analysts were optimistic about earnings developments through the remainder of 1996 and 1997. Further, while valuations were above those that prevailed during the 1980s, the current levels could be justified based upon the improved earnings quality. Finally, they also felt the dollar outlook would be helpful to earnings and valuation.

TABLE 19.6   **EXCHANGE RATE TRENDS 1994–1996E[a]**

		DM Strength		SFr Strength		FFr Strength		DFL Strength		Sterling Strength		
		vs US$ %	Trade-Weighted %	vs US$ %	Trade-Weighted %	vs US$ %	Trade-Weighted %	vs US$ %	Trade-Weighted %	vs US$ %	vs DM %	Trade-Weighted %
1994	Q1	−6	−3	+4	+8	−6	−2	−5	−1	+1	+6	+5
	Q2	−2	—	—	+7	−4	+1	−2	—	−2	+1	—
	Q3	+7	+2	+12	+7	+8	+2	+7	+2	+3	−4	−3
	Q4	+8	+2	—	+5	+9	+2	+9	+1	+6	−3	−1
1995	Q1	+14	+6	+15	+5	+9	+6	+14	+5	+6	−9	−4
	Q2	+16	+7	+18	+9	+14	+3	+16	+6	+7	−11	−5
	Q3	+7	+4	+10	+5	+8	+3	+8	+3	+2	−7	−4
	Q4	+8	+4	+11	+8	+7	+3	+8	+3	−1	−9	—
1996	Q1E[b]	+1	—	+4	+4	+6	+2	+1	—	−3	−4	−4
	Q2E[b]	−6	−2	−4	+1	−2	+1	−5	−2	−5	−1	−1
	Q3E[b]	−3	−1	−1	+2	−2	—	−3	−1	+3	—	−1
	Q4E[b]	−4	−2	−4	−1	−2	—	−4	−1	−2	+2	—

[a]Year-on-year percentage changes.
[b]Projections at 31 March 1996 rates of DM1.48/$, SFr1.19/$, FFr5.03/$, DFL1.65/$, $1.53/£ and DM2.25/£.

Source: Charles K. Brown, Mark Tracey, and Paul Krikler, "The Major European Chemicals/Pharma Groups—Share Price Surge" (London: Goldman, Sachs International Ltd., April 1996). Reprinted by permission of Goldman, Sachs & Co.

The rest of the report discussed the major chemical firms and made specific recommendations regarding each of them. This segment of the report on individual companies will be considered in our next chapter on company analysis.

Summary

- Several studies have examined industry performance and risk. They have found wide dispersion in the performance of alternative industries during specified time periods, implying that industry analysis can help identify superior investments. They also showed inconsistent industry performance over time, implying that looking at only past performance of an industry has little value in projecting future performance. Also, the performance by firms within industries typically is not very consistent, so you must analyze individual companies in an industry following the industry analysis.
- The analysis of industry risk indicated wide dispersion in the measures of risk for different industries, but a fair amount of consistency in the risk measure over time for individual industries. These results imply that risk analysis and measurement are useful in selecting industries. The good news is that past risk measures may be of some value when estimating future risk.
- The two-step approach to estimating the value of an industry involves estimating earnings per share beginning with an estimate of sales. We consider three techniques that can be helpful when estimating sales: the industrial life cycle, input–output analysis, and the relationship of the industry sales to alternative economic series. Similarly, prior to a detailed discussion of estimating earnings per share, we considered the five factors suggested by Porter that determine the intensity of competition in an industry, which in turn affects its long-run profitability. We estimated earnings per share based on an estimate of the operating profit margin, depreciation expense, interest expense, and the industry tax rate. In the second half of the procedure, we estimated the earnings multiplier for the industry through macroanalysis and a microanalysis.
- Global industry analysis must evaluate the effects not only of world supply, demand, and cost components for an industry, but also different valuation levels due to accounting conventions, and finally the impact of exchange rates on the total industry and the firms within it.

Questions

1. Briefly describe the results of studies that examined the performance of alternative industries during specific time periods and discuss their implications for industry analysis.

2. Briefly describe the results of the studies that examined industry performance over time. Do these results complicate or simplify industry analysis?

3. Assume all the firms in a particular industry have consistently experienced similar rates of return. Discuss what this implies regarding the importance of industry and company analysis for this industry.

4. Discuss the contention that differences in the performance of various firms within an industry limit the usefulness of industry analysis.

5. Several studies have examined the difference in risk for alternative industries during a specified time period. Describe the results of these studies and discuss their implications for industry analysis.

6. What were the results when industry risk was examined during successive time periods? Discuss the implication of these results for industry analysis.

7. Assume the industry you are analyzing is in the fourth stage of the industrial life cycle. How would you react if your industry–economic analysis predicted that sales per share for this industry would increase by 20 percent? Discuss your reasoning.

8. Discuss at what stage in the industrial life cycle you would like to discover an industry. Justify your decision.

9. Give an example of an industry in stage two of the industrial life cycle. Discuss your reasoning for putting the industry in stage two and any evidence that caused you to select this industry.

10. Discuss an example of input–output analysis to predict the sales for the auto industry. Discuss how you would use input–output analysis to predict the costs of production for the computer industry.

11. Discuss the impact of the threat of substitute products on the steel industry's profitability.

Problems

1. Select three industries from the S&P *Analysts Handbook* with different demand factors. For each industry, indicate what economic series you would use to predict the growth for the industry. Discuss why the economic series selected is relevant for this industry.

2. Prepare a scatter plot for one of the industries in Problem 1 of industry sales per share and observations from the economic series you suggested for this industry. Do this for the most recent 10 years using information available in the *Analysts Handbook.* Based on the results of the scatter plot, discuss whether the economic series was closely related to this industry's sales.

3. Based on an analysis of the results in Problem 2, discuss the stage of your industry in its life cycle.

4. Evaluate your industry in terms of the five factors that determine an industry's intensity of competition. Based on this analysis, what are your expectations about the industry's profitability in the short run (one or two years) and the long run (5–10 years)?

5. Using the S&P *Analysts Handbook,* plot the latest 10-year history of the operating profit margin for the S&P 400 versus the S&P industry of your choice. Is there a positive, negative, or zero correlation?

6. Using the S&P *Analysts Handbook,* calculate the means for the following variables of the S&P 400 and the industry of your choice during the last 10 years:
   a. Price/earnings multiplier
   b. Retention rate
   c. Return on equity
   d. Equity turnover
   e. Net profit margin
   Briefly comment on how your industry and the S&P 400 differ for each of the variables.

7. Prepare a table listing the variables that influence the earnings multiplier for your chosen industry and the S&P 400 series for the most recent 10 years.
   a. Do the average dividend-payout ratios for your industry and the S&P 400 differ? How should the dividend payout influence the difference between the multipliers?

b. Based on the fundamental factors, would you expect the risk for this industry to differ from that for the market? In what direction, and why? Calculate the industry beta using monthly data for 5 years. Based on the fundamental factors and the computed systematic risk, how does this industry's risk compare to the market? What effect will this difference in risk have on the industry multiplier relative to the market multiplier?

c. Analyze and discuss the different components of growth (retention rate, total asset turnover, total assets/equity, and profit margin) for your chosen industry and the S&P 400 during the most recent 10 years. Based on this analysis, how would you expect the growth rate for your industry to compare with the growth rate for the S&P 400? How would this difference in expected growth affect the multiplier?

8. *CFA Examination II (1995)*

As a securities analyst you have been asked to review a valuation of a closely-held business, Wigwam Autoparts Heaven, Inc. (WAH) prepared by the Red Rocks Group (RRG). You are to give an opinion on the valuation and to support your opinion by analyzing each part of the valuation. WAH's sole business is automotive parts retailing.

The RRG valuation includes a section called "Analysis of the Retail Autoparts Industry," based completely on the data in Table 1 and the following additional information.

- WAH and its principal competitors each operated over 150 stores at year end 1994.
- The average number of stores operated per company engaged in the retail autoparts industry is 5.3.
- The major customer base for auto parts sold in retail stores consists of young owners of old vehicles. These owners do their own automotive maintenance out of economic necessity.

TABLE 1	SELECTED RETAIL AUTOPARTS INDUSTRY DATA									
	1994	1993	1992	1991	1990	1989	1988	1987	1986	1985
Population 18–29 Years Old (Percentage Change)	−1.8%	−2.0%	−2.1%	−1.4%	−0.8%	−0.9%	−1.1%	−0.9%	−0.7%	−0.3%
Number of Households with Income More Than $35,000 (Percentage Change)	6.0%	4.0%	8.0%	4.5%	2.7%	3.1%	1.6%	3.6%	4.2%	2.2%
Number of Households with Income Less than $35,000 (Percentage Change)	3.0%	−1.0%	4.9%	2.3%	−1.4%	2.5%	1.4%	−1.3%	0.6%	0.1%
Number of Cars 5–15 Years Old (Percentage Change)	0.9%	−1.3%	−6.0%	1.9%	3.3%	2.4%	−2.3%	−2.2%	−8.0%	1.6%
Automotive Aftermarket Industry Retail Sales (Percentage Change)	5.7%	1.9%	3.1%	3.7%	4.3%	2.6%	1.3%	0.2%	3.7%	2.4%
Consumer Expenditures on Automotive Parts and Accessories (Percentage Change)	2.4%	1.8%	2.1%	6.5%	3.6%	9.2%	1.3%	6.2%	6.7%	6.5%
Sales Growth of Retail Autoparts Companies with 100 or More Stores	17.0%	16.0%	16.5%	14.0%	15.5%	16.8%	12.0%	15.7%	19.0%	16.0%
Market Share of Retail Autoparts Companies with 100 or More Stores	19.0%	18.5%	18.3%	18.1%	17.0%	17.2%	17.0%	16.9%	15.0%	14.0%
Average Operating Margin of Retail Autoparts Companies with 100 or More Stores	12.0%	11.8%	11.2%	11.5%	10.6%	10.6%	10.0%	10.4%	9.8%	9.0%
Average Operating Margin of all Retail Autoparts Companies	5.5%	5.7%	5.6%	5.8%	6.0%	6.5%	7.0%	7.2%	7.1%	7.2%

a. One of RRG's conclusions is that the retail autoparts industry as a whole is in the stabilization stage of the industry life cycle. Discuss *three* relevant items of data from Table 1 that support this conclusion. [9 minutes]

b. Another RRG conclusion is that WAH and its principal competitors are in the growth stage of their life cycle.

Cite *three* relevant items of data from Table 1 that support this conclusion.

Explain how WAH and its principal competitors can be in a growth stage while their industry as a whole is in the stabilization stage. [11 minutes]

References

Aber, John. "Industry Effects and Multivariate Stock Price Behavior." *Journal of Financial and Quantitative Analysis* 11, no. 5 (November 1976).

Fruhan, William E., Jr. *Financial Strategy.* Homewood, IL: Richard D. Irwin, 1979.

Porter, Michael E. *Competitive Advantage: Creating and Sustaining Superior Performance.* New York: Free Press, 1985.

Porter, Michael E. "How to Conduct an Industry Analysis." In *The Financial Analysts Handbook.* 2d ed., edited by Sumner N. Levine. Homewood, IL: Dow Jones-Irwin, 1988.

Stewart, Samuel S. "Forecasting Corporate Earnings." In *The Financial Analysts Handbook.* 2d ed., edited by Sumner N. Levine. Homewood, IL: Dow Jones-Irwin, 1988.

The following are proceedings from industry analysis seminars sponsored by the Association for Investment Management and Research:

Balog, James (ed.) *The Health Care Industry* (Charlottesville, VA: Association for Investment Management and Research, 1993).

Bhatia, Sanjiv (ed.) *The Consumer Staples Industry* (Charlottesville, VA: Association for Investment Management and Research, 1995).

Bhatia, Sanjiv (ed.) *The Media Industry* (Charlottesville, VA: Association for Investment Management and Research, 1996).

Billingsley, Randall S. (ed.) *The Telecommunications Industry* (Charlottesville, VA: Association for Investment Management and Research, 1994).

Petrie, Thomas A. (ed.) *The Oil and Gas Industries* (Charlottesville, VA: Association for Investment Management and Research, 1993).

Shasta, Theodore (ed.) *The Automotive Industry* (Charlottesville, VA: Association for Investment Management and Research, 1994).

Chapter 19A
APPENDIX

PREPARING AN INDUSTRY ANALYSIS

WHAT IS AN INDUSTRY?[1]

Identifying a company's industry can be difficult in today's business world. Although airlines, railroads, and utilities may be easy to categorize, what about manufacturing companies with three different divisions and none of them are dominant? Perhaps the best way to test whether a company fits into an industry grouping is to compare the operating results for the company and an industry. For our purposes, an industry is a group of companies with similar demand, supply, and operating characteristics.

The following is a set of guidelines for preparing an industry appraisal, including the topics to consider and some specific items to include.

[1]Reprinted and adapted with permission of Stanley D. Ryals, CFA; Investment Council, Inc.; La Crescenta, CA 91214.

Characteristics to Study

1. Price history reveals valuable long-term relationships
   a. Price–earnings ratios
   b. Common stock yields
   c. Price–book value ratios
   d. Price–cash flow ratios
2. Operating data show comparisons of
   a. Return on total investment (ROI)
   b. Return on equity (ROE)
   c. Sales growth
   d. Trends in operating profit margin
   e. Evaluation of stage in industrial life cycle
   f. Book value growth
   g. Earnings per share growth
   h. Profit margin trends (gross, operating, and net)
   i. Evaluation of exchange rate risk from foreign sales
3. Comparative results of alternative industries show
   a. Effects of business cycles on each industry group
   b. Secular trends affecting results
   c. Industry growth compared to other industries
   d. Regulatory changes
   e. Importance of overseas operations

Factors in Industry Analysis

MARKETS FOR PRODUCTS

1. Trends in the markets for the industry's major products: historical and projected
2. Industry growth relative to GDP or other relevant economic series; possible changes from past trends
3. Shares of market for major products among domestic and global producers; changes in market shares in recent years; outlook
4. Effect of imports on industry markets; share of market taken by imports; price and margin changes caused by imports; outlook for imports
5. Effect of exports on their markets; trends in export prices and units exported; outlook for exports
6. Expectations for the exchange rates in major non-U.S. countries; historical volatility of exchange rates; outlook for the level and volatility of exchange rates

FINANCIAL PERFORMANCE

1. Capitalization ratios; ability to raise new capital; earnings retention rate; financial leverage
2. Ratio of fixed assets to capital invested; depreciation policies; capital turnover
3. Return on total capital; return on equity capital; components of ROE
4. Return on foreign investments; need for foreign capital

OPERATIONS

1. Degrees of integration; cost advantages of integration; major supply contracts
2. Operating rates as a percentage of capacity; backlogs; new order trends
3. Trends of industry consolidation
4. Trends in industry competition

5. New product development; research and development expenditures in dollars and as a percentage of sales
6. Diversification; comparability of product lines

MANAGEMENT

1. Management depth and ability to develop from within; organizational structure
2. Board of directors: internal versus external members; compensation package
3. Flexibility to deal with product demand changes; ability to identify and eliminate losing operations
4. Record and outlook of labor relations
5. Dividend policy and historical progression

SOURCES OF INDUSTRY INFORMATION

1. Independent industry journals
2. Industry and trade associations
3. Government reports and statistics
4. Independent research organizations
5. Brokerage house research
6. Financial publishers (S&P; Moody's; Value Line)

Chapter
20

Company Analysis and Stock Selection

This chapter answers the following questions:

- Why is it important to differentiate between company analysis and stock analysis?
- What is the difference between a growth company and a growth stock?
- What techniques are available for estimating company sales?
- What are the two competitive strategies that a firm can use to cope with the competitive environment in its industry?
- What are the steps in estimating the profit margins and earnings per share for a company?
- What are the procedures and factors considered when estimating the earnings multiplier for a firm?
- In addition to the earnings multiplier, what are some other relative valuation ratios?
- What are some value-added measures that can be used to evaluate the performance of a firm?
- What are the specific calculations required to compute economic value-added (EVA), market value-added (MVA), and the franchise value for a firm?
- How do these value-added measures compare to the traditional measures of performance such as ROA and ROE?
- What is the relationship between these value-added measures and changes in the market value of firms?
- What are some additional factors that should be considered when analyzing a company on a global basis?
- What is meant by a true growth company?
- Why is it inappropriate to use the standard dividend discount model to value a true growth company?
- What is the difference between no growth, simple growth, and dynamic growth?
- What is the growth duration model and what information does it provide when analyzing a true growth company and evaluating its stock?
- What is the flexible three-stage growth model and how would you describe the three stages?

At this point, you have made two decisions about your investment in equity markets. First, after analyzing the economy and stock markets for several countries, you have decided what percent of your portfolio should be invested in common stocks. Second, after analyzing a number of industries, you have identified those that offer above-average risk-adjusted performance over your investment horizon. You must now answer the final question in the fundamental analysis procedure: Which are the best companies within these desirable industries, and are their stocks underpriced? Specifically, is the value of the stock above its market value or is the expected rate of return on the stock equal to or greater than its required rate of return?

We begin this chapter with a discussion of the difference between company analysis and stock selection. We then present an analysis of a company using the technique that was employed in Chapters 18 and 19 to estimate the value of the stock market and an industry. Specifically, we use the dividend discount model to value Walgreen Company shares. This analysis involves an analysis of the company's competitive strategies within its industry. Following our DDM valuation example, we consider some other valuation measures used by investors to evaluate stock issues. This is followed by a presentation on some well-regarded value-added measures of performance that help analysts identify outstanding managers and possibly superior stocks. We then present an example of the analysis of foreign stocks. The final section in the chapter discusses the unique features of true growth companies and considers several models that can be used to determine the relative value of growth companies.

ANALYSIS OF COMPANIES VERSUS THE SELECTION OF STOCK

The title of this chapter, "Company Analysis and Stock Selection," is meant to convey the idea that *the common stocks of good companies are not necessarily good investments*. In our discussion of the firm value, we analyze a company and its internal characteristics. The analysis should give you opinions about the quality of the firm, its management, and its outlook for the future.

Remember, however, that the quality of the company need not reflect the desirability of the company's stock as an investment. As a final step, you must compare the intrinsic value of a stock to its market value to determine if you should invest in it. The stock of a wonderful firm with superior management and performance measured by sales and earnings growth can be priced so high that the value of the stock of an outstanding company is below its market price. Therefore, you would not want to buy the stock of this wonderful company. In contrast, the stock of a company with less success based on its sales and earnings growth may have a stock market price that is below its intrinsic value. In this case, although the company is not as good, its stock could be a good addition to your portfolio.

The classic confusion in this regard concerns growth companies versus growth stocks. The stock of a growth company is not necessarily a growth stock. Recognition of this difference is very important for successful investing.

GROWTH COMPANIES AND GROWTH STOCKS

Growth companies have historically been defined as companies that consistently experience above-average increases in sales and earnings. This definition has some limitations because many firms could qualify due to certain accounting procedures, mergers, or other external events.

In contrast, financial theorists define a growth company as a firm with the management ability and the opportunities to *make investments that yield rates of return greater than the firm's required rate of return*.[1] You will recall from financial management courses that this required rate of return is the firm's average cost of capital. For example, a growth company might be able to acquire capital at an average cost of 10 percent, and yet have the management ability and the opportunity to invest those funds at rates of return of 15 percent to 20 percent. As a *result* of these investment opportunities, the firm's sales and earnings grow more than those of other firms of equal risk or the overall economy. In addition, a growth

---

[1] Ezra Solomon, *The Theory of Financial Management* (New York: Columbia University Press, 1963), 55–68; and Merton Miller and Franco Modigliani, "Dividend Policy, Growth and the Valuation of Shares," *Journal of Business* 34, no. 4 (October 1961): 411–433.

company with above-average investment opportunities should, and typically does, retain a large portion of its earnings to fund these superior investment projects. The point is, the tendency for a high retention rate and a high growth rate of sales and earnings is the *result* of superior investment opportunities. Many observers describe growth companies in terms of the *results* of true growth, not its *causes*, which is the appropriate specification.

Growth stocks are not necessarily shares in growth companies. A **growth stock** is a stock with a higher rate of return than other stocks in the market with similar risk characteristics. The stock achieves this superior return because at some point in time the market undervalued it compared to other stocks. Although the stock market adjusts stock prices relatively quickly and accurately to reflect new information, available information is not always perfect or complete. Therefore, imperfect or incomplete information may cause a given stock to be undervalued or overvalued at a point in time.[2]

If the stock is undervalued, its price should eventually increase to reflect its true fundamental value when the correct information becomes available. During this period of price adjustment, the stock's realized returns will exceed the required returns for a stock with its risk, and it will be considered a growth stock in retrospect.

Identifying a future growth stock as a currently undervalued stock that has a high probability of being properly valued in the near term means that growth stocks are not necessarily limited to growth companies. In fact, if investors recognize a growth company and discount the future earnings stream properly, the current market price of the growth company's stock will reflect its future earnings stream. Thus, those who acquire the stock of a growth company at this *correct* market price will receive a rate of return consistent with the risk of the stock, even when the superior earnings growth is attained. In fact, in many instances investors tend to overprice the stock of a growth company. In turn, investors who acquire the stock of a growth company at such an inflated price will earn a rate of return below the risk-adjusted required rate of return despite the fact that the company fulfills its bright prospects. A future growth stock can be issued by any type of company; the stock need only be undervalued by the market.

The search for a stock that was a growth stock in the past is relatively easy because you only need to examine past rates of return relative to risk. The investor, however, must search for *future* growth stocks. One who uncovers growth stocks consistently is, by definition, a superior analyst or investor.[3] Several studies have examined the stock price performance for a sample of growth companies or "excellent" companies and have found an inverse relationship, that is, the stock of growth companies or excellent companies did poorly—i.e., they were non-growth stocks.[4]

Other Company– Stock Comparisons

DEFENSIVE COMPANIES AND STOCKS   **Defensive companies** are those whose future earnings are likely to withstand an economic downturn. One would expect them to have relatively low business risk and not excessive financial risk. Typical examples are public utilities or grocery chains—firms that supply basic consumer necessities.

There are two closely related concepts of a **defensive stock.** First, a defensive stock's rate of return is not expected to decline during an overall market decline, or not decline as

---

[2] As noted in Chapter 7, an analyst is more likely to find undervalued stocks outside the top tier of companies because these top-tier stocks are scrutinized by numerous analysts; in other words, look for "neglected" stocks.

[3] See the discussion in Chapter 7 on "Evaluating the Performance of Analysts."

[4] Michael Solt and Meir Statman, "Good Companies, Bad Stocks," *Journal of Portfolio Management* 15, no. 4 (Summer 1989): 39–44; and Hersh Shefrin and Meir Statman, "Making Sense of Beta, Size, and Book-to-Market," *Journal of Portfolio Management* 21, no. 2 (Winter 1995): 26–34.

much as the overall market. Second, our CAPM discussion indicated that an asset's relevant risk is its covariance with the market portfolio of risky assets, that is, an asset's systematic risk. According to this theory, a stock with low systematic risk (a small beta) would be considered a defensive stock.

CYCLICAL COMPANIES AND STOCKS   A **cyclical company's** sales and earnings will be heavily influenced by aggregate business activity. Such a company will do very well during economic expansions and very poorly during economic contractions. This volatile earnings pattern typically is a function of the firm's business risk and can be compounded by financial risk.

A cyclical stock will experience changes in its rates of return that are greater than changes in overall market rates of return. In terms of the CAPM, these are stocks that have high betas. The stock of a cyclical company, however, is not necessarily cyclical. A **cyclical stock** is the stock of any company that has returns that are more volatile than the overall market.

SPECULATIVE COMPANIES AND STOCKS   A **speculative company** is one whose assets involve great risk, but also has a possibility of great gain. A good example of a speculative firm is one involved in oil exploration.

A **speculative stock** has a high probability of low or negative rates of return and a low probability of normal or high rates of return. This can be the stock of a speculative company (e.g., a penny mining stock), or it can be the opposite of a growth stock. Specifically, a speculative stock is one that is overpriced, so there is a high probability that during the future period when the market adjusts the stock price to its true value, it will experience either very low or possibly negative rates of return. This might be the case for an excellent growth company whose stock is selling at an extremely high price/earnings ratio.

You must examine a company to determine its characteristics and derive an estimate of the value for the stock. Then you compare this derived, intrinsic value of the stock to its current market price to determine whether you should acquire it. Specifically, based on a comparison of the stock's estimated intrinsic value and its market place, will the stock provide a rate of return consistent with its risk?

ESTIMATING THE VALUE OF A COMPANY

The purpose of this section is to compute a value for a particular company and compare that value to the market price of its stock. To do this, we select a firm and examine its sales and earnings performance, as well as its strategies and policies, relative to its industry and the market. This analysis continues our example from Chapter 19 by evaluating a company in the retail drugstore industry.

We selected the Walgreen Company, the largest retail drugstore chain in the United States. It operates 2,085 drugstores in 29 states and Puerto Rico. General merchandise accounts for 25 percent of total sales and pharmacy generates 44 percent.

Although we limit our demonstration to Walgreen, your complete company analysis would cover all the firms in the retail drugstore industry to determine which stocks should perform the best. The objective is to estimate the expected return and risk for all the individual firms in the industry over your investment horizon.

Similar to the market and industry analysis, you estimate the stock's expected return by estimating its future value. You derive these future values by predicting the stock's earnings per share and expected earnings multiplier.

ESTIMATING
COMPANY
EARNINGS
PER SHARE

*COMPANY SALES
FORECAST*

Expected earnings per share is a function of the sales forecast and the estimated profit margin.

The sales forecast includes an analysis of the relationship of company sales to various relevant economic series and to the retail drugstore industry series. These comparisons tell us how the company is performing relative to the economy and its closest competition. Besides providing background on the company, these relationships can help us develop specific sales forecasts for Walgreen.

Table 20.1 contains data on sales for Walgreen from its annual report, sales per share for the retail drugstore industry, and several personal consumption expenditure (PCE) series for the period 1975 to 1995.

To examine the relationship of Walgreen sales to the economy, we considered several alternative series. The series that had the strongest relationship was personal consumption expenditure for medicine (PCE-medical care).[5] The scatter plot of Walgreen sales and the PCE-medical care expenditures contained in Figure 20.1 indicates a strong linear relation-

TABLE 20.1	**COMPARATIVE ANALYSIS OF SALES FOR WALGREEN COMPANY, THE RETAIL DRUGSTORE INDUSTRY, AND VARIOUS ECONOMIC SERIES: 1975–1995**					
Year	Sales Walgreen Company ($ Millions)	Retail Drugstore Industry (Sales per Share)	Personal Consumption Expenditures ($ Billions)	Personal Consumption Expenditures ($ per Capita)	Personal Consumption Expenditures— Medical Care ($ Billions)	Medical Care as a Percentage of PCE
1975	1,079.1	25.89	1,024.9	4,745.5	93.0	9.07
1976	1,169.8	36.40	1,143.1	5,242.7	106.2	9.29
1977	1,223.2	43.99	1,271.5	5,773.3	122.4	9.63
1978	1,192.9	49.87	1,421.2	6,400.2	139.7	9.83
1979	1,334.5	73.39	1,583.7	7,036.9	157.8	9.96
1980	1,530.7	84.82	1,748.1	7,676.3	181.3	10.37
1981	1,743.5	95.50	1,926.2	8,376.0	213.6	11.09
1982	2,039.5	109.22	2,059.2	8,868.7	240.5	11.68
1983	2,360.6	118.85	2,257.5	9,634.8	265.7	11.77
1984	2,744.6	135.15	2,460.3	10,409.7	290.6	11.81
1985	3,161.9	153.30	2,667.4	11,185.7	319.3	11.97
1986	3,660.6	157.74	2,850.6	11,854.5	346.4	12.15
1987	4,281.8	191.72	3,052.2	12,570.6	384.7	12.60
1988	4,883.5	217.80	3,296.1	13,452.3	427.7	12.98
1989	5,380.1	239.68	3,523.1	14,243.8	471.9	13.39
1990	6,047.5	265.77	3,761.2	15,050.2	526.2	13.99
1991	6,733.0	283.50	3,902.4	15,446.3	571.9	14.66
1992	7,475.0	309.78	4,136.9	16,197.3	628.3	15.19
1993	8,294.8	329.20	4,378.2	16,961.9	680.5	15.54
1994	9,235.0	363.71	4,627.0	17,751.7	727.1	15.71
1995[e]	10,395.1	396.43	4,830.6	18,650.0	777.7	16.10
Average Annual Rate of Growth (%)	11.99	14.62	8.06	7.08	11.20	2.91

[e] Estimates

Sources: Walgreen Company annual reports; *Economic Report of the President*, various issues.

---

[5] The relationship between Walgreen sales and total PCE or per capita PCE was significant but not as strong as PCE medical care.

ship, including the fact that Walgreen sales grew faster than PCE-medical care. During the period 1975 to 1995, Walgreen sales increased by about 863 percent compared to an increase in PCE-medical care of 736 percent. As a result, Walgreen sales have gone from about 1.16 percent of PCE-medical care to 1.34 percent.

The graph in Figure 20.2 that compares Walgreen sales and sales per share for the retail drugstore industry does not reflect as strong a relationship because of the exceptional growth of industry sales (over 2,000 percent).

FIGURE 20.1

SCATTER PLOT OF WALGREEN SALES AND PCE-MEDICAL CARE: 1975–1995

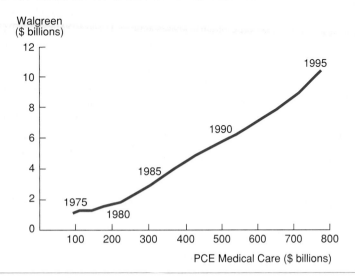

FIGURE 20.2

SCATTER PLOT OF WALGREEN SALES AND RSD INDUSTRY SALES: 1975–1995

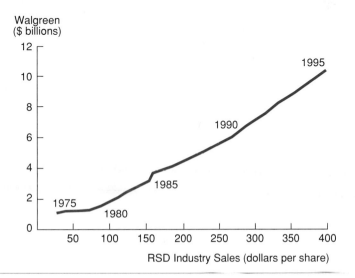

The figures in the last column of Table 20.1 indicate that during this period, the proportion of PCE allocated to medical care went from about 9 percent in 1975 to about 16.1 percent in 1995. The increasing proportion of PCE spent on medical care is a function of the growing proportion of the population over 65 and the rising cost of medical care. Because Walgreen sales are growing faster than medical expenditures, these increases should continue to be beneficial for Walgreen because 44 percent of its sales is prescriptions. Notably, these increases in medical care expenditures continued during the economic recessions in 1981–1982 and in 1990–1991.

As shown in Table 20.2, the internal sales growth for Walgreen resulted from an increase in the number of stores (from 633 in 1975 to 2,085 in 1995) and an increase in the annual sales per store because of the upgrading of stores. The net increase in stores includes numerous new, large stores and the closing of many smaller stores. As a result, the average size of stores has increased. More important, the firm has increased its sales per square foot, which is a critical value in the retailing industry.

SAMPLE ESTIMATE OF WALGREEN SALES   The foregoing analysis indicates that you should use the Walgreen–PCE-medical care graph. To estimate PCE-medical care, you should initially project total PCE and then determine how much would be included in the medical care component. As noted in Chapter 19 in connection with the industry analysis, economists were forecasting an increase in PCE of 5 percent during 1996, which implied a 1996 estimate of $5,125.6 billion. In addition, it was estimated that the percentage of PCE

TABLE 20.2	SALES, NUMBER OF STORES, AND SALES AREA FOR WALGREEN: 1975–1995					

Year	Sales ($ Millions)	Number of Stores	Annual Sales per Store ($ Millions)	Store Area (000 Square Feet)	Average Area per Store (000 Square Feet)	Sales per Thousand Square Feet
1975	1,079.1	633	1.70	5,133	8.11	210.23
1976	1,169.8	632	1.85	5,221	8.26	224.06
1977	1,223.2	626	1.95	5,188	8.29	235.77
1978	1,192.9	641	1.86	5,390	8.41	221.32
1979	1,334.5	688	1.94	5,851	8.50	228.08
1980	1,530.7	739	2.07	6,305	8.53	242.78
1981	1,743.5	821	2.12	7,209	8.78	241.85
1982	2,039.5	883	2.31	7,815	8.85	260.97
1983	2,360.6	941	2.51	8,402	8.93	280.96
1984	2,744.6	1,002	2.74	9,002	8.98	304.89
1985	3,161.9	1,095	2.89	10,010	9.14	315.87
1986	3,660.6	1,273	2.88	11,895	9.34	307.74
1987	4,281.8	1,356	3.16	12,844	9.47	333.37
1988	4,883.5	1,416	3.45	13,549	9.57	360.43
1989	5,380.1	1,484	3.63	14,272	9.62	376.97
1990	6,047.5	1,564	3.87	15,105	9.66	400.36
1991	6,733.0	1,646	4.09	15,877	9.65	424.07
1992	7,475.0	1,736	4.31	16,811	9.68	444.65
1993	8,294.8	1,836	4.52	17,950	9.78	462.11
1994	9,235.0	1,968	4.69	19,342	9.83	477.46
1995	10,395.1	2,085	4.99	20,731	9.94	501.43
Average Annual Rate of Growth (%)	12.0	6.1	5.5	7.2	1.0	4.4

Source: Walgreen Company annual reports.

spent on medical care in 1996 would be 16.1 percent. This implies an estimate for PCE-medical care of $825 billion, which is about a 13.5 percent increase from 1994. Based on the graph in Figure 20.1, which shows the historical relationship between these two variables, this would imply an 8 percent increase in Walgreen sales to about $11.23 billion ($10.395 billion × 1.08). Notably, this estimate is below the firm's recent growth in sales.

Firms in this industry provide data on square footage and the number of stores. This allows us to compute an alternative sales estimate using these company data in Table 20.2 to support the prior estimate that was based on macroeconomic data. If we assume an increase in store area during 1996 of about 1 million square feet (which is less than in 1993, 1994, and 1995), the firm's total sales area would be about 21.75 million square feet. As noted, sales per square foot have likewise increased. Assuming a continued increase to $525 of sales per square foot implies a sales forecast of about $11,420 million for 1996, a 9.86 percent increase over 1995 sales of $10,395 million.

Another internal estimate is possible by using the number of stores and sales per store. Walgreen is expected to open at least 150 stores during 1996. Assuming they close 35, this would be a net addition of 115 to 2,200 at the end of 1996. Assuming sales per store likewise continue to increase from $4.99 million to $5.20 million implies an estimate of $11,440 million (2,200 × $5.20 million), which is an increase of 10 percent over 1995.

Given the three estimates, the preference is for an estimate close to the high value of 10 percent because of the positive economic environment and the company's ability to increase sales between 11 and 12 percent during 1994 and 1995. Therefore, we will assume a 10 percent increase, which implies a final sales forecast for 1996 of $11,440 million.

ESTIMATING THE COMPANY PROFIT MARGIN

The next step in projecting earnings per share is to estimate the firm's net profit margin, which should include three considerations: (1) identification and evaluation of the firm's specific competitive strategy—i.e., either low cost or differentiation; (2) the firm's internal performance, including general company trends and consideration of any problems that might affect its future performance; and (3) the firm's relationship with its industry, which should indicate whether the company's past performance is attributable to its industry or if it is unique to the firm. These examinations should help us understand the firm's past performance, but should also provide the background to make a meaningful estimate for the future. In this analysis, we do not consider the company–economy relationship because the significant economywide profit factors are reflected in the industry results.

IDENTIFYING AND SELECTING COMPETITIVE STRATEGIES

In describing competition within industries, we identified five conditions that could affect the competitive structure and profits of an industry. They are (1) current rivalry, (2) threat of new entrants, (3) potential substitutes, (4) bargaining power of suppliers, and (5) bargaining power of buyers. Once you have determined the competitive structure of an industry, you should attempt to identify the *specific competitive strategy* used by each firm in the industry and evaluate these strategies in terms of the overall competitive structure of the industry. As an investor, you must understand the alternatives available, determine each firm's strategy, judge whether the strategy selected by a firm is reasonable for its industry, and finally, evaluate how successfully the firm implements its strategy.

Porter contends that there are two competitive strategies: *low-cost leadership* and *differentiation*.[6] These strategies dictate how a firm has decided to cope with the five competitive

---

[6] Michael Porter, *Competitive Advantage: Creating and Sustaining Superior Performance* (New York: Free Press, 1985).

conditions that define an industry's environment. Within each industry, the strategies available and the ways of implementing them differ.

LOW-COST STRATEGY

The firm that pursues the low-cost strategy is determined to become *the* low-cost producer and, hence, the cost leader in its industry. Cost advantages will vary by industry and might include economies of scale, proprietary technology, or preferential access to raw materials. To assert cost leadership, the firm must command prices near the industry average, which means that it must differentiate itself about as well as other firms. If the firm discounts price too much, it will erode the superior rates of return available because of its low cost. In the retail business, both Wal-Mart and Kmart are considered low-cost sources. They achieve this cost advantage by volume purchasing of merchandise and lower-cost operations. As a result, they charge less, but still enjoy higher profit margins and returns on capital than many of their competitors.

DIFFERENTIATION STRATEGY

With the differentiation strategy, a firm seeks to identify itself as *unique* in its industry in an area that is important to buyers. Again, the possibilities for differentiation vary widely by industry. A company can attempt to differentiate itself based on its distribution system (selling in stores, by mail order, or door-to-door), through some unique marketing approach (e.g., building significant brand loyalty such as Coca-Cola or Hershey), or by providing an important service to its customers such as very fast delivery. A firm using the differentiating strategy will enjoy above-average rates of return *only* if its price premium based on its differentiation exceeds the extra cost of being unique. Therefore, when you analyze this strategy, you must determine the cost of the differentiating strategy and whether the price premium derived from this uniqueness is greater than its cost. You must also determine if the differentiating factor is truly unique and sustainable.

FOCUSING A STRATEGY

Whichever strategy it selects, a firm must determine where to focus it. Specifically, a firm must select one or several segments in the industry and tailor its strategy to serve this specific group. For example, a cost focus typically would exploit cost advantages for certain segments of the industry such as being the low-cost producer for the expensive segment of the market. Similarly, a differentiation focus would attempt to serve the special needs of buyers in specific segments. For example, in the athletic shoe market, companies have attempted to develop shoes for unique sport segments such as tennis, basketball, aerobics, or walkers and hikers, rather than offering only shoes for runners. Firms thought that individuals involved in these other athletic endeavors needed shoes with different characteristics than those used by joggers. Equally important, they believed that these athletes would be willing to pay a premium for these special shoes. The firm must determine if (1) these special cost or need possibilities exist, (2) they are being served by another firm, and (3) whether these features can be priced to generate abnormal returns to the firm.

Next, you must determine which strategy is being pursued, whether the firm is successful at it, and if the strategies can be sustained. Finally, you should evaluate a firm's competitive strategy over time because strategies need to change as an industry evolves. Different strategies work during different phases of an industry's life cycle.

WALGREEN COMPETITIVE STRATEGIES

Over the years, has Walgreen pursued a low-cost strategy or has the firm attempted to differentiate itself from its competitors in some unique way? Based on its annual reports, Walgreen has pursued both strategies with different segments of its business. The firm's size and buying power allow it to be a cost leader for some of its nonprescription products such as liquor, ice cream, candy, and soft drinks. These items are advertised heavily to attract customer traffic and to build consumer loyalty. At the same time, Walgreen has attempted to build a very strong franchise in the medical prescription business based on differentiation in service. Its computer technology in the prescription area makes it possible to distinguish itself by providing outstanding service to its prescription customers. Specifically, the firm refers to itself as the nation's prescription druggist based on the number of prescriptions it fills and a nationwide computer system that allows customers to have their prescriptions filled at any of the 2,100 Walgreen drugstores in the country. This leadership in the growing medical field is a major goal.

THE INTERNAL PERFORMANCE   Profit margin figures for Walgreen and the retail drugstore industry are in Table 20.3. The profit margins for Walgreen increased from 1975 to the mid-1980s followed by a decline through 1988 and a recovery beginning in 1991. In contrast, the margins for the retail drugstore industry experienced a relatively steady decline throughout the 1980s and early 1990s. Overall, Walgreen experienced a positive trend in its operating and net profit mar-

TABLE 20.3   PROFIT MARGINS FOR WALGREEN COMPANY AND THE RETAIL DRUGSTORE INDUSTRY: 1975–1995

	WALGREEN COMPANY			RETAIL DRUGSTORES		
Year	Operating Profit Margin	NBT Margin	Net Profit Margin	Operating Profit Margin	NBT Margin	Net Profit Margin
1975	1.78	1.38	0.91	8.65	7.45	3.75
1976	2.97	2.51	1.46	9.18	8.19	4.09
1977	3.11	2.66	1.46	8.96	7.91	4.07
1978	3.86	3.73	2.16	8.78	7.74	4.03
1979	3.86	3.79	2.25	7.24	6.40	3.47
1980	3.56	3.52	2.27	7.07	6.27	3.47
1981	3.40	3.54	2.42	7.17	6.18	3.45
1982	4.32	4.20	2.75	7.30	6.22	3.44
1983	5.16	5.11	2.96	7.98	6.88	3.79
1984	5.57	5.46	3.11	7.19	5.53	3.03
1985	5.63	5.49	2.98	7.00	5.06	2.75
1986	5.37	5.13	2.82	7.37	5.67	3.11
1987	4.92	4.54	2.42	7.08	5.14	2.88
1988	4.59	4.28	2.64	6.70	4.71	2.89
1989	4.71	4.53	2.87	6.71	4.49	2.79
1990	4.70	4.65	2.89	6.71	4.68	2.89
1991	4.77	4.63	2.90	6.52	4.71	2.71
1992	4.80	4.72	2.95	6.35	4.59	2.89
1993*	4.90	4.82	2.96	6.25	4.56	3.22
1994	4.93	4.96	3.05	6.42	4.68	2.89
1995**	5.00	5.04	3.09	6.50	4.72	3.00
Averages:						
1975–1985	3.93	3.76	2.25	7.87	6.71	3.58
1986–1995	4.87	4.73	2.86	6.66	4.79	2.93
1975–1995	4.38	4.22	2.54	7.29	5.80	3.27

* Net profit margin for Walgreen excludes the effect of cumulative accounting change.
** Numbers for Retail Drugstores are expected.

Sources: Walgreen Company annual reports; *Standard & Poor's Analysts Handbook* (New York: Standard & Poor's Corporation, 1995). Reprinted by permission of Standard & Poor's Corp.

gins over the past 22 years, which has caused its net profit margin to be about equal to the industry. To predict future values, you need to determine the reason for the overall decline in the industry profit margin and, more important, what factors have caused Walgreen's strong positive performance.

INDUSTRY FACTORS   Industry profit margins have declined over the past two decades due to price discounting by aggressive regional drug chains.[7] The discussion in Chapter 19 suggested this as one of the competitive structure conditions that affect long-run profitability. Industry analysts have observed, however, that price cutting has subsided, and they currently foresee relative price stability. In addition, drugstores have tended toward a more profitable product mix featuring high profit margin items such as cosmetics, and this has had a positive influence on profit margins.

COMPANY PERFORMANCE   Walgreen's profit margin has showed consistent improvement, and a major reason has been the change in corporate structure. The outlook for profit margins is good because the firm has developed a strong position in the pharmacy business and has invested in service (including mail-order prescriptions) and inventory control technology that will help the firm experience strong margins on this business. The firm also has emphasized other big profit margin items such as greeting cards, photofinishing, and cosmetics.

Specific estimates for Walgreen's future margins typically would begin with an analysis of their relationship with drugstore industry margins using time-series plots such as those in Figure 20.3.[8] This time-series plot for the period 1975–1995 showed good results for Walgreen versus its industry. Specifically, the net profit margins for the company and industry have come together over time due to steady improvements by Walgreen. You also should consider any unique factors that would influence this long-run relationship, such as price wars that would be reported in business publications or an abnormal number of store openings or closings as reported by the firm in quarterly or annual earnings reports.

Following a consideration of the long-run company–industry profit margin relationship, you should analyze the firm's common size income statement for several years. As discussed in Chapter 12, the breakdown of the income statement depends on the consistent detail provided by the firm. Table 20.4 shows a common size income statement for Walgreen during the period 1992–1995. An analysis of the main items of interest—cost of goods sold and operating expense—was encouraging. The cost-of-sales percentage declined overall from 1992 to 1995. In addition, there was an overall decline in the percentage of SG&A expense through 1995. Interest expense has declined substantially in dollars and percentage through 1995, and interest income declined, but exceeded interest expense during 1993–1995. Finally, the tax rate remained between 38 and 39 percent during the last several years. Overall, the net profit margin experienced a small but steady increase over the four years.

NET PROFIT MARGIN ESTIMATE   The overall industry outlook is encouraging because of stable prices, an increase in mechanization within the industry, and the inclusion of more high profit margin items. Therefore, the industry profit margin is expected to increase during 1996. Because of Walgreen's strong relationship to the industry profit margin and

---

[7] For a more complete discussion, see "Retailing—Drug Stores," *Standard and Poor's Industry Surveys* (New York: Standard & Poor's, 1995).

[8] Both the operating margin and the net before tax margin were analyzed; the results indicated that the net profit margins yielded the best relationships. The long-run relationship cannot be very good because over the total period the industry margin was declining while Walgreen experienced fairly steady increases as shown in Figure 20.3.

FIGURE 20.3

TIME-SERIES PLOT OF NET PROFIT MARGIN FOR WALGREEN AND RSD INDUSTRY: 1975–1995

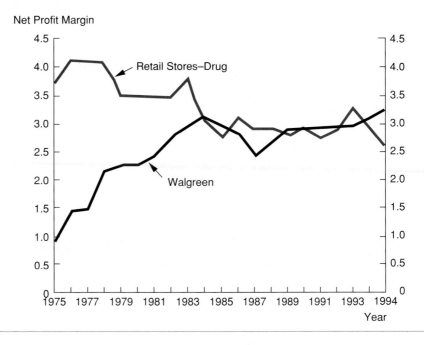

TABLE 20.4

WALGREEN COMPANY COMMON SIZE INCOME STATEMENT

	1995		1994		1993		1992	
	$ million	Percent	$ million	Percent	$ million	Percent	$ million	Percent
Net sales	10,395.1	100.00	9,235.0	100.00	8,294.8	100.00	7,475.00	100.00
Cost of sales	7,482.3	71.89	6,614.4	71.62	5,959.0	71.84	5,377.7	71.94
Gross profit	2,912.8	28.10	2,620.5	28.38	2,335.8	28.16	2,097.2	28.06
Selling, general, and administrative expense	2,392.7	23.02	2,164.9	23.44	1,929.6	23.26	1,738.8	23.26
Operating profit	520.1	5.08	455.6	4.93	406.2	4.90	358.5	4.80
Interest expense	1.2	0.01	2.6	0.03	6.5	0.08	15.7	0.21
Interest income	(4.9)	(0.05)	(5.4)	(0.06)	(6.7)	(0.08)	(10.2)	(0.14)
Extraordinary loss	—	—	—	—	—	—	—	—
Net before taxes	523.8	5.04	458.4	4.96	399.7	4.82	353.0	4.72
Tax excluding investment credit	203.0	1.95	176.5	1.91	154.4	1.86	132.4	1.77
Net earnings w/o acctg. changes	320.8	3.09	281.9	3.05	245.3	2.96	220.6	2.95
Tax rate	38.8%		38.5%		38.6%		37.5%	
Common shares outstanding (000)	246,141		246,141		246,141		246,141	
Net earnings per share	$1.30		$1.14		$0.99		$0.89	

the increase in its margin since 1992 as shown in Table 20.4, it is estimated that the firm will show a further increase during 1996 to 3.2 percent.

COMPUTING EARNINGS PER SHARE   This margin estimate, combined with the prior sales estimate of $11.44 billion, indicates net income of $366.1 million. Assuming about

246,141 million common shares outstanding, earnings should be about $1.49 per share for 1996, which is an increase of about 15 percent over the earnings of $1.30 per share in 1995. To find the value of Walgreen Company stock, our next step is to estimate its earnings multiplier.

ESTIMATING COMPANY EARNINGS MULTIPLIERS

As in our analysis of industry multipliers in Chapter 19, we use two approaches to estimate a company multiplier. First, we estimate the P/E ratio from the relationships among Walgreen, its industry, and the market. This is the macroanalysis. Second, we estimate a multiplier based on its three components: the dividend-payout ratio, the required rate of return, and the rate of growth. We then resolve the estimates derived from each approach and settle on one estimate.

MACROANALYSIS OF THE EARNINGS MULTIPLIER

Table 20.5 and Figure 20.4 show the mean earnings multiple for the company, the retail drugstore industry, and the aggregate market for the period 1975–1995. Walgreen's relationship to its industry has changed dramatically over time. During the late 1970s and early

---

TABLE 20.5

AVERAGE EARNINGS MULTIPLIER FOR WALGREEN, THE RETAIL DRUGSTORE INDUSTRY, AND THE STANDARD & POOR'S 400: 1975–1995

	WALGREEN COMPANY			RETAIL DRUGSTORE				S&P 400	
Year	EPS	Mean Price[a]	Mean P/E	EPS	Mean Price[a]	Mean P/E	Ratio Company/ Industry	Mean P/E	Ratio Company/ Market
1975	0.05	0.37	8.01	0.97	13.92	14.35	0.56	10.79	0.74
1976	0.07	0.47	6.73	1.49	19.86	13.33	0.50	10.41	0.65
1977	0.07	0.52	7.17	1.79	18.93	10.58	0.68	9.55	0.75
1978	0.10	0.73	7.07	2.01	22.2	11.05	0.64	8.21	0.86
1979	0.14	0.92	6.50	2.55	22.38	8.78	0.74	7.11	0.91
1980	0.16	1.06	6.60	2.94	24.57	8.36	0.79	8.44	0.78
1981	0.18	1.46	8.27	3.29	34.62	10.52	0.79	8.45	0.98
1982	0.23	2.52	10.85	3.76	41.58	11.06	0.98	10.37	1.05
1983	0.29	4.15	14.56	4.50	56.70	12.60	1.16	11.84	1.23
1984	0.33	4.61	13.86	4.10	58.30	14.22	0.97	9.92	1.40
1985	0.38	6.47	16.91	4.22	68.28	16.18	1.05	13.68	1.24
1986	0.42	8.69	20.68	4.90	83.78	17.10	1.21	17.42	1.19
1987	0.42	8.74	20.80	5.53	98.93	17.89	1.16	20.68	1.01
1988	0.52	8.13	15.63	6.30	93.05	14.77	1.06	11.35	1.38
1989	0.63	10.00	15.87	6.69	107.46	16.06	0.99	13.79	1.15
1990	0.71	11.63	16.37	7.67	114.53	14.93	1.10	15.83	1.03
1991	0.79	15.88	20.09	8.26	139.70	16.91	1.19	25.65	0.79
1992	0.89	18.75	21.07	8.96	159.62	17.81	1.18	25.90	0.81
1993	0.90	19.82	22.02	7.09	162.19	22.88	0.96	23.72	0.93
1994	1.14	20.24	17.75	10.51	162.67	15.48	1.15	16.21	1.10
1995	1.30	26.55	20.42	11.80	214.14	18.15	1.13	17.50	1.17
Means:									
1975–1995	NM	NM	14.15	NM	NM	14.43	0.95	14.12	1.01
1975–1984	NM	NM	8.96	NM	NM	11.48	0.78	9.51	0.93
1985–1995	NM	NM	18.88	NM	NM	17.11	1.11	18.31	1.07

[a]The mean price is the average of the high price and low price for the year.
N.M. = Not meaningful.

Sources: Walgreen Company annual reports; Standard & Poor's *Analysts Handbook* (New York: Standard & Poor's Corporation, 1996). Reprinted by permission of Standard & Poor's Corp.

FIGURE 20.4

TIME-SERIES PLOT OF MEAN PRICE/EARNINGS RATIOS FOR WALGREEN, RSD INDUSTRY, AND S&P 400

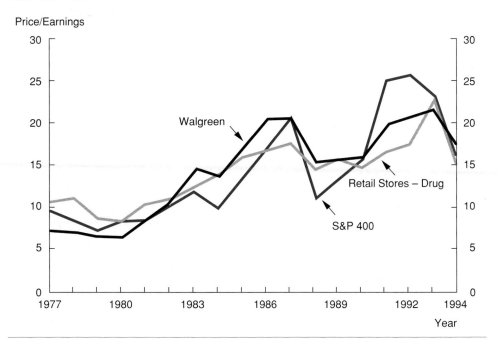

1980s, Walgreen's multiplier was consistently below the industry's. After 1985, the Walgreen multiplier typically has exceeded its industry by about 5 to 10 percent. Similarly, the Walgreen earnings multiplier typically was lower than the market multiplier until 1982 when it began exceeding it except for the period 1991–1993.

This pattern raises the question, is the recent premium of the Walgreen P/E relative to both its industry and the market that generally has prevailed since 1985 justified? The microanalyses should provide some insights regarding this question.

MICROANALYSIS OF THE EARNINGS MULTIPLIER   This historical data for the relevant series are contained in Table 20.6.[9] The relevant question is why has the earnings multiplier for Walgreen been above the market and industry earnings multiplier since the early 1980s? As before, we are looking for estimates of D/E, k, and g to find an earnings multiplier. We will use the historical data in Table 20.6 to determine patterns for the data and develop future projections.

COMPARING DIVIDEND-PAYOUT RATIOS   The dividend-payout ratio for Walgreen typically has been lower than its industry in recent years. The Walgreen–market comparison shows that Walgreen almost always had a lower payout. These payout results by themselves would produce a P/E ratio for Walgreen that is below the industry and the market P/E ratio.

ESTIMATING THE REQUIRED RATE OF RETURN   To find Walgreen's required rate of return (k), we should analyze the firm's fundamental risk characteristics (BR, FR, LR, ERR, and CR).

---

[9] Although some prior tables included data through 1995 using estimates for specific ratios, it is not possible to do this for all the variables in Table 20.6 as of early 1996. These data generally are not available until September.

TABLE 20.6 — VARIABLES THAT INFLUENCE THE EARNINGS MULTIPLIER FOR WALGREEN, RETAIL DRUGSTORES, AND THE STANDARD & POOR'S 400: 1977–1994

Year	WALGREEN COMPANY						RETAIL DRUG STORES						S&P 400					
	D/E	TAT	TAE	E/T	NPM	ROE	D/E	TAT	TAE	E/T	NPM	ROE	D/E	TAT	TAE	E/T	NPM	ROE
1977	45.80	3.81	2.39	9.08	1.27	11.56	20.11	2.84	1.53	4.34	4.07	17.68	43.23	1.27	2.15	2.73	5.11	13.95
1978	30.31	3.45	2.34	8.16	2.16	17.44	23.88	2.81	1.52	4.27	4.03	17.21	41.18	1.27	2.22	2.82	5.19	14.63
1979	30.33	3.53	2.30	8.18	2.25	18.27	27.45	3.00	1.68	5.02	3.47	17.49	36.34	1.30	2.28	2.96	5.57	16.51
1980	30.47	3.60	2.16	8.00	2.27	17.65	29.25	3.04	1.66	5.06	3.47	17.51	40.26	1.31	2.30	3.01	4.92	14.82
1981	30.42	3.60	2.08	7.62	2.42	18.12	31.00	3.03	1.65	4.99	3.45	17.25	41.88	1.28	2.32	2.97	4.86	14.43
1982	26.93	3.59	2.06	7.42	2.75	20.34	31.12	2.97	1.66	4.93	3.44	16.96	54.02	1.17	2.40	2.81	3.95	11.09
1983	26.33	3.54	2.04	7.25	2.96	21.38	29.33	2.85	1.68	4.81	3.79	18.15	49.56	1.15	2.37	2.73	4.42	12.05
1984	25.84	3.52	2.03	7.16	3.11	22.22	37.56	2.66	1.88	5.00	3.03	15.15	41.47	1.22	2.52	3.07	4.47	13.74
1985	28.68	3.39	2.16	7.08	2.98	21.82	40.76	2.70	2.04	5.50	2.75	15.15	51.51	1.15	2.54	2.92	3.92	11.45
1986	29.81	3.39	2.16	7.08	2.82	20.65	32.86	2.71	1.96	5.31	3.11	16.52	56.94	1.07	2.58	2.76	3.81	10.51
1987	32.08	3.35	2.19	7.28	2.42	17.75	31.65	2.80	2.04	5.71	2.88	16.45	43.00	1.08	2.62	2.83	4.77	13.51
1988	28.59	3.40	2.12	7.32	2.64	19.03	30.63	2.82	2.07	5.84	2.89	16.87	38.54	0.98	3.03	2.96	5.51	16.32
1989	27.12	3.37	2.04	7.01	2.87	19.73	32.29	2.82	2.03	5.73	2.79	15.99	44.54	0.97	3.16	3.06	5.01	15.33
1990	28.19	3.16	2.02	6.38	2.89	18.45	31.68	2.82	2.00	5.64	2.89	16.28	51.27	0.97	3.26	3.16	4.26	13.44
1991	29.04	3.21	1.94	6.23	2.90	18.06	32.81	2.85	1.83	5.23	2.91	15.25	73.98	0.94	3.24	3.06	2.97	9.09
1992	29.21	3.15	1.92	6.06	2.95	17.89	33.59	2.83	1.82	5.15	2.89	14.89	68.29	0.95	3.55	3.38	3.27	11.05
1993	33.52	3.27	1.84	6.02	2.67	16.08	46.83	2.79	1.88	5.23	2.15	11.27	59.55	0.92	3.76	3.45	3.73	12.86
1994	29.82	3.17	1.85	5.87	3.05	17.92	33.78	2.63	2.00	5.25	2.89	15.17	39.60	0.91	3.51	3.20	5.35	17.14
Means:	30.14	3.42	2.09	7.16	2.63	18.58	32.03	2.83	1.83	5.17	3.16	16.18	48.62	1.11	2.77	2.99	4.50	13.44

D/E = Dividend payout, equal to dividends/earnings.
TAT = Total asset turnover, equal to sales/total assets.
TAE = Leverage ratio, equal to total assets/equity.
E/T = (Equity turnover) Equity turnover ratio, equal to sales/equity.
NPM = Net profit margin, equal to net income/sales.
ROE = Return on equity, equal to net income/equity.

Walgreen should have relatively low business risk due to its stable sales growth compared to its industry and the aggregate economy. Notably, several measures of sales volatility did not support this expectation due to measurement problems. The coefficient of variation of sales that adjusts for absolute size indicated that Walgreen sales were less volatile than its industry, but more volatile than the market. It also is necessary to adjust for trend because a high growth trend will cause a larger standard deviation due to the growth. To adjust for growth, we computed the standard deviation of annual percentage changes, which indicated that sales for Walgreen were less volatile. Therefore, after adjusting for size and trend, the results indicated that Walgreen sales were less volatile, which indicates lower business risk.

Several financial risk variables for Walgreen, its industry, and the aggregate market are shown in Table 20.7. The firm's financial leverage ratio (total assets/equity) has recently been less than 2.00, which is comparable to the industry and definitely lower than the aggregate market. Walgreen has an interest coverage ratio in excess of 10, a cash flow/long-term debt ratio of over 300 percent, and a cash flow/total debt ratio of about 30 percent. These financial risk ratios indicate that Walgreen has comparable financial risk to its industry and substantially lower financial risk than the aggregate stock market.

The firm's liquidity risk is quite low compared to its industry and the average firm in the market. Indicators of market liquidity are (1) the number of stockholders, (2) the number of shares outstanding, (3) the number of shares traded, and (4) institutional interest in the stock. As of January 1, 1996, Walgreen had 26,400 holders of common stock—a relatively large number. At the end of 1995, there were almost 250 million common shares outstanding with a market value of almost $8.25 billion. Clearly, Walgreen would qualify as an investment for institutions that require firms with large market value. Walgreen stock has an annual trading turnover of 36 percent, which is slightly below average. Financial institutions own about 115 million shares of Walgreen, which is about 46 percent of the outstanding shares. Therefore, Walgreen's large number of stockholders, fairly active trading of its stock, and strong institutional interest indicate that Walgreen has very little liquidity risk.

As discussed in Chapter 18, the exchange rate risk for companies depends on what proportion of sales and earnings are generated outside the United States and the volatility of the exchange rates in the specific countries. Walgreen has very little exchange rate risk or country risk because the firm has virtually no non-U.S. sales.

In summary, Walgreen has below-average business risk, very low financial risk, low liquidity risk, and virtually no exchange rate and country risk. This implies that—based on fundamental factors—the overall risk for Walgreen should be lower than the market.

In addition to the consideration of fundamental factors, one should also consider market-determined risk (beta) based on the CAPM. The stock's beta derived from 5 years of monthly data relative to the S&P 500 for the period 1991 to 1995 is as follows:

$$R_{w,t} = 0.003 + 0.360\ R_{m,t}$$

$$\text{(t-value)}\quad (0.11)\quad (7.45)$$

$$R^2 = 0.49$$

These results, which indicate a beta of 0.36, are very consistent with those derived from an analysis of the fundamental factors—both indicate that Walgreen's risk is quite low compared to the aggregate market. This means that the risk premium and the required rate of return for Walgreen stock should be lower than the market. By itself, this lower required rate of return would suggest an earnings multiplier above the market multiplier.

TABLE 20.7 FINANCIAL RISK RATIOS FOR WALGREEN COMPANY, THE RETAIL DRUGSTORE INDUSTRY, AND THE S&P 400: 1977–1994

Year	WALGREEN COMPANY				RETAIL DRUGSTORES				S&P 400			
	Total Assets/Equity	Interest Coverage	Cash Flow/Long-Term Debt[a]	Cash Flow/Total Debt[b]	Total Assets/Equity	Interest Coverage	Cash Flow/Long-term Debt[a]	Cash Flow/Total Debt[b]	Total Assets/Equity	Interest Coverage	Cash Flow/Long-Term Debt[a]	Cash Flow/Total Debt[b]
1977	2.39	6.91	0.36	0.13	1.53	28.9	1.76	0.41	2.08	8.0	0.63	0.22
1978	2.34	7.93	0.43	0.18	1.52	30.9	1.94	0.42	2.15	7.6	0.63	0.22
1979	2.30	8.83	0.50	0.19	1.68	21.2	1.21	0.34	2.20	7.7	0.70	0.22
1980	2.16	9.01	0.60	0.20	1.66	20.1	1.33	0.35	2.23	6.0	0.66	0.21
1981	2.08	10.44	0.91	0.22	1.65	16.2	1.74	0.36	2.25	5.0	0.63	0.21
1982	2.06	13.38	1.40	0.24	1.66	17.4	2.43	0.36	2.31	4.0	0.54	0.18
1983	2.04	19.61	1.76	0.26	1.68	20.2	3.24	0.35	2.28	4.6	0.61	0.19
1984	2.03	25.23	2.14	0.27	1.88	10.6	1.43	0.24	2.34	4.1	0.65	0.19
1985	2.00	28.65	1.79	0.27	2.04	7.8	0.75	0.22	2.54	4.2	0.51	0.16
1986	2.16	17.11	0.90	0.23	2.00	12.7	0.99	0.24	2.59	3.6	0.51	0.15
1987	2.19	11.76	0.94	0.21	2.04	9.4	0.93	0.23	2.57	4.4	0.58	0.17
1988	2.12	11.46	0.99	0.24	2.07	8.2	1.00	0.24	2.99	3.8	0.44	0.15
1989	2.04	13.94	1.21	0.25	2.00	7.1	0.61	0.23	3.16	3.7	0.43	0.13
1990	2.02	11.22	2.26	0.26	2.00	8.2	0.69	0.25	3.26	3.6	0.40	0.12
1991	1.92	18.18	1.83	0.28	1.83	10.3	0.96	0.27	3.24	3.4	0.34	0.10
1992	1.90	23.53	6.16	0.29	1.82	13.4	1.13	0.27	3.55	4.0	0.38	0.11
1993	1.82	15.59	3.15	0.28	1.88	15.8	0.82	0.21	3.76	4.5	0.40	0.10
1994	1.83	10.51	3.66	0.31	2.00	16.7	0.86	0.23	3.51	5.6	0.50	0.13

[a]Long-term debt does not include deferred taxes.
[b]Total debt is equal to total assets minus total equity, including preferred stock.

ESTIMATING THE EXPECTED GROWTH RATE   Recall that the expected growth rate (g) is determined by the firm's retention rate and its expected return on equity (ROE). We have already noted Walgreen's low dividend payout compared to the industry and the aggregate market, which implies a higher retention rate.

The firm's ROE is determined by the total asset turnover (TAT), financial leverage (total assets/equity), and the net profit margin. As shown in Table 20.6, the TAT for Walgreen has consistently been above its industry and the market. Walgreen's financial leverage ratio has been quite comparable to its industry, but significantly lower than the market. As a result, Walgreen's equity turnover was above the industry and substantially larger than the market. Walgreen's profit margin has been similar to its industry margin in recent years, but as expected for a retail firm has been consistently lower than the S&P 400 margin.

Combining the average values from Table 20.6 for the total asset turnover, leverage, and profit margin indicates the following ROEs for Walgreen, its industry, and the market:

	TAT	Total Assets/ Equity	Net Profit Margin	ROE
Walgreen	3.42	2.09	2.63	18.80
Retail drugstores	2.83	1.83	3.16	16.37
S&P 400	1.11	2.77	4.50	13.84

As before, this multiplication of the three components is done for demonstration purposes to show the different impact of the three components. In actual practice, an analyst would probably not use all the years back to 1977 to compute an average value but would concentrate more on deriving an estimate based on an *estimate* of the three components.

The demonstration can be extended by combining the average annual ROEs reported in Tables 20.6 and 20.8 and the average of the annual retention rates in Table 20.8 to derive expected growth rates:

	Retention Rate	ROE	Expected Growth Rate
Walgreen	.70	.1858	.1301
Retail drugstores	.68	.1618	.1100
S&P 400	.51	.1344	.0685

Taken alone, these higher expected growth rates for Walgreen would indicate that it should have a higher multiple than its industry and the market.

COMPUTING THE EARNINGS MULTIPLIER   Entering our estimates of D/E, k, and g into the equation for the P/E ratio, we find that Walgreen's earnings multiplier based on the microanalysis should be greater than the multiplier for its industry and the market. The dividend payout ratio points toward a lower multiplier for Walgreen, whereas both the risk analysis and the expected growth rate would indicate a multiplier for Walgreen above that of its industry and the market.

The macroanalysis indicated that Walgreen's multiplier typically has been above that of its industry and the market. As noted, the microanalysis supported this relationship. Assuming a market multiple of about 18 and a retail drugstore multiplier of about 19, the multiplier for Walgreen should be between 20 and 22, with a tendency toward the upper

TABLE 20.8									

EXPECTED GROWTH RATE COMPONENTS FOR WALGREEN COMPANY, THE RETAIL DRUGSTORE INDUSTRY, AND THE S&P 400: 1977–1994

	WALGREEN COMPANY			RETAIL DRUGSTORES			S&P 400		
Year	Retention Rate	ROE	Expected Growth Rate	Retention Rate	ROE	Expected Growth Rate	Retention Rate	ROE	Expected Growth Rate
1977	0.54	11.56%	6.27%	0.80	17.68%	14.13%	0.57	13.95%	7.92%
1978	0.70	17.44	12.15	0.76	17.21	13.10	0.59	14.63	8.61
1979	0.70	18.27	12.73	0.73	17.49	12.69	0.64	16.51	10.51
1980	0.70	17.65	12.27	0.71	17.51	12.39	0.60	14.82	8.86
1981	0.70	18.12	12.61	0.69	17.25	11.90	0.58	14.43	8.39
1982	0.73	20.34	14.86	0.69	16.96	11.68	0.45	11.09	5.10
1983	0.74	21.38	15.75	0.71	18.15	12.82	0.50	12.05	6.08
1984	0.74	22.22	16.48	0.62	15.15	9.46	0.59	13.74	8.04
1985	0.71	21.82	15.56	0.59	15.15	8.97	0.48	11.45	5.55
1986	0.70	20.65	14.49	0.68	16.52	11.09	0.44	10.51	4.53
1987	0.68	17.75	12.06	0.68	16.45	11.24	0.57	13.51	7.70
1988	0.71	19.03	13.59	0.63	16.87	11.70	0.61	16.32	10.03
1989	0.73	19.78	14.38	0.68	15.99	10.83	0.55	15.33	8.50
1990	0.72	18.45	13.25	0.68	16.28	11.12	0.49	13.44	6.55
1991	0.71	18.06	12.80	0.67	15.25	10.25	0.26	9.09	2.37
1992	0.71	17.89	12.66	0.66	14.89	9.89	0.32	11.05	3.50
1993	0.66	16.08	11.21	0.53	11.27	5.99	0.40	12.86	5.20
1994	0.70	17.92	12.57	0.66	15.17	10.05	0.60	17.14	10.35
Mean:	0.70	18.58	13.09	0.68	16.18	11.07	0.51	13.44	7.10

end of the range. Alternatively, if we inserted fairly conservative values for D/E, k, and g into the P/E ratio formula, we would get a multiplier of about 20. Specifically, a payout ratio of .30, a k of about 13.50 percent given current market rates, and an expected growth rate (g) of 12 percent indicate the following

$$P/E = \frac{.30}{.135 - .12}$$

$$= \frac{.30}{.015} = 20X$$

ESTIMATE OF THE FUTURE VALUE FOR WALGREEN   Earlier, we estimated 1996 earnings per share for Walgreen of about $1.50 per share. Assuming multipliers of 18-20-22 implies the following estimated future values:

$$18 \times 1.50 = \$27.00$$
$$20 \times 1.50 = \$30.00$$
$$22 \times 1.50 = \$33.00$$

MAKING THE INVESTMENT DECISION

In our prior discussions of valuation, we set forth the investment decision in two forms:

1. Compute the estimated value for an investment using your required rate of return as the discount rate. If this estimated value is equal to or greater than the current market price of the investment, buy it.

2. Compute the estimated future value for an investment using your required rate of return as one of the components. Given this future value, compute the expected rate of return you would receive if you bought the asset at the current market price and held the investment during the future period, typically assumed to be a year. If this expected rate of return is equal to or greater than your required rate of return, buy the investment; if the expected return is below your required rate of return, do not buy it.

We can demonstrate how we would apply these two forms of the investment decision to Walgreen. We estimated three future values for Walgreen assuming a fairly conservative k of 13.5 percent: $27.00, $30.00, and $33.00. For the demonstration, we will use $30 a share as the future value and an estimated dividend over the next year of $0.45, which assumes a 30 percent payout of the earnings of $1.50.

COMPARING THE ESTIMATED VALUE TO THE CURRENT MARKET PRICE   Remember that the estimated value we have computed is a future value (at the end of 1 year). To compare it to a current market price, we must discount the ending price ($30) and the expected dividend ($0.45) by our required rate of return of 13.5 percent, which gives a current estimated value of[10]

$$\$30 \times .8811 = \$26.43$$
$$\$0.45 \times .8811 = \underline{\quad 0.40}$$
$$\text{Total value} = \$26.83$$

We would compare the current market price of Walgreen stock to this estimated value. For example, if Walgreen stock were currently priced at $20 a share, you would buy it; if it were currently priced at $30 a share, you would not buy it.

COMPARING EXPECTED RATE OF RETURN TO REQUIRED RATE OF RETURN   In past demonstrations of this decision rule, we have computed an expected rate of return using the expected value and dividend. Although we will again use this technique, we also will introduce another technique for computing an expected rate of return based on the dividend discount model (DDM).

We can compute the expected rate of return, $E(R_i)$, based on our expected future value using the formula

$$E(R_i) = \frac{EV - BV + Div}{BV}$$

where

EV = the estimated ending value of the stock
BV = the beginning value of the stock (typically its current market price)
Div = the expected dividend per share during the holding period.

In our case, these values would be

$$EV = \$30.00$$
$$BV = \text{(assume \$25 a share)}$$
$$Div = \$0.45$$

_____

[10] The computation of the value of the dividend payment is simplified and conservative since we have assumed the whole $0.45 is paid at the end of the year rather than $0.11 a quarter, which would have allowed for reinvestment to the end of the year.

Thus,

$$E(R) = \frac{\$30.00 - \$25.00 + \$0.45}{\$25.00}$$

$$= \frac{\$5.45}{\$25.00}$$

$$= .218 = 21.8\%$$

Based on the k of 13.5 percent used in the valuation section, we would buy this stock because its expected rate of return (21.8%) is larger than our required rate of return (13.5%).

The second technique used for deriving an expected rate of return is based on the dividend discount model. You will recall that the DDM states:

$$P_0 = \frac{D_1}{k - g}$$

Solving to estimate k:

$$k_i = \frac{D_1}{P_0} + g$$

In this equation, k serves as an estimate of the required rate of return when you assume that you know the firm's future growth rate. Alternatively, an investor can use this equation to estimate his or her long-run expected rate of return if you are estimating the future dividend and growth rate. For Walgreen, the P_0 would be the current price of the stock, D_1 would be the expected dividend during the investment horizon, and g would be the expected longer-run growth rate, as discussed in connection with Table 20.8.

As an example, assume a current price of $25, an expected dividend of $0.45 per share, and a growth rate of 12 percent which is the growth rate we used in the earlier micro-estimate of the multiplier. Notably, it is slightly below the g implied by the average values in Table 20.8. This would imply the following estimate of your expected rate of return on Walgreen common stock:

$$k = \frac{0.45}{25.00} + .120$$

$$= .017 + .120$$

$$= .137 = 13.7\%$$

This computation shows that you would expect a rate of return from investing in Walgreen stock of 13.7 percent. If your required rate of return was 13.5 percent, you would buy this stock.

ADDITIONAL
MEASURES OF
RELATIVE VALUE

The best-known measure of relative value for common stock is the price/earnings ratio or the earnings multiplier because it is derived from the dividend growth model and has stood the test of time as a useful measure of relative value. Although not rejecting the P/E ratio, analysts have begun to calculate two additional measures of relative value for common stocks—the price/book value ratio and the price/cash flow ratio.

PRICE/BOOK VALUE
(P/BV) RATIO

The relationship between the market price of a stock and its book value per share can be used as a relative measure of valuation because, under theoretically ideal conditions, the market value of a firm should reflect its book value. The *price/book value ratio* has been used extensively in the valuation of bank stocks because bank assets often have similar book values and market values. (Bank assets include investments in government bonds, high-grade corporate bonds or municipal bonds, along with commercial, mortgage, or personal loans that are generally expected to be collectible.) Under such ideal conditions, the price/book value (P/BV) ratio should be close to 1. Still, even in the banking industry the range of this ratio has increased. You can envision a P/BV ratio of less than 1 for a bank with a lot of problem loans. During certain years, this might include loans to firms in the oil industry, real estate loans in certain areas of the country, and loans to third-world countries. In contrast, you can envision a P/BV ratio above 1 for a bank with significant growth potential due to its location or because it is a desirable merger candidate. As a result, the P/BV ratios for different individual banks have ranged from 0.6 to over 2.0.

It is easy to see why the P/BV ratio of an industrial firm would exceed 1.0. The book value of assets, which are based on historical cost, will almost always be lower than either their current replacement value or the firm's breakup value. (Breakup value is the estimated market value of selling divisions of a firm to others.) An increase in the estimates of breakup value has caused the average P/BV ratio for industrial firms to experience a volatile increase over time. To demonstrate this relationship, the data are contained in Table 20.9. Figure 20.5 is a time-series plot of the historical P/BV ratio for the S&P 400, the retail drugstore industry, and Walgreen. Annual P/BV ratios are equal to the mean annual price/year-end book value.

FIGURE 20.5

TIME-SERIES PLOT OF PRICE/BOOK VALUE FOR WALGREEN, RSD INDUSTRY, AND S&P 400

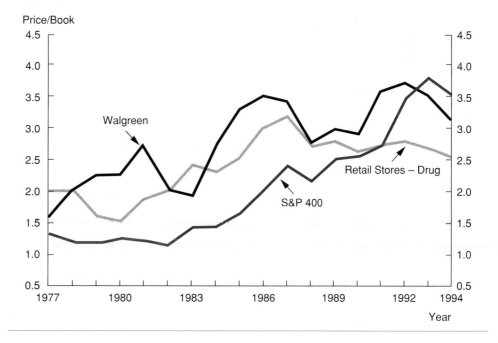

TABLE 20.3 PRICE/BOOK VALUE AND PRICE/CASH FLOW RATIOS FOR WALGREEN, RETAIL DRUGSTORES, AND THE S&P 400: 1977–1994

	WALGREEN COMPANY[1]					RETAIL DRUGSTORE							S&P 400						
Year	Mean Price	Book Value	P/BV	Cash Flow	P/CF	Mean Price	Book Value	P/BV	Company/ Industry Ratio	Cash Flow	P/CF	Company/ Industry Ratio	Mean Price	Book Value	P/BV	Company/ Market Ratio	Cash Flow	P/CF	Company/ Market Ratio
1977	0.52	0.33	1.57	0.06	8.97	18.93	9.35	2.02	0.78	2.20	8.60	1.04	109.40	82.21	1.33	1.18	19.94	5.49	1.63
1978	0.73	0.36	2.02	0.08	9.08	22.20	10.93	2.03	0.99	2.50	8.88	1.02	107.12	89.34	1.20	1.68	22.65	4.73	1.92
1979	0.92	0.4	2.25	0.10	9.46	22.38	13.95	1.60	1.40	3.26	6.87	1.38	115.79	98.71	1.17	1.92	27.06	4.28	2.21
1980	1.05	0.46	2.27	0.11	9.61	24.57	16.11	1.53	1.49	3.78	6.50	1.48	136.03	108.33	1.26	1.81	28.45	4.78	2.01
1981	1.45	0.53	2.75	0.13	11.64	34.62	18.45	1.88	1.46	4.31	8.03	1.45	141.48	116.06	1.22	2.25	30.52	4.64	2.51
1982	2.52	1.22	2.06	0.32	8.00	41.58	20.74	2.00	1.03	4.79	8.68	0.92	136.87	118.60	1.15	1.78	28.46	4.81	1.66
1983	4.15	2.15	1.93	0.58	7.18	56.70	23.34	2.43	0.79	5.90	9.61	0.75	174.90	122.32	1.43	1.35	30.41	5.75	1.25
1984	4.61	1.69	2.73	0.45	10.26	58.30	25.21	2.31	1.18	5.81	10.03	1.02	179.62	123.99	1.45	1.89	34.40	5.22	1.97
1985	6.47	1.96	3.30	0.52	12.32	68.28	26.82	2.55	1.30	6.24	10.94	1.13	208.99	125.89	1.66	1.99	33.44	6.25	1.97
1986	8.69	2.45	3.54	0.65	13.28	83.78	27.73	3.02	1.17	6.99	11.99	1.11	253.83	124.87	2.03	1.74	33.91	7.49	1.77
1987	8.74	2.54	3.44	0.64	13.60	98.93	30.79	3.21	1.07	8.16	12.12	1.12	324.30	134.19	2.42	1.42	40.46	8.02	1.70
1988	8.15	2.92	2.78	0.77	10.54	93.05	34.25	2.72	1.03	9.40	9.90	1.06	302.63	139.50	2.17	1.28	50.13	6.04	1.75
1989	10.00	3.33	3.00	0.90	11.15	107.46	38.31	2.81	1.07	10.07	10.67	1.04	364.58	145.34	2.51	1.20	50.02	7.29	1.53
1990	11.63	3.98	2.92	1.03	11.31	114.53	43.65	2.62	1.11	11.82	9.69	1.17	392.12	152.71	2.57	1.14	51.04	7.68	1.47
1991	15.88	4.39	3.61	1.14	13.98	139.70	50.94	2.74	1.32	12.29	11.37	1.23	428.81	157.05	2.73	1.32	44.41	9.66	1.45
1992	18.75	5.01	3.74	1.56	11.99	159.62	56.97	2.80	1.34	13.34	11.97	1.00	493.33	142.46	3.46	1.08	48.50	10.17	1.18
1993	19.82	5.60	3.54	1.75	11.32	162.19	60.04	2.70	1.31	11.84	13.70	0.83	520.21	136.91	3.80	0.93	50.61	10.28	1.10
1994	20.24	6.39	3.17	2.00	10.12	162.67	63.62	2.56	1.24	15.83	10.28	0.98	536.52	151.08	3.55	0.89	63.35	8.47	1.19

[1] Adjusted for stock splits.

The P/BV ratio for the S&P 400 was about 1.3 during 1977–1982. It subsequently has increased steadily to record levels in 1994 and 1995.

The retail drugstore industry P/BV ratio typically has followed the S&P P/BV ratio with a premium of about 30 percent pre-1990. A higher P/BV ratio for the retail drugstore industry appears reasonable because of the industry's higher ROE and its larger growth rate of book value.

Walgreen's P/BV ratio increased from about 1.60 in 1977 to over 3.5 in the mid-1980s. As a result, the ratio of the Walgreen P/BV ratio to the market P/BV ratio went from about 1.2 to a peak of over 2.0 in 1981. The company/market relationship of P/BV ratios has declined steadily since 1985 to the point of equality during 1992–1993. The ratio of Walgreen's P/BV ratio to its industry P/BV ratio varied from about 0.80 to a high of 1.49. In recent years, its P/BV ratio has been about 25–30 percent above its industry. One can explain the higher P/BV ratio for Walgreen relative to the market based on its higher growth rate of book value and its lower systematic risk. Walgreen's premium P/BV ratio relative to its industry's ratio is likewise a function of its higher ROE and expected growth rate.

THE P/BV RATIO AS A DECISION RULE   To use this ratio as part of an investment decision rule, some have suggested that stocks with low P/BV ratios should outperform high P/BV stocks, just as stocks with low P/E ratios outperform stocks with high P/E ratios. A study by Rosenberg, Reid, and Lanstein examined this strategy and found that stocks with low P/BV ratios experienced significantly higher risk-adjusted rates of return than the average stock.[11]

A study by Fama and French provided even greater support for this ratio as a useful measure of relative value.[12] The purpose of the study was to examine alternative variables that would explain the cross section of rates of return on common stock. One of the explanatory variables was the well-known beta coefficient. Their results did not provide much support for beta as an explanatory variable, but the results indicated that both the size of firms and the ratio of book value to market value (BV/MV) of equity were significant explanatory variables. Moreover, they contended that the BV/MV ratio was the single best variable.

A study by Harris and Marston showed that the P/BV ratio is positively impacted by future growth prospects and risk factors similar to the P/E ratio. The risk measure used is beta.[13] Along the same lines, using accounting information Fairfield showed that the P/B ratio is a function of the expected level of profitability on book value, which we know is related to ROE.[14] Again, this implies that the P/BV ratio is likewise impacted by growth expectations. Shefrin and Statman contend that the *Fortune* survey shows that the respondents believe that good companies are large companies with high P/BV ratios and they also believe that the stock of these companies will be good stocks.[15] As we know, these survey

---

[11] Barr Rosenberg, Kenneth Reid, and Ronald Lanstein, "Persuasive Evidence of Market Inefficiency," *Journal of Portfolio Management* 11, no. 3 (Spring 1985): 9–17. They examined the inverse of the ratio discussed here, that is, BV/P, but the interpretation is comparable; in other words, a high BV/P ratio is comparable to a low P/BV ratio.

[12] Eugene F. Fama and Kenneth R. French, "The Cross-Section of Expected Stock Returns," *Journal of Finance* 47, no. 2 (June 1992): 427–450. They likewise stipulated the ratio as book value/market value, but the interpretation is comparable.

[13] Robert S. Harris and Felicia C. Marston, "Value versus Growth Stocks: Book-to-Market, Growth and Beta," *Financial Analysts Journal* 50, no. 5 (September–October 1994): 18–24.

[14] Patricia Fairfield, "P/E, P/B and the Present Value of Future Dividends," *Financial Analysts Journal* 50, no. 4 (July–August 1994): 23–31.

[15] Hersh Shefrin and Meir Statman, "Making Sense of Beta, Size, and Book-to-Market," *Journal of Portfolio Management* 21, no. 2 (Winter 1995): 26–34.

results are inconsistent with the empirical results which show that stocks with high P/BV ratios are not good stocks in terms of risk-adjusted rates of return.

The P/BV ratio has become important as a measure of relative value for stocks. Analysts will discuss the stock's P/BV over time, examine it relative to a comparable market and industry ratio, and use this information as part of the investment decision. When using this ratio to make an investment decision, it is critical that its relative value be evaluated along with its relative growth rate and risk characteristics. This ratio also has been included as a component in other valuation models.

PRICE/CASH FLOW (P/CF) RATIO
Another measure of relative value, the *price/cash flow ratio,* is used to supplement the P/E ratio because a firm's cash flow typically is subject to less accounting manipulation than reported earnings. Also, cash flow has become an important measure of performance, value, and financial strength because numerous academic studies have shown that various cash flow measures can be used to predict both success and future problems.[16] Also, cash flow data have become more accessible because firms currently publish statements of cash flow, along with their income statements and balance sheets.

Developing benchmark values for these ratios is important because, similar to P/Es and P/BV ratios, they are relative measures of value. Therefore, you should understand the comparable values over time for the market as represented by the S&P 400 and the relevant industry. For demonstration purposes, availability of data leads us to define cash flow per share as net income per share plus depreciation expense per share. This traditional measure of cash flow is intended to reflect earnings plus noncash expenses; depreciation is the largest noncash expense that can be identified.

The historical P/CF ratios listed in Table 20.9 are plotted in Figure 20.6. These particular ratios are only available beginning in 1977 because the depreciation expense figure for the S&P 400 and individual S&P industries were not reported before this time. Again, both the retail drugstore industry and the Walgreen P/CF ratios are consistently higher than the market ratio until 1991 when they tended to merge. As before, these higher ratios for the industry and company are justified by the higher growth rate of cash flow during 1977–1994 for the industry versus the market and for the company versus the market.

USING THE P/BV AND P/CF RATIOS   As discussed, both of these ratios (P/BV and P/CF) are considered to be good supplements to the P/E ratio when you are engaged in fundamental valuation. Neither has the theoretical base that we have with the P/E ratio, but they can provide additional insights into relative valuation changes for a stock. In both instances, you should examine the company ratios over time relative to the same ratio for the market and for the firm's industry. You should look for: (1) relationships that are not justified by the fundamental differences in the growth rate of book value or cash flow and differences in risk, or (2) changes in the normal relationships that are not supported by changes in these fundamental factors.

As an example of the first case, assume that a firm's P/BV ratio was 0.8 compared to a market ratio of 3.0 and an industry ratio of 1.9. You would analyze the firm to see if these

---

[16]James A. Gentry, David T. Whitford, and Paul Newbold, "Predicting Industrial Bond Ratings with a Probit Model and Funds Flow Components," *The Financial Review* 23, no. 3 (August 1988): 269–286; James A. Gentry, Paul Newbold, and David T. Whitford, "Classifying Bankrupt Firms with Funds Flow Components," *Journal of Accounting Research* 23, no. 1 (Spring 1985): 146–160; and James A. Gentry, Paul Newbold, and David T. Whitford, "Predicting Bankruptcy: If Cash Flow Is Not the Bottom Line, What Is?" *Financial Analysts Journal* 41, no. 5 (September–October 1985): 47–58. A specific application to selecting common stocks is discussed in Kenneth S. Hackel and Joshua Livnat, *Cash Flow and Security Analysis,* 2d ed. (Burr Ridge, IL: Irwin Professional Publishing, 1996).

FIGURE 20.6   **TIME-SERIES PLOT OF PRICE/CASH FLOW FOR WALGREEN, RSD INDUSTRY, AND S&P 400**

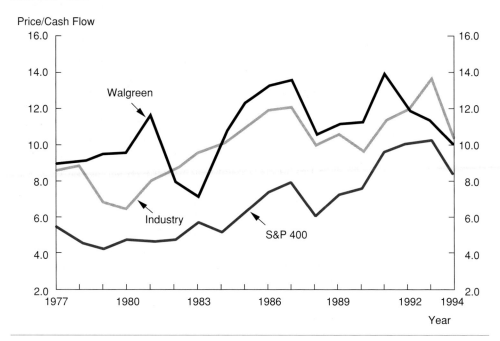

differences were justified. A difference that was not justified by differences in expected growth and risk might indicate an underpriced stock. As an example of an alternative case, assume a stock's P/BV ratio consistently had matched the market ratio, but recently the stock's P/BV ratio increased by 50 percent relative to the market with no change in the company's relative growth or risk. You would probably consider this a possible indicator of overvaluation. These examples would be only bits of evidence in a full-scale analysis, but they can be used as additional indicators of relative valuation.

MEASURES OF VALUE-ADDED[17]

In addition to the DDM, which feeds into the earnings–P/E ratio valuation technique and the supplementary P/BV and P/CF ratios, there has been growing interest in a set of performance measures referred to as "value-added." An appealing characteristic of these value-added measures of performance is that they are directly related to the capital budgeting techniques used in corporation finance. Specifically, they consider *economic profit*, which is analogous to the net present value (NPV) technique used in corporate capital budgeting. These value-added measures are mainly used to measure the performance of management based on their success in adding value to the firm. Notably, they also are being used by security analysts as possible indicators of future equity returns based on the logic that superior management performance should be reflected in a company's stock returns. In the subsequent discussion, we concentrate on two measures of value-added: **economic**

---

[17]This section benefited from Pamela P. Peterson and David Peterson, "Company Performance Measures of Value-Added" (Charlottesville, VA: The Research Foundation of the Institute of Chartered Financial Analysts, 1996).

value-added (EVA) and **market value-added (MVA)** pioneered by Stern and Stewart.[18] A discussion of the **franchise factor** developed by Leibowitz and Kogelman is also included.[19]

ECONOMIC VALUE-ADDED (EVA)[20]

As noted, this measure of value-added is closely related to the net present value (NPV) technique. Specifically, with the NPV technique you evaluate the expected performance of an investment by discounting the future cash flows from a potential investment at the firm's weighted average cost of capital (WACC) and compare this sum of discounted future cash flows to the cost of the project. If the discounted cash flows are greater than its cost, the project is expected to generate a positive NPV, which implies that it will add to the value of the firm and therefore it should be undertaken. In the case of EVA, you evaluate the annual performance of management by comparing the firm's net operating profit less adjusted taxes (NOPLAT) to the firm's total cost of capital in dollar terms, including the cost of equity. In this analysis, if the firm's NOPLAT during a specific year exceeds its dollar cost of capital, it has a positive EVA for the year and has added value for its stockholders. In contrast, if the EVA is negative, the firm has not earned enough during the year to cover its cost of capital and the value of the firm has declined. Notably, NOPLAT indicates what the firm has earned for all capital suppliers and the dollar cost of capital is what all the capital suppliers required—including the firm's equity holders. The following summarizes the major calculations:[21]

EVA =

	(A)	**Adjusted Operating Profits before Taxes**
minus	**(B)**	**Cash Operating Taxes**
equals	**(C)**	**Net Operating Profits Less Adjusted Taxes (NOPLAT)**
minus	**(D)**	**The Dollar Cost of Capital**
equals	*(E)*	*Economic Value-Added (EVA)*

In turn, these items are calculated as follows:

Operating Profit (after depreciation and amortization)

Add:	Implied Interest on Operating Leases
Add:	An Increase in the LIFO Reserve
Add:	Goodwill Amortization
Equals	*(A) Adjusted Operating Profits before Taxes*

---

[18] These concepts are described in detail in G. Bennett Stewart III, *The Quest for Value* (New York: Harper Business, 1991).

[19] Martin L. Leibowitz and Staley Kogelman, *Franchise Value and the Price-Earnings Ratio* (Charlottesville, VA: Research Foundation of the Institute of Chartered Financial Analysts, 1994).

[20] This is a registered trademark of Stern, Stewart, & Co.

[21] For a detailed discussion, see Stewart, *The Quest for Value*, or Peterson and Peterson, *Company Performance Measures of Value-Added*. For summary discussions, see Thomas P. Jones, "The Economic Value-Added Approach to Corporate Investments," in *Corporate Financial Decision Making and Equity Analysis* (Charlottesville, VA: Association for Investment Management and Research, 1995); T. J. Sheehan "To EVA or Not to EVA: Is That the Question?" *Journal of Applied Corporate Finance* 7, no. 2 (Summer 1994): 84–87, G. B. Stewart, "EVA: Fact and Fantasy," *Journal of Applied Corporate Finance* 7, no. 2 (Summer 1994): 71–84; and S. Tully, "The Real Key to Creating Wealth," *Fortune* (September 1993): 38–40, 44, 45, 48, 50.

Income Tax Expense

Add:	Decrease in Deferred Taxes
Add:	Tax Benefit from Interest Expenses
Add:	Tax Benefit from Interest on Leases
Less:	Taxes on Nonoperating Income
Equals	*(B) Cash Operating Taxes*

(A) minus **(B)** equals: **(C) Net Operating Profits Less Adjusted Taxes (NOPLAT)**

Capital Equals:	Net Working Capital (current assets less noninterest-bearing liabilities)
Plus:	LIFO Reserve
Plus:	Net Plant, Property, and Equipment
Plus:	Other Assets
Plus:	Goodwill
Plus:	Accumulated Goodwill Amortized
Plus:	Present Value of Operating Leases
Equals:	***Capital***

Weighted Average Cost of Capital (WACC) =

(Book Value of Debt/Total Book Value) × (the Market Cost of Debt) (1 − Tax Rate)

(Book Value of Equity/Total Book Value) × (Cost of Equity)

(Cost of equity is based on the CAPM using the prevailing 10-year Treasury bond as the RFR, a calculated beta, and a market risk premium between 3 and 6 percent.)

(D)	Dollar Cost of Capital = Capital × WACC
(E)	Economic Value-Added (EVA) =
(C)	Net Operating Profits Less Adjusted Taxes (NOPLAT)
Minus (D)	Dollar Cost of Capital

EVA RETURN ON CAPITAL   The prior calculations provide a positive or negative dollar value, which indicates whether the firm earned an excess above its cost of capital during the year analyzed. There are two problems with this annual dollar value for EVA. First, how does one judge over time if the firm is prospering relative to its past performance? Although you would want the absolute EVA to grow over time, the question is whether the *rate* of growth of EVA is adequate for the additional capital provided. Second, how does one compare alternative firms of different sizes? Both of these concerns can be met by calculating an EVA return on capital equal to:

EVA/Capital

You would want this EVA rate of return on capital for a firm to remain constant over time, or ideally grow. Also, using this ratio you can compare firms of different sizes and determine which firm has the largest *economic profit per dollar of capital.*

MARKET VALUE-ADDED (MVA) In contrast to EVA, which generally is an evaluation of internal performance, MVA is a measure of external performance—how the market has evaluated the firm's performance in terms of the market value of debt and market value of equity compared to the capital invested in the firm.

$$\begin{aligned}
\textbf{Market Value-Added (MVA)} = {} & (\text{Market Value of Firm}) - \text{Capital} \\
& - \text{Market Value of Debt} \\
& - \text{Market Value of Equity}
\end{aligned}$$

Again, to properly analyze this performance, it is necessary to look for positive changes over time—i.e., the percent change each year. It is important to compare these changes in MVA each year to those for the aggregate stock and bond markets because these market values can be impacted by interest rates and general economic conditions.

RELATIONSHIPS BETWEEN EVA AND MVA Although EVA is used primarily for evaluating management performance, it also is being used by external analysts to evaluate management with the belief that superior internal performance should be reflected in a company's stock performance. Several studies have attempted to determine the relationship between the two variables (EVA and MVA), and the results have been mixed. Although the stock of firms with positive EVAs has tended to outperform the stocks of negative EVA firms, the differences are typically insignificant and the relationship does not occur every year. This poor relationship may be due to the timing of the analysis (how fast EVA is reflected in stocks) or because the market values (MVAs) are affected by factors other than EVA—e.g., MVA can be impacted by market interest rates and by changes in *future* expectations for a firm not considered by EVA, i.e., it appears that EVA does an outstanding job of evaluating management's *past* performance in terms of adding value. While one would certainly hope that superior past performance will continue, there is nothing certain about this relationship.

THE FRANCHISE FACTOR The franchise factor concept is similar to EVA since it recognizes that, to add to the value of a firm, it is necessary to invest in projects that provide excess NPV—i.e., the firm must generate rates of return above its WACC. This technique is directly related to the valuation approach we have been using since the franchise value approach breaks a firm's observed P/E down into two components: (1) the P/E, based on the company's ongoing business (its base P/E); plus (2) a franchise P/E the market assigns to *the expected value of new and profitable business opportunities*. This can be visualized as:

$$\text{Franchise P/E} = \text{Observed P/E} - \text{Base P/E}$$

The base P/E is the reciprocal of the market discount rate K (it is $1/k$). For example, if the stock's market discount rate is 12 percent, the base P/E would be about 8.5X.

What determines the franchise P/E? Not surprising, it is a function of the relative rate of return on new business opportunities (the franchise factor) and the size of the superior return opportunities (the growth factor).

$$\text{Incremental Franchise P/E} = \text{Franchise Factor} \times \text{Growth Factor}$$
$$= \frac{R - k}{rk} \times G$$

where

> R = the expected return on the new opportunities
> k = the current cost of equity
> r = the current ROE on investment
> G = the present value of the new growth projects relative to the current value of the firm

The critical factors determining the franchise P/E are the difference between R and k and the size of these growth opportunities relative to the firm's current size.[22]

As will be shown in the subsequent discussion, this analysis of franchise value or the franchise P/E are very similar to the growth company valuation models.

GLOBAL COMPANY ANALYSIS

One of our goals in this book is to demonstrate investment techniques. We have shown that these techniques can be applied to foreign markets, industries, and companies. The major problem is getting the data required for the analysis.

In this section, we continue the analysis of the European chemical industry that we started in Chapter 19. The objective is to see how to select individual companies and specific stocks for your investment portfolio. As before, we will work with tables assembled by Goldman, Sachs and its global report. The tables contain data on several companies though the desired data are not always available for all firms.

EARNINGS PER SHARE ANALYSIS

Table 20.10 contains estimated earnings per share values for the major firms for 1996 and 1997 as of April 1996. This two-period comparison shows the outlook for these firms. Most estimates indicate continued growth for 1997. The dividend data indicate a fairly consistent range of payouts (i.e., about 28 percent to 48 percent).

TABLE 20.10 **EARNINGS AND DIVIDENDS PER SHARE FOR MAJOR EUROPEAN CHEMICAL FIRMS**

Company	Currency	EARNINGS PER SHARE		Dividends per Share (1996)	Dividend Payout (1996)
		1996E	1997E		
BASF	DM	40.0	46.0	15.0	0.375
Bayer	DM	38.0	44.0	16.5	0.434
Hoechst	DM	34.0	47.5	15.0	0.441
Ciba	SFr	86.3	97.7	24.0	0.278
AKZO	DFL	19.0	22.5	7.5	0.395
DSM[a]	DFL	24.3	29.5	9.0	0.370
Solvay[a]	BFr	1,552	1,982	600	0.387
L'Air Liquide	FFr	45.0	51.6	15.4	0.342
BOC	BP	56.5	62.8	27.0	0.478
AGA B	SKr	6.3	6.9	2.8	0.444
Rhone-Poulenc	FFr	8.6	12.4	3.8	0.442

[a]Before extraordinary items.
E = Estimate.

Source: Charles K. Brown, Mark Tracey and Paul Krikler, "The Major European Chemicals/Pharma Groups—Share Price Surge" (London: Goldman, Sachs International Ltd., April, 1996). Reprinted by permission of Goldman, Sachs.

---

[22] For further detail and examples of the application, see Leibowitz and Kogelman, *Franchise Value and the Price/ Earnings Ratio.*

TABLE 20.11	PROFITABILITY AND FINANCIAL STRENGTH FOR MAJOR EUROPEAN CHEMICAL FIRMS: 1995	
	NET INCOME/AVG. SHAREHOLDERS' EQUITY (%)	NET DEBT/SHAREHOLDERS' EQUITY (%)
	1995	1995
BASF	15	−19
Bayer	14	6
Hoechst	14	93
Ciba	13	−13
AKZO	20	55
L'Air Liquide	12	16
BOC	16	65
Rhone-Poulenc	5	153

Note: These figures are based on reported results and reflect differing accounting practices; they are intended to set out trends over time for the individual companies rather than provide a basis for comparisons between companies.

Sources: Company Reports, Goldman, Sachs Analysis; Charles K. Brown, Mark Tracey and Paul Krikler, "The Major European Chemicals/Pharma Groups—Share Price Surge" (London: Goldman, Sachs International Ltd., April, 1996). Reprinted by permission of Goldman, Sachs.

PROFITABILITY AND FINANCIAL STRENGTH

Table 20.11 contains information on profitability as measured by the return on equity (ROE) for the individual firms. The notes to the table caution that the analysis should concentrate on the performance for individual firms over time because the data are not adjusted for accounting differences between firms and countries. The results for 1995 reflect consistent performance in 1995 for all the firms relative to the results in 1994. This is probably a result of the economic expansion in Europe that generally started in 1994 and was continuing during 1996.

You also should examine the financial risk of the firms based on their debt/equity ratios. Again, you should limit your analysis to specific firms over time. The discussion makes it clear that the wide range of debt/equity ratios and the changes in these ratios over time reflect operating performance and financial strategy decisions as well as the effects of acquisitions by some firms.

COMMON STOCK STATISTICS

Given the prior analysis, Table 20.12 contains measures of absolute and relative stock performance for the firms in the industry. The absolute P/E ratios which range from 6.5 to 20.4 show the differences in the earnings multipliers among countries. The table contains some interesting information on the individual stock P/E ratios relative to the average P/E ratio in the local market. As an example, Bayer's P/E ratio is 13.7, which is only 97 percent of the average of all stocks in Germany. In contrast, AGA B has a P/E ratio of 16.7, which is moderately higher, but is 172 percent of the average for stocks in Sweden. This shows that two stocks with fairly similar P/E ratios could have different relative valuations in different countries due to variations in accounting conventions or social attitudes. Such differences in relative valuation among countries might be less in the future as accounting practices among countries become more consistent and global capital markets become more integrated.

The price/book value ratios likewise reflect major differences in relative valuation among countries. Again, these differences could be due to differences in valuation factors (growth and risk) or because of differences in accounting practices

	Currency	Shares Price[1]	12-Month Range High	Low	EPS (1996E)	EPS (1997E)	DPS (1996E)	P/E (1996E)	P/E-Relative (1996E)	P/CF (1996)	P/BV (1995)	Yield (1996E)
BASF[2]	DM	430	430	295	40.0	46.0	15.0	10.8	76	4.3	1.5	5.0%
Bayer[2]	DM	519	519	336	38.0	44.0	16.5	13.7	97	6.7	2.0	4.5
Hoechst[2]	DM	528	535	294	34.0	47.5	15.0	15.5	110	6.3	2.5	4.1
Ciba	SFr	1,436	1,507	744	86.3	97.7	24.0	15.9	91	9.9	2.4	1.8
AKZO	DFL	188	209	169	19.0	22.5	7.5	9.9	87	5.1	2.0	4.0
DSM	DFL	159	159	118	24.3	29.5	9.0	6.5	57	3.5	1.1	5.7
Solvay[3]	BFr	17,975	18,450	14,325	1,552	1,982	600	11.6	101	4.7	1.6	4.5
L'Air Liquide	FFr	916	938	753	45.0	51.6	15.4	20.4	149	10.0	2.6	2.5
BOC[4]	P	884	944	727	56.5	62.8	27.0	15.6	103	8.2	2.6	3.8
AGA B	SKr	105	105	79	6.3	6.9	2.8	16.7	172	8.7	2.6	2.7
Rhone-Poulenc	FFr	134	134	96	8.6	12.4	3.8	15.6	114	4.8	1.2	4.3

[1]Prices at 10 April 1996 all per share figures based on this price.
[2]EPS is on DVFA-adjusted basis, undiluted; potential dilution for BASF 3.5%, Bayer 2.5%.
[3]Before extraordinary items.
[4]Years to September.
E = Estimate.

Source: Charles K. Brown, Mark Tracey and Paul Krikler, "The Major European Chemicals/Pharma Groups—Share Price Surge" (London: Goldman, Sachs International Ltd., April, 1996). Reprinted by permission of Goldman, Sachs.

SHARE PRICE
PERFORMANCE

Table 20.13 compares the stock price changes for the major chemical firms. Here we can see the impact of exchange rates. Part A shows the stocks' absolute percentage changes and relative results compared to the stock's local market index over 1-, 3- and 5-year time horizons. The results indicate large differences in absolute and relative stock performances. In Part B, these stock returns are converted to U.S. dollars and compared to the U.S. market, which indicates the relative performance for a U.S. investor. This latter comparison is critical because it demonstrates the effect of international diversification and the necessity of considering exchange rate movements when making foreign investments. For example, looking at the results during the most recent year shows that basic exchange rates were a negative factor for most stocks based on a comparison of domestic returns in Part A and U.S. dollar returns in Part B. The results deteriorated further when compared to the S&P 500. In summary, during this particular period both the U.S. dollar and the U.S. stock market were strong, which hurt these relative comparisons.

TABLE 20.13   **SHARE PRICE PERFORMANCE FOR MAJOR EUROPEAN CHEMICAL FIRMS**

	ABSOLUTE CHANGE (%) OVER LAST			CHANGE RELATIVE TO LOCAL MARKET (%) OVER LAST		
	Year	3 Years	5 Years	Year	3 Years	5 Years
A: Domestic Currencies						
BASF	46	80	81	14	18	12
Bayer	52	88	92	19	23	19
Hoechst	76	114	115	37	40	33
Ciba	90	134	190	31	30	23
AKZO	5	24	68	−21	−25	−10
Solvay	24	41	38	2	10	7
L'Air Liquide	17	34	59	5	27	38
BOC	21	25	52	1	−8	−1
AGA B	30	68	91	6	−10	11
Rhone-Poulenc PICs	16	−10		4	−14	

	ABSOLUTE CHANGE (%) OVER LAST			CHANGE RELATIVE TO S&P 500 (%) OVER LAST		
	Year	3 Years	5 Years	Year	3 Years	5 Years
B: U.S. Dollars						
BASF	37	93	103	9	35	19
Bayer	43	101	115	14	40	27
Hoechst	65	129	140	32	60	41
Ciba	81	184	239	45	98	100
AKZO	−1	34	90	−21	−7	12
Solvay	16	51	55	−7	6	−9
L'Air Liquide	12	42	77	−10	−1	4
BOC	15	24	29	−8	−14	−24
AGA B	43	91	72	14	33	2
Rhone-Poulenc PICs	11			−11		

Source: Charles K. Brown, Mark Tracey and Paul Krikler, "The Major European Chemicals/Pharma Groups—Share Price Surge" (London: Goldman, Sachs International Ltd., April 1996). Reprinted by permission of Goldman, Sachs & Co.

TABLE 20.14

COMPANY AND STOCK PRICE DATA FOR BAYER

Price:	DM519	Price Relative to Market: 1 Month:	+6%
Market Value:	DM36.6bn	3 Months:	+19%
12-Month Range:	DM519–336	1 Year:	+19%
FT-A Germany:	135.3	3 Years:	+23%

Year to December	Pre-Tax Profit DMm	Net Profit DMm	EPS[a] DM	Net Div DM	Cash Flow/ Share[b] DM	P/E	P/E Rel %	Price/ Cash Flow	Gross Yield %
1993	2,354	1,327	22.5	11.0	72	23.1	72	7.2	3.0
1994	3,293	1,970	30.0	13.0	73	17.3	78	7.1	3.6
1995	4,188	2,394	34.0	15.0	77	15.3	87	6.7	4.1
1996E	4,700	2,685	38.0	16.5	78	13.7	97	6.7	4.5
1997E	5,650	3,225	44.0	18.0	82	11.8	92	6.3	5.0
1998E	6,250	3,580	49.0	18.0	89	10.6	87	5.8	5.0
1993–98E comp growth %	−8	−6	−8	—	−4				

| Options/Convertibles/Warrants: O/C/W | Reuters: BAYG.F |
| Listed ADRs: No | Quotron: BAYR.EU |

[a]DVFA undiluted–dilution approximately 2.5%.
[b]Undiluted.

Source: Charles K. Brown, Mark Tracey and Paul Krikler, "The Major European Chemical/Pharma Groups—Share Price Surge" (London: Goldman, Sachs International, Ltd., April 1996). Reprinted by permission of Goldman, Sachs.

INDIVIDUAL COMPANY ANALYSIS

The report concludes with a summary of the strengths and potential problems of each individual company. Table 20.14 summarizes the results for Bayer, a German firm considered to be one of the world's leading chemical companies. The discussion that accompanies the table considers the relatively strong performance during the early months of 1996 that they expect to continue throughout the year. The authors of the report base this on the outlook for this industry. Also, a stock price chart for Bayer (Figure 20.7) shows the absolute and relative movements for the firm's stock.

ANALYSIS OF GROWTH COMPANIES

Investment literature contains numerous accounts of the rapid growth of companies such as Wal-Mart, Cisco Systems, Intel, Merck, and Microsoft, along with stories about investors who became wealthy because of the timely acquisition of these stocks. These very high rates of return indicate that the proper valuation of true growth companies can be extremely rewarding. At the same time, for every successful Wal-Mart or Microsoft, there are numerous firms that did not survive. In addition, there are many instances where the stock price of a true growth company overcompensated for the firm's expected growth and the subsequent returns to the stockholder were below expectations. As noted earlier, the common stock of a growth company is *not* always a growth stock![23]

You are familiar with the dividend discount model and its basic assumptions, that is, that dividends are expected to grow at a *constant rate* for an *infinite time period*. As explained

---

[23] See Michael Solt and Meir Statman, "Good Companies, Bad Stocks," *Journal of Portfolio Management* 15, no. 4 (Summer 1989): 39–44.

FIGURE 20.7 BAYER SHARE PRICE PERFORMANCE, 1989–1998

Bayer

Price:	DM519
Market Value:	DM36.6bn
12 Month Range:	DM519-336
FT-A Germany:	135.3

Price Relative to Market:	1 Month: +6%
	3 Months: +19%
	1 Year: +19%
	3 Years: +23%

Year to December:	Pre-Tax Profit DMm	Net Profit DM	EPS[1] DM	Net Div DM	Cash Flow/ Share[2] DM	P/E	P/E Rel %	Price/ Cash Flow	Gross Yield %
1989	4,105	2,083	37.0	13.0	92	14.0	92	5.6	3.9
1990	3,366	1,881	30.0	13.0	84	17.3	135	6.2	3.9
1991	3,206	1,824	28.0	13.0	80	18.5	127	6.5	3.9
1992	2,693	1,516	25.0	11.0	74	20.8	125	7.0	3.3
1993	2,354	1,327	22.5	11.0	72	23.1	72	7.2	3.0
1994	3,293	1,970	30.0	13.0	73	17.3	78	7.1	3.6
1995	4,188	2,394	34.0	15.0	77	15.3	87	6.7	4.1
1996E	4,700	2,685	38.0	16.5	78	13.7	97	6.7	4.5
1997E	5,650	3,225	44.0	18.0	82	11.8	92	6.3	5.0
1998E	6,250	3,580	49.0	18.0	89	10.6	87	5.8	5.0
1989-98E comp growth %	5	6	3	4	-				

Options/Convertibles/Warrants: O/C/W
Listed ADRs: No

Reuters: BAYG.F

1. DVFA undiluted - dilution approx 2.5% in 1996; minimal thereafter 2. Undiluted.

Share Rating:

Next Report:
First Quarter Results
Thursday 25 April

Business Summary

Price Performance 1989-1996

PRICE (DM)
RELATIVE TO LOCAL MARKET(R.H.SCALE)
Source: DATASTREAM

Moderate Outperformer

Bayer's share price moved ahead sharply in recent months, driven by improved medium-term prospects and by interest stimulated by the on-going consolidation of the world's pharmaceutical industry, which has influenced the valuation for groups with large drug activities. However, based on increased confidence in higher medium-term earnings projections, we continue to see the shares as offering good value.

Bayer is one of the world's leading chemical companies with diverse operations and an international spread of business. In 1995, 53% of sales were made in Europe, 22% in North America, 19% in Asia (principally in Japan), Africa and Australia, and 6% in Latin America. Some 64% of operating profit was generated by businesses in Europe, 23% in North America, 5% in Latin America and 9% elsewhere.

Bayer's major speciality product areas are pharmaceuticals, imaging technologies (Agfa-Gevaert Group) and agrochemicals, which together accounted for around 67% of 1995 operating profit on 50% of sales. Other major product groups are industrial products (15% of profit on 19% of sales); polymers (11% on 18%) and organic products (7% on 13%). The product profile has a relatively limited weighting in bulk petrochemicals, does not include fertilisers and has only a small (2% of sales) exposure to fibres. The industrial products business comprises inorganic chemicals, polyurethanes, coating raw materials and speciality products and the H.C. Starck ceramics and metal products businesses.

The group's strategy is to build its business in areas of technical and market strength on an international basis, as reflected for example in its leading positions in such businesses as polyurethanes, polycarbonates and iron pigments. Research and development expenditure was 7.3% of sales in 1995.

in Chapter 13, although these assumptions are reasonable when evaluating the aggregate market and some large industries, they can be very tenuous when analyzing individual securities. *These assumptions are extremely questionable for a growth company.*

GROWTH COMPANY
DEFINED

A growth company has the opportunities and ability to invest capital in projects that generate rates of return greater than the firm's cost of capital. Such a condition is considered to be *temporary* because, in a competitive economy, all firms should produce at the point where marginal revenue equals marginal cost, which means that the returns to the producer will exactly compensate for the risks involved. If the returns earned in an industry are below what is expected for the risk involved, some participants will leave the industry. In contrast, if the rates of return for a given industry exceed the rates of return expected based on the risk involved, other companies will enter the industry, increase the supply, and eventually drive prices down until the rates of return earned are consistent with the risk involved, resulting in a state of equilibrium.

ACTUAL RETURNS
ABOVE EXPECTED
RETURNS

The notion of a firm consistently earning rates of return above its required rate of return requires elaboration. Firms are engaged in business ventures that offer opportunities for investment of corporate capital, and these investments entail some risk. Investors determine their required return for owning a firm based on the risk of its investments compared to the risk of other firms. Based on the CAPM, one would expect the difference in the required rate of return to be a function of the difference in the stock's systematic risk. This required rate of return is referred to as the firm's *cost of equity*. If the market is in a state of equilibrium, the rates of return earned on risky investments by the firm should equal the rates of return required by investors. If a firm earns returns above those required for the systematic risk involved, these excess returns are referred to as *pure profits*.

One of the costs of production is the cost of the capital used. Therefore, in a competitive environment, marginal revenue should equal marginal costs (including capital costs), and there would be no excess returns or pure profits. Excess profits are possible only in a noncompetitive environment. Assume that a medical equipment firm is able to earn 20 percent on its capital, while investors require only 15 percent from the firm because of its systematic risk. The extra 5 percent is defined as pure profit, and numerous companies would enter the medical equipment field to enjoy the excess profits. These competitors would increase the supply of equipment and reduce the price that producers could charge for the equipment until the marginal returns equaled the marginal costs.

Because many firms have derived excess profits for a number of years, these excess returns are probably not due to a temporary disequilibrium, but rather because of some noncompetitive factors that exist such as patents or copyrights that provide a firm or person with monopoly rights to a process or a manuscript for a specified period of time. During this period of protection from competition, the firm can derive above-normal returns without fear of competition. Also, a firm could possess other strategies, such as those discussed by Porter, that provide added profits (e.g., a unique marketing technique or other organizational characteristics). Finally, there may be significant barriers to entry such as capital requirements.

In a purely competitive economy with no frictions, true growth companies would not exist because competition would not allow continuing excess return investments. The fact is, our economy is not perfectly competitive (although this typically is the best model to use) because there are a number of frictions that restrict competition. Therefore, it is possible for *temporary* true growth companies to exist in our economy. The questions is, how long can they earn these excess profits?

GROWTH COMPANIES AND GROWTH STOCKS

Recall that a growth stock is expected to experience above-average risk-adjusted rates of return during some future period. This means that any undervalued stock can be a growth stock, regardless of the type of company. Alternatively, the stock of a growth company that is overvalued could be a speculative stock because the probability of below-normal returns would be very high.

In this section, we discuss models that are meant to help you evaluate the unique earnings stream of a growth company. As a result, you should derive a better estimate of the firm's value and be able to judge whether the stock of a growth company is: (1) a growth stock, (2) a properly valued stock, or (3) a speculative overvalued stock.

GROWTH COMPANIES AND THE DIVIDEND DISCOUNT MODEL

We know it is impossible for a true growth firm to exist for an infinite time period in a relatively competitive economy. Further, even in an economy with some noncompetitive factors, a true growth firm should not be able to exist for very long because patents and copyrights run out, unusual management practices can be copied, and competitors can enter the industry. Therefore, the constant growth dividend discount growth model is *not* appropriate for the valuation of growth companies, and we must consider special valuation models that allow for the finite periods of abnormal growth and for the possibility of different rates of growth. The rest of the chapter deals with models for valuing growth companies.

ALTERNATIVE GROWTH MODELS[24]

In this section, we consider the full range of growth models, from those of no growth and negative growth to dynamic true growth. Knowledge of the full range will help you understand why the dividend growth model is not always applicable. We assume the company is an all-equity firm to simplify the computations.

NO-GROWTH FIRM

The no-growth firm is a mythical company that is established with a specified portfolio of investments that generate a constant stream of earnings (E) equal to r times the value of assets. Earnings are calculated after allowing for depreciation to maintain the assets at their original value. Therefore

$$E = r \times \text{Assets}$$

It also is assumed that all earnings of the firm are paid out in dividends; if b is the rate of retention, $b = 0$. Hence,

$$E = r \times \text{Assets} = \text{Dividends}$$

Under these assumptions, the value of the firm is the discounted value of the perpetual stream of earnings (E). The discount rate (the required rate of return) is specified as k. In this case, it is assumed that $r = k$. The firm's rate of return on assets equals its required rate of return. The value of the firm is

$$V = \frac{E}{k} = \frac{(1-b)E}{k}$$

[24]The discussion in this section draws heavily from Ezra Solomon, *The Theory of Financial Management* (New York: Columbia University Press, 1963), 55–63; and M. Miller and F. Modigliani, "Dividend Policy, Growth, and the Valuation of Shares," *The Journal of Business* 34, no. 4 (October 1961): 411–433.

In the no-growth case, the earnings stream never changes because the asset base never changes, and the rate of return on the assets never changes. Therefore, the value of the firm never changes, and investors continue to receive k on their investment.

$$k = E/V$$

LONG-RUN GROWTH MODELS   Long-run models differ from the no-growth models because *they assume some of the earnings are reinvested*. The initial case assumes a firm retains a constant dollar amount of earnings and reinvests these retained earnings in assets that obtain a rate of return above the required rate.

In all cases, it is postulated that the market value (V) of an all-equity firm is the capitalized value of three component forms of returns discounted at the rate k.

- E = the level of (constant) net earnings expected from existing assets, without further net investments.
- G = the growth component that equals the present value of capital gains expected from reinvested funds. The return on reinvested funds is equal to r, which equals mk (m is the relative rate of return operator). If m is equal to one, then $r = k$. If m is greater than 1, the projects that generate these returns are considered true growth investments ($r > k$). If m is less than 1, the investments are generating returns (r) below the cost of capital ($r < k$).
- R = the reinvestment of net earnings (E) and is equal to bE, where b is a percent of retention between zero (no reinvestment) and unity (total reinvestment; no dividends).

SIMPLE GROWTH MODEL   This model assumes the firm has growth investment opportunities that provide rates of return equal to r, where r is greater than k (m is above 1). Further, it is assumed that the firm can invest R dollars a year at these rates and that $R = bE$; R is a *constant dollar amount* because E is the constant earnings at the beginning of the period.

The value of G, the capital gain component, is computed as follows: the first investment of bE dollars yields a stream of earnings equal to bEr dollars, and this is repeated every year. Each of these earnings streams has a present value, as of the year it begins, of bEr/k, which is the present value of a constant perpetual stream discounted at a rate consistent with the risk involved. Assuming the firm does this every year, it has a series of investments, each of which has a present value of bEr/k. The present value of *all* these series is $(bEr/k)/k$, which equals bEr/k^2. But because $r = mk$, this becomes

$$\frac{bEmk}{k^2} = \frac{bEm}{k} \text{ (Gross Present Value of Growth Investments)} \tag{20.1}$$

To derive these flows, the firm must invest bE dollars each year. The present value of these annual investments is equal to bE/k. Therefore, the *net* present value of growth investments is equal to

$$\frac{bEm}{k} - \frac{bE}{k} \text{ (Net Present Value of Growth Investments)} \tag{20.2}$$

The important variable is the value of m, which indicates the relationship of r to k. Combining this growth component with the capitalized value of the constant earnings stream indicates that the value of the firm is

$$V = \frac{E}{k} + \frac{bEm}{k} - \frac{bE}{k} \tag{20.3}$$

This equation indicates that the value of the firm is equal to the constant earnings stream plus a growth component equal to the *net* present value of reinvestment in growth projects. By combining the first and third terms in Equation 20.3, it becomes

$$V = \frac{E(1-b)}{k} + \frac{bEm}{k} \tag{20.4}$$

Because $E(1-b)$ is the dividend (D), this model becomes

$$V = \frac{D}{k} + \frac{bEm}{k} \quad \text{(Present Value of Constant Dividend plus the Present Value of Growth Investments)} \tag{20.5}$$

It can be stated as earnings only by rearranging Equation 20.3.

$$V = \frac{E}{k} + \frac{bE(m-1)}{k} \quad \text{(Present Value of Constant Earnings plus Present Value of Excess Earnings from Growth Investments)} \tag{20.6}$$

EXPANSION MODEL   The expansion model assumes a firm retains earnings to reinvest but receives a rate of return on its investments that is equal to its cost of capital ($m = 1$, so $r = k$). The effect of such a change can be seen in Equation 20.2, where the net present value of growth investments would be zero. Therefore, Equation 20.3 would become

$$V = \frac{E}{k} \tag{20.7}$$

Equation 20.4 would become

$$V = \frac{E(1-b)}{k} + \frac{bE}{k} = \frac{E}{k} \tag{20.8}$$

Equation 20.5 is still valid, but the present value of the growth investment component would be smaller because m would be equal to 1. Finally, the last term in Equation 20.6 would disappear.

   This discussion indicates that simply because a firm retains earnings and reinvests them, it is not necessarily beneficial to the stockholder *unless the reinvestment rate is above the required rate ($r > k$).* Otherwise, the investor in a tax-free world would be as well off with all earnings paid out in dividends.

NEGATIVE GROWTH MODEL   The negative growth model applies to a firm that retains earnings ($b > 0$) and reinvests these funds in projects that generate rates of return *below* the firm's cost of capital ($r < k$ or $m < 1$). The impact of this on the value of the firm can be seen from Equation 20.2, which indicates that with $m < 1$, the net present value of the growth investments would be *negative*. Therefore, the value of the firm in Equation 20.3 would be *less* than the value of a no-growth firm or an expansion firm. This also can be seen by examining the effect of $m < 1$ in Equation 20.6. The firm is withholding funds from the investor and investing them in projects that generate returns less than those available from comparable risk investments.

Such poor performance may be difficult to uncover because the firm's asset base will grow since it is retaining earnings and acquiring assets. Notably, the earnings of the firm will increase if it earns *any* positive rate of return on the new assets. *The earnings will not grow by as much as they should*, so the value of the firm will decline when investors discount this reinvestment stream at the firm's cost of capital.

WHAT DETERMINES THE CAPITAL GAIN COMPONENT?   These equations highlight the factors that influence the capital gain component. All the equations beginning with 20.1 suggest that the gross present value of the growth investments is equal to

$$bEm/k$$

Therefore, three factors influence the size of this capital gain term. The first is b, the percentage of earnings retained for reinvestment. The greater the proportion of earnings retained, the larger the capital gain component. The second factor is m, which is critical because it indicates the relationship between the firm's rate of return on investments and the firm's required rate of return (i.e., its cost of capital). A value of 1 indicates the firm is earning only its required return. A firm with an m greater than 1 is a true growth company. The important question is, how much greater than 1 is the return? The final factor is the time period for the superior investments. How long can the firm make these superior return investments? This time factor often is overlooked because we have assumed an infinite horizon to simplify the computations. However, when analyzing growth companies, this time estimate is clearly a major consideration. In summary, the three factors that influence the capital gain component are

1. The amount of capital invested in growth investments (b)
2. The relative rate of return earned on the funds retained (m)
3. The time horizon for these growth investments

DYNAMIC TRUE GROWTH MODEL   A dynamic true growth model applies to a firm that invests a constant *percentage* of *current* earnings in projects that generate rates of return above the firm's required rate ($r > k, m > 1$). In contrast to the simple growth model where the firm invests a *constant* dollar amount each year, in this model the amount invested is *growing* each year as earnings increase. As a result, the firm's earnings and dividends will grow at a *constant rate* that is equal to br (the percentage of earnings retained times the return on investments). In the current model, this would equal bmk, where m is greater than 1. Given these assumptions, the dynamic growth model for an infinite time period is the dividend discount model derived in the Appendix to Chapter 13:

$$V = \frac{D_1}{k - g}$$

Applying this model to a true growth company means that earnings and dividends are growing at a constant rate and *the firm is investing larger and larger dollar amounts in projects that generate returns greater than k*. Moreover, the DDM model implicitly assumes that the firm can continue to do this for *an infinite time period*. If the growth rate (g) is greater than k, the model blows up and indicates that the firm should have an infinite value. Durand considered this possibility and concluded that, although many firms had current growth rates above the normal required rates of return, very few of their stocks

TABLE 20.15	SUMMARY OF COMPANY DESCRIPTIONS		
		Retention	Return on Investments
No-Growth Company		$b = 0$	$r = k$
Long-Run Growth (assumes reinvestment)			
Negative growth		$b > 0$	$r < k$
Expansion		$b > 0$	$r = k$
Simple long-run growth		$b > 0$	
		(constant $)	$r > k$
Dynamic long-run growth		$b > 0$	
		(constant %)	$r > k$

were selling for infinite values.[25] He explained this by contending that investors expected the reinvestment rate to decline or they felt that the investment opportunities would not be available for an infinite time period. Table 20.15 contains a summary of the alternative company characteristics.

THE REAL WORLD   Because these models are simplified to allow us to develop a range of alternatives, several of them are extremely unrealistic. In the real world, companies may combine these models. Unfortunately, most firms have made some investments where $r < k$, and many firms invest in projects that generate returns about equal to their cost of capital. Finally, most firms invest in *some* projects that provide rates of return above the firm's cost of capital ($r > k$). The crucial questions are, how much is invested in these growth projects, and how long do these true growth opportunities last?

Given this understanding of growth companies and what creates their value, the rest of the chapter considers various models that help estimate specific values for these growth companies.

GROWTH DURATION   The purpose of the growth duration model is to help you *evaluate* the high P/E ratio for the stock of a growth company by relating the P/E ratio to the firm's rate and duration of growth. A stock's P/E ratio is a function of (1) the firm's expected rate of growth of earnings per share, (2) the stock's required rate of return, and (3) the firm's dividend-payout ratio. Assuming equal risk and no significant difference in the payout ratio for different firms, the principal variable affecting differences in the earnings multiple for two firms *is the difference in expected growth*. Further, the growth estimate must consider the *rate* of growth and how long it will last, that is, the *duration* of expected growth. As noted earlier, no company can grow indefinitely at a rate substantially above normal. For example, Wal-Mart cannot continue to grow at 20 percent a year for an extended period, or it will eventually become the entire economy. In fact, Wal-Mart or any similar growth firm will eventually run out of high-profit investment projects. Recall that continued growth at a constant rate requires that larger amounts of money be invested in high-return projects. Eventually competition will encroach on these high-return investments, and the firm's growth rate will decline to a rate consistent with the rate for the overall economy. Ascertaining the duration of a firm's high-growth period therefore becomes significant.

---

[25] David Durand, "Growth Stocks and the Petersburg Paradox," *Journal of Finance* 12, no. 3 (September 1957): 348–363.

COMPUTATION OF GROWTH DURATION   The growth duration concept was suggested by Holt, who showed that if you assume equal risk between a given security and a market security such as the S&P 400, you can concentrate on the differential past growth rates for the market and the growth firm as a factor causing the alternative P/E ratios.[26] This allows you to compute the market's *implied growth duration* for the growth firm.

If $E'(0)$ is the firm's current earnings, then $E'(t)$ is earnings in period t according to the expression

$$E'(t) = E(0)(1 + G)^t \qquad (20.9)$$

where G is the annual percentage growth rate for earnings. To adjust for dividend payments, it was assumed that all such payments are used to purchase further shares of the stock. This means the number of shares (N) will grow at the dividend rate (D). Therefore

$$N(t) = N(0)(1 + D)^t \qquad (20.10)$$

To derive the total earnings for a firm, $E(t)$, the growth rate in per share earnings and the growth in shares are combined as follows:

$$E(t) = E'(t)N(t) = E'(0)[(1 + G)(1 + D)]^t \qquad (20.11)$$

Because G and D are small, this expression can be approximated by

$$E(t) \simeq E'(0)(1 + G + D)^t \qquad (20.12)$$

Assuming the growth stock (g) and the nongrowth stock (a) have similar risk and payout, the market should value the two stocks in direct proportion to their earnings in year T, where T is the time when the growth company will begin to grow at the same rate as the market (i.e., the nongrowth stock). In other words, *current prices should be in direct proportion to the expected future earnings ratio that will prevail in year T.* This relationship can be stated

$$\left(\frac{P_g(0)}{P_a(0)} \right) \simeq \left(\frac{E_g(0)(1 + G_g + D_g)^T}{E_a(0)(1 + G_a + D_a)^T} \right) \qquad (20.13)$$

or

$$\left(\frac{P_g(0)/E_g(0)}{P_a(0)/E_a(0)} \right) \simeq \left(\frac{1 + G_g + D_g}{1 + G_a + D_a} \right)^T \qquad (20.14)$$

As a result, the *P/E ratios of the two stocks are in direct proportion to the ratio of composite growth rates raised to the Tth power.* You can solve for T by taking the log of both sides as follows:

$$\ln \left(\frac{P_g(0)/E_g(0)}{P_a(0)/E_a(0)} \right) \simeq T \ln \left(\frac{1 + G_g + D_g}{1 + G_a + D_a} \right) \qquad (20.15)$$

---

[26] Charles C. Holt, "The Influence of Growth Duration on Share Prices," *Journal of Finance* 7, no. 3 (September 1962): 465–475.

The growth duration model answers the question, how long must the earnings of the growth stock grow at the past rate, relative to the nongrowth stock, to justify its prevailing above-average P/E ratio? You must then determine whether the *implied* duration estimate is reasonable in terms of the company's potential.

Consider the following example. The stock of a well-known growth company is selling for $63 a share with expected per share earnings of $3.00 (its earnings multiple is 21). The growth firm's EPS growth rate during the past 5- and 10-year periods has been 15 percent a year, and its dividend yield has been 3 percent. In contrast, the S&P 400 Industrial Index has a current P/E ratio of 14, an average dividend yield of 4 percent, and an average growth rate of 6 percent. Therefore, the comparison looks as follows:

	S&P 400	Growth Company
P/E ratio	14.00	21.00
Average growth rate	.06	.15
Dividend yield	.04	.03

Inserting these values into Equation 20.15 yields the following:

$$\ln\left(\frac{21.00}{14.00}\right) = T\ln\left(\frac{1 + .15 + .03}{1 + .06 + .04}\right)$$

$$\ln(1.50) = T\ln\left(\frac{1.18}{1.10}\right)$$

$$\ln(1.500) = T\ln(1.073)$$

$$T = \ln(1.500)/\ln(1.073)$$

$$= .1761/.0306 \text{ (log base 10)}$$

$$= 5.75 \text{ years}$$

These results indicate the market is implicitly assuming that the growth company can continue to grow at this composite rate (18 percent) for almost six more years, after which it is assumed the growth company will grow at the same rate (10 percent) as the aggregate market (i.e., the S&P 400). You must now ask, can this growth rate be sustained by this growth company for at least this period? If the implied growth duration is greater than you believe is reasonable, you would advise against buying the stock. If the implied duration is below your expectations, you would recommend buying the stock.

INTRA-INDUSTRY ANALYSIS   Besides comparing a company to a market series, you can directly compare two firms. For an intercompany analysis, you should compare firms in the same industry because the equal risk assumptions of this model are probably more reasonable.

Consider the following example from the computer software industry:

	Company A	Company B
P/E ratios	21.00	15.00
Average annual growth rate	.1700	.1200
Dividend yield	.0250	.0300
Growth rate plus dividend yield	.1950	.1500
Estimate of T[a]		8.79 years

[a]Readers should check to see that they get the same answer.

These results imply that the market expects Company A to grow at an annual total rate of almost 20 percent for about 9 years, after which it will grow at Company B's rate of 15 percent. If you believe the implied duration is too long, you will prefer Company B; if you believe it is reasonable or low, you will recommend Company A.

AN ALTERNATIVE USE OF T Instead of solving for T and then deciding whether the figure derived is reasonable, you can use this formulation to compute a reasonable P/E ratio for a security relative to the aggregate market (or another stock) if the implicit assumptions are reasonable for the stock involved. Assume that you estimate the composite growth of a company to be about 20 percent a year compared to the market growth of 11 percent. Further, you believe that this firm can continue to grow at this above-normal rate for about 7 years. Using Equation 20.15, this becomes

$$\ln(X) = 7 \cdot \ln\frac{1.20}{1.11}$$

$$= 7 \cdot \ln(1.081)$$
$$= 7 \cdot (.033826)$$
$$= .236782$$

To determine what the P/E ratio should be given these assumptions, you must derive the antilog of 0.236782, which is approximately 1.725. Therefore, assuming the market multiple is 14.00, the earnings multiple for this growth company should be about 1.725 times the market P/E ratio, or 24.15.

Alternatively, if you expect that the firm can maintain this differential growth for only 5 years, you would derive the antilog for 0.16913 ($5 \times .033826$). The answer is 1.4761, which implies a P/E ratio of 20.66 for the stock.

FACTORS TO CONSIDER   When using the growth duration technique, remember the following factors: First, the technique assumes equal risk, which may be acceptable when comparing two large, well-established firms or relating them to a market proxy (e.g., IBM and Apple Computer to each other or to the S&P 400). It is probably *not* a valid assumption when comparing a small firm to the aggregate market.

Second, which growth estimate should be used? In the typical case, 5- and 10-year historical growth rates are used. Which time interval is most relevant if historical rates are used? It may be more appropriate to use the *expected* rate of growth based on the factors that affect g (i.e., the retention rate and the components of ROE).

Third, the growth duration technique assumes that stocks with higher P/E ratios have the higher growth rates. However, in many cases the stock with the higher P/E ratio does not have a higher historical growth rate, which generates a useless negative growth duration value. Inconsistency between growth and the P/E ratio could be attributed to one of four factors:

1. A major difference in the risk involved.
2. Inaccurate growth rate estimates. Possibly the firm with the higher P/E ratio is *expected* to grow faster in the future. Consider the historical growth rate used and whether you expect any changes in the firm's growth rate.
3. The stock with a low P/E ratio relative to its growth rate is undervalued. (Before you accept this possibility, consider the first two factors.)
4. The stock with a high P/E and a low growth rate is overvalued. (Before this is accepted, consider the second factor.).

The growth duration concept is valid, *given the assumptions made*, and can help you evaluate growth investments. It is not universally valid, though, because its answers are only as good as the data inputs (relative growth rates) and the applicability of the assumptions. The answer must be evaluated based on the analyst's knowledge.

The technique probably is most useful for helping spot overvalued growth companies with very high multiples. In such a case, the technique will highlight that the company must continue to grow at some very high rate for an extended period of time to justify its high P/E ratio (e.g., 15 to 20 years). Also, it can help you decide between two growth companies in the same industry by comparing each to the market, the industry, or directly to each other. Such a comparison has provided interesting insights wherein the new firms in an industry were growing faster than the large competitor, but their P/E ratios were *substantially* higher and implied that these new firms had to maintain this large growth rate superiority for *over 10 years* to justify the much higher P/E ratio.

A FLEXIBLE GROWTH STOCK VALUATION MODEL

Mao developed an investment opportunities growth model that incorporated some previous work on growth stock valuation by Solomon and by Miller and Modigliani.[27] These authors had recognized the true nature of a growth firm, but they assumed unrealistic infinite growth horizons to simplify the exposition, which meant the models were not applicable to practical problems.

Mao developed a three-stage valuation model that considered (1) *a dynamic growth period* during which the firm invests a constant percentage of current earnings in growth projects, (2) *a simple growth period* during which the firm invests a constant dollar amount in growth opportunities, and finally, (3) *a declining growth period* during which the amount invested in growth investments declines to zero. The model was theoretically correct and realistic but required difficult computations and was somewhat rigid in its assumptions about the parameters b (the retention rate), r (the return on growth investments), and k (the required rate of return on the stock). As a result, the model has not been applied as widely as expected. In this section, we discuss the flexible growth model, apply it to a growth company, and discuss the effects of varying the parameters.

THE VALUATION MODEL   Mao assumed that the price of the stock is equal to (1) the present value of current earnings, E, discounted to infinity at the required rate of return, k ($P = E/k$), plus (2) the net present value of growth opportunities, assuming three stages of growth.

The dynamic growth stage lasts for n_1 years during which the firm has opportunities to invest a given percentage of current earnings in growth projects where r is greater than k. Because b is a constant percentage of a growing earnings stream, the dollar amount invested in these growth projects grows at an exponential rate. The value of the dynamic investments is given by

$$\left(\frac{r-k}{k}\right)(bE)\sum_{t=1}^{n_1}\frac{(1+br)^{t-1}}{(1+k)^t} \quad \begin{matrix}\text{(Value of Dynamic}\\\text{Growth Opportunities)}\end{matrix} \qquad (20.16)$$

The simple growth stage lasts for n_2 years during which the firm invests a constant dollar amount in growth projects ($r > k$). The value of these projects is given by

---

[27] James C. Mao, "The Valuation of Growth Stocks: The Investment Opportunities Approach," *Journal of Finance* 21, no. 1 (March 1966): 95–102.

$$\left(\frac{r-k}{k}\right)(bE) \sum_{t=1}^{n_2} \frac{1}{(1+k)^t} \quad \begin{array}{l}\text{(Value of Simple} \\ \text{Growth Opportunities)}\end{array} \qquad (20.17)$$

During the final declining growth stage, which lasts n_3 years, the firm has opportunities to invest in growth projects, but the dollar amount declines steadily from bE to zero. The amount of the decline is steady at $1/n_3$ each year. As an example, if bE equals \$100,000 and n_3 is 20, then the amount invested in growth projects would decline by \$5,000 a year. The value of this component is

$$\left(\frac{r-k}{k}\right)(bE) \sum_{t=1}^{n_3} \frac{(n_3-t+1)}{n_3(1+k)^t} \quad \begin{array}{l}\text{(Value of Declining} \\ \text{Growth Opportunities)}\end{array} \qquad (20.18)$$

The complete model combines the no-growth component (E/k) plus the three growth components. If the final summation term in Equation 20.16 is designated A, the final term in Equation 20.17 is designated B, and the final term in Equation 20.18 is designated C, this formulation can be written as follows:

$$P = \frac{E}{k} + \left(\frac{r-k}{k}\right)(bE)\left[A + \frac{(1+br)^{n_1-1}}{(1+k)^{n_1}}B + \frac{(1+br)^{n_1-1}}{(1+k)^{n_1+n_2}}C\right] \qquad (20.19)$$

Tables were provided that contained values for A and C, given several combinations of the parameters. B is simply the present value of an annuity. Even with the tables and no change in the parameters, the computations are rather tedious.

FLEXIBLE PARAMETERS   The Mao model assumes (1) no change in the required rate of return (k), (2) the same rate of return on all growth projects (r), and (3) the same retention rate (b) during the three growth periods. Mao probably assumed constant parameters to avoid complicating a technique that already involved extensive computations. Still, there are indications that investors probably change their required return (k) during different phases of the firm's life cycle. Malkiel contends it is logical to require a higher return on high-growth stocks because the stream of returns is such that these stocks are inherently longer-duration securities.[28] At the other extreme, a firm may become more subject to cyclical variations during its declining years, which would indicate higher business risk and a higher required rate of return (k).

Regarding the return on investments (r), it could be too optimistic to assume that during the period of simple growth the firm can continue to earn very high rates, even on a stable dollar amount. Many analysts might prefer a longer n_2 period and a somewhat smaller r.

Finally, is it realistic to assume a constant retention rate (b) over the life of a firm? Most observers would expect a high retention rate during the early years when growth opportunities are abundant and capital is scarce, and a lower retention rate during the later years when growth investment opportunities are limited, the levels of earnings and cash flow are high, and outside capital is available. The model would be more useful and realistic if the parameters could be changed.

APPLICATION OF THE MODEL   A computer program that requires three statements for each case allows you to consider several alternative sets of parameters, including most

---

[28] Burton G. Malkiel, "Equity Yields, Growth, and the Structure of Share Prices," *American Economic Review* 53, no. 5 (December 1963): 1004–1031.

pessimistic, most optimistic, and most likely. For a high P/E stock, you should determine the required sets of estimates that justify the prevailing market price. When applying this technique to evaluate growth companies, you should consider the following suggestions:

1. The earnings figure (E) is assumed to be the figure for the coming year. A crude estimate is the actual earnings for the most recent year times the growth rate for the past 5 or 10 years. Practicing analysts would use their estimate of future growth.
2. The estimated retention rate (b) can be the average retention rate during the last several years.
3. The estimate of the return on investment (r) is obviously crucial.[29] You can compute the average ROE during the recent period or estimate the three components (total asset turnover, financial leverage, and the profit margin) and use the product of these three estimates. Alternatively, Mao suggested computing the increase in earnings per share during some period divided by the amount of earnings retained over a comparable period with a 1-year lag (e.g., the increase in earnings per share for the period 1994 to 1998 divided by the retained earnings for the period 1993 to 1997). This computation attempts to estimate the firm's current return on retained earnings rather than the traditional average ROE, which is current net earnings divided by current equity. This average ROE is heavily influenced by past performance and uses historical equity, which can become seriously distorted over time. The Mao estimate is akin to a marginal ROE.
4. The required return estimate (k) could be the actual return derived from all common stocks or the return experienced by the specific stock during some recent period. Alternatively, you could use a required rate of return based on the CAPM and the stock's beta. Because this model is *extremely sensitive to changes in k*, you definitely should consider a *range* of ks.

AN EXAMPLE   Assume the following for a firm that you consider to be a true growth company:

- Earnings: 1997 $2.50
            1998 (estimated) $2.88 ($2.50 × 1.15)
- Annual growth rate in EPS (1993–1997)   .15
- Retention rate (1993–1997)   .65
- Average return on equity (1993–1997)   .24
- Marginal return on equity (1993–1997)   .26
- Estimated r for analysis   .25

Given these estimates of the major parameters, you can derive a number of stock price values by simply changing the values for the three ns (n_1, n_2, n_3) and consider alternative required returns. You can change the values for each of these parameters for each growth period. In this example, they will be constant at these historical values to simplify the presentation. Subsequent estimates should consider alternative parameters. For the example, the initial estimates of the ns are relatively conservative (5, 5, 10) and are changed to more liberal estimates as follows:

A. $n_1 = 5$
   $n_2 = 5$
   $n_3 = 10$

---

[29] An article that discusses the components of growth is Guilford C. Babcock, "The Concept of Sustainable Growth," *Financial Analysts Journal* 26, no. 3 (May–June 1970): 236–242.

B. $n_1 = 5$
   $n_2 = 10$
   $n_3 = 15$
C. $n_1 = 10$
   $n_2 = 10$
   $n_3 = 15$
D. $n_1 = 15$
   $n_2 = 15$
   $n_3 = 20$

The ks considered ranged from 8 percent to 16 percent in increments of 2 percent. The results in Table 20.16 indicate a wide range of estimated values for this stock. You must select the best estimate of the three time periods and, most important, an estimate of k for this stock based on its systematic risk and the expected security market line (SML). Because almost all growth companies have above-average systematic risk (i.e., betas above 1.00), the required return typically will exceed the expected market return.

Assume the following estimates regarding the SML: RFR = .08; Rm = .12. If the stock has a beta of 1.5, the estimated required return would be

$$k = \text{RFR} + \beta_i(Rm - \text{RFR})$$
$$k = .08 + 1.5\,(.12 - .08)$$
$$k = .14$$

This would indicate further consideration of the .14 percent column and the adjoining columns. Comparing these prices to the current market price will indicate whether the stock should be included in the portfolio.

You can graph the stock values for a given set of n values and different ks. Using several sets of ns will produce a set of curves sloping downward to the right as shown in Figure 20.8. There are two ways to use this graph to examine the model results. First, compare the current market price to the range of computed values. The prevailing price should be within the total range, and you should get an indication of relative valuation depending on whether the current market price is at the upper or lower end of the valuation range. Second, determine the implied rate of return by drawing the current market price horizontally across the valuation curves. Because the valuation curves generally represent the full range of feasible parameters, the intersection of the current market price line with the curve to the right indicates the highest k that can be expected—with the most liberal parameters—if you buy the stock at the current market price. The curve to the left indicates the lowest k possible if you buy the stock at today's price.

TABLE 20.16

ESTIMATED VALUES FOR STOCK ASSUMING ALTERNATIVE TIME PERIODS AND REQUIRED RATES OF RETURN (E = \$2.88; b = .65; r = .25)

n_1	n_2	n_3	0.08	0.10	0.12	0.14	0.16
5	5	10	91.03	62.79	45.67	34.55	26.96
5	10	15	102.92	68.72	48.72	36.15	27.80
10	10	15	154.15	95.72	63.55	44.46	32.46
15	15	20	242.31	136.49	83.39	54.40	37.48

FIGURE 20.8   **ESTIMATED STOCK PRICES FOR A GROWTH COMPANY USING THE FLEXIBLE GROWTH MODEL**

Estimated Stock Price (in dollars)

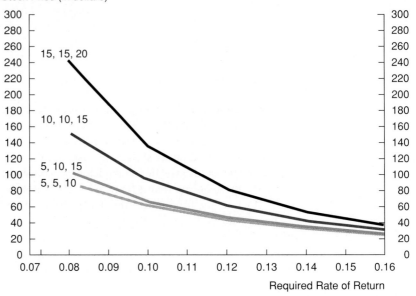

Required Rate of Return

Summary

- This chapter demonstrates how to complete the fundamental analysis process by analyzing a company and deciding whether you should buy its stock. This requires a separate analysis of a company and its stock. A wonderful firm can have an overpriced stock, or a mediocre firm can have an underpriced stock.
- Using Walgreen Company as an example, we demonstrate the DDM. We derive an estimate of expected value by computing an earnings per share estimate and the earnings multiplier.
- As part of this valuation process, we discuss the strategic alternatives available to firms in response to different competitive pressures in their industries. The alternative strategies include low-cost leadership or differentiation. Either of these should be focused toward alternative segments of the market and, if properly implemented, should help the company attain above-average rates of return.
- The investment decision is based on three comparisons. First, we compute the expected value of the stock discounted to the present and compare it to the prevailing market price. If the present value of the expected price exceeds the market price, we would buy the stock. Second, we compute the expected rate of return during our holding period on the basis of the expected value of the stock and the expected dividend. If this expected rate of return exceeds our required rate of return, we would buy it. Finally, we compute an expected long-run rate of return based on the expected dividend yield plus the expected growth rate and, again, if this expected return exceeds our required rate of return, we would buy the stock.
- We considered some additional relative valuation variables that affect the decisions of investors in the United States and abroad. Specifically, we compute and analyze the price/book value ratio and the price/cash flow ratio for the stock market, the retail drugstore industry, and Walgreen. This analysis provides some historical and current perspective for these ratios and Walgreen's relative position.
- Beyond these additional valuation variables, we consider several measures of value-added that are used by corporations to evaluate management. Specifically, the widely known concept of economic

profit, which is implied in the net present value (NPV) model of capital budgeting, has been formalized by Stern, Stewart, & Co. into economic value-added (EVA) and market value-added (MVA). Because these are well-regarded measures of management performance, they can be helpful in the overall valuation of a firm and its stock. The empirical tests provide some limited support for a relationship between EVA and MVA. Another helpful valuation concept that is consistent with our valuation approach is by Leibowitz and Kogelman. Specifically, they developed the franchise value approach, which breaks down the P/E assigned by the market into a P/E that is based on the company's ongoing business and its inherent risk (i.e., its base P/E), and the incremental P/E the market assigns to the company based on the expected value of new business opportunities that will generate returns above the firm's basic ROE. Awareness of the franchise value approach helps the analyst to recognize the importance of these growth investments and to understand how to estimate the impact they have on the stock's P/E.

- We continue our example of global analysis by applying the company analysis process to the European chemical industry. This demonstration shows the importance of differential demand and cost factors among countries, the significance of different accounting conventions, and the impact of exchange rate differences.

- We conclude the chapter with a discussion of how true growth companies are unique and temporary in a competitive economy. Because of the abnormal rates of return that are only available for a limited period, it is necessary to use a unique set of valuation models to help make the investment decision. One model used in this analysis is the growth duration model, which concentrates on the major concern of true growth companies: how long will this superior rate of growth last, and is this expectation consistent with the stock's implied growth duration? We also consider a three-step growth model, which provides a framework that considers the relevant growth variables.

- Because of the potential rewards from the superior analysis of growth companies, strong competition exists in the valuation process. The techniques presented in this chapter can help you derive an appropriate value for a growth firm, but *the estimated inputs are crucial*. The superior analyst for true growth companies is the one who derives the best estimates of the rate and duration of growth.

Questions

1. Give an example of a growth company and discuss why you identify it as such. Based on its P/E, do you think it is a growth stock? Explain.

2. Give an example of a cyclical stock and discuss why you have designated it as such. Is it issued by a cyclical company?

3. A biotechnology firm is growing at a compound rate of over 21 percent a year. (Its ROE is over 30 percent, and it retains about 70 percent of its earnings.) The stock of this company is priced at about 65 times next year's earnings. Discuss whether you consider this a growth company or a growth stock.

4. Select a company outside the retail drugstore industry and indicate what economic series you would use for a sales projection. Discuss why this is a relevant series.

5. Select a company outside the retail drugstore industry and indicate what industry series you would use in an industry analysis. (Use one of the industry groups designated by Standard & Poor's.) Discuss why this industry series is appropriate. Were there other possible alternatives?

6. Select a company outside the retail drugstore industry and, based on reading its annual report and other public information, discuss what you perceive to be its competitive strategy (i.e., low-cost producer or differentiation).

7. Discuss a company that is known to be a low-cost producer in its industry and consider what makes it possible for the firm to be a cost leader. Do the same for a firm known for differentiating.

8. What is the rationale for using the price/book value (P/BV) ratio as a measure of relative value?

9. What would you look for to justify a price/book value ratio of 3.0? What would you expect to be the characteristics of a firm with a P/BV ratio of 0.6?

10. Why has the price/cash flow (P/CF) ratio become a popular measure of relative value during the recent past? What factors would help explain a difference in this ratio for two firms?

11. Specify the major components for the calculation of economic value-added (EVA) and describe what a positive EVA signifies.

12. Discuss why you would want to use EVA return on capital rather than absolute EVA to compare two companies or to evaluate a firm's performance over time.

13. Differentiate between EVA and MVA and discuss the relatively weak relationship between these two measures of performance. Is this relationship surprising to you? Explain.

14. Discuss the two factors that determine the franchise value of a firm. Assuming a firm has a base cost of equity of 11 percent and does not have a franchise value, what will be its P/E?

15. You are told that a company retains 80 percent of its earnings, and its earnings are growing at a rate of about 8 percent a year versus an average growth rate of 6 percent for all firms. Discuss whether you would consider this a growth company.

16. It is contended by some that in a completely competitive economy, there would never be a true growth company. Discuss the reasoning behind this contention.

17. Why is it not feasible to use the dividend discount model in the valuation of true growth companies?

18. Discuss the major assumptions of the growth duration model. Why could these assumptions present a problem?

19. You are told that a growth company has a P/E ratio of 10 times and a growth rate of 15 percent compared to the aggregate market, which has a growth rate of 8 percent and a P/E ratio of 11 times. What does this comparison imply regarding the growth company? What else do you need to know to properly compare the growth company to the aggregate market?

20. Given the alternative companies described in the chapter (negative growth, simple growth, dynamic growth), indicate what your label would be for Walgreen Company. Justify your label.

21. Indicate and justify a label for General Motors.

22. What are the variables you must estimate if you want to use the Mao three-stage growth valuation model?

23. *CFA Examination I (1993)*
    Using book value to measure profitability and to value a company's stock has limitations. Discuss *five* such limitations from an accounting perspective. Be specific. [10 minutes]

24. *CFA Examination II (1995)*
    On your visit to Litchfield Chemical Corp. (LCC), you learned that the board of directors has periodically debated the company's dividend payout policy.
    a. Briefly discuss *two* arguments *for* and *two* arguments *against* a high dividend payout policy. [8 minutes]
    A director of LCC said that the use of dividend discount models by investors is "proof" that "the higher the dividend, the higher the stock price."
    b. Using a constant growth dividend discount model as a basis of reference, evaluate the above director's statement. [8 minutes]
    c. Explain how an increase in dividend payout would affect *each* of the following (holding all other factors constant):
       (i) Internal (implied, normalized, or sustainable) growth rate; and
       (ii) Growth in book value. [8 minutes]

Problems

1. Select two stocks in an industry of your choice, and perform a common size income statement analysis over a two-year period.
   a. Discuss which firm is more cost effective.
   b. Discuss the relative year-to-year changes in gross profit margin, operating profit margin, and net profit margin for each company.

2. Select a company outside the retail store industry, and examine its operating profit margin relative to the operating margin for its industry during the most recent 10-year period. Discuss the annual results in terms of levels and percentage changes.

3. Select any industry except chemicals and provide general background information on two *non-*U.S. companies from public sources (see Chapter 6). This background information should include their products, overall size (sales and assets), growth during the past 5 years (sales and earnings), ROE during the last 2 years, current stock price, and P/E ratio.

4. Given Hitech's beta of 1.75 and a risk-free rate of 7 percent, what is the expected rate of return assuming
   a. a 15 percent market return?
   b. a 10 percent market return?

5. Select three companies from any industry except retail drugstores.
   a. Compute their P/E ratios using last year's average price [(high plus low)/2] and earnings.
   b. Compute their growth rate of earnings over the last 5 years.
   c. Look up the most recent beta reported in *Value Line*.
   d. Discuss the relationships between P/E, growth, and risk.

6. What is the implied growth duration of Kayleigh Industries given the following:

	S&P 400	Kayleigh Industries
P/E ratios	16	24
Average growth	.06	.14
Dividend yield	.04	.02

7. Lauren Industries has an 18 percent annual growth rate compared to the market rate of 8 percent. If the market multiple is 14, determine P/E ratios for Lauren Industries, assuming its beta is 1.0 and you feel it can maintain its superior growth rate for
   a. the next 10 years.
   b. the next 5 years.

8. You are given the following information about two computer software firms and the S&P 400:

	Company A	Company B	S&P 400
P/E ratio	24.0	20.0	12.0
Average annual growth rate	.18	.15	.07
Dividend yield	.02	.03	.05

   a. Compute the growth duration of each company stock relative to the S&P 400.
   b. Compute the growth duration of Company A relative to Company B.
   c. Given these durations, what must you decide to make an investment decision?

9. *CFA Examination II (June 1981)*

   The value of an asset is the present value of the expected returns from the asset during the holding period. An investment will provide a stream of returns during this period, and it is necessary to discount this stream of returns at an appropriate rate to determine the asset's present value. A dividend valuation model such as the following is frequently used.

$$P_i = \frac{D_1}{(k_i - g_i)}$$

   where

   P_i = the current price of common stock i
   D_1 = the expected dividend in period 1
   k_i = the required rate of return on stock i
   g_i = the expected constant growth rate of dividends for stock i.

   a. *Identify* the three factors that must be estimated for any valuation model, and *explain* why these estimates are more difficult to derive for common stocks than for bonds. [9 minutes]

b. *Explain* the principal problem involved in using a dividend valuation model to value
   (1) Companies whose operations are closely correlated with economic cycles.
   (2) Companies that are of giant size and are maturing.
   (3) Companies that are of small size and are growing rapidly.
   Assume all companies pay dividends. [6 minutes]

 10. *CFA Examination I (June 1985)*

Your client is considering the purchase of $100,000 in common stock which pays no dividends and will appreciate in market value by 10 percent per year. At the same time, the client is considering an opportunity to invest $100,000 in a lease obligation that will provide the annual year-end cash flows listed in Table A. Assume that each investment will be sold at the end of 3 years and that you are given no additional information.

Calculate the present value of each of the two investments assuming a 10 percent discount rate, and state which one will provide the higher return over the 3-year period. Use the data in Table A, and show your calculations. [10 minutes]

TABLE A

Annual Cash Flow From Lease

End of Year	
1	$ -0-
2 Lease receipts	15,000
3 Lease receipts	25,000
3 Sale proceeds	$100,000

PRESENT VALUE OF $1

Period	6%	8%	10%	12%
1	.943	.926	.909	.893
2	.890	.857	.826	.797
3	.840	.794	.751	.712
4	.792	.735	.683	.636
5	.747	.681	.621	.567

 11. *CFA Examination I (1990)*

The constant growth dividend discount model can be used both for the valuation of companies and for the estimation of the long-term total return of a stock.

       Assume: $20 = the price of a stock today
                   8% = the expected growth rate of dividends
              $.60 = the annual dividend one year forward

a. Using *only* the above data, compute the expected long-term total return on the stock using the constant growth dividend discount model. Show calculations.
b. Briefly discuss *three* disadvantages of the constant growth dividend discount model in its application to investment analysis.
c. Identify *three* alternative methods to the dividend discount model for the valuation of companies. [10 minutes]

 12. *CFA Examination I (1992)*

Mulroney recalled from her CFA studies that the constant-growth discounted dividend model (DDM) was one way to arrive at a valuation for a company's common stock. She collected current dividend and stock price data for Eastover and Southampton, shown in Table 4.

a. Using 11% as the required rate of return (i.e. discount rate) and a projected growth rate of 8%, compute a constant-growth DDM value for Eastover's stock and compare the computed value for Eastover to its stock price indicated in Table 4. Show calculations. [10 minutes]

Mulroney's supervisor commented that a two-stage DDM may be more appropriate for companies such as Eastover and Southampton. Mulroney believes that Eastover and Southampton could grow more rapidly over the next three years and then settle in at a lower but sustainable rate of growth beyond 1994. Her estimates are indicated in Table 5.

b. Using 11% as the required rate of return, compute the two-stage DDM value of Eastover's stock and compare that value to its stock price indicated in Table 4. Show calculations. [15 minutes]

c. Discuss *two* advantages and *three* disadvantages of using a constant-growth DDM. Briefly discuss how the two-stage DDM improves upon the constant-growth DDM. [10 minutes]

TABLE 4

Current Information

	Current Share Price	Current Dividends Per Share	1992 EPS Estimate	Current Book Value Per Share
Eastover (EO)	$ 28	$ 1.20	$ 1.60	$ 17.32
Southampton (SHC)	48	1.08	3.00	32.21
S&P 500	415	12.00	20.54	159.83

TABLE 5

Projected Growth Rates

	Next 3 Years (1992, 1993, 1994)	Growth Beyond 1994
Eastover (EO)	12%	8%
Southampton (SHC)	13%	7%

13. *CFA Examination I (1992)*

In addition to the discounted dividend model (DDM) approach, Mulroney decided to look at the price/earnings ratio and price/book ratio, relative to the S&P 500, for *both* Eastover and Southampton. Mulroney elected to perform this analysis using 1987–1991 and current data.

a. Using the data in Tables 3 and 4 compute *both* the current and the 5-year (1987–1991) average relative price/earnings ratios and relative price/book ratios for Eastover and Southampton. Discuss *each* company's current relative price/earnings ratio as compared to its 5-year average relative price/earnings ratio and *each* company's current relative price/book ratio as compared to its 5-year average relative price/book ratio. [10 minutes]

b. Briefly discuss *one* disadvantage for *each* of the relative price/earnings and relative price/book approaches to valuation. [5 minutes]

TABLE 3

Eastover Company (EO)

	1986	1987	1988	1989	1990	1991
Earnings per share	$ 1.27	$ 2.12	$ 2.68	$ 1.56	$ 1.87	$ 0.90
Dividends per share	0.87	0.90	1.15	1.20	1.20	1.20
Book value per share	14.82	16.54	18.14	18.55	19.21	17.21
Stock price						
High	28	40	30	33	28	30
Low	20	20	23	25	18	20
Close	25	26	25	28	22	27
Average P/E	18.9x	14.2x	9.9x	18.6x	12.3x	27.8x
Average price/book	1.6x	1.8x	1.5x	1.6x	1.2x	1.5x

Southampton Company (SHC)

	1986	1987	1988	1989	1990	1991
Earnings per share	$ 1.66	$ 3.13	$ 3.55	$ 5.08	$ 2.46	$ 1.75
Dividends per share	0.77	0.79	0.89	0.98	1.04	1.08
Book value per share	24.84	27.47	29.92	30.95	31.54	32.21
Stock price						
High	34	40	38	43	45	46
Low	21	22	26	28	20	26
Close	31	27	28	39	27	44
Average P/E	16.6x	9.9x	9.0x	7.0x	13.2x	20.6x
Average price/book	1.1x	1.1x	1.1x	1.2x	1.0x	1.1x

S&P 500

	1986	1987	1988	1989	1990	1991	5-Year Average (1987–1991)
Average P/E	15.8x	16.0x	11.1x	13.9x	15.6x	19.2x	15.2x
Average price/book	1.8x	2.1x	1.9x	2.2x	2.1x	2.3x	2.1x

TABLE 4

Current Information

	Current Share Price	Current Dividends Per Share	1992 EPS Estimate	Current Book Value Per Share
Eastover (EO)	$ 28	$ 1.20	$ 1.60	$ 17.32
Southampton (SHC)	48	1.08	3.00	32.21
S&P 500	415	12.00	20.54	159.83

14. *CFA Examination I (1993)*

At year-end 1991, the Wall Street consensus was that Philip Morris' earnings and dividends would grow at 20% for five years after which growth would fall to a market-like 7%. Analysts also projected a required rate of return of 10% for the U.S. equity market.

a. Using the data in Table 1 and the multistage dividend discount model, calculate the intrinsic value of Philip Morris stock at year-end 1991. Assume a similar level of risk for Philip Morris stock as for the typical U.S. stock. Show all work. [7 minutes]

b. Using the data in Table 1, calculate Philip Morris' price/earnings ratio and the price/earnings ratio relative to the S&P 500 Stock Index as of December 31, 1991. [3 minutes]

c. Using the data in Table 1, calculate Philip Morris' price/book ratio and the price/book ratio relative to the S&P 500 Stock Index as of December 31, 1991. [3 minutes]

TABLE 1

Philip Morris Corporation
Selected Financial Statement and Other Data
Years Ending December 31
($ millions except per share data)

	1991	1981
Income Statement		
Operating revenue	$56,458	$10,886
Cost of sales	25,612	5,253
Excise taxes on products	8,394	2,580
Gross profit	$22,452	$ 3,053
Selling, general, and administrative expenses	13,830	1,741
Operating income	$ 8,622	$ 1,312
Interest expense	1,651	232
Pretax earnings	$ 6,971	$ 1,080
Provision for income taxes	3,044	420
Net earnings	$ 3,927	$ 660
Earnings per share	$4.24	$0.66
Dividends per share	$1.91	$0.25
Balance Sheet		
Current assets	$12,594	$ 3,733
Property, plant, and equipment, net	9,946	3,583
Goodwill	18,624	634
Other assets	6,220	1,230
Total assets	$47,384	$ 9,180
Current liabilities	$11,824	$ 1,936
Long-term debt	14,213	3,499
Deferred taxes	1,803	455
Other liabilities	7,032	56
Stockholders equity	12,512	3,234
Total liabilities and stockholders equity	$47,384	$ 9,180
Other Data		
Philip Morris:		
Common shares outstanding (millions)	920	1,003
Closing price common stock	$80.250	$6.125
S&P 500 Stock Index:		
Closing price	417.09	122.55
Earnings per share	16.29	15.36
Book value per share	161.08	109.43

15. *CFA Examination I (1993)*

   a. State *one* major advantage and *one* major disadvantage of *each* of the *three* valuation method-ologies you used to value Philip Morris stock in Question 14. [6 minutes]

   b. State whether Philip Morris stock is undervalued or overvalued as of December 31, 1991. Support your conclusion using your answers to previous questions and any data provided. (The past ten-year average S&P 500 Stock Index relative price/earnings and price/book ratios for Philip Morris were 0.80 and 1.61, respectively.) [9 minutes]

16. *CFA Examination II (1995)*

Your supervisor has asked you to evaluate the relative attractiveness of the stocks of two very similar chemical companies: Litchfield Chemical Corp. (LCC) and Aminochem Company

(AOC). AOC also has a June 30 fiscal year end. You have compiled the data in Table 1 for this purpose. Use a one-year time horizon and assume the following:

- Real gross domestic product is expected to rise 5%;
- S&P 500 expected total return of 20%;
- U.S. Treasury bills yield 5%; and
- 30 year U.S. Treasury bonds yield 8%.

a. Calculate the value of the common stock of LCC and AOC using the constant growth dividend discount model. Show your work. [5 minutes]

b. Calculate the expected return over the next year of the common stock of LCC and AOC using the Capital Asset Pricing Model. Show your work. [5 minutes]

c. Calculate the internal (implied, normalized, or sustainable) growth rate of LCC and AOC. Show your work. [5 minutes]

d. Recommend LCC or AOC for investment. Justify you choice by using your answers to A, B and C and the information in Table 1. [10 minutes]

TABLE 1		Litchfield Chemical (LCC)	Aminochem (AOC)
Current stock price		$50	$30
Shares outstanding (millions)		10	20
Projected earnings per share (fiscal 1996)		$4.00	$3.20
Projected dividend per share (fiscal 1996)		$0.90	$1.60
Projected dividend growth rate		8%	7%
Stock beta		1.2	1.4
Investors' required rate of return		10%	11%
Balance sheet data (millions)			
Long-term debt		$100	$130
Stockholders' equity		$300	$320

References

Born, Jeffery, James Moses, and Dennis Officer. "Changes in Dividend Policy and Subsequent Earnings." *Journal of Portfolio Management* 14, no. 4 (Summer 1988).

Cottle, Sidney, Roger F. Murray, and Frank E. Block. *Graham and Dodd's Security Analysis.* 5th ed. New York: McGraw-Hill, 1988.

Hackel, Kenneth S. and Joshua Livnat. *Cash Flow and Security Analysis.* 2d ed. (Burr Ridge, IL: Irwin Professional Publishing, 1996).

Hassel, J. and Robert Jennings. "Relative Forecast Accuracy and the Timing of Earnings Forecast Announcements." *The Accounting Review* 61, no. 1 (January 1986).

Imhoff, Eugene and G. Lobo. "Information Content of Analysts Composite Forecast Revisions." *Journal of Accounting Research* 22, no. 3 (Autumn 1984).

Jaffe, Jeffery, Donald Keim, and Randolph Westerfield. "Earnings Yields, Market Values, Stock Returns." *Journal of Finance* 44, no. 1 (March 1989).

Jennings, Robert. *Reaction of Financial Analysts to Corporate Management Earnings per Share Forecasts.* New York: Financial Analysts Research Foundation, Monograph No. 20, 1984.

Johnson, R. S., Lyle Fiore, and Richard Zuber. "The Investment Performance of Common Stocks in Relation to Their Price-Earnings Ratios: An Update of the Basu Study." *Financial Review* 24, no. 3 (August 1989).

Levine, Sumner N., ed. *The Financial Analysts Handbook.* 2d ed. Homewood, IL: Dow Jones-Irwin, 1988.

Waymire, G. "Additional Evidence on the Information Content of Management Earnings Forecasts." *Journal of Accounting Research* 22, no. 3 (Autumn 1984).

Chapter
21

Technical Analysis[1]

This chapter answers the following questions:

- How does technical analysis differ from fundamental analysis?
- What are the underlying assumptions of technical analysis?
- What is the major assumption that causes a difference between technical analysis and the efficient market hypothesis?
- What are the major challenges to the assumptions of technical analysis and its rules?
- What are the major advantages of technical analysis compared to fundamental analysis?
- What are the major contrary opinion rules used by technicians and what is the logic for them?
- What are some of the significant rules used by technicians who want to follow the smart money and what is the logic of those rules?
- What is the breadth of market measures and what are they intended to indicate to the technician?
- What are the three types of price movements postulated in the Dow Theory and how are they used by a technician?
- Why is the volume of trading considered important by technicians and how do they use it in their analysis?
- What are support and resistance levels, when do they occur, and how are they used by technicians?
- What is the purpose of moving average lines and how does the technician use one or several of them to detect major changes in trends?
- What is the rationale behind the relative strength line for an industry or a stock and how is it interpreted?
- How are bar charts different from point-and-figure charts?
- What are some uses of technical analysis in foreign security markets?
- How is technical analysis used when analyzing bond markets?

> The market reacted yesterday to the report of a large increase in the short interest on the NYSE.
>
> Although the market declined today, it was not considered bearish because there was very light volume.
>
> The market declined today after 3 days of increases due to profit taking by investors.

These and similar statements appear daily in the financial news. All of them have as their rationale one of numerous technical trading rules. Technical analysts develop technical

---

[1]The author received very helpful comments and material for this chapter from Richard T. McCabe, Chief Market Analyst at Merrill Lynch Capital Markets.

trading rules from observations of past price movements of the stock market and individual stocks. This philosophy is in sharp contrast to the efficient market hypothesis that we studied, which contends that past performance has no influence on future performance or market values. It also differs from what we learned about fundamental analysis, which involves making investment decisions based on the examination of fundamental economic and company variables that lead to an estimate of value for an investment, which is then compared to the prevailing market price of the investment. In contrast to the efficient market hypothesis or fundamental analysis, **technical analysis** involves the examination of past market data such as prices and the volume of trading, which leads to an estimate of future price and, therefore, an investment decision. Whereas fundamental analysts use economic data that are usually separate from the market, the technical analyst believes that using data *from the market itself* is a good idea because "the market is its own best predictor." Therefore, technical analysis is an alternative method of making the investment decision and answering the questions: What securities should an investor buy or sell? When should these investments be made?

Technical analysts see no need to study the multitude of economic and company variables to arrive at an estimate of future value because past price movements will signal future price movements. Technicians also believe that a change in the price trend may predict a forthcoming change in the fundamental variables such as earnings and risk earlier than it is perceived or anticipated by most fundamental analysts. Are technicians correct? Many investors using these techniques claim to have experienced superior rates of return on many investments. In addition, many newsletter writers base their recommendations on technical analysis. Finally, even the major investment firms that employ a large number of fundamental analysts also employ technical analysts to provide investment advice. Numerous investment professionals as well as individual investors believe in and use technical trading rules to make their investment decisions. Therefore, you should have an understanding of the basic philosophy and reasoning behind these technical approaches. To help you understand technical analysis, we begin this chapter with an examination of the basic philosophy underlying all technical approaches to market analysis and company analysis. Subsequently, we consider the advantages and potential problems with the technical approach. Finally, we present and discuss a number of the alternative technical trading rules that are applicable to both the U.S. market and foreign securities markets.

UNDERLYING ASSUMPTIONS OF TECHNICAL ANALYSIS

Technical analysts base trading decisions on examinations of prior price and volume data to determine past market trends from which they predict future behavior for the market as a whole and for individual securities. They cite several assumptions that support this view of price movements.

1. The market value of any good or service is determined solely by the interaction of supply and demand.
2. Supply and demand are governed by numerous factors, both rational and irrational. Included in these factors are those economic variables relied on by the fundamental analyst as well as opinions, moods, and guesses. The market weighs all these factors continually and automatically.
3. Disregarding minor fluctuations, *the prices for individual securities and the overall value of the market tend to move in trends, which persist for appreciable lengths of time.*

4. Prevailing trends change in reaction to shifts in supply and demand relationships. These shifts, no matter why they occur, *can be detected sooner or later in the action of the market itself.*[2]

Certain aspects of these assumptions are controversial, leading fundamental analysts and advocates of efficient markets to question their validity. Those aspects are emphasized above.

The first two assumptions are almost universally accepted by technicians and nontechnicians alike. Almost anyone who has had a basic course in economics would agree that, at any point in time, the price of a security (or any good or service) is determined by the interaction of supply and demand. In addition, most observers would acknowledge that supply and demand are governed by many variables. The only difference in opinion might concern the influence of the irrational factors. A technical analyst might expect the irrational influence to persist for some time, whereas other market analysts would expect only a short-run effect with rational beliefs prevailing over the long run. Certainly, everyone would agree that the market continually weighs all these factors.

A stronger difference of opinion arises over the technical analysts' third assumption about the *speed of adjustment* of stock prices to changes in supply and demand. Technical analysts expect stock prices to move in trends that persist for long periods because new information that affects supply and demand does not come to the market at one point in time, but rather enters the market *over a period of time.* This pattern of information access occurs because of different sources of information or because certain investors receive the information or perceive fundamental changes earlier than others. As various groups ranging from insiders to well-informed professionals to the average investor receive the information and buy or sell a security accordingly, its price moves toward the new equilibrium. Therefore, technicians do not expect the price adjustment to be as abrupt as fundamental analysts and efficient market supporters do, but expect *a gradual price adjustment* to reflect the gradual flow of information.

Figure 21.1 shows this process. The figure shows that new information causes a decrease in the equilibrium price for a security, but the price adjustment is not rapid. It occurs as a *trend* that persists until the stock reaches its new equilibrium. Technical analysts look

| FIGURE 21.1 | **TECHNICIANS' VIEW OF PRICE ADJUSTMENT TO NEW INFORMATION** |

---

[2]These assumptions are summarized in Robert A. Levy, "Conceptual Foundations of Technical Analysis," *Financial Analysts Journal* 22, no. 4 (July–August 1966): 83.

for the beginning of a movement from one equilibrium value to a new equilibrium value. Technical analysts do not attempt to predict the new equilibrium value. They look for the start of a change so that they can get on the bandwagon early and benefit from the move to the new equilibrium by buying if the trend is up or selling if the trend is down. A rapid adjustment of prices would keep the ride on the bandwagon very short such that investors could not get onboard and benefit from the ride.

CHALLENGES TO TECHNICAL ANALYSIS

Those who question the value of technical analysis for investment decisions challenge this technique in two areas. First, they challenge some of its basic assumptions. Second, they challenge some of its specific trading rules and their long-run usefulness. In this section, we consider both of these challenges.

CHALLENGES TO TECHNICAL ANALYSIS ASSUMPTIONS

The major challenge to technical analysis is based on the efficient market hypothesis. As discussed in Chapter 7, for technical trading rules to generate superior risk-adjusted returns after taking account of transactions costs, the market would have to be slow to adjust prices to the arrival of new information, that is, it would have to be inefficient. (This is referred to as the weak-form efficient market hypothesis.) The vast majority of studies that have tested the weak-form efficient market hypothesis have found that prices do not move in trends based on statistical tests of autocorrelation and runs. These results support the efficient market hypothesis.

As discussed in Chapter 7, these critics acknowledge that numerous technical trading rules exist that have not been or cannot be tested. Still, most of the trading rules tested support the hypothesis.

CHALLENGES TO TECHNICAL TRADING RULES

An obvious challenge to technical analysis is that the past price patterns or relationships between specific market variables and stock prices may not be repeated. As a result, a technique that previously worked might miss subsequent market turns. This possibility leads most technicians to follow several trading rules and to seek a consensus of all of them to predict the future market pattern.

Other critics contend that many price patterns become self-fulfilling prophecies. For example, assume that many analysts expect a stock selling at $40 a share to go to $50 or more if it should rise above its current pattern and "break through" its channel at $45. As soon as it reaches $45, a number of technicians will buy, causing the price to rise to $50, exactly as predicted. In fact, some technicians may place a limit order to buy the stock at such a breakout point. Under such conditions, the increase will probably be only temporary and the price will return to its true equilibrium.

Another problem with technical analysis is that the success of a trading rule will encourage many investors to adopt it. This popularity and the resulting competition will eventually neutralize the value of the technique. If numerous investors focus on a specific technical trading rule, some of them will attempt to anticipate what will happen prior to the completed price pattern and either ruin the expected historical price pattern or eliminate profits for most users of the trading rule by causing the price to change faster than expected. For example, suppose it becomes known that technicians who invest on the basis of the amount of short selling have been enjoying very high rates of return. Based on this knowledge, other technicians will likely start using these data and thus accelerate the stock price pattern following changes in the amount of short selling. As a result, the trading rule that provided high rates of return previously may no longer be profitable after the first few investors react.

Further, as we will see when we examine specific trading rules, *they all require a great deal of subjective judgment.* Two technical analysts looking at the same price pattern may arrive at widely different interpretations of what has happened and, therefore, will come to different investment decisions. This implies that the use of various techniques is neither completely mechanical nor obvious. Finally, as we will discuss in connection with several trading rules, *the standard values that signal investment decisions can change over time.* Therefore, technical analysts must adjust the specified values that trigger investment decisions over time to conform to the new environment. In other cases, trading rules are abandoned because it appears they no longer work.

ADVANTAGES OF TECHNICAL ANALYSIS

Despite these criticisms, technical analysts see benefits in their approach compared to fundamental analysis. Most technical analysts admit that a fundamental analyst with good information, good analytical ability, and a keen sense of information's impact on the market should achieve above average returns. However, this statement requires qualification. According to technical analysts, the fundamental analysts can experience superior returns *only* if they obtain new information before other investors and process it correctly and quickly. Technical analysts do not believe the vast majority of investors can consistently get new information before other investors and consistently process it correctly and quickly.

Technical analysts claim that a major advantage of their method is that *it is not heavily dependent on financial accounting statements*—the major source of information about the past performance of a firm or industry. As you know from Chapters 19 and 20, the fundamental analyst evaluates such statements to help project future return and risk characteristics for industries and individual securities. The technician points out several major problems with accounting statements:

1. They do not contain a great deal of information needed by security analysts, such as details on sales and general expenses or information related to sales and earnings by product line and customers.
2. Corporations may choose among several procedures for reporting expenses, assets, or liabilities, and these alternative procedures can produce vastly different values for expenses, income, return on assets, and return on equity. As a result, an investor can have trouble comparing the statements of two firms in the same industry, much less firms in different industries.
3. Many psychological factors and other nonquantifiable variables do not appear in financial statements. Examples include employee training and loyalty, customer goodwill, and general investor attitude toward an industry. Investor attitudes could become important when investors become concerned about the risk from restrictions or taxes on products such as tobacco or alcohol or when firms do business in countries that have significant political risk.

Therefore, because technicians are suspicious of financial statements, they consider it advantageous not to depend on them. As we will show, most of the data used by technicians, such as security prices, volume of trading, and other trading information, are derived from the stock market itself.

Also, a fundamental analyst must process new information correctly and *very quickly* to derive a new intrinsic value for the stock or bond before the other investors can. Technicians, on the other hand, need only quickly recognize a movement to a new equilibrium value for whatever reason.

Finally, assume a fundamental analyst determines that a given security is under- or overvalued a long time before other investors. He or she still must determine when to make the purchase or sale. Ideally, the highest return would come from making the transaction just before the change in market value occurs. For example, assume that based on your analysis in February, you expect a firm to report substantially higher earnings in June. Although you could buy the stock in February, you would be better off waiting until about May to buy the stock so your funds would not be tied up for an extra 3 months but you may be reticent to wait that long. Because most technicians do not invest until the move to the new equilibrium is underway, they contend that they are more likely to experience ideal timing compared to the fundamental analyst.

TECHNICAL TRADING RULES AND INDICATORS

To help you understand the specific technical trading rules, Figure 21.2 shows a typical stock price cycle that could be an example for the overall stock market or for an individual stock. The graph shows a peak and trough, along with a rising trend channel, a flat trend channel, a declining trend channel, and indications of when a technical analyst would ideally want to trade.

The graph begins with the end of a declining (bear) market that finishes in a **trough** followed by an upward trend that breaks through the **declining trend channel.** Confirmation that the trend has reversed would be a buy signal. The technical analyst would buy stocks in general or an individual stock that showed this pattern.

The analyst would then look for the development of a **rising trend channel.** As long as the stock price stayed in this rising channel, the technician would hold the stock(s) for the upward ride. Ideally, you want to sell at the **peak** of the cycle, but you cannot identify a peak until after the trend changes.

If the stock (or the market) begins trading in a flat pattern, it will necessarily break out of its rising trend channel. At this point, some technical analysts would sell, but most would hold to see if the stock experiences a period of consolidation and then breaks out of the **flat trend channel** on the upside and begins rising again. Alternatively, if the stock were to

| FIGURE 21.2 | **TYPICAL STOCK MARKET CYCLE** |

break out of the channel on the downside, the technician would take this as a sell signal and would expect a declining trend channel. The next buy signal would come after the trough when the price breaks out of the declining channel and establishes a rising trend. Subsequently, we will consider strategies to detect these changes in trend and the importance of volume in this analysis.

There are numerous technical trading rules and a large number of interpretations for each of them. Almost all technical analysts watch many alternative rules. This section discusses most of the well-known techniques. The presentation on domestic indicators is divided into four sections based on the attitudes of technical analysts. The first group includes trading rules used by analysts who like to trade against the crowd using contrary-opinion signals. The second group of rules attempts to emulate very astute investors, that is, the smart money. The next section includes technical indicators that are very popular but not easily classified. The fourth section covers pure price and volume techniques, including the famous Dow Theory. The final sections describe how these technical trading rules have been applied to foreign securities markets and bond markets.

CONTRARY-OPINION
RULES

Many technical analysts rely on technical trading rules developed from the premise that the majority of investors are wrong as the market approaches peaks and troughs. Therefore, these technicians try to determine when the majority of investors is either very bullish or very bearish and then trade in the opposite direction.[3]

MUTUAL FUND CASH POSITIONS   Mutual funds hold some part of their portfolio in cash for one of several reasons. The most obvious reason is that they need cash to liquidate shares that fundholders sell back to the fund. Another reason is that the money from new investments in the mutual fund may not have been invested. A third reason might be the portfolio manager's bearish outlook for the market, inspiring an asset allocation decision to increase the fund's defensive cash position.

Mutual funds' ratios of cash as a percentage of the total assets in their portfolios (the *cash ratio* or *liquid asset ratio*) are reported in the press, including monthly figures in *Barron's*.[4] This percentage of cash has varied during the last decade from a low point of about 7 percent to a high point near 13 percent, although the range has increased during the last several years.

Contrary-opinion technicians consider the mutual funds to be a good proxy for the institutional investor. They also feel that mutual funds usually are wrong at peaks and troughs. Thus, they expect mutual funds to have a high percentage of cash near the trough of a market cycle, implying that they are bearish exactly at the time that they should be fully invested to take advantage of the impending market rise. At the market peak, technicians expect mutual funds to be almost fully invested with a low percentage of cash. This would indicate a bullish outlook by the mutual funds when they should be selling stocks and realizing gains for some part of their portfolios. Therefore, contrary-opinion technicians would watch for the mutual fund cash position to approach one of the extremes and act contrary to the mutual funds. Specifically, they would tend to buy when the cash ratio approaches 13 percent and to sell when the cash ratio approaches 7 percent.

---

[3] Prior editions of this book include the percentage of odd-lot purchases and sales or odd-lot short sales as a percentage of total odd-lot sales as contrary-opinion rules. They are no longer included because odd-lot volume has become a very small proportion of total trading volume. Thus, odd-lot trading is no longer considered a valid indication of small investor sentiment.

[4] *Barron's* is a prime source for numerous technical indicators. For a readable discussion of relevant data and their use, see Martin E. Zweig, *Understanding Technical Forecasting* (New York: Dow Jones & Co., 1987).

FIGURE 21.3

TIME-SERIES PLOT OF DOW JONES INDUSTRIAL AVERAGE AND MUTUAL FUND CASH-TO-ASSET RATIO (CASH/TOTAL ASSETS)

Source: *Where the Indicators Stand* (New York: Merrill Lynch, March 1996). Reprinted by permission of Merrill Lynch. All Rights Reserved.

Figure 21.3 contains a time-series plot of the Dow Jones Industrial Average (DJIA) and the mutual fund cash ratio. It shows apparent bullish signals in 1970, in late 1974, in 1982, and in late 1990 near market troughs. Bearish signals appeared in 1971, 1972 to 1973, and 1976 prior to market peaks. During 1995 the cash ratio fluctuated midway between the extremes while the market rose substantially.

A high mutual fund cash position also can be considered as a bullish indicator because of potential buying power. Whether the cash balances have built up because of stock sales completed as part of a selling program or because investors have been buying mutual funds (as in 1996), technicians believe these cash funds will eventually be invested and will cause stock prices to increase. Alternatively, a low cash ratio would mean that the institutions have bought heavily and are left with little potential buying power.

A couple of studies have examined this mutual fund cash ratio and its components as a predictor of market cycles. They concluded that the mutual fund liquid asset ratio was not as strong a predictor of market cycles as suggested by technical analysts.[5]

[5] Paul H. Mauney, "The Mutual Fund Liquidity Ratio: A Trap for the Unwary," *Journal of Portfolio Management* 5, no. 2 (Winter 1979): 18–21; and R. David Ranson and William G. Shipman, "Institutional Buying Power and the Stock Market," *Financial Analysts Journal* 37, no. 5 (September–October 1981): 62–68.

CREDIT BALANCES IN BROKERAGE ACCOUNTS   Credit balances result when investors sell stocks and leave the proceeds with their brokers, expecting to reinvest them shortly. The amounts are reported by the SEC and the NYSE in *Barron's*. Technical analysts view these credit balances as pools of potential purchasing power so they interpret a decline in these balances as bearish because it indicates lower purchasing power as the market approaches a peak. Alternatively, technicians view a buildup of credit balances as an increase in buying power and a bullish signal.

Note that the data used to interpret the market environment are stated in terms of an increase or decline in the credit balance series rather than comparing these balances to some other series. This assumption of an absolute trend could make interpretation difficult as market levels change.

INVESTMENT ADVISORY OPINIONS   Many technicians feel that if a large proportion of investment advisory services have a bearish attitude, it signals the approach of a market trough and the onset of a bull market. It is reasoned that most services tend to be trend followers, so the number of bears usually is greatest when market bottoms are approaching. They develop this trading rule from the ratio of the number of advisory services that are bearish as a percentage of the number of services expressing an opinion.[6] A "bearish sentiment index" of 60 percent indicates a pervasive bearish attitude by advisory services, and contrarians would consider this a bullish indicator. In contrast, a decline of this bearish sentiment index to below 20 percent indicates a pervasive bullish attitude by advisory services, which technicians would interpret as a bearish sign. Figure 21.4 shows a time-series plot of the DJIA and both the bearish sentiment index and the bullish sentiment index. As of early 1996, both indexes are trending toward the bearish boundary values.

OTC VERSUS NYSE VOLUME   Prior to the 1970s, the accepted measure of speculative trading activity was the ratio of AMEX volume to NYSE volume. This ratio is no longer considered useful because the ratio of AMEX to NYSE volume has gone from about 50 percent in the 1950s and 1960s to about 10 percent or less currently. Instead, technicians currently use the ratio of OTC volume on the NASDAQ system to NYSE volume as a measure of speculative trading. They consider speculative activity high when this ratio gets to 112 percent or more. Speculative trading typically peaks at market peaks. Technicians consider the market to be oversold, that is, investors are too bearish, when this relative volume ratio drops below 87 percent. Figure 21.5 contains a time-series plot of the NASDAQ Composite Average and the OTC/NYSE volume ratio.

Notably, the current decision ratios of 112 percent for peak and 87 percent for an oversold (trough) position have changed over the past seven years—they were 80 and 60 percent in 1990, 90 and 70 percent in 1992, and 100 and 80 percent in 1994. There are two reasons for this upward drift in the boundary values. First, individual investors have started accounting for a higher proportion of trading, and individual investors are more likely to trade the small firms on the OTC market that lack the size and liquidity required by institutions. Also, there is a tendency for an increase in relative NASDAQ volume because more firms are being added to the OTC market than to the NYSE. Although the number of firms listed on the NYSE has increased by about 25 percent over the past 15 years, the number on NASDAQ has increased by over 50 percent (that is, the firms listed on NASDAQ have gone from about 3,000 in 1981 to 4,800 in 1995). As of early 1996 the ratio of OTC to NYSE volume clearly exceeded the 112 percent peak ratio. This either indicates a market peak or the need to consider another change in the decision ratios.

---

[6] This ratio is compiled by Investors Intelligence, Larchmont, NY 10538.

FIGURE 21.4   TIME-SERIES PLOT OF DOW JONES INDUSTRIAL AVERAGE AND BULLISH AND BEARISH SENTIMENT INDEXES

Sources: "Where the Indicators Stand" (New York: Merrill Lynch, March 1996). Data: *Investors' Intelligence,* Larchmont, NY 10538.

THE CHICAGO BOARD OPTIONS EXCHANGE (CBOE) PUT/CALL RATIO   The CBOE put/call ratio is a relatively new tool of contrary-opinion technicians. They use put options, which give the holder the right to sell stock at a specified price for a given time period, as signals of a bearish attitude. The technicians reason that a higher put/call ratio indicates a more pervasive bearish attitude, which they consider a bullish indicator.

As shown in Figure 21.6, this ratio historically was in the range of .35 to .80 but is currently in the range of .70 to 1.00. It typically has been substantially less than 1 because investors tend to be bullish and avoid selling short or buying puts. The current decision rule states that a put/call ratio of .90, which means that 90 puts are traded for every 100 calls, is considered bullish, while a relatively low put/call ratio of .70 or less is considered a bearish sign. The value of the ratio in early 1996 was within the .90 to .70 band, with a movement toward the lower (bearish) boundary.

FUTURES TRADERS BULLISH ON STOCK INDEX FUTURES   Another relatively new measure used by contrary-opinion technicians is the percentage of speculators in stock index futures who are bullish. Specifically, an advisory service (*Market Vane*) surveys other firms that provide advisory services for the futures market along with individual

FIGURE 21.5   **TIME-SERIES PLOT OF NASDAQ COMPOSITE AVERAGE AND THE RATIO OF OTC VOLUME TO NYSE VOLUME (3-WEEK AVERAGE)**

traders involved in the futures market to determine whether these futures traders are bearish or bullish regarding stocks. A plot of the series in Figure 21.7 indicates that these technicians would consider it a bearish sign when over 70 percent of the speculators are bullish. In contrast, if the portion of bullish speculators declines to 30 percent or lower, it is a bullish sign. Again, as of early 1996 the series was within the specified boundaries, with a tendency toward the upper (bearish) limit.

As you can see, technicians who seek to be contrary to the market have several series that provide measures of how the majority of investors are investing. They then take the opposite action. They generally would follow several of these series to provide a consensus regarding investors' attitudes.

FOLLOW THE SMART MONEY   Some technical analysts use an alternative set of indicators that they expect to indicate the behavior of smart, sophisticated investors. After studying the market, these technicians have created indicators that tell what smart investors are doing and create rules to follow them. In this section, we discuss some of the more popular indicators of what smart investors are doing.

FIGURE 21.6 **TIME-SERIES PLOT OF DOW JONES INDUSTRIAL AVERAGE AND CBOE PUT/CALL RATIO (25-DAY AVERAGE)**

THE CONFIDENCE INDEX   Published by *Barron's*, the Confidence Index is the ratio of *Barron's* average yield on 10 top-grade corporate bonds to the yield on the Dow Jones average of 40 bonds. This index measures the difference in yield spread between high-grade bonds and a large cross section of bonds.[7] Because the yields on high-grade bonds always should be lower than those on a large cross section of bonds, this ratio should never exceed 100. It approaches 100 as the spread between the two sets of bonds gets smaller.

Technicians believe the ratio is a bullish indicator because, during periods of high confidence, investors are willing to invest more in lower-quality bonds for the added yield. This should cause a decrease in the average yield for the large cross section of bonds relative to the yield on high-grade bonds. Therefore, this ratio of yields, which is the Confidence Index, will increase. In contrast, when investors are pessimistic, they will avoid investing in low-quality bonds and increase their investments in high-grade bonds.

[7] Historical data for this series are contained in *The Dow Jones Investor's Handbook* (Princeton, NJ: Dow Jones Books, annual). Current figures appear in *Barron's*.

FIGURE 21.7 **TIME-SERIES PLOT OF DOW JONES INDUSTRIAL AVERAGE AND PERCENTAGE OF FUTURES TRADERS BULLISH ON STOCK INDEX FUTURES**

Source: *Market Vane* and *Where the Indicators Stand* (New York: Merrill Lynch, March 1996). Reprinted by permission of Merrill Lynch. All Rights Reserved.

This shift in investment preference will increase the yield spread between high-grade and average bonds, which causes the Confidence Index to decline.

Unfortunately, this interpretation of bond investor behavior is almost solely demand-oriented. Specifically, it assumes that changes in the yield spread are caused almost exclusively by changes in investor demand for different quality bonds. In fact, the yield differences have frequently changed because the supply of bonds in one of the groups increased. For example, a large issue of high-grade AT&T bonds could cause a temporary increase in yields on all high-grade bonds, which would reduce the yield spread and cause an increase in the Confidence Index without any change in investors' attitudes. Such a change in the supply of bonds can cause the series to generate a false signal of a change in confidence.

Advocates of the index believe that it reflects investor attitudes toward financial assets. Several studies have found that this index has not been very useful for predicting stock price movements.

T-BILL–EURODOLLAR YIELD SPREAD   An alternative measure of investor attitude or confidence on a global basis is the spread between T-bill yields and Eurodollar rates. It is reasoned that, at times of international crisis, this spread widens as money flows to safe-haven U.S. T-bills, which causes a decline in this ratio. The stock market has tended to reach a trough shortly thereafter.

SHORT SALES BY SPECIALISTS   Data for total short sales on the NYSE, along with those for the specialist on the exchange, appear weekly in *Barron's*. It should be no surprise after our discussion in Chapter 4 that technicians who want to follow smart money watch the specialist. Specialists regularly engage in short selling as a part of their market-making function, but they can exercise discretion in this area when they feel strongly about expected market changes.

The normal ratio of specialists' short sales to total short sales has been approximately 40 percent.[8] Technicians view a decline in this ratio below 30 percent as a bullish sign because it means that specialists are attempting to minimize their participation in short sales while a ratio above 50 percent is a bearish sign.

Note two points about this ratio. First, do not expect it to be a long-run indicator; the nature of the specialists' portfolio probably will limit it to short-run movements. Second, there is a two-week lag in reporting these data.

Although a graph of the specialist short sales ratio indicated some support for the ratio as a buying signal, when used as a trading rule it provided insignificant excess returns.[9]

DEBIT BALANCES IN BROKERAGE ACCOUNTS (MARGIN DEBT)   Debit balances in brokerage accounts represent borrowing (margin debt) by knowledgeable investors from their brokers. These balances indicate the attitude of a sophisticated group of investors who engage in margin transactions. Therefore, an increase in debit balances by this astute group would be a bullish sign. In contrast, a decline in debit balances would indicate selling as these sophisticated investors liquidate their positions and could indicate less capital available for investing. In either case, this would be a bearish indicator.

Monthly data on margin debt is reported in *Barron's*. Unfortunately, this series does not include borrowing by investors from other sources such as banks. Also, it is an absolute value that may be difficult to interpret over time.

OTHER MARKET ENVIRONMENT INDICATORS

In this section, we discuss several indicators that show overall market sentiment and that are used to make investment decisions related to the aggregate market.

BREADTH OF MARKET   Breadth of market measures the number of issues that have increased each day and the number of issues that have declined. It helps explain the cause of a change of direction in a composite market series such as the DJIA or the S&P 400 Index. As discussed in Chapter 5, the major stock-market series are heavily influenced by the stocks of large firms because most indexes are value-weighted. As a result, it is possible that a stock-market series will go up, but the majority of the individual issues will not increase. This divergence between the value for the aggregate index and its components is a problem because it means that most stocks are not participating in the rising market. Such a situation can be detected by examining the advance–decline figures for all stocks on the exchange, along with the overall market index.

A useful way to specify the advance–decline series for analysis is to create a cumulative series of net advances or net declines. Each day major newspapers publish figures on

[8] Notably, during the early 1970s the norm for this short sale ratio was about 55 percent, and it became about 45 percent pre-1981. Therefore, this is an example of another technique for which the decision ratio has changed over time.

[9] Frank K. Reilly and David Whitford, "A Test of the Specialists' Short Sale Ratio," *Journal of Portfolio Management* 8, no. 2 (Winter 1982): 12–18.

TABLE 21.1

DAILY ADVANCES AND DECLINES ON THE NEW YORK STOCK EXCHANGE

Day	1	2	3	4	5
Issues traded	2,608	2,641	2,659	2,651	2,612
Advances	1,710	1,650	1,108	1,661	1,725
Declines	609	650	1,149	633	594
Unchanged	289	341	402	357	293
Net advances (advances minus declines)	+1,101	+1,000	−41	+1,028	+1,131
Cumulative net advances	+1,101	+2,101	+2,060	+3,088	+4,219
Changes in DJIA	+20.47	+13.99	−8.18	+9.16	+15.56

Sources: New York Stock Exchange and *Barron's.*

the number of issues on the NYSE that advanced, declined, or were unchanged. The figures for a 5-day sample, as would be reported in *Barron's*, are shown in Table 21.1. These figures, along with changes in the DJIA at the bottom of the table, indicate a strong market advance to a technician because the DJIA was increasing and the net advance figure was strong, indicating that the market increase was broadly based and extended to most individual stocks. Even the results on Day 3, when the market declined 8 points, were somewhat encouraging. Although the market was down, it was a very small net decline and the individual stocks were split just about 50–50, which points toward a fairly even environment.

An alternative specification of the advance–decline series, a **diffusion index,** shows the daily total of stocks advancing plus one-half the number unchanged, divided by the total number of issues traded. To smooth the series, Merrill Lynch computes a 5-week moving average of these daily figures as shown in Figure 21.8.

Crossings from below to above 50 indicate the market's intermediate-term trend if the moving average series has turned from down to up. This advance–decline series also is used to measure intermediate trends and to signal overbought levels if it reaches very high levels of 56 to 60 or the market is considered oversold when it gets down to 40–44.

The usefulness of the advance–decline series is supposedly greatest at market peaks and troughs when the composite value-weighted market series might be moving either up or down, but the majority of individual stocks might be moving in the opposite direction. As an example, near a peak, the DJIA would be increasing, but the net advance–decline ratio would become negative, the cumulative advance–decline series would level off and decline and the diffusion index would go below 50 percent. The *divergence* between the trend for the market index and the various advance–decline series would signal a market peak.

In contrast, as the market approached a trough, the composite market index would be declining, but the daily advance–decline ratio would become positive, the cumulative advance–decline index would turn up and the diffusion index would rise above 50 percent before the aggregate market index increased.[10] In summary, a technician would look for the advance–decline series to indicate a change in trend before the composite stock-market series.[11]

---

[10] Ideally the performance of the series should work at both peaks and troughs. In fact, it appears to work best at peaks. Apparently at troughs, the secondary stocks, which make up most of the issues, may remain weak until the low point and keep the advance–decline figures negative.

[11] This series also has been used to evaluate non-U.S. indexes. See Linda Sandler, "Advance–Decline Line, a Popular Indicator, Warns of Correction in Tokyo Stock Market," *The Wall Street Journal,* August 26, 1988, C1.

FIGURE 21.8   **TIME-SERIES PLOT OF DOW JONES INDUSTRIAL AVERAGE AND 5-WEEK MOVING AVERAGE OF ADVANCE–DECLINE DIFFUSION INDEX**

Source: *Where the Indicators Stand* (New York: Merrill Lynch, March 1996). Reprinted by permission of Merrill Lynch. All Rights Reserved.

SHORT INTEREST   The short interest is the cumulative number of shares that have been sold short by investors and not covered. This means the investor has not purchased the shares sold short and returned them to the investor from whom they were borrowed. Technicians compute a short-interest ratio as the outstanding short interest divided by the average daily volume of trading on the exchange. For example, if the outstanding short interest on the NYSE was 1,500 million shares and the average daily volume of trading on the exchange was 350 million shares, the short-interest ratio would be 4.29 (1,500/350). This means the outstanding short interest equals about 4 days' trading volume.

Technicians probably interpret this ratio contrary to your initial intuition. Because short sales reflect investors' expectations that stock prices will decline, one would typically expect an increase in the short-interest ratio to be bearish. On the contrary, technicians consider a high short-interest ratio bullish because it indicates *potential demand* for the stock by those who previously sold short and have not covered the sale.

This is another example of a change in the decision value over time. Before 1994, the range was between 2.0 and 3.0. Based on recent experience, a technician would be bullish when the short-interest ratio approached 4.0 and bearish if it declined toward 3.0. The short-interest position is calculated by the stock exchanges and the NASD as of the 20th of each month and is reported about 2 days later in *The Wall Street Journal.*

FIGURE 21.9

PERCENTAGE OF NYSE COMMON STOCK ABOVE THEIR 200-DAY MOVING AVERAGE

Source: *Where the Indicators Stand* (New York: Merrill Lynch, March 1996). Reprinted by permission of Merrill Lynch. All Rights Reserved.

A number of studies have examined the short-interest series as a predictor of stock price movements with mixed results. For every study that supports the technique, another indicates that it should be rejected.[12] Technical analysts have pointed out that this ratio—and any ratio that involves short selling—has been affected by the new techniques for short selling such as options and futures.

STOCKS ABOVE THEIR 200-DAY MOVING AVERAGE   Technicians often compute moving averages of a series to determine its general trend. To examine individual stocks, the 200-day **moving average** of prices has been fairly popular. From these moving-average series for numerous stocks, Media General Financial Services calculates how many stocks currently are trading above their moving-average series, and this is used as an indicator of general investor sentiment. As shown in Figure 21.9, the market is considered to be *overbought* when more than 80 percent of the stocks are trading above their 200-day moving average. Technical analysts feel that an overbought market signals a consolidation or a negative correction. In contrast, if less than 20 percent of the stocks are selling above their 200-day moving average, the market is considered to be *oversold*, which means investors should expect a positive correction. As shown in Figure 21.9, as of early 1996, the percent of stocks selling above their 200-day moving average is very close to 80 percent which is a bearish signal.

BLOCK UPTICK–DOWNTICK RATIO   As we discussed in Chapter 4, about 50 percent of NYSE volume comes from block trading by institutions. The exchange can determine whether the price change that accompanied a particular block trade was higher or lower than the price of the prior transactions. If the block trade price is above the prior transaction price, it is referred to as an **uptick**; if the block trade price is below the prior transaction price, it is referred to as a **downtick.**

---

[12] See Joseph Vu and Paul Caster, "Why All the Interest in Short Interest?" *Financial Analysts Journal* 43, no. 4 (July–August 1987): 77–79.

FIGURE 21.10 **TIME-SERIES PLOT OF DOW JONES INDUSTRIAL AVERAGE AND NYSE BLOCK UPTICK–DOWNTICK RATIO (3-WEEK AVERAGE)**

Source: *Where the Indicators Stand* (New York: Merrill Lynch, March 1996). Reprinted by permission of Merrill Lynch. All Rights Reserved.

It is assumed that if the block trade was initiated by a buyer, you would expect an uptick; if it was initiated by a seller, you would expect a downtick. This led to the development of the **uptick (buyers)–downtick (sellers) ratio,** which indicates institutional investor sentiment. As shown in Figure 21.10, this ratio generally has fluctuated in the range of .70, which indicates heavy selling and a bearish sentiment, to about 1.20, which indicates more buying and a bullish sentiment.

STOCK PRICE AND VOLUME TECHNIQUES

In the introduction to this chapter, we examined a hypothetical stock price chart that demonstrated the market cycle and its peaks and troughs. Also, we considered rising and declining trend channels and breakouts from channels that signal new price trends or reversals of the price trends. Although these price patterns are important, most technical trading rules for the overall market and individual stocks consider *both* stock price movements and corresponding volume movements. Because technicians believe that prices move in trends that persist, they seek to predict future price trends from an astute analysis of past price trends along with changes in the volume of trading.

THE DOW THEORY Any discussion of technical analysis using price and volume data should begin with a consideration of the Dow Theory because it was among the earliest work on this topic and remains the basis for many technical indicators. In this section, we show how Charles Dow combined price and volume information to analyze both individual stocks and the overall stock market.

Charles Dow published *The Wall Street Journal* during the late 1800s.[13] Dow described stock prices as moving in trends analogous to the movement of water. He postulated three types of price movements over time: (1) major trends that are like tides in the ocean, (2) intermediate trends that resemble waves, and (3) short-run movements that are like ripples. Followers of the Dow Theory hope to detect the direction of the major price trend (tide), recognizing that intermediate movements (waves) may occasionally move in the opposite direction. They recognize that a major market advance does not go straight up, but rather shows deviations including small price declines as some investors decide to take profits.

Figure 21.11 shows the typical bullish pattern. The technician would look for every recovery to reach a new peak above the prior peak, and this price rise should be accompanied by heavy trading volume. Alternatively, each profit-taking reversal that follows an increase to a new peak should have a trough above the prior trough, with a relatively light volume of trading during the reversals, indicating that only a limited number of investors are interested in profit taking at these levels. When this pattern of price and volume movements changes, the major trend may be entering a period of consolidation or a major reversal. When using the Dow Theory to analyze the overall stock market, technicians also look for confirmation of peaks and troughs in the industrial stock price series by subsequent peaks and troughs in the transportation series. Such an "echo" indicates that the change in direction is occurring across the total market.

FIGURE 21.11   **SAMPLE BULLISH PRICE PATTERN**

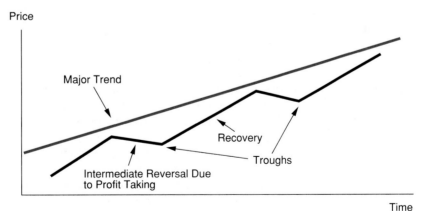

---

[13] A study that discusses the theory and provides support for it is David A. Glickstein and Rolf E. Wubbels, "Dow Theory Is Alive and Well," *Journal of Portfolio Management* 9, no. 3 (Spring 1983): 28–32. The Dow Jones Industrial Average celebrated its 100th anniversary in 1996. *The Wall Street Journal* published a special supplement on May 28, 1996 to commemorate the event.

IMPORTANCE OF VOLUME   As noted in the description of the Dow Theory, technicians watch volume changes along with price movements as an indicator of changes in supply and demand for individual stocks or stocks in general. A price movement in one direction means that the *net* effect on price is in that direction, but the price change alone does not tell us how widespread the excess demand or supply is at that time. Therefore, the technician looks for a price increase on heavy volume relative to the stock's normal trading volume as an indication of bullish activity while a price decline with heavy volume is very bearish. A generally bullish pattern would be when price increases are accompanied by heavy volume and small price reversals occur with light trading volume, indicating limited interest in selling and taking profits.

Technicians also use a ratio of upside–downside volume as an indicator of short-term momentum for the aggregate stock market. Each day the stock exchanges announce the volume of trading that occurred in stocks that experienced an increase divided by the volume of trading in stocks that declined. These data are reported daily in *The Wall Street Journal* and weekly in *Barron's*. Technicians consider this ratio to be an indicator of investor sentiment and use it to pinpoint excesses. Specifically, the ratio typically ranges between a value of 0.50 and 2.00. Technicians feel that a value of 1.50 or more indicates an overbought position and would be a bearish signal. Alternatively, a value of 0.70 and lower would reflect an oversold position and would be considered bullish.

SUPPORT AND RESISTANCE LEVELS   A **support level** is the price range at which the technician would expect a substantial increase in the demand for a stock. Generally, a support level will develop after a stock has enjoyed a meaningful price increase and the stock has begun to experience profit taking. Technicians reason that, at some price, other investors will buy who did not buy during the first price increase and have been waiting for a small reversal to get into the stock. When the price reaches this support price, demand surges and price and volume begin to increase again.

A **resistance level** is the price range at which the technician would expect an increase in the supply of stock and any price increase to reverse abruptly. A resistance level tends to develop after a stock has experienced a steady decline from a higher price level. It is reasoned that the decline in price leads some investors who acquired the stock at a higher price to look for an opportunity to sell it near their breakeven points. Therefore, the supply of stock owned by these investors is *overhanging* the market. When the price rebounds to the target price set by these investors, this overhanging supply of stock comes to the market and dramatically reverses the price increase on heavy volume. It is also possible to envision a resistance level for a stock in a rising trend wherein the resistance level is a price where a large number of holders feel it is appropriate to take a profit.

MOVING-AVERAGE LINES   Earlier, we discussed how technicians use a moving average of past stock prices as an indicator of the long-run trend and how they examine current prices relative to this trend for signals of a change. We also noted that a 200-day moving average is a relatively popular measure for individual stocks and the aggregate market. In this discussion, we want to add another 50-day moving-average price line and consider volume.

Figure 21.12 is a weekly, high-low-close price and volume chart for Cisco Systems, Inc., from the Bridge System for a two-year period ending in April 1996. It also contains a 50-day and 200-day moving-average (MA) line along with a line below reflecting relative strength compared to the S&P 500 index. As noted, MA lines are meant to reflect the overall trend for the price series, with the shorter MA series (50-day versus 200-day) reflecting shorter trends. Two comparisons involving the MA series are considered important. The first comparison is the specific prices to the shorter run MA series, which in this case is the 50-day MA series. If the overall price trend of a stock or the market has been down, the moving-average price line generally would lie above current prices. If prices reverse and break through the moving-average line *from below* accompanied by heavy trading volume, most technicians would consider this a very *positive* change and speculate that this breakthrough signals a reversal of the declining trend. In contrast, if the price of a stock had been rising, the moving-average line would also be rising, but it would be below current prices. If current prices broke through the moving-average line from above accompanied by heavy trading volume, this would be considered a bearish pattern that would signal a reversal of the long-run rising trend.

FIGURE 21.12

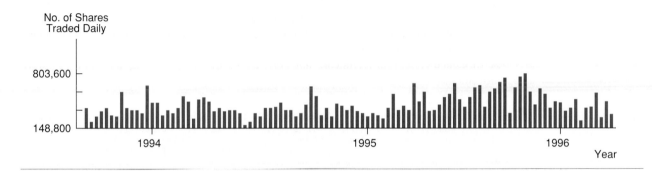

The second comparison is between the 50- and 200-day MA lines. Specifically, when these two lines cross, it signals a change in the overall trend. Specifically, if the 50-day MA line crosses the 200-day MA line from below on good volume, this would be a bullish indicator (buy signal) because it signals a reversal in trend from negative to positive. In contrast, when the 50-day line crosses the 200-day line from above, it signals a change to a negative trend and would be a sell signal.

Overall, for a *bullish* trend the 50-day MA line should be above the 200-day MA line as it is for Cisco Systems. Notably, if this positive gap gets too large (which happens with a fast run up in price similar to what happened in mid-1995), a technician might consider this an indication that the stock is temporarily overbought. A *bearish* trend is when the 50-day MA is always below the 200-day MA line. If the gap was very large on the downside, it might be considered a signal of an oversold stock.

RELATIVE STRENGTH   Technicians believe that once a trend begins, it will continue until some major event causes a change in direction. They believe this is also true of *relative* performance. If an individual stock or an industry group is outperforming the market, technicians believe it will continue to do so.

Therefore, technicians compute weekly or monthly **relative-strength (RS) ratios** for individual stocks and industry groups as the ratio of the price of a stock or an industry index relative to the value for some stock-market series such as the S&P 400. If this ratio increases over time, it shows that the stock or industry is outperforming the market, and a technician would expect this superior performance to continue. Relative-strength ratios work during declining as well as rising markets. In a declining market, if a stock's price does not decline as much as the market does, the stock's relative-strength ratio will continue to rise. Technicians believe that if this ratio is stable or increases during a bear market, the stock should do very well during the subsequent bull market.[14] The bottom line in Figure 21.12 shows that the RS line for Cisco Systems has been almost always increasing for the past year, which confirms the bullish MA line analysis.

Merrill Lynch publishes relative-strength charts for stocks and industry groups. Figure 21.13 describes how to read the charts.

BAR CHARTING   Technicians use charts that show daily, weekly, or monthly time series of stock prices. For a given interval, the technical analyst plots the high and low prices and connects the two points vertically to form a bar. Typically, he or she will also draw a small horizontal line across this vertical bar to indicate the closing price. Finally, almost all bar charts include the volume of trading at the bottom of the chart so that the technical analyst can relate the price and volume movements. A typical bar chart in Figure 21.14 shows data for the DJIA from *The Wall Street Journal* along with volume figures for the NYSE.

MULTIPLE INDICATOR CHARTS   Figure 21.12 is a fairly typical technical chart that contains several indicators that can be used together like the 50- and 200-day MA lines, but also contains the RS line, which can provide added support to the analysis. Technicians include as many price and volume series as are reasonable on one chart and, based on the performance of several technical indicators, try to arrive at a consensus about the future movement for the stock.

---

[14] A study that supports the technique is James Dohan, "Relative Strength: Further Positive Evidence," *Journal of Portfolio Management* 7, no. 1 (Fall 1981): 39–46. A study that rejects the technique is Robert D. Arnott, "Relative Strength Revisited," *Journal of Portfolio Management* 6, no. 3 (Spring 1979): 19–23. Finally, a study that combines it with modern portfolio theory is John S. Brush and Keith Boles, "The Predictive Power in Relative Strength and CAPM," *Journal of Portfolio Management* 9, no. 4 (Summer 1983) 20–23.

FIGURE 21.13

HOW TO READ INDUSTRY GROUP CHARTS

Industry Index

Relative Strength Ratio

Time

The industry group charts in this report display the following elements:
1. A line chart of the weekly close of the Standard & Poor's Industry Group Index for the last 9½ years, with the index range indicated to the left.
2. A line of the 75-week moving average of the Standard & Poor's Industry Group Index.
3. A relative-strength line of the Standard & Poor's Industry Group Index compared with the New York Stock Exchange Composite Index.
4. A 75-week moving average of relative strength.
5. A volatility reading that measures the maximum amount by which the index has outperformed (or underperformed) the NYSE Composite Index during the time period displayed.

Source: *Technical Analysis of Industry Groups* (New York: Merrill Lynch, monthly). Reprinted by permission of Merrill Lynch. All Rights Reserved.

POINT-AND-FIGURE CHARTS   Another graph that is popular with technicians is the point-and-figure chart.[15] Unlike the bar chart, which typically includes all ending prices and volumes to show a trend, the point-and-figure chart includes only significant price changes, regardless of their timing. The technician determines what price interval to record as significant (one point, two points, and so on) and when to note price reversals.

To demonstrate how a technical analyst would use such a chart, assume you want to chart a volatile stock that is currently selling for $40 a share. Because of its volatility, you believe that anything less than a two-point price change is not significant. Also, you consider anything less than a four-point reversal, meaning a movement in the opposite direction, quite minor. Therefore, you would set up a chart similar to the one in Figure 21.15, which starts at 40 and progresses in two-point increments. If the stock moves to 42, you would place an X in the box above 40 and do nothing else until the stock rose to 44 or

<hr />

[15] Daniel Seligman, "The Mystique of Point-and-Figure," *Fortune* (March 1962): 113–115.

FIGURE 21.14   **A TYPICAL BAR CHART**

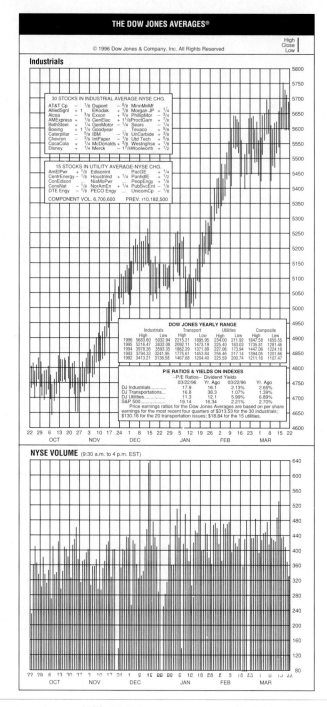

Source: "The Dow Jones Averages," *The Wall Street Journal*, March 25, 1996.

FIGURE 21.15

SAMPLE POINT-AND-FIGURE CHART

50									
48									
46			X						
44			X						
42	X	X	X						
40	X	X	X						
38		X	X						
36		X	X						
34		X	X						
32									
30									

dropped to 38 (a four-point reversal from its high of 42). If it dropped to 38, you would move a column to the right, which indicates a reversal in direction, and begin again at 38 (fill in boxes at 42 and 40). If the stock price dropped to 34, you would enter an X at 36 and another at 34. If the stock then rose to 38 (another four-point reversal), you would move to the next column and begin at 38, going up (fill in 34 and 36). If the stock then went to 46, you would fill in more Xs as shown and wait for further increases or a reversal.

Depending on how fast the prices rise and fall, this process might take anywhere from 2 to 6 months. Given these figures, the technical analyst would attempt to determine trends just as with the bar chart.

As always, you look for breakouts to either higher or lower price levels. A long horizontal movement with many reversals but no major trends up or down would be considered *a period of consolidation.* The technician would speculate that the stock is moving from buyers to sellers and back again with no strong support from either group that would indicate a consensus about its direction. Once the stock breaks out and moves up or down after a period of consolidation, analysts anticipate a major move because previous trading set the stage for it.

Point-and-figure charts differ from bar charts by providing a compact record of movements because they only consider significant price changes for the stock being analyzed. Therefore, some technicians prefer point-and-figure charts because they are easier to work with and give more vivid pictures of price movements.

This section discussed widely used technical indicators. As noted on several occasions, technical analysts generally do not concentrate on only a few indicators or even general categories, but seek to derive an overall feel for the market or a stock based on a *consensus of numerous technical indicators.*

TECHNICAL ANALYSIS OF FOREIGN MARKETS

Our discussion thus far has concentrated on U.S. markets, but as numerous analysts and firms have discovered, these techniques apply to foreign markets as well. Merrill Lynch, for instance, prepares separate technical analysis publications for individual countries such as Japan, Germany, and the United Kingdom as well as a summary of all world markets. The examples that follow show that when analyzing non-U.S. markets, many techniques are limited to price and volume data rather than using the more detailed market information described for the U.S. market. This emphasis on price and volume data is necessary because the more detailed information that is available on the U.S. market through the

SEC, the stock exchanges, the NASDAQ system, and various investment services is not always available in other countries.

FOREIGN STOCK MARKET SERIES   Figure 21.16 contains the daily time-series plot and near-term momentum series for the Mexican IPC Index. This chart shows the generally rising trend by the Mexican stock market during the period July 1995–March 1996.

In the written analysis, the market analyst at Merrill Lynch estimated support and resistance levels for the Mexican Stock Exchange series and commented on the medium-term outlook for the Mexican stock market.

Merrill Lynch publishes similar charts and discussions for 10 other countries and a summary release that compares the countries and ranks them by stock and currency performance. The next section discusses the technical analysis of currency markets.

| FIGURE 21.16 | MERRILL LYNCH GRAPH AND SUMMARY COMMENTS ON THE MEXICAN STOCK MARKET |

Mexico (The IPC Index: 2,844.10)

Support:	2,700; 2,600; 2,500
Resistance:	2,900; 3,102
52-Week Range:	3,102–1,590
Near Term:	Oversold
Medium Term:	Still negative

Source: Merrill Lynch, "The Global Technician," March 18, 1996.

TECHNICAL ANALYSIS OF FOREIGN EXCHANGE RATES   On numerous occasions, we have discussed the importance of changes in foreign exchange rates and their impact on the rates of return on foreign securities. Because of the importance of these relationships, technicians who trade bonds and stocks in world markets examine the time-series data of various individual currencies such as the British pound. They also analyze the spread between currencies such as the difference between the Japanese yen (¥) and the German deutschemark (DM). Finally, an analysis of the composite dollar performance over time, as shown in Figure 21.17, is very useful.

TECHNICAL ANALYSIS OF BOND MARKETS   Thus far, we have described technical tools for the analysis of the stock market in the United States and the world. Although we have emphasized the use of technical analysis in stock markets, you should be aware that technicians also apply these techniques to the bond market. The theory and rationale for technical analysis of bonds is the same as for stocks and many of the same trading rules are used. As with stocks, the techniques apply to an individual bond, several bonds, or a bond index. A major difference is that it is generally not possible to consider the volume of trading of bonds because these data generally are not available because most bonds are traded OTC, where volume is not reported.

FIGURE 21.17   **TIME-SERIES PLOT OF U.S. DOLLAR–TRADE WEIGHTED EXCHANGE RATES**

High 96.93 12-31-93
Low 79.01 9-4-92
Last 86.97

Sources: Datastream and Merrill Lynch, "The Global Technician," March 18, 1996.

| FIGURE 21.18 | TECHNICAL ANALYSIS OF THE WORLD BOND MARKETS, INCLUDING RELATIVE STRENGTH AND MOVING AVERAGES |

Source: Datastream and Merrill Lynch, "The Global Technician," March 18, 1996.

Figure 21.18 contains a table that summarizes the medium-term relative strength for six major U.S. trading partners compared to a world bond series (A is average; BA is below average). The top graph is a time-series plot for world bond yields that also contains a 55-day moving average line to reflect the trend. The bottom graph reflects the relative strength index (RSI) for this bond yield index series. Both technical series point toward higher bond yields for global bonds, which is bearish for bond investors.

These examples show how technical analysis can be and is applied to the bond market as well as the stock market.

Summary • Whether you want to base your investment decisions on fundamental analysis, technical analysis, or a belief in efficient markets, you should be aware of the principles and practice of technical analysis. Numerous investors believe in and use technical analysis, the large investment houses provide extensive support for technical analysis, and a large proportion of the discussion related to securities markets in the media is based on a technical view of the market. Now that you are aware of technical analysis principles, techniques, and indicators, you will recognize this tendency of security market commentators.

- Two main differences separate technical analysts and those who believe in efficient markets. The first, related to the information dissemination process, is concerned with whether one assumes that everybody gets the information at about the same time. The second difference is concerned with how quickly investors adjust security prices to reflect new information. Technical analysts believe that the information dissemination process differs for different people. They believe that news takes time to travel from the insider and expert to the individual investor. They also believe that price adjustments are not instantaneous. As a result, they contend that security prices move in trends that persist and, therefore, past price trends and volume information along with other market indicators can help you determine future price trends.
- We discussed technical trading rules under four general categories: contrary-opinion rules, follow-the-smart-money tactics, other market indicators, and stock price and volume techniques. These techniques and trading rules also can be applied to foreign markets and to the analysis of currency exchange rates. In addition, technical analysis has been used to determine the prevailing sentiment in the bond market.
- Most technicians follow several indicators and decision rules at any point in time and attempt to derive a consensus decision to buy, sell, or do nothing.[16] Many technicians often conclude to do nothing.

Questions

1. Technical analysts believe that one can use past price changes to predict future price changes. How do they justify this belief?
2. Technicians contend that stock prices move in trends that persist for long periods of time. What do technicians believe happens in the real world to cause these trends?
3. Briefly discuss the problems involved with fundamental analysis that are considered to be advantages for technical analysis.
4. Discuss some disadvantages of technical analysis.
5. If the mutual fund cash position were to increase close to 12 percent, would a technician consider this cash position bullish or bearish? Give two reasons why the technical analyst would feel this way.
6. Assume a significant decline in credit balances at brokerage firms. Discuss why a technician would consider this to be bearish.
7. If the bearish sentiment index of advisory service opinions were to increase to 61 percent, discuss why a technician would consider this to be bullish or bearish.
8. Suppose the ratio of specialists' short sales to total short sales increases to 70 percent. Discuss why a technician would consider this to be bullish or bearish.
9. Why is an increase in debit balances considered bullish?
10. Describe the Dow Theory and its three components. Which component is most important? What is the reason for an intermediate reversal?
11. Describe a bearish price and volume pattern, and discuss why it is considered bearish.
12. Discuss the logic behind the breadth of market index. How is it used to identify a peak in stock prices?
13. During a 10-day trading period, the cumulative net advance series goes from 1,572 to 1,053. During this same period of time, the DJIA goes from 3,257 to 3,407. As a technician, discuss what this set of events would mean to you.
14. Explain the reasoning behind a support level and a resistance level.

---

[16] An analysis using numerous indicators is Jerome Baesel, George Shows, and Edward Thorp, "Can Joe Granville Time the Market?" *Journal of Portfolio Management* 8, no. 3 (Spring 1982): 5–9.

15. What is the purpose of computing a moving-average line for a stock? Describe a bullish pattern using a 50-day moving-average line and the stock volume of trading. Discuss why this pattern is considered bullish.
16. Assuming a stock price and volume chart that also contains a 50-day and a 200-day MA line, describe a bearish pattern with the two MA lines and discuss why it is bearish.
17. Explain how you would construct a relative-strength series for an individual stock or an industry group. What would it mean to say a stock experienced good relative strength during a bear market?
18. Discuss why most technicians follow several technical rules and attempt to derive a consensus.

Problems

1. Select a stock on the NYSE and construct a daily high, low, and close bar chart for it that includes its volume of trading for 10 trading days.
2. Compute the relative-strength ratio for the stock in Problem 1 relative to the S&P 500 Index. Prepare a table that includes all the data and indicates the computations as follows:

	Closing Price		Relative-Strength Ratio
Day	Stock	S&P 500	Stock Price/S&P 500

3. Plot the relative-strength ratio computed in Problem 2 on your bar chart. Discuss whether the stock's relative strength is bullish or bearish.
4. Currently Charlotte Art Importers is selling at $32 per share. Although you are somewhat dubious about technical analysis, you feel that you should know how technicians who use point-and-figure charts would view this stock. You decide to note one-point movements and three-point reversals. You gather the following price information:

Date	Price	Date	Price	Date	Price
4/1	23½	4/18	33	5/3	27
4/4	28½	4/19	35⅜	5/4	26½
4/5	28	4/20	37	5/5	28
4/6	28	4/21	38½	5/6	28¼
4/7	29¾	4/22	36	5/9	28⅛
4/8	30½	4/25	35	5/10	28¼
4/11	30½	4/26	34¼	5/11	29⅛
4/12	32⅛	4/27	33⅛	5/12	30¼
4/13	32	4/28	32⅞	5/13	29⅞

Plot the point-and-figure chart using Xs for uptrends and Os for downtrends. How would a technician evaluate these movements? Discuss why you would expect a technician to buy, sell, or hold the stock based on this chart.

References

Colby, Robert W. and Thomas A. Mayers. *The Encyclopedia of Technical Market Indicators*. Homewood, IL: Dow Jones-Irwin, 1988.

Dines, James. *How the Average Investor Can Use Technical Analysis for Stock Profits*. New York: Dines Chart Corporation, 1974.

Edwards, R. D. and John Magee, Jr. *Technical Analysis of Stock Trends*. 5th ed. Springfield, MA: John Magee, 1988.

Fosback, Norman G. *Stock Market Logic*. Fort Lauderdale, FL: The Institute for Economic Research, 1976.

Grant, Dwight. "Market Timing: Strategies to Consider." *Journal of Portfolio Management* 5, no. 4 (Summer 1979).

Hardy, C. Colburn. *Investor's Guide to Technical Analysis.* New York: McGraw Hill, 1978.

Levy, Robert A. *The Relative Strength Concept of Common Stock Price Forecasting.* Larchmont, NY: Investors Intelligence, 1968.

Murphy, John J. *Technical Analysis of the Futures Markets.* 2d ed. New York: McGraw Hill, 1985.

Pring, Martin J. *Technical Analysis Explained.* 2d ed. New York: McGraw Hill, 1985.

Shaw, Alan R. "Market Timing and Technical Analysis." In *The Financial Analysts Handbook,* 2d ed., edited by Sumner N. Levine. Homewood, IL: Dow Jones-Irwin, 1988.

Sweeney, Richard J. "Some New Filter Rule Tests: Methods and Results." *Journal of Financial and Quantitative Analysis* 23, no. 3 (September 1988).

Zweig, Martin E. *Winning on Wall Street.* New York: Warner Books, 1986.

Chapter
22
Equity Portfolio Management Strategies

This chapter answers the following questions:

- What are the two generic equity portfolio management styles?
- What are three techniques for constructing a passive index portfolio?
- How does the goal of a passive equity portfolio manager differ from the goal of an active manager?
- What are the three themes that active equity portfolio managers can use?
- What techniques are used by active managers in an attempt to outperform their benchmark?
- What are four asset allocation strategies?
- How can futures and options be used to help manage an equity portfolio?

Recent chapters have reviewed how to analyze industries and companies, how to estimate a stock's intrinsic value, and how technical analysis can assist in stockpicking. Some equity portfolios are constructed one stock at a time. Research staffs analyze the economy, industries, and companies; evaluate firms' strategies and competitive advantages; and recommend individual stocks for purchase or for sale.

Other equity portfolios are constructed using a computer-intensive, rather than analyst-intensive, method. Computers analyze relationships between stocks and market sectors to identify undervalued stocks. Quantitative "screens" and factor models are used to construct portfolios of stocks with attributes such as low P/E ratios, low price/book ratios, small capitalization, high dividend yield, those neglected by analysts, or stocks whose returns are strongly correlated with economic variables such as interest rates. Computer programs detect trading patterns and place buy-and-sell orders depending on past price movements. Computers also examine pricing relationships between the stock, options, and futures markets and place orders across these markets to arbitrage small price differences.

Similar to bond portfolios, equity portfolio return profiles can be modified by the use of futures and options. It is possible to trade futures contracts on major indexes, as well as acquire options on stock market indexes, on selected industry groups, and on individual stocks. These derivative securities can assist the portfolio manager in shifting a portfolio's exposure to systematic and unsystematic risk.

PASSIVE VERSUS ACTIVE MANAGEMENT

Equity portfolio management styles fall into either a passive or an active category. Unlike the immunization of bond portfolios, no middle ground exists between active and passive equity management strategies. Some argue that "hybrid" active/passive equity portfolio management styles exist, but such styles really reflect active management philosophies. Similar to traditional active management, "hybrid"-style managers invest to find undervalued sectors or securities. The following discussion reviews the traditional meaning of the terms *passive* and *active* portfolio management.

Passive equity portfolio management is a long-term buy-and-hold strategy. Usually stocks are purchased so the portfolio's returns will track those of an index over time. Because of the goal of tracking an index, it is generally referred to as "indexing." Occasional rebalancing is needed as dividends must be reinvested and because stocks merge or drop out of the target index and other stocks are added. Notably, the purpose of an indexed portfolio is not to "beat" the target index, but to match its performance. A manager of an equity index portfolio is judged on how well he or she tracks the target index—i.e., minimizes the tracking error similar to the bond index portfolio manager.

Active equity portfolio management is an attempt by the manager to outperform, on a risk-adjusted basis, a passive benchmark portfolio.[1] A *benchmark portfolio* is a passive portfolio whose average characteristics (including factors such as beta, dividend yield, industry weighting, and firm size) match the risk–return objectives of the client.

In the next sections, we examine more closely the mechanics of passive and active equity portfolio management.

AN OVERVIEW OF PASSIVE EQUITY PORTFOLIO MANAGEMENT STRATEGIES

Passive equity portfolio management attempts to design a portfolio to replicate the performance of a specific index. The key word here is *replicate*. As discussed in Chapter 2, the portfolio manager who earns higher returns by violating the client's policy statement should be fired; a passive manager who isn't really passive should likewise be dismissed. A passive manager earns his or her fee by constructing a portfolio that closely tracks the performance of a specified equity index (referred to as the *benchmark index*) that meets the client's needs and objectives. If the manager attempts to outperform the index selected, he or she violates the passive premise of the portfolio.

In Chapter 7, we presented several reasons for investing in a passive equity portfolio. Strong evidence indicates that the stock market is fairly efficient. For most active managers, the costs of actively managing a portfolio (1 to 2 percent of the portfolio's assets) are difficult to overcome. As noted in Chapters 7 and 26, the S&P 500 index typically outperforms most equity mutual funds on an annual basis. Note that, although the S&P 500 is the most popular index to track, a client can choose from among about 30 different indexes.[2]

Chapter 5 contained a summary description of many different market indexes. Domestic U.S. equity indexes include the S&P 500, 400, and 100; the Value Line index; and the Wilshire 5000. *The Wall Street Journal* publishes the daily values of indexes for the organized exchanges, the OTC market, and various industry groups. Indexes exist for small capitalization stocks (Russell 2000), for value- or growth-oriented stocks (Russell Growth index and the Russell Value index), for numerous world regions (such as the EAFE index), as well as for smaller regions, individual countries, and types of countries (emerging markets). As passive investing has growth in popularity, money managers have created an index fund for virtually every broad market category.[3]

The goal of a passive portfolio is to track the index as closely as possible. But because of cash inflows and outflows and company mergers and bankruptcies, securities must be

---

[1] Evaluating the risk-adjusted performance of a portfolio is the subject of Chapter 27.

[2] The growing popularity of index funds is discussed in Jeffrey M. Laderman, "The Stampede to Index Funds," *Business Week* (April 1, 1996): 78–79.

[3] For a detailed discussion of selecting a benchmark for a bond portfolio, see Chris P. Dialynas, "The Active Decisions in the Selection of Passive Management and Performance Bogeys," in *The Handbook of Fixed-Income Securities*, 4th ed., edited by Frank J. Fabozzi and T. Dessa Fabozzi (Burr Ridge, IL: Irwin Professional Publishing, 1995).

bought and sold, which means that there necessarily will be tracking errors over time. In addition, even though index funds generally attempt to minimize turnover and the resultant transactions fees, they necessarily have to do some rebalancing as noted, which means that the long-run return performance of index funds will lag the benchmark index. Certainly, substantial or prolonged deviations of the portfolio's returns from the index's returns would be a cause for concern.

INDEX FUND CONSTRUCTION TECHNIQUES   There are three basic techniques for constructing a passive index portfolio: full replication, sampling, and quadratic optimization or programming. The most obvious technique is **full replication** wherein all the securities in the index are purchased in proportion to their weights in the index. This technique helps ensure close tracking, but it may be suboptimal for two reasons. First, the need to buy many securities will increase transaction costs that will detract from performance. Second, the reinvestment of dividends will also result in high commissions when many firms pay small dividends at different times in the year.

The second technique, **sampling**, addresses the problem of numerous stock issues. Statisticians have taught us that we don't need to ask everyone in the United States for his or her opinion to determine who may win an election. Thus, opinion pollsters query only a small sample of the population to gauge public sentiment. Sampling techniques also can be applied to passive portfolio management. With sampling, a portfolio manager would only need to buy a representative sample of stocks that comprise the benchmark index. Stocks with larger index weights are purchased according to their weight in the index; smaller issues are purchased so their aggregate characteristics (e.g., beta, industry distribution, and dividend yield) approximate the underlying benchmark. With fewer stocks to purchase, larger positions can be taken in the issues acquired, which should lead to proportionately lower commissions. Further, the reinvestment of dividend cash flows will be less problematic because fewer securities need to be purchased to rebalance the portfolio. The disadvantage of sampling is that portfolio returns will almost certainly not track the returns for the benchmark index as closely as with full replication.

Figure 22.1 estimates the **tracking error** that occurs from sampling.[4] For example, full replication of the S&P 500 would (in theory) have almost no tracking error. As smaller samples are used to replicate the S&P's performance, the potential tracking error increases. There must be an analysis of the costs (larger tracking errors) and the benefits (easier management, lower trading commissions) of using smaller samples.

Rather than obtaining a sample based on industry or security characteristics, **quadratic optimization** or programming techniques can be used to construct a passive portfolio. With quadratic programming, historical information on price changes and correlations between securities are input to a computer program that determines the composition of a portfolio that will minimize tracking error with the benchmark. A problem with this technique is that it relies on *historical* price changes and correlations, and, if these factors change over time, the portfolio may experience very large tracking errors.

Some passive portfolios are not based on a published index. Sometimes "customized" passive portfolios, called **completeness funds**, are constructed to complement active portfolios that do not cover the entire market. For example, a large pension fund may allocate some of its holdings to active managers expected to outperform the market. Many times these active portfolios are overweighted in certain market sectors or stock types. In this

---

[4] When the goal of a portfolio is to mimic an index, the portfolio's returns should closely follow or "track" those of the index. The quality of an index portfolio is not measured by the magnitude of its returns; rather, it is measured by its *tracking error*, or the degree to which the portfolio's returns deviate from those of the benchmark index.

FIGURE 22.1

EXPECTED TRACKING ERROR BETWEEN THE S&P 500 INDEX AND PORTFOLIOS COMPRISED OF SAMPLES OF LESS THAN 500 STOCKS

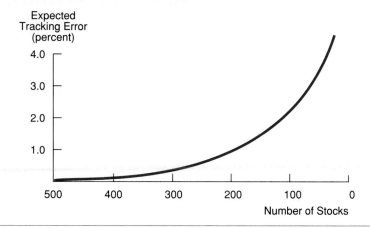

case, the pension fund manager may want the remaining funds to be invested passively to "fill the holes" left vacant by the active managers. The performance of the completeness fund will be compared to a customized benchmark that incorporates the characteristics of the stocks not covered by the active managers.

For example, suppose a pension fund hires three active managers to invest part of the fund's money. One manager emphasizes small capitalization U.S. stocks, the second invests only in Pacific Rim countries, and the third invests in U.S. stocks with low P/E ratios. To ensure adequate diversification, the pension fund may want to passively invest the remaining funds in a completeness fund that will have a customized benchmark that will include large- and mid-capitalization U.S. stocks, U.S. stocks with normal to high P/E ratios, and international stocks outside the Pacific Rim.

Still other passive portfolios and benchmarks exist for investors with certain unique needs and preferences.[5] Some investors may want their funds to be invested only in stocks that pay dividends or in a company that produces a product or service that the investor deems socially responsible. Benchmarks can be produced that reflect these desired attributes, and passive portfolios can be constructed to track the performance of the customized benchmark over time so investors' special needs can be satisfied.[6]

AN OVERVIEW OF ACTIVE EQUITY PORTFOLIO MANAGEMENT STRATEGIES

The goal of active portfolio management is to earn a portfolio return that exceeds the return of a passive benchmark portfolio, net of transaction costs, on a risk-adjusted basis. An important issue for active managers and their clients to resolve is the selection of an appropriate benchmark (sometimes called a "normal" portfolio).[7] The benchmark should incorporate the average qualities of the portfolio strategy of the client. Thus, an active portfolio manager who invests mainly in small capitalization stocks with low P/E ratios

---

[5] Recall our discussion in Chapter 2 on investors' objectives and constraints; two of the constraints were legal and regulatory requirements and unique needs and preferences.

[6] For further discussion on indexing related to bonds, see Sharmin Mossquer-Rahmani, "Indexing Fixed-Income Assets," in *The Handbook of Fixed-Income Securities*, 4th ed., edited by Frank J. Fabozzi and T. Dessa Fabozzi (Burr Ridge, IL: Irwin Professional Publishing, 1995).

[7] The construction of benchmark portfolios is discussed in Chapter 27.

because the client specified this strategy should not have his performance compared to a broad market index such as the S&P 500.

A first step in constructing the normal benchmark portfolio for the manager above may be to include, on an equally weighted basis, all stocks with market capitalizations under $500 million and P/E ratios less than 80 percent of the S&P 500 P/E ratio. Computerized databases allow the construction of such passive benchmarks so you can monitor the returns over time. This benchmark portfolio will be the standard by which the small stock, low P/E manager is evaluated.

The job of an active equity manager is not easy. If transaction costs total 1.5 percent of the portfolio's assets annually, the portfolio has to earn a return 1.5 percentage points above the passive benchmark just to keep pace with it. If the manager's strategy involves over-weighting specific market sectors in anticipation of price increases, the risk of the active portfolio will exceed that of the passive benchmark, so the active portfolio's return will have to exceed the benchmark by an even wider margin to compensate for its higher risk.

Thus, active managers must overcome two difficulties relative to the benchmark. First, an actively managed portfolio will have higher transaction costs. Second, active portfolios typically will have higher risk than the passive benchmark.

One key to success is for active managers to *be consistent* in their area of expertise. Market gyrations occur and investment styles go in and out of favor. Successful long-term investing requires that you maintain your investment philosophy and composure while others are panicking.

Another key to success is to *minimize the trading activity* of the portfolio. Attempts to time price movements over short horizons will result in lower profits because of growing commissions.

Active managers use three generic themes to time the market and add value to their portfolios in comparison to the benchmark. First, they can try to time the equity market by shifting funds into and out of stocks, bonds, and T-bills depending on broad market fore-casts and estimated risk premiums. Second, they can shift funds among different equity sectors and industries (financial stocks, consumer cyclicals, durable goods, and so on) or among investment styles (large capitalization, small capitalization, value, growth, and so on) to catch the next "hot" concept before the rest of the market does. Third, equity managers can do stockpicking, looking at individual issues in an attempt to find under-valued stocks—i.e., buy low and sell high. The following discussion describes some of the strategies used to implement these investment themes.

Global portfolios can apply the economic analysis discussed in Chapter 14 to identify different countries whose equity markets are potentially undervalued or overvalued. The global portfolio can then overweight or underweight those countries relative to a global benchmark portfolio as shown in Chapter 14.

Some global portfolio managers emphasize industry analysis rather than a country allocation.[8] As competition is becoming more global, some analysts examine industries and firms while disregarding country boundaries. For example, Caterpillar and Komatsu compete globally in the heavy equipment industry and Boeing, McDonnell Douglas, and Airbus compete globally in the airline manufacturing industry. The global automobile market is obvious by noting the home country of the cars on the street. These global portfolio managers analyze economic trends, industry competitive forces, and company strengths and strategies with a global perspective. The analyses of financial statements

---

[8] For example, see Robert Steiner, "Stock Pickers Slice Up Asia by Sector," *The Wall Street Journal*, October 21, 1993, C1, C23.

(Chapter 12), industries (Chapter 19), and companies (Chapter 20) are applied in a global, rather than a national, setting in order to identify undervalued industrial sectors and firms.

A **sector rotation strategy** is generally used by managers who invest in domestic equities. It involves positioning the portfolio to take advantage of the market's next move. Often this means emphasizing or overweighting (relative to the benchmark portfolio) certain economic sectors or industries in response to the next expected phase of the business cycle. Figure 22.2 contains suggestions on how sector rotators may position their portfolios to take advantage of stock market trends during the economic cycle.

"Sector" also can include different stock attributes. Because the market seems to favor some attributes more than others over time, sector rotation may involve overweighting stocks with certain characteristics such as small or large capitalization stocks, high or low P/E stocks, or stocks classified as "value" or "growth" stocks. A standard measure of a value stock is one with a below-average P/E ratio or price/book ratio. The low market ratios indicate that the stocks are potentially undervalued. Growth stocks are those whose earnings are expected to grow at a high rate. As a result, they typically have above-average P/Es, P/BV and P/CF ratios, and high ROEs.

During the last several years, there has been a growing interest in the growth versus value stock orientation—i.e., money management firms describe themselves as "value stock managers" or "growth stock managers." At this time, most of the evidence has favored the value stock results. Figure 22.3 shows the annual return results for the competing styles and documents the 10-year superiority for the value style. This is enforced by the longer-term results in Figure 22.4 for the period 1973–1995, which shows that value investing provided a much larger wealth value for both small-cap and large-cap stocks.

Earnings momentum and **price momentum** strategies are used because the market at times seems to reward the stocks of companies whose earnings have steady, above-average growth, or whose prices are rising because of market optimism.

The existence of computer databases has encouraged the use of computer screening and other quantitatively based methods of evaluating stocks. These screening methods search

---

FIGURE 22.2   **THE STOCK MARKET AND THE BUSINESS CYCLE**

*As of March 1994.

FIGURE 22.3

WILSHIRE SMALL CAP "VALUE" VERSUS SMALL CAP "GROWTH" (ANNUAL RETURNS ENDING DECEMBER 31)

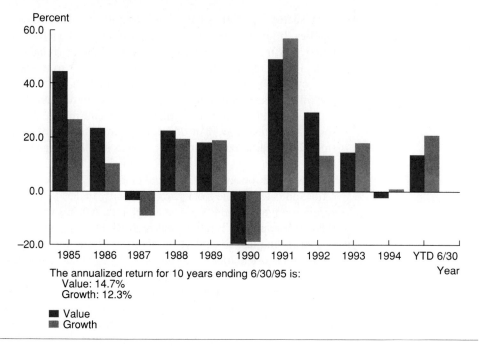

The annualized return for 10 years ending 6/30/95 is:
Value: 14.7%
Growth: 12.3%

■ Value
■ Growth

Source: Wilshire Associates.

for portfolios of stocks with certain characteristics rather than examining individual stocks to determine whether they are underpriced.

The simplest computer screens identify groups of stocks based on a set of attributes. Screens also are used to narrow the list of thousands of stocks to a manageable few that can then be evaluated using more traditional analytical means. Stocks can be screened on many company and stock price characteristics. For example, it is possible to generate a list of "value" stocks with at least a 20 percent return on equity, stable or growing dividends over the past 10 years and below market P/E ratios.

More complicated quantitative strategies are available that are similar in some ways to sector rotation. Factor models, similar to those used in the APT, can identify stocks whose earnings or prices are sensitive to economic variables such as exchange rates, inflation, interest rates, or consumer sentiment. With this information, portfolios can be "tilted" by trading those stocks most sensitive to the analyst's economic forecast. The manager can try to improve the portfolio's relative performance in a recession by purchasing stocks that are *least* sensitive to the analyst's pessimistic forecast.

Some quantitatively oriented portfolio managers use what is called a long–short approach to investing.[9] In the long–short approach, stocks are passed through a number of screens and assigned a rank. Stocks at the top of the ranking are purchased; stocks at the bottom are sold short. Such a strategy can be neutral on the overall market, since the value

---

[9] James A. White, "How Jacobs and Levy Crunch Stocks for Buying—and Selling." *The Wall Street Journal*, March 20, 1991, C1, C8.

FIGURE 22.4   **DOMESTIC COMMON STOCK INDEXES (MARCH 31, 1973–MARCH 31, 1995)**

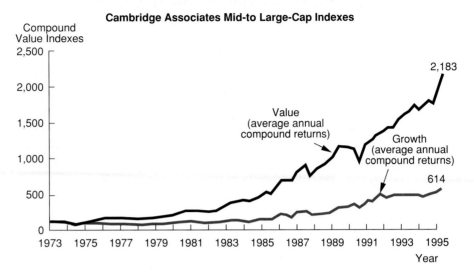

Cambridge Associates Mid-to Large-Cap Indexes

Cambridge Associates Small-Cap Indexes

Note: March 31, 1973 = 100

Source: Calculated from data provided by Standard & Poor's Compustat.

of the long position can approximate that of the short position. The performance of the top-ranked stocks is expected to exceed that of the lower-ranked stocks, regardless of whether the overall stock market rises, falls, or trades in a narrow range.

How do managers know that these quantitative models have the potential to offer above-average risk-adjusted returns? The answer is that they hope the future will be similar to the past because these quantitative strategies have been **backtested**. This involves using computers to examine the composition and returns of portfolios based on historical data to determine if the strategy would have worked successfully in the past. The risk of testing an investment strategy in this way is that relationships that existed in the past are not guaranteed to hold in the future.

Some managers let the computers do all the work. Neural networks are computer programs that attempt to imitate the thinking patterns of the human brain. They use vast databases and artificial intelligence capabilities to find cause-and-effect patterns in stock returns.[10] The computer attempts to discover undervalued securities by identifying abnormal risk-adjusted return patterns and "learning" what stock attributes drive the market.

Active managers also use quadratic programming to solve the efficient frontier optimization problem of Markowitz (see Chapter 8). The manager's expectations about returns, risk, and correlations are used by the optimizer to select portfolios that offer the optimal risk–return trade-off.

Linear programming techniques can be used to construct portfolios that maximize an objective (such as expected return) while satisfying linear constraints dealing with items such as the portfolio's beta, dividend yield, and diversification. As with almost all models, the output is only as good as the inputs, which in this case are expectations (estimates) of return, standard deviations, and correlations among alternative assets and the aggregate market.

USING FUTURES AND OPTIONS IN EQUITY PORTFOLIO MANAGEMENT

Irrespective of the active portfolio management strategy employed, there has been growing recognition that various derivative instruments are ideal for accomplishing a myriad of changes in a portfolio irrespective of the specific strategy of the manager. For example, the systematic and unsystematic risk of equity portfolios can be modified by using futures and options derivatives, as can the portfolio mix between equities and other assets. Cash inflows and outflows can be hedged through appropriate derivative strategies. Due to the cost, risk, and restrictions of short selling, selling futures contracts and purchasing puts are attractive alternatives to short selling for long–short managers.

MODIFYING PORTFOLIO RISK AND RETURN: A REVIEW

As discussed in Chapter 11, futures and options can affect the risk and return distribution for a portfolio. Generally, a dollar-for-dollar relationship exists between the changes in the price of the underlying security and the price of the corresponding futures contract. In effect, buying (selling) futures is identical to subtracting (adding) cash from the portfolio. Purchasing futures has the effect of increasing the exposure of the portfolio to the asset; selling futures decreases the portfolio's exposure. Suppose Figure 22.5A represents a portfolio's probability distribution of returns. *Buying* futures on the portfolio's underlying asset *increases* the portfolio's exposure (or sensitivity) to price changes of the asset. As shown in Figure 22.5B, as a result, the return distribution widens, indicating a larger return variance. Selling futures has the effect of decreasing the portfolio's sensitivity to the underlying asset. Figure 22.5C shows the effect on the portfolio if futures are sold. In this case, the variance of returns declines, causing a "narrower" return distribution.

Figure 22.5 illustrates that futures have a symmetrical impact on portfolio returns, since their impact on the portfolio's upside and downside return potential is the same. This is because of the close relationship between changes in the price of the futures contract and changes in the price of the underlying asset.

[10]Robert McGough, "Fidelity's Bradford Lewis Takes Aim at Indexes with His 'Neural Network' Computer Program," *The Wall Street Journal*, October 27, 1992, C1, C23; Delvin D. Hawley, John D. Johnson, and Dijjotam Raina, "Artificial Neural Systems: A New Tool for Financial Decision-Making," *Financial Analysts Journal* 46, no. 6 (November/December 1990): 63–72; and George S. Swales, Jr., and Young Yoon, "Applying Artificial Neural Networks to Investment Analysis," *Financial Analysts Journal* 48, no. 4 (September/October 1992): 78–80.

FIGURE 22.5 **HOW RETURN DISTRIBUTIONS ARE MODIFIED WHEN FUTURES CONTRACTS ARE PURCHASED OR SOLD**

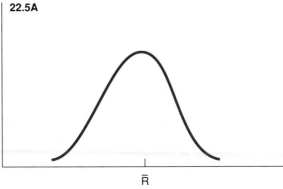

22.5A

$\bar{R}$

Portfolio without Futures

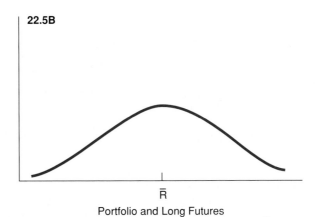

22.5B

$\bar{R}$

Portfolio and Long Futures

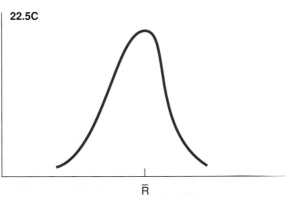

22.5C

$\bar{R}$

Portfolio and Short Futures

A futures contract represents an obligation to buy or sell the underlying asset unless cancelled by an offsetting transaction. In contrast, options give their owner the right (but not the obligation) to buy or sell the underlying asset. Because options provide this choice of whether or not to exercise the option, it means that options do not have a symmetrical impact on returns. For example, as will be shown in Chapter 24, buying a call option limits losses; buying a put when the investor owns the underlying security has the effect of controlling downside risk, as shown in Figure 22.6B. Writing a covered call, on the other hand, limits upside returns while not affecting loss potential, as seen in Figure 22.6C; writing a put option has the same effect.

THE USE OF FUTURES IN ASSET ALLOCATION

In times of changing market conditions, shifting a portfolio's asset allocation must be done quickly to take advantage of the manager's forecast. Such changes are costly since securities must be identified and then sold and bought to facilitate the reallocation. Commissions and the market impact of large trades can harm the portfolio's return potential.

Rather than identifying specific securities for sale and purchase, and then issuing large buy-and-sell orders, the portfolio manager can use futures to accomplish the change in asset allocation. Buying and selling appropriate futures contracts can quickly and easily change the portfolio's asset mix at lower transaction costs than trading large quantities of securities. Subsequently, if the manager wants to, he or she can identify specific assets to buy and sell so the trading will not have an adverse market impact.

Futures also can be used to achieve a proper stock/bond mix in a multiple-manager environment. Many medium and large pension funds divide the portfolio among different individual managers to exploit their specialized expertise in managing different asset classes (e.g., small-cap growth, emerging stock markets, high-yield debt). In such an environment, the overall pension fund manager can use futures to maintain the desired asset allocation; otherwise he or she would have to disrupt the specialized managers by adding or removing funds from them because of reallocation.

Futures also can be used to gain exposure to international markets. As noted in Table 22.1, many major stock markets have futures traded where the value of the futures contract is based on a major stock price index. Exposure to different currencies also can be managed by using currency futures contracts and currency options as discussed in Chapters 23 and 24.

THE USE OF DERIVATIVES IN EQUITY PORTFOLIOS

Regardless of whether the equity portfolio is passively or actively managed, futures and options can be used to help control cash inflows and outflows from the portfolio. In reality, most options used to modify portfolio risk are options whose underlying "security" is another derivative security—a futures contract. These options are called futures options or options on futures, which are discussed in Chapter 24.

HEDGING PORTFOLIO INFLOWS

When a large sum of money is deposited with a manager, the fund's asset composition changes; the lump-sum cash inflow has the effect of reducing the portfolio's exposure to equities since a larger proportion of the portfolio's assets are currently in cash. A potential problem is that, if the portfolio manager wants to quickly invest the funds in the market, he or she may purchase inappropriate securities. Also, large purchases can lead to sizeable commissions and a price-pressure impact on the stocks purchased.

A better strategy would be to use part of the cash inflow to purchase stock index futures contracts so the total contract value approximates the size of the inflow. Alternatively, you could purchase index call options. As a result, the money is immediately invested in stocks with lower commissions and a smaller price impact than if the stocks had been purchased

FIGURE 22.6

EXAMPLES OF TRUNCATED RETURN DISTRIBUTIONS WHEN OPTIONS ARE USED TO MODIFY PORTFOLIO RISK

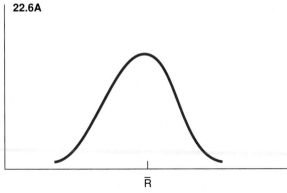

22.6A

$\overline{R}$

Portfolio without Options

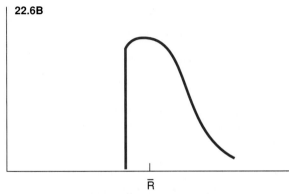

22.6B

$\overline{R}$

Portfolio and Put Option

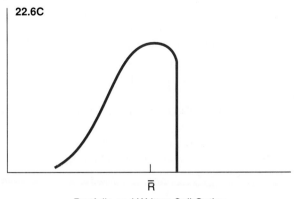

22.6C

$\overline{R}$

Portfolio and Written Call Option

| TABLE 22.1 | LIST OF COUNTRIES WITH STOCK INDEX FUTURES |

Country	Percent of FT-Actuaries World Index
Australia[a]	1.3%
Canada[a]	1.8
Denmark	0.3
France[a]	3.3
Germany	3.3
Hong Kong	1.4
Japan[a]	25.4
The Netherlands	1.5
New Zealand	0.1
Spain	0.9
Sweden	0.7
Switzerland	2.0
United Kingdom[a]	10.5
United States[a]	42.8
Total as of December 31, 1992	95.3%

[a]Approved for use by U.S. investors.

Source: Roger G. Clarke, "Application of Derivative Strategies in Managing Global Portfolios." Reprinted with permission, from *Derivative Strategies for Managing Portfolio Risk.* Copyright © 1993, Association for Investment Management and Research, Charlottesville, VA. All Rights Reserved.

outright. Once the futures are purchased, the manager has time to decide what assets to buy, and the specific stocks can be acquired in an orderly manner. The smaller purchases over time will reduce the price pressure. As these purchases are made, the futures contracts can be sold.

HEDGING PORTFOLIO OUTFLOWS

A large planned withdrawal from a portfolio usually is done by selling securities over time so that when the withdrawal date occurs, the needed funds are available for transfer. Similar to a cash deposit, the sale of securities causes an increase in cash holdings, which reduces the portfolio's equity exposure. A possible strategy to counterbalance the effect of a larger cash position is to buy futures contracts or call options as securities are sold. The net effect is to maintain the portfolio's overall exposure to stocks while accumulating cash. When the cash is withdrawn, the futures contracts can be sold such that the portfolio's operations have not been disrupted.

THE STANDARD & POOR'S 500 INDEX FUTURES CONTRACT

We will discuss futures contracts in this initial review of derivative securities in equity portfolio management because futures, and options on the futures, are the derivative tools typically used by portfolio managers.[11]

While a complete review of the numerous futures contracts is discussed in Chapter 23, in this initial review we will use the Chicago Mercantile Exchange's (CME) S&P 500 index futures contract to illustrate the use of futures.

Purchasers of the index futures contract must place funds in a margin account. Initial margin requirements are $6,000 for those buying the futures for speculative purposes and $2,500 for investors buying futures for hedging purposes. Hedgers must show that they

---

[11] In addition to futures, options, and options on futures, swaps are another derivative security that can be used in portfolio management. These are discussed in detail in Chapter 25.

currently own an equity portfolio whose market value approximates that of the futures traded.

The value of the S&P 500 futures contract is equal to $500 times the value of the index, so each one point change in the index leads to a $500 change in the value of the contract. When the S&P 500 futures contract expires, delivery or settlement of the contract is *not* made in the shares of 500 different stocks, but in cash. Every day, the contract is *marked to market*, which means its change in value is added to or subtracted from the investors' margin account. When investors close out their position, or when the futures contract expires, they receive the funds in their margin accounts. The difference between the funds in their account when it is closed and their initial margin deposit represents their profit or loss, which equals the change in value of the futures contract over the holding period.

There is one exception to this typical contract scenario. Should the funds in the investors' margin account become too low because of adverse price movements that reduced the money in the investor's account, the investor will receive a margin call. Maintenance margin requires that the account balance be increased to at least $2,500 for speculators and $1,500 for hedgers using the CME's S&P 500 index futures contract.

Prior to discussing how portfolio managers buy and sell S&P 500 futures, we need to discuss how managers determine the appropriate number of S&P 500 futures to buy or sell—i.e., the hedge ratio. We'll examine two examples.

DETERMINING HOW MANY CONTRACTS TO TRADE TO HEDGE A DEPOSIT OR A WITHDRAWAL   As discussed, futures can be used to maintain the desired exposure to stocks when the portfolio experiences a cash inflow or outflow. The number of futures contracts to be traded will equal:

$$\frac{\text{Cash Flow}}{\text{Value of 1 Contract}} \times \text{Portfolio Beta}$$

The value of one contract is the price of the S&P 500 index times $500. If the price of the S&P 500 futures contract is quoted as 476.60, the value of the contract will be $238,300.

The beta of the underlying futures index is taken to be 1.0. To determine the portfolio's beta to be used in the hedge ratio formula, portfolio returns are regressed on those of the underlying index as follows:

$$R_{portfolio} = \alpha + \beta R_{index}$$

The resulting slope estimate is the relative volatility of the portfolio's returns compared to those of the underlying index. We multiply the number of contracts by beta so the value of the futures position will change in value with the value of the portfolio.

Given several stock index futures contracts, a way to determine which contract is best for a particular portfolio is to examine the coefficient of determination (R^2) from estimating the equation above with different indexes. The index with the highest R^2 is the one that best follows the variations in the portfolio over time, which indicates it may be the most appropriate index. Generally, R^2 will be higher for well-diversified portfolios.

For example, to determine the appropriate number of futures contracts, assume an equity portfolio manager will receive a $5 million cash inflow today. The beta of the portfolio, measured against the S&P 500, is 1.15. The value of the contract is $238,300. The number of S&P 500 futures contracts that should be purchased to hedge this cash inflow of $5 million is equal to:

$$\frac{\$5 \text{ million}}{\$238,300} \times 1.15 = 24.13 \text{ contracts}$$

Since fractional contracts do not exist, managers typically round this number to the nearest integer and would purchase 24 contracts to hedge the cash inflow. These 24 contracts will be sold over time as the $5 million in cash is invested in stocks.

DETERMINING HOW MANY CONTRACTS TO TRADE TO ADJUST PORTFOLIO BETA　In Chapter 7, we learned the beta of a stock portfolio equals the weighted average of its components' betas. We use this concept to determine how many futures contracts are to be bought or sold to increase or decrease a portfolio's beta.

Suppose a $25 million equity portfolio has $22.5 million invested in stocks and $2.5 million invested in Treasury bills. The equity component of the portfolio has a beta of 0.95. Assume the manager expects rising stock prices, so he or she wants to increase the beta of the portfolio to 1.10. As above, we'll assume the value of a futures contract is $238,300. The beta of the cash or T-bill component of a portfolio usually is assumed to be zero, which means that we can ignore it in the analysis.

Currently, the weight of the equity component of the portfolio is $22.5 million/$25 million or 0.90; its beta is 0.95. The beta of the futures contract is 1.0. The weight of the futures component of the portfolio will be $(F \times \$238,300)/\$25$ million, where F represents the number of futures contracts to be traded. Since the target beta for the entire portfolio is 1.10, the weighted average of the portfolio's components must equal 1.10:

$$1.10 \quad = \quad 0.90 \times 0.95 \quad + \frac{F \times \$238,300}{\$25 \text{ million}} \times 1.0$$

$$\text{Target Beta} = \frac{\text{Contribution of}}{\text{Current Stock Portfolio}} + \frac{\text{Contribution of the}}{\text{Futures Component}}$$

Solving for F, we find that 25.70 contracts must be purchased to attain the target beta. Rounding to the nearest integer, 26 contracts will be bought.

If the manager forecasts a falling market and wants to reduce the beta of the portfolio to 0.80, the number of futures contracts required is determined as follows:

$$0.80 \quad = \quad 0.90 \times 0.95 \quad + \frac{F \times \$238,300}{\$25 \text{ million}} \times 1.0$$

$$\text{Target Beta} = \frac{\text{Contribution of}}{\text{Current Stock Portfolio}} + \frac{\text{Contribution of the}}{\text{Futures Component}}$$

Solving for F, we find the answer is −5.77. The negative sign indicates that futures contracts must be *sold* to *reduce* the portfolio beta to 0.80. Rounding to the nearest integer, the manager will sell 6 contracts to attain the desired portfolio beta. Option contracts *cannot* be used to adjust a portfolio's beta because they have a nonsymmetrical effect on a portfolio's return distribution.

USING FUTURES IN PASSIVE EQUITY PORTFOLIO MANAGEMENT　A passive investment strategy generally seeks to buy and hold a portfolio of equity securities. As noted earlier, a popular passive portfolio strategy is to replicate a stock market index. A passive strategy will not try to change a portfolio's beta based on an economic forecast.

With a passive investment strategy, the manager is expected to manage cash inflows and outflows without harming the ability of the portfolio to track its target index. The prior example on hedging a cash inflow or outflow is directly applicable to passive portfolio management. Instead of investing all cash inflows in the index or a subsample of the index, the manager can purchase an appropriate number of futures contracts to maintain the portfolio's structure and reduce the portfolio's tracking error relative to the index during the time period when the manager invests the funds in the index stocks. Similarly, anticipated cash outflows can be hedged when the portfolio manager is liquidating part of the portfolio over time. The hedge maintains the portfolio's exposure to the market through the use of futures contracts.

Options can be used to a limited extent in passive management. When cash rebalancing is imperfect and an index fund becomes overweighted in a sector or in individual stocks relative to its index, it is possible to sell call options on the individual stocks or on industry groups to correct the portfolio's weights.

USING FUTURES IN ACTIVE EQUITY PORTFOLIO MANAGEMENT

Active management often attempts to adjust the portfolio's systematic risk, unsystematic risk, or both. Systematic risk is a portfolio's exposure to price fluctuations caused by changes in the overall stock market. Unsystematic risk includes the portfolio's exposure to industries, sectors, or firms that is different from the benchmark.

MODIFYING SYSTEMATIC RISK   An equity portfolio's systematic risk is the sensitivity of the portfolio's value to changes in the benchmark index measured by the portfolio's beta. If a rising market is expected, active portfolio managers will want to increase their portfolio's beta while expectations of a falling market will invite managers to reduce their portfolio's betas.

Traditionally, when the market was expected to rise, active managers would sell low-beta stocks and buy high-beta stocks to raise the portfolio's weighted average beta. Alternatively, the use of futures provides a quicker and cheaper way to change the portfolio's beta with less disruption to the traits of the portfolio.[12] As discussed previously, buying or selling futures allows the manager to increase or decrease a portfolio's beta.

MODIFYING UNSYSTEMATIC RISK   Opportunities exist for controlling the unsystematic risk in an equity portfolio. Futures and options on futures exist for a limited number of sectors, while there are options for numerous components of the equity market. There are option contracts on market indexes such as the S&P 100 and S&P 500; for stock groups such as consumer goods and cyclicals; and for selected industries such as banks, utilities, pharmaceuticals, and mining. There also are options on over 1,400 individual stocks. Thus, even when industry option contracts don't exist, portfolio managers can buy or sell individual stock options for the industry to modify their exposure.

Unfortunately, we cannot determine the number of option contracts to be traded for a given effect because options truncate the return profile, which will affect the portfolio's beta and its responsiveness to market changes.

Options trading can be used to take advantage of the portfolio manager's forecasts for certain sectors and industries, by trading either sector options or options of firms in the industry. Options on index futures also can be used to exploit anticipated market changes. Because of their truncation effect on return distributions, options on index futures can affect both a portfolio's systematic and unsystematic risk.

---

[12] This is an important advantage; should the active managers feel they have expertise in identifying mispriced or undervalued securities, they may want to continue holding these individual securities in spite of predictions of an adverse market move.

For example, a manager can buy call options when anticipating a rise in the market, in a sector or industry, or in a group of individual stocks. The lower call premiums can provide more leverage than buying futures, and options contracts can allow greater precision in targeting sectors of the market rather than an entire index. The maximum loss for such strategies is limited to the call premium.

Similarly, investors can buy put options on an index future, a sector, or group of stocks in anticipation of a decline in value. Calls can be written on the market and subsets of the market when declining or stable values are forecast. Writing put options on the market and its subsectors can generate income when the portfolio managers expect the value of the market or subsectors to be stable or to rise.

MODIFYING THE
CHARACTERISTICS OF
AN INTERNATIONAL
EQUITY PORTFOLIO

Futures and options can be used to modify or hedge positions in international equity portfolios. As noted, international portfolios represent positions in both the securities and the currencies of the countries involved. Futures and options contracts on major currencies allow the portfolio manager to manage the risks of each of these components separately. Currency futures and options on currency futures can be used to modify the currency exposure of an international stock portfolio without affecting the actual holdings of the portfolios. For example, a portfolio manager may be bullish on German stocks but also may believe that the deutschemark is currently overvalued relative to the U.S. dollar. He or she can purchase the German securities and then adjust the overall currency exposure of the portfolio through the use of currency options and futures.

Consider the following example. Assume a stock portfolio has the equivalent of $30 million invested: $9 million in the United States; $12 million in Germany; the remainder in the United Kingdom. Thus, the current allocation across countries and currencies is: 30 percent United States, 40 percent Germany, and 30 percent United Kingdom. Assume the manager believes that the deutschemark is overvalued and expects a strengthening pound. Given this currency outlook, the manager wishes to reduce his or her exposure to the deutschemark by $4.5 million (or −15 percent of the portfolio) while increasing his or her exposure to the pound by $4.5 million (or +15 percentage points). In other words, the desired *currency* allocation is: 30 percent U.S. dollar, 25 percent German deutschemark, and 45 percent U.K. pound.

Traditional currency rebalancing would require rebalancing the country allocation whereby the manager would lose the chance to participate in security markets thought to be undervalued. Also, such security rebalancing would be costly and time consuming. Such a rebalancing scenario would cause the portfolio manager to ignore what presumably he or she does best, namely identify undervalued markets and securities. The point is, he or she would be forced to make stock allocation decisions based on currency forecasts.

Currently, the manager can maintain the country stock exposure while modifying the currency exposure. Assume the futures dollar/pound exchange rate is £1 = $1.48. Since the pound futures contract calls for the delivery of £62,500, the value of one contract is 1.48 $/£ × £62,500 = $92,500. If the deutschemark/dollar futures exchange rate is DM 1 = $0.57 and the deutschemark contract calls for the delivery of DM 125,000, the value of the deutschemark futures contract is 0.57 $/DM × DM 125,000 = $71,250.

If our manager wants to reduce the deutschemark exposure of the portfolio by $4.5 million, this is accomplished by selling $4,500,000/$71,250 = 63.16 (rounded off to 63) futures contracts on the deutschemark. The portfolio's exposure to the pound can be increased by $4.5 million by purchasing $4,500,000/$92,500 = 48.65 (or 49) British pound futures contracts.

Following these transactions, the security allocation across these countries remains as before: 30 percent United States, 40 percent Germany, 30 percent United Kingdom. Alternatively, through the use of currency hedging, the portfolio's exposure to the (presumably overvalued) deutschemark is only 25 percent, while exposure to the (presumably undervalued) pound is 45 percent. The use of derivatives allows the portfolio manager to shift currency exposures in a quicker, less costly manner than reallocating stocks across countries, while allowing the manager to maintain the desired exposure to undervalued securities.

ASSET ALLOCATION STRATEGIES

An equity portfolio does not stand in isolation; rather it is part of an investor's overall investment portfolio. Many times the equity portfolio is part of a balanced portfolio that contains holdings in various long- and short-term debt securities (such as bonds and Treasury bills) in addition to equities.

In such situations, the portfolio manager must consider more than just the composition of the equity or the bond component of the portfolio. The manager also must determine the appropriate mix of asset categories in the entire portfolio. There are four general strategies for determining the asset mix of a portfolio as follows: the integrated, strategic, tactical, and insured asset allocation methods.

INTEGRATED ASSET ALLOCATION

The integrated asset allocation strategy separately examines (1) capital market conditions and (2) the investor's objectives and constraints. These factors are then combined as inputs to an optimizer (such as that used to derive the Markowitz efficient frontier), which determines the portfolio asset mix that offers the best opportunity for meeting the investor's needs given the capital market forecast. The actual returns from the portfolio are then used as inputs to an iterative process in which changes over time in the investor's objectives and constraints are noted along with changes in capital market expectations. The optimizer then selects a new asset mix based on this update of investor needs and capital market expectations.

STRATEGIC ASSET ALLOCATION

Strategic asset allocation is used to determine the long-term policy asset weights in a portfolio. Typically, long-term average asset returns, risk, and covariances are used as estimates of future capital market results. Efficient frontiers are generated using this historical return information and the investor decides which asset mix is appropriate for his or her needs during the planning horizon. This results in *a constant-mix asset allocation with periodic rebalancing to adjust the portfolio to the specified asset weights.*

For example, assume an investor determines her stock/bond portfolio should have a 50/50 mix. Subsequently, stocks rise 10 percent in value while bonds fall 10 percent, making the mix 55/45. To adjust the portfolio mix back to the desired level, some stocks will have to be sold and the proceeds used to purchase bonds.

TACTICAL ASSET ALLOCATION

In tactical asset allocation, the investor's risk tolerance and constraints are assumed to be constant over time and *it is changing capital market conditions that lead to changes in the portfolio's stock-bond mix.* Tactical asset allocation models sometimes are driven by risk premium estimates; the proportion of equity in the overall portfolio rises (falls) when the equity risk premium appears to be large (small) relative to the bond risk premium. As such, tactical asset allocation strategies are somewhat contrarian in nature.

INSURED ASSET ALLOCATION

Insured asset allocation likewise results in continual adjustments in the portfolio allocation. Insured asset allocation assumes that expected market returns and risks are constant over time, while the investor's objectives and constraints change as his or her wealth position changes. For example, rising portfolio values increase the investor's wealth and consequently his or her ability to handle risk, which means the investor can increase his or her exposure to risky assets. Declines in the portfolio's value lowers the investor's wealth, consequently decreasing his or her ability to handle risk, which means the portfolio's exposure to risky assets must decline. Often, insured asset allocation involves only two assets, such as common stocks and T-bills. As stock prices rise, the asset allocation increases the stock component. As stock prices fall, the stock component of the mix falls while the T-bill component increases. This is opposite of what would happen under tactical asset allocation.

SELECTING AN ALLOCATION METHOD

Which asset allocation strategy is used depends on the perceptions of the variability in the client's objectives and constraints and the perceived relationship between past and future capital market conditions. If one believes that capital market conditions are relatively constant over time, you would use strategic or insured asset allocation. If you believe that the client's goals, risk preferences, and constraints are constant, you would likewise use tactical or strategic asset allocation. Integrated asset allocation assumes that both the investor's needs and capital market conditions are variable and therefore must be constantly monitored. Under these conditions, the portfolio mix must be updated constantly to reflect current changes in these parameters.

Summary

- Passive equity portfolios attempt to track the returns of an established benchmark, such as the S&P 500, or some other benchmark that meets the investor's needs. Active portfolios attempt to add value relative to their benchmark by market timing and/or by seeking to buy undervalued stocks.
- There are several methods for constructing and managing a passive portfolio, including full replication of a benchmark or sampling. Also, several active management strategies exist, including sector rotation, the use of factor models, quantitative screens, and linear programming methods.
- We also examine the use of derivative securities in equity portfolio management. Futures can be used to hedge against portfolio cash inflows and outflows; to keep a passive portfolio fully invested and help minimize tracking error; and to change an actively managed portfolio's beta. Alternatively, options can be used to modify a portfolio's unsystematic risk. Finally, derivatives can be used in managing currency exposures in international equity portfolios.
- Since equity portfolios typically are used with other assets in an investor's overall portfolio, we reviewed several common asset allocation strategies, including integrated asset allocation, strategic asset allocation, tactical asset allocation, and insured asset allocation. The basic difference between these strategies is whether they rely on current market expectations or long-run projections, and whether the investor's objectives and constraints remain constant over the planning horizon or change with market conditions.

Questions

1. Why have passive portfolio management strategies increased in use over time?
2. What is meant by an indexing portfolio strategy and what is the justification for this strategy? How might it differ from another passive portfolio?
3. Briefly describe four techniques considered active equity portfolio management strategies.
4. Describe several techniques for constructing a passive portfolio.
5. Discuss three strategies active managers can use to add value to their portfolios.
6. How do trading costs and market efficiencies affect the active manager? How may an active manager try to overcome these obstacles to success?
7. Discuss how the four asset allocation strategies differ from each other.

8. Describe the two components of risk in an equity portfolio.
9. What is a hedge ratio? How is it used?
10. Why might it be easier to construct a bond-market index than a stock-market index portfolio?
11. What are the trade-offs involved when constructing a portfolio using a full replication versus a sampling method?
12. Because of inflationary expectations, you expect natural resource stocks such as mining companies and oil firms to perform well over the next 3 to 6 months. As an active portfolio manager, describe the various methods available to take advantage of this forecast.

Problems

1. You have a portfolio with a market value of $50 million and a beta (measured against the S&P 500) of 1.2. If the market rises 10 percent, what value would you expect your portfolio to have?
2. Given the monthly returns below, how well did the passive portfolio track the S&P 500 benchmark? Find the R^2, alpha, and beta of the portfolio. Compute the average tracking error with and without sign.

Month	Portfolio Return	S&P 500 Return
January	5.0%	5.2%
February	−2.3	−3.0
March	−1.8	−1.6
April	2.2	1.9
May	0.4	0.1
June	−0.8	−0.5
July	0.0	0.2
August	1.5	1.6
September	−0.3	−0.1
October	−3.7	−4.0
November	2.4	2.0
December	0.3	0.2

3. Using the Ibbotson data on asset returns from Chapter 3 (Table 3.6), what percentage of the equity risk premium is consumed by trading costs of 1.5 percent? Assuming a normal distribution of returns, what is the probability that an active manager can earn a return that will overcome these trading costs?
4. Assume you actively manage a $100 million portfolio, 95 percent invested in equities, with a portfolio beta of 1.05. Your passive benchmark is the S&P 500. The current S&P 500 index value is 470.50.
   a. You anticipate a $3 million cash inflow from a pension fund next week. How many futures contracts should be bought or sold to mitigate the effect of this inflow on the portfolio's performance?
   b. Rather than a cash inflow, suppose you expected a cash outflow of $8 million. How many futures contracts should be bought or sold to mitigate the effect of this outflow on the portfolio's performance?
5. You manage the portfolio described in Problem 4. How many S&P 500 futures contracts must be bought or sold to:
   a. increase the portfolio beta to 1.15?
   b. increase the portfolio beta to 1.30?
   c. reduce the portfolio beta to 0.95?
   d. reduce the portfolio beta to zero?
6. You own a stock portfolio worth $1.5 million with a beta of 1.3. The current value of the S&P 500 index is 493.45.
   a. What is the value of one S&P 500 futures contract traded on the Chicago Mercantile Exchange?

    b. How many futures contracts must be bought or sold if you want to completely hedge the value of the portfolio against an expected market decline?

    c. Suppose the market, as measured by the S&P 500, declines by 10 percent over the course of the next several months.

       i. What is the profit or loss on your futures position?

       ii. What is the expected profit or loss for your stock portfolio (unhedged)?

       iii. What is the overall impact of the market decline on your hedged portfolio?

    d. Suppose the market, as measured by the S&P 500, increases by 10 percent over the course of the next several months.

       i. What is the profit or loss on your futures position?

       ii. What is the expected profit or loss for your stock portfolio (unhedged)?

       iii. What is the overall impact of the market rise on your hedged portfolio?

7. You own a stock portfolio worth $2.3 million with a beta of 1.1. The current value of the S&P 500 index is 477.75.

    a. What is the value of one S&P 500 futures contract traded on the Chicago Mercantile Exchange?

    b. How many futures contracts must be bought or sold if you want to hedge the portfolio against an expected market decline?

    c. Suppose the market, as measured by the S&P 500, drops by 10 percent over the course of the next several months, but your portfolio, because of unsystematic risk, falls 13 percent in value.

       i. What is the profit or loss on your futures position?

       ii. What is the profit or loss for your stock portfolio (unhedged)?

       iii. What is the overall impact of the market decline on your hedged portfolio? Why is this number not closer to zero?

    d. Suppose the market, as measured by the S&P 500, increases by 10 percent over the course of the next several months while your stock portfolio rises 15 percent.

       i. What is the profit or loss on your futures position?

       ii. What is the profit or loss for your stock portfolio (unhedged)?

       iii. What is the overall impact of the market rise on your hedged portfolio? Why is this number not closer to zero?

References

Bhatia, Sanjiv, ed. *Global Equity Investing*. Charlottesville, VA: Association for Investment Management and Research, May 1996.

Bhatia, Sanjiv, ed. *Managing Assets for Individual Investors*. Charlottesville, VA: Association for Investment Management and Research, March 1995.

Brown, Keith C., ed. *Derivative Strategies for Managing Portfolio Risk*. Charlottesville, VA: Association for Investment Management and Research, 1993.

Levine, Sumner N., ed. *The Financial Analysts Handbook*. 2d ed. Homewood, IL: Dow Jones–Irwin, 1988.

Maginn, John L. and Donald L. Tuttle, eds. *Managing Investment Portfolios*. 2d ed. Boston, MA: Warren, Gorham, and Lamont, Inc., 1990.

Peavy, John W. III, ed. *Managing Emerging Market Portfolios*. Charlottesville, VA: Association for Investment Management and Research, September 1993.

Squires, Jan R., ed. *Global Portfolio Management*. Charlottesville, VA: Association for Investment Management and Research, May 1996.

Squires, Jan R., ed. *Performance Evaluation, Benchmarks and Attribution Analysis*. Charlottesville, VA: Association for Investment Management and Research, November 1994.

Squires, Jan R., ed. *Value and Growth Styles in Equity Investing*. Charlottesville, VA: Association for Investment Management and Research, February 1995.

Part
6

DERIVATIVE SECURITY ANALYSIS

Chapter 23   Forward and Futures Contracts

Chapter 24   Option Contracts

Chapter 25   Swap Contracts, Convertible Securities, and Other Embedded Derivatives

*I*n recent years, it has been difficult to read the financial press without encountering at least a passing reference to an economic scandal attributed to trading in derivative securities. Procter & Gamble's ill-fated swap transactions with Banker's Trust and the equity index futures trades that brought down Barings Bank give the casual reader the impression that derivatives are highly volatile instruments used only by those investors interested in placing speculative "bets." Of course, nothing could be further from the truth. Although it is true that the companies in question either miscalculated or misunderstood the nature of their investment positions, the vast majority of derivative transactions are used by individuals and institutions seeking to reduce the risk exposures generated by their other business ventures.

Derivatives, in their many forms, have become a vital part of modern security markets, trailing only stocks and bonds in terms of importance. Unlike stocks and bonds, however, their widespread use is a relatively recent phenomenon, and misconceptions still exist about how derivatives work and the proper way for investors to trade them. The chapters in this section address this concern by providing the investor with a framework for understanding how derivatives are valued and used in practice. Building on the introduction to the topic in Chapter 11, this material considers the mechanics of the two basic contract forms—forwards and options—as well as several of the more sophisticated ways in which derivatives are used in combination with other securities.

Chapter 23 analyzes forward and futures contracts—the most prevalent form of derivative instrument. The similarities and differences between forward and futures contracts are described, with particular emphasis on the creation of (and subsequent adjustments to) margin accounts and the concept of basis risk. In addition, the calculation of the optimal hedge ratio and the arbitrage-free approach to determining the contract's delivery price are discussed. The chapter concludes with an examination of the features of forward and futures contracts that are designed to offset financial (as opposed to commodity) risk exposures, including interest rate, equity, and currency price movements. Applications and investment strategies involving each of these contract types illustrate this discussion.

In Chapter 24, the focus turns to option contracting. The discussion begins with a consideration of how option markets are organized and how both puts and calls are quoted and traded. Several different option-based investment and hedging strategies are described as well as how these contracts can be used in conjunction with other securities to create customized payoff distributions. The chapter concludes with a formal treatment of how option contracts are valued in an efficient market. Starting with the simple two-state option pricing model, which contains the essence of the basic valuation argument, the discussion progresses to include state-of-the-art approaches such as the binomial and the Black-Scholes models. In this development, special attention is paid to the role that price volatility plays in the valuation process.

Chapter 25, the last chapter of this section, considers three additional classes of derivative products. First, the rapidly developing market for swap, cap, and floor agreements is examined. After describing how these instruments are related to typical forward and option contracts, the discussion concentrates on the many ways in which investors and corporate risk managers use these new products in practice. In particular, applications involving four different exposures—interest rates, exchange rates, commodity prices, and equity prices—are developed. Second, the fundamentals of warrants and convertible securities are described. The emphasis of this discussion is on the option-like features of these instruments and how they alter the risk–return dynamics of traditional debt and equity products. Finally, the chapter concludes with an examination of the market for structured notes—instruments that can be viewed as "straight" bond issues into which derivatives have been embedded.

Chapter
23

Forward and Futures Contracts

This chapter answers the following questions:

- What are the differences in the way forward and futures contracts are structured and traded?
- How are the margin accounts on a futures contract adjusted for daily changes in market conditions?
- How can an investor use forward and futures contracts to hedge an existing risk exposure?
- What is a hedge ratio and how should it be calculated?
- What economic functions do the forward and futures markets serve?
- How are forward and futures contracts valued after origination?
- What is the relationship between futures contract prices and the current and expected spot price for the underlying commodity or security?
- How can an investor use forward and futures contracts to speculate on a particular view about changing market conditions?
- How do agricultural futures contracts differ from those based on financial instruments such as stock indexes, bonds, and currencies?
- How can forward and futures contracts be designed to hedge interest rate risk?
- How are implied forward rates and actual forward rates related?
- What is stock index arbitrage and how is it related to program trading?
- How can forward and futures contracts be designed to hedge foreign exchange rate risk?
- What is interest rate parity and how would you construct a covered interest arbitrage transaction?

As we saw in Chapter 11, forward and futures contracts are the most straightforward form of *derivative instrument* because they allow an investor to lock in the purchase or sales price of a transaction that will not be completed until a later date. Having laid the foundation for why these contracts exist and how they are used, in this chapter we continue our discussion along several lines. First, we take a closer look at the contract terms and trading mechanics of forwards and futures. In particular, we examine the important differences that exist between the two markets and describe the process by which futures contracts are **marked to market** on a daily basis. Further, we discuss how these contracts are used to hedge the price risk inherent in an existing or anticipated position and how **hedge ratios** are computed.

Second, we consider how forward and futures contracts are priced in an efficient capital market. Given that these instruments are not really securities in the same sense that stocks and bonds are, the notion of traditional security valuation is not quite appropriate in this market. Instead, valuation involves specifying the proper relationship between the forward contract price and the spot price for the underlying position. In general, we develop the "no arbitrage" result that the forward contract price should be equal to the spot price plus the cumulative costs of transporting the underlying security or commodity from the present to the future delivery date. These carrying costs can be either positive or negative; therefore, the correct forward contract price can be either higher or lower than the spot price.

Finally, we demonstrate several applications and strategies in which an investor can use forward and futures contracts. This demonstration concentrates on a class of contracts—*financial forward and futures*—that are particularly useful to investors. The underlying securities in financial futures include stock indexes, Treasury bonds, bank deposits, and foreign currencies. The use of these financial futures will be illustrated in a series of applications designed to demonstrate the connections between cash and futures markets.

AN OVERVIEW OF FORWARD AND FUTURES TRADING

Forward contracts are agreements negotiated directly between two parties in the OTC (i.e., nonexchange-traded) markets. A typical participant in a forward contract is a commercial or investment bank that, serving the role of the market maker, is contacted directly by the customer (although customers can form an agreement directly with one another). Forward contracts are individually designed agreements, and can be tailored to the specific needs of the ultimate end-user. Futures contracting, on the other hand, is more complicated. An investor wishing either to buy or to sell in the futures market gives his order to a broker (a *futures commission merchant*), who then passes it to a trader on the floor of an exchange (the *trading pit*). After a trade has been agreed on, details of the deal are passed to the **exchange clearinghouse**, which catalogs the transaction. The ultimate end-users in a futures contract never deal with each other directly. Rather, they always transact with the clearinghouse, which is also responsible for overseeing the delivery process, settling daily gains and losses, and guaranteeing the overall transaction. Figure 23.1 highlights the differences in how these contracts are created.[1]

For example, consider the traditional agricultural commodity futures that have been traded for more than a century, beginning with the creation of the Chicago Board of Trade (CBT). Since that development, futures contracts based on a wide array of commodities and securities have been created and now trade on numerous exchanges. Figure 23.2 shows price and trade activity data for a representative sample of commodity futures contracts. (Financial futures will be described in detail later in the chapter.) Notice that each of these commodity contracts is standardized in terms of the amount and type of the commodity involved and the available dates on which it can be delivered. As we will see, this standardization can lead to an important source of risk that may not exist in forward contracts.

To interpret the display in Figure 23.2, consider the gold futures contract traded on the Commodity Exchange (COMEX), a division of the New York Mercantile Exchange (NYM). Each contract calls for the long position to buy, and the short position to sell, 100 troy ounces of gold in the appointed months. With commodity futures, it usually is the case that delivery can take place any time during the month at the discretion of the short position. Contracts are available with settlement dates every other month for the next 18 months and then twice a year for another three years. An investor committing on this particular date to a long position in the June 1996 contract is obligated to buy 100 ounces of gold six months later for the contract price of $392.50 per ounce. The volume statistics show that more than 22,000 gold contracts changed hands on the last reported trading day.

---

[1] For a more detailed discussion of the futures trading process, see Roger G. Clarke, *Options and Futures: A Tutorial* (Charlottesville, VA: Research Foundation of the Institute of Chartered Financial Analysts, 1992). Some of this discussion is based on this book.

FIGURE 23.1

FORWARD AND FUTURES TRADING MECHANICS

A. Forward Contracts

B. Futures Contracts

Open interest—the total number of outstanding contracts of any maturity—was 138,727, down 185 contracts from the previous day.[2]

Another important difference between forward and futures contracts is how the two types of agreements account for the possibility that a counterparty will fail to honor its obligation. Forward contracts usually do not require either counterparty to post collateral, meaning that each is exposed to the potential default of the other during the entire life of the contract. In contrast, the futures exchange requires each customer to post an *initial* **margin account** in the form of cash or government securities when the contract is originated. (The futures exchange, as a well-capitalized corporation, does not post collateral to protect customers from its potential default.) This margin account is then adjusted, or marked to market, at the end of each trading day according to that day's price movements. All outstanding contract positions are adjusted to the **settlement price**, which is set by a committee to reflect the midpoint of the closing price range.

The marked-to-market process effectively credits or debits each customer's margin account for daily trading gains or losses as if the customer had closed out his position, even though the contract remains open. For example, Figure 23.2 indicates that the settlement price of the June 1996 gold contract increased by $0.90 per ounce from the previous trading day. This price increase benefits the holder of a long position by $90 (= $0.90 per ounce × 100 ounces). Specifically, if she had entered into the contract yesterday, she would have a commitment to buy gold for $391.60, which she could now sell for $392.50. Accordingly, her margin account will be increased by $90. Conversely, any party who is short June gold futures will have his margin account reduced by $90 per contract. To ensure that the exchange always has enough protection, collateral accounts are not allowed to fall

---

[2] New contracts are created when a new customer comes to the exchange at a time when no existing contract holder wishes to liquidate his position. On the other hand, if an existing customer wants to close out her short position and there is not a new customer to take her place, the contract price will be lowered until an existing long position is enticed to sell back his agreement, thereby canceling the contract and reducing open interest by one.

FIGURE 23.2

COMMODITY FUTURES QUOTATIONS

Source: *The Wall Street Journal*, December 19, 1995.

FIGURE 23.2 COMMODITY FUTURES QUOTATIONS (CONTINUED)

COCOA (CSCE)-10 metric tons; $ per ton.

	Open	High	Low	Settle	Change	Lifetime High	Lifetime Low	Open Int
Mr96	1,290	1,293	1,270	1,274	− 25	1,676	1,270	37,856
May	1,313	1,315	1,294	1,295	− 25	1,642	1,294	13,989
July	1,336	1,336	1,315	1,316	− 25	1,595	1,315	5,510
Sept	1,355	1,355	1,339	1,339	− 23	1,557	1,339	9,567
Dec	1,383	1,383	1,366	1,366	− 22	1,578	1,366	8,087
Mr97	1,411	1,400	1,399	1,392	− 22	1,518	1,400	2,777
May	....	....	....	1,412	− 22	1,526	1,431	1,036

Est vol 17,555; vol Fr 4,037; open int 78,822, −24.

COFFEE (CSCE)-37,500 lbs.; cents per lb.

	Open	High	Low	Settle	Change	Lifetime High	Lifetime Low	Open Int
Dec	106.00	108.00	103.00	100.90	− 7.70	242.00	103.00	109
Mr96	106.70	107.10	101.50	102.10	− 5.65	203.50	100.75	18,416
May	105.25	105.50	100.40	101.05	− 5.05	181.60	99.70	3,946
July	105.00	105.25	100.90	101.40	− 4.35	183.00	99.50	1,466
Sept	100.50	105.50	100.50	101.50	− 4.60	184.00	99.50	925
Dec	104.50	102.00	100.50	100.50	− 5.50	148.90	99.90	614
Mr97	....	....	....	100.25	− 5.50	122.00	99.25	213

Est vol 7,265; vol Fr 5,194; open int 25,696, −304.

SUGAR-WORLD (CSCE)-112,000 lbs.; cents per lb.

	Open	High	Low	Settle	Change	Lifetime High	Lifetime Low	Open Int
Mar	11.41	11.44	11.25	11.29	− .14	13.39	9.45	83,202
May	11.00	11.01	10.85	10.89	− .10	13.25	9.65	24,552
July	10.47	10.48	10.35	10.40	− .09	12.91	9.62	17,136
Oct	10.21	10.21	10.10	10.13	− .11	12.50	9.51	18,734
Mr97	9.95	9.95	9.88	9.86	− .09	10.57	9.48	10,984
May	9.83	9.83	9.78	9.71	− .12	10.37	9.85	1,465
July	....	....	....	9.48	− .12	10.34	8.88	499

Est vol 13,868; vol Fr 8,787; open int 156,580, −804.

SUGAR-DOMESTIC (CSCE)-112,000 lbs.; cents per lb.

	Open	High	Low	Settle	Change	Lifetime High	Lifetime Low	Open Int
Mar	22.65	22.65	22.65	22.65	− .01	22.66	21.75	2,558
May	22.76	22.79	22.77	22.79	+ .03	22.79	21.80	2,060
July	22.78	22.82	22.81	22.83	+ .02	22.82	21.88	2,479
Sept	....	....	....	22.70	....	22.72	21.90	1,928
Nov	....	....	....	22.17	....	22.18	21.25	592
Ja97	....	....	....	22.07	....	22.09	22.00	189

Est vol 91; vol Fr 343; open int 9,826, +211.

CATTLE-FEEDER (CME) 50,000 lbs.; cents per lb.

	Open	High	Low	Settle	Change	Lifetime High	Lifetime Low	Open Int
Jan	64.00	64.00	63.35	63.37	− .77	71.52	62.75	3,796
Mar	62.40	62.40	61.72	61.75	− .67	68.00	61.27	4,824
Apr	61.95	61.95	61.50	61.52	− .52	66.25	61.10	2,202
May	61.85	61.85	61.35	61.37	− .55	64.50	60.80	1,595
Aug	63.30	63.30	62.90	63.15	− .35	64.00	62.05	1,545
Sept	62.65	62.75	62.65	62.75	− .45	63.50	62.05	205
Oct	62.95	62.95	62.75	62.75	− .40	63.45	62.55	110

Est vol 1,578; vol Fr 2,035; open int 14,293, +69.

CATTLE-LIVE (CME) 40,000 lbs.; cents per lb.

	Open	High	Low	Settle	Change	Lifetime High	Lifetime Low	Open Int
Dec	67.60	67.65	67.25	67.27	− .32	69.25	61.75	4,486
Fb96	67.80	67.90	67.30	67.55	− .25	68.85	62.80	28,894
Apr	67.60	67.60	67.10	67.27	− .52	68.45	63.90	16,305
June	63.40	63.45	63.10	63.20	− .35	64.17	60.95	9,006
Aug	62.10	62.15	61.95	62.00	− .17	62.90	60.05	4,132
Oct	63.17	63.37	63.17	63.32	+ .12	63.40	61.30	3,531
Dec	64.25	64.40	64.20	64.40	+ .12	64.90	63.65	923

Est vol 10,157; vol Fr 12,173; open int 67,277, −1,534.

HOGS (CME) 40,000 lbs.; cents per lb.

	Open	High	Low	Settle	Change	Lifetime High	Lifetime Low	Open Int
Dec	47.90	48.75	47.85	48.67	+ .67	48.75	39.00	2,124
Fb96	50.00	50.35	49.80	50.25	+ .20	51.00	41.00	16,338
Apr	49.50	50.02	49.45	49.97	+ .32	50.32	40.55	7,451
June	54.30	54.80	54.25	54.77	+ .27	55.35	45.20	5,151
July	53.75	53.95	53.60	53.90	+ .15	54.60	44.70	2,322
Aug	52.60	52.75	52.45	52.70	− .02	53.20	44.65	1,824
Oct	47.65	47.70	47.55	47.70	+ .07	54.65	41.00	907
Dec	48.30	48.35	48.25	48.32	+ .02	49.57	41.90	355

Est vol 4,153; vol Fr 6,256; open int 36,472, −270.

PORK BELLIES (CME) 40,000 lbs.; cents per lb.

	Open	High	Low	Settle	Change	Lifetime High	Lifetime Low	Open Int
Feb	61.32	61.50	60.30	60.85	− .17	64.30	39.80	5,148
Mar	61.25	61.52	60.40	61.05	− .10	63.95	39.80	1,028
May	62.50	62.50	61.50	61.70	− .32	64.80	47.60	485
July	63.00	63.00	61.90	62.75	+ .10	69.85	48.50	597
Aug	60.50	60.50	60.00	60.20	− .15	62.70	51.00	174

Est vol 2,473; vol Fr 2,192; open int 7,432, +275.

---

below a predetermined *maintenance* level, typically about 75 percent of the initial level. If this $90 adjustment reduced the short position's account beneath the maintenance margin, he would receive a **margin call** and be required to restore the account to its full initial level or face involuntary liquidation.

To summarize, the main trade-off between forward and futures contracts is *design flexibility* versus *credit and liquidity risks*, as highlighted by the following comparison.

	Futures	Forwards
Design flexibility:	Standardized	Can be customized
Credit risk:	Clearinghouse risk	Counterparty risk
Liquidity risk:	Depends on trading	Negotiated exit

These differences represent extremes; some forward contracts, particularly in foreign exchange, are quite standard and liquid while some futures contracts now allow for greater flexibility in the terms of the agreement. Also, forwards require less managerial oversight and intervention—especially on a daily basis—because of the lump-sum settlement at delivery (i.e., no margin accounts or marked-to-market settlement), a feature that is often important to unsophisticated or infrequent users of these products.

HEDGING WITH FORWARDS AND FUTURES

HEDGING AND THE BASIS

The goal of a *hedge* transaction is to create a position that, once added to an investor's portfolio, will offset the price risk of another, more fundamental holding. The word "offset" is used here rather than "eliminate" because the hedge transaction attempts to neutralize an exposure that remains on the balance sheet. In Chapter 11, we expressed this concept with the following chart, which assumes that the underlying exposure results from a long commodity position:

Economic Event	Actual Commodity Exposure	Desired Hedge Exposure
Commodity prices fall	Loss	Gain
Commodity prices rise	Gain	Loss

In this case, a short position in a forward contract based on the same commodity would provide the desired negative price correlation. By virtue of holding a short forward position against the long position in the commodity, the investor has entered into a **short hedge**. A **long hedge**, on the other hand, is created by supplementing a short commodity holding with a long forward position.

The basic premise behind either a short or a long hedge is that as the price of the underlying commodity changes, so too will the price of a forward contract based on that commodity. Further, the implicit hope of the hedger is that the spot and forward prices change in a predictable way relative to one another. For instance, the short hedger in the last example is hoping that if commodity prices fall and reduce the value of her underlying asset, the forward contract price also will fall by the same amount to create an offsetting gain on the derivative. Thus, a critical feature that affects the quality of a hedge transaction is the way in which the spot and forward prices change over time.

To understand better the relationship between spot and forward price movements, it is useful to develop the concept of the **basis**. At any date t, the basis is the spot price minus the forward price for a contract maturing at date T:

$$B_{t,T} = S_t - F_{t,T}.$$

where

S_t = **the date t spot price**
$F_{t,T}$ = **the date t forward price for a contract maturing at date T.**

Potentially, a different level of the basis may exist on each trading date t. Two facts always are true, however. First, the *initial basis* at date 0 ($B_{0,T}$) always will be known since both the current spot and forward contract prices can be observed. Second, the *maturity basis* at date T ($B_{T,T}$) always is zero whenever the commodity underlying the forward contract matches the asset held exactly. If this is the case, the forward price must *converge* to the spot price as the contract expires ($F_{T,T} = S_T$).

Consider again the investor who hedged her long position in a commodity by agreeing to sell it at date T through a short position in a forward contract. The value of the combined position is ($F_{0,T} - S_0$). If the investor decides to liquidate her entire position (including the hedge) prior to maturity, she will not be able to deliver the commodity to satisfy her forward obligation as originally intended. Instead, the investor will have to (1) sell her commodity position on the open market for S_t, and (2) "buy back" her short forward position for the new contract price of $F_{t,T}$.[3] The profit from the short hedge liquidated at date t is:

$$B_{t,T} - B_{0,T} = (S_t - F_{t,T}) - (S_0 - F_{0,T}).$$

The term $B_{t,T}$ often is called the *cover basis* because that is when the forward contract is closed out, or covered.

---

[3] The mechanics of liquidating a forward or futures contract prior to maturity will be described in the next section.

This equation highlights an important fact about hedging. Once the hedge position is formed, the investor no longer is exposed to the absolute price movement of the underlying asset alone. Instead, she is exposed to **basis risk** because the terminal value of her combined position is defined as the cover basis minus the initial basis. Notice, however, that only the cover basis is unknown at date 0, and so her real exposure is to the *correlation* between future changes in the spot and forward contract prices. If these movements are highly correlated, the basis risk will be quite small. In fact, it is usually possible to design a forward contract based on a specific underlying asset and deliverable on exactly the desired future date. This sort of customized design reduces basis risk to zero, since $F_{T,T} = S_T$. Conversely, basis risk is a possibility when contract terms are standardized, and is most likely to occur in the futures market where standardization is the norm.

To illustrate the concept of basis risk, suppose the investor wishes to hedge a long position of 100,000 pounds of cotton that she is planning to sell in April. Figure 23.2 shows that cotton futures contracts do exist, but with delivery months in either March or May. With each contract requiring the delivery of 50,000 pounds of cotton, she decides to short two of the May contracts, specifically intending to liquidate her position a month early. Suppose that on the date she initiates her short hedge, the spot cotton price was $0.7945 per pound and the May futures contract price was $0.8232 per pound. This means that her initial basis was −2.87 cents, which she hopes will move toward zero in a smooth and predictable manner. Suppose, in fact, that when she closes out her combined position in April, cotton prices have declined so that $S_t = \$0.7660$ and $F_{t,T} = \$0.7753$, leaving a cover basis of −0.93 cent. This means the basis has increased in value, or *strengthened*, which is to the short hedger's advantage. The net April selling price for her cotton is $0.8139 per pound, which is equal to the spot price of $0.7660 plus the net futures profit of $0.0479 (= 0.8232 − 0.7753). Notice that this is lower than the original futures price but considerably higher than the April spot price. Thus, the short hedger has benefited by exchanging pure price risk for basis risk.

Although it is difficult to generalize, substantial indirect evidence exists that minimizing basis risk is the primary goal of most hedgers. For example, Brown and Smith noted that the phenomenal growth of OTC products to manage interest rate risk—despite the existence of exchange-traded contracts—is a response to the desire to create customized solutions.[4] Further, a survey by Jesswein, Kwok, and Folks showed that corporate risk managers preferred to hedge their firms' foreign exchange exposure with forward contracts rather than with futures by a ratio of about five to one.[5] Finally, Edwards and Canter chronicled the severe difficulties the German firm Metallgesellschaft A.G. had in trying to hedge the energy-related positions on its balance sheet with exchange-traded futures positions.[6]

CALCULATING THE OPTIMAL HEDGE RATIO

In the preceding example, the decision to short two cotton futures contracts was a simple one because the investor held exactly twice as much of the same commodity as was covered by a single contract. In most cases, calculating the appropriate hedge ratio, or the number of futures contracts per unit of the spot asset, is not that straightforward. The

[4] Keith C. Brown and Donald J. Smith, *Interest Rate and Currency Swaps: A Tutorial* (Charlottesville, VA: Research Foundation of the Institute of Chartered Financial Analysts, 1995).

[5] Kurt Jesswein, Chuck C. Y. Kwok, and William R. Folks, "What New Currency Risk Products Are Companies Using and Why?" *Journal of Applied Corporate Finance* 8, no. 3 (Fall 1995), pp. 103–114.

[6] Franklin R. Edwards and Michael S. Canter, "The Collapse of Metallgesellschaft: Unhedgeable Risks, Poor Hedging Strategy, or Just Bad Luck?" *Journal of Applied Corporate Finance* 8, no. 1 (Spring 1995), pp. 86–105.

approach suggested by Johnson and Stein is to choose the number of contracts that minimizes the variance of net profit from a hedged commodity position. The determination of the required number of contracts can be established as follows.[7]

Consider the position of a short hedger who is long one unit of a particular commodity and short N forward contracts on that commodity. Rewriting the previous equation for the profit from a short hedge and allowing for a variable number of contracts, the net profit (Π_t) of this position at date t can be written:

$$\Pi_t = (S_t - S_0) - (F_{t,T} - F_{0,T})(N) = (\Delta S) - (\Delta F)(N).$$

The variance of this value is then given as:

$$\sigma_\Pi^2 = \sigma_{\Delta S}^2 + (N^2)\sigma_{\Delta F}^2 - 2(N)\text{COV}_{\Delta S, \Delta F},$$

where

COV = the covariance of changes in the spot and forward prices.

Minimizing this expression and solving for N leaves:

$$N^* = \frac{\text{COV}_{\Delta S, \Delta F}}{\sigma_{\Delta F}^2} = \left(\frac{\sigma_{\Delta S}}{\sigma_{\Delta F}} \right) \rho$$

where

ρ = the correlation coefficient between the spot and forward price changes.[8]

The optimal hedge ratio (N^*) can be interpreted as the ratio of the spot and forward price standard deviations multiplied by the correlation coefficient between the two series. Recalling from Chapter 1 that standard deviation is a measure of a position's *total* risk, this means that the optimal number of contracts is determined by the ratio of total volatilities deflated by ρ to account for the *systematic* relationship between the spot and forward prices. (It is, in fact, identical to the beta coefficient of a common stock.) An important implication of this is that the best contract to use in hedging an underlying spot position is the one that has the highest value of ρ. What if, for instance, a clothing manufacturer wanted to hedge the eventual purchase of a large quantity of wool, a commodity for which no exchange-traded futures contract exists? The expression for N^* suggests that it may be possible to form an effective **cross hedge** if prices for a contract based on a related commodity (e.g., cotton) are highly correlated with wool prices. In fact, the expected basis risk of such a cross hedge can be measured as $(1 - \rho^2)$. Finally, note that the value for N^* also can be calculated as the slope coefficient of a regression using ΔS and ΔF as the dependent and independent variables, respectively. In the regression context, ρ^2 is called

---

[7] Leland L. Johnson, "The Theory of Hedging and Speculation in Commodity Futures," *Review of Economic Studies* 27 (1959–60), pp. 139–160 and Jerome L. Stein, "The Simultaneous Determination of Spot and Futures Prices," *American Economic Review* 51, no. 5 (December 1961), pp. 1012–1025.

[8] Given data for spot and forward prices, σ_Π^2 in the variance equation is a function of just one variable, N. Thus, differentiating this equation with respect to N leaves $[d\sigma_\Pi^2/dN] = 2(N)\sigma_{\Delta F}^2 - 2\text{COV}_{\Delta S, \Delta F}$, which can be set equal to zero and solved for N^*. It is easily confirmed that the second derivative of this function is positive and so N^* is a minimizing value.

the coefficient of determination or, more commonly, R^2. Several examples of these calculations are presented in subsequent sections.

FORWARD AND FUTURES CONTRACTS: BASIC VALUATION CONCEPTS

Forward and futures contracts are not securities but rather *trade agreements* that enable both buyers and sellers of an underlying commodity or security to lock in the eventual price of their transaction. As such, they typically require no front-end payment from either the long or short position to motivate the other's participation and, consequently, the contract's initial market value usually is zero. Once the terms of the agreement are set, however, any change in market conditions will likely increase the value of the contract to one of the participants. For example, an obligation made in November to purchase soybeans in March for $220 per ton is surely quite valuable in January if soybean prices in the spot market are already $250 and no additional harvest is anticipated in the next month. The valuation of these agreements, which is different for futures and forward contracts, is described below.

VALUING FORWARDS AND FUTURES

Suppose that at date 0 you had contracted in the forward market to buy Q ounces of gold at date T for $F_{0,T}$. At date t, prior to the maturity date T, you decide that this long position is no longer necessary for your portfolio and you want to get rid of the future price risk it entails. Accordingly, you want to **unwind** your original obligation. One way to do this is to take a short position in a date t forward contract designed to offset the terms of the first. That is, at date t you would agree to sell Q ounces of gold at date T for the price of $F_{t,T}$. This is shown in the upper panel of Figure 23.3. Notice that because you now have contracts to buy and sell Q ounces of gold, you have no exposure to gold price movements between dates t and T. The profit or loss on this pair of forward contracts is $(Q)[F_{t,T} - F_{0,T}]$, or the difference between the selling and purchase prices multiplied by the quantity involved. However, this amount would not be received (if $F_{t,T} > F_{0,T}$) or paid until date T, meaning that the value of the original long forward position when it is sold on date t (its unwind value) would be the *present value* of $(Q)[F_{t,T} - F_{0,T}]$, or:

$$V_{t,T} = (Q)[F_{t,T} - F_{0,T}] \div (1 + i)^{(T - t)}$$

where

i = the appropriate annualized discount rate.

This equation expresses the date t value of a long forward contract maturing at date T. Notice two things about this amount. First, $V_{t,T}$ can be either positive or negative depending on whether $F_{t,T}$ is greater or less than the original contract price, $F_{0,T}$. This means that any forward contract carries the potential for symmetric payoffs to both participants. Second, the value of the short side of the same contract is just $(Q)[F_{0,T} - F_{t,T}] \div (1 + i)^{(T - t)}$, reinforcing the fact that forward contracts are *zero-sum games* since whatever the long position gains, the short position loses, and vice versa. For example, if you had originally agreed to a long position in a six-month gold forward at $F_{0,0.5} = \$400$, and after three months the new forward contract price is $F_{0.25,0.5} = \$415$, the value of your position would be $\$1,464.68$ ($= (100)(415 - 400) \div (1.1)^{0.25}$), assuming a 10 percent discount rate. Conversely, the value of the original short position would then have to be $-\$1,464.68$. Finally, notice that as date t approaches date T, the value of the contract simply becomes $(Q)(F_{t,T} - F_{0,T})$.

Valuing a futures contract is conceptually similar to valuing a forward contract with one important difference. As we saw earlier, futures contracts are marked to market on a daily

FIGURE 23.3

UNWIND VALUES FOR FORWARD AND FUTURES CONTRACTS

```
├───────────────────────────┼───────────────────────────┤
Date 0                      Date t                      Date T
(Origination)               (Unwind)                    (Maturity)
```

A. Forward Contract

- Long Forward ($F_{0,T}$)   • Short Forward ($F_{t,T}$)
     • Contract Unwind Value: $V_{t,T} = (Q)[F_{t,T} - F_{0,T}] \div (1 + i)^{(T-t)}$

B. Futures Contract

- Long Futures ($F^*_{0,T}$)   • Short Futures ($F^*_{t,T}$)
     • Contract Unwind Value: $V^*_{t,T} = (Q)[F^*_{t,T} - F^*_{0,T}]$

basis, and this settlement amount was not discounted to account for the temporal difference between dates t and T. That is, the date t value of the futures contract is simply the undiscounted difference between the futures prices at the origination and unwind (or cover) dates, multiplied by the contract quantity, as shown in the bottom panel of Figure 23.3. Thus, the forward contract valuation equation can be adapted for futures as:

$$V^*_{t,T} = (Q)(F^*_{t,T} - F^*_{0,T})$$

where

> $*$ = the possibility that forward and futures prices for the same commodity at the same point in time might be different.

Cox, Ingersoll, and Ross showed that $F^*_{0,T}$ and $F_{0,T}$ would be equal if short-term interest rates (i in the forward valuation equation) are known, but need not be the same under other circumstances.[9]

Typically, for commodities and securities that support both forward and futures markets, differences between $F^*_{0,T}$ and $F_{0,T}$ exist but are relatively small. For instance, Cornell and Reinganum established few economically meaningful differences between forward and futures prices in the foreign exchange market, while Park and Chen found that certain agricultural and precious metal futures prices were significantly higher than the analogous forward prices.[10] Finally, note once again that $V^*_{t,T}$ can be either positive or negative depending on how contract prices have changed since inception.

THE RELATIONSHIP BETWEEN SPOT AND FORWARD PRICES

In many respects, the relationship between the spot and forward prices at any moment in time is a more challenging question than how the contract is valued. We can understand the intuition for this relationship with an example: You have agreed at date 0 to deliver 5,000

---

[9] John Cox, Jonathan Ingersoll, and Stephen Ross, "The Relation between Forward Prices and Futures Prices," *Journal of Financial Economics* 9, no. 4 (December 1981), pp. 321–346.

[10] Bradford Cornell and Marc R. Reinganum, "Forward and Futures Prices: Evidence from Foreign Exchange Markets," *Journal of Finance* 36, no. 5 (December 1981), pp. 1035–1045, and H. Y. Park and Andrew H. Chen, "Differences between Forward and Futures Prices: A Further Investigation of Marking to Market Effects," *Journal of Futures Markets* 5, no. 7 (February 1985), pp. 77–88.

bushels of corn to your counterparty at date T. What is a "fair" price ($F_{0,T}$) to charge? Recognizing that the contract price can be anything that two parties agree to, one way to look at this question is to consider how much it will cost you to fulfill your obligation. If you wait until date T to purchase the corn on the spot market, you have a *speculative* position since your purchase price (S_T) will be unknown when you commit to a selling price.

Alternatively, suppose you buy the corn now for the current cash price of S_0 per bushel and store it until you have to deliver it at date T. Under this scheme, the forward contract price you would be willing to commit to would have to be high enough to cover: (1) the present cost of the corn, and (2) the cost of storing the corn until contract maturity. In general, these storage costs, denoted here as $SC_{0,T}$, can involve several things, including commissions paid for the physical warehousing of the commodity ($PC_{0,T}$) and the cost of financing the initial purchase of the underlying asset ($i_{0,T}$) but less any cash flows received ($D_{0,T}$) by owning the asset between dates 0 and T. Thus, in the absence of arbitrage opportunities, the forward contract price should be equal to the current spot price plus the **cost of carry** necessary to transport the asset to the future delivery date:

$$F_{0,T} = S_0 + SC_{0,T} = S_0 + (PC_{0,T} + i_{0,T} - D_{0,T}).$$

Notice that even if the funds needed to purchase the commodity at date 0 are not borrowed, $i_{0,T}$ accounts for the opportunity cost of committing one's own financial capital to the transaction.

This cost of carry model is useful in practice because it fits a wide variety of situations. For some commodities, such as corn or oil, physical storage is possible but the costs are enormous. Also, neither of these assets pays periodic cash flows in the traditional sense of the term. On the other hand, common stock is costless to store but often pays a dividend. The presence of this cash flow makes it possible for the basis to be positive (i.e., $F_{0,T} < S_0$), meaning that $SC_{0,T}$ can be negative. There is another reason why $SC_{0,T}$ might be less than zero. For certain storable commodities that do not pay a dividend, $F_{0,T} < S_0$ can occur when there is effectively a "premium" placed on currently owning the commodity. This premium, called a **convenience yield**, results from a small supply of the commodity at date 0 relative to what is expected at date T after, say, a crop harvest. Although it is extremely difficult to quantify, the convenience yield can be viewed as a potential storage cost that works in a manner similar to $D_{0,T}$.

An immediate implication of the cost of carry model is that there should be a direct relationship between contemporaneous forward and spot prices; indeed, this positive correlation is the objective of any well-designed hedging strategy. A related question involves the relationship between $F_{0,T}$ and the spot price expected to prevail at the time the contract matures (i.e., $E(S_T)$). There are three possibilities. First, the *pure expectations* hypothesis holds that, on average, $F_{0,T} = E(S_T)$, so that futures prices serve as unbiased forecasts of future spot prices. When this is true, futures prices serve an important *price discovery* function for participants in the applicable market. Conversely, $F_{0,T}$ could be less than $E(S_T)$, a situation that Keynes and Hicks argued would arise whenever short hedgers outnumber long hedgers.[11] In that case, a risk premium in the form of a lower contract price would be necessary to attract a sufficient number of long speculators. For reasons that are not entirely

---

[11] John Maynard Keynes, *A Treatise on Money* (London: Macmillan, 1930), and John Hicks, *Value and Capital* (Oxford: Clarendon Press, 1939).

clear, this situation is termed *normal backwardation*. Finally, a *contango* market occurs when the opposite is true, specifically, when $F_{0,T} > E(S_T)$.[12]

FINANCIAL FORWARDS AND FUTURES: APPLICATIONS AND STRATEGIES

Originally, forward and futures markets were organized largely around trading agricultural commodities such as corn and wheat. Although markets for these products remain strong, the most significant recent developments in this area have involved the use of financial securities as the asset underlying the contract, as indicated in Figure 23.4. In this section, we take a detailed look at three different types of financial forwards and futures: interest rate, equity index, and foreign exchange.

INTEREST RATE FORWARDS AND FUTURES

Interest rate forwards and futures were among the first derivatives to specify a financial security as the underlying asset. The earliest versions of these contracts were designed to lock in the forward price of a particular fixed-coupon bond, which in turn locks in its yield.

FIGURE 23.4

GROWTH IN THE USE OF FINANCIAL FUTURES CONTRACTS

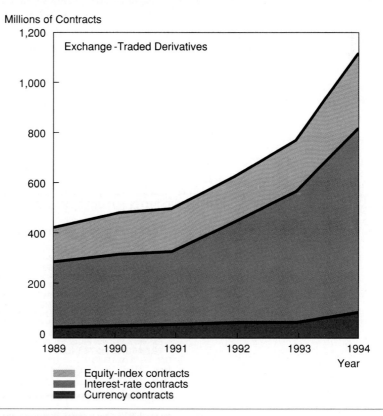

Source: Federal Reserve Bank of Cleveland.

---

[12] The existence of a risk premium in the futures market is a hotly debated topic. For a good review of this extensive literature, see Avraham Kamara, "The Behavior of Futures Prices: A Review of Theory and Evidence," *Financial Analysts Journal* 40, no. 4 (July–August 1984), pp. 68–75.

As we will see in Chapter 25, this market has progressed to where contracts such as *forward rate agreements* and *interest rate swaps* now fix the desired interest rate directly without reference to any specific underlying security. To understand the nuances of the most popular exchange-traded instruments, it is useful to separate them according to whether they involve long- or short-term rates.

LONG-TERM INTEREST RATE FUTURES

TREASURY BOND AND NOTE CONTRACT MECHANICS   The U.S. Treasury bond and note contracts at the Chicago Board of Trade (CBT) are among the most popular of all the financial futures contracts; in fact, in terms of average daily volume, the T-bond contract has historically been the most frequently traded futures contract of any kind. A similar T-bond contract is available at the London International Financial Futures Exchange (LIFFE) and a smaller version—one-half the delivery amount—at the MidAmerica Commodity Exchange (MCE). Delivery dates for both note and bond futures fall in March, June, September, and December. Figure 23.5 shows a representative set of quotes for these contracts.

Both the T-bond and the longer-term T-note contracts traded at the CBT call for the delivery of $100,000 face value of the respective instruments. For the T-bond contract, any Treasury bond that has at least 15 years to the nearest call date or to maturity (if non-callable) can be used for delivery. Bonds with maturities ranging from 6.5 to 10 years and 4.25 to 5.25 years can be used to satisfy the 10-year and 5-year T-note contracts, respectively. Delivery can take place on any day during the month of maturity, with the last trading day of the contract falling seven business days prior to the end of the month.

Mechanically, the quotation processes for T-bond and T-note contracts work the same way. For example, the settlement price of 118–11 for the March '96 T-bond contract on the CBT represents 118 and $11/32$ percent of the face amount, i.e., $118,343.75. The price went down by 46 "**ticks**" (−46) from the previous day's settlement, meaning that the short side

---

FIGURE 23.5   **TREASURY BOND AND NOTE FUTURES QUOTATIONS**

TREASURY BONDS (CBT)-$100,000; pts. 32nds of 100%

	Open	High	Low	Settle	Change	Lifetime High	Lifetime Low	Open Interest
Dec	119-26	119-26	118-18	118-19	− 45	121-20	93-27	34,173
Mr96	119-20	119-20	118-10	118-11	− 46	121-12	93-13	375,730
June	118-20	119-00	117-28	118-29	− 47	120-29	93-06	16,857
Sept	118-08	118-10	117-15	117-15	− 47	120-12	93-05	2,278
Mr97	117-13	117-13	117-00	117-00	− 47	119-13	99-26	760

Est vol 360,000; vol Fri 215,740; op int 429,925, −2,098.

TREASURY BONDS (MCE)-$50,000; pts. 32nds of 100%

	Open	High	Low	Settle	Change	Lifetime High	Lifetime Low	Open Interest
Dec	119-14	119-17	118-19	118-19	− 44	121-28	97-20	331
Mr96	119-10	119-10	118-09	118-11	− 42	120-31	98-00	7,723

Est vol 3,500; vol Fri 2,789; open int 8,064, +412.

TREASURY NOTES (CBT)-$100,000; pts. 32nds of 100%

	Open	High	Low	Settle	Change	Lifetime High	Lifetime Low	Open Interest
Dec	113-00	113-03	112-16	112-18	− 20	114-06	96-30	19,531
Mr96	113-07	113-12	112-22	112-24	− 23	114-12	98-20	215,482
June	112-15	112-18	112-02	112-04	− 23	113-22	102-10	17,659

Est vol 94,194; vol Fri 54,717; open int 252,827, +2,512.

5 YR TREAS NOTES (CBT)-$100,000; pts. 32nds of 100%

	Open	High	Low	Settle	Change	Lifetime High	Lifetime Low	Open Interest
Dec	109-08	109-08	109-00	109-00	− 13	109-30	05-095	33,264
Mr96	109-15	109-18	09035	109-04	− 16	110-03	106-03	132,739
June	09065	09065	108-28	08285	− 16	109-27	107-30	6,975

Est vol 55,000; vol Fri 45,212; open int 173,943, +3,378.

2 YR TREAS NOTES (CBT)-$200,000, pts. 32nds of 100%

	Open	High	Low	Settle	Change	Lifetime High	Lifetime Low	Open Interest
Dec	104-09	104-09	04077	04082	− 5.2	104-18	10245	236
Mr96	104-15	104-15	04107	04112	− 5.5	04222	103-19	17,371

Est vol 1,000; vol Fri 1,028; open int 17,622, −726.

Source. *The Wall Street Journal,* December 19, 1995.

had its margin account increased by $^{46}/_{32}$ percent of $100,000—or $1,437.50—where each $^{1}/_{32}$ equals $31.25 (i.e., 1,000 ÷ 32).

Although T-bond and T-note futures contracts are called interest rate futures, what the long and short positions actually agree to is the price of the underlying bond. Once that price is set, the yield will be locked in. When a yield is quoted, it is for reference only and typically assumes a coupon rate of 8 percent and 20 years to maturity. For the March 1996 bond contract, the settlement yield would be 6.3656 percent, which can be established by solving for the internal rate of return in the following "bond math" problem:

$$\$1,183.438 = \sum_{t=1}^{40} \frac{\$40}{(1 + i/2)^t} + \frac{\$1000}{(1 + i/2)^{40}}$$

This pricing formula takes into account that Treasury bonds pay semiannual interest. So, a 20-year, 8 percent bond makes 40 coupon payments of 4 percent each. Thus, the long position in this contract has effectively agreed in December to buy a 20-year T-bond in March priced to yield 6.37 percent. If, in March, the actual yield on the 20-year bond is below 6.37 percent (i.e., the bond's price is greater than $118,343.75), the long position will have made a wise decision. Thus, the long position in this contract gains as prices rise and rates decrease and loses as increasing rates lead to lower bond prices.

Because the bond and note futures contracts allow so many different instruments to qualify for delivery, the seller would naturally choose to deliver the least expensive bond if there were no adjustments made for varying coupon rates and maturity dates. To account for this, the CBT uses **conversion factors** to correct for the differences in the deliverable bonds. The conversion factor is based on the price of a given bond if its yield is 8 percent at the time of delivery and the face value is $1. For example, the March 1996 conversion factor for the 9 percent T-bond maturing in November 2018 would be 1.1036, calculated as:

$$1.1036 = \sum_{t=1}^{45} \frac{0.045}{(1 + .04)^t} + \frac{1}{(1 + .04)^{45}}$$

The actual delivery price, or invoice price, for that Treasury bond would be the quoted futures price, $118,343.75, multiplied by the conversion factor, 1.1036, for a total of $130,604.1625 (plus accrued interest). The buyer must pay more than $118,343.75 because the seller is delivering "more valuable" bonds since their coupon rate exceeds 8 percent.

The conversion factors used by the CBT are technically correct only when the Treasury yield curve is flat at 8 percent. Therefore, there usually will be a *cheapest to deliver* bond that maximizes the difference between the invoice price (the amount received by the short) and the cash market price (the amount paid by the short to acquire the delivery bond). Market participants always know which bond is the cheapest to deliver. Therefore, the T-bond futures contract trades as if this particular security were the actual underlying delivery bond. In fact, the cheapest to deliver security usually is the T-bond with the longest duration when yields are above 8 percent, and the one with the shortest duration for yields less than 8 percent.

A DURATION-BASED APPROACH TO HEDGING   In Chapter 16, we stressed that the main benefit of calculating the duration statistic was its ability to link interest rate changes to bond price changes by the formula:

$$\left(\frac{\Delta P}{P}\right) \approx -D\left(\frac{\Delta(1 + i/n)}{(1 + i/n)}\right)$$

We also saw that a more convenient way to write this expression is:

$$\left(\frac{\Delta P}{P}\right) \approx -\left(\frac{D}{(1 + i/n)}\right)\Delta(1 + i/n) = -D_{\text{mod}}\,\Delta(i/n)$$

where

D_{mod} = **the bond's modified duration, combining the Macaulay duration and its periodic yield into a single measure.**

Earlier in this chapter, we noted that the objective of hedging was to select a hedge ratio (N) such that $\Delta S - \Delta F(N) = 0$, where S is the current spot price of the underlying asset and F is the current futures contract price. Rewriting this leaves:

$$N^* = \frac{\Delta S}{\Delta F}$$

Using the modified duration relationship, this optimal hedge ratio can now be expanded as follows:

$$N^* = \frac{\Delta S}{\Delta F} = \frac{\left(\dfrac{\Delta S}{S}\right)}{\left(\dfrac{\Delta F}{F}\right)} \times \frac{S}{F} = \frac{-D_{\text{modS}} \times \Delta(i_S/n)}{-D_{\text{modF}} \times \Delta(i_F/n)} \times \frac{S}{F}$$

or

$$N^* = \frac{D_{\text{modS}}}{D_{\text{modF}}} \times \beta_i \times \frac{S}{F}$$

where

β_i = **the "yield beta."**

The yield beta is also called the ratio of changes in the yields applicable to the two instruments where n is the number of payment periods per year (e.g., $n = 2$ for semiannual coupon bonds).[13]

As a general example of the duration-based approach to setting hedge ratios, consider the following fixed-income securities, each making annual payments (i.e., $n = 1$):

Instrument	Coupon	Maturity	Yield
A	8%	10 years	10%
B	10%	15 years	8%

---

[13] Gerald Gay, Robert Kolb, and Raymond Chiang, "Interest Rate Hedging: An Empirical Test of Alternative Strategies," *Journal of Financial Research* 6, no. 3 (Fall 1983), pp. 187–197, tested the duration-based hedge ratio against several other more naive approaches and found that it reduced the risk of the underlying bond position by the greatest amount.

How much of instrument B is necessary to hedge A? This question can be answered in three steps. First, using the method shown in Chapter 16 (and summarized in Appendix 23A), the duration statistics for each position are:

$$D_A = 7.0439 \text{ so } D_{modA} = (7.0439) \div (1.10) = 6.4036 \text{ years,}$$

$$D_B = 8.8569 \text{ so } D_{modB} = (8.8569) \div (1.08) = 8.2009 \text{ years.}$$

Second, we will assume that yield beta is unity (i.e., $\beta_i = 1$). In general, this is calculated by observing historical yield curve movements across the 10- and 15-year maturities. Finally, current prices are easily confirmed to be 87.71 for security A and 117.12 for security B assuming par value of 100. Thus, the duration-based hedge ratio is:

$$N^* = \left(\frac{6.4036}{8.2009}\right)(1)\left(\frac{87.71}{117.12}\right) = 0.5847,$$

or 0.5847 unit of B short for every one unit of A held long.

TREASURY FUTURES APPLICATIONS

Hedging a future funding commitment   In late July, the treasurer of a U.S.-based company begins to arrange the details of an anticipated 15-year, $100 million funding. He feels that the company will be ready to launch its new debt issue in mid- to late-September, but is concerned that between July and September interest rates may rise, thereby increasing the company's funding cost. Consequently, he decides to hedge this exposure in the T-bond futures market. In this case, he will need to take a *short* position in the futures market, which will appreciate in value if interest rates increase, thereby offsetting the higher payments that will be required on the underlying debt.

The treasurer feels that if the bond issue was placed today, the credit standing of the firm would lead to a funding cost of 8.25 percent for the 15-year period. He knows that a September T-bond futures contract is trading at a price of 103–02 to yield 7.70 percent. He is also aware that bond yields beyond 10 years to maturity tend to move in a parallel fashion to one another so he is comfortable that a yield beta of one is appropriate. Further, the treasurer is aware that T-bond futures can't hedge for changes in the firm's risk premium over the risk-free rate; he will have to live with this source of basis risk.

If he plans to launch his new issue at par value, how many T-bond futures contracts would he need to short today? Assuming semiannual coupons for both the Treasury and corporate issues, their durations can be calculated using the closed-form equation shown in Appendix 23A:

$$D_{corp} = \frac{1.04125}{.04125} - \frac{1.04125 + [30(.04125 - .04125)]}{.04125[(1.04125)^{30} - 1] + .04125} = 17.74 \text{ periods}$$

and

$$D_{trsy} = \frac{1.0385}{.0385} - \frac{1.0385 + [40(.04 - .0385)]}{.04[(1.0385)^{40} - 1] + .0385} = 20.86 \text{ periods}$$

These statistics are denominated in "half years" so that the hedge ratio will be expressed in the same terms used to price the bonds. With these statistics we can calculate the modified durations as follows: $D_{modC} = 17.04 \ (= 17.74 \div 1.04125)$ and $D_{modT} = 20.09 \ (= 20.86 \div$

1.0385). Finally, since each T-bond futures contract is standardized to a denomination of $100,000, the treasurer can calculate the optimal number of contracts to short as:

$$(\text{Number of Contracts}) = \frac{(17.04)}{(20.09)} \times (1.0) \times \frac{(\$100,000,000)}{(\$103,062.50)} = 822.97, \text{ or } 823 \text{ contracts.}$$

*A **T-bond/T-note (NOB) futures spread*** Frequently, speculators in the bond market will have a clear view on a change in the overall shape of the yield curve but be less certain as to the actual direction in future rate movements. Suppose, for instance, you think the yield curve—which is currently upward sloping across all maturities—will flatten, but you're not sure in which of several ways this might occur:

- Short-term rates rise and long-term rates fall.
- Short- and long-term rates both rise, but short-term rates rise by more.
- Short- and long-term rates both fall, but short-term rates fall by less.

Clearly, taking a long or short position in a single futures contract linked to a single point on the yield curve is too speculative, given your view; you could be right about the shape shift but guess wrong about direction. One way to mitigate this unwanted risk while investing (based on your view) is to go both long and short in contracts representing different points on the yield curve. This is known as the Treasury "Notes over Bond" **spread** (or "NOB" spread) strategy.

Suppose in mid-February you observe the following price quotes (along with their implied yields to maturity) for T-bond and T-note futures contracts maturing in June:

Contract	Settle Price	Implied Yield
20-yr, 8% T-bond	103–02	7.70%
10-yr, 8% T-note	104–02	7.42%

Notice that your expectation of a flattening yield curve is identical to the view that the 28 basis point yield gap (= 0.0770 − 0.0742) between the longer- and shorter-term contracts will shrink. If you also feel this will occur by mid-June, the appropriate strategy would be:

- Go long in one Treasury bond futures.
- Go short in one Treasury note futures.

The net profit from this joint position when you close out the two contracts is calculated as the sum of the profits on the short T-note position and the long T-bond contract, or:

$$\left[\frac{104.0625 - \text{Sept T-Note Price}}{100} + \frac{\text{Sept T-Bond Price} - 103.0625}{100}\right](\$100,000)$$

To see how this combined position would pay off if your view is correct, consider two scenarios in which the yield curve flattens to where there is no difference between 10- and 20-year rates by the time you close your positions in June:

1. Rates increase to 8.00 percent by June

In this case, both futures contracts will sell at par and so your net profit will be:

$$\text{Net Profit} = [0.040625 - 0.030625](\$100,000) = \$1,000.$$

Notice that this same calculation can be done on a "price tick" basis:

$$\text{Net Profit} = \{[(104\text{--}02) - (103\text{--}02)] - [(100\text{--}00) - (100\text{--}00)]\}(\$31.25)$$
$$= (32 \text{ ticks})(\$31.25) = \$1,000$$

which is equivalent to the change in the number of ticks in the NOB spread multiplied by the dollar value of a tick.

2. Rates decrease to 7.00 percent by June

Except when both bonds trade at par, it is generally not the case that two bonds with different maturities—but the same coupon and same yield—will trade at the same price. Consequently, the settlement prices on the two futures contracts will be:

$$P_{\text{T-note}} = \sum_{t=1}^{20} \frac{\$4}{(1 + .035)^t} + \frac{\$100}{(1 + .035)^{20}} = \$107.11 \approx 107\text{--}04$$

and

$$P_{\text{T-bond}} = \sum_{t=1}^{40} \frac{\$4}{(1 + .035)^t} + \frac{\$100}{(1 + .035)^{40}} = \$110.68 \approx 110\text{--}22$$

so that the net profit from the NOB spread will be:

$$\text{Net Profit} = \{[(104\text{--}02) - (103\text{--}02)] - [(107\text{--}04) - (110\text{--}22)]\}(\$31.25)$$
$$= (32 + 114)(\$31.25) = \$4,562.50.$$

Interpreting this outcome differently, you made \$7,625.00 on your long position in the T-bond contract (i.e., [(110–22) – (103–02)] (31.25)), but you lost \$3,062.50 on your short T-note position (= [(104–02) – (107–04)](31.25)) for a net gain of \$4,562.50.

These results show that the futures spread allows speculators to separate their views on yield curve shape from an explicit forecast of a change in the curve's position. When using this strategy, however, the investor must realize that, because the duration of the T-bond is greater than that of the T-note, the former will be more sensitive to a given rate change.

SHORT-TERM INTEREST RATE FUTURES   Short-term interest rate futures have become the most rapidly expanding segment of the exchange-traded market. Currently, investors can hedge their exposures to several different money market rates (e.g., T-bill, LIBOR, Banker's Acceptance) denominated in a multitude of currencies (e.g., U.S. dollar, Swiss franc, British sterling). In the following analysis, we concentrate on two of these contracts: Eurodollar and Treasury bill.

EURODOLLAR AND TREASURY BILL CONTRACT MECHANICS   The Eurodollar contract traded at the International Monetary Market (IMM) on the Chicago Mercantile Exchange (CME, or "Merc"), as well as a comparable contract traded on the LIFFE, has become enormously successful since it was launched in the early 1980s. Delivery dates follow the March, June, September, December cycle (the so-called IMM dates) and now extend 10 years into the future. The final trading and settlement date is the second London business day before the third Wednesday of the delivery month. A representative set of quotes is shown in Figure 23.6. Also traded on the LIFFE (although not shown here) are similar contracts for hedging Eurosterling, Euromark, Eurolira, and Euroswiss rates.

FIGURE 23.6   **EURODOLLAR AND TREASURY BILL FUTURES QUOTATIONS**

EURODOLLAR (CME)-$1 million; pts of 100%

	Open	High	Low	Settle	Chg	Yield Settle	Chg	Open Interest
Dec	94.20	94.20	94.19	94.19	− .02	5.81	+ .02	258,791
Ja96	94.37	94.38	94.35	94.36	− .04	5.64	+ .04	23,941
Feb	94.51	94.51	94.48	94.48	− .05	5.52	+ .05	10,028
Mar	94.61	94.61	94.55	94.56	− .05	5.42	+ .05	431,429
June	94.83	94.83	94.75	94.76	− .07	5.24	+ .07	391,905
Sept	94.84	94.84	94.74	94.75	− .10	5.25	+ .10	231,630
Dec	94.74	94.74	94.63	94.64	− .11	5.36	+ .11	222,348
Mr97	94.70	94.70	94.58	94.59	− .12	5.41	+ .12	156,167
June	94.57	94.57	94.45	94.47	− .13	5.53	+ .13	143,141
Sept	94.47	94.47	94.32	94.36	− .14	5.64	+ .14	112,525
Dec	94.30	94.31	94.17	94.20	− .14	5.80	+ .14	87,357
Mr98	94.23	94.27	94.13	94.13	− .17	5.87	+ .17	75,674
June	94.14	94.17	94.03	94.06	− .14	5.94	+ .14	63,830
Sept	94.05	94.09	93.96	93.98	− .14	6.02	+ .14	50,001
Dec	93.96	93.97	93.84	93.86	− .14	6.14	+ .14	40,910
Mr99	93.91	93.95	93.84	93.84	− .14	6.16	+ .14	34,123
June	93.84	93.88	93.77	93.77	− .14	6.23	+ .14	29,049
Sept	93.82	93.82	93.71	93.71	− .14	6.29	+ .14	24,978
Dec	93.68	93.71	93.60	93.61	− .13	6.39	+ .14	20,911
Mr00	93.69	93.71	93.60	93.60	− .14	6.40	+ .14	19,577
June	93.63	93.65	93.54	93.54	− .14	6.46	+ .14	16,730
Sept	93.58	93.60	93.49	93.49	− .14	6.51	+ .14	13,200
Dec	93.51	93.51	93.40	93.40	− .14	6.60	+ .14	9,854
Mr01	93.51	93.51	93.40	93.40	− .14	6.60	+ .14	7,754
June	93.47	93.47	93.36	93.36	− .14	6.64	+ .14	8,048
Sept	93.43	93.43	93.32	93.32	− .14	6.68	+ .14	8,519
Dec	93.36	93.36	93.25	93.25	− .14	6.75	+ .14	8,126
Mr02	93.37	93.37	93.26	93.26	− .14	6.74	+ .14	6,765
June	93.33	93.33	93.22	93.22	− .14	6.78	+ .14	4,648
Sept	93.28	93.28	93.17	93.17	− .14	6.83	+ .14	4,360
Dec	93.21	93.21	93.12	93.10	− .14	6.90	+ .14	4,037
Mr03	93.20	93.20	93.12	93.10	− .14	6.90	+ .14	3,951
June	93.16	93.16	93.08	93.06	− .12	6.94	+ .12	3,498
Sept	93.12	93.12	93.04	93.02	− .12	6.98	+ .12	5,460
Dec	93.03	93.03	92.95	92.95	− .14	7.05	+ .14	3,776
Mr04	....	....	....	92.95	− .14	7.05	+ .14	4,479
June	....	....	....	92.91	− .14	7.09	+ .14	4,521
Sept	....	....	....	92.88	− .14	7.12	+ .14	4,234
Dec	....	....	....	92.80	− .14	7.20	+ .14	3,898
Mr05	....	....	....	92.81	− .14	7.19	+ .14	3,522
June	....	....	....	92.76	− .14	7.24	+ .14	2,586
Sept	....	....	....	92.71	− .14	7.29	+ .14	1,958

Est vol 284,471; vol Fr 278,224; open int 2,562,239, +9,575.

TREASURY BILLS (CME)-$1 mil.; pts. of 100%

	Open	High	Low	Settle	Chg	Discount Settle	Chg	Open Interest
Mar	95.04	95.05	95.01	95.01	− .04	4.99	+ .04	7,662
June	95.25	95.25	95.19	95.20	− .07	4.80	+ .07	2,304

Est vol 1,181; vol Fr 1,037; open int 10,002, +103.

LIBOR-1 MO. (CME)-$3,000,000; points of 100%

	Open	High	Low	Settle	Chg	Discount Settle	Chg	Open Interest
Dec	94.09	94.09	94.07	94.09	....	5.91	....	18,914
Ja96	94.33	94.34	94.29	94.30	− .04	5.70	+ .04	16,231
Feb	94.46	94.46	94.40	94.41	− .05	5.59	+ .05	11,510
Mar	94.54	94.54	94.53	94.52	− .05	5.48	+ .05	1,597
Apr	94.64	94.64	94.63	94.63	− .05	5.37	+ .05	....

Est vol 7,378; vol Fr 11,413; open int 49,142, +4,583.

Source: *The Wall Street Journal,* December 19, 1995.

Hypothetically, the Eurodollar contract requires the long position to make a $1,000,000, 90-day bank deposit with the short position at the maturity date. Unlike the Treasury bond and note futures just described, however, this contract requires all outstanding obligations to be settled in cash. This provision is necessary because the contract nominally requires the long position to make, and the short position to receive, a 90-day Euro-time deposit, something that the short position can't legally do unless it is a financial institution chartered for such business. The underlying interest rate is the three-month (i.e., 90-day) LIBOR that is quoted on a 360-day bank add-on basis. As we will see, arbitrage trading should drive the sequence of Eurodollar (or LIBOR) futures rates to equal the forward rates implied by the yield curve for interbank lending in the cash market. That is, in an efficient market, the futures rates should be close to the comparable implied forward rates.

In Figure 23.6, the quoted contract price for the March 1996 contract is 94.56, which is not an actual purchase price but merely an index calculated as 100 minus the settlement yield of 5.42 (percent). Eurodollar futures use this settlement price index because it conveniently preserves the inverse relation between price and yield. Thus, a long position in this contract can still be thought to "win" when prices rise—and the short position wins with falling prices—even though it is the opposite movement in the underlying interest rate that matters.

The minimum price change, or "tick," for this contract is one basis point and equals a $25 change in the value of the contract. Therefore, the *basis point value* of the contract is

$25 (= $1,000,000 × .0001 × 90/360). Thus, the five tick (−.05) decline in the price of the March contract means that LIBOR increased by five basis points from the prior day's settlement. This would benefit a person who acquired a short position at the close of the prior day inasmuch as he would have a locked-in borrowing cost for the 90-day period from March to June 1996 that is now five basis points lower than the market level. In fact, all sellers of this contract gained $125 per contract (i.e., $25 per tick times five ticks) in their margin accounts.

Finally, notice that the trading volume on the Eurodollar contract is less than that of the T-bond contract (shown in Figure 23.5), but the total open interest for all delivery months is over five times as great. Also, the Eurodollar open interest is spread over the various delivery dates to a greater extent than for the T-bond contract. In fact, the Eurodollar contract is the "deepest" financial futures contract available with, as noted, maturities going out 10 years. This makes it possible to hedge a LIBOR-based exposure a decade into the future. Brown and Smith interpreted these trading patterns as suggesting that T-bond futures are used in the market more as a speculative trading contract and that Eurodollar futures are used more frequently as a buy-and-hold hedging instrument.[14]

Figure 23.6 also lists quotes for the available Treasury bill futures traded at the IMM. This contract requires the long position to buy, and the short position to sell, a 90-day Treasury bill at maturity and can be settled in cash or with a physical exchange. Similar to the Eurodollar derivative, the T-bill contract is standardized to an amount of $1,000,000 so that each basis point change in the price (or rate) is worth $25 per contract. Again, the quoted price is a price index, 100 minus the settlement discount rate. In the absence of arbitrage, the T-bill futures rates should be close to the implied forward discount rates calculated from the cash market T-bill rates.

The T-bill contract at the IMM has lost much of its market share in recent years because it is dominated by competing contracts in two important applications. First, because many more corporate and banking transactions are tied to LIBOR—which can be viewed as a risk-free rate plus a credit spread—than to the T-bill rate, more end-users prefer the Eurodollar contract for hedging their interest rate exposures. Indeed, T-bill open interest is less than 1 percent that of the Eurodollar contract. Second, the T-bill contract is seldom used for speculative purposes in lieu of T-bond futures because the duration of the underlying instrument (a three-month T-bill) in the T-bill contract is so much shorter than that of the latter (a 20-year bond), meaning that its price will increase by less if the anticipated rate change is realized. Nevertheless, the following examples will show that T-bill futures play an important (if limited) economic role in financial markets.

SHORT-TERM INTEREST RATE FUTURES APPLICATIONS

Altering bond duration with futures contracts   An investor currently holds a six-month (i.e., 182-day) Treasury bill. Because of a fear that inflationary pressures will increase interest rates toward the end of the coming quarter, she would like to reduce her exposure by converting this position into a three-month T-bill. There are two ways to do this. First, she could sell her current holding and buy the shorter-term instrument she desires, a strategy that might entail nontrivial transaction costs. Second, she could accomplish the same change synthetically by supplementing her six-month bill with a short position in a T-bill futures contract maturing in 92 days. This is what she decides to do.

---

[14] Keith C. Brown and Donald J. Smith, "Recent Innovations in Interest Rate Risk Management and the Reintermediation of Commercial Banking," *Financial Management* 17, no. 4 (Winter 1988), pp. 45–58.

FIGURE 23.7

USING INTEREST RATE FUTURES TO ADJUST DURATION

Figure 23.7 shows the net effect of combining the long position in the 182-day T-bill with a short position in the T-bill futures (ignoring for simplicity the margin account on the derivative). In this illustration, the discount yield for the cash market instrument is 7.91 percent, leading to a price of $96 (per par value of 100). Also, the futures discount yield is 8 percent, that is, the investor is committed to deliver a 90-day T-bill at a price of $98 when the contract matures. The display assumes that she settles her futures obligation by giving up the remaining 90 days of her original T-bill in exchange for $98. This indicates that the combined position is equivalent to a 92-day Treasury bill with a current price of $96 and a "face" value of $98. Thus, shorting the futures contract has effectively converted a six-month holding into a three-month instrument with an implied discount yield of 7.99 percent (= [(98 − 96) ÷ 98][360 ÷ 92]).

Because Treasury bills, as zero-coupon securities, have durations equal to their maturities, a different way of interpreting this example is that the short position in a T-bill futures contract has allowed the investor to *reduce* the duration of her holding from six to three months. Conversely, although not shown in Figure 23.7, a long futures position can lengthen duration. For example, had the investor held a 92-day T-bill and supplemented it with a long T-bill futures contract maturing at the same date, she would have locked in her reinvestment rate for another 90-day T-bill position. Consequently, being long in the 92-day bill and long in the bill futures is equivalent to being long in a 182-day T-bill, which *increases* her investment duration from three to six months.[15]

Creating a synthetic fixed-rate funding with a Eurodollar strip Suppose that on March 15 a senior loan officer for a large regional bank is considering an investment scheme for lending $2,000,000 in temporary cash balances to a "large cap" manufacturing

---

[15] For a related discussion, see Jess B. Yawitz and William J. Marshall, "The Use of Futures in Immunized Portfolios," *Journal of Portfolio Management* 11, no. 2 (Winter 1985), pp. 51–58.

firm. The plan would last for one year and have the payment rate reset on a quarterly basis at LIBOR. At the planning stage, the LIBOR yield curve appears as follows:

90-day LIBOR	5.00%
180-day LIBOR	5.10
270-day LIBOR	5.20
360-day LIBOR	5.30

Given the debt market convention that the funding rates on floating-rate deal structures always are determined in advance and paid in arrears, she knows that her loan receipt for the first three months would be based on the prevailing 5.00 percent rate and be receivable in 90 days. Her concern is what her receipts might be in the subsequent three quarters and, specifically, she is worried that they may fall to an unacceptable level. Accordingly, she considers using the Eurodollar futures market to hedge her exposure.

As a prelude to checking futures contract price quotes, she calculates the forward rates implied by the current yield curve. Using money-market implied forward rate formulas shown in Appendix 23B, these computations generate:

$$_{180}IFR_{90} = \left[\frac{(.051)(180) - (.050)(90)}{(180 - 90)} \right] \left[\frac{1}{1 + \left(\frac{(90)(.050)}{360} \right)} \right] = 5.14\%$$

$$_{270}IFR_{180} = \left[\frac{(.052)(270) - (.051)(180)}{(270 - 180)} \right] \left[\frac{1}{1 + \left(\frac{(180)(.051)}{360} \right)} \right] = 5.27\%$$

$$_{360}IFR_{270} = \left[\frac{(.053)(360) - (.052)(270)}{(360 - 270)} \right] \left[\frac{1}{1 + \left(\frac{(270)(.052)}{360} \right)} \right] = 5.39\%$$

She checks with her trading desk for quotes on the relevant Eurodollar futures contracts and receives the following information:

Contract Expiration	Settlement Price
June	94.86
September	94.73
December	94.61

The futures settlement prices indicate LIBOR contract rates that are identical to the implied forward rates, suggesting there is no arbitrage potential between the cash and futures markets on this date.

To lock in her receipts for the $2,000,000 loan, the banker would go long a *strip* of Eurodollar futures contracts. That is, she takes long positions in two June contracts, two September contracts, and two December contracts. (Recall that the long position in a Eurodollar contract gains when the price index rises with a falling LIBOR; this is the protection she is seeking.) With these positions, her quarterly interest receipts will be fixed at the following levels:

$$\text{June Receipt} = (\$2{,}000{,}000)\left[\frac{(.0500)(90)}{360}\right] = \$25{,}000$$

$$\text{September Receipt} = (\$2{,}000{,}000)\left[\frac{(.0514)(90)}{360}\right] = \$25{,}700$$

$$\text{December Receipt} = (\$2{,}000{,}000)\left[\frac{(.0527)(90)}{360}\right] = \$26{,}350$$

$$\text{March (Next Year) Receipt} = (\$2{,}000{,}000)\left[\frac{(.0539)(90)}{360}\right] = \$26{,}950$$

Although these cash inflows are fixed in advance, they clearly differ in amount from quarter to quarter. To get a better indication of her overall return, the banker asks herself the following question: What quarterly annuity payment does this sequence of receipts imply? This amount can be calculated as the solution to:

$$\frac{\$25{,}000}{\left[1 + \frac{(.050)(90)}{360}\right]} + \frac{\$25{,}700}{\left[1 + \frac{(.051)(180)}{360}\right]} + \frac{\$26{,}350}{\left[1 + \frac{(.052)(270)}{360}\right]} + \frac{\$26{,}950}{\left[1 + \frac{(.053)(360)}{360}\right]}$$

$$= \frac{\text{Annuity}}{\left[1 + \frac{(.050)(90)}{360}\right]} + \frac{\text{Annuity}}{\left[1 + \frac{(.051)(180)}{360}\right]} + \frac{\text{Annuity}}{\left[1 + \frac{(.052)(270)}{360}\right]} + \frac{\text{Annuity}}{\left[1 + \frac{(.053)(360)}{360}\right]}$$

Solving this formula for "Annuity" gives a value of \$25,989.38, where the discount rates are from the prevailing cash market LIBOR curve. Finally, notice that annuity payment, when expressed on a full 360-day percentage basis, is:

$$\left[\frac{\$25{,}989.38}{\$2{,}000{,}000}\right]\left[\frac{360}{90}\right] = 5.198\%$$

which is a time-weighted average of the 90-day spot LIBOR and the series of three implied forward rates.

Creating a TED spread   As noted earlier, one of the features that makes the Eurodollar futures contract such a popular hedging vehicle is the rate it is based on—three-month LIBOR. This rate can be thought of as equivalent to the three-month T-bill yield *plus* a risk premium (i.e., credit spread). Sometimes, bond traders will have a view on future movements in this credit spread; for example, a trader might believe the current difference between the LIBOR and T-bill yield is too narrow and that it will soon widen. The problem with trying to play this view with a short position in the Eurodollar contract alone, however, is even if the trader is right about the spread, the general level of interest rates could still decline by more than enough to offset any spread gains.

The solution to this dilemma is to isolate the credit spread component in LIBOR through a strategy known as the *TED* (Treasury/EuroDollar) *spread*. The TED spread is created by taking simultaneous, but opposite, positions in both a Eurodollar and T-bill futures contract having the same maturity. In the parlance of the market, we have the following definitions.

Long a TED Spread = (Long T-Bill Futures) + (Short Eurodollar Futures)

Short a TED Spread = (Short T-Bill Futures) + (Long Eurodollar Futures)

Notice that a long position in a TED spread will gain when the credit spread increases; the short TED spread benefits from a narrowing of the credit spread.

To see this, consider the following example. Suppose that in early August you observe the following prices in the Eurodollar and T-bill futures markets:

	T-Bill	Eurodollar	Spread
September contracts	95.24	94.80	44 bp
December contracts	94.68	94.11	57 bp
March contracts	94.42	93.86	56 bp

Recall that the difference between the T-bill and Eurodollar price indexes is the credit spread built into the Eurodollar contract for a particular maturity.

If you believe the economy will remain sluggish for an extended period of time and that credit spreads currently are too narrow in the short-term contract, you would want to take a long TED spread position (i.e., short the Eurodollar futures and buy the T-bill contract). After you establish this position using the September contracts, the Federal Reserve Board tightens rates again so that by mid-September the following prices prevail when you unwind the strategy:

New September T-bill contract	94.55
New September Eurodollar contract	93.95
New spread	0.60

This new spread is more closely aligned with the December and March contracts. The profit on your transaction is calculated as (New TED spread) − (Original TED spread), or (94.55 − 93.95) − (95.24 − 94.80) = 16 basis points.

With each contract standardized so that a basis point is worth $25, the profit per contract-pair from this trade would be (16 × $25) = $400. Another way to see this profit is that you made an 85 basis point profit on the short position in the Eurodollar contract (= 94.80 − 93.95) but lost 69 basis points on the long T-bill contract (= 94.55 − 95.24). However, if both rates had declined, you still would have made money if the T-bill yield had fallen by more than LIBOR.

STOCK INDEX FUTURES   Another important form of financial futures contracting specifies an equity index as the underlying asset. In this section, we consider the basics of stock index futures trading and discuss two applications for these instruments, including a popular form of computer-assisted trading known as stock index arbitrage.

STOCK INDEX FUTURES CONTRACT FUNDAMENTALS   Like interest rate futures, stock index futures were originally intended to provide a hedge against movements in an underlying financial asset. We have just seen that some interest rate futures can be settled with either a cash or physical transfer. As detailed in Chapter 5, however, the underlying financial asset for a stock index futures contract is a hypothetical creation that does not exist in practice and therefore cannot be delivered to settle a contract. Thus, stock index futures can only be settled in cash, similar to the Eurodollar (i.e., LIBOR) contract.

Stock index futures are intended to provide general hedges against stock market movements and can be applied to either whole (i.e., diversified) portfolios or individual stocks. Hedging an individual stock with an index futures contract is done in an attempt to isolate the unsystematic portion of that security's risk. Additionally, stock index futures often are

FIGURE 23.8   **STOCK INDEX FUTURES QUOTATIONS**

S&P 500 INDEX (CME) $500 times index

	Open	High	Low	Settle	Chg		High	Low	Open Interest
Mr96	622.25	622.60	611.35	611.60	−	11.15	629.70	511.00	186,971
June	625.00	625.00	616.90	617.00	−	11.15	635.05	554.25	6,374
Sept	625.50	627.50	621.50	621.70	−	11.20	639.75	589.95	1,973

Est vol 119,909; vol Fr 75,734; open int 264,299, −489.
Indx prelim High 616.32; Low 606.13; Close 606.81−9.53

S&P MIDCAP 400 (CME) $500 times index

Mr96	213.70	213.70	210.40	211.45	−	4.25	224.30	186.90	10,576

Est vol 1,143; vol Fr 1,221; open int 15,749, +343.
The index: High 212.43; Low 208.13; Close 208.23−4.26

NIKKEI 225 STOCK AVERAGE (CME)-$5 times index

Mar	19530.	19380.	19220.	19315.	−	155	19665.	14605.	25,614
June	19450.	19450.	19330.	19355.	−	155	19450.	14655.	259

Est vol 1,841; vol Fr 1,325; open int 25,901, +674.
The index: High 19298.92; Low 19311.08; Close 19311.08 35.47

GSCI (CME)-$250 times nearby index

Feb	191.30	193.30	191.30	192.90	+	1.50	191.90	177.30	13,745

Est vol 510; vol Fr 495; open int 13,745, +31.
The index: High 198.20; Low 195.33; Close 197.93+2.22

CAC-40 STOCK INDEX (MATIF)-FFr 200 per index pt.

Dec	1872.5	1872.5	1825.0	1826.0	−44.0	1924.0	1732.5	36,249
Jan	1880.5	1880.5	1833.0	1833.5	−44.0	2038.0	1745.0	6,944
Fb96	1880.0	1888.0	1865.5	1841.5	−43.5	2030.0	1809.0	746
Mar	1894.0	1894.0	1850.5	1849.0	−44.0	2043.0	1779.0	8,606
Sept	1864.0	1864.0	1864.0	1842.0	−44.5	1924.0	1777.0	6,201

Est vol 22,450; vol Fri 29,731 ; open int 52,545, −1,085.

FT-SE 100 INDEX (LIFFE)-£25 per index point

Mr96	3658.0	3664.0	3592.0	3597.0	−	60.0	3721.0	3490.0	66,199
June	....	....	....	3598.0	−	60.0	3707.0	3492.5	1,116

Est vol 13,283; vol Fri 15,489; open int 67,315, +2,468.

Source: *The Wall Street Journal,* December 19, 1995.

used to convert entire stock portfolios into synthetic riskless positions to exploit an apparent mispricing between stock in the cash and futures markets. This strategy, commonly called **stock index arbitrage**, is the most prominent example of a wider class of computer-assisted trading schemes known as *program trading.*

Figure 23.8 lists quotes for futures contracts on both U.S. and foreign stock indexes, including the Standard & Poor's 500, the Standard & Poor's Midcap 400, the Nikkei (Japan) 225, the CAC (France) 40, and the FT-SE (England) 100. For instance, a person entering the long position of the March 1996 S&P 500 contract at the settlement price of 611.60 obligates himself to the theoretical purchase of 500 "shares" of the S&P 500 on the third Friday of March for \$305,800 (= 611.60 × 500). The minimum contract price movement is 0.05 point, which equals \$25. Thus, if the actual level of the S&P index on the contract settlement date turned out to be 610.55, the long position would lose \$525, or \$25 times 21 "ticks" [(611.60 − 610.55) ÷ 0.05)].

STOCK INDEX FUTURES VALUATION AND INDEX ARBITRAGE   Earlier we established that the key to understanding the pricing of futures contracts is the concept of arbitrage. To see how this works for index contracts, suppose that at date 0 an investor takes the following positions: (1) purchases a portfolio of stock representing the underlying stock index for S_0, and (2) goes short a stock index future (with an expiration date of T) for $F_{0,T}$. Assume further that in order to avoid making any investment at date 0, the funds for the long position are borrowed at the risk-free rate of RFR. Upon unwinding this position at date t, the net profit (Π) is given by:

$$\Pi = (F_{0,T} - F_{t,T}) + (S_t - S_0 - S_0 RFR_t + S_0 d_t) = (F_{0,T} - F_{t,T}) + [S_t - S_0 (1 + RFR_t - d_t)]$$

where

d_t = the dividend yield accruing to the stocks comprising the index between dates 0 and t.

In other words, the profit you make on this short hedge in stock index futures will consist of two components: the net difference in the futures position and the net difference in the underlying index position (after adding borrowing costs and subtracting dividends received from the initial purchase).

Now assume the long position in the stock portfolio is held until the expiration of the futures contract (i.e., date $t = T$). The advantage of doing this is that the cash settlement feature of the stock index futures contract ensures that the futures price and index level will converge. That is, at date T we will have $F_{t,T} = S_T$, which means that the short hedge profit (Π) equation can be written:

$$\Pi = [F_{0,T} - S_0 - S_0(RFR_t - d_T)].$$

As before, $RFR_t - d_T$ is called the net cost of carry and represents the difference between the borrowing cost paid and the dividend received.

If the dividend yield is known at date 0, this position is riskless and requires no initial investment. Thus, buying and selling among arbitrageurs trading in both the stock and futures markets should ensure that $\Pi = 0$. Thus, the futures price set at date 0 will be:

$$F_{0,T} = S_0 + S_0(RFR_t - d_T).$$

As in the cost of carry model discussed earlier, the futures price could be set below the spot level of the index if $(RFR_t - d_T) < 0$. That is, the index futures contract will be priced lower than the current level of the stock price whenever the dividends received by holding stock exceed the borrowing cost.

To see how this parity relationship helps establish the appropriate level of the stock index futures price, assume that one "share" of the S&P 500 index can be purchased for 605 and that the dividend yield and risk-free rate over the holding period are 1.5 percent and 2.5 percent, respectively. Under these conditions, the contract price on a six-month S&P 500 futures should be $F_{0,0.5} = 605 + 605(.025 - .015) = 611.05$. Now suppose you construct a short hedge position by: (1) purchasing the index at 605, and (2) selling the futures at 611.05. If the position is held to expiration, your profit at various expiration date levels of the S&P will be as shown in Table 23.1. Notice that your net profit remains constant no matter the level of the index at the expiration date. More importantly, this net profit can be expressed as $15.13 \div 605 = 2.5$ percent, which is the assumed cost of borrowing.

IMPLEMENTING AN INDEX ARBITRAGE STRATEGY   What if the parity condition between the stock index and the stock index futures price does not hold? Could you design a portfolio to take advantage of the situation? Suppose that in the last example the actual contract price on a six-month S&P 500 futures was 613.05 ($F_{0,T} > S_0 + S_0(RFR_t - d_T)$). You could then implement the following arbitrage transaction: (1) short the stock index future at 613.05, (2) borrow money at 2.5 percent to purchase the stock index at 605, and (3) hold the position until maturity, collecting 9.08 in dividends and then selling the stock to repay your loan. Your net profit at maturity would be $613.05 - 605 - 605(.025 - .015) = 2.00$. However, since this strategy was riskless (i.e., the sales price of the stock and the dividends were known in advance) and none of your own capital was used, it is an arbitrage profit.

TABLE 23.1   **STOCK INDEX FUTURES VALUATION EXAMPLE**

	S&P AT EXPIRATION IS:				
	590	600	610	620	630
Net futures profit	21.05	11.05	1.05	(9.95)	(19.95)
Net index profit	(15.00)	(5.00)	5.00	15.00	25.00
Dividend	9.08	9.08	9.08	9.08	9.08
Net profit	15.13	15.13	15.13	15.13	15.13

This is *stock index arbitrage*, which is possible whenever the index futures price is set at a level sufficiently different from the theoretical value for $F_{0,T}$ to account for trading costs. For example, if the actual level of $F_{0,T} < S_0 + S_0(RFR_t - d_T)$, the previous strategy could be reversed: (1) buy the stock index future at a price of $F_{0,T}$, (2) lend money at RFR_t and short the stock index at S_0, and (3) cover the position at the expiration date of the futures contract. Indeed, index arbitrage is a very popular form of trading. Figure 23.9 reports that about 40 percent of all computer-assisted program trading used this strategy. Further, program trading accounted for about a third of trading volume on the New York Stock Exchange, a figure that is about twice as large as normal because this period includes the expiration date of the December contract.

One important side effect of this sort of trading activity is that stock index futures prices tend to stay close to the theoretical levels expressed by the preceding valuation equation. To see why this occurs, notice that the arbitrage "prescription" for a futures settlement price that is too low (too high) is to go long (short) in the contract which, when done in sufficient volume, adjusts the price in the proper direction. The empirical evidence tends to support this view, particularly after transaction costs and other trading realities are considered. Cornell, for instance, found that stock index futures prices tracked their model values more closely as the market matured, although Keim and Smirlock detected some temporal (i.e., day-of-the-week, January) pricing patterns.[16] In response to the allegation that index arbitrage caused the worldwide stock market crash of October 1987, Roll documented that countries with the greatest level of program trading activity experienced less pronounced price declines.[17] This finding is consistent with the notion that index arbitrage reduces volatility by stabilizing cash and futures prices.

A STOCK INDEX FUTURES APPLICATION

Isolating the unsystematic risk of an individual stock   In Chapter 11, we demonstrated how stock index futures could alter the systematic risk of an otherwise well-diversified portfolio. When the holding is an individual stock, this process can isolate the unique attributes of the company. Recall from Chapter 1 that:

$$\text{Total Stock Risk} = \text{Systematic Risk} + \text{Unsystematic Risk}$$

[16] Bradford Cornell, "Taxes and the Pricing of Stock Index Futures: Empirical Results," *Journal of Futures Markets* 5, no. 1 (1985), pp. 89–101, and Donald B. Keim and Michael Smirlock, "Pricing Patterns in Stock Index Futures," in *The Handbook of Stock Index Futures and Options*, edited by F. Fabozzi and G. Kipnis (Homewood, IL: Dow Jones-Irwin, 1989).

[17] Richard Roll, "The International Crash of October 1987," *Financial Analysts Journal* 44, no. 5 (September–October 1988), pp. 19–35.

| FIGURE 23.9 | PROGRAM TRADING AND STOCK INDEX ARBITRAGE |

PROGRAM TRADING

NEW YORK — Program trading in the week ended Dec. 15 accounted for 30.9%, or an average 137.2 million daily shares, of New York Stock Exchange volume. This included program trading associated with the Dec. 15 quarterly expiration of stock-index options and futures.

Brokerage firms executed an additional 98.8 million daily shares of program trading away from the Big Board, mostly on foreign markets. Program trading is the simultaneous purchase or sale of at least 15 different stocks with a total value of $1 million or more.

Of the program total, 39.8% involved stock-index arbitrage, up from 26.5% the previous week. In this strategy, traders dart between stocks and stock-index options and futures to capture fleeting price differences.

Some 42.6% of trading reflected firms' trading for their own accounts, or principal trading, while 54.3% involved trading for customers. Another 3.1% was designated as customer facilitation, in which firms use principal positions to facilitate customer trades.

Of the five most-active firms, Morgan Stanley, First Boston and Nomura Securities did most of their trading for their own accounts; Susquehanna Brokerage Services and First Options traded all for customers.

NYSE PROGRAM TRADING
Volume (in millions of shares) for the week ending Dec. 15, 1995

Top 15 Firms	Index Arbitrage	Derivative-Related*	Other Strategies	Total
Morgan Stanley	1.0	...	97.6	98.6
First Boston	52.0	...	31.1	83.1
Susquehanna Bkrg. Srvs.	66.3	...	3.5	69.8
Nomura Securities	24.1	...	23.6	47.7
First Options	5.6	32.6	3.1	41.3
Bear Stearns	27.5	...	12.8	40.3
Salomon Bros.	...	0.4	33.2	33.6
Goldman Sachs	...	...	31.2	31.2
Lehman Bros.	13.7	0.2	14.2	28.1
Spear Leeds	13.9	...	14.0	27.9
Guzman & Co.	...	...	22.7	22.7
Deutsche Bank	22.1	...	...	22.1
Merrill Lynch	...	...	20.5	20.5
Thomas Williams	8.1	...	12.3	20.4
Smith Barney	...	...	12.7	12.7
OVERALL TOTAL	272.9	33.3	379.9	686.1

*Other derivative-related strategies besides index arbitrage
Source: New York Stock Exchange

Source: *The Wall Street Journal,* December 22, 1995.

with the systematic component representing about 25–30 percent of the total risk for the typical firm. Thus, using stock index futures to adjust the stock's beta to zero effectively isolates the unsystematic portion of risk.

To see how this might work, suppose that in mid-December you own 50,000 shares of Merck, a multinational pharmaceutical firm. The current price of Merck stock is $64.875, and you calculate the company's beta at 1.15. You like the stock as an investment because of the quality of its management and some other unique attributes of the firm, but you are concerned that during the first two quarters of the new year the aggregate stock market might undergo a sizable correction that could more than offset any firm-specific gains.

To protect yourself, you decide to sell June S&P 500 futures contracts, which are currently trading at a settlement price of 617.00. At this price, the implied dollar value of a single contract is $308,500. The current value of your Merck stock is $3,243,750. Since the stock's beta is defined as $\rho \, [\sigma_{\Delta S} \div \sigma_{\Delta F}]$, the optimal hedge ratio formula developed earlier can be adapted to provide the appropriate hedge ratio:

$$N^* = \left[\frac{\text{Market Value of Spot Position}}{\text{Value Implied by Futures Contract}} \right] \beta$$

$$= [(\$3,243,750) \div (\$308,500)] \, (1.15) = 12.09$$

So, you decide to short 12 contracts.

Now suppose that by mid-June when your futures position expires, the S&P 500 index settles at a level of 607.00 while the price of Merck stock has increased to $65.875. Although you have made a modest profit on your common stock holding (i.e., $50,000, or 1.54 percent), you will also benefit from a trading profit on the futures position of $60,000 (= (12)(617 − 607)($500)). As a result, your total return is $110,000, which expressed as a percentage of your original investment of $3,243,750 is equivalent to an unsystematic appreciation in Merck's stock of 3.4 percent. Notice that the difference between this amount and the gross increase of 1.54 percent on Merck stock is approximately equal to the 1.6 percent (= (607 ÷ 617) − 1) that the stock market fell.

CURRENCY FORWARDS AND FUTURES

Whether in the spot or forward markets, foreign exchange (FX) transactions often involve a confusing blend of unique terminology and market conventions. Although these conventions are easily assimilated, they represent an initial barrier to understanding how FX deals work. Thus, we begin our analysis of currency derivatives with a brief overview of some of the fundamental features of these products.

THE MECHANICS OF CURRENCY TRANSACTIONS   The market for foreign currency is no different than any other market in that buyer and seller negotiate for the exchange of a certain amount of a predetermined commodity at a fixed cash price. The challenge in FX transactions is that the "commodity" involved is someone else's currency. This means that the transaction can be viewed in two ways. For example, suppose that Company A agrees to pay 100 U.S. dollars to Company B in exchange for 67 British pounds. In this case, is Company A buying sterling (GBP) or selling dollars (USD)?[18] Similarly, is Company B selling pounds or buying dollars? The answer is that both are correct, depending on one's point of view.

Because of this dual interpretation, the price for all FX transactions also can be quoted in two ways. Assuming that Company A is a U.S.-based firm, it would probably think of the transaction as the purchase of 67 pounds at a cost of 100 dollars, which would yield the price of USD 1.4925/GBP (= 100/67). This method of quoting FX prices is called the *direct*, or *American*, convention. Notice that under this convention, the pound (i.e., the foreign currency from the U.S. firm's perspective) is treated as the commodity, and its price per unit is expressed in terms of dollars. On the other hand, if Company B is a British corporation, its managers would likely think of prices in terms of the amount of sterling they have to pay to acquire dollars. Here that amount translates into a price of GBP 0.67/USD. Treating the dollar as the commodity yields the *indirect*, or *European*, quotation method. Of course, the direct and indirect quotes are just *reciprocals* of one another, as they describe the same transaction from two different perspectives.

Figure 23.10 shows a representative set of FX quotes. Four prices are listed beside each currency. The first two columns report the current and previous days' dollar price, respec-

---

[18] Currency traders often use three letter abbreviations to denote a particular currency. Some of the more common abbreviations include USD (U.S. dollars), CAD (Canadian dollars), GBP (British pounds), JPY (Japanese yen), CHF (Swiss franc), DEM (German mark), FRF (French franc), and ECU (European currency unit). For a more complete listing, see Gary L. Gastineau, *Dictionary of Financial Risk Management* (Chicago, IL: Probus Publishing, 1992).

FIGURE 23.10   **SPOT AND FORWARD CURRENCY QUOTATIONS**

EXCHANGE RATES

Monday, December 18, 1995

The New York foreign exchange selling rates below apply to trading among banks in amounts of $1 million and more, as quoted at 3 p.m. Eastern time by Bankers Trust Co., Dow Jones Telerate Inc. and other sources. Retail transactions provide fewer units of foreign currency per dollar.

Country	U.S. $ equiv. Mon	Fri	Currency per U.S. $ Mon	Fri
Argentina (Peso)	1.0002	1.0000	.9998	1.0000
Australia (Dollar)	.7406	.7428	1.3502	1.3463
Austria (Schilling)	.09910	.09846	10.091	10.156
Bahrain (Dinar)	2.6527	2.6525	.3770	.3770
Belgium (Franc)	.03401	.03370	29.399	29.673
Brazil (Real)	1.0347	1.0334	.9665	.9677
Britain (Pound)	1.5415	1.5374	.6487	.6504
30-Day Forward	1.5382	1.5354	.6501	.6513
90-Day Forward	1.5381	1.5337	.6502	.6520
180-Day Forward	1.5354	1.5312	.6513	.6531
Canada (Dollar)	.7282	.7287	1.3732	1.3724
30-Day Forward	.7263	.7288	1.3768	1.3722
90-Day Forward	.7260	.7286	1.3773	1.3725
180-Day Forward	.7251	.7279	1.3791	1.3739
Chile (Peso)	.002462	.002464	406.25	405.80
China (Renminbi)	.1202	.1202	8.3180	8.3171
Colombia (Peso)	.001013	.001012	987.50	987.80
Czech. Rep. (Koruna) .				
Commercial rate	.03751	.03747	26.658	26.691
Denmark (Krone)	.1806	.1787	5.5385	5.5950
Ecuador (Sucre)				
Floating rate	.0003423	.0003429	2921.50	2916.50
Finland (Markka)	.2322	.2304	4.3065	4.3411
France (Franc)	.2033	.2014	4.9185	4.9655
30-Day Forward	.2033	.2016	4.9182	4.9600
90-Day Forward	.2034	.2017	4.9167	4.9568
180-Day Forward	.2034	.2019	4.9155	4.9538
Germany (Mark)	.7000	.6927	1.4285	1.4436
30-Day Forward	.7009	.6939	1.4267	1.4412
90-Day Forward	.7029	.6959	1.4227	1.4369
180-Day Forward	.7061	.6991	1.4162	1.4304
Greece (Drachma)	.004229	.004198	236.48	238.23
Hong Kong (Dollar)	.1293	.1293	7.7347	7.7348
Hungary (Forint)	.007195	.007183	138.99	139.21
India (Rupee)	.02859	.02861	34.980	34.955
Indonesia (Rupiah)	.0004374	.0004376	2286.00	2285.00
Ireland (Punt)	1.5950	1.5865	.6270	.6303
Israel (Shekel)	.3212	.3206	3.1135	3.1187
Italy (Lira)	.0006274	.0006271	1594.00	1594.73
Japan (Yen)	.009852	.009804	101.50	102.00
30-Day Forward	.009899	.009851	101.02	101.51
90-Day Forward	.009984	.009936	100.16	100.64
180-Day Forward	.01011	.01006	98.900	99.370
Jordan (Dinar)	1.4104	1.4104	.7090	.7090
Kuwait (Dinar)	3.3389	3.3333	.2995	.3000
Lebanon (Pound)	.0006260	.0006258	1597.50	1598.00
Malaysia (Ringgit)	.3932	.3932	2.5435	2.5430
Malta (Lira)	2.8243	2.8185	.3541	.3548
Mexico (Peso)				
Floating rate	.1294	.1291	7.7300	7.7450
Netherland (Guilder)	.6252	.6188	1.5996	1.6160
New Zealand (Dollar)	.6527	.6525	1.5322	1.5326
Norway (Krone)	.1583	.1569	6.3190	6.3746
Pakistan (Rupee)	.02923	.02923	34.216	34.216
Peru (new Sol)	.4322	.4315	2.3140	2.3175
Philippines (Peso)	.03817	.03814	26.200	26.220
Poland (Zloty)	.3966	.3948	2.5217	2.5330
Portugal (Escudo)	.006666	.006605	150.01	151.40
Russia (Ruble) (a)	.0002159	.0002159	4632.00	4632.00
Saudi Arabia (Riyal)	.2666	.2666	3.7504	3.7506
Singapore (Dollar)	.7072	.7062	1.4140	1.4160
Slovak Rep. (Koruna)	.03355	.03355	29.810	29.810
South Africa (Rand)	.2728	.2727	3.6662	3.6672
South Korea (Won)	.001296	.001296	771.75	771.65
Spain (Peseta)	.008204	.008133	121.89	122.95
Sweden (Krona)	.1517	.1509	6.5912	6.6257
Switzerland (Franc)	.8715	.8593	1.1474	1.1638
30-Day Forward	.8747	.8622	1.1433	1.1598
90-Day Forward	.8799	.8678	1.1365	1.1523
180-Day Forward	.8881	.8757	1.1259	1.1419
Taiwan (Dollar)	.03657	.03661	27.342	27.317
Thailand (Baht)	.03977	.03975	25.145	25.160
Turkey (Lira)	.00001767	.00001771	56582.00	56449.50
United Arab (Dirham)	.2723	.2723	3.6731	3.6730
Uruguay (New Peso)				
Financial	.1418	.1420	7.0500	7.0400
Venezuela (Bolivar)	.003453	.003453	289.62	289.63
SDR	1.4859	1.4839	.6730	.6739
ECU	1.2836	1.2731	....	....

Special Drawing Rights (SDR) are based on exchange rates for the U.S., German, British, French, and Japanese currencies. Source: International Monetary Fund.

European Currency Unit (ECU) is based on a basket of community currencies.

a-fixing, Moscow Interbank Currency Exchange

Source: *The Wall Street Journal,* December 19, 1995.

tively, for trading one unit of that currency (i.e., direct quotes). For instance, the prevailing price of a Norwegian krone on that date was USD 0.1583, which was 0.14 cent higher than the day before. The last two columns express these same prices in indirect terms (e.g., NKR 6.3190/USD = 1 ÷ USD 0.1583/NKR). Thus, the terms of a spot FX transaction can be structured to meet the particular needs of the counterparties involved.

Another important aspect of the FX markets highlighted by this display is that although many currencies trade in the spot market, relatively few also quote prices for forward transactions. In this list, only the British, Canadian, French, German, Japanese, and Swiss currencies have forward contracts. These contracts, which are negotiated in the OTC market with a currency dealer (Banker's Trust in this case), carry maturities one, three, and six months into the future. For example, an investor wishing to buy Swiss francs would pay USD 0.8715 per franc if the transaction was completed immediately, USD 0.8747 if the transaction was negotiated now but consummated in 30 days, and USD 0.8799 or USD 0.8881 for exchanges completed in 90 or 180 days, respectively.

In the situation where it costs increasingly more dollars to buy the same franc the farther out in the future it is delivered, the dollar is said to be trading at a **forward discount** to the franc. Conversely, the franc is at a **forward premium** to the dollar. Notice that this relationship depends on the currencies being compared. In this set of quotes, the U.S. dollar is trading at a forward discount to the French franc, German mark, Japanese yen, and Swiss franc, while it is at a forward premium to the British pound and Canadian dollar. It should come as no surprise by now that the relationship between the spot and forward FX rates is not a random one. In fact, we will see shortly that whether a particular currency trades at a discount or a premium to another depends on the relative level of the investment rates in the two countries.

Figure 23.11 lists quotes for a sample of exchange-traded currency futures contracts. These specific instruments are traded at the International Monetary Market at the CME. Each contract follows the convention that the U.S. dollar is the native monetary unit and the foreign currency is the commodity, meaning that all prices are quoted using the direct method. Also, notice that these contracts are standardized to deliver a set number of units of the foreign currency on a specific date in the future. For instance, the March Mexican peso contract negotiated on that date required the long position to purchase—and the short position to deliver—500,000 pesos at the price of USD 0.11660 per peso. By convention, all currency futures on the IMM mature on the third Wednesday of the stated delivery

---

FIGURE 23.11   **CURRENCY FUTURES QUOTATIONS**

	Open	High	Low	Settle	Change	Lifetime High	Low	Open Interest
JAPAN YEN (CME)-12.5 million yen; $ per yen (.00)								
Dec	.9840	.9849	.8930	.9832	+ .0038	1.2813	.8930	21,830
Mr96	.9925	.9992	.9925	.9983	+ .0055	1.2990	.9800	55,538
June	1.0100	1.0110	1.0100	1.0109	+ .0056	1.3130	.9950	730
Sept	....	....	....	1.235	+ .0057	1.2085	1.0095	157
Est vol 11,079; vol Fr 28,040; open int 78,334, −7.								
DEUTSCHEMARK (CME)-125,000 marks; $ per mark								
Dec	.6960	.6976	.6930	.6971	+ .0042	.7490	.6580	26,554
Mr96	.6972	.7030	.6967	.7028	+ .0068	.7505	.6250	49,029
June	.7020	.7058	.7017	.7060	+ .0068	.7315	.6765	2,756
Sept	....	....	....	.7088	+ .0067	.7312	.6812	1,085
Est vol 19,724; vol Fr 25,573; open int 79,424, −2514.								
CANADIAN DOLLAR (CME)-100,000 dlrs.; $ per Can $								
Dec	.7283	.7287	.7258	.7260	− .0021	.7530	.6895	16,156
Mr96	.7285	.7290	.7255	.7257	− .0021	.7512	.6900	30,464
June	.7282	.7282	.7249	.7250	− .0021	.7500	.6930	2,048
Sept	.7240	.7250	.7240	.7240	− .0021	.7490	.7170	654
Dec	.7255	.7257	.7239	.7230	− .0021	.7460	.7130	630
Est vol 4,621; vol Fr 8,023; open int 50,028, −259.								
BRITISH POUND (CME)-62,500 pds.; $ per pound								
Dec	1.5380	1.5400	1.5366	1.5376	+ .0004	1.6440	1.5240	27,317
Mr96	1.5352	1.5390	1.5334	1.5378	+ .0034	1.6140	1.5200	34,977
Est vol 9,140; vol Fr 13,060; open int 62,320, +424.								
SWISS FRANC (CME)-125,000 francs; $ per franc								
Dec	.8674	.8692	.8665	.8670	+ .0075	.9145	.7834	16,737
Mr96	.8684	.8811	.8684	.8797	+ .0119	.9220	.8240	35,527
June	.8820	.8889	.8820	.8876	+ .0120	.9120	.8228	821
Est vol 15,820; vol Fr 13,012; open int 53,187, −616.								
AUSTRALIAN DOLLAR (CME)-100,000 dlrs.; $ per A.$								
Dec	.7415	.7425	.7415	.7425	+ .0009	.7660	.7025	8,728
Mr96	.7381	.7390	.7375	.7380	− .0005	.7610	.7080	4,265
Est vol 943; vol Fr 1,578; open int 13,033, +216.								
MEXICAN PESO (CME)-500,000 new Mex. peso, $ per MP								
Dec	.12850	.12920	.12850	.12920	+ .0050	.15000	.11400	1,980
Mr96	.11700	.11720	.11650	.11660	+ .0010	.14170	10280	8,750
June	.10750	.10850	.10710	.10810	+ .0090	.13400	.09020	3,435
Sept	.10040	.10050	.10040	.10010	− .0040	.12700	.08600	644
Est vol 920; vol Fr 984; open int 14,809, −155.								

Source: *The Wall Street Journal,* December 19, 1995.

month and can be settled with a wire transfer of the foreign currency. Notice that the dollar traded at a substantial forward premium to the peso at this point in time.

INTEREST RATE PARITY AND COVERED INTEREST ARBITRAGE   A key concept in FX risk management is **interest rate parity**, a condition that specifies the "no arbitrage" relationship between spot and forward FX rates (as priced into the futures contracts) and the level of interest rates in each currency. This connection is best seen through an example. Suppose that an institutional investor has USD 100,000 to invest for one year and is considering two different riskless alternatives. The first strategy entails the purchase of a U.S. Treasury bill. Assume that under current market conditions, the effective U.S. dollar risk-free interest rate is 4.50 percent per annum for a one-year maturity, so that a direct T-bill investment would return USD 104,500 at the end of the 12 months.

For the second strategy, suppose that the investor also can sell the USD 100,000 in the spot market at the current exchange rate of DEM 1.70/USD (or, equivalently, USD 0.5882/DEM) to obtain a total of 170,000 German marks. We assume that that amount can then be invested in a German risk-free security (i.e., bund) at an annualized rate of 7.00 percent, returning DEM 181,900 at the end of the year. Of course, to make this return comparable to the dollar-denominated proceeds from the first strategy, the marks will have to be converted back into U.S. currency. If this translation is negotiated at the end of the investment, however, the investor will be subjected to foreign exchange risk in that he will not know at date 0 what the DEM/USD exchange rate will be at date T. Thus, to make the second strategy riskless, the investor must enter into a forward contract to exchange marks back into dollars at the end of the year. The question then is what would the exchange rate priced into a one-year forward contract have to be at date 0 to leave the investor indifferent between these two strategies?

These investments are depicted in Figure 23.12. The essence of the arbitrage argument is that the one-year forward FX rate must be such that USD 104,500 equals DEM 181,900. Otherwise, an arbitrage opportunity would exist, or at least a dominating investment choice. Therefore, the forward contract rate consistent with interest rate parity is DEM 1.7407/USD (= 181,900 ÷ 104,500) on an indirect basis, or USD 0.5745/DEM quoted directly. Notice that this is a breakeven value in the sense that it allows the 4.50 percent

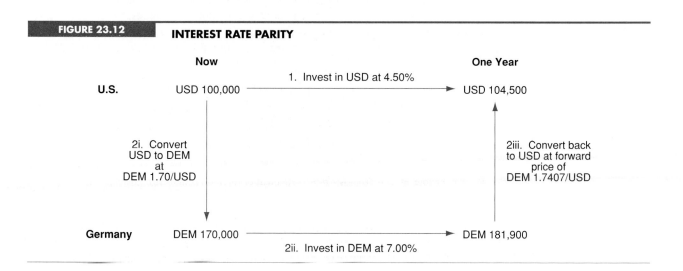

FIGURE 23.12   **INTEREST RATE PARITY**

investment return in the United States to be equal to the 7.00 percent available in Germany when the two are converted to the same currency. That is, the German return must be "deflated" by 250 basis points to leave the investor indifferent between the two strategies. This reduction occurs because, to invest in the mark-denominated security, the investor buys marks at a price of USD 0.5882/DEM but must sell them back in the forward market at the lower price of USD 0.5745/DEM. Thus, the loss on the roundtrip currency translation required in the second strategy adjusts its net return down to the 4.50 percent available on the direct dollar investment.[19]

If the actual one-year forward contract FX rate were higher than this breakeven level—say, for instance, DEM 1.77/USD—the currency translation loss would be greater than 250 basis points, leaving the dollar-based strategy the more profitable choice. Given that there is now a difference between the returns to two otherwise comparable riskless investments, arbitrage is possible. In this case, an arbitrageur could enter the following transactions:

(1) Borrow DEM 170,000 at 7.00 percent, agree to repay DEM 181,900 in one year;
(2) Sell the marks on the spot market at DEM 1.70/USD, receive USD 100,000;
(3) Invest the USD 100,000 at 4.50 percent, receive USD 104,500 in one year;
(4) Sell USD 104,500 forward at DEM 1.77/USD, agree to receive DEM 184,965;
(5) Repay the DEM loan, collect net profit of DEM 3,065.

If, on the other hand, the actual one-year forward rate was lower than breakeven—for instance, DEM 1.71/USD—the arbitrageur would implement the opposite trade:

(1) Borrow USD 100,000 at 4.50 percent, agree to repay USD 104,500 in one year;
(2) Sell the dollars on the spot market at DEM 1.70/USD, receive DEM 170,000;
(3) Invest the DEM 170,000 at 7.00 percent, receive DEM 181,900 in one year;
(4) Buy USD 104,500 forward at DEM 1.71/USD, agree to pay DEM 178,695;
(5) Repay the dollar loan, collect net profit of DEM 3,205.

These strategies are known as **covered interest arbitrage** because the arbitrageur will always hold the security denominated in the currency that is the least expensive to deliver in the forward market. In this sense, the arbitrage position is hedged, or covered, against adverse foreign exchange movements while receiving the largest amount of net interest income. In practice, traders involved in covered interest arbitrage strategies utilize bank rates (e.g., LIBOR) for borrowing and lending, which injects a slight amount of credit risk into the scheme. After surveying the empirical evidence, Solnik has concluded that the ability to take these arbitrage positions keeps interest rate parity a viable description of the way spot and forward prices are set for the world's major currencies.[20]

With exchange rates quoted on an *indirect basis* (i.e., foreign currency (FC) per U.S. dollar), the general formula for the forward rate implied by interest rate parity is:

$$\text{Forward} = \text{Spot} \times \left(\frac{1 + (\text{Foreign Interest Rate})\left(\frac{T}{365}\right)}{1 + (\text{U.S. Interest Rate})\quad \left(\frac{T}{365}\right)} \right)$$

where

T = **the number of days from the joint settlement of the futures and cash positions until they mature.**

---

[19] Under these conditions, the actual currency loss is calculated as $0.5745/0.5882 - 1 = -2.33$ percent. This, in turn, means the dollar-denominated return to the second strategy is $(1 + 0.07) \times (1 - 0.233) - 1 = 4.50$ percent.

[20] Bruno Solnik, *International Investments*, 3d ed. (Reading, MA: Addison-Wesley Publishing, 1996).

In the last example, $T = 365$ so that DEM 1.7407/USD = DEM 1.70/USD × (1.07/1.045). This formula also assumes that the rates in question are quoted on a 365-day basis. If U.S. money market rates such as LIBOR are used, then the equation should be adjusted to a 360-day year.

Letting S_0 and $F_{0,T}$ once again denote the current spot and forward prices for an instrument that matures at date T, the above expression can be rewritten as:

$$\frac{F_{0,T}}{S_0} = \left(\frac{1 + (RFR_{FC})\left(\frac{T}{365}\right)}{1 + (RFR_{USD})\left(\frac{T}{365}\right)} \right)$$

where

RFR_{USD} = the annualized risk-free rate in the United States
RFR_{FC} = the annualized risk-free rate in the foreign markets.

This equation defines the relationship between four different prices, all of which are determined at date 0: spot foreign exchange rate, forward foreign exchange rate, U.S. investment rate, and foreign investment rate. Importantly, notice that, if the markets are aligned properly, $F_{0,T}$ will be greater than S_0 whenever RFR_{FC} is greater than RFR_{USD}, with the opposite holding when $RFR_{FC} < RFR_{USD}$. With indirect currency quotes, $F_{0,T} > S_0$ implies that the foreign currency is at a forward discount to the dollar. In other words, the country with the *lowest* investment rate should see its currency trade at a forward premium. The intuition behind this is that to keep investment capital from flowing to the country with the highest returns, the currency translation must adjust accordingly. Thus, the high-interest country will suffer from a weaker forward value for its currency.[21]

A CURRENCY FUTURES APPLICATION

Calculating implied world investment rates   Suppose you are the cash manager for a multinational company and you have $1,000,000 in short-term balances that you can invest in sovereign-issued paper for the next two months. On Monday, December 18, 1995, you obtain the following quotes for spot and futures exchange rates for several currencies:

Currency	Spot (USD/FC)	March 1996 Futures (USD/FC)
German mark	0.7000	0.7028
Swiss franc	0.8715	0.8797
Canadian dollar	0.7282	0.7257
British pound	1.5415	1.5378

If you enter into any of these transactions, they will settle on Wednesday, December 20 (i.e., two business days later). The futures contracts mature on Wednesday, March 20, 1996, which leaves a 91-day investment window from settlement to maturity.

You also observe that a U.S. Treasury bill maturing at virtually the same time (i.e., March 21) pays a bond equivalent (i.e., 365-day) yield of 5.30 percent. Before checking the

---

[21] When using direct quotes (i.e., USD/FC), the interest rate parity condition must be adjusted by taking the reciprocal of the ratio on the left-hand side: $[S_0 \div F_{0,T}] = [(1 + RFR_{FC} (T \div 365)) \div (1 + RFR_{USD} (T \div 365))]$. In the above example, with the direct quotes for the spot and forward being USD 0.5882/DEM (= 1/1.70) and USD 0.5745/DEM, respectively, we have S_0 = USD 0.5882/DEM = USD 0.5745/DEM × (1.07/1.045).

actual quotes for government paper from these other countries, you first calculate the investment rates implied by the interest rate parity relationship. Specifically, for the four countries listed above, you compute:

$$\text{Implied Rate} = \left[\left(\frac{\text{Spot}}{\text{Futures}}\right)\left(1 + (\text{U.S. Interest Rate})\left(\frac{91}{365}\right)\right) - 1\right]\left(\frac{365}{91}\right)$$

which is just the parity relationship rearranged to use direct currency quotes and to isolate the foreign interest rate. Notice that the direct parity formulation is the correct one to use because of the quotation convention prevailing in the U.S. currency futures market. For British sterling, this calculation generates an implied 91-day investment rate of:

$$\left[\left(\frac{1.5415}{1.5378}\right)\left(1 + (0.0530)\left(\frac{91}{365}\right)\right) - 1\right]\left(\frac{365}{91}\right) = 0.06278 = 6.28\%.$$

This means that with the current spot and futures prices for exchanging dollars and pounds, you would be indifferent to either receiving a three-month investment rate of 5.30 percent in the United States or 6.28 percent in England.

Summarizing this calculation for all of the countries leaves:

Country	Implied 91-Day Rate
Great Britain	6.28%
Germany	3.68
Switzerland	1.51
Canada	6.70

You can now compare these figures to the actual investment rates in each of the countries to determine if a futures-based synthetic foreign bond strategy is warranted. If, for instance, the actual British three-month gilt rate was 6.50 percent, you could exceed the 5.30 percent dollar-denominated T-bill return by (1) exchanging your dollars for pounds in the spot market at USD 1.5415/GBP, (2) investing for three months in the sterling-based security at 6.50 percent, and (3) translating your proceeds back into dollars at maturity using the futures rate of USD 1.5378/GBP.

Finally, notice that the countries with implied investment rates higher than 5.30 percent (i.e., Canada and Great Britain) are those whose currencies sold at a forward discount to the U.S. dollar over this 91-day window. Conversely, Germany and Switzerland had currencies at a forward premium to the dollar and thus had implied investment rates less than 5.30 percent. One caution necessary in interpreting these yields properly is that it is imperative that the futures and spot FX quotes were obtained simultaneously and pertain to the same investment denomination. In this example, these conditions were more than likely violated to some extent.

Summary

- There is no question that forward and futures contracts have become an important feature of the modern investment landscape. As the most fundamental type of derivative instruments available, they greatly increase the alternatives that investors have to create and manage their portfolios and establish new trading opportunities. In this chapter, we discuss how these contracts work and the ways they are used in practice. As different mechanisms for accomplishing the same goals, forwards and futures differ primarily in the areas of design flexibility and collateralization. Specifically, forward agreements generally are more flexible but carry more credit risk, while the process of marking margin accounts to market on a daily basis makes futures contracts more secure (to the exchange, at least) even as the standardization of contract terms makes them less adaptable.

- We also show that hedging is key to understanding forward-based contracting and that the basis is the most important concept in understanding hedging. In particular, the basis, which is defined as the difference between spot and forward prices at any point in time, contains the essence of a short hedge position so that the hedger effectively trades the price risk of the underlying asset for the basis risk inherent in the spot-forward combination. This notion also leads to the calculation of an optimal hedge ratio, which specifies the appropriate number of contracts by minimizing the amount of basis (i.e., correlation) risk in the combined position.

- Although forward and futures contracts are not securities, their contract settlement prices still must follow certain regularities for these markets to remain efficient. For instance, the cost of carry model suggests that in order to avoid arbitrage, the forward price should be equal to the spot price plus the cost of transporting the underlying asset to the future delivery date. These carrying costs can include commissions for physical storage, an opportunity cost for the net amount of invested capital, and a premium for the convenience of consuming the asset now. When forward prices are set in this manner, the market value of a new contract should be zero, although this value can become either positive or negative as the contract matures under changing market conditions.

- Finally, we illustrate these concepts with detailed examinations of three types of financial futures contracts: interest rate, equity index, and foreign exchange. In addition to describing the dynamics of each of these markets, we discuss different applications, including those involving hedging, speculation, and arbitrage. These applications produce some useful adaptations of the basic concepts, such as duration- and beta-based hedge ratios for interest rate and stock index futures as well as the currency futures version of the cost of carry model known as interest rate parity. Although no such list of applications could ever be complete, they should provide an understanding of why these instruments have become so important in financial markets.

Questions

1. *CFA Examination III (June 1989)*

   The World Ecosystem Consortium (WEC) pension trust holds $100 million in long-term U.S. Treasury bonds. To reduce interest rate risk you, as an independent advisor to the WEC, suggest that the trust diversify by investing $30 million in German government bonds (Bunds) for six months. You point out that a fixed currency futures hedge (shorting a fixed number of contracts) could be used by WEC's pension trust to protect the $30 million in Bunds against exchange rate losses over the six months.

   Explain how a fixed currency futures hedge could be constructed for the WEC trust by shorting currency futures contracts to protect against exchange rate losses. Describe one characteristic of this hedge that WEC's investment committee might deem undesirable.

2. A multinational corporation is about to embark on a major financial restructuring program. One critical stage will be the issuance of seven-year Eurobonds sometime within the next month. The CFO is concerned with recent instability in capital markets and with the particular event that market yields rise prior to issuance, forcing the corporation to pay a higher coupon rate on the bonds. It is decided to hedge that risk by selling 10-year Treasury note futures contracts. Notice that this is a classic cross hedge wherein 10-year Treasury notes are used to manage the risk of seven-year Eurobonds.

   Describe the nature of the basis risk in the hedge. In particular, what specific events with respect to the shape of the Treasury yield curve and the Eurobond spread over Treasuries could render the hedge ineffective? In other words, under what circumstances would the hedge fail and make the corporation worse off?

3. It is often stated that a stock index arbitrage trade is easier to implement when the stock index futures contract price is above its theoretical level than when it is below that value. What institutional realities might make this statement true? Describe the steps involved in forming the arbitrage transaction in both circumstances. To the extent that the statement is valid, what does it suggest about the ability of the stock index futures market to remain efficient?

4. Explain why the currency of Country A, whose interest rates are twice as great as those in Country B, must trade at a forward discount. If there was no difference between the spot and forward exchange rates in this interest rate environment, what arbitrage trade could be constructed to take advantage of the situation?

5. "Hedgers trade price risk for basis risk." What is meant by this statement? In particular, explain the concept of the basis in a hedge transaction and how forward and futures contracts can be selected to minimize risk.

6. Suppose you are a derivatives trader specializing in creating customized commodity forward contracts for clients and then hedging your position with exchange-traded futures contracts. Your latest position is an agreement to deliver 100,000 gallons of unleaded gasoline to a client in three months.

   a. Explain how you can hedge your position using gasoline futures contracts.

   b. In calculating your hedge ratio, how must you account for the different valuation procedures used for forward and futures contracts? That is, what difference does it make that forward contracts are valued on a discounted basis while futures contracts are marked to market without discounting?

   c. If the only available gasoline futures contracts call for the delivery of 42,000 gallons and mature in either two or four months, describe the nature of the basis risk involved in your hedge.

7. Eurodollar futures contracts are based on LIBOR, an add-on yield, while Treasury bill futures contracts are based on the T-bill rate, a discount yield. Despite different quotation conventions, these contracts use the same "discount" price index (100 − Yield). Explain the function of this price index and why the same design can be used for both contracts.

8. There are currency futures contracts that allow for the exchange of Mexican pesos and U.S. dollars, while other contracts allow for the exchange of Swiss francs and U.S. dollars. If I am an investor based in Zurich, explain how I could use these contracts to convert the payoff to a peso-denominated asset back into francs in two months.

9. We have futures contracts on Treasury bonds, but we do not have futures contracts on individual corporate bonds. We have cattle and pork belly futures but no chicken futures. Explain why the market has developed in this manner. What do you think are the most important characteristics for the success of a new futures contract concept?

10. *CFA Examination II (June 1991)*

    Four factors affect the value of a futures contract on a stock index. Three of these factors are: the current price of the stock index, the time remaining until the contract maturity (delivery) date, and the dividends on the stock index. Identify the fourth factor and explain how and why changes in this factor affect the value of the futures contract.

11. You own an equally weighted portfolio of 50 different stocks worth about $5,000,000. The stocks are from several different industries, and the portfolio is reasonably well diversified. Which do you think would provide you with the best overall hedge: a single position in an index futures or 50 different positions in futures contracts on the individual stocks? What are the most important factors to consider in making this decision?

Problems

1. It is March 9 and you have just entered into a short position in a soybean meal futures contract. The contract expires on July 9 and calls for the delivery of 100 tons of soybean meal. Further, because this is a futures position, it requires the posting of a $3,000 initial margin and a $1,500 maintenance margin; for simplicity, however, assume that the account is marked to market on a monthly basis. Assume the following represent the contract delivery prices (in dollars per ton) that prevail on each settlement date:

March 9 (initiation)	$173.00
April 9	179.75
May 9	189.00
June 9	182.50
July 9 (delivery)	174.25

a. Calculate the equity value of your margin account on each settlement date, including any additional equity required to meet a margin call. Also compute the amount of cash that will be returned to you on July 9, and the gain or loss on your position, expressed as a percentage of your initial margin commitment.

b. Assuming that the underlying soybean meal investment pays no dividend and requires a storage cost of 1.5 percent (of current value), calculate the current (i.e., March 9) spot price for a ton of soybean meal, and the implied May 9 price for the same ton. In your calculations, assume that an annual risk-free rate of 8 percent prevails over the entire contract life.

c. Now suppose that on March 9 you also entered into a long forward contract for the purchase of 100 tons of soybean meal on July 9. Assume further that the July forward and futures contract prices always are identical to one another at any point in time. Calculate the cash amount of your gain or loss if you unwind both positions in their respective markets on May 9 and June 9, taking into account the prevailing settlement conditions in the two markets.

2. It is March 1 and you are a new derivatives trader making a market in forward contracts in Commodity W. One month ago (February 1), you began your operations with the following transactions, which are described from your perspective:

- With Client A: (1) Short a June 1 forward for 10,000 units at a contract price of $25.50/unit,
                   (2) Long a September 1 forward for 15,000 units at a contract price of $26.20/unit.

- With Client B: (3) Short a September 1 forward for 25,000 units at a contract price of $26.40/unit.

Your current (i.e., March 1) contract price quotes are as follows:

Contract	Bid	Ask
June	$24.95	$25.15
September	25.65	25.85

The appropriate discount rate is 9 percent per annum.

a. If Client A just called you wanting to unwind both of its contracts, calculate a fair cash amount that can be used in settlement today. Would you pay or receive this amount?

b. If these contracts had been exchange-traded futures contracts instead of OTC forward contracts, how would this settlement amount need to be adjusted (assuming the same March 1 contract prices)?

c. Calculate the dollar amount you would lose if Client B called you to default its contractual obligation. (Hint: Compute this amount in the same manner you calculated the net settlement in Part a.)

d. At the time you negotiated the three original agreements (i.e., February 1), did you have any price exposure on the September contracts? If so, what type of future price movements would be harmful to your net profit on the expiration date?

3. You are a coffee dealer anticipating the purchase of 82,000 pounds of coffee in three months. You are concerned that the price of coffee will rise, so you take a long position in coffee futures. Each contract covers 37,500 pounds and so, rounding to the nearest contract, you decide to go long in two contracts. The futures price at the time you initiate your hedge is 55.95 cents per pound. Three months later, the actual spot price of coffee turns out to be 58.56 cents per pound and the futures price is 59.20 cents per pound.

a. Determine the effective price at which you purchased your coffee. How do you account for the difference in amounts for the spot and hedge positions?

b. Describe the nature of the basis risk in this long hedge.

4. *CFA Examination III (June 1983)*

In February 1983, the United American Company is considering the sale of $100 million in 10-year debentures that will probably be rated AAA like the firm's other bond issues. The firm is anxious to proceed at today's rate of 10.5 percent.

As Treasurer, you know that it will take about 12 weeks (May) to get the issue registered and sold. Therefore, you suggest that the firm hedge the pending issue using Treasury bond futures contracts. (Each Treasury bond contract is for $1,000,000.)

Explain how you would go about hedging the bond issue, and describe the results, assuming that the following two sets of future conditions actually occur. (Ignore commissions and margin costs, and assume a 1-to-1 hedge ratio.) Show all calculations.

	Case 1	Case 2
Current Values—February 1983		
Bond Rate	10.5%	10.5%
June 1983 Treasury bonds	78.875	78.875
Estimated Values—May 1983		
Bond Rate	11.0%	10.0%
June 1983 Treasury bonds	75.93	81.84
Present Value of a $1 Annuity		
10 years at 10.5 percent	6.021	6.021

5. The corporate treasurer of XYZ Corp. manages the firm's pension fund. On February 15, 1993, the treasurer is informed that the pension fund will be required to sell its $100 million (face value) Treasury bond portfolio on August 15, 1993, because of a pending change in the structure of the plan.

The portfolio consists entirely of a single bond issue with a maturity date of August 2019. The bond pays coupons of $7\frac{1}{4}$ percent and is currently priced at 97–12. This corresponds to a yield of 7.479 percent. These T-bonds were originally purchased at par so the current price reflects a modest capital loss. The treasurer is concerned that further weakness in the dollar could raise market rates and exacerbate this loss before the August sale date.

Your task is to construct a hedge using T-bond futures to offset, or at least reduce, the risk exposure. Assume an August 1993 futures contract exists with the quoted price of 101–04 and a reference yield to maturity of 7.887 percent (based on an 8 percent coupon and 20 years to maturity). To complete the task, construct a numerical example to show the optimal number of contracts necessary to provide the desired price protection.

a. Assuming that interest rates do not change between February and August 1993, what will be the value of the T-bond portfolio? Briefly explain why this differs from the current value of $97.375 million.

b. As of August 1993, calculate the respective durations of the bond issue in the portfolio and the bond underlying the futures contract. Using the current yields to maturity, translate these into modified duration form. (Note: In your computation, recall that T-bonds pay semiannual interest.)

c. Assuming that the yield beta (β_j) between the instruments is equal to one, calculate the number of futures contracts required to form the optimal hedge. In this calculation, keep in mind that the face value of the bond underlying the futures contract is $100,000.

6. A bond speculator currently has positions in two separate corporate bond portfolios: a long holding in Portfolio 1 and a short holding in Portfolio 2. All of the bonds have the same credit quality. Other relevant information on these positions includes:

Portfolio	Bond	Market Value (mil.)	Coupon Rate	Compounding Frequency	Maturity	Yield to Maturity
1	A	$ 6.0	0%	Annual	3 yrs.	7.31%
	B	4.0	0	Annual	14 yrs.	7.31
2	C	11.5	4.6	Annual	9 yrs.	7.31

Treasury bond futures (based on $100,000 face value of 20-year T-bonds having an 8 percent semiannual coupon) with a maturity exactly six months from now are currently priced at 109–24 with a corresponding yield to maturity of 7.081 percent. The "yield betas" between the futures contract and bonds A, B, and C are 1.13, 1.03, and 1.01, respectively. Finally, the modified duration for the T-bond underlying the futures contract is 10.355 years.

    a. Calculate the modified duration (expressed in years) for each of the two bond portfolios. What will be the *approximate* percentage change in the value of each if all yields increase by 60 basis points on an annual basis?

    b. Without performing the calculations, explain which of the portfolios will *actually* have its value impacted to the greatest extent (in absolute terms) by the shift in yields. (Hint: This explanation requires knowledge of the concept of *bond convexity*.)

    c. Assuming the bond speculator wants to hedge her *net* bond position, what is the optimal number of futures contracts that must be bought or sold? Start by calculating the optimal hedge ratio between the futures contract and the two bond portfolios separately and then combine them.

7. Consider a hypothetical Euromarket security simply called "paper." "Paper" trades and is quoted on a discount yield basis, the same as U.S. Treasury bills and commercial paper. Listed below are the current rate quotes for "paper" issues of two different maturities, each having a face value of $100,000:

90-day	7.50%
180-day	7.50

Suppose further that a futures market also exists in 90-day "paper" and that you have just obtained a quote on a contract that matures in exactly 90 days from now at 7.50 percent. Assuming you can either buy or sell any of these securities (including the futures contract) at the quoted rates, show that a financial arbitrage opportunity exists. Calculating the implied forward discount rate will be useful. Demonstrate the sequence of transactions necessary to generate this arbitrage profit and indicate how much profit you would make. In these calculations, you may ignore the marked to market effects on the futures contract, assuming the exchange will hold any long position as collateral instead of cash.

8. As a relationship officer for a money-center commercial bank, one of your corporate accounts has just approached you about a one-year loan for $1,000,000. The customer would pay a quarterly interest expense based on the prevailing level of LIBOR at the beginning of each three-month period. As is the bank's convention on all such loans, the amount of the interest payment would then be paid at the end of the quarterly cycle when the new rate for the next cycle is determined. You observe the following LIBOR yield curve in the cash market:

90-day LIBOR	4.60%
180-day LIBOR	4.75
270-day LIBOR	5.00
360-day LIBOR	5.30

    a. If 90-day LIBOR rises to the levels "predicted" by the implied forward rates, what will the dollar level of the bank's interest receipt be at the end of each quarter during the one-year loan period?

    b. If the bank wanted to hedge its exposure to falling LIBOR on this loan commitment, describe the sequence of transactions in the futures markets it could undertake.

    c. Assuming the yields inferred from the Eurodollar futures contract prices for the next three settlement periods are equal to the implied forward rates, calculate the annuity value that would leave the bank indifferent between making the floating-rate loan and hedging it in the futures market, and making a one-year fixed-rate loan. Express this annuity value in both dollar and annual (360-day) percentage terms.

9. Suppose that one day in early April, you observe the following prices on futures contracts maturing in June: 93.35 for Eurodollar and 94.07 for T-bill. These prices imply three-month LIBOR and T-bill settlement yields of 6.65 percent and 5.93 percent, respectively. You think that over the next quarter the general level of interest rates will rise while the credit spread built into LIBOR will narrow. Demonstrate how you can use a TED (Treasury/Eurodollar) spread, which is a simultaneous long (short) position in a Eurodollar contract and short (long) position in the T-bill contract, to create a position that will benefit from these views.

10. An investment bank engages in stock index arbitrage for its own and customer accounts. On a particular day, the S&P index at the New York Stock Exchange is 602.25 when the futures contract for delivery in 90 days is 614.75. If the annualized 90-day interest rate is 8.00 percent and the (annualized) dividend yield is 3 percent, would program trading involving stock index arbitrage possibly take place? If so, describe the transactions that should be undertaken and calculate the profit that would be made per each "share" of the S&P 500 index used in the trade.

11. The treasurer of a middle market, import-export company has approached you for advice on how to best invest some of the firm's short-term cash balances. The company, which has been a client of the bank that employs you for a few years, has $250,000 that it is able to commit for a one-year holding period. The treasurer is currently considering two alternatives: (1) invest all the funds in a one-year U.S. Treasury bill offering a bond equivalent yield of 4.25 percent, and (2) invest all the funds in a Swiss government security over the same horizon, locking in the spot and forward currency exchanges in the FX market. A quick call to the bank's FX desk gives you the following two-way currency exchange quotes:

	Swiss Francs per U.S. Dollar	U.S. Dollar per Swiss Franc
Spot	1.5035	0.6651
One-year CHF futures	—	0.6586

a. Calculate the one-year bond equivalent yield for the Swiss government security that would support the interest rate parity condition.

b. Assuming the actual yield on a one-year Swiss government bond is 5.50 percent, which strategy would leave the treasurer with the greatest return after one year?

c. Describe the transactions that an arbitrageur could use to take advantage of this apparent mispricing and calculate what the profit would be for a $250,000 transaction.

References

Chance, Don M. *An Introduction to Derivatives.* 3d ed. Fort Worth, TX: Dryden Press, 1995.

Duffie, Darrell. *Futures Markets.* Englewood Cliffs, NJ: Prentice-Hall, 1989.

Ederington, Louis H. "The Hedging Performance of the New Futures Market." *Journal of Finance* 34, no. 1 (March 1979).

Hull, John C. *Introduction to Futures & Options Markets.* 2d ed. Englewood Cliffs, NJ: Prentice-Hall, 1995.

Kolb, Robert W. *Financial Derivatives.* Miami, FL: Kolb Publishing, 1993.

Rendleman, Richard J. and Christopher Carabini. "The Efficiency of the Treasury Bill Futures Market." *Journal of Finance* 44, no. 4 (September 1979).

Siegel, Daniel and Diane F. Siegel. *Futures Markets.* Hinsdale, IL: The Dryden Press, 1990.

Smithson, Charles W., Clifford W. Smith, Jr., and D. Sykes Wilford. *Managing Financial Risk.* Burr Ridge, IL: Richard D. Irwin, 1995.

Telser, Lester G. "Futures Trading and the Storage of Cotton and Wheat." *Journal of Political Economy* 66 (June 1958).

Working, Holbrook. "Economic Functions of Futures Markets." In *Selected Writings of Holbrook Working*. Chicago, IL: Chicago Board of Trade, 1977.

Chapter 23A
APPENDIX

A CLOSED-FORM EQUATION FOR CALCULATING DURATION

To calculate the duration statistic, it helps to think of a bond that pays a fixed coupon for a finite maturity as being just a portfolio of zero-coupon cash flows. Duration is then the weighted average of the payment (i.e., maturity) dates of those zero-coupon cash flows. What the duration statistic essentially does is convert a bond with any given coupon and maturity into what it would look like if it had been a zero-coupon bond. Thus, a bond's duration is its *zero-coupon equivalent maturity*.

To see how this calculation works, consider a nonamortizing, five-year bond with a face value of $1,000 making annual coupon payments of $120 (i.e., 12 percent). Assuming a current yield-to-maturity of 10 percent, this bond will trade at a premium and its weighted average payment date (i.e., duration) is 4.074 years, as shown in Table 23A.1. Interpreting the coupon bond as a portfolio of zero-coupon cash flows, the duration of 4.0740 years is the weighted average maturity of that portfolio, where the weights are the respective shares of market value (e.g., the one-year zero-coupon cash flow is 10.14 percent of the value of the portfolio, the five-year zero 64.64 percent).

This five-year coupon bond with a duration of 4.0740 years is "equivalent" in terms of price risk to a zero-coupon bond having a maturity of 4.0740 years. As we saw in Chapter 16, this suggests that when the interest rate increases by one percent above its original level (i.e., $[\Delta(1 + i) \div (1 + i)] = 0.01$), then the price of this bond will decline by about 4.074 percent.

The Macaulay duration can be calculated with the following formula:

$$
D = \frac{\dfrac{1 \times C}{\left(1 + \dfrac{Y}{n}\right)^1} + \dfrac{2 \times C}{\left(1 + \dfrac{Y}{n}\right)^2} + \dfrac{3 \times C}{\left(1 + \dfrac{Y}{n}\right)^3} + \ldots + \dfrac{(n \times T) \times (C + F)}{\left(1 + \dfrac{Y}{n}\right)^{n \times T}}}{\dfrac{C}{\left(1 + \dfrac{Y}{n}\right)^1} + \dfrac{C}{\left(1 + \dfrac{Y}{n}\right)^2} + \dfrac{C}{\left(1 + \dfrac{Y}{n}\right)^3} + \ldots + \dfrac{(C + F)}{\left(1 + \dfrac{Y}{n}\right)^{n \times T}}}
$$

TABLE 23A.1

A DURATION CALCULATION

Year	Cash Flow	PV at 10%	PV ÷ Price	Year × (PV ÷ Price)
1	$ 120	$ 109.09	0.1014	0.1014
2	120	99.17	0.0922	0.1844
3	120	90.16	0.0838	0.2514
4	120	81.96	0.0762	0.3047
5	1,120	695.43	0.6464	3.2321
		Price = $1,075.82		Duration = 4.0740 years

where

    C = the periodic coupon payment
    F = the face value at maturity
    T = the number of years until maturity
    n = the payments per year
    Y = the yield to maturity.

Note that the denominator of this equation is just P, the price of the security. The numerator is the present value of the cash flows weighted by the time the payment is made; the first by 1, the second by 2, and so forth. With some algebraic manipulation, this formula reduces to the following closed-form equation:

$$D = \frac{1 + \dfrac{Y}{n}}{\dfrac{Y}{n}} - \frac{1 + \dfrac{Y}{n} + \left[(n \times T)\left(\dfrac{C}{F} - \dfrac{Y}{n}\right)\right]}{\dfrac{C}{F}\left[\left(1 + \dfrac{Y}{n}\right)^{n \times T} - 1\right] + \dfrac{Y}{n}}$$

where

    C/F = the coupon rate per period.

Note that the duration statistic in this equation is calculated on the basis of the underlying periodic cash flows even though it is often annualized when reporting the statistic by dividing it by n.

In the numerical example above, $Y = .10$, $n = 1$, $T = 5$, $C/F = .12$, and $Y/n = .10$. The bond's duration can therefore be solved as:

$$D = \frac{1 + .10}{.10} - \frac{1 + .10 + 5\,(.12 - .10)}{.12\,[(1 + .10)^5 - 1] + .10} = 4.0740$$

As a second example of this formula, what is the duration of a 30-year Treasury bond with a 7⅝ percent coupon and a stated yield to maturity of 7.72 percent? Here you need to recall that T-bonds pay semiannual interest and so the appropriate definitions of the variables are: $C/F = 0.038125$, $T = 30$, $n = 2$, and $Y/n = .0386$. Therefore:

$$D = \frac{1 + 0.0386}{0.0386} - \frac{1 + 0.0386 + 60(0.038125 - 0.0386)}{(0.038125)[(1 + 0.0386)^{60} - 1] + 0.0386} = 24.18 \text{ periods}$$

or 12.09 years. Although the method summarized by Table 23A.1 always will work for any nonamortizing bond, the closed-form expression is considerably quicker when a large number of coupon payments are involved.

Chapter 23B
APPENDIX

CALCULATING MONEY MARKET IMPLIED FORWARD RATES

Implied forward rates are an essential factor in understanding how short-term interest rate futures contracts are priced. In our discussion of the expectations hypothesis of the yield curve in Chapter 16, we saw that implied forward rates represented the sequence of future short-term rates that were built into the yield to maturity of a longer-term security. However, implied forward rates can have another interpretation. Consider an investor who is deciding between the following strategies for making a two-year investment: (1) buy a single two-year, zero-coupon bond yielding 6 percent per annum; or (2) buy a one-year, zero-coupon bond with a 5 percent yield and replace it at maturity with another one-year instrument. An implied forward rate is the answer to the following question: At what rate must the investor be able to reinvest the interim proceeds from the second strategy to exactly equal the total return from the first investment? In other words, the implied forward rate is a *breakeven* reinvestment rate. In the notation of Chapter 16, we want to solve for $_2r_1$ in the following equation:

$$(1 + .06)^2 = (1 + .05)(1 + {_2r_1})$$

or $_2r_1 = [(1 + .06)^2 \div (1 + .05)] - 1 = 7\%$. An alternative interpretation is that investing for two years with a return of 6 percent per year is exactly the same as investing for one year at 5 percent, with the principal and interest then reinvested for a second year at 7 percent.

Implied forward money market rates can be interpreted in the same way as bond yields, but they must be calculated differently because of differences in the quotation methods for the various rates. For example, T-bill rates are quoted on a *discount* yield (DY) basis using the following pricing formula:

$$P = F - \left[F \times DY \times \frac{T}{360} \right] = F \left[1 - DY \times \frac{T}{360} \right]$$

where

F = the face value of the underlying instrument
P = the current price of the underlying instrument
T = the number of days to maturity.

For example, a Treasury bill with 91 days to maturity, a $10,000 face value, and a discount yield of 4.67 percent would sell for a current price of:

$$P = \$10,000 \left[1 - (.0467) \times \frac{91}{360} \right] = \$9,881.95.$$

On the other hand, we have seen that LIBOR is a bank *add-on yield* (AY) that is used to figure out how much money an investor will have at maturity given an initial investment of P (i.e., interest is "added on"):

$$F = P + \left[P \times AY \times \frac{T}{360} \right] = P \left[1 + AY \times \frac{T}{360} \right].$$

With this expression, a 60-day investment of $50,000 in a bank deposit paying LIBOR equal to 5.30 percent would be worth $50,441.67 at maturity. Notice that both the T-bill discount rate and LIBOR are based on a presumed 360-day year, the standard U.S. money market practice.

With these quotation conventions, Smith has shown that the implied forward rate between two money market instruments quoted on an add-on basis (e.g., LIBOR) can be calculated as:

$$_BAY_A = \left[\frac{(B \times AY_B) - (A \times AY_A)}{B - A}\right]\left[\frac{1}{1 + \left(\dfrac{A \times AY_A}{360}\right)}\right]$$

where AY_A and AY_B are add-on yields for A and B days from settlement to maturity, with $B > A$.[22] The implied forward rate ($_BAY_A$) also is on an add-on basis and has a maturity of $(B - A)$ days. That is, $_BAY_A$ corresponds to the time period between date A and date B. For money market instruments quoted on a discount yield basis (e.g., T-bill), a slightly different formula applies:

$$_BDY_A = \left[\frac{(B \times DY_B) - (A \times DY_A)}{B - A}\right]\left[\frac{1}{1 - \left(\dfrac{A \times DY_A}{360}\right)}\right]$$

where DY_A and DY_B are discount yields for A and B days from settlement to maturity, and $B > A$. The implied forward rate ($_ADY_B$) also is on a discount yield basis and has a maturity of $(B - A)$ days, assuming a 360-day year. Notice that these formulas have a common structure, differing only in that the add-on formula has a "plus" sign in the denominator of the second term while the discount yield has a "minus."

As an example of these calculations, consider the following short-term yield curves for T-bills and LIBOR:

Maturity	T-bill	LIBOR
30 days	4.00%	4.15%
60 days	4.10	4.25
90 days	4.20	4.35

What is the implied forward T-bill rate between days 30 and 60? Using $DY_A = 0.0400$, $DY_B = 0.0410$, $A = 30$ days, and $B = 60$ days for T-bills, we have:

$$_{60}DY_{30} = \left[\frac{(60 \times .0410) - (30 \times .0400)}{60 - 30}\right]\left[\frac{1}{1 - \left(\dfrac{30 \times .0400}{360}\right)}\right] = 4.21\%.$$

This means that buying a 30-day T-bill at 4.00 percent and then again at 4.21 percent in another 30 days would have the same total return as the 60-day T-bill at 4.10 percent.

As a second example, what is the implied forward LIBOR between days 60 and 90? Using $AY_A = 0.0425$, $AY_B = 0.0435$, $A = 60$ days, and $B = 90$ days for LIBOR, we have:

$$_{90}AY_{60} = \left[\frac{(90 \times .0435) - (60 \times .0425)}{90 - 60}\right]\left[\frac{1}{1 - \left(\dfrac{60 \times .0425}{360}\right)}\right] = 4.52\%.$$

---

[22] Donald J. Smith, "The Calculation and Use of Money Market Implied Forward Rates," *Journal of Cash Management* 98, no. 5 (September/October 1989), pp. 46–49.

That is, investing in a 60-day bank deposit at 4.25 percent and then a 30-day deposit at 4.52 percent would have the same total return (or cost of funds) as the 90-day deposit at 4.35 percent. This can be confirmed by examining the cash flows on the transactions. For example, the total return on a $100,000, 60-day deposit at 4.25 percent would be $100,708. This amount reinvested in a 30-day deposit at 4.52 percent would provide a total of $101,087, equaling the payoff on a $100,000, 90-day deposit at 4.35 percent.

Chapter

24

Option Contracts

This chapter answers the following questions:

- How are options traded on exchanges and in OTC markets?
- How are options for stock, stock indexes, foreign currency, and futures contracts quoted in the financial press?
- How can investors use option contracts to hedge an existing risk exposure?
- How do investors use options in combination with one another to create payoff structures tailored to a particular need or view of future market conditions?
- What differentiates a spread from a straddle, a strangle, or a range forward?
- What are the three steps in establishing the fundamental "no arbitrage" value of an option contract?
- What is the binomial (or two-state) option pricing model and in what way is it an extension of the basic valuation approach?
- What is the Black-Scholes option pricing model and how does it extend the binomial valuation approach?
- What is the relationship between the Black-Scholes and the put-call parity valuation models?
- How does the payment of a dividend by the underlying asset impact the value of an option?
- How can models for valuing stock options be adapted to other underlying assets such as stock indexes, foreign currency, or futures contracts?
- How do American- and European-style options differ from one another?
- What is implied volatility and what is its role in the contract valuation process?

Broken down to the most basic level, only two kinds of derivative contracts exist: forwards, which fix the price or rate of an underlying asset; and options, which allow holders to decide at a later date whether such a fixing is in their best interest. With our initial examination of forward and futures now complete, this chapter turns our attention to issues concerning the trading and valuation of option contracts. We develop the discussion in four parts. First, the contract terms and trading mechanics for both call and put options are considered. Options trade on exchanges as well as in OTC dealer markets and can be based on a wide array of securities and commodities. To focus this discussion, we concentrate on options that have financial instruments as underlying securities, including options on individual stocks, stock indexes, foreign currency, and futures contracts. A formal discussion of options on interest rates is highlighted in the next chapter.

Second, several option-based investment and hedging strategies are examined. Building from a base of the protective put and covered call strategies developed in Chapter 11, we demonstrate how options can be used in combination with one another to create risk-reward tradeoffs that do not otherwise exist in financial markets. In this sense, options can be used as building blocks to help investors design customized payoff schemes. We consider three broad classes of option combination strategies: **straddles,** which involve the purchase and sale of puts and calls; **spreads,** in which investors simultaneously buy one call (or put) while selling another; and **range forwards,** which require the purchase of a call and the concurrent sale of a put, or vice versa.

The third topic we explore is how option contracts are valued in an efficient capital market. We show that, at least intuitively, this can be viewed as a simple, three-step process: (1) creating a riskless hedge portfolio combining options with the underlying security, (2) invoking a no-arbitrage assumption about the rate of return such a portfolio should earn, and (3) solving for the option value consistent with the first two steps. We show that several of the most widely used valuation models, including the **binomial** and the **Black-Scholes,** are consistent with this approach. In this analysis, it is important to keep in mind that we will be *valuing* options and not *pricing* them. Indeed, prices are established through the actions of buyers and sellers; investors and analysts use valuation models to estimate what those prices should be.

Finally, we consider several extensions and advanced topics in option valuation. In particular, we show how the Black-Scholes model for call options on stock can be adapted to value put options as well as other financial assets used commonly as underlying assets. We describe how the payment of dividends affects an option's value and how the model can be adjusted accordingly. We discuss the practical differences between the European and American styles of contracting, and we examine price, or return, volatility—the role it plays in the valuation process and the ways an investor can estimate it.

AN OVERVIEW OF OPTION MARKETS AND CONTRACTS

In Chapter 23, we discussed the primary difference between forward and futures contracts: Futures are standardized and trade on exchanges while forward contracts have negotiable terms and therefore must be arranged in the OTC market. With the development of organized option exchanges during the past three decades, option contracts offer investors similar trading alternatives. The most important features of how these contracts are traded and quoted in the financial press are highlighted below.

OPTION MARKET CONVENTIONS

Option contracts have been traded for centuries in the form of separate agreements or embedded in other securities. Malkiel, for example, tells the story of how call options were used to speculate on flower prices during the tulip bulb frenzy of seventeenth century Holland.[1] Then, and for most of the time until now, options have been arranged and executed in private transactions. Collectively, these private transactions represent the OTC market for options. Like forward contracts, OTC option agreements can be structured around any terms or underlying asset to which two parties can agree. This has been a particularly useful mechanism when the underlying asset is too illiquid to support a widely traded contract. Also, credit risk is a paramount concern in this market because OTC agreements typically are not collateralized. This credit risk is one-sided with an option agreement because the buyer worries about the seller's ability to honor his obligations, but the seller has received everything he will get up front and is not concerned about the buyer's creditworthiness.

As in all security markets, OTC options ultimately are created in response to the needs and desires of the corporations and individual investors who use these products. Financial institutions such as money-center banks and investment banks serve as market makers by facilitating the arrangement and execution of these deals. Over the years, various trade

---

[1] See Burton G. Malkiel, *A Random Walk Down Wall Street* (New York: Norton, 1990).

associations of broker-dealers in OTC options have emerged (and, in some cases, faded), including the Put and Call Brokers and Dealers Association, which helped arrange private stock option transactions, and the International Swap and Derivatives Association, which monitors the activities of market makers for interest rate and foreign exchange derivatives. These trade groups create a common set of standards and language to govern industry transactions.

In April 1973, the Chicago Board of Trade changed the dynamics of option trading when it opened the Chicago Board Options Exchange (CBOE). Specializing in stock and stock index options, the CBOE has introduced two important aspects of market uniformity. Foremost, contracts offered by the CBOE are standardized in terms of the underlying common stock, the number of shares covered, the delivery dates, and the range of available exercise prices. This standardization, which increases the possibility of basis risk, was meant to help develop a secondary market for the contracts. The rapid increase in trading volume on the CBOE and other options exchanges suggests that this feature is desirable compared to OTC contracts that must often be held to maturity due to a lack of liquidity.

The centralization of the trading function also necessitated the creation of the **Options Clearing Corporation** (OCC), which acts as the guarantor of each CBOE-traded contract. Therefore, end-users in option transactions ultimately bear the credit risk of the OCC. For this reason, even though the OCC is independent of the exchange, it demands the option seller to post margin to guarantee future performance. Again, the option buyer will not have a margin account because a future obligation to the seller is nonexistent. Finally, this central market structure makes monitoring, regulation, and price reporting much easier than in the decentralized OTC markets.

PRICE QUOTATIONS FOR EXCHANGE-TRADED OPTIONS

EQUITY OPTIONS   Options on the common stock of individual companies have traded on the CBOE since 1973. Several other markets including the American (AMEX), Philadelphia (PHLX), and Pacific (PSE) Stock Exchanges began trading their own contracts shortly afterwards. The CBOE remains the largest exchange in terms of the number of companies for which options are listed with a market share of about 40 percent, but the AMEX is now a close second with just under 35 percent of the total listings. Options on each of these exchanges are traded similarly, with a typical contract for 100 shares of stock. Because exchange-traded contracts are not issued by the company whose common stock is the underlying asset, they require secondary transactions in the equity if exercised.[2]

Figure 24.1 displays price quotations for a sample of equity options and lists of the most actively traded contracts on January 23, 1996. To interpret this exhibit, suppose that an investor wanted to buy an option on AT&T common stock, the fifth company listed on the chart. The first column indicates that AT&T shares closed that day at $64.75, while the next two columns list the exercise prices and expiration months for the available contracts. By convention, stock options expire on the Saturday following the third Friday of the designated month. The next two columns show the volume (number of contracts traded) and closing price, respectively, for AT&T calls; the final two columns provide similar information for AT&T puts.

Assume this investor wanted to buy an April AT&T call with a striking price of $60. This contract would cost a total of $587.50, calculated as the stated "per share" price of $5.875 multiplied by 100 shares. In exchange for that payment, the holder of this American-style call would then be able to exercise the option in mid-April—or any time

---

[2] Call options issued directly by the firm whose common stock is the underlying asset are called *warrants*. We discuss the use and valuation of these contracts in Chapter 25.

FIGURE 24.1   **STOCK OPTION QUOTATIONS**

Tuesday, January 23, 1996

Composite volume and close for actively traded equity and LEAPS, or long-term options, with results for the corresponding put or call contract. Volume figures are unofficial. Open interest is total outstanding for all exchanges and reflects previous trading day. Close when possible is shown for the underlying stock on primary market. **CB**-Chicago Board Options Exchange. **AM**-American Stock Exchange. **PB**-Philadelphia Stock Exchange. **PC**-Pacific Stock Exchange. **NY**-New York Stock Exchange. **XC**-Composite. **p**-Put.

MOST ACTIVE CONTRACTS

Option/Strike		Vol	Exch	Last	Net Chg	a-Close	Open Int
Compaq	Feb 50	16,885	PC	2⁵⁄₁₆	+ ⁷⁄₁₆	49⅝	10,363
Tex In	Feb 50	7,443	CB	1⅛	− 1⁵⁄₁₆	46¼	12,648
I B M	Feb 105	5,995	CB	1¹³⁄₁₆	...	102⅞	9,851
Arakis	Jul 5	5,286	XC	¾	− ⅜	4	1,463
ReadRt	Feb 25	4,666	XC	⁷⁄₁₆	− 1³⁄₁₆	20½	7,556
AppleC	Feb 35	4,636	AM	¾	− ³⁄₁₆	31⅝	5,311
Compaq	Feb 50 p	4,408	PC	2⁹⁄₁₆	− 1³⁄₁₆	49⅝	5,810
Tex In	Feb 40	4,349	CB	½	+ ¹⁄₁₆	46¼	1,201
MicrTc	Feb 35	4,314	XC	1	− ¹⁄₁₆	32	13,365
I B M	Feb 100	4,294	CB	4⅝	+ ⅜	102⅞	8,457
I B M	Feb 100 p	3,766	CB	1¹¹⁄₁₆	− ⅜	102⅞	7,605
Citicp	Jan 97 60 p	3,555	CB	2½	− ¼	69½	1,532
MicrTc	Feb 30	3,388	XC	1³⁄₁₆	− ¹⁄₁₆	32	12,280
I B M	Feb 110	3,124	CB	¹¹⁄₁₆	...	102⅞	1,006
OfceDp	Apr 25	2,850	AM	½	+ ¼	19¼	1,156
AppleC	Feb 35 p	2,840	AM	3⅜	− 3	31⅝	2,959
SynMic	Feb 50	2,663	PC	1³⁄₁₆	− 1⁵⁄₁₆	44¼	4,706
TelBrasl	Feb 55	2,618	XC	2⅜	− ⅛	55	6,782
Oracle	Mar 50	2,584	CB	1⁹⁄₁₆	+ ¹⁄₁₆	46¼	3,754
MicrTc	Jul 40	2,528	XC	3	...	32	3,301

Option/Strike		Vol	Exch	Last	Net Chg	a-Close	Open Int
Compaq	Feb 45 p	2,514	PC	¾	− ⁹⁄₁₆	49⅝	4,565
BarickG	Feb 30	2,511	AM	¾	− ⅛	29½	7,204
TelMex	Feb 30 p	2,509	XC	¼	− ¹⁄₁₆	33¾	6,567
GnMotr	Jan 97 50 p	2,433	CB	4¼	− ⅛	50	11,905
Dig Eq	Feb 70	2,415	XC	3⅛	+ ⅛	70	5,034
I B M	Feb 95 p	2,404	CB	⅝	− ⅛	102⅞	5,714
Compaq	Feb 55	2,329	PC	¾	+ ⅛	49⅝	4,501
Intel	Feb 55	2,320	AM	1¹¹⁄₁₆	+ ³⁄₁₆	52¹¹⁄₁₆	15,809
AppleC	Feb 32½	2,297	AM	1⅝	+ ¹⁄₁₆	31⅝	3,313
Arakis	Apr 5 p	2,279	XC	1⅞	+ ⁵⁄₁₆	4	478
TelMex	Feb 35	2,216	XC	¹³⁄₁₆	− ³⁄₁₆	33¾	17,236
BarickG	Apr 30	2,199	AM	1⁹⁄₁₆	− ¼	29½	7,704
Dig Eq	Feb 75	2,188	XC	1⁷⁄₁₆	...	70	
Motrla	Apr 50 p	2,096	AM	2³⁄₁₆	+ ³⁄₁₆	53	3,666
Intel	Feb 45	2,087	AM	¼	− ¹⁄₁₆	52¹¹⁄₁₆	2,006
Chase	Jan 97 55	2,075	AM	2½	− ⅛	63¼	1,829
AppleC	Feb 30	2,055	AM	1⅛	− ⅞	31⅝	3,836
Cirrus	Jun 25	2,030	XC	2¼	...	20⁷⁄₁₆	588
TelBrasl	Mar 55	2,015	XC	3⅝	...	55	
TelBrasl	Feb 55 p	2,013	XC	2¹⁄₁₆	− ⁹⁄₁₆	55	3,936

(Stock option quotation tables — detailed Call/Put listings for individual issues ADC Tel through Gandlf and EmrsEl through Gandlf.)

Source: *The Wall Street Journal*, January 24, 1996.

before then—by paying $6,000 (= $60 × 100) and receive 100 AT&T shares from the option seller, who is obligated to make that exchange at the buyer's request. That request will only be rational if the mid-April price of AT&T is greater than $60. If the price closes below $60, the investor will simply let the call expire without acting on the option; that is her right as the derivative buyer. Finally, with the January share price of $64.75, the investor could immediately recover $4.75 of the $5.875 she paid for the contract. Thus, her time premium of $1.125 (= $5.875 – $4.75) preserves her right to buy AT&T stock at $60 for the next three months even if the market value of those shares moves higher.[3]

Consider another investor who sells the "April 60" AT&T put. In return for an upfront receipt of $75 (= $0.75 × 100), he now must stand ready to buy 100 shares of stock in mid-April for $6,000 if the option holder chooses to exercise his option to sell. The stock price will, of course, have to fall from its current level before this would occur. The investor has sold an out-of-the-money contract and hopes that it will stay out of the money through expiration, letting the passing of time "decay" the time premium to zero. As we saw earlier, the front-end premium is all that sellers of put or call options ever receive, and they hope to retain as much of it as possible. Like the long position in the call, the short put position benefits from an increase in AT&T share prices.

STOCK INDEX OPTIONS   Options on stock indexes such as Standard & Poor's 100 or 500 are patterned closely after equity options; however, they differ in one important way: Index options can only be settled in cash. This is because of the underlying index, which is a hypothetical portfolio that would be quite costly to duplicate in practice. First traded on the CBOE in 1983, index options are popular with investors for the same reason as stock index futures: They provide a relatively inexpensive and convenient way to take an investment or hedging position in a broad-based indicator of market performance. Index puts are particularly useful in portfolio insurance applications such as the protective put strategy described in Chapter 11.

Prices for three of the more widely traded contracts are listed in Figure 24.2. They are interpreted in the same way as equity option prices, with each contract demanding the transfer of 100 "shares" of the underlying index. For example, the March S&P 500 index call and put contracts with an exercise price of 600 could be purchased for $2,000 (= $20 × 100) and $600 ($6 × 100), respectively. On the expiration date, which will be the third Friday of the month, the holder of the call would exercise the contract to "buy" $60,000 worth of the index if the prevailing S&P 500 level is greater than 600, with the put being exercised at index levels less than 600.

FOREIGN CURRENCY OPTIONS   Foreign currency options are structurally parallel to the currency futures contracts discussed in Chapter 23. That is, each contract allows for the sale or purchase of a set amount of foreign (i.e., non-U.S. dollar) currency at a fixed exchange (FX) rate. A currency call option is like the long position in the currency futures since it permits the contract holder to buy the currency at a later date. (Of course, unlike futures, options do not require that this exchange be made.) A currency put is therefore the option analog to being short in the futures market. These contracts exist for several major currencies, including French francs, Japanese yen, German deutschemarks, British pounds, and Swiss francs. The majority of currency options trading, which began in 1982, occurs

---

[3] Recall from Chapter 11 that a call option's value can be divided into two components: the *intrinsic value*, which is the greater of either zero or the stock price minus the exercise price, and the *time premium*. In this example, the AT&T call is said to be *in the money* because it has positive intrinsic value, whereas an option with no intrinsic value is *out of the money*.

FIGURE 24.2   STOCK INDEX OPTION QUOTATIONS

S & P 100 INDEX (OEX)

Exp	Strike	Vol	Last	Net Chg	Open Int
Feb	500 c	6	86	+ 1½	11
Feb	500 p	166	3/16	+ 1/16	3,685
Feb	505 p	1,030	3/16	...	2,432
Feb	510 p	4,333	¼	...	5,611
Mar	510 c	7	78	+ 11 7/8	133
Mar	510 p	100	5/8	...	1,707
Feb	515 c	400	5/16	...	1,996
Mar	515 c	3	73	+ 6¼	330
Mar	515 p	250	11/16	− 1/16	340
Feb	520 p	3,137	3/8	+ 1/8	3,130
Mar	520 c	2	67	+ 7½	13
Mar	520 p	12	13/16	+ 1/16	1,286
Feb	525 p	200	7/16	+ 1/16	2,878
Mar	525 c	7	61½	+ 4 3/8	10
Mar	525 p	186	11/16	+ 3/16	274
Feb	530 p	675	7/16	...	5,599
Mar	530 p	5	13/16	+ 1/16	2,083
Feb	535 p	1,012	9/16	...	4,031
Feb	535 c	58	53	+ 4¾	35
Mar	535 p	104	1½	+ 1/8	1,440
Apr	535 c	1	54¾	...	...
Apr	535 p	1	2¾	...	...
Feb	540 c	1,916	11/16	...	12,750
Mar	540 c	66	47½	− 1	53
Mar	540 p	37	1 13/16	+ 1/8	2,045
Apr	540 c	2	51¾	+ 7½	13
Apr	540 p	122	2 7/8	+ 4 3/8	3,381
May	540 p	20	4 1/8	+ 1/8	13
Feb	545 p	532	¾	− 1/16	9,889
Mar	545 c	8	42	+ 2¾	2
Mar	545 p	112	2 1/8	+ 3/16	3,330
Apr	545 p	2	3 5/8	...	...
Feb	550 c	6	35	− 1½	300
Feb	550 p	2,776	1	− 1/16	14,754
Mar	550 p	193	2 3/8	− 1/8	3,257
Apr	550 p	43	4	...	783
May	550 p	50	4¾	− 5/8	56
Feb	555 c	2,420	13/16	− 3/16	23,267
Mar	555 c	2	35¾	+ 5½	11
Mar	555 p	434	2 7/8	− ¼	6,515
Apr	555 p	1	5 1/8	+ ½	377
Feb	560 c	20	28	...	932
Feb	560 p	2,308	1 9/16	− ¼	13,822
Mar	560 p	175	3 3/8	+ 1/8	3,111
Apr	560 p	18	5½	+ ¼	507
May	560 c	2	36 7/8	...	...
May	560 p	7	7	+ ½	25
Feb	565 c	1	23 1/8	− ¼	332
Feb	565 p	2,978	2 1/16	− 3/8	18,379
Mar	565 c	3	27¼	...	...
Mar	565 p	405	4 3/8	− 1/8	2,355
Apr	565 p	13	7	+ 3/8	34
Feb	570 c	391	18 5/8	− 7/8	4,296
Feb	570 p	5,275	2¾	− ½	19,926
Mar	570 p	586	5¼	− 1/8	4,085
Apr	570 p	10	7 3/8	− 3/8	647
May	570 c	6	28½	− 1	6
May	570 p	7	8 5/8	− 3/8	26
Feb	575 c	105	14¼	− ¾	8,238
Feb	575 p	9,324	3 5/8	− ¾	24,315
Mar	575 c	101	18 7/8	− 3/8	575
Mar	575 p	410	6 3/8	− ¼	1,267
Apr	575 p	70	8½	...	185
Feb	580 c	4,263	11¾	+ ¾	17,315
Feb	580 c	16,837	4 7/8	− ½	34,471
Mar	580 c	503	15	− 1 1/8	3,473
Mar	580 p	1,047	7 7/8	− ¼	5,898
Apr	580 c	51	20½	+ 2¼	660

S & P 500 INDEX-AM (SPX)

Exp	Strike	Vol	Last	Net Chg	Open Int
Feb	400 c	208	213	+ 1	6,772
Feb	400 p	200	1/8	+ 1/16	550
Mar	450 p	726	1/16	...	6,719
Mar	475 p	200	1/8	− 1/16	17,361
Feb	500 p	350	1/16	...	5,697
Mar	500 c	30	114	+ 6¼	2,378
Mar	500 p	318	3/16	− 1/16	19,414
Feb	520 p	500	1/8	...	650
Feb	525 c	400	90 5/8	+ 1¼	7,670
Feb	530 p	1,550	3/16	...	600
Feb	540 p	5	¾	...	9,784
Feb	550 p	40	3/8	+ 1/16	3,300
Mar	550 c	204	64½	+ 3	16,046
Mar	550 p	155	11/16	+ 1/16	21,808
Apr	550 p	158	1 7/8	...	...
Feb	555 p	201	57¼	...	1,950
Mar	555 p	5	1¼	+ 1/8	1,553
Feb	560 p	100	1½	...	9,695
Mar	560 p	101	1¼	− 1/16	15,624
Feb	565 p	1,190	9/16	+ 1/16	15,039
Feb	570 c	1	43	+ 3¼	158
Feb	570 p	475	¾	+ 1/16	17,252
Mar	570 p	2,202	1 15/16	− 1/8	12,521
Feb	575 p	63	7/8	− 1/8	14,736
Mar	575 p	650	2 1/8	− ¼	19,649
Apr	575 p	104	3½	...	254
Feb	580 p	807	11/16	− 1/16	7,511
Mar	580 p	2,852	2½	− 1/8	13,118
Apr	580 p	115	4½	...	...
Feb	585 c	367	1 3/8	...	5,824
Mar	585 p	45	3½	+ 1/8	42,334
Feb	590 c	1,200	25 7/8	+ 1 3/8	1,867
Feb	590 p	1,873	½	+ 1/8	16,954
Mar	590 p	328	3¾	− 1/8	10,336
Apr	590 p	200	4 7/8	+ ¼	100
Feb	595 c	10	21¼	+ 1	683
Feb	595 p	932	2 3/8	− 1/8	22,636
Mar	595 c	5	23½	+ 1 5/8	1,628
Mar	595 p	140	4¾	...	4,024
Feb	600 c	257	17¼	+ 1 1/8	18,028
Feb	600 p	2,299	3 1/8	− 3/8	37,286
Mar	600 c	100	20	− 1¼	7,933
Mar	600 p	468	6	...	17,639
Apr	600 c	5	24¾	...	...

NASDAQ-100 (NDX)

Exp	Strike	Vol	Last	Net Chg	Open Int
Feb	500 p	25	1¾	...	11,835
Mar	500 p	6	4½	− 4	549
Apr	500 p	140	8	...	...
Feb	510 p	10	2¼	...	105
Feb	520 p	65	2¾	− 5/8	3,153
Feb	525 p	60	3	− 7/8	155
Feb	530 p	71	4	− ¾	4,601
Mar	530 p	16	10	− 8	517
Feb	535 p	130	4½	− 6	293
Feb	540 p	20	6¼	− ½	2,627
Feb	545 p	289	7	− ½	324
Feb	550 c	6	27	− 4	895
Feb	550 p	16	9	+ ¾	840
Mar	550 p	3	16	+ ½	220
Feb	555 c	2	24½	+ 1½	275
Feb	555 p	25	11	+ ¾	218
Feb	560 c	1	21 5/8	− 2 5/8	209
Feb	560 p	289	11 7/8	− 1 1/8	446
Feb	565 c	47	18½	...	43
Mar	565 p	3	20 7/8	...	...
Feb	570 c	60	15½	− 1 1/8	731
Feb	570 p	27	15½	− 1	471
Mar	570 c	10	26¾	+ 3½	940
Apr	570 c	30	32	...	...
Feb	575 p	17	18¼	− ¾	199
Feb	580 c	134	10	− 1¼	738
Feb	580 p	21	20 1/8	− 1 7/8	1,173
Mar	580 c	5	19 5/8	+ 7/8	90
Feb	585 c	127	8¾	− 1¼	2,422
Feb	585 p	50	26	+ 1 3/8	210
Feb	590 p	100	27¼	− 1¼	537
Feb	595 c	50	7¼	+ ¾	278
Feb	600 c	111	4	− ½	612
Mar	600 p	4	40½	− 16½	404
Apr	600 c	140	18½	...	...
Mar	605 c	10	10 3/8	...	...
Feb	610 c	3	2	− 1	513
Feb	615 c	25	1¼	− 7/16	1,448
Feb	620 c	550	1 1/8	+ 1/8	8,600
Mar	630 c	10	4¼	...	21
Mar	645 c	10	1 7/8	...	...

Source: *The Wall Street Journal*, January 24, 1996.

on the PHLX. Figure 24.3 shows quotes from a sample of the available contracts, along with the spot foreign exchange rates for the same trading day.

Like the FX futures market, all of the prices are quoted from the perspective of U.S.-based investors. Consider, for example, an investor who lives in New York and holds Canadian dollar–denominated provincial government bonds in his portfolio. It is January, and when the bonds come due in two months, he will need to convert the proceeds back into U.S. dollars, which exposes him to a possible weakening in the Canadian currency. Accordingly, he buys the March put on the Canadian dollar with an exercise price of USD 0.77/CAD for a total price of USD 1,965.00 (= 50,000 × .0393). This option would allow the holder to sell CAD 50,000 in March for a total price of USD 38,500 (= 50,000 × 0.77). Obviously, our investor will only exercise the contract if the spot USD/CAD price

FIGURE 24.3

FOREIGN CURRENCY OPTION QUOTATIONS

	Calls Vol. Last	Puts Vol. Last
FFranc		**197.53**
250,000 French Franc EOM-European style.		
19¾ Jan	... ...	775 0.44
JYen		**94.47**
6,250,000 Japanese Yen-100ths of a cent per unit.		
90 Jun	... ...	2 0.80
91 Mar	... ...	1 0.26
92 Jun	... ...	1 1.25
94 Mar	... ...	10 1.05
95 Feb	40 0.84	... ...
97 Mar	50 0.87	... ...
105 Mar	600 0.06	... ...
DMark		**67.61**
62,500 German Mark EOM-European style.		
69 Feb	250 0.38	... ...
62,500 German Marks EOM-European style.		
66½ Feb	... ...	250 0.32
Australian Dollar		**73.47**
50,000 Australian Dollars-European Style.		
72 Jun	... ...	30 1.12
74 Mar	20 0.53	... ...
75 Mar	30 0.30	... ...
50,000 Australian Dollars-cents per unit.		
73 Feb	... ...	10 0.46
74 Mar	... ...	6 1.45
British Pound		**151.51**
31,250 British Pound EOM-cents per unit.		
152 Jan	10 0.27	... ...
31,250 British Pounds-European Style.		
137½ Mar	... ...	20 1.10
153 Feb	32 0.48	... ...
155 Mar	14 0.63	... ...
31,250 British Pounds-cents per unit.		
150 Mar	... ...	5 1.40
151 Feb	... ...	10 1.02
153 Feb	10 0.54	... ...
153 Mar	65 1.12	... ...

	Calls Vol. Last	Puts Vol. Last
155 Feb	... ...	10 3.77
British Pound-GMark		**224.12**
31,250 British Pound-German Mark cross.		
224 Feb	32 1.28	... ...
226 Mar	32 1.06	... ...
Canadian Dollar		**73.11**
50,000 Canadian Dollars-cents per unit.		
73 Mar	... ...	41 0.53
73 Jun	... ...	96 1.02
73½ Feb	... ...	3 0.71
73½ Mar	100 0.34	... ...
74 Feb	250 0.10	... ...
77 Mar	... ...	25 3.93
French Franc		**197.53**
250,000 French Francs-10ths of a cent per unit.		
20¾ Feb	... ...	7 10.12
GMark-JYen		**71.57**
62,500 German Mark-Japanese Yen cross EOM.		
72 Jan	15 0.12	... ...
62,500 German Mark-Japanese Yen cross.		
74 Feb	16 0.07	... ...
German Mark		**67.61**
62,500 German Marks EOM-cents per unit.		
66 Mar	... ...	1000 0.54
67 Jan	... ...	30 0.11
68 Mar	40 0.11	... ...
62,500 German Marks-European Style.		
66½ Feb	... ...	20 0.25
67 Feb	... ...	40 0.35
67 Mar	... ...	250 0.64
67½ Feb	... ...	20 0.56
68 Feb	... ...	20 0.75
68½ Feb	32 0.35	... ...
62,500 German Marks-cents per unit.		
64 Jun	... ...	300 0.49
66 Mar	... ...	1000 0.42
67 Feb	... ...	30 0.45

	Calls Vol. Last	Puts Vol. Last
67 Mar	... ...	20 0.75
67½ Feb	25 0.99	12 0.49
67½ Feb	... ...	100 0.91
68 Mar	... ...	10 1.20
68 Jun	... ...	4 1.74
68½ Feb	10 0.40	... ...
69 Feb	... ...	200 1.56
69 Mar	... ...	1 1.62
69½ Mar	2 0.52	... ...
70 Mar	2 0.44	... ...
71 Mar	... ...	6 3.36
71½ Feb	10 0.04	... ...
Japanese Yen		**94.47**
92½ Mar	... ...	30 0.56
92½ Mar	... ...	40 0.59
6,250,000 Japanese Yen-European Style		
120 Mar	... ...	10 24.50
120 Jun	... ...	10 23.05
6,250,000 Japanese Yen-European Style.		
94 Feb	... ...	100 0.52
96 Feb	10 0.59	... ...
Swiss Franc		**84.11**
62,500 Swiss Francs-European Style.		
80 Jun	5 6.12	... ...
82 Feb	5 2.77	... ...
83 Feb	... ...	30 0.41
83 Jun	... ...	50 1.46
88 Mar	60 0.44	... ...
62,500 Swiss Francs-cents per unit.		
81 Jun	... ...	50 0.98
82 Jun	... ...	97 1.28
84 Feb	10 1.09	... ...
85 Mar	20 1.40	... ...
85½ Mar	20 1.21	... ...
86 Mar	12 0.89	... ...
Call Vol 3,824		**Open Int ... 156,181**
Put Vol 5,635		**Open Int ... 187,493**

Key Currency Cross Rates   Late New York Trading Jan 23, 1996

	Dollar	Pound	SFranc	Guilder	Peso	Yen	Lira	D-Mark	FFranc	CdnDlr
Canada	1.3681	2.0720	1.1510	.82610	.18426	.01295	.00086	.92502	.27022	....
France	5.0630	7.6679	4.2596	3.0572	.68189	.04792	.00317	3.4233	....	3.7008
Germany	1.4790	2.2399	1.2443	.89306	.19919	.01400	.00093	....	.29212	1.0811
Italy	1595.0	2415.6	1341.9	963.11	214.81	15.097	....	1078.4	315.03	1165.9
Japan	105.65	160.01	88.886	63.794	14.229	....	.06624	71.433	20.867	77.224
Mexico	7.4250	11.245	6.2468	4.4834	....	.07028	.00466	5.0203	1.4665	5.4272
Netherlands ..	1.6561	2.5082	1.3933	....	.22304	.01568	.00104	1.1197	.32710	1.2105
Switzerland ...	1.1886	1.8001	....	.71771	.16008	.01125	.00075	.80365	.23476	.86880
U.K.	.66028	....	.55551	.39870	.08893	.00625	.00041	.44644	.13041	.48263
U.S.	....	1.5145	.84133	.60383	.13468	.00947	.00063	.67613	.19751	.73094

Source: Dow Jones Telerate Inc.

Source: *The Wall Street Journal*, January 24, 1996.

prevailing in March is less than 0.77 (i.e., if the Canadian dollar weakened relative to the U.S. currency). Finally, because the spot rate is USD 0.73094/CAD, this option is deep in the money, that is, the contract price of 0.0393 consists of 0.03906 (= 0.77 − 0.73094) of intrinsic value and 0.00024 of time premium.

OPTIONS ON FUTURES CONTRACTS   Although they have existed for decades in the OTC markets, options on futures contracts have only been exchange-traded since 1982. Also known as futures options, they give the holder the right, but not the obligation, to enter into a futures contract on an underlying security or commodity at a later date and at a predetermined price. Purchasing a call on a futures allows for the acquisition of a long position in the futures market, while exercising a put would create a short futures position. On the other hand, the seller of the call would be obligated to enter into the short side of the futures contract if the option holder decided to exercise the contract, while the seller of the put might be forced into a long futures position. Figure 24.4 lists quotations for options

FIGURE 24.4 — FUTURES OPTION QUOTATIONS

AGRICULTURAL

CORN (CBT)
5,000 bu.; cents per bu.

Strike Price	Calls-Settle Mar	May	Jly	Puts-Settle Mar	May	Jly
340	21¼	27½	28	¾	3¾	9½
350	12½	20½	22¼	2⅜	6½	13¾
360	6¾	14¾	18½	6	10¾	19
370	2⅞	10¼	14	12	16½	25
380	1	7	11	20½	23	31¾
390	⅜	4½	8½	29	....	....

Est vol 25,000 Mn 10,996 calls 6,278 puts
Op int Mon 205,156 calls 195,516 puts

SOYBEANS (CBT)
5,000 bu.; cents per bu.

Strike Price	Calls-Settle Mar	May	Jly	Puts-Settle Mar	May	Jly
700	38¼	46	52¼	⅞	4	8½
725	18⅛	31	38	5⅜	12¾	19
750	5⅞	19	28½	18	26¼	34
775	1¾	12¼	21	38¾	44	50½
800	¾	8½	16¾	62¾	64½	71
825	⅜	5½	12½	....	87	....

Est vol 19,000 Mn 11,747 calls 6,085 puts
Op int Mon 123,676 calls 86,623 puts

SOYBEAN MEAL (CBT)
100 tons; $ per ton

Strike Price	Calls-Settle Mar	May	Jly	Puts-Settle Mar	May	Jly
220	17.00	19.90	21.30	.30	1.20	2.25
230	7.75	11.90	14.10	1.00	3.00	4.90
240	2.20	6.75	9.25	5.50	8.00	....
250	.45	3.85	6.30	13.60	15.00	....
260	.20	2.25	4.40	23.25	23.20	....
270	.10	1.40	3.25	....	....	....

Est vol 1,200 Mn 494 calls 699 puts
Op int Mon 24,051 calls 20,496 puts

SOYBEAN OIL (CBT)
60,000 lbs.; cents per lb.

Strike Price	Calls-Settle Mar	May	Jly	Puts-Settle Mar	May	Jly
2350	.600	....	....	.150	.300	.350
2400	.320	.830	1.170	.340	.500	.530
2450	.130	.590	....	.650	.750	.780
2500	.080	.450	.750	1.100	1.100	1.080
2550	.040	....	.580	1.560	1.450	1.430

Est vol 550 Mn 274 calls 465 puts
Op int Mon 12,593 calls 12,415 puts

WHEAT (CBT)
5,000 bu.; cents per bu.

Strike Price	Calls-Settle Mar	May	Jly	Puts-Settle Mar	May	Jly
470	24¼	16½	10	2½	22¼	....
480	16½	12	8	4½	28	....
490	11	9½	6½	8¾	35	64½
500	6⅝	7½	5	14¼	43	....
510	3¾	4½	....	21¼	50¼	....
520	2	3½	2¾	29½	59	....

Est vol 5,000 Mn 2,307 calls 1,927 puts
Op int Mon 57,842 calls 42,345 puts

INDEX

S&P 500 STOCK INDEX (CME)
$500 times premium

Strike Price	Calls-Settle Feb	Mar	Jun	Puts-Settle Feb	Mar	Jun
605	14.75	17.75	....	3.65	6.70	12.25
610	11.10	14.35	25.20	4.95	8.25	13.80
615	7.90	11.30	22.00	6.75	10.15	15.50
620	5.35	8.60	19.05	9.20	12.40	17.45
625	3.30	6.35	16.40	12.10	15.15	19.70
630	2.00	4.50	13.90	15.80	18.25	22.05

Est vol 12,821 Mn 7,867 calls 16,085 puts
Op int Mon 85,846 calls 160,102 puts

OIL

CRUDE OIL (NYM)
1,000 bbls.; $ per bbl.

Strike Price	Calls-Settle Mar	Apr	May	Puts-Settle Mar	Apr	May
1700	1.18	1.04	.95	.12	.37	.48
1750	.80	.78	.70	.24	.56	.70
1800	.46	.51	.50	.40	.84	1.03
1850	.24	.34	.34	.68	1.17	....
1900	.12	.22	.23	1.06	1.54	1.75
1950	.05	.14	.16	1.49	....	....

Est vol 17,540 Mn 5,316 calls 7,361 puts
Op int Mon 190,785 calls 120,662 puts

HEATING OIL No.2 (NYM)
42,000 gal.; $ per gal.

Strike Price	Calls-Settle Feb	Mar	Apr	Puts-Settle Feb	Mar	Apr
51	.0208	.0210	.0130	.0013	.0128	.0272
52	.0125	.0165	.0100	.0030	.0183	.0341
53	.0068	.0120	.0075	.0073	.0238	.0416
54	.0030	.0090	.0058	.0135	.0307	.0498
55	.0011	.0068	.0042	.0216	.0385	....
56	.0007	.0050	.0032	.0312	.0466	....

Est vol 3,901 Mn 5,749 calls 1,201 puts
Op int Mon 59,805 calls 35,304 puts

GASOLINE-Unlead (NYM)
42,000 gal.; $ per gal.

Strike Price	Calls-Settle Feb	Mar	Apr	Puts-Settle Feb	Mar	Apr
52	.0184	.0241	.0446	.0018	.0123	.0095
53	.0107	.0186	....	.0041	.0168	....
54	.0049	.0146	.0314	.0083	.0228	.0162
55	.0025	.0111	.0260	.0159	.0292	.0207
56	.0009	.0084	.0210	.0243	.0365	.0257
57	.0004	.0062	.0172	.0338	.0443	.0318

Est vol 2,925 Mn 978 calls 519 puts
Op int Mon 21,688 calls 12,820 puts

NATURAL GAS (NYM)
10,000 MMBtu.; $ per MMBtu.

Strike Price	Calls-Settle Feb	Mar	Apr	Puts-Settle Feb	Mar	Apr
230	.177	.111	.033	.032	.291	....
235	.141	.096	....	.046	.326	....
240	.108	.083	.018	.062	.363	....
245	.080	.072	....	.085	....	....
250	.060	.062	.011	.115	.442	....
255	.045	.053	....	.150	.483	....

Est vol 9,964 Mn 4,390 calls 5,368 puts
Op int Mon 98,164 calls 81,574 puts

CURRENCY

DEUTSCHEMARK (CME)
125,000 marks; cents per mark

Strike Price	Calls-Settle Feb	Mar	Apr	Puts-Settle Feb	Mar	Apr
6700	1.11	1.46	....	0.29	0.65	0.80
6750	0.78	1.15	....	0.46	0.84	1.00
6800	0.52	0.90	1.38	0.70	1.08	1.23
6850	0.33	0.69	1.14	1.01	1.36	1.49
6900	0.20	0.52	0.94	1.38	1.69	1.78
6950	0.12	0.39	0.76	1.80	2.06	....

Est vol 10,142 Mn 4,005 calls 4,909 puts
Op int Mon 47,244 calls 54,768 puts

CANADIAN DOLLAR (CME)
100,000 Can.$, cents per Can.$

Strike Price	Calls-Settle Feb	Mar	Apr	Puts-Settle Feb	Mar	Apr
7200	....	1.20	....	0.05	0.16	....
7250	0.68	0.85	....	0.13	0.30	....
7300	0.36	0.56	0.66	0.31	0.51	0.65
7350	0.15	0.34	....	0.60	0.79	....
7400	0.05	0.19	....	1.00	1.13	....
7450	0.02	0.10	....	1.47	1.54	....

Est vol 154 Mn 38 calls 196 puts
Op int Mon 7,007 calls 5,785 puts

BRITISH POUND (CME)
62,500 pounds; cents per pound

Strike Price	Calls-Settle Feb	Mar	Apr	Puts-Settle Feb	Mar	Apr
14900	2.62	3.18	....	0.36	0.94	....
15000	1.86	2.52	2.88	0.60	1.26	....
15100	1.22	1.96	....	0.96	1.68	2.36
15200	0.74	1.46	....	1.48	2.20	....
15300	0.40	1.10	....	2.14	2.82	3.54
15400	0.26	0.78	....	3.00	5.50	....

Est vol 23,899 Mn 24,213 calls 16,-273 puts
Op int Mon 40,498 calls 56,289 puts

METALS

COPPER (CMX)
25,000 lbs.; cents per lb.

Strike Price	Calls-Settle Feb	Mar	Apr	Puts-Settle Feb	Mar	Apr
114	1.75	3.85	3.50	.50	2.60	4.80
116	.65	2.75	2.70	1.30	3.50	6.00
118	.30	2.00	2.10	3.00	5.75	7.30
120	.10	1.35	1.60	4.75	6.10	8.80
122	.05	.45	.70	9.70	10.20	13.00
124	.05	.25	.35	14.70	15.00	17.70

Est vol 300 Mn 151 calls 181 puts
Op int Mon 4,157 calls 3,135 puts

GOLD (CMX)
100 troy ounces; $ per troy ounce

Strike Price	Calls-Settle Mar	Apr	Jun	Puts-Settle Mar	Apr	Jun
380	26.50	26.80	28.30	.20	.40	1.40
390	16.70	17.10	20.20	.50	1.20	2.80
400	8.40	10.20	13.80	2.00	3.80	5.80
410	3.20	5.30	8.60	6.70	8.90	10.70
420	1.20	3.00	5.80	14.60	16.60	17.80
430	.40	1.80	4.40	23.90	23.90	26.00

Est vol 12,500 Mn 8,530 calls 1,693 puts
Op int Mon 179,561 calls 57,576 puts

SILVER (CMX)
5,000 troy ounces; cts per troy ounce

Strike Price	Calls-Settle Mar	Apr	May	Puts-Settle Mar	Apr	May
500	57.5	63.0	64.5	0.3	0.8	2.8
525	33.4	40.7	44.4	1.0	3.4	7.5
550	14.4	23.3	29.1	6.9	10.8	16.8
575	5.8	12.5	19.2	23.3	24.9	31.5
600	2.9	7.1	13.2	45.3	44.3	50.0
625	1.5	4.2	9.2	68.5	66.2	70.5

Est vol 5,300 Mn 2,664 calls 802 puts
Op int Mon 55,649 calls 22,009 puts

INTEREST RATE

T-BONDS (CBT)
$100,000; points and 64ths of 100%

Strike Price	Calls-Settle Mar	Jun	Sep	Puts-Settle Mar	Jun	Sep
118	2-36	3-35	4-05	0-31	1-58	2-63
119	1-56	....	0-50	....	....	....
120	1-19	2-32	3-06	1-14	2-53	3-60
121	0-53	....	....	1-47	....	....
122	0-33	1-43	2-20	2-27	3-63	....
123	0-19	....	3-13	....	....	....

Est. vol. 115,000;
Mn vol. 38,584 calls; 34,072 puts
Op. int. Mon 367,116 calls; 275,734 puts

T-NOTES (CBT)
$100,000; points and 64ths of 100%

Strike Price	Calls-Settle Mar	Jun	Sep	Puts-Settle Mar	Jun	Sep
112	2-21	2-37	....	0-08	0-60	1-30
113	1-33	1-61	2-35	0-19	1-20	1-55
114	0-56	1-28	2-04	0-41	1-50	2-21
115	0-27	1-02	1-40	1-13	2-23	....
116	0-11	0-46	1-18	1-60	....	....
117	0-05	0-31	0-62	....	....	....

Est vol 38,000 Mn 15,969 calls 13,-033 puts
Op int Mon 282,771 calls 218,551 puts

5 YR TREAS NOTES (CBT)
$100,000; points and 64ths of 100%

Strike Price	Calls-Settle Mar	Jun	Sep	Puts-Settle Mar	Jun	Sep
10900	1-25	1-42	2-01	0-06	0-37	0-63
10950	0-63	1-22	1-45	0-12	0-48	1-11
11000	0-41	1-04	....	0-22	0-62	....
11050	0-25	0-53	....	0-37	1-14	....
11100	0-14	0-40	1-00	0-58	....	1-59
11150	0-07	0-30	....	1-19	....	....

Est vol 6,800 Mn 4,539 calls 4,531 puts
Op int Mon 68,342 calls 66,667 puts

EURODOLLAR (CME)
$ million; pts. of 100%

Strike Price	Calls-Settle Feb	Mar	Apr	Puts-Settle Feb	Mar	Apr
9400	....	0.69	....	0.00	0.00	....
9425	....	0.44	....	0.00	0.00	....
9450	0.20	0.21	....	0.01	0.02	....
9475	0.04	0.06	....	0.10	0.12	0.04
9500	0.00	0.02	0.14	....	0.32	0.11
9525	0.00	0.00	0.05	....	0.56	....

Est. vol. 71,986;
Mn vol. 22,648 calls; 12,021 puts
Op. int. Mon 783,864 calls; 887,640 puts

Source: *The Wall Street Journal*, January 24, 1996.

based on a wide variety of underlying assets, including agricultural, metal, and energy commodities; treasury bonds and notes; foreign currencies; and stock indexes. Consistent with the trading patterns for the futures contracts we examined earlier, futures options on financial assets represent the largest part of the market.

To understand how these contracts work, consider a commodity futures option. The March call option on copper with an exercise price of $1.18 per ounce would cost the buyer $0.0200 per ounce covered by the futures position. Since each copper futures contract on the Commodity Exchange (COMEX) requires the transfer of 25,000 ounces of the metal, the total purchase price for this futures call is $500 (= 25,000 × $0.02). Also, because the March copper futures price on this day was $1.1525, this contract was out of the money; its per ounce price of two cents was purely a time premium.

As with any call position, the holder will only exercise at the expiration date if the prevailing price of the underlying asset exceeds the exercise price; she will let it expire worthless otherwise. This payoff structure might fit the need of an electronic appliance manufacturer exposed to higher copper prices as a factor of production or a speculator bullish on copper prices. In this example, suppose that on the expiration date of the option, the contract price of the March copper futures has risen to $1.21. At this point, she will exercise her option and assume a long position in a March futures with a contract price of $1.18 per ounce, which will require posting a margin account. Her new position will immediately be marked-to-market, however, and $750 (= ($1.21 − $1.18) × 25,000) will be added to her margin account. Alternatively, she may decide to unwind her "below market" futures contract immediately and take the $750 in cash.

The primary attraction of this derivative is the leverage it provides investors. In this example, the call buyer has been able to control 25,000 pounds of copper for two months for an investment of $500. Had she purchased the copper, it would have cost $28,812.50 (= 25,000 × $1.1525), assuming that the spot and futures prices were the same. Further, even if it required only a 5 percent margin, a long position in the copper futures contract would require a cash outlay of $1,440.63. Since leverage is the driving force behind this market, in most cases the option is set up to expire at virtually the same time as the underlying futures contract. This indicates that acquiring a futures position is not a primary concern of the option users.

OPTION TRADING STRATEGIES

The introductory analysis in Chapter 11 highlighted two ways investors use options. First, the asymmetrical payoff structures they possess as stand-alone positions allowed investors to isolate the benefits of an anticipated change in the value of an underlying security while limiting the downside risk of an adverse price movement. Options are a leveraged alternative to making a direct investment in the asset on which the contract is based. Second, options could be used in two important ways in conjunction with an existing portfolio to modify its risk or enhance its return. Specifically, the purchase of a protective put option, the most direct form of portfolio insurance, limited the portfolio's loss potential, while the sale of a covered call generated income for the investor in an otherwise static market environment.

This section introduces a third way options are used: in *combination* with one another to create customized payoff distributions that do not exist in more fundamental securities, like stocks or bonds. In designing such a combination, the investor usually attempts to exploit a specific view about future economic conditions. For example, he may believe that a particular company's stock returns will be extraordinarily volatile, but have no clear impression as to the price movement direction. On the other hand, he may feel that another company's

TABLE 24.1

HYPOTHETICAL SAS CORPORATION STOCK AND OPTION PRICES

Instrument	Exercise Price	Market Price	Intrinsic Value	Time Premium
Stock:	—	$40.00	—	—
Call: #1	$35.00	8.07	$5.00	$3.07
#2	40.00	5.24	0.00	5.24
#3	45.00	3.24	0.00	3.24
Put: #1	35.00	1.70	0.00	1.70
#2	40.00	3.67	0.00	3.67
#3	45.00	6.47	5.00	1.47

shares will trade within a very narrow range around their current price during the next few months. In developing these strategies, we return to the example in Chapter 11 of SAS Corporation, which has exchange-traded common stock as well as call and put options. Current prices for SAS stock and six different derivatives, all of which expire at the same time, are reproduced in Table 24.1.

STRADDLES, STRIPS, AND STRAPS   A straddle is the simultaneous purchase (or sale) of a call and a put option with the same underlying asset, exercise price, and expiration date. More precisely, a long straddle requires the purchase of the put and the call, while a short straddle sells both contracts. The long straddle takes positions in both a call and a put, giving the investor a combination that will appreciate in value whether stock prices rise or fall in the future. Buying two options increases the initial cost; that is, to profit from this investment, stock price movements must be more pronounced than if the investor had predicted changes in a single direction. In this sense, a straddle is a *volatility* play; the buyer expects stock prices to move strongly one way or the other, while the seller hopes for lower-than-normal volatility.

To illustrate this combination, suppose the investor purchases a put and a call on SAS stock, each with an exercise price of $40. The cost of this purchase will be the combined prices of call #2 and put #2, or $8.91 (= $5.24 + $3.67). Recalling that the terminal values of the options are $\max[0, S_T - 40]$ and $\max[0, 40 - S_T]$, respectively, the expiration date payoffs to the straddle position (net of the initial cost, unadjusted for the time value differential) are shown in Table 24.2. These are illustrated in Figure 24.5, which also depicts the payoff to the seller of the straddle. The breakeven points on this graph occur at $31.09 (= $40 - $8.91) and $48.91 (= $40 + $8.91).

TABLE 24.2

EXPIRATION DATE PAYOFFS TO A LONG STRADDLE POSITION

SAS Stock Price at Expiration	Value of Calls	Value of Puts	Cost of Options	Net Profit
$20.00	$ 0.00	$20.00	$−8.91	$11.09
25.00	0.00	15.00	−8.91	6.09
30.00	0.00	10.00	−8.91	1.09
35.00	0.00	5.00	−8.91	−3.91
40.00	0.00	0.00	−8.91	−8.91
45.00	5.00	0.00	−8.91	−3.09
50.00	10.00	0.00	−8.91	1.09
55.00	15.00	0.00	−8.91	6.09
60.00	20.00	0.00	−8.91	11.09

FIGURE 24.5   **THE STRADDLE ILLUSTRATED**

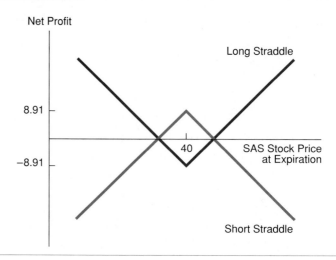

Not surprisingly, the expiration date values to the long and short positions are mirror images of each other; if the individual options themselves are zero-sum games, so too must be any combination of contracts. In particular, the buyer of the straddle is hoping for a dramatic event—such as a company-specific technological breakthrough or the impending judgment in a major lawsuit—that will either increase or decrease the stock price from its present $40 by at least $8.91. Conversely, the best result for the straddle seller is for SAS stock to continue to trade at its current price through the expiration date (i.e., no volatility at all) so that both options expire worthless. The seller's position is particularly interesting because it demonstrates that it is possible to make money in the stock market even when prices do not change.

The long straddle position assumes implicitly that the investor has no intuition about the likely direction of future stock price movements. A slight modification of this format is overweighting either the put or call position to emphasize a directional belief while maintaining a contract that would profit from a price movement the other way. A long *strap* position is the purchase of two calls and one put with the same exercise price, suggesting an investor who thinks stock prices are more likely to increase. An investor with a more "bearish" view could create a long *strip* position by purchasing two puts and only one call. The terminal payoffs to both of these combinations are listed in Table 24.3, which again assumes the use of the two at-the-money SAS contracts.

Panel A of the table shows that for the higher up-front payment of $14.15 (= (2 × $5.24) + $3.67), the strap will accelerate the payoff in a rising market relative to the straddle. The settlement payment when SAS stock finishes above $40 on the expiration date is twice as great because the strap has doubled the investor's number of calls. The gross payoff when the price falls below $40 remains the same; however, the net amount received is considerably lower because the extra contract the investor purchased would then be out of the money. The net terminal value of the strip position tells a similar story, only with the acceleration of the profit generated by falling stock prices. The strap is more expensive than the strip under these conditions because SAS is a nondividend-paying common stock that is expected to increase in price to provide the investor with a positive expected return.

TABLE 24.3   **EXPIRATION DATE PAYOFFS TO LONG STRAP AND LONG STRIP POSITIONS**

A. Strap Position (Two Calls and One Put)

SAS Stock Price at Expiration	Value of Calls	Value of Puts	Cost of Options	Net Profit
$20.00	$ 0.00	$20.00	$−14.15	$ 5.85
25.00	0.00	15.00	−14.15	0.85
30.00	0.00	10.00	−14.15	−4.15
35.00	0.00	5.00	−14.15	−9.15
40.00	0.00	0.00	−14.15	−14.15
45.00	10.00	0.00	−14.15	−4.15
50.00	20.00	0.00	−14.15	5.85
55.00	30.00	0.00	−14.15	15.85
60.00	40.00	0.00	−14.15	25.85

B. Strip Position (Two Puts and One Call)

SAS Stock Price at Expiration	Value of Calls	Value of Puts	Cost of Options	Net Profit
$20.00	$ 0.00	$40.00	$−12.58	$ 27.42
25.00	0.00	30.00	−12.58	17.42
30.00	0.00	20.00	−12.58	7.42
35.00	0.00	10.00	−12.58	−2.58
40.00	0.00	0.00	−12.58	−12.58
45.00	5.00	0.00	−12.58	−7.58
50.00	10.00	0.00	−12.58	−2.58
55.00	15.00	0.00	−12.58	2.42
60.00	20.00	0.00	−12.58	7.42

STRANGLES   One final variation on the straddle theme is an option combination known as a *strangle*. Like the straddle, a strangle is the simultaneous purchase or sale of a call and a put on the same underlying security with the same expiration date. Unlike the straddle, however, the options used in the strangle do not have the same exercise price; instead, they are chosen so that both are out of the money. By buying two out-of-the-money contracts, the investor reduces the original straddle position's initial cost. Offsetting this reduced cost, though, is that stock prices will have to change in either direction by a greater amount before the strangle becomes profitable. Thus, the strangle can be viewed as having a more modest risk–reward structure than the straddle.

As an example, suppose the investor purchased call #3 and put #1 for a combined price of $4.94 (= $3.24 + $1.70). If the price of SAS stock remained between the put exercise price of $35 and the call exercise price of $45, both contracts would expire worthless and the investor would lose his entire initial investment. Accordingly, prices would have to decline to $30.06 (= $35 − $4.94) or increase to $49.94 (= $45 + $4.94) before the investor would break even on the position. Figure 24.6 shows that these breakeven points for the strangle are outside those for the straddle described earlier. Thus, among the set of "volatility bets," the strangle costs less to implement than the straddle but requires greater movement in the underlying security's price before it generates a positive return. Finally, by varying the exercise prices on the two options—which is possible in the OTC market—the investor can create a strangle position that offers the exact tradeoff between initial cost and future expected profit that he desires.

FIGURE 24.6   **COMPARING THE LONG STRANGLE AND LONG STRADDLE POSITIONS**

CHOOSER OPTIONS   The straddle is a special case of a wider class of option contracts sometimes called *chooser* options. With a chooser option, the investor selects an exercise price and expiration date but doesn't have to decide if the option should be a put or a call until after the contract is purchased. That is, the straddle is just a chooser option for which the decision can be deferred until the expiration date. Rubinstein has shown that the value of a chooser option will depend on when the investor has to make the put or call choice.[4]

At one extreme, if the decision has to be made immediately, the buyer will select the option most likely to be in the money at expiration. In the previous example, with $X = \$40$, we have seen that this will be the call. Thus, a chooser option in this case is worth $5.24. At the other extreme, a chooser option that allows the holder to defer the decision until expiration is, as noted above, equivalent to holding both a put and a call for the entire time to expiration. Consequently, the straddle price of $8.91 is the upper bound of the chooser option value struck at $40. The usual design for the chooser contract requires the holder to make a choice after the initial purchase but before expiration, which would create a position worth somewhere between $5.24 and $8.91.

SPREADS   As described by Black, option spreads are the purchase of one contract and the sale of another, where the options are alike in all respects except for one distinguishing characteristic.[5] For example, in a *money* spread, the investor would sell an out-of-the-money call and purchase an in-the-money call on the same stock and expiration date. Alternatively, a *calendar* (or time) spread requires the purchase and sale of two calls—or two puts—with the same exercise price but different expiration dates. Option spreads are often used when one contract is perceived to be misvalued relative to the other. For instance, if an investor determines that a call option with an exercise price of X_1 and an expiration date T is selling at too high a price in the market, he can short it, thereby speculating on an eventual

[4] See Mark Rubinstein, "Options for the Undecided," in *From Black-Scholes to Black Holes* (London, England: Risk Magazine, 1992).

[5] See Fischer Black, "Fact and Fantasy in the Use of Options," *Financial Analysts Journal* 31, no. 4 (July–August 1975), pp. 36–41, 61–72.

TABLE 24.4   **EXPIRATION DATE PAYOFFS TO A BULL MONEY SPREAD POSITION**

SAS Stock Price at Expiration	Value of Call #1	Value of Call #3	Cost of Options	Net Profit
$20.00	0.00	$ 0.00	$-4.83	$-4.83
25.00	0.00	0.00	-4.83	-4.83
30.00	0.00	0.00	-4.83	-4.83
35.00	0.00	0.00	-4.83	-4.83
40.00	5.00	0.00	-4.83	0.17
45.00	10.00	0.00	-4.83	5.17
50.00	15.00	-5.00	-4.83	5.17
55.00	20.00	-10.00	-4.83	5.17
60.00	25.00	-15.00	-4.83	5.17

correction. However, if a broad-based increase in the stock market occurs before this contract-specific correction, he stands to lose a great deal because the short call position has unlimited liability. Thus, when he sells the first option, he can hedge some or all of the risk by buying a call with an exercise price of X_2 and expiring at T.

Returning to the data for SAS options, suppose the investor purchases the in-the-money call (call #1) and sells the contract that is out of the money (call #3). In this case, the option he buys is more valuable than the one he sells, leading to a net cash outlay of $4.83 (= $8.07 − $3.24). At the common expiration date, three price ranges should be considered. If SAS stock settles below $35, both options will expire worthless, and the investor will lose all of his initial investment. With a SAS price above $45, both contracts will be exercised, meaning that the investor must sell at $45 the share he bought for $35, leaving a $10 gross profit. Finally, if SAS prices fall between the two exercise prices, the investor's option will be in the money while the contract he sold will not. This situation is summarized by the net payoff calculations shown in Table 24.4.

This combination is sometimes called a *bull* money spread because it will be profitable when stock prices rise. Specifically, with the initial cost of $4.83, the investor's breakeven point occurs when the stock price rises to $39.83 (= $35 + $4.83). His benefit stops increasing if SAS shares reach $45 since this is where the short position in call #3 becomes a liability. Figure 24.7 contrasts this situation with the outright purchase of the in-the-money call. This contract would cost $8.07 initially, leading to the higher breakeven price of $43.07. It would not have a constraint on the upside profit potential, however, so once a share price of $48.24 is reached (= 45 + (8.07 − 4.83)), it would become the preferable alternative. Thus, in exchange for a lower initial purchase price, the bull spread investor is giving up the benefits of rising SAS prices after some point—a strategy that makes sense only if he expects the share price to settle within a reasonably narrow range.

The profit for a *bear* money spread (the purchase of call #3 and the sale of call #1) is the opposite of that for the bull money spread. That is, buying a bear spread is equivalent to selling a bull spread. Consequently, a long bear spread position might be used by an investor who believed stock prices might decline, but did not want to be short in the stock. Notice that a spread transaction also can be created using put options. For instance, suppose a new investor undertakes the simultaneous purchase of put #3 and sale of put #1. Her net cost to acquire the position would be $4.77 (= $6.47 − $1.70), which would then generate the terminal payoffs displayed in Figure 24.8. If SAS stock settled at $45 or higher, both puts would be worthless and the investor would lose all of her initial investment. If the expiration date share price was $35 or less, both options would be in the

FIGURE 24.7

COMPARING THE BULL MONEY SPREAD AND LONG CALL POSITIONS

FIGURE 24.8

A BEAR MONEY SPREAD WITH PUT OPTIONS

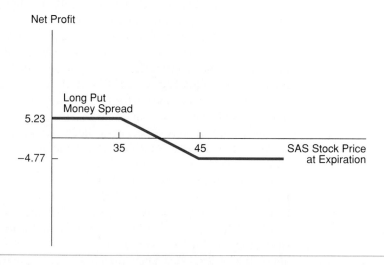

money, leaving the investor with a net position of $5.23 (= $45 − $35 − 4.77). Thus, this is the put option version of a bear money spread.

A final extension of this concept is the *butterfly* spread. Suppose an investor designed the following portfolio of SAS options: long one call #1, short two calls #2, and long one call #3. This position is equivalent to holding:

- A bull money spread (i.e., buy call #1 and sell call #2), and
- A bear money spread (i.e., buy call #3 and sell call #2).

The net purchase price for these transactions is $0.83 (= ($8.07 − $.5.24) + ($3.24 − $5.24)). The expiration date payoffs are listed in Table 24.5 and show that the value of the position peaks at a stock price of $40 and that the investor can lose, at most, her initial

TABLE 24.5					

EXPIRATION DATE PAYOFFS TO A BUTTERFLY SPREAD

SAS Stock Price at Expiration	Value of Bull Spread	Value of Bear Spread	Cost of Options	Net Profit
$20.00	$0.00	$ 0.00	$−0.83	$−0.83
25.00	0.00	0.00	−0.83	−0.83
30.00	0.00	0.00	−0.83	−0.83
35.00	0.00	0.00	−0.83	−0.83
40.00	5.00	0.00	−0.83	4.17
45.00	5.00	−5.00	−0.83	−0.83
50.00	5.00	−5.00	−0.83	−0.83
55.00	5.00	−5.00	−0.83	−0.83
60.00	5.00	−5.00	−0.83	−0.83

FIGURE 24.9	

COMPARING THE BUTTERFLY SPREAD AND SHORT STRADDLE POSITIONS

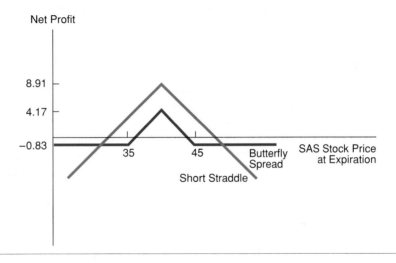

investment. The breakeven stock prices are $35.83 and $44.17. This form of the butterfly spread is equivalent to a hedged version of a short straddle position. That is, in exchange for receiving a smaller potential payoff (i.e., $4.17 versus $8.91) from a view on low volatility, the investor has limited her losses if SAS's stock price is more explosive than she expected. This tradeoff is shown in Figure 24.9.

RANGE FORWARDS

Despite a name that suggests otherwise, range (or "flexible") forwards are combinations of two option positions. They most often are used in hedging (as opposed to direct investment) applications, particularly in the management of foreign currency risk.[6] To see what they are and how they might be used in this context, suppose that the treasurer of a U.S. multinational corporation knows today that he will have a bill for imported goods that

---

[6] For a more complete discussion of range forward applications, see Roger G. Clarke and Mark P. Kritzman, *Currency Management: Concepts and Practices* (Charlottesville, VA: Research Foundation of the Institute of Chartered Financial Analysts, 1996); and Charles Smithson, Clifford W. Smith, Jr., and D. Sykes Wilford, *Managing Financial Risk* (Burr Ridge, IL: Richard D. Irwin, 1995).

TABLE 24.6				

HYPOTHETICAL DEM DERIVATIVE PRICES AND TERMS

Derivative	Contract/Striking Price (USD/DEM)	Expiration	DEM Amount	Price (USD/DEM)
Forward:	$0.67	3 months	1,000,000	—
Calls:	0.64	3 months	1,000,000	0.034
	0.67	3 months	1,000,000	0.015
	0.70	3 months	1,000,000	0.004
Puts:	0.64	3 months	1,000,000	0.004
	0.67	3 months	1,000,000	0.015
	0.70	3 months	1,000,000	0.034

must be paid in three months. This bill, denominated in German marks and requiring a payment of DEM 1,000,000, presents a challenge for a dollar-based company because it must buy the marks it needs rather than generate them in the natural flow of business. As shown in Chapter 23, this is a classic opportunity to use derivatives to hedge the firm's FX exposure.

After contacting a number of dealers in the OTC market, the treasurer establishes prices and terms for several DEM forward and option contracts. These are listed in Table 24.6, which states prices on a direct (i.e., USD/DEM) basis. The treasurer could lock in a three-month forward rate of USD 0.67/DEM without cost in two ways. First, he could commit to a long position in the DEM forward with a contract amount of DEM 1,000,000. Second, he could buy the DEM call option struck at USD 0.67/DEM and pay for it by selling the DEM put at the same exercise rate. As shown in Chapter 11, the put-call parity model indicates that buying a call and selling a put with the same exercise rate is equivalent to a long forward position. Further, this second strategy would generate a zero-cost forward (i.e., $C_0 = P_0$) only when the common exercise rate is set equal to the prevailing forward rate.

As a third alternative, what if the treasurer: (1) bought the 0.70 call for USD $0.004 per mark, and (2) sold the 0.64 put for the same price? Once again, this would be a costless combination of options; however, since the two options do not have a common exercise price, this combination is not equivalent to the actual forward—it is a range forward. At the expiration date, one of three things will happen: (1) if the spot FX rate is greater than USD 0.70/DEM, the treasurer will exercise his call and buy marks at that level; (2) if the spot FX rate is less than USD 0.64/DEM, the dealer to whom the treasurer sold the put will force him to buy marks for USD 0.64 per mark, and (3) if the spot FX rate is in between these extremes, both options will finish out of the money and the treasurer will buy the required currency at the regular market price. This payoff scheme is contrasted with the regular forward contract in Figure 24.10.

If the treasurer takes a long position in the regular forward contract, he will buy his marks at USD 0.67/DEM, whether or not the prevailing exchange rate in three months is above or below this level. Thus, although he is protected against a weakening dollar, he cannot benefit if the domestic currency strengthens. With a long position in the range forward, though, in exchange for worse FX "insurance"—namely, a maximum purchase price of USD 0.70/DEM—he could pay as little as USD 0.64/DEM if the dollar gets stronger. Finally, many zero-cost range forwards could be created; for any desired out-of-the-money call option, there will be an out-of-the-money put at some exercise price that has the same price. In fact, the actual forward contract can be viewed as a zero-cost range forward for which the put and the call options are both struck at USD 0.67/DEM.

FIGURE 24.10

COMPARING LONG POSITIONS IN REGULAR AND RANGE FORWARDS

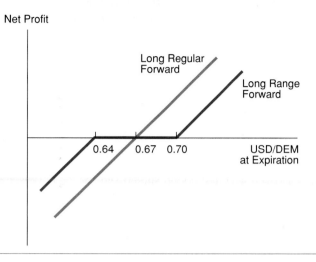

THE
FUNDAMENTALS
OF OPTION
VALUATION

Although we know that options can be used by investors to anticipate future levels of security prices, the key to understanding how they are valued comes from recognizing that they also are risk reduction tools. Specifically, in this section we show that an option's theoretical value depends on combining it with its underlying security to create a *synthetic risk-free portfolio*. That is, it always is theoretically possible to use the option as a perfect *hedge* against fluctuations in the value of the asset on which it is based.

Recall that this was essentially the same approach we used in Chapter 11 to establish the put-call parity relationships. The primary differences between put-call parity and what follows are twofold. First, the portfolio implied by the put-call parity transaction did not require special calibration; it simply consisted of one stock long, one put long, and one call short—a mixture that required no adjustment prior to the expiration date. However, hedging an underlying asset position's risk with a single option position—whether it is a put or a call—often involves using multiple contracts and frequent changes in the requisite number to maintain the riskless portfolio. Second, the put-call parity paradigm did not demand a forecast of the underlying asset's future price level whereas the following analysis will. Indeed, we will see that *forecasting the volatility of future asset prices* is the most important input the investor must provide in determining option values.

THE BASIC APPROACH

While the mathematics associated with option valuation can be complex, the fundamental intuition behind the process is straightforward and can be illustrated quite simply. Suppose you have just purchased a share of stock in WYZ Corp. for $50. The stock is not expected to pay a dividend during the time you plan to hold it, and you have made the following forecast of what the stock will be worth in one year:

Today		One Year
		65
50		
		40

Suppose further that you can either buy or sell a call option on WYZ stock with an exercise price of $52.50. If this is a European-style contract that expires in exactly one year, it will have the following possible expiration date values:

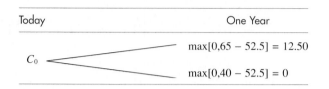

Today	One Year
	$\max[0, 65 - 52.5] = 12.50$
C_0	
	$\max[0, 40 - 52.5] = 0$

Although you do not know what the call option is worth today, you know what it is worth at expiration, given your forecast of future WYZ stock prices. The dilemma is establishing what the option should sell for today (i.e., C_0).

This question can be answered in three steps. First, design a hedge portfolio consisting of one share of WYZ stock held long and some number of call options (i.e., h), so that the combined position will be riskless. The number of call options needed can be established by ensuring that the portfolio has the same value at expiration no matter which of the two forecasted stock values occurs, or:

$$65 + (h)(12.50) = 40 + (h)(0)$$

leaving:

$$h = \frac{(65 - 40)}{(0 - 12.5)} = -2.00.$$

There are both *direction* and *magnitude* dimensions to this number. That is, the negative sign indicates that, in order to create the necessary negative correlation between two assets that are naturally positively correlated, call options must be *sold* to hedge a long stock position. Further, given that the range of possible expiration date option outcomes (i.e., $12.5 - 0$) is only half as large as the range for WYZ stock (i.e., $65 - 40$), twice as many options must be sold as there is stock in the hedge portfolio. The value h is known as the *hedge ratio*.[7] Thus, the risk-free hedge portfolio can be created by purchasing one share of stock and selling two call options.

The second step in the option valuation process assumes capital market efficiency. Specifically, suppose no arbitrage possibilities exist in these markets so that all riskless investments are priced to earn the risk-free rate over the time until expiration. That is, the hedge portfolio costing $[50 - (2)(C_0)]$ today would "grow" to the certain value of $40 by the following formula:

$$[50 - (2.00)(C_0)](1 + RFR)^T = 40$$

where

  RFR = the annualized risk-free rate
  T = the time to expiration (i.e., one year).

---

[7] In some valuation models (e.g., Black-Scholes), the hedge ratio is expressed as the option's potential volatility divided by that for the stock. In this example, that would be $(0 - 12.5) \div (65 - 40) = -0.5$, meaning that the option is half as volatile in dollar terms as the share of stock. Of course, this alternative calculation is just the reciprocal of the value of $h = -2.00$.

Two unknown values exist in this formula: C_0 and *RFR*. Finding a suitable estimate for *RFR* seldom is a problem because the investor can use as a proxy the yield-to-maturity on a U.S. Treasury security of appropriate length. For example, if the one-year T-bill yield is 8 percent, the formula for C_0 can be solved as follows:

$$C_0 = \frac{50 - 40/1.08}{2.00} = \$6.48.$$

This bit of algebraic manipulation is the third and final step in establishing the call's fair market value. That is, \$6.48 represents the fundamental value of a one-year call option on WYZ stock, given both the prevailing market prices for two other securities (i.e., stock and T-bills) and the investor's forecast of future share values. Of course, since the security prices are observable, the investor's share value forecast becomes the critical element in determining if this value is a reasonable estimate. Finally, since the call option is currently out of the money, this amount is purely a time premium.

IMPROVING FORECAST ACCURACY

Because it is unrealistic to assume only two possible outcomes for future WYZ share prices, the quality of the preceding valuation is highly suspect. To improve the accuracy of this process, the expiration date forecast of stock prices can be expanded to allow for numerous possibilities. For example, consider the following revised forecast, which includes two more potential prices in between the previous extreme values:

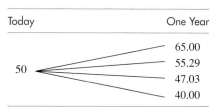

The three-step riskless hedge approach to calculating C_0 remains conceptually valid; however, the exact methodology must be modified because it is now impossible to calculate a hedge ratio that simultaneously accounts for all four date T possibilities. That is, several different hedge ratios are defined by each distinct pair of future share prices, which, in turn, means that it is impossible for the preceding valuation process to consider all four possible stock outcomes at once.

The solution to this problem requires that the time to expiration be divided into as many *subintervals* as necessary so that at any point in time the subsequent price can only move up or down. In this example, two subintervals are needed. Figure 24.11 shows how the WYZ stock price forecast might be embellished in this manner. This illustration, sometimes called a *stock price tree*, indicates that before the current stock price can reach, say, \$65 in one year, it must first move up to \$54.57 and \$59.56 in subperiods S1 and S2, respectively, before moving up a third time to its final value of \$65. Similarly, the lower extreme of \$40 only can be reached by three consecutive "down" price changes. On the other hand, three different paths exist to the two terminal outcomes in the middle: two ups and a down for \$55.29 and two downs and an up for \$47.03.

Once the investor fills in the details in this price tree, the call option's value can be solved by working backwards on each pair of possible outcomes from the future. If, for

FIGURE 24.11   **FORECASTED STOCK PRICE TREE**

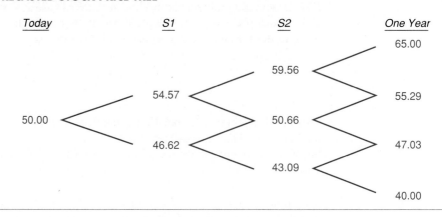

instance, two consecutive up movements left the price of WYZ stock at $59.56, a price change over the remaining subperiod could be characterized as:

The change in the value of the call option from this uppermost state of subinterval S2 (i.e., C_{21}) can then be shown as:

With $X = 52.50$, the call option would certainly be in the money for both expiration date stock values. This suggests a hedge ratio of:

$$h = \frac{(65.00 - 55.29)}{(2.79 - 12.50)} = -1.00$$

meaning that the riskless hedge portfolio at this point would contain one share of stock long and one call short. The intermediate option value is then found by solving:

$$[59.56 - (1.00)(C_{21})](1.08)^{0.33} = 52.50$$

or

$$C_{21} = \frac{59.56 - 52.50/1.026}{1.00} = \$8.39.$$

Here, 1.026 (= $(1.08)^{0.33}$) is roughly one-third of the annual risk-free rate since the original one-year holding period was divided into three equal subintervals.

After determining the value for C_{21}, the value for the option corresponding to an S2 share price of \$50.66 (i.e., C_{22}) can be established by the same three-step procedure with the stock and option price trees truncated as follows:

and:

The hedge ratio implied at this stage, reached after one up and one down price change, is:

$$h = \frac{(55.29 - 47.03)}{(0.00 - 2.79)} = -2.96$$

so that approximately three calls would be needed to hedge the single share of WYZ. Recalling that the hedge ratio after two up moves was one-to-one, notice that the composition of the riskless hedge portfolio varies with the underlying asset's prevailing price and must be adjusted after every movement. C_{22} is then given by:

$$C_{22} = \frac{50.66 - 47.03/1.026}{2.96} = \$1.63.$$

These intermediate calculations have little meaning to the investor who cares only about the current value of the option. They are, however, a necessary evil: C_0 cannot be established before determining C_{11} and C_{12}, which in turn depend on C_{21}, C_{22}, and C_{23}. Repeating the valuation process in a recursive fashion for each previous pair of stock prices results in the option price tree shown in Figure 24.12. In this case, the additional potential outcomes included in the stock price forecast have reduced the call option's value from \$6.48 to \$3.60. This valuation can become even more precise as more terminal share price outcomes are included in the forecast. At the same time, the number of pairwise calculations and the number of necessary subperiods also will increase. Consequently, although the three-step valuation method is flexible, a tradeoff exists between realism and the volume of required calculations.

THE BINOMIAL OPTION PRICING MODEL   A crucial element of this basic approach to option valuation is that future changes in the underlying asset's price always can be simplified to one of two possibilities: an up movement or a down movement. For that reason, this analytical development is part of a more

FIGURE 24.12

TREE OF CALCULATED OPTION VALUES

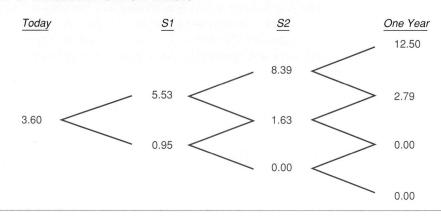

general valuation methodology known as the *two-state option pricing model*.[8] One difficulty with the preceding example, however, is that it required the investor to specify cash amounts for each of the future potential stock prices in all of the subperiods demanded by the forecast. This can be a rather daunting task as the number of terminal outcomes is allowed to grow larger with the time to expiration of the contract.

To simplify this forecasting process, suppose an investor focuses her estimates on how stock prices change from one subperiod to the next, rather than on the dollar levels. That is, beginning with today's known price for a stock, for the next subperiod she forecasts: (1) one plus the percentage change associated with an up (*u*) movement, and (2) one plus the percentage change associated with a down (*d*) movement. Further, to limit the number of required forecasts, suppose she also assumes that the same values for *u* and *d* apply to every up and down price change in all subsequent subperiods. With these assumptions, the investor need only forecast three things: *u, d,* and *N*—the total number of subperiods.

Figure 24.13 shows the effect that these modifications—which represent the essence of the **binomial option pricing model**—have on the forecasted stock price and option value trees. Consistent with the preceding example, this illustration allows for three subperiods (i.e., *N* = 3). The upper panel of the display shows that after an up and a down movement during the first two subperiods, the initial stock price of *S* will have changed to (*ud*)*S*. Of course, the values (*ud*)*S* and (*du*)*S* are equal, meaning that the forecast does not depend on whether the stock price begins its journey by rising or falling. As before, once *u, d,* and *N* are determined, the expiration date payoffs to the option (i.e., C_{uuu}, C_{uud}, C_{udd}, and C_{ddd}) are established.

The initial value for the call, C_0, can be solved by working backwards through the tree and solving for each of the remaining intermediate option values. Another distinct advantage of the binomial model relative to the basic three-step approach is that these intermediate values are much easier to compute. In fact, in the *j*th state in any subperiod, the value of the option can be calculated by:

[8] See Richard J. Rendleman, Jr., and Brit J. Bartter, "Two-State Option Pricing," *Journal of Finance* 34, no. 5 (December 1979), pp. 1093–1110, and John C. Cox, Stephen A. Ross, and Mark Rubinstein, "Option Pricing: A Simplified Approach," *Journal of Financial Economics* 7, no. 3 (September 1979), pp. 229–264.

| FIGURE 24.13 | **BINOMIAL MODEL FORECAST TREES** |

A. Stock Price Forecasts

B. Option Value Forecasts

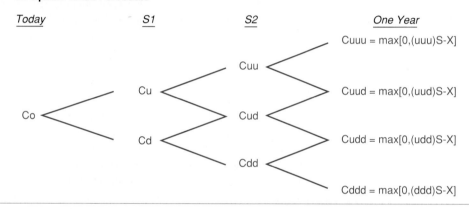

$$C_j = \frac{(p)C_{ju} + (1-p)C_{jd}}{r}$$

where:

$$p = \frac{r-d}{u-d}$$

and

r = one plus the risk-free rate over the subperiod.

If p is interpreted as the probability of an up movement in the security's price, which would then mean that $(1-p)$ is the probability of a down move, then the formula for C_j has an intuitively appealing interpretation. That is, the option's value at any point in time can be viewed as its expected value one subperiod hence discounted back to the current time. Further, although p was not an explicit part of the investor's forecast, it is nevertheless generated by the model. In this sense, p is referred to as the *implied probability* of an upward price movement. To ensure that this interpretation holds, the binomial model requires that $d < r < u$, a condition that is quite reasonable in practice.

This equation can be extended to a more useful format by recognizing that the value for C_j it generates is one of the inputs for valuing the option in the preceding subperiod. Thus, the formula for an option in subperiod t can be inserted into the right-hand side of the formula for subperiod $t - 1$. Carrying this logic all the way back to date 0, the binomial option valuation model becomes:

$$C_0 = \left\{ \sum_{j=0}^{N} \frac{N!}{(N-j)!j!} \, p^j(1-p)^{N-j} \max[0,(u^j d^{N-j})S - X] \right\} \div r^N$$

where

$N! = [(N)(N-1)(N-2) \ldots (2)(1)].$

To interpret this formula, the ratio $[N! \div (N - j)! \, j!]$ is the "combinatorial" way of stating how many distinct paths lead to a particular terminal outcome, $p^j(1-p)^{N-j}$ is the probability of getting to that outcome, and $\max[0,(u^j d^{N-j})S - X]$ is the payoff associated with that outcome. Letting m be the smallest integer number of up moves guaranteeing that the option will be in the money at expiration (i.e., $(u^m d^{N-m})S > X$), this formula can be reduced further to:

$$C_0 = \left\{ \sum_{j=m}^{N} \frac{N!}{(N-j)!j!} \, p^j(1-p)^{N-j} [(u^j d^{N-j})S - X] \right\} \div r^N.$$

As an example of how this model works, assume the investor has gathered contract terms and price data and has made her forecasts as follows: $S = 50.00$, $X = 52.50$, $T =$ one year, $RFR = 8$ percent (through expiration), $u = 1.09139$, $d = 0.92832$, and $N = 3$. By these forecasts, the investor has divided the one-year life of the option into three subperiods and estimated that the probability of up and down moves during any subperiod as slightly greater than 9 and 7 percent, respectively. Also, the values for r and p implied by these forecasts are $1.026 (= (1.08)^{0.33})$ and $0.599 (= [1.026 - 0.92832] \div [1.09139 - 0.92832])$. By the second binomial equation, which ignores the two terminal option outcomes in the first that are equal to zero, the value of a one-year European-style call option with an exercise price of $52.50 is:

$$C_0 = \frac{(3)(0.599)^2(0.401)(2.79) + (1)(0.599)^3(12.50)}{(1.026)^3} = \$3.60.$$

It is not surprising that this is the same value the three-step approach produced in the previous example because the forecasted stock price tree in Figure 24.11 was generated with these same values of u and d (e.g., $(uu)S = (1.09139)^2(50) = \$59.56$). We also can confirm that the tree of forecasted option values illustrated in Figure 24.12 may be replicated through repeatedly calculating the "state j" equation.[9] Finally, with this notation, the hedge ratio for any state j becomes:

$$h_j = \frac{(u-d)S_j}{(C_{jd} - C_{ju})}$$

---

[9] For example, $C_{uu} = [(0.599)(12.50) + (0.401)(2.79)] \div (1.026) = \$8.39.$

Thus, a share of stock held long could be hedged initially by shorting 1.78 call options (= (1.09139 − 0.92832)(50) ÷ (0.95 − 5.53)), a position that would be rebalanced to 1.32 calls after one subperiod if the first price change was positive.

THE BLACK-SCHOLES
VALUATION MODEL

The binomial model is a *discrete* method for valuing options because it allows security price changes to occur in distinct upward or downward movements. It also can be assumed that prices change *continuously* throughout time. This was the approach taken by Black and Scholes in developing their celebrated equation for valuing European-style options.[10] This is not a more realistic assumption because it presumes that security prices change when markets are closed (e.g., at night, on weekends). The advantage of the Black-Scholes approach—identical in spirit to the basic three-step, riskless hedge method outlined earlier—is that it leads to a relatively simple, closed-form equation that is capable of valuing options accurately under a wide array of circumstances.

Specifically, the Black-Scholes model assumes that stock price movements can be described by a statistical process known as *geometric Brownian motion*. Ultimately, this process is summarized by a volatility factor, σ, which is analogous to the investor's stock price forecasts in the previous models. Formally, the stock price process assumed by Black and Scholes is:

$$\frac{\Delta S}{S} = \mu[\Delta T] + \sigma\varepsilon[T]^{1/2}$$

That is, a stock's return ($\Delta S/S$) from the present through any future period T has both an expected component ($\mu[\Delta T]$) and a "noise" component ($\sigma\varepsilon[T]^{1/2}$), where μ is the mean return and ε is the lognormally distributed random error term.[11]

Assuming the continuously compounded risk-free rate and the stock's variance (i.e., σ^2) remain constant until the expiration date T, Black and Scholes used the riskless hedge intuition to derive the following formula for valuing a call option on a nondividend-paying stock:

$$C_0 = S\,N(d_1) - X\,(e^{-(RFR)T})\,N(d_2)$$

where $e^{-(RFR)T}$ is the discount function for continuously compounded variables,

$$d_1 = [(\ln(S/X) + (RFR + 0.5\sigma^2)[T])] \div (\sigma[T]^{1/2})$$

and

$$d_2 = d_1 - \sigma[T]^{1/2}$$

with $\ln(\cdot)$ being the natural logarithm function. The variable $N(d)$ represents the cumulative probability of observing a value drawn from the standard normal distribution (i.e., one with

[10] See Fischer Black and Myron Scholes, "The Pricing of Options and Corporate Liabilities," *Journal of Political Economy* 81, no. 2 (May–June 1973), pp. 637–654. For an interesting related discussion of this model, see Fischer Black, "How We Came Up with the Option Formula," *Journal of Portfolio Management* 15, no. 2 (Winter 1989), pp. 4–8.

[11] A rate of return follows a lognormal distribution if the logarithm of one plus that return follows a normal distribution. This is a reasonable characterization for stock price movements because it does not allow share prices to fall below zero. For a detailed analysis of the mathematics underlying the Black-Scholes model, see John Hull, *Options, Futures, and Other Derivatives*, 3d ed. (Englewood Cliffs, NJ: Prentice-Hall, 1997).

a mean of zero and a standard deviation of one) equal to or less than d. As the standard normal distribution is symmetric around zero, a value of $d = 0$ would lead to $N(d) = 0.5000$; positive values of d would then have cumulative probabilities greater than 50 percent, with negative values of d leading to cumulative probabilities of less than one-half.

Values for $N(d)$ can be established in two ways. First, an investor can use a table of calculated values for the standard normal distribution, such as the one shown in Appendix D at the end of the book. For example, if the value of d_1 is 0.65, $N(d_1)$ could be established by finding the entry corresponding to the 0.6 row and the 0.05 column, or 0.7422. This means that 74.22 percent of the observations in the standard normal distribution have a value of 0.65 or less. Notice also that if d_1 had been -0.65, the value of $N(-d_1) = 1 - N(d_1) = 1 - 0.7422 = 0.2578$, which must be the case since the distribution is symmetric.

A second approach to calculating cumulative normal probabilities is approximating them with the following formula:

$$N(d) \approx \begin{cases} 0.5e^{-(d^2)/2 \, - \, 281/(83 \, -351/d)} & \text{if } d < 0 \\ \\ 1 - 0.5 \; e^{-(d^2)/2 \, - \, 281/(83 \, + \, 351/d)} & \text{if } d \geq 0 \end{cases}$$

For example, with $d = 0.65$, we have an approximate probability of:

$$N(0.65) \approx 1 - 0.5 \; e^{-(0.65^2)/2 \, - \, 281(83 \, + \, 351/0.65)} = 0.7422.$$

This matches the actual value to the fourth decimal place, and will likely lead to reasonable valuations.[12]

The **Black-Scholes valuation model** has several attractive features. A joint examination of the expressions for C, d_1, and d_2 reveals that the option's value is a function of five variables:

1. current security price
2. exercise price
3. time to expiration
4. risk-free rate
5. security price volatility

Functionally, the Black-Scholes model holds that $C = f(S, X, T, RFR, \sigma)$. The first and fourth factors are observable market prices, and the second and third variables are defined by the contract itself. Thus, the only variable an investor must provide in the Black-Scholes framework is the volatility factor. As noted earlier, the estimate of σ embeds the investor's forecast of future stock prices.

The value of the call option will rise with increases in each of the five factors *except* the exercise price. Figure 24.14 summarizes these relationships. Specifically, the middle column of the figure shows what will happen to the value of the call when one of the five factors increases. The intuition behind the first three of these relationships is straightforward. In particular, an increase in the underlying asset's price (i.e., S) will increase the call's intrinsic value; a larger exercise price (i.e., X) will reduce the intrinsic value. Also, the longer the option has until it expires, the more valuable the time premium component. This is because a greater opportunity exists for the contract to finish in the money. On the

---

[12] For more on this approximation method, as well as how it can be written into a program usable on a hand-held financial calculator, see Peter Carr, "A Calculator Program for Option Values and Implied Standard Deviations," *Journal of Financial Education* 17, no. 1 (Fall 1988), pp. 89–93.

| FIGURE 24.14 | FACTORS AFFECTING BLACK-SCHOLES OPTION VALUES |

| | **WILL CAUSE AN INCREASE/DECREASE IN THE:** | |
An Increase in the:	Call Value	Put Value
Security price (S)	Increase	Decrease
Exercise price (X)	Decrease	Increase
Time to expiration (T)	Increase	Increase or decrease
Risk-free rate (RFR)	Increase	Decrease
Security volatility (σ)	Increase	Increase

other hand, the relationships between C, RFR, and σ are less obvious. An increase in RFR will increase the call's value because this reduces the present value of X, an expense that the call holder must pay at expiration to exercise the contract. Similarly, when the volatility of the underlying asset's price increases, the call becomes more valuable since this increases the probability that the option will be deeper in the money at expiration.[13]

Another useful facet of the Black-Scholes model is that the hedge ratio at any moment in time is simply $N(d_1)$, the partial derivative of the call's value with respect to the stock price (i.e., $\delta C/\delta S$). Under this interpretation, $N(d_1)$ is the change in the option's value given a one dollar change in the underlying security's price. For this reason, $N(d_1)$ often is called the option's **delta**, and it indicates the number of stock shares that can be hedged by a single call—the exact reciprocal of the previous interpretation of the hedge ratio, h. Finally, although the Black-Scholes model was developed several years before the binomial framework, the former can be viewed as an extension of the latter. Specifically, as the number of subperiods (i.e., N) is allowed to approach infinity, the up or down price movements begin to occur on a continuous basis. If the values of u and d are then set equal to $e^{\sigma[\Delta T]^{1/2}}$ and $e^{-\sigma[\Delta T]^{1/2}}$, respectively, the binomial model collapses to become the Black-Scholes formula.

As an example of Black-Scholes valuation, consider the following values for the five input variables: $S = 40$, $X = 40$, $T =$ one year, $RFR = 9$ percent, and $\sigma = 0.30$. To calculate the fundamental value of a European-style call option under these conditions, which again will be purely time premium, first calculate:

$$d_1 = (\ln(40/40) + (.09 + 0.5(0.3)^2)[1]) \div (0.3[1]^{1/2}) = 0.45$$

and

$$d_2 = 0.45 - 0.3[1]^{1/2} = 0.15.$$

so that

$$N(d_1) = 1 - 0.5 \ e^{-(0.45^2)/2 - 281/(83 + 351/0.45)} = 0.6736$$

and

$$N(d_2) = 1 - 0.5 \ e^{-(0.15^2)/2 - 281/(83 + 351/0.15)} = 0.5596.$$

Thus,

$$C_0 = (40)(0.6736) - 40(e^{-.09})(0.5596) = \$6.49.$$

---

[13] In more technical terms, these relationships can be summarized as $\delta C/\delta S > 0$, $\delta C/\delta RFR > 0$, $\delta C/\delta T > 0$, $\delta C/\delta \sigma > 0$, and $\delta C/\delta X < 0$.

TABLE 24.7

EXAMPLE OF BLACK-SCHOLES VALUATION

Stock Price	Call Value	Hedge Ratio
$25	$ 0.44	0.1321
30	1.51	0.3054
35	3.53	0.5020
40	6.49	0.6736
45	10.19	0.8003
50	14.42	0.8837
55	18.98	0.9347

Note: Assumes $X = 40$, $T = 1$ year, $RFR = 9\%$, and $\sigma = 0.30$.

FIGURE 24.15

BLACK-SCHOLES VALUES

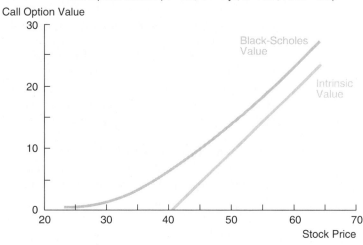

Call Option Values ($X = 40$, $T = 1$ yr, $\sigma = .30$, $RFR = .09$)

$N(d_1)$ says that the call option will change in value by about 67 cents for every dollar of change in the underlying asset which, in turn, suggests a hedge ratio of one-and-a-half calls short for every stock share held long. Table 24.7 shows how both the option's value and $N(d_1)$ change as the security's value changes—with the other factors held constant. Notably, the hedge ratios range in value from 0 to 1, and increase as stock prices increase. Therefore, the deeper in the money the option is, the closer its price movements will come to duplicating those of the stock itself. The relationship between stock prices and call option prices for this example is shown in Figure 24.15. The delta, or hedge ratio, associated with a given stock price is simply the slope of a line tangent to the call option price curve.

ESTIMATING VOLATILITY   Just as the growth rate of dividends (i.e., g) was a crucial element in establishing the fundamental value of common stock using the dividend discount model, option valuation depends critically on an accurate forecast of the underlying asset's future price level. Of course, in the Black-Scholes framework, this means selecting the proper σ. From the description of the geometric Brownian motion process, it should be clear that σ is equiva lent to the standard deviation of returns to the underlying asset. This value can be estimated in two ways. First, it can be calculated in the traditional manner using historical returns. Specifically, calculate the day *t price relative* as $R_t = \ln(P_t \div P_{t-1})$. If a series of price relatives are then calculated for a sequence of N days in the recent past, the mean and standard deviation of this series can be calculated as:

$$\bar{R} = \left(\frac{1}{N}\right) \sum_{t=1}^{N} R_t \quad \text{and} \quad \sigma^2 = \left(\frac{1}{N-1}\right) \sum_{t=1}^{N} (R_t - \bar{R})^2.$$

The factor σ is expressed in terms of daily price movements. To annualize this value, σ can be multiplied by the square root of the number of trading days in the year (usually assumed to be 250), which then becomes the estimate of volatility employed in the Black-Scholes formula. The advantage of historical volatility is that it is easy to compute and requires no prior assumption about stock market efficiency; its disadvantage is its presumption that stock price behavior in the future will continue as it has in the past, a sometimes dubious assumption in a rapidly changing world.[14]

An alternative to relying on historical price movements is a second volatility estimation approach that involves the Black-Scholes equation. Recall that if we know all five input factors—S, X, T, RFR, and σ—we can solve for the value of the call option. However, because σ is the only unobservable input, and if we know the current price of the option (call it C^*) and the four other variables, we can calculate the level of σ that forces the Black-Scholes value to equal C^*. That is, the volatility implied by current market prices is established by finding σ^* such that $C^* = f(S, X, T, RFR, \sigma^*)$. Accordingly, the value σ^* is known as the **implied volatility**. No simple closed-form solution exists for performing this calculation; it must be done by trial and error.

Implied volatility is advantageous because it calculates the same volatility forecast investors use to set option prices. The disadvantage of implied volatility is its presumption that markets are efficient in that the option price set in the market corresponds directly to that generated by the Black-Scholes equation. Beckers has shown that implied volatilities do a better job than historical volatilities of predicting future stock price movements; however, Figlewski cautions that σ^* can be "noisy" because it picks up not only the true level of volatility but any misestimate inherent in the valuation process.[15]

As an example of this calculation, Brown, Harlow, and Tinic estimated the volatilities implied by the S&P 500 index call option contract for the 121-day period surrounding the stock market crash in October 1987.[16] These calculations are reproduced in Figure 24.16. In this display, the time variable is denominated relative to "Black Monday" [i.e., Day 0], which occurred on October 19, 1987. To see how much market risk changed with the crash, the *average* implied volatility measure for the period Day −60 to Day −5 (i.e., the period

---

[14] For a good discussion of how stock price volatility has changed over time, see Charles P. Jones and Jack W. Wilson, "Is Stock Price Volatility Increasing?" *Financial Analysts Journal* 45, no. 6 (November–December 1989), pp. 20–26.

[15] See Stan Beckers, "Standard Deviations Implied in Option Prices as Predictors of Future Stock Price Variability," *Journal of Banking and Finance* 5, no. 3 (September 1981), pp. 363–381, and Stephen Figlewski, "What Does an Option Pricing Model Tell Us about Option Prices?" *Financial Analysts Journal* 45, no. 5 (September–October 1989), pp. 12–15. For an exhaustive review of the literature on this topic, see Stewart Mayhew, "Implied Volatility," *Financial Analysts Journal* 51, no. 4 (July–August 1995), pp. 8–20.

[16] See Keith C. Brown, W. V. Harlow, and Seha M. Tinic, "How Rational Investors Deal with Uncertainty (Or, Reports of the Death of Efficient Market Theory Are Greatly Exaggerated)," *Journal of Applied Corporate Finance* 2, no. 3 (Fall 1989), pp. 45–58.

FIGURE 24.16   **IMPLIED VOLATILITIES AND THE STOCK MARKET CRASH OF 1987**

beginning approximately two and a half months before the crash) was 18.9 percent. The comparable statistic for the period Day +5 to Day +60 was 43.3 percent. Moreover, on Black Monday itself, the implied volatility rose to 145 percent, more than seven and a half times its pre-crash level!

Implied volatilities also have been useful in determining if the fundamental values produced by the Black-Scholes model match the traded prices for option contracts. In one of the earliest empirical tests of the Black-Scholes equation, MacBeth and Merville showed for a sample of six stocks that implied volatilities tended to be overly large when the associated call options were in the money and too small for out-of-the-money contracts.[17] Assuming that at-the-money options are priced fairly, this suggested that in-the-money options were priced higher than their Black-Scholes values, with the opposite being true for out-of-the-money contracts. Thus, for the authors' sample of stocks, the Black-Scholes model overvalued out-of-the-money call options and undervalued in-the-money contracts. Interestingly, using a different set of data, Rubinstein found evidence that both supported and contradicted these results.[18]

OPTION VALUATION: EXTENSIONS AND ADVANCED TOPICS

The preceding discussion has concentrated on the valuation of European-style call options having a nondividend-paying stock as the underlying asset. Many other conditions and underlying assets exist for which options need to be valued. This section explores several extensions of the basic approach as well as other important topics relevant to the valuation process.

VALUING EUROPEAN-STYLE PUT OPTIONS

The put-call-spot parity model of Chapter 11 held that, in an efficient market, the value of a European-style put on a nondividend-paying security should be equivalent to a portfolio short in the security while long in both a call option and a Treasury bill having a face value

---

[17] See James D. MacBeth and Larry J. Merville, "An Empirical Examination of the Black-Scholes Call Option Pricing Model," *Journal of Finance* 34, no. 5 (December 1979), pp. 1173–1186.

[18] See Mark Rubinstein, "Nonparametric Tests of Alternative Options Pricing Models Using All Reported Trades and Quotes on the 30 Most Active CBOE Options Classes from August 23, 1976 through August 31, 1978," *Journal of Finance* 40, no. 2 (June 1985), pp. 455–480.

equal to the common exercise price X. Converting the discounting process for the T-bill to be a continuous function, this relationship can be expressed:

$$P_0 = C_0 + X\ (e^{-(RFR)T}) - S.$$

This formula implies that if we know the prices of the security, the call option, and the T-bill, we can solve for the value of the put option. Alternatively, if the Black-Scholes value for C is inserted into this expression, we have:

$$P_0 = [S\ N(d_1) - X\ (e^{-(RFR)T})\ N(d_2)] + X\ (e^{-(RFR)T}) - S,$$

which can be manipulated to equal:

$$P_0 = X\ (e^{-(RFR)T})\ N(-d_2) - S\ N(-d_1)$$

where all the notation is the same as before. This is the Black-Scholes put option valuation model.

The comparative statics of put option valuation were shown in the final column of Figure 24.14. In particular, the value of the put will increase with higher levels of X but decline with an increase in S because of the effect these movements have on the contract's intrinsic value. Like the call option, the put's value benefits from an increase in σ since this increases the likelihood that the contract will finish deep in the money. Also, an increase in the risk-free rate reduces the present value of X, which hurts the holder of the put who receives the striking price if the contract is exercised. Finally, the sign of $\delta P/\delta T$ could be either positive or negative depending on the tradeoff between the longer time over which the security price could move in the desired direction and the reduced present value of the exercise price received by the seller at expiration.

In the preceding example, we had the following inputs: $S = 40$, $X = 40$, $T =$ one year, $RFR = 9$ percent, and $\sigma = 0.30$. With these assumptions, d_1 and d_2 still are 0.45 and 0.15, respectively, but now we need to compute $N(-0.45) = 1 - 0.6736 = 0.3264$ and $N(-0.15) = 1 - 0.5596 = 0.4404$. Thus:

$$P_0 = 40(e^{-.09})\ (0.4404) - 40(0.3264) = \$3.04.$$

Finally, the hedge ratio for the put option in this model is $[N(d_1) - 1]$, which in this case is -0.3264 and indicates that the put option's value will *decrease* by approximately 33 cents for every dollar *increase* in S.

VALUING OPTIONS ON
DIVIDEND-BEARING
SECURITIES

We learned in Chapter 11 that the put-call parity relationship required an adjustment when the underlying asset common to both the put and call options paid a dividend. This adjustment is needed because the payment of the dividend reduces the asset's market value, converting the investor's return from capital appreciation to cash flow. Thus, other than the tax implications of this conversion, the underlying asset's owner should not lose any overall net worth over the payment of the dividend. On the other hand, the problem for the prospective call option owner is that he will not receive the dividend; therefore, the reduction in the present value of the stock will reduce the value of his derivative contract. Being rational, he will reduce the price he is willing to pay for the call option on the dividend-bearing security. Consequently, dividends become a sixth factor in the option valuation process.

The original Black-Scholes valuation model can be modified to incorporate dividend payments in two ways. The most straightforward and most accurate approach is reducing the current share price by the present value of the dividends paid during the option's life and then using this amount in place of the actual stock price. That is, replace S in the model with $S' = S - PV$(dividends). For example, for the case of the one-year, at-the-money call option with an exercise price of $40 that we saw earlier, assume that a dividend payment of $1 is made in six months, with another $1 paid just prior to expiration. Recalling that the continuously compounded risk-free rate and volatility factors were 9 percent and 30 percent, respectively, we would then have:

$$S' = 40 - (1)e^{-(.09)(0.5)} - (1)e^{-(.09)(1.0)} = \$38.13.$$

When inserted into the formulas for d_1 and d_2, this S' would generate values of 0.29 and −0.01, respectively.

With these inputs, the Black-Scholes valuation then becomes:

$$C_0 = (38.13)\ N(0.29) + (40)e^{-.09}\ N(-0.01) = (38.13)(0.6141) - (36.56)(0.4960) = \$5.28.$$

This amount can be compared to the $6.49 contract value for an otherwise identical call on a nondividend-paying share that we estimated earlier. In particular, the reduction in option value (i.e., $1.21) is not as great as the present value of the dividends (i.e., $1.87). This is due to the possibility that the option would have expired out of the money even without the dividend payment, meaning that the dividend-induced stock price reduction will not always affect the contract's terminal payoff. Also, the hedge ratio in the above formula is reduced from its original level of 0.6736 to 0.6141.

The second approach to adjusting the option valuation process for dividend payments involves modifying the model itself rather than the stock price input. This requires expressing the dividend in *yield* form, defined as the annual payment divided by the current stock price, and assuming that this yield is paid continuously. Merton first showed that the Black-Scholes model can be rewritten as:

$$C_0 = (e^{-(D)T})\ S\ N(d_1) - X(e^{-(RFR)T})\ N(d_2)$$

with

$$d_1 = [(\ln((e^{-(D)T})S/X) + RFR + 0.5\sigma^2)[T]] \div (\sigma[T]^{1/2})$$

and

$$d_2 = d_1 - \sigma[T]^{1/2}$$

where

D = the annualized dividend yield.[19]

[19]See Robert C. Merton, "Theory of Rational Option Pricing," *Bell Journal of Economics and Management* 4, no. 1 (Spring 1973), pp. 141–183.

The yield appears as a "discount" factor to the current stock value in two places in these equations. If we set $S' = (e^{-(D)T})S$, this second dividend adjustment is seen as just a continuous version of the first.

Extending the original example, we now have six factors to include: $S = 40$, $X = 40$, $T =$ one year, $RFR = 9$ percent, $\sigma = 30$ percent, and $D = (2/40) = 5$ percent. Plugging these into the model, we get values of 0.28 for d_1 and -0.02 for d_2 so that:

$$C_0 = (e^{-.05}) (40) N(0.28) - (e^{-.09}) (40) N(-0.02)$$
$$= (38.05)(0.6103) - (36.56)(0.4920) = \$5.23.$$

This amount differs from the first adjustment process amount because the assumption of a continuous dividend stream does not match the reality of how these payments are made. However, by modifying the model's structure instead of the input level, this approach is often much more convenient.

VALUING AMERICAN-STYLE OPTIONS

The preceding valuation discussion assumed European-style options. If the contract had been American-style—that is, its exercise is not limited to the expiration date—how would the valuation process change? The uncertainty over the possibility of early exercise makes the derivation of an exact closed-form analog to the Black-Scholes equation an elusive goal. Instead, Roll, Geske, and Whaley have designed elaborate approximation procedures for estimating the value of American-style calls, which have proven quite useful in practice.[20] Further, Johnson and Baroni-Adesi and Whaley, among others, have taken different approaches to address the issue of American put valuation.[21]

A formal summary of these models is beyond the scope of this discussion; however, we can consider several fundamental properties. Most important is that an American put or call has to be at least as valuable as its European-style counterpart because, by definition, the American option gives the holder more choices than the simpler contract. In other words, the American contract holder can exercise at the same time as the European option owner (i.e., at expiration) as well as any point prior to that terminal date. Since we have seen that an option's value ultimately derives from the choice to exercise the agreement or not, a better set of terms for that decision means a more valuable contract. Letting C_a and C_e represent the values of American and European calls, this relationship can be expressed as:

$$S \geq C_a(S,T,X) \geq C_e(S,T,X) \geq \max[0, S - Xe^{-(RFR)T}] \geq \max[0, S - X] \geq 0.$$

This expression says that (1) the American call is at least as valuable as the European contract, (2) neither call can be more valuable than the underlying stock, and (3) both contracts are at least as valuable as their intrinsic values, expressed on both a nominal and discounted basis. For puts, a similar boundary condition would be:

[20] The development of what is commonly called the Roll-Geske-Whaley model can be found in three separate articles: Richard Roll, "An Analytic Valuation Formula for Unprotected American Call Options on Stocks with Known Dividends," *Journal of Financial Economics* 5, no. 2 (November 1977), pp. 251–258; Robert Geske, "A Note on an Analytical Valuation Formula for Unprotected American Call Options on Stocks with Known Dividends," *Journal of Financial Economics* 7, no. 4 (June 1979), pp. 375–380; and Robert E. Whaley, "On the Valuation of American Call Options on Stocks with Known Dividends," *Journal of Financial Economics* 9, no. 2 (June 1981), pp. 207–212.

[21] See H. E. Johnson, "An Analytic Approximation for the American Put Price," *Journal of Financial and Quantitative Analysis* 18, no. 1 (March 1983), pp. 143–151, and Giovanni Barone-Adesi and Robert E. Whaley, "The Valuation of American Call Options and the Expected Ex-Dividend Stock Price Declines," *Journal of Financial Economics* 17, no. 1 (September 1986), pp. 91–112.

$$X \geq P_a(S,T,X) \geq P_e(S,T,X) \geq \max[0, Xe^{-(RFR)T} - S] \geq 0.^{22}$$

For a stock that does not pay dividends, C_a and C_e will be equal to one another. At any point prior to expiration, the above relationship shows that $C_a(S,T,X) - \max[0, S - X] > 0$, and $\max[0, S - X]$ is the value the investor would extract from the option's exercise. Therefore, without the depression in the stock's price caused by the dividend payment, an investor wishing to liquidate his American call position would sell it rather than exercise it so as not to surrender the contract's time premium. Thus, in the absence of dividends to consider during the life of the option, the American call offers choices that the investor neither wants nor will be willing to pay for. This result implies that the Black-Scholes model for C_e can be used to value C_a as well.

When the stock pays dividends, however, this situation changes. Suppose an investor holds an American call option on a stock just prior to its ex-dividend date. On the ex-date—call it date t—the value of the stock will decline by about the dividend amount, leaving $S_t = S_{t-1} - (\text{dividend})_t$ assuming no other new information impacted the share's value from the previous day. The value of the option will decline accordingly, from $C(S_{t-1})$ to $C(S_t)$. Of course, selling the contract on the day prior to the ex-date will not be possible since rational buyers will know what will happen the following day. Therefore, the investor must decide on date $t - 1$ whether he should exercise his contract and receive only the intrinsic value of $\max[0, S_{t-1} - X]$. This will be the proper choice if the loss of the option's time premium is less than $C(S_{t-1}) - C(S_t)$, which will likely occur when the option is close to maturity (and, hence, the time premium is low) and the stock's dividend is large. Because the American option allows the investor the possibility of preserving value when the European contract cannot, we must have $C_a > C_e$ for almost all cases.

Deciding to exercise a put prior to maturity does not depend on the presence of dividends. Indeed, dividend payments increase a put's value because they reduce the underlying common stock's value without an offset in the exercise price. Instead, the relevant issue is the limited liability of the stock itself. For example, suppose an investor holds an American put on a nearly bankrupt company. The contract, which is struck at $50, has three more months before it expires, and the stock is currently selling for $1. In this case, the option holder would evaluate the tradeoff between exercising the contract today to capture the $49 intrinsic value or waiting three months and hoping the stock becomes worthless. That is, she must decide whether she would rather have $49 now or the present value of the possibility of receiving $50. Depending on the discount rate and the estimated recovery probability, it is quite likely that she will exercise now.

On the other hand, the European put does not offer the investor this choice. Further, since the stock's expected return is positive, an efficient capital market would predict that the price of the nondividend-paying stock will be higher in three months, thereby reducing the expiration date value of the contract below $49. Consequently, without the ability to exercise the put prior to expiration, the European put sometimes can be worth less than its intrinsic value—unadjusted for the time value of money—which always is a lower bound for the American contract. Thus, P_e can be either greater or less than $\max[0, X - S]$, with the latter situation most likely to occur at extremely low values of S and large values of T. The above boundary condition shows that P_e must only be greater than the discounted version of the intrinsic value formula, or $\max[0, Xe^{-(RFR)T} - S]$. These relationships are illustrated in Figure 24.17.

---

[22] For a complete development of these boundary conditions, see Don M. Chance, *Introduction to Derivatives,* 3d ed. (Fort Worth, TX: Dryden Press, 1995).

FIGURE 24.17   **COMPARING AMERICAN AND EUROPEAN PUT VALUES**

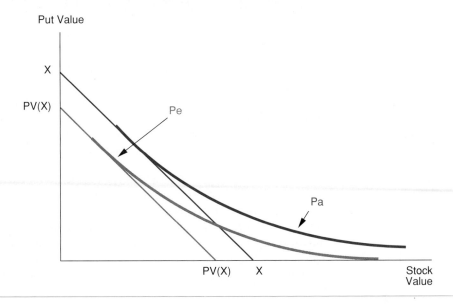

OTHER EXTENSIONS OF THE BLACK-SCHOLES MODEL

The dividend-adjusted Black-Scholes model is also quite useful in valuing options for underlying assets other than common stock. Three of the more important applications along these lines follow.

STOCK INDEX OPTIONS   As we have discussed, stock index options are fundamentally no different than regular stock options. That is, it is reasonable to assume that the index levels follow geometric Brownian motion just as the stock itself does. The primary difference is that, as a hypothetical creation, the stock index cannot be delivered to settle the contract and so it must be settled in cash. Beyond that, because it is a well-diversified portfolio, the volatility of the stock index's price usually is quite a bit lower than the typical stock. Finally, the applicable dividend yield can be assumed to be the average annualized yield on the index during the option's life, which is likely to be known to investors at least one calendar quarter into the future.

Suppose the Standard & Poor's 100 currently is at a level of 601.40 and a call option or the index with an exercise price of 600 is being offered at a price of $17.75. An investor wants to determine whether the fair value of this contract is above or below the market price. The option is set to expire in exactly 61 days, which translates to 0.1671 (= 61/365) year. The dividend yield on the S&P 100 is 2.00 percent, and the annualized yield on a 61-day Treasury bill is 5.70 percent. The investor forecasts the index's volatility to be 18 percent, and establishes that:

$$d_1 = [\ln(601.40e^{-(.02)0.1671}/600) + (.057 + 0.5(.18)^2)[0.1671]] \div (.18[0.1671]^{1/2}) = 0.1525$$

and

$$d_2 = 0.1525 - .18[0.1671]^{1/2} = 0.0789.$$

Using the cumulative normal probability approximation function, this leads to $N(d_1) = 0.5607$ and $N(d_2) = 0.5315$. Thus, she estimates the call's value to be:

$$C_0 = (599.39)(0.5607) - (600)(e^{-(.057)0.1671})(0.5315) = \$20.20.$$

Since this is higher than the market price of the option (i.e., $17.75), the contract appears undervalued. This is not necessarily an arbitrage opportunity, however, as the investor's valuation was based on two assumptions that may not match the consensus view of other market participants: (1) the Black-Scholes framework is appropriate, and (2) the index's volatility is 18 percent and not something lower. This, of course, is always the challenge confronting investors in an uncertain world.

FOREIGN CURRENCY OPTIONS   Recall that prices for exchange-traded currency options are quoted in U.S. cents per unit of foreign currency, reflecting that a call option is the right to buy a fixed amount of foreign currency with U.S. dollars. Let RFR_f and RFR_d be the risk-free rates in the foreign and U.S. domestic markets, respectively. Further, let σ be the volatility of the exchange rate between the United States and the foreign country, denominated in USD per unit of FC. Garman and Kohlhagen showed that the Black-Scholes model for European-style calls and puts under these conditions can be written as:[23]

$$C_0 = (e^{-(RFR_f)T})\, S\, N(d_1) - X\, (e^{-(RFR_d)T})\, N(d_2)$$
$$P_0 = X\, (e^{-(RFR_d)T})\, N(-d_2) - (e^{-(RFR_f)T})\, S\, N(-d_1)$$

where

$d_1 = [\ln((e^{-(RFR_f)T})S/X) + (RFR_d + 0.5\sigma^2)[T]] \div (\sigma[T]^{1/2})$
$d_2 = d_1 - \sigma[T]^{1/2}.$
$S =$ **the spot exchange rate quoted on a direct (i.e., USD/FC) basis.**

Again, this formula is equivalent to the dividend-adjusted Black-Scholes model for stock options when RFR_f is interpreted as the "dividend yield" on the foreign currency. As an example of valuing FX options, suppose the spot exchange rate between the U.S. dollar and the British pound is USD 1.50/GBP, and the risk-free rates in the United States and England are 4.5 percent and 9 percent, respectively. With these market conditions, interest rate parity holds that the dollar should trade at a forward premium relative to the pound. To the extent that forward FX rates "predict" future spot rates, this suggests that the dollar price of sterling will fall. Thus, an at-the-money put option should be more valuable to an investor than an at-the-money sterling call. To see if this is the case, consider the valuation of six-month contracts where $S = 1.50$, $X = 1.50$, $RFR_d = 4.5$ percent, $RFR_f = 9$ percent, $\sigma = 13$ percent, and $T = 0.5$. With these inputs, $S' = S(e^{-(.09)0.5}) = 1.434$ so that:

$$d_1 = [\ln(1.434/1.50) + (.045 + 0.5(.13)^2)[0.5]] \div (.13[0.5]^{1/2}) = -0.20$$

and

$$d_2 = -0.20 - .13[0.5]^{1/2} = -0.29.$$

[23] See Mark B. Garman and Steven W. Kohlhagen, "Foreign Currency Option Values," *Journal of International Money and Finance* 2, no. 3 (December 1983), pp. 231–237, as well as Nahum Biger and John Hull, "The Valuation of Currency Options," *Financial Management* 12, no. 1 (Spring 1983), pp. 24–28.

Therefore, the option values are:

$$C_0 = (1.434)(0.4207) - (1.50)(e^{-(.045)0.5})(0.3859) = \$0.037$$

and

$$P_0 = (1.50)(e^{-(.045)0.5})(0.6141) - (1.434)(0.5793) = \$0.070,$$

as expected.

FUTURES OPTIONS   In the last chapter, we showed that in the absence of physical storage costs or dividends, the futures contract price (F) should simply be the spot price (S) of the underlying asset carried forward to date T at the risk-free rate. With continuous yields, this can be written as $F = S\ e^{(RFR)T}$. Black showed that substituting F for S in the Black-Scholes formula for call options leaves:[24]

$$C_0 = [e^{-(RFR)T}\ F]\ N(d_1) - (e^{-(RFR)T})\ X\ N(d_2)$$
$$= (e^{-(RFR)T})\ [F\ N(d_1) - X\ N(d_2)].$$

where

$$d_1 = (\ln(F/X) + 0.5\sigma^2[T]) \div (\sigma[T]^{1/2})$$
$$d_2 = d_1 - \sigma[T]^{1/2}.$$

In the expressions for d_1 and d_2, the risk-free rate factor drops out because a risk-free hedge portfolio with futures and call options requires no initial investment since futures contracts require no front-end payment. Also, here σ represents the futures price volatility, which normally is assumed to be equal to the underlying asset volatility. Put options on futures contracts can then be valued like the call options described above.

Summary

- Along with forwards and futures, options represent another basic form of derivative contracting. Like the forward positions to which they are linked, puts and calls are used as either stand-alone investments or as supplements to an existing collection of assets. In the latter application, they provide investors with a convenient and inexpensive way to restructure the risk–reward tradeoff in a portfolio. The flexibility of this form of contracting permits investors to create unique payoff structures by combining different options in various ways. Option straddles, for instance, allow the holder to take advantage of a view on the underlying asset's volatility while remaining neutral about the direction of future price movements. Forward contracts can be viewed as a specifically chosen pair of options; and these contracts are special cases of option combinations known as range forwards.
- We consider how option contracts are valued in an efficient market. Although the mathematics of some valuation models can be formidable, the intuition behind the process is not. Each of three models we discuss—the two-state, the binomial, and the Black-Scholes—is based on the same three-step evolution. The first step is combining options with the underlying asset in order to create a riskless position. Invariably, this synthetic risk-free portfolio requires the sale (purchase) of multiple calls (puts) to offset to the full cash exposure of a single share of stock held long. This hedge ratio changes with movements in the underlying asset's price and the passage of time; therefore, the riskless hedge portfolio needs to be rebalanced frequently. Once it is formed, how-

[24] See Fischer Black, "The Pricing of Commodity Contracts," *Journal of Financial Economics* 3, no. 1/2 (January–March 1976), pp. 167–179.

ever, the option's value can be established by assuming that the hedge portfolio should earn the risk-free rate (i.e., the "no arbitrage" condition) and solving for the option value that makes this assumption true.

- The Black-Scholes model is extremely flexible. Although originally created for European-style call options on nondividend-bearing stock, this model extends easily to valuing put options and options on dividend-paying stocks. The payment of dividends decreases the value of an otherwise identical call option, but not by the amount of the dividend itself. We also discuss how volatility, the only user-provided variable in the valuation model, is either estimated directly from a historical series of asset prices or implied from option prices themselves.

- Finally, we discuss the process for valuing American-style puts and calls and how this differs from the valuation of their European counterparts. We conclude with an explanation of how the Black-Scholes model could be adapted to value options on other underlying assets such as stock indexes, foreign currency, or commodity futures contracts.

Questions

1. Straddles have been described as "volatility plays." Explain what this means for both long and short straddle positions. Given the fact that volatility is a primary factor in how options are priced, under what conditions might an investor who believes that markets are efficient ever want to create a straddle?

2. Put-call-forward parity and range forward positions both involve the purchase of a call option and the sale of a put option (or vice versa) on the same underlying asset. Describe the relationship between these two trading strategies. Is one a special case of the other?

3. *CFA Examination II (June 1993)*

   Michelle Industries issued a Swiss-franc denominated five-year discount note for CHF 200 million. The proceeds were converted to U.S. dollars to purchase capital equipment in the U.S. The company wants to hedge this currency exposure and is considering the following alternatives:

   (i) At-the-money Swiss Franc call options

   (ii) Swiss franc forwards

   (iii) Swiss franc futures

   Contrast the essential characteristics of each of these three derivative instruments. Evaluate the suitability of each in relation to Michelle's hedging objective, including both advantages and disadvantages.

4. *CFA Examination III (June 1991)*

   Six factors affect the value of call options on stocks. Three of these factors are: the current price of the stock, the time remaining until the option expires. and the dividend on the stock. Identify the other three factors and explain how and why changes in each of these three factors affect the value of call options.

5. "Although options are risky investments, they are valued by virtue of their ability to convert the underlying asset into a synthetic risk-free security." Explain what this statement means, being sure to describe the basic three-step process for valuing option contracts.

6. In valuing currency options with the Black-Scholes model, we saw that the risk-free rate on the foreign currency was equivalent to the dividend yield when an individual stock or stock index was the underlying asset. Discuss the appropriateness of this analogy. What sort of transaction involving foreign currency would be required to make this parallel exact?

7. Describe the condition under which it would be rational to exercise both an American-style put and call stock option before the expiration date. In both cases, comment specifically on the role that dividends play.

8. Explain why a change in the time to expiration (i.e., T) can have either a positive or negative impact on the value of a European-style put option. In this explanation, it will be useful to contrast the put's reaction with that of a European-style call, for which an increase in T has an unambiguously positive effect.

9. Currency option traders often speak of "buying low volatility (or 'vol') and selling high vol" rather than buying or selling the option itself. What does this mean exactly? From this perspective, what is the real underlying asset: volatility or foreign currency?

10. On October 19, 1987, the stock market (as measured by the Dow Jones Industrial Average) lost almost one-quarter of its value in a single day. Nevertheless, some traders made a profit buying call options on the stock index and then liquidating their positions before the market closed. Explain how this is possible, assuming that it was not a case of the traders taking advantage of spurious upward "ticks" in stock prices.

Problems

1. In March, a derivatives dealer offers you the following quotes for June British pound option contracts (expressed in U.S. dollars per GBP):

		MARKET PRICE OF CONTRACT	
Contract	Strike Price	Bid	Offer
Call	USD 1.40	0.0642	0.0647
Put		0.0255	0.0260
Call	1.44	0.0417	0.0422
Put		0.0422	0.0427
Call	1.48	0.0255	0.0260
Put		0.0642	0.0647

a. Assuming each of these contracts specifies the delivery of GBP 31,250 and expires in exactly three months, complete a table similar to the following (expressed in dollars) for a portfolio consisting of the following positions:
   (i) Long a 1.44 call
   (ii) Short a 1.48 call
   (iii) Long a 1.40 put
   (iv) Short a 1.44 put

June USD/GBP	Net Initial Cost	Call 1.44 Profit	Call 1.48 Profit	Put 1.40 Profit	Put 1.44 Profit	Net Profit
1.36	—	—	—	—	—	—
1.40	—	—	—	—	—	—
1.44	—	—	—	—	—	—
1.48	—	—	—	—	—	—
1.52	—	—	—	—	—	—

b. Graph the total net profit (i.e., cumulative profit less net initial cost, ignoring time value considerations) relationship using the June USD/GBP rate on the horizontal axis (be sure to label the break-even point(s)). Also, comment briefly on the nature of the currency speculation represented by this portfolio.

c. If in exactly one month (i.e., in April) the spot USD/GBP rate falls to 1.385 and the effective annual risk-free rates in the United States and England are 5 percent and 7 percent, respectively, calculate the equilibrium price differential that should exist between a long 1.44 call and a short 1.44 put positions. (Hint: Consider what sort of forward contract this option combination is equivalent to and treat the British interest rate as a dividend yield.)

2. *CFA Examination III (June 1986)*
   An institutional bond portfolio manager wants to increase the return on his existing holding of $1.0 million par value Government 11% bonds due June 1, 2006. The current market price of the bonds is 111. The manager has decided on June 1, 1986 to implement a covered option writing program on the portfolio. Available option information is listed below:

Options on Government 11% Bonds Due 2006 Expiring in 1986	Current Market Price of Option	Par Value of Bonds on Underlying Option	Option Commission $100 Par Value
December 112　CALLS	$1.65	$25,000	.05
December 109½　PUTS	$2.25	$25,000	.05

Standard deviation of the price of Government 11% bonds due in 2006 over six-month holding periods has been 10%.

a. Design a "straddle-like" option-writing strategy for the manager.

b. Calculate the break-even market prices for the underlying Government bond as a result of the "straddle-like" option-writing strategy.

c. Comment on the potential for a "straddle" option-writing strategy to add return to the portfolio.

3. In mid-May, there are two outstanding call option contracts available on the stock of ARB Co.:

Call #	Exercise Price	Expiration Date	Market Price
1	$50	August 19	$8.40
2	60	August 19	3.34

a. Assuming that you form a portfolio consisting of *one* call #1 held long and *two* calls #2 held short, complete the following table showing your intermediate steps. In calculating net profit, be sure to include the net initial cost of the options.

Price of ARB Stock at Expiration	Profit on Call #1 Position	Profit on Call #2 Position	Net Profit on Total Position
$40	—	—	—
45	—	—	—
50	—	—	—
55	—	—	—
60	—	—	—
65	—	—	—
70	—	—	—
75	—	—	—

b. Graph the net profit relationship in Part a, using stock price on the horizontal axis. What is (are) the break-even stock price(s)? What is the point of maximum profit?

c. Under what market conditions will this strategy (which is known as a *call ratio spread*) generally make sense? Does the holder of this position have limited or unlimited liability?

4. In developing the butterfly spread position, we showed that it could be broken down into two call option money spreads. Using the price data for SAS stock options from Table 24.1, demonstrate how a butterfly payoff structure similar to that shown in Figure 24.9 could be created using put options. Be specific as to the contract positions involved in the trade and show the expiration date net payoffs for the combined transaction.

5. *CFA Examination III (June 1987)*

You are considering the sale of a call option with an exercise price of $100 and one year to expiration. The underlying stock pays no dividends, its current price is $100, and you believe it will either increase to $120 or decrease to $80. The risk-free rate of interest is 10%.

a. Describe the specific steps involved in applying the binomial option pricing model to calculate the option's value.

b. Compare the binomial option pricing model to the Black-Scholes option pricing model.

6. *CFA Examination III (June 1992)*

You have decided to buy protective put options to protect the U.S. stock holdings of one of Global Advisers Company's (GAC) portfolios from a potential price decline over the next three months. You have researched the stock index options available in the U.S. and have assembled the following information:

Stock Index Option	Current Index Value	Underlying Value of One Put	Strike Price of Put	Put Premium	Average Daily Trading Volume of Puts
S&P 100	$365.00	$100 times index	365	$10.25	10,000
S&P 500	390.00	$100 times index	390	11.00	4,000
NYSE	215.00	$100 times index	215	6.25	1,000

(For each stock index option, the total cost of one put is the put premium times 100.)

	Beta vs. S&P 500	Correlation with Portfolio
Portfolio	1.05	1.00
S&P 100	0.95	0.86
S&P 500	1.00	0.95
NYSE	1.03	0.91

a. Using all relevant data from the above tables, calculate for each stock index option both the number and cost of puts required to protect a $7,761,700 diversified equity portfolio from loss. Show all calculations.

b. Recommend and justify which stock index option to use to hedge the portfolio, including reference to two relevant factors other than cost.

You know that it is very unlikely that the current stock index values will be exactly the same as the put strike prices at the time you make your investment decision.

c. Explain the importance of the relationship between the strike price of the puts and the current index values as it affects your investment decision.

d. Explain how an option pricing model may help you make an investment decision in this situation.

7. Assuming that a one-year call option with an exercise price of $38 is available for the stock of the DEW Corp., consider the following price tree for DEW stock over the next year:

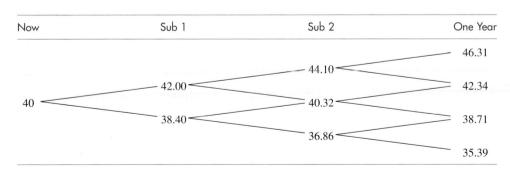

Now	Sub 1	Sub 2	One Year
40	42.00	44.10	46.31
			42.34
	38.40	40.32	38.71
		36.86	35.39

a. If the sequence of stock prices that DEW stock follows over the year is 40.00, 42.00, 40.32, and 38.71, describe the composition of the initial riskless portfolio of stock and options you would form and all of the subsequent adjustments you would have to make to keep this portfolio riskless. Assume the one-year risk-free rate is 6 percent.

b. Given the initial DEW price of $40, what are the probabilities of observing each of the four terminal stock prices in one year? (Hint: In arriving at your answer, it will be useful to consider (i) the number of different ways that a particular terminal price could be achieved and (ii) the probability of an up or down movement.)

c. Use the binomial option model to calculate the present value of this call option.

d. Calculate the value of a one-year put option on DEW stock having an exercise price of $38; be sure your answer is consistent with the correct response to Part c.

8. Consider the following questions on the pricing of options on the stock of ARB Inc.:

   a. A share of ARB stock sells for $75 and has a standard deviation of returns equal to 20 percent per year. The current risk-free rate is 9 percent and the stock pays two dividends: (i) a $2 dividend just prior to the option's expiration day, which is 91 days from now (i.e., exactly one quarter of a year); and (ii) a $2 dividend 182 days from now (i.e., exactly one half of a year). Calculate the Black-Scholes value for a European-style call option with an exercise price of $70.

   b. What would be the price of a 91-day European-style put option on ARB stock having the same exercise price?

   c. Calculate the change in the call option's value that would occur if ARB's management suddenly decided to suspend dividend payments and this action had no effect on the price of the company's stock.

   d. Briefly describe (without calculations) how your answer in Part a would differ under the following separate circumstances: (i) the volatility of ARB stock increases to 30 percent, and (ii) the risk-free rate decreases to 8 percent.

9. Suppose the current contract price of a futures contract on Commodity Z is $46.50 and the expiration date is in exactly six months (i.e., $T = 0.5$). The annualized risk-free rate over this period is 5.45 percent and the volatility of futures price movement is 23 percent, which is equal to that of the underlying commodity.

   a. Calculate the values for both a call option and a put option or this futures contract, assuming both have an exercise price of $46.50 and a six-month expiration date.

   b. Suppose the market prices for these contracts agree with the values you computed in Part a. You decide to buy the call option and sell the put option. What sort of position have you just created? Under what circumstances (i.e., for what view of subsequent market conditions) would it make sense for an investor to create such a position?

10. Suppose the current value of the Standard & Poor's 500 index is 653.50 and the dividend yield on the index is 2.8 percent. Also, the yield curve is flat at a continuously compounded rate of 5.5 percent.

    a. If you estimate the volatility factor for the index to be 16 percent, calculate the value of an index call option with an exercise price of 670 and an expiration date in exactly three months.

    b. If the actual market price of this option is $17.40, calculate its implied volatility coefficient.

    c. Besides volatility estimation error, explain why your valuation and the option's traded price might differ from one another.

11. Consider the following price data for TanCo stock in two different subperiods:

    Subperiod A: 168.375; 162.875; 162.5; 161.625; 160.75; 157.75; 157.25; 157.75; 161.125; 162.5; 157.5; 156.625; 157.875; 155.375; 150.5; 155.75; 154.25; 155.875; 156; 152.75; 150.5; 150.75

    Subperiod B: 122.5; 124.5; 121.875; 120.625; 119.5; 118.125; 117.75; 119.25; 122.25; 121.625; 120; 117.75; 118.375; 115.625; 117.75; 117.5; 118.5; 117.625; 114.625; 110.75

    a. For each subperiod, calculate the annualized historical measure of stock volatility that could be used in pricing an option for TanCo. In your calculations, you may assume that there are 250 trading days in a year.

b. Suppose now that you decide to gather additional data for each subperiod. Specifically, you obtain information for a call option with a current price of $12.25 and the following characteristics: $X = 115$; $S = 120.625$; time to expiration = 62 days; RFR = 7.42 percent; and dividend yield = 3.65 percent. Here the risk-free rate and dividend yields are stated on an annual basis. Use the volatility measure from subperiod B and the Black-Scholes model to obtain the "fair value" for this call option. Based on your calculations, is the option currently priced as it should be? Explain.

References

Black, Fischer. "How to Use the Holes in Black-Scholes." *Journal of Applied Corporate Finance* 1, no. 4 (Winter 1989).

Bookstaber, Richard M. *Option Pricing and Investment Strategies.* Chicago, IL: Probus Publishing, 1989.

Brenner, Menachem, Georges Courtadon, and Marti Subrahmanyam. "Options on the Spot and Options on Futures." *Journal of Finance* 40, no. 5 (December 1985).

Cox, John C. and Mark Rubinstein. *Option Markets.* Englewood Cliffs, NJ: Prentice-Hall, 1985.

Dubofsky, David A. *Options and Financial Futures: Valuation and Uses.* New York: McGraw-Hill, 1992.

Gastineau, Gary. *The Options Manual.* 3d ed. New York: McGraw-Hill, 1988.

Kolb, Robert W. *Options: An Introduction.* Miami, FL: Kolb Publishing, 1991.

Rao, Ramesh K. S. "Modern Option Pricing Models: A Dichotomous Classification." *Journal of Financial Research* 4, no. 1 (Spring 1981).

Shastri, Kuldeep and Kishore Tandon. "Options on Futures Contracts: A Comparison of European and American Pricing Models." *Journal of Futures Markets* 6, no. 4 (Winter 1986).

Smith, Clifford W., Jr. "Option Pricing: A Review." *Journal of Financial Economics* 3, no. 1/2 (January–March 1976).

Stoll, Hans R. and Robert E. Whaley. *Futures and Options: Theory and Applications.* Cincinnati, OH: South-Western Publishing, 1993.

Chapter
25

Swap Contracts, Convertible Securities, and Other Embedded Derivatives

This chapter answers the following questions:

- What are forward rate agreements and how can they be used to reduce the interest rate exposure of a borrower or investor?
- What are interest rate swaps and how can they transform the cash flows of a fixed or floating rate security?
- How does the swap market operate and how are swap contracts quoted and priced?
- How can swaps be interpreted as a pair of capital market transactions and how does this aid in the swap valuation process?
- How is credit risk measured in the interest rate swap market?
- What are interest rate caps and floors and how are they related to interest rate swaps?
- What is an interest rate swaption and how can it be used to "monetize" an otherwise nonmarketable asset?
- How does a currency swap differ from a "plain vanilla" interest rate swap and what is it used for?
- How can the swap contracting concept be adapted to manage equity and commodity price risk?
- How do the derivatives in convertible securities and warrant issues differ from traditional exchange-traded products?
- What are the similarities and differences between convertible preferred stock and convertible bonds?
- What are structured notes and what factors make their existence possible?
- How can securities with embedded derivatives reduce the funding cost of a corporate borrower?

Although derivatives only come in two basic "flavors"—forwards and options—the preceding chapters have shown that they can be used in a virtually unlimited number of situations by simply changing the contract terms or the nature of the underlying asset. In this chapter, we discuss several more ways in which these instruments can be modified to the specific needs of a particular end-user. Invariably, these modifications involve combining derivatives with other assets or liabilities to create the most highly valued cash flow pattern. We look at two general approaches to forming these combinations: "packages" of derivatives such as **interest rate swaps,** caps, and floors; and derivatives that have been "embedded" in more fundamental assets such as equity or debt issues.

To begin, we consider the market for OTC interest rate agreements—one of the fastest-growing segments of the derivatives industry in the past 20 years. In this examination, we once again focus on the differences between forward-based and option-based agreements while exploring the connection between the two. We then extend our discussion of swap contracting to include agreements based on foreign exchange, equity, and commodity price movements. Finally, we conclude the chapter with an overview of the myriad ways in which forwards and options are incorporated into other financial instruments. This includes an analysis of convertible securities, **warrants,** and **structured notes.** These innovations allow investors to acquire any of four different exposures—interest rate, currency, equity, or commodity price risk—in a creative and cost-effective manner.

OTC INTEREST RATE AGREEMENTS

In addition to futures and options contracts, an extremely active OTC market exists for products designed to manage an investor's or an issuer's interest rate risk. In describing strategies involving these instruments, it is useful to classify them as either forward-based or option-based contracts.[1]

FORWARD-BASED INTEREST RATE CONTRACTS

FORWARD RATE AGREEMENTS   The **forward rate agreement** (FRA) is the most basic of the OTC interest rate contracts. In an FRA, two parties agree today to a future exchange of cash flows based on two different interest rates. One of the cash flows is tied to a yield that is fixed at the deal's origination (the fixed rate); the other is determined at some later date (the floating rate). On the contract's settlement date, the difference between the two interest rates is multiplied by the FRA's **notional principal** (the "scale" of the transaction) and prorated to the length of the holding period. As the London Interbank Offer Rate (LIBOR) is frequently used as the floating rate index, FRAs are the OTC equivalent of the Eurodollar futures contracts traded at the Chicago Mercantile Exchange, with two important exceptions: (1) FRAs typically require no collateral account, and (2) they are not marked to market on a daily basis.

An FRA's settlement date and maturity are defined by its name: a 3×6 FRA allows the investor to lock in three-month LIBOR, three months forward; a 12×18 FRA locks in six-month LIBOR, one year forward, and so forth. FRA market makers quote a bid–offer spread on a rate basis. For example, suppose the FRA rates for three-month LIBOR shown in Table 25.1 prevail in the market at date zero, with current three-month LIBOR assumed to be 4.50 percent. This means that on a 3×6 FRA, the market maker is prepared to pay a fixed rate of 4.81 percent for receipt of three-month LIBOR and to receive a fixed rate of 4.85 percent for payment of LIBOR. In either case, there will be no payment until LIBOR is revealed in month 3. Settlement can then be made in arrears at month 6 or in advance at

---

TABLE 25.1

INDICATIVE BID–OFFER QUOTES ON 3-MONTH FORWARD RATE AGREEMENTS

Period	Bid	Offer
3×6	4.81%	4.85%
6×9	5.20	5.24
9×12	5.64	5.68
12×15	6.37	6.41
15×18	6.78	6.82
18×21	7.10	7.14
21×24	7.36	7.40

---

[1] Some of the discussion in this section is based on Keith C. Brown and Donald J. Smith, *Interest Rate and Currency Swaps: A Tutorial* (Charlottesville, VA: Research Foundation of the Institute of Chartered Financial Analysts, 1995).

month 3. If in arrears, the settlement flow will be adjusted to the actual number of days in the holding period and calculated by the following formula:

$$[\text{LIBOR} - \text{Fixed Rate}] \times [\text{Notional Principal}] \times \left[\frac{\text{Number of Days}}{360} \right]$$

recalling that in the U.S. market, LIBOR is based on a 360-day year. The advance settlement amount is calculated as the present value of the in-arrears amount, using the prorated level of the realized LIBOR as the discount rate. Notice that this settlement occurs on a net basis, i.e., only a single check for the rate differential will be written.

To see how an FRA might be used, suppose that Company Z decides to borrow financial capital for a six-month period, in two three-month installments. Because of the "set in advance, pay in arrears" convention for interest rate determination used in most debt markets, the firm finds itself exposed to rising interest rates over the next three months because the level of its second interest payment will not be established until the end of that period. (The amount of Company Z's first three-month payment would be known at origination.) To solve this problem, the firm can acquire a 3 × 6 FRA whereby it pays the dealer's quoted fixed rate of 4.85 percent in exchange for receiving three-month LIBOR at the settlement date. This is illustrated on the right-hand side of Figure 25.1, which depicts both the borrowing and derivative transactions.

Once the dealer has committed to the FRA with Company Z, two things occur. First, Company Z no longer is exposed to a rising funding cost because it now has a forward contract that obligates the dealer to "sell" it the LIBOR it needs in month 3 at a "price" of 4.85 percent. Second, the dealer now is exposed to rising LIBOR because it will be obligated to make the net settlement payment if LIBOR exceeds 4.85 percent three months from now. That is, Company Z has effectively used the FRA to transfer its interest rate exposure to the dealer. Unless the dealer wishes to hold this position as a speculation that rates will subsequently fall, the exposure can be hedged by "buying" LIBOR from another counterparty for its bid rate of 4.81 percent. This alternative is shown on the left-hand side of Figure 25.1 as a second FRA with Company Y, which is assumed to be an investor in a variable-rate asset who is naturally concerned about falling rates.

Now suppose that three-month LIBOR is 5.00 percent on the rate determination date in month 3 and that the deals with Companies Y and Z were negotiated to have a notional

---

FIGURE 25.1   **A MATCHED PAIR OF 3 × 6 FRA TRANSACTIONS**

principal of $10 million. If its contract specified settlement in arrears at month 6, Company Y would be obligated to pay the market maker $4,750, calculated as:

$$[.0500 - .0481] \times [10,000,000] \times \left[\frac{90}{360} \right]$$

assuming there are 90 days between months 3 and 6. If settled in advance, the month 3 payment would be:

$$4,750 \div \left[1 + \frac{90 \times 0.0500}{360} \right] = \$4,691.36.$$

Similarly, the payment from the dealer to Company Z would be $3,750 (= [.0500 − .0485] × [10,000,000] × [90/360]) in month 6, or $3,703.70 if accelerated to month 3. By matching the FRAs, the market maker is fully hedged from interest rate risk. Its spread of four basis points, which translates into $1,000, compensates for the costs (e.g., transaction costs, credit risk) of making a market in these contracts.

Finally, although the terms "buy" and "sell" are awkward, they are commonly used when describing FRA transactions. Since the FRA has an initial value of zero and therefore is neither an asset nor a liability, a counterparty doesn't really buy or sell anything. Instead, the parties to the transaction enter into a contract that may obtain a positive or a negative value—depending on the direction of future interest rate level changes. Nevertheless, this language is consistent with interpreting LIBOR as the "commodity" involved in the deal. In that case, the fixed rate is then the price paid or received in exchange for LIBOR, so that the payer of the fixed rate (Company Z) is said to be buying LIBOR, with the fixed-rate receiver (Company Y) selling LIBOR.

INTEREST RATE SWAPS   Although FRAs are quite useful, they represent a "one time only" solution to an interest rate risk management problem since they have a single settlement date. In fact, both investors and borrowers are routinely exposed to interest rate movements at regular intervals over an extended period of time, such as for the buyer and seller of a **floating rate note** that resets its coupon rate twice annually for several years according to movements in six-month LIBOR.[2] In that case, several "exposure dates" would need to be hedged, which could be accomplished with a series of FRAs. For example, suppose that an investor holding a one-year FRN paying quarterly coupons of three-month LIBOR becomes concerned that rates may fall in the future, thereby depressing the level of her last three coupons. (Recall that by convention her first coupon, payable in three months, is based on current LIBOR, which was assumed to be 4.50 percent.) Accordingly, she offsets this exposure by agreeing to receive the fixed rate on three separate FRA contracts: the 3 × 6, the 6 × 9, and the 9 × 12. Given the bid rates quoted in Table 25.1, these positions transform the cash flows on the floating-rate asset as shown in Figure 25.2.

This series of FRAs locks in the coupon levels, but they are at different fixed rates and require three separate contracts. This may be inconvenient to the investor, who might prefer a single contract that covers all of the future coupon dates and the same fixed rate.

---

[2] As we discussed briefly in Chapter 15, a floating (or variable) rate note is a debt instrument that is similar to a fixed-income bond in that it pays coupons at regular (e.g., semiannual) dates during its life. The difference is that the floating-rate note, or FRN, pays a coupon that is adjusted in a predetermined way with changes in some reference rate. For instance, a typical payment formula might be to reset the coupon every six months at LIBOR + 0.25 percent, meaning that the coupon amount would vary directly with LIBOR. Do not confuse the two acronyms FRA and FRN: the former is an over-the-counter forward contract; the latter is a bond.

FIGURE 25.2   **CONVERTING A FLOATING RATE NOTE WITH A SERIES OF FRAs**

A. Long One-Year FRN Paying LIBOR Quarterly

B. Series of Receive-Fixed FRAs

C. Combined Position

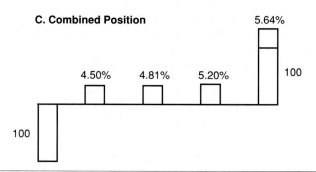

This is exactly what an interest rate swap does. Specifically, the swap contract can be viewed as a prepackaged series of FRAs to buy or sell LIBOR at the same fixed rate. Alternatively, an FRA can be viewed as a one-date interest rate swap. Of course, for the swap and FRA markets to remain efficient, the single fixed rate on the swap would have to be the appropriate average of 4.50 percent, 4.81 percent, 5.20 percent, and 5.64 percent. For simplicity, assume that each quarterly settlement period is exactly 0.25 year. This average can be approximated by solving for the internal rate of return on the hedged FRN:

$$100 = \frac{4.50 \times (0.25)}{(1 + IRR)^1} + \frac{4.81 \times (0.25)}{(1 + IRR)^2} + \frac{5.20 \times (0.25)}{(1 + IRR)^3} + \frac{100 + [5.64 \times (0.25)]}{(1 + IRR)^4}$$

or IRR = 1.258 percent. Thus, 5.03 percent (1.258 × 4) would be the fixed rate on a one-year, receive-fixed swap consistent with the forward rate agreements listed in Table 25.1.[3]

---

[3] See Vipul K. Bansal, M. E. Ellis, and John F. Marshall, "The Pricing of Short-Dated and Forward Interest Rate Swaps," *Financial Analysts Journal* 49, no. 2 (March/April 1993), pp. 82–87.

Although interest rate swaps are priced off the LIBOR forward yield curve, they are quoted off the Treasury bond yield curve. That is, the fixed rate side of a U.S. dollar–based swap generally is broken down to two components for trading purposes: (1) the yield of a Treasury bond with a maturity comparable to that of the swap; and (2) a risk premium term known as the **swap spread**. Because the floating rate side of the agreement typically is based on LIBOR "flat" (i.e., without any adjustment), the swap dealer can incorporate his bid–ask profit margin directly into this swap spread. Table 25.2 lists a representative set of fixed-rate quotes for U.S. dollar swaps, both in absolute and swap spread terms. Each of the swaps represented in this table assumes semiannual settlement dates with six-month LIBOR as the floating rate. For example, the swap dealer would be willing to pay the fixed rate of 5.95 percent on a five-year contract, a rate that is 29 basis points greater than the five-year T-bond yield. Notice that swaps with maturities as long as 30 years are quoted, although most contracts are transacted with maturities of 10 years or less.

With the fixed rate on the swap linked to a bond (i.e., 365-day) yield and the floating rate as a money market (360-day in the U.S. market) yield, the swap settlement cash flows are calculated in a slightly different manner than for FRAs. Specifically, while the swap is still

TABLE 25.2

INTEREST RATE SWAP AND SWAP SPREAD QUOTES

A. Absolute (i.e., T-Bond + Swap Spread) Basis

SECURITY	TIME	BID	ASK	CHANGE	OPEN	HIGH	LOW	PRV CLS
US$ SWAPS ABSOLUTE								
1) $SWAP2 Index	7:05	5.48	5.51	−.12	5.58	5.58	5.46	5.63
2) $SWAP3 Index	7:05	5.67	5.70	−.12	5.78	5.78	5.67	5.82
3) $SWAP4 Index	7:05	5.83	5.86	−.13	5.93	5.93	5.83	5.99
4) $SWAP5 Index	7:05	5.95	5.98	−.13	6.05	6.05	5.95	6.11
5) $SWAP7 Index	7:05	6.18	6.21	−.10	6.25	6.25	6.18	6.31
6) $SWAP10 Index	7:05	6.44	6.47	−.08	6.51	6.51	6.43	6.55
7) $SWAP15 Index	7:05	6.65	6.69	−.10	6.74	6.74	6.65	6.79
8) $SWAP20 Index	7:05	6.76	6.80	−.10	6.85	6.85	6.76	6.90
9) $SWAP30 Index	7:05	6.78	6.82	−.07	6.86	6.86	6.77	6.89

SEMI-ANN (ACT/ACT)
VS 6-MO US$ LIBOR

B. Swap Spread Basis

SECURITY	TIME	BID	ASK	CHANGE	OPEN	HIGH	LOW	PRV CLS
DLR-DLR SWAP SPREAD								
1) $$SWAP2 Index	7:05	15	18	—	17	18	17	18
2) $$SWAP3 Index	7:05	22	25	+1	24	25	24	24
3) $$SWAP4 Index	7:05	27	30	−1	30	30	30	31
4) $$SWAP5 Index	7:05	29	32	−1	33	33	32	33
5) $$SWAP7 Index	7:05	36	39	+1	38	39	38	38
6) $$SWAP 10 Index	7:05	38	42	+2	41	42	41	40
7) $$SWAP15 Index	7:05	60	64	—	64	64	64	64
8) $$SWAP20 Index	7:05	71	75	—	75	75	75	75
9) $$SWAP30 Index	7:05	35	39	—	39	39	39	39

SPREAD OFF U.S.
TREASURY
NOTE: 20YR SPREAD
OFF 10YR NOTE

Source: Bloomberg, March 1, 1996.

a net settlement contract, the date t fixed- and floating-rate payments are determined separately as:

$$(\text{Fixed-Rate Payment})_t = (\text{Swap Fixed Rate}) \times \left(\frac{\text{Number of Days}}{365} \right) \times (\text{Notional Principal})$$

and

$$(\text{Floating-Rate Payment})_t = (\text{Reference Rate})_{t-1} \times \left(\frac{\text{Number of Days}}{360} \right) \times (\text{Notional Principal}).$$

In these equations, the fixed rate never changes and the floating reference rate (i.e., LIBOR) always is determined at the beginning of a given settlement period. As an example of these calculations, assume that Counterparty A agreed to pay the fixed rate on a three-year swap with Counterparty B (i.e., the swap dealer). The terms of this transaction would be summarized as follows:

- Origination Date: March 1, 1996
- Maturity Date: March 1, 1999
- Notional Principal: $30 million
- Fixed-Rate Payer: Counterparty A
- Swap Fixed Rate: 5.70 percent (semiannual, actual/365 bond basis)
- Fixed-Rate Receiver: Counterparty B (i.e., the swap dealer)
- Floating Rate: Six-month LIBOR (money market basis)
- Settlement Dates: March 1 and September 1 of each year
- LIBOR Determination: Set in advance, paid in arrears

This "fixed-for-floating" transaction—the most basic form of a swap—is often called a *plain vanilla* agreement. Table 25.3 lists the settlement cash flows from the perspective of Counterparty A for a hypothetical time series of six-month LIBOR. In this display, the fixed-rate payer makes the net settlement payment when the day count–adjusted level of LIBOR is less than 5.70 percent; the fixed-rate receiver makes the settlement payment when LIBOR exceeds 5.70 percent.

Plain vanilla swaps generally are used for the same reason as FRAs: namely, to restructure the cash flows of an interest-sensitive asset or liability. For example, Counterparty A in the previous example could have been an institutional investor who owned a three-year, $30 million fixed-rate bond, but thought that interest rates were going to rise. Conse-

| **TABLE 25.3** | SETTLEMENT CASH FLOWS FOR A THREE-YEAR "PLAIN VANILLA" INTEREST RATE SWAP (FIXED-PAYER'S PERSPECTIVE) |

Settlement Date	Number of Days	Current LIBOR	Fixed-Rate Payment	Floating-Rate Receipt	Net Payment (Receipt)
3/1/96	—	5.30%	—	—	—
9/1/96	184	5.60	862,027	812,667	49,361
3/1/97	181	6.15	847,973	844,667	3,306
9/1/97	184	6.30	862,027	943,000	(80,973)
3/1/98	181	5.90	847,973	950,250	(102,277)
9/1/98	184	5.50	862,027	904,667	(42,639)
3/1/99	181	5.65	847,973	829,583	18,389

quently, he might want to convert his fixed-rate asset to an FRN so that his coupons would rise with future LIBOR increases. We saw in Chapter 11 that making this change synthetically with derivatives—rather than through a physical rebalancing of the portfolio—is the more cost-effective method. Assuming that A's bond currently pays a coupon of 7 percent, the net annualized cash flow he will receive after accounting for the swap position will be:

$$
\begin{array}{llll}
\text{Fixed-Rate Bond Coupon Receipt} & = (7.00\%) \times (360/365) & = 6.90\% \\
\text{Swap: (i) LIBOR Receipt} & = & = \text{LIBOR} \\
\qquad \text{(ii) Fixed Payment} & = [(5.70\%) \times (360/365)] & = \underline{(5.62\%)} \\
\text{Net Cost of Funds} & & = \text{LIBOR} + 1.28\%
\end{array}
$$

where this amount has been adjusted to a 360-day year. Thus, the net impact of combining the swap with the fixed-rate bond is to convert the fixed-rate bond into a variable-rate asset paying a coupon of LIBOR plus 128 basis points.

There is another important way of viewing this swap transaction. With the swap agreement, Counterparty A is effectively paying the fixed-rate coupons he receives from his bond in exchange for receiving floating-rate coupons. That is, the pay-fixed swap position can be viewed as equivalent to holding a portfolio consisting of: (1) a long position in a par-value FRN paying semiannual coupons of LIBOR, and (2) a short position in a par-value fixed-rate note paying semiannual coupons of 5.70 percent. This capital market interpretation is illustrated in Figure 25.3. Notice that by essentially buying and selling two different par-value instruments, no net principal amount exists at origination or maturity; this is what allows the swap's principal to be notional (i.e., not actually exchanged). Thus, all the swap agreement really does is transform the nature of the coupon payments.

FIGURE 25.3   **A CAPITAL MARKET INTERPRETATION OF AN INTEREST RATE SWAP**

Long in a Par-Value FRN and Short in a Par-Value, 5.70% Coupon Bond:

Equals a "Pay Fixed, Receive Floating" Plain Vanilla Swap:

The immediate consequence of this interpretation is that at any point in time the value of the pay-fixed swap position can be calculated as the present value of the floating-rate cash flows held as an asset minus the present value of the fixed-rate bond cash flows that is a liability, or:

(PV of Pay-Fixed Swap) = (PV of FRN Paying LIBOR) − (PV of Fixed-Rate Bond Paying 5.70%).

For example, suppose that one year after this swap was originated, yields have generally risen so that the fixed rate on a new two-year swap (i.e., the remaining time until the original maturity) is 6.70 percent. The value of this swap under these conditions can be established in two steps. First, on any settlement date, the FRN will be valued at par since its coupon always is reset according to current market conditions. Second, the market value of a bond paying a coupon of only 5.70 percent will fall, which benefits Counterparty A to whom this is a liability. Thus, using the new swap rate as a discount factor, A's position in the agreement (which as a forward contract had no value at origination) is now worth:

$$100 - \left[\sum_{t=1}^{4} \frac{(5.70/2)}{(1 + .067/2)^t} + \frac{100}{(1 + .067/2)^4} \right] = 1.8431$$

or 1.8431 percent of notional principal. Therefore, if Counterparty A chose to unwind his contract at this time, the dealer would be willing to pay as much as \$552,929 (= 0.018431 × \$30 million) and then find a new swap counterparty who would pay the now current fixed rate of 6.70 percent. The \$552,929 is considered to be the marked-to-market value of the swap. Given that interest rates have risen since inception, the original contract is now an asset to the fixed-rate payer (i.e., Counterparty A) and a liability to the fixed-rate receiver (i.e., the dealer).

An important characteristic of the swap agreement is that it becomes an *asset* to one participant and a *liability* to the other as soon as market conditions change after the terms of the contract are set. This means that swaps entail credit risk. To see why, consider what would happen to Counterparty A if, on a particular settlement date when LIBOR was 10 percent, the swap dealer was unable to make the net settlement payment. In that case, the investor would receive only the 7 percent coupon from his bond rather than the 11.28 percent (= LIBOR + 1.28 percent) coupon he expected from his synthetic FRN. The possibility that the swap counterparty either cannot or will not honor its obligation means that the synthetic floating-rate note carries *more* credit risk than the actual fixed-rate bond. Further, notice that the swap dealer also will be concerned about the ability of Counterparty A to perform on the agreement when LIBOR is less than 5.70 percent. Thus, like any forward arrangement, the credit risk on a swap runs two ways.

What would it cost Counterparty A if, with exactly two years remaining on the contract described above, the swap dealer suffered bankruptcy and defaulted on the remainder of the agreement? To retain his synthetic FRN, the investor would have to find a new swap dealer to replace the old contract. Unfortunately, with the change in market conditions, Counterparty A will now have to pay 6.70 percent to receive LIBOR over the next two years, implying an additional cost of 50 basis points (times 30 million) each settlement period. Thus, the economic consequence to A of the dealer's default can be measured as:

$$\sum_{t=1}^{4} \frac{(0.067/2 - 0.057/2) \times (30,000,000)}{(1 + 0.067/2)^t} = \$552,929$$

which, of course, is the same amount as the marked-to-market value of the swap. Thus, this figure represents the current potential default loss for the counterparty to whom the swap is an asset.[4]

Finally, although interest rate swaps have been in existence since 1981, very little empirical evidence exists on how they are priced in the marketplace because of the non-public nature of the information about these contracts. The available evidence includes Kim and Koppenhaver's investigation of commercial bank activity in the swap market; Sun, Sundaresan, and Wang, who examined the consistency of bid–ask quotes issued by two swap dealers with different credit grades; and Brown, Harlow, and Smith, who tested several theoretical relationships designed to explain the historical pattern of variation in the swap spread component.[5] Although each of the studies examined a different aspect of the swap contracting process, the collective evidence they present is consistent with the notion that this market works in an orderly and efficient manner. Further, the mechanics of swap pricing, which have matured over time, seem to be integrated with other affiliated securities such as Treasury notes and bills and Eurodollar futures contracts.

OPTION-BASED INTEREST RATE CONTRACTS   In this section, we discuss three types of OTC interest rate option arrangements as well as their relationship with interest rate swaps: (1) caps and floors, the two most basic option-based products; (2) collars, special combinations of caps and floors; and (3) options that allow the holder to enter into a swap contract at a later date.

CAPS AND FLOORS   Interest rate cap and floor agreements are equivalent to portfolios of interest rate option contracts, with each contract corresponding to a different settlement period. A **cap agreement** is a series of cash settlement interest rate options, typically based on LIBOR. The seller of the cap, in return for the option premium that is usually paid at origination, is obliged to pay the difference between LIBOR and the exercise, or cap, rate (times the fraction of the year, times the notional principal) whenever that difference is positive. The seller of a **floor agreement** makes settlement payments only when LIBOR is below the floor rate. No payment is made if LIBOR is above the floor or below the cap rate. As with swaps and FRAs, settlement can be either in advance or in arrears. Payment in arrears is more common because these contracts usually are used to hedge exposure to floating-rate bank loans and notes, which typically settle in arrears.

From these descriptions, the date t settlement payments on cap and floor agreements can be written as follows:

$$Cap\ Settlement: \text{(Notional Principal)} \times \left(\frac{\text{Number of Days}}{360} \right) \times \max[\text{LIBOR}_{t-1} - X_c, 0]$$

and

$$Floor\ Settlement: \text{(Notional Principal)} \times \left(\frac{\text{Number of Days}}{360} \right) \times \max[X_f - \text{LIBOR}_{t-1}, 0]$$

---

[4] For an interesting discussion of credit risk in the swap market, see Eric H. Sorensen and Thierry F. Bollier, "Pricing Interest Rate Swap Default Risk," *Financial Analysts Journal* 50, no. 3 (May–June 1994), pp. 23–33.

[5] See Sung-Hwa Kim and Gary D. Koppenhaver, "An Empirical Analysis of Bank Interest Rate Swaps," *Journal of Financial Services Research* 7, no. 1 (January 1993), pp. 57–72; Tong-sheng Sun, Suresh Sundaresan, and Ching Wang. "Interest Rate Swaps: An Empirical Investigation," *Journal of Financial Economics* 34, no. 1 (August 1993), pp. 77–99; and Keith C. Brown, W. V. Harlow, and Donald J. Smith, "An Empirical Analysis of Interest Rate Swap Spreads," *Journal of Fixed Income* 3, no. 3 (March 1994), pp. 61–78.

where

X_c = the cap exercise rate
X_f = the floor exercise rate.

(Recall once again that a 360-day year is used because of the quotation convention for U.S. dollar LIBOR.) For example, consider a three-year, semiannual settlement, 8 percent cap on six-month LIBOR. The buyer of the cap pays the writer an up-front premium, quoted as a percentage of the notional principal. Assuming the cost is 120 basis points and the notional principal is $100 million, the cost of the cap is $1,200,000.[6] Suppose that settlement dates are on the 15th of May and November of each year and that LIBOR on one particular May 15th is 9⅛ percent. The holder of the cap will receive settlement in arrears the following November in the amount of $575,000, calculated as (9.125 percent − 8 percent) × $100 million × (184/360).

The payoff relationships for caps and floors can be illustrated using traditional, option-style diagrams. Figure 25.4 portrays an 8 percent cap and a 4 percent floor on LIBOR. Notice that the payoff diagram for the cap looks like a typical call option on a commodity and the floor takes the form of a put option. Indeed, following the convention where LIBOR is the commodity, caps are referred to as "calls on LIBOR" and floors as "puts on LIBOR." Alternatively, a cap agreement on LIBOR is a series of put options on an underlying Eurodollar time deposit. In effect, the owner of the option has the right, but not the obligation, to sell to the cap writer a time deposit having a coupon rate equal to the cap rate in the amount of the notional principal of the contract. The owner exercises that option if current LIBOR exceeds the cap rate, thus selling a relatively low coupon deposit at par value. The proceeds of that sale can then be used to buy a time deposit that earns the higher market rate. The gain on those hypothetical transactions is equivalent to the payoff on the cap agreement. Whether one interprets a cap as a call on LIBOR or a put on a time deposit (and, similarly, a floor as a put on LIBOR or a call on a time deposit) is purely a matter of semantic preference.[7]

COLLARS   An **interest rate collar** is a combination of a cap and a floor, a long position in one and a short position in the other. To buy a 4 percent–8 percent collar on LIBOR is to buy an 8 percent cap and to write a 4 percent floor. The buyer will receive cash payments when LIBOR exceeds 8 percent, make payments when LIBOR is below 4 percent, and neither receive nor pay if LIBOR is between 4 percent and 8 percent. Often the motive for a firm to buy a collar is to reduce the initial cost of acquiring the protection from higher levels of LIBOR, as the up-front receipt from selling the floor can be used to offset the cost of buying the cap.

A special interest rate collar occurs when the initial premiums on the cap and the floor are equal and therefore offset each other. For instance, suppose that the premium on a three-year, 4 percent floor is 120 basis points, which matches the premium on the 8 percent

---

[6] In practice, interest rate caps and floors are quoted by market makers on a volatility basis, for instance, 18.5 percent bid and 19.5 percent offered. That measure of volatility (stated as a standard deviation), plus the exercise rate, the current term structure of interest rates, and the time-frame for the contract, are then entered into an option pricing model to obtain the actual amount of the premium. Hull has shown that this amount can be established by adapting Black's model for valuing futures options to price each separate option in the contract (i.e., "caplets" and "floorlets"), and then summing them up across all settlement dates. See John C. Hull, *Options, Futures, and Other Derivatives,* 3d ed. (Englewood Cliffs, NJ: Prentice-Hall, 1997).

[7] A good review of these instruments can be found in Peter A. Abken, "Interest Rate Caps, Collars, and Floors," Federal Reserve Bank of Atlanta *Economic Review* 74 (November–December 1989), pp. 2–24.

| FIGURE 25.4 | PAYOFF DIAGRAMS FOR BUYING AND WRITING AN INTEREST RATE CAP AND FLOOR |

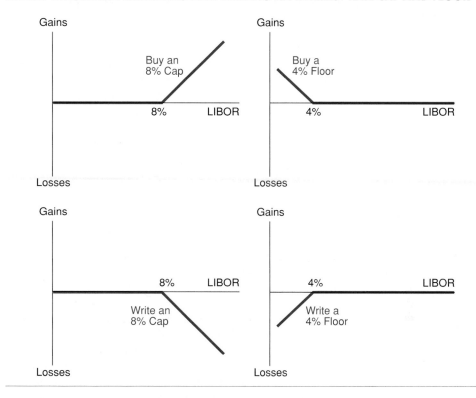

cap. The combination is known as zero-cost, or zero-premium, collar. This is a useful concept because it is easy to show that an interest rate swap is just a special case of a zero-cost interest rate collar. To see this, consider again the 4 percent–8 percent zero-cost collar on LIBOR that was constructed from buying the 8 percent cap and selling the 4 percent floor. Now tighten the collar by lowering the cap rate to 7 percent. The up-front premium paid by the buyer must go up; an insurance policy providing protection whenever LIBOR exceeds 7 percent has to cost more than a policy that pays off only when LIBOR moves above 8 percent. Suppose that premium is 200 basis points (times the notional principal). To keep the collar at a zero initial cost, the written floor must then generate additional premium for the seller as well. This will require a higher floor rate because a contract in which the seller makes settlement payments whenever LIBOR is less than 5 percent certainly will be worth more than one with a floor rate of 4 percent. If we keep tightening the collar at some exercise rate common to both the cap and the floor, say 6 percent, the combination will be zero-cost. That will be the pay-fixed swap fixed rate that prevails in the market. This is illustrated in Figure 25.5.

To summarize, buying a 6 percent cap and writing a 6 percent floor on LIBOR is equivalent in terms of settlement cash flows to an interest rate swap paying a fixed rate of 6 percent and receiving LIBOR. When LIBOR is above 6 percent, the net settlement receipt on the swap is the same as the receipt on the in-the-money cap that is owned. When LIBOR is below 6 percent, the net settlement payment on the swap is the same as the payment on the in-the-money floor that has been sold. Similarly, writing a cap and buying a floor at the same exercise rate is identical to a receive-fixed interest rate swap. Notice that a cap-floor

FIGURE 25.5 **AN ILLUSTRATION OF CAP-FLOOR-SWAP PARITY**

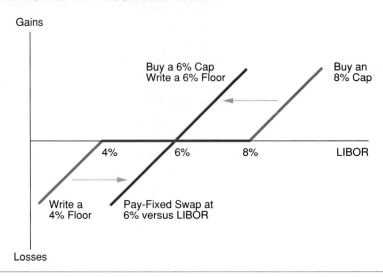

combination at the same exercise rate always has the same payoffs as a swap contract. However, only when the combination also nets to a zero initial cost does that common rate match the prevailing swap fixed rate. This relationship is known as *cap-floor-swap parity*, and is the swap market analog to the put-call-forward parity formula first discussed in Chapter 11 and extended to the range forward strategy in Chapter 24.

Along with the "portfolio of FRAs" and "pair of bonds" ways of viewing a swap contract, cap-floor-swap parity shows that a third interpretation exists: the swap can be viewed as a pair of option positions. This can be used to test the internal consistency of credit risk and valuation models for swaps. For example, because selling a cap and buying a floor at the same exercise rate can offer the same cash flows as a receive-fixed swap, the projected credit risk on the swap must be comparable to the credit risk on the floor agreement. (Note that a firm bears the counterparty's credit risk on purchased options, and not on written options, because only with purchased options is the firm relying on the other party's future performance.) This parity relationship also implies that variations of the option valuation models discussed in Chapter 24 can be used in the valuation of swap contracts.[8]

SWAP OPTIONS ("SWAPTIONS")   A **swaption** gives the holder of the option the right, but not the obligation, to enter into an interest rate swap having a predetermined fixed rate at some later date. As with all options, there are two types of these agreements: *receiver* and *payer* swaptions. A receiver swaption gives the buyer the right, but not the obligation, to enter into a swap on prearranged terms (fixed rate, maturity, notional principal, floating rate index, settlement periods, documentation, etc.) as the fixed-rate receiver. The seller of the option, in return for the up-front premium, must enter the swap as the fixed-rate payer on demand of the buyer. Naturally, the buyer will only exercise the receiver swaption if the market swap rate is less than the strike rate at the maturity of the option; that is, if she can receive an above-market fixed rate while paying LIBOR.

---

[8] The relationship between swap, cap, and floor agreements is described in Rudy Yaksick, "Swaps, Caps, and Floors: Some Parity and Price Identities," *Journal of Financial Engineering* 1, no. 1 (1992), pp. 105–115.

On the other hand, a payer swaption gives the buyer the right, but not the obligation, to enter into a swap on prearranged terms as the fixed-rate payer, with the seller of the option obligated to receive the fixed rate at the buyer's request. Holders of a payer swaption will only exercise the receiver swaption if the market pay-fixed swap rate prevailing at the option exercise date is higher than the strike rate, thereby entitling them to pay a below-market fixed rate while receiving LIBOR.

Swaptions are most useful to those firms who presently are not sure if they will be exposed to future interest rate movements. An example would be a bond portfolio manager who may be forced to liquidate part of his holdings in a year's time. In such a situation, the bond manager might like to have the option of fixing the future interest rate at the levels priced into today's yield curve.

Brown and Smith have shown how swaptions also can be used in the management of callable debt.[9] Suppose that three years ago, Company XYZ issued 15-year, fixed-rate callable debt with a coupon rate of 12 percent. Now, interest rates for XYZ's credit grade have fallen to 8 percent, but the outstanding debt issue still has two years before its call deferment period is over. Clearly, the issuing company would call the debt today if it could (i.e., it would rather make 8 percent coupon payments than 12 percent); the call option it implicitly holds on the bond it issued is currently in the money. However, it must wait for two years to exercise the call, during which time interest rates may rise back above 12 percent. Further, because the option cannot be detached from the original bond, it cannot be sold separately in today's market.

One solution to this dilemma involves the use of swaptions. Consider what would happen if the issuing firm entered into the following transaction today: Sell a two-year receiver option on a 10-year swap, giving the buyer the choice to receive the fixed rate of 12 percent. The benefit of doing this is that the company will receive a premium for selling the swaption at origination. This receipt of cash, which is illustrated in Figure 25.6, is analogous to what the company would have received if it had been able to sell the call feature embedded in the underlying bond directly in the marketplace.

To see what this will cost the company, consider what happens in two years when the swaption expires and the bond can be called. If interest rates are 12 percent or greater, neither the bond option nor the swap option will be exercised and they both expire out of the money. The issuing company continues to pay a 12 percent coupon for the next 10

FIGURE 25.6

CALL MONETIZATION WITH SWAPTIONS: ORIGINATION

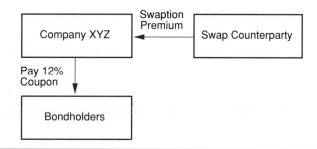

---

[9] See Keith C. Brown and Donald J. Smith, "Forward Swaps, Swap Options, and the Management of Callable Debt," *Journal of Applied Corporate Finance* 2, no. 4 (Spring 1990), pp. 59–71.

FIGURE 25.7	CALL MONETIZATION WITH SWAPTIONS: EXPIRATION DATE

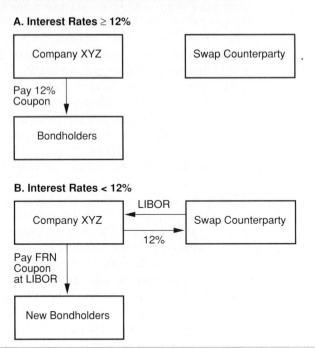

years. This is shown in panel A of Figure 25.7. Conversely, if interest rates are less than 12 percent, both the bond option and swap option will be exercised by their respective holders. To Company XYZ, this means: (1) it can refinance its original debt with a 10-year FRN (assumed to pay LIBOR), and (2) it will be forced to pay a fixed rate of 12 percent as per the terms of the swaption. Thus, the net effect is that the issuing company will continue to pay a 12 percent coupon for the next 10 years. (Panel B of Figure 25.7 illustrates this set of transactions.)

The key point here is that, by selling the swaption today, the company has committed itself to paying a 12 percent coupon for the remaining life of the original bond. This was done in exchange for an up-front swaption premium received at origination. Thus, even though the bond's call option could not be sold directly, it has been effectively "monetized" in the swaption market. Not surprisingly, this strategy is often referred to as *call monetization*.

One important caution is that swap rates and bond rates do not necessarily move in the same fashion. This will create basis risk in that a swap market instrument is being used as a substitute for a capital market instrument (i.e., the bond's call feature). In this example, the worst-case result for the company would have been if the fixed-rate on a 10-year swap was below 12 percent in two years, but its debt refunding rate in the capital market was above 12 percent. This result, which could occur if Company XYZ's credit quality deteriorates over the next two years, would mean that the company would be forced to enter into a swap it doesn't want (or unwind the position at a disadvantage) and not be able to refinance its borrowing profitably.

SWAP CONTRACTING EXTENSIONS

Although interest rate swaps are by far the most prevalent OTC rate contract, three other important extensions of this concept have developed recently. All these agreements, which preserve the essential feature of a swap contract by exchanging cash flows based on two different rates or prices, include (1) currency (i.e., foreign exchange) swaps, (2) equity index–linked swaps, and (3) commodity swaps.

CURRENCY SWAPS

Like the plain vanilla swap agreements, a **currency swap** is an agreement wherein two counterparties make periodic cash flow exchanges based on two different interest rates.[10] These contracts, also known as cross-currency swaps, differ from the single-currency version in two ways. First, because the associated cash flows are denominated in different monetary units, the principal amounts usually are exchanged at the origination and maturity dates of the contract. Second, because there are two currencies involved, the interest rates defining the transaction can be expressed on either a fixed- or floating-rate basis in either or both currencies. Assuming that the U.S. dollar is one of the currencies involved in the deal, this leaves the following four possibilities: (1) a fixed rate in the foreign currency versus a fixed rate in U.S. dollars, (2) a fixed rate in the foreign currency versus a floating rate in U.S. dollars, (3) a floating rate in the foreign currency versus a fixed rate in U.S. dollars, and (4) a floating rate in the foreign currency versus a floating rate in U.S. dollars. Although all of these formats are available, the predominant currency swap exchanges a fixed rate in the foreign currency for U.S. dollar LIBOR. This structure is shown in Figure 25.8.

FIGURE 25.8

A BASIC CURRENCY SWAP TRANSACTION

A. At Origination

Foreign Currency Principal

Counterparty D ← Counterparty E

U.S. Dollar Principal →

B. On Each Settlement Date (Including Maturity)

Foreign Currency Fixed-Coupon Rate

Counterparty D → Counterparty E

U.S. Dollar LIBOR ←

C. At Maturity

Foreign Currency Principal

Counterparty D → Counterparty E

U.S. Dollar Principal ←

---

[10] A good collection of readings on both the currency swap market and applications of these instruments can be found in Carl R. Beidleman, ed., *Cross Currency Swaps* (Homewood, IL: Business One-Irwin, 1992).

This diagram shows that two distinct types of exchanges exist: principal at both origination and maturity and coupon interest on all of the settlement dates. It is customary that both principal exchanges be executed at the spot foreign exchange (FX) rate prevailing at the initiation date, regardless of subsequent market FX rates. Further, similar to the interest rate swap, the floating-rate side of the coupon exchanges in the standard currency swap usually is quoted flat. Thus, the dollar cash flow paid by Counterparty E on each settlement date is determined by multiplying the relevant LIBOR (which would have been determined at the previous settlement date) by the U.S. dollar principal amount, adjusted by the day count factor. The periodic cash flow that Counterparty D is obligated to pay is the product of the quoted fixed rate and the foreign currency–based principal amount. Because the cash flows differ in denomination, currency swaps do not settle on a net basis.

To see how these conventions translate into cash flows, suppose Counterparty D has agreed to pay Counterparty E 8.65 percent on a four-year, British pound swap. Assume further that the transaction can be summarized as follows:

- Origination Date: November 15, 1996
- Maturity Date: November 15, 2000
- Notional Principal: GBP 20 million and USD 34.4 million
- Fixed-Rate Payer: Counterparty D
- Swap Fixed Rate: 8.65 percent in pounds sterling (semiannual bond basis)
- Fixed-Rate Receiver: Counterparty E
- Floating Rate: Six-month LIBOR in U.S. dollars (money market basis)
- Settlement Dates: November 15th and May 15th of each year
- LIBOR Determination: Set in advance, paid in arrears

The initial and ultimate principal exchanges are based on the spot exchange rate of USD 1.72/GBP that is assumed to have prevailed at the swap origination date. Given the rate conventions in each country, the pound-denominated coupon settlement payments are computed as [0.0865 × (Number of days ÷ 365) × GBP 20 million] while the dollar-based cash flows are determined by [LIBOR × (Number of days ÷ 360) × USD 34.4 million]. These amounts are shown in Table 25.4 from the perspective of Counterparty D (i.e., the fixed-rate payer).[11]

As an example of why such a transaction might be used, suppose that Counterparty E is a British pension fund that would like to invest GBP 20 million in a fixed-rate note making semiannual coupon payments for the next four years. Given the current pricing in the market, however, the coupon on sterling-denominated, par-value fixed-rate bonds issued by companies with an acceptable Aa credit rating is 8.40 percent. Suppose, on the other hand, that the pension fund buys a four-year floating rate note from an Aa-rated American corporation paying LIBOR flat for USD 34.4 million. In this case, the pension manager could purchase the dollar-denominated FRN and enter into the "pay USD floating/receive GBP fixed" swap outlined above. The combination of these two transactions, shown in

---

[11] Although the most typical form of a currency swap is this fixed foreign currency/floating dollar structure, that is not always the most useful way to package cash flows. If, for instance, Counterparty D had wanted to pay a fixed rate in U.S. dollars (USD), instead of LIBOR, in exchange for fixed sterling (GBP) receipts, the standard fixed/floating currency swap can be easily repackaged by combining it with a floating/fixed U.S. dollar interest rate swap. As a practical matter, if both of these transactions were executed simultaneously with the same market maker, the corporate end-user (i.e., Counterparty D) would not undertake two separate transactions. Rather, to minimize the requisite documentation and bookkeeping, the swap intermediary in this case would undoubtedly offer the counterparty a direct, blended quote of "receive fixed USD, pay fixed GBP," leaving LIBOR out altogether. These fixed/fixed swaps were once known as CIRCUS swaps, standing for "combined interest rate and currency swaps."

| TABLE 25.4 | SETTLEMENT CASH FLOWS FOR A U.S. DOLLAR/BRITISH POUND CURRENCY SWAP |

Settlement Date	Number of Days	Assumed Current LIBOR	Fixed-Rate Payment	Floating-Rate Receipt
A. Initial Exchange of Principal				
11/15/96	—	5.75%	USD 34.400	GBP 20.000
B. Coupon Exchanges				
5/15/97	181	6.00%	GBP 0.858	USD 0.994
11/15/97	184	6.25%	0.872	1.055
5/15/98	181	6.70%	0.858	1.087
11/15/98	184	7.25%	0.872	1.178
5/15/99	181	7.00%	0.858	1.254
11/15/99	184	6.75%	0.872	1.187
5/15/00	182	5.50%	0.863	1.167
C. Final Coupon and Principal Exchange				
11/15/00	184	5.75%	GBP 0.872 and GBP 20.000	USD 0.967 and USD 34.400

Figure 25.9, would leave the investor with the equivalent of owning a pound-denominated bond paying a fixed rate of 8.65 percent in sterling, a yield "pickup" of 25 basis points relative to the direct issue market. Thus, by using the swap to transform both the rate sensitivity and currency denomination of the dollar FRN, the pension fund has created a more desirable package of cash flows than was otherwise available. In this sense, we can view any financial security as a substitute for any other financial security, once the appropriate repackaging has been accomplished.[12]

As with plain vanilla interest rate swaps, currency swaps can be viewed as a pair of bond transactions. Specifically, panel B of Figure 25.9 shows that, from Counterparty E's perspective, the swap can be interpreted as a portfolio containing: (1) a long position in a fixed-rate, pound-denominated bond and (2) a short position in a USD FRN. This intuition is useful in calculating the value of the agreement after origination, which is:

$$\text{Value of Currency Swap (in GBP)} = (\text{PV of GBP fixed cash flows}) \\ - [(\text{PV of USD FRN}) \div (\text{Spot USD/GBP})].$$

There are two important features of this equation. First, the swap's value depends on changes in three fundamental factors: British interest rates, U.S. interest rates, and the USD/GBP exchange rate. Second, on any given settlement date, the floating rate note should once again be valued at par, which assumes no change in counterparty creditworthiness. This simplifies the swap valuation calculation tremendously.

Suppose, for example, that exactly two years (i.e., four settlement dates) after this agreement was originated, the fixed rate on a new two-year "receive GBP fixed, pay USD LIBOR" swap has fallen to 7.65 percent while the prevailing exchange rate has moved to

---

[12] An important mitigating factor that must once again be considered with any swap-based investment scheme is the credit risk of the swap counterparty. Whether the presence of this additional exposure in this case explains the 25 bp investment advantage would, of course, depend on an assessment of the likelihood that Counterparty D would default on the swap agreement under adverse market conditions. For a theoretical discussion on this topic, see Ian A. Cooper and Antonio S. Mello, "The Default Risk of Swaps," *Journal of Finance* 46, no. 2 (June 1991), pp. 597–620.

FIGURE 25.9   **TRANSFORMING A BOND INVESTMENT WITH A CURRENCY SWAP**

A. Purchase USD Floating Rate Note

LIBOR x (1/2) x (USD 34.4)

USD 34.4

USD 34.4

B. Enter Pay USD Floating, Receive GBP Fixed Currency Swap

USD 34.4

(0.0865) x (1/2) x (GBP 20.0)

GBP 20.0

USD 34.4

LIBOR x (1/2) x (USD 34.4)

GBP 20.0

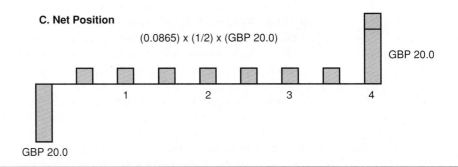

C. Net Position

(0.0865) x (1/2) x (GBP 20.0)

GBP 20.0

GBP 20.0

USD 1.82/GBP. Assuming, for the ease of computation, that all of the remaining GBP cash flows on the existing contract are 0.865 million (= (0.0865) × (1/2) × (20.0 million)), Counterparty E's position in the swap is worth:

$$\left[\sum_{t=1}^{4} \frac{GBP\ 0.865}{(1 + 0.0765/2)^t} + \frac{GBP\ 20.0}{(1 + 0.0765/2)^4} \right] - \frac{USD\ 34.4}{(USD\ 1.82/GBP)}$$

$$= (20.364) - (18.901) = GBP\ 1.463\ million.$$

Of course, this amount also represents a liability to Counterparty D; like any derivative a currency swap is a zero sum game. Finally, notice that both the GBP rate decline and the exchange rate increase have changed the swap's value in the same direction by increasing the value of the pound-denominated asset and reducing the translated value of the dollar liability, respectively. Thus, even though the swap was originally negotiated to have no net value to either counterparty, it will become an asset to one and a liability to the other as soon as market conditions change.

EQUITY INDEX–LINKED SWAPS

Similar in form to interest rate swaps, **equity** index–linked **swaps** are equivalent to portfolios of forward contracts calling for the exchange of cash flows based on two different investment rates: (1) a variable debt rate (e.g., three-month LIBOR) and (2) the return to an equity index (e.g., Standard & Poor's 500). The index-linked payment is based on either the total return (i.e., dividends plus capital gain or loss) or just the percentage index change for the settlement period plus a fixed spread adjustment, which is expressed in basis points and can be negative. The floating-rate payments typically are based on LIBOR flat. Like interest rate and currency swaps, equity swaps are traded in the OTC markets and can have maturities out to 10 years or beyond.

In addition to the S&P 500, equity swaps can be structured around foreign indexes such as TOPIX (Japan), FT-SE 100 (Great Britain), DAX (Germany), CAC 40 (France), TSE 35 (Canada), EOE (Netherlands), and Hang Seng (Hong Kong). These agreements also can be designed so that the cash flows are denominated in the same currency or in two different currencies. The equity index–based cash flow typically is denominated in the currency of the index's country of origination, but the swap can be designed so that this payment is automatically hedged into a different currency. Further, these agreements specify a notional principal that is not exchanged at origination but serves the purpose of converting percentage returns into cash flows. This notional principal can either be variable or fixed during the life of the agreement, but the same notional principal applies to both sides of the transaction.

There are several reasons why the equity swap market has developed. First, these agreements allow investors to take advantage of overall price movements in a specific country's stock market without having to purchase the equity securities directly.[13] This has the advantage of reducing both the transaction costs and tracking errors associated with assembling a portfolio that mimics the index as well as allowing the investor to avoid dividend withholding taxes normally associated with cross-border investing. Second, creating a direct equity investment in a foreign country may be difficult for some companies where prohibited by law or operating policy. Finally, an investment fund wanting to accumulate foreign index returns denominated in their domestic currency may not be able or legally permitted to obtain sufficient exchange-traded futures or option contracts to hedge a direct equity investment. The equity swap can be structured so that there is no need for separate hedging transactions.

The most common application for an equity swap involves a counterparty that receives the index-based payment in exchange for making the floating rate payment. For example, consider a pension fund that currently has a substantial portion of its asset portfolio invested in floating rate notes paying quarterly coupons based on LIBOR. If the manager of this fund wants to alter his existing asset allocation by converting some of these debt-based cash flows into equity-based receipts, he has two ways to do so. First, he can sell the existing floating rate notes and purchase a portfolio of equities directly in the market. Alternatively, the manager can enter into an equity swap with an initial notional principal

---

[13] For a more detailed analysis of the uses and development of this product, see Julie A. Allen and Janet L. Showers, "Equity-Index Linked Derivatives: A User's Guide" (New York: Salomon Brothers, 1991).

FIGURE 25.10 ALTERING AN ASSET ALLOCATION POSITION WITH AN EQUITY SWAP

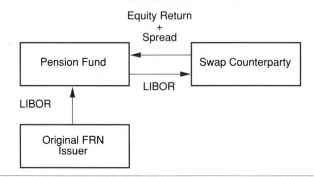

equal to the amount of the existing debt holdings he wants to convert. As we have seen, from the standpoint of reducing transaction costs, the second alternative is clearly preferable. The mechanics of this arrangement are illustrated in Figure 25.10.

The net return to the fund in this example is simply the return on the equity index plus the spread adjustment. Further, if the floating rate notes held as an asset yield more than LIBOR, this incremental amount would serve to increase the overall net return. Assuming that both cash flows are denominated in the same currency, the net settlement payment on the equity swap from the company's standpoint can be calculated as the difference between the variable-rate outflow and the equity-linked inflow, where:

$$\text{Payment} = [\text{LIBOR} - \text{Spread}] \times [\text{Notional Principal}] \times \left[\frac{(\text{Number of days})}{360} \right]$$

and

$$\text{Receipt} = \left[\frac{\text{Index}_{new} - \text{Index}_{old}}{\text{Index}_{old}} \right] \times [\text{Notional Principal}]$$

where Index_{new} and Index_{old} represent the index levels occurring on the current and immediate past settlement dates, assuming all dividends are reinvested. Notice here that to minimize calculations, the settlement payment is computed using (LIBOR − Spread) rather than adding a separate inflow for the equity spread itself. Gastineau investigated indicative spread quotes as of 1992 for various indexes throughout the world and found that, while some were positive (e.g., 90 bp for DAX, 25 bp for FT-SE), others were negative (e.g., −10 bp for S&P 500, −60 bp for Hang Seng).[14] However, he noted that the equity swap quotations methods are not standardized across all dealers; therefore, the quoted values may not be directly comparable.

Another way to view the effect of this swap-based cash flow transformation is shown in Figure 25.11. Here, it should be clear that equity swaps differ from interest rate and currency swaps in one important way. Specifically, because there is no guarantee that the equity index will appreciate in value from one settlement period to the next, it is possible

---

[14] See Gary L. Gastineau, "Using Swaps in Equity Portfolios," in *Derivative Strategies for Managing Portfolio Risk,* edited by K. Brown (Charlottesville, VA: Association for Investment Research and Management, 1993).

FIGURE 25.11   **CONVERTING A BOND WITH AN EQUITY SWAP**

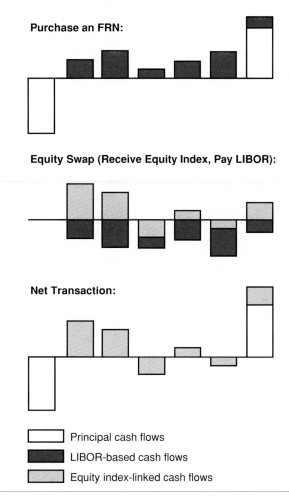

Purchase an FRN:

Equity Swap (Receive Equity Index, Pay LIBOR):

Net Transaction:

☐ Principal cash flows
■ LIBOR-based cash flows
▨ Equity index-linked cash flows

that the company receiving the equity index will have to make a double payment. First, the usual debt-related cash flow, based on LIBOR, will have to be paid. Second, whenever $Index_{new}$ is less than $Index_{old}$, the company will make an equity index–based payment to (i.e., "receive" a negative payment from) its counterparty. Thus, rather than netting one cash flow against the other, the company will pay both when the value of the equity index declines. (Examples of this situation are represented by the third and fifth payments in the figure.)

COMMODITY SWAPS   The preceding equity example demonstrates that the swap contracting mechanism can be applied to economic variables other than interest and exchange rates. In particular, a fast-growing market exists for OTC derivative agreements designed to hedge exposures to commodity prices. To date, these **commodity swaps** have been used mostly by corporate liability managers to fix the level of one or more of the firm's production costs, with the most active markets in energy, precious metals, and base metals. As in the rate swap markets, the growth of commodity swaps primarily has been attributable to the constraints imposed on hedgers and speculators by the rigid standardization of exchange-traded futures contracts.

A commodity swap effectively fixes the price of a commodity over a certain time period in the same way that an interest rate swap fixes the value of LIBOR. That is, on each settlement date, the two counterparties exchange cash flows based on: (1) a fixed commodity price that does not change over the life of the agreement and (2) a variable commodity price that does. The equivalent of the floating rate index in a commodity swap is the price of a commodity index (e.g., West Texas Intermediate Oil index, COMEX gold index), which is periodically reset over the contract's life. The agreement also sets a notional amount of the commodity on which the periodic cash exchanges are based, but no physical delivery ever takes place.

To illustrate how a commodity swap works and who might benefit, consider the following situations for two different corporations. Company OIL is an independent oil producer with production limited to 250,000 barrels a month. Because of high production costs, OIL needs to guarantee that it receives an average price of at least $18.50 per barrel. On the other hand, Company CHM uses a monthly average of 250,000 barrels of West Texas Intermediate (WTI) crude oil in the production of its petrochemicals. Because of the competitive nature of its business and the highly elastic demand for its products, CHM's operations will lose financial viability if oil prices rise above $19.50 per barrel over the next three years.

Clearly, OIL and CHM are concerned about falling and rising oil prices, respectively. As such, they are good candidates for a three-year oil swap with monthly settlement and a "notional principal" of 250,000 barrels. Suppose, therefore, that working through a swap dealer, they arrange the transactions illustrated in Figure 25.12, where the monthly WTI index value is determined as the average of the daily settlement prices for the crude oil futures contract traded on the New York Mercantile Exchange (NYMEX). By their agreements with the swap dealer, OIL is effectively fixing the price of its oil sales at $19.00 per barrel and CHM is fixing the price of its purchase at $19.10. Examples of the actual settlement transactions are as follows:

- If average oil futures settlement price is $20.15:
  OIL pays to Dealer: ($20.15 − $19.00) × (250,000 barrels) = $287,500
  CHM receives from Dealer: ($20.15 − $19.10) × (250,000 barrels) = $262,500.
- If average oil futures settlement price is $18.40:
  OIL receives from Dealer: ($19.00 − $18.40) × (250,000 barrels) = $150,000
  CHM pays to Dealer: ($19.10 − $18.40) × (250,000 barrels) = $175,000.

FIGURE 25.12   **ILLUSTRATION OF AN OIL-ORIENTED COMMODITY SWAP**

Thus, barring default of one of the counterparties, the swap dealer in this matched transaction has no exposure to crude oil prices and simply collects the spread of $25,000 each month.

Using commodity swaps to maintain the economic viability of a high-cost project such as oil drilling or gold mining is not merely a matter of convenience. Because reopening an oil field or a mine can be quite costly, there typically will be a limited period of time during which it pays to keep them running at a loss. Thus, it often is prudent for producers (e.g., Company OIL) to enter into received-fixed commodity swaps to remove price volatility at times when the operation is particularly vulnerable. Commodity swaps also can be used to reverse forward positions previously transacted if the counterparty to those agreements changed its view of future prices. For example, airlines often use forward contracts to lock in the price of jet fuel two or three years out. If a carrier felt that prices would decrease to a level below the contracted price, a swap could neutralize the long forward positions allowing the user effectively to pay the market price.[15]

WARRANTS AND CONVERTIBLE SECURITIES

A popular investment strategy in recent years has involved the creation of security "packages" in which derivatives are combined with, or embedded into, more basic instruments such as stock shares or bonds. In this section, we take a detailed look at two important variations on this theme: (1) bonds with warrants that give the investor the right to buy additional shares of the company's common stock; and (2) securities, such as debt or preferred stock, that the investor can convert into other securities.

WARRANTS

By its most commonly used definition, a **warrant** is an equity call option issued directly by the company whose stock serves as the underlying asset. The key feature that distinguishes it from an ordinary call option is that, if exercised, the company will create new shares of stock to give to the warrantholder. Thus, the exercise of a warrant will increase the total number of outstanding shares, which reduces the value of each individual share. Because of this dilutive effect, the warrant will not be as valuable as an otherwise comparable option contract. Indeed, the valuation of warrants is complicated by many factors, such as how and when the number of outstanding warrants will be exercised, what the company's current capital structure looks like, and what the company plans to do with the new capital it will receive if and when the warrant is exercised.

Galai and Schneller proposed a simple warrant valuation model in which a firm is presently financed with all equity and the warrants it issues are European-style.[16] On its expiration date T, the warrant will be worth:

$$W_T = \max\left[\frac{V_T + N_W X}{N + N_W} - X, 0 \right]$$

where

N = the current number of outstanding shares
N_W = the number of new shares created if the warrants are exercised
V_T = the value of the firm before the warrants are exercised
X = the exercise price.

[15] For more on how commodity swaps and other derivative products can be used to hedge oil price movements, see Keith C. Brown and Robert F. Semmens, "Perspectives on Integration in the Oil Industry: Innovations from the Financial Market," in *Oil in the New World Order*, edited by K. Gillespie and C. Henry (Gainesville, FL: University of Florida Press, 1994).

[16] See Dan Galai and Meir I. Schneller, "Pricing Warrants and the Value of the Firm," *Journal of Finance* 33, no. 5 (December 1978), pp. 1333–1342.

They show that this terminal value can be rewritten as:

$$W_T = \left[\frac{1}{1 + (N_W/N)} \right] C_T$$

where

C_T = the expiration date value of a regular call option with otherwise identical terms as the warrant.

Consequently, at any point prior to expiration, the value of the warrant should be equal to the value of the call deflated (i.e., diluted) by the factor $[1 + (N_W/N)]^{-1}$.

Although warrants can be issued as stand-alone instruments, more frequently a company will attach them to a bond issue to lower its initial funding cost. Warrants created in this manner usually can be detached from the debt instrument by the buyer and traded separately. Suppose, for example, a firm with 1,000,000 shares of common stock outstanding at a current share price of $100 attempts to raise an additional $10 million by issuing a 10-year bond paying annual coupons. Given its current credit rating, assume further that the yield it would have to pay for a straight debt issue is 8.50 percent. The firm could lower this borrowing cost by attaching to the bond European-style equity warrants that mature in exactly one year and have an exercise price of $115 per share. Assuming the firm eventually hopes to raise an additional $5.75 million with these warrants, it will have to create new derivative contracts to cover 50,000 shares ($5.75 million ÷ $115).

Assuming that the one-year risk-free rate is 7 percent and the volatility of the firm's common stock is 25 percent, the Black-Scholes value for a one-year call option to buy one share at $X = \$115$ can be calculated as $7.09. In turn, this means that the warrants are worth $6.75 (= 7.09 ÷ [1 + (50,000/1,000,000)]) per share. If each warrant allows for the purchase of one share and the face value of a single bond is $1,000, the firm will issue 10,000 bonds with five warrants attached to each. Assuming it pays an 8.50 percent coupon, the total proceeds it would generate from the sale of each bond with the warrants attached would be $1,033.75, or $1,000 for the bond and $33.75 (= 5 × $6.75) for the warrants. Thus, the firm can reduce its funding cost to 8.00 percent—the solution to the yield-to-maturity in the following bond calculation:

$$1033.75 = \sum_{t=1}^{10} \frac{85}{(1 + y)^t} + \frac{1000}{(1 + y)^{10}}.$$

Packaging warrants with bonds to reduce debt expenses can be done in a variety of ways. In particular, a recent trend in financial markets is for a firm to attach to its bonds an option that is based on an underlying asset other than the company's own stock. To date, alternative structures have included foreign exchange and stock index transactions. For instance, Rogalski and Seward detail the development of the market for *foreign currency exchange warrants*, which give the holder the right, but not the obligation, to purchase a predetermined number of U.S. dollars for a price denominated in a foreign currency.[17] Although called warrants, these contracts are closer in form to traditional call options on the dollar (or, equivalently, put options on the foreign currency) because they do not result

[17] See Richard J. Rogalski and James K. Seward, "Corporate Issues of Foreign Currency Warrants," *Journal of Financial Economics* 30, no. 2 (December 1991), pp. 347–366.

in any direct change to the issuing firm's capital structure. That is, no dilutive valuation effect exists for these derivatives since there are no new shares of stock issued. Beyond that, these instruments generally can only be settled in cash but can be detached and traded separately from the original bond.

CONVERTIBLE
SECURITIES

A convertible security gives its owner the right, but not the obligation, to convert the existing investment into another form. Typically, the original security is either a bond or a share of preferred stock, which can be exchanged into common stock according to a predetermined formula. From this description, it should be clear that a convertible security is a hybrid issue consisting of a regular bond or preferred stock holding and a call option that allows for the conversion. Similar to warrants, they have been popular with issuers because they generally lead to a lower initial borrowing cost and represent a future supply of equity capital. In fact, Pinches noted that these securities often are used in connection with mergers because they generate capital without immediately diluting the equity base of the acquiring firm.[18] On the other hand, investors in convertibles gain the upside potential of common stock while actually holding a less risky asset.

CONVERTIBLE
PREFERRED STOCK

To see how convertible securities work, let us consider the dynamics of convertible preferred stock. As suggested above, owning a share of convertible preferred is equivalent to holding a portfolio long in a normal share of preferred stock and long in a call option on the firm's common stock that can be exercised by surrendering the preferred stock. There generally is no waiting period before the conversion can be made, and the conversion privilege usually never expires. This means that the *minimum value of the convertible* issue must be:

$$max[\text{Preferred Stock Value, Conversion Value}]$$

where the **conversion value** is the value of the common stock into which the preferred issue can be exchanged.

Suppose that for a $1,000,000 investment, an institutional investor could purchase 25,000 shares of a convertible preferred issue with the following terms (per share):

- Current Convertible Share Price: $40.00
- Annual Convertible Dividend: $ 3.00
- Convertible Yield: 7.50% (= $3 ÷ $40)
- Regular Preferred Yield: 10.00%
- Current Common Stock Price: $20.00
- Conversion Ratio: 1.75

With these conditions, the share value of a regular preferred stock issue paying a $3 dividend would be $30.00 (= $3 ÷ 0.10 percent), or the perpetual dividend amount divided by the prevailing regular yield. This means that the convertible issue sells at a 33 percent premium to the regular preferred. Also, given the **conversion ratio** of 1.75 shares of common to each share of preferred, the conversion value of the convertible issue is $35 (= 1.75 × $20). Thus, the minimum price of the convertible security would be $35, the greater of the regular preferred price and the conversion value. Since the market price of the convertible still is above this level, this implies a **conversion premium** of 14.29

---

[18] See George E. Pinches, "Financing with Convertible Preferred Stock, 1960–1967," *Journal of Finance* 25, no. 1 (March 1970), pp. 53–63.

| TABLE 25.5 | **MINIMUM CONVERTIBLE PREFERRED STOCK VALUES AS A FUNCTION OF REGULAR PREFERRED YIELDS AND COMMON STOCK PRICES** | | |

		COMMON STOCK PRICES		
		15	20	25
Yield	8%:	37.50	37.50	43.75
	10%:	30.00	35.00	43.75
	12%:	26.25	35.00	43.75

percent (= [$40 − $35] ÷ $35), meaning that the convertible currently is selling based on its option value.

The future value of the convertible issue will depend on two events: (1) interest rate movements, which directly affect the yield on the regular preferred stock component, and (2) changes in common stock prices, given the 1.75 conversion ratio. Consider the matrix of minimum values for various levels of these two variables, shown in Table 25.5. In this situation, the value of the convertible preferred stock will likely be driven by its conversion value when interest rates and common stock prices are high and its preferred stock value when rates and share prices are low.

CONVERTIBLE BONDS   Like convertible preferred stock, a convertible bond can be viewed as a prepackaged portfolio containing two distinct securities: a regular bond and an option to exchange the bond for a prespecified number of shares of the issuing firm's common stock. Thus, a convertible bond represents a hybrid investment involving elements of both the debt and equity markets. Conversely, the issuer of a convertible bond increases the company's leverage while providing a potential source of equity financing in the future. Figure 25.13 shows a portion of a page from *Moody's Bond Record* summarizing the pertinent details of a sample of outstanding convertible bonds issued by U.S.-based companies.

As an example of how one such issue is structured and priced, consider the 7⅝ percent coupon convertible subordinated debentures (c.s.d.) issued by Beverly Enterprises, an S&P 500–listed firm that operates nursing care facilities, pharmacies, and retirement centers. The listing for this issue, which is scheduled to mature in March of 2003, is shown on the fifth line from the bottom. After showing the issue's CUSIP identifier, contract terms, and default rating (i.e., B2), the entry in the fourth column indicates that this bond pays interest semiannually on March 15 and September 15. The bond issue has $67.92 million outstanding and is callable at par until maturity. At the time of this report (i.e., March 1996), the listed price of the debenture was 96.50 percent of par and the share price of Beverly Enterprises common stock was $12.125. Additional details of this security are shown in Figure 25.14, which was generated by Bloomberg.

As spelled out at the top of Figure 25.14—and approximated in the ninth column of Figure 25.13—each $1,000 of face value of this bond can be converted into 48.852 shares of Beverly common stock. As in the convertible preferred example, this statistic is called the instrument's **conversion ratio.** At the listed share price of $12.125, an investor exercising her conversion option would have received only $592.33 (= $12.125 × 48.852) worth of stock, an amount considerably below the current market value of the bond. In fact, the **conversion parity price** (i.e., the common stock price at which immediate conversion would make sense) is equal to $19.75, which is the bond's price of $965.00 divided by the conversion ratio of 48.852. The prevailing market price of $12.125 is far below this parity level,

FIGURE 25.13

CONVERTIBLE BOND INFORMATION SUMMARY

U.S. Convertible Bonds

CUSIP	ISSUE	MOODY'S RATING	INT. DATES	ANN. S.F. THOUS.	CURR. CALL PRICE	AMT. OUTS. MILL.	CONV. PRICE‡	SHS. $1,000 DEB	CURRENT PRICE — COM.	DEB.	DEB. YIELDS CURR.	DEB. YIELDS MAT.	DEB. CONV. VALUE	ANTIC. COM. PRICE	1996 RANGE COM.	1996 RANGE DEB	LAT. ANN. PER EARNS	COM. ANN. DIV. RATE
000945AC	•ADT Operations, Inc. LYONS .00 2010[1]	Ba3 r	N.P.	None	599.46	675 [2]	—	28.23	—	47¼	—	5.3	—	—	48¾ - 45	—	Nil	
00130HAA	AES Corporation cv.deb. 6.50 2002	Ba3 r	A&O 1	None	[3]105.00	50.0	26.21	38.14	■24½	107¼b	6.1	5.1	93¾	28	25 - 21	107¼ -100¾	—	Nil
001250AA	AG Services of America cv.sub.deb. 7.00 2003	N.R.	M31&N30	None	108.00	12.0	18.50	54.05	■10⅞	116b	6.0	4.4	58¾	21¾	12⅛ - 8⅞	125 -109	0.66	Nil
008474AA	Agnico-Eagle Mines Ltd. cv.sr.deb. 3.50 2004	B1	J&J 27	None	887.18	110	17.93	55.76	■16¾	101¾b	3.4	3.2	94	18¼	17¾ -12½	105¼ -83¼	—	0.10
009058AA	Air & Water Technologies cv.sd. 8.00 2015	B3 r	M&N 15	75%-'00	104.80	115	30.00	33.33	●6½	87½b	9.1	9.4	21¾	26¼	8⅛ - 6⅛	89½ -84¼	d0.35	Nil
009104AB	♦Air Express Int'l Corp. c.s.d. 6.00 2003	B1 r	J&J 15	None	104.20	74.75	22.71	44.03	■24½	113¼	5.3	3.8	107¾	25¾	25½ - 20	115 -102	1.58	0.16
009236AA	Air Wis Services, Inc. c.s.d. 7.75 2010	B3 r	J&D15	1,750-'96	100.78	35.0	259.07	03.86	—	89¾b	8.7	9.1	—	232½	— - —	92½ - 86	—	Nil
009266AC	•Airborne Freight Corp. c.s.d. 6.75 2001	Ba1 r	F&A 15	None	104.20	100	35.50	28.16	●27¾	103	6.6	6.1	78¾	36¼	28¾ - 25	103 -101	—	0.30
011659AD	•Alaska Air Group, Inc. cv.sr.deb. 6.50 2005	Ba3 r	J&D 15	None	104.33	115	21.50	46.51	●22¼	116¼	5.6	4.3	103¾	25	22¾ -15¾	116¼ -105	—	Nil
011659AA	c.s.d. 7.75 2010	Ba3 r	J&D 15	None	100.00	25.1	28.25	35.39	●22¼	91½b	8.5	8.8	78¾	25¾	22¾ -15¾	92½ -88¼	—	Nil
011659AB	• c.s.d. 6.875 2014	Ba3 r	J&D 15	4%-'99	102.75	75.0	33.02	29.76	●22¼	90	7.6	7.9	67¼	29¾	22¾ -15¾	90 - 82	—	Nil
012348AA	•Albany Int'l Corp. cv.deb. 5.25 2002	Ba3	M&S 15	None	091.54	135	23.00	38.08	●19¾	91¼	5.8	7.1	84¼	20¾	20¼ -17¼	92 - 88	—	0.35
018800AA	Alliant Computer Systems c.s.d. 7.25 2012	Ca r	[5]-15-92	5%-'98	101.45	50.0	39.75	25.16	—	19f	—	—	—	7½	1¼ - 1¼	— - —	—	Nil
020047AA	•Allwaste, Inc. c.s.d. 7.25 2014	B2 r	J&D 1	5%-'99	102.90	30.0	11.94	83.75	● 4¾	87¾	8.3	8.6	36¾	10¾	5½ - 4½	89¾ - 82	—	Nil
021441AA	Altera Corp. cv. sub. nts. 5.75 2002	B2				197.8	51.17	19.54	■65¼	143b	4.0	—	127¾	73¼	77 -42½	160¾ -115¼	1.91	2.00
022815AC	•ALZA Corp. LYONS .00 2014	Baa3r	N.P.	None	459.63	35.47	—	12.98	●31¼	47¼	—	4.1	—	—	34⅞ -24¼	48¼ - 41	0.88	Nil
025143AA	Amer. City Bus Journal c.s.d. 6.00 2011	B3	J30&D31	None			39.41	16.75	62.69	■ —	175b	3.4	—	—	29¼	— - —	182 -100	—	Nil
027446AA	American Medical Response cv. sub. nts. 5.25 2001	B1	F&A 1	None		110	—	—	—	—	—	—	—	—	— - —	— - —	—	Nil
001765AY	•AMR Corp. cv.sub.cap.nts. B 6.125 2024[6]	Ba2 r	FMA&N1	None	104.20		79.00	12.65	●87¾	113¼	5.4	5.2	111	89¾	89¾ - 68	116 - 99	2.48	Nil
032161AA	•Ameco International, Inc. step-up c.s.d. 8.00 2007	Ba3 r	A&O 15	None		110	30.10	33.22	■15¾	96b	6.8	7.3	51¾	28¾	16 -13¼	96½ - 95	0.97	Nil
032375AC	•Anacomp, Inc. c.s.d. 13.875 2002	Ca r	J&J 15	3,750-'92	100.00	42.7	17.50	57.14	¼₆	10¼b	—	½	1¾	¼ - 1/16	10 - 9	d5.22	Nil	
032654AB	Analog Devices, Inc. cv. sub. nts. 3.50 2002	Ba1	J&D 1	None		200	—	—	200	—	—	—	—	—	— - —	— - —	—	Nil
033352AA	•Andal Corp. c.s.d. 5.50 1997[8]	Caa r	M&S15	2,000-'82	100.00	1.825	450.45	02.22	—	—b	—	—	—	—	— - —	— - —	•	Nil
035229AJ	Anheuser-Busch Cos., Inc. c.s.d. 8.00 1996	A1	A&O 1	None	N.C.	241	[10]47.60	21.01	●67¾	—	—	—	141¾	—	71¾ -65¾	— - —	—	1.60
037904AA	Apollo Computer Inc. c.s.d. 7.25 2011[11]	Aa3	F&A1	5%-'97	100.00	100	[12] —	—	●100¾	99b	7.3	7.4	—	—	104⅛ -73¾	99 -89¼	4.63	0.80
002040AA	•ARAMARK Services, Inc. c.s.d. 4.625 1996[13]	Ba3 r	J&D15	2,400-'82	100.00	09.02 [14]	—	—	—	—	—	—	—	—	— - —	— - —	—	Nil
040228AA	•Argosy Gaming Corp. cv. sub. nts. 12.00 2001	B3 r	J&D 1	None	106.00	100	17.70	56.49	■ 9	92¾b	12.9	14.0	50¾	16¾	9¼ - 6¾	95¼ -89¾	0.29	Nil
043339AF	Arvin Industries c.s.d. 7.50 2014	Ba3 r	M31&S30	None	103.00	97.53	28.50	35.08	●22¼	104	7.2	7.1	77½	29¾	22¼ -16¾	104 -99¼	—	0.76
044204AA	•Ashland, Inc. cv.sub.deb. 6.75 2014	Baa2r	J&J 1	5%-'00	102.70	200	51.34	19.47	●36¾	101	6.7	6.7	71¼	51¾	39½ -34¼	103 -90¾	0.08	1.10
044540AJ	•Ashland Oil, Inc. c.s.d. 6.75 2014	Baa2r	J&J 1	5%-'00	103.37	200	51.34	19.48	—	90¼b	7.5	7.8	—	46¼	— - —	92 -89¾	—	Nil
046003EL	Associates Corp. N.A. nts. 6.00 2000	Aa3	J&D 15	None		300	—	—	—	99½b	6.0	6.1	—	—	— - —	101¾ -99¼	—	Nil
001907AB	AST Computer, Inc. LYONS 2013	B2	N.P.	None		275	—	12.99	● 6⅝	32¾b	18.3	—	—	9 - 6¼	34 -32¼	d3.07	Nil	
	Au Bon Pain Co., Inc. cv. sub. nts. 4.75 2001 [16]	B2	J&J 1	None		30.0	25.50	39.21	—	—	—	—	—	—	— - —	— - —	—	Nil
050753AA	Audiotronics Corp. c.s.d. 10.25 2002[4]	N.R.r	A&O 21	7.5%-'92	107.70	5.371	3.12	320.00	—	—	—	—	—	—	— - —	— - —	—	Nil
050757AA	AUDIOVOX Corp. cv.sr.deb. 6.25 2011[16]	Caa	M&S 15	None	100.00	65.0	5.34	56.49	● 5¼	64¾b	9.6	16.9	98¼	3¾	6¼ - 4¾	66¼ - 63	—	Nil
053015AC	•Automatic Data Processing LYONS .00 2012	Aa3	[17]N.P.	None	459.63	700	—	06.46	●38¾	51½	—	4.2	—	—	43¾ -35¾	55¼ -47¾	1.38	0.20
056180AA	Baby Superstore, Inc. cv. sub. nts. 4.80 2000	B3 r	A&O 1	None	102.44	100	53.87	18.56	■42¼	—	—	—	78¼	—	57¾ -28¼	— - —	—	Nil
057224AH	•Baker Hughes Inc. LYONS .00 2008	A2	N.P.	None	070.68	385.2	—	18.59	●26¾	64	—	3.7	—	—	27¾ -22¾	64 - 63	0.67	0.46
05873CAC	Bally Entertainment Corp. cv.sr.sub.deb. 8.00 2000[16]	B3	J&D 15	None		13.59	—	—	—	116¾	6.4	4.1	—	—	— - —	118¼ -108	—	Nil
058732AB	• c.s.d. 10.00 2006	Caa r	[19]•12-15-90	5,000-'91	100.62	100	32.68	30.60	—	87fb	flat	flat	—	28¾	— - —	100¾ -88½	—	Nil
05873CAB	cv.sub.deb. 10.00 2006	B3	J&D 15	None	100.62	86.96	32.68	30.60	●15¼	98¾	10.1	10.2	47¾	32¼	16¼ -12¾	100 - 93	—	Nil
064057AK	•Bank of NY Co. Inc. cv.deb. 7.50 2001	A3 r	F&A 15	None	103.75	250	19.55	51.15	●51¾	265¼b	2.8	—	265¼	51¾	55¼ -43¼	240 -240	4.57	1.28
077903AA	Bell Sports Corp. cv. sub. nts. 4.25 2000	B2 r	M&N 15	None	102.43	86.25	54.06	18.49	■ 7¾	70½b	6.0	12.8	13¾	38¼	9¼ - 7¼	75 -69¾	d0.42	Nil
082484AA	Benson Eyecare Corp. cv. sub. nts. 8.00 2001	B3	M&N 15	None	104.57	40.0	9.05	110.41	● 8¾	106¼b	7.5	6.6	97¾	9¼	9¾ - 7¾	119 -105¾	—	Nil
083739AC	•Bergen Brunswig Corp. c.s.d. 6.875 2011	Baa2r	J&J 15	2,150-'96	101.69	10.9 [20]	—	00.00	●24¼	95¾	7.2	7.3	—	—	27¾ -24¼	95¾ - 92	1.61	0.48
087851AB	•Beverly Enterprises, Inc. c.s.d. 7.625 2003	B2 r	M&S 15	7,500-'93	100.00	87.92	20.47	48.85	●12¼	96¼	7.9	8.3	59¼	19¾	12¾ -10½	96¼ - 94	d0.16	Nil
087851AJ	• LYONS .00 2003	Ba3 r	N.P.	None	100.00	1.99	—	13.32	●12¼	53b	—	8.8	—	—	12¾ -10½	— - —	d0.16	Nil
087851AK	cv.sub.deb. 5.50 2018	B3	F&A 1	None		150	—	—	—	100	5.5	5.5	—	—	— - —	102 -94¼	—	Nil
088891AA	Big B, Inc. c.s.d. 6.50 2003	B2 r	M&S 15	None	105.20	35.0	24.40	81.96	■11¼	104½b	6.2	5.7	45¼	25¼	11¾ -9¾₆	107¼ -98¼	•	0.16
090324AB	Bindley Western Indus. c.s.d. 6.50 2002	Ba3	A&O 1	None	103.90	65.0	19.82	50.44	● 17	104½b	6.2	5.7	85¾	20¾	21 -15¾	111 -102¼	1.42	0.08

Source: *Moody's Bond Record*, March 1996, p. 93.

meaning that the conversion option is currently out of the money. Of course, if the conversion parity price ever fell below the market price for the common stock, an astute investor could buy the bond and immediately exchange it into stock with a greater market value.

As indicated in the sixth column of Figure 25.13, most convertible bonds are also callable by the issuer. Of course, a firm will never call a bond selling for less than its call price (which is the case with the Beverly Enterprises debenture). In fact, firms often wait until the bond is selling for significantly more than its call price before calling it.[19] If the company calls the bond under these conditions, investors will have an incentive to convert the bond into stock that is worth more than they would receive from the call price; this situation is referred to as *forcing conversion*. Two other factors also increase the investors' incentive to convert their bonds. First, some instruments have conversion prices that step

[19] An empirical study of this issue revealed that almost all of the convertible securities studied were called later than the theoretically optimal time. See Jonathan E. Ingersoll, Jr., "An Examination of Corporate Call Policies on Convertible Securities," *Journal of Finance* 32, no. 2 (May 1977), pp. 463–478.

FIGURE 25.14   DETAILS OF BEVERLY ENTERPRISES' CONVERTIBLE BOND ISSUE

```
BEVERLY ENTERPR   BEV7 5 8 03/15/03
CONV TO          48.8520 SHRS(PER    1000.0)BEV  (UNKN) $11 3 8 (      )DP 100%
CONVERTIBLE UNTIL   3/14/ 3                 ISSUER INFORMATION
 SECURITY INFORMATION                       NAME BEVERLY ENTERPRISES
 CPN FREQ        SEMI-AN                     TYPE INDUSTRIAL
 CPN TYPE        FIXED             IDENTIFICATION #'S    REDEMPTION INFO
 MTY/REFUND TYP CV/CALL/SINK       CUSIP    087851AB7   MATURITY DT    3/15/ 3
 CALC TYP( 49) CONVERTIBLE         MLNUM A19C3          REFUNDING DT
 DAY COUNT( 5) 30/360                                   NEXT CALL DT   5/ 8/96
 MARKET ISS     US DOMESTIC                             WORKOUT DT     3/15/ 3
 COUNTRY/CURR   USA /DOL                                RISK FACTOR    5.3053
 COLLATERAL TYP DEBENTURES          ISSUANCE INFO
 AMT ISSUED          100000 (M)    ANNOUNCE DT   3/10/83      RATINGS
 AMT OUTSTAND         67924 (M)    1ST SETTLE DT 3/17/83  MOODY    B2
 MIN PC/INC     1000/     1000     1ST CPN DT    9/15/83  S & P    B
 PAR AMT            1000.00        INT ACCRUE DT 3/15/83  COMP     B2
 LEADMGR/UWRTR DREXEL BURNHAM      PRICE @ ISSUE 100      DCR      B+
 EXCHANGE       NEW YORK                                 FITCH    NA
                                                         HLX      44
 NOTES:  HAVE PROSPECTUS, DTC, SAMEDAY
CONV SUB DEB. CO ENDED REPURCHASE PROGRAM 1/29/88. CO OMITTED 2ND & 3RD QTR STK
DIVS (5/17/88). TRUSTEE: CHEMICAL BANK NYC.              O/S: 12/31/94.
```

Source: Bloomberg, April 8, 1996.

up over time according to a predetermined schedule. Since a stepped-up conversion price leads to a lower number of shares received, it becomes more likely that investors will exercise their option just before the conversion price increases. Second, a firm can help to encourage conversion by increasing the dividends on the stock, thereby making the income generated by the shares more attractive relative to the income from the bond.

Another important characteristic when evaluating convertible bonds is the **payback** or *break-even time*, which measures how long the higher interest income from the convertible bond (compared to the dividend income from the common stock) must persist to make up for the difference between the price of the bond and its conversion value (i.e., the conversion premium). The calculation is as follows:

$$\text{Payback} = \frac{\text{Bond Price} - \text{Conversion Value}}{\text{Bond Income} - \text{Income from Equal Investment in Common Stock}}.$$

For instance, the annual coupon yield on the Beverly Enterprises convertible bond is $76.25, while the firm's dividend yield, which suspended payment of cash dividends in February 1988, is zero. Thus, assuming you sold the bond for $965 and used the proceeds to purchase 79.588 shares (= $965.00/$12.125) of Beverly stock, the payback period would be:

$$\frac{\$965.00 - \$592.33}{\$76.25 - \$0.00} = 4.89 \text{ years.}$$

It also is possible to calculate the combined value of the investor's conversion option and issuer's call feature that are embedded in the debenture. In the Beverly Enterprises example, with a market price of $965, the convertible's yield-to-maturity can be calculated as the solution to:

$$\$965.00 = \sum_{t=1}^{14} \frac{38.125}{(1 + y/2)^t} + \frac{1038.125}{(1 + y/2)^{14}},$$

or $y = 8.29$ percent (reported as 8.3 percent in the thirteenth column of Figure 25.13). This computation assumes 14 semiannual coupon payments of $38.125 (= $76.25 ÷ 2). Since the yield for a similar seven-year Beverly debt issue with no embedded options on this date was 9.25 percent, the present value of a "straight" fixed-income security with the same cash flows would be:

$$917.61 = \sum_{t=1}^{14} \frac{38.125}{(1 + .04625)^t} + \frac{1038.125}{(1 + .04625)^{14}}.$$

This means that the net value of the combined options is $47.39, or $965.00 minus $917.61. Using the Black-Scholes valuation model, it is easily confirmed that a seven-year call option to buy *one* share of Beverly Enterprises stock—which does not pay a dividend—at an exercise price of $19.75 (i.e., the conversion parity value) is equal to $3.46.[20] Thus, the value of the investor's conversion option—which allows for the acquisition of 48.852 shares—must be $169.03 (= 48.852 × $3.46). This means that the value of the issuer's call feature under these conditions must be $121.64 (= $169.03 − $47.39).

Figure 25.15 illustrates the value of a convertible bond in a more general way. The horizontal axis plots the value of the firm, which establishes an upper bound for the value of a convertible since it cannot sell for more than the firm's assets. Thus, there is a firm value line that bisects the plane and the value of the convertible must be below that line. Note that the line for the bond value is relatively flat for a wide range of firm values because higher firm values do not increase the value of the bond since bondholders receive only their promised payments. In contrast, at fairly low firm values, the value of the bond drops off as bankruptcy becomes more likely. Conversion value rises directly with the value of the firm. The figure shows that for low firm values, the bond value will be the minimum value of the convertible, whereas the convertible's price will be driven by its conversion potential for high firm values. Finally, the line for the value of the convertible shows that when the firm value is low, the convertible will act more like a bond, trading for only a slight premium over the bond value (as is the case with the Beverly Enterprises debenture discussed earlier). Alternatively, when firm values are high, the convertible will act more like a stock, selling for only a slight premium over the conversion value. In the fairly wide middle range, the convertible will trade as the hybrid security that acts somewhat like a bond and somewhat like a stock.

OTHER EMBEDDED DERIVATIVES

For many years, the nature of borrowing and lending in securitized capital markets remained quite stable, with companies typically issuing bonds at par value and paying either a fixed or floating rate of interest in the same currency in which the money was borrowed. With few exceptions, the choice of maturity or coupon structure was driven by the eco-

[20] This calculation assumes the following input values: $S = 12.125$, $X = 19.75$, $T = 7.00$, $RFR = 0.06$, $\sigma = 0.30$, and $D = 0.00$.

FIGURE 25.15   **ILLUSTRATING THE VALUE OF A CONVERTIBLE BOND**

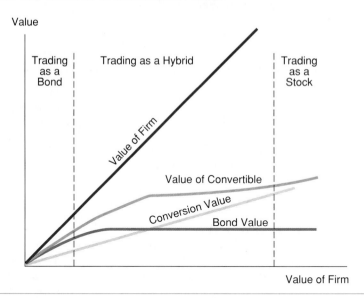

nomic situation faced by the borrower, rather than the investor. Over the past decade, however, this scenario has greatly changed with the development of the *structured note* market. Generally speaking, structured notes are debt issues that have their principal or coupon payments linked to some other underlying variable. Examples include bonds whose coupons are tied to the appreciation of an equity index such as the S&P 500, or a zero-coupon bond with a principal amount tied to the appreciation of an oil price index.

Crabbe and Argilagos have pointed out several common features that distinguish structured notes from regular fixed-income securities, two of which are important for our discussion.[21] First, structured notes are designed for and targeted to a specific investor with a very particular need. That is, these are not "generic" instruments, but products tailored to address an investor's special constraints, which often are themselves created by tax, regulatory, or institutional policy restrictions. Second, after structuring the financing to meet the investor's needs, the issuer typically will hedge that unique exposure with swaps or exchange-traded derivatives. Inasmuch as the structured note most likely required an embedded derivative to create the desired payoff structure for the investor, this unwinding of the derivative position by the issuer generates an additional source profit opportunity for the bond underwriter.

The growth of this market has been quite rapid. From its ostensible origin in the mid-1980s, Crabbe and Argilagos report that just under $100 billion of these notes were issued in 1994. Equally impressive is the wide variety of economic risks that have been embedded and the maze of new acronyms that has accompanied these innovations (e.g., FLAG, LYON, SPEL, STEER, PERCS, and ICON). We will take a detailed look at four such

---

[21] See Leland E. Crabbe and Joseph D. Argilagos, "Anatomy of the Structured Note Market," *Journal of Applied Corporate Finance* 7, no. 3 (Fall 1994), pp. 85–98. Also see Ira G. Kawaller, "Understanding Structured Notes," *Derivatives Quarterly* 1, no. 3 (Spring 1995).

structures representative of the major exposures an investor might desire: currency, equity, commodity, and interest rates.

DUAL CURRENCY BONDS

A dual currency bond is a debt instrument that has coupons denominated in a different currency than its principal amount. They have been popular funding instruments, particularly in the Euromarkets, for more than a decade and have been designed to include virtually all of the world's major currencies. These bonds can be viewed as a combination of two simpler financial instruments: (1) a single-currency fixed-coupon bond, and (2) a forward contract to exchange the bond's principal into a predetermined amount of a foreign currency. They often are sold to investors who are willing to "take a view" over the longer term in the foreign exchange markets. By having the currency forward attached to the bond, fixed-income portfolio managers who might otherwise be restricted from trading in FX have the potential to enhance their performance if their beliefs about future market conditions prove correct.

To demonstrate a structure typical of these products, consider a five-year bond paying an annual coupon of 9 percent in U.S. dollars and redemption amount of JPY 110,000. The initial price of the bond is USD 1,020, relative to a par value of USD 1,000. Assuming further that a regular five-year, dollar-denominated bond of comparable risk yielding 9 percent could have been issued at par, this means that the forward contract portion of the dual currency instrument is "off market" because it carries a present value of USD 20. Table 25.6 shows the cash flows for this structure from the investor's point of view. It also demonstrates how it can be assembled from its more basic component parts.

Notice that the embedded forward contract allows the bondholder to exchange the USD 1,000 for JPY 110,000, generating an implied *nominal* exchange rate of JPY 110/USD (or, equivalently, USD 0.0091/JPY). However, given that the investor has to pay an additional USD 20 today for this future transaction, this is not the *effective* exchange rate that the investor faces. Indeed, the fact that the investor is willing to pay the additional USD 20 suggests that JPY 110/USD is a favorable price to purchase yen forward. The effective exchange rate built into this transaction can be established by dividing JPY 110,000 by the sum of USD 1,000 and the future value (in year 5) of USD 20. Calculating this latter amount as 30.77 $(= 20 \times (1.09)^5)$, the effective exchange rate becomes JPY 106.72/USD $(= 110,000 \div (1,000 + 30.77))$.

There are at least two reasons why this dual currency bond might trade at a premium over a single-currency 9 percent coupon bond of comparable creditworthiness. First, it is possible that the five-year forward exchange rate between yen and dollars is JPY 106.72/

TABLE 25.6						
CASH FLOWS FOR A DUAL CURRENCY BOND FROM INVESTORS' PERSPECTIVE						

	YEAR					
Transaction	0	1	2	3	4	5
1. Long 9% USD bond	−USD 1,000	+USD 90	+USD 90	+USD 90	+USD 90	+USD 1,090
2. Long yen forward (pay USD, receive JPY)	−USD 20	—	—	—	—	+JPY 110,000 and −USD 1,000
3. Long dual currency bond (Transaction 1 + Transaction 2)	−USD 1,020	+USD 90	+USD 90	+USD 90	+USD 90	+JPY 110,000 and +USD 90

USD, meaning that at USD 1,020, the bond is priced properly. The more likely possibility, though, is that the five-year forward rate actually is JPY 110/USD, and that investors are "paying up" for a desirable FX exposure that they cannot acquire in any other way. If this is true, the issuer—who is effectively short the regular dollar bond and short in the yen forward—can unwind its derivative position at a profit, thereby reducing its funding cost below 9 percent. That is, the issuer's commitment to "sell" JPY 110,000 to the investor in year 5 can be offset by a long position in a separate yen forward (which, once again, is usually done with the bond's underwriter as the counterparty) at the market forward exchange rate of JPY 110/USD. Thus, the issuer's net borrowing cost can be calculated by solving for the yield as follows:

$$1{,}020 = \sum_{t=1}^{5} \frac{90}{(1+y)^t} + \frac{1000}{(1+y)^5},$$

or $y = 8.49$ percent. This 51 basis-point differential from the "plain vanilla" borrowing rate of 9 percent represents the issuer's compensation for creating an investment vehicle that is tailored to the needs of the investor.

EQUITY INDEX–LINKED NOTES

In July of 1992, Merrill Lynch & Co. raised $77,500,000 by issuing 7,750,000 units of an S&P 500 Market Index Target-Term Security (MITTS) at a price of $10 per unit.[22] These MITTS units had a maturity date of August 29, 1997, making them comparable in form to a five-year bond even though they traded on the New York Stock Exchange. Indeed, Merrill Lynch issued them as a series of Senior Debt Securities making no coupon payments prior to maturity. At maturity, a unitholder received the original issue price plus a "supplemental redemption amount," the value of which depended on where the Standard & Poor's 500 index settled relative to a predetermined initial level. Given that this supplemental amount could not be less than zero, the total payout to the investor at maturity can be written:

$$10 + \max\left[0, \left\{10 \times \left(\frac{\text{Final S\&P Value} - \text{Initial S\&P Value}}{\text{Initial S\&P Value}}\right) \times 1.15\right\}\right]$$

where the initial S&P value was specified as 412.08. The cover page from the prospectus for this deal is shown in Figure 25.16.

From the preceding description, recognize that the MITTS structure combines a five-year, zero-coupon bond with an S&P index call option, both of which were issued by Merrill Lynch. Thus, the MITTS investor essentially owns a "portfolio" that is (1) long in a bond and (2) long in an index call option position. This particular security was designed primarily for those investors who wanted to participate in the equity market but, for regulatory or taxation reasons, were not permitted to do so directly. For example, the manager of a fixed-income mutual fund might be able to enhance her return performance by purchasing this "bond" and then hoping for an appreciating stock market. Notice that the use of the call option in this design makes it fairly easy for Merrill Lynch to market to its institutional customers because it is a "no lose" proposition; the worst-case scenario for the investor is that she simply gets her money back without interest in five years. (Of course, the customer carries the company's credit risk for this period.) Thus, unlike the dual

---

[22] We would like to thank Jim Spilman and Scott Soules of Merrill Lynch for their insights into the creation and trading of this security.

FIGURE 25.16

PROSPECTUS FOR MERRILL LYNCH'S MITTS ISSUE

PROSPECTUS SUPPLEMENT
(To Prospectus dated July 14, 1992)

7,750,000 Units

Merrill Lynch & Co., Inc.

S&P 500 Market Index Target-Term Securities^{SM} due August 29, 1997

"MITTS^{SM}"

An aggregate principal amount of $77,500,000 of S&P 500 Market Index Target-Term Securities^{SM} due August 29, 1997 (the "Securities" or "MITTS^{SM}") of Merrill Lynch & Co., Inc. (the "Company") are being offered hereby. Each $10 principal amount of Securities will be deemed a "Unit" for purposes of trading and transfer at the Securities Depository described below. Units will be transferable by the Securities Depository, as more fully described below, in denominations of whole Units.

The Securities are being offered at an original issue price of 100% of the principal amount thereof, will bear no periodic payments of interest and will mature on August 29, 1997. At maturity, a Holder of a Security will be entitled to receive, with respect to each Security, the principal amount thereof, plus a contingent interest payment (the "Supplemental Redemption Amount"), if any, if the Final Value (as defined herein) of the S&P 500 Composite Stock Price Index (the "S&P 500 Index") exceeds 412.08 (the "Initial Value"). If the Final Value does not exceed the Initial Value, a Holder of a Security will be repaid the principal amount of the Security, but the Holder will not receive any Supplemental Redemption Amount. The Securities are to be issued as a series of Senior Debt Securities under the Senior Indenture described herein. The Securities are not redeemable prior to maturity.

The Supplemental Redemption Amount, if any, payable with respect to a Security at maturity will equal the product of (A) the principal amount of the applicable Security, and (B) the quotient of the Final Value less the Initial Value, divided by the Initial Value, and (C) 115%. The calculation of the Final Value, as more fully described herein, will be based upon certain values of the S&P 500 Index during the ten Business Days prior to the maturity date of the Securities.

For information as to the calculation of the Supplemental Redemption Amount, if any, which will be paid at maturity, the calculation and the composition of the S&P 500 Index and certain tax consequences to holders of the Securities, see "Description of Securities," "The Standard & Poor's 500 Index," and "Certain United States Federal Income Tax Considerations" in this Prospectus Supplement. **For other information that should be considered by prospective investors, see "Special Considerations" in this Prospectus Supplement.**

Ownership of the Securities will be maintained in book-entry form by or through the Securities Depository. Beneficial owners of the Securities will not have the right to receive physical certificates evidencing their ownership except under the limited circumstances described herein.

The Securities have been approved for listing on the New York Stock Exchange under the symbol "MIT".

THESE SECURITIES HAVE NOT BEEN APPROVED OR DISAPPROVED BY THE SECURITIES AND EXCHANGE COMMISSION OR ANY STATE SECURITIES COMMISSION NOR HAS THE SECURITIES AND EXCHANGE COMMISSION OR ANY STATE SECURITIES COMMISSION PASSED UPON THE ACCURACY OR ADEQUACY OF THIS PROSPECTUS SUPPLEMENT OR THE PROSPECTUS. ANY REPRESENTATION TO THE CONTRARY IS A CRIMINAL OFFENSE.

	Price to Public	Underwriting Discount	Proceeds to the Company(1)
Per Unit	$10	$.25	$9.75
Total(2)	$77,500,000	$1,937,500	$75,562,500

(1) Before deduction of expenses payable by the Company.
(2) The Company has granted an option to the Underwriter, exercisable within 30 days after the date of this Prospectus Supplement, to purchase up to an additional 1,162,500 Units of the Securities upon the same terms and conditions as set forth above to cover over-allotments, if any. If the option is exercised in full, the total Price to Public, Underwriting Discount and Proceeds to the Company will be $89,125,000, $2,228,125 and $86,896,875, respectively. See "Underwriting."

The Securities are offered by the Underwriter, subject to prior sale, when, as and if issued by the Company and accepted by the Underwriter and subject to certain other conditions. The Underwriter reserves the right to reject orders in whole or in part. It is expected that delivery of the Securities will be made in New York, New York on or about July 30, 1992.

This Prospectus Supplement and the accompanying Prospectus may be used by the Underwriter in connection with offers and sales related to market-making transactions in the Securities. The Underwriter may act as principal or agent in such transactions. Such sales will be made at prices related to prevailing market prices at the time of sale.

Merrill Lynch & Co.

The date of this Prospectus Supplement is July 23, 1992.
^{SM}"MITTS" and "Market Index Target-Term Securities" are service marks of Merrill Lynch & Co., Inc.

currency bond where the investor could either gain or lose from changing exchange rates, at origination the MITTS issue had no downside exposure to stock price declines.

The call option embedded in this structure is actually a partial position. To see this, we can rewrite the option portion of the note's redemption value as:

$$\max\left[0,\ \left\{10 \times \left(\frac{\text{Final S\&P} - 412.08}{412.08}\right) \times 1.15\right\}\right] = \max\left[0,\ \left\{\left(\frac{11.50}{412.08}\right)(\text{Final S\&P} - 412.08)\right\}\right]$$

or

$$(0.0279)\ \{\max[0,\ (\text{Final S\&P} - 412.08)]\}.$$

Thus, given that a regular index call option would have a terminal payoff of $\max[0,\ (\text{Final S\&P} - X]$, where X is the exercise price, the derivative in the MITTS represents 2.79 percent of this amount. The terminal payoffs to the MITTS embedded option are shown in Table 25.7, along with those to a regular index call option for several potential August 1997 levels of the S&P 500 index. Notice that although the MITTS and regular options become in the money at the same point (i.e., 412.08), only the latter produces a "dollar-for-dollar" payoff with increasing values of the index beyond this point. The payoff call feature in the structured note still rises for any S&P level above 412.08, but gains only $0.0279 for every one point gained by the index.

Rewriting the redemption value in this fashion also makes valuing the MITTS issue a more transparent process. This can be accomplished by recognizing that the value of the entire structure simply should be the value of the bond portion plus the value of the option

---

TABLE 25.7

TERMINAL PAYOFFS TO MITTS EMBEDDED CALL OPTION AND REGULAR INDEX CALL OPTION (X = 412.08)

Terminal S&P Value	Regular Index Call	MITTS Call
350	0.00	0.00
370	0.00	0.00
390	0.00	0.00
410	0.00	0.00
430	17.92	0.50
450	37.92	1.06
470	57.92	1.62
490	77.92	2.17
510	97.92	2.73
530	117.92	3.29
550	137.92	3.85
570	157.92	4.41
590	177.92	4.97
610	197.92	5.52
630	217.92	6.08
650	237.92	6.64
670	257.92	7.20
690	277.92	7.76
710	297.92	8.31
730	317.92	8.87
750	337.92	9.43

component; any price "synergy" for the packaging will be a market-driven phenomenon. Specifically, on February 28, 1996, the closing price for the MITTS issue was $15.625, while the S&P 500 closed at 644.75. Further, the semiannually compounded yield of a zero-coupon (i.e., "stripped") Treasury bond on this date was 5.35 percent. Assuming a credit spread of 30 basis points is appropriate for Merrill Lynch's credit rating (i.e., A+ and A1 by Standard & Poor's and Moody's, respectively) and the remaining time to maturity (i.e., one-and-a-half years, or three half-years), the bond portion of the MITTS issue should be worth:

$$\text{MITTS Bond Value: } \frac{10}{\left(1 + \frac{.0565}{2}\right)^3} = \$9.20.$$

This means that the investor is paying $6.43 (= $15.63 − $9.20) for the embedded index call.

Whether $6.43 represents a fair price for the MITTS call depends on the value of the regular index option, which, as we saw in Chapter 24, can be calculated with the dividend yield–adjusted version of the Black-Scholes model. To perform this computation, some additional inputs are needed. First, the S&P dividend yield on February 28, 1996, was 2.20 percent. Second, the number of days between February 28, 1996, and August 29, 1997, is 548. Third, the continuously compounded equivalent of the quoted risk-free rate is 5.28 percent.[23] Finally, the volatility of the S&P 500 index returns over the time to the MITTS issue's maturity is assumed to be 14.5 percent, a level approximated from the prevailing implied volatilities for exchange-traded index options on that date.

The value of an index call option with an exercise price of 412.08 can now be generated by the Black-Scholes formula using the following inputs: $S = 644.75$, $X = 412.08$, $T = 1.50$ (= 548/365), $RFR = 0.0528$, $D = 0.022$, and $\sigma = 0.145$. Under these conditions, we have:

$$d_1 = [\ln(644.75e^{-(.022)1.5}/412.08) + (.0528 + 0.5(.145)^2)(1.5)] \div (.145[1.5]^{1/2}) = 2.97$$

and

$$d_2 = 2.97 - .145[1.5]^{1/2} = 2.79$$

so that $N(d_1) = 0.9985$ and $N(d_2) = 0.9974$. Thus, the index call's Black-Scholes value is:

$$C_0 = (623.82)(0.9985) - (412.08)(e^{-(.0528)1.5})(0.9974) = 243.19.$$

The value of the embedded MITTS call is then established by multiplying 243.19 by 0.0279, which leaves a value of 6.78. Thus, on this particular date the MITTS issue was priced in the market below its theoretical value, presenting investors with a potential buying opportunity depending on their transaction costs. In fact, the embedded call is actually priced below the index option's adjusted intrinsic value of 6.49 (= [644.75 − 412.08] × 0.0279), making the issue that much more attractive to investors.

---

[23] This value can be established by solving for r in the following equation:

$$e^r = (1 + (.0535/2))^2$$

or

$$r = \ln[(1 + (.0535/2))^2] = 0.0528.$$

Besides linking their payoffs to currency or equity indexes, fixed-income securities can be designed to give an investor exposure to commodity price movements as well. As with the commodity swaps we saw earlier, the commodities involved in these structures are seldom exchanged but instead represented in the form of "cash settlement only" derivatives. Thus, virtually no theoretical limit exists to the number of different underlying assets that can be embedded into a bond issue. However, recall that innovation in the structured note market is dictated by investor demands, which to date has tended to concentrate on either oil or precious metals. As in the previous examples, the primary attractions to the investor of gaining the desired exposure through the purchase of structured notes are their convenience and their ability to avoid restrictions on taking commodity positions directly.

A particularly interesting form of the commodity-linked bond is the so-called bull and bear note. This structure gets its name from a bond that is issued in two portions: a bull tranche, whose principal redemption amount increases directly with the price of the designated commodity; and a bear tranche, whose principal refunding declines with increasing commodity prices. One of the first issues of this kind occurred in October 1986 when the Kingdom of Denmark raised $120 million in two separate $60 million tranches, each having a different payoff structure depending on the movement of an index of gold prices.[24] Both of these gold-linked note tranches had a seven-year maturity, paid an annual coupon of 3 percent, and were issued at a price of 100.125 percent of par value. The principal redemptions for each $1,000 of face value for the two tranches were:

Bull Redemption: ($1,000) × [1.158 × (Index at Redemption ÷ Initial Index)],

and

Bear Redemption: ($1,000) × {2.78 − [1.158 × (Index at Redemption ÷ Initial Index)]}.

Finally, for both tranches, maximum and minimum redemption levels of $2,280 and $500, respectively, were set.

Table 25.8 shows the redemption amount that the Kingdom of Denmark is obligated to pay on each tranche for a series of gold index levels relative to the initial level, which was set at 426.50. The final column of this display shows what the average redemption value was when the two tranches are considered together. Notice that this average amount does not vary, i.e., *the issuer has no net exposure to gold price movements.* Unlike the dual currency bond example considered earlier, which required the issuer to adopt an offsetting derivative position to offset the instrument's inherent FX exposure, the virtue of this two-tranche approach is that the commodity exposure is neutralized internally. That is, the Kingdom of Denmark is effectively both long and short gold in equal amounts across the bear and bull segments, respectively. An immediate consequence of this is that they have a fixed funding cost for the full $120 million issue, calculated by solving:

$$1001.25 = \sum_{t=1}^{7} \frac{30}{(1+y)^t} + \frac{1390}{(1+y)^t},$$

---

[24] Additional details of this example are explained in Julian Walmsley, *The New Financial Instruments* (New York: John Wiley & Sons, 1988), which also contains descriptions of an exhaustive set of such deals. It is recommended reading for anyone wishing to learn more about the development of these innovative products.

TABLE 25.8	REDEMPTION VALUES FOR THE "BULL AND BEAR" GOLD-LINKED NOTE (IN U.S. DOLLARS)			

Terminal Gold Index	Bull Tranche	Bear Tranche	Average
100	500	2,280	1,390
150	500	2,280	1,390
200	543	2,237	1,390
250	679	2,101	1,390
300	815	1,965	1,390
350	950	1,830	1,390
400	1,086	1,694	1,390
450	1,222	1,558	1,390
500	1,358	1,422	1,390
550	1,493	1,287	1,390
600	1,629	1,151	1,390
650	1,765	1,015	1,390
700	1,901	879	1,390
750	2,036	744	1,390
800	2,172	608	1,390
850	2,280	500	1,390
900	2,280	500	1,390

or $y = 7.42$ percent. At the time this deal was launched, a regular seven-year, par-value debt issue would have required a yield of about 8 percent, a fact that underscores the Kingdom of Denmark's incentive to create this structure in the first place.

The attraction for the investors, of course, is the ability to purchase a fixed-income security that also allows for participation in gold price movements. In exchange for accepting a lower-than-market coupon, buyers of the bull (bear) tranche will receive a redemption value that exceeds their purchase price if the gold index increases (declines). Figure 25.17, which shows the redemption values for the two tranches in a graphical form, suggests that the commodity derivatives embedded in this transaction are not simple forward or option positions. Rather, the minimum and maximum principal payoffs effectively convert the gold exposure into a call option money spread—a bull spread for the bull tranche, a bear for the bear—as described in Chapter 24. The investors, who undoubtedly will be different people for the two portions, pay for this spread position through a reduction in their average yield-to-maturity relative to the regular bond.

SWAP-LINKED NOTES   As we have seen, interest rate swaps are efficient mechanisms for transforming the cash flows of existing debt issues. They also are quite useful in the new-issue market when the desired rate exposures of the borrower and lender do not coincide naturally. Imagine, for example, that Company LMN wishes to raise $50 million by issuing a fixed-rate note with semiannual coupon payments over a three-year period. Having floated a similar issue in the capital markets recently, however, LMN finds that little "appetite" exists for another one of its fixed-rate notes. On the other hand, a large institutional investor is willing to accept LMN's credit risk on a privately placed loan, providing that the deal can be structured to its satisfaction. In particular, the fund manager for this investment company thinks that interest rates are going to decline substantially over the next few years and wants to design the loan contract to take advantage of that possibility. Accordingly, she wants the semiannual coupon on the note to move inversely with the level of some variable interest rate index,

FIGURE 25.17   REDEMPTION VALUES FOR THE "BULL AND BEAR" GOLD-LINKED NOTE

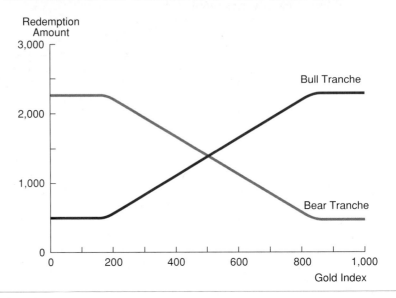

such as LIBOR. This sort of arrangement is known as a *reverse floating rate* contract; the coupon rate changes as the general level of interest rates moves, but in the opposite direction.

Suppose the specific structure that LMN and the investor agree on resets the coupon on a semiannual basis at a level equal to 12 percent minus LIBOR. Thus, if six-month LIBOR on a particular settlement date is 7.5 percent, the coupon payment will be 4.5 percent (times one-half times $50 million). Conversely, a LIBOR of only 3.75 percent would generate a coupon of 8.25 percent. In this way, the investor gains the desired benefit from falling rates and does so in a convenient form that entails less credit risk than if it had transformed a regular bond issue with a derivative on its own. In addition, the reverse floater will actually benefit more from a rate decline than would a fixed-rate note of identical maturity. Specifically, while the price of a fixed-rate bond paying constant coupons will appreciate when yields fall, the reverse floater will increase the investor's periodic cash flow as well.

Unfortunately, although this design satisfies the investor's requirements, it does not do the same for the issuer. This discrepancy can be easily remedied, though, by combining Company LMN's debt position with a swap in which it receives the fixed rate and pays LIBOR. This is illustrated in Figure 25.18, assuming a three-year fixed swap rate of 6.5 percent against six-month LIBOR. One helpful way to see how a swap must be written to fix the coupon on this reverse rate structure is to notice that paying a coupon of 12 percent minus LIBOR is equivalent to paying a coupon of 12 percent and receiving one of LIBOR. Thus, to neutralize LMN's floating rate exposure, it must pay out LIBOR on the swap.

Figure 25.18 also shows that the net synthetic fixed-rate funding cost to Company LMN is 5.5 percent (assuming the swap fixed rate has been converted to a 360-day year basis). This will only be true, however, whenever LIBOR does not exceed 12 percent. If LIBOR is greater than 12 percent, the benefit from paying lower coupons to the investor will stop—the coupon rate can never go negative—but LMN will continue having to make the higher net settlement payment on the swap, which raises the effective borrowing cost above 5.5

| FIGURE 25.18 | CONVERTING A RESERVE FLOATING RATE NOTE WITH A SWAP |

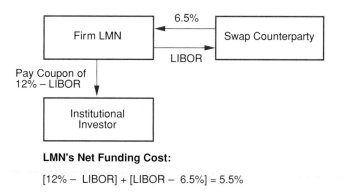

LMN's Net Funding Cost:

[12% − LIBOR] + [LIBOR − 6.5%] = 5.5%

percent. Consequently, because there is an implicit cap on LIBOR built into the reverse floating rate contract, Company LMN will need to offset this by purchasing an actual cap agreement with an exercise rate of 12 percent and a notional principal of $50 million. This option will not be expensive because it is quite far out of the money but it will not be free, which means the net funding cost will be somewhat greater than 5.5 percent.

Earlier in the chapter, we saw that an interest rate swap can be interpreted as a pair of capital market transactions. In this particular case, a "receive 6.5 percent fixed, pay LIBOR" swap can be viewed as a portfolio long in a fixed-rate note paying 6.5 percent and short in a LIBOR-based floating rate note. Recalling that "+" represents a long position and " −" represents a short position, the synthetic fixed-rate issue from Company LMN's perspective can be written as follows:

$$
\begin{aligned}
- \text{(Synthetic Fixed Rate Bond at 5.5\%)} = &- \text{(Reverse Floater at 12\% − LIBOR)} \\
&+ \text{(Receive 6.5\%, Pay LIBOR Swap)} \\
&+ \text{(Cap at 12\% Exercise Rate)} \\
= &- \text{(Reverse Floater at 12\% − LIBOR)} \\
&- \text{(FRN at LIBOR)} + \text{(Fixed Rate Bond at 6.5\%)} \\
&+ \text{(Cap at 12\% Exercise Rate)}.
\end{aligned}
$$

As in the previous examples, this sort of structured solution would only make sense to the issuer if it could ultimately obtain a funding cost that was lower than a direct fixed-rate loan. The biggest reason for this is that while a direct fixed-rate loan would carry no credit risk for Company LMN, the structured loan would because of the swap and cap positions. Thus, the swap-based borrowing is never as good as a direct approach, and therefore requires a lower cost to entice the issuer.

As a final extension of this concept, consider what would have happened if the institutional investor decided to take an even more aggressive view of falling interest rates and requested that the coupon reset the formula to 18.4 percent minus (2 × LIBOR). Such a design is called a *leveraged* floating rate note, with the leverage coming from the fact that the coupon increases twice as fast as the decline in yields. Figure 25.19 indicates that to convert this to a fixed-rate issue, Company LMN would have to enter into two $50 million receive-fixed swaps (or, more practically, one contract with a notional principal of $100 million). As before, to fix its funding cost completely, it also would have to purchase two $50 million cap agreements with a cap rate of 9.2 percent (= 18.4 percent ÷ 2). This

FIGURE 25.19   **CONVERTING A LEVERAGED RESERVE FLOATER WITH TWO SWAPS**

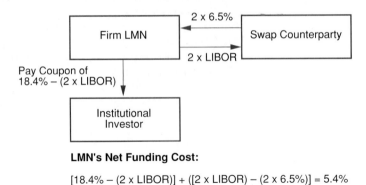

LMN's Net Funding Cost:

$$[18.4\% - (2 \times \text{LIBOR})] + ([2 \times \text{LIBOR}) - (2 \times 6.5\%)] = 5.4\%$$

converted position, which would have a net funding cost of 5.4 percent before factoring in the cost of the caps, can be represented as:

$$
\begin{aligned}
-\,(\text{Synthetic Fixed Rate Bond at } 5.4\%) = {} & -\,(\text{Reverse Floater at } 18.4\% - 2 \times \text{LIBOR}) \\
& +\,(2 \text{ Receive } 6.5\%, \text{ Pay LIBOR Swaps}) \\
& +\,(2 \text{ Caps at } 9.2\% \text{ Exercise Rate}) \\
= {} & -\,(\text{Reverse Floater at } 18.4\% - 2 \times \text{LIBOR}) \\
& -\,(2 \text{ FRNs at LIBOR}) + (2 \text{ Fixed Rate Bonds at } 6.5\%) \\
& +\,(2 \text{ Caps at } 9.2\% \text{ Exercise Rate}).
\end{aligned}
$$

Although the net coupon on this swapped leveraged structure is lower than on the swapped unleveraged reverse floater, the cost of the required options will be more than twice as expensive since two contracts must be purchased at a lower cap rate.[25]

Summary

- The genius of modern financial markets is that they continuously provide new products and strategies to meet the constantly changing needs of anyone willing to pay the required price. In this chapter, we explore several ways in which derivatives can aid in that development process. In particular, we see that innovation sometimes takes the form of creating a new set of instruments, such as interest rate and currency swaps, while at other times it involves packaging existing securities in a creative way. Structured notes, which combine bonds with a derivative position based on a different sort of underlying asset, are a good example of this latter approach. It is important to keep in mind that the ultimate purpose of this financial engineering is to help borrowers and lenders control one of four types of potential exposures: interest rate, currency, equity, or commodity price risk.
- We begin our discussion with an examination of the market for OTC interest rate agreements. Although forward rate agreements are the most basic product in this category, interest rate swaps are the most popular. Swap contracts can be interpreted in three unique ways: as a series of FRAs, as a portfolio of bond positions, or as a zero-cost collar, which consists of a pair of cap and floor agreements. We then extend the "plain vanilla" swap concept to include contracts designed to handle other exposures such as currency, equity, and commodity swaps, as well as the growing market for swap options. Since all of these agreements are traded off of the organized exchanges, they are extremely flexible in the terms available—the primary appeal to investors and issuers.

---

[25] For a more complete examination of how swaps can be used to create structured investment payoffs, see Keith C. Brown and Donald J. Smith, "Structured Swaps," in *Yearbook of Fixed Income Investing,* edited by J. Pinnerty and M. Pridson (Burr Ridge, IL: Irwin Professional Publishing, 1995).

- We conclude with an analysis of several ways in which derivatives can be embedded into other securities to create customized payoff distributions. Because these hybrid structures often are designed to the specific needs of a particular investor, the investor must "pay up" for the customization. Warrants, which are call options on common stock issued directly by the company itself, can be attached to a debt issue to offer investors the upside potential of equity with the safety of a bond. Further, bonds and preferred stock issues can be set up to allow for conversion into common stock at the investor's option. In both cases, the issuing firm will likely end up with a lower front-end funding cost because of the options they have implicitly sold. Finally, a class of instruments known as structured notes carries this concept even further by embedding into bonds derivatives that often are based on exposures that may not appear on the issuer's balance sheet. These instruments epitomize how much value derivatives can add when they are used properly and are indicative of the ways in which investors are likely to see them appear in the market for years to come.

Questions

1. *CFA Examination III (June 1994)*

    Several Investment Committee members for the pension fund you work for have asked about Interest Rate Swap agreements and how they are used in the management of domestic fixed-income portfolios.

    a. Define an interest rate swap and briefly describe the obligation of each party involved.

    b. Cite and explain two examples of how interest rate swaps could be used by a fixed-income portfolio manager to control risk or improve return.

2. Explain how an interest rate swap can be viewed as either a series of forward rate agreements, a pair of bond transactions, or a pair of option agreements. To make your description more precise, take the point of view of the fixed-rate receiver in the swap.

3. "When the yield curve is upward sloping, the fixed rate on a multiyear swap must be higher than the current level of LIBOR. With a downward sloping yield curve, the opposite will occur." Explain what is meant by this statement and why it must be true.

4. Three years ago, you entered into a five-year interest rate swap agreement by agreeing to pay a fixed rate of 7 percent in exchange for six-month LIBOR. If your counterparty were to default today when the fixed rate on a new two-year swap was 6.5 percent, would you experience an economic loss? Explain.

5. If the fixed rate on a five-year, plain vanilla swap is currently 8 percent, what would happen if you: (1) bought a five-year cap agreement with an exercise rate of 7 percent, and (2) sold a five-year, 7 percent floor agreement? Use the concept of cap-floor-swap parity to describe the kind of position you have created and discuss whether or not a front-end cash payment would be necessary and whether you or your counterparty would receive it.

6. *CFA Examination III (June 1995)*

    A colleague has asked you about the effects of using interest rate swaptions in a fixed-income portfolio.

    a. Explain how the purchase of an interest rate receiver's swaption would modify:

     (i) the risk characteristics of a fixed-income portfolio; and

     (ii) the return characteristics of a fixed-income portfolio.

    b. Explain two potential disadvantages of using swaptions to help manage risk in a fixed-income portfolio.

7. *CFA Examination III (June 1995)*

    The manager of Bontemps International (BI) defined-benefit pension plan's fixed-income portfolio has shown exceptional security selection skills, and has produced returns consistently above those on BI's fixed-income benchmark portfolio. The Board wants to allocate more money to this manager to enhance further the fund's alpha. This action would increase the proportion allocated to fixed income and decrease the proportion in equities. However, the Board wants to keep the present fixed income/equity proportions unchanged.

    a. Identify two distinct strategies using derivative financial instruments that the Board could use to increase the fund's allocation to the fixed-income manager without changing the present fixed-income/equity proportions. Briefly explain how each of these two strategies would work. (Note: Make sure that equity swaps are one of the two strategies that you choose.)

b. Briefly discuss one advantage and one disadvantage of each of the strategies you identified in Part a above. Present your discussion in terms of the effect(s) of these advantages and disadvantages on the portfolio's:

(i) risk characteristics; and

(ii) return characteristics.

8. *CFA Examination III (June 1995)*

The Board of Bontemps International (BI) will substantially increase the company's defined-benefit pension fund's allocation to international equities in the future. However, the Board wants to retain the ability to reduce temporarily this exposure without making the necessary transactions in the cash markets. You develop a way to meet the Board's condition:

> "BI enters into a swap arrangement with Bank A for a given notional amount and agrees to pay the EAFE (Europe, Australia, and Far East) Index return (in U.S. dollars) in exchange for receiving the LIBOR interest rate plus 0.2% (20 basis points).
>
> On the same notional amount, BI arranges another swap with Bank B under which BI receives the return on the S&P 500 Index (in U.S. dollars) in exchange for paying the interest rate on the U.S. Treasury bill plus 0.1% (10 basis points).
>
> Both swaps would be for a one-year term."

From BI's perspective, identify and briefly describe:

(i) the major risk that this transaction would eliminate;

(ii) the major risk that this transaction would not eliminate (i.e., retain), and:

(iii) three risks that this transaction would create.

9. We have seen that equity warrants are not as valuable as an otherwise identical call option on the stock of the same company. Explain why this must be the case. Also, what is the incentive for a firm to issue a warrant rather than issuing stock directly?

10. Bonds and preferred stock that are convertible into common stock are said to provide investors with both upside potential and downside protection. Explain how one security can possess both attributes. What implications do these features have for the way a convertible security is priced?

11. Describe the conditions necessary for a structured note issue to be successful. How can an issuer come to know what the particular economic needs of a potential investor happen to be?

Problems

1. With the interest rate swap quotations shown in Table 25.2, calculate the swap cash flows from the point of view of the fixed-rate receiver on a two-year swap with a notional principal of $22.5 million. You may assume the relevant part of the settlement date pattern and the realized LIBOR path shown in Table 25.3 for the three-year agreement. Also, calculate the fixed-rate payments on a 365-day basis and the floating-rate payments on a 360-day basis.

2. Suppose that on March 1, 1996, the treasurer for Company W wishes to restructure the coupon payments of one of her outstanding debt issues. The bond in question is scheduled to pay semiannual interest on March 1 and September 1 each year until March 1, 2001, and has a coupon rate of 6.50 percent with a face value of $35 million. On the same day, the treasurer for Company X wants to restructure the interest payments on his $50 million, four-year floating-rate note having its coupon reset each March 1 and September 1 to a reference rate of LIBOR flat. The maturity of this floating-rate bond is March 1, 2000.

a. Using the plain vanilla interest rate swap quotes in Table 25.2, describe how both treasurers, working with a dealer, can use a swap agreement to alter synthetically their current cash flow obligations. Specifically, assume that Company W wishes to wind up with floating-rate exposure while Company X desires fixed-rate debt.

b. Assuming that the dealer negotiates these swap transactions simultaneously, will they represent a matched book? If not, describe two remaining sources of market exposure that the dealer still faces.

3. The treasurer of a British brewery is planning to enter a plain vanilla, three-year, quarterly settlement interest rate swap to pay a fixed rate of 8 percent and to receive three-month sterling LIBOR. But first he decides to check various cap-floor combinations to see if any might be preferable. A market maker in British pound sterling OTC options presents the treasurer with the following price list for three-year, quarterly settlement caps and floors:

	INTEREST RATE CAPS		INTEREST RATE FLOORS	
Strike Rate	Buy	Sell	Buy	Sell
7%	582 bp	597 bp	320 bp	335 bp
8	398	413	401	416
9	205	220	502	517

The prices are in basis points, which when multiplied by the notional principal give the actual purchase or sale price in pounds sterling. These quotes are from the perspective of the market maker, not the firm. That is, the treasurer could buy a 9 percent cap from the market maker for 220 bp, or sell one for 205 bp. The strike rates are quoted on a 365-day basis, as is sterling LIBOR.

   In financial analysis of this sort, the treasurer assumes that the three-year cost of funds on fully amortizing debt would be about 8.20 percent (for quarterly payments). Should another structure be considered in lieu of the plain vanilla swap?

4. Corporation XYZ seeks $50 million, five-year fixed-rate funding. The firm is confident that it can issue a 9½ percent coupon bond (semiannual payments) at par value. Since the five-year Treasury issue yields 8.25 percent, this funding could be attained at 125 basis points over Treasuries—a reasonable spread given XYZ's credit rating. The corporate treasurer would like to explore the possibility of issuing an FRN, possibly an innovative type, and using the interest rate swap market to create synthetic fixed-rate funding. According to XYZ's capital markets group, the following FRNs could be launched:

Type	Reset Formula
"Traditional" floater	LIBOR + 0.25%
"Bull" (i.e., reverse) floater	18.40% − LIBOR
"Bear" floater	(2 × LIBOR) − 9.10%

Assume that each FRN could be placed at par value and that the flotation costs for the fixed-rate bond and various variable rate issues are the same (and can therefore be ignored in the comparison). Note that the FRNs are quoted on a money market (360-day) basis and reset the coupon rate semiannually based on the prevailing six-month LIBOR. A quick canvassing of the swap market generates the following representative quotes on a five-year swap with semiannual settlements:

Dealer's Bid	Dealer's Ask
T + 85	T + 95

a. What specific swap transactions are needed to transform each FRN into a synthetic fixed rate? What synthetic fixed rate can be attained by each of the structures? Is the rate fixed for all possible levels of LIBOR? (Note: Calculate all synthetic funding rates on a 365-day basis.)

b. What would the funding cost be if XYZ raised the desired $50 million by issuing $25 million of a traditional FRN and $25 million of a bull floater?

c. Which structure would you recommend for XYZ?

d. What types of investors might be interested in acquiring a bull floater? If the motive was speculative, what would be the investor's view on the future path for LIBOR?

e. What types of investors might be interested in acquiring a bear floater? If an investor's motive was to hedge exposure to LIBOR, what might its balance sheet look like?

5. As a swap dealer, you have just been contacted by a prospective corporate counterparty who wishes to do a three-year "fixed/fixed" yen/sterling currency swap. In particular, the corporation needs to pay a fixed interest rate in Japanese yen and to receive a fixed rate in British pound sterling. Your current spot FX and three-year currency swap quotes (versus six-month U.S. dollar LIBOR) are as follows:

		Japanese Yen	British Pound Sterling
Spot Exchange Rate		JPY127.47/USD	USD1.82/GBP
Currency Swap:	Bid	4.85%	9.83%
	Offer	4.92	9.93

These quotes imply that you would be willing to pay 4.85 percent in yen to receive U.S. dollar LIBOR, but you would need to receive 4.92 percent in yen when paying LIBOR. Your bid–offer spread is seven basis points in yen. Note that the bid–offer spread is higher in sterling because each basis point is not worth as much (since sterling would be at a forward discount to yen).

a. Describe the sequence of transactions necessary to construct this swap from the counterparty's perspective, including your quotes for both of the fixed rates.

b. Construct a chart similar to Table 25.4 summarizing the cash flow exchanges on each exchange date, again adopting the end user's viewpoint. In this analysis, assume that the deal is to be scaled to a transaction size of USD 25 million and that the number of days in the settlement payments alternates between 182 and 183, starting with 183 days between the origination date and the first settlement date.

6. Suppose that on April 15, 1987, a French corporation entered into an annual-settlement, three-year currency swap to receive 12.72 percent in U.S. dollars (USD) and to pay 14.88 percent in French francs (FRF). Suppose that the spot market exchange rate was FRF 8.4435/USD at the time, or USD 0.118433/FRF. The principal on the swap was USD 100 million, which equals FRF 844.35 million. The scheduled cash flows on the swap from the perspective of the French corporation were the following:

	Receive	Pay
April 15, 1988	USD 12,720,000	FRF 125,639,280
April 15, 1989	USD 12,720,000	FRF 125,639,280
April 15, 1990	USD 112,720,000	FRF 969,989,280

On April 15, 1988, just after the initial coupon exchange, the corporation decides to cancel the remainder of its swap position and negotiate a lump-sum settlement with its counterparty. On that date, plain vanilla two-year fixed/fixed currency swaps were quoted by a number of dealers at 10.20 percent in USD versus 12.78 percent in FRF. The spot market exchange rate was FRF 9.4829/USD, or USD 0.105453/FRF.

a. Calculate the amount of the swap unwind payment (in FRF) suggested by these new market conditions.

b. Would the French corporation pay or receive this amount? Explain.

7. On December 2, the manager of a tactical asset allocation fund that is currently invested entirely in floating-rate debt securities decides to shift a portion of her portfolio to equities. To effect this change, she has chosen to enter into the "receive equity index" side of a one-year equity swap based on movements in the S&P 500 index plus a spread of 10 basis points. The swap is to have quarterly settlement payments with the floating-rate side of the agreement pegged to three-month LIBOR denominated in U.S. dollars. At the origination of the swap, the value of the S&P 500 index was 463.11 and three-month LIBOR was 3.50 percent. The notional principal of the swap is set for the life of the agreement at $50 million, which matches the amount of debt holdings in the fund that she would like to convert to equity.

   a. Calculate the net cash receipt or payment—from the fund manager's perspective—on each future settlement date, assuming the value for the S&P 500 index (with all dividends reinvested) and LIBOR are as follows:

Settlement Date	Number of Days	S&P Level	LIBOR Level
December 2 (initial year)	—	463.11	3.50%
March 2 (following year)	90	477.51	3.25%
June 2	92	464.74	3.75%
September 2	92	480.86	4.00%
December 2	91	482.59	—

   b. Explain why the fund manager might want the notional principal on this swap to vary over time and what the most logical pattern for this variation would be.

8. *CFA Examination III (June 1996)*

On June 30, 1996, Help for Students (HFS) Foundation owns $10 million (face amount) of 6% coupon SteelCo. bonds, currently priced at par, which it must hold to maturity on June 30, 1998, two years from now. John Ames, HFS's fixed income manager, expects that the yield curve, now normal in shape (i.e., positively sloped), will undergo an upward shift and invert sometime prior to maturity. He wishes to enter into a swap on the $10 million notional amount of the holding to take advantage of this yield curve forecast. Assume that HFS's policy permits such action.

SELECTED JUNE 30, 1996 MARKET DATA

	Price	Yield
September 1996 Eurodollar Future	94.9	5.1%
2-year swap fixed rate	n/a	5.5%

   a. Identify and explain an interest rate swap arrangement that could achieve Ames' goal in this particular instance. Base your response only on the data above and assume quarterly cash flows.

   b. Describe the direction and calculate the amount of the first quarterly cash flow (on September 30, 1996) under this arrangement. [*Note: Assume that 90-day spot LIBOR on June 30, 1996 equals the September 1996 Eurodollar futures contract settlement yield.*]

   c. Explain the effect of the interest rate swap created in Part a above on the sensitivity of HFS's portfolio value to interest rate changes.

   d. Describe the role of the Eurodollar forward rate curve in pricing the fixed rate payment side of the interest rate swap created in Part a above.

   e. Identify a strategy that would use options to replicate the position of a fixed rate payer in a swap and explain how this strategy would accomplish its purposes. (Assume no transactions costs.)

9. A Spanish pension fund is considering buying a five-year floating-rate note named "El Oso Grande." El Oso Grande would have a coupon reset formula of three times six-month (Spanish peseta) LIBOR minus 24 percent, subject to a minimum coupon rate of 0 percent if peseta LIBOR were to fall below 8 percent. Currently, six-month peseta LIBOR is 11.20 percent, so the initial coupon would be based on a rate of 9.60 percent. The five-year, semiannual payment, 100 million peseta floating-rate note can be bought at par value. The pension fund intends to use derivative instruments to convert El Oso Grande into a synthetic fixed-rate asset. Quotes for five-year, semiannual settlement interest rate swaps, caps, and floors on six-month Spanish peseta LIBOR are obtained from a Madrid commercial bank specializing in derivative products.

Interest Rate Swaps: The pension fund can pay a fixed rate of 13.50 percent and receive six-month peseta LIBOR, or the fund can receive a fixed rate of 13.35 percent and pay six-month peseta LIBOR.

Interest Rate Caps:

Strike Rate	The Fund Buys the Cap	The Fund Writes the Cap
24%	125 bp	90 bp

Interest Rate Floors:

Strike Rate	The Fund Buys the Floor	The Fund Writes the Floor
8%	175 bp	140 bp

(Recall that the premiums on the caps and floors are quoted as a percentage of the notional principal.)

a. Indicate the specific combination of transactions that provides a synthetic fixed-rate asset to the pension fund.

b. Calculate the "all-in," fixed rate of return. Assume that Spanish peseta LIBOR, the coupon rate on El Oso Grande, the swap fixed rate, and the strike rate on the caps and floors are all stated on a semiannual bond basis.

10. In July of 1986, Guinness Finance B.V. placed a three-year, $100 million Eurobond issue known as *Stock Performance Exchange Linked* (SPEL) bonds. The concept of the SPEL is that the bond has its principal redemption amount tied to the level of the NYSE composite index at maturity (i.e., NY_3) by the following formula:

$$\text{Variable Redemption Amount} = \max\{100, 100 \times (1 + [(NY_3 - 166) \div 166])\}$$

Notice that the investor is guaranteed redemption at par as a minimum. The bond also pays an annual coupon of 3 percent, which is 0.5 percent below the average annual dividend yield of shares on the NYSE. At the time the SPEL was launched, the NYSE composite index stood at 134.

a. Demonstrate that the SPEL is a combination of a regular debt issue and an equity option by analyzing the pattern of annual cash flows generated by the issue. In your work, assume a par value of 100.

b. The SPEL bonds were issued at a price of 100.625. Assuming that Guinness would ordinarily have to pay a borrowing cost of 7.65 percent on a three-year "straight" bond (i.e., one with no attached options), calculate the implicit dollar price of the equity index option embedded in this issue. How much of this amount represents intrinsic value and how much is time premium?

11. A firm has 100,000 shares of stock outstanding priced at $35 per share. The firm has no debt and does not pay a dividend. To raise more capital, it plans to issue 10,000 warrants, each allowing for the purchase of one share of stock at a price of $50. The warrants are European-style and expire in five years. The standard deviation of the firm's common stock is 34 percent and the continuously compounded, five-year risk-free rate is 5.2 percent.

   a. Estimate the fair value of the warrants, first using the relevant information to calculate the Black-Scholes value of an analogous call option.

   b. Determine the stock price at expiration, assuming the warrants are exercised if the value of the firm is at least $5,200,000.

   c. Using the information in Parts a and b about initial and terminal warrant and stock prices, discuss the relative merits of these two ways of making an equity investment in the firm.

References

Beidleman, Carl R., ed. *Interest Rate Swaps*. Homewood, IL: Business One-Irwin, 1991.

Bicksler, James and Andrew H. Chen. "An Economic Analysis of Interest Rate Swaps." *Journal of Finance* 41, no. 3 (July 1986).

Campbell, Tim S. and William A. Kracaw. *Financial Risk Management*. New York: HarperCollins, 1993.

Constantinides, George M. "Warrant Exercise and Bond Conversion in Competitive Markets." *Journal of Financial Economics* 13, no. 3 (September 1984).

Dattareya, Ravi E., Raj E. S. Venkatesh, and Vijaya Venkatesh. *Interest Rate & Currency Swaps*. Chicago, IL: Probus Publishing, 1994.

Eckl, S., J. N. Robinson, and D. C. Thomas. *Financial Engineering: A Handbook of Derivative Products*. Cambridge, MA: Basil Blackwell, 1991.

Finnerty, John D. "An Overview of Corporate Securities Innovation." *Journal of Applied Corporate Finance* 4, no. 4 (Winter 1992).

Ingersoll, Jonathan E., Jr. "A Contingent Claims Valuation of Convertible Securities." *Journal of Financial Economics* 4, no. 3 (May 1977).

Litzenberger, Robert H. "Swaps: Plain and Fanciful." *Journal of Finance* 47, no. 3 (July 1992).

Marshall, John F. and Kenneth R. Kapner. *The Swaps Market*. 2d ed. Miami, FL: Kolb Publishing, 1993.

Smithson, Charles, Clifford W. Smith, Jr., and D. Sykes Wilford. *Managing Financial Risk*. Burr Ridge, IL: Richard D. Irwin, 1995.

Wall, Larry D. and John J. Pringle. "Alternative Explanations of Interest Rate Swaps: A Theoretical and Empirical Analysis." *Financial Management* 18, no. 2 (Summer 1989).

Part

7

INVESTMENT COMPANIES AND EVALUATING PORTFOLIO PERFORMANCE

Chapter 26   *Investment Companies*

Chapter 27   *Evaluation of Portfolio Performance*

This final section of the book contains two chapters: the first deals with investment companies, and the second is concerned with the evaluation of portfolio performance. The investment company chapter is mainly of concern to individual investors, while both individual and institutional investors need to be aware of how one evaluates the performance of a portfolio.

Because many individual investors employ investment companies (also referred to as mutual funds) for the bulk of their investments, Chapter 26 is an important wrap-up to their asset allocation and portfolio construction process. After a basic explanation of the concept of investment companies and a description of the major forms, we examine the numerous types of funds available including money market funds, REITs, high-growth companies, international stocks and bonds, high-yield (junk) bonds, and municipal bonds. It is demonstrated that almost any investment objective can be met by investing in one or several investment companies. There is an extensive discussion of the numerous studies that have examined the performance of funds. The results of these studies indicate that, on average, investment companies have not been able to outperform the aggregate market, although there is some recent evidence of performance persistence. It is noted that even with the average performance shortfall, investment companies are capable of fulfilling a number of functions that are important to investors. The chapter concludes with a discussion of sources of information that provide support for investors making choices among the growing number of funds available.

We conclude the book with a chapter dealing with the evaluation of portfolio performance. After a discussion of what is required of a portfolio manager, we review in detail the major risk-adjusted portfolio performance models including a recent performance attribution model that, in turn, is capable of evaluating a global portfolio that necessarily includes the effect of currency allocation. We also consider how the alternative models relate to each other. This is followed by a demonstration of their use with a sample of mutual funds.

As always, it is important to understand potential problems with a technique or models. Therefore, we consider potential problems with the performance measures including a review of Roll's benchmark problem and its effect on these performance models. It is demonstrated that this benchmark problem has become more significant with the growth of global investing. Finally, because the factors that determine success in bonds differ from what is important in equities, we review and evaluate several alternative models used to evaluate the performance of bond portfolio managers.

Chapter
26
Investment Companies

This chapter answers the following questions:

- What are investment companies and how are they started?
- Who manages the investment company portfolio and how are its managers compensated?
- How do you compute the net asset value (NAV) for investment companies?
- What is the difference between a closed-end and an open-end investment company?
- What is the difference between the NAV and the market price for a closed-end fund?
- What is the growth pattern for open-end investment companies?
- What is the difference between a load and a no-load open-end fund?
- What is a 12b-1 plan fund and how does it affect an investor?
- What are fund management fees, how do they affect fund investors, and how do they influence fund management companies?
- What are the two major means of fund distribution and what has been the pattern of growth for each approach?
- Given the breakdown of all funds by investment objectives, which groups have experienced relative growth or decline?
- What has been the risk-adjusted performance of domestic equity mutual funds relative to alternative market indexes?
- What has been the risk-adjusted performance of international stock and bond funds relative to appropriate benchmarks?
- What has been the ability of fund managers to correctly time the market and perform consistently?
- Given a desire to have a personal portfolio manager perform certain functions for you, how do investment companies help fulfill these needs?
- What are some of the major sources of information on the performance of funds and the costs associated with investment companies?

So far, we have discussed how to analyze the aggregate market, alternative industries, and individual companies as well as their stocks and bonds in order to build a portfolio that is consistent with your investment objectives. Part 6 centered on alternative instruments such as options, warrants, convertibles, and futures that provide additional risk–return possibilities beyond those available from a straight stock–bond portfolio. This chapter introduces another investment opportunity: investment companies that sell shares in portfolios of stocks, bonds, or some combination of securities. Investment companies can make up part of a larger portfolio along with investments in individual stocks and bonds, or investment companies can be your total portfolio.

Efficient market studies have indicated that few individual investors outperform the aggregate market averages. This makes managed investment companies an appealing alternative to direct investments because they provide several services. Many different types of investment companies offer a wide variety of investment instruments with a range of risk and return characteristics.

The initial sections in this chapter explain investment companies with examples and discuss the management organizations for investment company groups. Subsequently, we discuss how they are traded in the secondary market and how they charge for their services. The next section divides investment companies into types based on their investment objectives and the types of securities in their portfolios. As noted, there are some unusual types of instruments as well as securities from around the world.

To choose among almost 5,000 investment companies available, you need to understand how to evaluate their performance. After discussing some major studies of what features are important and how to examine them, we consider the implications of these results for investors. We conclude the chapter with a presentation on some sources of information on investment companies that can help you to make an investment decision that considers the growing availability of investment companies that invest in stocks and bonds from around the world.

WHAT IS AN INVESTMENT COMPANY?

An **investment company** invests a pool of funds belonging to many individuals in a portfolio of individual investments such as stocks and bonds. For example, suppose an investment company sells 10 million shares to the public at $10 a share for a total of $100 million. If this common stock fund emphasized blue-chip stocks, the manager would invest the proceeds of the sale ($100 million less any commissions) in the stock of companies such as AT&T, Standard Oil, IBM, Xerox, and General Electric. Therefore, each individual who bought shares of the investment company would own a percentage of the investment company's total portfolio.

The value of these investment company shares depends on what happens to the investment company's portfolio of stocks. With no further transactions, if the total market value of the stocks in the portfolio increased to $105 million, then each original share of the investment company would be worth $10.50 ($105 million/10 million shares). This per-share value is the **net asset value (NAV)** of the investment company. It equals the total market value of all its assets divided by the number of fund shares outstanding.

MANAGEMENT OF INVESTMENT COMPANIES

The investment company typically is a corporation that has as its major assets the portfolio of marketable securities referred to as a fund. The management of the portfolio of securities and most of the other administrative duties are handled by a separate **investment management company** hired by the board of directors of the investment company. This legal description oversimplifies the typical arrangement. The actual management usually begins with an investment advisory firm that starts an investment company and selects a board of directors for the fund. Subsequently, this board of directors hires the investment advisory firm as the fund's portfolio manager.

The contract between the investment company (the portfolio of securities) and the investment management company indicates the duties and compensation of the management company. The major duties of the investment management company include investment research, the management of the portfolio, and administrative duties such as issuing securities and handling redemptions and dividends. The management fee is generally stated as a percentage of the total value of the fund and typically ranges from one-quarter to one-half of 1 percent, with a sliding scale as the size of the fund increases.

To achieve economies of scale, many management companies start numerous funds with different characteristics. The variety of funds allows the management group to appeal to many investors with different risk–return preferences. In addition, it allows investors to switch among funds as economic or personal conditions change. This "family of funds" promotes flexibility and increases the total capital managed by the investment firm.

CLOSED-END VERSUS OPEN-END INVESTMENT COMPANIES

Investment companies begin like any other company—someone sells an issue of common stock to a group of investors. An investment company, however, uses the proceeds to purchase the securities of other publicly held companies rather than buildings and equipment. An open-end investment company (often referred to as a **mutual fund**) differs from a closed-end investment company (typically referred to as a *closed-end fund*) in the way each operates *after* the initial public offering.

CLOSED-END INVESTMENT COMPANIES

A **closed-end investment company** operates like any other public firm. Its stock trades on the regular secondary market, and the market price of its shares is determined by supply and demand. The typical closed-end investment company offers no further shares and does not repurchase the shares on demand. Thus, if you want to buy or sell shares in a closed-end fund, you must make transactions in the public secondary market. The shares of many of these funds are listed on the NYSE. No new investment dollars are available for the investment company unless it makes another public sale of securities. Similarly, no funds can be withdrawn unless the investment company decides to repurchase its stock, which is quite unusual.

The closed-end investment company's NAV is computed twice daily based on prevailing market prices for the portfolio securities. The *market price* of the investment company shares is determined by the relative supply and demand for the investment company stock in the public secondary market. When buying or selling shares of a closed-end fund, you pay or receive this market price plus or minus a regular trading commission. You should recognize that *the NAV and the market price of a closed-end fund are almost never the same!* Over the long run, the market price of these shares has historically been from 5 to 20 percent below the NAV (i.e., closed-end funds typically sell at a discount to NAV). Figure 26.1 is a list of closed-end stock funds, including general equity funds; specialized equity funds; convertible securities, dual-purpose funds; and world equity funds as quoted in *Barron's*. The figure also contains a listing of closed-end bond funds, including loan participation funds, high-yield bond funds, world income funds, national municipal bond funds, and single state municipal bond funds.

Table 26.1 shows the dramatic growth in the number and value of closed-end stock funds based on new fund issues sales from 1981 to 1995. Another growth indicator is that as of 1986, there were eight diversified common stock funds and 18 specialized and convertible funds listed in *Barron's*. By 1995, the number had grown to 57 general and specialized equity funds, 93 world equity funds, and 16 convertible securities and dual-purpose funds. The growth of closed-end bond funds has been even more dramatic. After many years of relative stability, the number of bond funds listed in *Barron's* has increased from about 20 in 1986 to over 300 in 1995. We discuss several international bond funds later in the chapter.

At the time of the quotes in Figure 26.1, most of the funds were selling at discounts to their NAV. This typical relationship has prompted questions from investors: Why do these funds sell at a discount? Why do the discounts differ between funds? What are the returns available to investors from funds that sell at large discounts? This final question arises

FIGURE 26.1   **CLOSED-END FUNDS**

CLOSED-END FUNDS

Closed-end funds sell a limited number of shares and invest in securities. Unlike open-end mutual funds, closed-ends generally do not buy their shares back from investors who wish to sell. Instead, shares trade on a stock exchange. The following list, provided by Lipper Analytical Services, shows the exchange where each fund trades (A: American; C: Chicago; N: NYSE; O: Nasdaq or other over-the-counter; T: Toronto; z: The fund does not trade on an exchange). The data also include the fund's most recent net asset value, (NAV), as well as its closing share price on the day that NAV was calculated, and the percentage difference between the market price and NAV (commonly known as the premium or discount). For equity funds, the final column provides 52-week returns based on market prices plus dividends; for bond funds, the past 12 months' income distributions as a percentage of the current market price. Footnotes: a: The Net Asset Value and the market price of this closed-end fund are ex dividend. c: NAV, market price and premium or discount are as of Thursday's close. d: NAV market price and premium or discount are as of Wednesday's close. v: NAV is converted at the commercial Rand rate. w: Convertible Note-NAV (not market) conversion value. y: NAV and market price are in Canadian dollars. N/A: Information is not available or is not applicable.

Fund Name	Stock Exch	NAV	Market Price	Prem /Disc	52 week Market Return
Friday, March 22, 1996					
General Equity Funds					
Adams Express	N	22.35	19⅛	−14.4	26.9
Alliance All-Mkt	N	23.30	20⅝	−11.5	34.2
Avalon Capital	O	10.40	9¾	−6.3	N/A
Baker Fentress	N	22.86	18¼	−20.2	29.8
Bergstrom Cap	A	135.76	121¼	−10.3	39.3
Blue Chip Value	N	9.19	8⅜	−8.9	40.1
Central Secs	A	21.83	22⅝	+3.6	43.4
Corp Renaissance -c	O	10.35	8⅞	−14.3	−17.4
Engex	A	17.03	12⅜	−27.3	59.7
Equus II	A	22.98	16⅛	−29.8	43.6
Gabelli Equity	N	10.12	9½	−6.1	8.3
General American	N	25.62	21¾	−15.1	27.2
Inefficient Mkt	A	12.87	10⅝	−17.4	28.3
Librty AllStr Eq	N	11.51	11⅛	−3.3	26.9
Librty AllStr Gr	N	11.16	9⅜	−16.0	19.2
MicroCap Fund	O	N/A	4⅞	0.0	−2.5
Morgan FunShares -c	O	9.94	8⁷⁄₁₆	−15.1	19.1
Morgan Gr Sm Cap	N	12.55	10½	−16.3	38.4
Specialized Equity Funds					
Alliance Gl Env	N	14.61	12	−17.9	39.4
C&S Realty	A	8.90	9½	+6.7	14.4
C&S Total Rtn	N	13.48	13⅜	−0.8	11.3
Centrl Fd Canada -c	A	5.02	5⅛	+2.1	11.0
Counsellors Tand	N	19.09	17½	−8.3	31.1
Delaware Gr Div	N	14.51	15	+3.4	30.2
Delaware Grp Gl	N	14.40	14⅞	+3.3	30.6
Duff&Ph Util Inc	N	8.44	9⅛	+8.1	17.7
Emer Mkts Infra	N	12.68	11	−13.2	20.0
Emer Mkts Tel	N	19.25	16⅞	−12.3	8.2
First Financial	N	13.60	12½	−8.1	31.5
Gabelli Gl Media	N	8.16	6¾	−17.3	1.7
Global Health	N	23.13	18⅛	−21.6	55.9
Convertible Sec's. Funds					
Bancroft Conv	A	26.21	22⅝	−13.7	21.3
Castle Conv	A	28.63	25	−12.7	15.9
Ellsworth Conv	A	11.19	9¹¹⁄₁₆	−13.4	23.0
Gabelli Conv Sec	N	11.25	10¼	−8.9	N/A
Lincoln Conv -c	N	20.25	17¼	−14.8	18.1
Putnam Conv Opp -a	N	26.40	22⅛	−16.2	N/A
Putnam Hi Inc Cv -a	N	9.54	10	+4.8	14.2
TCW Conv Secs	N	8.81	9⅛	+3.6	19.0
VKAC Cv Sec	N	24.59	20⅞	−15.1	17.4
Dual-Purpose Funds					
Conv Hold Cap	N	14.15	12¼	−13.4	30.9
Conv Hold Inc	N	9.59	10⅛	+5.6	12.0
Gemini II Cap	N	28.40	26¼	−7.6	50.9
Gemini II Inc	N	9.39	10⅜	+10.5	12.0
Quest Value Cap	N	36.14	33⅝	−6.3	38.4
Quest Value Inc	N	11.60	11¾	+1.3	8.1
World Equity Funds					
ASA Limited -cv	N	43.56	45⅜	+4.2	3.0
All Seasons Glbl	O	5.21	4	−23.2	6.7
Anchor Gold&Curr	C	6.59	6	−9.0	11.6
Argentina	N	12.40	12⅞	+3.8	21.4
Asia Pacific	N	14.97	14⅜	−4.0	7.4
Asia Tigers	N	13.37	12⅝	−5.6	37.6
Austria	N	10.83	8⅝	−20.4	13.1
BGR Prec Metals -cy	T	23.04	19	−17.5	38.2
Brazil -c	N	22.97	21⅞	−4.8	−2.9
Brazilian Equity -c	N	14.12	14	−0.8	4.7
Cdn Genl Inv -cy	T	47.14	35⅞	−23.9	30.5
Cdn Wrld Fd Ltd -cy	T	5.13	4¼	−17.2	11.8
Central Eur Eqty	N	22.59	17⅞	−20.9	22.7
Chile	N	25.33	23⅝	−6.7	20.6

Fund Name	Stock Exch	NAV	Market Price	Prem /Disc	12 Mo Yield 2/29/96
Loan Participation Funds					
EV Classic Sr -a	z	9.99	N/A	0.0	N/A
EV Prime Rate	z	10.01	N/A	0.0	N/A
Merrill Sen Fl	z	10.01	N/A	0.0	N/A
Pilgrim Pr Rate	N	9.59	9⅜	−2.2	9.0
Prime Income	z	9.99	N/A	0.0	N/A
VKAC Prime	z	N/A	N/A	0.0	N/A
High Yield Bond Funds					
CIGNA High Inc	N	7.26	8	+10.2	10.3
CIM High Yld	N	7.36	7¾	+5.3	10.1
Colonial Intmdt	N	6.77	7	+3.4	9.9
Corp Hi Yld	N	13.63	13⅝	0.0	10.7
Corp Hi Yld II	N	12.62	12⅜	−1.9	10.7
Franklin Univ -c	N	9.66	8⅞	−8.1	9.2
High Inc Adv	N	5.27	5¾	+9.1	10.2
High Inc Adv II	N	5.96	6	+0.7	10.9
High Inc Adv III	N	6.36	6⅞	+8.1	10.3
High Inc Opp	N	11.61	11	−5.3	9.9
High Yld Income	N	7.24	7⅞	+8.8	11.0
High Yld Plus	N	8.51	8⅞	+4.3	9.9
Kemper High Inc	N	8.86	9½	+7.2	9.4
World Income Funds					
Americas Inc Tr -c	N	8.14	6⅞	−15.5	0.7
BlckRk North Am -c	N	11.14	9½	−14.7	1.5
Dreyfus Str Govt	N	10.38	9⅛	−12.1	8.2
Emer Mkts Float	N	13.85	13½	−2.5	12.2
Emer Mkts Inc	N	15.53	15⅞	+2.2	10.5
Emer Mkts Inc II	N	12.42	13½	+8.7	12.3
First Aust Prime	A	9.44	8¹¹⁄₁₆	−5.3	9.1
First Commonwlth	N	13.02	11⅝	−10.7	8.8
Global Hi Inc $ -a	N	12½		0.0	10.0
Kleinwort Aust	N	10.06	9¼	−6.8	9.5
Lat Am $ Income	N	12.95	13¼	+2.3	11.3
Morg St Em Debt	N	13.14	13½	+2.7	12.8
Morgan St Glbl	N	13.43	13¼	−1.3	12.1
Op Fd Multi-Gov	N	8.01	7¼	−11.0	8.7
Salomon SBG	N	8.37	8⅜	+0.1	10.2
Salomon SBW	N	12.46	12⅝	+1.3	11.1
National Muni Bond Funds					
ACM Muni Secs	N	12.31	13	+5.6	6.3
Amer Muni Income -c	N	13.37	12⅛	−9.3	6.6
Amer Muni Tm II -c	N	11.35	10⅝	−6.4	5.7
Amer Muni Tm III -c	N	10.63	10⅜	−2.4	6.5
Amer Muni Tm Tr -c	N	11.55	11	−4.8	5.8
Apex Muni	N	10.01	9¼	−8.8	7.3
BlckRk Ins 2008	N	15.60	14	−10.3	6.2
BlckRk Ins Muni	N	10.71	10	−6.6	6.1
BlckRk Inv Q Mun	N	14.21	12¼	−13.8	6.4
BlckRk Muni Tgt	N	10.87	10¼	−6.9	5.4
Colonial Hi Inc	N	8.35	8¼	−2.7	7.2
Colonial Inv Gr	N	10.60	10	−5.7	6.2
Single State Muni Bond					
BlckRk CA Ins 08	N	15.42	14	−9.2	6.0
BlckRk CA Inv	A	13.71	12¾	−7.0	6.1
BlckRk FL Ins 08	N	15.53	15	−3.4	5.7
BlckRk FL Inv	N	13.70	12¾	−6.9	6.0
BlckRk NJ Inv	A	13.14	11⅝	−11.5	6.2
BlckRk NY Ins 08	N	15.61	14¾	−5.5	5.8
BlckRk NY Inv	A	13.48	12¾	−5.4	6.2
Dreyfus CA Inc	A	9.31	8⁹⁄₁₆	−10.7	6.1
Dreyfus NY Inc	A	9.95	10¼	+3.0	5.7
Greenwich St CA	A	13.20	11¾	−11.0	5.9
InterCap CA Ins	N	13.12	11½	−12.3	6.2
InterCap CA Qual	N	12.53	10⅞	−13.2	6.4
InterCap Ins CA	N	14.69	13½	−8.1	5.3
InterCap NY Qual	N	12.74	11¼	−10.7	6.3

TABLE 26.1

NUMBER OF CLOSED-END FUND INITIAL PUBLIC OFFERINGS AND NEW FUNDS RAISED

Year	Number of Funds	Amount Raised
1981	1	$ 62 million
1982	0	—
1983	4	58 million
1984	4	106 million
1985	3	614 million
1986	28	5 billion
1987	34	9 billion
1988	66	20 billion
1989	39	9 billion
1990	38	6 billion
1991	43	11 billion
1992	98	18 billion
1993	126	19 billion
1994	41	7 billion
1995	3	480 million

Source: Thomas J. Herzfeld Advisors, Inc., P.O. Box 161465, Miami, Florida 33116. Reprinted by permission of Thomas J. Herzfeld Advisors, Inc.

because an investor who acquires a portfolio at a price below market value (i.e., below NAV) expects an above-average dividend yield. Still, the total rate of return on the fund depends on what happens to the discount during the holding period. If the discount relative to the NAV declines, the investment should generate positive excess returns. If the discount increases, the investor will likely experience negative excess returns. The analysis of these discounts remains a major question of modern finance.[1]

CLOSED-END FUND INDEX   The interest in closed-end funds has led Thomas J. Herzfeld Advisors, a firm that specializes in closed-end funds, to create an index that tracks the market price performance of a sample of U.S. closed-end funds that invest principally in U.S. equities. The following is a list of the funds in the average:

- The Adams Express Company
- Baker, Fentress and Company
- Bergstrom Capital Corporation
- Blue Chip Value Fund, Inc.
- Central Securities Corporation
- The Charles Allmon Trust, Inc.
- Engex, Inc.
- The Gabelli Equity Trust, Inc.
- General American Investors Company, Inc.
- The Inefficient-Market Fund, Inc.

---

[1] Studies over the years include Charles Lee, Andrei Shleifer, and Richard Thaler, "Investor Sentiment and the Closed-End Fund Puzzle," *Journal of Finance* 46, no. 1 (March 1991): 76–110; Michael Barclay, Clifford Holderness, and Jeffrey Pontiff, "Private Benefits from Block Ownership and Discounts on Closed-End Funds," *Journal of Financial Economics* 33, no. 3 (June 1993): 263–292; and Burton Malkiel, "The Structure of Closed-End Fund Discounts Revisited," *Journal of Portfolio Management* 21, no. 4 (Summer 1995): 32–38. For a discussion of bond funds, see Malcolm Richards, Donald Fraser, and John Groth, "The Attractions of Closed-End Bond Funds," *Journal of Portfolio Management* 8, no. 2 (Winter 1982): 56–61. For a discussion of performance and opportunities in closed-end funds, see Thomas J. Herzfeld, "Battered Beauties?" *Barron's*, August 13, 1990, and Thomas J. Herzfeld, "Finding Value in Closed-End Funds," *Investment Advisor*, July 1990.

FIGURE 26.2   **HERZFELD CLOSED-END FUND AVERAGE**

The Herzfeld Closed-End Average measures 17 equally-weighted closed-end funds based in the U.S. that invest principally in American equities. The net asset value is a weighted average of the funds' NAVs. *The net asset value and % discount charts lag the market by one week. Source: Thomas J. Herzfeld Advisors Inc., Miami. 305-271-1900

Source: *Barron's,* April 1, 1996. Copyright © 1996 Dow Jones & Company, Inc. Reprinted by permission of Barron's. All Rights Reserved Worldwide.

- Liberty All-Star Equity Fund
- Morgan Grenfell SMALLCap Fund, Inc.
- Royce Value Trust
- The Salomon Brothers Fund, Inc.
- Source Capital Inc.
- Tri-Continental Corporation
- The Zweig Fund, Inc.

The funds are listed on either the NYSE or AMEX, and one trades on NASDAQ. The price-weighted index is based on fund market values rather than NAVs. In addition to its market price index, Herzfeld also computes the average discount from NAV. The graph in Figure 26.2 indicates that the average discount from NAV changes over time and has a major impact on the market performance of the index. For example, during the first quarter of 1996, the average discount increased to almost 12 percent. As a result, the performance of the Herzfeld closed-end average during this quarter was relatively flat, although the DJIA was increasing steadily.

OPEN-END INVESTMENT COMPANIES **Open-end investment companies,** or mutual funds, continue to sell and repurchase shares after their initial public offerings. They stand ready to sell additional shares of the fund at the NAV, with or without sales charge, or to buy back (redeem) shares of the fund at the NAV, with or without redemption fees.

Open-end investment companies have enjoyed substantial growth since World War II, as shown by the figures in Table 26.2. Clearly, open-end funds account for a substantial portion of invested assets, and they provide a very important service for almost 54 million accounts.

TABLE 26.2

OPEN-END INVESTMENT COMPANIES: NUMBER AND VALUE OF ASSETS: 1945–1995

	Number of Reporting Funds	Assets ($Billions)		Number of Reporting Funds	Assets ($Billions)
1945	73	$ 1.3	1985	1,071	$ 251.7
1950	98	2.5	1986	1,356	424.2
1955	125	7.8	1987	1,781	453.8
1960	161	17.0	1988	2,109	472.3
1965	170	35.2	1989	2,253	553.9
1970	361	47.6	1990	2,362	568.5
1975	390	42.2	1991	2,603	853.1
1980	458	58.4	1992	2,984	1,100.1
1981	486	55.2	1993	3,638	1,510.1
1982	539	76.8	1994	4,394	1,550.5
1983	653	113.6	1995	4,764	2,067.3
1984	820	137.8			

Note: Does not include money market and short-term bond funds.

Sources: *1975 Mutual Fund Fact Book, 1981 Mutual Fund Fact Book,* and *1996 Mutual Fund Fact Book* (Washington D.C.: Investment Company Institute). Reprinted by permission of Investment Company Institute.

LOAD VERSUS NO-LOAD OPEN-END FUNDS   One distinction of open-end funds is that some charge a sales fee for share sales. The offering price for a share of a *load fund* equals the NAV of the share plus a sales charge, which typically is 7.5 to 8.0 percent of the NAV. A fund with an 8 percent sales charge (load) would give an individual who invested $1,000 shares in the fund that are worth $920. Such funds generally charge no redemption fee, which means the shares can be redeemed at their NAV. These funds typically are quoted with an NAV and an offering price. The NAV price is the redemption (bid) price, and the offering (ask) price equals the NAV divided by 1.0 minus the percent load. For example, if the NAV of a fund with an 8 percent load is $8.50 a share, the offering price would be $9.24 ($8.50/0.92). The 74-cent differential is really 8.7 percent of the NAV. The load percentage typically declines with the size of the order.

A **no-load fund** imposes no initial sales charge so it sells shares at their NAV. Some of these funds charge a small redemption fee of about one-half of 1 percent. In *The Wall Street Journal,* quotes for these no-load funds list bid prices as the NAV with the designation "NL" (no-load) for the offering price, i.e., the bid and offer are the same.

The number of no-load funds has increased substantially in recent years. *The Wall Street Journal* lists more than 350 no-load funds, and *Barron's* lists more than 800. A directory of no-load funds is available from an industry association.[2]

Between the full-load fund and the pure no-load fund, several important variations exist. The first is the **low-load fund,** which imposes a front-end sales charge when the fund is bought, but it is typically in the 3 percent range rather than 7 to 8 percent. Generally, low-load funds are used for bond funds or equity funds offered by management companies that also offer no-load funds. For example, most Fidelity Management funds were no-load prior to 1985, but several of their newer funds have carried a low load of 3 percent. Alternatively, some funds—previously charging full loads—have reduced their loads.

The second major innovation is the **12b-1 plan,** named after a 1980 SEC ruling. This plan permits funds to deduct as much as 1.25 percent of average net assets *per year* to cover

---

[2] No-Load Mutual Fund Association, Inc., 11 Penn Plaza, New York, NY 10001. The cost of the directory is $10.

distribution costs such as advertising, brokers' commissions, and general marketing expenses. A large and growing number of no-load funds are adopting these plans, as are a few low-load funds. You can determine if a fund has a 12b-1 plan only by reading the prospectus or using an investment service that reports charges in substantial detail.

Finally, some funds have instituted **contingent, deferred sales loads** in which a sales fee is charged when the fund is sold if it is held for less than some time period, perhaps 3 or 4 years.

FUND MANAGEMENT FEES

In addition to selling charges (loads or 12b-1 charges), all investment firms charge annual **management fees** to compensate professional managers of the fund. Such a fee typically is a percentage of the average net assets of the fund varying from about 0.25 to 1.00 percent. Most of these management fees are on sliding scales that decline with the size of the fund. For example, a fund with assets under $1 billion might charge 1 percent, funds with assets between $1 billion and $5 billion might charge 0.50 percent, and those over $5 billion would charge 0.25 percent.

These management fees are a major factor driving the creation of new funds. More assets under management generate more fees, but the costs of management do not increase at the same rate as the managed assets because substantial economies of scale exist in managing financial assets. Once the research staff and management structure have been established, the incremental costs do not rise in line with the assets under management. For example, the cost of managing $1 billion of assets is *not* twice the cost of managing $500 million.

TYPES OF INVESTMENT COMPANIES BASED ON PORTFOLIO MAKEUP

COMMON STOCK FUNDS

Some funds invest almost solely in common stocks; others invest in preferred stocks, bonds, and so forth. Within common stock funds, wide differences are found in emphasis, including funds that focus on growth companies, small cap stocks, companies in specific industries (e.g., Chemical Fund, Oceanography Fund), certain classes of industry (e.g., Technology Fund), or even geographic areas (such as the Northeast Fund or international funds). Different common stock funds can suit almost any taste or investment objective. Therefore, you must decide whether you want a fund that invests only in common stock; then you must consider the type of common stock you desire.

BALANCED FUNDS

Balanced funds diversify outside the stock market by combining common stock with fixed-income securities, including government bonds, corporate bonds, convertible bonds, or preferred stock. The ratio of stocks to fixed-income securities will vary by fund, as stated in each fund's prospectus.

BOND FUNDS

Bond funds concentrate on various types of bonds to generate high current income with minimal risk. They are similar to common stock funds; however, their investment policies differ. Some funds concentrate on U.S. government or high-grade corporate bonds, others hold a mixture of investment-grade bonds, and some concentrate on high-yield (junk) bonds. Management strategies also can differ, ranging from buy-and-hold to extensive trading of the portfolio bonds.

In addition to government, mortgage, and corporate bond funds, a change in the tax law in 1976 caused the creation of numerous municipal bond funds. These funds provide investors with monthly interest payments that are exempt from federal income taxes, although some of the interest may be subject to state and local taxes. To avoid the state tax, some municipal bond funds concentrate on bonds from specific states such as the New

TABLE 26.3	STATISTICS ON MONEY MARKET FUNDS			
	Total Number of Funds	Total Accounts Outstanding	Average Maturity (Days)	Total Net Assets ($Millions)
1975	36	208,777	93	$ 3,695.7
1980	96	4,745,572	24	74,447.7
1985	348	14,425,386	42	207,535.3
1986	360	15,653,595	40	228,345.8
1987	389	16,832,666	31	254,676.4
1988	432	17,630,528	28	272,293.3
1989	463	20,173,265	38	358,719.2
1990	508	21,577,559	41	414,733.3
1991	553	21,863,351	50	452,559.2
1992	585	21,770,692	51	451,353.4
1993	628	21,586,862	49	461,903.9
1994	644	23,338,196	34	500,427.8
1995	672	27,852,374	52	629,729.1

Source: *1996 Mutual Fund Fact Book* (Washington, D.C.: Investment Company Institute). Reprinted by permission of Investment Company Institute.

York Municipal Bond Fund, which allows New York residents to avoid most state taxes on the interest income.

MONEY MARKET FUNDS

Money market funds were initiated during 1973 when short-term interest rates were at record levels. These funds attempt to provide current income, safety of principal, and liquidity by investing in diversified portfolios of short-term securities such as Treasury bills, banker certificates of deposit, bank acceptances, and commercial paper. They typically are no-load funds and impose no penalty for early withdrawal. Also, they generally allow holders to write checks against their account.[3] Table 26.3 documents the significant growth of these funds. Changes in their growth rate usually are associated with investor attitudes toward the stock market. When investors are bullish toward stocks, they withdraw funds from their money market accounts to invest; when they are uncertain, they shift from stocks to the money funds. Because of the interest in money market funds, Monday editions of *The Wall Street Journal* provide a special section within the mutual fund section titled "Money Market Funds."

BREAKDOWN BY FUND CHARACTERISTICS

Table 26.4 groups funds by their method of sale and by investment objectives. The two major means of distribution are (1) by a sales force and (2) by direct purchase from the fund or direct marketing. Sales forces would include brokers such as Merrill Lynch, commission-based financial planners, or dedicated sales forces such as those of IDS Financial. Almost all mutual funds acquired from these individuals charge sales fees (loads) from which salespeople are compensated.

Investors typically purchase shares of directly marketed funds through the mail, telephone, bankwire, or an office of the fund. These direct sales funds usually impose a low sales charge or none at all. In the past, because they had no sales fee, they had to be sold

---

[3] For a list of names and addresses of money market funds, write to Investment Company Institute, 1775 K Street N.W., Washington, DC 20006. A service that concentrates on money market funds is *Donoghue's Money Letter,* 770 Washington Street, Holliston, MA 01746. An analysis of performance is contained in Michael G. Ferri and H. Dennis Oberhelman, "How Well Do Money Market Funds Perform?" *Journal of Portfolio Management* 7, no. 3 (Spring 1981) 18–26.

TABLE 26.4   **TOTAL NET ASSETS BY FUND CHARACTERISTICS ($MILLIONS)**

	1995		1994		1993		1992	
	Dollars	Percent	Dollars	Percent	Dollars	Percent	Dollars	Percent
Total net assets	$2,067,337.3	100.0	$1,550,490.4	100.0	$1,510,047.3	100.0	$1,056,310.0	100.0
Method of Sale								
Sales force	1,117,451.5	54.1	878,546.1	56.6	876,474.4	58.0	659,446.7	62.4
Direct marketing	700,727.3	33.9	505,324.0	32.6	487,811.4	32.3	341,588.0	32.3
Variable annuity	247,753.0	12.0	165,492.6	10.7	144,566.6	9.6	53,776.0	5.1
Not offering shares	1,405.5	0.0	1,127.7	0.1	1,194.9	0.1	1,479.3	0.2
Investment Objective								
Aggressive growth	190,822.3	9.2	110,407.1	7.7	123,734.5	8.2	83,365.3	7.9
Growth	354,235.0	17.1	228,761.2	14.8	167,145.2	11.1	133,175.3	12.6
Growth and income	429,202.7	20.8	292,906.1	18.9	276,952.0	18.3	168,321.0	15.9
Precious metals	4,727.5	0.2	5,237.8	0.3	5,564.6	0.4	2,143.8	0.2
International	120,736.3	5.8	101,744.6	6.6	71,024.8	4.7	22,916.5	2.2
Global equity	76,001.6	3.8	60,175.6	3.9	43,269.7	2.9	22,987.4	2.2
Flexible portfolio	52,435.9	2.5	44,338.3	2.9	34,973.6	2.3	14,836.8	1.4
Balanced	81,288.0	3.9	59,209.6	3.8	58,031.2	3.8	31,865.2	3.0
Income equity	93,314.1	4.5	67,215.9	4.3	61,262.5	4.1	42,466.5	4.0
Income—mixed	77,404.4	3.7	57,939.5	3.7	53,934.3	3.6	34,720.7	3.3
Income—bond	66,111.2	3.2	53,038.7	3.4	55,467.1	3.7	39,742.6	3.8
U.S. government income	87,926.7	4.3	86,950.4	5.6	116,448.7	7.7	120,067.4	11.4
Ginnie Mae	55,257.0	2.7	53,695.6	3.5	73,200.5	4.9	57,513.4	5.4
Global bond	33,412.3	1.6	31,395.6	2.0	38,235.2	2.5	31,633.5	3.0
Corporate bond	31,731.9	1.5	25,217.6	1.6	27,517.1	1.8	20,033.3	1.9
High-yield bond	59,715.9	2.9	45,055.7	2.9	48,708.5	3.2	34,258.6	3.2
Long-term municipal bond	135,789.0	6.6	122,400.6	7.9	140,999.4	9.3	110,846.4	10.5
Long-term state municipal bond	117,225.5	5.7	104,800.2	6.8	113,578.4	7.5	85,416.3	8.1

Sources: *1995 Mutual Fund Fact Book* and *1996 Mutual Fund Fact Book* (Washington, DC.: Investment Company Institute). Reprinted by permission of Investment Company Institute.

directly because a broker had no incentive to sell a no-load fund. This has changed recently because some brokerage firms, most notably Charles Schwab & Co., have developed agreements with specific no-load funds whereby they will sell these funds to their clients and collect a fee from the fund. As of April 1996, Schwab had a list of about 300 funds that they would sell no-load, no-fee, plus another 750 that were no-load, but Schwab charged a small transaction fee. As seen in Table 26.4, the division between these two major distribution channels is currently about 54 to 34 percent in favor of the sales force method, although there has been a steady shift toward direct marketing. Given the investor preference for no-load funds and the increasing availability through firms like Charles Schwab, this trend toward direct marketed funds should continue.

The breakdown by investment objective indicates the investment companies' response to a shift in investor emphasis. The growth of an alternative investment objective category reflects not only the overall growth of the industry, but also the creation of new funds in response to the evolving demands of investors. For example, aggressive growth, growth, and growth and income funds have continued to grow and generally increased their percentages. The growing desire for international diversification that is heavily espoused in this book is reflected in strong relative growth in international and global equity funds.[4]

PERFORMANCE OF INVESTMENT COMPANIES

A number of studies have examined the historical performance of mutual funds because (1) these funds reflect the performance of professional money managers and (2) data on the funds are available for a long period. Two of the three major portfolio evaluation techniques that are discussed in Chapter 27 were derived in connection with mutual fund performance studies.

ANALYSIS OF OVERALL PERFORMANCE

When Sharpe evaluated the performance of mutual funds for a total period, only 32 percent of the funds outperformed the DJIA.[5] Further, comparing the ranks of the funds between the first and second half of the sample period led Sharpe to conclude that past performance was not the best predictor of future performance.

An examination of the relationship between performance and the expense ratio indicated that good performance was associated with low expense ratios. Finally, analysis of *gross* performance, with expenses added back to the returns, indicated that 56 percent of the funds did better than the DJIA. Therefore, Sharpe concluded that the average mutual fund manager selected a portfolio at least as good as the DJIA, but after deducting the operating costs of the fund, most achieved *net* returns below those of the DJIA.

The results of a study by Jensen indicated that on average the funds earned 1.1 percent less per year than they should have earned for their level of risk.[6] Analysis of gross returns with expenses added back indicated that 42 percent did better than the overall market on a risk-adjusted basis, whereas the analysis of net returns indicated that only 34 percent of the funds outperformed the market. The gross returns indicate the forecasting ability of the funds because these results do not penalize the funds for operating expenses (only brokerage commissions). Jensen concluded that on average these funds could not beat a buy-and-hold policy.

Mains questioned several of Jensen's estimates, which apparently biased the results against mutual funds.[7] After adjusting for these biases, he contended that the net returns indicated neutral performance, whereas the gross returns indicated that most fund managers outperformed the market.

Carlson examined the overall performance of mutual funds with emphasis on the effects of the market series used for comparison and the time period.[8] The results depended heavily on which market series were used: the S&P 500, the NYSE composite, or the DJIA. For the total period, most fund groups outperformed the DJIA, but only a few had gross returns better than the S&P 500 or the NYSE composite. Using net returns, *none* of the groups outperformed the S&P 500 or the NYSE composite. Analysis of the perfor-

---

[4] International funds only invest in non-U.S. stocks or bonds, whereas global funds can invest in securities from anywhere in the world, including the United States.

[5] William F. Sharpe, "Mutual Fund Performance," *Journal of Business* 39, no. 1, Part 2 (January 1966): 119–138.

[6] Michael C. Jensen, "The Performance of Mutual Funds in the Period 1945–1964," *Journal of Finance* 23, no. 2 (May 1968): 389–416.

[7] Norman E. Mains, "Risk, the Pricing of Capital Assets, and the Evaluation of Investment Portfolios: Comment," *Journal of Business* 50, no. 3 (July 1977): 371–384.

[8] Robert S. Carlson, "Aggregate Performance of Mutual Funds, 1948–1967," *Journal of Financial and Quantitative Analysis* 5, no. 1 (March 1970): 1–32.

mance factors indicated consistency over time for return or risk alone, but no consistency in the risk-adjusted performance. Less than one-third of the funds that performed above average during the first half did so in the second half. Lehmann and Modest likewise found substantial differences between benchmarks, but also concluded that average performance was consistently inferior to the overall market performance.[9] A study by Grinblatt and Titman examined performance using portfolio holdings which does not require a market benchmark.[10] Notably, using this technique they find that portfolio managers who manage aggressive growth stocks earned significantly positive risk-adjusted returns during 1976–1985.

All of the early studies were concerned with evaluating the performance of U.S. equity funds. Given the growing tendency toward global stock and bond investing, several authors have examined the performance of international equity and fixed income funds.

Cumby and Glen examined the performance of international funds compared to the Morgan Stanley world equity index and a U.S. index.[11] Using two risk-adjusted performance measures, they found no evidence that the performance of the funds surpassed that of a broad international index during the sample period. Bailey and Lim examined the performance of country funds (e.g., France, Germany, Korea, Spain) to see if these funds helped investors attain international diversification.[12] They found that country fund returns often resembled domestic U.S. stock returns more than returns from foreign stock portfolios, that is, these funds would not provide the expected benefits of diversification.

Blake, Elton, and Gruber examined the performance of bond mutual funds and found that the bond funds generally underperformed relevant bond indexes.[13] Because the underperformance was about equal to the management fees, it is suggested that these funds performed about equal to the indexes—before expenses. They also found no evidence that past performance could predict future performance.

Cornell and Green examined the performance of low-grade (high yield) bond funds and found that the returns on low-grade bond funds for the total period were about equal to the return on high-grade bonds.[14] They used a two-factor risk model that allowed for the impact of interest rates and stock returns. After adjusting for risk using this two-factor model, they concluded that the returns on low-grade bonds were not statistically different from the returns on high-grade bonds.

IMPACT OF FUND OBJECTIVES

A fund investor needs to know whether the fund's performance is consistent with its stated objective. For example, does the performance of a balanced fund reflect less risk and lower return than an aggressive growth fund? To answer this, several studies have examined the relationship between funds' stated objective and their measures of risk and return.

---

[9] Bruce N. Lehmann and David M. Modest, "Mutual Fund Performance Evaluations: A Comparison of Benchmarks and Benchmark Comparisons," *Journal of Finance* 42, no. 2 (June 1987): 233–265.

[10] Mark Grinblatt and Sheridan Titman, "Performance Measurement without Benchmarks: An Examination of Mutual Fund Returns," *Journal of Business* 66, no. 1 (January 1993): 47–68.

[11] Robert E. Cumby and Jack D. Glen, "Evaluating the Performance of International Mutual Funds," *Journal of Finance* 45, no. 2 (June 1990): 497–522.

[12] Warren Bailey and Joseph Lim, "Evaluating the Diversification Benefits of the New Country Funds," *Journal of Portfolio Management* 18, no. 3 (Spring 1992): 74–80.

[13] Christopher R. Blake, Edwin J. Elton, and Martin J. Gruber, "The Performance of Bond Mutual Funds," *The Journal of Business* 66, no. 3 (July 1993): 371–403.

[14] Bradford Cornell and Kevin Green, "The Investment Performance of Low-Grade Bond Funds," *Journal of Finance* 46, no. 1 (March 1991): 29–48.

McDonald examined the overall performance of a sample of mutual funds relative to their stated objectives and found a positive relationship between stated objectives and measures of risk, with risk measures increasing as objectives become more aggressive.[15] Beyond finding a positive relationship between return and risk, the risk-adjusted performance indicated that the more aggressive funds outperformed the more conservative funds during this period. Martin, Keown, and Farrell examined mutual funds representing five investment objectives and found definite differences in the abnormal variability for the funds in alternative classifications.[16]

MARKET TIMING
ABILITY

As noted, one way to achieve superior performance is through market timing wherein you invest aggressively prior to strong markets and become very conservative prior to weak or declining markets. Several studies have examined the ability of fund portfolio managers to increase the relative volatility of their portfolios in anticipation of a bull market and reduce its volatility prior to a bear market. The results of these studies indicated that the funds were not able to time market changes and change risk levels accordingly.[17] Veit and Cheney concluded that mutual funds do not successfully alter their risk characteristics *consistently* with timing strategies.[18] In fact, no change occurred in the characteristic lines over the market cycle.

Kon and Jen examined the ability of mutual funds to time the market and select undervalued securities.[19] Although many of the funds experienced a significant change in risk during the test period (implying superior timing ability), no individual fund *consistently* generated superior results. Shawky found that risk was consistent with fund objectives, but most funds had inferior performance although it appeared that the funds improved the diversification of their portfolios.[20]

Chang and Lewellen tested for market timing ability and found little successful market forecasting.[21] After finding neither skillful market timing nor clever security selection, they concurred with the conclusion of prior studies that mutual funds cannot outperform a passive investment strategy.

When Henriksson tested for the ability to enjoy consistent success, he found little evidence of market timing ability, and the results for each fund for two subperiods were independent.[22] He found that managers could not forecast large changes, and those who were good at stock selection apparently had negative market timing ability. Chan and Chen analyzed the timing performance of asset allocation funds and found no evidence of market

---

[15] John G. McDonald, "Objectives and Performance of Mutual Funds, 1960–1969," *Journal of Financial and Quantitative Analysis* 9, no. 3 (June 1974): 311–333.

[16] John D. Martin, Arthur J. Keown, Jr., and James L. Farrell, "Do Fund Objectives Affect Diversification Policies?" *Journal of Portfolio Management* 8, no. 2 (Winter 1982): 19–28.

[17] Jack L. Treynor and Kay K. Mazuy, "Can Mutual Funds Outguess the Market?" *Harvard Business Review* 44, no. 4 (July–August 1966): 131–136; and Frank J. Fabozzi and Jack C. Francis, "Mutual Fund Systematic Risk for Bull and Bear Markets," *Journal of Finance* 34, no. 5 (December 1979): 1242–1250.

[18] E. Theodore Veit and John M. Cheney, "Are Mutual Funds Market Timers?" *Journal of Portfolio Management* 8, no. 2 (Winter 1982): 35–42.

[19] Stanley J. Kon and Frank C. Jen, "The Investment Performance of Mutual Funds: An Empirical Investigation of Timing, Selectivity, and Market Efficiency," *Journal of Business* 52, no. 2 (April 1979): 263–289.

[20] Hany A. Shawky, "An Update on Mutual Funds: Better Grades," *Journal of Portfolio Management* 8, no. 2 (Winter 1982): 29–34.

[21] Eric C. Chang and Wilbur G. Lewellen, "Market Timing and Mutual Fund Investment Performance," *Journal of Business* 57, no. 1, Part 1 (January 1984): 57–72.

[22] Roy D. Henriksson, "Market Timing and Mutual Fund Performance: An Empirical Investigation," *Journal of Business* 57, no. 1, Part 1 (January 1984): 73–96.

timing abilities.[23] Also, the total performance of these funds suggested inferior performance compared to the benchmark portfolio.

CONSISTENCY OF
PERFORMANCE

Although several studies have considered consistency along with overall performances, some studies have concentrated on it. When Klemkosky examined rankings of risk-adjusted performance for adjacent time periods, he found some consistency between the 4-year periods, but relatively low consistency between the adjacent 2-year periods.[24] Klemkosky concluded that investors should not use past performance to predict short-run future performance.

Dunn and Theisen examined institutional portfolios over a 10-year period looking for consistent success.[25] After finding that historical results give little help in explaining future results, they concluded that historical performance should be given very little weight when selecting a manager. Ang and Chua examined the consistency of performance of funds with different objectives and found that various funds met their stated objectives, but they did not do it consistently.[26]

In contrast to these past studies, several more recent studies have found persistence in fund performance. Grinblatt and Titman used a multiple portfolio benchmark and found that differences between funds persisted over time and therefore, past performance is useful information.[27] Similarly, Hendricks, Patel, and Zeckhauser found persistence in the short run in terms of relative performance with the strongest evidence for a one-year evaluation horizon.[28] Rather than examine calendar periods, Bauman and Miller attempted to predict performance rankings when the measurement period encompassed full stock market cycles.[29] They found the correlations of portfolio performance rankings from one full market cycle to the next was positive and meaningful. Brown and Goetzmann examined performance persistence with specific concern for survivorship bias.[30] They found evidence of performance persistence, but acknowledged that it was strongly dependent on the time period of study and also correlation across winning funds due to common themes. Elton, Gruber, and Blake also found evidence of persistent performance, and this is repeated in Gruber.[31] Finally, Malkiel provides very insightful mixed results.[32] Specifically, he found evidence of performance

[23] Anthony Chan and Carl R. Chen, "How Well Do Asset Allocation Mutual Fund Managers Allocate Assets?" *Journal of Portfolio Management* 18, no. 3 (Spring 1992): 81–91.

[24] Robert C. Klemkosky, "How Consistently Do Managers Manage?" *Journal of Portfolio Management* 3, no. 2 (Winter 1977): 11–15.

[25] Patricia C. Dunn and Rolf D. Theisen, "How Consistently Do Active Managers Win?" *Journal of Portfolio Management* 9, no. 4 (Summer 1983): 47–50.

[26] James S. Ang and Jess H. Chua, "Mutual Funds: Different Strokes for Different Folks?" *Journal of Portfolio Management* 8, no. 2 (Winter 1982): 43–47.

[27] Mark Grinblatt and Sheridan Titman, "The Persistence of Mutual Fund Performance," *Journal of Finance* 47, no. 5 (December 1992): 1977–1984.

[28] Darryl Hendricks, Jayendu Patel, and Richard Zeckhauser, "Hot Hands in Mutual Funds: Short-Run Persistence of Relative Performance, 1974–1988," *Journal of Finance* 48, no. 1 (March 1993): 93–130.

[29] W. Scott Bauman and Robert E. Miller, "Can Managed Portfolio Performance Be Predicted?" *Journal of Portfolio Management* 20, no. 4 (Summer 1994): 31–40.

[30] Stephen J. Brown and William N. Goetzmann, "Performance Persistence," *Journal of Finance* 50, no. 2 (June 1995): 679–698.

[31] Edwin Elton, Martin J. Gruber and Christopher Blake, "The Persistence of Risk-Adjusted Mutual Fund Performance," *Journal of Business* 69, no. 2 (April 1996): 133–157; and Martin J. Gruber, "Another Puzzle: The Growth in Actively Managed Mutual Funds," *Journal of Finance* 51, no. 3 (July 1996): 783–809.

[32] Barton G. Malkiel, "Returns from Investing in Equity Mutual Funds: 1971 to 1991," *Journal of Finance* 50, no. 2 (June 1995): 549–572.

persistence in the 1970s, but the persistence rules did *not* work during the 1980s. Notably, these time period effects are consistent with Brown and Goetzmann.

WHAT PERFORMANCE
STUDIES MEAN TO YOU
What functions would you want your own personal portfolio manager to perform for you? The list would probably include:

1. Determine your risk–return preferences and develop a portfolio that is consistent with them.
2. Diversify your portfolio to eliminate unsystematic risk.
3. Maintain your portfolio diversification and your desired risk class while allowing flexibility so you could shift between alternative investment instruments as desired.
4. Attempt to achieve a risk-adjusted performance that is superior to aggregate market performance. As noted, this can be done either by consistently selecting undervalued stocks or by superior asset allocation that is properly timed for markets around the world. Some investors may be willing to sacrifice diversification for superior returns in limited segments of their portfolios.
5. Administer the account, keep records of costs, provide timely information for tax purposes, and reinvest dividends if desired.

Although the performance studies typically reviewed only risk-adjusted performance, all of these functions should be considered to put performance into perspective. Therefore, let us consider each of these functions and discuss how mutual funds fulfill them.

Mutual funds do not determine your risk preference. However, once you determine your risk–return preferences, you can choose a mutual fund from a large and growing variety of alternative funds designed to meet almost any investment goal. Recall that the empirical studies indicated that the funds generally were consistent in meeting their stated goals for investment strategies, risk, and returns.

Diversifying your portfolio to eliminate unsystematic risk is one of the major benefits of mutual funds. They provide *instant diversification*. This is especially beneficial to small investors who do not have the resources to acquire 100 shares of 10 or 12 different issues required to reduce unsystematic risk. By initiating an investment in a fund with about $1,000 you can participate in a portfolio of securities that is correlated about 0.90 with the market portfolio, which means that it is about 90 percent diversified. Although diversification varies among funds, typically about three-quarters of the funds have a correlation with the market above 0.90. Therefore, most funds provide excellent diversification, especially if they state this as an objective.

The third function of your portfolio manager is to maintain the diversification and your desired risk class. It is not too surprising that mutual funds have generally maintained the stability of their correlation with the market because few change the makeup of reasonably well-diversified portfolios substantially. Strong evidence exists regarding the consistency of the risk class for individual funds even when there was inconsistency in risk-adjusted performance.

Mutual funds have met the desire for flexibility to change investment instruments by the initiation of numerous funds within a given management company. Typically, investment groups such as T. Rowe Price or Fidelity Investments will allow you to shift among their funds without a charge simply by calling the fund. Therefore, you can shift among an aggressive stock fund, a money market fund, and a bond fund for much less than it would cost you in time and money to buy and sell numerous individual issues.

The fourth function of your portfolio manager is to provide risk-adjusted performance that is superior to the aggregate market, which implies that it is superior to a naive buy-and-hold policy. As indicated in the prior discussion, the majority of empirical evidence indicates that on average fund managers' results in selecting undervalued securities or timing the market are about as good as, or only slightly better than, the results of a naive buy-and-hold policy. This conclusion is based on *gross* returns. Unfortunately, the evidence from *net* returns, after research and trading costs, indicates that most funds do not do as well as a naive buy-and-hold policy. Notably, some recent studies indicate that there *is* some persistence in performance. The shortfall in performance of about 1 percent a year roughly matches the average cost of research and trading commissions.

In response to these findings, several investment management firms have started index funds based on the philosophy, "if you can't beat 'em, join 'em." These *market index funds* do not attempt to beat the market, but merely try to match the composition, and therefore, the performance of some specified market index such as the S&P 500 Index. Because these index funds have no research costs and minimal trading expenses, their returns typically have correlated with the chosen indexes at rates in excess of .99 with very low expenses. Also, their management fees are substantially below those charged by active managers.[33]

Although institutions have used index funds for many years, such funds were not generally available for individual investors until 1989 when several major investment company sponsors initiated such funds. Currently, six or seven equity index funds are available.

The final function of a portfolio manager is account administration. This is another significant benefit of most mutual funds because they allow automatic reinvestment of dividends with no charge and consistently provide records of total cost. Further, each year they supply statements of dividend income and capital gain distribution that can be used to prepare tax returns.

In summary, as an investor, you probably want your portfolio manager to perform a set of functions. Typically, mutual funds can help you accomplish four of the five functions at a lower cost in terms of time and money than doing the work on your own. This convenience and service have, on average, cost about 1 percent a year in terms of performance.

The theme of an article by Gruber is that, while the average investor in mutual funds experiences inferior performance, because there is performance persistence, there will be some investors who take advantage of the persistence and they appear to have experienced positive risk-adjusted returns.[34] He also indicates some evidence of poor performing funds disappearing.

Notably, assuming that you decide to build your portfolio with mutual funds, it is important to minimize your trading. A study by Nesbitt showed that individual investors who attempt to time the market generally buy into asset categories near their peaks and sell after they level off or fall.[35] This results in an underperformance of about 1 percent a year.

SOURCES OF INFORMATION

Because a wide variety of funds are available, you should examine the performance of various funds over time to understand their goals and management philosophies. Daily quotations for numerous open-end funds appear in *The Wall Street Journal*. These quotations and the information provided have been enhanced dramatically since 1992 when the *Journal* began providing historical returns and rankings for alternative periods on Fridays. (A description of the performance data provided is shown in Figure 26.3.)

---

[33] For a discussion of the reasoning behind these index funds (both economic and legal) and their development, see A. F. Ehrbar, "Index Funds—An Idea Whose Time Is Coming," *Fortune*, June 1976, 146–148.

[34] Martin J. Gruber, "Another Puzzle: The Growth in Actively Managed Mutual Funds," *Journal of Finance* 51, no. 3 (July 1996): 783–809.

[35] Stephen L. Nesbitt, "Buy High, Sell Low: Timing Errors in Mutual Fund Allocations," *Journal of Portfolio Management* 22, no. 1 (Fall 1995): 57–60.

FIGURE 26.3   **DESCRIPTION OF DAILY MUTUAL FUND QUOTATIONS IN *THE WALL STREET JOURNAL* FOR FRIDAYS**

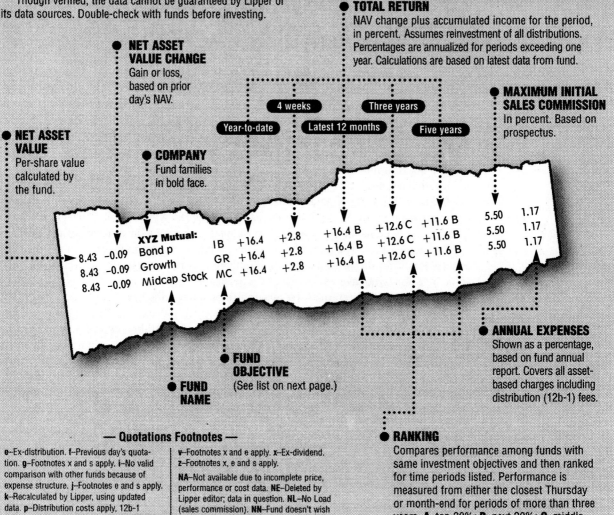

How to Read These Tables

Data come from two sources. The daily Net Asset Value (NAV) and Net Change calculations are supplied by the National Association of Securities Dealers (NASD). The NASD requires a mutual fund to have at least 1,000 shareholders or net assets of $25 million before being listed. Performance and cost data come from **Lipper Analytical Services Inc.**

Though verified, the data cannot be guaranteed by Lipper or its data sources. Double-check with funds before investing.

Performance calculations assume reinvestment of all distributions, and are after subtracting annual expenses. But figures don't reflect sales charges ("loads") or redemption fees.

These expanded tables appear Fridays. Other days, you'll find net asset value and the daily change and year-to-date performance.

● **TOTAL RETURN**
NAV change plus accumulated income for the period, in percent. Assumes reinvestment of all distributions. Percentages are annualized for periods exceeding one year. Calculations are based on latest data from fund.

● **NET ASSET VALUE CHANGE**
Gain or loss, based on prior day's NAV.

● **NET ASSET VALUE**
Per-share value calculated by the fund.

● **COMPANY**
Fund families in bold face.

● **MAXIMUM INITIAL SALES COMMISSION**
In percent. Based on prospectus.

4 weeks · Three years · Year-to-date · Latest 12 months · Five years

				4 weeks	Year-to-date	Latest 12 months	Three years	Five years			

XYZ Mutual:

8.43	−0.09	Bond p	IB	+16.4	+2.8	+16.4 B	+12.6 C	+11.6 B	5.50	1.17
8.43	−0.09	Growth	GR	+16.4	+2.8	+16.4 B	+12.6 C	+11.6 B	5.50	1.17
8.43	−0.09	Midcap Stock	MC	+16.4	+2.8	+16.4 B	+12.6 C	+11.6 B	5.50	1.17

● **FUND OBJECTIVE**
(See list on next page.)

● **FUND NAME**

● **ANNUAL EXPENSES**
Shown as a percentage, based on fund annual report. Covers all asset-based charges including distribution (12b-1) fees.

— Quotations Footnotes —

e–Ex-distribution. **f**–Previous day's quotation. **g**–Footnotes x and s apply. **i**–No valid comparison with other funds because of expense structure. **j**–Footnotes e and s apply. **k**–Recalculated by Lipper, using updated data. **p**–Distribution costs apply, 12b-1 **r**–Redemption charge may apply. **s**–Stock split or dividend. **t**–Footnotes p and r apply.

v–Footnotes x and e apply. **x**–Ex-dividend. **z**–Footnotes x, e and s apply.

NA–Not available due to incomplete price, performance or cost data. **NE**–Deleted by Lipper editor; data in question. **NL**–No Load (sales commission). **NN**–Fund doesn't wish to be tracked. **NS**–Fund didn't exist at start of period.

● **RANKING**
Compares performance among funds with same investment objectives and then ranked for time periods listed. Performance is measured from either the closest Thursday or month-end for periods of more than three years. **A**=top 20%; **B**=next 20%; **C**=middle 20%; **D**=next 20%; **E**=bottom 20%.

A comprehensive weekly list of quotations with data on dividend income and capital gain for the previous 12 months is carried in *Barron's*. In addition, *Barron's* publishes quarterly updates on the performance of several funds over the previous 10 years. As shown earlier in Figure 26.1, *Barron's* lists closed-end stock and bond funds with their current net asset values, current market quotes, and the percentage of difference between the two figures.

A major source of comprehensive historical information is *Investment Companies,* an annual publication issued by Arthur Wiesenberger Services. This book contains statistics for over 600 mutual funds. Arranged alphabetically, it describes each major fund including a brief history, investment objectives and portfolio analysis, statistical history, special services available, personnel, advisors and distributors, sales charges, and a chart of the value of a hypothetical $10,000 investment over 10 years. Figure 26.4 shows a sample page for the Phoenix Tax Exempt Bond A fund. The Wiesenberger book also contains a summary list with annual rates of return and price volatility measures for a number of additional funds.

Wiesenberger has two other services. Every three months, the firm publishes *Management Results,* which updates the long-term performance of more than 400 mutual funds, arranged alphabetically and grouped by investment objective. The firm's monthly publication, *Current Performance and Dividend Record,* reports the dividend and short-run performance of more than 400 funds, listed alphabetically with objectives indicated.[36]

Another source of analytical historical information of funds is *Forbes*. This biweekly financial publication typically discusses individual companies and their investment potential. In addition, the magazine's August issue contains an annual survey of mutual funds. A sample page in Figure 26.5 demonstrates the survey reports on annual average 10-year returns and last 12 month returns. The survey also provides information regarding each fund's yield, its sales charge, and its annual expense ratio. Notably, they include a separate section on foreign stock funds as shown.

Business Week publishes a "Mutual Fund Scoreboard." Figure 26.6 contains a sample of this scoreboard for open-end equity funds. The magazine publishes a comparable one for closed-end, fixed-income funds and equity funds. Besides information on performance (both before-tax and after-tax returns for 1–3–5–10 years), sales charges (including those for 12b-1 plans), expenses, portfolio yield and rank within objective, the table also contains portfolio information and telephone numbers for all the funds.

United Business Service Company publishes a semimonthly report called *United Mutual Fund Selector.* In the first issue of each month, a four-page supplement entitled "Investment Company Performance Comparisons" gives recent and historical changes in NAV for load and no-load funds.[37]

Morningstar is a well-regarded information service for mutual funds. Its basic service is "Morningstar Mutual Funds," which provides an informative one-page sheet that evaluates the performance of open-end mutual funds (1,240 funds). An example sheet for a fund is included as Figure 26.7. This sheet provides up-to-date information on the fund's objective and its risk-adjusted performance relative to an appropriate benchmark. There is also an analysis of performance and investment strategy based on an interview with the fund manager. The one-page sheet is best described as a *Value Line* sheet for a mutual fund. A similar service evaluates 268 closed-end funds.

---

[36] These services are currently published by Wiesenberger Investment Companies Services, Warren, Gorham and Lamont, 210 South St., Boston, MA 02111.

[37] This service is available from United Business Service Company, 210 Newbury St., Boston, MA 02116.

FIGURE 26.4 **SAMPLE PAGE FROM *INVESTMENT COMPANIES***

Phoenix Tax Exempt Bond A

Municipal Bond (MBD)

12/31/95 CDA Rating **26**
(99 = lowest, 1 = highest)

Overview

The Phoenix Tax-Exempt Bond fund seeks the production of as high a level of current income exempt from federal income taxation as is consistent with the preservation of capital. Under normal conditions, it intends to invest at least 80% of its net assets in municipal securities that are rated within the four highest grades as determined by Moddy's Aaa, Aa, A or Baa or by Standard & Poor's AAA, AA, A or BBB, or are judged by the advisor to be of equivalent quality to municipal securities so rated. While the portfolio may not invest more than 20% of its total assets in unrated municipal securities under normal conditions, it may invest up to 100% in taxable fixed income obligations for temporary defensive purposes.

Portfolio Characteristics as of 12/95

Sector	No. Iss.	Value (mil$)	PctBy Value			
Industrial	-	-	-	Yield to Maturity		-
Utility	-	-	-	Coupon		6.1
Finance	-	-	-	Years to Maturity		11.7
Government	-	-	-	Duration		7.2
Mtg-Backed	-	-	-			
Miscellaneous	-	-	-			
Total	-	-	-			

Quality	AAA	AA	A	BBB	BB	B	Other
Percent	30.4	12.8	19.4	9.2	1.5	0.0	18.3

Administration

Directors: C. Duane Blinn; Catherine Dudley; E. Virgil Conway; Harry Dalzell-Payne; Herbert Roth, Jr.; James D. Wehr; James M. Dolan; James M. Oales; Leroy Keith, Jr.; Philip R. McLoughlin; Philip R. Reynolds; Richard E. Seagerson; Robert Chesek, Pres.; William R. Moyer
Portfolio Manager(s): James Wehr since 1988
Investment Advisor: Phoenix Investment Counsel
Maximum Management Fee (%): 0.540
Distributor: Phoenix Equity Planning Corp.
Fiscal Year End / Ticker Symbol: November / PHTBX

Shareholder Information

Minimum initial investment: $500
Minimum subsequent investment: $25
Max. Front-End Sales Charge: 4.75%
Max. Annual 12b-1 Fee: 0.25
Transfer Agent: Phoenix Equity Planning Corp
Qualified for Sale: In all states and PR
Address: 101 Munson Street; Greenfield, MA 01301
Telephone: (800) 243-1574; (203) 253-1000

Statistical History

Year	Net Assets (mil$)	# of Accounts (000s)	NAV ($)	Yield (%)	Csh Eqv	Bds Pfds	Com Stks	Inc. Divs ($)	Cap. Gains ($)	Exp. Ratio (%)	Total Return	+/-% LB Gvt/ Corp
1995	148.6	4.3	11.43	0.1	8	92	0	0.60	0.00	-	18.2	-1.0
1994	140.5	4.6	10.21	0.1	2	98	0	0.64	0.04	0.94	-7.4	-3.9
1993	174.5	5.0	11.75	0.1	0	100	0	0.61	0.00	0.50	13.4	2.4
1992	39.1	1.0	10.92	0.1	0	100	0	0.69	0.28	0.53	10.6	3.1
1991	27.5	0.6	10.78	0.1	1	99	0	0.65	0.09	0.94	11.3	-4.8
1990	20.6	0.4	10.38	0.1	1	99	0	0.65	0.00	1.00	6.3	-2.0
1989	17.4	0.3	10.40	0.1	-	-	-	0.68	0.31	1.00	11.0	-3.2
1988	13.3	-	10.29	2.7	-	-	-	0.29	0.02	1.00	-	-

Commenced Operations: 07/15/88

Performance as of 12/31/95

Ann'lzd Total Return	Fund	Avg. MBD	LB Gvt/ Corp
1 Yr.	18.2	14.8	19.2
3 Yr.	7.5	6.7	8.5
5 Yr.	8.9	8.0	9.8
10 Yr.	-	8.1	9.7
Bull*	56.9	50.7	65.5
Bear*	2.1	2.2	3.6

MPT Stats.	Fund	Avg. MBD	LB Gvt/ Corp
Alpha	-0.79	-0.64	-
Beta	1.15	0.92	-
Std Dev	6.66	5.35	4.66

Risk-to-Reward

Fd (Δ) vs. all MBD; Intersect: LB Gvt/ Corp

Performance on $10,000 Investment

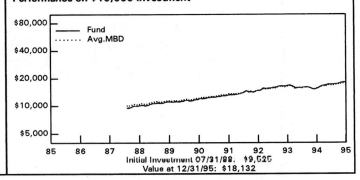

Initial Investment 07/31/88: $9,525
Value at 12/31/95: $18,132

FIGURE 26.5   **SAMPLE FUND RATING PAGE FROM *FORBES***

FUND SURVEY

Stock funds

Pay close attention to the down market grades in this table. If the recent "correction" is the start of a bear market, preservation of capital will be far more important than sexy 12-month returns. Funds with the best bull market grades are often heavily weighted with high growth and high-risk stocks, and, thus, fare poorly in bear markets. FORBES rates stock funds through three up-and-down market cycles; to be graded, a fund must have been in existence for at least two full cycles, dating back to Nov. 30, 1987. Stock funds' last down period—May 31, 1996 to July 16—is only six weeks, but could signal what's ahead in an extended bear market.

The Standard & Poor's 500 price index, scaled so that July 31, 1984 is 100, shows the market cycles against which FORBES measures U.S. stock fund performance.

Performance UP / DOWN —markets—		Fund/distributor	7/31/84 to 7/16/96	last 12 months	5-year	Assets 6/30/96 ($mil)	Weighted average P/E	Median market cap ($bil)	Maximum sales charge	Annual expenses per $100
			—Annualized total return—							
		Standard & Poor's 500 stock average	16.4%	15.1%	13.3%					
		Forbes stock fund composite	14.5%	10.6%	13.2%		18.5	$10.3		$1.20
■D	■A	AAL Capital Growth/AAL	—*	11.5%	10.3%	$1,421	18.4	$24.3	4.75%	$1.12
		AAL Mid Cap Stock¹/AAL	—*	9.9	—*	440	28.1	1.5	4.75	1.39
		AAL Utilities Fund/AAL	—*	12.9	—*	124	15.3	17.1	4.75	1.20
■C	D	AARP Growth–Capital Growth/Scudder	—*	8.6	10.9	798	12.9	10.5	none	0.91
■D	A	AARP Growth–Growth & Income/Scudder	—*	16.4	14.8	3,952	15.7	9.7	none	0.70
A	C	Acorn Fund/Acorn	17.2%	12.9	17.7	2,813	14.7	1.2	none	0.57
■D	B	Addison Capital Shares/Addison	—*	14.5	12.0	51	14.6	7.9	none	1.97
■D	A	AIM Blue Chip²/AIM	—*	14.7	11.8	79	22.9	15.7	5.50	1.30a
A+	F	AIM Equity–Aggressive Growth/AIM	16.8	5.8	25.9	2,917	24.5	0.8	†	1.08a
C	A	AIM Equity–Charter-A/AIM	15.3	9.1	10.4	2,839	18.5	22.8	5.50	1.17
A+	F	AIM Equity–Constellation-A/AIM	19.8	1.4	17.8	10,349	22.7	3.9	5.50	1.20a
B	C	AIM Equity–Weingarten-A/AIM	16.7	4.8	9.4	5,029	19.2	8.6	5.50	1.20a

Note: Last 12-month return 7/18/95-7/16/96; 5-year return 7/31/91-7/16/96. ■Fund rated for two periods only; maximum allowable grade A. *Fund not in operation or did not meet asset minimum for full period. †Closed to new investors. §Distributor may impose redemption fee whose proceeds revert to the fund. a: Net of absorption of expenses by fund sponsor. b: Includes back-end load that reverts to distributor. ¹Formerly AAL Smaller Company Stock. ²Formerly Baird Blue Chip.
Sources: Forbes; Lipper Analytical Services; Morningstar, Inc.

Rules, page 148. Distributor table, page 233.

Source: "1996 Mutual Fund Survey," *Forbes,* August 26, 1996, pp. 149, 186. Copyright © Forbes, Inc., 1996. Reprinted by permission of FORBES magazine.

FIGURE 26.5　**(CONTINUED)**

FUND SURVEY

Foreign stock funds

Foreign stocks haven't done well recently. Morgan Stanley Capital International Europe, Australasia and Far East index has a five-year compound annual total return (in dollars) of 10%, to 15.7% for the U.S. market. Over long stretches, however, foreign stocks have displayed an ability to dampen the volatility of a U.S. portfolio. Given the hazards (such as exchange losses and political instability), it makes sense to buy overseas via a fund, in order to gain diversification. We measure most foreign funds against the up and down market cycles of the EAFE index. Emerging market funds are measured against Morgan's Emerging Markets index.

Rising markets		7/31/84 to 8/31/87		10/31/87 to 12/31/89			10/31/92 to 6/30/96	
Declining markets	3/31/84 to 7/31/84		8/31/87 to 10/31/87		12/31/89 to 10/31/92			

Morgan Stanley's Europe, Australasia and Far East stock index, scaled so that Mar. 31, 1984 is 100, determines the market cycles against which foreign equity funds are measured. This dollar-denominated index reflects both stock prices and currency values.

–18%　+301%　–16%　+44%　–29%　+59%

Performance UP DOWN —markets—		Fund/distributor	3/84 to 6/96	Annualized total return last 12 months	5-year	Assets 6/30/96 ($mil)	Weighted average P/E	Median market cap ($bil)	Maximum sales charge	Annual expenses per $100
		Morgan Stanley Capital Intl EAFE index	15.0%	13.3%	10.0%					
		Forbes foreign stock fund composite	8.6%	16.2%	10.8%		25.2	$5.0		$1.55
		Acorn International Fund/Acorn	—*	24.6%	—*	$1,625	22.8	$0.7	none	$1.20
		AIM Intl–Equity-A/AIM	—*	21.8	—*	1,285	27.2	3.9	5.50%	1.67a
A	C	Alliance International Fund-A/Alliance	12.8%	15.8	9.9%	295	31.9	9.5	4.25	1.86
		Alliance New Europe-A/Alliance	—*	16.4	15.3	130	18.4	6.9	4.25	2.02
		Alliance Worldwide Privatization/Alliance	—*	19.2	—*	758	19.0	4.1	4.25	1.78
		Babson-Stewart Ivory Intl/Jones & Babson	—*	18.7	12.6	80	28.1	2.3	none	1.30
		Bartlett Value International/Legg Mason	—*	14.2	11.8	79	17.3	4.0	none	1.84
		Bernstein International Value/Bernstein	—*	23.0	—*	2,923	24.8	3.7	none	1.35
		Wm Blair–International Growth/Wm Blair	—*	17.7	—*	101	25.2	1.9	none	1.48
		Blairlogie Emerging Markets-Inst/Pimco Advisors	—*	7.7	—*	81	29.2	2.8	none	1.35
		Brinson Non-US Equity/Fund/Plan	—*	23.6	—*	212	26.8	10.8	none	1.00a
		Colonial Intl Fund for Growth-A/Colonial	—*	16.4	—*	111	28.0	6.4	5.75	1.74
■B	B	Colonial Newport Tiger-A/Colonial	—*	10.2	19.1	918	NA	NA	5.75	1.78
		Columbia International Stock/Columbia	—*	25.1	—*	125	33.3	8.3	none	1.50
		Dean Witter European Growth/Dean Witter	—*	21.6	17.7	1,089	18.4	3.7	5.00b	2.15
		Dean Witter Intl SmallCap/Dean Witter	—*	20.8	—*	147	30.0	0.6	5.00	2.78
		Dean Witter Pacific Growth/Dean Witter	—*	7.3	13.4	1,777	23.9	4.0	5.00b	2.45
		Delaware Group Intl Equity-A/Delaware	—*	17.6	—*	85	18.5	6.2	4.75	1.85a
		Dreyfus International Equity/Dreyfus	—*	13.8	—*	103	28.7	4.7	none	1.92

■Fund rated for two periods only; maximum allowable grade A. *Fund not in operation or did not meet asset minimum for full period. §Distributor may impose redemption fee whose proceeds revert to the fund. a: Net of absorption of expenses by fund sponsor. b: Includes back-end load that reverts to distributor. NA-Not applicable or not available.
Sources: Forbes; Lipper Analytical Services; Morningstar, Inc.
Rules, page 148. Distributor table, page 233.

FIGURE 26.6 | **MUTUAL FUND SCOREBOARD**

MUTUAL FUND SCOREBOARD

FUND	RATING	OBJECTIVE	SIZE		FEES		1995 RETURNS (%)			RANK WITHIN OBJECTIVE
			ASSETS $MIL.	% CHG. 1994-5	SALES CHARGE (%)	EXPENSE RATIO (%)	PRE-TAX	AFTER-TAX	YIELD	
DEAN WITTER HEALTH SCIENCES		Health care	360.8	48	5.00**	2.30†	62.3	59.4	0.0	1/9
DEAN WITTER INTL. SMALL CAP		Foreign	109.2	12	5.00**	2.90†	2.9	2.9	0.0	55/66
DEAN WITTER MID-CAP GROWTH		Growth	203.1	130	5.00**	2.21†	41.3	38.0	0.0	17/229
DEAN WITTER NAT. RESOURCE DEV. SEC.	♦♦	Natural resources	149.9	10	5.00**	1.90†	23.4	21.6	0.3	6/11
DEAN WITTER PACIFIC GROWTH	♦♦	Pacific	1467.1	3	5.00**	2.41†	4.0	3.2	2.3	10/22
DEAN WITTER STRATEGIST	AVG	Asset allocation	1262.7	65	5.00**	1.63†	24.3	21.0	1.9	17/34
DEAN WITTER UTILITIES	AVG	Utilities	3323.0	17	5.00**	1.64†	28.4	26.9	3.8	13/26
DEAN WITTER VALUE-ADDED MKT. EQTY.	♦	Growth/income	806.8	63	5.00**	1.64†	29.0	28.4	1.0	108/138
DEAN WITTER WORLD WIDE INVMNT. ☖	♦♦	World	498.2	-13	5.00**	2.41†	4.6	4.6	0.0	41/41
DELAWARE A		Balanced	510.7	15	4.75	0.97†	25.9	22.9	3.1	26/57
DELAWARE DECATUR INCOME A	AVG	Equity-income	1404.4	21	4.75	0.81†	32.9	28.9	3.6	9/34
DELAWARE DECATUR TOTAL RET. A	AVG	Growth/income	550.0	36	4.75	1.26†	36.5	32.5	2.3	26/138
DELAWARE DELCAP A	♦♦	Growth	860.5	5	4.75	1.35†	29.8	25.4	0.0	149/229
DELAWARE TREND A ♣	♦	Maximum growth	399.3	49	4.75	1.36†	42.5	40.3	0.0	6/34
DELAWARE VALUE A ☖	♦	Small company	180.5	3	5.75	1.46†	23.5	21.8	1.0	73/99
DG EQUITY		Growth	359.9	55	3.50	0.95†	35.0	33.1	1.2	86/229
DODGE & COX BALANCED	♦♦	Balanced	1800.3	148	No load	0.58	28.0	25.9	3.9	13/57
DODGE & COX STOCK	♦	Growth/income	1227.9	126	No load	0.61	33.4	31.2	2.0	54/138
DREYFUS ☖	♦	Growth/income	2654.7	8	No load	0.74	23.8	13.4	1.5	132/138
DREYFUS APPRECIATION	AVG	Growth	460.7	97	No load	0.96	37.9	37.2	1.6	48/229
DREYFUS BALANCED		Balanced	196.3	112	No load	1.04	25.0	22.1	3.5	33/57
DREYFUS CAP. VALUE A (PREMIER)	♦♦♦	Multi-asset global	250.5	-30	4.50	1.21	-3.1	-4.4	4.4	18/18
DREYFUS CORE VALUE INV.	AVG	Growth	402.2	26	No load	1.11†	35.6	31.9	1.4	76/229
DREYFUS GLOBAL GROWTH	♦	World	108.9	-21	3.00	1.40	12.1	12.1	0.0	28/41
DREYFUS GROWTH & INCOME		Growth/income	1860.1	15	No load	1.14	25.0	23.2	2.3	128/138
DREYFUS GROWTH OPPORTUNITY ☖	♦♦	Growth	408.6	12	No load	1.10	28.4	23.5	1.2	165/229
DREYFUS INTL. EQUITY ☖		Foreign	107.2	-33	No load	1.92†	0.7	0.7	0.0	59/66
DREYFUS MIDCAP INDEX (h)		Growth	128.6	72	1.00*	0.40	30.3	28.2	1.5	145/229
DREYFUS NEW LEADERS ♣	♦	Small company	608.2	55	1.00*	1.16	29.8	27.0	0.2	53/99
DREYFUS S&P 500 INDEX (i)		Growth/income	365.4	56	1.00*	0.61	36.7	35.6	1.7	20/138
DREYFUS THIRD CENTURY	♦	Growth	419.3	20	No load	1.12	35.8	33.1	0.5	70/229
ECLIPSE FINANCIAL ASSET EQUITY	AVG	Small company	174.8	-10	No load	1.12	19.7	18.3	0.5	85/99
ENTERPRISE CAPITAL APPREC A	♦	Growth	121.3	20	4.75	1.66†	25.7	22.4	0.0	197/229
ENTERPRISE GROWTH A ♣	♦	Growth	122.4	38	4.75	1.60†	40.0	38.5	0.0	26/229
EUROPACIFIC GROWTH ♣	♦	Foreign	10922.3	32	5.75	0.97†	12.9	11.9	2.1	15/66
EV MARATHON GREATER CHINA GROWTH		Pacific	304.3	46	5.00**	2.38†	3.2	3.2	0.0	13/22
EV TRADITIONAL GROWTH	♦♦	Growth	135.5	13	4.75	0.95†	29.2	27.9	0.3	153/229
EV TRADITIONAL INVESTORS	♦	Balanced	236.6	18	4.75	0.91†	29.7	27.1	3.0	6/57
EV TRADITIONAL STOCK	♦	Growth/income	99.2	18	4.75	0.98†	32.8	28.4	1.7	63/138
EV TRADITIONAL TOTAL RETURN ☖	♦	Utilities	456.7	2	4.75	1.18†	27.4	25.1	4.3	16/26
EVERGREEN BALANCED B (j)		Balanced	109.0	9	5.00**	1.48†	25.5	23.2	3.0	29/57
EVERGREEN UTILITY A (k) ☖		Utilities	108.2	NM	4.75	0.53†	30.7	27.7	3.9	10/26
EVERGREEN VALUE A (l)	AVG	Growth	292.4	55	4.75	0.93†	31.8	29.3	2.4	128/229
EXCELSIOR EQUITY (m)	♦	Growth	172.0	49	4.50	1.05	28.9	25.6	0.4	156/229
EXCELSIOR INCOME & GROWTH (n)	♦♦♦	Growth/income	118.9	21	4.50	1.06	30.0	28.9	2.2	97/138
FAM VALUE	♦♦♦	Small company	266.3	27	No load	1.39	19.7	18.9	0.8	84/99
FEDERATED GROWTH STRATEGIES A (o)		Growth	245.5	-13	5.50	0.99	40.0	32.1	0.6	25/229
FEDERATED INDEX MINI-CAP		Small company	134.2	31	No load	0.73	26.4	24.1	1.1	67/99
FEDERATED INTL. EQUITY A (p) ☖	♦♦♦	Foreign	182.9	-26	5.50	1.61	6.5	3.3	0.5	47/66
FEDERATED STOCK ♣	♦	Growth/income	665.4	20	No load	0.97	35.6	32.5	1.4	37/138
FIDELITY	♦	Growth/income	3213.7	70	No load	0.64	32.8	29.9	1.7	62/138
FIDELITY ADVISOR EQUITY GROWTH A		Growth	2099.8	131	3.50	1.70†	39.1	37.2	0.2	31/229
FIDELITY ADVISOR EQUITY INCOME A		Equity-income	956.3	369	3.50	1.64†	32.5	31.2	1.6	10/34
FIDELITY ADVISOR GLOBAL RESOURCES A	♦	Natural resources	315.7	63	3.50	2.07†	28.7	27.5	0.0	3/11
FIDELITY ADVISOR GROWTH OPPORT. A	♦♦♦	Growth	10946.2	127	3.50	1.62†	33.0	32.1	1.3	113/229
FIDELITY ADVISOR INCOME & GROWTH A	♦♦	Balanced	3488.5	10	3.50	1.58†	14.1	12.7	3.9	57/57
FIDELITY ADVISOR OVERSEAS A	♦	Foreign	803.4	22	3.50	1.90†	8.6	8.4	0.6	39/66
FIDELITY ADVISOR STRAT. OPPTY. A	♦	Growth	615.0	63	3.50	1.84†	38.1	36.6	1.5	45/229
FIDELITY ASSET MANAGER	♦♦	Multi-asset global	11165.4	1	No load	0.97	18.2	17.1	2.9	13/18
FIDELITY ASSET MANAGER: GROWTH		Multi-asset global	2894.6	1	No load	1.15	20.0	19.4	1.5	10/18
FIDELITY ASSET MANAGER: INCOME		Asset allocation	600.7	26	No load	0.79	16.7	15.1	4.6	32/34
FIDELITY BALANCED	♦♦	Balanced	4880.1	-2	No load	0.90	14.9	13.4	4.2	56/57
FIDELITY BLUE CHIP GROWTH	♦♦	Growth	7801.9	137	3.00	1.02	28.4	25.5	0.4	164/229
FIDELITY CANADA	♦♦	Foreign	174.7	-48	4.00*	1.57	19.4	19.2	0.4	5/66
FIDELITY CAPITAL APPRECIATION	AVG	Maximum growth	1669.1	3	3.00	1.06	18.8	16.1	2.2	32/34
FIDELITY CONTRAFUND	♦♦♦	Growth	14831.7	71	3.00	1.00	36.3	33.3	0.2	61/229
FIDELITY DESTINY I ♣	♦♦♦	Growth	4278.7	33	8.24	0.68	37.0	34.5	2.2	54/229
FIDELITY DESTINY II ♣	♦♦♦	Growth	2207.5	50	8.24	0.80	36.0	34.1	2.0	68/229
FIDELITY DISCIPLINED EQUITY	♦	Growth	2145.6	85	No load	0.93	29.0	25.0	1.3	155/229
FIDELITY DIVERSIFIED INTERNATIONAL		Foreign	340.7	11	No load	1.25	18.0	16.4	1.7	7/66

*Includes redemption fee. **Includes deferred sales charge. †12(b)-1 plan in effect. ‡Not currently accepting new accounts. §Less than 0.5% of assets. NA=Not available. NM=Not meaningful. (h) Formerly Peoples S&P MidCap Index. (i) Formerly Peoples Index. (j) Formerly First Union Balanced C Invmt. (k) Formerly First Union Utility B Invmt. (l) Formerly First Union Value B Invmt. (m) Formerly UST Master Equity. (n) Formerly UST Master Income & Growth. (o) Formerly Federated Growth. (p) Formerly FT International Equity A.

Source: "Mutual Fund Scoreboard," p. 110. Copyright © 1996 by McGraw-Hill, Inc. Reprinted from February 5, 1996, issue of *Business Week* by special permission.

FIGURE 26.6   *(CONTINUED)*

Equity Funds

3 YEARS PRETAX	3 YEARS AFTERTAX	5 YEARS PRETAX	5 YEARS AFTERTAX	10 YEARS PRETAX	10 YEARS AFTERTAX	TURNOVER	%CASH	P-E RATIO	STYLE	UNTAXED GAINS (%)	LARGEST HOLDING COMPANY (% ASSETS)	RISK	TOLL-FREE (800)	IN-STATE
17.0	16.3					High	0	40	SG	27	IDEXX Laboratories(3)		869-3863	NY 212-392-2550
New fund, not rated							7	27	SB	-8	Kiekert(1)		869-3863	NY 212-392-2550
New fund, not rated							6	33	MG	22	Analog Devices(2)		869-3863	NY 212-392-2550
12.8	10.7	10.3	8.5	10.8	9.1	Average	2	25	LB	12	Exxon(5)	High	869-3863	NY 212-392-2550
18.6	17.7	16.0	15.3			Low	1	23	MG	5	Hutchison Whampoa(3)	Very high	869-3863	NY 212-392-2550
9.6	7.6	13.3	11.6			Very high	3	22	LB	17	Cisco Systems(1)	Low	869-3863	NY 212-392-2550
9.3	7.7	11.0	9.4			Very low	1	17	LV	16	AT&T(2)	Low	869-3863	NY 212-392-2550
13.3	12.7	16.7	16.2			Very low	4	20	MV	24	Burlington Northern Santa Fe()	Average	869-3863	NY 212-392-2550
11.0	10.2	8.1	7.3	10.0	7.8	Average	7	28	LG	5	Nokia Cl A(1)	High	869-3863	NY 212-392-2550
10.8	8.4	13.1	10.4	11.3	8.0	High	6	20	LB	15	Philip Morris(3)	Low	523-4640	PA 215-988-1333
15.0	11.6	15.0	12.0	12.3	8.9	High	2	19	LV	15	JC Penney(2)	Low	523-4640	PA 215-988-1333
16.0	12.5	15.2	12.2			Average	2	19	LV	18	DuPont(3)	Low	523-4640	PA 215-988-1333
11.2	8.8	14.8	13.3			Low	5	29	MG	37	Bay Networks(3)	High	523-4640	PA 215-988-1333
16.2	13.6	27.4	25.0	16.6	14.3	Average	5	28	SG	23	Central Sprinkler(3)	High	523-4640	PA 215-988-1333
10.9	10.1	18.8	17.6			Very low	16	18	SV	15	FNMA(3)	Low	523-4640	PA 215-988-1333
13.2	12.1					Very low	11	22	LB	23	Hewlett-Packard(4)		748-8500	
14.9	13.0	15.1	13.4	13.6	11.1	Low	5	19	LV	15	Digital Equipment(2)	Very low	621-3979	
18.4	16.6	17.4	15.8	15.0	13.0	Very low	7	19	LV	26	General Motors(3)	Average	621-3979	
8.0	3.7	11.2	8.0	10.8	6.9	Low	4	21	LB	28	Texaco(4)	Average	645-6561	MA 718-895-1206
12.9	12.2	15.7	15.1	13.8	12.4	Very low	2	20	LG	27	Coca-Cola(6)	Average	645-6561	MA 718-895-1206
13.0	11.1					Average	1	19	LB	12	Olin(2)		645-6561	MA 718-895-1206
1.6	0.7	-0.4	-1.5	7.6	5.9	Average	18	41	MG	-35	Placer Dome(4)	High	554-4611	MA 718-895-1396
16.6	13.5	15.2	12.4	12.3	8.5	Average	3	18	LV	23	IBM(3)	Average	645-6561	MA 718-895-1206
8.1	8.1	7.6	7.6			High	0	22	LG	28	Hutchison Whampoa(3)	Low	645-6561	MA 718-895-1206
12.0	10.8					High	6	21	LB	11	DuPont(3)		645-6561	MA 718-895-1206
7.0	1.6	12.2	8.7	10.7	7.0	Very high	2	21	LB	14	BBC Brown Boveri (Reg)(3)	High	645-6561	MA 718-895-1206
New fund, not rated						Average	6	26	LV	2	Lucas Industries(2)		645-6561	MA 718-895-1206
12.4	10.6					Low	9	22	MB	17	First Bank System(1)		645-6561	MA 718-895-1206
14.9	12.2	19.3	16.5	13.9	12.1	High	5	23	SB	22	Integrated Silicon Solution(2)	Average	645-6561	MA 718-895-1206
14.7	12.5	16.1	14.4			Low	6	20	LB	22	General Electric(2)	Average	645-6561	MA 718-895-1206
9.8	6.8	13.2	11.1	11.6	8.4	High	3	21	LG	25	EMC(3)	Average	645-6561	MA 718-895-1206
10.1	7.5	15.9	13.8			High	5	17	SV	18	Arrow Electronics(2)	Average	872-2710	GA 770-631-0414
8.7	7.2	16.6	15.7			Average	8	28	LG	34	Nokia Cl A (ADR)(5)	High	432-4320	GA 404-396-8118
15.3	13.7	18.3	16.1	14.7	11.5	Average	3	25	LG	37	Cisco Systems(5)	Average	432-4320	GA 404-396-8118
15.7	14.6	13.4	12.5	15.5	13.8	Very low	14	22	LB	17	ANZ Banking Group(1)	Average	421-4120	CA 213-486-9200
New fund, not rated						Low	4	18	LB	-3	Jardine Matheson Holdings(3)		225-6265	MA 617-482-8260
6.4	4.9	12.1	10.1	11.1	8.4	High	7	23	LB	19	American International Group(4)	Average	225-6265	MA 617-482-8260
12.3	9.7	12.8	10.1	11.0	7.5	Low	3	19	LB	27	Astra Cl A Free(3)	Very low	225-6265	MA 617-482-8260
9.9	6.5	11.5	8.1	11.7	7.9	Average	5	19	LV	26	Eastman Kodak(3)	Average	225-6265	MA 617-482-8260
7.0	4.7	10.1	7.2	10.3	7.0	High	7	16	MV	15	Frontier(5)	Average	225-6265	MA 617-482-8260
New fund, not rated						Low	3	17	LV	19	Avnet(1)		807-2940	
New fund, not rated						Low	2	18	LV	7	GTE(4)		807-2940	
13.6	11.4	14.7	12.4	13.2	11.1	Average	12	17	LV	17	American General(4)	Low	807-2940	
14.5	12.8	18.7	17.3	13.4	11.8	Low	4	24	LB	30	Mellon Bank(3)	Average	446-1012	MA 617-451-1912
14.1	12.8	17.7	16.4			Average	4	24	MB	17	John Wiley(3)	Very low	446-1012	MA 617-451-1912
8.6	7.9	18.8	17.8			Very low	7	20	SV	19	Conmed(9)	Low	932-3271	NY 518-234-7400
9.6	6.7	14.1	11.7	13.9	11.3	Average	5	22	MB	39	USA Waste Services(2)	Average	245-5051	PA 412-288-1561
12.3	10.6					Low	12	23	SB	13	Altera()		245-5040	PA 412-288-1900
12.0	10.3	7.3	6.2	10.8	8.0	Average	1	27	LG	13	BBC Brown Boveri (Br)(2)	High	245-5051	PA 412-288-1561
14.9	13.0	17.0	14.6	12.2	9.7	Low	2	17	LV	36	Hewlett-Packard(3)	Average	245-5040	PA 412-288-1900
17.3	14.1	16.8	14.0	14.1	10.7	High	5	21	LB	16	Philip Morris(2)	Low	544-8888	
16.6	15.4					High	11	24	LG	23	Intel(5)		522-7297	MA 617-439-6793
18.6	17.6					High	15	18	LV	12	Philip Morris(4)		522-7297	MA 617-439-6793
20.1	19.2	17.6	15.9			High	4	21	MB	10	Alcan Aluminium(1)	High	522-7297	MA 617-439-6793
18.7	17.4	22.4	20.6			Average	15	19	LV	16	FNMA(5)	Low	522-7297	MA 617-439-6793
9.0	7.7	13.7	11.9			Very high	1	23	MV	2	Union Camp(1)	Very low	522-7297	MA 617-439-6793
16.3	16.1	9.8	9.5			Average	10	26	LV	8	Deutsche Bank(1)	High	522-7297	MA 617-439-6793
15.6	13.8	16.5	13.9			High	0	18	MG	21	i-STAT(7)	Low	522-7297	MA 617-439-6793
10.8	9.3	13.7	12.0			High	21	22	LB	8	FNMA(1)	Very low	544-8888	
12.0	11.1					High	2	23	LB	8	IBM(2)		544-8888	
9.9	8.3					High	38	22	LB	4	Philip Morris(1)		544-8888	
9.1	7.3	12.2	10.0			Very high	1	13	MV	-1	Jefferson Smurfit(1)	Very low	544-8888	
20.6	17.8	23.6	21.6			Very high	10	19	MB	14	General Motors(4)	Average	544-8888	
9.7	9.6	8.5	8.1			Average	1	25	MB	4	Barrick Gold (Canada)(6)	High	544-8888	
17.6	14.7	15.8	12.5			Average	7	20	MV	14	Centerior Energy(7)	Low	544-8888	
17.8	16.1	24.1	22.1	19.4	17.4	Very high	10	22	MB	24	IBM(3)	Average	544-8888	
21.8	17.8	23.7	19.4	18.1	13.9	Average	5	20	LV	32	FNMA(6)	Low	752-2347	MA 617-439-0547
21.7	18.7	24.1	20.5	22.6	19.5	Average	8	19	LV	26	FNMA(5)	Average	752-2347	MA 617-439-0547
14.8	12.5	18.5	10.0			Very high	11	22	LD	20	Coca Cola(3)	Average	544-8888	
17.7	16.6					High	8	24	LV	18	Hitachi(2)		544-8888	

DATA: MORNINGSTAR, INC., CHICAGO, IL.

FIGURE 26.7 **SAMPLE PAGE FROM MORNINGSTAR MUTUAL FUNDS**

Fidelity Magellan

	Ticker	Load	NAV	Yield	SEC Yield	Assets	Objective
	FMAGX	3.00%	$87.22	0.6%	---	$55429.9 mil	Growth

Fidelity Magellan Fund seeks capital appreciation. The fund invests primarily in common stocks and convertible securities, with up to 20% of assets invested in debt securities of all types and qualities. It features domestic corporations operating primarily in the United States, domestic corporations that have significant activities and interests outside the U.S., and foreign companies. No limitations are placed on total foreign investment, but no more than 40% of assets will be invested in companies operating exclusively in one foreign country.

The fund closed to new investment in 1965 and reopened in 1981.

Portfolio Manager(s)

Jeffrey N. Vinik, CFA. Since 7-92. BS'81 Duke U.; MBA'85 Harvard U. Vinik is a portfolio manager with Fidelity Investments. He joined the company in 1986 as an analyst covering the energy and computer-services industries. Previously, he was an equity block trader with First Boston. He began his investment career in 1981 as a securities analyst with Value Line.

Performance 01-31-96

	1st Qtr	2nd Qtr	3rd Qtr	4th Qtr	Total
1991	20.23	-0.14	9.06	7.70	41.03
1992	-0.70	0.65	1.73	5.25	7.02
1993	8.62	6.42	8.21	-0.34	24.66
1994	-1.59	-4.49	5.43	-0.90	-1.81
1995	8.44	15.77	10.60	-1.46	36.82

Trailing	Total Return %	+/- S&P500	+/- Wil 5000	% Rank All	% Rank Obj	Growth of $10,000
3 Mo	2.58	-7.43	-6.20	84	83	10,258
6 Mo	2.67	-11.86	-10.21	91	86	10,267
1 Yr	40.22	1.61	3.08	6	16	14,022
3 Yr Avg	18.29	2.00	2.84	6	8	16,553
5 Yr Avg	19.10	2.73	2.31	8	15	23,964
10 Yr Avg	17.14	1.94	2.77	4	7	48,643
15 Yr Avg	21.16	5.79	6.50	1	1	178,051

Most Similar Funds in MMF

Fidelity Contrafund	Strong Fit
Fidelity Stock Selector	Strong Fit
Fidelity Growth Company	Strong Fit

Tax Analysis	Tax-Adj Return %	% Pretax Return
3 Yr Avg	15.65	85.5
5 Yr Avg	15.80	82.7
10 Yr Avg	13.84	80.7
Potential Capital Gain Exposure		26% of assets

Historical Profile

Return High
Risk Average
Rating ★★★★★ Highest

	92%	90%	97%	81%	84%	93%	93%	68%

Investment Style History
Equity
Average Stock %

Growth of $10,000
IIII Investment Value ($000) of Fund
— Investment Value ($000) S&P 500
▼ Manager Change
▽ Partial Manager Change
► Mgr Unknown After
◄ Mgr Unknown Before

Performance Quartile (Within Objective)

	1985	1986	1987	1988	1989	1990	1991	1992	1993	1994	1995	01-96	History
	45.21	48.69	40.10	48.32	59.85	53.93	68.61	63.01	70.85	66.80	85.98	87.22	NAV
	43.11	23.74	1.00	22.77	34.58	-4.51	41.03	7.02	24.66	-1.81	36.82	1.44	Total Return %
	11.37	5.07	-4.26	6.16	2.90	-1.39	10.54	-0.60	14.60	-3.13	-0.71	-1.96	+/- S&P 500
	10.55	7.65	-1.36	4.82	5.41	1.67	6.82	-1.96	13.38	-1.74	0.38	-1.24	+/- Wilshire 5000
	1.94	0.90	1.65	2.27	2.22	1.51	2.18	2.00	1.12	0.19	0.77	0.00	Income Return %
	41.17	22.85	-0.65	20.50	32.36	-6.02	38.85	5.01	23.54	-2.00	36.05	1.44	Capital Return %
	4	10	51	9	8	69	14	58	12	34	7	38	Total Rtn %Rank All
	2	7	63	13	20	52	32	58	6	52	19	69	Total Rtn %Rank Obj
	0.65	0.46	0.72	0.90	1.24	0.83	1.30	1.25	0.75	0.13	0.59	0.00	Income $
	1.78	6.84	9.02	0.00	3.82	2.42	5.43	8.82	6.50	2.64	4.69	0.00	Capital Gains $
	1.12	1.08	1.08	1.14	1.08	1.03	1.06	1.05	1.00	0.99	0.96	---	Expense Ratio %
	2.79	1.95	1.18	1.33	2.13	2.54	2.47	1.57	2.11	1.07	0.39	---	Income Ratio %
	126	96	96	101	87	82	135	172	155	132	120	---	Turnover Rate %
	4136.0	7405.5	.7800.1	8971.1	12699.6	12325.7	19257.1	22268.9	31705.1	36441.5	53702.3	55429.9	Net Assets ($mil)

Risk Analysis

Time Period	Load-Adj Return %	Risk %Rank All	Risk %Rank Obj	Mstar Return	Score Risk	Morningstar Risk-Adj Rating
1 Yr	36.02					
3 Yr	17.10	77	52	1.46	0.88	★★★★
5 Yr	18.38	75	44	1.43	0.83	★★★★
10 Yr	16.78	69	40	1.82	0.89	★★★★★
Average Historical Rating	(122 months)				5.0	★s

¹1=low, 100=high

Other Measures		Standard Index S&P500	Best Fit Index SPMid400
Standard Deviation	11.11	Alpha	1.7	4.7
Mean	17.53	Beta	1.03	1.03
Sharpe Ratio	1.20	R-Squared	58	78

Portfolio Analysis 09-30-95

Share Chg (03-95) 000	Amount 000	Total Stocks: 452 / Total Fixed-Income: 39	Value $000	% Net Assets
8732	12947	Hewlett-Packard	1079439	2.03
16180	19961	Chrysler	1057949	1.99
5205	11769	Micron Technology	935667	1.76
-3893	12217	Motorola	933073	1.76
6396	11370	Texas Instruments	908187	1.71
12458	12458	Nokia CI A	874938	1.65
	760	US Treasury Bond 7.625%	860737	1.62
6823	14484	Caterpillar	823749	1.55
3192	16888	Columbia/HCA Healthcare	821184	1.55
-37	7692	Applied Materials	786497	1.48
6810	12803	LSI Logic	739396	1.39
-2625	15687	General Motors	735312	1.39
245	6815	FNMA	705301	1.33
-8072	16936	Oracle	649911	1.22
929	7602	CSX	639476	1.21
5859	11451	Travelers	608315	1.15
-331	9064	Merrill Lynch	566519	1.07
2617	7127	FHLMC	492619	0.93
-1117	7666	Intel	460906	0.87
315	7429	DSC Communications	440162	0.83
-391	9636	Digital Equipment	439624	0.83
1447	5224	Deere	425316	0.80
-1343	6040	Conrail	415223	0.78
3348	9013	3Com	410078	0.77
1320	11784	Silicon Graphics	405068	0.76

Investment Style

Style
Value Blend Growth
Size Large Med Small

	Stock Portfolio Avg	Rel S&P500	Rel Objective
Price/Earnings Ratio	21.2	0.96	0.89
Price/Book Ratio	3.9	0.89	0.90
5 Yr Earnings Gr %	20.8	2.04	1.22
Return on Assets %	10.2	1.26	1.12
Debt % Total Cap	23.5	0.85	0.91
Med Mkt Cap ($mil)	4697	0.25	0.64

Analysis by Kathleen Hartman 02-16-96

Fidelity Magellan Fund is not as unpredictable as the weather, but it still stymies its critics.

In late 1995, manager Jeff Vinik's three-year love of technology and semiconductor stocks came to an abrupt end. This dramatic move was widely publicized for two reasons. Vinik had touted certain tech stocks in a September shareholder report, then halved the fund's tech stake in November. While Vinik merely represented the stocks as having performed particularly well, this awkward incident instigated price-manipulation lawsuits, and subsequently silenced public stock discussions by Fidelity's fund managers.

What really took the investment public by surprise was that Vinik sold most of the fund's 45% tech position without sending the sector sprawling, or arousing the suspicion of the legions of Magellan watchers who strive to uncover the fund's every move.

Such has been the story of Vinik's tenure at Magellan. Seemingly oblivious to the fund's soap-operatic role, Vinik continues to make some remarkably assertive moves. At the close of 1995, he had just 68% of assets in equities; the rest was split between cash and long Treasuries. Instead of technology, he has now turned his attention to industrial cyclicals.

These rapid-fire moves are hardly out of character. Upon arrival in 1992, he revamped the $21 billion fund in less than six months. He jettisoned millions of shares in consumer nondurables in favor of energy stocks, and raised cash and bonds to about 24% of assets. Although the fund took a lot of heat for its lackluster results in 1992, it went on to wallop the average growth fund in 1993. It's also worth noting that Vinik's decision to raise cash paid off nicely at Contrafund in 1990.

Although critics have recently charged him with market-timing, Vinik's reasoning has proved sound in the past, and is hardly worth second-guessing when the market is at record-breaking levels.

Address	82 Devonshire Street Boston, MA 02109
Telephone	800-544-8888
Advisor	Fidelity Management & Research
Subadvisor	FMR (U.K.)/FMR (Far East)
Distributor	Fidelity Distributors
States Available	All
Report Grade	A+
Income Distrib	Semiannually

Minimum Purchase	$2500	Add: $250	IRA: $500
Min Auto Inv Plan	$2500	Systematic Inv: $100	
Date of Inception	05-02-63		

Expenses & Fees		
Sales Fees	3.00%L	
Management Fee	.30%+.52% max./.27% min.(G)+(-).2%P	
Actual Fees	Mgt: 0.75% Dist: ---	
Expense Projections	3Yr: $60 5Yr: $81 10Yr: $144	
Annual Brokerage Cost	0.26%	

Special Securities % of assets

● Private/Illiquid Securities		Trace
○ Structured Notes		0
● Emerging-Markets Secs		Trace
○ Options/Futures/Warrants		No

Composition % of assets 12-31-95

Cash	15.5
Stocks	67.9
Bonds	16.6
Other	0.0

Index Allocation % of stocks

S&P 500	57.6
S&P Mid	17.9
US Sm Cap	20.1
Foreign	5.6

Sector Weightings

	% of Stocks	Rel S&P
Utilities	1.2	0.10
Energy	1.7	0.18
Financials	15.3	1.21
Industrial Cyclicals	17.8	1.06
Consumer Durables	8.1	1.97
Consumer Staples	0.3	0.03
Services	14.5	1.45
Retail	2.4	0.52
Health	2.4	0.23
Technology	36.4	4.41

Source: "Morningstar Mutual Funds," Morningstar, Inc., February 20, 1996. Reprinted by permission of Morningstar, Inc.

In addition, the firm publishes an annual source book that provides a year-end profile of 2,400 open-end funds, a source book for 370 closed-end funds, a monthly performance report (similar to the stock guide) on 2,500 mutual funds, and an annual reference publication of the elite 500 open- and closed-end funds.[38]

GLOBAL INVESTMENT COMPANIES

As discussed throughout this text, serious thought should be given to global diversification of your investment portfolio. Funds that invest in non-U.S. securities are generally called *foreign funds*. More specific designations include either *international funds* or *global funds*. International funds include only non-U.S. stocks from countries such as Germany, Japan, Singapore, and Korea. Global funds contain both U.S. and non-U.S. securities. Ideally, a global fund should invest in a large number of countries. Both international and global funds fall into familiar categories: money funds, long-term government and corporate bond funds, and equity funds. In turn, an international equity fund might limit its focus to a segment of the non-U.S. market such as the European Fund or Pacific Basin Fund, or to a single country such as Germany, Italy, Japan, or Korea. In the chapter on global investing, there was an extensive discussion about investing in emerging markets. Given the need to invest in a diversified portfolio of emerging markets, an emerging market mutual fund that contains a number of them is an ideal vehicle for this asset allocation.

Although most global or international funds are open-end funds (either load or no-load), a significant number are closed-end funds, including most of the single country and the emerging market funds. These funds have opted to be closed-end because being closed-end, they are not subject to major investor liquidations that require the sale of stocks in the portfolio on an illiquid foreign stock exchange. Because of the growth and popularity of foreign funds, most sources of information include separate sections on foreign stock or bond funds.

Summary

- An investment company can be defined as a pool of funds from many individuals that is invested in a collection of individual investments such as stocks, bonds, and other publicly traded securities. Investment companies can be classified as closed-end or open-end; the latter can have either load or no-load funds. A wide variety of funds are available, so you can find one to match almost any investment objective or combination of objectives.
- Numerous studies have examined the historical performance of mutual funds. Most found that less than half the funds matched the risk-adjusted net returns of the aggregate market. The results with gross returns generally indicated average risk-adjusted returns about equal to the market's, with about half of the funds (more than half for some studies) outperforming the market. Interestingly, some recent studies have found evidence of performance persistence.
- Although the returns received by the average individual investor on funds managed by investment companies will probably not be superior to the average results for a specific U.S. or international market, several other important services are provided by investment companies. Therefore, you should give serious consideration to these funds as an important alternative to investing in individual stocks and bonds in the United States or worldwide. For the vast majority of investors, the ideal way to invest internationally is through mutual funds for a country, a region, or a sector of the world (e.g., emerging markets).

[38] These services are available from Morningstar, 53 West Jackson Boulevard, Chicago, IL 60604.

Questions

1. Discuss the difference between an open-end and a closed-end investment company.
2. What two prices are provided for a closed-end investment company? What is the typical relationship between these prices?
3. What is the difference between a load fund and a no-load fund?
4. Discuss the risk–return differences between a common stock fund and a balanced fund?
5. Do you care about how well a mutual fund is diversified? Why or why not?
6. Discuss why the stability of a risk measure for a mutual fund is important to an investor. Are mutual funds' risk measure generally stable?
7. Discuss why the performance of mutual funds should be judged on a risk-adjusted basis. Use examples.
8. Define the net return and gross return for a mutual fund. Discuss how you would compute each, and which is relevant to you.
9. As an investigator evaluating how well mutual fund managers select undervalued stocks or project market returns, discuss whether net or gross returns are more relevant.
10. Based on the numerous tests of mutual fund performance, you believe that only about half of the funds do better than a naive buy-and-hold policy. Does this mean you would forget about investing in investment companies? Why or why not?
11. You are told that Fund X experienced *above-average* performance over the past two years. Do you think it will continue over the next two years? Why or why not?
12. You are told that Fund Y experienced consistently *poor* performance over the past two years. Do you think this performance will continue over the next two years? Why or why not?
13. You see advertisements for two mutual funds indicating that they have investment objectives that are consistent with yours.
    a. How would you get a quick view of these two funds' performance over the past two or three years?
    b. Where would you find longer-term and more in-depth information on the funds?

Problems

1. Suppose ABC Mutual fund had no liabilities and owned only four stocks as follows:

Stock	Shares	Price	Market Value
W	1,000	$12	$12,000
X	1,200	15	18,000
Y	1,500	22	33,000
Z	800	16	12,800
			$75,800

The fund began by selling $50,000 of stock at $8.00 per share. What is its NAV?

2. Suppose you are considering investing $1,000 in a load fund that charges a fee of 8 percent, and you expect your investment to earn 15 percent over the next year. Alternatively, you could invest in a no-load fund with similar risk that charges a 1 percent redemption fee. You estimate that this no-load fund will earn 12 percent. Given your expectations, which is the better investment and by how much?

3. In *Barron's,* look up the NAVs and market prices for five closed-end funds. Compute the difference between the two values for each fund. How many are selling at a premium to NAV? How many are selling at a discount to NAV? What is the average premium or discount? How does this compare to the Herzfeld chart published in *Barron's* that tracks the average discount on a sample of closed-end funds over time?

References

Anderson, Seth Copeland. "Closed-End Funds vs. Market Efficiency." *Journal of Portfolio Management* 13, no. 1 (Fall 1986).

Bekaert, Geert and Michael S. Urias. "Diversification, Integration and Emerging Market Closed-End Funds." *Journal of Finance* 51, no. 3 (July 1996).

Brealey, Richard A. "How to Combine Active Management with Index Funds." *Journal of Portfolio Management* 12, no. 2 (Winter 1986).

Ferson, Wayne E. and Rudi W. Schadt. "Measuring Fund Strategy and Performance in Changing Economic Conditions." *Journal of Finance* 51, no. 2 (June 1996).

Simonds, Richard R. "Mutual Fund Strategies for IRA Investors." *Journal of Portfolio Management* 12, no. 2 (Winter 1986).

Thaler, Richard. "Investor Sentiment and the Closed-End Fund Puzzle." *Journal of Finance* 46, no. 1 (March 1991).

Weiss, Kathleen. "The Post Offering Performance of Closed-End Funds." *Financial Management* 18, no. 3 (Autumn 1989).

Chapter
27

Evaluation of Portfolio Performance

This chapter answers the following questions:

- What major requirements do clients expect from their portfolio managers?
- What can a portfolio manager do to attain superior performance?
- What is the Treynor portfolio performance measure?
- What is the Sharpe portfolio performance measure?
- What is the critical difference between the Treynor and Sharpe portfolio performance measures?
- What is the Jensen portfolio performance measure and how does it relate to the Treynor measure?
- When evaluating a sample of portfolios, how do you determine how well diversified they are?
- What is the bias found regarding the composite performance measures?
- What is the Fama portfolio performance measure and what information does it provide beyond other measures?
- What is attribution analysis and how can it be used to distinguish between a portfolio manager's market timing and security selection skills?
- What is the Roll benchmark error problem and what are the two factors that are affected when computing portfolio performance measures?
- What is the impact of global investing on the benchmark error problem?
- How do bond portfolio performance measures differ from equity portfolio performance measures?
- In the Wagner and Tito bond portfolio performance measure, what is the measure of risk used?
- What are the components of the Dietz, Fogler, and Hardy bond portfolio performance measure?
- What are the sources of return in the Fong, Pearson, and Vasicek bond portfolio performance measure?
- What are customized benchmarks?
- What are the important characteristics that any benchmark should possess?

Investors always are interested in evaluating the performance of their portfolios. It is both expensive and time-consuming to analyze and select securities for a portfolio, so an individual, company, or institution must determine whether this effort is worth the time and money invested in it. Investors managing their own portfolios should evaluate their performance as should those who pay one or several professional money managers. In the latter case, it is imperative to determine whether the investment performance justifies the service's cost.

This chapter outlines the theory and practice of evaluating the performance of an investment portfolio. In the first section, we consider what is required of a portfolio manager. We pinpoint what to look for before we discuss techniques to evaluate portfolio managers.

In section two, we briefly discuss how performance was evaluated before portfolio theory and the CAPM were developed. The rest of the section contains a detailed discussion of three portfolio performance evaluation techniques (referred to as *composite performance measures*) that consider return and risk.

The third section applies these composite measures to gauge the performance of a selected sample of mutual funds. This demonstration analyzes how these measures relate to each other. Although some redundancy exists among the measures, each of them provides unique perspectives, so they are best viewed as complementary measures. We also consider a fourth measure that evaluates the components of performance. Because some observers have contended that these three composite measures of performance are biased in favor of low-risk portfolios, we examine their arguments and the evidence for and against these contentions. The section concludes with an examination of attribution analysis, a measurement technique designed to establish the source of a portfolio manager's skill.

Section four identifies factors to consider when applying these measures. This includes the work of Roll, which questioned any evaluation technique that depends on the CAPM and a market portfolio. This controversy is referred to as the *benchmark problem*. We also discuss why this benchmark problem becomes larger when you begin investing globally. Notably, it affects both your measures of risk and your portfolio performance measures. The section concludes with a description of studies that have evaluated how reliable the composite measures are at predicting future performance.

In the final section, we discuss how factors that determine the performance of a bond portfolio differ from those that affect common stocks. Therefore, we consider several models developed to evaluate the performance of bond portfolios.

WHAT IS REQUIRED OF A PORTFOLIO MANAGER?

There are two major requirements of a portfolio manager:

1. The ability to derive above-average returns for a given risk class
2. The ability to diversify the portfolio completely to eliminate all unsystematic risk

In terms of return, the first requirement is obvious, but the need to consider *risk* in this context was generally not apparent before the 1960s, when work in portfolio theory showed its significance. In modern theory, superior risk-adjusted returns can be derived through *either* superior timing or superior security selection.

An equity portfolio manager who can do a superior job of predicting the peaks or troughs of the equity market can adjust the portfolio's composition to anticipate market trends, holding a completely diversified portfolio of high-beta stocks through rising markets and favoring low-beta stocks and money market instruments during declining markets. Bigger gains in rising markets and smaller losses in declining markets give the portfolio manager above-average risk-adjusted returns.

A fixed-income portfolio manager with superior timing ability changes the portfolio's duration in anticipation of interest rate changes by increasing the duration of the portfolio in anticipation of falling interest rates and reducing the duration of the portfolio when rates are expected to rise. If properly executed, this bond portfolio management strategy likewise provides superior risk-adjusted returns.

As an alternative strategy, a portfolio manager and his or her analysts may try consistently to select undervalued stocks or bonds for a given risk class. Even without superior market timing, such a portfolio would likely experience above-average risk-adjusted returns.

The second factor to consider in evaluating a portfolio manager is the ability to diversify completely. As noted in Chapter 9, the market rewards investors only for bearing systematic (market) risk. Unsystematic risk is not considered when determining required returns because it can be eliminated in a diversified market portfolio. Because they can expect no reward for bearing this uncertainty, investors often want their portfolios completely diversified, which means they want the portfolio manager to eliminate most or all unsystematic risk. The level of diversification can be judged on the basis of the correlation between the portfolio returns and the returns for a market portfolio. A completely diversified portfolio is perfectly correlated with the fully diversified market portfolio.

These two requirements of a portfolio manager are important because some portfolio evaluation techniques take into account one requirement but not the other. Other techniques implicitly consider both factors, but do not differentiate between them.

COMPOSITE PORTFOLIO PERFORMANCE MEASURES

PORTFOLIO EVALUATION BEFORE 1960

At one time, investors evaluated portfolio performance almost entirely on the basis of the rate of return. They were aware of the concept of risk, but did not know how to quantify or measure it, so they could not consider it explicitly. Developments in portfolio theory in the early 1960s showed investors how to quantify and measure risk in terms of the variability of returns. Still, because no single measure combined both return and risk, the two factors had to be considered separately as researchers had done in several early studies.[1] Specifically, the investigators grouped portfolios into similar risk classes based on a measure of risk (such as the variance of return) and then compared the rates of return for alternative portfolios directly within these risk classes.

This section describes in detail the three major composite equity portfolio performance measures that combine risk and return performance into a single value. We describe each measure and its intent, and then demonstrate how to compute it and interpret the results. We also compare two of the measures and discuss how they differ and why they rank portfolios differently.

TREYNOR PORTFOLIO PERFORMANCE MEASURE

Treynor developed the first **composite measure** of portfolio performance that included risk.[2] He postulated two components of risk: (1) risk produced by general market fluctuations and (2) risk resulting from unique fluctuations in the portfolio securities. To identify risk due to market fluctuations, he introduced the *characteristic line,* which defines the relationship between the rates of return for a portfolio over time and the rates of return for an appropriate market portfolio, as we discussed in Chapter 9. He noted that the characteristic line's slope measures the *relative volatility* of the portfolio's returns in relation to returns for the aggregate market. As we also know from Chapter 9, this slope is the portfolio's beta coefficient. A higher slope (beta) characterizes a portfolio that is more sensitive to market returns and that has greater market risk.

Deviations from the characteristic line indicate unique returns for the portfolio relative to the market. These differences arise from the returns on individual stocks in the portfolio. In a completely diversified portfolio, these unique returns for individual stocks should

---

[1] Irwin Friend, Marshall Blume, and Jean Crockett, *Mutual Funds and Other Institutional Investors* (New York: McGraw-Hill, 1970).

[2] Jack L. Treynor, "How to Rate Management of Investment Funds," *Harvard Business Review* 43, no. 1 (January–February 1965): 63–75.

cancel out. As the correlation of the portfolio with the market increases, unique risk declines and diversification improves. Because Treynor was not concerned about this aspect of portfolio performance, he gave no further consideration to the diversification measure.

TREYNOR'S COMPOSITE PERFORMANCE MEASURE   Treynor was interested in a measure of performance that would apply to all investors—regardless of their risk preferences. Building on developments in capital market theory, he introduced a risk-free asset that could be combined with different portfolios to form a straight portfolio possibility line. He showed that rational, risk-averse investors would always prefer portfolio possibility lines with larger slopes because such high-slope lines would place investors on higher indifference curves. The slope of this portfolio possibility line (designated T) is equal to[3]

$$T = \frac{\overline{R_i} - \overline{RFR}}{\beta_i}$$

where

$\overline{R_i}$ = the average rate of return for portfolio i during a specified time period
$\overline{RFR}$ = the average rate of return on a risk-free investment during the same time period
β_i = the slope of the fund's characteristic line during that time period (this indicates the portfolio's relative volatility).

As noted, a larger T value indicates a larger slope and a better portfolio for all investors (regardless of their risk preferences). Because the numerator of this ratio ($\overline{R_i} - \overline{RFR}$) is the *risk premium* and the denominator is a measure of risk, the total expression indicates the portfolio's *risk premium return per unit of risk*. All risk-averse investors would prefer to maximize this value. Note that the risk variable beta measures systematic risk and tells us nothing about the diversification of the portfolio. It *implicitly assumes* a completely diversified portfolio, which means that systematic risk is the relevant risk measure.

Comparing a portfolio's T value to a similar measure for the market portfolio indicates whether the portfolio would plot above the SML. Calculate the T value for the aggregate market as follows:

$$T_m = \frac{\overline{R_m} - \overline{RFR}}{\beta_m}$$

In this expression, β_m equals 1.0 (the market's beta) and indicates the slope of the SML. Therefore, a portfolio with a higher T value than the market portfolio plots above the SML, indicating superior risk-adjusted performance.

DEMONSTRATION OF COMPARATIVE TREYNOR MEASURES   To understand how to use and interpret this measure of performance, suppose that during the most recent 10-year period, the average annual total rate of return (including dividends) on an aggregate market portfolio such as the S&P 500 was 14 percent ($\overline{R_m} = 0.14$) and the average nominal rate of return on government T-bills was 8 percent ($\overline{RFR} = 0.08$). Assume that, as administrator of a large pension fund that has been divided among three money managers during the past 10

---

[3] The terms used in the formula differ from those used by Treynor but are consistent with our earlier discussion. Also, our discussion is concerned with general *portfolio* performance rather than being limited to mutual funds.

years, you must decide whether to renew your investment management contracts with all three managers. To do this, you must measure how they have performed.

Assume you are given the following results.

Investment Manager	Average Annual Rate of Return	Beta
W	0.12	0.90
X	0.16	1.05
Y	0.18	1.20

You can compute T values for the market portfolio and for each of the individual portfolio managers as follows:

$$T_m = \frac{0.14 - 0.08}{1.00} = 0.060$$

$$T_w = \frac{0.12 - 0.08}{0.90} = 0.044$$

$$T_x = \frac{0.16 - 0.08}{1.05} = 0.076$$

$$T_y = \frac{0.18 - 0.08}{1.20} = 0.083$$

These results indicate that investment manager W not only ranked the lowest of three managers, but did not perform as well as the aggregate market. In contrast, both X and Y beat the market portfolio, and manager Y performed somewhat better than manager X. In terms of the SML, both of their portfolios plotted above the line, as shown in Figure 27.1.

FIGURE 27.1	**PLOT OF PERFORMANCE ON SML (T MEASURE)**

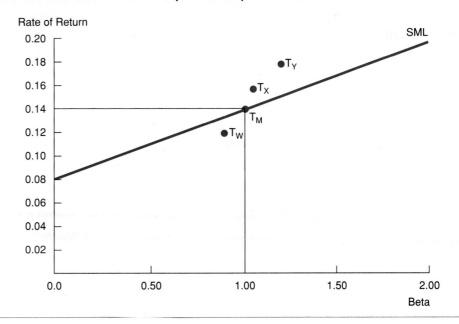

Very poor return performance or very good performance with very low risk may yield negative T values. An example of poor performance is a portfolio with both an average rate of return below the risk-free rate and a positive beta. For instance, in the preceding case assume that a fourth portfolio manager, Z, had a portfolio beta of 0.50, but an average rate of return of only 0.07. The T value would be

$$T_z = \frac{0.07 - 0.08}{0.50} = -0.02.$$

Obviously, this performance would plot below the SML in Figure 27.1.

A portfolio with a *negative* beta and an average rate of return above the risk-free rate of return would likewise have a negative T value. In this case, however, it indicates exemplary performance. As an example, assume that portfolio manager G invested heavily in gold mining stocks during a period of great political and economic uncertainty. Because gold typically has a negative correlation with most stocks, this portfolio's beta could be negative. If you were examining this portfolio after gold prices increased in value as a result of the uncertainty, you might find excellent returns. Assume that our gold bug portfolio G had a beta of −0.20 and yet experienced an average rate of return of 10 percent. The T value for this portfolio would then be

$$T_g = \frac{0.10 - 0.08}{-0.20} = -0.100.$$

Although the T value is −0.100, if you plotted these results on a graph, it would indicate a position substantially above the SML in Figure 27.1.

Because negative betas can yield T values that give confusing results, it is preferable either to plot the portfolio on an SML graph or to compute the expected return for this portfolio using the SML equation and then compare this expected return to the actual return. This comparison will reveal whether the actual return was above or below expectations. In the preceding example for portfolio G, the expected return would be

$$
\begin{aligned}
E(R_g) &= RFR + \beta_i(R_m - RFR) \\
&= 0.08 + (-0.20)(0.06) \\
&= 0.08 - 0.012 \\
&= 0.068.
\end{aligned}
$$

Comparing this expected (required) rate of return of 6.8 percent to the actual return of 10 percent shows that portfolio manager G has done a superior job.

SHARPE PORTFOLIO PERFORMANCE MEASURE

Sharpe likewise conceived of a composite measure to evaluate the performance of mutual funds.[4] The measure followed closely his earlier work on the capital asset pricing model (CAPM), dealing specifically with the capital market line (CML).

The **Sharpe measure** of portfolio performance (designated S) is stated as follows:

$$S_i = \frac{\overline{R}_i - \overline{RFR}}{\sigma_i}$$

---

[4] William F. Sharpe, "Mutual Fund Performance," *Journal of Business* 39, no. 1, Part 2 (January 1966): 119–138.

where

$\overline{R}_i$ = the average rate of return for portfolio i during a specified time period
$\overline{RFR}$ = the average rate of return on risk-free assets during the same time period
σ_i = the standard deviation of the rate of return for portfolio i during the time period.

This composite measure of portfolio performance clearly is similar to the Treynor measure; however, it seeks to measure the *total risk* of the portfolio by including the standard deviation of returns rather than considering only the systematic risk summarized by beta. Because the numerator is the portfolio's risk premium, this measure indicates the *risk premium return earned per unit of total risk*. In terms of capital market theory, this portfolio performance measure uses total risk to compare portfolios to the CML, whereas the Treynor measure examines portfolio performance in relation to the SML.

DEMONSTRATION OF COMPARATIVE SHARPE MEASURES

The following examples use the Sharpe measure of performance. Again, assume that $\overline{R}_m$ = 0.14 and $\overline{RFR}$ = 0.08. Suppose you are told that the standard deviation of the annual rate of return for the market portfolio over the past 10 years was 20 percent (σ_m = 0.20). Now you want to examine the performance of the following portfolios:

Portfolio	Average Annual Rate of Return	Standard Deviation of Return
D	0.13	0.18
E	0.17	0.22
F	0.16	0.23

The Sharpe measures for these portfolios are as follows:

$$S_m = \frac{0.14 - 0.08}{0.20} = 0.300$$

$$S_d = \frac{0.13 - 0.08}{0.18} = 0.278$$

$$S_e = \frac{0.17 - 0.08}{0.22} = 0.409$$

$$S_f = \frac{0.16 - 0.08}{0.23} = 0.348$$

The D portfolio had the lowest risk premium return per unit of total risk, failing even to perform as well as the aggregate market portfolio. In contrast, portfolios E and F performed better than the aggregate market: portfolio E did better than portfolio F.

Given the market portfolio results during this period, it is possible to draw the CML. If we plot the results for portfolios D, E, and F on this graph, as shown in Figure 27.2, we see that portfolio D plots below the line, whereas the E and F portfolios are above the line, indicating superior risk-adjusted performance.

TREYNOR VERSUS SHARPE MEASURE   The Sharpe portfolio performance measure uses the standard deviation of returns as the measure of risk, whereas the Treynor performance measure uses beta (systematic risk). The Sharpe measure, therefore, evaluates the portfolio manager on the basis of both rate of return performance and diversification.

For a completely diversified portfolio, one without any unsystematic risk, the two measures give identical rankings because the total variance of the completely diversified

FIGURE 27.2

PLOT OF PERFORMANCE ON CML (S MEASURE)

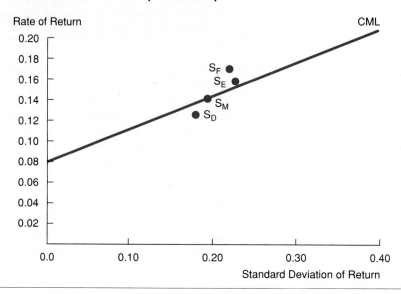

Therefore, these two performance measures provide complementary yet different information, and both measures should be used. If you are dealing with a group of well-diversified portfolios, as many mutual funds are, the two measures provide similar rankings.

portfolio is its systematic variance. Alternatively, a poorly diversified portfolio could have a high ranking on the basis of the Treynor performance measure but a much lower ranking on the basis of the Sharpe performance measure. Any difference in rank would come directly from a difference in diversification.

Therefore, these two performance measures provide complementary yet different information, and both measures should be used. If you are dealing with a group of well-diversified portfolios, as many mutual funds are, the two measures provide similar rankings.

A disadvantage of the Treynor and Sharpe measures is that they produce relative, but not absolute, rankings of portfolio performance. That is, the Sharpe measures for portfolios E and F illustrated in Figure 27.2 show that both generated risk-adjusted returns above the market. Further, F's risk-adjusted performance measure is larger than E's. What we cannot say with certainty, however, is whether any of these differences are statistically significant.

JENSEN PORTFOLIO PERFORMANCE MEASURE

The **Jensen measure** is similar to the measures already discussed because it is based on the capital asset pricing model (CAPM).[5] All versions of the CAPM calculate the expected one-period return on any security or portfolio by the following expression:

$$E(R_j) = RFR + \beta_j[E(R_m) - RFR]$$

where

$E(R_j)$ = the expected return on security or portfolio j
RFR = the one-period risk-free interest rate
β_j = the systematic risk (beta) for security or portfolio j
$E(R_m)$ = the expected return on the market portfolio of risky assets

[5] Michael C. Jensen, "The Performance of Mutual Funds in the Period 1945–1964," *Journal of Finance* 23, no. 2 (May 1968): 389–416.

The expected return and the risk-free return vary for different periods. Consequently, we are concerned with the time series of expected rates of return for security or portfolio j. Moreover, assuming the asset pricing model is empirically valid, you can express the expectations formula in terms of *realized* rates of return as follows:

$$R_{jt} = RFR_t + \beta_j[R_{mt} - RFR_t] + U_{jt}$$

This equation states that the realized rate of return on a security or portfolio during a given time period should be a linear function of the risk-free rate of return during the period, plus a risk premium that depends on the systematic risk of the security or portfolio during the period plus a random error term.

Subtracting the risk-free return from both sides, we have

$$R_{jt} - RFR_t = \beta_j[R_{mt} - RFR_t] + U_{jt}$$

This shows that the risk premium earned on the jth portfolio is equal to β_j times a market risk premium plus a random error term. In this form, an intercept for the regression is not expected if all assets and portfolios were in equilibrium.

Alternatively, superior portfolio managers who forecast market turns or consistently select undervalued securities earn higher risk premiums than those implied by this model. Specifically, superior portfolio managers have consistently positive random error terms because the actual returns for their portfolios consistently exceed the expected returns implied by this model. To detect and measure this superior performance, you must allow for an intercept (a nonzero constant) that measures any positive or negative difference from the model. Consistent positive differences cause a positive intercept, whereas consistent negative differences (inferior performance) cause a negative intercept. With an intercept or nonzero constant, the earlier equation becomes

$$R_{jt} - RFR_t = \alpha_j + \beta_j[R_{mt} - RFR_t] + U_{jt}$$

In this equation, the α_j value indicates whether the portfolio manager is superior or inferior in market timing and/or stock selection. A superior manager has a significant positive α (or "alpha") value because of the consistent positive residuals. In contrast, an inferior manager's returns consistently fall short of expectations based on the CAPM model giving consistently negative residuals. In such a case, the nonzero constant α_j is a significant negative value.

The performance of a portfolio manager with no forecasting ability but not clearly inferior equals that of a naive buy-and-hold policy. In the equation, because the rate of return on such a portfolio typically matches the returns you expect on the basis of the CAPM, the residual returns generally are randomly positive and negative. This gives a constant term that differs insignificantly from zero, indicating that the portfolio manager basically matched the market on a risk-adjusted basis.

Therefore, the α_j represents how much of the rate of return on the portfolio is attributable to the manager's ability to derive above-average returns adjusted for risk. Superior risk-adjusted returns indicate that the manager is good at either predicting market turns, or selecting undervalued issues for the portfolio, or both.

APPLYING THE JENSEN MEASURE   The Jensen measure of performance requires using a different *RFR* for each time interval during the sample period. For example, to examine the performance of a fund manager over a 10-year period using yearly intervals, you must examine the fund's annual returns less the return on risk-free assets for each year, and relate this to the annual return on the market portfolio less the same risk-free rate. This contrasts with the Treynor and Sharpe composite measures, which examine the *average* returns for the total period for all variables (the portfolio, the market, and the risk-free asset).

Also, like the Treynor measure, the Jensen measure does not evaluate the portfolio manager's ability to diversify because it calculates risk premiums in terms of systematic risk. As noted earlier, to evaluate the performance of a group of well-diversified portfolios such as mutual funds, this is likely to be a reasonable assumption. Jensen's analysis of mutual fund performance showed that complete diversification was a fairly reasonable assumption because the funds typically correlated with the market at rates above 0.90.

APPLICATION OF PORTFOLIO PERFORMANCE MEASURES

To apply these measures, we selected 20 open-end mutual funds and used monthly data for the 5-year period from 1988 to 1992. The monthly rates of return for the first fund (Aim Constellation Fund) and the S&P 500 are contained in Table 27.1. The total rate of return for each month is computed as follows:

$$R_{it} = \frac{EP_{it} + Div_{it} + Cap.Dist._{it} - BP_{it}}{BP_{it}}$$

where

R_{it} = the total rate of return on fund i during month t
EP_{it} = the ending price for fund i during month t
Div_{it} = the dividend payments made by fund i during month t
$Cap.Dist._{it}$ = the capital gain distributions made by fund i during month t
BP_{it} = the beginning price for fund i during month t

These return computations do not take into account any sales charges by the funds. Given the monthly results for the fund and the aggregate market (as represented by the S&P 500), you can compute the composite measures presented in Table 27.1.

The arithmetic average annual rate of return for Aim Constellation Fund was 26.40 percent versus 15.71 percent for the market, and the fund's beta was greater than 1.00 (1.351). Using the average annual rate of T-bills of 6.20 percent as the $\overline{RFR}$, the Treynor measure for the Aim Constellation Fund (T_i) was substantially greater than the comparable measure for the market (T_m) (14.949 versus 9.508). Likewise, the standard deviation of returns for Aim Constellation was greater than the market's (20.67 versus 13.25). Even with the higher standard deviation, the Sharpe measure for the fund (S_i) was larger than the measure for the market (S_m) (0.977 versus 0.717).

Finally, a regression of the fund's annual risk premium ($R_{it} - RFR_t$) and the market's annual risk premium ($R_{mt} - RFR_t$) indicated a positive intercept (constant) value of 0.610, but was not statistically significant. If this intercept value had been significant, Aim Constellation's risk-adjusted annual rate of return would have averaged about .61 percent above the market on a reliable basis.

TOTAL SAMPLE RESULTS   The overall results in Table 27.2 generally are consistent with the findings of earlier studies. Our sample was rather casually selected because we intended it for demonstration purposes only. The mean annual return for all the funds was quite close to the market return (15.45 versus 15.71). Considering only the rate of return, 7 of the 20 funds outperformed the market.

TABLE 27.1   **EXAMPLE OF PORTFOLIO EVALUATION MEASURES COMPUTATION USING AIM CONSTELLATION FUND, INC.**

	R_{it}	R_{mt}	RFR_t	$R_{it} - RFR_t$	$R_{mt} - RFR_t$
Jan. 1988	−1.00	4.27	0.49	−1.49	3.78
Feb. 1988	9.50	4.70	0.47	9.03	4.23
Mar. 1988	0.60	−3.02	0.47	0.13	−3.49
Apr. 1988	3.50	1.08	0.49	3.01	0.59
May 1988	−2.00	0.78	0.52	−2.52	0.26
Jun. 1988	12.00	4.64	0.54	11.46	4.10
Jul. 1988	−3.00	−0.40	0.50	−3.50	−0.90
Aug. 1988	−5.00	−3.31	0.53	−5.53	−3.84
Sep. 1988	4.50	4.24	0.54	3.96	3.70
Oct. 1988	0.00	2.73	0.61	−0.61	2.12
Nov. 1988	−3.00	−1.42	0.64	−3.64	−2.06
Dec. 1988	3.80	1.81	0.67	3.13	1.14
⋮	⋮	⋮	⋮	⋮	⋮
⋮	⋮	⋮	⋮	⋮	⋮
⋮	⋮	⋮	⋮	⋮	⋮
Jan. 1992	2.10	−1.86	0.32	1.78	−2.18
Feb. 1992	1.60	1.28	0.32	1.28	0.96
Mar. 1992	−3.00	−1.96	0.34	−3.34	−2.30
Apr. 1992	−5.00	2.91	0.32	−5.32	2.59
May 1992	0.70	0.54	0.31	0.39	0.24
Jun. 1992	−5.00	−1.45	0.31	−5.31	−1.76
Jul. 1992	6.00	4.03	0.27	5.73	3.76
Aug. 1992	−3.00	−2.02	0.26	−3.26	−2.28
Sep. 1992	3.70	1.15	0.25	3.45	0.90
Oct. 1992	6.20	0.36	0.24	5.96	0.12
Nov. 1992	8.20	3.37	0.26	7.94	3.11
Dec. 1992	4.00	1.31	0.27	3.73	1.04
Mean	26.40	15.71	6.20		
Standard Deviation	20.67	13.25	0.50		
Beta	1.351				
S_i	0.977				
S_m	0.717				
T_i	14.949				
T_m	9.508				
Jensen Intercept	0.610				
Beta j	1.355				
R_{lm}^2	0.752				

The R^2 for a portfolio with the market can serve as a measure of diversification. The closer the R^2 is to 1.00, the more completely diversified the portfolio. The average R^2 for our sample was not very high at 0.766, and the range was quite large, from 0.284 to 0.948. This indicates that many of the funds were not well-diversified. Of the 20 funds, 11 had R^2 values less than 0.80.

The two risk measures (standard deviation and beta) also show a wide degree of dispersion, but generally are consistent with expectations. Specifically, 7 of the 20 funds had larger standard deviations than the market, and the mean standard deviation was smaller (12.12 versus 13.25). Only 5 of the funds had a beta above 1.00; the average beta was 0.799.

TABLE 27.2	PERFORMANCE MEASURES FOR 20 SELECTED MUTUAL FUNDS						
	Average Annual Rate of Return	Standard Deviation	Beta	R^2	Treynor	Sharpe	Jensen
Aim Constellation Fund, Inc.	26.40	20.67	1.351	0.751	14.949 (6)	0.977 (7)	0.610 (2)
Dean Witter Developing Growth Fund	13.72	9.51	0.594	0.605	5.650 (19)	0.332 (19)	−0.430 (20)
Dreyfus Growth Opportunity Fund	13.22	14.20	0.905	0.713	7.764 (15)	0.495 (16)	−0.134 (15)
Fasciano Fund, Inc.	17.66	12.53	0.757	0.641	15.144 (5)	0.915 (8)	0.355 (5)
Fidelity Magellan Fund	18.46	14.32	1.048	0.941	11.699 (10)	0.856 (9)	0.192 (9)
Fidelity Puritan Fund	15.24	9.12	0.645	0.878	14.029 (7)	0.992 (6)	0.240 (8)
Gabelli Asset Fund	17.42	9.51	0.594	0.686	18.888 (2)	1.180 (4)	0.463a (4)
Guardian Park Avenue Fund	16.04	12.91	0.828	0.723	11.883 (9)	0.762 (11)	0.160 (10)
IDS Mutual Fund	11.88	9.17	0.662	0.916	8.584 (13)	0.620 (13)	−0.053 (12)
Income Fund of America, Inc.	14.68	6.98	0.458	0.758	18.504 (3)	1.216 (2)	0.342a (6)
Investment Company of America Fund	16.88	10.68	0.785	0.948	13.615 (8)	1.000 (5)	0.296a (7)
Janus Venture Fund	22.54	13.45	0.889	0.768	18.374 (4)	1.215 (3)	0.657a (1)
Kemper Technology Fund	13.70	17.05	1.106	0.739	6.780 (17)	0.440 (18)	−0.253 (17)
Lindner Dividend Fund	15.06	5.64	0.227	0.285	39.064 (1)	1.573 (1)	0.555a (3)
Oppenheimer Fund	12.42	12.32	0.818	0.818	7.603 (16)	0.505 (15)	−0.149 (16)
Putnam Fund for Growth and Income A	14.26	9.77	0.700	0.902	11.514 (11)	0.825 (10)	0.117 (11)
Templeton World Fund	12.86	12.32	0.810	0.810	8.224 (14)	0.541 (14)	−0.100 (14)
T. Rowe Price Growth Stock Fund	12.94	14.49	1.033	0.893	6.525 (18)	0.465 (17)	−0.258 (18)
Value Line Special Situations Fund	11.00	17.53	1.033	0.609	4.651 (20)	0.274 (20)	−0.418 (19)
Vanguard Wellington Fund	12.66	10.20	0.745	0.939	8.668 (12)	0.634 (12)	−0.053 (13)
Mean	15.45	12.12	0.799	0.766	12.606	0.791	0.107
S&P 500	15.71	13.25	1.000	1.000	9.508	0.717	0.000
90-Day T-Bill Rate	6.20	0.50					

aSignificant at the 0.05 level.

Alternative measures ranked the performance of individual funds consistently. Using the Sharpe or the Treynor measure, 11 of the 20 funds had a value that was better than the market. The Jensen measure indicated that 11 of the 20 had positive intercepts, but only 5 of these were statistically significant (none of the negative intercepts were significant). The mean values for the Sharpe and Treynor measures were greater than the aggregate market figure. These results indicate that, on average, and without considering transaction costs, this sample of funds had slightly better results than the market during this time period.

You should analyze the individual funds and consider each of the components: rate of return, risk (both standard deviation and beta), and the R^2 as a measure of diversification. One might expect the best performance by funds with low diversification because they apparently are attempting to beat the market by being unique in their selection or timing. This seems to be true for the top performing funds such as Lindner Dividend Fund and Gabelli Asset Fund as well as some unsuccessful funds that had poor diversification but low returns such as Value Line Special Situations Fund.

POTENTIAL BIAS OF ONE-PARAMETER MEASURES   Friend and Blume pointed out that, theoretically, the three composite measures of performance should be independent of alternative measures of risk because they are *risk-adjusted* measures.[6] An analysis of the relationship between the composite measures of performance and two measures of risk

---

[6] Irwin Friend and Marshall Blume, "Measurement of Portfolio Performance under Uncertainty," *American Economic Review* 60, no. 4 (September 1970), 561–575.

FIGURE 27.3

SCATTER DIAGRAM OF JENSEN'S PERFORMANCE MEASURE[a] ON RISK: JANUARY 1960 TO JUNE 1968

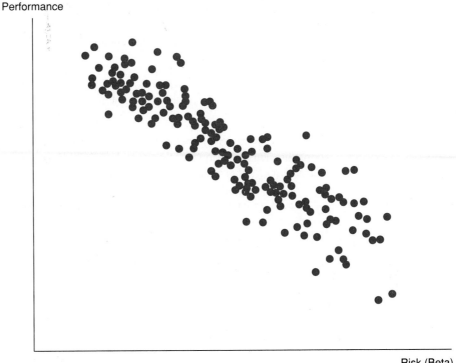

Performance

Risk (Beta)

[a]Using log relatives.

Source: Irwin Friend and Marshall Blume, "Measurement of Portfolio Performance under Uncertainty," *American Economic Review* 60, no. 4 (September 1970): 567. Reprinted by permission.

(standard deviation and beta) for 200 random portfolios from the NYSE indicated a significant *inverse* relationship (the risk-adjusted performance of low-risk portfolios was better than the comparable performance for high-risk portfolios). The results for the Jensen performance measure are shown in Figure 27.3.

Subsequently, Klemkosky examined the relationship between composite performance measures and risk measures using actual mutual fund data in contrast to the random portfolio data used by Friend and Blume.[7] Beyond the three composite measures, the author derived two measures that computed the excess return above the risk-free rate relative to the semistandard deviation and relative to the mean absolute deviation as risk measures. The results indicated a positive bias—that is, a *positive* relationship between the composite performance measures and the risk involved. This was especially true for the Treynor and Jensen measures. The performance measures that used the mean absolute deviation and the semistandard deviation as risk proxies were less biased than the three standard performance measures. He concluded that although a bias might exist, one could not be certain of its direction.

[7]Robert C. Klemkosky, "The Bias in Composite Performance Measures," *Journal of Financial and Quantitative Analysis* 8, no. 3 (June 1973): 505–514.

COMPONENTS OF
INVESTMENT
PERFORMANCE

Following the work of Treynor, Sharpe, and Jensen, Fama suggested a somewhat finer breakdown of performance.[8] Fama's evaluation model likewise assumes that the returns on managed portfolios can be judged relative to those of naively selected portfolios with similar risk levels. The technique uses the simple one-period version of the two-parameter model, all the perfect market assumptions, and derives the *ex ante* market line, which indicates the following equilibrium relationship between expected return and risk for any security j:

$$E(\hat{R}_j) = RFR + \left[\frac{E(\hat{R}_m) - RFR}{\sigma(\hat{R}_m)}\right] \frac{\text{Cov}(\hat{R}_j, \hat{R}_m)}{\sigma(\hat{R}_m)}$$

$\text{Cov}(R_j, R_m)$ is the covariance between the returns for security j and the return on the market portfolio. This equation indicates that the expected return on security j is the riskless rate of interest, RFR, plus a risk premium that is $[E(\bar{R}_m) - RFR]/\sigma(\bar{R}_m)$, called the *market price per unit of risk*, times the risk of asset j, which is $[\text{Cov}(\bar{R}_j, \bar{R}_m)]/\sigma(\bar{R}_m)$.

This *ex ante* market line relationship should hold for portfolios as well as for individual assets and assumes completely efficient markets in which prices fully reflect all available information. If a portfolio manager believes that the market is not completely efficient and that she can make better judgments than the market, then an *ex post* version of this market line can provide a benchmark for the manager's performance. Given that the risk variable, $\text{Cov}(R_j, R_m)/\sigma(R_m)$, can be denoted β_x, the *ex post* market line is as follows:

$$R_x = RFR + \left(\frac{R_m - RFR}{\sigma(R_m)}\right)\beta_x$$

This *ex post* market line provides the benchmark used to evaluate managed portfolios in a sequence of more complex measures.

EVALUATING SELECTIVITY   You can measure the return due to selectivity as follows:

$$\text{Selectivity} = R_a - R_x(\beta_a)$$

where

R_a = the return on the portfolio being evaluated
$R_x(\beta_a)$ = the return on the combination of the riskless asset and the market portfolio m that has risk β_x equal to β_a, the risk of the portfolio being evaluated.

As shown in Figure 27.4, selectivity measures how well the chosen portfolio performed relative to a naively selected portfolio of equal risk. This measure indicates any difference from the *ex post* market line and is quite similar to Treynor's measure.

Also, you can examine *overall performance* in terms of selectivity (which was just shown) and the returns from assuming risk as follows:

$$\begin{array}{ccc} \text{Overall} \\ \text{Performance} = & \text{Selectivity} & + & \text{Risk} \\ [R_a - RFR] = & [R_a - R_x(\beta_a)] & + & [R_x(\beta_a) - RFR] \end{array}$$

---

[8] Eugene F. Fama, "Components of Investment Performance," *Journal of Finance* 27, no. 3 (June 1972); 551–567.

| FIGURE 27.4 | AN ILLUSTRATION OF THE PERFORMANCE MEASURES |

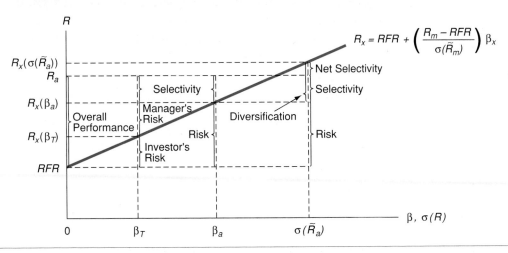

Source: Eugene F. Fama, "Components of Investment Performance," *Journal of Finance* 27, no. 3 (June 1972): 588. Reprinted by permission.

Figure 27.4 shows that overall performance is the total return above the risk-free return and includes the return that *should* have been received for accepting the portfolio risk (β_a). This expected return for accepting risk (β_a) is equal to $[R_x(\beta_a) - RFR]$. Any excess over this expected return is due to selectivity.

EVALUATING DIVERSIFICATION   If a portfolio manager attempts to select undervalued stocks and in the process gives up some diversification, it is possible to measure the added return necessary to justify this diversification decision. The portfolio's *gross selectivity* is made up of *net selectivity* plus *diversification* as follows:

$$\underset{\text{Selectivity}}{R_a - R_x(\beta_a)} = \text{Net Selectivity} + \underset{\text{Diversification}}{[R_x(\sigma(R_a)) - R_x(\beta_a)]}$$

or

$$\begin{aligned}\text{Net Selectivity} &= \underset{\text{Selectivity}}{R_a - R_x(\beta_a)} - \underset{\text{Diversification}}{[R_x(\sigma(R_a)) - R_x(\beta_a)]}\\ &= R_a - R_x(\sigma(R_a)),\end{aligned}$$

where

$R_x(\sigma(R_a))$ = **the return on the combination of the riskless asset and the market portfolio that has return dispersion equivalent to that of the portfolio being evaluated.**

Therefore, the diversification measure indicates the *added return* required to justify any loss of diversification in the portfolio. The term emphasizes that diversification is the elimination of all unsystematic variability. If the portfolio is completely diversified so that total risk (σ) is equal to systematic risk (β), then the $R_x(\sigma(R_a))$ would be the same as $R_x(\beta_a)$, and the diversification term would equal zero.

Because the diversification measure always is nonnegative, net selectivity will always be equal to or less than gross selectivity. The two will be equal when the portfolio is completely diversified. If the investor is not concerned with the diversification of the portfolio, this particular breakdown will not be important, and only selectivity will be considered.

EVALUATING RISK   Assuming the investor has a target level of risk for the portfolio equal to β_T, the overall performance due to risk (the total return above the risk-free return) can be assessed as follows:

$$\text{Risk} = \text{Manager's Risk} + \text{Investor's Risk}$$
$$[R_x(\beta_a) - RFR] = [R_x(\beta_a) - R_x(\beta_T)] + [R_x(\beta_T) - RFR]$$

where

$R_x(\beta_T)$ = the return on the naively selected portfolio with the target level of market risk (β_T).

If the portfolio risk is equal to the target risk ($\beta_a = \beta_T$), then the manager's risk does not exist. If there is a difference between β_a and β_T, then the manager's risk is the return she must earn due to the decision to accept risk (β_a), which is different from the risk desired by the investor (β_T). The investor's risk is the return expected because the investor stipulated some positive level of risk. This evaluation is possible only if the client has specified a desired level of market risk, which is typical of pension funds and profit-sharing plans. Generally, it is not possible to compute this measure for *ex post* evaluations because the desired risk level is typically not available.

APPLICATION OF FAMA MEASURES   Several of these performance components can be used in *ex post* evaluation, as shown in Table 27.3. Overall performance is the return derived above the risk-free return (i.e., the return above 6.20 percent as shown in Table 27.2). All of these mutual funds experienced positive overall performance. Next, determine how much the portfolio (fund) *should* receive for its systematic risk using the following expected return equation for this period (15.71 percent is the return on the S&P 500 during this period, as shown in Table 27.2):

$$E(R_i) = 6.20 + \beta_i (15.71 - 6.20)$$
$$= 6.20 + \beta_i (9.51)$$

The required return for risk simply is the latter term in this expression: $\beta_i(9.51)$. The required return for risk for Aim Constellation Fund was $1.351(9.51) = 12.85$ percent (its total required return is $6.20 + 12.85 = 19.05$). The return for selectivity is the difference between overall performance ($26.40 - 6.20 = 20.20$) and the required return for risk (12.85). If the overall performance exceeds the required return for risk, the portfolio has experienced a positive return for selectivity. The results indicate that Aim Constellation had an average annual return of 7.35 percent for selectivity ($20.20 - 12.85$). Eleven funds had positive returns for selectivity. In contrast, several funds had positive overall performance, but their required return for risk exceeded this figure, giving them negative returns for selectivity (e.g., Kemper Technology Fund).

The next two columns in Table 27.3 indicate the effect of diversification on performance. The diversification term indicates the required return for not being completely diversified (i.e., having total risk above systematic risk). If a fund's total risk is equal to its

TABLE 27.3   COMPONENTS OF PERFORMANCE FOR 20 SELECTED MUTUAL FUNDS

	Average Rate of Return	Standard Deviation	Beta	R^2	Overall Performance	Risk	Selectivity	Diversification	Net Selectivity
Aim Constellation Fund, Inc.	26.40	20.67	1.351	0.751	20.20	12.85	7.35	1.99	5.36 (2)
Dean Witter Developing Growth Fund	13.72	22.68	1.331	0.605	7.52	12.66	−5.14	3.62	−8.76 (20)
Dreyfus Growth Opportunity Fund	13.22	14.20	0.905	0.713	7.02	8.61	−1.59	1.59	−3.17 (16)
Fasciano Fund, Inc.	17.66	12.53	0.757	0.641	11.46	7.20	4.26	1.79	2.47 (8)
Fidelity Magellan Fund	18.46	14.32	1.048	0.941	12.26	9.97	2.29	0.31	1.98 (9)
Fidelity Puritan Fund	15.24	9.12	0.645	0.878	9.04	6.13	2.91	0.41	2.49 (7)
Gabelli Asset Fund	17.42	9.51	0.594	0.686	11.22	5.65	5.57	1.18	4.39 (4)
Guardian Park Avenue Fund	16.04	12.91	0.828	0.723	9.84	7.87	1.97	1.39	0.57 (11)
IDS Mutual Fund	11.88	9.17	0.662	0.916	5.68	6.30	−0.62	0.29	−0.90 (13)
Income Fund of America, Inc.	14.68	6.98	0.458	0.758	8.48	4.36	4.12	0.65	3.47 (5)
Investment Company of America Fund	16.88	10.68	0.785	0.948	10.68	7.47	3.21	0.20	3.01 (6)
Janus Venture Fund	22.54	13.45	0.889	0.768	16.34	8.45	7.89	1.20	6.69 (1)
Kemper Technology Fund	13.70	17.05	1.106	0.739	7.50	10.52	−3.02	1.72	−4.74 (18)
Lindner Dividend Fund	15.06	5.64	0.227	0.285	8.86	2.16	6.70	1.89	4.81 (3)
Oppenheimer Fund	12.42	12.32	0.818	0.818	6.22	7.78	−1.56	1.06	−2.62 (15)
Putnam Fund for Growth and Income A	14.26	9.77	0.700	0.902	8.06	6.66	1.40	0.36	1.05 (10)
Templeton World Fund	12.86	12.32	0.810	0.810	6.66	7.70	−1.04	1.14	−2.18 (14)
T. Rowe Price Growth Stock Fund	12.94	14.49	1.033	0.893	6.74	9.82	−3.08	0.58	−3.66 (17)
Value Line Special Situations Fund	11.00	17.53	1.033	0.609	4.80	9.82	−5.02	2.76	−7.78 (19)
Vanguard Wellington Fund	12.66	10.20	0.745	0.939	6.46	7.08	−0.62	0.24	−0.86 (12)
S&P 500	15.71	13.25							
90-Day T-Bill Rate	6.20	0.50							

systematic risk, then the ratio of its total risk to the market's total risk will equal its beta. If this is not the case, then the ratio of the fund's total risk for the fund relative to the market will be greater than its beta, which implies an added return required because of incomplete diversification. For Aim Constellation, the ratio of total risk was

$$\frac{\sigma_i}{\sigma_m} = \frac{20.67}{13.25} = 1.56$$

This total risk ratio compares to the fund's beta of 1.351, indicating that the fund is not completely diversified, which is consistent with its R^2 of 0.751. The fund's required return, given its standard deviation, is

$$R_i = 6.20 + 1.56(9.51)$$
$$= 21.04$$

Recall that the fund's required return for systematic risk was 19.05 [= 6.20 + 1.351(9.51)]. The difference of 1.99 (= 21.04 − 19.05) is the added return required because of less than perfect diversification. This fairly large required return for diversification is in contrast to Fidelity Magellan Fund, which has an R^2 with the market of 0.941 and a required return for diversification of 0.31 percent.

This required return for diversification is subtracted from the selectivity return to arrive at net selectivity. Aim Constellation had a return for selectivity of 7.35 percent and net selectivity of 5.36 percent. This indicates that, even accounting for the added cost of incomplete diversification, the fund's performance was above the market line. Thirteen funds had positive net selectivity returns.

RELATIONSHIP AMONG PERFORMANCE MEASURES   Table 27.4 contains the matrix of the rank correlation coefficients among the Treynor, Sharpe, Jensen, and Fama measures. Although the various measures provide alternative insights regarding performance, *the overall ranks are very similar.* Notably, the Treynor measure appears to have the strongest relationship with the other performance measures.

PERFORMANCE ATTRIBUTION ANALYSIS

As noted earlier, portfolio managers can add value to their investors in either of two ways: selecting superior securities or demonstrating superior market timing skills by allocating funds to different asset classes or market segments. **Attribution analysis** attempts to distinguish which of these factors is the source of the portfolio's overall performance. Specifically, this method compares the total return to the manager's actual investment holdings to the return for a predetermined benchmark portfolio and decomposes the differ-

TABLE 27.4   **CORRELATIONS AMONG ALTERNATIVE PORTFOLIO PERFORMANCE MEASURES**

	Treynor	Sharpe	Jensen	Fama
Treynor	—			
Sharpe	.97	—		
Jensen	.96	.94	—	
Fama (net selectivity)	.97	.98	.94	—

ence into an *allocation effect* and a *selection effect*. The most straightforward way to measure these two effects is as follows:

$$\text{Allocation Effect} = \Sigma_i[(w_{ai} - w_{pi}) \times (R_{pi} - R_p)]$$
$$\text{Selection Effect} = \Sigma_i[(w_{ai}) \times (R_{ai} - R_{pi})]$$

where

w_{ai}, w_{pi} = the investment proportions given to the *i*th *market segment* (e.g., asset class, industry group) in the manager's actual portfolio and the benchmark portfolio, respectively.
R_{ai}, R_{pi} = the investment return to the *i*th market segment in the manager's actual portfolio and the benchmark portfolio, respectively.
R_p = the total return to the benchmark portfolio.

Computed in this manner, the allocation effect measures the manager's decision to over- or underweight a particular market segment (i.e., $[w_{ai} - w_{pi}]$) in terms of that segment's return performance relative to the overall return to the benchmark (i.e., $[R_{pi} - R_p]$). Good timing skill is therefore a matter of investing more money in those market segments that end up producing greater than average returns. The selection effect measures the manager's ability to form specific market segment portfolios that generate superior returns relative to the way in which the comparable market segment is defined in the benchmark portfolio (i.e., $[R_{ai} - R_{pi}]$), weighted by the manager's actual market segment investment proportions. When constructed in this manner, the manager's total value-added performance is the sum of the allocation and selection effects.[9]

ASSET CLASS ATTRIBUTION ANALYSIS: AN EXAMPLE

As an example of this process, consider an investor whose top-down portfolio strategy consists of two dimensions. First, he decides on a broad allocation of his investment dollars across three asset classes: U.S. stocks, U.S. long-term bonds, and cash equivalents such as U.S. Treasury bills or certificates of deposit. Once this judgment is made, the investor's second general decision is choosing which stocks, bonds, and cash instruments to buy. As a benchmark for his investment prowess, he selects a hypothetical portfolio with a 60 percent allocation to the Standard & Poor's 500 index, a 30 percent investment in the Lehman Corporate Long Bond index, and a 10 percent allocation to three-month Treasury bills.

Suppose that at the start of the investment period, the investor believes equity values are somewhat inflated and is not optimistic about the near-term performance of the stock market. Compared to the benchmark, he therefore decides to underweight stocks and overweight bonds and cash in his actual portfolio. The investment proportions he chooses are 50 percent in equity, 38 percent in bonds, and 12 percent in cash. Further, instead of selecting a broad portfolio of equities, he decides to concentrate on the interest rate–sensitive sectors such as utilities and financial companies, while deemphasizing the technology and consumer durables sectors. Finally, he resolves to buy shorter duration bonds of a higher credit quality than are contained in the benchmark bond index and to buy commercial paper rather than Treasury bills.

[9] Wainscott has argued that a better way to measure the selection effect is to multiply the market segment return differential by the benchmark weight for that segment, or $\Sigma_i[(w_{pi}) \times (R_{ai} - R_{pi})]$. A drawback of this approach, however, is that the allocation and selection effects no longer sum to the total value-added return. To balance the equation, he calculates an *interaction effect* as $\Sigma_i[(w_{ai} - w_{pi}) \times (R_{ai} - R_{pi})]$ to measure the residual performance. See Craig B. Wainscott, "Attribution Analysis for Equities," in *Performance Evaluation, Benchmarks, and Attribution Analysis*, edited by J. Squires (Charlottesville, VA: Association for Investment Management and Research, 1995).

TABLE 27.5 **ASSET CLASS PERFORMANCE ATTRIBUTION ANALYSIS**

Asset Class	INVESTMENT WEIGHTS			RETURNS		
	Actual	Benchmark	Excess	Actual	Benchmark	Excess
Stock	0.50	0.60	−0.10	9.70%	8.60%	1.10%
Bonds	0.38	0.30	0.08	9.10%	9.20%	−0.10%
Cash	0.12	0.10	0.02	5.60%	5.40%	0.20%

In this example, the manager has made active investment decisions involving both the allocation of assets and the selection of individual securities. To determine if either (or both) of these decisions proved to be wise ones, at the end of the investment period he can calculate his overall and segment-specific performance. Table 27.5 summarizes these hypothetical returns for the investor's actual and benchmark asset class portfolios as well as the investment weightings for each. The overall actual and benchmark returns can be computed as follows:

$$\text{Overall Actual Return} = (0.50 \times 0.097) + (0.38 \times 0.091) + (0.12 \times 0.056)$$
$$= 8.98\%$$

and

$$\text{Overall Benchmark Return} = (0.60 \times 0.086) + (0.30 \times 0.092) + (0.10 \times 0.054)$$
$$= 8.46\%.$$

Thus, the manager beat the benchmark by 52 basis points (= 0.0898 − 0.0846) over this particular investment horizon.

The goal of attribution analysis is to isolate the reason for this value-added performance. The manager's allocation effect can be computed by multiplying the excess asset class weight by that class's relative investment performance:

$$[(-0.10) \times (0.086 - 0.0846)] + [(0.08) \times (0.092 - 0.0846)] +$$
$$[(0.02) \times (0.054 - 0.0846)] = -0.02\%.$$

This shows that if the investor had made just his market timing decisions and not picked different securities than those represented in the benchmark, his performance would have lagged the target return by two basis points. This total allocation effect can be broken down further into an equity allocation return of −2 basis points (= [(−0.10) × (0.086 − 0.0846)]), a bond allocation return of 6 basis points (= [(0.08) × (0.092 − 0.0846)]), and a cash allocation return of −6 basis points (= [(0.02) × (0.054 − 0.0846)]). Therefore, the decision to underweight stock and overweight cash (asset classes that generated returns above and below the benchmark, respectively) resulted in diminished performance that was more than enough to offset the benefit of emphasizing bonds.

Since the investor knows that he outperformed the benchmark overall, a negative allocation effect necessarily implies that he exhibited positive security selection skills. His selection effect can be computed as:

$$[(0.50) \times (0.097 - 0.086)] + [(0.38) \times (0.091 - 0.092)] + [(0.12) \times (0.056 - 0.054)] = 0.54\%.$$

In this example, the investor formed superior stock and cash portfolios, although his bond selections did not perform quite as well as the Lehman Long Bond index. One important caveat in this analysis is that, because the returns are not risk-adjusted, it is possible that the asset class portfolios formed by the investor are riskier than their benchmark counterparts. If this is the case, which is almost certainly true for a cash portfolio that holds short-term corporate debt obligations instead of Treasury bills, the investor should expect a higher return that has nothing to do with his skill. Finally, notice that the investor's total incremental return of 52 basis points can be decomposed as:

$$\text{Total Value-Added} = \text{Allocation Effect} + \text{Selection Effect}$$
$$= (-0.02\%) + (0.54\%) = 0.52\%.$$

Using a procedure similar to the one just described, Brinson, Hood, and Beebower examined the return performance of a group of 91 large U.S. pension plans over the decade from 1974 to 1983.[10] They established that the mean annual return for this sample was 9.01 percent, compared to 10.11 percent for their benchmark. Thus, they documented that active management cost the average plan 110 basis points of return per year. This "value subtracted" return increment consisted of a −77 basis point allocation effect and a −33 basis point selection effect. Further, they concluded that a plan's initial strategic asset allocation choice, rather than any of its active management decisions, was the primary determinant of portfolio performance. In a followup study, Brinson, Singer, and Beebower reached a similar conclusion for a different group of 82 pension plans over the 1977–1987 period.[11] For this new sample, however, they showed that the total active return shortfall had fallen to −7 basis points, which was divided into an 18 basis point selection effect and a −25 basis point allocation effect.

PERFORMANCE ATTRIBUTION EXTENSIONS

Although the preceding example concentrated partly on an investor's ability to time broad asset class movements, the attribution methodology can be used to distinguish security selection skills from any of several other decisions that an investor might make. For instance, the manager of a broad-based, all-equity portfolio must decide what economic sectors (e.g., basic materials, consumer nondurables, transportation) to under- and overweight before she can choose her preferred companies in those sectors. In such cases, performance attribution analysis is still applicable, with a "sector rotation" effect replacing the market timing effect. To see how this might work, Table 27.6 summarizes the performance of The MBA Investment Fund, L.L.C., a privately funded investment portfolio managed by a group of graduate students at the University of Texas. During the time of this analysis, which covered the one-year period from the Fund's inception on January 17, 1995, through January 16, 1996, the managers were restricted to investing in U.S.-traded equities and ADRs only. Because the Fund's investment mandate was to beat the return on the Standard & Poor's 500, the managers had two basic decisions to make: which sectors to emphasize and which individual stocks to buy within those sectors.

Over the course of the year, the overall returns to the S&P 500 and the Fund were 29.63 percent and 29.54 percent, respectively. The second and third columns of Table 27.6 document the actual and benchmark weights for the 10 economic sectors comprising the

[10] Gary P. Brinson, L. Randolph Hood, and Gilbert L. Beebower, "Determinants of Portfolio Performance," *Financial Analysts Journal* 42, no. 4 (July–August 1986): 39–44.

[11] Gary P. Brinson, Brian D. Singer, and Gilbert L. Beebower, "Determinants of Portfolio Performance II: An Update," *Financial Analysts Journal* 47, no. 3 (May–June 1991): 40–48.

TABLE 27.6				

MBA INVESTMENT FUND SECTOR PERFORMANCE ATTRIBUTION ANALYSIS

| S&P 500 Sector | INVESTMENT WEIGHTS | | | EXCESS RETURNS |
	Actual	S&P 500	Excess	S&P Sector—Overall S&P
Basic materials	0.0331	0.0670	−0.0339	−15.15%
Capital equipment and technology	0.2544	0.1841	0.0703	−3.31
Consumer services	0.0208	0.0692	−0.0484	6.95
Consumer durables	0.0588	0.0353	0.0235	−21.34
Consumer nondurables	0.2752	0.2851	−0.0099	5.85
Energy	0.1170	0.0935	0.0235	−7.08
Financial	0.1619	0.1249	0.0370	7.15
Transportation	0.0199	0.0172	0.0027	−1.72
Utilities	0.0590	0.1000	−0.0410	1.91
Miscellaneous	0.0000	0.0242	−0.0242	−13.15

S&P 500 index, with the Fund's excess weightings (i.e., $[w_{ai} - w_{pi}]$) listed in the fourth column. The entries in the last column show the benchmark sector return relative to the overall S&P return (i.e., $[R_{pi} - R_p]$). Thus, the sector allocation effect can be calculated by summing the product of the entries in the last two columns:

$$[(-0.0339) \times (-0.1515)] + [(0.0703) \times (-0.0331)]$$
$$+ \ldots + [(-0.0242) \times (-0.1315)] = -0.28\%.$$

With an overall return difference of −9 basis points (= 0.2954 − 0.2963), this means that the Fund's managers generated a security selection effect of 19 basis points (= (−0.0009) − (−0.0028)). Consequently, although the student managers virtually matched the strong performance of the entire stock market, it appears they were better at picking stocks than forecasting broader economic trends.

This general attribution analysis methodology has been extended to other specific asset classes as well. Kuberek showed that producing fixed-income attributions for bond portfolio managers is quite straightforward once the relevant decision variables have been specified.[12] He noted that these decision variables might include allocations to different countries, foreign exchange effects, individual bond selections, and other risk factors such as the portfolio's term structure positioning. Karnosky and Singer have developed a comprehensive, unified framework for attributing performance in a global asset management context.[13] In particular, they have added both active and hedged currency allocation returns to the single-currency attribution model of Brinson, Hood, and Beebower to allow for the intricacies of cross-border investing. In a comparison of the performance of one of their global investment portfolios relative to the MSCI World Equity Index during 1989, they demonstrated that the combined effect of the currency selection decision accounted for 563 basis points of the 7.66 percent return advantage that the portfolio enjoyed.

[12] Robert C. Kuberek, "Attribution Analysis for Fixed Income," in *Performance Evaluation, Benchmarks, and Attribution Analysis*, edited by J. Squires (Charlottesville, VA: Association for Investment Management and Research, 1995).

[13] Denis S. Karnosky and Brian D. Singer, *Global Asset Management and Performance Measurement* (Charlottesville, VA: Research Foundation of the Institute of Chartered Financial Analysts, 1994). See also Ernest M. Ankrim and Chris R. Hensel, "Multicurrency Performance Attribution," *Financial Analysts Journal* 50, no. 2 (March–April 1994): 29–35.

MEASURING
MARKET TIMING
SKILLS

Tactical asset allocation (TAA) is a portfolio management strategy in which a manager attempts to produce active value-added returns solely through allocation decisions. Specifically, instead of trying to pick superior individual securities, TAA managers adjust their asset class exposures based on perceived changes in the relative valuations of those classes. A typical TAA fund shifts money between three asset classes—stocks, bonds, and cash equivalents—although many definitions of these categories (e.g., large cap versus small cap, long term versus short term) are used in practice. Of course, this means that the relevant performance measurement criterion for a TAA manager is how well he is able to time broad market movements. There are two reasons why attribution analysis is ill-suited for this task. First, by design, a TAA manager indexes his actual asset class investments and so the selection effect is not relevant. Second, a TAA approach to investing might entail dozens of changes to asset class weightings during an investment period, which could render meaningless an attribution effect computed on the average holdings. Because of these problems, many analysts consider a regression-based method for measuring timing skills to be a superior approach.

Weigel tested the market timing skills of a group of 17 U.S.-based managers using the TAA approach.[14] His methodology was motivated by the pioneering work of Merton and Hendriksson and assumed that perfect market timing ability was equivalent to owning a look-back option that pays at expiration the return to the best performing asset class.[15] That is, for any given investment period t, a manager with perfect market timing skills would have a return (R_{pt}) equal to:

$$R_{pt} = RFR_t + \max[R_{st} - RFR_t, R_{bt} - RFR_t, 0]$$

where R_{st} and R_{bt} are the period t returns to the stock and bond benchmark portfolios, respectively. Thus, controlling for stock and bond price movements in a manner comparable to Jensen's method, the following regression equation can be calculated:

$$(R_{pt} - RFR_t) = \alpha + \beta_b(R_{bt} - RFR_t) + \beta_s(R_{st} - RFR_t) + \gamma\{\max[R_{st} - RFR_t, R_{bt} - RFR_t, 0]\} + U_t.$$

Weigel showed that the samplewide average value for γ, which measures the proportion of the perfect timing option that the TAA managers were able to capture, was 0.30. This value was statistically significant, meaning that this group of managers had reliable, if not perfect, market timing skills. He also demonstrated that the average alpha was −0.5 percent per quarter, indicating that these same managers had negative nonmarket timing skills (e.g., hedging strategies).

Many other studies have examined the market timing ability of portfolio managers who are not exclusively TAA practitioners. Several of the investigations discussed in Chapter 26, as typified by Kon and Chang and Lewellen, concluded that mutual fund managers

---

[14] Eric J. Weigel, "The Performance of Tactical Asset Allocation," *Financial Analysts Journal* 47, no. 5 (September–October 1991): 63–70.

[15] Robert C. Merton, "On Market Timing and Investment Performance: An Equilibrium Theory of Value for Market Forecasts," *Journal of Business* 54, no. 3 (July 1981): 363–406, and Roy D. Hendriksson and Robert C. Merton, "On Market Timing and Investment Performance: Statistical Procedures for Evaluating Forecasting Skills," *Journal of Business* 54, no. 4 (October 1981): 513–534. See also Carl R. Chen, Anthony Chan, and Nancy J. Mohan, "Asset Allocation Managers' Investment Performance," *Journal of Fixed Income* 3, no. 3 (December 1993): 46–53 for another application of this methodology.

generally possess negative market timing skills.[16] Coggin, Fabozzi, and Rahman carried this analysis further by looking at both the timing and selectivity skills of a group of U.S. equity pension fund managers.[17] Using a regression-based model with monthly return data from January 1983 to December 1990, they demonstrated that their sample of managers possessed positive, but small, selection skills and negative timing skills. From these studies, it is reasonable to conclude that only those managers explicitly trying to time market movements have a chance of doing so.

FACTORS THAT AFFECT USE OF PERFORMANCE MEASURES

All of the performance measures just described are only as good as their data inputs. You must be careful when computing the rates of return to take proper account of all inflows and outflows. More importantly, you should use judgment and be patient in the evaluation process. It is not possible to evaluate a portfolio manager on the basis of a quarter or even a year. Your evaluation should extend over several years and cover at least a full market cycle. This will allow you to determine whether the manager's performance differs during rising and declining markets.[18] Beyond these general cautions, several specific factors should be considered when using these measures.

Although we discussed Roll's contentions regarding the measurement problem in Chapter 10, it is useful at this point to recall the problem, discuss the implications of a global capital market on this problem, and put it in perspective. With the exception of attribution analysis, all the equity portfolio performance measures we have discussed are derived from the CAPM. They assume the existence of a market portfolio at the point of tangency on the Markowitz efficient frontier. Theoretically, the market portfolio is an efficient, completely diversified portfolio because it is on the efficient frontier. We also noted that this market portfolio must contain all risky assets in the economy, so that it will be completely diversified, and that all components are market-value weighted.

The problem arises in finding a realistic proxy for this theoretical market portfolio. As noted previously, analysts typically use the Standard & Poor's 500 Index as the proxy for the market portfolio because it contains a fairly diversified portfolio of stocks, and the sample is market-value weighted. Unfortunately, it does not represent the true composition of the market portfolio. Specifically, it includes only common stocks and most of them are listed on the NYSE. Notably, it excludes many other risky assets that theoretically should be considered such as numerous AMEX and OTC stocks, foreign stocks, foreign and domestic bonds, real estate, coins, precious metals, stamps, and antiques.

This lack of completeness always has been recognized but was not highlighted until several articles by Roll detailed the problem with the market proxy and pointed out its implications for measuring portfolio performance.[19] Although a detailed discussion of

---

[16] Stanley J. Kon, "The Market-Timing Performance of Mutual Fund Managers," *Journal of Business* 56, no. 3 (July 1983): 323–347, and Eric C. Chang and Wilbur G. Lewellen, "Market Timing and Mutual Fund Investment Performance," *Journal of Business* 57, no. 1 (1984): 57–72.

[17] T. Daniel Coggin, Frank J. Fabozzi, and Shafiqur Rahman, "The Investment Performance of U.S. Equity Pension Fund Managers: An Empirical Investigation," *Journal of Finance* 48, no. 3 (July 1993): 1039–1055.

[18] In this regard, see Robert C. Kirby, "You Need More than Numbers to Measure Performance," paper presented at Institute of Chartered Financial Analysts Seminar, Chicago, April 2, 1976. For a formal presentation related to the importance of the time element, see Mark Kritzman, "How to Detect Skill in Management Performance," *Journal of Portfolio Management* 12, no. 2 (Winter 1986): 16–20.

[19] Richard Roll, "A Critique of the Asset Pricing Theory's Tests," *Journal of Financial Economics* 4, no. 4 (March 1977): 129–176; Richard Roll, "Ambiguity When Performance Is Measured by the Securities Market

Roll's critique will not be repeated here, we need to consider his major problem with the measurement of the market portfolio, which he refers to as a **benchmark error.**

When evaluating portfolio performance, various techniques use the market portfolio as the benchmark, and we use the market portfolio to derive our risk measures (betas). Roll showed that if the proxy for the market portfolio is not a truly efficient portfolio, then the SML using this proxy may not be the true SML—the true SML could have a higher slope. In such a case, a portfolio plotted above the SML and derived using a poor benchmark could actually plot below the SML that uses the true market portfolio. Also, the beta could differ from that computed using the true market portfolio. For example, if the true beta were larger than the beta computed using the proxy, the true position of the portfolio would shift to the right. In an empirical test, Brown and Brown documented a considerable amount of "ranking reversal" when the definition of the market portfolio was changed in a Jensen's alpha analysis of a sample of well-established mutual funds.[20] In more recent work, Grinblatt and Titman attempted to avoid the problem altogether by developing a performance measurement process that did not require benchmarks.[21]

BENCHMARK ERRORS AND GLOBAL INVESTING

The concern with the benchmark error increases with global investing. The studies on international diversification discussed in Chapter 3 state clearly that adding non-U.S. securities to the portfolio universe almost certainly will move the efficient frontier to the left because including foreign securities reduces risk. You will recall that this reduction in risk continues as you add countries that have less economic interaction with the United States, such as some Asian and third-world countries. Also, some of these additions increase the expected returns of the universe so that the efficient frontier moves up as well as leftward. The efficient frontier will almost certainly change when you invest in foreign securities.

The extent of the shift in the efficient frontier depends on the relationships among countries, and these relationships are changing dramatically. Because our trade with European and Asian countries will continue its rapid growth from recent years, the interdependence of our economies and the correlation of our financial markets should increase. Also, individual European countries have become more interdependent after 1992, when numerous barriers to trade and travel in the European Economic Community were eliminated. A paper by Brinson and Fachler discusses the performance measurement problem for non-U.S. equities, while a subsequent paper by Brinson, Diermeier, and Schlarbaum describes a multiple markets index (MMI) that includes U.S. stocks and bonds, non-U.S. stocks, non-dollar bonds, venture capital, and real estate.[22]

Line," *Journal of Finance* 33, no. 4 (September 1978): 1051–1069; Richard Roll, "Performance Evaluation and Benchmark Error I," *Journal of Portfolio Management* 6, no. 4 (Summer 1980): 5–12; and Richard Roll, "Performance Evaluation and Benchmark Error II," *Journal of Portfolio Management* 7, no. 2 (Winter 1981): 17–22.

[20] Keith C. Brown and Gregory D. Brown, "Does the Composition of the Market Portfolio Really Matter?" *Journal of Portfolio Management* 13, no. 2 (Winter 1987): 26–32.

[21] Mark Grinblatt and Sheridan Titman, "Performance Measurement without Benchmarks: An Examination of Mutual Fund Returns," *Journal of Business* 66, no. 1 (January 1993): 47–68.

[22] Gary P. Brinson and Nimrod Fachler, "Measuring Non-U.S. Equity Portfolio Performance," *Journal of Portfolio Management* 11, no. 3 (Spring 1985): 73–76. It discusses the problems with developing an appropriate index and considers market selection (country) and stock selection within countries. The multiple markets index (MMI) is described in Gary P. Brinson, Jeffrey J. Diermeier, and G. G. Schlarbaum, "A Composite Portfolio Benchmark for Pension Plans," *Financial Analysts Journal* 42, no. 2 (March–April 1986): 15–24. This index also is discussed with changes in asset weights in Roger G. Ibbotson and Gary P. Brinson, *Global Investing* (New York: McGraw-Hill, 1993): 18–19.

A DEMONSTRATION OF THE GLOBAL BENCHMARK PROBLEM

To illustrate the impact of the benchmark problem in an environment of global capital markets, Reilly and Akhtar demonstrated what happens to the individual measures of risk (beta) and the SML when the world equity market is employed.[23] Table 27.7 contains the parameters of the characteristic line for the 30 stocks in the Dow Jones Industrial Average (DJIA) using the S&P 500, which is the typical proxy, and the Morgan Stanley World Stock Index, which is a market value–weighted index that contains stocks from around the world. These findings were calculated using monthly returns from the five-year period from 1989–1994. The major differences are reflected in the betas and the R^2 of the regres-

TABLE 27.7

PARAMETERS OF THE CHARACTERISTIC LINES FOR THE DOW JONES 30 INDUSTRIALS, MONTHLY DATA: 1989–1994

Stock	Standard Deviation	S&P 500			WORLD		
		Intercept	Beta	R^2	Intercept	Beta	R^2
Alcoa	0.066	−0.004	1.115	0.394	0.007	0.411	0.056
Allied Signal	0.067	0.002	0.984	0.277	0.011	0.439	0.066
American Express	0.089	−0.006	1.104	0.191	0.003	0.546	0.055
AT&T	0.062	0.000	0.944	0.292	0.007	0.671	0.199
Bethlehem Steel	0.111	−0.013	1.531	0.241	−0.001	0.872	0.101
Boeing	0.068	0.001	0.917	0.227	0.007	0.679	0.168
Chevron	0.054	0.005	0.514	0.105	0.009	0.384	0.077
Coca-Cola	0.061	0.012	1.048	0.401	0.021	0.786	0.307
DuPont	0.065	0.001	0.941	0.263	0.009	0.576	0.129
Eastman Kodak	0.062	0.000	0.582	0.104	0.004	0.366	0.051
Exxon	0.036	0.000	0.507	0.251	0.003	0.406	0.221
General Electric	0.059	0.001	1.227	0.571	0.011	0.721	0.263
General Motors	0.081	−0.004	0.718	0.093	0.001	0.479	0.051
Goodyear	0.098	−0.012	1.067	0.142	−0.003	0.448	0.024
IBM	0.075	−0.009	0.512	0.047	−0.005	0.321	0.019
International Paper	0.066	−0.003	1.124	0.369	0.006	0.651	0.163
McDonald's	0.071	0.005	0.942	0.227	0.012	0.628	0.133
Merck	0.075	0.000	1.182	0.318	0.009	0.732	0.161
Minnesota M&M	0.044	0.001	0.809	0.430	0.007	0.488	0.208
Navistar	0.126	−0.022	1.136	0.095	−0.011	0.378	0.002
Philip Morris	0.073	0.003	1.041	0.258	0.011	0.644	0.131
PA	0.096	−0.009	1.814	0.458	0.006	0.931	0.157
Procter & Gamble	0.065	0.006	1.002	0.304	0.014	0.548	0.117
Sears	0.068	−0.006	0.988	0.266	0.001	0.617	0.136
Texaco	0.046	−0.002	0.488	0.136	0.001	0.472	0.181
USX	0.094	−0.004	1.028	0.146	0.005	0.559	0.051
Union Carbide	0.111	0.008	0.925	0.079	0.014	0.695	0.059
United Technologies	0.081	−0.002	1.079	0.231	0.006	0.719	0.136
Westinghouse	0.079	−0.018	1.071	0.228	−0.009	0.471	0.051
Woolworth	0.085	−0.018	1.344	0.319	−0.007	0.805	0.151
Mean	0.074	−0.003	0.991	0.249	0.005	0.581	0.121

Source: Frank K. Reilly and Rashid A. Akhtar, "The Benchmark Error Problem with Global Capital Markets," *Journal of Portfolio Management* 22, no. 1 (Fall 1995): 33–52.

[23] Frank K. Reilly and Rashid A. Akhtar, "The Benchmark Error Problem with Global Capital Markets," *Journal of Portfolio Management* 22, no. 1 (Fall 1995): 33–52.

sion lines. Specifically in each case, the beta was *smaller* when measured against the world index than against the S&P 500 Index, and the average beta (0.991 versus 0.581) was about 41 percent lower. The impact also is reflected in the R^2, which was likewise almost always lower with the world index and had an average (0.249 to 0.121) that was 51 percent smaller. These results imply a fairly significant impact on the individual measures of risk with a clear tendency for a decline in the measure. You will recall from the discussion in Chapter 9 that beta is equal to the covariance between an asset and the market portfolio divided by the variance of the market portfolio. It is shown that the world portfolio has a lower variance than the S&P 500 (as expected), but the covariance was much lower, which caused the decline in beta.

The effect of the choice of a benchmark on global performance measurement can be seen in Figure 27.5, which plots the SMLs for six different indexes over three time horizons: 1983–1988, 1989–1994, and 1983–1994. Four country-specific benchmarks—the S&P 500 (United States), the Nikkei (Japan), the FT-All Shares (England), the FAZ (Germany)—and two aggregate benchmarks—M-S World and Brinson GSMI—were used in the analysis. The results indicate that using alternative market proxies for different countries or alternative composite series will generate SMLs that differ substantially during a given time period, and that these SMLs tend to be very unstable over time. For instance, the Nikkei SML goes from the largest risk premium during 1983–1988 to a negative risk premium during 1989–1994, which clearly is contrary to capital market theory. Notice, however, that this volatility would be masked by anyone looking at Japanese performance over the entire 1983–1994 period, during which the Nikkei SML assumed a more "normal" shape. Finally, the S&P 500 provided investors with the biggest performance hurdle over the whole sample period, which was mostly due to the high risk premiums in the United States during 1989–1994.

IMPLICATIONS OF THE
BENCHMARK PROBLEMS

Several points are significant regarding this benchmark criticism. First, the benchmark problems noted by Roll, which are increased with global investing, do not negate the value of the CAPM as a *normative* model of equilibrium pricing; the theory is still viable. The problem is one of *measurement* when using the theory to evaluate portfolio performance.

You need to find a better proxy for the market portfolio or to adjust measured performance for benchmark errors. In fact, Roll made several suggestions to help overcome this problem.[24] From Chapter 5, we know that new comprehensive stock market and bond market series are being developed that will be available as market portfolio proxies. Finally, the multiple markets index (MMI), developed by Brinson, Diermeier, and Schlarbaum and maintained monthly by Brinson Partners, Inc., is a major step toward a truly comprehensive world market portfolio.

Alternatively, you might consider giving greater weight to the Sharpe portfolio performance measure because it does not depend heavily on the market portfolio. Recall that this measure relates excess return to the *standard deviation* of return, that is, to total risk. Although this evaluation process generally uses a benchmark portfolio as an example of an unmanaged portfolio for comparison purposes, the risk measure for the portfolio being evaluated does not directly depend on a market portfolio. Also, recall that the portfolio

---

[24] Richard Roll, "Performance Evaluation and Benchmark Error II," *Journal of Portfolio Management* 7, no. 2 (Winter 1981): 17–22. Several more recent papers on this topic include Jeffrey V. Bailey, "Are Manager Universes Acceptable Performance Benchmarks?" *Journal of Portfolio Management* 18, no. 3 (Spring 1992): 9–13; and Richard C. Grinwold, "Are Benchmark Portfolios Efficient?" *Journal of Portfolio Management* 19, no. 1 (Fall 1992): 34–40.

FIGURE 27.5

SECURITY MARKET LINES FOR S&P 500, NIKKEI, FT-ALL SHARES, FAZ, M-S WORLD, AND BRINSON GSMI INDEXES

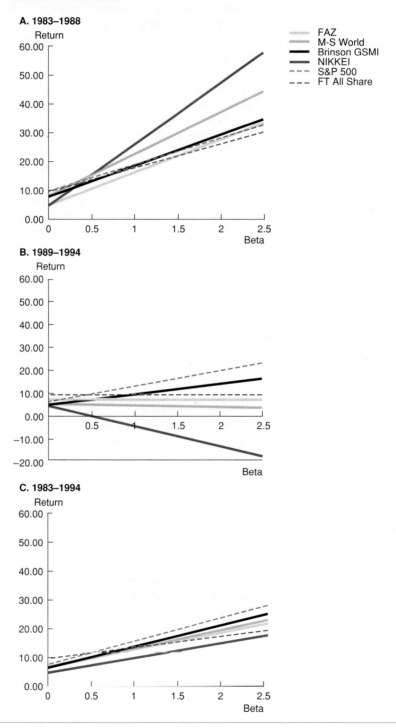

Source: Frank K. Reilly and Rashid A. Akhtar, "The Benchmark Error Problem with Global Capital Markets," *Journal of Portfolio Management* 22, no. 1 (Fall 1995): 33–52.

rank from the Sharpe measure typically correlates very highly with the ranks derived from alternative performance measures (see Table 27.4).

RELIABILITY OF PERFORMANCE MEASURES

Another concern is how reliably these measures rank managers and indicate their ability to significantly outperform the market. French and Henderson examined the performance measures under ideal conditions and showed that when you eliminate the random noise, these measures of performance do an excellent job of ranking portfolios consistently with their true ranking.[25] At the same time, the random noise in stocks and portfolio data complicates detecting performance that statistically is superior or inferior to the market portfolio. A manager must be much better or worse than average before a difference shows up. This difficultly in projecting future performance based on past performance is consistent with the results discussed for mutual funds in Chapter 26.

EVALUATION OF BOND PORTFOLIO PERFORMANCE

As discussed, the analysis of risk-adjusted performance for equity portfolios started in the late 1960s following the development of portfolio theory and the capital asset pricing model (CAPM). The common stock risk measures have been fairly simple—either total risk (the standard deviation of returns) or systematic risk (betas). No such development has simplified analysis for the bond market, where numerous and complex factors can influence portfolio returns. One reason for this lack of development of bond portfolio performance measures was that prior to the 1970s most bond portfolio managers followed buy-and-hold strategies, so their performance probably did not differ much. A reason for this buy-and-hold strategy is that interest rates were very stable, so one could gain little from the active management of bond portfolios.

The environment in the bond market changed dramatically in the late 1970s and especially in the 1980s when interest rates increased dramatically and became more volatile. This created an incentive to trade bonds, and this trend toward more active management led to substantially more dispersed performance by bond portfolio managers. This dispersion in performance in turn created a demand for techniques that would help investors evaluate the performance of bond portfolio managers.

As with the equity market, the critical questions are: (1) How did performance among portfolio managers compare to the overall bond market? and (2) What factors explain or contribute to superior or inferior bond portfolio performance? In this section, we present various attempts to develop bond portfolio performance evaluation systems that consider multiple-risk factors.[26]

A BOND MARKET LINE

Wagner and Tito attempted to apply asset pricing techniques to the evaluation of bond portfolio performance.[27] A prime factor needed to evaluate performance properly is a measure of risk such as the beta coefficient for equities. This is difficult to achieve because a bond's maturity and coupon have a significant effect on the volatility of its prices.

[25] Dan W. French and Glenn V. Henderson, Jr., "How Well Does Performance Evaluation Perform?" *Journal of Portfolio Management* 11, no. 2 (Winter 1985): 15–18.

[26] An overview of this area and a discussion of the historical development is contained in H. Gifford Fong, "Bond Management: Past, Current, and Future," in *The Handbook of Fixed-Income Securities,* 4th ed., edited by Frank J. Fabozzi and T. Dessa Fabozzi (Burr Ridge, IL: Irwin Professional Publishing, 1995).

[27] Wayne H. Wagner and Dennis A. Tito, "Definitive New Measures of Bond Performance and Risk," *Pension World* (May 1977): 17–26; and Dennis A. Tito and Wayne H. Wagner, "Is Your Bond Manager Skillful?" *Pension World* (June 1977): 10–16.

FIGURE 27.6   **SPECIFICATION OF BOND MARKET LINE USING LEHMAN BROTHERS BOND INDEX**

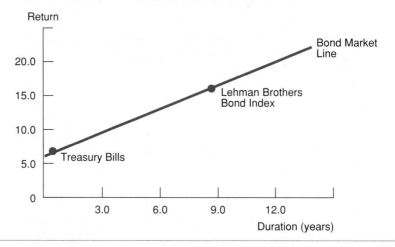

Source: Wayne H. Wagner and Dennis A. Tito, "Definitive New Measures of Bond Performance and Risk," *Pension World* (May 1977): 17–26. Reprinted with permission.

You know from our discussion in Chapter 15 that an appropriate composite risk measure indicates the relative price volatility for a bond compared to interest rate changes in the bond's *duration*. Using this as a measure of risk, the authors derived a bond market line much like the security market line used to evaluate equity performance. Duration simply replaces beta as the risk variable. The bond market line in Figure 27.6 is drawn from points defined by returns on Treasury bills to the Lehman Brothers Government-Corporate Bond Index rather than the S&P 500 index.[28] The Lehman Brothers Index gives the market's average annual rate of return during some common period, and the duration for the index is the value-weighted duration for the individual bonds in the index.

Given the bond market line, this technique divides the portfolio return that differs from the return on the Lehman Brothers Index into four components: (1) a **policy effect,** (2) a **rate anticipation effect,** (3) an **analysis effect,** and (4) a **trading effect.** When the latter three effects are combined, they are referred to as the **management effect.** These effects are portrayed in Figure 27.7.

The policy effect measures the difference in the expected return for a given portfolio because of a difference in policy regarding the duration of this portfolio compared to the duration of the Lehman Brothers Index. It is assumed that the duration of an unmanaged portfolio would be equal to the Lehman Brothers Index.[29] The duration of a portfolio being evaluated that differs from the index duration indicates a basic policy decision regarding relative risk (measured by duration), and there should be a difference in expected return consistent with that risk policy decision. For example, assume the duration and return for the Lehman Brothers Index is 9.0 years and 8.25 percent, respectively. If your portfolio has

---

[28] As you know from the presentation in Chapter 5, it would be equally reasonable to use a comparable bond-market index series from Merrill Lynch, Salomon Brothers, or the Ryan Index.

[29] Notably, the duration of the various bond-market indexes has changed over time (i.e., the duration of the corporate bond series has declined, whereas the duration of the government bond series has increased slightly). For a presentation and discussion of this phenomenon, see Frank K. Reilly, Wenchi Kao, and David J. Wright, "Alternative Bond Market Indexes," *Financial Analysts Journal* 48, no. 3 (May–June 1992): 44–58.

| FIGURE 27.7 | GRAPHIC DISPLAY OF BOND PORTFOLIO PERFORMANCE BREAKDOWN |

Manage effect is the improvement in investment performance of a passive strategy through active bond management. It is the difference between total bond portfolio return and the expected return at the long-term average duration.

Policy effect is the difference between long-term duration of a bond portfolio and the duration of a bond market index resulting from long-term investment policy. Measured as the return at the long-term average less the return on the Lehman Brothers Index.

Bond market line is a straight line drawn through the return/duration of treasury bills and the return/duration of the Lehman Brothers Index.

Trading effect is the result of the current quarter's trading, either through effective trade-desk operation or short-term selection abilites. It is the difference between total management effect and the effects attributable to analysis and interest rate anticipation.

Analysis effect, attributable to the selection of issues with better than average long-term prospects, is the difference between the actual return of the buy-and hold portfolio at the beginning of the quarter and the expected return of that buy-and-hold portfolio.

Interest rate anticipation effect is attributable to changes in portfolio duration resulting from attempts to profit from and ability to predict bond market movements. It is the difference between the expected return at the actual portfolio duration and the expected return at the long-term duration.

Actual Return on Portfolio

Actual Return on Buy-and-Hold Portfolio

Long Term

Rate of Return

Expected Return on Buy-and-Hold Portfolio

Lehman Brothers Index

Expected Return at Actual Duration of Portfolio

Treasury Bills

Duration

Buy-and Hold portfolio is the composition of the portfolio at the beginning of the quarter. Used to differentiate between trading gains secured within a quarter and long-term analysis gains.

Duration, a measure of the average time to receipt of cash flows from an investment. It is a measure of the sensitivity of a bond's price to changes in interest rates.

Source: Wayne H. Wagner and Dennis A. Tito, "Definitive New Measures of Bond Performance and Risk," *Pension World* (May 1977): 17–26. Reprinted with permission.

a duration of 9.5 years, according to the prevailing bond market line, your return should be about 8.60 percent. In this example, the policy effect is 0.5 year and 0.35 percent (35 basis points). Specifically, the higher duration implies that your portfolio should have a higher average return of 0.35 percent (this positive relationship assumes the typical upward-sloping yield curve).

Given the expected return and duration for this long-term portfolio, all deviations from the index portfolio are attributable to the remaining management effect components. The interest rate anticipation effect attempts to measure the differential return from changing the duration during this period compared to the portfolio's long-term duration. Hopefully, the manager would increase the duration of the portfolio during periods of declining interest rates to increase the price volatility (price appreciation) of your portfolio and reduce duration during periods of rising interest rates to minimize the price decline. Therefore, you would determine the duration of the actual portfolio during the period and compare this to the duration of the long-term portfolio. Then you would determine the difference in expected return for these portfolios and their two durations using the bond market line. For example, assume the duration for the long-term portfolio is 9.5 years, which implies an expected return of 8.60 percent, and that the prevailing duration for the portfolio being evaluated is 10.0 years, which implies an expected return of 9.00 percent using the bond market line. Therefore, the rate anticipation effect during this period is 0.40 percent (9.00 − 8.60).

The difference between this expected return based on the portfolio's duration and the actual return for the portfolio during this period is a combination of an analysis effect and a trading effect. The analysis effect is the differential return attributable to acquiring bonds that are temporarily mispriced relative to their risk level. To measure the analysis effect, compare the *expected* return for the portfolio held at the beginning of the period (using the bond market line) to the *actual* return of this same portfolio. If the actual return is greater than the expected return, it implies that the portfolio manager acquired some underpriced issues that became properly priced and thus provided excess returns during the period. For example, if the portfolio at the beginning of the period had a duration of 10 years, this might indicate that the portfolio's expected return was 9.00 percent for the period. In turn, if the actual return for this buy-and-hold portfolio was 9.40 percent, it would indicate an analysis effect of 40 basis points.

Finally, the trading effect occurs due to short-run changes in the portfolio during the period. It is measured as the residual after taking account of the analysis effect from the total excess return based on duration. For example, assume the total actual return is 10.50 percent with a duration of 10.0 years. The prevailing bond market line indicates an expected return of 9 percent for a portfolio with a 10-year duration. Thus, the combination of the analysis and trading effects is 1.50 percent (= 10.50 − 9.00). Previously, we determined that the analysis effect was 0.40 percent, so the trading effect must be 1.10 percent. In summary, for this portfolio manager, the actual return was 10.50 percent, compared to a return for the Lehman Brothers Index of 8.25 percent. This total excess of 2.25 percent would be divided as follows:

- 0.35 percent policy effect due to higher long-term duration
- 0.40 percent interest rate anticipation effect due to increasing the duration of the current portfolio above the long-term portfolio duration
- 0.40 percent analysis effect—the impact of superior selection of individual issues in the beginning portfolio
- 1.10 percent trading effect—the impact of trading the issues *during* the period

This technique breaks down the return based on the duration as a comprehensive risk measure. The only concern is that *it does not consider differences in the risk of default*. Specifically, the technique does not differentiate between an Aaa bond with a duration of 8 years and a Baa bond with the same duration. This could clearly affect the performance. A portfolio manager that invested in Baa bonds, for example, could experience a very positive analysis effect simply because the bonds were lower quality than the average quality implicit in the Lehman Brothers Index. The only way to avoid this would be to construct differential market lines for alternative ratings or construct a benchmark line that matches the quality makeup of the portfolio being evaluated.[30]

DECOMPOSING PORTFOLIO RETURNS   Dietz, Folger, and Hardy set forth a technique to decompose the bond portfolio returns into maturity, sector, and quality effects.[31] The total return for a bond during a period of time is

[30] This problem is briefly discussed in Frank K. Reilly and Rupinder Sidhu, "The Many Uses of Bond Duration," *Financial Analysts Journal* 36, no. 4 (July–August 1980): 58–72. See also Arthur Gudikunst and Joseph McCarthy, "Determinants of Bond Mutual Fund Performance," *Journal of Fixed Income* 2, no. 1 (June 1992): 95–101.

[31] Peter O. Dietz, H. Russell Fogler, and Donald J. Hardy, "The Challenge of Analyzing Bond Portfolio Returns," *Journal of Portfolio Management* 6, no. 3 (Spring 1980): 53–58.

composed of a known **income effect** (due to normal yield-to-maturity factors) and an unknown **price change effect** (due to an interest rate effect, a sector/quality effect, and a residual effect). It is graphed as follows:

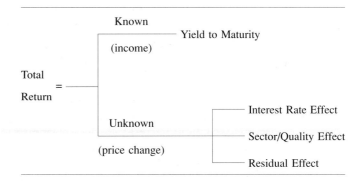

The yield-to-maturity (income) effect is the return an investor would receive if nothing had happened to the yield curve during the period. That is, the investor would receive the interest income, a price change relative to par, and any price change due to the passage of time and the shape of the yield curve.

The **interest rate effect** measures what happened to each issue because of changes in the term structure of interest rates during the period. Each bond is valued based on the Treasury yield curve at its maturity and takes account of its normal premium relative to Treasury yields. Assume a normal risk premium spread of 30 basis points and that yields on Treasury bonds with the maturity of your bond go from 8.50 percent to 9.25 percent. To determine the interest rate effect, you would compute the value of your bond at 8.80 percent (8.50 + 0.30) and at 9.55 percent (9.25 + 0.30) and then compute the price change. This is the price change caused by a change in market interest rates.

The **sector/quality effect** measures the expected impact on the returns because of the sector of the bonds (corporates, utilities, financial, GNMA, etc.) and also the quality of the bonds (Aaa, Aa, A, Baa). The authors determined the average impact of these sets of variables by deriving a matrix of sector/quality returns for all bonds on the Telstat pricing tapes as follows (i.e., you would fill in this table with the appropriate yields):

	SECTOR/QUALITY RETURNS (VALUE-WEIGHTED)			
	Aaa	Aa	A	Baa
Corporates				
Utilities				
Financial				
Telephone				
Foreign				
GNMA				
Agencies				

Given this matrix, you can determine what happened to bonds in each cell after taking account of the yield to maturity and the interest rate effect. As an example, during a given period you might find that an average Aa utility had negative excess returns of −0.50 percent after taking account of the yield to maturity and the interest rate effect, whereas an

A-rated corporate bond experienced a comparable positive excess return of 0.30 percent. Therefore, the sector/quality effect would be −0.50 and 0.30 for these sets of bonds.

The **residual effect** is what remains after taking account of the three prior factors—yield to maturity, interest rate effect, and the sector/quality effect. It is computed as follows:

$$\begin{array}{c}\text{Total} \\ \text{Return}\end{array} - \begin{array}{c}\text{Yield to} \\ \text{Maturity} \\ \text{Effect}\end{array} - \begin{array}{c}\text{Interest} \\ \text{Rate Effect}\end{array} - \begin{array}{c}\text{Sector/Quality} \\ \text{Effect}\end{array} = \text{Residual}$$

The presence of a consistently large positive residual would indicate superior bond selection capabilities. Specifically, a positive residual indicates that after taking account of all market effects from interest rate changes and sector/quality, it is still possible the bond manager has helped provide positive returns due to bond selection. Alternatively, large positive interest rate effects during periods of declining interest rates and small negative interest rate effects during periods of rising interest rates would indicate a bond manager with good skills at interest rate anticipation. Consistently positive sector/quality effects would indicate the ability to make proper allocations and to anticipate shifts in this area over time.

ANALYZING SOURCES OF RETURN

Fong, Pearson, and Vasicek proposed a performance evaluation technique that likewise divides the total returns into several components that affect bond returns.[32] Their intent was to measure total realized return and attribute the return to its sources (i.e., what factors contributed to the total return?). The first breakdown divides the total return (R) between the effect of the external interest rate environment (I), which is beyond the control of the portfolio manager, and the contribution of the management process (C). Thus:

$$R = I + C$$

In turn, I is broken down into two parts. The first is the *expected* rate of return (E) on a portfolio of default-free securities, assuming no change in forward rates (i.e., no change in future one-period rates). This expected return also is referred to as the *market's implicit forecast*. The second component of I is U, the *unexpected* return on the Treasury index that is due to actual changes in forward rates. Thus:

$$I = E + U$$

For example, assume that at the beginning of a quarter, the expected annual return on a portfolio of Treasury bonds is 11 percent. (This expected return assumes no change in the term structure of bonds during this year.) At the end of the year, you determine that the actual return on this portfolio of Treasury bonds was 11.75 percent. This would imply an E of 11 percent and a U of .75 percent.

In turn, C (the management contribution) is composed of three factors:

- M = return from maturity management
- S = return from spread/quality management
- B = return attributable to the selection of specific securities

---

[32] Gifford Fong, Charles Pearson, and Oldrich Vasicek, "Bond Performance: Analyzing Sources of Return," *Journal of Portfolio Management* 9, no. 3 (Spring 1983): 46–50.

The return from *maturity management, M,* is determined by how well the portfolio manager changes maturity (duration) in anticipation of interest rate changes. The component is measured by computing the default-free price of every security (at the beginning and end of the period) based on the spot rate for its maturity, as indicated by the Treasury yield curve. The total return over the evaluation period is derived from these prices, while maintaining all actual trading activity. Given this total return based on maturity yields, subtract the actual return on the Treasury index (assumed earlier to be 11.75 percent) to arrive at the maturity return. For example, if the total return for the portfolio based on the pricing computations was 12.25 percent, the maturity management return would be 0.50 percent, assuming the Treasury index return of 11.75 percent.[33]

The *spread/quality management* component indicates the effect on return due to the manager's selection of bonds from various sectors and qualities. It is measured by pricing each bond at the beginning and end of the period using yields appropriate for its specific sector and quality and then computing the rate of return given these prices. This total return less the return for Treasury bonds, considering the maturity effect (assumed to be 12.25 percent), indicates the return attributable to sector/quality selection. If this sector/quality pricing indicates a total return of 12.0 percent, it would imply a negative 0.25 percent for sector/quality management (12.00 − 12.25).

The *selectivity component (B)* is the remaining return. It is attributable to the selection of specific bonds after considering the maturity and sector/quality decisions—specifically, what individual bonds were selected to carry out these decisions. It is measured as the difference between the actual total return on the portfolio and the prior total return that considered maturity and sector/quality. Continuing our example, if the actual total return on the portfolio was 13.00 percent, the selectivity component would be 1.00 percent because the return for maturity and sector/quality above was 12.00 percent. To summarize the results:

$$R = \quad I \quad + \quad C$$
$$= (E + U) + (M + S + B)$$

where

E = **expected Treasury yield**		**11.00**
U = **unexpected Treasury yield**		.75
M = **maturity management**		.50
S = **spread/quality management**		(.25)
B = **selectivity**		1.00
Total return		**13.00**

This analysis indicates that the portfolio manager was quite good at maturity (duration) decisions and at selecting individual bonds but did not do well in terms of sector/quality decisions. As before, you should do a similar breakdown for some market index series as a basis of comparison to an unmanaged portfolio. Also, examine these components over time to determine any consistent strengths or weaknesses for the portfolio manager.

---

[33] A subsequent article suggests a possible refinement of the maturity management effect by considering the separate effects of duration, convexity, and yield curve "twist." See Gifford Fong, Charles Pearson, Oldrich Vasicek, and Theresa Conroy, "Fixed-Income Portfolio Performance: Analyzing Sources of Return," in *The Handbook of Fixed-Income Securities,* 3d ed., edited by Frank J. Fabozzi (Homewood, IL: Business One Irwin, 1991).

CONSISTENCY OF PERFORMANCE

Numerous investigators have documented performance inconsistency for managers of equity portfolios. Kritzman considered this question for bond managers by examining the ranking for 32 bond managers employed by AT&T.[34] He divided a 10-year period into two 5-year periods, determined each manager's percentile ranking in each period, and correlated the rankings. The results revealed *no relationship* between performance in the two periods. A further test also revealed *no relationship* between past and future performance even among the best and worst performers. Based on these results, Kritzman concluded that it would be necessary to examine something besides past performance to determine superior bond portfolio managers.

REQUIRED CHARACTERISTICS OF BENCHMARKS

Previously, the benchmark problem was described as being related to finding a proxy for the theoretical market portfolio, especially given the trend toward global capital markets. Concurrent with this search for a global market portfolio, there has also been a search for appropriate **normal portfolios,** which are customized benchmarks that reflect the specific styles of alternative managers. Bailey, Richards, and Tierney consider this a critical need of pension plans and endowments who hire multiple managers with widely divergent styles.[35] They point out that if a broad market index is used rather than a specific benchmark portfolio, it is implicitly assumed that the portfolio manager does not have an investment style, which is quite unrealistic. Also, it does not allow the plan sponsors to determine if the money manager is consistent with his or her stated investment style. The authors contend that any useful benchmark should have the following characteristics:

- *Unambiguous*. The names and weights of securities comprising the benchmark are clearly delineated.
- *Investable*. The option is available to forgo active management and simply hold the benchmark.
- *Measurable*. It is possible to calculate the return on the benchmark on a reasonably frequent basis.
- *Appropriate*. The benchmark is consistent with the manager's investment style or biases.
- *Reflective of current investment opinions*. The manager has current investment knowledge (be it positive, negative, or neutral) of the securities that make up the benchmark.
- *Specified in advance*. The benchmark is constructed prior to the start of an evaluation period.

If a benchmark does not possess all of these properties, it is considered flawed as an effective management tool. One example of a flawed benchmark is the use of the median manager from a broad universe of managers or even a limited universe of managers. This criticism is spelled out in detail by Bailey, who argues that the manager universe is inadequate on almost every characteristic.[36]

---

[34] Mark Kritzman, "Can Bond Managers Perform Consistently?" *Journal of Portfolio Management* 9, no. 4 (Summer 1983): 54–56.

[35] Jeffrey V. Bailey, Thomas M. Richards, and David E. Tierney, "Benchmark Portfolios and the Manager/Plan Sponsor Relationship," *Current Topics in Investment Management* (New York: Harper & Row, 1990). For a discussion of who shall construct a customized benchmark, see Jeffrey V. Bailey and David E. Tierney, "Gaming Manager Benchmarks," *Journal of Portfolio Management* 19, no 4 (Summer 1993): 37–40.

[36] Jeffrey V. Bailey, "Are Manager Universes Acceptable Performance Benchmarks?" *Journal of Portfolio Management* 18, no. 3 (Spring 1992): 9–13. For a general discussion of what to look for in a benchmark, see Jeffrey V. Bailey, "Evaluating Benchmark Quality," *Financial Analysts Journal* 48, no. 3 (May–June 1992): 33–39. For a discussion of fixed-income benchmarks, see Chris P. Dialynas, "The Active Decisions in the Selection of Passive Management and Performance Bogeys," and Daralyn B. Peifer, "A Sponsor's View of Benchmark Portfolios,"

In summary, because of a growing desire to evaluate aggregate performance and identify what factors contribute to superior or inferior performance, benchmarks must be selected at two levels: (1) a *global* level that contains the broadest mix of risky assets available from around the world, and (2) a fairly specific level consistent with the management style of an individual money manager (i.e., a customized benchmark). When searching both levels, the set of characteristics suggested by Bailey, Richards, and Tierney should be kept in mind.

Summary

- The first major goal of portfolio management is to derive rates of return that equal or exceed the returns on a naively selected portfolio with equal risk. The second goal is to attain complete diversification. Several techniques have been derived to evaluate equity portfolios in terms of both risk and return (composite measures) based on the CAPM. The Treynor measure considers the excess returns earned per unit of systematic risk. The Sharpe measure indicates the excess return per unit of total risk. Jensen likewise evaluated performance in terms of the systematic risk involved and showed how to determine whether the difference in risk-adjusted performance (good or bad) is statistically significant. Additional work in equity portfolio evaluation has been concerned with models that indicate what components of the management process contributed to the results. A model by Fama divided the composite return into measures related to total risk, systematic risk, diversification, and selectivity, in addition to measuring overall performance. Finally, attribution analysis seeks to establish whether market timing or security selection skills (or both) are the source of a manager's performance.
- Roll challenged the validity of all techniques that assume a market portfolio that theoretically includes all risky assets when actually investigators use a proxy such as the S&P 500 that is limited to U.S. common stocks. This criticism does not invalidate the normative asset pricing model, only its application because of measurement problems related to the proxy for the market portfolio. It is demonstrated that the measurement problem is increased in an environment where global investing is the norm. The good news is that more comprehensive indexes are feasible and are currently being developed.
- Although the techniques for evaluating equity portfolio performance have been in existence for almost 35 years, comparable techniques for examining bond portfolio performance were initiated more recently. Notably, the evaluation models for bonds typically consider separately the several important decision variables related to bonds: the overall market factor, the impact of maturity-duration decisions, the influence of sector and quality factors, and the impact of individual bond selection. A study indicated a lack of consistency over time for a sample of bond managers similar to results for equity managers.
- In conclusion, investors need to evaluate their own performance and the performance of hired managers. The various techniques we discuss provide theoretically justifiable measures that differ slightly. Although there is high rank correlation among the alternative measures, *all the measures should be used* because they provide different insights regarding the performance of managers. Finally, an evaluation of a portfolio manager should be done many times over different market environments before a final judgment is reached regarding the strengths and weaknesses of a manager.[37]

both in *The Handbook of Fixed-Income Securities,* 4th ed., edited by Frank J. Fabozzi and T. Dessa Fabozzi (Burr Ridge, IL: Irwin Professional Publishing, 1995).

[37] For a general discussion of portfolio evaluation, see Peter O. Dietz and Jeannette R. Kirschman, "Evaluating Portfolio Performance," in *Managing Investment Portfolios,* 2d ed., edited by John L. Maginn and Donald L. Tuttle (Boston: Warren Gorham and Lamont, 1990). For a detailed discussion of the equity portfolio evaluation techniques, see Ray Shulka and Charles Trzcinka, "Performance Measurement of Managed Portfolios," in *Financial Markets, Institutions and Investments,* Vol. 1, no. 4 (New York: New York University Salomon Center, 1992). For a general discussion of bond portfolio evaluation, see Frank J. Fabozzi, *Bond Markets, Analysis and Strategies,* 3d ed. (Upper Saddle River, NJ: Prentice-Hall, 1996), Chapter 20.

Questions

1. Describe two major factors that a portfolio manager should consider before designing an investment strategy. What types of decisions can a manager make to achieve these goals?

2. Compare and contrast three prominent approaches to measuring investment performance on a risk-adjusted basis. In developing your answer, comment on the conditions under which each measure will be most useful.

3. The Sharpe and Treynor performance measures both calculate a portfolio's average excess return per unit of risk. Under what circumstances would it make sense to use both measures to compare the performance of a given set of portfolios? What additional information is provided by a comparison of the rankings achieved using the two measures?

4. Describe how the Jensen measure of performance is calculated. Under what conditions should it give a similar set of portfolio rankings as the Sharpe and Treynor measures? Is it possible to adjust the Jensen measure so that a portfolio's alpha value is measured relative to an empirical form of the arbitrage pricing theory rather than the capital asset pricing model? Explain.

5. A fund had an overall performance value of −0.50 percent using the Fama performance technique. Discuss whether the manager of this fund could have experienced a positive selectivity value and under what conditions that value might have occurred.

6. A portfolio has an R^2 with the market of 0.95 and a selectivity value of 2.5 percent. Would you expect this portfolio to have a positive or a negative net selectivity value? Explain.

7. *CFA Examination I (June 1991)*
   a. Explain why the asset allocation decision is the primary determinant of total portfolio performance over time.
   b. Describe three reasons why successful implementation of asset allocation decisions is even more difficult in practice than in theory.

8. Performance attribution analysis is an attempt to divide a manager's "active" residual return into an allocation effect and a selection effect. Explain how these two effects are measured and why their sum must equal the total value-added return for the manager. Is this analysis valid if the actual portfolio in question is riskier than the benchmark portfolio to which it is being compared?

9. *CFA Examination III (June 1991)*
   A number of different management "styles" are utilized by investment managers. Performance evaluation, however, is not standardized either within or across management styles. One development aimed at mitigating this problem is the emergence of the "benchmark portfolio" concept.

   Against this background, comment on the role of benchmark portfolios in evaluating a manager's investment performance and contrast the suitability of benchmark portfolios for this purpose with that of the "median manager" approach often employed. Include *four* elements of comparison in your discussion.

10. *CFA Examination III (June 1981)*
    Richard Roll, in an article on using the capital asset pricing model (CAPM) to evaluate portfolio performance, indicated that it may not be possible to evaluate portfolio management ability if there is error in the benchmark used.
    a. In evaluating portfolio performance, describe the general procedure, with emphasis on the benchmark employed.
    b. Explain what Roll meant by the benchmark error and identify the specific problem with this benchmark.
    c. Draw a graph that shows how a portfolio that has been judged as superior relative to a "measured" security market line (SML) can be inferior relative to the "true" SML.
    d. Assume that you are informed that a given portfolio manager has been evaluated as superior when compared to the DJIA, the S&P 500, and the NYSE Composite Index. Explain whether this consensus would make you feel more comfortable regarding the portfolio manager's true ability.

e. While conceding the possible problem with benchmark errors as set forth by Roll, some contend this does not mean the CAPM is incorrect, but only that there is a measurement problem when implementing the theory. Others contend that because of benchmark errors, the whole technique should be scrapped. Take and defend one of these positions.

11. It has been contended that the derivation of an appropriate model for evaluating the performance of a bond manager is more difficult than an equity portfolio evaluation model because more decisions are required. Discuss some of the specific decisions that need to be considered when evaluating the performance of a bond portfolio manager.

12. *CFA Examination III (June 1982)*

During a quarterly review session, a client of Fixed Income Investors, a pension fund advisory firm, asks Fred Raymond, the portfolio manager for the company's account, if he could provide a more detailed analysis of their portfolio performance than simply total return. Specifically, the client had recently seen a copy of an article by Dietz, Fogler, and Hardy on the analysis of bond portfolio returns that attempted to decompose the total return into the following four components:

a. Yield-to-maturity effect
b. Interest rate effect
c. Sector/quality effect
d. Residual

Although he does not expect you to be able to provide such an analysis this year, he asks you to explain each of these components to him so he will be better prepared to understand such an analysis when you do it for his company's portfolio next year. Explain each of these components.

Problems

1. *CFA Examination III (June 1985)*

You have been asked to evaluate the performance of two portfolios: Good Samaritan Hospital's endowment assets and estate fund of the recently deceased Mrs. Mary Atkins, which has just been transferred in a bequest to Good Samaritan. The existing Good Samaritan endowment assets (excluding the Atkins' estate) have been managed by an investment counseling firm with an income objective of approximately 5% annually. The returns from this portfolio and from Mrs. Atkins' portfolio are shown in the table below.

	Latest Fiscal Year Total Return	Beta
Good Samaritan existing endowment assets		
– equity only	11.8%	1.20
– total portfolio	8.4	
Mrs. Atkins' Portfolio		
– equity only	10.7%	1.05
– total portfolio	5.1	
S&P 500 Index	9.9%	
Lehman Bond Index	3.4	
90-day Treasury Bills	7.8	
Municipal Bond Index	1.4	

a. Calculate the risk-adjusted return of each of the two equity-only portfolios. Compare these returns to each other and to the S&P 500, and explain the significance of any differences.

b. List and briefly comment on three factors which could account for the difference in reported performance between Mrs. Atkins' and Good Samaritan's total portfolios.

2. The portfolios identified below are being considered for investment. During the period under consideration, $RFR = 0.07$.

Portfolio	Return	Beta	σ_i
P	.15	1.0	.05
Q	.20	1.5	.10
R	.10	0.6	.03
S	.17	1.1	.06
Market	.13	1.0	.04

a. Compute the Sharpe measure for each portfolio and the market portfolio.

b. Compute the Treynor measure for each portfolio and the market portfolio.

c. Rank the portfolios using each measure, explaining the cause for any differences you find in the rankings.

3. *CFA Examination I (June 1994)*

An analyst wants to evaluate Portfolio X, consisting entirely of U.S. common stocks, using both the Treynor and Sharpe measures of portfolio performance. The table below provides the average annual rate of return for Portfolio X, the market portfolio (as measured by the Standard & Poor's 500 Index), and U.S. Treasury bills (T-bills) during the past 8 years.

	Annual Average Rate of Return	Standard Deviation of Return	Beta
Portfolio X	10%	18%	0.60
S&P 500	12	13	1.00
T-bills	6	n/a	n/a

n/a = not applicable

a. Calculate both the Treynor measure and the Sharpe measure for both Portfolio X and the S&P 500. Briefly explain whether Portfolio X underperformed, equaled, or outperformed the S&P 500 on a risk-adjusted basis using both the Treynor measure and the Sharpe measure.

b. Based on the performance of Portfolio X relative to the S&P 500 calculated in Part a, briefly explain the reason for the conflicting results when using the Treynor measure versus the Sharpe measure.

4. You have been assigned the task of comparing the investment performance of five different pension fund managers. After gathering 60 months of excess returns (i.e., returns in excess of the monthly risk-free rate) on each fund as well as the monthly excess returns on the entire stock market, you perform the regressions of the form:

$$(R_{fund} - RFR)_t = \alpha + \beta (R_{mkt} - RFR)_t + U_t$$

You have prepared the following summary of the data, with the standard errors for each of the coefficients listed in parentheses.

Portfolio	REGRESSION DATA:			(R_{fund} – RFR):	
	α	β	R^2	Mean	σ
ABC	0.192	1.048	94.1%	1.022%	1.193%
	(0.11)	(0.10)			
DEF	0.053	0.662	91.6	0.473	0.764
	(0.19)	(0.09)			
GHI	0.463	0.594	68.6	0.935	0.793
	(0.19)	(0.07)			
JKL	0.355	0.757	64.1	0.955	1.044
	(0.22)	(0.08)			
MNO	0.296	0.785	94.8	0.890	0.890
	(0.14)	(0.12)			

a. Which fund had the highest degree of diversification over the sample period? How is diversification measured in this statistical framework?

b. Rank these funds' performance according to the Sharpe, Treynor, and Jensen measures.

c. Since you know that according to the CAPM the intercept of these regressions (i.e., alpha) should be zero, this coefficient can be used as a measure of the value-added provided by the investment manager. Which funds have statistically outperformed and underperformed the market using a two-sided 95 percent confidence interval? (Note: The relevant t-statistic using 60 observations is 2.00.)

5. You have decided to undertake an evaluation of the performance of the Cirrus International Fund (CIF) for your Investment Club. After collecting the following data:

$$R_a = 0.15$$
$$RFR = 0.05$$
$$\beta_a = 1.20$$
$$R_m = 0.10$$

a. Draw the security market line.

b. Calculate CIF's overall performance.

c. Calculate CIF's selectivity.

d. Calculate CIF's risk.

6. *CFA Examination III (June 1995)*

Your discussion with a client has turned to the measurement of investment performance, particularly with respect to international portfolios.

PERFORMANCE AND ATTRIBUTION DATA: ANNUALIZED RETURNS FOR 5 YEARS ENDED 12/31/94

International Manager/Index	Total Return	Country/Security Return	Currency Return
Manager A	−6.0%	2.0%	−8.0%
Manager B	−2.0	−1.0	−1.0
EAFE Index	−5.0	0.2	−5.2

a. Assume that the data in the above table for Manager A and Manager B accurately reflect their investment skills and that both managers actively manage currency exposure. Briefly describe one strength and one weakness for each manager.

b. Recommend and justify a strategy that would enable the Fund to take advantage of the strengths of each of the two managers while minimizing their weaknesses.

7. Consider the following performance data for two portfolio managers (A and B) and a common benchmark portfolio:

	BENCHMARK		MANAGER A		MANAGER B	
	Weight	Return	Weight	Return	Weight	Return
Stock	0.6	−5.0%	0.5	−4.0%	0.3	−5.0%
Bonds	0.3	−3.5	0.2	−2.5	0.4	−3.5
Cash	0.1	0.3	0.3	0.3	0.3	0.3

a. Calculate: (i) the overall return to the benchmark portfolio; (ii) the overall return to Manager A's actual portfolio; and (iii) the overall return to Manager B's actual portfolio. Briefly comment on whether these managers have under- or outperformed the benchmark fund.

b. Using attribution analysis, calculate (i) the *selection effect* for Manager A, and (ii) the *allocation effect* for Manager B. Using these numbers in conjunction with your results from Part a, comment on whether these managers have added value through their selection skills, their allocation skills, or both.

8. *CFA Examination III (June 1985)*

A U.S. pension plan hired two off-shore firms to manage the non-U.S. equity portion of its total portfolio. Each firm was free to own stocks in any country market included in Morgan Stanley/ Capital International's Europe, Australia, and Far East Index (EAFE) and free to use any form of dollar and/or non-dollar cash or bonds as an equity substitute or reserve. After three years had elapsed, the records of the managers and the EAFE Index were as shown below:

SUMMARY: CONTRIBUTIONS TO RETURN

	Currency	Country Selection	Stock Selection	Cash/Bond Allocation	Total Return Recorded
Manager A	(9.0%)	19.7%	3.1%	0.6%	14.4%
Manager B	(7.4)	14.2	6.0	2.81	5.6
Composite of					
A & B	(8.2)	16.9	4.5	1.71	5.0
EAFE Index	(12.9)	19.9	—	—	7.0

You are a member of the plan sponsor's Pension Committee, which will soon meet with the plan's consultant to review manager performance. In preparation for this meeting, you go through the following analysis:

a. Briefly describe the strengths and weaknesses of each manager, relative to the EAFE Index data.

b. Briefly explain the meaning of the data in the "Currency" column.

9. Reggie Portmus has made a performance evaluation of his bond holdings. He has misplaced some of the values and has asked for your help in calculating the remaining ones. At present he holds 10-year AA, 5-year A, and 25-year B bonds, and the following information has been recovered:

I = external interest rate environment:	11.00
E = expected return:	10.00
U = unexpected return:	?
M = maturity:	0.2%/year in the first 5 years, 0.1%/year thereafter
S = spread/quality:	−0.2%/rank (AAA, AA, A, BBB, etc.)
B = specific selection:	0.25, 0.50, 075, respectively
C:	?
R:	?

10. *CFA Examination III (June 1994)*

To illustrate for the Investment Committee of the profit-sharing plan to which you are a consultant on some of the issues that arise in measuring performance, you have identified three U.S. fixed-income management firms whose investment approaches are representative of general practice. Each firm's approach is described below.

Firm A: An enhanced index fund manager that seeks to add value by superior security selection while maintaining portfolio duration and sector weights equal to the overall bond market.

Firm B: An active duration manager investing only in the government and corporate bond sectors. The firm uses futures to manage portfolio duration.

Firm C: An active manager seeking to add value by correctly anticipating changes in the shape of the yield curve, while maintaining portfolio duration and sector weights roughly equal to the overall bond market.

You have provided the Committee with the following additional information about these firms, derived from a consultant's data base.

**ANNUALIZED TOTAL RETURN DATA
(PAST FIVE YEARS)**

	Firm A	Firm B	Firm C
Reported Returns	9.2%	9.3%	9.0%

	Aggregate Index	**INDEX SECTORS**			
		Governments	Corporates	Government/ Corporate	Mortgages
Index Return	8.7%	9.0%	9.8%	9.5%	8.3%

	CONSULTANT'S MANAGER UNIVERSE		
	All Managers	Managers Using the Aggregate Index as Their Benchmark	Managers Using the Govt./Corp. Sector as Their Benchmark
Return 5th percentile	6.0%	7.7%	8.4%
25th percentile	7.1	8.1	8.9
50th percentile	8.0	8.6	9.4
75th percentile	8.6	9.1	9.9
95th percentile	9.3	13.1	13.9

a. Evaluate the performance of each of these three firms relative to its appropriate Index and to the manager universe. Use only the data from the descriptions and the above table, even though other information would be required for a more complete and accurate appraisal. To provide additional guidance to the Committee, you decide to do an attribution analysis on the returns produced by Firm A and Firm C and have prepared the following table:

**PERFORMANCE ATTRIBUTION ANALYSIS
(PAST FIVE YEARS—ANNUALIZED TOTAL RETURNS)**

	RETURN ATTRIBUTED TO				
	Total Return =	Duration Decisions +	Yield Curve Decisions +	Sector Weighting Decisions +	Security Selection Decisions & Residuals
Firm A					
Total Return	9.20%	8.00%	0.80%	0.00%	0.40%
Benchmark Index Return	8.70	7.00	0.50	0.70	0.50
Difference	0.50	1.00	0.30	−0.70	−0.10
Firm C					
Total Return	9.00%	7.03%	0.80%	0.71%	0.46%
Benchmark Index Return	8.70	7.00	0.50	0.70	0.50
Difference	0.30	0.03	0.30	0.01	−0.04

b. Evaluate the performance of Firm A and of Firm C based on all the information previously provided and your interpretation of the data in this new table.
c. Based solely on the attribution analysis you performed in Part b above, state which firm produced the better result and justify your conclusion.

References

Brown, Stephen J., William Goetzmann, Roger G. Ibbottson, and Stephen A. Ross. "Survivorship Bias in Performance Studies." *Review of Financial Studies* 5, no. 4 (December 1992).

Dybvig, Philip H. and Stephen A. Ross. "The Analytics of Performance Measurement Using a Security Market Line." *Journal of Finance* 40, no. 2 (June 1985).

Elton, Edwin J. and Martin J. Gruber. *Modern Portolio Theory and Investment Analysis.* 5th ed. New York: John Wiley & Sons, 1995.

Grinblatt, Mark and Sheridan Titman. "Mutual Fund Performance: An Analysis of Quarterly Portfolio Holdings." *Journal of Business* 62, no. 3 (1989).

Grinold, Richard C. and Ronald N. Kahn. *Active Portfolio Management.* Burr Ridge, IL: Irwin, 1995.

Kon, Stanley J. and Frank C. Jen. "Estimation of Time-Varying Systematic Risk and Performance of Mutual Fund Portfolios: An Application of Switching Regression." *Journal of Finance* 33, no. 2 (May 1978).

Maginn, John L. and Donald L. Tuttle, eds. *Managing Investment Portfolios: A Dynamic Process.* 2d ed. Boston, MA: Warren, Gorham, & Lamont, 1990.

Radcliffe, Robert, Robert Brooks, and Haim Levy. "Active Asset Allocation Decisions of Professional Equity Managers." *Review of Financial Services* 2, no. 1 (1992/1993).

Sharpe, William F. "Asset Allocation: Management Style and Performance Measurement." *Journal of Portfolio Management* 18, no. 2 (Winter 1992).

Squires, Jan, ed. *Performance Evaluation, Benchmarks, and Attribution Analysis.* Charlottesville, VA: Association for Investment Management and Research, 1995.

As mentioned in the section on career opportunities, the professional designation of Chartered Financial Analyst (CFA) is becoming a significant requirement for a career in investment analysis and/or portfolio management. For that reason, this section presents the history and objectives of the Institute of Chartered Financial Analysts and general guidelines for acquiring the CFA designation. If you are interested in the program, you can write to the Institute for more information.

The Institute of Chartered Financial Analysts (ICFA) was formed in 1959 in Charlottesville, Virginia. The CFA candidate examinations were first offered in 1963. The ICFA, along with the Financial Analysts Federation, form the Association for Investment Management and Research (AIMR).

The Institute of Chartered Financial Analysts (ICFA) was organized to enhance the professionalism of those involved in various aspects of the investment decision-making process and to recognize those who achieve a high level of professionalism by awarding the designation of Chartered Financial Analyst (CFA).

The basic missions and purposes of the AIMR/ICFA are

- To develop and keep current a "body of knowledge" applicable to the investment decision-making process. The principal components of this knowledge are financial accounting, economics, both fixed-income and equity securities analysis, portfolio management, ethical and professional standards, and quantitative techniques.
- To administer a study and examination program for eligible candidates, the primary objectives of which are to assist the candidate in mastering and applying the body of knowledge and to test the candidate's competency in the knowledge gained.
- To award the professional CFA designation to those candidates who have passed three examination levels (encompassing a total of 18 hours of testing over a minimum of three years), who meet stipulated standards of professional conduct, and who otherwise are eligible for membership in the ICFA.
- To provide a useful and informative program of continuing education through seminars, publications, and other formats that enable members, candidates, and others in the investment constituency to be more aware of and to better utilize the changing and expanding body of knowledge.
- To sponsor and enforce a *Code of Ethics and Standards of Professional Conduct* that apply to enrolled candidates and to all members.

A college degree is necessary to enter the program. A candidate may sit for all three examinations without having had investment experience *per se* or having joined a constituent Society of the Financial Analysts Federation. However, after passing the three examination levels, the CFA Charter will not be awarded unless or until the candidate

- has at least three years of experience as a financial analyst, which is defined as a person who has spent and/or is spending a substantial portion of his/her professional time collecting, evaluating, and applying financial, economic, and related data to the investment decision-making process, and
- has applied for membership or is a member of a constituent Society of the Financial Analysts Federation, if such a Society exists within 50 miles of the candidate's principal place of business.

The curriculum of the CFA study program covers:

1. Ethical and Professional Standards
2. Financial Accounting
3. Economics
4. Fixed-Income Securities Analysis
5. Equity Securities Analysis
6. Portfolio Management
7. Quantitative Techniques

Members and candidates are typically employed in the investment field. From 1963 to 1991, over 13,000 charters have been awarded. More than 13,000 individuals currently are registered in the CFA Candidate Program. If you are interested in learning more about the CFA program, the Institute has a booklet that describes the program and includes an application form. The address is Institute of Chartered Financial Analysts, P.O. Box 3668, Charlottesville, Virginia 22903.

Source: Reprinted with permission from The Financial Analysts Federation and The Institute of Chartered Financial Analysts, Charlottesville, Virginia.

THE STANDARDS OF PROFESSIONAL CONDUCT

I. Obligation to Inform Employer of Code and Standards

The financial analyst shall inform his employer, through his direct supervisor, that the analyst is obligated to comply with the Code of Ethics and Standards of Professional Conduct, and is subject to disciplinary sanctions for violations thereof. He shall deliver a copy of the Code and Standards to his employer if the employer does not have a copy.

II. Compliance with Governing Laws and Regulations and the Code and Standards

A. Required Knowledge and Compliance

The financial analyst shall maintain knowledge of and shall comply with all applicable laws, rules, and regulations of any government, governmental agency, and regulatory organization governing his professional, financial, or business activities, as well as with these Standards of Professional Conduct and the accompanying Code of Ethics.

B. Prohibition Against Assisting Legal and Ethical Violations

The financial analyst shall not knowingly participate in, or assist, any acts in violation of any applicable law, rule, or regulation of any government, governmental agency, or regulatory organization governing his professional, financial, or business activities, nor any act which would violate any provision of these Standards of Professional Conduct or the accompanying Code of Ethics.

C. Prohibition Against Use of Material Nonpublic Information

The financial analyst shall comply with all laws and regulations relating to the use and communication of material nonpublic information. The financial analyst's duty is generally defined as to not trade while in possession of, nor communicate, material nonpublic information in breach of a duty, or if the information is misappropriated.

Duties under the Standard include the following: (1) If the analyst acquires such information as a result of a special or confidential relationship with the issuer or others, he shall not communicate the information (other than within the relationship), or take investment action on the basis of such information, if it violates that relationship. (2) If the analyst is not in a special or confidential relationship with the issuer or others, he shall not communicate or act on material nonpublic information if he knows, or should have known, that such information (a) was disclosed to him, or would result in a breach of a duty, or (b) was misappropriated.

If such a breach of duty exists, the analyst shall make reasonable efforts to achieve public dissemination of such information.

D. Responsibilities of Supervisors

A financial analyst with supervisory responsibility shall exercise reasonable supervision over those subordinate employees subject to his control, to prevent any violation by such persons

*Masculine personal pronouns, used throughout the Code and Standards to simplify sentence structure, shall apply to all persons, regardless of sex.

of applicable statutes, regulations, or provisions of the Code of Ethics or Standards of Professional Conduct. In so doing the analyst is entitled to rely upon reasonable procedures established by his employer.

III. Research Reports, Investment Recommendations and Actions

A. Reasonable Basis and Representations

1. The financial analyst shall exercise diligence and thoroughness in making an investment recommendation to others or in taking an investment action for others.

2. The financial analyst shall have a reasonable and adequate basis for such recommendations and actions, supported by appropriate research and investigation.

3. The financial analyst shall make reasonable and diligent efforts to avoid any material misrepresentation in any research report or investment recommendation.

4. The financial analyst shall maintain appropriate records to support the reasonableness of such recommendations and actions.

B. Research Reports

1. The financial analyst shall use reasonable judgment as to the inclusion of relevant factors in research reports.

2. The financial analyst shall distinguish between facts and opinions in research reports.

3. The financial analyst shall indicate the basic characteristics of the investment involved when preparing for general public distribution a research report that is not directly related to a specific portfolio or client.

C. Portfolio Investment Recommendations and Actions

1. The financial analyst shall, when making an investment recommendation or taking an investment action for a specific portfolio or client, consider its appropriateness and suitability for such portfolio or client. In considering such matters, the financial analyst shall take into account (a) the needs and circumstances of the client, (b) the basic characteristics of the investment involved, and (c) the basic characteristics of the total portfolio. The financial analyst shall use reasonable judgment to determine the applicable relevant factors.

2. The financial analyst shall distinguish between facts and opinions in the presentation of investment recommendations.

3. The financial analyst shall disclose to clients and prospective clients the basic format and general principles of the investment processes by which securities are selected and portfolios are constructed and shall promptly disclose to clients any changes that might significantly affect those processes.

D. Prohibition Against Plagiarism

The financial analyst shall not, when presenting material to his employer, associates, customers, clients, or the general public, copy or use in substantially the same form material prepared by other persons without acknowledging its use and identifying the name of the author or publisher of such material. The analyst may, however, use without acknowledgement factual information published by recognized financial and statistical reporting services or similar sources.

E. Prohibition Against Misrepresentation of Services

The financial analyst shall not make any statements, orally or in writing, which misrepresent (1) the services that the analyst or his firm is capable of performing for the client, (2) the qualifications of such analyst or his firm, or (3) the expected performance of any investment.

The financial analyst shall not make, orally or in writing, explicitly or implicitly, any assurances about or guarantees of any investment or its return except communication of accurate information as to the terms of the investment instrument and the issuer's obligations under the instrument.

F. Performance Presentation Standards

1. The financial analyst shall not make any statements, oral or written, which misrepresent the investment performance that the analyst or his firm has accomplished or can reasonably be expected to achieve.

2. If an analyst communicates directly or indirectly individual or firm performance information to a client or prospective client, or in a manner intended to be received by a client or prospective client ("Performance Information"), the analyst shall make every reasonable effort to assure that such performance information is a fair, accurate and complete presentation of such performance.

3. The financial analyst shall inform his employer about the existence and content of the Association for Investment Management and Research's Performance Presentation Standards, and this Standard III F, and shall encourage his employer to adopt and use the Performance Presentation Standards.

4. If Performance Information complies with the Performance Presentation Standards, the analyst shall be presumed to be in compliance with III F 2 above.

5. An analyst presenting Performance Information may use the following legend on the Performance Information presentation, but only if the analyst has made every reasonable effort to assure that such presentation is in compliance with the Performance Presentation Standards in all material respects:

This Report has been prepared and presented in compliance with the Performance Presentation Standards of the Association for Investment Management and Research.

This Standard shall take effect January 1, 1993.

G. Fair Dealing with Customers and Clients

The financial analyst shall act in a manner consistent with his obligation to deal fairly with all customers and clients when (1) disseminating investment recommendations, (2) disseminating material changes in prior investment advice, and (3) taking investment action.

IV. Priority of Transactions

The financial analyst shall conduct himself in such a manner that transactions for his customers, clients, and employer have priority over transactions in securities or other investments of which he is the beneficial owner, and so that transactions in securities or other investments in which he has such beneficial ownership do not operate adversely to their interests. If an analyst decides to make a recommendation about the purchase or sale of a security or other investment, he shall give his customers, clients, and employer adequate opportunity to act on this recommendation before acting on his own behalf.

For purposes of these Standards of Professional Conduct, a financial analyst is a "beneficial owner" if he directly or indirectly, through any contract, arrangement, understanding, relationship or otherwise, has or shares a direct of indirect pecuniary interest in the securities or the investment.

V. Disclosure of Conflicts

The financial analyst, when making investment recommendations, or taking investment actions, shall disclose to his customers and clients any material conflict of interest relating to him and any material beneficial ownership of the securities or other investments involved that could reasonably be expected to impair his ability to render unbiased and objective advice.

The financial analyst shall disclose to his employer all matters that could reasonably be expected to interfere with his duty to the employer, or with his ability to render unbiased and objective advice.

The financial analyst shall also comply with all requirements as to disclosure of conflicts of interest imposed by law and by rules and regulations of organizations governing his activities and shall comply with any prohibitions on his activities if a conflict of interest exists.

VI. Compensation

A. Disclosure of Additional Compensation Arrangements

The financial analyst shall inform his customers, clients, and employer of compensation or other benefit arrangements in connection with his services to them which are in addition to compensation from them for such services.

B. Disclosure of Referral Fees

The financial analyst shall make appropriate disclosure to a prospective client or customer of any consideration paid or other benefit delivered to others for recommending his services to that prospective client or customer.

C. Duty to Employer

The financial analyst shall not undertake independent practice which could result in compensation or other benefit in competition with his employer unless he has received written consent from both his employer and the person for whom he undertakes independent employment.

VII. Relationships with Others

A. Preservation of Confidentiality

A financial analyst shall preserve the confidentiality of information communicated by the client concerning matters within the scope of the confidential relationship, unless the financial analyst receives information concerning illegal activities on the part of the client.

B. Maintenance of Independence and Objectivity

The financial analyst, in relationships and contacts with an issuer of securities, whether individually or as a member of a group, shall use particular care and good judgment to achieve and maintain independence and objectivity.

C. Fiduciary Duties

The financial analyst, in relationships with clients, shall use particular care in determining applicable fiduciary duty and shall comply with such duty as to those persons and interests to whom it is owed.

VIII. Use of Professional Designation

The qualified financial analyst may use, as applicable, the professional designation "Member of the Association for Investment Management and Research", "Member of the Financial Analysts Federation", and "Member of the Institute of Chartered Financial Analysts", and is encouraged to do so, but only in a dignified and judicious manner. The use of the designations may be accompanied by an accurate explanation (1) of the requirements that have been met to obtain the designation, and (2) of the Association for Investment Management and Research, the Financial Analysts Federation, and the Institute of Chartered Financial Analysts, as applicable.

The Chartered Financial Analyst may use the professional designation "Chartered Financial Analyst", or the abbreviation "CFA", and is encouraged to do so, but only in a dignified and judicious manner. The use of the designation may be accompanied by an accurate explanation (1) of the requirements that have been met to obtain the designation, and (2) of the Association for Investment Management and Research, and the Institute of Chartered Financial Analysts.

IX. Professional Misconduct

The financial analyst shall not (1) commit a criminal act that upon conviction materially reflects adversely on his honesty, trustworthiness or fitness as a financial analyst in other respects, or (2) engage in conduct involving dishonesty, fraud, deceit or misrepresentation.

Amended - May 2, 1992, Standard III C, E, G, IV and VI C revised
Amended - May 2, 1992, Standard III F added

INTEREST TABLES

TABLE C.1 Present Value of $1: PVIF = $1/(1 + k)^t$

Period	1%	2%	3%	4%	5%	6%	7%	8%	9%	10%	12%	14%	15%	16%	18%	20%	24%	28%	32%	36%
1	.9901	.9804	.9709	.9615	.9524	.9434	.9346	.9259	.9174	.9091	.8929	.8772	.8696	.8621	.8475	.8333	.8065	.7813	.7576	.7353
2	.9803	.9612	.9426	.9246	.9070	.8900	.8734	.8573	.8417	.8264	.7972	.7695	.7561	.7432	.7182	.6944	.6504	.6104	.5739	.5407
3	.9706	.9423	.9151	.8890	.8638	.8396	.8163	.7938	.7722	.7513	.7118	.6750	.6575	.6407	.6086	.5787	.5245	.4768	.4348	.3975
4	.9610	.9238	.8885	.8548	.8227	.7921	.7629	.7350	.7084	.6830	.6355	.5921	.5718	.5523	.5158	.4823	.4230	.3725	.3294	.2923
5	.9515	.9057	.8626	.8219	.7835	.7473	.7130	.6806	.6499	.6209	.5674	.5194	.4972	.4761	.4371	.4019	.3411	.2910	.2495	.2149
6	.9420	.8880	.8375	.7903	.7462	.7050	.6663	.6302	.5963	.5645	.5066	.4556	.4323	.4104	.3704	.3349	.2751	.2274	.1890	.1580
7	.9327	.8706	.8131	.7599	.7107	.6651	.6227	.5835	.5470	.5132	.4523	.3996	.3759	.3538	.3139	.2791	.2218	.1776	.1432	.1162
8	.9235	.8535	.7894	.7307	.6768	.6274	.5820	.5403	.5019	.4665	.4039	.3506	.3269	.3050	.2660	.2326	.1789	.1388	.1085	.0854
9	.9143	.8368	.7664	.7026	.6446	.5919	.5439	.5002	.4604	.4241	.3606	.3075	.2843	.2630	.2255	.1938	.1443	.1084	.0822	.0628
10	.9053	.8203	.7441	.6756	.6139	.5584	.5083	.4632	.4224	.3855	.3220	.2697	.2472	.2267	.1911	.1615	.1164	.0847	.0623	.0462
11	.8963	.8043	.7224	.6496	.5847	.5268	.4751	.4289	.3875	.3505	.2875	.2366	.2149	.1954	.1619	.1346	.0938	.0662	.0472	.0340
12	.8874	.7885	.7014	.6246	.5568	.4970	.4440	.3971	.3555	.3186	.2567	.2076	.1869	.1685	.1372	.1122	.0757	.0517	.0357	.0250
13	.8787	.7730	.6810	.6006	.5303	.4688	.4150	.3677	.3262	.2897	.2292	.1821	.1625	.1452	.1163	.0935	.0610	.0404	.0271	.0184
14	.8700	.7579	.6611	.5775	.5051	.4423	.3878	.3405	.2992	.2633	.2046	.1597	.1413	.1252	.0985	.0779	.0492	.0316	.0205	.0135
15	.8613	.7430	.6419	.5553	.4810	.4173	.3624	.3152	.2745	.2394	.1827	.1401	.1229	.1079	.0835	.0649	.0397	.0247	.0155	.0099
16	.8528	.7284	.6232	.5339	.4581	.3936	.3387	.2919	.2519	.2176	.1631	.1229	.1069	.0930	.0708	.0541	.0320	.0193	.0118	.0073
17	.8444	.7142	.6050	.5134	.4363	.3714	.3166	.2703	.2311	.1978	.1456	.1078	.0929	.0802	.0600	.0451	.0258	.0150	.0089	.0054
18	.8350	.7002	.5874	.4936	.4155	.3503	.2959	.2502	.2120	.1799	.1300	.0946	.0808	.0691	.0508	.0376	.0208	.0118	.0068	.0039
19	.8277	.6864	.5703	.4746	.3957	.3305	.2765	.2317	.1945	.1635	.1161	.0829	.0703	.0596	.0431	.0313	.0168	.0092	.0051	.0029
20	.8195	.6730	.5537	.4564	.3769	.3118	.2584	.2145	.1784	.1486	.1037	.0728	.0611	.0514	.0365	.0261	.0135	.0072	.0039	.0021
25	.7798	.6095	.4776	.3751	.2953	.2330	.1842	.1460	.1160	.0923	.0588	.0378	.0304	.0245	.0160	.0105	.0046	.0021	.0010	.0005
30	.7419	.5521	.4120	.3083	.2314	.1741	.1314	.0994	.0754	.0573	.0334	.0196	.0151	.0116	.0070	.0042	.0016	.0006	.0002	.0001
40	.6717	.4529	.3066	.2083	.1420	.0972	.0668	.0460	.0318	.0221	.0107	.0053	.0037	.0026	.0013	.0007	.0002	.0001	*	*
50	.6080	.3715	.2281	.1407	.0872	.0543	.0339	.0213	.0134	.0085	.0035	.0014	.0009	.0006	.0003	.0001	*	*	*	*
60	.5504	.3048	.1697	.0951	.0535	.0303	.0173	.0099	.0057	.0033	.0011	.0004	.0002	.0001	*	*	*	*	*	*

*The factor is zero to four decimal places.

TABLE C.2 Present Value of an Annuity of $1 Per Period for n Periods:

$$PVIFA = \sum_{t=1}^{n} \frac{1}{(1+k)^t} = \frac{1 - \dfrac{1}{(1+k)^n}}{k}$$

Number of Payments	1%	2%	3%	4%	5%	6%	7%	8%	9%	10%	12%	14%	15%	16%	18%	20%	24%	28%	32%
1	0.9901	0.9804	0.9709	0.9615	0.9524	0.9434	0.9346	0.9259	0.9174	0.9091	0.8929	0.8772	0.8696	0.8621	0.8475	0.8333	0.8065	0.7813	0.7576
2	1.9704	1.9416	1.9135	1.8861	1.8594	1.8334	1.8080	1.7833	1.7591	1.7355	1.6901	1.6467	1.6257	1.6052	1.5656	1.5278	1.4568	1.3916	1.3315
3	2.9410	2.8839	2.8286	2.7751	2.7232	2.6730	2.6243	2.5771	2.5313	2.4869	2.4018	2.3216	2.2832	2.2459	2.1743	2.1065	1.9813	1.8684	1.7663
4	3.9020	3.8077	3.7171	3.6299	3.5460	3.4651	3.3872	3.3121	3.2397	3.1699	3.0373	2.9137	2.8550	2.7982	2.6901	2.5887	2.4043	2.2410	2.0957
5	4.8534	4.7135	4.5797	4.4518	4.3295	4.2124	4.1002	3.9927	3.8897	3.7908	3.6048	3.4331	3.3522	3.2743	3.1272	2.9906	2.7454	2.5320	2.3452
6	5.7955	5.6014	5.4172	5.2421	5.0757	4.9173	4.7665	4.6229	4.4859	4.3553	4.1114	3.8887	3.7845	3.6847	3.4976	3.3255	3.0205	2.7594	2.5342
7	6.7282	6.4720	6.2303	6.0021	5.7864	5.5824	5.3893	5.2064	5.0330	4.8684	4.5638	4.2883	4.1604	4.0386	3.8115	3.6046	3.2423	2.9370	2.6775
8	7.6517	7.3255	7.0197	6.7327	6.4632	6.2098	5.9713	5.7466	5.5348	5.3349	4.9676	4.6389	4.4873	4.3436	4.0776	3.8372	3.4212	3.0758	2.7860
9	8.5660	8.1622	7.7861	7.4353	7.1078	6.8017	6.5152	6.2469	5.9952	5.7590	5.3282	4.9464	4.7716	4.6065	4.3030	4.0310	3.5655	3.1842	2.8681
10	9.4713	8.9826	8.5302	8.1109	7.7217	7.3601	7.0236	6.7101	6.4177	6.1446	5.6502	5.2161	5.0188	4.8332	4.4941	4.1925	3.6819	3.2689	2.9304
11	10.3676	9.7868	9.2526	8.7605	8.3064	7.8869	7.4987	7.1390	6.8052	6.4951	5.9377	5.4527	5.2337	5.0286	4.6560	4.3271	3.7757	3.3351	2.9776
12	11.2551	10.5753	9.9540	9.3851	8.8633	8.3838	7.9427	7.5361	7.1607	6.8137	6.1944	5.6603	5.4206	5.1971	4.7932	4.4392	3.8514	3.3868	3.0133
13	12.1337	11.3484	10.6350	9.9856	9.3936	8.8527	8.3577	7.9038	7.4869	7.1034	6.4235	5.8424	5.5831	5.3423	4.9095	4.5327	3.9124	3.4272	3.0404
14	13.0037	12.1062	11.2961	10.5631	9.8986	9.2950	8.7455	8.2442	7.7862	7.3667	6.6282	6.0021	5.7245	5.4675	5.0081	4.6106	3.9616	3.4587	3.0609
15	13.8651	12.8493	11.9379	11.1184	10.3797	9.7122	9.1079	8.5595	8.0607	7.6061	6.8109	6.1422	5.8474	5.5755	5.0916	4.6755	4.0013	3.4834	3.0764
16	14.7179	13.5777	12.5611	11.6523	10.8378	10.1059	9.4466	8.8514	8.3126	7.8237	6.9740	6.2651	5.9542	5.6685	5.1624	4.7296	4.0333	3.5026	3.0882
17	15.5623	14.2919	13.1661	12.1657	11.2741	10.4773	9.7632	9.1216	8.5436	8.0216	7.1196	6.3729	6.0472	5.7487	5.2223	4.7746	4.0591	3.5177	3.0971
18	16.3983	14.9920	13.7535	12.6593	11.6896	10.8276	10.0591	9.3719	8.7556	8.2014	7.2497	6.4674	6.1280	5.8178	5.2732	4.8122	4.0799	3.5294	3.1039
19	17.2260	15.6785	14.3238	13.1339	12.0853	11.1581	10.3356	9.6036	8.9501	8.3649	7.3658	6.5504	6.1982	5.8775	5.3162	4.8435	4.0967	3.5386	3.1090
20	18.0456	16.3514	14.8775	13.5903	12.4622	11.4699	10.5940	9.8181	9.1285	8.5136	7.4694	6.6231	6.2593	5.9288	5.3527	4.8696	4.1103	3.5458	3.1129
25	22.0232	19.5235	17.4131	15.6221	14.0939	12.7834	11.6536	10.6748	9.8226	9.0770	7.8431	6.8729	6.4641	6.0971	5.4669	4.9476	4.1474	3.5640	3.1220
30	25.8077	22.3965	19.6004	17.2920	15.3725	13.7648	12.4090	11.2578	10.2737	9.4269	8.0552	7.0027	6.5660	6.1772	5.5168	4.9789	4.1601	3.5693	3.1242
40	32.8347	27.3555	23.1148	19.7928	17.1591	15.0463	13.3317	11.9246	10.7574	9.7791	8.2438	7.1050	6.6418	6.2335	5.5482	4.9966	4.1659	3.5712	3.1250
50	39.1961	31.4236	25.7298	21.4822	18.2559	15.7619	13.8007	12.2335	10.9617	9.9148	8.3045	7.1327	6.6605	6.2463	5.5541	4.9995	4.1666	3.5714	3.1250
60	44.9550	34.7609	27.6756	22.6235	18.9293	16.1614	14.0392	12.3766	11.0480	9.9672	8.3240	7.1401	6.6651	6.2402	5.5553	4.9999	4.1667	3.5714	3.1250

TABLE C.3   Future Value of $1 at the End of *n* Periods: $FVIF_{k,n} = (1 + k)^n$

Period	1%	2%	3%	4%	5%	6%	7%	8%	9%	10%	12%	14%	15%	16%	18%	20%	24%	28%	32%	36%
1	1.0100	1.0200	1.0300	1.0400	1.0500	1.0600	1.0700	1.0800	1.0900	1.1000	1.1200	1.1400	1.1500	1.1600	1.1800	1.2000	1.2400	1.2800	1.3200	1.3600
2	1.0201	1.0404	1.0609	1.0816	1.1025	1.1236	1.1449	1.1664	1.1881	1.2100	1.2544	1.2996	1.3225	1.3456	1.3924	1.4400	1.5376	1.6384	1.7424	1.8496
3	1.0303	1.0612	1.0927	1.1249	1.1576	1.1910	1.2250	1.2597	1.2950	1.3310	1.4049	1.4815	1.5209	1.5609	1.6430	1.7280	1.9066	2.0972	2.3000	2.5155
4	1.0405	1.0824	1.1255	1.1699	1.2155	1.2625	1.3108	1.3605	1.4116	1.4641	1.5735	1.6890	1.7490	1.8106	1.9388	2.0736	2.3642	2.6844	3.0360	3.4210
5	1.0513	1.1041	1.1593	1.2167	1.2763	1.3382	1.4026	1.4693	1.5386	1.6105	1.7623	1.9254	2.0114	2.1003	2.2878	2.4883	2.9316	3.4360	4.0075	4.6526
6	1.0615	1.1262	1.1941	1.2653	1.3401	1.4185	1.5007	1.5869	1.6771	1.7716	1.9738	2.1950	2.3131	2.4364	2.6996	2.9860	3.6352	4.3980	5.2899	6.3275
7	1.0721	1.1487	1.2299	1.3159	1.4071	1.5036	1.6058	1.7138	1.8280	1.9487	2.2107	2.5023	2.6600	2.8262	3.1855	3.5832	4.5077	5.6295	6.9826	8.6054
8	1.0829	1.1717	1.2668	1.3686	1.4775	1.5938	1.7182	1.8509	1.9926	2.1436	2.4760	2.8526	3.0590	3.2784	3.7589	4.2998	5.5895	7.2058	9.2170	11.703
9	1.0937	1.1951	1.3048	1.4233	1.5513	1.6895	1.8385	1.9990	2.1719	2.3579	2.7731	3.2519	3.5179	3.8030	4.4355	5.1598	6.9310	9.2234	12.166	15.916
10	1.1046	1.2190	1.3439	1.4802	1.6289	1.7908	1.9672	2.1589	2.3674	2.5937	3.1058	3.7072	4.0456	4.4114	5.2338	6.1917	8.5944	11.805	16.059	21.646
11	1.1157	1.2434	1.3842	1.5395	1.7103	1.8983	2.1049	2.3316	2.5804	2.8531	3.4785	4.2262	4.6524	5.1173	6.1759	7.4301	10.657	15.111	21.198	29.439
12	1.1263	1.2682	1.4258	1.6010	1.7959	2.0122	2.2522	2.5182	2.8127	3.1384	3.8960	4.8179	5.3502	5.9360	7.2876	8.9161	13.214	19.342	27.982	40.037
13	1.1381	1.2936	1.4685	1.6651	1.8856	2.1329	2.4098	2.7196	3.0658	3.4523	4.3635	5.4924	6.1528	6.8858	8.5994	10.699	16.386	24.758	36.937	54.451
14	1.1495	1.3195	1.5126	1.7317	1.9799	2.2609	2.5785	2.9372	3.3417	3.7975	4.8871	6.2613	7.0757	7.9875	10.147	12.839	20.319	31.691	48.756	74.053
15	1.1610	1.3459	1.5580	1.8009	2.0789	2.3966	2.7590	3.1722	3.6425	4.1772	5.4736	7.1379	8.1371	9.2655	11.973	15.407	25.195	40.564	64.358	100.71
16	1.1726	1.3728	1.6047	1.8730	2.1829	2.5404	2.9522	3.4259	3.9703	4.5950	6.1304	8.1372	9.3576	10.748	14.129	18.488	31.242	51.923	84.953	136.96
17	1.1843	1.4002	1.6528	1.9479	2.2920	2.6928	3.1588	3.7000	4.3276	5.0545	6.8660	9.2765	10.761	12.467	16.672	22.186	38.740	66.461	112.13	186.27
18	1.1961	1.4282	1.7024	2.0258	2.4066	2.8543	3.3799	3.9960	4.7171	5.5599	7.6900	10.575	12.375	14.462	19.673	26.623	48.038	85.070	148.02	253.33
19	1.2081	1.4568	1.7535	2.1068	2.5270	3.0256	3.6165	4.3157	5.1417	6.1159	8.6128	12.055	14.231	16.776	23.214	31.948	59.567	108.89	195.39	344.53
20	1.2202	1.4859	1.8061	2.1911	2.6533	3.2071	3.8697	4.6610	5.6044	6.7275	9.6463	13.743	16.366	19.460	27.393	38.337	73.864	139.37	257.91	468.57
21	1.2324	1.5157	1.8603	2.2788	2.7860	3.3996	4.1406	5.0338	6.1088	7.4002	10.803	15.667	18.821	22.574	32.323	46.005	91.591	178.40	340.44	637.26
22	1.2447	1.5460	1.9161	2.3699	2.9253	3.6035	4.4304	5.4365	6.6586	8.1403	12.100	17.861	21.644	26.186	38.142	55.206	113.57	228.35	449.39	866.67
23	1.2572	1.5769	1.9736	2.4647	3.0715	3.8197	4.7405	5.8715	7.2579	8.9543	13.552	20.361	24.891	30.376	45.007	66.247	140.83	292.30	593.19	1178.6
24	1.2697	1.6084	2.0328	2.5633	3.2251	4.0489	5.0724	6.3412	7.9111	9.8497	15.178	23.212	28.625	35.236	53.108	79.496	174.63	374.14	783.02	1602.9
25	1.2824	1.6406	2.0938	2.6658	3.3864	4.2919	5.4274	6.8485	8.6231	10.834	17.000	26.461	32.918	40.874	62.668	95.396	216.54	478.90	1033.5	2180.0
26	1.2953	1.6734	2.1566	2.7725	3.5557	4.5494	5.8074	7.3964	9.3992	11.918	19.040	30.166	37.856	47.414	73.948	114.47	268.51	612.99	1364.3	2964.9
27	1.3082	1.7069	2.2213	2.8834	3.7335	4.8223	6.2139	7.9881	10.245	13.110	21.324	34.389	43.535	55.000	87.259	137.37	332.95	784.63	1800.9	4032.2
28	1.3213	1.7410	2.2879	2.9987	3.9201	5.1117	6.6488	8.6271	11.167	14.421	23.883	39.204	50.065	63.800	102.96	164.84	412.86	1004.3	2377.2	5483.8
29	1.3345	1.7758	2.3566	3.1187	4.1161	5.4184	7.1143	9.3173	12.172	15.863	26.749	44.693	57.575	74.008	121.50	197.81	511.95	1285.5	3137.9	7458.0
30	1.3478	1.8114	2.4273	3.2434	4.3219	5.7435	7.6123	10.062	13.267	17.449	29.959	50.950	66.211	85.849	143.37	237.37	634.81	1645.5	4142.0	10143.
40	1.4889	2.2080	3.2620	4.8010	7.0400	10.285	14.974	21.724	31.409	45.259	93.050	188.88	267.86	378.72	750.37	1469.7	5455.9	19426.	66520.	•
50	1.6446	2.6916	4.3839	7.1067	11.467	18.420	29.457	46.901	74.357	117.39	289.00	700.23	1083.6	1670.7	3927.3	9100.4	46890.	•	•	•
60	1.8167	3.2810	5.8916	10.519	18.679	32.987	57.946	101.25	176.03	304.48	897.59	2595.9	4383.9	7370.1	20555.	56347.	•	•	•	•

*FVIFA > 99.999

TABLE C.4 — Sum of an Annuity of $1 Per Period for n Periods:

$$FVIFA_{k,n} = \sum_{t=1}^{n}(1+k)^{t-1} = \frac{(1+k)^{n}-1}{k}$$

Number of Periods	1%	2%	3%	4%	5%	6%	7%	8%	9%	10%	12%	14%	15%	16%	18%	20%	24%	28%	32%	36%
1	1.0000	1.0000	1.0000	1.0000	1.0000	1.0000	1.0000	1.0000	1.0000	1.0000	1.0000	1.0000	1.0000	1.0000	1.0000	1.0000	1.0000	1.0000	1.0000	1.0000
2	2.0100	2.0200	2.0300	2.0400	2.0500	2.0600	2.0700	2.0800	2.0900	2.1000	2.1200	2.1400	2.1500	2.1600	2.1800	2.2000	2.2400	2.2800	2.3200	2.3600
3	3.0301	3.0604	3.0909	3.1216	3.1525	3.1836	3.2149	3.2464	3.2781	3.3100	3.3744	3.4396	3.4725	3.5056	3.5724	3.6400	3.7776	3.9184	4.0624	4.2096
4	4.0604	4.1216	4.1836	4.2465	4.3101	4.3746	4.4399	4.5061	4.5731	4.6410	4.7793	4.9211	4.9934	5.0665	5.2154	5.3680	5.6842	6.0156	6.3624	6.7251
5	5.1010	5.2040	5.3091	5.4163	5.5256	5.6371	5.7507	5.8666	5.9847	6.1051	6.3528	6.6101	6.7424	6.8771	7.1542	7.4416	8.0484	8.6999	9.3983	10.146
6	6.1520	6.3081	6.4684	6.6330	6.8019	6.9753	7.1533	7.3359	7.5233	7.7156	8.1152	8.5355	8.7537	8.9775	9.4420	9.9299	10.980	12.135	13.405	14.798
7	7.2135	7.4343	7.6625	7.8983	8.1420	8.3938	8.6540	8.9228	9.2004	9.4872	10.089	10.730	11.066	11.413	12.141	12.915	14.615	16.533	18.695	21.126
8	8.2857	8.5830	8.8923	9.2142	9.5491	9.8975	10.259	10.636	11.028	11.435	12.299	13.232	13.726	14.240	15.327	16.499	19.122	22.163	25.678	29.731
9	9.3685	9.7546	10.159	10.582	11.026	11.491	11.978	12.487	13.021	13.579	14.775	16.085	16.785	17.518	19.085	20.798	24.712	29.369	34.895	41.435
10	10.462	10.949	11.463	12.006	12.577	13.180	13.816	14.486	15.192	15.937	17.548	19.337	20.303	21.321	23.521	25.958	31.643	38.592	47.061	57.351
11	11.566	12.168	12.807	13.486	14.206	14.971	15.783	16.645	17.560	18.531	20.654	23.044	24.349	25.732	28.755	32.150	40.237	50.398	63.121	78.998
12	12.682	13.412	14.192	15.025	15.917	16.869	17.888	18.977	20.140	21.384	24.133	27.270	29.001	30.850	34.931	39.580	50.894	65.510	84.320	108.43
13	13.809	14.680	15.617	16.626	17.713	18.882	20.140	21.495	22.953	24.522	28.029	32.088	34.351	36.786	42.218	48.496	64.109	84.852	112.30	148.47
14	14.947	15.973	17.086	18.291	19.598	21.015	22.550	24.214	26.019	27.975	32.392	37.581	40.504	43.672	50.818	59.195	80.496	109.61	149.23	202.92
15	16.096	17.293	18.598	20.023	21.578	23.276	25.129	27.152	29.360	31.772	37.279	43.842	47.580	51.659	60.965	72.035	100.81	141.30	197.99	276.97
16	17.257	18.639	20.156	21.824	23.657	25.672	27.888	30.324	33.003	35.949	42.753	50.980	55.717	60.925	72.939	87.442	126.01	181.86	262.35	377.69
17	18.430	20.012	21.761	23.697	25.840	28.212	30.840	33.750	36.973	40.544	48.883	59.117	65.075	71.673	87.068	105.93	157.25	233.79	347.30	514.66
18	19.614	21.412	23.414	25.645	28.132	30.905	33.999	37.450	41.301	45.599	55.749	68.394	75.836	84.140	103.74	128.11	195.99	300.25	459.44	700.93
19	20.810	22.840	25.116	27.671	30.539	33.760	37.379	41.446	46.018	51.159	63.439	78.969	88.211	98.603	123.41	154.74	244.03	385.32	607.47	954.27
20	22.019	24.297	26.870	29.778	33.066	36.785	40.995	45.762	51.160	57.275	72.052	91.024	102.44	115.37	146.62	186.68	303.60	494.21	802.86	1298.8
21	23.239	25.783	28.676	31.969	35.719	39.992	44.865	50.422	56.764	64.002	81.698	104.76	118.81	134.84	174.02	225.02	377.46	633.59	1060.7	1767.3
22	24.471	27.299	30.536	34.248	38.505	43.392	49.005	55.456	62.873	71.402	92.502	120.43	137.63	157.41	206.34	271.03	469.05	811.99	1401.2	2404.6
23	25.716	28.845	32.452	36.617	41.430	46.995	53.436	60.893	69.531	79.543	104.60	138.29	159.27	183.60	244.48	326.23	582.62	1040.3	1850.6	3271.3
24	26.973	30.421	34.426	39.082	44.502	50.815	58.176	66.764	76.789	88.497	118.15	158.65	184.16	213.97	289.49	392.48	723.46	1332.6	2443.8	4449.9
25	28.243	32.030	36.459	41.645	47.727	54.864	63.249	73.105	84.700	98.347	133.33	181.87	212.79	249.21	342.60	471.98	898.09	1706.8	3226.8	6052.9
26	29.525	33.670	38.553	44.311	51.113	59.156	68.676	79.954	93.323	109.18	150.33	208.33	245.71	290.08	405.27	567.37	1114.6	2185.7	4260.4	8233.0
27	30.820	35.344	40.709	47.084	54.669	63.705	74.483	87.350	102.72	121.09	169.37	238.49	283.56	337.50	479.22	681.85	1383.1	2798.7	5624.7	11197.9
28	32.129	37.051	42.930	49.967	58.402	68.528	80.697	95.338	112.96	134.20	190.69	272.88	327.10	392.50	566.48	819.22	1716.0	3583.3	7425.6	15230.2
29	33.450	38.792	45.218	52.966	62.322	73.639	87.346	103.96	124.13	148.63	214.58	312.09	377.16	456.30	669.44	984.06	2128.9	4587.6	9802.9	20714.1
30	34.784	40.568	47.575	56.084	66.438	79.058	94.460	113.28	136.30	164.49	241.33	356.78	434.74	530.31	790.94	1181.8	2640.9	5873.2	12940.	28172.2
40	48.886	60.402	75.401	95.025	120.79	154.76	199.63	259.05	337.88	442.59	767.09	1342.0	1779.0	2360.7	4163.2	7343.8	22728.	69377.	·	·
50	64.463	84.579	112.79	152.66	209.34	290.33	406.52	573.76	815.08	1163.9	2400.0	4994.5	7217.7	10435.	21813.	45497.	·	·	·	·
60	81.669	114.05	163.05	237.99	353.58	533.12	813.52	1253.2	1944.7	3034.8	7471.6	18535.	29219.	46057.	·	·	·	·	·	·

*FVIF > 99,999

Appendix D

STANDARD NORMAL PROBABILITIES

z	0.00	0.01	0.02	0.03	0.04	0.05	0.06	0.07	0.08	0.09
0.0	.5000	.5040	.5080	.5120	.5160	.5199	.5239	.5279	.5219	.5359
0.1	.5398	.5438	.5478	.5517	.5557	.5596	.5636	.5675	.5714	.5753
0.2	.5793	.5832	.5871	.5910	.5948	.5987	.6026	.6064	.6103	.6141
0.3	.6179	.6217	.6255	.6293	.6331	.6368	.6406	.6443	.6480	.6517
0.4	.6554	.6591	.6628	.6664	.6700	.6736	.6772	.6808	.6844	.6879
0.5	.6915	.6950	.6985	.7019	.7054	.7088	.7123	.7157	.7190	.7224
0.6	.7257	.7291	.7324	.7357	.7389	.7422	.7454	.7486	.7517	.7549
0.7	.7580	.7611	.7642	.7673	.7704	.7734	.7764	.7794	.7823	.7852
0.8	.7881	.7910	.7939	.7967	.7995	.8023	.8051	.8078	.8106	.8133
0.9	.8159	.8186	.8212	.8238	.8264	.8289	.8315	.8340	.8365	.8389
1.0	.8413	.8438	.8461	.8485	.8508	.8531	.8554	.8577	.8599	.8621
1.1	.8643	.8665	.8686	.8708	.8729	.8749	.8770	.8790	.8810	.8830
1.2	.8849	.8860	.8888	.8907	.8925	.8943	.8962	.8980	.8997	.9015
1.3	.9032	.9049	.9066	.9082	.9099	.9115	.9131	.9147	.9162	.9177
1.4	.9192	.9207	.9222	.9236	.9251	.9265	.9279	.9292	.9306	.9319
1.5	.9332	.9345	.9357	.9370	.9382	.9394	.9406	.9418	.9429	.9441
1.6	.9452	.9463	.9474	.9484	.9495	.9505	.9515	.9525	.9535	.9545
1.7	.9554	.9564	.9573	.9582	.9591	.9599	.9608	.9616	.9625	.9633
1.8	.9641	.9649	.9656	.9664	.9671	.9678	.9686	.9693	.9699	.9706
1.9	.9713	.9719	.9726	.9732	.9738	.9744	.9750	.9756	.9761	.9767
2.0	.9772	.9778	.9783	.9788	.9793	.9798	.9803	.9808	.9812	.9817
2.1	.9821	.9826	.9830	.9834	.9838	.9842	.9846	.9850	.9854	.9857
2.2	.9861	.9864	.9868	.9871	.9875	.9878	.9881	.9884	.9887	.9890
2.3	.9893	.9896	.9898	.9901	.9904	.9906	.9909	.9911	.9913	.9916
2.4	.9918	.9920	.9922	.9925	.9927	.9929	.9931	.9932	.9934	.9936
2.5	.9938	.9940	.9941	.9943	.9945	.9946	.9948	.9949	.9951	.9952
2.6	.9953	.9955	.9956	.9957	.9959	.9960	.9961	.9962	.9963	.9964
2.7	.9965	.9966	.9967	.9968	.9969	.9970	.9971	.9972	.9973	.9974
2.8	.9974	.9975	.9976	.9977	.9977	.9978	.9979	.9979	.9980	.9981
2.9	.9981	.9982	.9982	.9983	.9984	.9984	.9985	.9985	.9986	.9986
3.0	.9987	.9987	.9987	.9988	.9988	.9989	.9989	.9989	.9990	.9990

Glossary

Abnormal rate of return   The amount by which a security's return differs from the market's expected rate of return based on the market's rate of return and the security's relationship with the market.

Accumulation phase   Phase in the investment life cycle during which individuals in the early-to-middle years of their working career attempt to accumulate assets to satisfy short-term needs and longer-term goals.

Actuarial rate of return   The discount rate used to find the present value of a defined benefit pension plan's future obligations and thus determine the size of the firm's annual contribution to the plan.

American Depository Receipts (ADRs)   Certificates of ownership issued by a U.S. bank that represent indirect ownership of a certain number of shares of a specific foreign firm. Shares are held on deposit in a bank in the firm's home country.

American option   An option contract that can be exercised at any time until its expiration date.

Analysis effect   The difference in performance of a bond portfolio from that of a chosen index due to acquisition of temporarily mispriced issues that then move to their correct prices.

Anomalies   Security price relationships that appear to contradict a well-regarded hypothesis; in this case, the efficient market hypothesis.

Arbitrage   A trading strategy designed to generate a guaranteed profit from a transaction that requires no capital commitment or risk bearing on the part of the trader. A simple example of an arbitrage trade would be the simultaneous purchase and sale of the same security in different markets at different prices.

Arbitrage pricing theory (APT)   A theory concerned with deriving the expected or required rates of return on risky assets based on the asset's systematic relationship to several risk factors. This multifactor model is in contrast to the single-factor CAPM.

Arithmetic mean (AM)   A measure of mean return equal to the sum of annual holding period yields divided by the number of years.

Asset allocation   The process of deciding how to distribute an investor's wealth among different asset classes for investment purposes.

At-the-money   A special case of an out-of-the-money option where the exercise price and the price of the underlying asset are identical.

Attribution analysis   An assessment technique designed to establish whether a manager's performance relative to a benchmark resulted from market timing or security selection skills.

Autocorrelation test   A test of the efficient market hypothesis that compares security price changes over time to check for predictable correlation patterns.

Backtest   A method of testing a quantitative model in which computers are used to examine the composition and returns of portfolios based on historical data to determine if the selected strategy would have worked in the past.

Balance sheet   A financial statement that shows what assets the firm controls at a fixed point in time and how it has financed these assets.

Balanced fund   A mutual fund with, generally, a three-part investment objective: (1) to conserve the investor's principal, (2) to pay current income, and (3) to increase both principal and income. The fund aims to achieve this by owning a mixture of bonds, preferred stocks, and common stocks.

Basis   The difference between the spot price of the underlying asset and the futures contract price at any point in time (e.g., the *initial* basis at the time of contract origination, the *cover* basis at the time of contract termination).

Basis of an asset   For tax purposes, the cost of an asset.

Basis risk   The residual exposure to the price volatility of an underlying asset that results from a cross hedge transaction.

Bearer bond   An unregistered bond for which ownership is determined by possession. The holder receives interest payments by clipping coupons attached to the security and sending them to the issuer for payment.

Benchmark error   Situation where an inappropriate or incorrect benchmark is used to compare and assess portfolio returns and management.

Benchmark portfolio   A comparison standard of risk and assets included in the policy statement and similar to the investor's risk preference and investment needs, which can be used to evaluate the investment performance of the portfolio manager.

Beta   A standardized measure of systematic risk based upon an asset's covariance with the market portfolio.

Binomial option pricing model   A valuation equation that assumes the price of the underlying asset changes through a series of discrete upward or downward movements.

Black-Scholes option pricing model   A valuation equation that assumes the price of the underlying asset changes continuously through the option's expiration date by a statistical process known as *geometric Brownian motion*.

Bond price volatility   The percentage changes in bond prices over time.

Bond swap   An active bond portfolio management strategy that exchanges one position for another to take advantage of some difference between them.

Business risk   The variability of operating income arising from the characteristics of the firm's industry. Two sources of business risk are sales variability and operating leverage.

Buy-and-hold strategy   A passive bond portfolio management strategy in which bonds are bought and held to maturity.

Call market   A market in which trading for individual stocks only takes place at specified times. All the bids and asks available at the time are combined and the market administrators specify a single price that will possibly clear the market at that time.

Call option   Option to buy a firm's common stock within a certain period at a specified price called the *exercise price*.

Call premium   Amount above par issuer must pay to bondholder for retiring the bond before its stated maturity.

Call provisions   Specifies when and how a firm can issue a call for bonds outstanding prior to their maturity.

Cap agreement   A contract that on each settlement date pays the holder the greater of the difference between the reference rate and the cap rate or zero; it is equivalent to a series of call options on the reference rate.

Capital appreciation   A return objective in which the investor seeks to increase the portfolio value, primarily through capital gains, over time to meet a future need; generally a goal of an investor willing to take on risk to meet a goal.

Capital asset pricing model (CAPM)   A theory concerned with deriving the expected or required rates of return on risky assets based on the assets' systematic risk levels.

Capital market instruments   Fixed-income investments that trade in the secondary market.

Capital market line (CML)   The line from the intercept point that represents the risk-free rate tangent to the original efficient frontier; it becomes the new efficient frontier.

Capital preservation   A return objective in which the investor seeks to minimize the risk of loss; generally a goal of the risk-averse investor.

Certificates of deposit (CDs)   Instruments issued by banks and S&Ls that require minimum deposits for specified terms and that pay higher rates of interest than deposit accounts.

Characteristic line   Regression line that indicates the systematic risk.

Closed-end investment company   An investment company that issues only a limited number of shares, which it does not redeem (buy back). Instead, closed-end shares are traded in securities markets at prices determined by supply and demand.

Coefficient of variation (CV)   A measure of relative variability that indicates risk per unit of return. It is equal to: standard deviation divided by the mean value. When used in investments, it is equal to: standard deviation of returns divided by the expected rate of return.

Coincident indicators   A set of economic variables whose values reach peaks and troughs at about the same time as the aggregate economy.

Collateral trust bonds   A mortgage bond wherein the assets backing the bond are financial assets like stocks and bonds.

Collateralized mortgage obligation (CMO)   A debt security based on a pool of mortgage loans that provides a relatively stable stream of payments for a relatively predictable term.

Commission brokers   Employees of a member firm who buy or sell for the customers of the firm.

Commodity swap   A swap transaction in which one of the cash flows is tied to a fixed price for a commodity and the other is based on a fluctuating commodity index level.

Common size statements   The normalization of balance sheet and income statement items to allow for easier comparison of different-size firms.

Common stock   An equity investment that represents ownership of a firm, with full participation in its success or failure. The firm's directors must approve dividend payments.

Competitive environment   The level of intensity of competition among firms in an industry, determined by an examination of five competitive forces.

Competitive strategy   The search by a firm for a favorable competitive position within an industry, which affects evaluation of the industry's prospects.

Completely diversified portfolio   A portfolio in which all unsystematic risk has been eliminated by diversification.

Completeness fund   A specialized index used to form the basis of a passive portfolio whose purpose is to provide diversification to a client's total portfolio by excluding those segments in which the client's active managers invest.

Consolidation phase   Phase in the investment life cycle during which individuals who are typically past the midpoint of their career have earnings that exceed expenses and invest them for future retirement or estate planning needs.

Contingent deferred sales load   A mutual fund that imposes a sales charge when the investor sells or redeems shares. Also referred to as *rear-end loads* or *redemption charges*.

Continuous market   A market where stocks are priced and traded continuously either by an auction process or by dealers during the time the market is open.

Contract price   The transaction price specified in a forward or futures contract.

Convenience yield   An adjustment made to the theoretical forward or futures contract delivery price to account for the preference that consumers have for holding spot positions in the underlying asset.

Conversion factors   The adjustments made to Treasury bond futures contract terms to allow for the delivery of an instrument other than the standardized underlying asset.

Conversion parity price   The price at which common stock can be obtained by surrendering the convertible instrument at par value.

Conversion premium   The excess of the market value of the convertible security over its equity value if immediately converted into common stock. Typically expressed as a percentage of the equity value.

Conversion ratio   The number of shares of common stock for which a convertible security may be exchanged.

Conversion value   The value of the convertible security if converted into common stock at the stock's current market price.

Convertible bonds   A bond with the added feature that the bondholder has the option to turn the bond back to the firm in exchange for a specified number of common shares of the firm.

Convexity   A measure of the degree to which a bond's price–yield curve departs from a straight line. This characteristic affects estimates of a bond's price volatility.

Correlation coefficient   A standardized measure of the relationship between two series that ranges from -1.00 to $+1.00$.

Cost of carry The net amount that would be required to store a commodity or security for future delivery, usually calculated as physical storage costs plus financial capital costs less dividends paid to the underlying asset.

Counterparty A participant to a derivative transaction.

Country risk Uncertainty due to the possibility of major political or economic change in the country where an investment is located. Also called *political risk.*

Coupon Indicates the interest payment on a debt security. It is the coupon rate times the par value that indicates the interest payments on a debt security.

Coupon reinvestment risk The component of interest rate risk due to the uncertainty of the rate at which coupon payments will be reinvested.

Covariance A measure of the degree to which two variables, such as rates of return for investment assets, move together over time relative to their individual mean returns.

Covered call A trading strategy in which a call option is sold as a supplement to a long position in an underlying asset or portfolio of assets.

Covered interest arbitrage A trading strategy involving borrowing money in one country and lending it to another designed to exploit price deviations from the interest rate parity model.

Credit analysis An active bond portfolio management strategy designed to identify bonds that are expected to experience changes in rating. This strategy is critical when investing in high-yield bonds.

Cross hedge A trading strategy in which the price volatility of a commodity or security position is hedged with a forward or futures contract based on a different underlying asset or different settlement terms.

Crossover price The price at which it becomes profitable for an issuer to call a bond. Above this price, yield to call is the appropriate yield measure.

Cross-sectional analysis An examination of a firm's performance in comparison to other firms in the industry with similar characteristics to the firm being studied.

Currency swap A swap transaction in which the cash flows, which can be either fixed or variable, are denominated in different currencies.

Current income A return objective in which the investor seeks to generate income rather than capital gains; generally a goal of an investor who wants to supplement earnings with income to meet living expenses.

Current yield A bond's yield as measured by its current income (coupon) as a percentage of its market price.

Cyclical company A firm whose earnings rise and fall with general economic activity.

Cyclical stock A stock with a high beta; its gains typically exceed those of a rising market and its losses typically exceed those of a falling market.

Debentures Bonds that promise payments of interest and principal but pledge no specific assets. Holders have first claim on the issuer's income and unpledged assets. Also known as *unsecured bonds.*

Declining trend channel The range defined by security prices as they move progressively lower.

Dedication   A portfolio management technique in which the portfolio's cash flows are used to retire a set of liabilities over time.

Dedication with reinvestment   A dedication strategy in which portfolio cash flows may precede their corresponding liabilities. Such cash flows can be reinvested to earn a return until the date the liability is due to be paid.

Defensive company   Firms whose future earnings are likely to withstand an economic downturn.

Defensive stock   A stock whose return is not expected to decline as much as that of the overall market during a bear market.

Defined benefit pension plan   A pension plan to which the company contributes a certain amount each year and that pays employees an income after they retire. The benefit size is based on factors such as workers' salary and time of employment.

Defined contribution pension plan   A pension plan in which worker benefits are determined by the size of employees' contributions to the plan and the returns earned on the fund's investments.

Delta   The change in the price of the option with respect to a one dollar change in the price of the underlying asset; this is the option's *hedge ratio,* or the number of units of the underlying asset that can be hedged by a single option contract.

Derivative security   An instrument whose market value ultimately depends upon, or derives from, the value of a more fundamental investment vehicle called the underlying asset or security.

Diffusion index   An indicator of the number of stocks rising during a specified period of time relative to the number of stocks declining and not changing price.

Discount   A bond selling at a price below par value due to capital market conditions.

Dividend discount model (DDM)   A technique for estimating the value of a stock issue as the present value of all future dividends.

Downtick   A price decline in a transaction price compared to the previous transaction price.

DuPont system   A method of examining ROE by breaking it down into three component parts.

Duration   A composite measure of the timing of a bond's cash flow characteristics taking into consideration its coupon and term to maturity.

Duration strategy   A portfolio management strategy employed to reduce the interest rate risk of a bond portfolio by matching the modified duration of the portfolio with its investment horizon. For example, if the investment horizon is 10 years, the portfolio manager would construct a portfolio that has a modified duration of 10 years. This strategy is referred to as *immunization of the portfolio.*

Earnings momentum   A strategy in which portfolios are constructed of stocks of firms with rising earnings.

Earnings multiplier   Also known as the price/earnings ratio, it is a measurement of the relationship between a company's, or the aggregate stock market's, stock prices and earnings.

Earnings multiplier model   A technique for estimating the value of a stock issue as a multiple of its earnings per share.

Earnings surprise   A company announcement of earnings that differ from analysts' prevailing expectations.

Economic value-added (EVA)   Internal management performance measure that compares net operating profit to total cost of capital. Indicates how profitable company projects are as a sign of management performance.

Effective duration   Direct measure of the interest rate sensitivity of a bond (or any financial instrument).

Efficient capital market   A market in which security prices rapidly reflect all information about securities.

Ending-wealth value   The total amount of money derived from investment in a bond until maturity, including principal, coupon payments, and income from reinvestment of coupon payments.

Equipment trust certificates   Mortgage bonds that are secured by specific pieces of transportation equipment like boxcars and planes.

Equity swap   A swap transaction in which one cash flow is tied to the return to an equity portfolio position, often an index such as the Standard & Poor's 500, while the other is based on a floating-rate index.

Estimated rate of return   The rate of return an investor anticipates earning from a specific investment over a particular future holding period.

Eurobonds   Bonds denominated in a currency not native to the country in which they are issued.

European option   An option contract that can only be exercised on its expiration date.

Event study   Research that examines the reaction of a security's price to a specific company, world event, or news announcement.

Exchange clearinghouse   The functional unit attached to a futures exchange that guarantees contract performance, oversees delivery, serves as a bookkeeper, and calculates settlement transactions.

Exchange rate risk   Uncertainty due to the denomination of an investment in a currency other than that of the investor's own country.

Exercise price   The transaction price specified in an option contract; also known as the *strike* or *striking* price.

Expected rate of return   The return that analysts' calculations suggest a security should provide, based on the market's rate of return during the period and the security's relationship to the market.

Expiry   The expiration date of a derivative security.

Fiduciary   A person who supervises or oversees the investment portfolio of a third party, such as in a trust account, and makes investment decisions in accordance with the owner's wishes.

Filter rule   A trading rule that recommends security transactions when price changes exceed a previously determined percentage.

Financial risk The variability of future income arising from the firm's fixed financing costs, for example, interest payments. The effect of fixed financial costs is to magnify the effect of changes in operating profit on net income or earnings per share.

Fixed-income investments Loans with contractually mandated payment schedules from investors to firms or governments.

Flat trend channel The range defined by security prices as they maintain a relatively steady level.

Floating rate note (FRN) Short- to intermediate-term bonds with regularly scheduled coupon payments linked to a variable interest rate, most often LIBOR.

Floor agreement A contract that on each settlement date pays the holder the greater of the difference between the floor rate and the reference rate or zero; it is equivalent to a series of put options on the reference rate.

Floor brokers Independent members of an exchange who act as brokers for other members.

Forward contract An agreement between two counterparties that requires the exchange of a commodity or security at a fixed time in the future and at a predetermined price.

Forward discount A situation where, from the perspective of the domestic country, the spot exchange rate is smaller than the forward exchange rate with a foreign country.

Forward premium A situation where, from the perspective of the domestic country, the spot exchange rate is larger than the forward exchange rate with a foreign country.

Forward rate A yield for a future holding period implied by the spot market prices of two securities with different maturities.

Forward rate agreement (FRA) A transaction in which two counterparties agree to a single exchange of cash flows based on a fixed and floating rate, respectively.

Fourth market Direct trading of securities between owners, usually institutions, without any broker intermediation.

Franchise factor A firm's unique competitive advantage that makes it possible for a firm to earn excess returns (rates of return above a firm's cost of capital) on its capital projects. In turn, these excess returns and the franchise factor cause the firm's stock price to have a P/E ratio above its base P/E ratio that is equal to 1/k.

Free cash flow This cash flow measure equals cash flow from operations minus capital expenditures and dividends.

Full replication A technique for constructing a passive index portfolio in which all securities in an index are purchased in proportion to their weights in the index.

Fully taxable equivalent yield (FTEY) A yield on a tax-exempt bond that adjusts for its tax benefits to allow comparisons with taxable bonds.

Futures contract An agreement that provides for the future exchange of a particular asset at a specified delivery date in exchange for a specified payment at the time of delivery.

General obligation bond (GO) A municipal issue serviced from and guaranteed by the issuer's full taxing authority.

Generally accepted accounting principles (GAAP) Accounting principles formulated by the Financial Accounting Standards Board and used to construct financial statements.

Geometric mean (GM)   The nth root of the product of the annual holding period returns for n years minus 1.

Gifting phase   Phase in the investment life cycle during which individuals use excess assets to financially assist relatives or friends, establish charitable trusts, or construct trusts to minimize estate taxes.

Growth company   A company that consistently has the opportunities and ability to invest in projects that provide rates of return that exceed the firm's cost of capital. Because of these investment opportunities, it retains a high proportion of earnings, and its earnings grow faster than those of average firms.

Growth stock   A stock issue that generates a higher rate of return than other stocks in the market with similar risk characteristics.

Hedge   A trading strategy in which derivative securities are used to reduce or completely offset a counterparty's risk exposure to an underlying asset.

Hedge ratio   The number of derivative contracts that must be transacted to offset the price volatility of an underlying commodity or security position.

High-yield bond   A bond rated below investment grade. Also referred to as *speculative-grade bonds* or *junk bonds*.

Holding period return (HPR)   The total return from an investment, including all sources of income, for a given period of time. A value of 1.0 indicates no gain or loss.

Holding period yield (HPY)   The total return from an investment for a given period of time stated as a percentage.

Immunization   A bond portfolio management technique of matching modified duration to the investment horizon of the portfolio to eliminate interest rate risk.

Implied volatility   The standard deviation of changes in the price of the underlying asset that can be inferred from an option's market price in relation to a specific valuation model.

In-the-money   An option that has positive intrinsic value.

Income bonds   Debentures that stipulate interest payments only if the issuer earns the income to make the payments by specified dates.

Income effect   The known component of the total return for a bond during a period of time if the shape and position of the yield curve did not change.

Income statement   A financial statement that shows the flow of the firm's sales, expenses, and earnings over a period of time.

Indenture   The legal agreement that lists the obligations of the issuer of a bond to the bondholder including payment schedules, call provisions, and sinking funds.

Indexing   A passive bond portfolio management strategy that seeks to match the composition, and therefore the performance, of a selected market index.

Industry life cycle analysis   An analysis that focuses on the industry's stage of development.

Informationally efficient market   A more technical term for an efficient capital market that emphasizes the role of information.

Initial public offering (IPO)   A new issue by a firm that has no existing public market.

Interest-on-interest   Bond income from reinvestment of coupon payments.

Interest rate anticipation   An active bond portfolio management strategy designed to preserve capital or take advantage of capital gains opportunities by predicting interest rates and their effects on bond prices.

Interest rate anticipation effect   The difference in return because of changing the duration of the portfolio during a period as compared with the portfolio's long-term policy duration.

Interest rate collar   The combination of a long position in a cap agreement and a short position in a floor agreement, or vice versa; it is equivalent to a series of range forward positions.

Interest rate effect   The return on a bond portfolio caused by changes in the term structure of interest rates during a period.

Interest rate parity   The relationship that must exist in an efficient market between the spot and forward foreign exchange rates between two countries and the interest rates in those countries.

Interest rate risk   The uncertainty of returns on an investment due to possible changes in interest rates over time.

Interest rate swap   An agreement calling for the periodic exchange of cash flows, one based on an interest rate that remains fixed for the life of the contract and the other that is linked to a variable-rate index.

Internal rate of return (IRR)   The discount rate at which cash outflows of an investment equal cash inflows.

International domestic bonds   Bonds issued by a foreign firm, denominated in the firm's native currency, and sold within its own country.

Intrinsic value   The portion of a call option's total value equal to the greater of either zero or the difference between the current value of the underlying asset and the exercise price; for a put option, intrinsic value is the greater of either zero or the exercise price less the underlying asset price.

Investment   The current commitment of dollars for a period of time in order to derive future payments that will compensate the investor for the time the funds are committed, the expected rate of inflation, and the uncertainty of future payments.

Investment company   A firm that sells shares of the company and uses the proceeds to buy stock, bonds, or other financial instruments.

Investment decision process   Estimation of value for comparison with market price to determine whether or not to invest.

Investment horizon   The time period used for planning and forecasting purposes or the future time at which the investor requires the invested funds.

Investment management company   A company separate from the investment company that manages the portfolio and performs administrative functions.

Jensen measure   An absolute measure of a portfolio's risk-adjusted performance, computed as the intercept in a regression equation where the excess returns to a manager's portfolio and the market index are, respectively, the dependent and independent variables.

Lagging indicators   A set of economic variables whose values reach peaks and troughs after the aggregate economy.

Leading indicators   A set of economic variables whose values reach peaks and troughs in advance of the aggregate economy.

Limit order   An order that lasts for a specified time to buy or sell a security when and if it trades at a specified price.

Liquid   Term used to describe an asset that can be quickly converted to cash at a price close to fair market value.

Liquidity   The ability to buy or sell an asset quickly and at a reasonable price.

Liquidity risk   Uncertainty due to the ability to buy or sell an investment in the secondary market.

Long hedge   A long position in a forward or futures contract used to offset the price volatility of a short position in the underlying asset.

Long position   The buyer of a commodity or security or, for a forward contract, the counterparty who will be the eventual buyer of the underlying asset.

Long-term, high-priority goal   A long-term financial investment goal of personal importance that typically includes achieving financial independence, such as being able to retire at a certain age.

Low-load fund   A mutual fund that imposes a moderate front-end sales charge when the investor buys the fund, typically about 3 to 4 percent.

Lower-priority goal   A financial investment goal of lesser personal importance, such as taking a luxurious vacation or buying a car every few years.

Maintenance margin   The required proportion that the investor's equity value must be to the total market value of the stock. If the proportion drops below this percent, the investor will receive a margin call.

Management effect   A combination of the interest rate anticipation effect, the analysis effect, and the trading effect.

Management fee   The compensation an investment company pays to the investment management company for its services. The average annual fee is about 0.5 percent of fund assets.

Margin   The percent of cost a buyer pays in cash for a security, borrowing the balance from the broker. This introduces leverage, which increases the risk of the transaction.

Margin account   The collateral posted with the futures exchange clearinghouse by an outside counterparty to insure its eventual performance; the *initial* margin is the deposit required at contract origination while the *maintenance* margin is the minimum collateral necessary at all times.

Margin call   A request by an investor's broker for additional capital for a security bought on margin if the investor's equity value declines below the required maintenance margin.

Marked-to-market   The settlement process used to adjust the margin account of a futures contract for daily changes in the price of the underlying asset.

Market   The means through which buyers and sellers are brought together to aid in the transfer of goods and/or services.

Market order   An order to buy or sell a security immediately at the best price available.

Market portfolio   The portfolio that includes all risky assets with relative weights equal to their proportional market values.

Market risk premium   The amount of return above the risk-free rate that investors expect from the market in general as compensation for systematic risk.

Market value-added (MVA)   External management performance measure to compare the market value of the company's debt and equity with the total capital invested in the firm.

Maturity strategy   A portfolio management strategy employed to reduce the interest rate risk of a bond portfolio by matching the maturity of the portfolio with its investment horizon. For example, if the investment horizon is 10 years, the portfolio manager would construct a portfolio that will mature in 10 years.

Mean rate of return   The average of an investment's returns over an extended period of time.

Modified duration   A measure of Macaulay duration adjusted to help you estimate a bond's price volatility.

Money market   The market for short-term debt securities with maturities of less than 1 year.

Money market funds   Investment companies that hold portfolios of high-quality, short-term securities like T-bills. High liquidity and superior returns make them a good alternative to bank savings accounts.

Money market mutual fund   A fund that invests in short-term securities sold in the money market. (Large companies, banks, and other institutions also invest their surplus cash in the money market for short periods of time.) In the entire investment spectrum, these are generally the safest, most stable securities available. They include Treasury bills, certificates of deposit of large banks, and commercial paper (short-term IOUs of large corporations).

Mortgage bonds   Bonds that pledge specific assets such as buildings and equipment. The proceeds from the sale of these assets are used to pay off bondholders in case of bankruptcy.

Moving average   The continually recalculating average of security prices for a period, often 200 days, to serve as an indication of the general trend of prices and also as a benchmark price.

Mutual fund   An investment company that pools money from shareholders and invests in a variety of securities, including stocks, bonds, and money market securities. A mutual fund ordinarily stands ready to buy back (redeem) its shares at their current net asset value, which depends on the market value of the fund's portfolio of securities at the time. Mutual funds generally continuously offer new shares to investors.

National Association of Securities Dealers Automated Quotation (NASDAQ) system   An electronic system for providing bid-ask quotes on OTC securities.

Near-term, high-priority goal   A short-term financial investment goal of personal importance, such as accumulating funds for making a house down payment or buying a car.

Net asset value (NAV) per share   The market value of an investment company's assets (securities, cash, and any accrued earnings) after deducting liabilities, divided by the number of shares outstanding.

No-load fund A mutual fund that sells its shares at net asset value without adding sales charges.

Nominal yield A bond's yield as measured by its coupon rate.

Normal portfolio A specialized or customized benchmark constructed to evaluate a specific manager's investment style or philosophy.

Notes Intermediate-term debt securities with maturities longer than 1 year but less than 10 years.

Notional principal The principal value of a swap transaction, which is not exchanged but is used as a scale factor to translate interest rate differentials into cash settlement payments.

Objectives The investor's goals expressed in terms of risk and return and included in the policy statement.

Open-end investment company The more formal name for a mutual fund, which derives from the fact that it continuously offers new shares to investors and redeems them (buys them back) on demand.

Operating leverage The use of fixed-production costs in the firm's operating cost structure. The effect of fixed costs is to magnify the effect of a change in sales on operating profits.

Option clearing corporation (OCC) A company designed to guarantee, monitor margin accounts, and settle exchange-traded option transactions.

Option contract An agreement that grants the owner the right, but not the obligation, to make a future transaction in an underlying commodity or security at a fixed price and within a predetermined time in the future.

Option premium The initial price that the option buyer must pay to the option seller to acquire the contract.

Out-of-the-money An option that has no intrinsic value.

Overfunded plan A defined benefit pension plan in which the present value of the pension liabilities is less than the plan's assets.

Overweighted A condition in which a portfolio, for whatever reason, includes more of a class of securities than the relative market value alone would justify.

Payback The time required for the added income from the convertible relative to the stock to offset the conversion premium.

Peak The culmination of a bull market when prices stop rising and begin declining.

Perpetuity An investment without any maturity date. It provides returns to its owner indefinitely.

Personal trust An amount of money set aside by a grantor and often managed by a third party, the trustee; often constructed so one party receives income from the trust's investments and another party receives the residual value of the trust after the income beneficiaries' death.

Policy effect The difference in performance of a bond portfolio from that of a chosen index due to differences in duration, which result from a fund's investment policy.

Policy statement   A statement in which the investor specifies investment goals, constraints, and risk preferences.

Portfolio   A group of investments. Ideally, the investments should have different patterns of returns over time.

Preferred stock   An equity investment that stipulates the dividend payment either as a coupon or a stated dollar amount. The firm's directors may withhold payments.

Premium   A bond selling at a price above par value due to capital market conditions.

Price change effect   The unknown component of the total return for a bond portfolio during a period of time due to the interest rate effect, sector/quality effect, and residual effect.

Price continuity   A feature of a liquid market in which prices change little from one transaction to the next due to the depth of the market.

Price/earnings (P/E) ratio   The number by which earnings per share is multiplied to estimate a stock's value; also called the *earnings multiplier.*

Price momentum   A portfolio strategy in which you acquire stocks that have enjoyed above-market stock price increases.

Price risk   The component of interest rate risk due to the uncertainty of the market price of a bond caused by possible changes in market interest rates.

Price-weighted series   An indicator series calculated as an arithmetic average of the current prices of the sampled securities.

Primary market   The market in which newly issued securities are sold by their issuers, who receive the proceeds.

Principal (par value)   The original value of the debt underlying a bond that is payable at maturity.

Private placement   A new issue sold directly to a small group of investors, usually institutions.

Promised yield to call (YTC)   A bond's yield if held until the first available call date, with reinvestment of all coupon payments at the yield-to-call rate.

Promised yield to maturity (YTM)   The most widely used measure of a bond's yield that states the fully compounded rate of return on a bond bought at market price and held to maturity with reinvestment of all coupon payments at the yield to maturity rate.

Protective put   A trading strategy in which a put option is purchased as a supplement to a long position in an underlying asset or portfolio of assets; the most straightforward form of *portfolio insurance.*

Public bond   A long-term, fixed-obligation debt security in a convenient, affordable denomination for sale to individuals and financial institutions.

Pure cash-matched dedicated portfolio   A conservative dedicated portfolio management technique aimed at developing a bond portfolio that will provide payments exactly matching the specified liability schedules.

Put–call parity   The relationship that must exist in an efficient market between the prices for put and call options having the same underlying asset, exercise price, and expiration date.

Put options   Options to sell a firm's common stock within a certain period at a specified price.

Quadratic optimization   A technique that relies on historical correlations in order to construct a portfolio that seeks to minimize tracking error with an index.

Range forward   A trading strategy based on a variation of the put–call parity model where, for the same underlying asset but different exercise prices, a call option is purchased and a put option is sold (or vice versa).

Real estate investment trusts (REITs)   Investment funds that hold portfolios of real estate investments.

Real risk-free rate (RFR)   The basic interest rate with no accommodation for inflation or uncertainty. The pure time value of money.

Realized capital gains   Capital gains that result when an appreciated asset has been sold; realized capital gains are taxable.

Realized yield   The expected compounded yield on a bond that is sold before it matures assuming the reinvestment of all cash flows at an explicit rate. Also called *horizon yield*.

Refunding issue   Bonds that provide funds to prematurely retire another bond issue. These bonds can be either a junior or senior issue.

Registered bond   A bond for which ownership is registered with the issuer. The holder receives interest payments by check directly from the issuer.

Registered competitive market makers (RCMM)   Members of an exchange who are allowed to use their memberships to buy or sell for their own account within the specific trading obligations set down by the exchange.

Relative-strength ratio   The ratio of a stock price or an industry index value to a market indicator series, indicating performance relative to the overall market.

Required rate of return   The return that compensates investors for their time, the expected rate of inflation, and the uncertainty of the return.

Residual effect   The return on a bond portfolio after taking account of the three prior factors—yield to maturity, interest rate effect, and sector/quality effect.

Resistance level   A price at which a technician would expect a substantial increase in the supply of a stock to reverse a rising trend.

Revenue bond   A bond that is serviced by the income generated from specific revenue-producing projects of the municipality.

Rising trend channel   The range defined by security prices as they move progressively higher.

Risk   The uncertainty that an investment will earn its expected rate of return.

Risk averse   The assumption about investors that they will choose the least risky alternative, all else being equal.

Risk-free asset   An asset with returns that exhibit zero variance.

Risk premium   The increase over the nominal risk-free rate that investors demand as compensation for an investment's uncertainty.

Risky asset   An asset with uncertain future returns.

Runs test   A test of the weak-form efficient market hypothesis that checks for trends that persist longer in terms of positive or negative price changes than one would expect for a random series.

Sampling   A technique for constructing a passive index portfolio in which the portfolio manager buys a representative sample of stocks that comprise the benchmark index.

Secondary market   The market in which outstanding securities are bought and sold by owners other than the issuers.

Sector/quality effect   The return on a bond portfolio caused by changing yield spreads between bonds in different sectors and with different quality ratings.

Sector rotation strategy   An active strategy that involves purchasing stocks in specific industries or stocks with specific characteristics (low P/E, growth, value) that are anticipated to rise in value more than the overall market.

Secured (senior) bond   A bond backed by a legal claim on specified assets of the issuer.

Security-market indicator series   An index created as a statistical measure of the performance of an entire market or segment of a market based on a sample of securities from the market or segment of a market.

Security market line (SML)   The line that reflects the combination of risk and return of alternative investments.

Semistrong-form efficient market hypothesis   The belief that security prices fully reflect all publicly available information, including information from security transactions and company, economic, and political news.

Separation theorem   The proposition that the investment decision, which involves investing in the market portfolio on the capital market line, is separate from the financing decision, which targets a specific point on the CML based on the investor's risk preference.

Serial obligation bond   A bond issue that has a series of maturity dates.

Settlement price   The price determined by the exchange clearinghouse with which futures contract margin accounts are marked to market.

Sharpe measure   A relative measure of a portfolio's benefit-to-risk ratio, calculated as its average return in excess of the risk-free rate divided by its standard deviation.

Short hedge   A short position in a forward or futures contract used to offset the price volatility of a long position in the underlying asset.

Short position   The seller of a commodity or security or, for a forward contract, the counterparty who will be the eventual seller of the underlying asset.

Short sale   The sale of borrowed securities with the intention of repurchasing them later at a lower price and earning the difference.

Sinking fund   Bond provision that requires the bond to be paid off systematically over the term rather than in full at maturity.

Specialist   The major market maker on U.S. stock exchanges who acts as a broker or dealer to ensure the liquidity and smooth functions of the secondary stock market.

Speculative company   A firm with a great degree of business and/or financial risk, with commensurate high earnings potential.

Speculative stock   A stock that appears to be highly overpriced compared to its reasonable valuation.

Spending phase   Phase in the investment life cycle during which individuals' earning years end as they retire. They pay for expenses with income from social security and prior investments and invest to protect against inflation.

Spread   A trading strategy where long and short positions in two call (or two put) option contracts having the same underlying asset but different exercise prices or expiration dates are combined to create a customized return distribution.

Standard deviation   A measure of variability equal to the square root of the variance.

Statement of cash flows   A financial statement that shows the effects on the firm's cash flow of income flows and changes in its balance sheet.

Stock index arbitrage   A trading strategy involving a long position in a stock portfolio and a short position in a stock index futures contract (or vice versa) designed to exploit a mispricing in the futures contract relative to the underlying index.

Straddle   A trading strategy requiring the simultaneous purchase of a call option and a put option having the same exercise price, underlying asset, and expiration date. Variations of this theme include *strips, straps, strangles,* and *chooser options.*

Strong-form efficient market hypothesis   The belief that security prices fully reflect all information from both public and private sources.

Structured note   A bond with an embedded derivative designed to create a payoff distribution that satisfies the needs of a specific investor clientele.

Subordinated (junior) bonds   Debentures that, in case of default, entitle holders to claims on the issuer's assets only after the claims of holders of senior debentures and mortgage bonds are satisfied.

Support level   A price at which a technician would expect a substantial increase in price and volume for a stock to reverse a declining trend that was due to profit taking.

Sustainable growth rate   A measure of how fast a firm can grow using internal equity and debt financing to keep the capital structure constant over time.

Swap spread   A measure of the risk premium for an interest rate swap, calculated as the difference between the agreement's fixed rate and the yield on a Treasury bond with the same maturity.

Swaptions   Also known as *swap options,* these contracts give the holder the right, but not the obligation, to enter into an interest rate or currency swap on prearranged terms.

Systematic risk   The variability of returns that is due to macroeconomic factors that affect all risky assets. Because it affects all risky assets, it cannot be eliminated by diversification.

Technical analysis   Estimation of future security price movements based on past price and volume movements.

Term bond   A bond that has a single maturity date.

Term structure of interest rates   The relationship between term to maturity and yield to maturity for a sample of comparable bonds at a given time. Popularly known as the *yield curve.*

Term to maturity   Specifies the date or the number of years before a bond matures or expires.

Third market   Over-the-counter trading of securities listed on an exchange.

Tick   The minimum price movement for the asset underlying a forward or futures contract; for Treasury bonds, one tick equals $\frac{1}{32}$ of 1% of par value.

Time premium   The difference between an option's total market value and its intrinsic value.

Time-series analysis   An examination of a firm's performance data over a period of time.

Total return   A return objective in which the investor wants to increase the portfolio value to meet a future need by both capital gains and current income reinvestment.

Tracking error   The difference between the return of a portfolio that is constructed to replicate an index and the return on the index itself.

Trading effect   The difference in performance of a bond portfolio from that of a chosen index due to short-run changes in the composition of the portfolio.

Trading rule   A formula for deciding on current transactions based on historical data.

Trading turnover   The percentage of outstanding shares traded during a period of time.

Transaction cost   The cost of executing a trade. Low costs characterize an operationally efficient market.

Treasury bill   A negotiable U.S. government security with a maturity of less than 1 year that pays no periodic interest but yields the difference between its par value and its discounted purchase price.

Treasury bond   A U.S. government security with a maturity of more than 10 years that pays interest periodically.

Treasury note   A U.S. government security with maturities of 1 to 10 years that pays interest periodically.

Treynor measure   A relative measure of a portfolio's benefit-to-risk ratio, calculated as its average return in excess of the risk-free rate divided by its beta coefficient.

Trough   The culmination of a bear market at which prices stop declining and begin rising.

12b-1 fee   A fee charged by some funds, named after the SEC rule that permits it. Such fees pay for distribution costs, such as advertising, or for brokers' commissions. The fund's prospectus details any 12b-1 charges that apply.

Underfunded plan   A defined benefit pension plan in which the present value of the fund's liabilities to employees exceeds the value of the fund's assets.

Underweighted   A condition in which a portfolio, for whatever reason, includes less of a class of securities than the relative market value alone would justify.

Unrealized capital gains   Capital gains that reflect the price appreciation of currently held unsold assets; taxes on unrealized capital gains can be deferred indefinitely.

Unsystematic risk   Risk that is unique to an asset, derived from its particular characteristics. It can be eliminated in a diversified portfolio.

Unweighted index   An indicator series affected equally by the performance of each security in the sample regardless of price or market value. Also referred to as an equal-weighted series.

Unwind The negotiated termination of a forward or futures position before contract maturity.

Uptick An incremental movement upward in a transaction price over the previous transaction price.

Uptick–downtick ratio A ratio of the number of uptick block transactions (indicating buyers) to the number of downtick block transactions (indicating sellers of blocks). An indicator of institutional investor sentiment.

Valuation analysis An active bond portfolio management strategy designed to capitalize on expected price increases in temporarily undervalued issues.

Valuation process Part of the investment decision process in which you estimate the value of a security.

Value stocks Stocks that appear to be undervalued for reasons besides earnings growth potential. These stocks are usually identified based on low P/E ratios or low price-to-book ratios.

Value-weighted series An indicator series calculated as the total market value of the securities in the sample.

Variable-rate note A debt security for which the interest rate changes to follow some specified short-term rate, for example, the T-bill rate; see floating rate note.

Variance A measure of variability equal to the sum of the squares of a return's deviation from the mean, divided by n.

Warrant An instrument that allows the holder to purchase a specified number of shares of the firm's common stock from the firm at a specified price for a given period of time.

Weak-form efficient market hypothesis The belief that security prices fully reflect all security market information.

Yankee bonds Bonds sold in the United States and denominated in U.S. dollars but issued by a foreign firm or government.

Yield The promised rate of return on an investment under certain assumptions.

Yield illusion The erroneous expectation that a bond will provide its stated yield to maturity without recognizing the implicit reinvestment assumption related to coupon payments.

Yield spread The difference between the promised yields of alternative bond issues or market segments at a given time.

Zero coupon bond A bond that pays its par value at maturity, but no periodic interest payments. Its yield is determined by the difference between its par value and its discounted purchase price. Also called *minicoupon bonds* or *original issue discount (OID) bonds*.

Name Index

Abken, Peter A., 926n
Academy of Financial Services, 201
Adams Express Company, The, 970
Affleck-Graves, John, 238
AGA B, 744
Aim Constellation Fund, 1002–1003, 1008, 1010
Airbus, 806
Akhtar, Rashid A., 168n, 296n, 298, 320, 321n, 322n, 1018, 1020n
Aklarka, Matt, 239–240
Albright, S. Christian, 102n, 212n, 213n
Alexander, Gordon J., 627
Allen, J. D., 155n
Allen, Julie A., 935n
Altman, Edward I., 311, 421n, 514n, 596n, 597n, 598
American Economic Association, 202
American Finance Association, 200
American Municipal Bond Assurance Corporation (AMBAC), 507
American National Bank and Trust Company, 245
American Railroad Association, 189
American Stock Exchange (AMEX), 83, 113, 115, 116–117, 121, 135, 138, 183, 184, 191, 202, 224, 779, 874
American Telephone & Telegraph. See AT&T
AMEX. See American Stock Exchange (AMEX)
Amos Press, Inc., 88n
Ang, James S., 979
Ankrim, Ernest M., 1014n
Apilado, Vincent P., 467n
Apple Computer, 123–124
Arbel, Avner, 225–226
Archer, Stephen H., 285n
Archibald, T. Ross, 233n
Argilagos, Joseph D., 946
Ariel, Robert A., 222
Arnott, Robert D., 792n
Asquith, Paul, 597n
Association for Investment Management and Research (AIMR), 201, 679, 1037
AT&T, 120, 125, 202, 408, 874–876, 967
Atkinson, Thomas R., 624n

Babcock, Guilford C., 760n
Baesel, Jerome B., 310–311
Bailey, Jeffrey V., 1019n, 1028, 1029
Bailey, Warren, 86n, 977
Baker, Fentress and Company, 970
Baker, Kent, 232n
Ball, Ray, 215n, 218–219
Balvers, Ronald J., 217

Banker's Trust, 825, 855
Bank of America, 202
Bansal, Vipul K., 920n
Banz, R. W., 224
Barclay, Michael, 970n
Barings Bank, 825
Barone-Adesi, Giovanni, 905
Barry, Christopher B., 226
Bartter, Brit J., 894n
Basu, S., 223, 224
Battalio, Robert H., 136n
Batterymarch Financial Management Corporation, 245
Bauman, W. Scott, 979
Baumol, William J., 141n
Bavishi, Vinod B., 411–412, 415n
Bayer, 744, 747, 748
Beatty, Randolph, 230n
Beaver, William H., 233n
Beckers, Stan, 901
Beckman, Barry A., 463n, 464n
Beebower, Gilbert L., 56n, 240, 1013, 1014
Behn-Miller Publications, 88n
Beidleman, Carl R., 931
Belkaoui, Ahmed, 498n
Benavides, Rosario, 490n
Benderly, Jason, 462n
Benesh, Gary A., 243n
Benz, 82
Berger, Lisa, 45n
Berges, Angel, 221
Bergstrom Capital Corporation, 970
Berkman, Neil, 137n
Berkowitz, Stephen A., 240
Bernard, Victor L., 219
Bessembinder, H., 112n
Beverly Enterprises, 942–945
Bhandari, Laxims Chand, 314
Bhattasharya, Anand K., 602n
Bicksler, J., 298n, 323
Bierwag, G. O., 610–611
Biger, Nahum, 908n
Billingsley, R., 498n
Bishop, Graham, 501n
Black, Fischer, 237, 307, 309n, 312–313, 884, 897, 909
Blake, Christopher R., 977, 979
Bleakley, Fred R., 645n
Blitz, Steven, 500n
Blue Chip Value Fund, Inc., 970n
Blume, Marshall, 215n, 310, 995n, 1004, 1005
Boeing, 806
Bohan, James, 792n
Boles, Keith, 792n
Bollier, Thierry F., 925n
Bomberger, William A., 628n
Bonham, Howard B., Jr., 686n
Bookstaber, Richard M., 359n

Boston Stock Exchange, 120
Boyce, W. M., 534n
Bradford, David, 309n
Bradford, R. W., 88n
Branch, Ben, 220
Brannigan, Martha, 132n
Brauchli, Marcus W., 133n
Brealey, Richard A., 110n
Brennan, Michael J., 234n, 306n
Brigham, Eugene F., 20n, 398n
Brinson, Gary P., 56n, 98n, 149n, 150n, 240, 1013, 1014, 1017, 1019
Brinson Partners, Inc., 168, 606, 1019
Brown, Charles K., 706, 707n, 708n, 743n, 744n, 745n, 746n, 747n, 748n
Brown, Gregory D., 1017
Brown, Keith C., 355n, 358n, 832, 845, 901, 917n, 925, 929, 936n, 939n, 956n, 1017
Brown, Philip, 221, 225
Brown, Stephen J., 226, 329, 979, 980
Brush, John S., 215n, 792n
Bulldog Market, 82
Burger King, 433
Burmeister, Edwin, 328
Bush, Janet, 138n
Business Information Services, 203
Business International Corp., 203
Business Week, 983
Butler, H. L., Jr., 155n

Cagan, Phillip, 559n
Campbell, Harvey, 217n
Campbell, J., 213n
Campbell, John Y., 217n
Canes, Michael, 238–239
Canter, Michael S., 832
Cantor, Richard, 497n
Capital Guaranty Insurance Company (CGIC), 507
Carlson, Robert S., 976
Carpenter, Michael D., 311
Carr, Peter, 898n
Carroll, Thomas J., 119n
Carron, Andrew S., 504n, 508, 509n
Carter, E. E., 155n
Case, Carl, 95
Caster, Paul, 787n
Caterpillar, 806
CBOE. See Chicago Board Options Exchange (CBOE)
CBOT. See Chicago Board of Trade
Center for International Business Cycle Research (CIBCR, Columbia University), 462, 467–469

Center for Research in Security Prices (CRSP, University of Chicago), 202
Central Securities Corporation, 970n
Chalk, Andrew J., 230n
Chan, Anthony, 978–979, 1015n
Chan, K. C., 224
Chan, Kalok, 112n
Chan, Louis K., 227
Chance, Don M., 906n
Chang, Eric C., 221, 239, 978, 1015–1016
Chang, Kyun Chun, 220n
Charles Allmon Trust, Inc., The, 970
Charles Schwab & Co., 975
Chen, Andrew H., 835
Chen, Carl R., 978–979, 1015n
Chen, Nai-fu, 217n, 224, 300, 328, 472
Chen, Son-Nan, 311
Cheney, John M., 978
Chiang, Raymond, 840n
Chicago, University of, 202
Chicago Board of Trade (CBT, CBOT), 84, 85, 113, 827, 838, 839, 874
Chicago Board Options Exchange (CBOE), 780, 874, 876
Chicago Mercantile Exchange (CME, Merc), 85, 113, 814, 843, 856, 917
Chicago Stock Exchange, 120, 121
Cho, Chinhyang, 329n
Cho, D. Chinhyung, 326
Choi, Frederick D. S., 411–412, 415n, 416n, 417n
Chowdhuny, M., 236n
Christensen, Peter E., 608n, 615n
Christie, William G., 232n, 309n
Chrysler, 82, 706
Chua, Jess H., 979
Churchill, Dwight D., 605n
Cisco Systems, 747
Citicorp, 143
Clarke, Roger G., 359n, 814n, 827n, 887n
CME. See Chicago Mercantile Exchange
Coca-Cola, 256–259, 259–261, 293–297, 433, 722
Coggin, T. Daniel, 1016
Cohen, Abby Joseph, 471n, 472n, 473n
Cohen, K. J., 155n
Collier, Ian C., 502n
Columbia University, 462, 467
Commodity Exchange (COMEX), 827, 880
CompuServe, Inc., 203
Compustat, 203
Connie Lee Insurance Company, 507

Connor, Gregory, 329n
Conrad, Jennifer, 213n
Conroy, Theresa, 165n, 1027n
Cooper, Guy M., 293n, 312
Cooper, Ian A., 933n
Cooper, Richard V. L., 471n
Copeland, Thomas E., 237
Cornell, Bradford, 835, 852, 977
Cosimano, Thomas F., 217
Cox, John, 835, 894n
Crabbe, Leland E., 946
Cragg, John G., 243
Crain Communications, Inc., 196
Crockett, Jean, 995n
Cullity, John P., 434n, 461n
Cumby, Robert E., 977

Daimler, 82
Daiwa, 142, 187, 515
Daniells, P. M., 181n
Das, Sanjiv, 239–240
Data Resources, Inc. (DRI), 203
Dattatreya, Ravi E., 567n, 572n, 576n, 577n
Davidson, Lawrence S., 471n
De Caires, Bryan, 119n
Deere and Co., 433
Dennis, Patrick, 228, 317
Desai, Hemang, 238–239
Dharan, Bala G., 232
Dhrymes, Phoebus J., 300, 326, 327
Dialynas, Chris P., 165n, 547n, 561n, 593n, 601, 803n, 1028n
Dicks, G. R., 182
Diermeier, Jeffrey J., 1017, 1019
Dietz, Peter O., 1024, 1029n
Dimson, Elroy, 224, 226
Disclosure Information Group, 202
Dobrzynski, Judith H., 88n
Douglas, G. W., 312
Douglass, K. Scott, 597n
Dow, Charles, 789
Dow Jones and Company, 155, 184, 185, 203
Drexel Burnham Lambert, 511, 512
Droms, William G., 605n
Drzycimski, Eugene F., 132n, 229–230, 233, 682–683
DuBois, Peter C., 88n
Duff & Phelps, 497–499, 600
Dun & Bradstreet, 382
Dundaram, Sridhar, 228, 317
Dunetz, Mark L., 569n, 576n
Dunn, Patricia C., 979
Durand, David, 753–754
Dushkin Publishing Group, Inc., 183
Dybvig, Philip H., 329
Dyl, Edward A., 220, 548n

Eastern Finance Association, 201
Economist Newspaper, Inc., The, 197
Edens, Lynn, 504n
Ederington, L. H., 498n
Edington, David H., 547n, 561n, 601
Edmister, Robert, 226
Edwards, Franklin, 141n, 032
Ehrbar, A. F., 981n
Einhorn, Steven, 471
Elbaum, Bernard L., 87n
Elhabashi, Sahar, 500n
Ellis, Charles D., 42n, 43n
Ellis, M. E., 920n
Elton, Edwin J., 239–240, 309n, 326, 328, 500n, 977, 979
Emery, Kenneth, 467n

Engex, Inc., 970
Euromoney Publications PLC, 196
Evans, John L., 285n
Evans, Thomas G., 412n
Exxon, 256–259, 259–261
Ezzell, John R., 310

Fabozzi, Frank J., 109n, 112n, 132n, 165n, 232n, 359n, 494n, 500n, 504n, 506n, 507n, 508n, 510n, 511n, 514n, 515n, 540n, 546n, 548n, 549n, 551n, 567n, 572n, 576n, 577n, 593n, 595n, 596n, 597n, 598n, 602n, 605n, 608n, 615n, 803n, 805n, 852n, 978n, 1016, 1021n, 1027n, 1029n
Fabozzi, T. Dessa, 165n, 494n, 504n, 506n, 507n, 508n, 510n, 511n, 540n, 546n, 548n, 549n, 551n, 567n, 576n, 593n, 595n, 596n, 597n, 598n, 602n, 605n, 608n, 615n, 803n, 805n, 1021n, 1029n
Fachler, Nimrod, 1017
Fairchild Publications, 185
Fairfield, Patricia M., 228n, 660n, 737
Fama, Eugene F., 95n, 210–211, 212n, 215, 217, 226, 227, 228, 229, 244n, 305, 313, 315, 316n, 317, 476n, 737, 1006, 1007n
Farrell, James L., 978
Feldstein, Sylvan G., 109n, 506n, 507n
Ferri, Michael G., 548n, 974n
Ferris, Stephen P., 476n
Fiat, 82
Fidelity Investments, 980
Fielitz, Bruce, 310, 521n
Figlewski, Stephen, 901
Financial Analysts Federation, 1037
Financial Guaranty Insurance Company (FGIC), 507
Financial Management Association, 201
Financial Security Assurance (FSA), 507
Financial Services Information Company, 196
Finkel, Sidney R., 648, 650, 651
Finnerty, John D., 534n
Finnerty, Joseph E., 235n
Finney, Louis D., 240
First Boston, 112, 600
Fisher, Andrew, 118n, 143n
Fisher, Kenneth, 184
Fisher, Lawrence, 229, 569n, 610, 612
Fitch Investors Service, 497–499
Fixed Income Group (Kidder Peabody & Company), 187
Fogler, H. Russell, 243n, 1024
Folks, William R., 832
Fong, H. Gifford, 165n, 593n, 1021n, 1026, 1027n
Ford Motors, 82, 136, 706
Forman, Craig, 142n
Foster, F. D., 112n
Foster, George, 219
Francis, Jack C., 978n
Frankfort Stock Exchange, 143
Frank Russell Analytical Services, 240
Fraser, Donald, 970n
Frazer, W. J., 628n
French, Don W., 1021

French, Kenneth R., 217, 222, 226, 227, 228, 244n, 305, 315, 316n, 317, 737
Fridson, Martin S., 512n, 513n, 514n, 548n, 596n
Fried, Dov, 400n
Friedman, Milton, 252, 470–471
Friend, Irwin, 298n, 314, 323, 326, 327, 995n, 1004, 1005
Fromson, Brett Duval, 127n
Froyen, Richard T., 471n

Gabelli Asset Fund, 1004
Gabelli Equity Trust, Inc., The, 970
Galai, Dan, 939
Gapenski, Louis C., 20n
Garman, M. Christopher, 596n
Garman, Mark B., 908
Garner, C. Alan, 469, 546n
Gastineau, Gary, 854, 936
Gay, Gerald, 840n
General American Investors Company, Inc., 970
General Electric (GE), 126, 967
General Electric Information Service, 203
General Motors, 82, 109, 120, 706
Gentry, James A., 498n, 738n
Geske, Robert, 905
Gibbons, Michael R., 222, 308
Gillespie, K., 939n
Gladstein, Mathew L., 359n
Gleizes, Fiona, 142n
Glen, Jack D., 977
Glickstein, David A., 789n
Global Information, Inc., 196
Glosten, L., 213n
Goetzmann, William N., 87n, 95, 97n, 979, 980
Goldman, Sachs & Company (GS&Co.), 113, 136–137, 143, 186, 471, 477–483, 545n, 645n, 671, 706, 743
Goldman Sachs International Corporation, 186
Gombola, Michael J., 235
Goodman, David A., 223
Gordon, Myron J., 438n
Gordon, Roger, 309n
Goulet, Waldemar M., 232n
Grasso, Richard A., 141
Graven, Kathryn, 133n
Gray, H. Peter, 650
Green, Kevin, 977
Greene, Jason, 136n
Greshin, Adam, 494n, 605n
Griepentrog, Gary L., 311, 597n
Griffin, Paul A., 628
Grinblatt, Mark, 230, 977, 979, 1017
Grinwold, Richard C., 1019n
Grossman, Sanford J., 107n, 213n
Groth, John, 970n
Gruber, Martin J., 239–240, 309n, 326, 328, 500n, 977, 979, 981
Grundy, Kevin, 228n, 317
GTE Information Systems, Inc., 203
Gudikunst, Arthur, 1024n
Gulrajani, Deepak, 548n
Gultekin, Mustofa N., 327, 328
Gultekin, N. Bulent, 326, 327, 328

Hackel, Kenneth S., 738n
Hadzima, Margaret Darasz, 494n, 605n
Hafer, R. W., 471n, 546n

Hagerman, Robert L., 213n
Hagstrom, Robert G., Jr., 430n
Hamao, Yasushi, 227
Hamilton, James L., 136n, 140
Handa, Punect, 107n, 329n
Hanks, Sara, 111n
Hanley, Kathleen Weiss, 230n, 232
Hardy, Donald J., 1024
Hardy, Eric S., 87n
Harlow, W. V., 901, 925
Harrington, Diana R., 300n
Harris, Diane, 87n
Harris, Lawrence, 213n, 222
Harris, R. S., 534n
Harris, Robert S., 737
Hatfield, Kenneth, 230n
Hausman, W. H., 229
Hawawini, Gabriel, 246
Hawley, Delvin D., 810n
Hawthorne, Fran, 152n, 165n, 593n
Hayne, Lakhbir S., 504n
Heathcotte, Bryan, 467n
Henderson, Glenn V., Jr., 1021
Hendricks, Darryl, 979
Henriksson, Roy, 239, 978, 1015
Henriques, Diana, 88n
Henry, C., 939n
Hensel, Chris R., 1014n
Herman, Tom, 60n
Hershey, 722
Hertzberg, Marie P., 463n, 464n
Herzfeld, Thomas J., 970, 970n, 971
Hess, Patrick, 222
Hickman, W. Braddock, 492n, 498n, 624n
Hicks, John, 836
Hill, Joanne M., 355, 356
Hino, Hisaaki, 416n, 417n
Hoffmeister, Ronald, 83n
Holderness, Clifford, 970n
Holloway, Clark, 237
Holt, Charles C., 755
Holthausen, Robert W., 628
Holzmann, Oscar, 412n
Homa, Kenneth, 471n
Homer, Sidney, 531n, 534n, 562, 594n, 602n, 603n, 604n, 609n
Honda Motors, 82
Honolulu Stock Exchange, 120
Hood, L. Randolph, 240, 1013, 1014
Hoopes, David, 182
Hopewell, Michael H., 132n, 568n
Hourdouvelis, Gikas A., 560n
Howe, J. S., 236n
Howe, Jane Tripp, 514n, 595n, 596n, 597n, 598
Hradsky, G., 597n
Hsich, David A., 224
Hsueh, L. Paul, 497n
Huang, Roger D., 232n
Huberman, Gur, 238
Hudson-Wilson, Susan, 87n
Hulbert, Mark, 238
Hull, John C., 897n, 908n, 926n
Hynes, Joseph, 599

Ibbotson, Roger G., 58n, 87n, 89–90, 91, 95, 97n, 98n, 100n, 149n, 150n, 230n, 231n, 626n, 656n, 659, 668
Ibbotson Associates, 57n, 59n, 60n, 184, 624, 657
IDM, 125, 132, 408, 967
IFR Publishing, Ltd., 185
Ikenberry, David L., 232

Illinois, University of, 202
IMM. *See* International Monetary Market
Inefficient-Market Fund, Inc., The, 970
Ingersoll, Jonathan, 835, 943n
Institute of Chartered Financial Analysts (ICFA), 201, 1037
Institutional Investor, Inc., 201
Institutional Investors Systems, 196, 201
Intel, 82, 443, 747
Interactive Data Corporation, 203
Intermountain Stock Exchange, 120
International Federation of Stock Exchanges, 118–119
International Finance Corporation (IFC), 119, 183
International Monetary Fund, 182
International Monetary Market (IMM), 843, 845, 856
International Organization of Securities Commissions (IOSCO), 120n
International Swap and Derivatives Association, 874
Interstate Department Stores, 82
Investment Company Institute, 974n
Investors Intelligence, 779n
Investors Management Services, 202
Ippolito, Richard A., 239, 240n
Iron and Steel Institute, 189

Jacquillat, B., 311
Jaffe, Jeffrey F., 95n, 231n, 235, 476n
Jaffee, Dwight M., 471n, 624n
Jagannathan, Rari, 317
Jain, Prom C., 233, 238–239
JAI Press, 201
James, Christopher, 226
Japan Bond Research Institute, 514
Japan Credit Rating Agency, Ltd., 514
Jasen, Georgette, 131n
Jen, Frank C., 978
Jennings, Robert, 136n
Jensen, Michael C., 108n, 229, 234, 239n, 312–313, 976, 1000, 1006
Jesswein, Kurt, 832
Jobson, J. D., 329
Joehnk, Michael D., 548n, 625, 627
Johnson, Glenn L., 476n
Johnson, H. E., 905
Johnson, John D., 810n
Johnson, Leland L., 833
Jones, C. N., 112n
Jones, Charles P., 218, 219, 901n
Jones, Frank J., 546n
Jones, Thomas P., 740n
Jordan, James V., 549n
Jorion, Philippe, 21
Joy, O. Maurice, 218

Kadlec, Gregord, 232n
Kalotay, Andrew J., 534n, 548n, 576n
Kamara, Avraham, 347n, 837n
Kandel, Shmuel, 238
Kao, Wenchi, 165, 166n, 171n, 173n, 593, 623–624, 625, 1022n
Kaplan, Robert S., 233n, 498n
Karnosky, Denis S., 1014
Kat, Harry M., 357n
Katz, Steven, 628

Kaufman, George, 568n, 610–611
Kaul, Gantam, 112n, 213n
Kawaller, Ira G., 946n
Keim, Donald B., 217n, 220, 221, 222, 852
Kemper Technology Fund, 1008
Keown, Arthur J., Jr., 978
Keran, Michael W., 471n
Kerr, Halbert, 235
Kessel, Reuben A., 559n
Keynes, John Maynard, 836
Khandwala, Amit, 83n
Kidder Peabody & Company, 113, 186, 187, 545n, 599
Kidwell, David S., 109n, 497n, 507n
Kim, Sung-Hwa, 925
Kinney, William R., Jr., 221
Kipnis, G., 852n
Kirby, Robert C., 1016n
Kirschman, Jeannette R., 1029n
Kisaikai, 514
Klaffky, Thomas E., 616n
Kleidon, Allan W., 221, 225
Klemkosky, Robert C., 239, 979, 1005
Kmart, 722
Koenig, Evan, 467n
Kogelman, Staley, 740, 743n
Kohlhagen, Steven W., 908
Kolb, Robert, 840n
Komatsu, 806
Kon, Stanley J., 978, 1015–1016
Konajczyk, Robert A., 300n
Koppenhaver, Gary D., 925
Kopprasch, Robert W., Jr., 360n
Korajczyk, Robert, 329n
Kothari, S. P., 215n, 227–228, 317
Kraus, Alan, 314
Krikler, Paul, 706n, 707n, 708n, 743n, 744n, 745n, 746n, 747n, 748n
Kritzman, Mark, 357n, 887n, 1016n, 1028
Kuberek, Robert C., 1014
Kuhn, Susan E., 87n, 807n
Kulason, Robert A., 509n
Kwok, Chuck C., 832

Lachapelle, C. A., 230n
Laderman, Jeffrey M., 803n
Lakonishok, Josef, 221, 222n, 227, 229n
Lamy, R., 498n
Lanstein, Ronald, 226, 315n, 737
Largay, J. A., 229
Lascelles, David, 120n
Latané, H. A., 218, 219
Latimer, Mark J., 509n
Lee, Charles, 970n
Lee, Wayne Y., 235–236
Leftwich, Richard W., 628
Lehman Brothers, 113, 600
Lehmann, Bruce N., 977
Leibowitz, Martin L., 531n, 534n, 562, 580, 591n, 594n, 602n, 603n, 604n, 607n, 609n, 616n, 617, 619n, 620n, 621n, 622n, 740, 743n
Lev, Baruch, 229n
Levasseur, M., 311
Levi, Maurice, 222n
Levine, Caroline, 203n
Levine, Sumner N., 203n, 434n, 461n, 497n
Levis, M., 232n

Levy, Robert A., 310, 773n
Lewellen, Wilbur G., 239, 978, 1015–1016
Liberty All-Star Equity Fund, 971
LIFFE. *See* London International Financial Futures Exchange (LIFFE)
Lim, Joseph, 85n, 977
Lim, Kian-Guan, 314
Lin, J. C., 236n
Lin, Pu, 238–239
Lindner Dividend Fund, 1004
Linn, Scott C., 329n
Lintner, John, 280
Lipson, M. L., 112n
Litzenberger, Robert, 218, 309n, 314
Liu, P., 498n
Livingston, Miles, 682n
Livnat, Joshua, 738n
Lloyd-Davies, Peter, 238–239
Lo, Andrew W., 213n
Lofaso, Anthony, 615n
Logue, Dennis E., 230n, 240
London International Financial Futures Exchange (LIFFE), 838, 843
London Stock Exchange (LSE), 83, 118, 133–134, 141–142
Long, Robert, 597n
Longs Drug Stores, 683, 700
Lonski, John G., 624n
Lorie, James, 235n, 284n
Love, Kathryn S., 91, 100n
Lowenstein, Roger, 596n
LSE. *See* London Stock Exchange
Lucas, Douglas J., 597n, 624n

Ma, Christopher K., 132n
Ma, Zhewei, 231n
Macaulay, Frederick R., 565, 610
MacBeth, James, 212n, 902
MacBeth, R., 313, 315
MacKinley, A. Craig, 213n
McCabe, Richard T., 771n
McCarthy, Joseph, 1024n
McConnell, John J., 221, 232n
McCulloch, J. Huston, 559n
McCulloch, Robert, 329n
McDonald, Bill, 217
McDonald, John G., 978
McDonald's, 82, 433
McDonnell Douglas, 806
McElroy, Marjorie B., 328
McEnally, Richard W., 218, 314, 549n
McGoldrick, Beth, 111n
McGough, Robert, 135n, 810n
McGraw-Hill, 196
McKelvey, Edward, 462n
McNees, Stephen K., 628n
Madden, Gerald P., 235
Maginn, John L., 1029n
Mahoney, James M., 569n, 572n
Mains, Norman E., 976
Makhija, Anil K., 476n
Malkiel, Burton G., 141n, 228n, 243, 317, 562, 759, 873, 970n, 979
Mandel, Steven, 616n
Mandelker, Gershon, 95n, 476n
Mao, James S., 758, 759, 760
Markowitz, Harry, 22, 207, 253, 261, 277, 278, 279, 280, 810
Marr, M., 498n
Marsh, Paul, 226

Marsh, Terry A., 221, 225
Marshall, John F., 920n
Marshall, William, 548n, 846n
Marston, Felicia C., 737
Martin, John D., 978
Massey, Paul H., 778n
Masulis, Ronald W., 230
Matthur, Ike, 228, 317
Mayers, David, 237
Mayhew, Stewart, 901n
Mazuy, Kay K., 978n
MBA Investment Fund, L.L.C., 1013–1014
Media General Financial Services, Inc., 203, 787
Mello, Antonio S., 933n
Mendenhall, Richard R., 219, 238
Merc. *See* Chicago Mercantile Exchange
Merck, 747, 853–854
Merjos, Anne, 173n
Merrill Lynch, 44, 112, 113, 143, 167, 186, 292, 311, 545n, 599, 600, 645n, 785, 792, 795–798, 948–951, 974
Merrill Lynch Capital Markets Group, 187
Merrill Lynch, Pierce, Fenner & Smith. *See* Merrill Lynch
Merton, Robert C., 347n, 359n, 904, 1015
Merville, Larry J., 902
Metallgesellschaft A. G., 832
Meyers, Stephen L., 434n, 682n
Michaely, R., 230n
Microsoft, 82, 747
MidAmerica Commodity Exchange (MCE), 838
Mikuni's Credit Rating Company, 514
Milken, Michael, 512
Miller, Merton H., 66n, 107n, 309n, 312, 443n, 715n, 750n, 758
Miller, Robert E., 230n, 979
Miller, Thomas W., Jr., 347n
Milligan, John W., 111n
Min, Sang Kee, 416n, 417n
Mitchell, Constance, 507n
Modest, David M., 977
Modigliani, Franco, 443n, 715n, 750n, 758
Mohan, Nancy J., 1015n
Mohebbi, Cyrus, 504n
Moody's, 191, 194, 497–499, 514, 951
Moore, Geoffrey H., 434n, 461n, 463n, 464n, 469n
Moore, W. T., 498n
Morgan Grenfell SMALLCap Fund, Inc., 971
Morgan Stanley, 112, 113, 143, 186, 977
Morningstar, 200, 983, 990
Mossavar-Rahmani, Sharmin, 165n, 593n, 805n
Mossin, J., 280
Motorola, Inc., 790–792
Mueller, Gerhard G., 416n
Mullins, David W., Jr., 597n
Municipal Bond Insurance Association (MBIA), 521
Municipal Bond Investors Assurance (MBIA), 507
Munnell, Alicia, 240n
Murphy, Brian, 548n

Myer, C. F., 87n
Myers, Stewart C., 110n

Nam, Sang Oh, 416n, 417n
Nammacher, Scott A., 598
Napolitano, Gabrielle, 471n, 472n, 473n
NASDAQ, 84, 121, 122, 123–125, 183, 202, 779
National Association of Insurance Commissioners (NAIC), 53, 54
National Association of Securities Dealers Automatic Quotations. *See* NASDAQ
National Bureau of Economic Research (NBER), 461, 462–463, 466–467
National Consumer Finance Association, 190
Nemerever, William L., 615n
Nesbitt, Stephen L., 981
Netscape Communications Corp., 110
Neuberger, B. M., 230n
Newbold, Paul, 498n, 738n
New Orleans, University of, 202
New York Mercantile Exchange (NYM), 827
New York Stock Exchange (NYSE), 83, 113, 114, 115–116, 120, 121, 135, 137, 138, 139, 140, 141, 183, 184, 191, 202, 214, 224, 779, 784, 786, 852, 968
New York Stock Exchange Fixed Income Market, 112
New York Times Information Service, 203
Niederhoffer, Victor, 235n
Nikko, 142, 515
Nippon Investors Service, Inc., 514
Nissan, 82
No-Load Mutual Fund Association, Inc., 972n
Nomura, 142, 515
Nomura Research Institute (NRI), 187
Nomura Securities Company, Ltd., 187n
North Holland Publishing Company, 200, 202
Nunn, Kenneth P., Jr., 235
NYSE. *See* New York Stock Exchange

Oberhelman, H. Dennis, 974n
Officer, Dennis T., 83n
Officer, R. R., 284n
Ohlson, 230n
Olsen, Chris, 219
Options Clearing Corporation (OCC), 874
Oxford University Press, 201

Pacific Bell, 517, 519
Pacific Stock Exchange (PSE), 120, 121, 874
Packer, Frank, 497n
Pardee, Scott E., 68n
Paris Bourse, 142
Park, H. Y., 835
Patel, Jayendu, 979
Pathmark Corp., 519
Patterson, Jerry E., 88n

Paul, Richard, 434n
PBW Exchange, 120, 121
Pearson, Charles, 165n, 1026, 1027n
Peavy, John W., 223, 230n
Peers, Alexandra, 88n
Peifer, Daralyn B., 165n, 593n, 1028n
Penman, 230n
Penn Central, 82
Pepsico, 433
Percival, John, 624
Perfect, Steven, 228, 317
Perry, Kevin J., 512n
Pesaran, M. Hashem, 218
Peterson, David, 238, 739n, 740n
Peterson, Pamela P., 243n, 739n, 740n
Pettengill, Glenn, 228, 317
Pettit, R. Richardson, 235
Pflamm, Christopher C., 311
Philadelphia Stock Exchange (PHLX), 874, 877
PHLX. *See* Philadelphia Stock Exchange (PHLX)
Pier 1 Corp., 519
Pierce, Douglas, 233
Pierce, Phyllis S., 154n
Pinches, George E., 215n, 628, 941
Pinegar, J. Michael, 221
Pinnerty, J., 956n
Pitts, Mark, 567n, 572n, 576n, 577n
Pollack, I. M., 109n
Pontiff, Jeffrey, 970n
Porsche, 82
Porter, Michael E., 689, 690n, 707n, 721, 749
Porter, R. Burr, 310
Poterba, James M., 284n
Power, William, 44n, 127n, 129n, 138n
Pridson, M., 956n
Procter & Gamble, 825
Pruitt, Stephen W., 215n
PSE. *See* Pacific Stock Exchange
Put and Call Brokers and Dealers Association, 874
Putka, Gary, 127n
Pye, Gordon, 498n

Quaker Oats, 374, 375–381, 383–393, 393–398, 398–405, 407–408, 408–411
Quotron Systems, Inc., 203

Rahman, Shafiqur, 1016
Raina, Dijjotam, 810n
Ramaswamy, K., 309n
Ranson, R. David, 778n
Rashavan, Anita, 116n
Redington, F. M., 609
Reichenstein, William, 658
Reid, Kenneth, 226, 315n, 737
Reilly, Frank K., 69n, 73n, 94n, 96n, 132n, 137n, 165, 166n, 167, 168n, 169n, 171n, 173n, 229–230, 233, 292–293, 296n, 298, 312, 320, 321n, 322n, 476n, 514n, 567n, 580, 593, 595n, 596n, 597n, 598n, 623–624, 625, 626, 627, 659n, 682–683, 697n, 784n, 1018, 1020n, 1022n, 1024n

Reinganum, Marc R., 219, 221, 224, 225, 300, 327–328, 835
Rendleman, Richard J., Jr., 219, 894n
Rentzler, Joel, 309n, 328
Rhone-Poulenc, 706
Rich, Steven P., 658
Richards, Malcolm, 970n
Richards, Thomas M., 1028, 1029
Richmond, Richard D., 213n
Ritchie, John, 508n
Rite Aid, 683, 700
Ritter, Jay R., 230n, 231n, 232
Robert Morris Associates, 382
Rochester, University of, 200–201
Rock, K., 230n
Roenfeldt, Rodney L., 311
Rogalski, Richard J., 222, 940
Rogowski, Robert J., 111n
Roley, Vance, 233
Roll, Richard, 149n, 150n, 220, 224, 229, 233n, 297–298, 300, 305, 318, 322, 325, 326, 329, 472, 627, 852, 905, 994, 1016–1017, 1019
Rosenberg, Barr, 226, 315n, 737
Rosenberg, Michael R., 453n, 494n, 605n
Ross, Stephen A., 87n, 207, 298, 300, 305, 323, 325, 326, 329, 472, 835, 894n
Rossi, Peter, 329n
Royce Value Trust, 971
Rozeff, Michael S., 217, 221, 235n, 471n, 657
Rubinstein, Mark, 357n, 884, 894n, 902
Ryals, Stanley D., 711n

Salomon, Ezra, 443n
Salomon Brothers, Inc., 113, 143, 186, 187, 547n, 600, 616n, 971
Salwen, Kevin, 111n
Samurai Market, 82
Sandler, Linda, 785n
Sanvicente, Antonio Z., 628
Sargan, Nicholas, 500n
SAS Corporation, 338–340, 344, 346, 881, 882, 885
Sauvain, Harry, 508n
Savage, Leonard J., 252
Schatz, Eric A., 490n
Schering, 706
Schlarbaum, Gary G., 221, 1017, 1019
Schneller, Meir I., 939n
Schoenhotz, Kermit L., 500n
Scholes, Myron, 309n, 312–313, 359n, 897
Schramm, Sabine, 246n
Schwartz, Anna J., 470
Schwartz, Arthur L., Jr., 132n
Schwartz, Robert A., 107n
Schwert, G. William, 284n
Sears, R. Stephen, 314
Seligman, Daniel, 793n
Semmens, Robert F., 939n
Sender, Manny, 142n
Sequin, P. J., 112n
Seward, James K., 940
Seyhun, H. Nejat, 235, 236n
Shakla, Ravi, 329n
Shanken, Jay, 227–228, 300, 308, 317, 329

Sharpe, William F., 22, 207, 239n, 280, 293n, 300n, 312, 330n, 976, 998, 1006
Shaw, W. H., 230n
Shawky, Hany A., 978
Sheehan, T. J., 740n
Shefrin, Hersh, 228n, 716n, 737
Shellans, Steve, 434n
Sherbin, Robert, 22n
Shevlin, Terry, 219
Shiller, Robert, 95, 217
Shipman, William G., 778n
Shiskin, Julius, 463n
Shleifer, Andrei, 970n
Showers, Janet L., 935n
Shukla, Ravi, 239
Shulka, Ray, 1029n
Siconolfi, Michael, 82n, 111n, 129n
Sidhu, Rupinder, 567n, 580, 1024n
Siegel, Jeremy J., 461n
Siegel, Laurence B., 91, 100n
Simon, Babe E., 597n
Simon Graduate School of Management (University of Rochester), 200–201
Sindelar, Jody L., 230n
Singer, Brian D., 56n, 1013, 1014
Singleton, Clay, 628
Sinquefield, Rex A., 58n, 89–90, 91n, 626n, 656n, 659, 668
Slater, Karen, 129n
Sloan, Richard G., 227–228, 317
Smidt, Seymour, 221
Smirlock, Michael, 222, 852
Smith, Clifford W., Jr., 108n, 234, 887n
Smith, Donald J., 347n, 832, 845, 870n, 917n, 925, 929, 956n
Smith, Ralph E., 476n
Smith, Stanley D., 238–239
Smithson, Charles, 887n
Smyth, David, 119n
Snapple, 392
Snow, Karl, 228, 317
Society for Financial Studies, 201
Soldofsky, Robert M., 624, 625n
Solnik, Bruno, 76n, 858
Solof, Robert, 514n
Solomon, Ezra, 715n, 750n, 758
Solt, Michael, 235–236, 716n, 747n
Sondhi, Ashwinpaul C., 400n, 599n
Sorensen, Eric H., 109n, 111n, 507n, 925n
Sosin, Howard B., 312n
Soules, Scott, 948n
Source Capital, Inc., 971
Southern Finance Association, 201
Southwestern Finance Association, 201
Spilman, Jim, 948n
Spiro, Peter S., 284n
Spitzfaden, James, 232n
Spokane Stock Exchange, 120
Sprinkel, Beryl W., 471n
Squires, Jan B., 590n, 605n, 1011n, 1014n
Stacks, Laura, 222
Stambaugh, Robert F., 217n, 222, 308
Standard & Poor's Corporation, 184, 188, 189, 190, 191, 192, 193, 202, 240, 382, 497–499, 600, 645, 951

Standard Oil, 967
Statman, Meir, 228n, 285n, 292, 312, 358n, 490n, 716n, 737, 747n
Stein, Jerome L., 833
Steiner, Robert, 806n
Stern, Stewart, & Co., 740
Sternberg, Joel S., 347n
Stevens, Jerry L., 434n
Stewart, G. Bennett, III, 740
Stickel, Scott E., 237
Stoll, Hans R., 125n, 140n, 225, 347n
Stonehill, Arthur J., 416n, 417n
Strebel, Paul, 225–226
Summers, Lawrence H., 284n
Sun, Tong-sheng, 925
Sundaresan, Surech, 925
Sunder, Shyam, 233n
Swales, George S., Jr., 810n
Syed, Axmat A., 238–239

Taggart, Robert A., Jr., 512n
Taylor, Martin E., 412n
Thale, Richard, 970n
Theisen, Rolf D., 979
Theobald, Michael, 311
Thomas, Jacob K., 219
Thompson, Donald J., II, 23n
Thompson, T., 498n
Thomson, Robert, 142n
Throop, Adrian W., 628n
Tierney, David E., 1028, 1029
Time, Inc., 194, 196
Timmermann, Allann, 218
Tinic, Seha M., 221, 901
Titman, Sheridan, 230, 977, 979, 1017
Tito, Dennis A., 1021, 1022n, 1023n
Tobin, James, 286
Todd, Russell, 22n
Tokyo Stock Exchange (TSE), 85, 117–118, 121, 133, 142, 183
Tole, Thomas M., 285n, 310
Torres, Craig, 125n, 138n

Tracey, Mark, 706n, 707n, 708n, 743n, 744n, 745n, 746n, 747n, 748n
Treynor, Jack L., 239n, 978n, 995–996, 1006
Tri-Continental Corporation, 971
Trivoli, George W., 235
T. Rowe Price, 980
Trzcinka, Charles, 239, 329n, 1029n
TSE. *See* Tokyo Stock Exchange
Tully, S., 740n
Turner, John A., 240n
Tuttle, Donald L., 593n, 648, 650, 651, 1029n

Ujiie, Junichi, 416n, 417n
United Business Service Company, 983
Unlisted Securities Market (USM), 122–123
Upton, David E., 311
Urwitz, Gabrial, 498n
Ushman, Neal L., 490n

Value Line (VL), 194, 195, 200, 202, 203, 235, 236–238, 241, 292, 311
Vandell, Robert F., 434n
Van Eck, Tracy Hudson, 510n
Van Gogh, Vincent, 88
Van Horne, James C., 232n, 399n, 546n, 624n
Vasicek, Oldrich, 165n, 1026, 1027n
Veit, E. Theodore, 978
Venkatesh, P. C., 235
Viner, Aron, 500n, 515n
Viswanathan, S., 112n
VL. *See* Value Line
Vock, Thomas, 593n
Vu, Joseph, 787n

Wachowicz, J. M., 507n
Wagner, Jerry, 434n

Wagner, Wayne H., 1021, 1022n, 1023n
Wahab, Mahmoud, 83n
Wainscott, Craig B., 1011n
Waldman, Michael, 509n
Walgreen Company, 683, 700, 717–721, 722–739
Wall Street Journal, The, 185
Wal-Mart, 82, 443, 747, 754
Walmsley, Julian, 952n
Walter, John R., 470n
Wang, Ching, 925
Wang, J., 213n
Wang, Zhenyu, 317
Ward, David J., 597n
Warga, Arthur D., 113n
Warner, Jerald B., 234
Washington, University of, 201
Wasley, Charles, 215n
Wassel, David, 463n
Watts, Ross L., 219
Webb, James, 87n
Wei, John, 314
Weigel, Eric J., 1015
Weil, Roman L., 569n, 610, 612
Weinberger, Alfred, 616n, 617, 619n, 620n, 621n, 622n
Weinstein, Mark I., 329, 627, 628
Wells Fargo Bank, 245
Wells Fargo Investment Advisors, 245
West, Richard R., 221, 229
Westerfield, Randolph, 314
Whaley, Robert E., 225, 905
White, Gerald I., 400n
White, James A., 246n, 808n
White, Richard E., 215n
Whitford, David T., 498n, 738n, 784n
Widder, Pat, 138n
Wiesenberger, Arthur, Services, 198, 983
Wigmore, Barrie A., 596n

Wiles, Kenneth, 228, 317
Wilford, D. Sykes, 887n
Wilhelm, William J., Jr., 232
Williams, George O., 576n
Williams, J. B., 438n
Williams, Terry, 246n
Wilson, Jack W., 901n
Wilson, Richard, 508n, 511n
Winkelmann, Kurt, 576n
Wolff, Eric D., 597n
Wolkowitz, Benjamin, 546n
Womach, Kent L., 239
Won, David, 548n
Wong, Tom, 608n
Woolford, W. David, 546n
Woolridge, Randall, 659
Wright, David J., 69n, 73n, 137n, 165, 166n, 167, 169n, 171n, 173n, 292–293, 312, 593, 598n, 623–624, 625, 626, 659n, 1022n
W. T. Grant, 82
Wubbels, Rolf E., 789n
Wyatt, Edward A., 132n, 152n
WYX Corp., 889–893

Xerox, 125, 967

Yago, Glenn, 512n
Yaksick, Rudy, 928
Yamaichi, 142, 514
Yates, James W., Jr., 360n
Yawitz, Jess B., 548n, 846n
Yoon, Young, 810n

Zaman, Mir A., 235
Zarb, F. G., 109n
Zeckhauser, Richard, 979
Zeller, Thomas, 697n
Zhu, Yu, 608n
Zimmerman, Thomas A., 504n
Zisler, Randall, 87n
Zweig, Martin E., 185n, 777n
Zweig Fund, Inc., The, 971

Subject Index

Aaa bonds, 27
Abnormal rate of return, 216
ABS. *See* Asset-backed securities (ABS)
Academic journals, 200–202
Accounting
changes in, 233
principles of, 411–412, 414–415
Accounting statements, non-U.S. formats for, 411
Accrued interest, 540
fixed-income obligations and, 519
Accumulation phase, of investment life cycle, 39
Active bond portfolio management, 593–607
bond swaps as, 601–605
contingent procedures and, 616–622
credit analysis as, 595–600
global fixed-income strategy and, 605–607
interest anticipation as, 593–595
valuation analysis as, 595
yield spread analysis as, 600–601
Active equity portfolio management, 805–810
futures in, 817–818
trading activity in, 806
Actual rate of return, 52
ADRs. *See* American Depository Receipts (ADRs)
Advance-decline series, 785
Agencies, securities from U.S. and foreign governments, 79–81, 496. *See also* Information sources
Aggregated coefficients model, 224
Aggregate market analysis, with efficient capital markets, 242
Aggregate operating profit margin, 648–649
Aggregate security-market analysis, 182–187
brokerage firm reports, 186–187
commercial publications, 183–186
government publications, 182–183
Allocation, of assets, 37
Alternative bond portfolio strategies. *See* Bond portfolio management
Alternative trading systems, 114
AM. *See* Arithmetic mean
American Banker, The, 183, 186
American Banker Yearbook, 183
American convention method, 854
American Depository Receipts (ADRs), 83, 122
American options, 337
American shares, 83

American Stock Exchange (AMEX), 113, 115, 116–117. *See also* Stock exchanges
NYSE and, 779
options traded on, 874
American-style options, valuing, 905–906
AMEX. *See* American Stock Exchange (AMEX)
AMEX Fact Book, 183
Analysis. *See also* Company analysis; Industry analysis; Stock market analysis; Technical analysis
aggregate security-market information, 182–187
attribution, 1010–1014
country, 480–481
of country equity market growth, 672–674
cross-sectional, 382
fundamental, 242–244
growth, 406–408
of growth companies, 747–762
of individual stocks and bonds, 190–194
industry, 188–190, 679–680
of non-U.S. financial statements, 411–417
of ratios, 409–411
of risk, 396–405
of stock market, 640–641
technical, 241–242
theoretical and empirical, 200–202
time-series, 382–383
of world security markets, 477–483
Analysis effect, 1022
Analysts, evaluating, 243
Annual Report of the SEC, 182–183
Annual reports, 190
Annual security-market publications, 183–184
Anomalies, in EMH, 209
Antiques
historical risk/returns on, 94–95
investing in, 88
Approximate yield to call (AYC), 534–535
APT. *See* Arbitrage pricing theory (APT)
A-rated bonds, 498
Arbitrage, 334
covered interest, 858–859
stock index, 850
Arbitrage pricing theory (APT), 29, 278, 297–300
alternative testing techniques for, 329
and anomalies, 327–329
CAPM, 322–327

defined, 298
empirical tests of, 325
and inflation, 328–329
January effect and, 328
Roll-Ross study of, 325–326
Shanken challenge to, 329
Arbitrage trading, Eurodollar (or LIBOR) futures and, 844
Arithmetic mean (AM), 8
Art
historical risk/returns on, 94–95
investing in, 88
Asian Wall Street Journal, 185
Asset(s). *See also* Asset allocation; Risk; Risk-free asset; Turnover
basis of, 48
characteristic line of, 291
classes of, 77
correlations between returns on, 93
current, 383–385
financial, 77
global allocation of, 460–461
liquidity of, 47
liquidity risk and, 20–21
low liquidity investments as, 77
marketability of, 106
in portfolio, 252
real, 77
relative risk of, 93
return and risk on, 57–61, 91–92
risk premium for, 23
swap agreement as, 924
tactical allocation of, 354
undervalued and overvalued, 290–291
Asset allocation, 37
and cultural differences, 61, 62
equity swap and, 936
futures contracts in, 812
by institutional investors, 55–61
insured, 820
integrated, 819
real investment returns after taxes and costs, 56
by risk, 44
selecting method for, 820
strategic, 819–820
tactical, 819
worldwide, 482, 483
Asset-backed securities (ABS), 507, 510
Asset class attribution analysis, 1011–1014
Asset/equity, 665
ratio for foreign stocks, 455–456
Asset pricing models, 277–278. *See also* Capital asset pricing model (CAPM)
arbitrage pricing theory (APT) and, 297–300

capital asset pricing model (CAPM) and, 287–297
capital market theory and, 278–287
Asset turnover, 664
for foreign stocks, 455
Association for Investment Management and Research (AIMR), 679
Associations
for Chartered Financial Analyst, 1037
trade, 188–190
Asymmetric expiration date payoffs, 341
Attention, and neglect, 225–226
At-the-money, 337
Attribution analysis, 1010–1014
Auction market, 114
Auctions, on Treasury bills, notes, and bonds, 108
Autocorrelation tests, 212
AYC. *See* Approximate yield to call (AYC)

Baa ratings, 26, 27
Backtested strategies, 809
Balanced funds, 85, 973
Balance sheet, 375
comparative formats for, 412
quality of, 417–418
sample of, 377
Balance sheet ratios, financial risk and, 399–402
Bank(s)
information from, 182
institutional investments and, 54–55
publications of, 180–181
regulation of, 55
Bank accounts, for cash reserve, 38
Bank and Quotation Record, 198
Bank bonds, in Japan, 515
Bankers. *See* Investment bankers
Banking World, 185
Bank of Japan. *See* Japan
Bankruptcy, financial ratios and, 421
Banks for Cooperatives, 79
Bar charting, 792
Bargaining power
of buyers, 690–691
of suppliers, 691
Barriers to entry. *See* Entry barriers
Barriers to exit. *See* Exit barriers
Barron's, 155, 183, 184–185, 198
Confidence Index of, 782–783
mutual fund information from, 983
Basis
of asset, 48
defined, 831
hedging and, 830–832

Basis point value, of Eurodollar futures contract, 844–845
Basis risk, 832
Bearer bond, 491
Bearish sentiments, DJIA and, 780
Bear money spread, 885–886
Beginning-wealth value, 538–539
Benchmark, GSMI series and, 168n
Benchmark error, 318–322, 994
bond portfolio and, 1028
defined, 1017
and global investing, 1017–1019
implications of, 1019–1021
Benchmark index, sampling and, 804
Benchmark issue, in Japanese bonds, 501
Benchmark portfolio, 42, 803
as "normal" portfolio, 805–806
Benefits, in pension plans, 52–53
Best-effort basis, 110
Beta, 289. See also Risk
bond portfolio and, 624–625
for bonds, 627
comparability of published estimates of, 311–312
computation with selected indexes, 295
stability of, 310–311
time intervals and, 292–293
trading to adjust, 816
Bias, of one-parameter measures, 1004–1005
Bibliographies, 182
Big Bang, 141–142
Bills, Treasury, 197
Binomial valuation model, 873
of options, 893–897
Biweekly magazines, 196
"Black Monday," 901–902
Black-Scholes-Merton options pricing model, 627
Black-Scholes valuation model, 873, 897–900, 904
foreign currency options and, 908–909
futures options and, 909
stock index options and, 907–908
Block houses, 136
Block trades, 136–137
Block uptick-downtick ratio, 787–788
Blue-chip stocks, ratings of, 154–155
Blue List of Current Municipal Offerings, The, 198, 521
Bond(s), 490–491. See also Bond portfolio management; Bond price volatility; Bond valuation; Bond yields; Corporate bonds; Global bond market; High-yield bonds; Interest rates; Preferred stock; Yields
alternative issues of, 500–517
analysis of, 190–194, 525–526
bank, 515
bearer, 491
calculating future prices for, 536–541
callable, 576–577
collateral trust, 80
commercial publications about, 191–194
commodity-linked bull and bear, 952–953

company-generated information about, 190–191
convertible, 80, 942–945
corporate, 79–81, 109–111
currency swaps and, 934
cushion, 594
debentures, 80
deep discount, 511
domestic government, 500–502
dual currency, 947–948
equipment trust certificates, 80
Eurobond, 81
features of, 490–494
general obligation, 79, 109
high-yield, 511–514
historical risk/returns on, 89–91
income, 80
indenture provisions of, 492
information on, 197–198
interest rates and, 474–475
international, 81–82, 516–517
intrinsic features of, 491–492
junk, 511
maturities of, 492–493
mean rate of return and standard deviation of returns for, 626
minicoupon, 511
municipal, 79, 108–109
outstanding, by country, 495
price information for, 517–521, 522
quotations on, 517–521, 522
rates of return on, 493–494
ratings of, 26–27, 497–499
refunding issues, 492
registered, 491
revenue, 79, 492
secured (senior), 79–80, 492
serial obligation, 491
sources of quotes for, 198
speculative-grade, 511
subordinated (junior) debentures, 80, 492
tax-exempt, 540–541
term, 491
Treasury, 108
types of, 491–492
unsecured (debentures), 492
valuation of, 436–437, 525–526
warrants and, 80–81, 507
Yankee, 81–82
zero coupon, 81, 511
Bond Buyer, The, 186, 198
Bond Buyer Yearbook, The, 183–184
Bond convexity, 569–575
computation of, 574–575
determinants of, 573
modified duration and, 573
price-yield relationship and, 570–573
Bond duration, futures contracts and, 845–846
Bond funds, 85, 973–974
Bond indexes, correlations among monthly, 169, 170, 171
Bond market
global structure of, 494–499
international return-risk results, 71
returns in global, 69–70
secondary, 112–113
technical analysis of, 797–798
Bond-market efficiency, 627–628

Bond-market indicator series, 165–167. See also Stock-market indicator series (indexes)
global government bond market, 167
high-yield bond indexes, 167
investment-grade bond indexes, 165–166
Bond market line, 1021–1024
Bond portfolio. See also Bond portfolio management
correlation coefficient in rates of return, 73–74
EMH and, 627–628
global risk in, 73–74
risk-return tradeoff for international, 75
Bond portfolio analysis, performance consistency, 1028
Bond portfolio management, 591
active, 591, 593–607, 616–622
bond-market efficiency and, 627–628
capital market theory and, 624–627
contingent immunization and, 616, 617–622
contingent procedure (structured active management), 591
matched-funding techniques for, 591, 607–616
passive management strategies for, 591, 592–593
total portfolio theory and, 623–624
Bond portfolio performance, evaluation of, 1021–1029
Bond portfolio returns, decomposing, 1024–1026
Bond price volatility, 561–580
defined, 562
duration measures and, 565–568
modified duration and, 568–569
trading strategies and, 564
Bond rates of return, annual, 171–173
Bond ratings
description of, 498, 499
financial ratios and, 420
of Japanese bonds, 514
Bond swaps, 601–605
Bond valuation. See also Bond yields
interest rate determination and, 543–554
present value model for, 526–528
with spot rates, 541–543
yield model for, 528–530
Bond yield books, 541
Bond yields
computing, 529–536
current, 530
nominal, 528–530
promised yield to call and, 534–535
promised yield to maturity and, 530–534
realized (horizon) yield, 535–536
Books, for bond yields. See Bond yield books
Book-to-market equity, 315
Book-to-market value, CAPM and, 315
Book value-market value ratio, 226
Borrowers, 544
Borrowing rates, CAPM and, 306

B-rated bonds, 498
Breakeven time, 944
Brinson Partners Global Security Market Index (GSMI). See Global Security Market Index (GSMI)
Broker
commission, 126
floor, 126
investment banker as, 110
Brokerage accounts, credit balances in, 779
Brokerage firms, reports of, 186–187, 194
Bullish price pattern, 789
Bullish sentiments, DJIA and, 780
Bull money spread, 885–886
Bund bonds, 501–502
Business and Investment Almanac, 184
Business cycle
indicators of, 463–464
monitoring of, 461–462
NBER on, 462–463
performance measures and, 466
stock market and, 807
Business One Irwin Investor's Handbook, 184
Business risk, 20, 700
analysis of, 398–399
Business Statistics, 180
Business Week, 196–197, 200
Leading Indicator Series, 467, 468
"Mutual Fund Scoreboard," 983, 987–988
Butterfly spread, 886–887
Buy-and-hold strategy, 592
Buyers, as competitive force, 690–691
BV/MV ratio. See Book value-market value ratio

Calendar effects, 222–223
January anomaly and, 220–222
Calendar spread, 884
Call
covered, 354
margin, 130
markets, 114
option, 84
provisions, 79
Callable bonds
duration and convexity for, 576–577
value of, 601
Call monetization
defined, 930
with swaptions, 929, 930
Call options, 337. See also Option contracts
Black-Scholes model and, 873
currency, 876
European-style, 899
payoffs for, 341–344
portfolio payoffs and, 360–362
terminal payoffs to, 345
Call premium, 492
Canada. See Toronto Stock Exchange
Cap agreement, 916, 925, 927–928
Capital
EVA return on, 741–742
return on, 392
Capital appreciation, 46

Capital asset pricing model (CAPM), 29, 278, 287–297. *See also* Arbitrage pricing theory (APT)
arbitrage pricing theory and (APT), 322–327
benchmark errors and, 318–322
bond portfolio performance evaluation and, 1021
bonds and, 624–627
book-to-market value and, 315
defined, 287
and differential borrowing and lending rates, 306
empirical tests of, 310–312
Jensen performance measure and, 1000–1001
market portfolio concept and, 317–318
planning periods and, 309
quarterly earnings studies and, 218–219
risk, return, and, 312–317
risk variables of, 314
security market line and, 288–297
Capital gains
bonds and, 494
in long-run growth models, 753
realized, 48
unrealized, 48
Capital market(s). *See also* Efficient markets hypothesis (EMH)
changes in, 27
conditions of, 18
efficient, 208–209
expected inflation, security market line, and, 28
implications of efficient, 241–247
nominal risk-free rate and, 17
primary, 108–111
return on world, 92
securities in, 68–69
total investable, 69
Capital market instruments, 78–81
convertible bonds as, 80
corporate bonds as, 79–80
debentures as, 80
income bonds as, 80
municipal bonds as, 79
preferred stock as, 80–81
subordinated bonds as, 80
U.S. government agency securities as, 79
U.S. Treasury securities as, 78–79
warrants as, 80–81
Capital market line (CML), 283
optimal portfolio combinations in, 286
risk measure for, 286–287
and separation theorem, 285–286
Capital market theory, 22, 278–287
assumptions of, 279
and bond portfolio management, 624–627
Capital preservation, 46
CAPM. *See* Capital asset pricing model (CAPM)
Careers, Chartered Financial Analyst (CFA), 1037
CARs. *See* Certificates for automobile receivables (CARs)
Cash conversion, cycle of, 388
Cash flow
alternative measures of, 405

from bonds, 519
from financing activities, 380
from operations, 380–381
statement of, 376–380
Cash flow coverage ratio, 404
Cash flow/interest expense, 403–404
Cash flow/long-term debt ratio, 404–405
Cash flow ratios, 402–405
Cash flow/total debt ratio, 405
Cash-matching dedication, horizon matching and, 615
Cash positions, mutual fund, 777–778
Cash ratio, 386, 409, 777
Cash reserve, 38
CBOE. *See* Chicago Board Options Exchange (CBOE)
CBOT. *See* Chicago Board of Trade (CBOT)
CDs. *See* Certificates of deposit (CDs)
Center for International Business Cycle Research (CIBCR), 462
Leading Employment Index of, 469
Leading Inflation Index of, 469
Long-Leading Index of, 467–469
Centralized reporting, 137–138
Certificates for automobile receivables (CARs), 510
Certificates of deposit (CDs), 78
CFA. *See* Chartered Financial Analyst
Changes, rates and direction of, 466
Characteristic line
of asset, 291–293
computations of, 293–297
Charitable contributions, 53
Chartered Financial Analyst (CFA), 1037
Charts and charting
bar, 792
multiple indicator, 792
point-and-figure, 793–795
Cheapest to deliver bond, 839
Chicago Board of Trade (CBOT), 113
Chicago Board Options Exchange (CBOE) and, 874
financial futures and, 85
futures contracts and, 827
T-bonds and, 838
Chicago Board Options Exchange (CBOE), 874
options traded on, 874
put/call ratio of, 782
Chicago Mercantile Exchange (CME), 113, 843
financial futures and, 85
Chooser options, 884
CIBCR. *See* Center for International Business Cycle Research (CIBCR)
Classical immunization
application of, 614–615
example of, 611
and interest rate risk, 609–610
Clearinghouse, of futures exchange, 336
Closed-end investment company, 968–971

closed-end fund index and, 970–971
CME. *See* Chicago Mercantile Exchange (CME)
CML. *See* Capital market line (CML)
CMOs. *See* Collateralized mortgage obligations (CMOs)
Code of ethics, and professional conduct standards, 1039–1040
Coefficient, credit analysis and, 598. *See also* Correlation coefficient
Coefficient of variation, 15
business risk and, 398
computation of, 34–35
Coincident indicators, 464
Coins, investing in, 88–89
Collars, interest rate, 926–928
Collateral, 80. *See also* Margin
forward contracts and, 335
investor's equity and, 129
Collateralized mortgage obligations (CMOs), 508–509
Collateral trust bonds, 80, 508
Combined country investments, risk of, 71–77
COMEX. *See* Commodity Exchange (COMEX)
Commercial banks, information from, 181
Commercial bonds, in Germany, 515
Commingled Real Estate Funds (CREFs), 95
Commission brokers, 126
Commission rates, negotiated, 135–136
Commodity Exchange (COMEX), 827
Commodity exchanges, futures contracts on, 84–85
Commodity futures quotations, 829–830
Commodity-linked bull and bear bonds, 952–953
Commodity swaps, 937–939
Common size statements, 383
of income, 392
sample of, 384, 385
Common stock, 82–83. *See also* Stock; Stock valuation
calculating expected rate of return on, 669–674
correlation coefficients between price returns on, 75
dividend discount model and, 438–443
effective duration for, 580
foreign, 83–84
in global companies, 744, 745
income payouts from, 61
indexes for domestic, 809
infinite period model for valuing, 441–443
mean rate of return and standard deviation of returns for, 626
valuation of, 438
valuation over multiple-year holding period, 440–441
valuation over one-year holding period, 439–440
Common stock funds, 85, 973
Compact Disclosure, 202

Company
cyclical, 717
defensive, 716–717
earnings multipliers of, 726–734
earnings per share of, 718–721
estimating value of, 717
information on stocks and bonds from, 190–191
large, 222–223
neglected, and trading activity, 225–226
no-growth, 750–751
profit margin of, 721
sales forecast of, 718–721
size of, 224–225
small, 224–225
speculative, 717
Company analysis
defensive companies and defensive stock, 716–717
with efficient capital markets, 242–243
of growth companies and growth stocks, 715–716
individual, 747
and security valuation, 433
and stock selection, 714–715
Company and stock price data, for Bayer, 747
Company performance. *See also* Performance; Performance, industry; Portfolio performance
analytical measures of, 466
of European chemical industry, 706–708
evaluation of, 993–994
of investment companies, 976–981
operating, 388–396, 409
Comparative analysis, of ratios, 409–411
Competition
basic forces of, 689–691
environment of, 689–691
and expected industry returns, 689–696
foreign, 650–651
industry, 689
among market makers, 139–140
Competitive bid, for bond sales, 108
Competitive strategy, 689
for company analysis and stock selection, 721–722
of Walgreen, 722–726
Completely diversified portfolio, 284
Completeness funds, 804–805
Composite leading indicator index, 464–465
Composite performance measures, 994, 995–1002
of Treynor, 995–998
Composite series, and ratio of series, 464–465
Composite stock-bond indexes, 167–168
Brinson Partners Global Security Market Index (GSMI), 168
Merrill-Lynch U.S. Capital Markets Index (ML-WCMI), 168
Compound realized (horizon) rate of return, 539
Comptroller of the Currency, bank regulation by, 55

Computer, for portfolio management, 810
Computer-assisted Order Routing and Execution System (CORES), 133
Computerized data sources, 202–203
Conduct. *See* Code of ethics; Professional conduct standards
Conference Board Consumer Confidence Index, 470
Confidence Index, 782–783
Consolidation period, 795
Consolidation phase, of investment cycle, 39
Constant correlation, with changing weights, 266–268
Constant growth dividend discount model (DDM), 458–459
Constraints, on portfolio, 46–51
Consumer expectations, surveys of, 469–470
Consumer price, 451
changes in, 478
Consumption, saving and, 4–5
Contingent, deferred sales loads, 973
Contingent immunization, 616, 617–622
floor portfolio and, 621
Contingent procedures, as active management, 616–622
Continuous market, 114–115
Contract. *See* Forward contracts; Futures contracts; Option contracts
Contract price, 335
Contrary-opinion rules, 777–781
CBOE put/call ratio and, 779–780
credit balances in brokerage accounts and, 779
futures traders bullish on stock index futures and, 780–781
investment advisory opinions and, 779
mutual fund cash positions and, 777–778
Convenience yield, 836
Conversion factors, on futures contracts, 839
Conversion premium, 941–942
Conversion ratio, 941
Conversion value, 941
Convertible bonds, 80, 942–945
Convertible obligations, 507
Convertible securities, 941
Convertible stock, 941–942
Convexity, 569
of bonds, 569–575
of callable bonds, 577
computation of, 574–575
determinants of, 573
CORES. *See* Computer-assisted Order Routing and Execution System (CORES)
Corporate bonds, 79–81. *See also* Bonds
call provisions of, 79
collateral trust, 80
convertible, 80
debentures, 80
default rates on, 597
equipment trust, 80
in Germany, 515–516
income, 80

indenture and, 79
and inflation, 474
issues of, 109–111
in Japan, 514–515
mean rate of return and standard deviation of returns for, 626
mortgage, 80
preferred stock and, 81
quotes for, 517–519
secondary market for, 112–113
senior secured, 79–80
sinking fund provision of, 79
subordinated, 80
in United Kingdom, 516
in United States, 507–514
warrants and, 80–81
zero coupon, 81
Corporate events, effect on stock prices, 234
Corporate growth statistics, 672
Corporate insiders, 234
insider trading and, 235–236
Corporate net profits, alternative estimates of, 647–648
Corporate stocks, issues of, 109–111. *See also* Stock
Corporations, global bond markets and, 496
Correlation, 103–104
calculation of, 104
constant, with changing weights, 266–268
covariance and, 259–261
among international returns, 479–480
among monthly bond indexes, 169, 170, 171
among monthly equity price changes, 169
negative, 264
Correlation coefficient, 259
for art, antiques, stocks, bonds, and inflation (1976–1991), 96
in rates of return, 72, 73
Cost of carry, 836
Cost of equity, 749
Cost of funds, interest rate as, 18
Costs, transaction, 107
Counterparties, 335
Country analysis, 480–481
and global portfolio management, 806–807
Country real GDP growth and inflation, forecasts for, 671
Country (political) risk, 21–22, 453, 700
for combined country investments, 71–77
and return, 71
Coupon
of bond, 491
and bond price volatility, 563
and duration, 566
zero, 511
Coupon income, 491
Coupon reinvestment risk, 609
Covariance, 102–103, 255
calculation of, 103
and correlations, 259–261
of returns, 255–259
with risk-free asset, 280
Covariance of returns, computation of, 258

Coverage ratio, cash flow, 404
Covered calls, 354, 360–362
Covered interest arbitrage, 858–859
C-rated bonds, 498
Credit
leverage and, 128
margin requirement and, 129
Credit analysis
bond ratings and, 497–498
of defaulted debts, 597
of high-yield bonds, 600
models of, 598
Credit analysis strategy, 595–600
Credit balances, in brokerage accounts, 779
Credit card receivables, 510
Credit Markets, 185, 198
Credit risk
of CMOs, 509
forward contracts and, 335
Credit risk series, 657
CREFs. *See* Commingled Real Estate Funds (CREFs)
Cross hedge, 833
Crossover price, 534
Crossover yield, 534
Cross-sectional analysis, 382
Cross-sectional returns, 223–234
book value-market value ratio and, 226–228
neglected firms, trading activity, and, 225–226
price-earnings ratios and returns, 223
size effect and, 224–225
Cross-section distribution of returns, 215
Culture, asset allocation and, 61, 62
Currency, 470. *See also* Dual-currency bonds; Foreign currency options
Currency forwards, 854–860
quotations on, 855, 856
Currency futures, 854–860
application of, 859–860
Currency swap, 931–935
Current assets, 383–385
Current consumption, 5
Current income, 4, 46
Current liabilities, 383–385
Current Performance and Dividend Record (Arthur Wiesenberger Services), 199, 983
Current ratio, 383–385, 409
Current yield, 530
Curves, price-yield, 527–528. *See also* Yield curve
Cushion bond, 594
Cushion spread, 618
Cycle
business, 461–462
stock market, 776
Cyclical company, 717
Cyclical indicator approach, 462
analytical performance measures and, 466
Business Week leading indicator series, 467
to forecasting of economy, 462–470
international series and, 469
Leading Employment Index, 469
leading indicators and, 463–464

leading indicators and stock prices, 467
Leading Inflation Index, 469
limitations of, 466–467
Long-Leading Index, 467–470
surveys of sentiment and expectations, 469–470
Cyclical stock, 717

Daily security-market publications, 185–186
Daily Stock Price Records, 203
Databases, listing of on-line, 203
Data sources. *See also* Information sources
computerized, 202–203
data banks as, 202–203
DDM. *See* Dividend discount model (DDM)
Dealer market, 114
Debentures, 80, 492, 507
subordinated (junior), 492
Debt, defaulted, 597
Debt balances, in brokerage accounts, 784
Debt/equity ratio, 400–401
Debt instruments, floating rate note as, 919n
Debt ratios, financial risk and, 399–402
Decision rule, P/BV ratio as, 737–738
Declining trend channel, 776
Decomposing, of bond portfolio returns, 1024–1026
Dedicated portfolios, 607–615
Dedication, 607
with reinvestment, 608
Deep discount bonds, 511, 608
Default. *See also* Bonds
bonds and, 26
on corporate bonds, 597
Default bonds, 498
Default premium, 90
Default risk, forward contracts and, 335
Defensive companies, 716–717
Defensive stock, 716–717
Deferred call provision, 492
Defined benefit pension plans, 52
Defined contribution pension plans, 52
Delivery, of bonds, 839
Delta, 899
Demand, 544
Demand deposits, 470
Demographic Yearbook (United Nations), 181
Depreciation, industry, 692, 694
Depreciation expense, estimating, 652
Depth, in market, 107
Derivative markets, 334–337. *See also* Derivative securities
Derivative securities, 29, 333–334. *See also* Convertible securities; Forward contracts; Futures contracts; Interest rate swaps; Option contracts; Swaps; Warrants
commodity-linked bull and bear bonds, 952–953
covered calls and, 354

Derivative securities (*continued*)
  dual currency bonds, 947–948
  embedded, 945–956
  equity index-linked notes, 948–951
  in equity portfolios, 812
  forward contracts and, 354, 826
  futures contracts as, 826
  interest swaps as, 916
  investing with, 338–346
  in portfolio management, 354–362
  protective puts and, 354
  relationship between forward and
      option contracts, 347–354
  shorting forward contracts and,
      354
  Standard & Poor's 500 index
      futures contract and, 814–816
  structured notes as, 917
  swap-linked notes, 953–956
  warrants as, 917
Deutschemark bonds, 517
Developed markets, worldwide,
    148–149
Diamonds, investing in, 89
Differentiation strategy, 721, 722
Diffusion index, 466, 785
  advance and decline of, 786
Direct convention, 854
Direction of change approach, to
    estimating earnings multiplier,
    665–667
Disability insurance, 38
Discount, 528
  forward, 856
Discount bonds, 608
Discretionary account, 50
Disequilibrium, risk-free rates and,
    18
Dispersion, measures of, 34–35
Distribution, and municipal bond
    underwriting, 108–109
Distribution of wealth, asset
    allocation and, 37
Diversification
  benefits of, 60
  evaluating, 1007–1008
  international and global equity
      funds and, 976
  measuring, 284
  risk reduction through, 76
  standard deviation and, 76
  taxes and, 49
  and unsystematic risk, 284–285
Dividend-bearing securities, valuing
    options on, 903–905
Dividend discount model (DDM),
    438–443, 641
  derivation of constant growth,
      458–459
  growth companies and, 750
  infinite period, 443
  stock market valuation and, 642
Dividend growth, for foreign stocks,
    455–456
Dividend payout, active or residual
    decision about, 663–664
Dividend-payout ratio, 727
  estimating, 663
  for industry, 699
Dividends
  estimating growth rate of, 660–662
  growth rate of, 447–456
  per share, 743

preferred, 81
  put-call-spot parity and, 351–352
Dividends per share, 666
Dividend yield estimate, 657
DJIA. *See* Dow Jones Industrial
    Average
Dollar bonds, 521
Dow Jones Industrial Average
    (DJIA), 151, 153, 154–155
  advance-decline diffusion index
      and, 786
  benchmark problem and,
      1018–1019
  and CBOE put/call ratio, 782
  and futures traders bullish on stock
      index futures, 783
  and mutual fund cash ratio, 778
  and NYSE block uptick-downtick
      ratio, 788
  reports of, 155
Dow Jones World Stock Index, 162
  listings on, 164
Downtick, 787–788
Downward-sloping yield curve, 558
Dow Theory, 789
  volume and, 790
D-rated bonds, 498
Drugstore industry. *See* Retail stores-
    drug (RSD) industry
Dual currency bonds, 947–948
Duff and Phelps, ratings of, 497
Duff & Phelps Credit Decisions, 198
Dun & Bradstreet, financial ratio
    information from, 382
DuPont System, 393–394
  extended, 395–396, 397
Duration, 565
  of bond, 1022
  and bond price volatility, 568–569
  for callable bonds, 576–577
  classical immunization and,
      614–615
  closed-form equation for
      calculating, 867–868
  effective, 579–580
  to first call, 576
  growth, 754–758
  hedging and, 839–841
  interest rate anticipation and,
      593–594
  interest rate futures and, 846
  Macaulay, 565–568
  maturity and, 566, 567, 576
  measures of, 565–568
  modified, 565
  option-adjusted, 576–577
Duration strategy, 611–612
Dynamic true growth model,
    753–754

Earnings
  growth of, 406
  investment and, 4
  variability in, 398
Earnings before depreciation,
    interest, and taxes (EBDIT),
    391, 647–648
Earnings before taxes (EBT), 648
Earnings estimate, industry, 694–696
Earnings momentum, 807
Earnings multiplier, 642–645
  company, 726–734
  computing, 731–732

determinants of, 655–664, 665
  estimating, 665–669
  example of estimation, 665–669
  industry, 696–706
  and market multiple, 705
  microanalysis of, 727–732
  stock-market series, 655–669
  stock price movements and,
      643–645
  value for market series, 669
  variables influencing, 728
  Walgreen and, 726–734
Earnings multiplier model, 445–447
Earnings per share, 666
  calculating, 654–655
  of company, 718–721
  estimating expected, 645–655
  estimating for industry, 684–689
  forecasting of, 689
  in global company analysis, 743
Earnings ratios, 402–405
Earnings retention rate, for RSD
    industry, 701
Earnings surprises, 220
Earnings-to-book-equity, 228
EBDIT. *See* Earnings before
    depreciation, interest, and taxes
    (EBDIT)
EBT. *See* Earnings before taxes
    (EBT)
Economic factors, and interest rates,
    546–547
Economic forecasting. *See*
    Forecasting
Economic Indicators (publication),
    179
Economic information. *See*
    Information sources; Security-
    market indicators series
    (indexes)
*Economic Intelligence Unit, The
    (EIU)*, 181
Economic Report of the President,
    180
Economic series
  in NBER coincident and lagging
      indicator series, 464
  in NBER leading indicator group,
      463
Economic value-added (EVA),
    740–741
  and MVA, 742
Economic variables
  economy, stock prices, and,
      470–477
  in Germany, 674
Economist, The, 181, 197
Economy. *See also* Global asset
    allocation
  cyclical indicator approach to
      forecasting of, 462–470
  global asset allocation and,
      460–461
  industry and, 687
  investment opportunities and real
      RFR, 17
  money supply and, 470–471
  security markets and, 460,
      461–462
Educational institutions, contributions
    to, 53
Effective duration, 579–580
  for common stock, 580

greater than maturity, 580
  negative, 580
Efficiency
  external, 107
  informational, 107
  internal, 107
  operating, 388–390
Efficient capital markets, 208–209
  and fundamental analysis,
      242–244
  implications of, 241–247
  and technical analysis, 241–242
Efficient frontier, 270
  for alternative portfolios, 271
  and investor utility, 270–272
Efficient market, 29
  European, 246–247
  informationally, 209
  and portfolio management,
      244–246
Efficient markets hypothesis (EMH),
    208
  alternatives to, 210–212
  bonds and, 627–628
  event studies for testing, 228–234
  insider trading and, 235–236
  semistrong-form, 211, 215–234
  strong-form, 212, 234–241
  tests and results of alternative,
      212–241
  weak-form, 211, 212–215
Efficient markets hypothesis (EMH),
    size, P/E, leverage, and, 314
Efficient portfolio, 253
8-K SEC form, 190
Embedded derivative securities,
    945–956
Embedded option, 576
Emerging markets, 150
Emerging Stock Markets Factbook,
    183
EMH. *See* Efficient markets
    hypothesis (EMH)
Ending-wealth value, 531
Endowment funds, 53
Entry barriers, as competitive force,
    689–690
Environment
  competitive, 689–691
  portfolio strategies and, 61, 62
Equations. *See* equations by name
Equipment trust certificates, 80, 508
Equities International, 185
Equity
  correlations among monthly price
      changes, 169
  cost of, 749
  of investor, 129
  return on, 392–393
Equity call option, warrant as,
    939–941
Equity earnings, growth of, 406
Equity exchanges, 494
Equity indexes
  Dow Jones World Stock Index,
      162
  FT/S&P-Actuaries World Indexes,
      160, 161
  global, 160–162
  Morgan Stanley Capital
      International (MSCI) Indexes,
      162, 163
Equity index-linked notes, 948–951

Equity index-linked swaps, 935–937
Equity instruments
  acquiring foreign, 83–84
  common stock, 82–83
  futures contracts as, 84–85
  options as, 84
  special, 77
Equity investments, 77
Equity markets
  efficiency in European, 246–247
  growth of country, 672–674
  returns in global, 70–71
  secondary, 113–114
Equity portfolio, global risk in, 74–77
Equity portfolio management
  strategies, 802. See also Global
  portfolio management
  active, 805–810
  asset allocation strategies, 819–820
  futures and options in, 810–819
  passive, 803–805
  passive vs. active, 802–803
Equity risk, 59
  premium, 656–660
Equity turnover, 389–390
Equivalent taxable yield (ETY), 506
ERISA, 53
ERR. See Exchange rate risk (ERR)
Estimated rates of return, defined, 290
Estimated values
  and market prices, 435–436
  for market series, 669
Estimation risk, 269–270
Ethics, code of, 1039–1040
ETY. See Equivalent taxable yield
  (ETY)
Eurobond, 81, 496–497, 516
Eurodeutschemark bonds, 497
Eurodollar, T-bill yield spread and,
  783–784
Eurodollar bonds, 496–497, 516
Eurodollar contracts, mechanics of,
  843–845
Eurodollar strips, for synthetic fixed-
  rate funding, 846–848
Europe, efficient equity markets in,
  246–247
European chemical firms
  common stock statistics for, 744
  earnings and dividends per share
  in, 743
  profitability and financial strength
  for, 744
  profit performance of, 706–708
  share price performance for, 746
European options, 337
European quotation method, 854
European-style options
  American-style options and, 907
  call, 899
  put, 902 903
Eurostatistics, 181
Eurosterling bonds, 497, 517
Euro Week, 185
Euroyen bonds, 496–497, 516–517
EVA. See Economic value-added
  (EVA)
Evaluation, of portfolio performance,
  993–994. See also Performance
Event studies, 229
  to test EMH, 228–234
Ex ante market line relationship,
  1006

Exchange. See also Forward
  contracts; Futures contracts;
  Securities exchanges; Securities
  markets; Stock exchanges;
  exchanges by name
  American Stock Exchange
  (AMEX), 113
  block trades and, 136
  commodity, 84
  equity, 494
  futures, 336
  listing on national, 232–233
  for long forward and long call
  transactions, 339
  market makers and, 131–134
  membership in, 125–126
  option, 338
  options traded on, 874
  regional, 120–121
  for short forward and long put
  transactions, 341
  types of orders in, 126–131
Exchange clearinghouse, 827
Exchange markets, analysis of,
  125–134
Exchange rate
  forecasts of, against U.S. dollar,
  479
  inflation and, 477–479
  risk of global investing and, 548
  trends in, 708
  U.S. dollar-trade weighted, 797
Exchange rate risk (ERR), 21, 452,
  700
Exchange-traded options, quotations
  for, 874–876
Exercise price, 337
Exit barriers, competition and, 689
Expansion model, 752
Expectations hypothesis, yield curve
  and, 556–558
Expected earnings per share,
  estimated, 645–655
Expected growth rate, for RSD
  industry, 701–705
Expected inflation, changes in, 27
Expected interest rates, 593–595
Expected rates of return, 6, 254
  on common stocks, 669–674
  and required rate of return,
  733–734
  risk and, 11–14
  risk measurement for, 14–15
Expected return, 228
  of risk-free asset and risky
  portfolio, 280–281
  skewness and, 314
  stream of, 434–435
Expected return (fair game) model,
  210–211
Expiration date payoffs, 341–344
Export markets, profit margins in,
  650–651
Ex poste market line relationship,
  1006
Extended DuPont System, 395–396,
  397
External efficiency, 107
External market liquidity, 408–409

Factors, in APT study, 326–327
Fair game model, 210–211
Fama measures, application of, 1008

Fannie Mae. See Federal National
  Mortgage Association (FNMA,
  Fannie Mae)
FASB. See Financial Accounting
  Standards Board (FASB)
FDIC. See Federal Deposit Insurance
  Corporation (FDIC)
Federal agencies. See Government
  agency securities
Federal Deposit Insurance
  Corporation (FDIC), bank
  regulation by, 55
Federal Home Loan Bank (FHLB),
  79
  issues of, 503
Federal Home Loan Mortgage, issues
  of, 503
Federal Housing Administration
  (FHA), 79
Federal Land Banks (FLBs), 79
Federal National Mortgage
  Association (FNMA, Fannie
  Mae), 79
Federal Reserve Bulletin, 179
Federal Reserve System
  auctions of, 108
  bank regulation by, 55
  information from, 180
  money supply and, 470–471
  Regulations T and U of, 128–129
Federal Trade Commission (FTC),
  financial ratio information from,
  382
FHA. See Federal Housing
  Administration (FHA)
FHLB. See Federal Home Loan
  Bank (FHLB)
Fiduciary, 50
FIFO. See First-in-first-out (FIFO)
Filter rules, 214–215
Financial Accounting Standards
  Board (FASB), 375
Financial assets, defined, 77
Financial forward contracts. See
  Forward contracts
Financial futures contracts, 85, 113.
  See also Futures contracts
  growth in use of, 837
Financial issues, 507
Financial leverage
  of firm, 599
  for RSD industry, 703
Financial markets
  secondary, 111–120
  in United States, 68–69
Financial plan, insurance in, 38
Financial Planning, 196
Financial ratios. See also Ratio
  analysis of, 381–383
  and bond ratings, 420
  computation of, 383
  differences in aggregate, 416–417
  and insolvency (bankruptcy), 421
  limitations of, 421–422
  summary of, 410
  and systematic risk, 419, 420
  uses of, 418–422
Financial reports. See Information
  sources
Financial risk, 20, 409, 700
  analysis of, 399–405
  debt (balance sheet) ratios,
  399–402

for foreign securities, 452
Financial risk ratios, for Walgreen
  Company and RSD industry,
  730
Financial services, changes in
  industry, 143–144
Financial Services Week, 185
Financial statements
  alternate cash flow measurements
  and, 380–381
  analysis of, 375
  balance sheet and, 375
  cash flows statement and, 376–380
  external market liquidity and,
  408–409
  financial ratios and, 381–383,
  418–422
  generally accepted accounting
  principles (GAAP) and, 375
  growth potential analysis and,
  405–408
  income statement and, 375–376
  internal liquidity evaluation and,
  383–388
  non-U.S., 411–417
  operation performance evaluation
  and, 388–396
  quality of, 417–418
  ratio analysis and, 409–411
  risk analysis and, 396–405
  technicians and, 775
  value of analysis, 418
Financial Times, The, 155, 186
  actuaries share indices from, 159
  stock indexes and, 155, 157
Financial World, 196
Firm. See Company
First-in-first-out (FIFO), 233
First-mortgage issues, 507
Fiscal policy, 432
  risk-free rates and, 18
Fitch Investors Service
  Corporate Credit Analysis, 197
  Municipal Credit Analysis, 197
  Rating Register, 197
  ratings by, 497
Fixed charge coverages, 403
Fixed costs, as competitive force,
  689
Fixed exchange (FX) rate, 876
Fixed-for-floating transaction, 922
Fixed-income bond, floating-rate note
  and, 919n
Fixed-income investments, 77, 78–82
  capital market instruments as,
  78–81
  international bonds and, 81–82
  savings accounts as, 78
Fixed-income investment strategy,
  global, 605–607
Fixed-income obligations, accrued
  interest basis trading of, 519
Fixed-rate funding, synthetic,
  846–848
Flat bonds, 498
Flat trend channel, 776–777
Flat yield curve, 558
FLBs. See Federal Land Banks
  (FLBs)
Flexible forwards, 887
Flexible growth stock valuation
  model, 758–761, 762
  application of, 759–760

Flexible growth stock valuation model (*continued*)
  example of, 760–761
  parameters in, 759
Floating rate index, LIBOR as, 917
Floating rate (variable) note (FRN), 919
  leveraged, 955
  reverse, 954
  swap and, 955
  and two swaps, 956
Floor agreement, 916, 925, 927–928
Floor brokers, 126
Floor Order Routing and Execution System (FORES), of Tokyo Stock Exchange, 133
Floor portfolio, 621
Floor return, price behavior for, 619
FNMA. *See* Federal National Mortgage Association (FNMA, Fannie Mae)
Forbes, 196, 200
  fund information from, 983, 986
Forcing convention, 943
Forecasting
  for country real GDP growth and inflation, 671
  cyclical indicator approach to, 462–470
  of earnings per share, 689
  of industry profit margin, 691–694
  of interest rates, 544–545
  options contracts and, 891–893
  sales, 684–689
  for world economic activity, 477
Foreign bonds, 496–497, 516
Foreign common stock, 83–84
Foreign currency exchange warrants, 940–941
Foreign currency options, 876–878
  Black-Scholes valuation model and, 908–909
Foreign exchange rates, technical analysis of, 797
Foreign exchange (FX) transactions, 854
Foreign funds, 990
Foreign markets
  stock-market indexes available for, 160
  stock market series in, 796
  technical analysis of, 795–797
Foreign securities, required return for, 449–453
Foreign stocks and bonds
  direct purchase or sale of, 83–84
  estimating dividend growth for, 455–456
  importance of, in portfolio, 77
  listing on NYSE, 141
  net profit margin for, 455
  retention rates for, 455
  total asset/equity ratio, 455–456
  total asset turnover for, 455
FORES. *See* Floor Order Routing and Execution System (FORES)
Fortune, 196
Fortune Investment Information Directory, 183
Forward-based interest rate contracts, 917–925
  forward rate agreements as, 917–919

interest rate swaps as, 919–925
Forward contracts, 334–335, 826–827
  applications and strategies for, 837–860
  compared with options, 339–340
  currency, 854–860
  hedging with, 830–834
  interest rates, 837–838
  payoff diagrams for, 340–341
  relationship with option contracts, 347–354
  trading in, 827–830
  valuation concepts and, 834–837
Forward currency quotations, 855
Forward discount, 856
Forward premium, 856
Forward prices, spot prices and, 835–837
Forward rate, 550, 554
  calculating from spot-rate curve, 554–561
  implied, 556
  for money market, 868–871
Forward rate agreement (FRA), 917–919
  floating rate note (FRN) and, 919–920
401(k) plans, 49
403(b) plans, 49
Fourth market, 125
FRA. *See* Forward rate agreement (FRA)
Franchise factor, 742–743
Frankfurt Stock Exchange, 115, 118
  changes on, 143
Free cash flow, 381, 405
FRN. *See* Floating rate (variable) note
FTEY. *See* Fully taxable equivalent yield (FTEY)
FT/S&P-Actuaries World Indexes, 160, 161
Full replication, 804
Fully taxable equivalent yield (FTEY), 540–541
Fund. *See also* Closed-end investment company; Investment company; Mutual fund; Open-end investment company
  balanced, 85, 973
  bond, 85, 973–974
  characteristics of, 974–976
  closed-end index for, 970–971
  common stock, 85, 973
  endowment, 53
  management fees of, 973
  market (index), 245–246
  market timing ability and, 978–979
  money market, 85, 974
  mutual, 51
  pension, 51–53
  sources of information on, 981–990
  specialty, 143
  supply of, 546–547
  value of performance studies, 980–981
Fundamental analysis
  of common stock, 641

of efficient capital markets, 242–244
  technical analysis and, 776
Fundamental risk
  of security, 22
  and systematic risk, 23
Funding, synthetic fixed-rate, 846–848
Future bond prices, calculating, 536–541
Future consumption, 4–5
Future earnings, 642
Futures contracts, 29, 77, 84–85, 335–336, 826–827
  in active equity portfolio management, 817–818
  altering bond duration with, 845–846
  applications and strategies for, 837–860
  in asset allocation, 812
  commodities quotations, 829–830
  cost of carry and, 836
  currency, 854–860
  in equity portfolio management, 810–819
  examples of, 336
  financial, 113
  financial futures, 85
  in global markets, 812–814
  hedging with, 830–834
  interest rates, 837–838
  long-term interest rate futures, 838–843
  options on, 878–880
  in passive equity portfolio management, 816–817
  short-term interest rate, 843–849
  stock index, 849–854
  trading in, 827–830
  Treasury futures applications, 841–843
  valuation concepts and, 834–837
Futures exchange, 336
  examples of, 336
Futures options, Black-Scholes valuation model and, 909
Futures traders, bullish on stock index futures, 780–781, 783
Future value
  for industry, 705–706
  for stock market, 640
  for Walgreen, 732
FX transactions. *See* Fixed exchange (FX) rate; Foreign exchange (FX) transactions

GAAP. *See* Generally accepted accounting principles (GAAP)
GDP. *See* Gross domestic product (GDP)
Generally accepted accounting principles (GAAP), 375, 376
General obligation bonds (GOs), 79, 109, 505, 506
Geometric mean (GM), 8
German Securities Clearing System (*Kassenverein*), 502
Germany. *See also* Frankfurt Stock Exchange
  agency securities in, 505
  corporate bond market in, 515, 516
  equity market growth in, 672, 674

government bond issues by, 501–502
  international bonds in, 517
  municipal bonds in, 505
  portfolio strategies in, 61, 62
  regional exchanges in, 121
GICs. *See* Guaranteed insurance contracts (GICs)
Gifting phase, of investment life cycle, 40
"Gilt" market, 502
Ginnie Mae. *See* Government National Mortgage Association (GNMA, Ginnie Mae)
Glass-Steagall Act, bank regulation by, 55
Global asset allocation, 460–461
Global bond market
  bond ratings in, 497–499
  investors in, 497
  issuers in, 495–497
  structure of, 494–499
"Global Economic Outlook and Asset Allocation" (Salomon Brothers), 187
Global equity indexes, 160–162
"Global Equity Investment Strategy" (Salomon Brothers), 187
Global Finance, 196
Global fixed-income investment strategy, 605–607
"Global Fixed-Income Investment Strategy" (Salomon Brothers), 187
Global funds, 990
Global government bond market indexes, 167
Global industry analysis, 706–708
Global investment. *See also* Global portfolio management; Information sources
  benchmark error and, 1017–1019
  in bonds, 81–82
  choices for, 77–89
  currency forwards and futures, 854–860
  currency swaps and, 931–935
  domestic bonds, 82
  dual-currency bonds, 947–948
  equity instruments as, 82–84
  fixed-income investments as, 78–82
  foreign currency options and, 876–878
  futures contracts as, 84–85
  information on aggregate economic analysis, 179–182
  information sources on, 178–179
  investment companies as, 85–86
  low liquidity investments as, 87–89
  market security returns, 93
  mutual funds, 84
  options as, 84
  performance in, 91–93
  range forwards and, 887–888
  real estate as, 86–87
  reasons for making, 67–77
  taxation and, 47
  worldwide asset allocation and, 482, 483
Global investment companies, 990
Global Investor, 196

Global markets
  analysis of, 671–674
  bond market returns, 69–70
  futures in, 812–814
  investment selection for, 66–67
  portfolio bond portfolio risk and,
    73–74
  valuation matrix for, 673
  worldwide developed markets,
    148–149
  worldwide emerging, 150
Global portfolio management,
  806–810
  modifying portfolio characteristics,
    818–819
Global Security Market Index
  (GSMI), 168, 294, 321
Global security markets, analysis of,
  477–483
Global 24-hour market, 119–120
GM. See Geometric mean
GNMA. See Government National
  Mortgage Association (GNMA,
  Ginnie Mae)
GNP. See Gross national product
Goals. See Objectives
Goods and services. See Market
Good until canceled limit order, 127
GOs. See General obligation bonds
  (GOs)
Government. See also United States
  government; country by name
  domestic bond issues of, 500–502
  market for securities of, 496
  municipal bonds and, 79
Government agency securities
  characteristics of, 503
  in Germany, 505
  in global bond market, 496
  in Japan, 505
  quotations on, 519–521
  in United Kingdom, 505
  in United States, 79–81, 502–505
Government bonds, mean rate of
  return and standard deviation of
  returns for, 626
Government National Mortgage
  Association (GNMA, Ginnie
  Mae), 79
  issues of, 504
Government publications. See
  Information sources
Gross domestic product (GDP),
  growth worldwide, 477
Gross national product (GNP),
  estimating, 645–647
Gross profit margin, 390–391
Growth
  as competitive force, 689
  potential for, 406–408
  stock valuation and, 443–445
Growth analysis, 406–408, 411
Growth company, 443, 715–716
  actual returns above expected
    returns, 749
  alternative models for, 750
  analysis of, 747–762
  defined, 749
  and dividend discount model, 750
  estimated stock prices for,
    760–761
  example of, 760–761

flexible growth stock valuation
    model and, 758–760
  growth duration and, 754–758
  long-run, 751–754
  no-growth firm and, 750–751
  in real world, 754
Growth duration, 754–758
  computation of, 755
  factors in, 757–758
  intra-industry analysis and,
    756–757
Growth rate
  of dividends, 447–456, 660–662
  estimating, 704–705
  expected, 701–705
  real, 17
  for Walgreen and STD industry,
    732
Growth stock, 716
  vs. value stock, 807, 808
GSMI. See Global Security Market
  Index (GSMI)
Guaranteed insurance contracts
  (GICs), 54

Health insurance, 38
Hedge, 334
  cross, 833
  short and long, 831
  Treasury futures as, 841–842
Hedged returns, 452n
Hedge position, 354–355
Hedge ratio, 826, 890–893
  calculating, 832–834
Hedging. See also Black-Scholes
    valuation model; Hedge; Hedge
    ratio
  basis and, 830–832
  duration and, 839–841
  with forwards and futures,
    830–834
  futures contracts and, 814–816
  options and, 889–891
  of portfolio inflows, 812–813
  of portfolio outflows, 814
  with stock index futures, 849
Hedging pressure theory, 559
Herzfeld closed-end fund average,
  970–971
High grade bonds, 499
High-yield (junk) bonds, 511–514
  credit analysis of, 595–597
  distributions of ratings for,
    512–513
  indexes for, 167
  and investment grade bonds,
    626–627
  ownership of, 513–514
  research on, 599–600
Historical average annual returns
  (1926–1995), 58
Historical Chart Book, 180
Historical equity risk premium
  approach, 657
Historical rates of return, 6
  computing, 8–11
Historical risk/returns. See also
    Historical rates of return
  for art and antiques, 94–95
  on investments, 89–97
  for real estate, 95–97
  on stocks, bonds, and T-bills,
    89–91

for world capital market, 92, 93
  world portfolio performance and,
    91–93
Holding period return (HPR), 6–8
  for bond, 493
Holding period yield (HPY), 7–8
  stock indexes and, 157
Horizon matching, 615–616
Horizon premium, 90
Horizon yield. See Realized
  (horizon) yield
HPR. See Holding period return
  (HPR)
HPY. See Holding period yield
  (HPY)
Humped yield curve, 558
Hybrid active/passive equity
  portfolio management, 802

Ibbotson-Sinquefield technique, 657
  risk premium and, 668
IFC. See International Finance
  Corporation (IFC)
Immunization
  over beginning-to end-wealth
    position, 612–614
  contingent, 616, 617–622
  defined, 609
  horizon matching and, 615
Immunization strategies, 608–615
  application of, 610–611
  classical immunization as,
    614–615
  components of interest rate risk
    and, 608–609
  example of, 611–612
  and interest rate risk, 609–610
Immunized portfolio, monitoring,
  620–622
Implied forward rate, 556
Implied volatility, 901–902
Import-export sector, economic
  indicators and, 467
Income
  current, 4
  exempt, 49
  interest or coupon, 491
  of specialists, 132
Income bonds, 80, 507
Income payouts, from common
  stocks and Treasury bills, 61
Income statement, 375–376
  common size, 392
  comparative formats for, 411, 413
  quality of, 418
  sample of, 378
  for Walgreen, 725
Indenture, 79
  provisions of bonds, 492
Independence, statistical tests of,
  212–213
Index arbitrage, of futures, 850–852
Indexes. See also Bond-market
    indicator series; Cyclical
    indicator approach; Indicators;
    Security-market indicators series
    (indexes); Stock-market
    indicator series (indexes)
  comparison over time, 169–173
  Confidence, 782–783
  consumer sentiment measures and,
    469–470
  diffusion, 466, 785

of DJIA and bullish-bearish
    sentiments, 780
  domestic common stock, 809
  foreign stock-market, 177
  passive portfolio management and,
    803–804
  replicating, 803
Index funds, 245–246
  construction techniques for,
    804–805
Indexing, 592, 593
Indicators. See also Cyclical
    indicator approach; Indicator
    series
  coincident, 464
  lagging, 464
  leading, 463–464
  performance of, 465
  technical trading rules and,
    776–798
Indicator series
  composite and ratio of, 464–465
  performance of, 465
  selected, 464
Indirect quotation method, 854
Individual asset, variance for, 255
Individual investment, standard
    deviation of returns for,
    254–255
Individual investors, 38–50
Industrial life cycle, 684–686
Industrials, 507
Industry. See also Industry analysis
  depreciation in, 692
  drugstore, 724
  earnings estimate in, 694–696
  economy and, 687
  identifying, 711–713
  interest expense in, 692–693
  sources of information for, 713
  tax rate in, 693–694
Industry analysis, 679–680
  competition and expected industry
    returns, 689–697
  cross-sectional industry
    performance and, 681–682
  earnings multiplier and, 696–706
  earnings per share and, 684–689
  with efficient capital markets,
    242–243
  global, 706–708
  in global portfolio management,
    806–807
  industry performance over time,
    682
  industry risk difference, 682–683
  information on, 188–190
  performance of companies within
    industry, 682
  preparing, 711–713
  of rates of return, 683–684
  reasons for, 680–683
Industry influences, on security
    valuation, 432–433
Industry life cycle
  deceleration of growth and decline
    stage, 686
  mature growth stage, 685–686
  pioneering development stage, 684
  rapid accelerating growth stage,
    685
  stabilization and market maturity
    stage, 685–686

Industry multiplier
  macroanalysis of, 697–698
  and market multiplier, 699
  microanalysis of, 697–705
Industry returns, competition and, 689–696
Infinite period DDM, and growth periods, 443
Inflation, 432
  accounting methods and, 233
  APT and, 328–329
  changes in, 27
  and exchange rates, 477–479
  expected rate of, 18–20, 546
  forecasts for country, 671
  interest rates and, 473–474
  and investment returns, 57
  mean rate of return and standard deviation of returns for, 626
  nominal risk-free rate and, 17
  and profit margin, 650
Inflation rate, for foreign securities, 450–452
Inflows, hedging, 812–813
Information, returns and, 226
Informational efficiency, 107
  market and, 209
Information sources. See also Security-market indicators series (indexes)
  academic journals as, 200–202
  on aggregate economic analysis, 179–182
  for aggregate security-market analysis, 182–187
  bank publications as, 180–181
  bibliographies, 182
  on bonds, 197–198
  brokerage firm reports, 186–187
  computerized data sources, 202–203
  on financial ratios, 382
  on funds, 981–990
  on global investments, 178–179
  on high-yield bonds, 599–600
  individual stock and bond analysis, 190–194
  for industry, 713
  industry analysis, 188–190
  investment information listing, 204–206
  investment magazines, 194–197
  listing of, 204–206
  listing of on-line databases, 203
  on mutual funds, 198–200
  non-U.S. economic data, 181
  for theoretical and empirical analysis, 200–202
  U.S. government aggregate security-market analysis, 182–183
  U.S. government economic information, 179–180
Initial margin account, 828
Initial public offerings (IPOs), 109–110
  of closed-end funds, 970
  number of, initial return, and gross proceeds of, 231
  studies of, 230–233
Input-output analysis, sales forecasting and, 686
Insiders. See Corporate insiders

Insider trading, 235–236
Insolvency, financial ratios and, 421
Institutional Investor, The, 196, 679
Institutional investors, 51–55
  asset allocation by, 55–61
  banks and, 54–55
  endowment funds and, 53
  insurance companies and, 53–54
  mutual funds and, 51
  objects and constraints of, 51–55
  pension funds and, 51–53
Institutionalization, in securities markets, 134–135
Institutional theory, 559
Institutions, and stock price volatility, 136
Insurance
  in financial plan, 38
  life, 53–54
  on municipal bonds, 506–507
  nonlife, 54
  portfolio, 357–358
  terminal payoff to stock position and, 359
Insurance companies, institutional investment and, 53–54
Insured asset allocation, 820
Integrated asset allocation, 819
Interest
  on bonds, 493, 509
  risk-free rate of, 17–20
  short, 786–787
Interest expense, 695
  cash flow and, 403–404
  estimating, 652–653
  industry, 692–693
Interest income, 491
Interest-on-interest, 531, 532
Interest rate
  bank investments and, 54
  bond characteristics and, 547–548
  and bond prices, 474–475
  bond price volatility and, 561–562
  cost of funds and, 18
  determination of, 543–554
  expected, 594
  forecasting of, 478, 544–545, 673
  inflation and, 473–474
  price and yield determination and, 540
  and stock prices, 475–476
  term structure of, 544, 548–553, 554
  volatility of, 493–494
Interest rate agreements
  forward-based contracts, 917–925
  option-based contracts, 925–930
  OTC, 917–930
Interest rate anticipation, 593–595
Interest rate collar, 926–928
Interest rate contracts
  forward-based, 917–925
  option-based, 925–930
Interest rate effect, 1025
Interest rate forwards, 837–838
Interest rate futures, 837–838
  long-term, 838–843
  short-term, 843–849
Interest rate parity, 857
Interest rate risk
  components, 608–609
  defined, 609

Interest rate sensitivity, bond price volatility and, 564
Interest rate swaps, 916, 919–925
  option-based, 925–930
  swaption and, 928–930
Interest rate sways, swap contracting extensions, 931–939
Interest tables, 1041–1048
Intermarket spread swaps, 601
Intermarket trading system (ITS), 138–139
Internal characteristics, of assets, 435. See also Internal liquidity
Internal efficiency, 107
Internal liquidity, 409
  cash conversion cycle and, 388
  evaluating, 383–388
  ratios of, 383–388
Internal rate of return (IRR), 529
International bond market, return-risk results, 71
International bonds, 496–497, 516–517
  yields of, 545
International Federation of Stock Exchanges, 118–119
International Finance Corporation (IFC), 119
International Financial Statistics, 182
International Financing Review, 185
International fund, 990
International investments. See Global investment
International investors, asset allocation by, 61, 62. See also Global investments
International Marketing Data and Statistics, 181
International Monetary Fund, Balance of Payments Yearbook, 182
International Monetary Market (IMM), 843
International ratio analysis, 412–416
"International Report, The" (Kidder Peabody), 187
In-the-money, 337
Intrinsic value, of option, 337
Inventory
  accounting for, 233
  turnover of, 387–388
Investment(s), 4–5. See also Asset(s); Derivative securities; Global investment; Information sources
  calculating implied world futures rates, 859–860
  combined country, 71–77
  defined, 5–6
  equity, 77
  fixed-income, 77, 78–82
  futures contracts as, 77
  global, 66–67
  global asset allocation and, 460–461
  historical risk/returns on, 89–97
  long-term performance of, 9
  low-liquidity, 77, 87–89
  objectives, by age, 46
  portfolio of, 10–11
  risk and return characteristics of alternative, 98
  special equity instruments as, 77

three-step process for, 431–434
time horizon of, 47
valuation of alternative, 436–447
Investment advisory opinions, 779
Investment bankers, corporate issue underwriting and, 110
Investment Companies (Arthur Wiesenberger Services), 198, 983, 984
Investment company, 966–967
  balanced funds, 86
  bond funds, 86
  closed-end vs. open-end, 968–973
  common stock funds, 86
  defined, 967
  global, 990
  information sources about, 981–990
  management of, 967–968
  money market funds, 85–86
  performance of, 976–981
  specialization in, 143
  types, based on portfolio makeup, 973–976
Investment Dealers Digest, 197
Investment decision process, 429–430, 435–436, 732–734
Investment firms, as block houses, 136
Investment-grade bond indexes, 165–167
Investment-grade securities, 498
Investment horizon, 608–609
Investment information, list of sources for, 204–206
Investment magazines, 194–197
Investment management company, 967–968
Investment opportunities, real risk-free rate and, 17
Investment policy statement. See Policy statement
Investment risk, 5
Investment strategy, global fixed-income, 605–607
Investor
  evaluating, 243
  financial plans of, 38
  individual, 38–50
  institutional, 51–55
  needs and preferences of, 51
  policy of, 37
Investor Daily, 186
Investor life cycle, individual, 37
Investor's equity, 129
Investor utility, efficient frontier and, 270–272
IPOs. See Initial public offerings (IPOs)
IRR. See Internal rate of return (IRR)
ISL Daily Stock Price Tapes, 203
Issues. See Bonds; Corporate bonds; Corporate stocks; Municipal bonds; New issues
ITS. See Intermarket trading system (ITS)

January anomaly, 220–222
January effect, APT and, 328
Japan. See also Tokyo Stock Exchange (TSE)
  agency securities in, 505

bank bonds in, 515
corporate bond market in, 514–515
government bond issues by, 500–501
international bond market in, 516–517
municipal bonds in, 505
portfolio strategies in, 61, 62
regional exchanges in, 121
Japan Securities Exchange, 117
Jensen measure, of portfolio performance, 1000–1002, 1005
Journals, listing of academic, 200–202
Junk bonds. *See* High-yield bonds

Kassenverein, 502
Kisaikai, 514

Labor cost, unit, 649–650
Lagging indicators, 464
Land, investing in, 87
Large firms
calendar effects and, 222–223
size effect and, 224–225
Last-in, first-out (LIFO), 233
LBO. *See* Leveraged buyout (LBO) firms
Leading indicators, 463–464
Business Week Leading Indicator Series, 467, 468
CIBCR *Leading Inflation Index,* 469
CIBCR *Long-Leading Index,* 469
international, 469
NBER group, 463
and stock prices, 467
Legal factors, 50
Lehman Brothers Government-Corporate Bond Index, 1022
Lending, by banks, 54
Lending rates, CAPM and, 306
Leverage, and margin transactions, 128
Leveraged buyout (LBO) firms, 599
Leveraged floating rate note, 955
Liabilities. *See also* Taxes and taxation
current, 383–385
in portfolio, 252
swap agreement as, 925
Liability schedule, 607
LIBOR. *See* London Interbank Offer Rate (LIBOR)
Life cycle, investor, 37
Life cycle investment
goals of, 40
strategies for, 38–40
Life insurance, 38
Life insurance companies, institutional investment and, 53–54
LIFFE. *See* London International Financial Futures Exchange (LIFFE)
LIFO. *See* Last-in, first-out (LIFO)
Limit order, 126–127
Limit-order processing system, 141
Linear programming techniques, 810
Liquid asset, 47
Liquid asset ratio, 777
Liquidity
defined, 106

external, 408–409
forward contracts and, 335
internal, 383–388, 409
low-liquidity investments and, 77, 87–89
monetary, 462
secondary financial markets and, 111–112
and stock prices, 471–472
Liquidity needs, 47
of insurance companies, 54
Liquidity preference hypothesis, 558–559
Liquidity risk, 20–21, 700
Listed securities exchanges, 113
Load funds, 972–973
Loanable funds, 546–547
interest rates and, 544
Lock-out period, 510
London Interbank Offer Rate (LIBOR), and forward-based interest rate contracts, 917-919. *See also* Eurodollar contracts; Interest rate swaps; Swaps; Synthetic fixed-rate funding
London International Financial Futures Exchange (LIFFE), T-bond contracts at, 838
London Stock Exchange (LSE), 113, 115, 118, 133–134
changes on, 141–142
Long call transactions, exchanges for, 339
Long forward transactions, exchanges for, 339
Long hedge, 831
Long-leading Index, 467–469
Long position, 335
in regular and range forwards, 889
Long-run growth models, 751–754
capital gain component of, 753
dynamic true, 753–754
expansion model, 752
negative, 752–753
simple, 751–752
Long-term, high-priority goals, 40
Long-term buy-and-hold strategy, passive equity portfolio management as, 803
Long-term debt/total capital ratio, 401
Long-term interest rate futures, 838–843
Long-term performance, 9
Low-cost leadership strategy, 721, 722
Lower-priority goals, 40
Low-liquidity investment, 77, 87–89
antiques, 88
coins and stamps, 88–89
Low-load fund, 972
Low positive correlation, 72

M1 money supply, 470
M2 money supply, 470
Macaulay duration, 565–568. *See also* Duration
limitations of, 578–580
Macroanalysis
of earnings multiplier, 726–727
of industry multiplier, 697–698
Macroeconomic analysis, 470–477

Macroeconomic developments, security valuation and, 432
Magazines. *See also* Information sources
on industry, 188–190
investment, 194–197
Maintenance margin, 130
Management. *See* Portfolio management
Management effect, 1022
Management fees, 973
Management Results (Arthur Wiesenberger Services), 198–199, 983
Management strategies. *See* Bond portfolio management
Mandatory securities valuation reserve (MSVR), 53
Margin
in futures exchange, 336
in futures market, 336
safety, 618
Margin account, 828
Margin call, 130
Margin debt, 784
Margin requirement, 129
Margin transactions, 128–131
Marked-to-market, 336, 826
process of, 828
Market(s). *See also* Derivative markets; Derivative securities; Global markets; Over-the-counter (OTC) market; Securities markets
auction, 114
bond, 69–70, 494–499, 797–798
breadth of, 784–785
call, 114
capital, 69
characteristics of good, 106–107
continuous, 114–115
corporate bond, 507–514
dealer, 114
defined, 106
efficient, 29, 107
efficient capital, 208
equity, 70–71
fourth, 125
global, 66–67
global 24-hour, 119–120
high-yield bond, 511–514
informationally efficient, 209
negotiated, 122
for option contracts, 336–337, 873–880
primary, 107
primary capital, 108–111
secondary, 107
secondary financial, 111–120
third, 125
Unlisted Securities, 122–123
world security, 477–483
worldwide developed, 148–149
worldwide emerging, 150
Marketability, of asset, 106
Market cycles, mutual fund cash ratio and, 778
Market effects, adjustments for, 215–217
Market funds, 245
Market impact, 356
Market indexes, factors in constructing, 153. *See also*

Security-market indicators series (indexes)
Market line, bond, 1021–1024
Market liquidity, external, 408–409
Market makers, 131–134
Market multiplier
and earnings multiple, 705
industry multiplier and, 699
Market order, 126
Market order processing, of Super Dot, 140
Market portfolio, 278, 283–284
measures of, 1016
security market line and, 25
theory vs. practice and, 317–322
Market price
estimated values and, 435–436
of investment company shares, 968
per unit of risk, 1006
Market proxy, effect of, 293
Market risk premium, 289
change in, 27
security market line and, 25–26
Market series
estimate of value for, 669
estimating sales per share for, 645–647
Market's implicit forecast, 1026
Market timing skills
fund performance and, 978–979
measuring, 1015–1016
Market value, technical analysis and, 772
Market value-added (MVA), 740, 742
and EVA, 742
Market Vane advisory service, 780–781
Markowitz efficient investor, 278
Markowitz portfolio theory, 253–272
Matched-funding techniques, 591, 607–616
immunization strategies and, 608–615
Maturity. *See also* Duration
and bond price volatility, 563
of bonds, 491, 492–493
duration and, 566, 567
effective duration greater than, 580
time to, 491
Maturity spread, 541
Maturity strategy, 611–612
MCE. *See* MidAmerica Commodity Exchange (MCE)
Mean
arithmetic, 8
geometric, 8
Mean rates of return, 8–11
Measures. *See also* Analysis; Portfolio performance analysis
of market timing skills, 1015–1016
of performance, 466
of relative value, 734–739
of speculative trading activity, 779
of value-added, 739–743
Media General Data Bank, 203
Media General Financial Weekly, The, 197
Medium grade bonds, 498
Merc. *See* Chicago Mercantile Exchange (CME)

Merrill-Lynch U.S. Capital Markets Index (ML-WCMI), 168
Microanalysis
    of earnings multiplier, 727–732
    of industry multiplier, 697–705
MidAmerica Commodity Exchange (MCE), T-bonds and, 838
Minicoupon bonds, 511
Minimum commission schedule, 135
ML-WCMI. *See* Merrill-Lynch U.S. Capital Markets Index (ML-WCMI)
MMI. *See* Multiple markets index (MMI)
Modified duration, 565
    and bond price volatility, 568–569
    convexity and, 573
    limitations of, 578–580
Monday trading effect, 222
Monetary liquidity, 462
Monetary policy, 432
    risk-free rates and, 18
Monetary variables, economy, stock prices, and, 470–477
Monetization, call, 929, 930
Money magazine, 194
Money managers, 235
    performance of, 239–241
Money market, 491
    calculating implied forward rates for, 868–871
Money market funds, 85, 974
Money market mutual funds, for cash reserve, 38
Money market rates, for short-term interest rate futures, 843
Money spread, 884
Money supply, 462, 470–472
    economy and, 470–471
    and stock prices, 471
Monte Carlo simulation, 359–360
Monthly magazines, 194–196
Moody's
    Aaa corporate bonds, 474, 475
    bond ratings by, 26n
    corporate bond yield spreads of, 26
    ratings of, 497
    publications of, 191–197
Morgan Stanley Capital International (MSCI) Indexes, 162, 163
    World Equity Index, 1014
Morgan Stanley World Stock Index, 1018
Morningstar, fund information from, 983–984, 989
Morningstar Mutual Funds, information on, 200
Mortgage bonds, 80, 508
    in Germany, 515
Moving average, 787
Moving-average lines, 790–792
MSCI Indexes. *See* Morgan Stanley Capital International (MSCI) Indexes
MSVR. *See* Mandatory securities valuation reserve (MSVR)
M-S World Stock Index, 320
Multiple indicator charts, 792
Multiple Markets Index (MMI), 168n, 1017
Multiplier. *See also* Earnings multiplier

earnings, 642–645
industry, 697–705
Multiplier effect, 432
Municipal bonds, 79
    in Germany, 505
    insurance on, 506–507
    issues of, 108–109
    in Japan, 505
    quotations for, 521, 522
    secondary markets for, 112
    in United Kingdom, 505
    in United States, 505–507
Municipalities, global bond market and, 496
Mutual fund, 51. *See also* Open-end investment companies
    cash positions of, 777–778
    components of performance for, 1009
    defined, 968
    information on, 198–200
    international, 51
    performance measures for, 1004
    performance of, 976–981
    quotations for, 982
    "Mutual Funds" (Morningstar), 983, 989
    "Mutual Fund Scoreboard," 983, 987–988
MVA. *See* Market value-added (MVA)

NAIC. *See* National Association of Insurance Commissioners (NAIC)
NASDAQ composite average, OTC-NYSE volumes and, 781
NASDAQ Fact Book, 183
NASDAQ/NMS (National Market System) system, 121, 123
NASDAQ system, 118, 123
    listing requirements for, 123
    OTV vs. NYSE volume and, 779
    qualifications for inclusion in, 124
    trading on, 121–122
National Association of Insurance Commissioners (NAIC), 53
National Association of Securities Dealers Automated Quotation system. *See* NASDAQ system
National Bureau of Economic Research (NBER), 461, 462–463
    business cycle and, 462–463
    indicators of, 463–464
National investment differences, 61, 62
National Market System (NMS), 123, 137–140
    centralized quotation system and, 138–139
    centralized reporting and, 137–138
    central limit-order book (CLOB) and, 139
    and competition among market makers (Rule 390), 139–140
    qualifications for inclusion in, 124
National stock exchanges, 115
NAV. *See* Net asset value (NAV)
NBER. *See* National Bureau of Economic Research (NBER)
NBT profit margin. *See* Net before tax (NBT) profit margin

Near-term, high-priority goals, 40
Needs, of investors, 51
Negative correlation, 72
    of hedge position with payoffs, 355
    time patterns of returns for assets with, 264
Negative effective duration, 580
Negative growth model, 752–753
Neglected firms, and trading activity, 225–226
Negotiated bid, for municipal bonds, 109
Negotiated commission rates, 135–136
Negotiated market, OTC market as, 122
Negotiation, for bond sales, 108
Net asset value (NAV), 967
Net before tax (NBT) profit margin, 647
Net fixed asset turnover, 389
Net profit margin, 391–392
    estimating, 647
    for foreign stocks, 455
    for Walgreen and RSD industry, 725
Net profit margin estimate, for Walgreen, 724–726
New issues, 109
    seasoned, 110
New York Mercantile Exchange (NYM), 827
New York Stock Exchange (NYSE), 113, 115–116. *See also* Exchange; National Market System (NMS); Securities markets; Stock exchanges
    AMEX and, 779
    membership prices on, 117
    off-hours trading of, 141
    Rule 390 of, 140
New York Stock Exchange Fact Book, 183
Nikkei Average, 153
Nikkei-Dow Jones Average (Nikkei Stock Average Index), 155
9-K SEC form, 190
NMS system. *See* NASDAQ/NMS (National Market System) system; National Market System (NMS)
NOB (Notes over Bond) spread, 842
No-growth firm, 750–751
No-load fund, 972–973
Nominal GNP, 645
Nominal RFR, 546
    for major countries, 451
Nominal risk-free rate, 5, 656
    factors affecting, 17–20
Nominal yield, 491, 530
Nomura Investment Review (Nomura Research Institute), 187
Noncallable provision, of bond, 492
Nonlife insurance companies, 54
Nonparallel shift, in yield curve, 578
Nonrated bonds, 497
Nonrefunding provision, 492
Normal portfolio, 1028–1029
    benchmark portfolio as, 805–806
Notes, 491
    equity index-linked, 948–951

floating rate, 919
    structured, 917
    swap-linked, 953–956
    Treasury, 108
    variable-rate, 510–511
Notional principal, 917
NYM. *See* New York Mercantile Exchange (NYM)
NYSE. *See* New York Stock Exchange (NYSE)
NYSE Composite index, 153

OARS. *See* Opening automated report service (OARS)
Objectives
    in policy statement, 43–46
    of portfolio management, 41–42
    risk and, 59–60
Obligations. *See* Bonds
OCC. *See* Options Clearing Corporation (OCC)
Odd-lot sales, as contrary-opinion rules, 777n
Off-hours trading, on NYSE, 141
OID. *See* Original-issue discount (OID)
OLS. *See* Ordinary least squares (OLS) model
One-parameter measures, of portfolio performance, 1004–1005
One-period CAPM, 224
On-line databases, 203
On-the-run Treasury issues, 551
Open-ended limit order, 127
Open-end investment companies, 971–973
Opening automated report service (OARS), 140
Operating efficiency ratios, 388–390
Operating leverage, 399
Operating performance, 409
    evaluating, 388–396
Operating profitability, ratios for, 388–389, 390–396
Operating profit margin (OPM), 647, 691
    aggregate, 648–649
    foreign competition and, 650–651
Operations, cash flow from, 405
OPM. *See* Operating profit margin (OPM)
Optimal portfolio, 252, 272
    risk and, 271
Option-adjusted duration, 576–577
Option-based interest rate contracts, 925–930
Option contracts, 29, 84, 336–337, 872–873. *See also* Call options; Put option; Warrants
    American-style, 905–906
    call, 337
    chooser options, 884
    combinations of, 880–881
    compared with forwards, 339–340
    dividend-bearing securities and, 903–905
    embedded, 576
    in equity portfolio management, 810–819
    European-style, 899, 902–903
    examples of, 338
    forecasting and, 891–893
    foreign currency, 876–878

hedging and, 889–891
investment returns for, 346
markets and, 873–880
payoffs for, 344–346
for portfolio risk, 813
put, 337
quotations for exchange-traded,
    874–876
range forwards and, 887–888
spreads, 884–887
stock index, 876
straddles as, 881–882
strangles as, 883, 884
straps as, 881–882, 883
strips as, 881–882, 883
synthetic risk-free portfolio and,
    889
trading strategies for, 880–888,
    889
unsystematic risk and, 817–818
valuation of, 889–909
warrants and, 939–941
Option exchanges, examples of, 338
Option premium, 337
Options Clearing Corporation (OCC),
    874
Options pricing model, 627
Orders
    in exchanges, 126–131
    limit, 126–127
    market, 126
    stop buy, 128
    stop loss, 127
Ordinary least squares (OLS) model,
    224
    of portfolio betas, 311
*Organization for Economic
    Cooperation and Development,
    The (OECD),*
    publications of, 181
Original-issue discount (OID), 511
Origination
    and municipal bond underwriting,
        108
    of option contracts, 339
OTC market. *See* Over-the-counter
    (OTC) market
OTC Review, 196
Outflows, hedging, 814
Out-of-the-money, 337
Overfunded pension plans, 52
Overhanging, of market, 790
Over-the-counter (OTC) market, 113,
    121–125. *See also* Derivative
    securities
    forward contracts and, 334–335,
        827
    interest rate agreements and,
        917–930
    NASDAQ system and, 123
    and NYSE volume, 779
    operation of, 122
    option contracts and, 873
    third market and, 125
    Unlisted Securities Market (USM)
        and, 122–123
Overweighted country, 432

Paris, International Federation of
    Stock Exchanges in, 118
Paris Bourse, 115, 142
Parity
    cap-floor-swap, 928

interest rate, 857
put-call, 334, 347
put-call-forward, 352–354
Par value, of issue, 491
Passive equity portfolio management
    futures in, 816–817
    index fund construction techniques
        and, 804–805
    replication in, 803–804
    strategies for, 803–805
Passive management strategies,
    592–593
Pass the book, 119
Pass-through certificates, 504–505
Payback, 944
Pay-fixed swap, 923–924
Payoffs
    altering with call options, 360–362
    for call and put options, 341–344
    for forward contracts, 340–341
    for option contracts, 344–346
    terminal, 345
Payout ratio, time series plot of, 667
P/BV ratio. *See* Price book value
    (P/BV) ratio
PCE-medical care. *See* Retail stores-
    drug (RSD) industry
P/CF ratio. *See* Price/cash flow
    (P/CF) ratio
Peak, of cycle, 776
Pension and Investment Age, 196
Pension funds, 51–53
    defined contribution plans, 52
    defined definite plans, 52
    overfunded, 52
    underfunded, 52
P/E ratio. *See* Price/earnings (P/E)
    ratio
Performance, industry, 681–682
    of companies within industry, 682
    over time, 682
Performance, of Walgreen, 724. *See
    also* Performance, industry
Performance measures, 466. *See also
    Portfolio performance analysis
Periodicals. *See* Information sources;
    Magazines
Perpetuity, 437
Personal consumption expenditures
    (PCE), 686–689
Personal trust, time horizon and, 47
Pickup swap, pure yield, 603
PIK bond, 509
Plain vanilla swap, 922–923
Planning. *See* Objectives; Portfolio
    management
Planning periods, CAPM and, 309
Point-and-figure chart, 793–795
Point estimate of sales, 647
Policy effect, 1022
Policy statement
    asset allocation and, 55–56
    constructing, 51
    investment objectives in, 43–46
    need for, 41–42
    for portfolio management, 40–41
Political risk, 21–22, 432. *See also*
    Country risk
Portfolio. *See also* Bond portfolio
    management; Portfolio
    management; Portfolio
    performance; Stock indexes
    benchmark, 803

bond, 73–74
    completely diversified, 284
    dedicated, 607–615
    diversified, 67
    efficient, 253
    equity, 74–77
    estimation risk and, 269–270
    foreign stocks and bonds in, 77
    hedging inflows in, 812–813
    hedging outflows in, 814
    historical rates of return for, 10–11
    investment company types based
        on, 973–976
    of investments, 6
    market, 278, 283–284
    mixes, by country, 62
    options and, 889
    passive equity, 803–805
    protecting value with put options,
        356–360
    risk-free, 264
    standard deviation formula for,
        261–268
    stocks in, and standard deviation
        of return, 285
    theory vs. practice and, 317–322
    three-asset, 268–269
    trading to adjust beta, 816
    variance (standard deviation) of
        returns for, 255–259
    volatility of returns on, 59
    world performance in, 91–93
Portfolio insurance, 357–358
Portfolio management, 251
    benchmark portfolio and, 42
    derivatives in, 354–362
    efficient markets and, 244–246
    immunization strategies and,
        608–615
    investment constraints and, 46–51
    legal and regulatory factors in,
        50–51
    performance standard for, 42–43
    process of, 40–41
    return objectives and, 46
Portfolio management strategies,
    contingent immunization as,
    616, 617–622
Portfolio manager, 994–995
Portfolio performance
    components of, 1006–1010
    composite measures of, 994,
        995–1002
    factors affecting measures of,
        1016–1021
    Jensen measure of, 1000–1002
    measures of, 993–994, 1002–1010
    Sharpe measure of, 998–1000
    Treynor composite measure of,
        995–998
Portfolio performance analysis, of
    bond portfolio, 1021–1029
Portfolio theory, 22, 29. *See also*
    Capital market theory
    bond portfolio performance
        evaluation and, 1021
    of Markowitz, 253–272
Positive correlation, low, 72
Potential asset sales, 600
Potential return, 619–620
    concept of, 621
    contingent immunization and,
        619–620

Predictions
    of returns, 215
    of semistrong-form returns,
        217–218
Preferences, of investors, 51
Preferred habitat, 559
Preferred stock, 81
    convertible, 941–942
    valuation of, 434–435
Pre-investment needs
    cash reserve as, 38
    insurance as, 38
Premium, 528. *See also* Market risk
    premium; Options
    conversion, 941–942
    equity risk, 656–660
    forward, 856
    option, 337
    risk, 20
Present value model, 526–528
    price-yield curve and, 527–528
    yield model and, 528–529
Price. *See also* Stock price
    for bonds, 517–521, 522, 536–541
    consumer (retail), 451, 478
    crossover, 534
    leading indicators and, 467
    on noninterest dates, 540
    of option, 337
    spot and forward, 835–837
    stock, 471–472
Price adjustment, to new information,
    773–774
Price and volume data, technical
    analysis with, 788–795
Price behavior, floor return and, 619
Price book value (P/BV) ratio,
    735–738
Price/cash flow (P/CF) ratio, 736,
    738–739
Price continuity, 107
Price discovery function, futures
    prices and, 836
Price-driven system, 114
Price/earnings (P/E) ratio, 445–447
    earnings multiplier and, 642,
        655–656
    and returns, 223
Price momentum, 807
Price movements, of forward and
    futures contracts, 336
Price quotations. *See* Quotations
Price risk, 609
Price volatility, for bonds, 561–580
Price-weighted series, 153–155
    DJIA as, 154–155
    Nikkei-Dow Jones Average as,
        155
Price-yield relationship, 527–528
    for bonds, 570–573
    between noncallable and callable
        bonds, 577
Pricing theory. *See* Arbitrage pricing
    theory
Primary capital markets, 108–111
Primary financial markets. *See*
    Financial markets; Secondary
    financial markets
Primary market, 107
Principal, of issue, 491
Private placement
    defined, 111
    of municipal bonds, 108

Private placement (*continued*)
and Rule 144A, 111
Professional conduct standards, code
of ethics and, 1039–1040
Professional money managers, 235
performance of, 239–241
Profitability, of European chemical
industry, 706-708, 744. *See also*
Operating profitability
Profit margin, 647–648, 663
aggregate operating, 648–649
of company, 721
export markets and, 650–651
gross, 390–391
industry, 693
industry forecast, 691–694
inflation and, 650
net, 391–392
for Walgreen Company, 722
Profit takeouts, 601
Programming. *See* Computer
Program trading, and stock index
arbitrage, 853
Promised yields, and realized returns,
610
Promised yield to call (YTC),
534–535
computing, 534–535
Promised yield to maturity, 530–534
computing, 532–533
for zero coupon bond, 533–534
Protective put, 354, 357
expiration date value of, 358
Publications. *See* Information
sources; Magazines
Pure auction market, 114
Pure expectations hypothesis, cost of
carry model and, 836
Pure profits, 749
Pure rate of interest, 5
Pure time value of money, 5
Pure yield pickup swap, 602, 603
Put, protective, 354, 357
Put-call-forward parity, 352–354
Put-call parity, 334, 349–350
synthetic securities and, 350–351
Put/call ratio, of Chicago Board
Options Exchange (CBOE), 780
Put-call-spot parity, 348
adjusting for dividends, 351–352
European-style put options and,
902–903
Put option, 84, 337. *See also* Option
contract
currency, 876
European-style, 902–903
forward contracts and, 340
payoffs for, 341–344
protecting portfolio value with,
356–360
terminal payoffs to, 345

Quadratic optimization, 804
Quarterly earnings, studies of,
218–223
*Quarterly Financial Report, The
(QFR)*, 179–180
Quick ratio, 383–384, 409
Quotations
for agency securities, 519–521
on commodities futures, 829–830
for corporate bonds, 517–519

for currency forwards and futures,
854, 855, 856
for Eurodollar and Treasury bill
futures, 844
for exchange-traded options,
874–876
for futures options, 879
for interest rate swap and swap
spread, 921
for municipal bonds, 521, 522
for mutual funds, 982
stock index option, 877
for T-bonds and T-notes, 838

Rail and transportation issues, 507
Random walk hypothesis, 210
Range forwards, 873, 887–888, 889
Rate, calculating forward, 868–871
Rate anticipation effect, 1022
Rate of inflation, and profit margin,
650
Rate of interest, pure, 5
Rate of return. *See also* Required
rate of return; Return; Risk
actuarial, 52
estimated, 290
expected, 254
for major stock markets, 72
mean, 8
required, 6, 435
Rates of change, 466
Rates of return. *See also* Expected
rates of return
abnormal, 216
annualized, 240
of annual securities, 173
on bonds, 493–494
computation of monthly, 256
covariance of, 255
estimating for industry, 683–684
expected, 11–14
industry, 683–684
and risk, for major stock markets,
72
for stock price indicator series
(1972–1995), 172
Ratings
of bonds, 497–499
description of, 498, 499
financial ratios and, 420
of Japanese bonds, 514
Moody's and, 26n
Ratio
analysis of international, 412–416
asset/equity, 455–456
block uptick-downtick, 787–788
cash, 386, 409
cash flow, 403
cash flow coverage, 404
cash flow/interest expense,
403–404
cash flow/long-term debt,
404–405
cash flow/total debt, 405
common size, 383
comparative analysis of, 409–411
conversion, 941
current, 383–385, 409
debt, 399–402
debt/equity, 400–401
DuPont System and, 393–396
earnings or cash flow, 402–405
financial, 381–383

for fixed charge coverages, 403
for gross profit margin, 390–391
hedge, 826, 832–834, 890–893
of indicator series, 464–465
of internal liquidity, 383–388
long-term debt/total capital, 401
of Moody's corporate bond yields,
450
for net profit margin, 391–392
operating efficiency, 388–390
operating profitability, 388–389,
390–396
P/BV, 735–738
price/earnings, 223, 445–447
quick, 383–384, 409
relative-strength (RS), 792
return on owner's equity, 392–393
for return on total capital, 392
of series, 464–465
for total asset turnover, 393
total debt, 401–402
turnover, 386–388
uptick (buyers)-downtick (sellers),
788
uses of financial, 418–422
Raw land, investing in, 87
RCMMS. *See* Registered competitive
market makers (RCMMs)
Real assets, 77
Real estate, 86–87
compared with other asset classes,
97
direct investment in, 87
historical risk/returns on, 95–97
land development and, 87
raw land as, 87
rental property as, 87
Real estate investment trusts
(REITs), 86–87
Real GDP, 451
Real growth rate, 17
Real investment returns, after taxes
and costs, 56
Realized capital gains, 48
Realized returns, 228
promised yields and, 610
Realized (horizon) yield, 535–536,
602
with differential reinvestment
rates, 538–539
Real risk-free rate (RFR) of interest,
17, 546
equity risk premium and, 659–660
for major countries, 451
Receivables, turnover of, 386–387
Refunding issues, 492
Regional exchanges, 113, 120–121
Registered bonds, 491
Registered competitive market
makers (RCMMs), 126
Registration, of security issues,
110–111
Regression analysis, 691
Regulation, 50
of banks, 55
Regulation T, 128–129
Regulation U, 128–129
Reinvestment, dedication with, 608
Reinvestment rates, realized
(horizon) yield with, 538–539
REITs. *See* Real estate investment
trusts (REITs)
Relative-strength (RS) ratios, 792

Relative value
measures of, 734–739
price book value (P/BV) ratio,
735–738
for Walgreen and RSD industry,
735–738
Rental property, investing in, 87
Replication, in passive portfolio
management, 803, 804–805
Reports, SEC-required, 374–375. *See
also* Financial statements
Required rate, nominal risk-free rate
and, 5
Required rate of return, 6, 435,
447–449, 727
changes in, 27–28
determining, 16–24
estimating, 656
and expected rate of return,
733–734
for industry, 699–701
risk measures, sources, and, 23–24
security market line movements
and, 25
and valuation model process,
447–456
Required return, for foreign
securities, 449–453
Research, on high-yield bonds,
599–600
Reserve floating-rate note, swap and,
955
Residual effect, 1026
Resistance level, 790
Retail price, 451
changes in, 478
Retail stores-drug (RSD) industry.
See also Company analysis
as earnings estimate sample,
697–705
growth rate for, 732
sales forecasting for, 686–689
Walgreen's competitive strategies
and, 722–726
Retention rates, for foreign stocks,
455
Retirement, investment life cycle
and, 39
Retirement planning, pension funds
and, 51–53
Return(s). *See also* Historical risk/
returns; Markowitz portfolio
theory; Rate of return; Required
rate of return; Risk
bond portfolio sources of,
1026–1027
from common stocks and Treasury
bills, 61
competition and, 689–696
country risk and, 71
covariance of, 255–259
of different asset classes, 57–61
distributions of, 622
estimated rates of, 290
for foreign securities, 449–453
form of, 435
futures contracts and, 810–812
for growth company, 749
hedged and unhedged, 452n
historical and expected of, 6
historical average annual (1926–
1995), 58
for individual investment, 254–255

measuring, 6–11
for portfolio, 255–259, 810–812
on portfolios formed on size and
    book-to-market equity, 227
potential, 619–620
predicting, 215
real investment, 56
relationship among assets and, 252
required rate of, 6
risk and, 24–28, 253–254
security market line and, 24–28
systematic risk and, 312–317
time patterns of, 264, 435
uncertainty of, 435
variability of, 59–60
Return on assets, 662
Return on equity (ROE), 228
breakdown of, 454–455
and growth rate of dividends,
    660–662
increasing, 406
as return on investment, 228
for RSD industry, 702–704
Return on investment (ROI), 228
DuPont analysis of, 395
Return on owner's equity, 392–393
Return on total capital, 392
Revenue bonds, 79, 492, 505–506
municipal bonds as, 109
Reverse floating rate contract, 954
RFR. See Real risk-free rate of
    interest (RFR)
Rising trend channel, 776
Risk, 11–14. See also Beta; Global
    markets; Historical risk/returns;
    Return; Risk aversion; Security
    market line (SML); Systematic
    risk
bank investments and, 55
basis, 832
benchmark problem and,
    1018–1019
bond, 625–626
of bond swaps, 601–602
business, 20, 398–399
capital market theory and, 278
CML and, 286–287
complete measures of, 224
country (political), 21–22, 71–77
coupon reinvestment, 609
defined, 11, 253
of different asset classes, 57–61
equity, 59
estimation of, 269–270
evaluating, 1008
exchange rate, 21, 452
external market measure of, 22
financial, 20, 399–405, 409
hedge positions and, 355
hedge ratio and, 833
historical and expected rates of, 6
industry, 682–683
interest rate, 609
investment, 5
liquidity, 20–21
measures of, 6, 11–16, 59–60,
    253–254
Monte Carlo simulation and,
    359–360
optimal portfolio and, 271
options for, 813
political, 432
in portfolio, 810–812

price, 609
range of returns and, 253
rates of return and, for major stock
    markets, 72
real risk-free rate and, 17
reducing through diversification,
    76
required rate of return and,
    700–701
return and, 24–28, 262–264
return variability and, 59–60
security market line and, 24–28
systematic, 4, 22–23, 152–153,
    284
tolerance of, 45, 46
total, 4
unsystematic, 284, 852–854
yield curve, 578
Risk-adjusted returns, firm size and,
    224
Risk analysis, 396–405
business risk, 398–399
financial risk, 399–405
Risk aversion, 14, 252–253
Risk-bearing, and municipal bond
    underwriting, 108
Risk categories, and asset allocations,
    44
Risk-comfort scale, 45
Risk-free asset, 279–280
covariance with, 280
risky asset and, 279
and risky portfolio, 280–283
Risk-free investment, probability
    distribution for, 12
Risk-free portfolio, 264
with risky securities, 350
Risk-free rate, 17–20
nominal, 5, 656
Risk preferences, portfolio
    management and, 244–245
Risk premium, 5, 20, 90, 432,
    448–449, 547–548
equity, 656–660
factors affecting, 660
for foreign securities, 452
industry required rate of return
    and, 700
intermediate-term, 658
market, 289
systematic risk and, 22–23
Risk-return, for long-term securities,
    625
Risk-return combination, of risk-free
    asset and risky portfolio,
    281–282
Risk-return with leverage, of risk-
    free asset and risky portfolio,
    282–283
Risky asset, 279
expected rate of return for,
    289–290
Risky investments, probability
    distributions for, 13
Robert Morris Associates, financial
    ratio information from, 382
ROE. See Return on equity
ROI. See Return on investment
Rolling out, of cash-matched
    segment, 616
Roll-Ross study
of APT, 325–326
extensions of, 326–327

RSD. See Retail stores-drug (RSD)
    industry
RS ratios. See Relative-strength (RS)
    ratios
Rule 144A, private placements and,
    111
Rule 390, 139–140
Rule 415, security issue registration
    and, 110–111
Runs tests, 213

Safety margin, 618
for portfolio of 30-year bonds, 620
Saitori members, of Tokyo Stock
    Exchange, 118, 133
Sales forecasting
company, 718–721
demonstrating, 686–689
and industrial life cycle, 684–686
and industry-economy relationship,
    687
and input-output analysis, 686
Sales variability, 398
Sampling, 804
Samurai bonds, 496, 516
S&P. See Standard & Poor's
Saving, consumption and, 4–5
Savings accounts, 78
as fixed-income investments, 78
Savings and loan associations, asset/
    liability mismatch and, 55n
Schuldscheindarlehen, 515
SEAQ. See Stock Exchange
    Automated Quotations (SEAQ)
    International
Seasonal effects. See Calendar
    effects
Seasoned new issues, 110
SEC. See Securities and Exchange
    Commission (SEC)
Secondary bond markets, 112–113
Secondary equity markets
national stock exchanges and, 115
securities exchanges and, 113–115
Secondary financial markets,
    111–120
for corporate bonds, 112–113
equity markets, 113–114
financial futures and, 113
for government and municipal
    bonds, 112
Secondary market, 107
Sector/quality effect, 1025
Sector rotation strategy, 807
Secured (senior) bonds, 492
Securities. See also Bonds;
    Derivative securities; Global
    investment; Orders; Stocks
buying on margin, 128
convertible, 941
derivative, 338–346, 916–917
dividend-bearing, 903–905
foreign, 449–453
fundamental risk of, 22
investment-grade, 498
synthetic, 350–351
U.S. agency, 79–81
in world capital markets, 68–69
Securities and Exchange Commission
    (SEC)
financial reports and, 374–375
publications of, 182–183
Rule 144A and, 111

Securities and Exchange Commission
    (SEC) reports, as information
    sources, 190–191
Securities exchanges, 113–115
Securities markets. See also Stock
    market analysis; Stock markets
block trades and, 136–137
changes in, 134–144
economic activity and, 460,
    461–462
future developments in, 143–144
global asset allocation and,
    460–461
global market changes and,
    141–143
institutionalization in, 134–135
institutions and stock price
    volatility, 137
national market system (NMS)
    and, 137–140
negotiated commission rates in,
    135–136
new trading systems and, 140–141
organization and functioning of,
    105–106, 107–108
in United States, 68–69
worldwide, 477–483
Security analysis, recommendations
    of, 238–239
Security analysts, 236–239
Security-market indicators series
    (indexes), 151–152
bond-market indicators series,
    164–167
comparison of indexes over time,
    169–173
composite stock-bond indexes, 168
stock-market indicators series and,
    153–164
uses of, 152–153
Security market line (SML), 24–28,
    288–297, 1020
differential, 319, 320
movements along, 25
slope of, 25–27
transaction costs and, 308–309
with zero-beta portfolio, 307
Security-market publications. See
    also Aggregate security-market
    analysis; Information sources
annual, 183–184
daily, 185–186
weekly, 184–185
Security prices. See Stock price
Security prospectus, as information
    source, 190
Security valuation, 429–430
Segmented market hypothesis,
    559–561
Selected series
as business cycle indicators, 464
of indicators, 464
Selectivity
diversification and, 1007–1008
measuring, 1006–1007
Semistrong EMH, 211, 215–234, 628
Senior secured bonds, 79–80
Separation theorem
CML and, 285–286
defined, 286
Sequential distribution process, 509
Serial obligation bond, 491
Settlement price, 828

Share price performance
  for Bayer, 748
  for global companies, 746
Sharpe measure, of portfolio
    performance, 998–1000
Shelf registrations, 110
Short hedge, 831
Short interest, 786–787
Short position, 335
Short sales, 127
  by specialists, 784
Short-term interest rate futures,
    843–849
  applications of, 845–849
  Eurodollar and Treasury bill
      contract mechanics, 843–845
Simple growth model, 751–752
Singapore Stock Exchange, 122
Sinking fund, 492–493
  provision, 79
Size effect, 224–225
Skewness, expected returns and, 314
Slope
  of efficient frontier curve, 270
  of security market line, 25–27
  for stock returns, 316
Small firms, size effect and, 224–225
Small stock premium, 90
SML. See Security market line
    (SML)
Sotheby's indexes, rates of return
    and standard deviation for, 94
Sources of information. See
    Information sources
Specialists, 131
  income of, 132
  short sales by, 784
  stock exchange, 235, 236
Specific estimate approach, to
    estimating earnings multiplier,
    667–669
Speculative bonds, 498, 511
Speculative company, 717
Speculative stock, 717
Speculative trading activity, measures
    of, 779
Speed of adjustment, of stock prices,
    773
Spending, investment and, 4
Spending phase, of investment cycle,
    39
Split rating, 498
Spot currency quotations, 855
Spot parity, put-call, 348
Spot prices, forward prices and,
    835–837
Spot rates, 550
  bond valuation with, 541–543
Spot rate-yield curve, 551–553, 554
  calculating forward spots from,
    554–561
Spread, 53, 842, 873
  banks and, 54
  insurance companies and, 53
  options, 884–887
  swap, 921
  Treasury/Eurodollar (TED),
    848–849
  yield, 560–561
Square root of variance, standard
    deviation as, 14
Stamps, investing in, 88–89
Standard deviation, 14

computation of, 33–34, 260
diversification and, 76
formula for portfolio computation,
    261–268
of returns for individual
    investment, 254–255
of returns for portfolio, 255–259
of risk-free asset and risky
    portfolio, 280–281
as risk measure, 59, 71
Standardized unexpected earnings
    (SUE), 219
Standard & Poor's
  400 Index, 643, 644, 646, 652,
    662
  500 Index, 153, 1016, 1018
  500 Index futures contract,
    814–816
  financial ratio information from,
    382
  publications of, 184, 188–193, 197
  ratings of, 497
  Retail Store-Drug (RSD) index,
    683–684
Statement of cash flows, 376–380
  sample of, 379
Statistical Abstract of the United
    States, 180
Statistical tests, of independence,
    212–213
Stock. See also Common stock;
    Preferred stock
  above 200-day moving average,
    787
  analysis of individual, 190–194
  blue-chip, 154–155
  commercial publications about,
    191–194
  common, 82–83, 438
  company-generated information
    about, 190–191
  cyclical, 717
  defensive, 716–717
  with different returns and risk,
    264–266
  foreign common, 83–84
  growth, 750
  historical risk/returns on, 89–91
  investment returns for, 346
  issues of, 109–111
  preferred, 81, 434–435
  speculative, 717
Stock Exchange Automated
    Quotations (SEAQ)
    International, 142
Stock exchanges, 494. See also
    Exchange; National stock
    exchanges; Regional exchanges;
    Securities exchanges; Securities
    markets; Stock market;
    exchanges by name
  effects of listing on, 232–233
  national, 113
  purchase of foreign stock on,
    83–84
  regional, 113, 120–121
  Singapore, 122
Stock exchange specialists, 235, 236
Stock index arbitrage, 850
  program trading and, 853
Stock indexes, for German equity
    market, 674. See Market

indexes; Security-market
    indicators series (indexes)
Stock index futures, 849–854
  countries with, 814
  futures traders bullish on, 780–781
  index arbitrage and, 850–851
  to isolate unsystematic risk,
    852–854
  valuation of, 850–851, 852
Stock index options, 876
  Black-Scholes valuation model
    and, 907–908
  quotations for, 877
Stock market
  and business cycle, 807
  comparative statistics for, 479
  correlation coefficients between
    price returns on common
    stocks, 75
  correlations among returns,
    479–480
  Dow Theory and, 789
  estimated expected earnings per
    share and, 645–655
  in Mexico, 796
  rate of return for, 72
  rates of return and risk for, 72
  in United Kingdom, 482
  valuation model and, 641–645
  worldwide performance of, 481
Stock market analysis, 640–641
Stock market crash, of 1987,
    901–902
Stock market cycle, 776
Stock-market indicator series,
    153–164. See also Bond-market
    indicator series; Security-market
    indicators series (indexes)
  comparison of, 164–165
  data bank information, 159
  Dow Jones Industrial Average
    (DJIA) and, 152
  foreign indexes, 177
  global equity indexes, 160–162
  indexes in, 153
  price-weighted series, 153–155
  summary of indexes, 158
  unweighted price indicator series,
    153, 157
  value-weighted series, 153,
    156–157
Stock market series
  estimating earnings multiplier for,
    655–669
  in foreign markets, 796
  futures contracts on, 85
  value of, 641
Stock price
  adjustment to supply and demand
    change, 773
  annual changes in, 171
  corporate events and, 234
  by country, 480
  and economy, 461–462
  interest rates and, 475–476
  money supply and, 471
  responses to world or economic
    news, 233
  volatility in, 136
  and volume techniques, 788–795
Stock price indicator series, rates of
    return for (1972–1995), 172
Stock price tapes, 202–203

Stock price tree, forecasted, 892
Stocks, Bonds, Bills, and Inflation,
    184
Stock selection, company analysis
    and, 714–715. See also Growth
    company
Stock splits, studies of, 229–230
Stock valuation
  earnings multiplier model and,
    445–447
  financial ratios and, 419
  flexible growth model for,
    758–761, 762
  with temporary supernormal
    growth, 443–445
Stop buy order, 128
Stop loss order, 127
Straddles, 873, 881–882
Strangles, 883, 884
Straps, 881–882, 883
Strategic asset allocation, 819
Strategies. See Bond portfolio
    management; Competitive
    strategy; Equity portfolio
    management strategies; Portfolio
    management
Stream of expected returns, 434–435
Striking price, 337
Stripped coupon interest, 521
Stripped principal, 521
Strips. See also Treasury strips
  Eurodollar, 846–848
  options contracts and, 881–882,
    883
Strong-form EMH, 212, 234–241
Structured notes, 917
Subordinated bonds, 80
Subordinated (junior) debentures,
    492, 507
Substitute products, as competitive
    force, 690
Substitution swaps, 601, 602–603,
    604
SUE. See Standardized unexpected
    earnings (SUE)
Super Dot, 140
Suppliers, as competitive force, 691
Supply, 544
Supply and demand
  technical analysis and, 772
  trends and, 773
Support level, 790
Survey of Current Business, 179
Sustainable growth, 406, 408
Swap-linked notes, 953–956
Swaps
  bond, 601–605
  commodity, 937–939
  contracting extensions for,
    931–939
  currency, 931–935
  equity index-linked, 935–937
  interest rate, 916, 919–925
  plain vanilla, 922–923
  pure yield pickup, 602
  substitution, 601, 602, 604
  tax, 601, 603–605
Swap spread, 921
Swaption, 928–930
Synthetic fixed-rate funding,
    Eurodollar strips and, 846–848
Synthetic risk-free portfolio, options
    and, 889

Synthetic securities, put-call parity and, 350–351
Systematic risk, 4, 22–23, 152–153, 284. *See also* Risk; Unsystematic risk
    altering synthetically, 357
    beta and, 289
    bonds and, 625–626
    characteristic line and, 291–292
    computing, 700–701
    of equity portfolio, 817
    error in estimating, 319
    financial ratios and, 419, 420
    fundamental risk and, 23
    and return, 312–317

TAA. *See* Tactical asset allocation (TAA)
Tactical asset allocation (TAA), 354, 819, 1015–1016
TAT. *See* Total asset turnover (TAT)
Tax-deferred investments, 49–50
Taxes and taxation, 356
    diversification and, 49
    investment planning and, 47–50
    and investment returns, 56, 57
    on municipal bonds, 506
    on pass-through securities, 505
    planning periods and, 309
    reducing liabilities for, 49
Tax-exempt bonds
    municipals as, 79
    yield adjustments for, 540–541
Tax rate
    estimating, 653
    industry, 693–694, 696
Tax swaps, 601, 603–605
T-bill Eurodollar yield spread, 783–784
T-bills. *See* Treasury bills (T-bills)
T-bonds. *See* Treasury bonds (T-bonds)
Technical analysis, 771–772
    advantages of, 775–776
    assumptions of, 772–774
    of bond markets, 797–798
    challenges to assumptions of, 774
    defined, 772
    of efficient capital markets, 241–242
    of foreign exchange rates, 797
    of foreign markets, 795–797
    technical trading rules and, 774–775
Technical trading rules
    bar charting and, 792
    block uptick-downtick ratio and, 787–788
    breadth of market and, 784–785
    challenges to, 774–775
    Confidence Index and, 782–783
    contrary-opinion, 777–781
    Dow Theory and, 789–790
    and indicators, 776–798
    margin debt and, 784
    moving-average lines and, 790–792
    multiple indicator charts and, 792
    point-and-figure charts and, 793–795
    relative strength and, 792
    short interest and, 786–787
    short sales by specialists and, 784

smart investors and, 781–784
    stock price, volume technique, and, 788
    and stocks above 200-day moving average, 787
    support and resistance levels and, 790
    T-bill-Eurodollar yield spread and, 783–784
    volume and, 790
Technicians, stock market changes and, 152. *See* Treasury/Eurodollar (TED) spread
TED spread. *See* Treasury/Eurodollar (TED) spread
10-K report, 190, 375
10-Q report, 375
Term bond, 491
Term life insurance, 38
Term structure of interest rates, 544, 548–553
    trading implications of, 560
Term to maturity, 491, 527
    and Macaulay duration, 566
Tests
    autocorrelation, 212–213
    of efficient market hypothesis, 228–234
    of independence, 212–213
    of semistrong-form hypothesis, 215–234
    of trading rules, 213–214
    of weak-form hypothesis, 212–215
Third market, 125
    OTC market as, 121
Ticks, 838–839
Time horizon, of investments, 47
Time interval, systematic risk and, 292–293
Time pattern, of returns, 435
Time preference, risk and, 17
Time premium, of option, 337
Time-series analysis, 215, 382–383, 691. *See also* Forecasting
    quarterly earnings studies and, 218, 219
Time-series plot
    of "excess liquidity" in United States, 472
    of "excess liquidity" outside United States, 473
    of Moody's Aaa corporate bonds and inflation, 474
    of Moody's corporate bond yield spreads, 26, 449
Time-series returns, 257
Time value of money, pure, 5
Timing, of market, 1015–1016
T-notes. *See* Treasury notes (T-notes)
Tokyo Stock Exchange (TSE), 113, 115, 117–118
    changes on, 142
    market makers on, 133
    Nikkei-Dow Jones Average and, 155
Tokyo Stock Exchange Fact Book, 183
Tokyo Stock Market Quarterly Review, 187
Toronto Stock Exchange, 118
Total asset turnover (TAT), 389, 393, 702
Total debt, cash flow ratio with, 405
Total debt ratios, 401–402

Total portfolio theory, bonds and, 623–624
Total return, 46
Total risk, 4
Tracking error, 593, 804
Trade associations, information from, 188–190
Traders, futures, 780–781
Trading. *See also* Orders; Securities markets
    annual strategy for, 225
    average daily, 116
    block, 136–137
    changing dealer inventory and, 124–125
    insider, 235–236
    intermarket system for, 138–139
    new system of, 140
    off-hours, 141
    of options contracts, 880–888, 889
    sample of, 124–125
Trading effect, 1022
Trading rules, 213–214
    challenges to technical, 774–775
    simulations of, 214–215
    tests of, 213–214
Trading strategies
    and bond price volatility, 564
    with modified duration, 569
Trading systems, alternative, 114
Trading turnover, 409
Transaction cost, 107, 355
    and SML, 308–309
Transactions. *See* Exchange; Margin transactions; Orders; Trading
Treasury bills (T-bills), 78, 108
    historical risk/returns on, 89–91
    income payouts from, 61
    liquidity risk and, 19
    mean rate of return and standard deviation of returns for, 626
    mechanics of contracts, 843–845
    yields and inflation rates, 19
Treasury bonds (T-bonds), 108
    futures and, 838–839
    NOB spread and, 842
Treasury Bulletin, 197
Treasury/Eurodollar (TED) spread, 848–849
Treasury futures
    applications of, 841–843
    to hedge future funding commitment, 841–842
    T-bond/T-note (NOB) futures spread, 842
Treasury notes (T-notes), 108, 838
    NOB spread and, 842
Treasury securities, 78–79. *See also* Treasury securities by type
    quotations on, 519–521
    yield curves of, 549
Treasury strips, yield on, 542. *See also* Treasury securities
Treynor composite measure
    of portfolio performance, 995–998
    and Sharpe measure, 999–1000
Trigger point, 618
Trough, 776
Trust, personal, 47
Trust account, 50
TSE. *See* Tokyo Stock Exchange (TSE)

Turnover
    equity, 389–390
    net fixed asset, 389
    total asset, 389, 393
Turnover ratios
    for inventory, 387–388
    for receivables, 386–387
12b-1 plan, 972–973
200-day moving average, 787
Two-state pricing model, 894

Uncertainty, expected rates of return and, 11–14. *See also* Risk
Underfunded pension plans, 52
Underweighted country, 432
Underwriting
    of corporate issues, 110
    of municipal bonds, 108
Unhedged returns, 452n
United Kingdom. *See also* Global investment; London Interbank Offer Rate (LIBOR); London Stock Exchange (LSE)
    agency securities in, 505
    corporate bond market in, 516
    economic outlook for, 481
    government bond issues by, 502
    international bonds in, 517
    municipal bonds in, 505
    portfolio strategies in, 61, 62
    regional exchanges in, 121
    stock market performance for, 482
United Mutual Fund Selector, 983
United Nations Statistical Yearbook, 181
United Nations Yearbook of International Trade Statistics, 182
United Nations Yearbook of National Accounts Statistics, 182
United States
    corporate bonds in, 507–514
    financial markets in, 68–71
    government agency issues in, 502–505
    government bond issues by, 500
    international bond market in, 516
    market makers in, 131–132
    municipal bonds in, 505–507
    portfolio strategies in, 61, 62
    regional exchanges in, 120–121
    secondary markets for bond issues in, 112
United States government. *See also* Treasury listings
    agency securities, 79–81
    aggregate security-market analysis information from, 182–183
    economic information from, 179–180
United States International Trade Administration, International Economic Indicators, 181
United States Treasury securities. *See* Treasury securities
Unit labor cost, 649–650
Universal life insurance, 38
University of Chicago Stock Price Tapes, 202
University of Michigan, Consumer Sentiment Index, 470
Unlisted Securities Market (USM), 122–123

Unrealized capital gains, 48
Unsecured bonds (debentures), 492
Unsystematic risk, 284
  diversification and, 284–285
  of equity portfolio, 817–818
  stock index futures and, 852–854
Unweighted price indicator series, 157
Unweighted series, 153
Unwind values
  for forward and futures contracts, 835
  of obligation, 834
Upstairs traders, 136
Uptick, 787–788
Uptick (buyers)-downtick (sellers) ratio, 788
Uptick trade, 127
Upward-sloping yield curve, 558
USM. *See* Unlisted Securities Market (USM)
Utilities, in bond market, 507
Utility, investor, 270–272

Valuation. *See also* Bond valuation
  of alternative investments, 436–447
  of American-style options, 905–906
  Black-Scholes model, 873
  of bonds, 436–437, 526–536
  of common stock, 438
  of European-style put and call options, 899, 903–905
  flexible growth model for, 758–761, 762
  of forward and futures contracts, 834–837
  of options contracts, 889–909
  of preferred stock, 437–438
  required rate of return and, 447–456
  security, 429–430
  of stock index futures, 850–851, 852
Valuation analysis strategy, 595
Valuation model
  binomial, 873, 893–897
  Black-Scholes, 897–900
  stock market and, 641–645

Valuation process, 430–431
  general economic influences and, 431–432
  three-step, 431–434
Valuation theory, 434–436
  investment decision process and, 435–436
  required rate of return and, 435
  stream of expected returns and, 434–435
Value
  of company, 717
  components of, 642–645
Value-added
  economic, 740
  market, 740
  measures of, 739–743
Value Line, performance enigma and, 236–237
Value Line publications, 194, 195
  Data Base, 202
  Industry Survey, 188
  Investment Survey, 194
  OTC Special Situations Service, 194
Value stock, vs. growth stock, 807, 808
Value-weighted series, 153, 156–157
Variable life insurance, 38
Variable-rate notes, 510–511
Variables, for industry multiplier microanalysis, 698–699. *See also* Monetary variables
Variance, 14
  of annual rates of return, 59
  computation of, 33–34
  proof of, 275
  of returns for individual investment, 254–255
  of returns for portfolio, 255–259
Variation, coefficient of, 34–35
Volatility
  for bonds, 561–580
  implied, 901
  options and, 900–902
  of returns, 59
  in stock prices, 136
  of stocks vs. bonds, 657
Volume, importance and, 790. *See also* Price and volume data

Volume techniques, stock price and, 788–795

Wall Street Journal, The, 155, 185–186, 198
  in Asia, 185
  fund information in, 981, 982
  stock indexes and, 155, 157
Wall Street Transcript, The, 197
Wall Street Waltz, The, 184
Warrants, 80–81, 84, 874n, 939–941
  bonds and, 507
  defined, 917, 939
Wash sale, 604
Weak-form EMH, 211, 212–215, 628
Wealth
  asset allocation and, 37
  over lifetime, 39
  tax deferral and, 49
Weekend effect, 222
Weekly magazines, 196–197
Weekly security-market publications, 184–185
Weighting, of market indexes, 153
Wilshire small cap "value," vs. small cap "growth," 808
World Bank, IFC and, 119
"World Bond Market Monitor" (Merrill Lynch), 187
World Investment Strategy Highlights (Goldman Sachs), 186–187
World markets. *See* Global investment; Global markets
World security market. *See* Global security markets
Worldwide Economic Indicators, 181

Yankee bonds, 81–82, 496, 516
Yen. *See* Japan
Yield, 528. *See also* Bond price volatility; Yield curve
  adjustments for tax-exempt bonds, 540–541
  on alternative bonds, 16
  computing, 529–536
  convenience, 836
  crossover, 534
  current, 530
  of international government bonds, 545

  nominal, 491
  on noninterest dates, 540
  price-yield relationship and, 527–528
  promised to maturity, 530–534
  ratios of, 448–449
  realized (horizon), 535–536
Yield books, 541
Yield curve, 548–553. *See also* Term structure of interest rates
  expectations hypothesis and, 556–558
  liquidity preference hypothesis and, 558–559
  segmented market hypothesis and, 559–561
  shape of, 558
  spot-rate, 551–553, 554–561
  of Treasury securities, 549
  types of, 550
Yield curve risk, 578
Yield illusion, 531–532
Yield level, and bond price volatility, 564
Yield model, 528–529
Yield spread, 26, 560–561
  analysis of, 600–601
Yield to call, 534–535
Yield to maturity (YTM), 530–534. *See also* Promised yield to maturity
  future bond prices and, 536–538
  interest rates and, 543–544
  of zero coupon and deep discount bonds, 511
Yield to worst, 534
YTC. *See* Promised yield to call (YTC)
YTM. *See* Yield to maturity (YTM)

Z bond, 508
Zero-beta model, 307–308
Zero correlation, 72
Zero coupon bonds, 81, 511
Zero-sum games, 341
Zero variance, risk-free asset and, 279–280